PERSONAL FINANCIAL PLANNING

SEVENTH EDITION

Lawrence J. Gitman
San Diego State University

Michael D. Joehnk
Arizona State University

Larkin Integrated Case contributed by Vickie Hampton, *University of Texas, Austin*

End-of-Chapter Feature, "*Getting a Handle on Your Financial Future,*"
contributed by Robert W. McLeod, CFP, CFA, *University of Alabama*
and Saliba, Reinhart, McLeod & Company

The Dryden Press
Harcourt Brace College Publishers

Fort Worth Philadelphia San Diego New York Orlando Austin San Antonio
Toronto Montreal London Sydney Tokyo

Executive Editor: Mike Reynolds
Development Editor: Shana Lum
Project Editor: Jim Patterson
Art Director: Jeanette Barber
Production Manager: Eddie Dawson
Product Manager: Craig Johnson
Marketing Coordinator: Kelly Whidbee

Art & Literary Rights Editor: Louise Kartkouli
Proofreader: Roberta Kirchhoff
Indexer: Sylvia Coates
Text Type: 10/12 Garamond

Address for orders:
The Dryden Press
6277 Sea Harbor Drive
Orlando, FL 32887-6777
1-800-782-4479, or 1-800-433-0001 (in Florida)

Address for editorial correspondence:
The Dryden Press
301 Commerce Street, Suite 3700
Fort Worth, TX 76102

ISBN: 0-03-008457-1

Library of Congress Catalog Card Number: 95-67302

Printed in the United States of America

6 7 8 9 0 1 2 3 4 069 9 8 7 6 5 4 3 2

The Dryden Press
Harcourt Brace College Publishers

The Dryden Press Series in Finance

Amling and Droms
Investment Fundamentals

Berry and Young
Managing Investments: A Case Approach

Bertisch
Personal Finance

Brigham
Fundamentals of Financial Management
Seventh Edition

Brigham, Aberwald, and Gapenski
Finance with Lotus 1-2-3
Second Edition

Brigham and Gapenski
Cases in Financial Management: Dryden Request

Brigham and Gapenski
Cases in Financial Management: Module A

Brigham and Gapenski
Cases in Financial Management: Module C

Brigham and Gapenski
Financial Management: Theory and Practice
Seventh Edition

Brigham and Gapenski
Intermediate Financial Management
Fifth Edition

Brigham and Houston
Fundamentals of Financial Management: The Concise Edition

Chance
An Introduction to Derivatives
Third Edition

Clark, Gerlach, and Olson
Restructuring Corporate America

Cooley
Advances in Business Financial Management: A Collection of Readings
Second Edition

Cooley
Business Financial Management
Third Edition

Dickerson, Campsey, and Brigham
Introduction to Financial Management
Fourth Edition

Eaker, Fabozzi, and Grant
International Corporate Finance

Evans
International Finance: A Markets Approach

Fama and Miller
The Theory of Finance

Gardner and Mills
Managing Financial Institutions: An Asset/Liability Approach
Third Edition

Gitman and Joehnk
Personal Financial Planning
Seventh Edition

Greenbaum and Thakor
Contemporary Financial Intermediation

Harrington and Eades
Case Studies in Financial Decision Making
Third Edition

Hayes and Meerschwam
Financial Institutions: Contemporary Cases in the Financial Services Industry

Hearth and Zaima
Contemporary Investments: Security and Portfolio Analysis

Johnson
Issues and Readings in Managerial Finance
Fourth Edition

Kidwell, Peterson, and Blackwell
Financial Institutions, Markets, and Money
Fifth Edition

Koch
Bank Management
Third Edition

Leahigh
Pocket Guide to Finance

Maisel
Real Estate Finance
Second Edition

Martin, Cox, and MacMinn
The Theory of Finance: Evidence and Applications

Mayes and Shank
Financial Analysis with Lotus for Windows

Mayes and Shank
Financial Analysis with Microsoft Excel

Mayo
Financial Institutions, Investments, and Management: An Introduction
Fifth Edition

Mayo
Investments: An Introduction
Fourth Edition

Pettijohn
PROFIT+

Reilly
Investment Analysis and Portfolio Management
Fourth Edition

Reilly and Norton
Investments
Fourth Edition

Sears and Trennepohl
Investment Management

Seitz and Ellison
Capital Budgeting and Long-Term Financing Decisions
Second Edition

Siegel and Siegel
Futures Markets

Smith and Spudeck
Interest Rates: Principles and Applications

Stickney
Financial Reporting and Statement Analysis: A Strategic Perspective
Third Edition

Weston, Besley, and Brigham
Essentials of Managerial Finance
Eleventh Edition

The HB College Outline Series

Baker
Financial Management

Preface

"Consumer Prices Continue Their Slow Growth"
"Major Tax Overhaul Becomes Law"
"Short-Term Interest Rates Drop"
"Mortgage Rates Hit New High"
"Major Insurers Cut Rates in Price War"
"The DOW Continues to Hit New Highs"

During recent years we have seen numerous headlines similar to these. Continuous changes in the financial environment, along with changes in our own lives—family, health, job—make personal financial planning both necessary and challenging. This textbook, *Personal Financial Planning,* Seventh Edition, provides the framework and tools for preparing personal financial plans that serve as road maps for goal achievement. *Personal Financial Planning* emphasizes the dynamics of the personal financial planning process by considering the impact of life changes—birth, marriage, divorce, job and career, and death.

The book serves individuals who are, or will be, actively developing their own personal financial plans. It meets the needs of instructors and students in the first course in personal financial planning (often called "personal finance") offered at colleges and universities, junior and community colleges, professional certification programs, and continuing education courses. The experiences of individuals and families are used to demonstrate successes and failures in various aspects of personal financial planning. A conversational style and liberal use of examples and worksheets guide students through the material and emphasize important points. Clearly the benefits of the book's readability accrue not only to students but also to their instructors.

MAJOR CHANGES IN THE SEVENTH EDITION

The seventh edition has been thoroughly updated to reflect the cutting edge of contemporary personal financial planning. It reflects feedback from past users as well as nonusers, practicing financial planners, students, and our own research. It provides helpful new approaches, expanded coverage in certain areas and streamlined coverage in others, and enhanced pedagogy through the introduction of a state-of-the-art integrated learning system. At the same time, the basic organizational structure, topical coverage, superior readability, and useful instructional aids that marked the success of the first six editions have been retained. One notable addition is the chapter opening profiles that describe a person or family who is dealing with a financial planning issue related to the chapter content. This and other changes will be described first as general changes and then as specific chapter-by-chapter changes.

GENERAL CHANGES

- The *book has been shortened* to make it even more manageable and accessible for use at quarter and semester schools. Although the overall organization of the textbook remains very similar to that of earlier editions, it has been *reduced from 16 to 15 chapters.* This was accomplished by combining and streamlining Chapter 2 ("Measuring Your Financial Standing") and Chapter 3 ("Planning Your Financial Future") from the sixth edition. The result of this combination is a new, fully integrated Chapter 2, "Your Financial Statements and Plans." In addition, through small cuts in coverage and general streamlining of discussions, the entire textbook has been better focused and tightened without sacrificing its relevance and pedagogical effectiveness.
- New to this edition is *an emphasis on the important issue of change*—how life's changes, such as marriage, divorce, career switches, and so on, affect personal financial planning. This theme has been both integrated into relevant text discussion and further reinforced through the *addition of "Financial Shocks" boxes* interspersed throughout the text to highlight the causes, consequences, and remedies for unexpected changes in one's financial life. For example on page 56 in Chapter 2, the box titled

"Planning for Dependent Parents" gives guidelines for planning for an unexpected health problem that causes you to become responsible for a parent. Of course, the textbook continues to include "Smart Money" and "Issues in Money Management" boxes.

- An *integrated learning system* has been installed in this edition to help students anchor their study to a set of chapter learning goals. Now, each chapter begins with a list of six numbered *learning goals,* LG 1 through LG 6. The learning goal numbers are tied to first-level chapter headings and restated and reviewed point-by-point in the end-of-chapter summary. Another element of this system is the *Concept Check questions* that appear at the end of each section of the chapter (located ahead of the next first-level heading). As students read through the chapter, they can test their understanding of the material in each section. The numerous other advanced pedagogical features from the sixth edition—critical thinking passages, running glossary, exhibit and worksheet captions, and end-of-chapter questions, problems, and cases have been retained as part of the integrated learning system.
- *Each chapter now opens with an engaging profile* of an individual's or family's experience with an important financial planning issue related to the chapter content. These profiles, which replace the chapter-opening stories included in the sixth edition, involve both traditional and non-traditional family situations. In addition, several further highlight the "change" theme by describing how families and individuals adapt to change. The profiles provide interesting personal insights into the backgrounds, motivations, strategies, and outcomes of the personal financial planning process. A discussion question at the end of every chapter specifically tying the profile to the chapter will help students integrate real-life experience with the chapter concepts.
- The highly regarded *Worksheets* continue to be included with this edition. The expanded and revised worksheets are now separately labeled and numbered as "Worksheet X.Y." The new labels make text references to the worksheets much clearer. All end-of-chapter problems that can be solved using a given worksheet, provide the worksheet reference which directs the student to its application.
- In addition to the worksheets, each new copy of the seventh edition comes with *Financial Planning on the Personal Computer* (FP/PC), a software program developed by Jim Pettijohn and Joe Evans. Students will find that the chapter concepts, worksheets, cases, and problems that are accompanied by this symbol can be solved with the use of FP/PC. We feel that students using FP/PC will be more inclined to begin and continue *their own* financial planning given the ease of using this software program.
- *A completely new continuous case, The Larkin Case,* has been written for the seventh edition. It provides personal and financial information about a real-life person/family and challenges students with the task of developing a specific comprehensive financial plan. Unlike the Williams case from the previous edition, the Larkin case begins with Paul Larkin, a single person who subsequently gets married and experiences a number of other financial "shocks" as his story unfolds and the textual material progresses. This case, therefore, is consistent with the theme of change that is now integrated throughout the text.
- The final section of each chapter, titled "Getting a Handle on Your Financial Future," has been shortened and focuses more clearly on the topic of concern. These sections, prepared by a practicing financial planner, provide advice and checklists that help students, both those "just starting out" and those who are "thirty-something," to immediately apply the chapter concepts to their own financial planning.

SPECIFIC CHAPTER-BY-CHAPTER CHANGES

Because users often like to know where new material appears, the significant but less sweeping changes that have been made in the seventh edition are summarized below, on a chapter-by-chapter basis.

- *Chapter 1* on understanding the financial planning process has been reorganized to place greater emphasis on the ongoing nature of personal financial planning. It now includes recent data from a *Worth* magazine study of "Americans and Their Money" that provides useful insight into psychology and money goals. The chapter also includes life cycle financial data; new discussions of employee benefit planning, personal computers in financial planning, and how geographical factors influence personal income; and both a career planning checklist and a list of specific career strategies.

- *Chapter 2* on your financial statements and plans is the result of combining Chapter 2 and Chapter 3 from the sixth edition. It integrates the discussion of financial statements with the process of preparing financial plans and budgets. The chapter begins with an overview of the financial planning process that includes discussions of the use of professional financial planners and special planning concerns such as managing two incomes, managing employee benefits, and adapting to other major life changes. In addition, the discussion of keeping good records now focuses on proper organization and types of records to maintain, and the discussion of cash budgets now includes a list of 12 tips to balance your budget.
- *Chapter 3* on managing your taxes has been completely updated to reflect the latest tax laws, rates, and procedures. To provide more logical coverage, capital gains are now part of the discussion of gross income; tax credits are now covered as part of the tax calculation; and effective tax planning is now discussed earlier in the chapter, before the now-shortened discussion of forms of personal taxes (federal, state, and local).
- *Chapter 4* on managing your cash and savings includes the latest returns and institutional data that accurately reflect current rates and structure in the financial marketplace. Other changes in Chapter 4 include added coverage of the federal *Truth-In-Savings Act* and *annual percentage yield* (*APY*) to the discussion of checking and savings products; new coverage of the use of asset management accounts (AMA) as an alternative to traditional checking and savings accounts; simplified and clarified discussion of measuring the account balance qualified to earn interest; revised discussion of Series EE bonds reflecting the recently introduced method for determining the rate of interest paid by them; and a new section describing new money management services that are now offered by banks.
- *Chapter 5* on making housing and automobile decisions has been updated to reflect current real estate market conditions, costs, and procedures. Other improvements include a new major section on renting that includes an improved discussion of the rent-or-buy decision; new coverage on using a computer or phone to access real estate databases; discussion on remodeling an existing home as an option to purchasing new; and coverage of how to use a buyer's broker or facilitator. We have moved the discussion of prequalifying for a mortgage loan to the section on buying a home and created a separate major section on financing the home purchase transaction that includes an improved example of mortgage refinancing analysis. In addition, we have added references to computer programs and car buying guides and services that facilitate auto purchase and financing decisions; a major section on leasing your car that describes and demonstrates the leasing process and the lease versus purchase decision; and guidelines for what to do when a lease expires. We eliminated the discussion of furniture and appliance purchases.
- *Chapter 6* on borrowing on open account has undergone significant consolidation but still continues to emphasize the positive aspects of credit. One major change, for example, has been the coordinated coverage of both bank credit cards and retail charge cards, where the emphasis is placed more on the similarities in these two types of credit, rather than their differences. At the same time, we have judiciously expanded the material on obtaining and managing open account credit, using credit wisely, and ways to avoid credit problems; in addition, coverage of rebate (or co-branded) credit cards and prepaid cards has been added to this chapter. Finally, the discussion of credit bureaus has been modified to reflect their new responsibilities as mandated by the 1995 Amendment to the *Fair Credit Reporting Act*.
- *Chapter 7* on using consumer loans has been tightened up considerably and now contains substantially more information on managing credit. The material on student loans has been revised to reflect the latest requirements and limitations; in addition, we have added a *Financial Shocks* box on different ways of meeting the ever-increasing cost of a college education. Also new to this chapter is a discussion of prepayment penalties that are sometimes found on installment loans.
- *Chapter 8* on insuring your life has gone through a number of modifications that involved both consolidation and restructuring of material. Some

of the highly technical material has been condensed or removed in an attempt to make the coverage more user-friendly; at the same time, more attention has been devoted to the role of life insurance in both traditional and non-traditional family situations. We expanded the underwriting section to more fully describe the application review process, and added a section on "who needs insurance?" that also discusses life cycle issues. In addition, we created a new section on buying life insurance (including material on the comparative cost of life insurance policies), expanded the discussion of term versus permanent insurance, and updated the Social Security survivor's benefit data.

- *Chapter 9* on insuring your health has been thoroughly updated and completely reorganized to describe, first the various types of health care plans, next the providers of health care insurance, and finally the various types of medical expense coverages and policy provisions. In addition, major sections are now separately devoted to long-term care and disability income insurance. The final section is an updated guide to buying health care insurance that includes annotated questions to ask when choosing a health care plan. The chapter now clearly defines and differentiates between indemnity (fee-for-service) plans and managed care plans; includes a discussion of group versus individual health care insurance; describes special insurance coverages you *don't* need; includes an exhibit with suggestions on how to get insurance claims paid; and adds an annotated list of questions to consider along with guidelines for buying long-term care insurance. New tables include a schedule of disability income insurance premiums for both males and females for various benefit periods and a list of tips for buying disability income insurance policies.
- *Chapter 10* on protecting your property has been streamlined and updated throughout. As in previous editions, major attention is directed toward three types of insurance: homeowner's, automobile, and liability; however, the coverage has been condensed to provide a much tighter discussion of the topics. In addition, we have revised the coverage of personal property floaters, added a box on some of the shortcomings of replacement insurance, and added a new exhibit on the comparative costs of homeowner's insurance. We have also expanded the discussion of the factors that drive the cost of automobile insurance rates and added an exhibit on some of the top-rated property and liability insurers.
- *Chapter 11* on investing in stocks and bonds has been thoroughly updated to reflect security returns and market performance through 1994. In addition, we have expanded the discussion of different types of stocks to include the smaller segments of the market—the so-called *mid-cap and small-cap stocks.* We even added a box that discusses *micro-caps*, the really tiny stocks. In the bond segment of the chapter, the table of taxable equivalent yields has been updated to include the two additional federal tax brackets that were added in 1993; and the material on mortgage-backed securities has been dropped because of their growing complexity and riskiness.
- *Chapter 12* on making securities investments has also been thoroughly updated with the latest security quotes, returns, and market requirements. A new table on comparative broker commissions has been added, along with a new section on executing trades. Also, the coverage of annual reports was expanded to include some valuable suggestions on how to get the most from these reports; the material on market indexes was revised to include the newest S&P index, the SmallCap 600; and the bond quote exhibit now includes both corporate and Treasury bond quotes. In addition, a new section on the PC as a source of investment information was added to this edition to reflect the growing role that PC's play in the world of investing, even for individual investors; we also added a box on how to build a portfolio when you're just starting out, and have expanded the discussion of how life cycle changes can affect your investment portfolio.
- *Chapter 13* on investing in mutual funds now deals exclusively with one type of investment vehicle: mutual funds, which are, far and away, the most popular type of investment with individual investors. Because the entire chapter now focuses on this one type of investment, more attention can be given to the different types of mutual funds, as well as different investment strategies. For example, a new section has been added on closed-end investment companies and the discussion of fund loads and charges has been greatly expanded. In addition,

as far as different types of funds are concerned, we now also cover convertible bond funds, asset allocation funds, and life cycle funds. And finally, the section on making mutual fund investments has been greatly expanded, so that it covers everything from how to go about selecting funds to how to deal with fund load charges.

- *Chapter 14* on meeting retirement goals has not only been updated with the latest retirement program regulations and limitations, it also now includes expanded coverage of how changing lifestyles can impact retirement plans and goals. Also new to this chapter are sections on computer-based retirement planning and the role of variable annuities in a retirement program.
- *Chapter 15* on preserving your estate has a new introduction that includes a clear definition of estate planning. A discussion of other important estate planning documents such as power of attorney and living wills has been added to the section on wills. A new table that includes brief descriptions of six important trusts has been included in the trusts section, and all gift and estate tax rates and procedures have been clarified and updated in accordance with recent changes.

ORGANIZATION OF THE BOOK

Personal Financial Planning addresses all of the major personal financial planning problems that individuals and families encounter. It presents a model of the major elements of effective money management. All of the latest financial planning tools and techniques are discussed. Most of the profiles and widely used examples involve relatively young people so that the student reader may more easily identify with each situation.

This comprehensive text is written in a low-key, personal style and uses state-of-the-art pedagogy to present the key concepts and procedures used in sound personal financial planning and effective money management. The roles of various financial decisions in the overall personal financial planning process are clearly delineated.

The book is divided into six parts. Part One presents the foundations of personal financial planning, beginning with the financial planning process and then covering financial statements and plans, and taxes. Part Two concerns the management of basic assets, including cash and savings instruments, housing, and automobiles. Part Three covers credit management, including the various types of open account borrowing and consumer loans. Part Four deals with managing insurance needs, and considers life insurance, health care insurance, and property insurance. Part Five concerns investments, including stocks, bonds, and mutual funds, and how to make transactions in securities markets. Part Six is devoted to retirement and estate planning. All these parts are tied together via the *Larkin continuous case,* which begins at the end of Chapter 1 with an extensive inventory of personal and financial data. Additional elements of the Larkin's financial plans are then introduced at the ends of Parts One through Five, and Chapters 14 and 15 so that the students can deal with the unfolding elements of a complete personal financial plan.

PEDAGOGY

Each chapter opens with a *Profile,* a description of an individual's or family's experience with an important financial planning issue related to the chapter content. Along with the profile are six learning goals that link the material covered to specific learning outcomes and, as noted earlier, anchor the text's *integrated learning system.* In addition, each major section of the chapter begins with a *critical thinking question* designed to stimulate interest in the material that follows by challenging the student to relate it to his or her personal life. At the end of each of the major sections are *Concept Check* questions that allow the student to confirm their understanding of the material before moving on to the next section.

Each chapter contains two *boxes* set off from the text material and containing brief discussions of relevant personal financial planning material that serve to enrich the topical coverage. The boxes are of three possible types: "Financial Shocks" that address the issue of change, "Issues in Money Management" that present controversial issues, and "Smart Money" that provide advisory tips.

Worksheets, which are typically filled out and discussed, are included to simplify demonstration of various calculations and procedures and to provide students with helpful materials they can use in managing their own personal finances. The worksheets are numbered to provide convenient reference to them in the end-of-chapter problems, and they include descriptive captions. Numerous exhibits, each containing descriptive captions, are used throughout to more fully illustrate key points in the text.

Many chapters contain discussions and illustrations of how the personal computer can be used in various phases of personal financial planning and, where appropriate, brief descriptions of some of the more popular computer software are included. A running glossary provides brief definitions of key terms. End-of-chapter material includes a *summary* that restates each learning goal and follows it with a summary of the material related to it. *Financial Facts or Fantasies,* a series of six true-false questions concerning the material covered in the chapter, follow the summary. Answers to the *Financial Facts or Fantasies* are included in text Appendix E. The next element is *discussion questions and problems* that students can use to test their grasp of the material. Two or more *case problems* highlighting the important analytical topics and concepts are also supplied.

Following the cases is the financial advisory section, "Getting a Handle on Your Financial Future," which provides helpful checklists for students who are just starting out and for those who are more established. And, of course, as noted before, each part of the book ends with the *Larkin continuous case.*

SUPPLEMENTARY MATERIALS

Recognizing the importance of outstanding support materials to the instructor and the student, we have continued to improve and expand our supplement package.

WORKSHEETS

A packet containing *blank worksheets* identical to those presented and used in the text is included free of charge with each new copy of the book. Each worksheet provides a logical format for dealing with some aspect of personal financial planning such as preparation of a cash budget, home affordability analysis, or automobile lease versus purchase analysis.

INSTRUCTOR'S MANUAL AND TEST BANK

A comprehensive *Instructor's Manual and Test Bank* has been prepared to assist the teacher. For each chapter, the manual includes

- An outline
- Discussion of major topics
- A list of key concepts
- Solutions to all Concept Check questions, end-of-chapter discussion questions and problems, and cases
- *Outside projects* that can be assigned to students so that they can apply major concepts and techniques presented in the chapter (instructions for outside projects are printed on separate sheets to make duplication for classroom distribution a simple task)
- Solutions to all Larkin continuous case questions.
- Two additional integrative cases, each with a detailed solution. One of the cases deals with a young couple, and the other addresses the financial concerns faced by single parents.
- A complete test bank that has been revised, updated, and expanded by Carlene Creviston of Ball State University includes true-false and multiple-choice questions, as well as four to six short problems for nearly every chapter.

COMPUTERIZED TEST BANK

A computerized version of the printed test bank is available on a $3\frac{1}{2}$" IBM-compatible diskette, $3\frac{1}{2}$" Windows, or Macintosh featuring Dryden's computerized test bank program EXAMaster+. EXAMaster+ has many features that allow the instructor to modify test questions, select items by key words, scramble tests for multiple class sections, and test completely on-line.

WORKBOOK

Carlene Creviston of Ball State University has updated the *Workbook* to assist students in mastering the information and techniques presented in the text, and to serve as a resource manual as they develop personal financial plans. Specific components for each chapter include

- A thorough outline of concepts discussed
- Completion exercises that stress vocabulary

- Comprehensive case problems (with solutions) that demonstrate the application of chapter concepts and utilize the worksheets

Most chapters include both problem-solving exercises (with solutions) and comprehensive cases.

PERSONAL FINANCIAL PLANNING DISK

The computer-based problem-solver—*Financial Planning on the Personal Computer (FP/PC)*—was revised for this edition of the book by its author, Professor James B. Pettijohn of Southwest Missouri State University and Joe Evans. The disk performs like any of the widely used commercially available software packages and is completely interactive; best of all, being very user-friendly, it streamlines the recordkeeping and problem-solving activities presented in the text. A computer logo is used in the margin to identify sections of the book to which the disk is applicable. End-of-chapter problems and cases that can be solved with the disk are keyed with the same logo. Some worksheets used in the text are formatted on the disk to provide assistance in applying some of the more complex procedures, ranging from financial statement and budget preparation to tax estimation, investment management, and retirement planning. The software has been extensively tested to ensure its accuracy and ease of use.

PRESENTATION SOFTWARE

For instructors who enjoy working with computerized presentations, we have provided a complete lecture presentation in Microsoft Power Point. Each chapter's file includes an outline, appropriate numerical concepts, and key topics. Instructors can easily modify the presentations using Power Point's many features.

The Dryden Press will provide complementary supplements or supplement packages to those adopters qualified under our adoption policy. Please contact your sales representative to learn how you may qualify. If as an adopter or potential user you receive supplements you do not need, please return them to your sales representative or send them to:

Attn: Returns Department
Troy Warehouse
465 South Lincoln Drive
Troy, MO 63379

ACKNOWLEDGMENTS

In addition to the many individuals who made significant contributions to this book by their expertise, classroom experience, guidance, general advice, and reassurance, we also appreciate the students and faculty who used the book and provided valuable feedback on it, confirming our conviction that a truly teachable personal financial planning text could be developed.

Of course, we are indebted to all the academicians and practitioners who have created the body of knowledge contained in this text. We particularly wish to thank several people who gave the most significant help in developing and revising it. The first is Robert W. McLeod, CFP, CFA, of the University of Alabama and Saliba, Reinhart, McLeod & Company, for developing the end-of-chapter financial advisory sections, "Getting a Handle on Your Financial Future." In addition, we want to thank Vickie Hampton of the University of Texas at Austin for her intensive review of the entire manuscript and for her work on the continuous cases. Also, we want to thank Jim Pettijohn and Joe Evans for developing the state-of-the-art software. Larry A. Cox, CFP of the University of Georgia deserves thanks for his advice and work on the insurance chapters, particularly those on life and health insurance. Thanks is also due Robert J. Wright of Wright & Wright, CPAs, for his assistance in the chapter on taxes; and John C. Bost, Esq., of San Diego State University for his help in revising and updating the estate planning chapter.

The Dryden Press, which shared our objective of producing a truly teachable text, relied on the experience and advice of numerous excellent reviewers for the seventh edition: Larry A. Cox, University of Georgia; Carlene Creviston, Ball State University; Rosa Lea Danielson, College of DuPage; William B. Dillon, Carson-Newman College; Jeanette A. Eberle, Hardin-Simmons University; Alan Goldfarb, Financial Strategies Advisory Corporation; James Haltman, Wheaton College; Vickie L. Hampton, University of Texas at Austin;

Ted Jones, Jefferson Community College; William W. Jones, University of Central Florida; Peggy Keck, Western Kentucky University; Gary L. Killion, Jones College; David Manifold, William Carey College on the Coast; Charles W. McKinney, Whitworth College; Robert W. McLeod, University of Alabama; Charles O'Connor, Pacific University; Alan Raedels, Portland State University; Charles F. Richardson, Austin Peay State University; Kenneth H. St. Clair, Cedarville College; and Brent T. Sjaardema, Nyack University.

We also appreciate the many suggestions from previous reviewers, all of whom have had a significant impact on the earlier editions of this book. Our thanks go to the following: Linda Afdahl, Michael J. Ahern III, Robert J. Angell, H. Kent Baker, Catherine L. Bertelson, Steve Blank, Dan Casey, P. R. Chandy, Maurice L. Crawford, David Durst, Mary Ellen Edmundson, Ronald Ehresman, Jim Farris, Sharon Hatten Garrison, Carol Zirnheld Green, C. R. Griffen, John L. Grimm, Chris Hajdas, Forrest Harlow, Kendall P. Hill, Darrell D. Hilliker, Arlene Holyoak, Frank Inciardi, Kenneth Jacques, Dixie Porter Johnson, Karol Kitt, George Klander, Xymena S. Kulsrud, Carole J. Makela, Charles E. Maxwell, George Muscal, Robert Nash, Albert Pender, Franklin Potts, Fred Power, Arnold M. Rieger, Vivian Rippentrop, Gayle M. Ross, Rosemary Walker, Gary Watts, Grant J. Wells, Betty Wright, and R. R. Zilkowski. And, of course, the opening profiles would neither exist nor be as interesting and helpful to the reader were it not for the people who selflessly gave us their time and stories, including: Carol Adams, Steven and Elise Griffith, Terry and Sarah Joehnk, Jeff Kaiser, Don Maescher and Marlene Bellamy, Lori Rapuano, Annabelle Reitman, Bill Stanley, Steve and Kelly Stuart, Juanita Tippins, and Randy and Jan Walker.

Because of the wide variety of topics covered in this book, we called upon many experts for whose insight on recent developments we are deeply grateful. We would like to thank them and their firms for allowing us to draw on their knowledge and resources, particularly Robin Gitman, Willis M. Allen Co. Realtors; Craig Gussin, CLU, Gussin and Auerbach, La Jolla; Scott Knudten, State Farm Insurance; Trevor Morris, The Seidler Companies; Mark Nussbaum, Paine Webber, Inc.; Pat Rupp, CFP, IDS, Inc.; Bill Shaffer, Waysys, Inc.; Jeanine Volinski, La Jolla Insurance Services; Barbara Walchli, First Interstate Capital Management, Scottsdale, AZ; Fred Weaver, Great Western Bank; Flora Weston, Coldwell Banker Realtors; and Lynn Yturri, Bank One Investment Management, Phoenix, AZ.

We would like to thank our colleagues at San Diego State University and Arizona State University for their expertise, encouragement, and support. Also, we want to thank Marlene G. Bellamy of Writeline Communication Associates for preparing the profiles and boxes and her assistance in research and writing, and for preparation of the Instructor's Manual. Thanks is also due Amy Balser Blumenthal for her assistance with box preparation. Our thanks also go to Melissa Beede and Karyn Williams of Arizona State University for the research and editorial help they provided throughout various parts of this book. We would also like to express our appreciation to Carlene Creviston for her review and assistance in revising the *Test Bank* and *Workbook*. Special mention is due to Pam Hively, Frances Grieshaber, Sheryl McMaster, and Liz Rogers for their outstanding assistance, particularly in keyboarding the manuscript.

The editorial staff of The Dryden Press has been most cooperative. We wish to thank Eddie Dawson, production manager, Jeanette Barber, art director, and Louise Kartkouli, art and literary rights editor. Special thanks go to Mike Reynolds, acquisitions editor, and Shana Lum, development editor, without whose support this revision would not have been as lively and contemporary in approach as we believe it is and whose expert management of the writing and reviewing of the text proved invaluable. We are also grateful to Jim Patterson, project editor, who ably assured the book's timely and accurate production.

Finally, our wives, Robin and Charlene, have provided needed support and understanding during the writing of this book. We are forever grateful to them.

Lawrence J. Gitman
La Jolla, California

Michael D. Joehnk
Scottsdale, Arizona

October 1995

About the Authors

Lawrence J. Gitman is a professor of finance at San Diego State University. He received his bachelor's degree from Purdue University, his M.B.A. from the University of Dayton, and his Ph.D. from the University of Cincinnati. Professor Gitman is a prolific textbook author and has over 40 articles appearing in *Financial Management,* the *Financial Review,* the *Journal of Financial Planning,* the *Journal of Risk and Insurance,* the *Journal of Financial Research, Financial Practice and Education,* the *Journal of Financial Education,* and other publications. He currently serves as an associate editor of *Journal of Financial Planning, Journal of Financial Education, and Financial Practice and Education.*

His major textbooks include *Principles of Managerial Finance,* Seventh Edition, *Foundations of Managerial Finance,* Fourth Edition, *The World of Business,* Second Edition, which is coauthored with Carl McDaniel, and *Fundamentals of Investing,* Sixth Edition, which is coauthored with Michael D. Joehnk. Gitman and Joehnk also wrote *Investment Fundamentals: A Guide to Becoming a Knowledgeable Investor,* which was selected as one of 1988's ten best personal finance books by *Money* magazine.

An active member of numerous professional organizations, Professor Gitman is past president of the Academy of Financial Services, the Midwest Finance Association, and the FMA National Honor Society. In addition, he is a Certified Financial Planner (CFP). Gitman currently serves as President of the San Diego Chapter of the Financial Executives Institute and as a Director of the San Diego MIT Enterprise Forum. He lives with his wife and two children in La Jolla, California, where he is an avid bicyclist.

Michael D. Joehnk is a professor of finance at Arizona State University. He received his bachelor's and Ph.D. degrees from the University of Arizona and his M.B.A. from Arizona State University. A Chartered Financial Analyst (CFA), he has served as a member of the Candidate Curriculum Committee and the Council of Examiners of the Institute of Chartered Financial Analysts. He has also served as a Director of the Phoenix Society of Financial Analysts, a vice-president of the Financial Management Association, and secretary-treasurer of the Western Finance Association. And in 1995, he was elected to another term as a vice-president of FMA.

Professor Joehnk is the author (or coauthor) of some 50 articles, five books, and numerous monographs. His articles have appeared in *Financial Management,* the *Journal of Finance,* the *Journal of Bank Research,* the *Journal of Portfolio Management,* the *Journal of Consumer Affairs,* the *Journal of Financial and Quantitative Analysis,* the *AAII Journal,* the *Journal of Financial Research,* the *Bell Journal of Economics,* the *Daily Bond Buyer, Financial Planner,* and other publications. In addition to coauthoring several books with Lawrence J. Gitman, Professor Joehnk is the author of a highly successful paperback trade book, *Investing for Safety's Sake.* In addition, Dr. Joehnk was the editor of *Institutional Asset Allocation,* which was sponsored by the Institute of Chartered Financial Analysts and published by Dow Jones-Irwin. He also is a contributor to the *Handbook for Fixed Income Securities,* and *Investing and Risk Management*—Vol. 1 of the Library of Investment Banking; and he recently completed a 6-year term as executive co-editor of the *Journal of Financial Research.* He and his wife live in Scottsdale, Arizona, where they enjoy collecting Southwestern art.

Brief Contents

Contents

PART 5 *Managing Investments* 433

FOUNDATIONS OF FINANCIAL PLANNING

CHAPTER 1
UNDERSTANDING THE FINANCIAL PLANNING PROCESS

CHAPTER 2
YOUR FINANCIAL STATEMENTS AND PLANS

CHAPTER 3
MANAGING YOUR TAXES

CHAPTER 1

UNDERSTANDING THE FINANCIAL PLANNING PROCESS

Jo Ann's Good Start

Jo Ann Jones has big plans for the future. The 24-year-old graphic artist moved to Las Vegas, Nevada, in January 1994 because the area had many job opportunities. In a few years, she and a partner hope to use her design expertise and his computer knowledge to form their own company. Ideally, she'll buy a house in five years and retire by age 45. First, however, she wants to repay her debts as soon as possible—$16,000 in art school loans and $900 in credit card debt—and start an investment program.

To reach these personal financial goals, Jo Ann knows she has to manage her personal finances wisely and start investing soon so her money can grow. A personal finance class taught her the basics of money management and investments, and reading personal finance magazines like *Money* expands her knowledge. She learned the value of saving and investing firsthand when her dad was laid off in 1988. The stock he bought through his firm's payroll purchase plan provided the financial reserves the family needed until he found work. When she lost her job in September 1994, her savings gave her time to find a good job rather than taking the first offer.

To get a jump-start on her goals, Jo Ann has pared her living expenses to a minimum so she can pay off her loans and begin building for the future. "I'm very stingy about spending," she reports, "but eating out seems to be my weakness." She uses her monthly take-home pay of about $1,000 for housing and food costs (shared

Learning Goals

LG1. *Identify the benefits of using personal financial planning techniques to manage your finances.*

LG2. *Define your major financial goals and describe the personal financial planning process that will help you achieve them.*

LG3. *Explain why personal financial plans must change according to your life situation.*

LG4. *Describe how government, business, and consumer actions and changing economic conditions affect personal financial plans.*

LG5. *Evaluate the impact of age, gender, race, education, marital status, geographic location, and career choice on personal income.*

LG6. *Recognize the importance of career planning and its relationship to personal financial planning.*

with a roommate), $400; school and credit card debt repayment, $400; investments and reserve fund, $150; and other expenses, $50. Health insurance coverage starts after six months at her new job. She has car insurance and a low-cost, $50,000 term life insurance policy but no renter's coverage. Once she has an emergency fund covering six months' expenses in the bank, she'll look into certificates of deposit and mutual funds. She plans to buy stocks at this early stage, to earn a higher rate of return, and eventually add bonds. Right now she is learning how to select investments that meet her needs, to be ready when she has the funds.

Jo Ann realizes that owning her own business also takes good career planning. She learns the latest computer graphics programs and techniques at work and home. This makes her a more valuable employee and also leads to freelance opportunities that, coupled with savings, would provide for living expenses during the venture's start-up phase.

Establishing good personal financial planning habits when she is young gets Jo Ann off to a good start. Although she may have to adapt her plans if she gets married and has children, she now has a game plan to follow. "It's the only way to be financially independent," she says. "I don't want to work for someone else for the rest of my life; I want to enjoy life and let my money work for me." As you will see in the following chapters, personal financial planning provides the best tools to achieve Jo Ann's— and your— dreams.

THE REWARDS OF SOUND FINANCIAL PLANNING

LG1

A person's standard of living and patterns of consumption are related and can profoundly affect the accumulation of wealth. If your primary financial goal is to achieve maximum wealth accumulation, what kind of standard of living and consumption patterns would you exhibit? Before reading on, take a few moments to consider the tradeoffs among standard of living, consumption, and wealth accumulation.

We live in a complex, fast-paced world with rapidly changing social, economic, political, and technological environments. Developing personal strategies to improve our lifestyles becomes increasingly difficult, and we are faced with a bewildering array of choices—where to live, what career to follow, what car to buy, when to change jobs, how much to save or invest, to name just a few. Before we can evaluate our options and make informed decisions, we all need to set goals to give direction to our lives. As we move toward the twenty-first century, many of the financial goals our parents took for granted—home ownership, a college education, job security, building a substantial nest egg for retirement—are becoming harder to obtain. As a result, two incomes may be required to maintain an acceptable standard of living, and it may take longer to be able to afford a home.

Setting goals is extremely important in personal money management. Even if we're managing our personal finances pretty well today, we worry about the future. We want to maintain and improve our current lifestyle and also prepare for the future so we can send our children to college and have funds to retire comfortably.

The best way to achieve these and other financial objectives is through *personal financial planning*. It helps us define our short- and long-term financial goals and develop appropriate financial strategies to reach them. However, today's complex financial environment and volatile economy can be intimidating. And we can no longer depend on employee or government benefits like steady salary increases or enough funding from employer-paid pensions or social security to retire comfortably. We must plan our own financial security—a daunting task, indeed—but may not know where to start. The goal of this book is to take the mystery out of the personal financial planning process and provide the tools you need to take charge of your personal finances.

Because needs and goals change as personal circumstances change, personal financial planning is a lifelong activity. As you will learn, creating flexible plans and revising them on a regular basis is the key to building a sound financial future. Of course, planning alone does not guarantee success, but if used effectively and consistently, it can help you control your life and use your resources wisely. As a result, it will have a profound effect on your standard of living, consumption patterns, and ultimately, the amount of your accumulated wealth.

IMPROVING YOUR STANDARD OF LIVING

One of the major benefits of personal financial planning is that is helps us to acquire, use, and control our financial resources more efficiently. In essence, it allows us to gain more enjoyment from our income and thus improve our **standard of living**—the necessities, comforts, and luxuries we have or desire. The quality of our lives is, for most of us, closely tied to our standard of living. The presence or absence of certain material items—such as a home, cars, and jewelry—is commonly associated with quality of life. Large, expensive, or "fancy" items, for example, are viewed as components of a high standard of living. Having money for entertainment, health, education, art, music, and travel also contributes to the quality of life. Although many other factors—geographical location, public facilities, local cost of living, pollution, traffic, and population density—also affect the quality of an individual's life, wealth is commonly viewed as its primary determinant. Of course, many so-called wealthy people live "plain" lives, choosing to save or invest their money rather than spend it on luxuries and frills. Even so, their quality of life is probably no lower than that of a more flamboyant consumer.

One trend that has had a profound effect on our standard of living is the *two-income family*. What was relatively rare in the early 1970s has become commonplace today, and, in the process, the incomes of millions of families have risen sharply. Granted, two incomes increase the things we can afford to buy, but they also carry with them greater responsibilities for managing money wisely and coordinating the partners' financial and career goals and plans. This is where personal financial planning comes in: By carefully planning future purchases and financial activities, people can set goals consistent with their desired quality of life.

DETERMINING YOUR CONSUMPTION PATTERNS

Spending money more wisely is another payoff of financial planning. Basically, such planning gives you a better idea of what you should do with the money you make. Given a certain level of income, you can either spend it now or save a portion of it for future consumption. Determining both your current and future **consumption** patterns is an important part of the personal money management process. The goal, of course, is to plan how to spend your money to get the most satisfaction from your income dollar.

Current Consumption. Your current level of consumption is based on the necessities of life and your average propensity to consume. A minimum level of consumption would allow you to obtain only the **necessities of life:** food, clothing, and shelter. Although the quantity and types of food, clothing, and shelter purchased may differ among individuals depending on their wealth, some amount of these items is essential for survival. **Average propensity to consume** refers to the percentage of each dollar of income that is spent, on average, for current consumption rather than saved. People exhibiting high average propensities to consume may do so because their income is low and they must spend a large portion of it just for basic necessities. On the other hand, there are many "ultra consumers" who choose to splurge on a few items and scrimp elsewhere. Clearly these people also exhibit high average propensities to consume. Conversely, individuals earning large amounts quite often have low average propensities to consume, because the cost of necessities represents only a small proportion of their income. Still, it is not unusual to find two people with significantly different incomes but the same average propensity to consume due to differences in standard of living. The person making more money may believe it is essential to buy better-quality and/or more items and thus on average spend the same percentage of each dollar of income as the person making far less.

Future Consumption. In any carefully developed financial plan, a portion of current income will be set aside for deferred, or future, consumption. For example, we may want to put money aside to build up a retirement fund so that we can maintain a desirable standard of living in our later years. In this case, we fully intend to spend the money put aside, but not until we retire. Thus, we are deferring actual consumption to some time in the future. Other examples of deferred consumption include saving for a child's education, a primary residence or vacation home, a major acquisition (like a car or home entertainment center), or even a vacation. The money put aside for such deferred consumption is placed in various savings and/or investment vehicles to generate a return over the time it is held. The portion of our current income committed to future consumption will be a function of the amount of money we earn on the one hand and our level of current spending on the other. The more we earn and/or the less we devote to current consumption, the more we can commit to meeting future consumption needs. In any case, *some* portion of current income should be set aside *regularly* for future consumption purposes—this creates good saving habits.

ACCUMULATING WEALTH

A certain portion of current income is used to meet the everyday *expenses* of living: Food, clothing, insurance, utilities, entertainment, and so on. Another part is used to acquire *assets,* such as cars, a home, or stocks and bonds. For the most part, it

standard of living The necessities, comforts, and luxuries enjoyed or aspired to by an individual or group.

consumption The using up of goods or services in the satisfaction of wants.

necessities of life Items that are needed for survival—food, clothing, and shelter.

average propensity to consume The percentage of each dollar of income that a person spends, on average, for current consumption.

is our assets that determine how wealthy we are. Personal financial planning plays a critical role in the accumulation of wealth, as it helps us direct our financial resources to the most productive areas.

As a rule, a person's **wealth** at any point in time is a function of the total value of all the items he or she owns. Wealth consists of financial and tangible assets. **Financial assets** are intangible, paper assets, such as savings accounts and securities (stocks, bonds, mutual funds, and so forth). They are earning assets that are held for the returns they promise. **Tangible assets,** in contrast, are physical assets, such as real estate, that can be held for either consumption (like your home, car, artwork or jewelry) or investment purposes (like the duplex you bought for rental purposes). In general, the goal of most people is to accumulate as much wealth as possible while maintaining current consumption at a level that provides a desired standard of living.

Concept Check

1-1. What is a standard of living? What are the factors that affect quality of life?

1-2. Are consumption patterns related to quality of life? Explain.

1-3. What is average propensity to consume? Is it possible for two people with very different incomes to have the same average propensity to consume?

1-4. Discuss the various forms in which wealth can be accumulated.

PERSONAL FINANCIAL PLANNING

LG2

Assume that you have decided to take charge of your financial future through personal financial planning. Once you establish your financial goals, in what specific areas will you need to develop plans? Try to answer this question before reading on.

Personal financial planning is the key to achieving financial goals. No one is exempt from the need to develop personal financial plans—neither new college graduates, nor the growing number of single, mobile, urban professionals, nor single parents, midcareer married breadwinners, nor senior-level corporate executives. Knowing what you hope to accomplish financially and how you intend to do it clearly gives you an edge over someone who merely reacts to financial events as they unfold. For example, purchasing a new car immediately after graduation may be an important goal for you. Evaluating and possibly arranging financing before your shopping trip—as opposed to simply accepting the financing arrangement offered by an auto dealer—might save you a considerable amount of money. Moreover, because some dealers advertise low-interest loans but then charge higher prices for their cars, knowing all your costs in advance can help you identify the best deal. For most people, buying a car is a major expenditure involving a substantial up-front cash outlay. It also usually results in additional consumer debt to repay over time. Therefore, it warrants careful planning. Likewise, using personal financial planning concepts to reach other goals will bring similar positive benefits.

DEFINING YOUR FINANCIAL GOALS

What are your **financial goals?** Have you spelled them out, at least over the short run? The fact is, without financial goals it is difficult, if not impossible, to effectively manage your financial resources. We all need to know where we are going, in a financial sense, in order to direct the major financial events in our lives. Perhaps achieving financial independence at a relatively early age is important to you. If so, then things like saving, investing, and retirement planning will become an important part of your life. Whatever your financial goals or preferences, they must be stated in monetary terms, because money, and the *utility* (defined later) it buys, is an integral part of financial planning.

The Role of Money. **Money** is the common denominator by which all financial transactions are gauged. It is the medium of exchange used as a measure of value in our economy. Without the standard unit of exchange provided by the dollar, it would be difficult to set specific personal financial goals and to measure progress in achieving them. Money, as we know it today, is therefore the key consideration in establishing *financial* goals. Yet it is not money as such that most people want.

Rather, it is the utility that money makes possible. **Utility** refers to the amount of satisfaction a person receives from purchasing certain types or quantities of goods and services. Often the utility or satisfaction provided, rather than the cost, is the overriding factor in the choice between two items of differing price. A special feature may provide additional utility in one item, causing it to be the preferred one. For example, many people prefer to pay more to buy a car with a CD player rather than buy one with a "standard" cassette player. The added utility may result from the actual usefulness of the special feature, from the "status" it is expected to provide, or both. Regardless, different people receive varying levels of satisfaction from similar items that are not necessarily related to the cost of the items. When evaluating alternative qualities of life, consumption patterns, and forms of wealth accumulation, it is clear, therefore, that utility should be considered along with cost.

The Psychology of Money. Money and its utility are not only economic concepts, but are also closely linked to the psychological concepts of values, emotion, and personality. Your personal *value system*—the ideals and beliefs you hold important and use to guide your life—will also shape your attitudes toward money and wealth accumulation. If status and image are important to you, you may spend a high proportion of your current income to acquire luxuries. If you place a high value on family life, you may choose a career that offers regular hours and less stress or an employer with "flextime" rather than a higher-paying position requiring travel and lots of overtime. Clearly, your financial goals and decisions should be consistent with your values. Identifying your values allows you to formulate financial plans that provide greater personal satisfaction and quality of life.

People react differently to similar situations involving money. Depending upon timing and circumstances, emotional responses to money may be positive—such as love, happiness, and security—or negative—such as fear, greed, and insecurity. For example, some people, upon receipt of a paycheck, feel satisfaction in their work. Others feel relief in knowing that they can pay past-due bills. Still others worry over what to do with the money. In a survey on "Americans and Their Money," published in the June 1994 issue of *Worth* magazine, making the wrong investment choice ranked first in terms of causing anxiety. Money means different things to different people. For some, saving money for financial security is a high priority—security was important to 74 percent of *Worth* respondents—while others place greater emphasis on spending for pleasure (23 percent of those surveyed) or money as power (15 percent).

Money is a primary motivator of personal behavior. It has a strong effect on one's self-image. Therefore, each individual's unique personality and emotional makeup determine the importance and role of money in her or his life. You should become aware of your own attitudes toward money because they are the basis of your "money personality" and management style. Some questions to ask yourself are: How important is money to you? Why? What types of spending give you satisfaction? Are you a risk taker? Do you need large financial reserves to feel secure? Such an understanding is a prerequisite to the development of realistic and effective financial goals and plans. For example, if you are a person who prefers immediate satisfaction, you will find it more difficult to achieve long-term net worth or savings goals than if you

wealth The total value of all items owned by an individual, such as bank accounts, stocks, bonds, home, and automobiles.

financial assets Intangible assets, such as savings accounts and securities, that are acquired for some promised future return.

tangible assets Physical assets, such as real estate and automobiles, that can be held for either consumption or investment purposes.

personal financial planning Planning that covers the key elements of an individual's financial affairs and is aimed at achievement of his or her financial goals.

financial goals Short- and long-term results that an individual wants to attain, such as controlling living expenses, managing one's tax burden, establishing savings and investment programs, and meeting retirement needs.

money The medium of exchange used as a measure of value in financial transactions.

utility The amount of satisfaction an individual receives from purchasing certain types or quantities of goods and services.

are highly disciplined and primarily concerned with achieving a comfortable retirement at an early age. Clearly, tradeoffs between current and future benefits are strongly affected by values, emotion, and personality.

While this textbook emphasizes a rational, unemotional approach to personal financial planning, it is important to recognize that universally applicable financial plans do not exist. Every financial plan must not only consider the individual's wants, needs, and financial resources, but must also *realistically reflect* his or her personality and emotional reactions to money. Conflicts between personality, goals, and values must be resolved early in the planning process. Obviously, plans requiring high levels of annual savings to achieve future consumption goals will be inconsistent with a highly indulgent personality fueled by a need to consume. In this case, goals will have to be moderated to achieve an acceptable balance between current and future consumption. In all cases, a key to effective personal financial planning is a *realistic* understanding of the role of money and its utility in the individual's life. Effective financial plans are both economically and psychologically sound.

Money and Relationships. Money is one of the most emotional issues in any relationship. It is also one of the hardest subjects to discuss. Most people are uncomfortable doing so and therefore avoid talking about money matters, even with their partners. However, differing opinions of how a family's money should be spent can threaten the stability of a marriage or cause many arguments between parents and children. Learning to communicate about money with your partner and/or children is, therefore, a critical step in developing effective financial plans.

As we noted earlier, there are many distinct money personality types. One person may be analytical and see money as a means of control, another may view it as a way to express affection, and yet another may use it to boost his or her self-esteem. When couples have very different attitudes toward money—for example, if one person likes to prepare detailed budgets but the other is an impulse shopper—conflicts are bound to arise. The *Issues in Money Management* box on page 9 discusses how money attitudes affect relationships and provides a quiz to compare your money attitudes to your partner's.

The best way to resolve money disputes is to be aware of your partner's financial style, keep the lines of communication open, and be willing to compromise. It's highly unlikely that you can change your partner's style—or your own, for that matter—but you can work out your differences. Financial planning is an especially important part of the process of resolving conflict. You will gain a better understanding of your differences by working together to establish a set of financial goals that take into account each person's needs and values. For instance, you may be a risk taker who likes to speculate in the stock market, while your cautious partner believes that all your money should go into a savings account in case one of you loses your job. If you can agree on the amount of money you should have readily available in low-risk investments and savings accounts, you can then allocate a specific portion of your funds to riskier investments.

TYPES OF FINANCIAL GOALS

Financial goals cover a wide range of financial desires—from controlling living expenses to meeting retirement needs, from setting up a savings and investment program to minimizing the amount of taxes you pay. In the *Worth* survey cited earlier, participants considered the following four financial goals the most important: having enough money to live as well as possible now (37 percent of respondents), being financially independent (33 percent), sending children to college (31 percent), and providing for retirement (28 percent).

Your financial goals should be defined as *specifically* as possible and focus on the *results* you want to attain. Simply saying you want to save money next year is not a specific goal. How much do you want to save, and for what purpose? Formulating a goal such as "save 10 percent of my take-home pay each month to start an investment program" clearly states what you want to do and why.

Equally important, as mentioned earlier, your goals should be *realistically attainable,* because they form the basis on which your financial plans are established. If you set your savings goals too high—for example, 25 percent when your basic living expenses already account for 85 percent of your take-home pay—the goal becomes unattainable. If set too low, you may not accumulate enough funds

Issues in Money Management

Money Matters Can Make or Break a Relationship

Money—it's a loaded topic for today's couples. It gets to the very essence of how we view ourselves, bringing up issues like independence, power, security, and control. The increase in two-income households focuses greater attention on how money affects relationships. No longer is the man the sole wage earner who controls the family's finances. Typically, the more income a woman makes, the more input she wants in financial decision making. This can result in power struggles between partners, who may have very different money personalities. A *Worth* magazine survey of 2,000 Americans listed money as the number one source of fights between partners. And 89 percent rated compatibility in money values as essential or important to a successful relationship. When relationships end, money often represents loss of love and becomes a means of revenge.

Psychotherapists who work with couples find that partners who get along in most other areas often have major differences in attitudes toward money. A new breed of "financial psychology" specialists is trying to help couples resolve their money issues—issues that are likely to indicate deeper problems in the relationship. Take two major issues—independence and intimacy. Some people equate pooled bank accounts and joint financial decision making with intimacy; others may feel they signal loss of self. Kathleen Gurney, a pioneer in the field, warns against following the "opposites attract" maxim when it comes to money matters. She defines nine money personality types, some combinations of which spell disaster for couples—for example, pairing a "power/control baron" with a "compromiser." She advises couples to use her 28-question "Moneymax Profile" to evaluate their potential money compatibility. Here's a brief version that can help you and your partner compare money attitudes.

1. I am concerned that the financial and investment decisions I make are right for me.
2. I can't resist spending money whenever I have some.
3. I feel better if I am in charge of the money management.
4. I wish I were more confident in managing money and investments.
5. I wish I were more rational and less emotional in my use of money.
6. I prefer staying in charge of money and investments.

According to Gurney, questions 1 and 4 indicate whether you are confident or anxious about making financial decisions. Questions 2 and 5 deal with emotional versus rational spending habits, while questions 3 and 6 relate to the desire to control money decisions versus the ability to share or delegate money management. Taking this quiz won't give you all the answers, but it can start you on the road to a sound financial partnership.

Sources: Donald Katz, "The Last Taboo: Men, Women, and Money," *Worth*, June 1993, pp. 55-61; Louis Rukeyser, Tribune Media Services, Inc.; and Robert Sullivan, "Americans and Their Money," *Worth*, June 1994, pp. 60-61, 69.

for a meaningful investment program. Clearly, if the goals are little more than "pipe dreams," the integrity of the financial plans may be suspect as well (not to mention a possible source of frustration). Finally, financial goals should be ranked in order of priority and set with a definite time frame in mind—are they short-term goals, such as saving for a vacation, to be attained within the next year or long-term goals, such as purchasing a vacation home, not to be realized for many more years?

Worksheet 1.1 lists many different types of financial goals and provides a convenient way to summarize your own. It is not intended to be an exhaustive inventory of each and every kind of personal financial objective. Rather it represents some of the more common and important types of financial goals. Some individuals certainly could have other, more personal or more detailed goals in addition to those listed. Also, it is highly unlikely that anyone at any given point in time would be pursuing all of the listed goals at once. Instead, as we go through life, we'll find that some financial goals become more important than others. You will want to develop a set of personal financial goals that is meaningful to you at this particular stage of your life.

WORKSHEET 1.1

A Summary of Personal Financial Goals

It is important to set financial objectives carefully. They must be realistically attainable, because they are the basis for financial planning.

PERSONAL FINANCIAL GOALS

Name(s) ______________________ **Date** ______________

Type of Financial Goal	Brief Description	Degree of Priority (High, Medium, or Low)	Target Date	Cost
Increase income				
Gain control over living expenses				
Have more money left over for discretionary/entertainment purchases				
Set up an education fund for yourself, your spouse, and/or your children				
Establish an emergency fund to meet unexpected expenses				
Implement procedures to keep your tax burden to a minimum				
Put money aside for a home, car, and/or other major expenditures				
Pay off/reduce personal debt; reduce monthly debt service requirements				
Provide adequate protection against personal risk—life, disability, health, property, and liability insurance				
Start a general savings/investment program to accumulate capital and achieve financial security				
Start your own business				
Set up a retirement fund to supplement social security and employer-sponsored retirement programs				
Maximize the disposition/transfer of estate to heirs				
Other personal financial objectives and goals:				

THE PERSONAL FINANCIAL PLANNING PROCESS

How will you achieve the financial goals you set for yourself? The answer, of course, lies in the financial plans that you establish. Financial plans provide the direction necessary to achieve your objectives. The planning process, which results in a set of different yet interrelated plans, involves identifying your personal needs, evaluating your current situation, and setting realistic goals. Then you can develop and implement financial plans with specific strategies to achieve your goals. Periodically you must assess and revise your goals and plans to account for life-situation changes. Creating your financial plans requires a basic understanding of personal financial statements, budgets, and taxes (presented in Chapters 2 and 3, respectively).

Financial plans cover the most important financial dimensions of your life. Some deal with the more immediate aspects of money management, such as preparing budgets to help manage spending. Others focus on acquiring major assets such as a car or home. Liability plans control borrowing, insurance plans reduce financial risks, savings and investment plans provide for emergency funds and future wealth accumulation. An employee benefit plan will help you take advantage of and manage your employer-sponsored benefits and coordinate them with your other financial arrangements, and tax plans to minimize tax payments. You also need retirement plans to provide financial security when you stop working and estate plans to ensure the orderly and cost-effective transfer of assets to your heirs.

Concept Check

1-5. What is the role of money in setting financial plans? What is the relationship of money to utility?

1-6. Explain why financial plans must be psychologically as well as economically sound. What is the best way to resolve money disputes in a relationship?

1-7. Identify three financial goals that are important to you now. Why is it important to set realistically attainable financial goals? Explain using examples of realistic and unrealistic personal financial goals. Select one of your personal financial goals and develop a brief financial plan to reach it.

1-8. What types of financial planning concerns does a complete set of financial plans cover?

A LIFETIME OF PLANNING

LG3

To remain meaningful, your personal and financial goals and the plans you create to reach them must be revised to reflect changes in your life. How would you expect your current financial goals and plans to differ in five years, and why? Consider these questions briefly before you continue.

Financial planning is a dynamic process. As you move through different stages of your life, your needs and goals will change. While certain financial goals are important regardless of age—having extra resources to fall back on in an economic downturn should be a priority whether you are 25, 45, or 65—your goals and plans at each stage of life will vary based on your particular circumstances. Some of these changes—job changes, marriage, children, moving to a new area—may be part of your original plan. However, more often than not, you will face unexpected "financial shocks" during your life: loss of a job, divorce or death of a spouse, a long illness, or the need to support adult children or aging parents. These and other changing life situations make sound financial planning more important than ever. With careful planning you can get through tough times and prosper in good times. To cope with life's financial shocks, you need to plan ahead and take steps—for example, setting up an emergency fund or reducing monthly expenses—that will protect you and your family financially if a setback occurs.

The Life Cycle of Financial Plans. As we move from childhood to retirement age, we go through different life stages. Exhibit 1.1 illustrates the various components of a typical *financial planning life cycle* as it compares to these different life

EXHIBIT 1.1

The Personal Financial Planning Life Cycle

As people go through different stages in their lives, their income patterns change as do the types of financial plans they pursue.

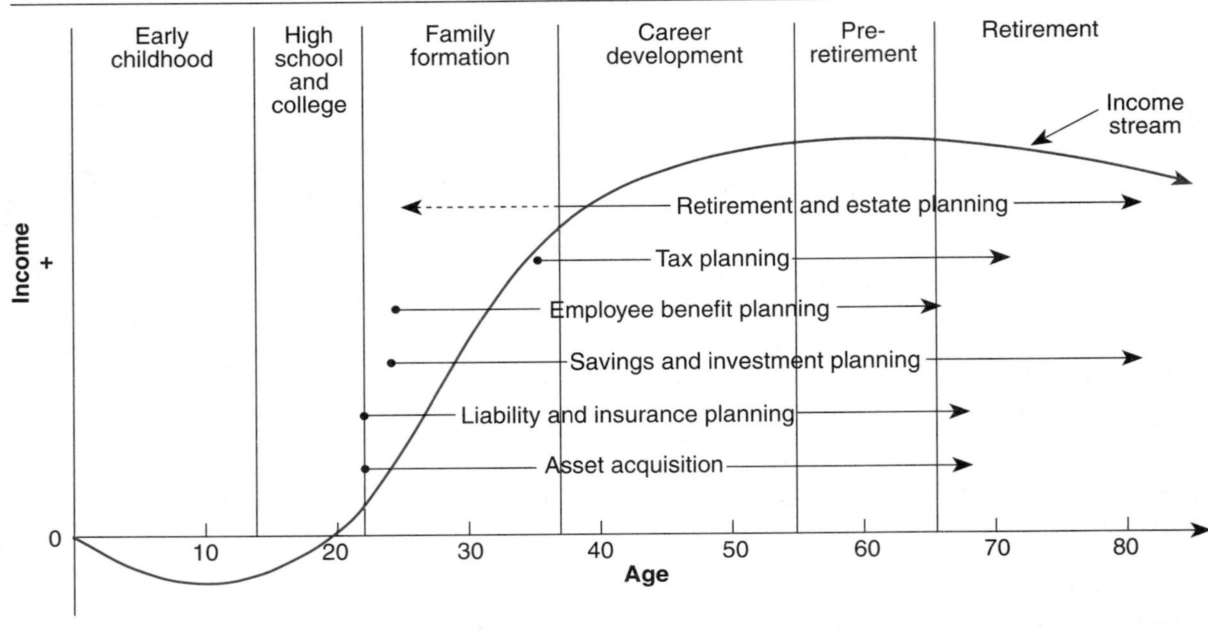

stages. It shows that as we pass from one state of maturation to the next, our patterns of income change simultaneously. From our early childhood days, when we relied on our parents for support, to our early adulthood, when we started our families and, very likely, held our first "real" jobs, we can see a noticeable change in income pattern. First, the negative income—in the form of reliance on our parents for money—is eventually replaced with a rapidly increasing positive stream of earnings as we embark on our chosen careers. Then, as we move from career development to preretirement years, our income becomes more stable. Finally, our income begins to trail off (ideally, only a bit) as we enter our retirement years. Thus, as our emphasis in life changes, so do the kinds of financial plans we pursue—that is, at various points in our lives, different types of financial goals and plans become more important than others.

Obviously, not everyone follows these typical patterns, and each life situation needs its own financial goals and plans. Today, many people in their 20s are waiting to marry and have children, focusing on their careers and building a financial base. Controlling expenses, managing credit, and saving for a new car may be goals when you are 25 and single. They may also be important goals for people in their 40s and 50s who lose their jobs due to corporate downsizing or early retirement and must cope with reduced income. New career strategies—planned and unplanned job changes, several different careers over a lifetime, for example—are common and may require revising financial plans. Families of women who interrupt their careers to stay home with their children, whether for six months or six years, need to plan for periods of reduced income.

A divorce or the death of a spouse can drastically change one's financial circumstances. Divorce can severely reduce the household income for one or both parties. Remarriage often involves a special type of financial plan, the prenuptial agreement, that spells out the disposition of assets each person brings into the marriage in case of divorce or death. Remarried couples may have children from their prior marriages and may start second

EXHIBIT 1.2

Life Cycle Financial Data

The finances of those in different stages of the life cycle vary. Income tends to increase and then decline over the life cycle, while home ownership and other assets tend to increase. Debts tend to increase and then taper off over the life cycle.

Age of Family Head	Average Household Income	Percent Who Own Home	Median Equity in Home	Median Value of Other Major Assets[1]	Median Debt Level[2]
Under 35	$33,800	37.0%	$17,000	$119,800	$26,300
35-44	52,300	64.1	36,000	186,500	39,100
45-54	62,100	75.5	53,000	324,100	64,200
55-64	55,200	77.9	57,000	348,300	46,600
65-74	34,600	78.9	53,000	342,600	27,900
75 and over	27,300	76.7	55,000	363,900	18,800

[1]Includes financial assets (bank accounts, CDs, and investment portfolios) plus other personal assets such as cars, business ownership, investment real estate.

[2]Excluding mortgage debt on principal residence.

Source: Arthur Kennickell and Martha Starr-McCluer, "Changes in Family Finances from 1989 to 1992: Evidence from the Survey of Consumer Finances," *Federal Reserve Bulletin*, Board of Governors of the Federal Reserve System, Washington, D.C., October 1994, pp. 863, 869, 873, 877.

families—situations that require revised financial goals and plans. Many people in their 30s, 40s, and 50s find themselves in the "sandwich generation," supporting their elderly parents while they are still raising their children and paying for college.

These and other changing life situations make sound financial planning more important than ever in the 1990s. Careful planning makes it possible to get through tough times and prosper in good times. Some financial goals are important regardless of age. For example, having a reservoir of funds to draw on in an emergency is an important and appropriate goal for all ages. Of course, other goals and plans at each stage of life will be based on your particular circumstances.

Exhibit 1.2 summarizes data that demonstrate life cycle differences in the finances of various age groups. Income tends to increase, then decline over the life cycle; home ownership and other assets tend to increase; debts tend to increase and then decline. Clearly those in the 45–64 age range tend to have more income and debts than those persons below age 45 and above and including age 65.

PLANS TO ACHIEVE YOUR FINANCIAL GOALS

As discussed earlier, financial goals can range from short-term goals like saving for a new stereo to long-term objectives such as saving enough to start your own business. Reaching your particular goals requires different types of financial plans. Let's take a brief look at what each major plan category includes.

Asset Acquisition Planning. One of the first categories of financial planning we typically encounter is asset acquisition. We accumulate *assets*—things we own—throughout our lives. These include *liquid assets* (cash, savings accounts, and money market funds) used for everyday expenses, *investments* (assets such as stocks, bonds, and mutual funds acquired to earn a return), *personal property* (movable property such as automobiles, household furnishings, appliances, clothing, jewelry, home electronics, and similar items), and *real property* (immovable property; land and anything fixed to it, such as a house). Chapters 4 and 5 focus on important considerations with regard to acquiring liquid assets and major assets such as housing and automobiles.

Liability and Insurance Planning. Another category of financial planning is liability planning. A *liability* is something we owe and is represented by the amount of debt we have incurred. We create liabilities by borrowing money. By the time most of us graduate from college, we have debts of some sort—education loans, car loans, credit card balances, and so on. Our borrowing needs typically increase as we acquire other assets—a home, furnishings, and appliances. Regardless of the source of credit, such transactions have one thing in common: *The debt must be repaid at some future time.* Using credit effectively requires careful planning and is the topic of Chapters 6 and 7. As we will see, how we manage our debt burden is just as important as how we manage our assets.

Obtaining adequate *insurance coverage* is also essential. Like borrowing money, it is generally something that is introduced at a relatively early point in our life cycle (usually early in the family formation stage). Insurance provides a means of reducing financial risk and protecting both income (life, health, and disability insurance) and assets (property and liability insurance). Most consumers regard insurance as absolutely essential—and for good reason. One serious illness or accident can wipe out everything that one has accumulated over years of hard work. However, overinsuring or misinsuring can be costly too. The appropriate types and amounts of insurance coverage are examined in Chapters 8, 9, and 10.

Planning Your Savings and Investment Programs. As your income begins to increase, so does the importance of savings and investment planning. People *save* initially in order to establish an emergency fund for meeting unexpected expenses. Eventually, however, they devote greater attention to *investing* excess income as a means of accumulating wealth, either for retirement or for major expenditures such as a child's college education. Wealth may be acquired through savings and subsequent investing of funds in various investment media—common or preferred stocks, government or corporate bonds, mutual funds, real estate, and so on. Success is determined by how profitably excess funds are invested.

The impact of alternative rates of return on accumulated wealth is illustrated in Exhibit 1.3. It shows that if you had $1,000 today and could keep it invested at 8 percent, you would accumulate a considerable sum of money over time. For example, at the end of 40 years you would have $21,725 from your original $1,000. Earning a higher rate of return has even greater rewards. Some might assume that earning, say, two percentage points more—that is, 10 rather than 8 percent—would not matter a great deal. But it certainly would! Note that if you could earn 10 percent over the 40 years, you would accumulate $45,259, or *more than twice as much* as what you would accumulate at 8 percent. Note also that *how long you invest* is just as important as *how much you earn* on your investments. As shown in Exhibit 1.3 with either rate of return, investing for 40 rather than 30 years results in more than two times as much accumulated capital. This is the magic of compound interest, which explains why it's so important to create strong savings and investment habits early in life. We will more fully examine savings in Chapter 4 and investments in Chapters 11, 12, and 13.

Employee Benefit Planning. Your employer may offer a wide variety of employee benefit plans, especially if you work for a large firm. These could include life, health, and disability insurance; tuition reimbursement programs for continuing education; pension and profit-sharing plans and 401(k) retirement plans; flexible spending accounts for child care and health care expenses; stock options; sick leave, personal time, and vacation days; and miscellaneous benefits such as employee discounts and subsidized meals or parking. (*Note:* Many of these plans will be more fully described in later chapters.)

Managing employee benefit plans and coordinating them with your other plans is an important part of the overall financial planning process. For example, benefits such as tax-deferred retirement plans and flexible spending accounts offer tax advantages; your contributions lower your taxable income. Some retirement plans allow you to borrow against them. Employer-sponsored insurance programs may need to be supplemented with personal policies. In addition, in today's volatile labor market, you can no longer assume that you will be working at the same company for many years. If you change jobs, your new company may not offer the same benefits. Your personal financial plans should include contingency plans to replace employer-provided benefits as required. We will discuss employee benefits in greater detail in Chapters 2 (planning); 3 (taxes); 8, 9, and 10 (insurance); and 14 (retirement).

Tax Planning. In spite of all the talk about tax reform and the sweeping tax revisions of 1986, 1993, and subsequent changes, our tax code remains highly complex. Some income is taxed as active (ordinary) income, some is treated as portfolio (investment) income, some is treated as passive income, some is tax free, and some is tax deferred. Then there are tax shelters, which use various aspects of the tax code (such as depreciation expenses) to legitimately reduce an investor's

EXHIBIT 1.3

How a $1,000 Investment Can Grow over Time

Differences in the rates of return earned on investments can have a dramatic impact on the amount of money you make from your investments, especially as the length of the investment period increases.

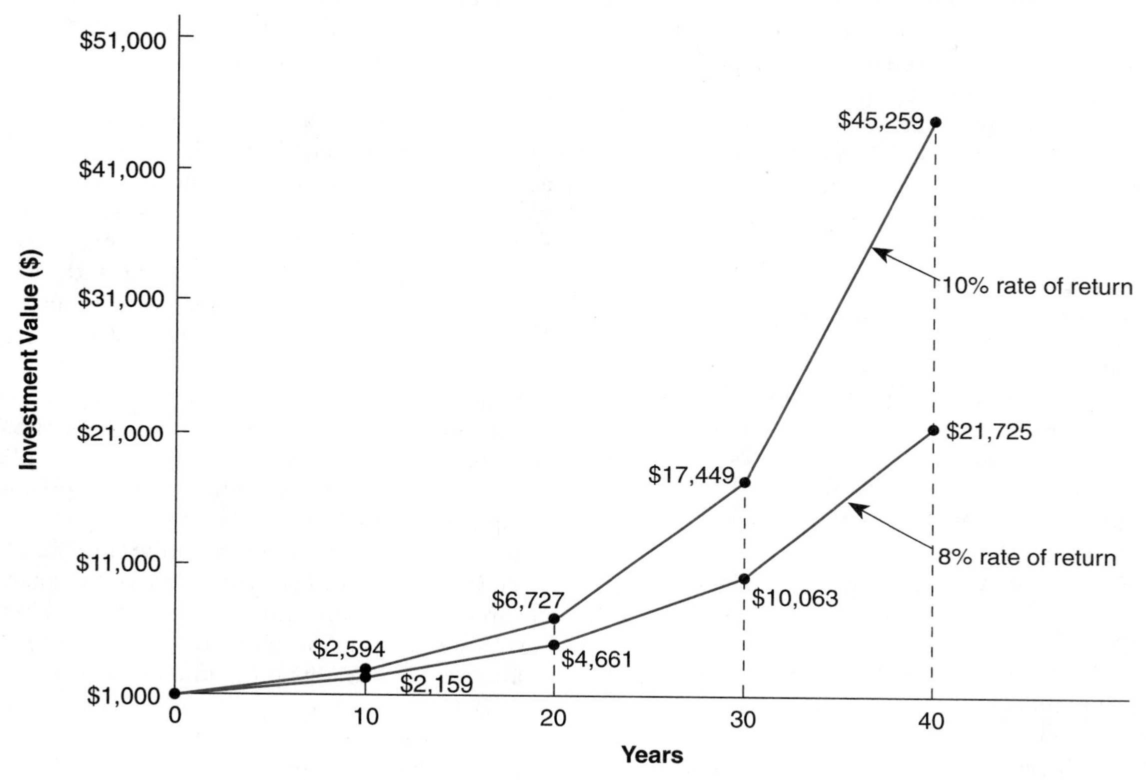

tax liability. *Tax planning* considers all these dimensions and more. It involves looking at an individual's current and projected earnings and developing strategies that will *defer* and/or *minimize taxes.* Tax plans should reflect the desired form in which returns are to be received—active income, portfolio income, passive income, capital gains, or tax-sheltered income. These plans are closely tied to investment plans and will often specify certain investment strategies. Although the use of tax planning is most common among individuals with high incomes, sizable savings can also result for people with lower levels of income. We will examine taxes and tax planning in Chapter 3.

Retirement and Estate Planning. While you are still working, you should be managing your finances to attain those goals you feel are important in old age. These might include extensive travel, plans for visiting children, dining out frequently at better restaurants, and perhaps a vacation home or boat. It is important to see that *retirement planning* begins long before you actually retire. As a rule, most people do not start thinking about retirement until well into their 40s or 50s. This is unfortunate, because it usually results in a *substantially reduced* level of retirement income. The sooner you start, the better off you will be. Take, for instance, the IRA (individual retirement account), in which certain wage earners are allowed to invest up to $2,000 per year. If you can earn 10 percent and put $2,000 per year in an IRA for 25 years (that is, start investing for retirement at age 40), your account will grow to $196,694. However, if you start your retirement program ten years earlier (at age 30), your IRA will grow to a whopping $542,049—even though you are investing a total of only $20,000 more ($2,000 per year for an extra ten years), your IRA will *nearly triple* in size. We will look at IRAs and other aspects of retirement planning in Chapter 14.

Accumulating assets to enjoy in retirement is only part of the long-run planning process. As people grow older, they eventually must consider how they can most effectively pass on their wealth to heirs—an activity called *estate planning*. We will examine this complex subject, which deals with such topics as wills, trusts, and the effects of gift, estate, and inheritance taxes, in Chapter 15.

THE PERSONAL COMPUTER IN FINANCIAL PLANNING

As it has in so many other aspects of our lives, the personal computer (PC) has found its way into financial planning. Indeed, financial planning is a natural application of the PC—what better way to handle all the number crunching involved in budgeting, tax planning, and investment management? These and other tasks include a good deal of time-consuming, analytical work and mathematical computations, all of which can be aided considerably by the personal computer.

A PC with personal finance software will dramatically reduce the time and effort needed to set up your financial plans and manage your money effectively. For example, a PC can be used to:

- Prepare detailed financial budgets and compare your monthly actual and budgeted figures.
- Prepare tax returns and perform complicated tax planning.
- Evaluate the financial benefits and costs of major purchases.
- Analyze borrowing alternatives.
- Keep a full inventory of all types of insurance coverage.
- Analyze the merits of various securities and investments.
- Track investment purchases and monitor the risk-and-return performance of a diversified investment portfolio.
- Evaluate alternative retirement plans and identify actions required to achieve a desired level of income at retirement.

Computer and software prices have dropped substantially in recent years, and reasonably sophisticated computer systems are quite affordable. In early 1995, you could buy a complete system (processor, hard disk, keyboard, and color monitor packaged with several software programs) for $1,500 to $2,000, depending on operating speed, amount of internal memory, and hard disk storage. Some packages also include a CD-ROM drive for multimedia capability. Printers range from about $250 to $450 for a good-quality inkjet model to $750 and up for a laser printer. A high-speed fax/modem, which allows you to transfer data and documents over telephone lines and provides access to many information and investment services, adds another $150. There are hundreds of reasonably-priced, "user-friendly" programs available for personal financial planning and money management. (See the *Smart Money* box in Chapter 2, page 70, for descriptions of some popular personal financial planning software.)

Just as the PC is widely used in the everyday world of financial planning, we believe it should be used in learning about personal financial planning. Accordingly, we will introduce the personal computer repeatedly throughout this book. In addition, a simple, menu-driven computer program has been developed for use with many of the analytical and computational procedures addressed in the text. Known as Financial Planning on the Personal Computer (FPPC), this program is written for IBM and IBM-compatible computers and is keyed to various sections of the textbook for use in performing many of the routine financial calculations and procedures presented. You will also find that the majority of the worksheets in the chapters can also be completed on FPPC. To help you recognize these sections, we have keyed the major text headings and selected end-of-chapter problems with the following symbol: FPPC

Concept Check

1-9. Discuss the relationship of life-cycle considerations to personal financial planning. What are some factors to consider when revising financial plans to reflect changes in a person's life cycle?

1-10. Mark Potter's investments over the past several years have not lived up to his full expectations. He is not really concerned, though, since the difference is only about two percentage points. Do you have any advice for Mark?

1-11. Describe employee benefit planning and tax planning. How do they fit into the financial planning framework?

1-12. There's no sense in worrying about retirement until you reach "middle age." Discuss this point of view.

1-13. What role can a personal computer play in personal financial planning?

THE PLANNING ENVIRONMENT

LG4

The financial planning environment is made up of a number of players and is affected by economic conditions and consumer prices. What effect do you think government, business, consumers, changing economic conditions, and consumer prices will have on your financial plans? Spend a few moments answering this question before reading on.

Financial planning is not carried out in isolation but in an economic environment created by the actions of business, government, and consumers. Your purchase, saving, investment, and retirement plans and decisions are influenced by both the present and future state of the economy. An understanding of the economic environment will thereby allow you to make better financial plans and decisions.

As an example, a strong economy can lead to big profits in the stock market, which can positively affect your investment and/or retirement programs. The economy can also affect the interest rates you pay on your mortgage and credit cards and those you earn on saving accounts and bonds. Periods of high inflation can lead to price increases that come so fast it is hard to make ends meet. It is important, therefore, to understand the environment in which you will carry out your financial plans and strategies. This section briefly looks at two key aspects of the planning environment: the major players in the environment and the economy.

THE PLAYERS

The financial planning environment contains various interrelated groups of players, each attempting to fulfill certain goals (see Exhibit 1.4). Although their objectives are not necessarily incompatible, they do impose some constraints on one another. There are three vital groups: the government, business, and consumers.

Government. The federal, state, and local governments provide us with many essential public goods and services, such as police and fire protection, national defense, highways, and health care. Government also plays a major role in establishing special policies that regulate business and consumers. The federal government plays a major role in regulating the level of economic activity, as discussed later in this chapter. In addition, government is a customer of business and an employer of consumers. As a result, it is a source of revenue for business and wages for consumers. The relationship between government and businesses and consumers is depicted in Exhibit 1.4. The two principal constraints from the perspective of personal financial planning are taxes and government regulations.

Taxation. The federal government levies taxes on income, state governments levy taxes on sales and income, and local governments levy taxes primarily on real estate and personal property. The largest tax bite for consumers is federal income taxes, which may take as much as 39.6 percent of earnings. These taxes are somewhat progressive, because (up to a point) the greater the taxable income, the higher the tax rate. Changes in tax rates and procedures will increase or decrease the amount of income consumers have to spend. Therefore, careful consideration should be given to the effects of taxes on personal money management activities. Due to the constraints of the tax structure and the potential magnitude of taxes, *financial decisions should be evaluated on an "after-tax" basis.* (Taxes are discussed in Chapter 3.)

Regulation. Federal, state, and local governments place many regulations on consumer- and citizen-related activities. Aimed at protecting the consumer from fraudulent and undesirable actions by sellers and lenders, these regulations require certain types of businesses to have licenses, maintain certain hygienic standards,

EXHIBIT 1.4

The Financial Planning Environment

Business, government, and consumers are the major participants in our economic system. They all interact with one another to produce the environment in which we carry out our financial plans.

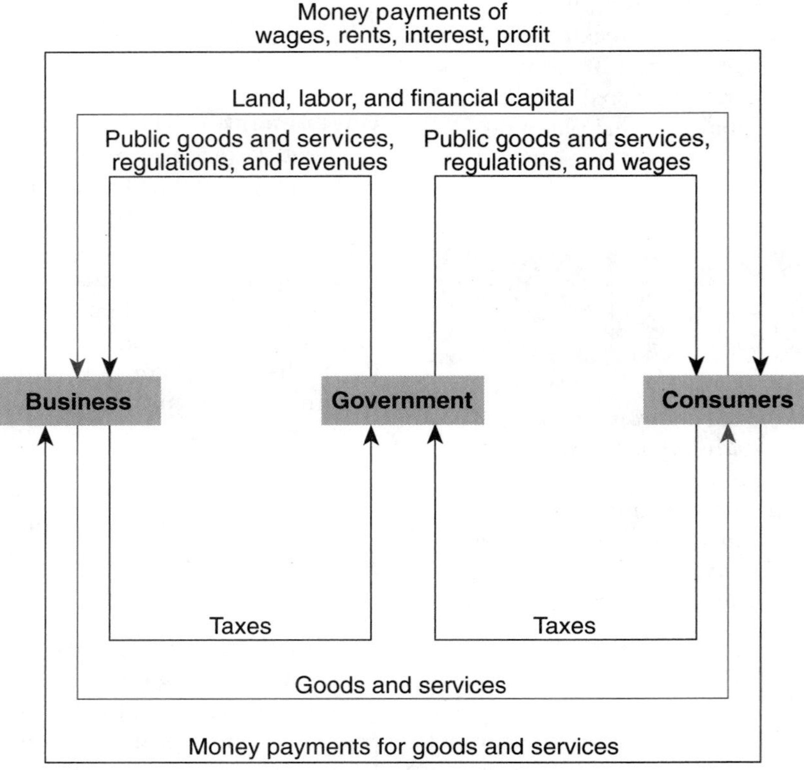

adequately disclose financial charges, and warrant their goods and services. Other laws protect sellers from adverse activities by consumers, for example, shoplifting and nonpayment for services rendered. Certainly, any decisions relating to achieving personal financial goals should take into consideration both the legal requirements that protect consumers and those that constrain their activities.

Business. As shown in Exhibit 1.4, business provides consumers with goods and services and in return receives payment in the form of money. To produce these goods and services, firms must hire labor and use land and capital (what economists refer to as *factors of production*). In return, firms pay out wages, rents, interest, and profits to the various factors of production. Thus, businesses are a key part of the circular flow of income that sustains our free enterprise system. In general, their presence creates a competitive environment in which consumers may select from an array of goods and services. There are, of course, certain industries, such as public utilities, in which the degree of competition or choice offered the consumer is limited, for economic reasons, by various regulatory bodies. As indicated in the preceding section, all businesses are limited in some way by federal, state, and/or local laws. An understanding of various business activities should permit consumers to make better purchases and help them determine with which firms to deal.

Consumers. The consumer is the central player in the financial planning environment. Consumer choices ultimately determine the kinds of goods and services businesses will provide. In addition, the consumer's choice of whether to spend or save has a direct impact on the present and future circular flows of income. A cutback in spending is usually associated with a decline in economic activity, while an increase helps the economy recover. Although consumers are often thought to have free choices in the marketplace, they must operate within an environment that interacts with government and business. While they can affect these parties through their elected officials and by their purchase actions, lobbyists and consumer groups are necessary for any real impact. The individual consumer should not expect to change government or business independently. As an *individual* consumer, you are best off accepting the existing environment and planning your transactions within it.

THE ECONOMY

Our economy is the result of interaction among government, business, and consumers, as well as the economic conditions in other nations. The government's goal is to regulate the economy and provide economic stability and high levels of employment through specific policy decisions. These government decisions have a major impact on the economic and financial planning environment. The federal government's *monetary policy,* programs for controlling the amount of money in circulation (the money supply), is used to stimulate or contract economic growth. For example, increases in the money supply tend to lower interest rates. This typically leads to a higher level of consumer and business borrowing—and spending—that increases overall economic activity. The reverse is also true. Reducing the money supply raises interest rates, thereby reducing consumer and business borrowing—and spending—and slowing economic activity.

The government's other principal tool for managing the economy is *fiscal policy,* its programs of taxation and spending. Increased spending for social services, education, defense, and other programs stimulates the economy while decreased spending slows economic activity. Increasing taxes, on the other hand, gives businesses and individuals less to spend and, as a result, negatively affects economic activity. Conversely, decreasing taxes stimulates the economy.

Economic Cycles. Although the government uses monetary and fiscal policy to regulate the economy and provide economic stability, the level of economic activity changes constantly. The upward and downward movement creates economic cycles (also called business cycles). These cycles vary in length and in how high or low the economy moves. An economic cycle typically contains four stages: **expansion, recession, depression,** and **recovery.** Exhibit 1.5 shows how each of these stages relates to employment and production levels, two key indicators of economic activity. The stronger the economy, the higher the levels of employment and production. Eventually a period of economic expansion will peak and begin to move downward, becoming a recession when the decline lasts more than six months. A depression occurs when a recession worsens to the point where economic activity is almost at a standstill. The recovery phase, with increasing levels of employment and production, follows either a recession or a depression. For more than 60 years, the government has been reasonably successful in keeping the economy out of a depression, although we have experienced periods of rapid expansion and high inflation followed by periods of deep recession.

Economic growth is measured by changes in the **gross domestic product (GDP),** the total of

expansion The phase of the economic cycle during which the levels of employment and economic activity/growth are both high; generally accompanied by rising prices for goods and services.

recession The phase of the economic cycle during which the levels of employment and economic activity/growth are both slowing down.

depression The phase of the economic cycle during which the employment level is low and economic activity and growth are at a virtual standstill.

recovery The phase of the economic cycle during which the employment level is improving and the economy is experiencing increased activity and growth.

gross domestic product (GDP) The total of all goods and services produced by workers located in a country; used to monitor economic growth.

EXHIBIT 1.5

The Economic Cycle

The economy goes through various stages over time, though real depressions are extremely rare. These stages tend to be cyclical and directly affect the levels of employment and production.

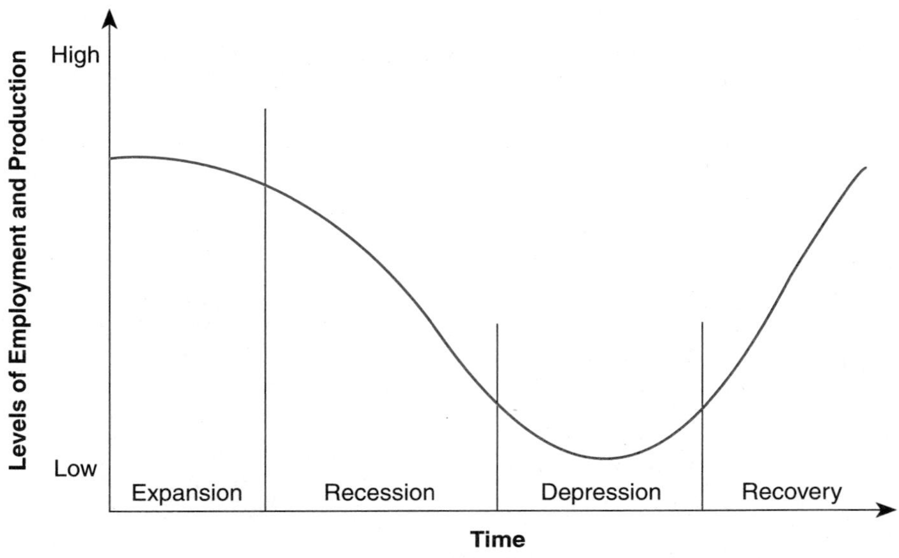

all goods and services produced by workers located within the country. The broadest measure of economic activity, it is reported quarterly and is used to compare trends in national output. A rising GDP means the economy is growing. The *rate* of GDP growth is also important. For example, although actual GDP rose steadily from 1982 to 1990 and again from 1992 to 1994, the percentage increase varied widely from year to year.

Another important yardstick of economic health is the unemployment rate. The swings in unemployment from one phase of the cycle to the next can be substantial. For example, during the Great Depression of the 1930s, U.S. unemployment reached a staggering 25 percent of the work force. In contrast, during the expansion in 1968, unemployment dropped to slightly less than 4 percent. More recently, the 1981–1982 recession—in which unemployment rose to over 10 percent—was the worst experienced in this country since the Great Depression. During the expansion that followed and lasted until late 1990, unemployment fell to 5.3 percent before rising to about 7.4 percent during the recessionary period of the early 1990s. By late 1994, unemployment had dropped to about 6.0 percent.

Unemployment, inflation, interest rates, bank failures, corporate profits, taxes, and government deficits are all examples of economic conditions that can have a direct and profound impact on our financial well-being, because they affect the very heart of our financial plans—our level of income, investment returns, interest earned and paid, taxes paid, and in general, prices paid for goods and services consumed.

Inflation, Prices, and Planning. As we just saw, our economy is based on the exchange of goods and services between businesses and their customers—consumers, government, and other businesses—for a medium of exchange called money. The mechanism that facilitates this exchange is a system of *prices*. Technically speaking, the price of something is *the amount of money the seller is willing to accept in exchange for a given quantity of some good or service*—for instance, $3 for a pound of meat or $10 for an hour of work. When the general level of prices *increases* over time, the economy is said to be experiencing a period of **inflation.** The most common measure of inflation is the **consumer price index (CPI),** an index based on the changes in the cost of a market basket of consumer goods and services. The United States has experienced a general rise in the level of prices for the past 40 years or so. And at times the rate of inflation has been fairly substantial—in 1980, for instance, prices went up by 13.5 percent. Fortunately, inflation has dropped dramatically in this country and the annual rate of inflation has remained below 5 percent in every year since 1983, except 1990 when it was 5.4 percent. Indeed, there is considerable hope that inflation is finally under control and will remain in the 3 to 5 percent range for the foreseeable future.

Inflation is of vital concern to financial planning. It affects not only what we pay for the various goods and services we consume but also what we earn in our jobs. Inflation tends to give an illusion of something that does not exist. That is, while we seem to be making more money, we really aren't. As prices rise, we need more income because our **purchasing power**—the amount of goods and services we can buy with our dollars—declines. For example, assume that you earned $30,000 in 1993 and received annual raises so that your salary was $34,000 by 1996. That represents an annual growth rate of 4.3 percent. If inflation averaged 5 percent per year, however, your purchasing power would have decreased, even though your income rose. You would require $34,729 just to keep pace with inflation. It is, therefore, important to look at what you can earn in terms of its purchasing power, not just in absolute dollars.

Inflation also directly affects interest rates. High rates of inflation drive up the cost of borrowing money, ultimately leading to higher mortgage payments, higher monthly car payments, and so on. High inflation rates also have a detrimental effect on stock and bond prices, generally causing them to go down. Finally, sustained high rates of inflation can have devastating effects on retirement plans and other long-term financial goals—indeed, for many people it can put such goals out of reach. Clearly, low inflation is good for the economy, for interest rates and stock and bond prices, and, in general, for financial planning.

Concept Check

1-14. Discuss the following statement: "It is the interaction among government, business, and consumers that determines the environment in which personal financial plans must be made."

1-15. What are the stages of an economic cycle? Explain their significance for one's personal finances.

1-16. What is inflation, and why should it be a concern in financial planning?

WHAT DETERMINES YOUR PERSONAL INCOME? LG5 LG6

The amount of money you make is a function of many factors, including your age, level of education, where you live, and career. What combination of age, educational level, geographic location, and career do you think will provide you with the best opportunity to make a lot of money? Take a moment to answer this question before reading on.

An obvious and important factor in determining how well we live is the amount of income we earn. In the absence of any inheritance or similar financial windfall, your income will depend in large part on demographic factors such as your age, gender, race, and marital status. Your education, geographic location, and choice of a career also influence your earning power. Making a lot of money is not easy.

inflation A state of the economy in which the general price level is rising due to excessive demand or rapidly rising production costs: usually occurs during the recovery and expansion phases of the economic cycle.

consumer price index (CPI) A measure of cost of living and inflation based on the changes in the cost of a market basket of consumer goods and services.

purchasing power The amount of goods and services each dollar buys at a given point in time.

EXHIBIT 1.6

How Age, Education, Gender, and Career Affect Annual Income

The amount of money you earn is closely tied to your age, education, gender, and career. Generally, the closer you are to middle age (35-55), the more education you have, and the more professionally or managerially oriented your career, the greater your income will be.

	Annual Income (Head of Household)					
	Under $25,000	$25,000-$34,999	$35,000-$49,999	$50,000-$74,999	Over $75,000	Median Income
Age	*Percent in Each Income Bracket by Age*					
15-24	67.5%	16.8%	10.4%	4.1%	1.2%	$18,313
25-34	38.7	18.3	21.6	14.7	6.6	30,842
35-44	27.5	15.7	21.8	21.3	13.6	39,349
45-54	25.5	13.3	18.2	23.7	19.2	43,751
55-64	37.3	14.8	17.9	16.1	14.0	33,304
65 and over	67.8	13.0	9.2	5.8	4.1	16,975
Education (highest level)	*Percent in Each Income Bracket by Education*					
Elementary						
Less than 9th grade	77.4%	10.5%	7.4%	3.4%	1.1%	$13,221
High School						
1–3 years	65.7	14.0	11.2	6.9	2.2	17,535
Graduate	43.1	17.8	19.5	14.2	5.4	28.487
College						
Some college, no degree	32.8	16.7	21.5	19.1	9.7	35,150
Associate degree	25.8	16.9	23.0	22.2	12.1	39,700
Bachelor's degree or more	15.6	12.4	19.0	24.9	28.1	52,270

	Median Income by Gender	
Career (full-time)	Women	Men
Executive, administrators, and managerial	$26,928	$41,635
Professional specialty	30,487	42,358
Technical and related support	22,497	32,029
Sales	17,254	30,597
Admin. support (incl. clerical)	19,444	27,037
Precision production, craft and repair	18,554	27,508
Machine operators, assemblers, and inspectors	14,965	23,604
Transportation and material moving	19,448	25,194
Handlers, equipment cleaners, helpers, and laborers	15,528	17,508
Service workers	12,148	19,533
Farming, forestry, and fishing	10,205	14,978

Source: U.S. Bureau of the Census, *Statistical Abstract of the United States, 1993* (113th edition) Washington, D.C., 1993. Table No. 673 (page 428) and No 713 (page 458).

But it can be done! A high level of income—whether derived from your job, your own business, or your investments—is within your reach if you are willing to provide the necessary dedication and hard work, along with a well thought-out set of financial plans. Exhibit 1.6 presents data relative to the effect of age, education, gender, and career on annual income. Looking at the median income shown in the far right column you can see that, as a rule, the closer you are to middle age, the more education you have, and the more professionally or managerially oriented your career, the greater your income will be.

YOUR AGE, GENDER, RACE, AND MARITAL STATUS

Although age, gender, and race are variables over which you have no control, it is interesting to look at their relationship to income. Typically, people with low incomes fall into the very young or very old age groups, while the period of highest earnings generally occurs between the ages of 35 and 55. This distribution results because those below age 35 are just developing their trades or beginning to move up in their jobs, while many over 55 are working only part-time or are completely retired. In the 25-34 age group, the median income of the heads of household is about $31,000; this jumps to about $43,750 for those in the 45-54 age group and then falls sharply in the 65-and-over group to about $17,000. It is very likely that your own income will vary over time; therefore, when setting financial goals and making financial plans, you should consider expected changes in earnings.

Gender and race also affect earning potential. Although the gap between the earnings of men and women has been narrowing, women still earn only on average about 70 percent as much as men. Until recently women tended to choose or be limited to jobs in lower-paying "traditional" fields—sales clerks, teaching, clerical work, for example. Women's salaries are also negatively affected when they take time off to raise their children. They lose seniority, miss out on training opportunities, and are generally unable to regain lost ground, regardless of the amount of time off they take.

Salaries of minority workers are below those of whites. On average, African-Americans earn only about 65 percent as much as white workers, and Hispanics, about 73 percent as much. The outlook is promising for both women and minorities, however, with the elimination of many barriers that prevented them from acquiring the education and skills necessary for higher-paying careers. Recent studies show that pay differences continue to decrease as women and minorities are better represented in managerial, high technology, and professional positions. In fact, earnings of women ages 25 to 33—who have benefited from greater accessibility to education and job training—are about 87 percent of men's.

Your income also depends on whether you are married or single. The median income of married-couple families is currently about $41,000, more than double that of single people. While many single individuals may be supporting only themselves, others have children or other dependents to support as well.

YOUR EDUCATION

Your level of formal education is a controllable factor that has a considerable effect on your income. This is not to say that all people with equivalent formal educations will earn similar incomes. Rather, formal education is simply a tool that, when properly applied, can lead to higher earnings. As Exhibit 1.6 illustrates, heads of household who have more formal education earn higher annual incomes than those with lesser degrees. According to recent census bureau data, the median salary of a high school graduate is about $28,500, compared to $48,700 for someone with a bachelor's degree. And a Ph.D. and other professional degrees add substantially to the earnings of a college graduate. Over a lifetime, these differences really add up! Although education alone cannot guarantee a high income, these statistics suggest that your earning potential is greatly enhanced when you start with a good formal education.

WHERE YOU LIVE

Geographic factors also affect your earning power. Salaries vary regionally and tend to be higher in the Northeast and West than in the South. Robert Half International's *1994 Salary Guide* lists average national salaries for accounting, finance, and computer positions and includes a table to adjust them for geographic variances—for example, Massachusetts, +2 percent; Hawaii, −5 percent. Typically, your salary will be higher if you live in a large metropolitan area than in a smaller one or in a rural area. Factors such as economic conditions, labor supply, and industrial base also affect salary levels in different areas. In addition, living costs vary considerably throughout the country. You would earn more in Los Angeles than Boise, Idaho, but your salary would probably not go as far due to the higher cost of living. However, you may decide that lifestyle considerations take priority over earning potential. Your local chamber of commerce can provide an intercity cost of living index (see Exhibit 1.7) that compares living costs in major cities, and serves as a useful resource for comparing jobs in different areas. The overall index is developed by tracking costs in six major categories—groceries, housing, utilities, transportation, health care, and miscellaneous goods and services.

YOUR CAREER

How much you earn over your lifetime depends also on your career. Your choice of a career is closely related to your level of education and determined by your particular skills, interests, lifestyle preferences, and personal values. In addition, social, demographic, economic, and technological trends may affect your decision as to what fields

EXHIBIT 1.7

Cost of Living Index for Selected Cities (First Quarter, 1994)

(Index of 100 = Average for All 298 Cities Surveyed)

City	All Items	City	All Items	City	All Items
Albany, NY	106.8	Denver, CO	107.8	Oklahoma City, OK	93.8
Albuquerque, NM	104.9	El Paso, TX	100.9	Omaha, NE	91.9
Anchorage, AK	127.4	Fargo, ND	95.9	Philadelphia, PA	129.7
Atlanta, GA	100.6	Ft. Wayne, IN	91.0	Phoenix, AZ	102.5
Baltimore, MD	103.8	Houston, TX	98.8	Portland, OR	108.5
Baton Rouge, LA	100.9	Jackson, MS	102.1	Rapid City, SD	96.7
Billings, MT	105.8	Kansas City, MO-KS	97.5	Richmond, VA	106.6
Boise, ID	105.0	Lansing, MI	103.5	Rochester, NY	113.0
Boston, MA	135.6	Las Vegas, NV	109.3	Rockford, IL	104.7
Buffalo, NY	118.5	Lawrence, KS	95.5	St. Louis, MO-IL	97.0
Cedar Rapids, IA	99.3	Little Rock, AR	89.8	St. Paul, MN	109.4
Charleston, SC	99.6	Los Angeles, CA	125.2	Salt Lake City, UT	95.7
Charlotte, NC	100.1	Louisville, KY	92.5	San Antonio, TX	97.4
Cheyenne, WY	96.4	Memphis, TN	98.3	San Diego, CA	127.5
Cincinnati, OH	103.8	Miami, FL	109.8	Spokane, WA	108.2
Cleveland, OH	105.2	Milwaukee, WI	107.0	Wheeling, WV	95.9
Dallas, TX	104.9	Mobile, AL	94.6	Wilmington, DE	111.8

Source: American Chamber of Commerce Researchers Association, Louisville, Kentucky.

offer the best opportunities for the future. While not a prerequisite for many types of careers, such as sales, service, and certain types of manufacturing and clerical work, formal education generally leads to greater decision-making responsibilities—and increased income potential—within a career. Exhibit 1.8 presents an alphabetical list of average salaries from entry-level, mid-level, and managerial positions for a variety of careers, compiled from *U.S. News and World Report*'s "1995 Career Guide." As shown in Exhibits 1.6 and 1.8, professional and managerial workers, who typically have a college degree, tend to earn the highest salaries. Clearly those careers requiring greater formal education or specialized skills typically result in higher incomes.

PLANNING YOUR CAREER

Career planning and personal financial planning are closely related activities, and the decisions you make in one area affect the other. Suppose you graduate with a computer science degree and accept a job with a software company. Your financial plan might include furnishing your apartment, saving for a vacation or new car, and starting an investment program. If five years later you decide to go to law school, your revised financial plan will have strategies to cover living expenses and finance your tuition.

Through career planning, you can improve your work situation to gain greater personal and professional satisfaction. Some of the steps are similar to the financial planning process described earlier:

- Identify your interests, skills, needs, and values
- Set specific long- and short-term career goals
- Develop and implement an action plan to achieve your goals
- Review and revise career plans as your situation changes

Your action plan will depend on your job situation. For example, if you are unemployed, it will focus on your job search. If you have a job but want to change careers it might include researching career options, networking to develop a broad base of contacts, listing companies to contact for information, and getting special training to prepare for your chosen career.

Making Career Decisions. The best career decisions start with self assessment. An awareness of your interests, abilities, needs, and values relating to work and to lifestyle will help you choose a personally satisfying job or a career. What types of work situations do you prefer—independent, team, high pressure, stable, physically or intellectually challenging, public contact? Why do you want to work—for monetary gain, to help others, to change society, for personal achievement, to gain expertise? Lifestyle values—where you want

EXHIBIT 1.8

Average Salaries for Selected Professions

Profession	Salary		
	Entry-level	Mid-level	Managerial
Accountant, public	$29,000	$51,500	$ 62,000
Architect	24,700	45,300	65,000
Bookkeeper	21,000	26,500	33,500
Bank branch manager	31,500	38,500	45,000
Computer programmer	27,000	38,500	62,000
Corporate finance attorney	34,000	80,000	130,000
Credit and collections analyst	23,500	32,000	49,000
Electrical engineer	33,100	59,300	78,200
Financial analyst	26,000	35,000	51,000
Human resources technical trainer	37,200	57,200	70,000
Industrial engineer	37,500	57,000	76,300
Information systems consultant	38,000	57,500	70,000
Medical assistant	16,250	23,000	29,000
Medical researcher	20,000	32,400	77,400
Sales representative	31,900	56,500	68,200
Social worker	23,500	29,000	40,000
Systems analyst	30,000	43,500	60,000
Teacher	22,000	36,500	65,000
Telecommunications network specialist	31,750	57,500	100,000

Sources: *1994 Salary Guide,* Robert Half International, Inc., and "20 Hot Job Tracks," *U.S. News & World Report: 1995 Career Guide,* October 31, 1994, pp. 110-122.

to live, importance of cultural or athletic activities, desire for travel, family considerations—may help you narrow your career options. For example, because of the great personal satisfaction you gain from helping children learn, you may accept limited salary potential to teach preschool children in a Head Start program. If you prefer living and working in a rural area rather than in a big city, you may have to accept a lower salary for your chosen career. The Career Planning Checklist in Exhibit 1.9 summarizes important steps to take and helps track your progress.

Like financial planning, career planning is a lifelong process that includes short- and long-term goals. You can no longer expect to stay in one field or remain with one company your whole life, and your career goals are likely to change several times. The ability to make good career decisions is critical to surviving in today's increasingly competitive job market. Most educational institutions have placement offices that can teach you how to make career decisions, and there are many good books about careers and the job search process. Government publications, particularly the *Occupational Outlook Handbook,* which is revised every two years, provide excellent career information. Magazines such as *Business Week, Money, Kiplinger's Personal Finance, Newsweek, Time,* and *U.S. News & World Report* often feature articles on the best job opportunities for the future.

Career planning is a complex process that involves analyzing many factors and often making compromises. Salary, while important, is only one element in the decision-making process. Employee benefits, as described earlier in the chapter, can substantially increase your total compensation package. Your personal motivation and work and lifestyle preferences should also be taken into account. Clearly you should consider all these factors when comparing career and employment opportunities.

Career Strategies for the 1990s. Today's workplace is considerably different than that of our parents. The average American starting his or her career in the mid-1990s can expect to have at least 10 jobs for five or more employers, and many of us will have three, four, or even more careers during our lifetimes. Some of these changes will be based on personal decisions; others may result from layoffs from corporate downsizings. Many of us may suddenly find ourselves unemployed and need to switch careers. For example, a production manager for an aerospace manufacturer who feels that his prospects for another job in that industry

EXHIBIT 1.9

A Career Planning Checklist

The following checklist will help you organize your career search.

Assess Yourself

- ☐ I have chosen the setting in which I would like to work (e.g., large industrial, small business, government, nonprofit).
- ☐ I have chosen one of the following locations: rural, urban, suburban.
- ☐ I have listed my three most useful job skills.
- ☐ I know what I am most successful doing.
- ☐ I have identified whether I want to work with people, data, or things.
- ☐ I know whether I want to be supervised or be the supervisor.
- ☐ I know if I want to work with others or work alone.
- ☐ I have listed several career areas that interest me.
- ☐ I know whether I like "doing" or "thinking" activities at work.
- ☐ I have listed my favorite activities (hobbies, sports, etc.).
- ☐ I know what values are most important to me (e.g., prestige, security, variety).
- ☐ I know what kind of rewards I need in a job (e.g., social, monetary, job flexibility).

Research Career Information

- ☐ I am familiar with the career information in the placement office or public library so I can explore my options.
- ☐ I have a list of career possibilities to research.
- ☐ I follow current trends in my field (salary, job requirements, growth).
- ☐ I have identified three or more employers in the fields I am considering.
- ☐ I have sought information and advice from at least three contacts in my field(s).

Try Work Options

- ☐ I have narrowed down the career options I am considering.
- ☐ I have identified the additional education or experience I need to prepare for my choices (e.g., course work, part-time work, extracurricular activities).
- ☐ I have discovered ways my academic work supports my career objective.
- ☐ I have participated in some work experience or internship program in my field of interest.
- ☐ I am aware of the daily realities of the occupational area I am approaching.
- ☐ I have visited several work sites being considered as my career choice.
- ☐ I have become an active member in at least one professional association to enhance my job awareness.

Source: Adapted from Richard M. Hodgetts, *Modern Human Relations at Work,* Fort Worth, TX: The Dryden Press, 1993, p. 498.

are slim may buy a quick-print franchise and become his own boss. Job security is practically a thing of the past, and corporate loyalty has given way to a more self-centered career approach requiring new career strategies. Even looking for a job today requires different techniques, as the *Smart Money* box on page 28 explains.

To protect your earning power during economic downturns and to develop it to its fullest potential during prosperous times, you should develop a personal portfolio of skills, both general and technical. Employers need flexible, adaptable workers as companies restructure and pare down their operations. The following strategies will help you succeed in the changing workforce.

- *Get as much education as possible.* Develop and upgrade your skills through on-the-job training programs and continuing education courses, and add new skills to keep up with changing technology and workplace requirements. Computer skills, knowledge of a foreign language, problem-solving abilities, and managerial skills also enhance your value as an employee. These will allow you to branch out from your first job into new directions and to new companies.
- *Take new assignments to gain a broader base of experience and skills.* These could be in the same field or company or involve transferring your skills to new areas. The more diverse your background (within reason), the better off you will be in terms of both promotability and employability.
- *Keep up with marketplace changes.* Broaden your contacts within your industry and among your professional colleagues, know which industries have potential and which are in trouble, and know what skills are in demand in your field.
- *Don't get locked into one industry.* Defining what you do in terms of your skills or profession allows you to uncover new opportunities. Suppose you are a human resources manager laid off by a financial services firm. Because financial services jobs have declined substantially in recent years, you need to find fields with

EXHIBIT 1.10

Organizational Model

This text emphasizes making financial decisions relative to assets, credit, insurance, investments, and retirement and estates in a fashion consistent with financial plans developed to achieve desired financial results.

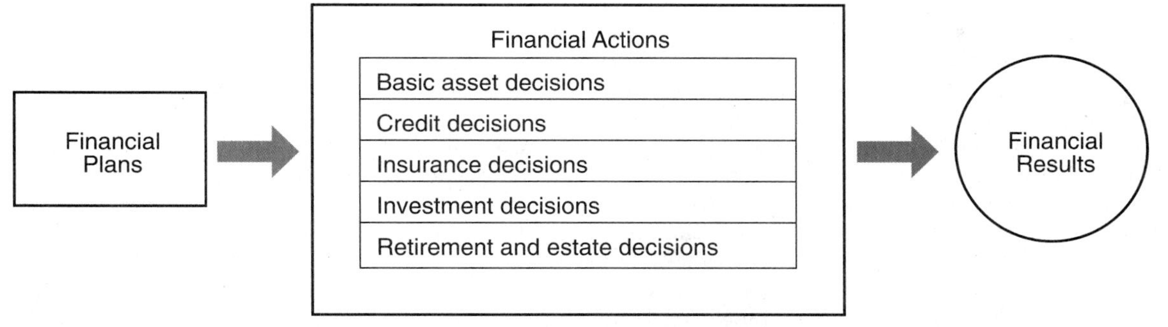

job growth. Your research might lead you to health care or telecommunications, fields that have expanded in recent years.

- *Hone your job search techniques.* Good job hunting skills will serve you well throughout your career. Learn how to research new career opportunities and investigate potential job opportunities. Develop a broad base of career resources, starting with your college placement office, public library, and personal contacts such as family and friends. Know how to market your qualifications to your advantage—in your resume and cover letters, on the phone, and in person during a job interview.

Clearly, the establishment of educational and career goals is closely related to personal financial planning. Only after such goals are identified can you develop realistic personal financial goals and plans.

Concept Check

1-17. "All people having equivalent formal education earn similar incomes." Do you agree or disagree with this statement? Explain your position.

1-18. Discuss the need for career planning throughout the life cycle and its relationship to financial planning. What are some of your personal career goals?

AN OVERVIEW OF THE TEXT

This text is divided into six parts, each devoted to the explanation of a different aspect of personal financial planning.

- **Part 1:** Foundations of Financial Planning
- **Part 2:** Managing Basic Assets
- **Part 3:** Managing Credit
- **Part 4:** Managing Insurance Needs
- **Part 5:** Managing Investments
- **Part 6:** Retirement and Estate Planning

The book is developed around the organizational model shown in Exhibit 1.10.

Our organizational scheme revolves around financial decision making that is firmly established on an operational set of financial plans. We believe that through sound financial plans, individuals can make financial decisions that will lead to desired financial results. Therefore, starting with Part 1, where we look at personal financial statements, plans, and taxes, we move successively through the various types of decisions that individuals make when implementing their financial plans.

To allow you to gain some hands-on financial planning experience, a continuous case is developed and presented at the end of various chapters and parts of the text. The case begins at the end of this chapter with an inventory of personal and financial data for Paul Larkin. With this data,

Smart Money

Hi-Tech Job Hunting

Want to increase your chances of finding a job? Hop onto the information superhighway and travel down more possible roads to employment than ever before.

Increasingly, both job seekers and employers use computers and on-line services to save time, money, and hassle in the employment process. Electronic résumé database systems allow employers to quickly search millions of résumés to identify and compare the qualifications of applicants who meet certain job criteria. Technical, medical, and managerial positions are among the easiest to find this way, because the necessary skills are easily defined. Some major database services are Cors, Job Bank USA, National Résumé Bank, and SkillSearch. Online Career Services, accessed through the Internet, lists résumés and also posts thousands of job openings. Online services (America Online, CompuServe, Genie, the Internet, and Prodigy) offer various services that may include classified ads, career advice forums, résumé posting, and job-networking message boards. Specialized electronic classified services include the Federal Opportunity Job Board and Career Connections (also on the Internet).

Before embarking on an electronic job search, you probably need to revise your résumé. Employers and recruiters use "key words" to search the databases to match applicants with job openings. These are usually nouns or noun phrases—for example, a job title or task (systems analyst, biotech research, UNIX programmer, budgeting, market research, public relations, problem solving, project management) or company name—rather than the action verbs—developed, coordinated, implemented—found in standard résumés. For example, the computer may only pick up "cost control" from the phrase "developed successful cost control system that reduced expenses 20 percent."

To improve your chances of attracting a potential employer's attention from among a database's thousands of résumés, you should develop a special résumé to describe your qualifications, work experience, and skills (such as proficiency in specific computer programs and foreign languages) in key word terms. Don't focus on writing style or fancy typefaces. Your goal is a straightforward, computer-friendly résumé that can be accurately scanned into the database. For best results, use sans serif typefaces (this is a sample of sans serif type), a simple layout, and avoid italic, boldface, script text, underlining, graphics, and similar items.

So how can you get your new résumé into a database? Check your college or university placement office, which may have no- or low-cost arrangements for graduating students and alumni with some of the major résumé databases. Many successful résumé services depend on fees from employers, so their listing fees are free or low. On-line services may include résumé listing services. America Online's Help Wanted-USA Worldwide Résumé/Talent Bank, for example, has 12,000 résumés on file and can be accessed via the Internet. For more advice on your high-tech job search, consult books like Tom Morrow and Joyce Lain Kennedy's *Electronic Job Search Revolution* and *Electronic Résumé Revolution* and *The Online Job Search Companion* by James C. Gonyea.

Sources: Joyce Lain Kennedy and Thomas J. Morrow, "Rules for Job Hunting Revised" and "Job Computers Adore One Thing in a Résumé: Simplicity," *The San Diego Union-Tribune,* February 9, 1994, pp. I–1, 2; Wayne M. Gonyea, "Keyword Résumés—Your New Hi-Tech Way to Get a Job!" America Online Career Center, September 1994; and Dan Moreau, "Cybersearching for a New Job," *Kiplinger's Personal Finance Magazine,* November 1994, pp. 99–105.

opportunities to develop various components of Larkin's financial plan appear at the end of Parts 1 through 5, Chapter 14, and Chapter 15. At each of these points, any additional data is presented, if needed, along with statements and questions aimed at directing the development of the aspect of Larkin's financial plan related to the material presented in that part or chapter of the text. Completion of all of these components will result in a comprehensive financial plan for Paul Larkin. Of course, depending on course objectives and time constraints, the preparation of Larkin's financial plan may or may not be required by your instructor.

SUMMARY

LG1. **Identify the benefits of using personal financial planning techniques to manage your finances.** Personal financial planning helps you to marshal and control your financial resources. It should allow you to get more enjoyment from your money, improve your standard of living, and spend money more wisely. By setting short- and long-term financial goals, you will enhance your quality of life both now and in the future. The ultimate result will be an increase in wealth.

LG2. **Define your major financial goals and describe the personal financial planning process that will help you achieve them.** Before you can manage your financial resources, you must *realistically* spell out your short- and long-term financial goals. Goals are essential to sound financial planning and should be stated in terms of the desired results. They should reflect your values and change as personal circumstances dictate. Once you define your goals, you can develop and implement an appropriate personal financial plan. A set of financial plans includes asset acquisition planning, liability and insurance planning, savings and investment planning, employee benefit planning, tax planning, and retirement and estate planning. These plans should be reviewed regularly and revised as required.

LG3. **Explain why personal financial plans must change according to your life situation.** Financial plans must be revised over time to include goals and strategies appropriate to each life-cycle stage. As you move through the various stages, income and expense patterns change. Changes in your life due to marriage, children, divorce, remarriage, and job status require adapting financial plans to meet current needs. Though these plans change over time, they provide the direction necessary to achieve your financial goals.

LG4. **Describe how government, business, and consumer actions and changing economic conditions affect personal financial plans.** Financial planning occurs in an environment where the government, business, and consumers are all influential participants. Government provides the structure within which businesses and consumers function and certain types of essential services. Businesses provide goods and services to consumers, whose choices influence the products and services businesses offer. Personal financial decisions are affected by economic cycles (expansion, recession, depression, and recovery) and the impact of inflation on prices, and, therefore, purchasing power and personal income.

LG5. **Evaluate the impact of age, gender, race, education, marital status, geographic location, and career choice on personal income.** Demographics, education, and career are all important factors that affect your income level. As a rule, people aged 35 to 55 tend to earn more than others, as do those in professional or managerial positions. Equally important, statistics show a direct correlation between level of education and income. Gender, race, and marital status also appear to affect earning potential. Where you live is another consideration; salaries are higher in some areas than others.

LG6. **Recognize the importance of career planning and its relationship to personal financial planning.** Career planning is a lifetime process that involves goal setting and career development strategies. These plans should provide for flexibility to adapt to new workplace requirements through continuing education and job training and job, employer, and career changes. When making career decisions, you must consider employee benefits, personal values, and lifestyle in addition to salary. Many career decisions have monetary implications. Therefore, you should coordinate your career plans with your personal financial plans.

FINANCIAL FACTS OR FANTASIES

Are the following statements financial facts (true) or fantasies (false)?

1. An improved standard of living is one of the payoffs of sound money management.
2. A savings account is an example of a real asset, as it represents something on deposit at a bank or S&L.
3. Personal financial planning involves the restatement of personal financial goals into specific plans and, ultimately, into financial arrangements that put those plans into action.
4. Over the long run, gaining an extra percent or two on an investment makes little difference in the amount of earnings generated.
5. Generally speaking, inflation has little effect on personal financial planning.
6. A high salary is the most important factor in choosing a particular job or career.

DISCUSSION QUESTIONS AND PROBLEMS

Discussion Question for Opening Profile

How would you evaluate Jo Ann's financial planning so far? What other advice would you give her?

1. ***Use Worksheet 1.1*** Describe your current status based on the personal financial planning life cycle shown in Exhibit 1.1. Fill out three versions of Worksheet 1.1, A Summary of Personal Financial Goals, that reflect:
   - **a.** your current situation.
   - **b.** your expected life situation in 5 years.
   - **c.** your expected life situation in 10 years.

   Discuss the reasons for the changes in your goals and how you will need to adapt your financial plans as a result. Which types of financial plans do you need for your current situation, and why?
2. Summarize the current and projected trends in the economy with regard to GDP growth, unemployment, and inflation. How should you use this information to make personal financial and career planning decisions?
3. Select a career field of interest to you and prepare a brief plan to gather information for your job search.
4. Assume you graduated from college with a major in marketing and took a job with a large consumer goods corporation. After three years, you are laid off when the company downsizes. Describe the steps you'd take to "repackage" yourself for another field.

CONTEMPORARY CASE APPLICATIONS

1.1 Neil's Need to Know: Personal Finance or Tennis?

During the Christmas break of his final year at Mountain View College, Neil Stone planned to put together his résumé in preparation for his actively seeking full-time employment as a medical technician during the spring semester. To help Neil prepare for the job interview process, his older brother arranged for him to meet with a friend, Marilyn Nave, who has been a practicing medical technician since her graduation from Mountain View two years earlier. Neil and Marilyn met for lunch, and Marilyn provided him with numerous pointers on résumé preparation, the interview process, job opportunities, and so on.

After answering Neil's many questions, Marilyn asked Neil to bring her up to date on a variety of topics related to Mountain View College. Of special interest to Marilyn were the many changes that had taken place in the faculty and curriculum of the medical technology department since her graduation. As they discussed courses, Marilyn indicated that of all the electives she had taken, she had found the course in personal financial planning most useful. Neil said that he still had one elective to take and had been giving some thought to personal financial planning, although he was currently leaning toward a beginning tennis course. Neil felt that since a number of his friends would be taking tennis, it would be a lot of fun. He pointed out that since he never expected to get rich and already knew how to balance his checkbook, the personal financial planning course did not seem well suited to his needs. Marilyn said that there is certainly much more to personal financial planning than balancing a checkbook and that the course was highly relevant regardless of income level. She strongly believed that the personal financial planning course would be more beneficial to Neil than beginning tennis—a course that she herself had taken while at Mountain View College.

Questions

1. Describe to Neil the goals and rewards of the personal financial planning process.
2. Explain to Neil what is meant by financial planning and why it is important regardless of income.
3. Describe the financial planning environment to Neil. Explain the role of the consumer in, and the impact of economic conditions on, this environment.
4. What arguments would you present to convince Neil that the personal financial planning course would be more beneficial for him than beginning tennis?

1.2 Sid's Dilemma: Finding a New Job

Sid Como, a 47-year-old retail store manager earning $45,000 a year, had worked for the same company during his entire 28-year career. Then came a major recession that resulted in massive layoffs throughout the retail industry. He was among the unlucky people who lost their jobs. Now, ten months later, he is still unemployed. Sid's ten months' severance pay and six months' unemployment compensation have run out. However, when he first became a store manager he had taken a personal financial planning course offered at the local university. Because he then adopted careful financial planning practices, he now has sufficient savings and investments to carry him through several more months of unemployment. Currently, his greatest financial need is to find a job.

Sid has actively sought work but finds himself overqualified for lower-paying jobs that are available and underqualified for higher-paying, more desirable positions. There have been no new openings for positions equivalent to the manager's job he lost. Although Sid attended college for two years after high school, he did not earn a degree. Sid is divorced and close to his two grown children who live in the same city.

The options facing Sid are:

- wait out the recession until another, equivalent retail store manager position opens up.
- move to another area of the country where store manager positions are still available.
- accept a lower-paying job for two or three years and go back to school evenings to finish his college degree and qualify for a better position.
- consider other types of jobs that could benefit from his managerial skills.

Questions

1. What important career factors should Sid consider when evaluating his options?
2. What important personal factors should Sid consider when deciding among his career options?
3. What recommendations would you give Sid in light of both the career and personal dimensions of his options noted in Questions 1 and 2 above?
4. What career strategies should today's workers employ in order to avoid Sid's dilemma?

GETTING A HANDLE ON YOUR FINANCIAL FUTURE

To achieve your financial goals, you must establish financial plans that point in the direction you want to go. The major types of financial plans include (1) asset acquisition, (2) liability and insurance, (3) savings and investment, (4) employee benefit, (5) tax, and (6) retirement and estate. As you might expect, people go through different stages in their lives, and, therefore, their income pattern and the financial goals they express may change. Remember, financial planning is a lifelong process, but the sooner you get started and the more effort you put into it, the better off you will be financially. So, let's get started!

If You Are Just Starting Out

The financial goals for someone just starting out are: record keeping, liability and insurance, savings, and investment. Rank these in order of priority and assign a definite time frame for realizing each goal.

Record Keeping:

1. Develop a good system of record keeping to monitor your progress. Software packages and spreadsheets can help you in this process.
2. Generate balance sheets on a periodic basis.
3. Analyze your current income and expenditures in order to gain control over spending.
4. Create a statement of projected income and expenses and analyze it for problems and opportunities.

Liabilities and Insurance:

1. Consider borrowing money for a worthwhile purpose to establish a credit history.
2. Consolidate your outstanding bills to reduce monthly payments.
3. Be sure you have adequate long-term disability, health, property, and liability insurance. If you are married and/or have dependents, you should also have additional life insurance.

Savings and Investment:

1. Set aside an emergency fund (usually three months' income) to cover unexpected expenses.
2. Establish a regular savings program.
3. Plan an investment portfolio, deciding on the proper mix of assets.
4. Review your investments and savings periodically to monitor performance.

If You Are Thirty-Something

As your income increases, you will hopefully have more excess funds that can be used to meet your financial goals and a greater ability to accept risks for higher expected returns. Among the areas that should be reviewed as you mature are insurance, real estate and other goals, investments, taxes, and retirement and estate planning.

Insurance:

1. Evaluate all your personal insurance plans to see if there are any gaps in coverage.
2. Adjust current levels to reflect changes in your income and net worth.
3. Consider professional liability insurance.

Investments:

1. If you are thinking of buying a home, set aside funds for the down payment and closing costs.
2. If you have or plan to have children, project your income and expenses to accommodate the additional cost of raising a child (day-care, education, and so on).
3. Review your investments to consider any changes in your attitude toward risk and your time frame for achieving your financial goals.

Tax Planning:

1. Plan for the implications of increased income and be aware of changes in the tax laws.
2. Evaluate your investments to see if they are achieving the best after-tax rate of return.
3. Determine if you are taking advantage of all applicable tax-savings techniques.

Retirement and Estate Planning:

1. Review your employer's retirement options to ensure that you have made proper elections.
2. Estimate expected retirement benefits and compare them to estimated expenditures.
3. Maintain an up-to-date will and powers of attorney.
4. Estimate the value of your estate and establish trusts where applicable.
5. Make sure guardians have been appointed for dependent children.

Paul Larkin is a computer programmer for a small software corporation. At age 29, he is making enough money to live comfortably as a single person with no children. In the six years since he graduated from college, he has not worried too much about how he was spending his earnings. However, a couple of his friends have recently had experiences (one lost her job and another's parent suffered a debilitating stroke) which have caused Paul to take a closer look at his own financial management. Paul has also been dating a young lady, Christine Stevens, for the past three years, and they are beginning to talk about marriage and children. All of this has made Paul a little more concerned than usual about the rising balances on his credit cards.

Paul and Christine have not really discussed their finances, but Paul is sometimes irritated by the way Christine "pinches pennies." Christine refuses to buy anything unless it's marked down, and she always shops and shops for the best prices . . . even on small purchases. Paul does not understand this behavior because he knows Christine makes more money and has fewer bills than he does. Paul likes to spend money. He gets pleasure from buying Christine expensive gifts and does not like it when she tells him he spent too much money on her. While he does not consider himself a spendthrift, he does enjoy the lifestyle money can buy. Paul collects good wines, likes fixing up old trucks, and stays in shape training for marathons. He travels two or three times a year to various cities to run in marathons.

Paul lives in a duplex he has been renting for the past four years. It is owned by Jack and Sarah Mathews, a couple in their mid fifties, who live in the other half of the duplex. The Mathews have treated Paul like a son ever since he started renting from them. Paul savors this relationship since his own parents divorced when he was young. His mother, Betty Larkin, now lives over 500 miles away, but they still talk often on the telephone and visit each other three to four times a year. The Mathews have two children—a son who is a 24-year-old graduate student and a daughter, age 31, who is married and has one child. Paul admires Jack and Sarah because they get along so well with each other and with their children.

Paul grew up as an only child. His mother worked and his father provided child support regularly, but the family still had to spend carefully to make ends meet. Since his graduation from college, Paul's mother has had money for a few luxuries and has begun to save for her own retirement. At age 50, she is now in very good health. However, Paul would like to be in a position to help her someday if she needs his financial support. Christine supports Paul's desire to help his mother as Christine has just finished helping her youngest brother with the costs of his college education.

Motivated by his financial concerns, Paul attended a three-part seminar on financial management at his local credit union. He received data gathering forms at the seminar and has filled them out as completely as possible. These forms are presented on the following pages. Read the information Paul has provided so that you can "get acquainted" with him. As you first read the case, you probably will not understand all the vocabulary or why certain information is even included on the forms. But remember, this is just Chapter 1 of the text. By the time you reach the end of the book, Paul, as well as his financial data, will be old friends, and you will feel very comfortable with what all of this means!

PERSONAL FINANCIAL INFORMATION

CLIENT INFORMATION

Name: Paul Andrew Larkin

Birth Date: June 7, 1967

Soc. Sec. No.: 428-55-3342

Business Phone: 309/555-6390

Residence Address: 1468B Bluebonnet Dr.

City, State & Zip: Jefferson, USA 60131

Home Phone: 309/555-5828

Wedding Date: Not applicable

SPOUSE INFORMATION

Name: Not applicable

Birth Date:

Soc. Sec. No.:

Business Phone:

CHILDREN

Name	Birth Date	Social Security Number	Grade
None			

EDUCATION

	School	Degree	Year Received
Paul	Northern State University	B.S. Computer Science	May 28, 1990

OCCUPATION

	Employer	Position	Years From	To
Paul	Tower Software	Computer Programmer	1992–present	

CONSULTANTS FOR FINANCIAL PLANNING

	Name	Address	Phone
Attorney	None		
Securities Broker	None		
Bank Officer	Jason Maxie	Community Credit Union Jefferson, USA 60131	555-2382
Insurance Agent	Sandra Ortez	The Independent Agency 125009 Jackson Road Jefferson, USA 60131	555-6722

LOCATION OF DOCUMENTS		
Wills/Trusts:	None	
Insurance:	Life	Group policy through Tower Software Information booklet in desk drawer at home
	Health	Group coverage through Tower Software Information booklet in desk drawer at home
	Dental	Group coverage through Tower Software Information booklet in desk drawer at home
	Disability income	None
	Auto	Policy in desk drawer at home
	Homeowners/Renters	None
Deeds:	Auto Truck	In desk drawer at home In desk drawer at home
Birth/Marriage/ Other Certificates:	Birth	Mother must still have it

ASSETS—January 1, 1996

	Location	Balance	Rate of Interest	Maturity
Checking	Jefferson National Bank[1] (minimum balance acct.)	$ 1,945	NA	N/A
Money Market Accounts/Funds:	Jefferson National Bank[1] (opened 1993)	$3,055	3.0%	N/A
	Fidelity Cash Reserves (opened 1994)	$2,534	5.2%	N/A
CD				
Savings Acct. (share account)	Community Credit Union[1] (opened 1970)	$ 670	2.5%	N/A
Cash on hand	Desk drawer at home	$ 430	N/A	
Life Insurance (cash value of policy)				
Vested Pension 401(k)-Tower Software	See Security Investments (below)		N/A	

Security Investments

Security	# Shares	Date Acquired	Cost Per Share	Cost Total	Current Value Per Share	Current Value Total
Physician's Corp. of America PCAM (ticker)	200	9/30/93	18-1/2	$ 3,700	26-3/4	$ 5,350
Fidelity Equity-Income II Mutual Fund (inherited) FEQTX (ticker)	1,465	11/20/90	$10.24	$15,000	$19.73	$28,904
Vested Pension 401(k)—Tower Software:			Average			
—Janus Mutual Fund JANSX (ticker)	272.786	Monthly purchases from 1993 to present	$20.21	$5,513	$22.13	$6,037
—Janus Venture Mutual Fund JAVTX	106.634		$51.70	$5,513	$53.35	$5,689
—Janus Mutual Fund	32.756	Reinvested dividends & capital gains distributions	$20.21	$ 662	$22.13	$ 725
—Janus Venture Mutual Fund	25.592		$51.70	$1,323	$53.35	$1,365

[1]Federally insured

REAL PROPERTY	**Year**	**Make**	**Model**	**Cost**	**Current Value**
Automobile:	1994	Pontiac	Firebird	$19,500	$14,600
Truck:	1982	Ford	Pickup	$ 2,000	$ 3,000

PERSONAL PROPERTY	**Market Value**	**Replacement Value**
Clothing	$ 3,500	$ 7,000
Furniture & appliances	$ 8,000	$12,000
Stereo, TVs, cameras, etc.	$ 4,500	$ 5,000
Computer, printer, & software	$ 3,500	$ 3,500
Exercise equipment	$ 1,750	$ 2,500
Wine collection	$ 1,500	$ 1,500
Miscellaneous household items and tools	$ 2,000	$ 3,500

LIABILITIES—January 1, 1996

LOANS:

To Whom Owed	Original Amount of Account	Property or Service Purchased	Interest Rate	Current Balance	Payment Amount	How Often Paid	Total Number of Payments	Date of First Payment
Community Credit Union	$23,000	Education (Stafford)	9.0%	$12,704	$291	monthly	120	7/1/90
GMAC	$16,500	Automobile	6.5%	$10,475	$391	monthly	48	6/10/94

LINE OF CREDIT:

Company	Number	Annual Fee	Interest Rate	Maximum Line of Credit	Outstanding Balance	Minimum Monthly Payment	Grace Period	Calculation Method
Community Credit Union	428-55-3342	$ 0	12.0%	$15,000	$ 0	2% of balance or $50, whichever is greater	no	Av. daily balance

CREDIT CARDS:

Company	Number	Annual Fee	Interest Rate	Maximum Line of Credit	Outstanding Balance
AT&T Universal MasterCard	4897 2301 5602 1927	$ 0	17.4%	$3,500	$1,293
Community Credit Union Visa	4310 4516 3100 3259	$ 0	14.0%	$5,000	$4,808
GM Gold MasterCard	3529 0317 2432 0917	$35	18.9%	$3,000	$2,061
American Express	2782 163539 62005	$55	—	—	$ 0
Optima True Grace	1626 5512 7111 66	$ 0	18.0%	$2,500	$ 893
Dillards	0 50186 96182 0	$ 0	19.8%	$5,000	$ 729
Discover	361 0589 1345	$ 0	17.9%	$2,600	$1,365

Company	Minimum Monthly Payment	Grace Period	Calculation Method
AT&T Universal MasterCard	2% of balance or $20, whichever is greater	yes[1]	Av. daily balance[2]
Community Credit Union Visa	2% of balance or $25, whichever is greater	yes	Av. daily balance[3]
GM Gold MasterCard	2% of balance or $20, whichever is greater	yes[1]	Av. daily balance[2]
American Express	Total balance	—	—
Optima True Grace	3% of balance or $25, whichever is greater	yes	Av. daily balance[3]
Dillards	3% of balance or $30, whichever is greater	yes[1]	Av. daily balance[2]
Discover	2% of balance or $25, whichever is greater	no	Two-cycle average daily balance[2]

Note: Paul has decided he will pay all new charges in full starting January 1996.

[1]Grace period only if total outstanding is paid monthly.

[2]Including new purchases and cash advances.

[3]Excluding new purchases, but including cash advances.

1995 INCOME

Salary	(Paul's)	$37,000
Bonuses		$ 0
Salary	(Spouse's)	N/A
Bonuses		N/A
Interest[1]		$ 107
Dividends[2]		$ 541
Capital gains distributions[3]		$ 787
Sale of assets[4]		$ 1,149
Prize money	(marathons)	$ 1,500

Monthly salary after tax deductions:

$3,083	gross salary
- 472	federal income tax withholding
- 77	state income tax withholding
- 236	social security tax withholding
$2,298	net salary

[1]Money market account ($90 a year, paid monthly), savings account ($17 a year, paid quarterly in March, June, September, and December).

[2]Fidelity Cash Reserves ($132 a year) and Fidelity Equity-Income II ($409 a year)—both paid quarterly in March, June, September, and December.

[3]Fidelity Equity-Income II ($272 a year, paid quarterly in March, June, September, and December) and Janus Venture ($515 a year, paid in December).

[4]Sold 100 shares of Fidelity Select Energy Services 6/1/95 for $11.49 a share. Paul had purchased these shares 6/13/93 for $12.63 which included a 3% load when he purchased.

1995 EXPENSES

	Cash Flow Monthly	Cash Flow Annually
Rent	$775	$9,300
Utilities (electricity and gas)	150	1,800
Telephone	65	780
Cable TV	25	300
Groceries	190	2,280
Food away from home	200	2,400
Auto loan payments	391	4,692
Auto maintenance (gas, repairs, licenses, etc.)	185	2,220
Medical/dental expenses (not covered by insurance)	65	780
Clothing	175	2,100
Insurance premiums paid through withholding	0	0
Contributions to 401(k) pension	215	2,580
Auto insurance (paid semi-annually in February and August)		725
Federal income tax withholding	472	5,664
Social security tax withholding	236	2,832
State income tax withholding	77	924
Appliance, furniture, and equipment purchases		1,535
Personal care	35	420
Entertainment	150	1,800
Vacations (marathon trips)		1,600
Wine collection	30	360
Charitable contributions	25	300
Gifts ($75/mo. Jan. through Oct., $500/mo. Nov. and Dec.)		1,750
Reinvested interest, dividends, and capital gains distributions		1,435
Education loan payments	291	3,492
Miscellaneous	100	1,200

EMPLOYEE BENEFIT INFORMATION

Tower Software offers a cafeteria benefit plan with the following choices. Tower pays $200 per month towards the premiums of the selected insurance coverages. If the employee wants more of the insurance coverages than the $200 premium Tower pays, the difference is deducted from the employee's monthly paycheck. No reimbursement is made if the employee selects less coverage than the $200 premium covers. Paul currently is covered by the group term life, the major medical, and the dental coverage. He is not participating in the company's flexible spending account.

LIFE INSURANCE

Type of life insurance	Group Term	Accidental Death and Dismemberment
Face amount	2, 3, or 4 times gross salary	Sold in multiples of $10,000 not to exceed 10 times gross salary
Monthly premium	$0.068 per $1,000 of coverage	$0.021 per $1,000 of coverage
Paul's current coverage	$74,000 (2 times gross salary)	None
Beneficiary	Betty Larkin (mother)	N/A
Owner	Paul	N/A
Monthly premium for coverage selected	$5.03	N/A

DISABILITY INSURANCE

Policy number		Employer group policy
Definition of disability		Own job
Monthly benefit		65% of gross monthly salary
Waiting period	Sick	90 days
	Accident	90 days
Benefit period	Sick	to age 65
	Accident	to age 65
Monthly premiums		$0.0373 per $100 of gross monthly salary
Paul's current coverage		None
Monthly premium for coverage selected		N/A

MEDICAL INSURANCE

*Type of Policy	Major Medical Option	HMO Option
Company	Metro Life	Health Care Plan (HMO)
Policy number	Group #063-111	Group # 168521 AGC
*Hospitalization Room Rate	80% of semi-private rate	100% of semi-private rate
Number of days	unlimited	unlimited
*Major Medical Maximum	$500,000/person/year	unlimited
Deductible/copayment	$500/person/year	$25 copayment/emergency room visit $15 copayment/doctor's visit $10 copayment/brand-name prescription $ 5 copayment/generic prescription
Participation percentage	80/20	—
Cap on participation	$1,000/person/year	—
Mental health	80% for up to 30 visits	$15 copayment per visit
Dental	not covered	not covered
Monthly premiums	$177 per person	$160 per person
Current coverage— Major medical	$177	N/A

*COMMENTS	
Major medical:	Prescription drugs are covered with a $5 copayment for generic prescriptions and a $15 copayment for brand-name prescriptions. Drug copayments cannot be included as part of the deductible or the participation cap.
HMO:	Must use HMO facilities and selected pharmacies and hospitals.

DENTAL INSURANCE

Policy Number	Group #063-112
Annual deductible	$25 (waived for 2 diagnostic and 2 preventative treatments a year)
Maximum annual benefit	$1,000
Diagnostic (oral exams and x-rays)	100%
Preventive (cleanings, fluoride, and sealants)	100%
Restorative—minor (fillings and stainless steel crowns)	80%
Restorative—major (porcelain, resin, and gold crowns)	50%
Endodontics (pulp caps and root canals)	80%
Periodontics (periodontal scaling, root planing, and treatment of gum disease)	80%
Prosthodontics (bridges and dentures)	50%
Oral surgery (extractions)	80%
Orthodontics (retainers and braces)	50% ($1,000 lifetime maximum)
Monthly premium for coverage selected	$18

OTHER BENEFITS

Sick leave: Employee earns 1 day per month. Sick days can be accumulated up to 90 days of leave. Paul currently has 23 days accumulated.

Personal days: 3 days of personal leave with pay are given each year after 1 year of employment. These days cannot be accumulated from year to year.

Vacation: Two weeks of vacation are given annually after 1 year of employment. Three weeks of vacation are given annually after 10 years of employment. Vacation days can be split, but they cannot be accumulated from year to year.

Tuition reimbursement: Up to $1,000 per year tuition and fee reimbursement for courses taken that improve job skills.

Flexible spending accounts: Up to $300 per month can be contributed to both a health care flexible spending account and a dependent care flexible spending account. Employees can contribute to one or both of these accounts, as needed.

PRIVATE INSURANCE

AUTO INSURANCE

DESCRIPTION	(1) 1994 Pontiac Firebird	(2) 1982 Ford Pickup
Company	AETNA Casualty	AETNA Casualty
Policy Number	156-88876-AOB6	same
Liability	$40,000 or (20/40/15)	$40,000 or (20/40/15)
Medical Payments	$2,500/person	$2,500/person
Uninsured Motorist	$40,000 or (20/40/15)	$40,000 or (20/40/15)
Collision	(Actual Cash Value)	
Deductible	$200	
Comprehensive	(Actual Cash Value)	
Deductible	$ 50	
Annual Premium	$490	$235
Comments	Paid semi-annually in February and August	Paid semi-annually in February and August

RETIREMENT INFORMATION

Type of pension plan	401(k) salary reduction plan
Employee contribution	Voluntary contribution. Maximum contribution is 15% of gross salary.
Employer contribution	Matches $0.50 for every $1.00 of employee contribution for the first 7% contributed by employee.
Vesting	Immediate
Investment choices	Employee can put money in a 5-year Guaranteed Investment Contract (GIC) and/or any of the Janus family of mutual funds. The 5-year GIC offered is paying a 6% rate of return.
Paul's current contribution	7% of gross salary
Current value of pension	$13,816
Beneficiary	Betty Larkin (mother)

FINANCIAL GOALS

Short range (1 year):

- Evaluate his financial situation and make necessary changes in spending and financial alternatives
- Get control of his finances
- Pay all new credit card charges in full upon billing

Intermediate range (2-5 years):

- Pay off all his credit cards
- Have an adequate emergency fund
- Purchase a house
- Save for a new car

Long term (over 5 years):

- Save for his retirement
- Provide funds for his mother if she needs financial support

OTHER INFORMATION

1. Are you able to save regularly? Only for retirement through my 401(k) and through reinvestment of interest, dividend, and capital gains distribution income.
2. How much are you able to save annually? $2,580 in the 401(k) and $1,435 of reinvested interest, dividend, and capital gains distribution income.
3. Do you invest regularly? Only through the 401(k).
4. Do you feel that you are financially organized? No, but I am working on it.
5. Do you budget your money? No, but I'm willing to start budgeting.
6. If you were to die, could your dependents handle their finances? I don't have any dependents. My mother, the beneficiary of my life insurance and pension plan, can handle her finances.
7. How do you feel about saving for retirement? It's important, but I have other goals that are also very important right now.
8. If you had an extra $5,000 what would you do with it? Pay off some of my credit card debt.
9. How do you feel about taking investment risks? I am comfortable with a moderate amount of risk.
10. How is your health? Very good except for an occasional injury. I am now seeing a doctor who specializes in sports medicine that is not associated with the HMO offered through my group benefit plan.
11. What is your single most important financial objective at this time? Get my spending under control and reduce my credit card debt.

Chapter 2

Your Financial Statements and Plans

The Breyers Learn to Budget

"Where does all the money go?" Ken and Rhonda Breyer wonder. "We can't seem to balance our budget, no matter how hard we try." In their early thirties with two daughters, ages five and three, the San Diego, California, couple struggles to live on Ken's $50,000 salary as a sheriff's detective, plus any extra from his seasonal tax-return business. Because most of Rhonda's salary would go for day care, they agreed she would stay home with the girls for now. The Breyers bought a home in the mid-1980s and also own 30 percent of a rental property that is just starting to show a profit. However, their personal debt from car loans and credit card spending is very high—$20,000—and they only have about $2,200 cash to cover living expenses and emergencies. They want to save but never seem to have extra money at the month's end. Ken and Rhonda won't be able to achieve their financial goals, which include buying a second car, establishing a savings/emergency fund, and paying for the girls' college. Ken would also like to finish his college degree and earn a graduate degree.

Realizing that they needed help to improve their finances, the Breyers consulted a financial planner for advice. She helped them clarify their goals and develop a plan with target dates for goal achievement. Her first recommendation was to develop a realistic budget and stick to it. Although Ken and Rhonda tracked their expenses with a personal finance program on their computer, they did not use the information as the basis for a budget and to find ways to cut spending. They should review several month's

Learning Goals

LG1. *Describe the financial planning process, including the role of professional financial planners, the need to address special planning concerns, and the relationship among financial statements, budgets, and financial plans.*

LG2. *Prepare a personal balance sheet.*

LG3. *Generate a personal income and expenditures statement.*

LG4. *Develop a good record keeping system and use ratios to interpret personal financial statements.*

LG5. *Set long- and short-term financial goals using time value of money concepts.*

LG6. *Construct a cash budget and use it to monitor and control spending.*

expenses to discover their spending habits and learn which expenses are fixed and which can be cut. Then they can set priorities—including a set amount to save each month—and arrive at a balanced budget by dropping or deferring lower-priority items.

Clearly, the Breyers need to become more disciplined when it comes to spending and saving. For example, they reduced the cost of their home mortgage by refinancing at a lower rate but increased the size of the loan to repay their consumer debt. While the mortgage refinancing was a good move, they spent rather than saved the funds it freed up, and once again have too much debt. Ken and Rhonda agreed to pay off their car loan as quickly as possible and put away their credit cards until they pay down their balances, and then only use them if they can pay off the amount each month. Next, they must make savings a budget priority by setting up an automatic savings plan with monthly direct deposits from Ken's paycheck and build up their emergency reserve fund to about $5,000 to $10,000. Their advisor recommended a money market fund rather than an easily-accessible bank savings account, to remove the temptation to spend.

For the Breyers, learning to budget was the first step toward taking control of their personal finances. Chapter 2 shows how they can use personal financial statements and budgets to achieve their goals.

Source: Based mostly on Mark Maynard, "Experts Offer Family Advice so as to Avert Fiscal Descent," *San Diego Union-Tribune,* January 4, 1993, pp. C–1,2.

MAPPING OUT YOUR FINANCIAL FUTURE: THE FINANCIAL PLANNING PROCESS

LG1

Financial plans, personal financial statements, and budgets work together to provide direction for future financial activities and to keep financial transactions on track. How might financial statements and budgets help you achieve your financial goals? Take a few moments to answer this question before reading on.

Financial planning helps you achieve greater wealth and financial security by means of well-defined plans and carefully developed and implemented strategies and controls. On the one hand, financial plans, financial statements, and budgets provide direction by helping you work toward specific financial goals; on the other, they provide control by bringing the various dimensions of your personal financial affairs into focus.

Many people erroneously assume that financial planning is only for the wealthy. Nothing could be further from the truth! Whether you have a lot of money or too little, you still need personal financial planning. If you have enough money, planning can help you spend and invest it wisely. If your income seems inadequate, taking steps to control your financial situation will lead to an improved lifestyle. This is what personal financial planning is all about: taking conscientious and systematic steps toward fulfilling your financial goals. To reap the full benefits of personal financial planning, though, you need well-defined financial goals and carefully prepared financial plans, personal financial statements, and cash budgets.

Before you can develop your financial plans and effectively manage your money, you must know where you stand financially. Two types of personal financial statements—the balance sheet and income and expenditure statement—are essential to developing and monitoring personal financial plans. They show your actual results, allowing you to gauge your financial position at specific times and track your progress toward your financial goals. Knowing how to prepare and interpret personal financial statements is a cornerstone of personal financial planning. Without some standards to measure your financial condition, establishing financial goals and evaluating your progress toward those goals is difficult, if not impossible.

On your journey to financial security, financial planning and budgeting are the road maps that show you the way, while personal financial statements are navigational aids to guide you to your destination. All are essential to sound personal financial management and achievement of personal financial goals.

THE FINANCIAL PLANNING PROCESS

Take a closer look at financial planning and you'll see that it is a process that translates personal financial goals into specific financial plans and then implements the plans through financial strategies. One way to achieve the goals in your financial plan is with **budgets,** detailed short-term financial forecasts that compare estimated income to estimated expenditures. Budgets monitor and control expenditures and purchases, thereby providing the mechanism to carry out your financial plans. Exhibit 2.1 summarizes the various financial statements and reports and their relationship to each other in the personal financial planning process. Note that while financial plans provide direction to annual budgets, success (or lack of it) in budget implementation directly affects your balance sheet and income and expenditure statement. As you move from plans to budgets to actual statements, you can see how financial statements provide essential feedback to your financial plans and budgets. They show your progress toward your financial goals and whether you are staying within your budget. The financial planning process generally involves the following steps:

1. Define financial goals.
2. Develop financial plans and strategies to achieve goals.
3. Implement financial plans and strategies.
4. Periodically develop and implement budgets to monitor and control progress toward goals.
5. Use financial statements to evaluate results of plans and budgets, taking corrective action as required.
6. Revise and replace goals as personal circumstances change.

EXHIBIT 2.1

The Interlocking Network of Financial Plans and Statements

Personal financial planning involves a whole network of financial reports that link future goals and plans with actual results. Such a network provides direction, control, and feedback.

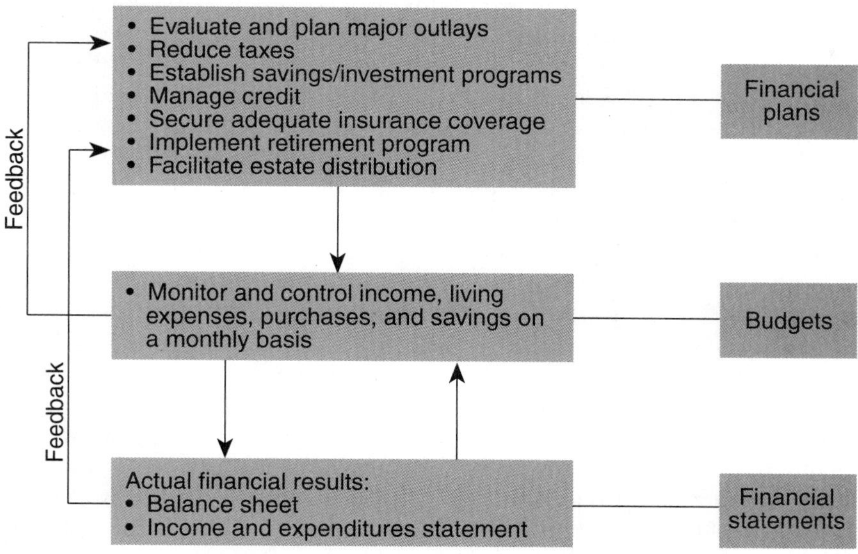

In effect, the financial planning process runs full circle. You start with financial goals, formulate and implement plans to reach them, monitor and control plans through budgets, and evaluate plan results. This leads you back to redefining your goals to better meet your current needs and revising your financial plans accordingly.

As noted earlier, discussing your personal financial goals and attitudes toward money with your partner are important to successful personal financial planning. You also must allocate the responsibility for money management tasks and decisions. Many couples divide routine financial decision-making on the basis of expertise and interest and make major decisions jointly. Each family should consider its members' interests, skills, and spending styles when developing a money management system consistent with its goals. Giving children an allowance is a good way to start teaching them to budget and save. Allowing them to participate in the personal financial planning process, whether at regular "financial meetings" or on a less formal basis, shows them where the household's money goes. By setting their own financial goals and taking steps to reach them, they will develop good money management skills.

Using Personal Financial Planners. Today, more people than ever recognize the importance of managing and controlling their personal finances. They get planning help from personal finance magazines like *Money, Kiplinger's Personal Finance, Smart Money,* and *Worth* and from personal finance software. With the increased variety and complexity of financial products offered, many people turn to **professional financial planners** for help in developing and carrying out personal financial plans. This field has experienced tremendous growth, and currently there are over 250,000 financial planners in the United States. Financial planners provide a wide range of services, including preparing

budget A detailed financial forecast used to monitor and control expenditures and purchases; it provides a mechanism for carrying out financial plans to achieve short-term financial goals.

professional financial planner An individual or firm that assists clients in establishing long- and short-term financial goals and in developing and implementing financial plans aimed at their achievement.

comprehensive financial plans that evaluate a client's total personal financial situation or abbreviated plans focusing on a specific concern—for example, investments or retirement planning—and managing clients' assets and investments. Some planners specialize in income tax planning.

Types of Planners. Most financial planners earn commissions on the financial products they sell, while others charge only a fee based on the complexity of the plan they prepare. In 1993, about 42 percent were paid both fees and commissions; 32 percent, commissions only; and 17 percent, fee only. Some financial planners are simply converted insurance salespeople or securities brokers who continue to sell the same financial products (life insurance, stocks, bonds, mutual funds, and annuities) but now call themselves "financial planners." Others work for large, established financial institutions who recognize the enormous potential in the field and train their planners to compete with the best financial planners. Independent planners offer only sound, high-quality advice for a flat fee or an hourly rate. Regardless of their affiliation, full-service financial planners help their clients articulate their long- and short-term financial goals and systematically plan for their financial needs.

In addition to one-on-one financial planning services, some institutions offer *computerized financial plans*. Ranging in price from $0 to about $500, Shearson Lehman, Merrill Lynch, IDS/American Express, T. Rowe Price, and other major investment firms provide these computerized plans to help clients develop plans to save for college or retirement, reduce taxes, or restructure investment portfolios. While these plans are relatively inexpensive, they tend to be somewhat impersonal. However, they are a good solution for those who need help getting started.

The cost of financial planning services depends on the type of planner, the complexity of your financial situation, and the services you want. A comprehensive plan is the most expensive; its median cost in 1993 was $950, but the range was a low of $250 to a high of $4,000. Abbreviated plans averaged $300. Plan implementation—managing assets or investments—usually costs 1 percent to 3 percent of the assets' value. These costs may be well worth the benefits, especially for people who have neither the time, inclination, discipline, nor expertise to plan on their own. Remember, however, that the best advice is worthless if you are not willing to change your financial habits.

Choosing a Financial Planner. Planners who have completed the required course of study and earned the Certified Financial Planner (CFP) or Chartered Financial Consultant (ChFC) designation are often a better choice than the many self-proclaimed financial planners. Of course, CPAs, attorneys, investment managers, and other professionals without such certifications in many instances do provide sound financial planning advice. Unfortunately, though, the field is still largely unregulated, and almost anyone can call himself or herself a financial planner. Most financial planners are honest and reputable, but there have been cases of fraudulent practices. It is therefore critical to thoroughly check out a potential financial advisor—and preferably interview two or three—using the tips in Exhibit 2.2. Choosing the wrong one could wipe out your hard-earned savings.

The way a planner is paid—fees, commissions, or both—should be one of your major concerns. Obviously, you need to be aware of potential conflicts of interest when using a planner with ties to a brokerage firm, insurance company, or bank. Many planners now provide clients with disclosure forms outlining fees and/or commissions for various transactions. In addition to asking questions, you should check with your state securities department (for those planners registered to sell securities) and the Securities and Exchange Commission to see if there are any pending lawsuits, complaints by state or federal regulators, personal bankruptcies, or convictions for investment-related crimes. However, even these agencies may not have accurate or current information; simply being properly registered and without a record of disciplinary actions provides no guarantee that the planner's track record is good. You may also want to do some additional checking about the planner within the local financial community. Clearly, you should do your homework before engaging the services of a professional financial planner.

A Comprehensive Financial Plan. To get an idea of what is involved in a **comprehensive personal financial plan,** let's look at a professionally prepared plan. Essentially, a comprehensive plan —whether you prepare it yourself or hire a professional—provides an individual or a family with a set of plans and recommendations to follow to reach a variety of specific financial goals. This plan is based on questionnaires and interviews about

EXHIBIT 2.2

Finding and Using a Financial Planner

The following suggestions will help you choose and work with a competent personal financial planner.

1. Decide what you want to accomplish with the planner: budgeting, insurance or tax planning, retirement planning, managing investments?
2. Get names of candidates from other financial advisors, family, and friends and interview several planners to make sure that you feel comfortable with the planner and any associates who will work with you.
3. Thoroughly investigate the planner's background: education, training, previous work experience, type and length of financial planning experience, continuing education programs, certification (International Board of Certified Financial Planners, CFP; the American Society, ChFC; American Institute of Certified Public Accountants, PFS), Securities and Exchange Commission registration. Check SEC Form ADV Part II for disciplinary actions taken by regulators.
4. Make sure the planner's areas of specialization and types of clients served fit *your* needs.
5. Review a sample financial plan and contact several client references to evaluate the quality and completeness of the advice.
6. Find out who will actually prepare your plan (the planner or a subordinate?) and the consultants (accountants, attorneys) the planner uses for specialized expertise.
7. Understand how you will pay for advisory services: flat fee, hourly fee, commission, or combination. Get a contract or agreement letter that specifies the services to be provided and compensation.
8. Once you select a planner, protect yourself from potential problems. If the adviser purchases insurance or securities for you, make sure you receive regular statements from the investment or insurance company as well as from the planner. Question anything you don't understand until you are satisfied with the response.

Source: Based on information from "Consumer Guide to Comprehensive Financial Planning" and "How to Protect Yourself against Fraud," International Association for Financial Planning, Atlanta, Georgia; Terence P. Paré, "How to Find a Financial Planner," *Fortune,* May 14, 1994, pp. 103–106.

personal and financial circumstances: family profile (health, age, education, and similar information for each member); household income, expenses, assets, investments, and debts; tax returns; insurance coverages; retirement programs; and estate plans. Other important information includes personal and family expectations, motivations, risk tolerances, and objectives.

With this information, the planner helps the client define and prioritize personal financial goals in general areas—for example, capital accumulation for specific goals (buying a home, children's education), reducing taxes, protecting against personal risk using insurance, managing investments, and maximizing the estate left to heirs. Such a professional plan could run 50 or more pages and includes the client's major financial goals, detailed strategies and recommendations for each, and expected results.

Exhibit 2.3 summarizes the recommendations from a real-life, 77-page, professionally prepared financial plan. It was prepared at a cost of $1,500 for a dual career couple with two children and a family income of $105,000. With this plan, the couple can now implement the recommended strategies and develop an annual budget to guide them to their established goals.

SPECIAL PLANNING CONCERNS

Throughout your life, you will face changes in your personal circumstances that call for special attention during the personal financial planning process. Changing job status, relocation to a new state, getting married, having children, losing a spouse through divorce or death, retirement, taking responsibility for dependent parents—these and other stressful events are "financial shocks" that require reevaluation of your financial goals and plans.

However, you should avoid making major financial decisions at such times, when you are most vulnerable. It's important to postpone any action until you have had time to recover from the event and evaluate all your options carefully. This can be difficult, because financial salespeople rush

comprehensive personal financial plan
A set of detailed plans and recommendations for achieving specific financial goals, as compiled from a family profile; information on current income, expenses, and financial condition; tax returns; insurance coverages; retirement programs; and estate plans.

EXHIBIT 2.3

Summary of the Recommendations from a Comprehensive, Professionally Prepared Financial Plan

Professionally prepared, comprehensive financial plans are custom-tailored to provide detailed recommendations aimed at the achievement of specific personal financial goals. However, to be effective, the financial plans and recommendations must be implemented—they should be viewed as a launching pad, not a landing strip! The following recommendations are given for a dual-career couple in their 40s with two children.

Education of Children

■ Recommendation:	Engage in a systematic program of prefunding the children's education by putting $60,000 in a custodial account or by setting aside $9,500 annually for the next nine years.
■ Desired result:	Savings of $200,000 in a custodial account at the end of nine years.

Income for Disability

■ Recommendation:	Make no change to present disability program.
■ Desired result:	Adequate income provided in the event of long-term disability.

Medical Insurance

■ Recommendation:	Increase major medical insurance to at least $500,000.
■ Desired result:	Adequate insurance coverage in the event of serious illness.

Property and Liability Insurance

■ Recommendation 1:	Reduce liability coverage under present insurance to the suggested minimum and purchase an excess liability policy in the amount of $2 million.
■ Recommendation 2:	Confirm that the dwelling coverage is at least 80 percent of its replacement value.
■ Desired result:	Adequate overall insurance protection.

Proper Disposition of Estate

■ Recommendation 1:	Purchase $250,000 of universal life insurance on husband's life at an annual cost of approximately $3,000 to provide both insurance and tax-free accumulation.
■ Desired result:	Provide capital for projected survivor income shortages.
■ Recommendation 2:	New wills should first place the unified credit amount in trust for the surviving spouse; the balance of each spouse's estate should qualify for the unlimited marital deduction.
■ Desired result:	Estate tax savings of $80,000 and $45,000, respectively.
■ Recommendation 3:	Consider the use of a testamentary trust in their wills for the benefit of their children.
■ Desired result:	Protection and management of assets until minor children have completed school.

Retirement Income

■ Recommendation:	Follow systematic investment program (described in detail).
■ Desired result:	Monthly income in first year of retirement will be $10,500.

Investment Program

■ Recommendation:	Over a period of time to be determined by tax advice, couple should: Place $20,000 in commercial real estate Place $12,000 in a cash reserve account Place $16,000 in a tax-deferred annuity Place $10,000 in municipal bonds Place $15,000 in growth stock Place $12,500 in an exploratory oil and gas partnership Invest excess cash flow annually
■ Desired result:	Write-offs will save $10,500 in income taxes; capital at retirement will be $725,000.

to contact you in these circumstances. For example, when you have a child, insurance agents, financial planners, and stockbrokers will contact you to buy insurance and start investing in a college fund. While these are valid objectives, don't be pushed into any expensive decisions. People who get large sums of money—from severance packages, retirement benefits, or insurance policies when a loved one dies—are also likely to hear from financial salespeople eager to help them invest the funds. This is another time to wait. These brokers may have a greater interest in selling their own products than advising you on the best strategy for your needs.

Managing Two Incomes. Today, dual income couples account for about 60 percent of U.S. households. Many depend on the second income to make ends meet, while for others it provides financial security and a way to afford "extras." Often, however, the second income does not add as much as expected to the bottom line. With it may come higher expenses—such as child care, taxes, clothing, dry cleaning, transportation, and lunches—that consume a large portion of the second paycheck. Worksheet 2.1 allows you to assess the net monthly income of a second paycheck, both without and with the impact of employer-paid benefits. Be sure to include only those expenses that are directly related to the second job; some personal expenses would exist in the absence of a second job. In addition, couples should coordinate their employee benefits to obtain the needed coverage at a minimum cost.

When analyzing a second income, you must also consider the intangible costs (additional demands on your life, less time with family, and higher stress) and benefits (career development, job satisfaction, and sense of worth). For instance, taking a part-time job while the children are young may not add much to household income, but it could keep the spouse on a career track and ease the transition to full-time work later. Clearly, you should consider personal circumstances and goals when you are assessing the costs and benefits of a second income.

For this reason, two-income families should develop financial plans that consider the possibility of the loss of one income for any reason, including a spouse's staying at home with young children, going back to school, or losing a job. In some cases, couples use the second income to meet the basic expenditures associated with their luxurious lifestyles. They should analyze past income and expenditure statements to study spending patterns and identify areas where expense reductions are possible. Such reductions would then be incorporated into the budgeting process (described later in this chapter).

The dual-income situation often complicates the establishment of a money management system. Spouses need to decide how to allocate income to household expenditures, family financial goals, and personal spending goals. Some options include placing all income into a single joint account; having each spouse contribute equal amounts into a joint account that is used to make expenditures consistent with achievement of their joint goals, while retaining individual discretion over each spouse's remaining income; or contributing a proportional share of each income to finance joint expenditures and goals. Couples may experiment with different strategies until they find one that works best for them. Consideration, of course, must be given to the amount each spouse earns and various emotional and behavioral factors in their relationship. Regardless of the money management system, each spouse needs to have some money of his or her own that he or she can spend without accountability.

Managing Employee Benefits. As we discussed in Chapter 1, if you hold a full-time job, your employer probably provides a variety of employee benefits, ranging from health and life insurance to pension plans. Most people rely on their employee benefit plans for a large part of their financial security. For example, the majority of American families depend solely on company-sponsored *group plans* for their health insurance coverage as well as a big piece of their life insurance coverage and retirement needs.

Actually, today's well-defined employee benefits packages cover a full spectrum of benefits that may include:

- Health and life insurance
- Disability insurance
- Pension and profit-sharing plans
- Supplemental retirement programs, like 401(k) plans
- Dental and vision care
- Child-care and educational assistance programs
- Subsidized employee food services

Each company's benefit package is different; some companies and industries are known for generous benefit plans, while others offer far less attractive packages; in general, large firms can afford more benefits than small ones. Because employee benefits can increase your total compensation by *30 percent or more,* it is *critical* that you thoroughly investigate your employee benefits to choose those appropriate for your personal situation. Such a

WORKSHEET 2.1

Analyzing the Benefit of a Second Income

Use this worksheet to estimate the contribution of a second paycheck. Your employer should be able to estimate your noncash benefits. Without the employer-paid benefits of $816 (line 2) the Diaz's would realize net monthly income of $904 (line 1 – line 3) and with them their net monthly income would be $1,720 (line 4). Note that even though the social security tax shows up as a job-related expense, it is buying future benefits.

Second Income Analysis

Name(s) Ariana and Marcos Diaz   Dated December 31, 1995

MONTHLY CASH INCOME	
Gross pay	$2,500
Pretax contributions (401(k) plans, dependent-care-reimbursement accounts)	200
Additional job-related income (bonuses, overtime, commissions)	0
(1) Total Cash Income	$2,700
EMPLOYER-PAID BENEFITS	
Health insurance	$ 275
Life insurance	50
Pension contributions	300
Thrift-plan contributions	0
Social security	191
Profit sharing	0
Other deferred compensation	0
(2) Total Benefits	$ 816
MONTHLY JOB-RELATED EXPENSES	
Federal income tax	$ 750
Social security tax	191
State income tax	125
Child care	320
Clothing; personal care; dry cleaning	200
Meals away from home	100
Public transportation	0
Auto-related expenses (gas, parking, maintenance)	110
Other	0
(3) Total Expenses	$ 1,796
(4) Net Income (Deficit) [(1) + (2) – (3)]	$ 1,720

Source: Adapted from Kevin McManus, "How to Get the Most from Two Incomes," *Changing Times*, July 1989, p. 24.

sizable amount warrants good planning—not only when considering a job offer but also on an annual basis, because your needs will change over time. Companies change their benefit packages frequently and today are shifting more costs to employees. While the employer pays for some benefits in full, typically the employee pays for a portion of the cost of group health insurance coverage on his or her family, supplemental life insurance, and participation in voluntary retirement programs.

Many employers today are replacing traditional programs, where the company sets the type and amount of benefits with **flexible-benefit plans,** in which the employee selects the benefits most desirable to him or her. These programs are better suited to today's employees, whose financial security needs vary greatly with age, marital status, number of dependent children, level of income, and so forth. In flexible-benefit programs, the employer allocates a certain amount of money to each employee and then lets the employee "spend" that money to pick and choose from a variety of benefits, usually covering everything from child-care to retirement benefits. These plans usually offer several levels of health and life insurance coverage and have some limits on the minimum and maximum amount of coverage. But within these constraints, you can select the benefits that do you the most good. In some plans, you can even take a portion of the benefits in the form of more take-home pay or extra vacation time!

Along with greater choice comes the responsibility to manage these benefits carefully, whether you're covered by a traditional or flexible-benefit plan. You should periodically assess the benefits package you have at work relative to your own individual/family needs. Make sure you have the coverage or protection you need; if there is a shortfall in your company benefits package, try to supplement it with personal coverage. Except perhaps for group medical coverage, *don't rely on your employer as the sole source of financial security.* Your coverage may disappear if you change jobs or become unemployed, and, especially with life insurance and retirement plans, you'll find that your employee benefits fall short of your total financial needs.

As you can see, integrating employee benefit planning into your financial plans should be an ongoing process. In later chapters, you'll see how to assess your life insurance, disability insurance, and pension programs to see if they meet your needs and if not, how to bring your coverage up to a desirable standard.

Adapting to Other Major Life Changes. Other situations that require special consideration include changes in marital status and the need to support grown children and/or elderly relatives. The accompanying *Financial Shocks* box discusses planning steps that help if you must assume responsibility for your parents' care. Marriage, divorce, or death of a spouse result in the need to revise financial plans and money management strategies.

As discussed earlier, couples should discuss their money attitudes and financial goals and decide how to manage joint financial affairs before they get married. Marriage may create a two-income household, raising the concerns addressed above. It's important to take an inventory of your financial assets and liabilities, including savings and checking accounts; credit card accounts and outstanding bills; auto, health, and life insurance policies; and investment portfolios. You may want to eliminate some credit cards if there is overlap; too many cards can hurt your credit rating, and most people only need one or two. Each partner should have a card in his or her name to establish a credit record. Compare employee benefit plans to figure out the lowest-cost source of health insurance coverage and coordinate other benefits. Change the beneficiary on your life insurance policies. If you don't yet have life insurance, consider buying term insurance, perhaps from your employer. Because you move into a different filing category when you marry, estimate annual income tax payments and adjust withholding amounts as necessary based on your new filing category.

In the event of divorce, income may decrease because alimony and/or child support payments

flexible-benefit plans A type of employee benefit plan wherein the employee, rather than the employer, picks the type of benefit coverage received from a menu covering everything from child-care to health and life insurance to retirement benefits.

Financial Shocks

Planning for Dependent Parents

The phone rings in the middle of the night with a serious message: your mother has had a stroke and is in the hospital, unconscious. The doctors tell you that it is unlikely that she will be able to live on her own once she recovers. Or perhaps the problem appears more gradually. Your father is becoming increasingly forgetful and needs constant supervision that your mother can't provide. Becoming responsible for our parents or other relatives ranks high among life's financial shocks, and as life expectancy increases, the odds are high that you'll have to contend with this situation. Today over 8 million Americans help elderly relatives by managing personal affairs, providing financial assistance, or selecting the right housing and health care options. This additional emotional and financial burden often comes when you are financially stressed as well—raising young children, paying for their college education, or trying to save for your own retirement. Often family members do not agree on a course of action, creating additional tension.

While it's difficult to eliminate the emotional stress, you can minimize the financial concerns by careful planning before a crisis occurs. Start by having a candid discussion with your parents while they are still healthy. They may be reluctant to confront issues like their financial situation, insurance coverage, medical treatment, and the type of living situation they prefer when they can no longer live independently. You'll also want to start researching retirement communities and nursing homes before they are needed; the better ones typically have waiting lists. Emphasize that this information will help you make decisions in compliance with their wishes if they become mentally or physically incapacitated.

You'll need to know where they keep important personal, financial, and legal information, including bank and investment account statements, names of financial advisors and attorneys, medical information, insurance policy records, trust agreements and wills, and similar items. Make sure they have written wills and encourage them to meet with estate planning professionals to set up trusts if appropriate. Discuss obtaining durable powers of attorney for financial matters and health care. These important documents designate someone to make decisions on their behalf if they are incapable of doing so. If possible, meet your parents' advisors (banker, stockbroker, attorney, accountant) and get authorization (joint signature card or power of attorney) to be informed of unusual transactions. To simplify money management tasks, help your parents set up automatic bill payment and automatic deposit of social security and pension checks. Often elderly people forget to pay bills or have difficulty getting to the bank to make deposits.

Making decisions about your elderly relatives' care is even harder when you live far away. You feel guilty that you can't provide emotional and physical support in person, and you probably don't know what resources and services are available. Again, advance planning pays off. The National Association of Area Agencies on Aging's Eldercare Locator Services (800-677-1116) and a phone book for your relative's city can guide you to local agencies and senior services like day care and home help providers. Churches and synagogues often have special programs for seniors and volunteer groups who will check up on or visit your homebound relative. There are also many organizations, both local and national, to assist you.

Sources: Jonathan D. Pond, *The ABCs of Managing Your Money*. Denver, CO: National Endowment for Financial Education, 1993, pp. 222–227; Mary Rowland, "Assistance from a Distance," *Worth*, December/January 1994, pp. 103–104; Grace W. Weinstein, "Helping Your Parents Cope," *Kiplinger's Personal Finance Magazine*, March 1994, pp. 69–72.

cause one salary to be divided between two households. Single parents may have to stretch limited financial resources further to meet added expenses such as child care. Remarriage brings additional financial considerations, including decisions involving children from prior marriages and managing the assets each spouse brings to the marriage. Some couples find it helpful to develop a prenuptial contract that sets forth their agreement on financial matters, such as the control of assets, their disposition in the event of death or divorce, and other important money issues.

Death of a spouse is another change that greatly affects financial planning. The surviving spouse is typically faced with decisions on how to receive and invest life insurance proceeds and manage other assets. In families where the deceased made most of the financial decisions with little or no involvement of the surviving spouse, the survivor may be overwhelmed by the need to take on financial responsibilities. Advance planning can minimize many of these problems. Couples should, on a regular basis, review all aspects of their finances. Each spouse should understand what is owned and owed, participate in formulating financial goals and investment strategies, and fully understand estate plans (covered in detail in Chapter 15).

THE ROLE OF FINANCIAL STATEMENTS IN FINANCIAL PLANNING

Clearly, in order to set realistic personal financial plans and strategies, we must know where we stand financially. Once the plans and strategies are in place, we then need a system for monitoring our progress. Personal financial statements can help in both stages by defining your current financial condition and enabling you to track changes in your financial position over time.

To begin with, the *balance sheet* describes financial position—the assets you hold, debts you owe, and your net worth—at a given point in time. Then it helps you track the progress you're making toward your goals, in building up your assets and/or reducing your debt. Thus, it is indispensable in setting, monitoring, and revising financial plans. Also, by revealing the changes taking place in your financial position, it helps you know when it is time to alter your financial plans.

In contrast, the *income and expenditures statement* measures financial performance over time. It tracks income earned, as well as expenditures made, over a given period of time (usually a year). A key ingredient in financial planning is gaining budgetary control over expenses and purchases. Without such control, you could find yourself without the funds necessary to carry out your financial plans. A statement of income and expenditures provides a way to check actual expenses and purchases against the amounts budgeted. Corrective action can then be taken when discrepancies exist between the actual and budgeted amounts.

The primary function of financial statements, therefore, is to summarize your financial position as it *actually* exists and report on various financial transactions that have *really* occurred. On the other hand, financial plans deal with mapping out the *future* and, at first glance, may appear to be incompatible with financial statements because of their different time references. Yet the whole planning system would indeed collapse without statements to provide feedback on your financial progress. Somewhere along the line, you must look at how actual results compare with your plans.

Think of financial statements as *planning tools* that provide an up-to-date evaluation of your financial well-being, help you identify potential financial problems, and in general help you make better-informed financial decisions. The following sections take a detailed look at the basic personal financial statements, starting with the balance sheet.

Concept Check

2-1. What is the difference between a budget and a financial plan? Does a budget play any role in a financial plan?

2-2. Identify the six key steps involved in the financial planning process. What role should partners and/or families play in this process?

2-3. What is a professional financial planner? Does it make any difference whether the financial planner earns money from commissions made on products sold, or on the fees he or she charges?

2-4. Describe a comprehensive financial plan. How are such plans constructed, and what kind of information do they contain?

2-5. Discuss briefly how the following situations affect personal financial planning:
- **a.** major life changes such as the birth of a child or loss of a job
- **b.** being part of a dual-income couple
- **c.** changes in marital status

2-6. How do financial statements fit into the personal financial planning process?

EXHIBIT 2.4

Commonly Held Personal Assets

The specific types and amounts of personal assets held will vary from one person or family to another. Most households will likely hold some liquid assets, possibly even some investments, and real and personal property.

Liquid Assets	Investments	Real Property
Cash On hand In checking account **Savings accounts** At banks, S&Ls At other thrift institutions Money market deposits and funds Certificates of deposit (< 1 year maturity)	**Stocks and bonds** Common stock Preferred stock Corporate bonds Government and municipal bonds **Certificates of deposit** (> 1 year maturity) **Investment companies** Closed-end funds Mutual funds **Real estate** **Business ownership** **Cash value of life insurance** **Cash value of pensions** **Retirement fund, investments** IRA, 401(k) plans **Other investment vehicles** Commodities and financial futures Options Precious minerals Collectibles Annuities and limited partnerships	Primary residence Vacation home **Personal Property** Automobiles Recreational equipment Household items Jewelry and artwork

THE BALANCE SHEET: A STATEMENT OF YOUR FINANCIAL CONDITION FPPC LG2

A balance sheet reports the things you own, on the one hand, relative to the money you owe and your financial worth, on the other. What do you currently own and owe? List and evaluate all items you own and owe, noting their current dollar value, before reading on.

The **balance sheet**—or *statement of financial position*—summarizes a person's (or family's) financial condition at a certain point in time. Think of a balance sheet as a snapshot taken of a person's financial position on one day out of the year. Technically, you could have a (slightly) different balance sheet each day of the year. A balance sheet represents a summary of what you own—your *assets*—balanced against what you owe—your *liabilities,* or debts—and what you are worth—your *net worth.* The accounting relationship between these three categories is called the *balance sheet equation* and is expressed as follows:

$$\text{Total assets} = \text{Total liabilities} + \text{Net worth}$$

ASSETS: THE THINGS YOU OWN

Assets are the items you own. They are mostly tangible, although in certain instances they may also be intangible. An item is classified as an asset regardless of whether it was purchased for cash or financed with debt. In other words, even if an asset has not been fully paid for, it is considered owned by the individual and should be listed on the balance sheet. An item that is leased, in contrast, is not shown as an asset, because it is actually owned by someone else.

Assets can be grouped in a variety of ways. One useful procedure is to group them on the basis of their underlying characteristics and uses, as shown in Exhibit 2.4. This results in four broad categories: Liquid assets, investments, real property, and personal property. As of 1992, the average household's assets consisted of about 32.3 percent financial assets (liquid assets and investments), 44.3 percent real property (including housing), and 23.4 percent other nonfinancial assets (business assets and personal property).

Regardless of their type, all assets are recorded on the balance sheet at their current **fair market value,** which may differ considerably from their original purchase price. Fair market value is either the actual value of the asset (such as money in a checking account) or the price that the asset can reasonably be expected to sell for in the open market (like a used car or a home).

Liquid Assets. **Liquid assets** are those low-risk financial assets that are held in the form of cash or can readily be converted to cash with little or no loss in value. These assets are held to meet the everyday needs of life. Cash can be held either in the form of cash on hand or in a *demand deposit* (checking account). Savings are also part of one's liquid assets and can be held in such financial instruments as *time deposits* (savings accounts), money market deposit accounts, money market mutual funds, or certificates of deposit that mature within one year.

Investments. **Investments** are assets that are acquired in order to earn a return rather than provide a service. These assets, which typically consist largely of intangible *financial assets* (stocks, bonds, and other types of securities), tend to be held for the anticipated future benefit they offer. Popular investments assets include common and preferred stocks and corporate, government, and municipal bonds. Certificates of deposit with maturities of greater than one year, shares in investment companies—especially mutual funds—and real estate are also popular. Business ownership, the cash value of life insurance and pensions, retirement funds such as IRAs and 401(k) plans, and other investment vehicles such as commodities and financial futures, and options represent still other forms of investment assets. (With regard to retirement fund accounts, *only those balances that are eligible to be withdrawn should be shown as an asset on the balance sheet.*) Investment assets tend to be acquired to achieve long-run personal financial goals. They vary in marketability (the ability to sell quickly) from high (stocks and bonds) to low (real estate and business ownership investments).

Real and Personal Property. Real and personal property are categories of tangible assets that are used in our everyday lives and provide support for our activities. **Real property** refers to immovable property: land and anything fixed to it, such as a house. Real estate may *appreciate,* or increase in value. **Personal property** is movable property such as automobiles, recreational equipment, household furnishings and appliances, clothing, jewelry, home electronics, and similar items. Except for some kinds of older collectible cars, and perhaps jewelry and artwork, most types of personal property *depreciate,* or decline in value, shortly after being put into use. In fact, the resale value of clothing and furniture quickly drops to a fraction of their original cost.

balance sheet A key financial statement that summarizes a person's assets, liabilities, and net worth, measured at a specified point in time.

assets Items that one owns.

fair market value The price that an asset can reasonably be expected to sell for in the open market.

liquid assets Assets that are held in the form of cash or can be readily converted to cash with minimal or no loss in value; used to meet living expenses, make purchases, pay bills and loans, and provide for emergencies and unexpected opportunities.

investments Assets like stocks, bonds, and mutual funds that are acquired for the purpose of earning a return rather than providing a service.

real property Tangible assets that are immovable, such as land and anything fixed to it, such as a house; generally have relatively long lives and high costs.

personal property Tangible assets that are movable and used to provide the general comforts of life; includes automobiles, household furnishings, and jewelry.

EXHIBIT 2.5

Common Types of Personal Liabilities

The type of debt you have can include everything from current liabilities such as unpaid utility bills and credit card balances to long-term liabilities such as mortgages and consumer loans. Regardless of the type, they all have one thing in common—they are obligations that must be paid off in the future.

Current Liabilities	Long-Term Liabilities
Utility bills	Home (primary residence) mortgage
Rent	Other residence (second home) mortgages
Insurance premiums	Real estate investment mortgages
Taxes	Automobile loans
Medical/dental bills	Appliance and furniture loans
Repair bills	Home improvement loans
Bank credit card balances	Single-payment bank loans
Department store credit card balances	Education loans
Travel and entertainment card balances	Margin loans (on securities)
Gas and other credit card balances	Other loans
Bank line of credit balances	
Other current liabilities	

LIABILITIES: THE MONEY YOU OWE

Liabilities represent an individual's or family's debts. They could result from department store charges, bank credit card charges, installment loans, or mortgages on housing and other real estate. A given liability, regardless of its source, is something that is owed and must be repaid in the future. Liabilities are generally classified as either current or long term. A **current,** or **short-term, liability** is any debt due within one year of the date of the balance sheet. A **long-term liability** is a debt due one year or more from the date of the balance sheet. Exhibit 2.5 lists some common types of liabilities that may appear on a personal balance sheet. The level and status of an individual's liabilities are given careful consideration by potential lenders because very high levels of debt and overdue debts are both viewed with a great deal of disfavor.

Current Liabilities. One type of current liability arises from charges for the purchase of consumable goods and services. Utility bills, rent, insurance premiums, taxes, medical bills, repair bills, and all similar debts fall into this category. Typically, these bills are due to be paid in full upon receipt or by a specified date, usually within one month of the billing date. Include these bills as liabilities only if you owe the funds now (an unpaid bill). Do not include something you may owe in the future, such as next month's utility bill.

A second type of current liability is **open account credit obligations**—the balances outstanding against preestablished credit lines, which are used to purchase various types of goods and services. For most people, such credit means the use of "plastic"—that is, a credit card. The balances on some credit cards (like bank and department store credit cards) can be paid off over time with small "minimum payments"; however, others, like gas or most travel and entertainment cards (American Express, for example), require payment in full upon receipt of the monthly statement. Another type of open account credit is the *line of credit* offered by most banking institutions, which provides a preauthorized amount of credit. Rather than use a credit card, you access the line of credit by writing a check against either your regular checking account or a special credit line set up at your bank or financial institution. The amount of the liability on open account credit obligations is the *total balance outstanding,* not the monthly payment; the outstanding balance will be printed on your monthly statement.

Long-Term Liabilities. Debt obligations with final repayment dates more than one year from the date of the balance sheet are classified as *long-term liabilities.* They typically include real estate mortgages, most consumer installment loans, education loans, and margin loans used to purchase securities. **Real estate mortgages** are loans associated with housing and other real estate purchases; they normally have lives of 15 years or more. They most commonly result from the purchase of a home but sometimes arise from real estate investments such as apartments or office buildings. Real estate mortgages are normally paid on an installment basis. **Consumer installment loans** include all debts (other than mortgages) for which a series of payments are required over a specified period of time. Installment loans are generally used to finance such purchases as automobiles, appliances, furniture, and boats. Other types of long-term liabilities include single-payment bank loans, education loans, and margin loans on securities.

All types of loans must be shown on the balance sheet. Although most loans will fall into the category of long-term liabilities, *any loans that come due within a year should be shown as current liabilities.* Examples of such short-term loans include a six-month, single-payment bank loan or a nine-month consumer installment loan for a refrigerator. Regardless of the type of loan, *only the latest outstanding loan balance should be shown as a liability on the balance sheet* because at any given point in time it is the *latest* balance still due—not the initial loan balance—that matters. Another important and closely related point is that *only the principal portion of a loan or mortgage* should be listed as a liability on the balance sheet. In other words, you should not include the interest portion of your payments as part of your balance sheet debt. The principal actually defines the amount of debt you owe at a given point in time and does not include any future interest payments. You may have to contact the lender or refer to a *loan amortization table* for the loan in order to determine the amount of this liability.

NET WORTH: A MEASURE OF YOUR FINANCIAL WORTH

Net worth is the amount of actual wealth or **equity** an individual or family has in owned assets. It can be viewed as the amount of money that would remain after selling all owned assets at their estimated fair market values and paying off all liabilities (assuming there are no transaction costs). As noted earlier, every balance sheet must "balance" so that total assets equals total liabilities plus net worth. Rearranging this equation, we get net worth equals total assets minus total liabilities. Once the fair market value of assets and the level of liabilities have been established, net worth is easily calculated by subtracting total liabilities from total assets. If net worth is less than zero, the family is *technically insolvent.* While this form of **insolvency** does not mean that the family will end up in bankruptcy proceedings, it does reflect the absence of adequate financial planning.

Net worth typically increases over the life cycle of an individual or family. For example, the balance sheet of a college student will probably be fairly simple. Assets would include modest liquid assets (cash, checking and savings accounts) and personal property, which may include a car. Liabilities might include utility bills, perhaps some open account credit obligations, and automobile and education loans. At this point in life, net worth would typically be very low, because assets are small in comparison to liabilities. A 29-year-old, single financial analyst would have more liquid assets and personal property, may have started an investment program, and may have purchased a condominium. Net worth would be rising but may still be low due to the increased liabilities associated with real and

liabilities Debts, such as credit card charges, installment loan balances, and real estate mortgages.

current (short-term) liability Any debt due within one year of the date of the balance sheet.

long-term liability Any debt due in one year or more from the date of the balance sheet.

open account credit obligations Current liabilities that represent the balances outstanding against preestablished credit lines, which are used to purchase various types of goods and services.

real estate mortgages Loans associated with housing and other real estate purchases; they normally have lives of 15 years or more.

consumer installment loans Loans (other than mortgages) that are repaid in a series of fixed, scheduled payments.

net worth An individual's or family's actual wealth; determined by subtracting total liabilities from total assets.

equity The actual ownership interest in a specific asset or group of assets.

insolvency The financial state in which net worth is less than zero.

personal property purchases. The higher net worth of a two-career couple in their late 30s with children would reflect a greater proportion of assets relative to liabilities as they save for college expenses and retirement.

In the long-term financial planning process, the level of net worth is important. Once a family has established a goal of accumulating a certain level or type of wealth, progress toward that goal is best analyzed by monitoring net worth.

BALANCE SHEET FORMAT AND PREPARATION

Worksheet 2.2 presents a hypothetical balance sheet prepared for Fred and Denise Weaver on December 31, 1995. Assets are listed on the left side and liabilities on the right. The net worth entry is shown on the right side of the statement just below the liabilities. The subheadings included in Exhibits 2.4 and 2.5 may be used to break the statement into various categories. Regardless of how the various assets and liabilities are categorized, the statement should *balance*. Total assets equal the sum of total liabilities and net worth, as shown in the balance sheet equation.

You should prepare your personal balance sheet at least once a year, preferably every three to six months. Begin by listing your assets at their fair market value as of the date you are preparing the balance sheet, using the categories in Exhibit 2.4 as a guide. To determine the fair market value of assets, use checking and savings account records, bills of sale, investment account statements, and similar sources of information to get their original costs. For most personal property, values are then adjusted for the age of the item. The values of investments, a home, and a car are easier to estimate, because there are published sources of information such as stock and bond quotations, advertisements for comparable homes, and the *Blue Book* for used car values. Certain items—for example, homes, jewelry, and artwork—may appreciate, or increase, in value over time. The values of other assets—cars and most other types of personal property—depreciate, or decrease in value, over time.

Next, list all current and long-term liabilities, using the categories in Exhibit 2.5 as a starting point. *You should show all outstanding charges—even if you have not received the bill—as current liabilities on the balance sheet.* For example, assume that on June 23 you used your Visa card to charge $240 for a set of tires. You typically receive your Visa bill around the tenth of the following month. If you were preparing a balance sheet dated June 30, the $240 should be shown on it as a current liability—even though the bill won't arrive until July 10. Remember to list only the principal balance of any loan obligation.

The final step in the preparation of your balance sheet is to calculate net worth. Subtracting your total liabilities from your total assets results in your net worth, which reflects the equity you have in your assets.

A BALANCE SHEET FOR FRED AND DENISE WEAVER

The relationship between assets, liabilities, and net worth and the general format of the balance sheet is perhaps best illustrated with an example. Toward that end, we will now examine the financial statements of Fred and Denise Weaver, a young couple whose balance sheet as of December 31, 1995, appears as Worksheet 2.2.

Fred and Denise live in a midwestern suburb, were married in 1992, and currently have no children. Fred is 28 years old and has just completed his fifth year as a marketing representative for a large soap manufacturer. Denise is 26 and holds a bachelor's degree in primary education. After teaching one year, she realized that a career in education was not for her, so she went back to school full-time and earned a master's degree in business administration (M.B.A.). In June 1995 she began working at a local advertising agency. The Weavers live in their own condominium, which they purchased in October 1993. Fred and Denise love to travel and ski. They plan to have children in a few years, but for now they want to devote their efforts toward developing some degree of financial stability and independence.

Given their ages, the Weavers' asset position looks quite good. Their dominant asset is their condo, and they also have $5,750 in investments and retirement funds and appear to have adequate liquid assets to meet their bill payments and cover small, unexpected expenses. But their financial position cannot be accurately measured without examining their debts.

The Weavers' primary liability is the $62,000 mortgage on their condo. Their *equity,* or actual ownership interest, in the condo is approximately

WORKSHEET 2.2

The Weavers' Balance Sheet

A balance sheet is set up to show what you own on one side (your assets) and how you paid for them on the other (debt or net worth).

BALANCE SHEET

Name(s) Fred and Denise Weaver Dated December 31, 1995

ASSETS

Liquid Assets		
Cash on hand	$ 90	
In checking	575	
Savings accounts	760	
Money market funds and deposits	800	
Certificates of deposit (<1 yr. to maturity)		
Total Liquid Assets		$ 2,225
Investments		
Stocks	$ 1,250	
Bonds Corp.	1,000	
Certificates of deposit (>1 yr. to maturity)		
Mutual funds	1,500	
Real estate		
Retirement funds, IRA	2,000	
Other		
Total Investments		$ 5,750
Real Property		
Primary residence	$70,000	
Second home		
Other		
Total Real Property		$70,000
Personal Property		
Auto(s): '93 Toyota Corolla	$ 8,500	
Auto(s): '90 Ford Escort	4,000	
Recreational vehicles		
Household furnishings	3,700	
Jewelry and artwork	1,500	
Other		
Other		
Total Personal Property		$ 17,700
(I) Total Assets		$ 95,675

LIABILITIES AND NET WORTH

Current Liabilities		
Utilities	$ 120	
Rent		
Insurance premiums		
Taxes		
Medical/dental bills	75	
Repair bills		
Bank credit card balances	395	
Dept. store credit card balances	145	
Travel and entertainment card balances	125	
Gas and other credit card balances		
Bank line of credit balances		
Other current liabilities	45	
Total Current Liabilities		$ 905
Long-Term Liabilities		
Primary residence mortgage	$62,000	
Second home mortgage		
Real estate investment mortgage		
Auto loans	4,250	
Appliance/furniture loans	800	
Home improvement loans		
Single-payment loans		
Education loans	3,800	
Other long-term loans (from parents)	4,000	
Total Long-Term Liabilities		$74,850
(II)Total Liabilities		$75,755
Net Worth [(I) – (II)]		$19,920
Total Liabilities and Net Worth		$95,675

$8,000 ($70,000 market value minus $62,000 outstanding mortgage loan). Their current liabilities, most of which must be paid over the next month, total $905. Other debts total $12,850 and include auto, furniture, and education loans, plus a personal loan from their parents toward the down payment on their home. Comparing the Weavers' total liabilities of $75,755 to their total assets or $95,675 provides a more realistic view of their current wealth position.

The Weavers' net worth (from Worksheet 2.2) is $19,920—a respectable figure considering their ages. By calculating their net worth at specified points in time, they can measure how their financial plans and decisions affect their wealth position. As you'd expect, a large or increasing wealth position is preferable to a low or declining one.

Concept Check

2-7. Describe the balance sheet, its components, and how you would use it in personal financial planning. Differentiate between investments and real and personal property.

2-8. What is the balance sheet equation? Explain when a family may be viewed as technically insolvent.

2-9. Explain two ways in which net worth could increase (or decrease) from one period to the next. Which way would make the change in net worth more likely to occur? Why?

THE INCOME AND EXPENDITURES STATEMENT: A MEASURE OF YOUR FINANCIAL PERFORMANCE

FPPC LG3

An income and expenditures statement provides a summary of the income you received and the money you spent over a given period of time, usually one year. Do you know how much you received and spent during the last year? Before reading on, make a list of each item and amount of your income and expenditures during the most recent year.

While the balance sheet describes a person's or family's financial position at a given point in time, the **income and expenditures statement** captures the various financial activities that have occurred over time—normally over the course of a year, although it technically can cover any time period (monthly, quarterly, and so on). Think of this statement as a motion picture that not only shows actual results over time but allows for their comparison to budgeted financial goals as well. Equally important, the statement evaluates the amount of saving and investing that has taken place during the time period covered.

The income and expenditures statement consists of three major parts: *income, expenditures,* and *cash surplus (or deficit).* A cash surplus (or deficit) is merely the difference between income and expenditures. The statement is prepared on a **cash basis,** which means that *only transactions involving actual cash receipts or actual cash outlays are recorded.* In effect, the statement describes a person's or family's financial activities in terms of the cash inflows and outflows. (As a point of clarification, the term *cash* is used in this case to include not only coin and currency but also checks drawn against demand deposits and certain types of savings accounts.)

Income and expenditure patterns change depending on where an individual or family is in the life cycle. Both income and spending levels rise steadily to a peak in the 45–54 age bracket. On average, persons in this age group, whose children are typically in college or no longer at home, generally have the highest level of income; they also spend more than other age groups on entertainment, dining out, transportation, education, insurance, and charitable contributions. Families in the 35–44 age bracket have slightly lower average levels of income and expenditures but very different spending patterns. Because they tend to have school-age children, they spend more on food at home, housing, clothing, and other personal needs. The average percentage of income spent, however, is about the same—85 to 87 percent—for all age brackets through age 55, when it drops slightly to 82 percent. It rises sharply to 98 percent, however, for persons age 65 and over.

INCOME: THE AMOUNT OF CASH IN

Income includes earnings received as wages, salaries, self-employment income, bonuses, and

EXHIBIT 2.6

Sources of Income

For most gainfully employed people, the vast majority of total income is made up of wages and salaries.

- Wages and salaries
- Self-employment income
- Bonuses and commissions
- Pensions and annuities
- Investment income:
  - Interest received
  - Dividends received
  - Proceeds from sale of securities
  - Rents received from leased assets
- Alimony and child support received
- Scholarships and grants received
- Social security received
- Other income:
  - Proceeds from sale of assets
  - Tax refunds
  - Miscellaneous (gifts, royalties, and so on)

commissions; interest and dividends received from savings and investments; and proceeds from the sale of assets, such as stocks and bonds or an auto. Other income items include pension or annuity income, rent received from leased assets, alimony and child support, scholarships, grants, and social security received, tax refunds, and other miscellaneous types of income. As noted above, only income that has actually been received should be shown. This approach forces an honest representation of the way things were during the year, not the way they were expected to be. Note also that the proper figure to use is *gross* wages, salaries, and commissions, which constitute the amount of income you receive from your employer *before* taxes and other payroll deductions are taken out. You should not use *take-home* pay, because it will understate your income by the amount of these deductions. Common sources of income which should be shown on the income and expenditures statement are listed in Exhibit 2.6.

EXPENDITURES: THE AMOUNT OF CASH OUT

Expenditures represent money used for outlays. Due to the many different kinds of expenditures, it is perhaps easiest to categorize them by the types of benefits they provide, as shown in Exhibit 2.7: (1) *living expenses* (such as rent, food, medical expenses, repairs, insurance, and utilities), (2) *asset purchases* (like autos, stereos, furniture, appliances, and clothing), (3) *tax payments,* and (4) *debt payments* (on mortgages, installment loans, credit cards, and so on). Some are **fixed expenditures** that usually are contractual, predetermined, and involve equal payments each period (typically each month). Examples include mortgage and installment loan payments, insurance premiums, professional or union dues, club dues, monthly savings or investment programs, and cable television fees.

income and expenditures statement A key financial statement that presents one's income, expenditures, and cash surpluses or deficits over a designated time period.

cash basis A method of preparing financial statements in which only cash income and cash expenditure items are recorded.

income Earnings received as wages, salaries, bonuses and commissions, interest and dividends received from savings and investments, and proceeds from the sale of assets.

expenditures Money spent on living expenses, to purchase assets, pay taxes, and/or repay debt.

fixed expenditures Expenditures involving equal payments each period (typically each month).

EXHIBIT 2.7

Common Types of Household Expenditures

Classifying expenses into major categories, such as those shown below, simplifies record-keeping and statement preparation. The percentages represent the estimated average annual expenditures by major categories as a percentage of average before-tax household income.

Housing (19%)

Mortgage payments
Rent
Repairs and additions
Household services

Utilities (7%)

Gas and electric
Garbage service
Telephone
Water
Cable TV

Food (13%)

Groceries
Dining out

Transportation (16%)

Purchase or loan payments
Gas and oil
License fees
Repairs
Lease payments
Other transportation

Health Care (5%)

Doctor bills
Dental bills
Hospital bills
Health insurance

Clothing, Shoes, and Accessories (5%)

Personal Insurance and Pensions (8%)

Life insurance
Disability income insurance
Pensions and Social Security

Taxes (9%)

Income
Property

Appliances, Furniture, or Other Assets (3%)

Purchases
Installment payments
Repairs and maintenance

Personal Care (1%)

Laundry and dry cleaning
Cosmetics
Hairdresser

Recreation, Entertainment, and Vacation (6%)

Admissions
Alcoholic beverages
Hobby supplies
Cigarettes and tobacco
Sports equipment
Records and tapes
Vacation and travel

Other Items (8%)

Postage and stationery
Personal allowance
Books and magazines
Tuition
Legal fees
Interest expenses
Dues and club memberships
Gifts
Church and charity
Pets
Child care
Miscellaneous unclassified expenditures

Source: "Consumer Expenditures in 1993," *News Release,* 94–546, Washington, D.C., Bureau of Labor Statistics, November 7, 1994.

Others (such as food, clothing, utilities, entertainment, and medical expenses) are **variable expenditures,** because their amounts are always changing.

Just as only the amounts of cash actually received are shown as income, only the amounts of money actually paid out in cash are listed as expenditures. If an item—particularly an asset—is acquired through borrowing, only the net or actual dollar amount of money paid out (that is, purchase price minus amount borrowed) is included as an expenditure. In effect, the financed portion of such an outlay is not viewed as an expenditure until debt payments are actually made. Instead, credit purchases of this type are shown as an asset and corresponding liability *on the balance sheet.* Payments against these loans are shown on the income and expenditures statement in the period they are actually made: In other words, cash expenditures include actual *payments* against loans but not the amounts of the loans themselves. For example, assume you purchase a new car for $15,000 in September. You make a down payment of $3,000 and finance the remaining $12,000 with a four-year, 10.5 percent installment loan. Your September 30 income statement would show a cash expenditure of $3,000, and each subsequent monthly income statement would include your monthly loan payment of $307. Your September 30 balance sheet would show the car as an asset valued at $15,000 and the loan balance as a $12,000 long-term liability. The market value of the car and the loan balance would be adjusted on future balance sheets.

Finally, when developing your list of expenditures for the year, remember to include the amount of income and social security taxes withheld from your paycheck as well as any other payroll deductions taken out, such as for health insurance, savings plans, retirement and pension contributions, and professional/union dues. These deductions (from *gross* wages, salaries, and commissions) represent personal expenditures even if they do not involve the *direct* payment of cash.

CASH SURPLUS (OR DEFICIT)

The third component of the income and expenditures statement captures the net result of the period's financial activities. The cash surplus (or deficit) for the period is obtained by subtracting total expenditures from total income and allows you to determine at a glance how you did financially over the period. The figure can be zero, positive, or negative. A value of zero indicates that expenditures were exactly equal to income for the period. A positive figure indicates that the expenditures were less than income and therefore a **cash surplus** resulted. A negative value indicates that the period's expenditures exceeded income, thereby resulting in a **cash deficit.**

A cash surplus can be used for savings or investment purposes, to acquire assets, or reduce (that is, make payments on) debt. Additions to savings or investments (it is hoped) will result in increased future income, while payments on debt will have a favorable effect on cash flow by reducing future expenditures. In contrast, when a cash deficit occurs, the shortfall must be covered by either drawing your savings or investments down, reducing assets, or borrowing. Either strategy will have undesirable effects on your financial future. One final point: The cash surplus (or deficit) figure does not necessarily indicate that funds are simply lying around waiting to be used. Because the income and expenditures statement reflects what has actually occurred, the disposition of the surplus (or deficit) is reflected in the asset, liability, and net worth accounts on the balance sheet. For example, if the surplus were used to make investments, it would be represented by an increase in the asset account. If it were used to pay off a loan, it would be represented by a reduction in that liability account. Of course, if the surplus were used to increase cash balances, the funds would be available for use.

Balance Sheet Effects of a Cash Surplus or Deficit. The effect of a cash surplus on the income and expenditures statement is to *increase* the net worth account on the balance sheet. This increase results because an asset account increases without a corresponding increase in any liability. Note that this could be *any* asset, from a savings or investment account to a new car or room addition. In order for the balance sheet equation to balance, an increase in assets without any increase in liabilities must result in an increase in net worth. Even if the cash surplus is used to reduce a liability, *an increase in net worth will still result.* For example, if the Weavers have a $1,500 cash surplus in 1996, their net worth at December 31, 1996 would be $21,420 (1995 net worth of $19,920, from Worksheet 2.2, plus $1,500). Whether they used the funds to increase assets or repay a debt, their net worth increases by the amount of the surplus ($1,500).

While surpluses add to net worth, deficits *reduce* it. Again, this must be the case for the balance sheet equation to balance, whether the shortfall is financed by reducing an asset (for example, drawing down a savings account) or by borrowing. Assume the Weavers have a $1,500 cash deficit for 1996. Their December 31, 1996, balance sheet would show net worth of $18,420 ($19,920 net worth, from Worksheet 2.2, less $1,500), with either

variable expenditures Expenditures that involve payments of varying amounts from one time period to the next.

cash surplus An excess amount of income over expenditures that can be used for savings or investments and to acquire assets or reduce debt. Results in increased net worth.

cash deficit An excess amount of expenditures over income resulting in insufficient funds that must be made up either by drawing down savings or investments, reducing assets, or through borrowing. Results in decreased net worth.

a decrease in assets or increase in liabilities to cover the deficit.

In summary, cash surpluses, regardless of how used, result in increases in net worth and cash deficits, regardless of how covered, result in decreases. Increases in net worth are associated with *growing* financial strength; obviously, cash deficits indicate *declining* financial strength.

PREPARING THE INCOME AND EXPENDITURES STATEMENT

As shown in Worksheet 2.3, the income and expenditures statement is dated to define the period covered. The first set of entries includes all income items and a total income figure. Next, the expenditures are listed and totaled. Although not essential, the statement's readability is greatly enhanced by including various income and expenditure category headings. These not only permit a better understanding of the general nature of the income and expenditure items but also greatly simplify the budget control process (described later in this chapter). The final entry, representing the cash surplus (or deficit), is the result of subtracting total expenditures from total income. This entry constitutes the *bottom line* of the statement and basically is a summary of the *net cash flow* that resulted from the financial activities during the designated period.

Preparing an income and expenditures statement is not as difficult as it seems. Although this statement should be prepared at least annually, it's useful to prepare quarterly or semiannual statements. The first step is to determine your income from all sources for the chosen time period. If you are like most people, you probably have a very good idea of how much you make at work. But if you are unsure, you can always look at your check stubs for the amount of your *gross* pay. Regardless of the procedure you use, you should not overlook bonuses, commission checks, and overtime pay. Bank statements provide information on interest earned on savings accounts, and statements from brokerage houses, mutual funds, and so on provide information on securities bought and sold, dividends received, and other investment matters. You should also keep a running list of other income sources such as rents, tax refunds, and sales of assets.

Next, establish meaningful expenses categories, such as those listed in Exhibit 2.7, breaking down fixed and variable expenses. Information on monthly house (or rent) payments, loan payments, and other fixed payments (such as insurance premiums and cable TV), is readily available from either the payment book or your checkbook (or, in the case of payroll deductions, your check stubs). (Note: Be careful with so-called *adjustable-rate loans,* because the amount of monthly loan payments will change when the interest rate changes.) Variable expenses are undoubtedly the toughest expenditures to keep track of. Because trying to keep receipts for each and every transaction usually does not work too well, most people tend to rely on their check registers and credit card statements for information on these items. In many cases, the figures that show up on the income and expenditures statement amount to little more than educated "guesstimates" of the amount of money spent on the various categories of expenses, such as entertainment, clothing, and so on. While some of this is obviously necessary and appropriate, too much guesswork can lead to unreliable numbers that will greatly reduce the usefulness of these statements.

The final step is to subtract total expenditures from total income. This gives the cash surplus (a positive number) or deficit (a negative number).

Fortunately, there are a number of good computer software packages available that simplify the job of preparing personal financial statements and doing other personal financial planning tasks. The *Smart Money* box on page 70 explains how some popular personal finance software can help you.

AN INCOME AND EXPENDITURES STATEMENT FOR FRED AND DENISE WEAVER

Fred and Denise Weaver's income and expenditures statement for the year ended December 31, 1995, is provided in Worksheet 2.3 and illustrates the relationship among total income, total expenditures, and cash surplus (or deficit). This statement, which was prepared using the background material presented earlier, along with the Weavers' balance sheet (Worksheet 2.2) is best evaluated by separately analyzing their income, expenditures, and cash surplus (or deficit).

Fred's wages clearly represent the family's chief source of income, although Denise has finished her M.B.A. and will now be making a major contribution. Other sources of income include $195 in interest received on their savings accounts and bond investments and $120 in dividends received on

WORKSHEET 2.3

The Weavers' Income and Expenditures Statement

The income and expenditures statement essentially shows what you earned, how you spent your money, and how much you were left with (or, if you spent more than you took in, how much you went "in the hole").

Income and Expenditures Statement

Name(s) Fred and Denise Weaver

For the Year Ending December 31, 1995

INCOME		
Wages and salaries	Name: Fred Weaver	$ 35,000
	Name: Denise Weaver	15,450
	Name:	
Self-employment income		
Bonuses and commissions	Fred—sales commissions	2,275
Pensions and annuities		
Investment income	Interest received	195
	Dividends received	120
	Rents received	
	Sale of securities	
	Other	
Other income		
	(I) Total Income	$ 53,040
EXPENDITURES		
Housing	Rent/mortgage payment (include insurance and taxes, if applicable)	$ 6,864
	Repairs, maintenance, improvements	1,050
Utilities	Gas, electric, water	1,750
	Phone	480
	Cable TV and other	240
Food	Groceries	2,425
	Dining out	3,400
Autos	Loan payments	2,520
	License plates, fees, etc.	250
	Gas, oil, repairs, tires, maintenance	2,015
Medical	Health, major medical, disability insurance (payroll deductions or not provided by employer)	1,200
	Doctor, dentist, hospital, medicines	305
Clothing	Clothes, shoes, and accessories	1,700
Insurance	Homeowner's (if not covered by mortgage payment)	425
	Life (not provided by employer)	260
	Auto	695
Taxes	Income and social security	15,430
	Property (if not included in mortgage)	1,000
Appliances, furniture, and other major purchases	Loan payments	800
	Purchases and repairs	450
Personal care	Laundry, cosmetics, hair care	700
Recreation and entertainment	Vacations	2,000
	Other recreation and entertainment	2,630
Other items	Tuition and books: Denise	1,400
	Gifts	215
	Loan payments: Education loans	900
	Loan payments: Parents	600
	(II) Total Expenditures	$ 51,704
	CASH SURPLUS (OR DEFICIT) [(I)-(II)]	$ 1,336

Smart Money

Using Personal Financial Planning Software

Managing your personal finances used to be a tedious, time-consuming job. Now, however, you can streamline the financial planning process with one of the many affordable, easy-to-use personal finance software programs. The following brief descriptions of some popular general money management software will help you decide if you can benefit from computerized financial planning. These and similar programs range in price from about $29 to $60.

Quicken (Intuit/Microsoft) and *Managing Your Money* (MECA) are the most popular general money management programs and come in DOS, Windows, and Macintosh versions. Both track expenses and bank and credit card accounts, write checks, balance your checkbook, pay bills electronically, prepare financial statements and budgets, help with tax planning, set up savings programs to reach certain goals, monitor and/or recommend investments, perform loan, mortgage, and lease analyses, and generate various reports and graphs. *Quicken* does a good job of integrating your personal finances and is especially easy to learn because it is based on electronic versions of the familiar checkbook and check register. Both programs automatically put the transactions entered in the appropriate categories, making it easy to monitor and control expenses. You can prepare cash forecasts and ask "what if" questions to evaluate different financial strategies.

Tracking your stock, bond, and mutual fund investments now takes only minutes a day, and you can also calculate rates of return on your investments. The programs update portfolio values whenever you enter a new securities transaction or update price quotes (manually or from various on-line services). *Managing Your Money (MYM)* also discusses financial planning and investment principles and performs more complex financial planning analysis, such as calculating life insurance needs and developing savings plans for college costs and retirement. Its investment analysis capabilities include suggestions for diversifying your investments among various categories.

WealthBuilder (Reality Technologies and Money Magazine, DOS and Macintosh) is a more sophisticated planning program—it won't handle the day-to-day tasks like check-writing—that focuses on personal financial planning strategies. First you describe your current financial situation and develop a budget (you can transfer data from *Quicken* or *MYM*). Then you establish financial goals, including a timetable and the amounts needed and already saved, and the program calculates the monthly savings and rate of return required to reach the goal. This program gives you a comprehensive plan tied to your goals. By changing assumptions you can see the effect of different strategies on your overall financial plan. *WealthBuilder* also has a portfolio manager to track investments and suggests the best types of investments for your goals and personal risk preferences. One of its best features is an easy-to-use communications package that lets you access on-line securities and mutual fund quotes, research, and financial news updates.

their common stock holdings. The Weavers' total income for the year ended December 31, 1995, amounts to a very respectable $53,040.

The Weavers' major expenditures are their home mortgage, food, clothing, and income and social security taxes. Other sizable expenditures during the year included home repairs and additions, gas and electricity, auto loan and expenses, insurance, tuition, and education loan payments. Total expenditures for the year were $51,704. Your expense categories should be set up in a manner most suitable to your requirements. Note that expenditure items represent actual cash outlays made by the Weavers during the year ended December 31, 1995.

The Weavers end the year with a cash surplus of $1,336, found by subtracting the total expenditures of $51,704 from the total income of $53,040. This surplus could be used to increase savings, invest in stocks, bonds, or other vehicles, or make payments on some outstanding debts. The correct strategy depends on their financial goals. If a cash deficit had resulted, the Weavers would have had to withdraw savings, liquidate investments, or borrow an amount equal to the deficit in order to meet their financial commitments (that is, "make ends meet"). With their *surplus* of $1,336, the Weavers have made a positive contribution of their net worth.

Concept Check

2-10. What is an income and expenditures statement? What role does it serve in personal financial planning? Name its three components, some major sources of income, and the four basic types of expenditures.

2-11. Explain what cash basis means in the following statement: "An income and expenditures statement should be prepared on a cash basis." How and where are credit purchases shown when statements are prepared on a cash basis?

2-12. Distinguish between fixed and variable expenditures and give examples of each.

2-13. Is it possible to have a cash deficit on an income and expenditures statement? If so, how?

2-14. Explain the role the personal computer can play in the personal financial planning process. Briefly discuss the capabilities of some of the popular personal financial planning software.

USING YOUR PERSONAL FINANCIAL STATEMENTS

FPPC LG4

Personal financial statements can be used to assess your progress toward achievement of long-term financial goals. How would you use your personal financial statements to do this? Take a few moments to answer this question before reading on.

Your financial statements—the balance sheet and the income and expenditures statement—should provide the information you need to examine your financial position, monitor your financial activities, and track the progress you're making toward your financial goals. Very likely, your financial statements are like those of most other people—not a lot of substance at present perhaps, but certainly no shortage of potential. Regardless of the particulars surrounding your situation, it should be clear that a thorough understanding of your current financial status will enable you to better direct your financial plans and activities toward your personal financial goals.

KEEPING GOOD RECORDS

You should prepare financial statements at least once each year, ideally when you draw up your budget. Many people update their financial statements every three or six months. To simplify the preparation process, you should set up a **ledger,** or financial record book, that you update continuously. It summarizes all your financial transactions in sections for assets, liabilities, sources of income, and expenditures that contain separate accounts for each item in the section. Whenever any accounts change, make an appropriate ledger entry. For example, if you buy a VCR for $300 cash, record it as both an asset and an expenditure. Then you'd show the VCR on your balance sheet as an asset (at its fair market value) and as a $300 expenditure on your income and expenditures statement. If you borrowed to pay for the VCR, the loan amount would be a liability on the balance sheet and any loan payments made during the period are shown on the income statement. You'd keep similar records for asset sales, loan repayment, income sources, and so on.

Organizing Your Records. A good record-keeping system helps you manage and control your personal financial affairs. Up-to-date records are essential for preparing accurate personal financial statements and budgets. With organized financial records, you'll pay less to your tax preparer, not miss any tax deductions, and save taxes when you sell a home or securities or withdraw retirement

ledger A financial record book summarizing financial transactions in sections for assets, liabilities, sources of income, and expenditures.

funds. Also, good records make it easier for a spouse or relative to manage your financial affairs in an emergency. To that end, you should prepare a comprehensive list of these records, their locations, and your key advisors (financial planner, banker, accountant, attorney, doctors) for family members.

Your system doesn't have to be fancy to be effective. You'll need a bank safe deposit box, the ledger book described earlier, and a set of files with general categories such as banking and credit cards, home, insurance, investments, and retirement accounts. Tax planning records for income (paycheck stubs, interest on savings accounts, and so on) and deductions need separate files, as do individual mutual fund and brokerage account records. Hard-to-replace records go in the safe deposit box, with photocopies and a list of what's in the box at home. These include securities certificates, home deed, purchase and sale documents on all homes owned, birth and marriage certificates, divorce/alimony/custody records, military service records, and powers of attorney. Written inventories, appraisals, photos or videos of your home and its contents also belong in your safe deposit box, to verify its condition in the event of damage. Once you set up your files, be sure to go through them at least once a year and throw out unnecessary items.

Types of Records to Keep. Here are some guidelines for the types of records to keep, and how long to retain them.

Banking and credit cards: Keep a list of bank accounts and one year's account statements; a list of credit card numbers protects you if your cards are lost or stolen. Credit card statements help track expenses, but toss them after a year unless you need them for tax purposes.

Home: Document major home improvement expenditures, which increase the cost of your home for tax purposes and reduce your taxable gain when you sell it. Keep home-related documents at least six years after you sell your home.

Insurance: Keep current policies and discard expired ones unless you think there may be a claim later. Put a list of policies and insurance agents in your safe deposit box.

Taxes: The better your income and deduction files, the easier it is to prepare your tax returns. Save time each month by filing checks and receipts that relate to tax deductions or major purchases in appropriate folders, like charitable contributions, medical expenses, or home improvements. Keep returns with supporting documentation for the current year plus the past six years, the maximum time for IRS audits unless fraud is suspected. Some financial planners suggest keeping old returns (without backup records) as reminders of past financial actions.

Investment and retirement accounts: Designate a folder for each mutual fund, partnership investment, or brokerage account. Keep security purchase and sale confirmations and records of stock splits for tax reporting for at least three years after you sell a security. Toss monthly mutual fund and brokerage statements if your year-end statements are cumulative. Keep retirement fund records (pension plans, IRAs, and so on) indefinitely to know which portions of them are tax-deferred and which aren't subject to tax.

Trusts and wills: Trust agreements and wills should *not* go in your safe deposit box because it may be sealed at death, making the information unavailable to your heirs. Keep copies at home and give the original to your attorney. Destroy prior wills; they may cause later confusion and disputes.

Other records: In case of emergency, you should have photos and fingerprints of your children. Medical records are also good to keep.

TRACKING FINANCIAL PROGRESS: RATIO ANALYSIS

Each time you prepare your financial statements, you should analyze them to see how well you are doing in light of your financial goals. For example, with an income and expenditures statement, you can compare actual financial results to budgeted figures to make sure you have your spending under control. Likewise, comparing a set of financial plans to a balance sheet will reveal if you are meeting your savings and investment goals, reducing your debt, or building up a retirement reserve. In addition to assessing your future, financial statements help you track your progress over time—that is, you can compare current to historical performance to find out if things are improving or getting worse.

You can usually do this by calculating certain financial ratios to evaluate your financial performance over time. Moreover, if you apply for a loan, the lender probably will look at these ratios to judge your ability to carry additional debt. Four important money management ratios are (1) solvency ratio, (2) liquidity ratio, (3) savings ratio, and (4) debt service ratio. The first two are associated primarily with the balance sheet, while the last two relate primarily to the income and expenditures statement.

Balance Sheet Ratios. When evaluating your balance sheet, you should be most concerned with your net worth at a given point in time. As explained earlier in this chapter, you are technically insolvent when your total liabilities exceed your total assets—that is, when you have a negative net worth. The **solvency ratio** shows, in percentages, the extent to which you are exposed to insolvency, or how much "cushion" you have as a protection against insolvency. It is calculated as follows:

$$\text{Solvency ratio} = \frac{\text{Total net worth}}{\text{Total assets}}$$

The Weavers' solvency ratio in 1995 is

$$\frac{\$19{,}920}{\$95{,}675} = 0.21, \text{ or } 21 \text{ percent}$$

This tells us that Fred and Denise could withstand only about a 21 percent decline in the market value of their assets before they would be insolvent. The low value for this ratio suggests they should consider improving it in the future.

While the solvency ratio gives an indication of the potential to withstand financial problems, it does not deal directly with the ability to pay current debts. This issue is addressed with the **liquidity ratio,** which shows how long you could continue to pay current liability expenditures with existing liquid assets in the event of income loss. It is calculated by dividing liquid assets by total current debts; "current" in this case means any bills or charges that must be paid *within one year*. The ratio is computed as follows:

$$\text{Liquidity ratio} = \frac{\text{Liquid assets}}{\text{Total current debts}}$$

The Weavers' liquid assets (see Worksheet 2.2) total \$2,225. Their current liabilities of bills and open account credit balances total \$905. The portions of their loan payments due within one year total \$11,684 (\$6,864 in mortgage payments + \$2,520 in auto loan payments + \$800 in furniture loan payments + \$900 in education loan payments + \$600 in loan payment to parents)—all found on the income and expenditures statement in Worksheet 2.3. Adding their total current liabilities (\$905) to the current portion of their loans (\$11,684) yields total current debts of \$12,589. Thus, the Weavers have a liquidity ratio of:

$$\frac{\$2{,}225}{\$12{,}589} = 0.18 \text{ or } 18 \text{ percent}$$

This ratio indicates that the Weavers can cover only about 18 percent of their existing one-year debt obligations with their current liquid assets. In other words, they have slightly over two months (one month is 1/12, or 8.3 percent) of coverage. If an unexpected event curtailed their income, their liquid reserves would be exhausted very quickly. While there is no hard and fast rule as to what this ratio should be, it seems low for the Weavers. They should consider strengthening it along with their solvency ratio. They should be able to add to their cash surpluses now that Denise is working full-time.

The amount of liquid reserves will vary with your personal circumstances and "comfort level." Another useful liquidity guideline is to have a reserve fund equal to three to six months of after-tax income available to cover living expenses. The Weavers' after-tax income for 1995 was \$3,134 per month ([\$53,040 − \$15,430] ÷ 12). Therefore, this guideline suggests they should have between \$9,402 and \$18,804 in liquid assets—considerably more than the \$2,225 on their latest balance sheet. If you feel that your job is secure and/or you have other potential sources of income, you may be comfortable with three or four months in reserve. If you tend to be very cautious financially, you may want to build a larger fund. In troubled economic times, you may want to keep six months or more of income in this fund as protection should you lose your job.

Income and Expenditures Statement Ratios. When evaluating your income and expenditures statement, you should be concerned with the *bottom line,* which shows the cash surplus (or deficit)

solvency ratio Total net worth divided by total assets; measures solvency.

liquidity ratio Liquid assets divided by total current debts; measures ability to pay current debts.

resulting from the period's activities. You can relate it to income by calculating a **savings ratio,** which is done most effectively with after-tax income, as follows:

$$\text{Savings ratio} = \frac{\text{Cash surplus}}{\text{Income after taxes}}$$

For the Weavers, the savings ratio is

$$\frac{\$1{,}336}{\$53{,}040 - \$15{,}430} = \frac{\$1{,}336}{\$37{,}610} = \begin{array}{l}0.036, \text{ or}\\ 3.6 \text{ percent}\end{array}$$

Fred and Denise saved about 3.6 percent of their after-tax income, which is a bit on the low side (American families, on average, normally save about 5 to 8 percent). How much to save is a personal choice. Some families would plan much higher levels, particularly if they are saving to achieve an important goal, such as buying a home.

While maintaining an adequate level of savings is obviously important to personal financial planning, so is the ability to pay debts promptly. In fact, debt payments have a *higher* priority: The **debt service ratio** allows you to make sure you can comfortably meet your debt obligations. It is calculated as follows:

$$\text{Debt service ratio} = \frac{\text{Total monthly loan payments}}{\text{Monthly gross (before-tax) income}}$$

This ratio excludes current liabilities and considers only mortgage, installment, and personal loan obligations. On an *annual* basis, the Weavers' obligations total $11,684 ($6,864 in mortgage payments, $2,520 in auto loan payments, $800 in furniture loan payments, $900 in education loan payments, $600 in loan payments to parents from Worksheet 2.3). The Weavers' total *monthly* loan payments are about $974 ($11,684 ÷ 12 months). Dividing the Weavers' *annual* gross income, also found in Worksheet 2.3, of $53,040 by 12 equals $4,420 monthly ($53,040/12). The Weavers' debt service ratio is calculated as follows:

$$\frac{\$974}{\$4{,}420} = 0.22, \text{ or } 22 \text{ percent}$$

Monthly loan payments account for about 22 percent of Fred and Denise's gross income. This relatively low debt service ratio indicates that the Weavers should have little difficulty in meeting their monthly loan payments. From a financial planning perspective, you should try to keep your debt service margin somewhere under 35 percent or so, since that's generally viewed as a manageable level of debt—and, of course, the lower the debt service ratio, the easier it is to meet loan payments as they come due.

Concept Check

2-15. How can accurate records and control procedures be used to ensure effectiveness in the financial planning process?

2-16. Describe some of the areas or items you would consider when evaluating your balance sheet. Cite several ratios that could help in this effort.

DEFINING YOUR FINANCIAL GOALS

LG5

The financial planning process begins by defining both long- and short-term financial goals. These goals provide direction for financial plans and budgets. Have you set long-term and short-term financial goals? Before reading on, spend a few moments formulating and listing them.

As noted earlier, setting financial goals is the first step in the personal financial planning process. Once set, these goals provide direction for your financial plans. But just as you cannot prepare plans for attaining goals that are not yet formulated, neither can you start the financial planning process without knowing your current financial position. This is accomplished using your personal financial statements. After evaluating your current financial position, you can establish both long-term and short-term financial goals. Your goals will, of course, depend on your personal situation and where you are in the life cycle. Some long-term goals, such as saving for retirement, may not change as you move through life, while others will vary. Short-term goals, by their nature, will change frequently. Exhibit 2.8 presents some typical short- and long-term goals of persons in different life situations.

EXHIBIT 2.8

How Financial Goals Change over the Life Cycle

Financial goals are not static but change continually over an individual's or family's lifetime. Here are listed some typical long-term and short-term goals for a number of different personal situations.

Personal Situation	Long-Term Goals	Short-Term Goals
College senior	Repay college loans Begin an investment program Buy a condominium	Find a job Rent an apartment Get a bank credit card Buy a car
Single, mid-20s	Begin law school Build an investment portfolio Start a retirement fund	Prepare a budget Buy a new television and VCR Get additional job training Build an emergency fund Take a Caribbean vacation Reduce expenses 10%
Married couple with children, late 30s	Buy a second car Increase college fund contributions Buy a larger home Diversify investment portfolio	Trade in car Repaint house Get braces for children Increase second income: from part-time to full-time job Review life and disability insurance
Married couple with grown children, mid-50s	Decide whether to relocate upon retirement Retire at age 62 Sell house and buy smaller residence Travel to Europe and the Orient	Buy new furniture Shift investment portfolio into income producing securities Review skills Take cruise vacation

As noted earlier, it is important to involve your immediate family in the goal-setting process in order to eliminate potential future conflicts. By having each family member effectively "buy into" these plans, a cooperative team effort should result, thereby improving the family's chances of achieving its goals. Once your goals have been defined and approved, appropriate cash budgets can be prepared. Normally, long-term financial goals are set first, followed by a series of corresponding short-term goals.

SETTING LONG-TERM FINANCIAL GOALS

Long-term financial goals should indicate the individual's or family's wants and desires for the next 2 to 5 years on out to the next 30 or 40 years. Of course, many people find it difficult to pinpoint exactly what they will want 30 or so years from now; however, if they at least give some thought to the matter, they should be able to establish some tentative long-term financial goals. Recognize, though, that many long-term goals will change over time. For example, an individual might set a goal of retiring at age 55 with a net worth of $400,000. At age 50, this same person might decide to purchase a condominium in Florida and retire at age 62 with a net worth of $500,000. Although this individual's long-term goal is changed, note that his short-term goals will remain pretty much the same: to make substantial, regular contributions to savings or investments to accumulate the desired net worth.

Putting a Dollar Value on Financial Goals. Some financial goals can be defined in rather general terms. Others should be defined more precisely, perhaps with fairly specific dollar values.

savings ratio Cash surplus divided by after-tax income; indicates relative amount of cash surplus achieved.

debt service ratio Total monthly loan payments divided by monthly gross (before-tax) income; provides a measure of ability to pay monthly loan payments in a prompt and timely fashion.

long-term financial goals Goals that are set well into the future, typically to retirement and sometimes beyond.

Consider, for example, the goal of buying your first home in six years. The first question is how much to spend. Let's say that you have done some "window shopping" and feel that, *taking future inflation into consideration,* you will have to spend about $90,000 to get the kind of house you like. Of course, you will not need the full amount, but given a 20 percent down payment ($90,000 × .20 = $18,000) plus closing costs, you estimate that you will need around $20,000. You now have a fairly well-defined long-term financial goal: *to accumulate $20,000 in six years to buy a home costing about $90,000.*

The next question is how to get all that money. You will probably accumulate it by saving or investing a set amount each month or year. You can easily estimate how much to save or invest each year if you know your goal and what you expect to earn on your savings or investments. In this case, if you have to start from scratch (that is, have nothing saved today) and estimate that you can earn about 10 percent on your money, you will have to save or invest about $2,600 per year for each of the next six years to accumulate $20,000 over that time period. Now you have another vital piece of information: *You know what you must do over the next six years in order to reach your financial goal.*

The Time Value of Money. To correctly compare dollar values occurring at different points in time, you need to understand the **time value of money,** the idea that a dollar today is worth more than a dollar received in the future. As long as you can earn a positive rate of return on your investments (ignoring taxes and other behavioral factors), in a strict financial sense you should always prefer to receive equal amounts of money sooner rather than later. The two key time value concepts, *future value* and *present value* are discussed separately below. (*Note:* Although the following time value discussions and demonstrations rely on the use of financial tables, many inexpensive business calculators have these tables built into them and therefore can be conveniently used to make time value calculations.)

Future Value. The **future value** is the value to which an amount today will grow if it earns a specific rate of interest over a given period of time. Assume, for example, that you make annual deposits of $2,000 into a savings account that pays 5 percent interest per year. At the end of 20 years, your deposits would total $40,000 (20 × $2,000). If you made no withdrawals, your account balance would have increased to $66,132! This growth in value occurs not only as a result of earning interest, but because of **compounding**—the interest earned each year is left in the account and becomes part of the balance (or principal) on which interest is earned in subsequent years.

To demonstrate future value, let's return to the goal of accumulating $20,000, for a down payment to buy a home in six years. You might be tempted to solve this problem by simply dividing the $20,000 goal by the six-year period: $20,000/6 = $3,333. Unfortunately, this procedure would be incorrect, because it would fail to take into account the *time value of money.* The correct way to approach this problem is to use the future value concept. For instance, if you can invest $100 today at 10 percent, you will have $110 in a year: You will earn $10 on your investment ($100 × .10 = $10), plus get your original $100 back. Once you know the length of time *and* rate of return involved, you can find the future value of any investment by using the following simple formula:

$$\text{Future value} = \text{Amount invested} \times \text{Future value factor}$$

Tables of future value factors simplify the computations in this formula (see Appendix A). The table is very easy to use: Simply find the factor that corresponds to a given year *and* interest rate. Referring to Appendix A, you will find the future value factor for a six-year investment earning 10 percent is 1.772 (the factor that lies at the intersection of six years and 10 percent).

Returning to the problem at hand, let's say you already have accumulated $5,000 toward the purchase of a new home. To find the future value of that investment in six years earning 10 percent, you can use the above formula as follows:

$$\text{Future value} = \$5{,}000 \times 1.722 = \underline{\underline{\$8{,}860}}$$

The $8,860 is how much you will have in six years if you invest the $5,000 at 10 percent. Because you feel you are going to need $20,000, you are still $11,140 short of your goal. How are you going to accumulate an additional $11,140?

Again you can utilize the future value concept, but this time you will employ an annuity factor. An

annuity is an equal cash flow that occurs annually—for example, $1,000 per year for each of the next five years with payment to be made at the end of each year. To find out how much you have to save each year to accumulate a given amount, use the following equation:

$$\text{Yearly savings} = \frac{\text{Amount of money desired}}{\text{Future value annuity factor}}$$

When dealing with an annuity you will have to use a different table of factors, such as that in Appendix B. Note that it is very much like the table of future value factors and, in fact, is used in exactly the same way: The proper future value annuity factor is the one that corresponds to a given year *and* interest rate. As an example, you'll find in Appendix B that the future value annuity factor for six years and 10 percent is 7.716. Using this factor in the above equation, you can find out how much to save each year to accumulate $11,140 in six years given a 10 percent rate of return, as follows:

$$\text{Yearly savings} = \frac{\$11{,}140}{7.716} = \underline{\underline{\$1{,}443.75}}$$

You will have to save about $1,445 a year to reach your goal. Note in the example that you must add $1,445 a year to the $5,000 you already have in order to build up a pool of $20,000 in six years. At a 10 percent rate of return, the $1,445 per year will grow to $11,140 and the $5,000 will grow to $8,860 so that in six years you will have $11,140 + $8,860 = $20,000.

How much, you may ask, would you have to save each year if you did not have the $5,000 to start with? In this case, your goal would still be the same (to accumulate $20,000 in six years), but, because you would be starting from scratch, the full $20,000 would have to come from yearly savings. Assuming you can still earn 10 percent over the six-year period, you can use the same future value annuity factor (7.716) and compute the amount of yearly savings as follows:

$$\text{Yearly savings} = \frac{\$20{,}000}{7.716} = \underline{\underline{\$2{,}592.02}}$$

or approximately $2,600. Note that this amount corresponds to the $2,600 figure cited earlier.

Using the future value concept, you can readily find either the future value to which an investment will grow over time or the amount that you must save each year to accumulate a given amount of money by a specified future date. In either case, the procedures allow you to put monetary values on long-term financial goals.

Present Value. The **present value,** on the other hand, is the value *today* of an amount to be received in the future. It is the amount you would have to invest today at a given interest rate over the specified time period to accumulate the future amount. The process of finding present value is called **discounting.** It is the inverse of *compounding* to find future value. For instance, assume that you are 35 years old and wish to accumulate a retirement fund of $300,000 by the time you are age 60 (25 years from now). You estimate that you can earn 7 percent annually on your investments during the next 25 years. Assuming you wish to create the retirement fund (future value) by making a single lump-sum deposit today, you can use the following formula:

$$\text{Present value} = \text{Future value} \times \text{Present value factor}$$

time value of money The concept that a dollar today is worth more than a dollar received in the future; it exists as long as one can earn a positive rate of return (interest rate) on investments.

future value The value to which an amount today will grow if it earns a specific rate of interest over a given period of time. It can be used to find the yearly savings needed to accumulate a given future amount of money.

compounding When interest earned each year is left in the account and becomes part of the balance (or principal) on which interest is earned in subsequent years.

annuity An equal cash flow that occurs annually.

present value The value today of an amount to be received in the future; it is the amount that would have to be invested today at a given interest rate over a specified time period to accumulate the future amount.

discounting The process of finding present value; the inverse of compounding to find future value.

Tables of present value factors (see Appendix C) make this calculation easy. First, find the present value factor for a 25-year investment at a 7 percent discount rate (the factor that lies at the intersection of 25 years and 7 percent) in Appendix C; it is .184. Then, substitute the future value of $300,000 and the present value factor of .184 into the formula as follows:

$$\text{Present value} = \$300{,}000 \times .184 = \underline{\underline{\$55{,}200}}$$

The $55,200 represents the amount you would have to deposit today into an account paying 7 percent annual interest in order to accumulate $300,000 at the end of 25 years.

Present value techniques can also be used to determine how much you can withdraw from your retirement fund each year over a specified time horizon. Assume that at age 55 you wish to begin making equal annual withdrawals over the next 30 years from your $300,000 retirement fund. At first, you might think you could withdraw $10,000 per year ($300,000/30 years). However, the funds still on deposit would continue to earn 7 percent annual interest. To find the amount of the equal annual withdrawal, you again need to consider the time value of money. Specifically, you would use the following formula:

$$\text{Annual withdrawal} = \frac{\text{Initial deposit}}{\text{Present value annuity factor}}$$

The present value annuity factors for various numbers of years and rates are given in Appendix D. To find the annual withdrawal (or payment), which is an *annuity,* substitute the $300,000 initial deposit and the present value annuity factor for 30 years and 7 percent of 12.409 (from Appendix D) into the equation above to get:

$$\text{Annual withdrawal} = \frac{\$300{,}000}{12.409} = \underline{\underline{\$24{,}176}}$$

You can withdraw $24,176 each year for 30 years. This value is clearly much larger than the $10,000 annual withdrawal mentioned earlier.

Furthermore, present value techniques can be used to analyze investments. Suppose you have an opportunity to purchase an annuity investment that promises to pay you $700 per year for five years. You know that you will receive a total of $3,500 ($700 × 5 years) over the five-year period. However, you wish to earn a minimum annual return of 8 percent on your investments. What is the most you should pay for this annuity today? You can answer this question by rearranging the terms in the equation above to get:

$$\text{Initial deposit} = \text{Annual withdrawal} \times \text{Present value annuity factor}$$

In terms of the equation, the "initial deposit" would represent the maximum price to pay for the annuity; the "annual withdrawal" would represent the annual annuity payment of $700. The present value annuity factor for five years and 8 percent (found in Appendix D) is 3.993. Substituting this into the equation, you get:

$$\text{Initial deposit} = \$700 \times 3.993 = \underline{\underline{\$2{,}795.10}}$$

The most you should pay for the $700, five-year annuity given your 8 percent annual return is $2,795.10. At this price you would earn exactly 8 percent on the investment.

By using the present value concept, you can easily determine the present value of a sum to be received in the future, equal annual future withdrawals available from an initial deposit, and the initial deposit that would generate a given stream of equal annual withdrawals. These procedures, like future value concepts, allow you to place monetary values on long-term financial goals.

Putting Target Dates on Financial Goals. Financial goals are most effective when set in reference to certain goal dates. *Goal dates* are target points in the future at which time certain financial activities are expected to be concluded; they may serve as checkpoints in the progress toward some financial goals or as deadlines for the achievement of others. For example, one goal may be to purchase a boat in 1997 (the goal date) and another to accumulate a net worth of $200,000 by 2014, with goal dates of 2000 and 2005 set as checkpoints for the attainment of net worth of $10,000 and $110,000, respectively. It is usually helpful to set goal dates at intervals of two to five years for the first ten years or so and at five- to ten-year intervals thereafter. As time passes, adjustments to the financial plans may have to be made; or, as desired financial outcomes are realized, goals may also have to be changed. In other words, the person or family may recognize that the goals were set either too high or too low. If the goals appear to be too high, they must be revised and made more realistic. If they are too low, they should be evaluated and set at a level that will force the individual or family to make financially responsible decisions rather than squandering surplus funds.

GOALS FOR THE SHORT TERM

Short-term financial goals are set each year; they cover a 12-month period and should be consistent with established long-term goals. These short-term goals become the key input for the *cash budget*—a tool used to plan for short-term income and expenditures. The individual's or family's immediate goals, expected income for the year, and long-term financial goals must all be taken into account when defining short-term goals. In addition, consideration must be given to the latest financial position, as reflected by the current balance sheet, and spending in the year immediately preceding, as reflected in the income and expenditures statement for that period. Short-term planning should also include establishing an emergency fund with three to six months' worth of income. This special savings account serves as a safety valve in case of financial emergencies—for example, a temporary loss of income.

The degree of effectiveness in reaching short-term goals significantly affects the ability to achieve long-term goals. If short-term goals are not attained, the likelihood of achieving long-term goals is greatly reduced. In setting short-term goals, current desires should not override the requirements for long-term goals. The general tendency to prefer current consumption over future consumption may be the greatest challenge when setting short-term goals. Short-term sacrifices may be necessary to provide for a comfortable future; realizing this fact 10 or 20 years too late may make some important financial goals unattainable.

THE FINANCIAL GOALS OF FRED AND DENISE WEAVER

Earlier in this chapter, we met Fred and Denise Weaver, whose financial data were used to develop their financial statements. We continue to use their financial data to illustrate various aspects of financial planning and budgeting. The Weavers' long- and short-term financial goals, which they set in December of 1995, are described in the following sections.

Because Fred and Denise are 28 and 26 years old, respectively, they have set their longest-term financial goal 33 years from now, when they want to retire. The top portion of Worksheet 2.4 presents a summary of the Weavers' long-term financial goals. They have set their goal dates arbitrarily at 1998, 2003, 2008, 2013, 2018, 2023, and 2028. As time passes, they will probably adjust both the goals and the dates. Although most of their goals do not have dollar amounts attached, Fred and Denise can still use them to lend general direction to their short-term financial plans. In the planning process, the Weavers have made estimates of the costs of achieving their various long-term goals and then set the short-term goals necessary for attaining them.

In the final week of December 1995, Fred and Denise set their short-term financial goals for the coming year. They considered three factors: (1) their current financial condition as reflected in their balance sheet (Worksheet 2.2); (2) their latest income and expenditures statement (Worksheet 2.3), from which they were able to evaluate their spending requirements for 1996, and (3) their *long-term* financial goals (top of Worksheet 2.4), which provided the framework for the Weavers' short-term goals. The Weavers' short-term financial goals for the coming year, along with the dollar outlay required to achieve each of them, are given in the bottom portion of Worksheet 2.4.

To simplify the process of eliminating expenditures in the event that sufficient funds are not available, the Weavers have assigned priorities to their short-term goals. The first three items are considered necessities, and the fourth is associated with their long-term net worth goal. (Note that because of the many interactions affecting it, the dollar outlay required to achieve the net worth goal cannot be clearly specified.) The remaining items are extras, or luxuries, that the Weavers would like to acquire during the year but probably can do without. Once they have prepared their budget, the Weavers will be able to determine which of their short-term goals they can afford during the coming year.

short-term financial goals Goals that are set each year and cover a 12-month period; they should be consistent with established long-term goals.

WORKSHEET 2.4

The Weavers' Summary of Long-Term and Short-Term Personal Financial Goals

It is important to establish long-term financial goals in order to lend a general sense of direction to the financial decisions and activities we undertake. Short-term financial goals support the long-term goals by specifying what we hope to achieve in the next year or so; they specify the dollar outlay required for their achievement as well as relative priority.

Personal Financial Goals

Name(s) Fred and Denise Weaver Date December 27, 1995

LONG-TERM GOALS

Goal Date	Goal Description
1998	Pay off all loans other than mortgage.
	Save money for new home.
	Increase investment portfolio.
	Start family.
	Buy new car (trade Escort).
2003	Begin college fund.
	Save money for new home.
	Buy minivan (trade every 4 years).
	Diversify and increase investments.
	Review life and disability insurance.
2008	Buy new $185,000 home.
	Purchase new furniture.
	Increase annual contribution to college funds.
2013	Increase investments, retirement funds.
	Purchase sailboat.
	Take European vacation.
	Accumulate net worth of $80,000.
2018	Children in college.
	Buy third car for children.
	Remodel home.
	Accumulate net worth of $110,000.
	Take Australian vacation.
2023	Children finish college.
	Build retirement funds.
	Investigate where to live upon retirement.
	Accumulate net worth of $175,000.
2028	Retire from jobs.
	Sell home, buy condominium.
	Travel to Orient.
	Accumulate net worth of $275,000.

SHORT-TERM GOALS (for the coming year)

Priority	Goal Description	Dollar Outlay
1	Buy new tires, brakes for Escort.	$ 425
2	Buy career clothes for Denise.	1,500
3	Buy suit & sport jacket for Fred.	650
4	Accumulate net worth of $25,000.	—
5	Buy electric garage door opener.	350
6	Take two-week vacation to Hawaii.	4,000
7	Buy workshop equipment.	1,500
8	Take ski trip to Colorado.	1,800
9	Replace stereo system components.	1,450
10		

Concept Check

2-17. Distinguish between long-term and short-term financial goals. Be sure to mention:

a. personal situation and stage of life cycle

b. flexibility

c. inflation considerations

d. goal dates

e. the key input to the cash budget

2-18. Why is it important to use time value of money concepts in setting personal financial goals? When might you use future value? Present value?

SETTING UP A CASH BUDGET

FPPC 1

LG6

Cash budgets are prepared from schedules of estimated income and expenditures for the coming year and provide a system of disciplined spending. How would you go about estimating your income and expenditures for the coming year? Before reading on, spend a few moments answering this question.

Once you define your short-term financial goals, you can prepare a cash budget for the coming year. Recall that a budget is a short-term financial planning report that helps you achieve your short-term financial goals. As such, it also makes a positive contribution toward the achievement of your *long-term* financial goals.

By taking the time to evaluate your current financial situation, spending patterns, and goals, you can develop a realistic budget consistent with your personal lifestyle, family situation, and values. As you go through the budgeting process, you will have to decide how to allocate your income to reach your financial objectives. The resulting budget will be a valuable money management tool that provides the necessary information to monitor and control your finances in a fashion consistent with goal achievement. If carefully followed, your budget will help you accomplish two very important objectives: Implementing a system of *disciplined spending*—as opposed to just existing from one paycheck to the next—and reducing *needless spending* so you can increase the funds allocated to savings and investments.

Just as your goals change over your lifetime, so will your budget. Typically, the number of income and expense categories increases as you accumulate more assets and debts, and you have more family responsibilities. For example, the budget of a college student would be quite simple, with limited income from part-time jobs, parental contributions, and/or scholarships and grants. Expenses might include basic living expenses, clothes, books, auto expenses, and entertainment. Once the student graduates and goes to work full-time, his or her budget will cover additional expenses such as rent, insurance, work clothes, and commuting costs. Clearly, as you move through the life cycle your financial situation will become increasingly more complex, thereby further increasing the importance of financial planning activities such as budgeting. Not until retirement can you expect this process to begin to simplify.

Like the income and expenditures statement, a *budget should be prepared on a cash basis;* thus, we call this document a **cash budget.** A cash budget deals with cash receipts and cash expenditures that are expected to occur in the coming year. For budgeting purposes, it makes no difference whether money is being spent on living expenses or on loan payments; in either case, an outflow of cash is involved, and therefore the amounts would be included in the cash budget. On the other hand, an asset purchased on credit would not be included, at least not until loan payments were made. Basically, a cash budget contains annual estimates of income and expenditures, including savings and investments. It is usually divided into monthly intervals, although in some cases other time intervals may be more convenient.

The cash budget preparation process has three stages: estimating income, estimating expenditures, and finalizing the budget. When estimating income and expenditures, you should take into account any anticipated changes in the cost of living and their impact on your budget components. If your

cash budget A budget that takes into account estimated monthly cash receipts and cash expenditures for the coming year.

income is fixed—not expected to change over the budgetary period—increases in various items of expenditure will probably cause the purchasing power of your income to deteriorate.

ESTIMATING INCOME

The first step in the cash budget preparation process is to prepare a **schedule of estimated income** for the coming year. Because bills are most commonly rendered and paid monthly, it is best to estimate income as well as expenditures using monthly intervals. The income forecast takes into consideration all income expected for the year—for example, the take-home pay of both spouses, expected bonuses or commissions, pension or annuity income, and interest, dividend, rental and security sale income. Many families find it useful to use a schedule like the one in Worksheet 2.5 to project their income.

When estimating income, keep in mind that *any item expected to be received for which repayment is required is not considered income.* For instance, a loan is treated not as a source of income but as a *liability* for which scheduled repayments are required. Note also that unlike the income and expenditures statement, it is *take-home pay* that generally should be used on the cash budget rather than gross income before deductions and withholdings. This makes sense, because in a cash budget you want to direct your attention to those areas over which you have some control—and most people certainly have little, if any, control over things like taxes withheld, contributions to company insurance and pension plans, and the like. In effect, take-home pay represents the amount of *disposable income* you receive from your employer.

ESTIMATING EXPENDITURES

The second step in the cash budgeting process is by far the most difficult: Preparing a **schedule of estimated expenditures** for the coming year. This is usually done using actual expenditures from previous years (as found on income and expenditures statements and in supporting information for those periods), along with predetermined short-term financial goals. Good financial records, as discussed earlier, make it easier to develop realistic expense estimates. If you do not have past expenditure data, you could reexamine old checkbook registers and credit card statements to approximate expenditures. Families without past expenditure data could also use a "needs approach" to develop spending forecasts; that is, needs are projected and dollar values attached to them to estimate future expenditures. Pay close attention to expenditures associated with medical disabilities, divorce and child support, and similar special circumstances.

Regardless of whether historical information is available, it is important that you *become aware of your expenditure patterns and how you spend money.* In the absence of spending data, you can develop useful information by keeping track of your expenses over several months. Carefully study your spending habits to see if you are doing things that should be eliminated (like writing too many small, frivolous checks or using credit cards too freely). In addition, you will probably find it easier to budget expenditures if you group them into several general categories, rather than trying to estimate each and every item. An example of one such grouping scheme—patterned after the categories used in the income and expenditures statement—is provided in Worksheet 2.6. Included on the budget expenditures form are suggested spending guidelines for each major category. The percentage that you allocate depends on your age, lifestyle, and where you live. For instance, housing costs vary depending on location; it costs considerably more to buy a home in San Diego than in Indianapolis. Dining out generally is more expensive in metropolitan than rural areas; if you live in the suburbs, your commuting expenses may be higher than those for city-dwellers.

Initially, achievement of all short-term goals should be built into your expenditure estimates. To do this effectively, estimate the cost of achieving the goals as well as the timing of the expenditures. Any current or short-term contributions toward achievement of long-term goals should also be quantified and appropriately scheduled into the

schedule of estimated income A part of the cash budget that shows an item-by-item breakdown of the estimated income for each month of the coming year.

schedule of estimated expenditures A part of the cash budget that shows an item-by-item breakdown of the estimated expenditures for the coming year.

WORKSHEET 2.5

The Weavers' Schedule of Estimated Income for 1996

The Weavers' income will increase substantially now that Denise is working full-time and they are a two-career, two-income family.

Cash Budget: Estimated Income

Name(s) Fred and Denise Weaver

For the Year Ending December 31, 1996

SOURCES OF INCOME		Jan.	Feb.	Mar.	April	May	June	July	Aug.	Sep.	Oct.	Nov.	Dec.	Total for the Year
Take-home pay	Name: Fred	$2,250	$2,250	$2,250	$2,440	$2,440	$2,440	$2,440	$2,440	$2,440	$2,440	$2,440	$2,440	$28,710
	Name: Denise	1,525	1,525	1,525	1,525	1,525	1,700	1,700	1,700	1,700	1,700	1,700	1,700	19,525
	Name:													
Bonuses and commissions							1,350						1,300	2,650
Pensions and annuities														
Investment income	Interest			55			55			55			55	220
	Dividends			35			35			35			35	140
	Rents													
	Sale of securities													
	Other													
Other Income														
	TOTAL INCOME	$3,775	$3,775	$3,865	$3,965	$3,965	$5,580	$4,140	$4,140	$4,230	$4,140	$4,140	$5,530	$51,245

WORKSHEET 2.6

The Weavers' Initial Schedule of Estimated Annual Expenditures for 1996

The initial schedule of estimated expenditures is usually prepared on an annual basis, because some of the numbers are probably going to have to be changed anyway; preparing the schedule this way saves a lot of time if the budget does not balance. (Note: the parenthetical numbers provide suggested guidelines of how much of the average family's income is spent in each major category.)

Cash Budget: Estimated Expenditures

Name(s) Fred and Denise Weaver

For the Year Ending December 31, 1996

	EXPENDITURE CATEGORIES	**Annual Amounts**
Housing (12–30%)	Rent/mortgage payment (include insurance and taxes, if applicable)	$ 6,864
	Repairs, maintenance, improvements	1,550
Utilities (4–8%)	Gas, electric, water	1,850
	Phone	500
	Cable TV and other	300
Food (15–25%)	Groceries	3,000
	Dining out	3,900
Autos (5–18%)	Loan payments	2,520
	License plates, fees, etc.	250
	Gas, oil, repairs, tires, maintenance	2,375
Medical (2–10%)	Health, major medical, disability insurance (payroll deductions or not provided by employer)	
	Doctor, dentist, hospital, medicine	375
Clothing (3–8%)	Clothes, shoes, and accessories	3,500
Insurance (4–8%)	Homeowner's (if not covered by mortgage payment)	450
	Life (not provided by employer)	300
	Auto	740
Taxes (N/A)	Income and social security	
	Property (if not included in mortgage)	1,100
Appliances, furniture, and other major purchases (2-8%)	Loan payments	150
	Purchases and repairs Workshop equipment	1,500
	Other: New stereo equipment	1,450
Personal care (1–3%)	Laundry, cosmetics, hair care	1,200
Recreation and entertainment (2-8%)	Vacations Hawaii & Colorado	5,800
	Other recreation and entertainment	2,750
Savings and investments (3–10%)	Savings, stocks, bonds, etc.	4,500
Other expenditures (1–10%)	Charitable contributions	450
	Gifts	500
	Education loan payment	900
	Subscriptions, magazines, books	185
	Other: Loan payment–parents	900
	Other: Misc.	600
Fun money (1–5%)		3,000
	TOTAL EXPENDITURES	$ 53,459

budget. Equally important are scheduled additions to savings and investments, because *planned savings* should be high on everyone's list of goals. If the inclusion of all these items will not allow the budget to balance, you may have to remove some from the final budget. Base estimated expenditures on current price levels and then increase them by a percentage that reflects the anticipated rate of inflation. For example, if you estimate the monthly food bill at $350 and expect 4 percent inflation, you should budget your monthly food expenditure at $364—or $350 + $14 ($350 × 4 percent). You should also include an allowance for *fun money,* which family members spend as they wish. This gives each person a degree of financial independence and helps provide a healthy family budget relationship.

FINALIZING AND PREPARING THE CASH BUDGET

After you estimate both income and expenditures, you can finalize your budget by comparing projected income to projected expenditures on month-to-month and annual bases. A **balanced budget** results when the total income for the year equals or exceeds total expenditures. Budget preparation is complete once all monthly deficits are resolved and the total annual budget balances.

The Budget Format. The **budget summary** combines and summarizes the schedules of estimated income and expenditures and adds a third section, the difference between them—the surplus or deficit. Usually the budget shows monthly figures as well as the annual total for each income and expenditure item. When you have many income and expense categories, breaking the budget into the separate income, expense, and summary schedules shown here actually simplifies budget preparation. Admittedly, there is a lot of "number crunching" in personal cash budgeting. As discussed earlier, personal financial planning software can greatly streamline the budget preparation process.

Dealing with Monthly Deficits. Even if the annual budget balances, in certain months expenditures may exceed income, causing a monthly **budget deficit**. Likewise, a **budget surplus** occurs when income in some months exceeds expenditures. Two remedies exist:

- Shift expenditures from months with budget deficits to months with surpluses (or, conversely, transfer income if possible from months with surpluses to those with deficits).
- Use savings, investments, or borrowing to cover temporary deficits.

Because the budget balances for the year, the need for funds to cover shortages is only temporary. In months with budget surpluses, you should return funds taken from savings or investments or repay loans. Either remedy is feasible for curing a monthly budget deficit in a balanced annual budget, although the second is probably more practical.

What to Do If You End the Year in the Red. Three approaches exist to resolve the more difficult problem of an annual budget deficit. The first is to either *liquidate enough savings and investments or borrow enough* to meet the total budget shortfall for the year. Obviously, this action is not recommended, because it violates the objective of budgeting—to set expenditures at a level that allows you to enjoy a reasonable standard of living while making progress toward your long-term goals. Reducing savings and investments or increasing debt to balance the budget reduces net worth. People who use this approach are *not* living within their means.

A second—and preferred—approach is to *cut low priority expenditures* from the budget to bring it into balance. This method balances the budget

balanced budget A budget in which total income for the year equals or exceeds total expenditures.

budget summary A statement that summarizes and combines projections of estimated income, estimated expenditures, and the difference between them, which may be either a surplus or a deficit.

budget deficit A situation that occurs when the expenditures exceed the income in a cash budget.

budget surplus A situation that occurs when the income exceeds the expenditures in a cash budget.

EXHIBIT 2.9

Tips to Balance Your Budget

The following tips are ways to reduce discretionary spending so you can live within your means.

1. Cancel your credit cards, or at least put them where you can't use them until you get your spending under control.
2. Stop your cable TV service or reduce the number of premium services you get.
3. Reduce your phone bill by making long distance phone calls when evening, weekend, and holiday discount rates are in effect, and investigate special calling plans.
4. Take public transportation to work or school if it's cheaper than driving, or carpool.
5. Become a savvy comparison shopper. Do your research first to curb impulse buying, and be sure you're getting the best price when you must buy an item.
6. Use coupons when you grocery shop, and look for stores that offer double coupon savings.
7. Keep a daily spending diary. Writing down every cent you spend keeps you from forgetting those little expenses that really add up.
8. Take your lunch and snacks from home. You'd be surprised how much eating out can cost.
9. Joining a local food cooperative can save hundreds of dollars a year on grocery bills.
10. Use the library instead of buying books or renewing magazine subscriptions.
11. Consider lowering auto and homeowners insurance premiums by raising deductibles.
12. Don't carry extra cash; you'll be tempted to spend it.

Sources: Adapted from Tershia d'Elgin, "How to Save $100," *Price Club Journal,* March 1993, p. 6; "Ways to Start Saving Today," *Parents Magazine,* September 1993, p. 189.

without using external funding sources. Low-priority items are those associated with your least important short-term goals. These are flexible, or discretionary, expenditures for nonessential items (such as recreation, entertainment, and some clothing) that can be reduced or cut to balance the budget. Exhibit 2.9 presents some ways to spend less.

The third approach is to *increase income* by finding a higher paying job or perhaps a second, part-time job. This is obviously the most difficult technique and may bring a significant change in leisure activities and lifestyle. However, individuals who have no savings or investments to liquidate, cannot borrow funds, and cannot cover necessary expenditures may have to choose this route to balance their budgets.

A CASH BUDGET FOR FRED AND DENISE WEAVER

Using their short-term financial goals (bottom of Worksheet 2.4) and past financial statements (Worksheets 2.2 and 2.3), Fred and Denise Weaver have prepared their cash budget for the 1996 calendar year. They have used the separate income, expenditure, and summary schedules.

Worksheet 2.5 shows the Weavers' estimated total 1996 annual income—$51,245–by source for each month. By using take-home pay, they eliminate the need to show taxes, social security payments, and other payroll deductions as expenditures. Both Fred and Denise expect to receive salary increases, Fred in April and Denise in June. Their initial schedule of estimated annual expenditures for 1996 (Worksheet 2.6) is self-explanatory. They anticipate a slight amount of inflation and have factored some price increases into their expense projections. They have also allocated $4,500 to savings and investments, a wise budgeting strategy. They will divide the $250 monthly fun money between them.

This first estimate of expenditures is designed to achieve all the Weavers' short-term goals. Comparing this initial expenditure estimate of $53,459 (Worksheet 2.6) to estimated income of $51,245 (Worksheet 2.5), it is clear that their budget does not balance and has a $2,214 deficit. To balance their budget, Fred and Denise must cut some low-priority goals, reschedule some loan payments, or reduce their fun money. After discussing their options, they decide to: replace only the stereo speakers, saving $700; purchase $600 less in workshop equipment; shorten their Hawaii vacation, saving $1,000; reschedule $200 of loan repayment to parents; and reduce fun money by $20 per month, or $240 annually. These reductions of $2,740 lower the total scheduled expenditures to $50,719, balancing the budget on an annual basis.

The Weavers can now prepare the schedule of estimated monthly expenditures, Worksheet 2.7, that reflects the adjusted expenditure totals. Of course, the Weavers may decide that the $526 budget surplus ($51,245 − $50,719) does not adequately allow for unexpected expenses, and they therefore may further reduce other discretionary expenditures.

The Weavers' final step is to combine the monthly income and expense schedules to create the monthly cash budget summary (Worksheet 2.8). This allows them to analyze monthly surpluses and deficits to see whether they should use savings, investments, or borrowing to cover monthly shortages. The summary shows monthly cash surpluses and deficits that total $526 for the year. They can use this surplus to increase savings or investments or repay part of a loan. The bottom line of the budget summary lists the cumulative, or running, totals of monthly cash surpluses and deficits.

Although monthly deficits occur throughout the year, they result in a cumulative deficit for the months of February through August—primarily due to their March Hawaiian vacation. To cover these deficits, Fred and Denise have arranged an interest-free loan from their parents. If they had used their savings to finance the deficits, they would have lost some interest earnings, included as income. If they want to reduce the deficits more quickly, they can postpone purchasing the stereo and delay clothing and entertainment expenses until later in the year. If they could not obtain funds to cover the deficits, they would have to reduce expenditures further or increase income.

COMPARING ACTUAL RESULTS TO BUDGETED FIGURES

In the final analysis, a cash budget has value only if (1) you use it and (2) you keep careful records of actual income and expenditures. These records show whether you are staying within budget limits. Record this information in a *budget record book* often enough so that you don't overlook anything of significance, yet not so often that it becomes a nuisance. A looseleaf binder with separate pages for each income and expenditure category works quite well. Rounding entries to the nearest dollar simplifies the arithmetic.

At the beginning of each month, record the budgeted amount for each category and enter income received and money spent on the appropriate pages. At month-end, total each account and calculate the surplus or deficit. With the exception of certain income accounts (like salary) and fixed expense accounts like mortgage or loan payments, most categories will end the month with a positive or negative variance, indicating a cash surplus or deficit.

This monthly comparison makes it easy to identify major budget categories where income falls far short or spending far exceeds desired levels (variances of 5 to 10 percent or more). Once you pinpoint these areas, you can take corrective action to keep your budget on course. However, it is not enough to simply determine the size of the variances. You should analyze them, particularly the larger ones, to find out why they occurred. An account deficit that occurs in only one period is obviously less of a problem than one that occurs in several periods. If recurring deficits indicate that an account was underbudgeted, you may need to adjust the budget to cover the outlays, reducing overbudgeted or nonessential accounts. Only in exceptional situations should you finance budget adjustments with savings and investments or borrowing.

Control is important not only in individual categories but also in the total monthly budget. By examining end-of-month totals for all accounts, you can discover whether you have a net budget surplus or deficit and take appropriate action to maintain a balanced budget for the rest of the year.

The Weavers' **budget control schedule** (Worksheet 2.9) shows how their actual income and expenditures compare to the various budget categories and where variances exist. Such periodic feedback is essential for budgetary control and to ensure that actual income and expenditures stay within the budgeted amounts. This schedule allows you to identify problems and take steps to bring individual accounts and/or the whole budget into balance. Looking at the Weavers' budget, we see that actual income and expenditure levels are reasonably close to their targets with a positive variance for the months shown (their surpluses exceed

budget control schedule A summary that shows how actual income and expenditures compare to the various budget categories and where surpluses or deficits exist.

WORKSHEET 2.7

The Weavers' Final Schedule of Estimated Monthly Expenditures for 1996

When put on a monthly basis, the schedule of estimated expenditures shows in detail projected month-by-month spending patterns; you can tell at a glance where most of your money is going each month.

Cash Budget: Estimated Expenditures

Name(s) *Fred and Denise Weaver*

For the *Year* Ending *December 31, 1996*

EXPENDITURE CATEGORIES		Jan.	Feb.	Mar.	April	May	June	July	Aug.	Sep.	Oct.	Nov.	Dec.	Total for the Year
Housing	Rent/mortgage payment (include insurance and taxes, if applicable)	$ 572	$ 572	$ 572	$ 572	$ 572	$ 572	$ 572	$ 572	$ 572	$ 572	$ 572	$ 572	$ 6,864
	Repairs, maint., improvements	100	450	100	100	100	100	100	100	100	100	100	100	1,550
Utilities	Gas, electric, water	180	180	180	110	110	135	165	180	140	130	160	180	1,850
	Phone	40	40	40	40	45	45	40	40	40	40	45	45	500
	Cable TV and other	25	25	25	25	25	25	25	25	25	25	25	25	300
Food	Groceries	250	250	250	250	250	250	250	250	250	250	250	250	3,000
	Dining out	325	325	325	325	325	325	325	325	325	325	325	325	3,900
Autos	Loan payments	210	210	210	210	210	210	210	210	210	210	210	210	2,520
	License plates, fees, etc.				170						80			250
	Gas, oil, repairs, tires, maintenance	160	410	160	160	160	160	365	160	160	160	160	160	2,375
Medical	Health, major medical, disability insurance (not provided by employer)		paid by employers and payroll deductions											
	Doctor, dentist, hospital, medicines	30	30	30	30	30	45	30	30	30	30	30	30	375
Clothing	Clothes, shoes, and accessories	150	150	500	400	200	200	300	500	200	300	300	300	3,500
Insurance	Homeowners (if not covered by mortgage payment)				225						225			450
	Life (not provided by employer)							300						300
	Auto					370						370		740
Taxes	Income and social security		assumed equal to amounts withheld from paycheck											
	Property (if not included in mortgage)		550						550					1,100
Appliances, furniture, and other	Loan payments	60	60	30										150
	Purchases and repairs						750			300	300	300		1,650
Personal care	Laundry, cosmetics, hair care	100	100	100	100	100	100	100	100	100	100	100	100	1,200
Recreation and entertainment	Vacations *Hawaii, Colorado*			3,000									1,800	4,800
	Other recreation and entertainment	250	250	200	200	200	300	300	200	200	200	200	250	2,750
Savings and investments	Savings, stocks, bonds, etc.	375	375	375	375	375	375	375	375	375	375	375	375	4,500
Other expenditures	Charitable contributions		100			100			150			100		450
	Gifts			100		25	25			100			250	500
	Education loan payment	75	75	75	75	75	75	75	75	75	75	75	75	900
	Subscriptions, magazines, books	10	25	10	10	10	30	10	10	20	10	30	10	185
	Other: *Loan payment—parents*					350						350		700
	Other: *Misc.*	50	50	50	50	50	50	50	50	50	50	50	50	600
Fun Money		230	230	230	230	230	230	230	230	230	230	230	230	2,760
	TOTAL EXPENDITURES	$3,192	$4,457	$6,562	$3,657	$3,912	$4,002	$3,822	$4,132	$3,502	$3,787	$4,357	$5,337	$50,719

WORKSHEET 2.8

The Weavers' Monthly Cash Budget Summary

The Weavers' cash budget summary shows several months in which substantial cash deficits are expected to occur; they can use this information to develop plans for covering these monthly shortfalls.

Cash Budget: Monthly Summary

Name(s) Fred and Denise Weaver

For the Year Ending December 31, 1996

INCOME	**Jan.**	**Feb.**	**Mar.**	**April**	**May**	**June**	**July**	**Aug.**	**Sep.**	**Oct.**	**Nov.**	**Dec.**	**Total for the Year**
Take-home pay	$3,775	$3,775	$ 3,775	$ 3,965	$ 3,965	$ 4,140	$ 4,140	$4,140	$ 4,140	$4,140	$4,140	$ 4,140	$48,235
Bonuses and commissions						1,350						1,300	2,650
Pensions and annuities													
Investment income			90			90			90			90	360
Other income													
(I) Total Income	$3,775	$3,775	$ 3,865	$ 3,965	$ 3,965	$5,580	$ 4,140	$4,140	$4,230	$4,140	$4,140	$5,530	$ 51,245
EXPENDITURES													
Housing	$ 672	$1,022	$ 672	$ 672	$ 672	$ 672	$ 672	$ 672	$ $672	$ 672	$ 672	$ 672	$ 8,414
Utilities	245	245	245	175	180	205	230	245	205	195	230	250	2,650
Food	575	575	575	575	575	575	575	575	575	575	575	575	6,900
Autos	370	620	370	540	370	370	575	370	370	450	370	370	5,145
Medical	30	30	30	30	30	45	30	30	30	30	30	30	375
Clothing	150	150	500	400	200	200	300	500	200	300	300	300	3,500
Insurance				225	370		300			225	370		1,490
Taxes		550						550					1,100
Appliances, furniture, and other	60	60	30			750			300	300	300		1,800
Personal care	100	100	100	100	100	100	100	100	100	100	100	100	1,200
Recreation and entertainment	250	250	3,200	200	200	300	300	200	200	200	200	2,050	7,550
Savings and investments	375	375	375	375	375	375	375	375	375	375	375	375	4,500
Other expenditures	135	250	235	135	610	180	135	285	245	135	605	385	3,335
Fun Money	230	230	230	230	230	230	230	230	230	230	230	230	2,760
(II) Total Expenditures	$3,192	$4,457	$ 6,562	$ 3,657	$ 3,912	$4,002	$3,822	$4,132	$3,502	$3,787	$4,357	$5,337	$ 50,719
CASH SURPLUS (OR DEFICIT) [(I) – (II)]	$ 583	$(682)	$(2,697)	$ 308	$ $53	$ 1,578	$ 318	$ 8	$ 728	$ 353	$ (217)	$ 193	$ 526
CUMULATIVE CASH SURPLUS (OR DEFICIT)	$ 583	$ (99)	$(2,796)	$(2,488)	$(2,435)	$ (857)	$ (539)	$ (531)	$ 197	$ 550	$ 333	$ 526	$ 526

WORKSHEET 2.9

The Weavers' Budget Control Schedule for January, February, and March 1996

The budget control schedule provides important feedback on how the actual cash flow is stacking up to the forecasted cash budget. If the variances are significant enough and/or continue month after month, the Weavers should consider altering either their spending habits or their cash budget.

Budget Control Schedule

Name(s) Fred and Denise Weaver

For the 3 Months Ending March 31, 1996

	Month: January				Month: February				Month: March			
INCOME	**Budgeted Amount (1)**	**Actual (2)**	**Monthly Variance (3)**	**Year-to-Date Variance (4)**	**Budgeted Amount (5)**	**Actual (6)**	**Monthly Variance (7)**	**Year-to-Date Variance (8)**	**Budgeted Amount (9)**	**Actual (10)**	**Monthly Variance (11)**	**Year-to-Date Variance (12)**
Take-home pay	$3,775	$3,792	$ 17	$ 17	$3,775	$3,792	$ 17	$ 34	$ 3,775	$ 3,792	$ 17	$ 51
Bonuses and commissions												
Pensions and annuities												
Investment income									90	86	(4)	(4)
Other income												
(I)Total Income	$3,775	$3,792	$ 17	$ 17	$3,775	$3,792	$ 17	$ 34	$3,865	$3,878	$ 13	$ 47
EXPENDITURES												
Housing	$ 672	$ 672	$ 0	$ 0	$1,022	$1,022	$ 0	$ 0	$ 672	$ 672	$ 0	$ 0
Utilities	245	237	(8)	(8)	245	252	7	(1)	245	228	(17)	(18)
Food	575	559	(16)	(16)	575	548	(27)	(43)	575	450	(125)	(168)
Autos	370	385	15	15	620	601	(19)	(4)	370	310	(60)	(64)
Medical	30	0	(30)	(30)	30	45	15	(15)	30	0	(30)	(45)
Clothing	150	190	40	40	150	135	(15)	25	500	475	(25)	0
Insurance												
Taxes					550	550	0	0				0
Appliances, furniture, and other	60	60	0	0	60	60	0	0	30	30	0	0
Personal care	100	85	(15)	(15)	100	120	20	5	100	75	(25)	(20)
Recreation and entertainment	250	210	(40)	(40)	250	240	(10)	(50)	3,200	3,285	85	35
Savings and investments	375	375	0	0	375	375	0	0	375	375	0	0
Other expenditures	135	118	(17)	(17)	250	245	(5)	(22)	235	200	(35)	(57)
Fun Money	230	200	(30)	(30)	230	225	(5)	(35)	230	230	0	(35)
(II) Total Expenditures	$3,192	$3,091	$(101)	$(101)	$4,457	$4,418	$(39)	$(140)	$6,562	$6,330	$(232)	$(372)
CASH SURPLUS (OR DEFICIT) [(I) – (II)]	$ 583	$ 701	$ 118	$ 118	$ (682)	$ (626)	$ 56	$ 174	$(2,697)	$(2,452)	$ 245	$ 419
CUMULATIVE CASH SURPLUS (OR DEFICIT)	$ 583	$ 701			$ (99)	$ 75			$(2,796)	$(2,377)		

Key: Col. (3) = Col. (2) – Col. (1); Col. (7) = Col. (6) – Col. (5); Col. (11) = Col. (10) – Col. (9); Col. (4) = Col. (3); Col. (8) = Col. (4) + Col. (7); Col. (12) = Col. (8) + Col. (11)

the budgeted surplus amounts). The biggest variances were in food and auto expenses, but neither was far off the mark. Thus, for the first three months of the year, the Weavers seem to be doing a good job of controlling their income and expenditures. They have, in fact, achieved a cumulative cash deficit $419 smaller than budget (actual of −$2,377 versus budget of −$2,796) by cutting discretionary spending.

Concept Check

2-19. Describe the cash budget and its income and expenditure schedules. How does a budget deficit differ from a budget surplus?

2-20. The Smith family has prepared their annual cash budget for 1996. They have divided it into 12 monthly budgets. Although only one monthly budget balances, they have managed to balance the overall budget for the year. What remedies are available to the Smith family for meeting the monthly budget deficits?

2-21. Why is it important to analyze actual budget surpluses or deficits at the end of each month?

SUMMARY

LG1. Describe the financial planning process, including the role of professional financial planners, the need to address special planning concerns, and the relationship among financial statements, budgets, and financial plans. Personal financial planning provides a logical framework for making financial decisions that are consistent with your long- and short-term financial goals. Sound financial planning involves not only defining financial goals and objectives, but also developing, implementing, and controlling plans and strategies for putting goals into action. Professional financial planners can help you with the planning process. Investigate a prospective financial planner's background carefully and understand how he or she is paid (fees and/or commissions). Situations that require special attention include the timing of financial decisions (especially during periods of personal stress or major life changes), managing two incomes, and adapting to changes in your personal situation such as marital status or taking responsibility for elderly relatives' care. Preparing and using personal financial statements is important to financial planning, because they allow you to keep track of your current financial position and to monitor your progress toward your financial goals.

LG2. Prepare a personal balance sheet. A balance sheet reports on your financial position at a given point in time. It provides a summary of the things you own (assets), the money you owe (liabilities), and your financial worth (net worth). Assets include liquid assets, investments, and real and personal property. Liabilities include current liabilities that are due in less than one year (unpaid bills, open account credit obligations), and long-term liabilities (real estate mortgages, consumer installment loans, education loans). Net worth represents your actual wealth and is the difference between your total assets and total liabilities.

LG3. Generate a personal income and expenditures statement. The income and expenditures statement summarizes the income you received and the money you spent over a given time period. It is prepared on a cash basis and, as such, reflects your actual cash flow. Expenditures consist of cash outflows to (1) meet living expenses, (2) purchase various kinds of assets, (3) pay taxes, and (4) reduce debts. The cash surplus (or deficit) is the difference between income and expenditures. A cash surplus can be used to increase assets and/or reduce debts. This has a positive effect on the balance sheet's net worth account. A cash deficit, in contrast, reduces assets and/or increases debts, acting to reduce net worth.

LG4. **Develop a good record keeping system and use ratios to interpret personal financial statements.** Good records facilitate the preparation of accurate personal financial statements. Organized records also simplify tax return preparation and provide the necessary documentation for tax deductions. Ratio analysis allows you to interpret your personal financial statements to assess how well you are doing relative to your past performance. Four important financial ratios are the solvency, liquidity, savings, and debt service ratios.

LG5. **Set long- and short-term financial goals using time value of money concepts.** Long-term financial goals should provide general direction for the long haul, while short-term goals should be more specific in nature and consistent with established long-term goals. Both types of financial goals will change depending on personal circumstances and stage in the life cycle. When putting a dollar value on your financial goals, be sure to consider the *time value of money* and, if appropriate, use the notion of *future value* or *present value* when preparing your estimates. These techniques explicitly recognize that a dollar today is worth more than a dollar in the future.

LG6. **Construct a cash budget and use it to monitor and control spending.** A cash budget will help you implement a system of disciplined spending. By curbing needless spending, it can increase the amount of funds allocated to savings and investments. Household budgets should be set up on a cash basis. They identify planned monthly cash receipts and cash expenditures for the coming year. The objective is to take in more money than you spend so that you'll save money and add to your net worth over time. The final step in the budgeting process is to compare actual receipts and expenditures to budgeted figures to learn if, in fact, you are living within your budget and if not, to take appropriate corrective actions.

FINANCIAL FACTS OR FANTASIES

Are the following statements financial facts (true) or fantasies (false)?

1. Financial plans are set up after the annual budget is prepared.
2. Since financial statements are used to record actual results, they're really not that important in personal financial planning.
3. You would list a leased car as an asset on your personal balance sheet.
4. When evaluating your income and expenditures statement, primary attention should be given to the top line income received.
5. Defining financial goals is the first step in the personal financial planning process.
6. If a budget shows a cash deficit for the year, then you have no choice but to borrow enough money to make up the shortfall.

DISCUSSION QUESTIONS AND PROBLEMS

Discussion Question for Opening Profile

Why did the financial planner recommend that the Breyers first prepare a detailed budget? What additional advice would you give the Breyers to help them improve their personal financial planning? Are there any steps they can take to reach their goals more quickly?

1. Chris Jones is preparing his balance sheet and income and expenditures statement for the year ending June 30, 1995. He is having difficulty classifying six items and asks for your help. Which, if any, of the following transactions are assets, liabilities, income, or expenditure items?
   a. He rents a house for $400 a month.

b. On June 21, 1995, he bought a diamond ring for his wife and charged it to his VISA card. The ring cost $600, but he has not yet received the bill.

c. He borrowed $2,000 from his parents last fall but so far has made no payments.

d. He makes monthly payments of $120 on an installment loan, about half of which is interest and the balance repayment of principal. He has 20 payments left totaling $2,400.

e. He paid $1,200 in taxes during the year and is due a tax refund of $450, which he has not yet received.

f. He invested $1,800 in some common stock.

2. Put yourself ten years into the future. Construct a fairly detailed and realistic balance sheet and income and expenditures statement reflecting what you would like to achieve by that time.

FPPC **3.** ***Use Worksheet 2.2.*** Elizabeth Walker has been asked by her banker to submit a personal balance sheet as of June 30, 1995, in support of an application for a $3,000 home improvement loan. She has come to you for help in preparing it. So far, she has prepared a list of her assets and liabilities as follows:

Cash on hand		$ 70
Balance in checking account		180
Balance in money market deposit account with Mid-American Savings		650
Bills outstanding:		
Telephone	$ 20	
Electricity	70	
Charge account balance	190	
Visa	180	
MasterCard	220	
Taxes	400	
Insurance	220	1,300
Home and property		68,000
Home mortgage loan		52,000
Automobile:		
1991 Honda Accord		6,000
Installment loan balances:		
Auto loans	$3,000	
Furniture loan	500	3,500
Personal property:		
Furniture	$1,050	
Clothing	900	1,950
Investments:		
U.S. government savings bonds	$ 500	
Stock of WIMCO Corporation	3,000	3,500

From the data given, prepare Elizabeth Walker's balance sheet, dated June 30, 1995 (follow the balance sheet form shown in Worksheet 2.2). Then evaluate her balance sheet relative to the following factors: (a) solvency, (b) liquidity, and (c) equity in her dominant asset.

FPPC **4.** ***Use Worksheet 2.3.*** Chuck and Judy Schwartz are about to construct their balance sheet and income and expenditures statement for the year ending December 31, 1995. They have put together the following information:

Judy's salary	$37,000
Reimbursement for travel expenditures	1,950
Interest on:	
Savings account	110
Bonds of Alpha Corporation	70
Groceries	4,150
Rent	9,600
Utilities	960
Gas and auto expenditures	650
Chuck's tuition, books, and supplies	3,300
Books, magazines, and periodicals	280
Clothing and other miscellaneous expenditures	2,700
Cost of photographic equipment purchased with charge card	2,200
Amount paid to date	1,600
Judy's travel expenditures	1,950
Purchase of a new car (cost)	9,750
Outstanding loan balance on car	7,300
Purchase of bonds in Alpha Corporation	4,900

Using the information provided, prepare an income and expenditures statement for the Schwartzes for the year ending December 31, 1995 (follow the form shown in Worksheet 2.3).

FPPC **5.** Over the past several years, Helen Chang has been able to save regularly; as a result, today she has $14,188 in savings and investments. She wants to establish her own business in five years and feels she will need $50,000 to do so.

a. If she can earn 12 percent on her money, how much will her $14,188 savings/investments be worth in five years? Will Helen have the $50,000 she needs? If not, how much more money will she need?

b. Given your answer to part a, how much will Helen have to save each year over the next five years to accumulate the additional money assuming she can earn interest at a rate of 12 percent?

c. If Helen can afford to save only $2,000 a year, given your answer to part a, will she have the $50,000 she needs to start her own business in five years?

FPPC **6.** Bill Shaffer wishes to have $200,000 in a retirement fund 20 years from now. He can create the retirement fund by making a single lump-sum deposit today.

a. If he can earn 10 percent on his investments, how much must Bill deposit today to create the retirement fund? If he can only earn 8 percent on his investments? Compare and discuss the results of your calculations.

b. If upon retirement in 20 years Bill plans to invest the $200,000 in a fund that earns 11 percent, what is the maximum annual withdrawal he can make over the following 15 years?

c. How much would Bill need to have on deposit at retirement to annually withdraw $35,000 over the 15 years if the retirement fund earns 11 percent?

d. In order to achieve his annual withdrawal goal of $35,000 calculated in part c, how much more than the amount calculated in part a must Bill deposit today in an investment earning 10 percent annual interest in order to create the retirement fund in 20 years?

FPPC **7.** Use future or present value techniques to solve the following problems.

a. Starting with $10,000, how much will you have in 10 years if you can earn 15 percent on your money? If you can earn only 8 percent?

b. If you inherited $25,000 today and invested all of it in a security that paid a 10 percent rate of return, how much would you have in 25 years?

c. If the average new home costs $125,000 today, how much will it cost in 10 years if the price increases by 5 percent each year?

d. You feel that in 15 years it will cost $75,000 to give your child a college education. Will you have enough if you take $25,000 *today* and invest it for the next 15 years at 8 percent? If you start *from scratch*, how much will you have to save each year to have $75,000 in 15 years if you can earn an 8 percent rate of return on your investments?

e. If you can earn 12 percent, how much will you have to save each year if you want to retire in 35 years with $1 million?

f. You plan to have $750,000 in savings and investments when you retire at age 60. Assuming you earn an average of 9 percent on this portfolio, what is the maximum annual withdrawal you can make over a 25-year period?

8. Dave and Betty Williamson are preparing their 1996 budget. Help the Williamsons reconcile the following differences, giving reasons to support your answers:

a. Their only source of income is Dave's salary, which amounts to $2,000 a month before taxes. Betty wants to show the $2,000 as their monthly income, whereas Dave argues that his take-home pay of $1,650 is the correct value to show.

b. Betty wants to make a provision for fun money, an idea that Dave cannot understand. He asks, "Why do we need fun money when everything is provided for in the budget?"

FPPC **9.** Below is a portion of Jeffrey Cook's budget record for April 1996. Fill in the blanks in columns 6 and 7.

FPPC **10.** ***Use Worksheet 2.6.*** Prepare a record of your income and expenditures for the last 30 days; then prepare a personal budget for the next month (using the schedule of estimated expenditures in Worksheet 2.6). Use the budget to control and regulate your expenditures during the month. Discuss the impact of the budget on your spending behavior as well as any differences between your expected and actual spending patterns.

Item Number (1)	Item (2)	Amount Budgeted (3)	Amount Expended (4)	Beginning Balance (5)	Monthly Surplus (Deficit) (6)	Cumulative Surplus (Deficit) (7)
1	Rent	$350	$360	$20	$____	$____
2	Utilities	150	145	15	____	____
3	Food	310	275	−15	____	____
4	Auto	25	38	−5	____	____
5	Recreation and entertainment	50	60	−50	____	____

CONTEMPORARY CASE APPLICATIONS

2.1 The Sullivans' Version of Financial Planning

John and Irene Sullivan are a married couple in their mid-20s. John is a computer analyst and Irene works as a sales representative. Since their marriage four years ago, John and Irene have been living comfortably. Their income has exceeded their expenditures, and they have accumulated a net worth of nearly $25,000—$15,000 represents equity in their home, cars, furniture, and other personal belongings, and the other $10,000 is held in the form of savings accounts and common stock investments. Because their income has always been more than adequate to allow them to live in the fashion they desire, the Sullivans have done no financial planning.

Irene has just learned that she is two months pregnant and is concerned about how they will make ends meet if she quits work after their child is born. Each time she and John discuss the matter, John tells her not to worry because "we have always managed to pay our bills on time." Irene cannot understand this, as her income will be completely eliminated. In order to convince Irene that there is no need for concern, John points out that their expenditures for necessities last year were $24,885, which just about equaled his take-home pay of $26,480, and with an anticipated 10 percent pay raise, his income next year should exceed this amount. John also points out that they can reduce luxuries (trips, recreation, and entertainment) and can always draw down their savings or sell some of their stock if they get in a bind. When asked about the long-run implications of their finances, John replies that there will be "no problems" because his boss has assured him of a bright future with the company. John also emphasizes that in a few years Irene can go back to work if necessary.

In spite of John's somewhat convincing arguments, Irene still feels uncomfortable with their rather matter-of-fact approach to financial planning—she knows there has to be a better way—and has gathered the following financial information for the year ending December 31, 1995:

Salaries	Take-home	Gross Salary
John	$26,480	$38,350
Irene	18,090	26,000

Expenditure	Amount
Food	$ 4,200
Clothing	2,300
Mortgage payments, including property taxes ($1,400)	9,400
Travel and entertainment card balances	2,000
Gas, electric, water expenses	1,990
Household furnishings	4,500
Telephone	640
Auto loan balance	2,650
Common stock investments	7,500
Bank credit card balances	675
Income taxes	16,940
Credit card loan payments	2,210
Cash on hand	85
1991 Nissan Sentra	4,000
Medical expenses (nonreimbursed)	600
Homeowner's insurance premiums paid	400
Checking account balance	485
Auto insurance premiums paid	800
Transportation	2,800
Cable television	480
Estimated value of home	85,000
Trip to Europe	5,000
Recreation and entertainment	4,000
Auto loan payments	2,150
Money market account balance	2,500
Purchase of common stock	7,500
Addition to money market account	500
Mortgage on home	70,000

Questions

1. Using this information and Worksheets 2.2 and 2.3, construct the Sullivans' December 31, 1995, balance sheet and income and expenditures statement for the year ending December 31, 1995.
2. Comment on the Sullivans' financial condition with respect to (a) solvency, (b) liquidity, (c) savings, and (d) ability to pay debts promptly. If the Sullivans continue to manage their finances as described, what do you expect the long-run consequences to be? Discuss.
3. Critically evaluate the Sullivans' approach to financial planning. Point out any fallacies in John's arguments, and be sure to mention (a) implications for the long term, (b) the potential impact of inflation, and (c) the impact on their net worth. What procedures should they use to get their financial house in order? Be sure to discuss the role that long- and short-term financial plans and budgets might play.

2.2 Joe Garcia Learns to Budget

Joe Garcia graduated from college in 1994 and moved to Atlanta to take a job as a market research analyst. He was pleased to be financially independent and was sure that, with his $25,000 salary, he could cover his living expenses and also have plenty of money left over to furnish his studio apartment and enjoy the wide variety of social and recreational activities available in Atlanta. He opened several department store charge accounts and also obtained a bank credit card.

For a while Joe managed pretty well on his monthly take-home pay of $1,450, but by the end of 1995 he was having trouble fully paying all his credit card charges each month. Concerned that his spending had gotten out of control and that he was barely making it from paycheck to paycheck, he decided to compile a list of his expenses for the past calendar year and develop a budget. He hoped not only to reduce his credit card debts but also to begin a regular savings program.

He prepared the following summary of expenses for 1995:

Item	Annual Expenditure
Rent	$6,000
Auto insurance	520
Auto loan payments	2,340
Clothing	1,200
Installment loan for stereo	540
Personal care	240
Phone	300
Cable TV	240
Gas and electricity	720
Medical care	120
Dentist	70
Groceries	1,500
Dining out	1,200
Car expenses (gas, repairs, fees, and so on)	780
Furniture purchases	900
Recreation and entertainment	1,020
Other expenses	600

After reviewing his 1995 expenses, he made the following assumptions about his expenses for 1996:

1. All expenses remain at the same levels, with the following exceptions:
   a. Auto insurance, auto expenses, gas and electricity, and groceries will increase 5 percent.
   b. Clothing purchases will decrease to $1,000.
   c. Phone and cable TV will increase $5 per month.
   d. Furniture purchases will decrease to $660, most of which is for a new television.
   e. He will take a one-week vacation to Lake Tahoe in July at a cost of $1,100.
2. All expenses will be budgeted in equal monthly installments except for the vacation and the following:
   a. Auto insurance is paid in two installments due in June and December.
   b. He plans to replace the brakes on his car in February at a cost of $120.
   c. Visits to the dentist will be made in March and September.
3. He will eliminate his bank credit card balance by making extra monthly payments of $75 during each of the first six months.

With regard to his income, he has just received a raise so that his take-home pay will be $1,575 per month.

Questions

1. a. Prepare an estimated annual expense schedule for Joe for the year ending December 31, 1996, using the format shown in Worksheet 2.6.
   b. Compare Joe's estimated expenses to his expected income and make recommendations that will help him balance his budget.
2. After making any necessary adjustments, prepare Joe's estimated monthly expenditures and monthly cash budget summary for the year ending December 31, 1996, using the format shown in Worksheets 2.7 and 2.8.
3. Analyze the budget and advise Joe on his financial situation. Suggest some long- and short-term financial goals for Joe and discuss some steps he can take to reach them.

GETTING A HANDLE ON YOUR FINANCIAL FUTURE

The most important aspect of financial planning is actually implementing your plan. If you do nothing, nothing will happen. In order to achieve your goals, you must establish a system of monitoring and controlling your expenditures, and, if necessary, revise and replace your goals. This evaluation involves the development and use of financial statements and plans.

If You Are Just Starting Out

The use of your personal financial statements and cash budgets will help you monitor your progress toward achieving your goals. The following suggestions and recommendations will help you get started.

Constructing Financial Statements:

1. Choose an appropriate time period for the analysis, usually the most recent year.
2. Realistically determine the fair market value of your real and personal property. You don't want to overestimate your financial position.
3. Include your credit card balances in the revolving credit section of your balance sheet.
4. Use gross wages before taxes in your income statement, since taxes are treated later as expenditures. And don't forget to include tax refunds as a source of income.
5. Remember to include any withholdings from your pay as expenditures (like social security, income taxes, health insurance).

Financial Goals:

1. Set goals in monetary terms along with anticipated dates for achievement.
2. Where possible, prioritize your goals.
3. Set your short-term goals each year, making sure they are consistent with your long-term goals.
4. Don't let short-term desires jeopardize achieving your long-term goals.
5. Set checkpoints for long-term goals to monitor progress.

Cash Budgets:

1. Be sure to use net or take-home pay as income.
2. Any item for which repayment is required is not considered income. Therefore, a loan would be considered a liability.
3. Base all expenditures on current price levels and then adjust for inflation.
4. Don't forget to include planned savings in your expenditures.

If You Are Thirty-Something

As you get older and your work life expectancy gets shorter, financial planning becomes even more important. If you make a mistake, you have less time to recover from it. As a result, you need to monitor your progress more closely and be willing to make changes more quickly. The following suggestions will help you in this process.

Financial Statements:

1. Be sure to adjust your older assets to their true market value—failure to do so can overstate your assets and net worth.
2. Your net worth should be increasing as long as your income exceeds your expenditures or the value of your assets is growing at a faster rate than your liabilities.
3. Your real growth in earnings may level off or decline, but this should be offset by investment income.
4. As your marital and family situation changes, plan for changes in your expenditures.

Financial Goals:

1. Pay greater attention to managing your tax liability.
2. Adjust your investments more frequently to achieve your goals, if appropriate.
3. Protecting your assets becomes more important as you accumulate more wealth.

Cash Budget:

1. Your pattern of expenditures should be set. This will aid in planning.
2. You should be running a surplus in your budget that could be reallocated to help achieve your financial goals.
3. If long-term goals are in jeopardy, take immediate action with your expenditures.
4. Pay closer attention to deviations in actual versus budgeted expenditures.

CHAPTER 3

MANAGING YOUR TAXES

Tax Planning by the Griffiths

For Steven & Elise Griffith, managing their personal finances is a joint effort, from checking and bill-paying to planned purchases, investments, and year-round tax planning. "Having a well-organized money management system really pays off, especially when it's time to prepare our tax returns," notes Elise. "Our taxes are complicated because I am a freelance writer and own a small business—Leese's Pieces, a desktop publishing and promotional writing firm. We also had some interesting tax consequences when Steve joined MCI as a senior program architect in 1993 and our family (we have two sons, ages 7 and 2) relocated to Colorado from Texas."

The Griffiths' tax planning starts with good record keeping to document their eligible deductions. All receipts (gas, office supplies, postage, large purchases, and so on) go in a special desk drawer and are periodically sorted by business or expense category. Currently, their deductions are mostly business expenses such as Elise's home office costs, computer equipment, postage and printing costs, office supplies, and advertising.

Elise stresses the importance of not waiting until the last minute to think about taxes. "In October to December of the previous year, gather your receipts and tax information and do some preliminary calculations of medical or miscellaneous expenses. Then you can shift the timing to group them in one tax year to exceed the thresholds," she advises. Tax software—the Griffiths use CA Simply Tax—allows them to do

Learning Goals

LG1. *Discuss the basic principles of income taxes and determine your filing status.*

LG2. *Classify the various types of gross income, differentiate between itemized and standard deductions and exemptions, and calculate taxable income.*

LG3. *Prepare a basic tax return using the appropriate tax forms and rate schedules.*

LG4. *Explain who needs to pay estimated taxes, when to file your return, how to handle an audit, and where to get help with your taxes.*

LG5. *Implement a tax planning strategy.*

LG6. *Describe the other major forms of personal taxes.*

their own taxes, saving hundreds of dollars in tax preparation fees. Elise adds, "Because we've done our homework, it takes about three hours to finalize our returns when income information arrives in January or February."

Reducing taxes is part of the Griffiths' financial planning. They owned a house in Texas that provided deductions in the form of mortgage interest and property taxes. Because they couldn't sell it until a year after they moved—and then at a loss—they did not have the down payment for another house. Saving to buy a house is therefore a top priority, both for tax and personal reasons. Other strategies include making sure they take every allowable deduction and investing before-tax dollars in Steven's 401(k) plan to build tax-deferred funds for retirement. Elise sometimes shifts client invoices into the next tax year to lower current-year income. She can also deduct costly office equipment, furnishings, and job-related education for her business.

In some years, however, even the best advance planning doesn't help. "With the move, our income—and tax bill—jumped," Steven recalls. "We had a moving allowance from MCI, rental income from the house until we sold it, and a payment for voluntarily resigning as part of my former employer's downsizing program." That year aside, the Griffiths manage and plan their taxes well. In Chapter 3, you will learn the basics of tax preparation and planning, a key part of the personal financial planning process.

PRINCIPLES OF FEDERAL INCOME TAXES

LG1

The amount of income you report for tax purposes and the way you file your returns both have significant bearing on the amount of taxes you must pay. Why must we pay federal income taxes, and what procedures must we follow when preparing and filing federal income tax returns? Before reading on, spend a few moments answering these questions.

A typical American family currently pays *about one-third of its gross income in taxes:* federal income and social security taxes and numerous state and local income taxes, sales taxes, and property taxes. It is, therefore, no surprise that tax planning is an important aspect of personal financial planning. It is a year-round activity; tax consequences must be considered both when making major financial decisions and when developing and revising your financial plans.

The overriding objective of tax planning is very simple: to maximize the amount of money you keep by minimizing the amount of taxes you pay. As long as it done honestly and within the tax codes, there is nothing immoral, illegal, or unethical about trying to minimize your tax bill. Most tax planning centers on ways to minimize income and estate taxes. Chapter 15 considers estate taxes. This chapter concentrates on income taxes paid by individuals, particularly the federal income tax, the largest and most important tax for the individual or family.

Taxes are dues we pay for membership in our society; they are the cost of living in this country. Federal, state, and local tax receipts fund government activities and a wide variety of public services, from national defense to local libraries. We cannot directly control the tax laws because they are established by the legislators we elect. However, with good tax planning, especially with regard to federal income taxes, you will have more money to spend and invest.

The federal income tax law was outlined in the *Internal Revenue Code of 1939.* In 1954 this code was revised to further clarify and more precisely state its provisions. Since then, a number of amendments have been added to the code that have attempted to simplify it, eliminate infrequently used provisions, and repeal and modify other provisions. The code's various sections and amendments deal with the tax effects of practically all personal and business transactions. The administration and enforcement of federal tax laws is the responsibility of the *Internal Revenue Service (IRS),* which is part of the U.S. Department of the Treasury. The IRS is responsible for making sure that people pay their taxes as required by the various tax codes.

Without a doubt, the biggest and perhaps most controversial piece of tax legislation to come out of Congress in the last 50 years was the *Tax Reform Act of 1986.* (The *Technical and Miscellaneous Revenue Act of 1988* later refined and clarified a number of the 1986 act's provisions.) The purpose of this act was threefold: (1) to simplify the tax code for individual taxpayers; (2) to reduce taxpayer abuses by closing many existing loopholes; and (3) to shift a significant amount of the tax burden from individuals to corporations. The net result of this legislation was far-reaching, as it removed millions of low-income families from the tax rolls, reduced the number of tax brackets from fifteen down to just three, eliminated some popular tax deductions, did away with the preferential treatment of capital gains, and sharply curbed the ability of individual taxpayers to generate tax-sheltered income. In 1993, two additional tax brackets were added, for a current total of five. However, the U.S. tax code remains so complex that taxpayers who itemize their deductions often require costly professional help just to file a return.

The provisions of the tax code may change annually with regard to tax rates, amounts and types of deductions and personal exemptions, and similar items. Often these changes are not finalized until late in the year. The tax tables, calculations, and sample tax returns presented in this chapter are based on the tax laws applicable to calendar 1994—those in effect at the time this book went to press. Any known changes for 1995 are shown parenthetically. *Although tax rates and other provisions will change, the basic procedures will remain the same.* Before preparing your tax returns be sure to review the current regulations; IRS publications and other tax preparation guides should be helpful in this regard.

THE ECONOMICS OF INCOME TAXES

It should come as little surprise to learn that most people simply do not like to pay taxes! Some of this feeling undoubtedly stems from the widely held perception that a lot of government spending amounts to little more than bureaucratic waste. But a good deal of it is probably also due to the fact that taxpayers really get nothing tangible in return for their money. After all, paying taxes is not like spending $7,000 on a car, boat, or European vacation. The fact is, we too often tend to overlook or take for granted the many services that are provided by the taxes we pay—public schools and state colleges, roads and highways, and parks and recreational facilities, not to mention police and fire protection, retirement benefits, and many other health and social services.

Income taxes provide the major source of revenue for the federal government. Personal income taxes are scaled on progressive rates. To illustrate how this **progressive tax structure** works, we will use the following data for single taxpayers filing 1994 returns:

Taxable Income	Tax Rate
$0 to $22,750	15%
$22,751 to $55,100	28%
$55,101 to $115,000	31%
$115,001 to $250,000	36%
Over $250,000	39.6%

Now consider three possible taxable incomes: (1) $15,000, (2) $30,000, and (3) $60,000. The tax liability on these incomes would be:

(1) $2,250—i.e., $15,000 × .15
(2) $5,443—i.e., [($30,000 − $22,750) × .28] + [$22,750 × .15]
(3) $13,990—i.e., [($60,000 − $55,100) × .31] + [($55,100 − $22,750) × .28] + [$22,750 × .15]

Notice that as income moves from a lower to a higher bracket, the higher rate applies *only to the additional income in that bracket* and not to the entire income. For example, you pay the 28 percent rate only on that portion of the $30,000 in income that exceeds $22,750. As a result of this kind of progressive scale, the more money you make, the progressively more you pay in taxes. Note also that the progressive tax structure actually results in total taxes that are lower than implied by the stated tax rates; when you relate the amount of taxes paid to the level of income earned, the tax rate drops considerably.

Returning to the three income levels illustrated above, we can see what happens to the **average tax rate:**

Taxable Income	Tax Liability	Stated Tax Rate	Average Tax Rate
(1) $15,000	$2,250	15%	15% ($2,250/$15,000)
(2) $30,000	$5,443	28%	18.1% ($5,443/$30,000)
(3) $60,000	$13,990	31%	23.3% ($13,990/$60,000)

Clearly, taxes are still progressive, but the size of the bite is not as bad as the stated tax rate might suggest.

The Economic Recovery Tax Act (ERTA) of 1981 attempted to mitigate the impact of inflation on our income taxes, often referred to as **bracket creep.** Here, even when the rate of increase in your income matches the rate of inflation, you may still wind up losing to inflation if your additional income is taxed at higher rates. If this occurs, the growth in your after-tax income will fall short of the inflation rate. The progressive nature of taxes is at the core of bracket creep and, when combined with inflation, can have a cruel effect on family income. Inflation leads to a higher level of income, which pushes you into a higher tax bracket and causes you to pay even more taxes, resulting in your take-home pay going up at a slower rate than inflation. In an attempt to keep bracket creep in check, one of the provisions of ERTA was to *index* the tax brackets, standard deductions, and personal exemptions to the consumer price index. In this way, as inflation increased, so, too, would both the income-level steps in each tax bracket and the personal exemption amounts. The Tax Reform Act of

income taxes A type of tax levied on taxable income by the federal government as well as many state and local governments.

progressive tax structure A tax structure in which the larger the amount of taxable income, the higher the rate at which it is taxed.

average tax rate The rate at which each dollar of taxable income is taxed on average; calculated by dividing tax liability by taxable income.

bracket creep A situation in which increases in income are taxed at higher rates, causing the growth in after-tax income to fall short of the inflation rate.

1986 further curtailed the effects of bracket creep by *reducing* the number of tax brackets and *widening* the income levels within each bracket. Thus, a jump to a higher tax bracket occurs less often today than it did in the past, and it takes a much larger increase in income to trigger a jump to a new bracket.

YOUR FILING STATUS

The taxes you pay depend in part on your *filing status*, the category that identifies you based on your marital status and family situation. Filing status is an important factor in determining whether you are required to file an income tax return, the amount of your standard deduction, and your tax rate. Your filing status is based on your status on the last day of your tax year (usually December 31). If you have a choice of filing status, you should calculate taxes both ways and choose the status that results in the lower tax liability. There are five different filing status categories.

Single taxpayers are unmarried or legally separated from their spouses by either a separation or final divorce decree. *Married filing jointly* refers to married couples who combine their income and allowable deductions and file one tax return. *Married filing separately*, the next category, occurs when each spouse files his or her own return, reporting only his or her income, exemptions, and deductions. *Head of household* refers to a taxpayer who is unmarried or considered unmarried and pays more than half of the cost of keeping up a home for himself or herself and an eligible dependent child or relative. The final category is *qualifying widow or widower with dependent child*, which applies to persons whose spouses died within two years of the tax year (for example, in 1992 or 1993 for the 1994 tax year) and support a dependent child. They may use joint return tax rates and are eligible for the highest standard deduction. (After the two-year period, they may file under the head of household status if they qualify.)

In general, married taxpayers who file jointly have a lower tax liability than if they file separately. However, sometimes these married couples pay more in total taxes than if they were single taxpayers. Combining the two incomes results in *bracket creep*—it pushes the couple into a higher tax bracket resulting in a "marriage tax." The amount of the extra tax depends on the level of each spouse's earnings and usually occurs when the smaller of the two partner's taxable income is equal to at least 30 percent of the couple's total taxable income. As an example, compare the taxes (calculated using the 1994 Tax Rate Schedule, Exhibit 3.5 on page 114) owed by a married couple *filing jointly* with total taxable income of $110,000 to those owed by *two single taxpayers* with taxable incomes of $55,000 each:

Filing Status	**Total Tax Due**
Married couple filing jointly	$26,405
Two single taxpayers: taxes of $12,442.50 each	−24,885
"Marriage tax"	$ 1,520

Combining their incomes pushes the married couple into the 31 percent tax bracket and results in a tax liability that is $1,520 higher than the amount paid by the two *single* taxpayers, who fall into the 28 percent tax bracket. It is illegal, however, for married individuals to use the single filing status. But a couple planning a December wedding may reap considerable tax savings by postponing their wedding until January of the next year.

The tax brackets (rates) and payments for married couples filing separately are typically higher than for joint filers because the spouses rarely account for equal amounts of taxable income. In some cases, however, it may be advantageous for spouses to file separate returns. For instance, if one spouse has a moderate income and substantial medical expenses and the other has a low income and no medical expenses, filing separately may provide a tax savings. It's worth your time to calculate your taxes under both scenarios to see which results in lower taxes.

Every individual or married couple who earns a specified level of income is required to file a tax return. Exhibit 3.1 provides a list of some of the more common filing requirements that existed in 1994. Like the personal tax rates, these minimums are adjusted annually based on the annual rate of inflation. Note that if your income falls below the prevailing minimum levels, you are not required to file a tax return. However, if you had any tax withheld during the year, you must file a tax return—even if your income falls *below* minimum filing amounts—in order to receive a refund of these taxes.

EXHIBIT 3.1

Income Tax Filing Requirements (1994)

Individuals and married couples are required to file tax returns only if their incomes meet or exceed minimum levels. These minimums vary depending upon the taxpayer's filing status.

Filing Status	Minimum Income
Single individual, under 65	$16,250[a]
Single individual, 65 or older	7,200
Married couple, joint return, both under 65	11,250
Married couple, joint return, one spouse 65 or older	12,000
Married couple, joint return, both 65 or older	12,750
Married couple, separate return, any age	2,450
Head of household, under 65	8,050
Head of household, 65 or older	9,000
Qualifying widow(er) with dependent child, under 65	8,800
Qualifying widow(er) with dependent child, 65 or older	9,550

[a]Anyone who is claimed as a dependent on someone else's return (such as a student or elderly parent) must file a return if his or her gross income exceeds $600 and includes some unearned income (such as interest and dividends) or if his or her earned income (such as wages and salary) exceeds $3,800.

YOUR TAKE-HOME PAY

Income taxes are usually collected on a **pay-as-you-go basis,** under which your employer withholds (deducts) a portion of your income every pay period and periodically sends it to the Internal Revenue Service on a scheduled basis. Self-employed persons must likewise deduct and forward a portion of their income to the Internal Revenue Service each quarter. After the close of the taxable year, you calculate the taxes you owe and file your tax return. At the time of filing, you receive full credit for the amount of taxes withheld from your income during the year. Depending on whether the amount of taxes withheld is larger or smaller than the actual taxes you incurred, you will either (1) receive a refund from the Internal Revenue Service (if too much tax was withheld from your paycheck) or (2) have to pay additional taxes (when the amount withheld was not enough to cover your tax liability). Withholdings are normally made not only for federal income taxes, but also for FICA (or social security) taxes and, if applicable, state and local income taxes. In addition to taxes, you may have other deductions for items such as life and health insurance, savings plans, retirement programs, professional or union dues, and/or charitable contributions—all of which lower your take-home pay. Your *take-home pay* is what you are left with after subtracting the amount withheld from your *gross earnings.*

Federal Withholding Taxes. The amount of **federal withholding taxes** deducted from your gross earnings each pay period depends on both the level of your earnings and the number of withholding allowances you have claimed on a form called a W-4, that you must complete for your employer(s). Obviously, given the progressive nature of federal income taxes, the more you make, the more you can expect to have withheld from your paycheck. Withholding allowances are based, for the most part, on the number of people your income supports and act to reduce the amount of taxes withheld from your income. A taxpayer is entitled to one for himself or herself, one for the spouse (if filing jointly), and one for each dependent claimed. In addition, a *special allowance* can be taken by those (1) who are single and have one

pay-as-you-go basis A method of paying income taxes in which the employer (or self-employed person) withholds (deducts) a portion of income every pay period (or quarter) and sends it to the IRS.

federal withholding taxes Taxes—based on the level of earnings and the number of withholding allowances claimed—that are deducted by an employer from the employee's gross earnings each pay period.

job; (2) who are married, have only one job, and have a nonworking spouse; or (3) whose wages from a second job or whose spouse's wages (or the total of both) are $1,000 or less. *Additional withholding allowances* can be claimed by (1) heads of households, (2) those with at least $1,500 of child or dependent-care expenses for which they plan to claim to credit, and (3) those with an unusually large amount of deductions. Of course, you can elect to have your employer withhold amounts greater than those prescribed by the withholding tables.

If you know you will work less than eight months during a year—as you would if you are a college graduate starting your first job in the summer—you can ask your employer to calculate withholding using the part-year method. This method bases withholding on what you actually earn in the tax year, rather than your annual salary. For example, a single person who began a $30,000 per year job in September would have $292 withheld from $2,500 monthly pay, or $1,168 for the four months. The part-year plan would withhold nothing in September and October and a total of $360 for November and December.

FICA (or Social Security Taxes). All employed workers (except certain federal employees) have to pay a combined old-age, survivor's, disability, and hospital insurance tax under provisions of the **Federal Insurance Contributions Act (FICA).** Known more commonly as the **social security tax,** it is applied to a stipulated amount of every employee's wages as mandated by Congress. This tax is paid equally by employer and employee. In 1994, the total social security tax rate was 15.3 percent, which was levied against the first $60,600 of an employee's earnings. Therefore, in 1994 7.65 percent would have been deducted from your paycheck until you earned more than $60,600, with a 1.45 percent Medicare surcharge on amounts in excess of $60,600. Self-employed persons pay the full tax—15.3 percent in 1994—and can deduct 50 percent of it on their tax returns.

The social security tax rate changes (that is, rises) over time, as does the tax base, which is linked to the cost of living. As with income taxes, your employer is required by law to withhold social security taxes from your paycheck. However, unlike income taxes, you have to pay social security only up to a stipulated maximum amount. In 1994, as noted above, once your salary went over $60,600, you stopped paying social security taxes for the balance of that year (the 1.45 percent Medicare surcharge was paid on earned income over $60,600). Finally, while the number of withholding allowances you claim has a bearing on the amount of income taxes withheld, it has absolutely no effect on the amount of social security taxes you pay. Everybody pays the same rate on the same amount of earnings, regardless of the number of dependents claimed. The amount of federal income tax withheld depends on both your level of earnings and the number of withholding allowances claimed.

State and Local Income Taxes. Unlike federal income taxes, state and local income taxes differ from state to state. If levied, these taxes are generally tied to the individual's level of earnings. While state and local income taxes that have been withheld (or paid) are deductible on federal returns, federal taxes may or may not be deductible on the state or local return, depending on state and local laws. Especially in large cities, local income taxes can amount to as much as 2 percent of income—and in some states, the state income tax can be 15 percent or more.

Concept Check

3-1. Discuss the following items and explain their significance with respect to personal taxes: (a) Internal Revenue Code of 1939, (b) the IRS, (c) federal withholding taxes, and (d) FICA. What was the purpose of the Tax Reform Act of 1986?

3-2. What is a progressive tax structure? What is the economic rationale underlying the notion of progressive income taxes?

3-3. Mo Huang has an opportunity to earn $2,000 working overtime during the Christmas season. He thinks he will turn it down, however, because the extra income would put him in a higher tax bracket and the government would probably get most of it. Discuss Mo's reasoning.

3-4. Briefly define the five filing categories available to taxpayers. When might married taxpayers choose to file separately?

3-5. Distinguish between gross earnings and take-home pay. What does the employer do with the difference?

3-6. What two factors determine the amount of federal withholding taxes that will be deducted from gross earnings each pay period? Explain.

IT'S TAXABLE INCOME THAT MATTERS

LG2

Taxable income *is the actual amount on which we pay taxes and is calculated by subtracting certain allowable items from* gross income. *Can you name some sources of income and several types of deductible expenses? Give some thought to these questions before reading on.*

Various sections of the Internal Revenue Code define the key components of **taxable income.** Unfortunately, because of the numerous conditions and exceptions surrounding the tax treatment and/or deductibility of certain income and expense items, the actual amount of taxable income is often difficult to determine. In its simplest form, taxable income can be found according to the following procedure:

	Gross income
Less:	Adjustments to (gross) income
Equals:	Adjusted gross income (AGI)
Less:	Larger of itemized or standard deductions
Less:	Exemptions
Equals:	**Taxable income**

The preceding explanation looks simple enough—just subtract certain adjustments, deductions, and exemptions from your gross income, and you will get taxable income. As we will see, however, there are a number of problems that arise in defining what is included in these items.

GROSS INCOME

Basically, **gross income** includes any and all income that is subject to federal taxes. Some of the more common forms of gross income include:

- Wages and salaries
- Bonuses, commissions, and tips
- Interest and dividends received
- Alimony received
- Business and farm income
- Gains from the sale of assets
- Income from pensions and annuities
- Income from rents and partnerships
- Prizes, lottery, and gambling winnings

In addition to these sources of income, there are other types that are considered to be *tax exempt* and as such are excluded—totally or partially—from gross income. Tax-exempt income does not even have to be listed on the tax return. A partial list of different types of tax-exempt income is shown in Exhibit 3.2.

Three Kinds of Income. One of the major provisions of the 1986 Tax Reform Act was the creation of three basic categories of income, devised as a way to limit write-offs from tax-sheltered investments: (1) active (ordinary "earned") income, (2) portfolio (investment) income, and (3) passive income. *Active income* is the broadest category and consists of everything from wages and salaries to bonuses, tips, pension income, and alimony. It is made up of income earned on the job, as well as most other forms of *noninvestment* income. *Portfolio income*, in contrast, is comprised of the earnings generated from various types of investment holdings—in fact, this category of income covers most (but not all) types of investments, from savings accounts, stocks, bonds, and mutual funds to commodities and stock options. For the most

Federal Insurance Contributions Act (FICA); social security tax The law establishing the combined old-age, survivor's, disability, and hospital insurance tax levied on both employer and employee, also called the *social security tax.*

taxable income The amount of income that is subject to taxes; calculated by subtracting adjustments, the larger of standard or itemized deductions, and exemptions from gross income.

gross income The total of all income (before any adjustments, deductions, and/or exemptions) generated by a taxpayer; it includes active, portfolio, and passive income.

EXHIBIT 3.2

Common Types of Tax-Exempt Income

On some forms of income, you do not have to pay any taxes at all, because they can be totally or partially excluded from gross income.

Child support payments
Compensation from accident, health, and life insurance policies
Disability payments (limited in some cases)
Employee fringe benefits (limited to certain items)
Federal income tax refunds
Gifts
Inheritances
Interest on state or local government obligations
Military allowances
Return of original investment capital
Scholarships and fellowships (limited as to amount and time)
Social security benefits (amount exempted depends on total income)
Stock rights and stock dividends
Veterans' benefits
Welfare and other public assistance benefits
Workers' compensation payments

part, portfolio income consists of interest, dividends, and capital gains (that is, the profit on the sale of an investment). Finally, there is *passive income*, a special category of income that is comprised chiefly of income derived from real estate, limited partnerships, and other forms of tax shelters.

The key feature of these categories is that they limit the amount of deductions and write-offs that can be taken, particularly with regard to portfolio and passive income. Specifically, the amount of allowable, deductible expenses associated with portfolio and passive income *is limited to the amount of income derived from these two sources.* For example, if you had a total of $380 in portfolio income for the year, you could write off no more than $380 in portfolio-related interest expense. Note, however, that if you have more portfolio expenses than income, you can "accumulate" the difference and write it off in later years (when you have sufficient portfolio income) or when you finally sell the investment. Likewise, the same rules generally apply to passive income and related expenses (with a few notable exceptions, which will be discussed later in this chapter). Thus, if you own limited partnerships that generate no income, you cannot write off the losses from those partnerships (at least not in the year in which they occur—as with investment expenses, you can "accumulate" these losses and write them off later).

It is important to understand that for deduction purposes, the portfolio and passive income categories cannot be mixed and/or combined with each other or with active income. *Investment-related expenses can be used only with portfolio income,* and with a few exceptions, *passive investment expenses can be used only to offset the income from passive investments.* As it turns out, therefore, all the other allowances and deductions (as described below) are written off against the total amount of *active* income generated by the taxpayer. In essence, the taxpayer's income from wages, salaries, bonuses, tips, pensions, alimony, and so on is all added up, and it is against this amount that the various deductions are subtracted to arrive at adjusted gross income and, ultimately, the amount of taxable income.

Capital Gains. Technically, a *capital gain* occurs whenever an asset (such as a stock, bond, or real estate) is sold for more than its original cost. Thus, if you purchased stock for $50 per share and sold it for $60, you'd have a capital gain of $10 per share. As of early 1995, capital gains are taxed at a maximum rate of 28 percent. Therefore, only taxpayers in the 31, 36, or 39.6 percent bracket (in 1994, single filers with taxable income over $55,100 and married couples filing jointly with taxable income over $91,850) benefit from a lower tax rate on capital gains. To qualify for the 28 percent rate, taxpayers in the higher tax brackets must have long-term capital gains (gains on assets held more than one year) in excess of any short-term *capital losses.* (In contrast to a capital gain, a *capital loss* occurs when an asset is sold for less than its original cost.) The reinstatement of more attractive (lower) capital gains tax rates is being considered by Congress.

As a rule, most capital gains will probably be included as part of the taxpayer's *portfolio income*, by adding any capital gains (actually realized) to the amount of dividends, interest, and rents generated by the taxpayer to arrive at total investment income. While there are no limits on the amount of capital gains taxpayers can generate, there are some IRS-imposed restrictions on the amount of capital losses that can be taken in a given year. Specifically, a taxpayer can write off capital losses, dollar for dollar, against any capital gains. For example, if a taxpayer has $10,000 in capital gains, she can write off up to $10,000 in capital losses. After that, no more than $3,000 in additional capital losses can be written off against other (active, earned) income. Thus, in our example, if the taxpayer had $18,000 in capital losses, she could only write off $13,000 of it in the current year; $10,000 against the capital gains she generated in that year and another $3,000 against her active income. Anything left ($5,000 in this case) would have to be written off in later years in the same order as indicated above: first against any capital gains and then up to $3,000 against active income. (Note: to qualify as a deductible item, the capital loss *must result from the sale of some income-producing asset*, such as stocks and bonds. The capital loss on a nonincome-producing asset, such as a car or TV set, does *not* qualify for tax relief.)

The Special Case of Selling Your Home. Homeowners, for a variety of reasons, are given special treatment in the tax codes, and the way capital gains are taxed on the sale of a home is no exception. Essentially, the tax on any gain you make from the sale of your home can be *deferred* almost indefinitely as long as you buy another home of equal or greater value within a stipulated time period. Note that this provision applies only to your *principle residence* and not to any other homes or real estate you may own. Here is how it works: If you sell your home and purchase and use a new one within 24 months, any gain made on the sale of the old home will not be taxable as long as the amount paid for the new home is equal to or greater than the sale proceeds from the old home. (Note that the home you purchase need not be a new home in order to qualify for this special tax treatment; it only needs to be "new" to you and, as such, can be a previously occupied, older house.) If a new home is not purchased within 24 months from the date of the sale of the old home, taxes must be paid on all capital gains realized from the sale of this *and any previous homes*.

If the price of the new home is lower than the sale price of the old home, the amount by which the price of the old residence exceeds that of the new one is subject to tax. For instance, assume that you sell your first home, which you purchased for $70,000 three years ago, for $83,000. In this case you will have a capital gain of $13,000 ($83,000 − $70,000). Further, suppose that within 24 months of the sale of your old home you purchase and use a new one costing $80,000. As a result, you have to pay taxes on the $3,000 in profits that you pocketed. In contrast, if the new home cost $90,000, no taxes will be due in the current year, because the $90,000 purchase price exceeds the $83,000 for which the old home was sold.

While you can sell and buy homes over and over again and defer the taxes on all profits literally to the day you die, there is a provision in the tax code that allows people 55 or older to take a one-time exclusion of $125,000 in capital gains earned from the sale of principal residences. For married couples filing joint returns, it requires merely that one of the spouses be 55 or older and that the couple have owned and lived in the house as their principal residence for three years out of the five-year period ending on the date of sale. This feature provides a real break for homeowners, allowing them a one-time chance to earn up to $125,000 of tax-free income.

To illustrate, consider the case of Homer and Lucile Greenman, who are both 58 years old and have decided to retire in sunny Arizona. They purchased their first house 30 years ago for $25,000 and have since owned three other homes, each higher priced than the last. They have been offered $250,000 for their present home, for which they paid $100,000 in the late 1970s. Their records show that they realized $40,000 in profits from their first three houses. When this is added to the $150,000 gain they will realize on their present home, they will have to declare $190,000 in capital gains if they decide to retire into a rental unit. However, because of their ages, they are eligible for the $125,000 tax-free exclusion. Thus, they will have to pay taxes on only $65,000 of their gain (that is, $190,000 − $125,000). On the other hand, if the Greenmans decide to buy another home when they retire, all they have to do is buy one for $125,000 (the $250,000 sale price of their current home less the one-time exclusion of $125,000) and they can keep $125,000—*tax-free*—and avoid any taxes altogether.

ADJUSTMENTS TO (GROSS) INCOME

Adjustments to gross income are allowable deductions from gross income that include certain employee and personal retirement, insurance, and support expenses. Most of these deductions are nonbusiness in nature. The following list, though not exhaustive, includes items that can be treated as adjustments to income:

- IRA deductions (limited)
- Self-employment tax deduction (limited to 50 percent of amount paid)
- Self-employed health insurance deduction (limited to 25 percent of amount paid)
- Keogh retirement plan and self-employed SEP deduction (limited)
- Penalty on early withdrawal of savings
- Alimony paid
- Moving expenses (some limits)

There are some important restrictions that were placed on IRA deductions in the 1986 Tax Reform Act that taxpayers should be aware of. In particular, contributions to IRA accounts (of up to $2,000 for a wage earner and $250 for a nonworking spouse) are tax deductible *only* if the taxpayer is not covered by a qualified company-sponsored retirement program, or if the taxpayer's annual income is below a specified minimum: *$40,000 for married couples, $25,000 for single individuals.* (Note that if one spouse is covered by an employer plan, then *both* individuals' IRA contributions are restricted as a tax deduction depending on their income.) In essence, a taxpayer can be covered by an employer pension plan and also deduct contributions to his or her own IRA account so long as the income constraints are not violated. Note that allowable tax deductible IRA contributions are phased out between $40,000 and $50,000 for married couples (and $25,000–$35,000 for individuals) so that a married worker earning, say, $45,000 a year would be able to deduct an IRA contribution of only $1,000 (plus $125 for a nonworking spouse); workers earning more than $50,000 (or $35,000 if single) who are covered by a company pension plan would not be allowed any deduction. (The income limitations apply only to workers who are covered by employer-provided retirement plans; there is no income limitation on workers who are not covered by company programs.) When the total of any IRA contributions and any other allowable adjustments to income are subtracted from gross income, you are left with **adjusted gross income (AGI),** which in itself is an important calculation, because certain itemized deductions are limited by its amount.

DEDUCTIONS: ITEMIZED OR STANDARD?

The next step in calculating your taxes is to subtract allowable deductions from your adjusted gross income to determine taxable income. This is perhaps the most complex part of the tax preparation process. You have two options: list your *itemized deductions* (specified tax-deductible personal expenses) or take the *standard deduction*, a blanket deduction that depends on your filing status. Obviously, you should use the method that results in larger allowable deductions.

Itemized Deductions. Deducting **itemized expenses** allows taxpayers to reduce their AGI by the amount of their allowable personal expenditures. The Internal Revenue Code defines the types of nonbusiness items that can be deducted from adjusted gross income. Some of the more common ones are as follows:

- Medical and dental expenses (in excess of 7.5 percent of AGI)
- State, local, and foreign income and property taxes; and state and local personal property taxes
- Residential mortgage interest and investment interest (limited)
- Charitable contributions (limited to 50 percent, 30 percent, or 20 percent of AGI depending on certain factors)
- Casualty and theft losses (in excess of 10 percent of AGI)
- Moving expenses (some restrictions; also deductible for those who don't itemize)
- Job and other expenses (in excess of 2 percent of AGI)

Beginning in 1991, taxpayers with AGI in excess of $100,000 ($50,000 for marrieds filing separately) lost part of their itemized deductions. (In 1994 the base level of AGI rose to $111,800; $55,900 for marrieds filing separately.) This phaseout applies to certain categories of deductions, including taxes, home mortgage interest, charitable contributions, moving expenses, unreimbursed employee expenses, and other miscellaneous deductions subject to the 2 percent limit. Medical expenses, casualty and theft losses, and investment interest are exempt from this phaseout, and the amount of the total reduction in itemized deductions cannot be more than 80 percent of the total deductions to which the phaseout applies. These total itemized deductions are reduced by 3 percent of AGI over $111,800 (or $55,900 for married taxpayers filing separately). As an example, assume your AGI is $150,000, deductions (in excess of any specified percentages of AGI) affected by the income limitation total $45,000, and other deductions total $10,000. You must reduce deductions by $1,146 [($150,000 AGI − $111,800) × .03 = $1,146]. Therefore, you would subtract $1,146 from your $55,000 total itemized deductions, for an allowed deduction of $53,854. This loss of itemized deductions has the effect of raising the tax rate applied to your top bracket (in this case) from 31 percent to 31.93 percent [31.00% + (3% × 31%)]. Married taxpayers with combined income over $111,800 and high itemized deductions that can be allocated to one spouse (such as medical expenses) may find that filing separately will allow them to avoid this phaseout.

A deduction is allowed for medical and dental expenses paid during the taxable year; however, it is limited to the amount by which such expenditures *exceed*, not equal, 7.5 percent of adjusted gross income. Medical insurance premiums and any expenses incurred in the diagnosis, cure, mitigation, and treatment of disease and injury or in the prevention of disease may be counted as medical and dental expenses. Specifically, they include costs related to doctors, dentists, hospitals, corrective devices such as eyeglasses, transportation, medicine and drugs, education for the physically or mentally handicapped, and the cost of medical insurance. Surgery for purely cosmetic reasons is not deductible. Of course, you cannot deduct any item for which you are reimbursed by medical insurance. The Internal Revenue Code also allows taxpayers to deduct certain taxes from AGI, including state, local, and foreign income taxes; state, local, and foreign real property taxes; and state and local personal property taxes.

Another deduction is permitted for interest paid on first and second mortgages. These mortgages must be on the taxpayer's principal residence or second home such as a summer cabin or vacation condo. In most cases, you can deduct all of your home mortgage interest. There are some limitations, however, depending in the date of the mortgage, the amount of the mortgage, and how you used the proceeds. Interest on mortgages of any amount acquired before October 13, 1987, is fully deductible. After October 13, 1987, mortgages taken out in order to buy, build, or improve your home are fully deductible if these mortgages, together with any mortgages taken out before October 13, 1987, total $1 million or less. Interest on mortgages taken out for uses other than to buy, build, or improve your home (called *home equity loans* and described more fully in Chapter 6) is deductible on loans up to $100,000. (These items are halved for married taxpayers filing separately.) If a home equity loan exceeds $100,000, interest on the portion used for home improvements or for educational or medical purposes is tax deductible up to the $1 million total mortgage interest limit. Exhibit 3.3 employs a simple illustration to summarize and clarify the treatment of interest expense on home equity loans.

As explained in the preceding discussion of *gross income*, interest may also be deductible when incurred for investment purposes as long as such interest expense does not exceed the amount of *portfolio income* reported by the taxpayer. The deduction for interest paid on consumer loans, allowed for decades, was eliminated in 1991.

adjustments to (gross) income Allowable deductions from gross income that include certain employee and personal retirement, insurance, and support expenses.

adjusted gross income (AGI) The amount of income remaining after subtracting adjustments to income from gross income.

itemized expenses Personal expenditures that can be deducted from adjusted gross income when determining taxable income.

Financial Shocks

With Good Planning, You Can Avoid a Tax Audit

Not only is it a financial shock, but it's everyone's worse fear: the dreaded envelope saying that the Internal Revenue Service wants more information or, worse yet, is auditing your tax return. In fact, this "fear of filing" keeps many people honest—and also may prevent them from claiming valid deductions. While the number of returns the IRS audits is quite small—less than 1 percent—going through an audit is not a pleasant experience. You can take steps, however, to prepare your tax return so that it's less likely to attract the IRS's keen eye.

With its sophisticated computer system, the IRS can now catch things that would have escaped notice in the past, such as understated income or excessive deductions. These may not trigger a full audit, but at the very least the IRS will request verification of such items. It can quickly match your reported income against documentation (W-2, 1098, and 1099 forms) from employers and financial institutions. Underreporting income cost taxpayers $1.8 billion in taxes, fines, and interest in 1993. If you receive interest from several sources, don't lump all interest together on Schedule B but list each institution's payments, as shown on your 1099-INT forms, separately. The IRS computer looks for each payor and flags your return if it doesn't find them. If you receive an incorrect 1099 or W-2 form, get the *issuer* to correct it; don't try to explain it yourself. The self-employed may also be asked to prove that they have reported all income; bank deposit records help document income received.

Deductions are a big concern for those who itemize. Certain categories are more likely to trigger an audit than others—the home office deduction, high entertainment, travel, or casualty loss deductions, passive losses, and complex tax shelters are a few examples. And deductions that exceed IRS ceilings send up red flags for IRS examiners. For example, the IRS wouldn't expect a couple with adjusted gross income (AGI) of $40,000 to have over $1,315 in charitable contributions. Does this mean that you should omit deductions that fall outside of IRS norms or may increase your chances of an audit? Not at all, say tax experts. Just be sure that you understand the IRS regulations, qualify for the deduction, and can document the amount claimed. Keep *meticulous* records of legitimate deductions (such as mortgage interest, charitable donations, medical expenses, business-related travel and publications, job-search expenses, and so on; see IRS Publication 529 for a complete list). Because people often overstate property damage and theft losses, including Form 4684 to explain the loss along with any appraisals, police, or fire department records will answer IRS questions. To take the home office deduction, keep a log that shows that the space claimed is your only regular place of business. And any charitable contribution of $250 or more requires a receipt from the recipient.

What if your deductions seem over the usual limits—perhaps your son had several operations so that medical expenses jumped, or your deductions look high compared to income because you lost your job during the year? "If something is confusing but correct, explain it in a statement attached to your return. Be direct and concise," advises Robert J. Garner, Ernst and Young's national director of personal financial counseling.

Another area that can flag your return for an audit is failing to pay the penalty for early withdrawals from retirement accounts. If you tap a retirement account before age 59½ and don't reinvest the funds in a similar account within 60 days, you owe a 10 percent penalty. The withdrawal is reported as income on line 16a of Form 1040; the penalty, on Form 5329. Forgetting to do this may cost you 7 percent interest, plus another 5 percent failure-to-pay penalty.

Sources: Adapted from Stephen Advokat, "A Few Tips on Avoiding that IRS Audit," *The San Diego Union-Tribune,* February 14, 1994, p. C-1; Deborah Lohse, "Bulletproof Your Income Tax Return to Avoid Becoming an IRS Target," *The Wall Street Journal,* February 25, 1994, pp. C1, C18; and Elizabeth M. MacDonald, "Avoid the Audit Red Flags as You File Your Tax Return," *Money,* January 1994, pp. 78–79.

To encourage charitable giving, a deduction is allowed for the amount of such contributions up to a maximum of 50 percent of adjusted gross income. (*Note*: A maximum contribution limit of 30 percent or 20 percent may apply in certain cases.) Contributions must be made to qualified organizations outlined by the IRS. Contributions over $250 require substantiation from the charity. They

EXHIBIT 3.3

Some Interest Is Deductible, Some Is Not

Because interest paid on first and second mortgages on a principal residence and a second home is the only form of noninvestment interest that can be deducted for tax purposes, borrowing against home equity has become popular in recent years. To be deductible, these loans must conform to rather rigid ground rules, which are illustrated in the following example.

Here's a hypothetical example of how the new rules on deductibility of *mortgage interest expense* would affect the tax return of a married couple who want to borrow against the value of their home, which is now worth $350,000:

Original first mortgage loan, taken out in 1988	$220,000
Current balance owed on first mortgage loan	193,000

The couple took out a home equity loan of $120,000 and used $75,000 to renovate their house and $45,000 for other purposes. They can deduct all of the interest on both mortgages:

- The first mortgage was taken out after October 13, 1987.
- Even though the home equity line (second mortgage) was over $100,000, all of the interest is deductible because:

  1. The total of the proceeds used for home improvements ($75,000) plus the current balance on the first mortgage ($193,000) is $268,000, which is below the $1 million limit.

  2. The portion *not* used for home improvement ($45,000) is below the $100,000 limit.

Their remaining unrestricted borrowing power for tax purposes is:

- Up to $37,000 for any purpose ($82,000 limit [$350,000 home value − $268,000 mortgage balance used to buy, build, or improve home] less $45,000 from existing home equity line *not* used for home improvements).
- Up to $82,000 for tuition and/or medical expenses ($350,000 home value − $268,000 mortgage balance).
- Whatever it costs (up to the $1 million limit) to make any home improvements and/or buy a second home.

include contributions of money and property, but contributions of labor are not deductible. Another deduction that can be taken is for any personal casualty or theft losses, such as those suffered from fire, storms, vandalism, or robbery. These deductions are limited to the amount of each loss above $100 and then only to that portion in excess of 10 percent of adjusted gross income.

Another category of allowable deductions is for job and other expenses. This catchall category includes everything from unreimbursed employee expenses such as job travel, union and professional association dues, and job related subscriptions to professional journals to safe deposit box rental and tax preparation fees. (The amount of allowable deductions for business-related meals and entertainment is limited to 50 percent of the amount actually spent on them.) The total of all these job and other expenses is deductible *only to the extent that it exceeds 2 percent of adjusted gross income.* Thus, if you have an AGI of $25,000, your total job and other expense deductions would have to exceed $500 (which is 2 percent of the AGI, or .02 × $25,000 = $500); if expenses amounted to $800, for instance, you would write off $300 in these deductions: $800 − $500 = $300. The *Financial Shocks* box on page 110 provides useful suggestions to help you prepare and document a return that is less likely to trigger an audit.

Standard Deduction. Instead of itemizing personal deductions, a taxpayer can take the **standard deduction,** which is a type of blanket deduction that is meant to capture the various deductible expenses that taxpayers normally incur. People who don't want to itemize their deductions take the stipulated standard deduction, which varies depending on the taxpayer's filing status (single, married filing jointly, and so on), age (65 or older), and vision (blind). In 1994 the standard deduction varied from $3,800 to $9,350. Exhibit 3.4 includes

> **standard deduction** A blanket deduction that depends on the taxpayer's filing status, age, and vision and can be taken by a taxpayer instead of itemizing deductions.

EXHIBIT 3.4

Calculating Standard Deduction Amounts under Various Filing Alternatives (1994)

The standard deduction for taxpayers depends on filing status, age, and vision. The following IRS form can be used to estimate your allowable standard deduction.

STEP 1. Check the correct number of boxes below.

You	65 or older _____	Blind _____
Your spouse	65 or older _____	Blind _____

Total number of boxes you checked . . . . ______

STEP 2. Find your standard deduction.

If your filing status is:	and number of boxes checked in Step 1 above are:	your standard deduction is:
Single	0	$3,800
	1	4,750
	2	5,700
Married filing jointly or Qualifying widow(er) with dependent child	0	$6,350
	1	7,100
	2	7,850
	3	8,600
	4	9,350
Married filing separately[a]	0	$3,175
	1	3,925
	2	4,675
	3	5,425
	4	6,175
Head of household	0	$5,600
	1	6,550
	2	7,500

[a]If your spouse itemizes deductions on a separate return, you must also itemize deductions rather than take the standard deduction.

the 1994 table that can be used to calculate your standard deduction. Each year the standard deduction amounts are adjusted in response to changes in the cost of living.

Choosing the Best Option. The decision to itemize deductions or take the standard deduction may be changed from year to year, or even in the same year. Taxpayers who find they have chosen the wrong option and paid too much may recompute their tax using the other method and claim a refund for the difference. As an example, suppose you computed and paid your taxes, which amounted to $2,450, using the standard deduction. A few months later you find that had you itemized your deductions, your taxes would have been only $1,950. Using the appropriate forms, you can file an *amended return (Form 1040X)* showing a $500 refund ($2,450 - $1,950). To avoid having to file an amended return as a result of using the wrong deduction technique, you should estimate your deductions using both the itemized and standard deduction amounts and then choose the alternative that results in lower taxes. Interestingly, most taxpayers use the standard deduction; generally homeowners who pay home mortgage interest and property taxes itemize, however, because those expenses alone typically exceed the allowable standard deduction.

EXEMPTIONS

Deductions based on the number of persons supported by the taxpayer's income are called **exemptions.** A taxpayer can claim an exemption for himself or herself, his or her spouse, and any *dependents*—which include children or other relatives earning less than a stipulated level of income ($2,450 in 1994) and for whom the taxpayer provides at least half of their total support. This income limitation is waived for children under the age of 24 who are full-time students. Therefore, a college student, for example, could earn $8,000 and still be claimed as an exemption by his or her parents as long as all other dependency requirements are met. In 1994 each exemption claimed was worth $2,450. The personal exemption amount is tied to the cost of living and will change annually in line with the prevailing rates on inflation.

Exemptions are phased out and eliminated altogether for taxpayers with high levels of AGI. The phaseout provision was introduced in 1991. After adjustment for inflation, it applies to single taxpayers with 1994 AGI over $111,800 and married couples filing jointly with 1994 AGI over $167,700. This phaseout, together with the itemized deduction phaseout, raises the effective tax rate for a single taxpayer with AGI over $111,800 and one exemption to about 33 percent and for a married couple with two children, to more than 34 percent.

Moreover, a personal exemption can be claimed only once. If a child is *eligible* to be claimed as an exemption by his or her parents, then the child does not have the choice of using a personal exemption on his or her own tax return regardless of whether or not the parents use the child's exemption.

In 1994 a family of four could take total exemptions of $9,800—that is, 4 × $2,450. Subtracting the amount claimed for itemized deductions (or the standard deduction) and exemptions from AGI results in the amount of your *taxable income,* which is the basis on which your taxes are figured. A taxpayer who makes $40,000 a year may have only, say, $25,000 in taxable income after adjustments, deductions, and exemptions. It is the *lower,* taxable income figure that determines how much tax an individual must pay.

Concept Check

3-7. Define and differentiate between gross income and adjusted gross income (AGI). What is *passive income?* Name several types of tax exempt income.

3-8. Define what is meant by capital gains and capital losses. What is the tax treatment of capital gains?

3-9. If you itemize your deductions, certain expenses may be included as part of your itemized deductions. Discuss five types of deductions and the general rules that apply to them.

3-10. Larry Tolle was married on January 15, 1995. His wife, Rebecca, is a full-time student at the university and earns $125 a month working in the library. How many personal exemptions will Larry and Rebecca be able to claim on their joint return? Would it make any difference if Rebecca's parents paid for more than 50 percent of her support? Explain.

CALCULATING AND FILING YOUR TAXES

FPPC

LG3

The amount of taxes you pay depends on the amount of taxable income you have and the rate at which your income is taxed. On average, what percent of every dollar of your income do you pay out in taxes? Try to estimate this percentage before reading on.

Now that we have reviewed the general principles of federal income taxes and the components of taxable income, we can direct our attention to calculating the amount of income tax due. To do this, we will need to address several key aspects of measuring taxable income and taxes: (1) the tax rates applicable to various types of personal income, (2) tax credits, (3) the basic tax forms and schedules, and (4) the procedures for determining tax liability.

TAX RATES

As we saw earlier in this chapter, the amount of *taxable income* is found by subtracting itemized deductions (or the standard deduction for nonitemizers) *and* personal exemptions from adjusted

exemptions Deductions from adjusted gross income based on the number of persons supported by the taxpayer's income.

EXHIBIT 3.5

Tax Rate Schedules (1994)

Tax rates levied on personal income vary with the amount of reported taxable income and the taxpayer's filing status.

Single

Taxable Income	Tax Rate	Taxes Due
$0 to $22,750	15%	15% of reported taxable income
$22,751 to $55,100	28%	$3,412.50 *plus* 28% of the amount over $22,750
$55,101 to $115,000	31%	$12,470.50 *plus* 31% of the amount over $55,100
$115,001 to $250,000	36%	$31,039.50 *plus* 36% of the amount over $115,000
Over $250,000	39.6%	$79,639.50 *plus* 39.6% of the amount over $250,000

Married Filing Jointly or Qualifying Widow(er)

Taxable Income	Tax Rate	Taxes Due
$0 to $38,000	15%	15% of reported taxable income
$38,001 to $91,850	28%	$5,700 *plus* 28% of the amount over $38,000
$91,851 to $140,000	31%	$20,778 *plus* 31% of the amount over $91,850
$140,001 to $250,000	36%	$35,704.50 *plus* 36% of the amount over $140,000
Over $250,000	39.6%	$75,304.50 *plus* 39.6% of the amount over $250,000

Married Filing Separately

Taxable Income	Tax Rate	Taxes Due
$0 to $19,000	15%	15% of reported taxable income
$19,001 to $45,925	28%	$2,850 *plus* 28% of the amount over $19,000
$45,926 to $70,000	31%	$10,389 *plus* 31% of the amount over $45,925
$70,001 to $125,000	36%	$17,852.25 *plus* 36% of the amount over $70,000
Over $125,000	39.6%	$37,652.25 *plus* 39.6% of the amount over $125,000

Head of Household

Taxable Income	Tax Rate	Taxes Due
$0 to $30,500	15%	15% of reported taxable income
$30,501 to $78,700	28%	$4,575 *plus* 28% of the amount over $30,500
$78,701 to $127,500	31%	$18,071 *plus* 31% of the amount over $78,700
$127,501 to $250,000	36%	$33,199 *plus* 36% of the amount over $127,500
Over $250,000	39.6%	$77,299 *plus* 39.6% of the amount over $250,000

gross income. This procedure is used for *both itemizers and nonitemizers* and is a key calculation in determining your tax liability because the amount of income subject to federal income taxes is specified by the amount of taxable income you report. Once you know the amount of your taxable income, you can refer to *tax rate tables* to find the amount of taxes you owe. (When actually filing a tax return, taxpayers with taxable income of more than $50,000 must use the tax rate schedules.)

Tax rates vary not only with the amount of reported taxable income but also with filing status. Thus, there are different tax rate schedules for each filing category, as shown in Exhibit 3.5. The vast majority of taxpayers—perhaps 90 percent or more—fall into the first two brackets and are subject to tax rates of either 15 or 28 percent.

To see how the tax rates in Exhibit 3.5 work, consider two single taxpayers: one has taxable income of $12,500, the other has $29,600 in taxable income. We would calculate their respective tax liabilities as follows:

- for taxable income of $12,500—
  $12,500 × .15 = $1,875
- for taxable income of $29,600—
  $3,412.50 + [($29,600 − $22,750) × .28] =
  $3,412.50 + $1,918 = $5,330.50

As we can see, the income of $12,500 is taxed at the 15 percent tax rate, and the $29,600 is taxed first at 15 percent and then at 28 percent. Keep in mind that the same procedures would be used whether the taxpayer itemizes or not. In order to show how the amount of tax liability will vary with the level

EXHIBIT 3.6

Taxable Income and the Amount of Income Taxes Due (1994)

Given the progressive tax structure that exists in this country, it follows that the larger your income, the more you can expect to pay in taxes.

Taxable Income	Taxes Due: Individual Returns	Taxes Due: Joint Returns
$ 500	$ 75*	$ 75*
1,000	150	150
1,500	225	225
2,000	300	300
2,500	375	375
5,000	750	750
7,500	1,125	1,125
10,000	1,500	1,500
12,500	1,875	1,875
15,000	2,250	2,250
20,000	3,000	3,000
25,000	4,043**	3,750
30,000	5,443	4,500
35,000	6,843	5,380
40,000	8,243	6,260**
50,000	11,043	9,060
60,000	13,990***	11,860
75,000	18,640	16,060
100,000	26,390	23,305***
150,000	43,640****	39,305****

* Income is taxed at 15%.

** 28% tax rate now applies.

*** 31% tax rate now applies.

**** 36% tax rate now applies.

of taxable income, Exhibit 3.6 lists the taxes due on a range of taxable incomes from $500 to $150,000 for both single and married taxpayers.

Recall from our earlier discussions that the *average tax rate* is found by dividing your tax liability by the amount of reported taxable income. Returning to our example involving the taxpayer with an income of $29,600, we see that this individual had an average tax rate of $5,330.50 ÷ $29,600 = 18%, which is considerably *less* than the stated tax rate of 28 percent. Actually, the 28 percent represents the taxpayer's **marginal tax rate**—it is the rate at which the next dollar of taxable income is taxed. Notice in our calculations that the 28% tax rate applies only to that portion of the income that exceeds $22,750. Thus, the first $22,750 in income is taxed at 15 percent—only the balance ($29,600 − $22,750 = $6,850) is subject to the marginal tax rate of 28 percent.

Some taxpayers are subject to the *alternative minimum tax (AMT),* currently 26 percent of the first $175,000 and 28 percent of the excess. A taxpayer's tax liability is the higher of the AMT or the regular tax. The AMT was originally designed to ensure that high-income taxpayers with many deductions pay their fair share of taxes. Prior to its passage in 1978, the effective use of tax shelters (investments providing attractive tax write-offs) by many taxpayers allowed them to reduce their taxable incomes to near zero. The AMT includes in taxable income certain types of deductions otherwise allowed, such as state and local income and property taxes, miscellaneous itemized deductions, unreimbursed medical expenses, and depreciation. Therefore, taxpayers with moderate levels of taxable income, including those living in states with high tax rates and self-employed persons with depreciation deductions, may be subject to the AMT.

marginal tax rate The rate at which the next dollar of taxable income is taxed.

TAX CREDITS

Once taxable income has been determined and the *tax liability,* or amount of taxes owed, calculated, there is one final step to determine the amount of taxes due. Some taxpayers are allowed to take certain deductions, known as **tax credits,** directly from their tax liability.

A tax credit is much more valuable than a deduction or an exemption, because it directly reduces, dollar for dollar, the amount of *taxes due,* whereas a deduction or an exemption merely reduces the amount of *taxable income.* For example, assume that a single taxpayer in the 28 percent tax bracket has $1,000 in deductions and another in the same bracket has a $1,000 tax credit. Look at what happens to the amount of taxes paid:

		$1,000 Deduction	$1,000 Tax Credit
	Gross income	$38,000	$38,000
Less:	Other deductions/ exemptions	6,000	6,000
Less:	$1,000 deduction	1,000	—
	Taxable income	$31,000	$32,000
	Tax liability*	$ 5,723	$ 6,003
Less:	$1,000 tax credit	—	1,000
	Taxes paid	$ 5,723	$ 5,003

***Note:** The tax liability is figured as follows: the first $22,750 of taxable income taxed at 15%, the balance at 28%.

In effect, the tax credit in this example has reduced taxes (and therefore *increased* after-tax income) by over $700.

A frequently used tax credit is for child- and dependent-care expenses. This credit is based on the amount spent for dependent care while a taxpayer (and spouse, if married) works or goes to school. The qualifying dependent must be less than 13 years old, except in the case of a disabled dependent or spouse. The base amount of the credit is limited to $2,400 for one dependent and $4,800 for two or more dependents. The actual amount of the credit is a percentage of the amount spent or of the limit, whichever is less. The percentages range from 20 to 30 percent, depending on the taxpayer's AGI. For example, a couple with AGI of $30,000 who spent $3,000 on child care expenses for their two young children would receive a dependent care credit of $600 (.20 × $3,000).

An important credit for lower-income workers is the earned income credit. In 1994 this credit is worth $2,038 for taxpayers with one qualifying child living with them in their home, in the United States ($2,557 with two qualifying children; $306 for taxpayers between 25 and 65 years old with no qualifying children). The credit is gradually phased out for taxpayers with earned income (from wages) and AGI in excess of $11,000 ($5,000 if there is no qualifying child). It is phased out completely when earned income or AGI reaches $23,755 for one qualifying child; ($25,295 for two qualifying children; $9,000 for none). The amount of the credit for taxpayers with qualifying children is currently scheduled to increase annually until 1996. Other common tax credits include:

- Credit for the elderly or the disabled
- Foreign tax credit
- Credit for prior year minimum tax
- Mortgage interest credit
- Credit for fuel from a nonconventional source
- General business credit

To receive one of these credits, the taxpayer must file a return, along with a separate schedule in support of the tax credit claimed.

TAX FORMS AND SCHEDULES

The Internal Revenue Service requires taxpayers to file their returns using certain specified tax forms. As noted earlier, these forms and a variety of instruction booklets on how to prepare them are available to taxpayers free of charge. Generally, all persons who filed tax returns in the previous year are automatically sent a booklet containing tax forms and instructions for preparation of returns for the current year. Inside the booklet is a form that can be used to obtain additional tax forms for filing various tax-related returns and information. Exhibit 3.7 provides a list of some of the more commonly used tax forms.

Variations of Form 1040. All individuals use some variation of Form 1040 to file their tax returns. Form 1040EZ is a simple, one-page form. You qualify to use this form if you are single or married filing a joint return; under age 65 (both if filing jointly); not blind; do not claim any dependents; have taxable income of less than $50,000 only from wages, salaries, tips, or taxable scholarships or grants; have interest income of less than $400; and do not itemize deductions or claim any tax credits. Worksheet 3.1 shows the Form 1040EZ filed in 1994 by Mohammed Akbar, a full-time graduate stu-

EXHIBIT 3.7

Commonly Used Tax Forms

A number of types of 1040 tax return forms are available. If the standard Form 1040 is used, one or more forms (listed below the 1040s) may be included with the tax return, depending on the amount and types of deductions claimed.

1040	Standard tax return, used with itemized deductions
1040A	Short-form tax return
1040EZ	Short-form tax return for single persons with no dependents
1040-ES	Estimated tax payments
1040X	Amended tax return
2106	Employee business expenses
2119	Sale or exchange of principal residence
2441	Credit for child and dependent care expenses
3903	Moving expenses
4562	Depreciation and amortization expenses
4684	Casualties and thefts
4868	Application for automatic filing extension
8829	Expenses for business use of your home

dent at Anystate University. His sources of income include a $5,000 scholarship, of which $1,200 was used for room and board, $5,500 earned from part-time and summer jobs, and $75 interest earned on a savings account deposit. Because scholarships used for tuition and fees are not taxed, he must include as income only the portion used for room and board. He had a total of $250 withheld for federal income taxes during the year.

To use Form 1040A, a two-page form, your income must be less than $50,000 and derived only from specified sources. Using this form you may deduct certain IRA contributions and claim certain tax credits, but you cannot itemize your deductions. If your income is over $50,000 or you itemize deductions, you must use the standard Form 1040 along with appropriate schedules, briefly described as follows:

Schedule	Description
A	For itemized deductions
B	For interest and dividend income of more than $400 each
C	For profit (or loss) from a personally owned business
D	For capital gains and losses
E	For supplemental income and losses from rents, royalties, partnerships, estates, trusts, etc.
F	For income and expense from farming
R	For credit for the elderly or disabled
SE	For reporting social security self-employment tax

The use of these schedules, which provide detailed guidelines for calculating certain entries on the first two pages of Form 1040, varies among taxpayers depending on the relevance of these entries to their situations. Pages 1 and 2 of Form 1040 summarize all items of income and deduction detailed on the accompanying schedules and are used to determine and report the taxable income and associated tax liability.

THE 1994 TAX RETURN OF TERRY AND EVELYN BECKER

Terry and Evelyn Becker are both 35 years old. They have been married for 11 years and have three children—Tom (age 9), Dick (age 7), and Harriet (age 3). Terry is a staff accountant for a major oil company headquartered in their hometown of Anytown, Anystate. Evelyn Becker, who has one-and-a-half years of college, works part-time as a sales clerk in a major department store. During 1994, Terry's salary totaled $30,415 while Evelyn earned $3,750. Terry's employer withheld taxes of $3,560 and Evelyn's $550. During the year, the Beckers earned $500 interest on their joint savings account, received $750 in cash dividends on stock they owned jointly, and realized $850 in capital gains on the sale of securities. In addition, Terry kept the books for his brother's car dealership, from which he netted $3,600 during the year. Because no taxes were withheld from any of their outside

tax credits Deductions from a taxpayer's tax liability that directly reduce his or her taxes due rather than taxable income.

Worksheet 3.1

1994 Tax Return for Mohammed Akbar (Form 1040EZ) FPPC

Form 1040EZ is very easy to use, and most of the instructions are printed right on the form itself. Mohammed Akbar qualifies to use it because he is single, under age 65, not blind, and meets its income and deduction restrictions.

Form **1040EZ** Department of the Treasury—Internal Revenue Service
Income Tax Return for Single and Joint Filers With No Dependents **1994** (B)

OMB No. 1545-0675

Use the IRS label (See page 12.) Otherwise, please print.

LABEL HERE

Print your name (first, initial, last): **Mohammed Akbar**

If a joint return, print spouse's name (first, initial, last):

Home address (number and street). If you have a P.O. box, see page 12.: **1000 State University Dr** Apt. no. **14A**

City, town or post office, state and ZIP code. If you have a foreign address, see page 12.: **Anytown, Anystate 10100**

Your social security number: 987 | 65 | 3210

Spouse's social security number:

See instructions on back and in Form 1040EZ booklet.

Presidential Election Campaign (See page 12.)
Note: *Checking "Yes" will not change your tax or reduce your refund.*

	Yes	No
Do you want $3 to go to this fund? ▶	☒	☐
If a joint return, does your spouse want $3 to go to this fund? ▶	☐	☐

Income

Attach Copy B of Form(s) W-2 here. Enclose, but do not attach, any payment with your return.

Note: *You must check Yes or No.*

Line	Description	Dollars	Cents
1	Total wages, salaries, and tips. This should be shown in box 1 of your W-2 form(s). Attach your W-2 form(s).	6,700	00
2	Taxable interest income of $400 or less. If the total is over $400, you cannot use Form 1040EZ.	75	00
3	Add lines 1 and 2. This is your **adjusted gross income.** If less than $9,000, see page 15 to find out if you can claim the earned income credit on line 7.	6,775	00
4	Can your parents (or someone else) claim you on their return? ☐ **Yes.** Do worksheet on back; enter amount from line G here. ☒ **No.** If **single,** enter 6,250.00. If **married,** enter 11,250.00. For an explanation of these amounts, see back of form.	6,250	00
5	Subtract line 4 from line 3. If line 4 is larger than line 3, enter 0. This is your **taxable income.** ▶	525	00

Payments and tax

Line	Description	Dollars	Cents
6	Enter your Federal income tax withheld from box 2 of your W-2 form(s).	250	00
7	**Earned income credit** (see page 15). Enter type and amount of nontaxable earned income below. Type ____ $ ____		
8	Add lines 6 and 7 (don't include nontaxable earned income). These are your **total payments.**	250	00
9	**Tax.** Use the amount on **line 5** to find your tax in the tax table on pages 28–32 of the booklet. Then, enter the tax from the table on this line.	81	00

Refund or amount you owe

Line	Description	Dollars	Cents
10	If line 8 is larger than line 9, subtract line 9 from line 8. This is your **refund.**	169	00
11	If line 9 is larger than line 8, subtract line 8 from line 9. This is the **amount you owe.** See page 20 for details on how to pay and what to write on your payment.		

Sign your return

Keep a copy of this form for your records.

I have read this return. Under penalties of perjury, I declare that to the best of my knowledge and belief, the return is true, correct, and accurately lists all amounts and sources of income I received during the tax year.

Your signature: *Mohammed Akbar* Spouse's signature if joint return

Date: *3/12/95* Your occupation: *Grad. Student* Date Spouse's occupation

For IRS Use Only—Please do not write in boxes below.

For Privacy Act and Paperwork Reduction Act Notice, see page 4. Cat. No. 11329W Form 1040EZ (1994)

income, during the year they made estimated tax payments totaling $500. The Beckers' records indicate that they had $8,613 of itemized deductions during the year. Finally, Terry Becker plans to contribute $2,000 to his IRA account, something he's been doing for the past six years. He does this each year without fail, not only to reap immediate tax benefits but also because he strongly feels that such investments are an important part of sound retirement planning.

Finding the Beckers' Tax Liability: Form 1040. An examination of the Beckers' 1994 tax return will show the basic calculations required in preparing Form 1040. Although the supporting schedules are not included here, the basic calculations they require are illustrated. The Beckers have kept detailed records of their income and expenditures, which they use not only for tax purposes but as an important input into their budgeting process. Using this information, the Beckers intend to prepare their 1994 tax return in a fashion that will allow them to reduce their tax liability as much as possible. A hypothetical 1994 tax return for the Beckers is given in Worksheet 3.2. Like most married couples, the Beckers file a *joint return*.

Gross Income. The Beckers' gross income in 1994 amounted to $39,865; this is the amount shown as "Total Income" on line 22 of their tax return. Their income is composed of both *active income* and *portfolio income,* as follows:

Active Income		
Terry's earnings	$30,415	
Evelyn's earnings	3,750	
Terry's business income (net)	3,600	
Total active income		$37,765
Portfolio Income		
Interest from savings account	$ 500	
Stock dividends	750	
Capital gains realized	850	
Total portfolio income		2,100
Total income		$39,865

They have no investment expenses to offset their portfolio income, so they'll be liable for taxes on the full amount of portfolio income. Because they have portfolio income, the Beckers will have to file Schedule B (for their interest and dividend income—each of which is in excess of $400) with the Form 1040. In addition, Terry will have to file Schedule C, detailing the income earned and expenses incurred in his bookkeeping business, and Schedule D to report capital gains income.

Adjustments to Gross Income. The Beckers have only two adjustments to income: Terry's IRA contribution and 50 percent of the self-employment tax on Terry's net business income. Because the Beckers fall below the $40,000 income ceiling (just barely), they can deduct all of their $2,000 contribution to an IRA account even if Terry and/or Evelyn are already covered by a company-approved retirement program. Even though they could put more money into the IRA, they have chosen to stick with Terry's $2,000 contribution (see line 23a). Terry's self-employment tax will be 15.3 percent of his $3,600 net business income, and he will be able to deduct one-half that amount—$275 [(.153 × $3,600)/2]—on line 25.

Adjusted Gross Income. After deducting the $2,000 IRA contribution and the $275 self-employment tax from their gross income, the Beckers are left with an adjusted gross income of $37,590, as reported on lines 31 and 32.

Itemized Deductions or Standard Deduction? The Beckers are filing a joint return and neither is over age 65 or blind, so according to Exhibit 3.4 (married filing jointly with zero boxes checked), they are entitled to a standard deduction of $6,350. However, they want to evaluate their itemized deductions before deciding which type of deduction to take—obviously they'll take the highest deduction, because it will result in the lowest amount of taxable income and keep their tax liability to a minimum. Their preliminary paperwork resulted in the following deductions:

Medical and dental expenses	$ 723
State income and property taxes paid	960
Mortgage interest	5,193
Charitable contributions	475
Job and other expenses	1,262
Total	$8,613

The taxes, mortgage interest, and charitable contributions are deductible in full; so at the minimum, the Beckers will have itemized deductions that amount to $6,628 ($960 + $5,193 + $475). However, to be deductible, the medical and dental expenses and job and other expenses must exceed stipulated minimum levels of adjusted gross income (AGI)—only that portion which exceeds the specified minimum levels of AGI can be included as part of their itemized deductions. For medical and dental expenses, the minimum is 7.5 percent of AGI and for job and other expenses it

Worksheet 3.2

1994 Tax Return (Form 1040) for the Beckers FPPC

Because they itemize deductions, the Beckers use standard Form 1040 to file their tax return. When filed with the IRS, their return will include not only Form 1040 but also other schedules and forms that provide details on many of the expenses and deductions claimed by the Beckers. *Note:* The Form 1040 depicted here is the one used in 1994; it is expected that there will be slight modifications in this form in subsequent years.

Form **1040** Department of the Treasury—Internal Revenue Service **U.S. Individual Income Tax Return** (O) **1994** IRS Use Only—Do not write or staple in this space.

For the year Jan. 1–Dec. 31, 1994, or other tax year beginning , 1994, ending , 19 OMB No. 1545-0074

Label (See instructions on page 12.) **Use the IRS label.** Otherwise, please print or type. LABEL HERE

Your first name and initial: Terry B. — Last name: Becker — Your social security number: 123 : 45 : 6789

If a joint return, spouse's first name and initial: Evelyn A. — Last name: Becker — Spouse's social security number: 987 : 65 : 4321

Home address (number and street). If you have a P.O. box, see page 12.: 123 Laughing Lane — Apt. no.

City, town or post office, state, and ZIP code. If you have a foreign address, see page 12.: Anytown, Anystate 10100

For Privacy Act and Paperwork Reduction Act Notice, see page 4.

Presidential Election Campaign (See page 12.)

	Yes	No
Do you want $3 to go to this fund?	✓	
If a joint return, does your spouse want $3 to go to this fund?	✓	

Note: *Checking "Yes" will not change your tax or reduce your refund.*

Filing Status (See page 12.) Check only one box.

1 ☐ Single
2 ☑ Married filing joint return (even if only one had income)
3 ☐ Married filing separate return. Enter spouse's social security no. above and full name here. ▶
4 ☐ Head of household (with qualifying person). (See page 13.) If the qualifying person is a child but not your dependent, enter this child's name here. ▶
5 ☐ Qualifying widow(er) with dependent child (year spouse died ▶ 19). (See page 13.)

Exemptions (See page 13.)

6a ☑ **Yourself.** If your parent (or someone else) can claim you as a dependent on his or her tax return, **do not** check box 6a. But be sure to check the box on line 33b on page 2 — No. of boxes checked on 6a and 6b: 2

b ☑ **Spouse**

c **Dependents:**

If more than six dependents, see page 14.

(1) Name (first, initial, and last name)	(2) Check if under age 1	(3) If age 1 or older, dependent's social security number	(4) Dependent's relationship to you	(5) No. of months lived in your home in 1994
Tom T. Becker		456 : 01 : 2347	son	12
Richard L. Becker		012 : 34 : 5678	son	12
Harriet M. Becker		234 : 56 : 7890	daughter	12

No. of your children on 6c who: • lived with you: 3 • didn't live with you due to divorce or separation (see page 14): — Dependents on 6c not entered above: —

d If your child didn't live with you but is claimed as your dependent under a pre-1985 agreement, check here ▶ ☐

e Total number of exemptions claimed — Add numbers entered on lines above ▶ 5

Income

Attach Copy B of your Forms W-2, W-2G, and 1099-R here.

If you did not get a W-2, see page 15.

Enclose, but do not attach, any payment with your return.

Line	Description		Amount
7	Wages, salaries, tips, etc. Attach Form(s) W-2	7	34,165 00
8a	**Taxable** interest income (see page 15). Attach Schedule B if over $400	8a	500 00
b	**Tax-exempt** interest (see page 16). DON'T include on line 8a — 8b		
9	Dividend income. Attach Schedule B if over $400	9	750 00
10	Taxable refunds, credits, or offsets of state and local income taxes (see page 16)	10	
11	Alimony received	11	
12	Business income or (loss). Attach Schedule C or C-EZ	12	3,600 00
13	Capital gain or (loss). If required, attach Schedule D (see page 16)	13	850 00
14	Other gains or (losses). Attach Form 4797	14	
15a	Total IRA distributions — 15a — b Taxable amount (see page 17)	15b	
16a	Total pensions and annuities — 16a — b Taxable amount (see page 17)	16b	
17	Rental real estate, royalties, partnerships, S corporations, trusts, etc. Attach Schedule E	17	
18	Farm income or (loss). Attach Schedule F	18	
19	Unemployment compensation (see page 18)	19	
20a	Social security benefits — 20a — b Taxable amount (see page 18)	20b	
21	Other income. List type and amount—see page 18	21	
22	Add the amounts in the far right column for lines 7 through 21. This is your **total income** ▶	22	39,865 00

Adjustments to Income

Caution: See instructions ▶

Line	Description		Amount		Total
23a	Your IRA deduction (see page 19)	23a	2,000 00		
b	Spouse's IRA deduction (see page 19)	23b			
24	Moving expenses. Attach Form 3903 or 3903-F	24			
25	One-half of self-employment tax	25	275 00		
26	Self-employed health insurance deduction (see page 21)	26			
27	Keogh retirement plan and self-employed SEP deduction	27			
28	Penalty on early withdrawal of savings	28			
29	Alimony paid. Recipient's SSN ▶	29			
30	Add lines 23a through 29. These are your **total adjustments** ▶			30	2,275 00

Adjusted Gross Income

Line	Description		Amount
31	Subtract line 30 from line 22. This is your **adjusted gross income.** If less than $25,296 and a child lived with you (less than $9,000 if a child didn't live with you), see "Earned Income Credit" on page 27 ▶	31	37,590 00

Cat. No. 11320B — Form **1040** (1994)

Worksheet 3.2

Continued

Form 1040 (1994) Page **2**

Section	Line	Description		Line	Amount	Cents
Tax Computation (See page 23.)	32	Amount from line 31 (adjusted gross income)		32	37,590	00
	33a	Check if: ☐ **You** were 65 or older, ☐ Blind; ☐ **Spouse** was 65 or older, ☐ Blind. Add the number of boxes checked above and enter the total here ▶ 33a				
	b	If your parent (or someone else) can claim you as a dependent, check here ▶ 33b ☐				
	c	If you are married filing separately and your spouse itemizes deductions or you are a dual-status alien, see page 23 and check here ▶ 33c ☐				
	34	Enter the **larger** of your: **Itemized deductions** from Schedule A, line 29, **OR** **Standard deduction** shown below for your filing status. **But if you checked any box on line 33a or b,** go to page 23 to find your standard deduction. If you checked **box 33c,** your standard deduction is zero. • Single—$3,800 • Head of household—$5,600 • Married filing jointly or Qualifying widow(er)—$6,350 • Married filing separately—$3,175		34	7,138	00
	35	Subtract line 34 from line 32		35	30,452	00
	36	If line 32 is $83,850 or less, multiply $2,450 by the total number of exemptions claimed on line 6e. If line 32 is over $83,850, see the worksheet on page 24 for the amount to enter		36	12,250	00
If you want the IRS to figure your tax, see page 24.	37	**Taxable income.** Subtract line 36 from line 35. If line 36 is more than line 35, enter -0-		37	18,202	00
	38	Tax. Check if from a ☐ Tax Table, b ☐ Tax Rate Schedules, c ☐ Capital Gain Tax Worksheet, or d ☐ Form 8615 (see page 24). Amount from Form(s) 8814 ▶ e		38	2,730	00
	39	Additional taxes. Check if from a ☐ Form 4970 b ☐ Form 4972		39		
	40	Add lines 38 and 39 ▶		40	2,730	00
Credits (See page 24.)	41	Credit for child and dependent care expenses. Attach Form 2441	41			
	42	Credit for the elderly or the disabled. Attach Schedule R	42			
	43	Foreign tax credit. Attach Form 1116	43			
	44	Other credits (see page 25). Check if from a ☐ Form 3800 b ☐ Form 8396 c ☐ Form 8801 d ☑ Form (specify)	44			
	45	Add lines 41 through 44		45	0	00
	46	Subtract line 45 from line 40. If line 45 is more than line 40, enter -0- ▶		46	2,730	00
Other Taxes (See page 25.)	47	Self-employment tax. Attach Schedule SE		47	551	00
	48	Alternative minimum tax. Attach Form 6251		48		
	49	Recapture taxes. Check if from a ☐ Form 4255 b ☐ Form 8611 c ☐ Form 8828		49		
	50	Social security and Medicare tax on tip income not reported to employer. Attach Form 4137		50		
	51	Tax on qualified retirement plans, including IRAs. If required, attach Form 5329		51		
	52	Advance earned income credit payments from Form W-2		52		
	53	Add lines 46 through 52. This is your **total tax** ▶		53	3,281	00
Payments	54	Federal income tax withheld. If any is from Form(s) 1099, check ▶ ☐	54: 4,110 00			
	55	1994 estimated tax payments and amount applied from 1993 return	55: 500 00			
Attach Forms W-2, W-2G, and 1099-R on the front.	56	**Earned income credit.** If required, attach Schedule EIC (see page 27). Nontaxable earned income: amount ▶ and type ▶	56			
	57	Amount paid with Form 4868 (extension request)	57			
	58	Excess social security and RRTA tax withheld (see page 32)	58			
	59	Other payments. Check if from a ☐ Form 2439 b ☐ Form 4136	59			
	60	Add lines 54 through 59. These are your **total payments** ▶		60		
Refund or Amount You Owe	61	If line 60 is more than line 53, subtract line 53 from line 60. This is the amount you **OVERPAID** ▶		61	4,610	00
	62	Amount of line 61 you want **REFUNDED TO YOU** ▶		62	1,329	00
	63	Amount of line 61 you want **APPLIED TO YOUR 1995 ESTIMATED TAX** ▶	63		1,329	00
	64	If line 53 is more than line 60, subtract line 60 from line 53. This is the **AMOUNT YOU OWE.** For details on how to pay, including what to write on your payment, see page 32		64		
	65	Estimated tax penalty (see page 33). Also include on line 64	65			

Sign Here Keep a copy of this return for your records.

Under penalties of perjury, I declare that I have examined this return and accompanying schedules and statements, and to the best of my knowledge and belief, they are true, correct, and complete. Declaration of preparer (other than taxpayer) is based on all information of which preparer has any knowledge.

Your signature	Date	Your occupation
Terry A. Becker	4-1-95	*Accountant*
Spouse's signature. If a joint return, BOTH must sign.	Date	Spouse's occupation
Evelyn A. Becker	4-1-95	*Sales Clerk*

Paid Preparer's Use Only

Preparer's signature	Date	Check if self-employed ☐	Preparer's social security no.
Firm's name (or yours if self-employed) and address		E.I. No.	
		ZIP code	

Printed on recycled paper

is 2 percent of AGI. Because 7.5 percent of the Beckers' AGI is $2,819 (.075 x $37,590), they cannot deduct any medical and dental expenses—they fall short of the minimum. In contrast, because 2 percent of the Beckers' AGI is $752 (.02 × $37,590), they can deduct any job and other expenses that exceed that amount, or $1,262 − $752 = $510. Adding the amount of their allowable job and other expenses ($510) to their other allowable deductions ($6,628) results in total itemized deductions of $7,138. This amount exceeds the standard deduction by a comfortable margin, so the Beckers itemize their deductions. The details of these deductions would be provided on Schedule A and attached to the Beckers' Form 1040. (The total amount of itemized deductions is listed on line 34 of the 1040 Form).

Personal Exemptions. The Beckers are entitled to claim two exemptions for themselves and another three exemptions for their three dependent children, so they can claim a total of five exemptions. Because each exemption is worth $2,450, they receive a total personal exemption of $12,250 (5 × $2,450), which is the amount listed on line 36 of their Form 1040.

The Beckers' Taxable Income and Their Tax Liability. Taxable income is found by subtracting itemized deductions *and* personal exemptions from adjusted gross income. Thus, in the Beckers' case, taxable income amounts to $37,590 − $7,138 − $12,250 = $18,202. This is the amount shown on line 37. Given this information, the Beckers can now refer to the tax rate schedule (like the one in Exhibit 3.5) to find their appropriate tax rate and, ultimately, the amount of taxes they'll have to pay. [Note: Because the Beckers' taxable income is less than $50,000, they should use the *tax tables* (not shown) to find their tax. For clarity and convenience, the schedules are used here.] As we can see, the Beckers' $18,202 in taxable income places them in the lowest (15 percent) tax bracket. Note in the tax rate schedule that joint returns with taxable incomes of up to $38,000 fall into the 15 percent tax bracket. At this point, all the Beckers have to do is multiply their taxable income by 15 percent to find their tax liability. $18,202 × .15 = $2,730; this amount is entered on line 38. (Note: Had the tax tables been used, the tax would have been $2,734.) Because they have no additional taxes and no tax credits, they also enter this tax liability on lines 40 and 46, respectively. However, the Beckers do owe self-employment (social security) tax on Terry's $3,600 net business income. This will increase their tax liability by $551 (.153 × $3,600) and would be reported on Schedule SE and entered on line 47 of Form 1040. (Remember 50 percent of this amount—$275—was deducted on line 25 as an adjustment to gross income.) The Beckers' total tax liability is $3,281 ($2,730 + $551) and is entered on line 53.

Do They Get a Tax Refund? Because the total amount of taxes withheld of $4,110 ($3,560 from Terry's salary and $550 from Evelyn's wages) shown on line 54 plus estimated tax payments of $500 shown on line 55 total $4,610, the Beckers' total tax payments exceed their tax liability, and, as a result, they are entitled to a refund. (About 65 percent of all taxpayers receive refunds each year.) The amount of the refund is found by subtracting the tax liability (on line 53) from total tax payments (on line 60): $4,610 − $3,281 = $1,329 in tax refund shown on lines 61 and 62. Instead of paying the IRS, they'll be getting money back. (Generally it takes one to two months after a tax return has been filed to receive a refund check.) All the Beckers have to do now is sign their completed 1040 and send it, along with any supporting forms and schedules, to the nearest IRS district office on or before April 17, 1995 (because April 15 falls on a Saturday that year). As a final point here, in light of the fact that the Beckers are going to receive such a large tax refund, they might want to stop making estimated tax payments because their combined withholdings more than cover the amount of taxes they owe. Another option is to adjust withholding to reduce the amount withheld. Note that if total tax payments had been less than the Beckers' tax liability, they would have owed the IRS money—the amount owed is found by subtracting total tax payments made from the tax liability. A check in this amount would then be included with Form 1040 when they filed their tax return.

Concept Check

3-11. Define and differentiate between the average tax rate and marginal tax rate. How does a tax credit differ from an itemized deduction?

3-12. Explain how the following are used in filing a tax return: (a) Form 1040, (b) various schedules that accompany Form 1040, and (c) tax rate schedules.

OTHER FILING CONSIDERATIONS

LG4

When filing your tax return you must also consider estimated payments, extensions, amendments, audits, tax preparation services, or computer-based tax returns. Why are each of these considerations important when filing your return? Before reading on, give some thought to this question.

The preparation and filing of tax returns is not quite as easy as filling out and filing a tax return on or before April 15. Other related considerations include the need to pay estimated taxes, file for extensions, or amend the return; the possibility of a tax audit; and whether to use a tax preparation service or computer software to assist in preparing your return. Here we give attention to each of these filing considerations.

ESTIMATES, EXTENSIONS, AND AMENDMENTS

There are several factors to consider when filing your tax return. If you have income that is not subject to withholding you may be required to file a declaration of estimated taxes with your return and to pay taxes on a quarterly basis. The normal filing deadline is April 15, but, if necessary, taxpayers can seek an extension of this deadline. In addition, you can file an amended return to correct a previously filed return.

Estimated Taxes. Because federal withholding taxes are taken only from income earned on a regular basis, such as that paid in the form of wages, the Internal Revenue Service requires certain people to pay **estimated taxes** on income earned from other sources. This requirement allows the principle of "pay as you go" to be applied not only to wages subject to withholding but also to other sources of income. The payment of estimated taxes is most commonly required of investors, consultants, lawyers, business owners, and various other professionals who are likely to receive income in a form that is not subject to withholding. Generally, if all of your income is subject to withholding, you probably do not need to make estimated tax payments.

Suppose you figure that your estimated tax in the coming year will be $500 or more, while the total amount of income tax withheld and your tax credits will be less than the smaller of (1) 90 percent of the tax to be shown on your coming year's income tax return or (2) 100 percent of the tax shown on your prior year's tax return (assuming it covered 12 months). (If your AGI exceeds $150,000, tax withheld and tax credits must be at least 110 percent of the tax shown on your prior year's tax return.) In this case you should file a declaration of estimated taxes (Form 1040-ES) and make estimated tax payments. When the total of tax withheld and estimated payments does not meet the 100 percent (or 110 percent, if applicable) guideline, you must pay estimated taxes consistent with the actual income earned in the immediately preceding quarter to avoid penalties. Each estimated tax payment equals the tax payable on income earned in the preceding quarter, or one-fourth of the amount paid in taxes during the immediately preceding year (or 100 percent of these taxes), less the amount of tax withheld during the preceding quarter.

The declaration of estimated taxes is normally filed with the tax return. The amount of estimated taxes must be paid in four quarterly installments on April 15, June 15, and September 15 of the current year, and January 15 of the following year. Failure to estimate and pay these taxes can result in a penalty levied by the IRS. If the total taxes paid through withholdings and quarterly estimated payments is less than both 90 percent of your actual tax liability and 100 (or 110) percent of the tax shown on your prior year's tax return, the 90 percent test is applied and a penalty is levied if it is not met.

April 15: Filing Deadline. At the end of each tax year, those taxpayers who are required to file a return must determine the amount of their *tax liability*—the amount of taxes that they owe as a result of the past year's activities. The tax year corresponds to the calendar year and covers the period January 1 through December 31. Taxpayers are asked to file their returns as soon after the end of the tax year as possible and *must* do so by no

estimated taxes Quarterly tax payments required on income not subject to withholding.

later than April 15 of the year immediately following the tax year (or by the first business day after that date if it falls on a weekend or federal holiday). Some single taxpayers in certain states who file Form 1040EZ can file their returns by touch-tone phone. (Qualifying individuals receive special tax packages.) In other states, returns can be filed via the *CompuServe* on-line service. Depending on whether the total of taxes withheld and any estimated tax payments is greater or less than the computed tax liability, the taxpayer will either receive a refund or have to pay additional taxes. As an example, assume that you had $2,000 withheld and paid estimated taxes of $1,200 during the year. After filling out the appropriate tax forms, you find your tax liability amounts to only $2,800. In this case, you have overpaid your taxes by $400 ($2,000 + $1,200 − $2,800) and will receive a $400 refund from the IRS. On the other hand, if your tax liability had amounted to $4,000, you would owe the IRS an additional $800 ($4,000 − $2,000 − $1,200).

Filing Extensions and Amended Returns. It is possible to receive an extension of time for filing your federal tax return. You can apply for an automatic four-month **filing extension,** which makes the due date August 15, simply by submitting Form 4868. In filing for an extension, however, the taxpayer must estimate the taxes due and remit that amount with the application. The extension does *not* give taxpayers more time to pay their taxes. Beyond the four-month automatic extension other extensions can be requested, but before granting them the IRS must be convinced that they are justified.

After filing a return, you may discover that you overlooked some income or a major deduction or made a mistake and as a result paid too little or too much in taxes. You can easily correct this by filing an **amended return** (Form 1040X), which will show the corrected amount of income or deductions and the amount of taxes that should have been paid, along with the amount of any tax refund or additional taxes owed. You generally have three years from the date your original return was filed or two years from the date the taxes were paid, whichever is later, to file an amended return. If your amended return is properly prepared and filed and reflects nothing out of the ordinary, it generally will not trigger an audit. By all means, do not "correct" an oversight in one year by "adjusting" next year's tax return—the IRS frowns on that.

AUDITED RETURNS

Because taxpayers themselves provide the key information and fill out the necessary tax forms, the IRS has no proof that taxes have been correctly calculated. Therefore, it more or less randomly selects some returns for a **tax audit**—an examination to validate the return's accuracy. The odds of being audited are actually quite low. In 1993, the IRS audited about 1 million individual taxpayers, under 1 percent of the 115 million returns filed. However, higher-income earners tend to have a greater chance of audit. For example, those with incomes between $25,000 and $50,000 have less than a 1 percent chance of being audited, but the chance of audit jumps to nearly 5 percent for those with incomes over $100,000. The outcome of an audit is not always owing more taxes to the IRS. In fact, about 5 percent of all audits result in a refund to the taxpayer, and in 15 percent of all audits the returns are found to be correctly prepared.

IRS audits attempt to confirm the validity of filed returns by carefully examining the data reported in them. In the course of an audit, the IRS may arrange a meeting at which the taxpayer is asked to explain and document some of the deductions taken. Even when the documentation is provided, the IRS examiner may still question the legitimacy of the deductions. If the taxpayer and the IRS examiner cannot informally agree on the disputed items, the taxpayer can meet with the examiner's supervisor to discuss the case further. If there is still disagreement, the taxpayer can appeal through the IRS Appeals Office. Finally, if satisfaction is not obtained from the hearing before the Appeals Office, the case can be brought before the U.S. Tax Court, the U.S. Claims Court, or a U.S. District Court.

It is important to keep satisfactory and thorough tax records, because some day you may be audited by the IRS. Although the IRS does not specify any type of recordkeeping system, you should keep track of the source or use of all cash receipts and cash payments. Notations with respect to the purpose of the expenditures are important, as well as proof that you actually made the expenditures for which you have claimed deductions. Typically, audits question both (1) whether all income received has been properly reported and (2) the amounts and legitimacy of deductions taken. The IRS can take as many as three years from the date of filing to audit your return—and in some cases an unlimited period of time—so records and receipts used in preparing returns are best kept on hand for several years. Severe financial penalties—even prison sentences—can result from violating tax laws.

In sum, while you should take advantage of all legitimate deductions in order to minimize your tax liability, you must also be sure to properly report all items of income and expenditure as required by the Internal Revenue Code.

TAX PREPARATION SERVICES: GETTING HELP ON YOUR RETURNS

Many people prepare their own tax returns. These "do-it-yourselfers" typically have fairly simple returns that can be prepared without a great deal of difficulty. Of course, some taxpayers with quite complicated financial affairs may also invest their time in preparing their own returns. IRS informational publications that are helpful when preparing your tax return can be ordered directly from the IRS by mail or by calling its toll-free number (1-800-829-3676 or special local numbers in some areas). An excellent (and free) comprehensive tax preparation reference book is IRS Publication 17, *Your Federal Income Tax*. Recently, the IRS added an information service called Tele-Tax that provides recorded phone messages on selected tax topics. The toll-free telephone number for this service is 1-800-829-4477, and special local numbers are available in some areas.

Help from the IRS. The Internal Revenue service, in addition to issuing various publications for use in preparing tax returns, also provides direct assistance to taxpayers. The IRS will compute taxes for those whose adjusted gross income is not more than $50,000 and who do not itemize deductions. Persons who use this IRS service are required to fill in certain data, sign and date the return, and send it to the IRS on or before April 15 of the year immediately following the tax year. The IRS attempts to calculate taxes to result in the "smallest" tax bite. Taxpayers are then sent a refund, if their withholding exceeds their tax liability, or a bill, if their tax liability is greater than the amount of withholding. People who either fail to quality for or do not want to use this total tax preparation service can still obtain IRS assistance in preparing their returns from a toll-free service. Consult your telephone directory for the toll-free number of the IRS office closest to you.

It is important to recognize that the IRS sometimes makes mistakes. It may not always correctly answer your tax questions. In a 1992 survey by *Money* magazine, IRS representatives were correct only 86 percent of the time. To increase your chances of getting correct information, use Publication 17 and other resources to research your question before calling, state your question as clearly as you can, and make sure that the IRS representative fully understands your question. Remember: *You are liable for any underpayment of taxes, including interest and penalties, that results from incorrect information provided by the IRS over the phone.* As an alternative, you may put the question in writing and receive a written response from the IRS. If the written answer is incorrect, and as a result you underpay your taxes, you will have to pay the additional taxes and interest due, but no penalties.

Private Tax Preparers. About 46 percent of all taxpayers prefer to use professional *tax preparation services* because (1) they are concerned about accuracy and minimizing their tax liability as much as possible and (2) they believe the complexity of the tax forms makes preparation too difficult and/or time consuming. Taxpayers who do not wish to prepare their returns and have relatively common types of income and expenditures might consider using a *national tax service,* like H&R Block. Many *local tax preparation services* are also available. Caution is recommended when selecting a tax preparation service, however, as differing levels of competence exist. The fees charged by professional tax preparers range from $15 to $25 for very simple returns to $1,000 or more for complicated returns that include many itemized deductions, partnership income or losses, or self-employment income.

filing extension An extension of time beyond the April 15 deadline during which taxpayers, with the approval of the IRS, can file their returns without incurring penalties.

amended return A tax return filed to correct errors or adjust for information received after the filing date of the taxpayer's original return.

tax audit An examination by the IRS to validate the accuracy of a given tax return.

Taxpayers with more complex finances often employ an enrolled agent, an attorney with tax training, or a *certified public accountant (CPA)*. These professionals know the various technical points and are able to advise the taxpayer on how to defer income, qualify for deductions, and generally minimize tax liability. *Enrolled agents (EAs)* are federally-licensed individual tax practitioners who have demonstrated their competence in the area of taxation through a grueling, two-day, IRS-administered exam. They are fully qualified to handle tax preparation at various levels of complexity. *Tax attorneys* generally counsel taxpayers on tax planning, while CPAs not only provide tax counseling but also prepare the actual returns. Because the services provided by EAs, tax attorneys, and CPAs can be expensive, they are usually best used only by those taxpayers with relatively complicated financial situations.

As with any financial planning professional, choose your tax preparer carefully. Bad or fraudulent advice can cost plenty. Although attorneys and CPAs are state-licensed and EAs have federal licenses, no license or certification is required to call oneself a tax preparer. Before hiring a tax professional, ask about the preparer's qualifications, what fields he or she specializes in (divorce, complex investments, and so on), and how you will be charged. He or she should carry malpractice insurance and pay for penalties and interest resulting from an accounting error. Make sure the adviser can give you the level of advice you need—someone who is basically a return preparer is not the best person to help you do complex tax planning—and that you get impartial advice. A tax adviser should make recommendations but not earn fees or commissions from tax-sheltered investments you buy. You must also be comfortable with the adviser's suggestions, especially with regard to strategies that involve gray areas of the tax law.

Taxpayers should check completed returns carefully before signing them. Remember that *taxpayers themselves must accept primary responsibility for the accuracy of their returns*. The IRS requires professional tax preparers to sign each return as the preparer, enter their own social security number and address, and provide the taxpayer with a copy of the return being filed. Tax preparers with the necessary hardware can electronically file their clients' tax returns, thereby permitting eligible taxpayers to more quickly receive refunds. (There is a surcharge of about $25 for electronic filing, so it may not make sense for everyone.) In 1994 about 13.5 million taxpayers filed their returns electronically.

There is no guarantee that your professional tax preparer will correctly determine your tax liability. About 97 percent of the 1993 penalties assessed by the IRS against tax preparers involved unlicensed practitioners. But even the best may not have all the answers at their fingertips. In *Money* magazine's annual tax return test for 1994, none of the 50 experienced tax preparers they contacted answered all 10 questions about the 1993 tax law revisions correctly, and only 34 got half or more right. To reduce the chance of error, you should become familiar with the basic tax principles and regulations, check all documents (such as W-2s and 1099s) for accuracy, maintain good communication with your tax preparer, and request an explanation of any entries on your tax return that you do not understand.

COMPUTER-BASED TAX RETURNS

Many people use their personal computers to help with tax planning and tax return preparation. Several good tax software packages will save hours of figuring out the forms and schedules involved in filing tax returns. These computer programs are not for everyone, however. Very simple returns do not require them. And for very complex returns, there is no substitute for the skill and expertise of an attorney or tax accountant. Those who itemize deductions but do not need tax advice are most likely to find the computer helpful.

Basically there are two kinds of software: tax planning and tax preparation. Planning programs like *Managing Your Money* (discussed in Chapter 2) let you experiment with different strategies to see their effects on the amount of taxes you must pay. The other category of tax software focuses on return preparation. (Of course, you can do planning with any of these tax preparation programs by doing "what if" analysis—changing various income and expense entries and preparing the return to find the tax liability associated with each planning alternative.) Popular tax preparation programs for federal tax returns include Andrew Tobias's or Kiplinger's *TaxCut* (similar programs), *TurboTax/MacInTax*, and *Personal Tax Edge*. These software packages are revised annually for tax code changes, so their final versions may not be available until late February or early March. Most of these programs have separate versions for selected states. The programs generally cost under $40 and vary in ease of use, sophistication, and features. Upgrades to the current version at a reduced price are available to those who already own the program.

With tax preparation programs, you can input income, expenses, and other information required by most or all major tax forms and schedules. Some programs have an interview format that, based on your responses to its questions, guides you to the appropriate forms and suggests deductions. These programs make all the necessary tax calculations for you and then print out completed forms and schedules formatted in a manner acceptable to the IRS. The major software packages even offer an electronic filing option. Of course, because no program can answer all your tax questions, you should research the tax laws in order to make sure that you have taken all allowed deductions.

Concept Check

3-13. Define estimated taxes, and explain under what conditions such tax payments are required.

3-14. What is the purpose of a tax audit? Describe some things you can do to be prepared if your return is audited.

3-15. Briefly discuss the tax preparation services available from (a) the IRS, (b) national or local tax preparation services, (c) an enrolled agent (EA), (d) tax attorneys and CPAs, and (e) tax preparation computer software. Discuss the relative costs of each. When is each of these preferred, and how should you choose a tax preparer?

EFFECTIVE TAX PLANNING

LG5

Comprehensive tax planning is aimed at reducing taxes immediately as well as in the long run; it involves several activities that are closely tied to other areas of financial planning. How might you go about preparing your immediate and long-run tax plans? Try to answer this question before reading on.

A key ingredient of personal financial planning is *tax planning*. The overriding objective of effective tax planning is to maximize total after-tax income by reducing, shifting, or deferring taxes to as low a level as is legally possible.

Keep in mind that *avoiding* taxes is one thing, but *evading* them is another matter altogether. By all means, don't confuse tax avoidance with **tax evasion,** which includes illegal activities such as omitting income or overstating deductions. Tax evasion, in effect, involves a failure to fairly and accurately report income and/or expenses, and, in extreme cases, a failure to pay taxes altogether. Persons found guilty of tax evasion are subject to severe financial penalties and even prison terms. **Tax avoidance,** in contrast, is concerned with reducing taxes in ways that are legal and compatible with the intent of Congress.

FUNDAMENTAL OBJECTIVES OF TAX PLANNING

Tax planning basically involves the use of various investment vehicles, retirement programs, and estate distribution procedures to (1) reduce, (2) shift, or (3) defer taxes. You can *reduce* taxes, for instance, by using techniques that create tax deductions or credits, or that receive preferential tax treatment—such as investments that produce depreciation (like real estate) or that generate tax-free income (like municipal bonds). You can *shift* taxes by using gifts or trusts to shift some of your income to other family members who are in lower tax brackets and to whom you intend to provide some level of support anyway, such as a retired, elderly parent.

The idea behind *deferring* taxes is to reduce or eliminate your taxes today by postponing them to some time in the future when you may be in a lower tax bracket. Perhaps more important, *deferring taxes gives you use of the money that would otherwise go to taxes*—which you can invest to

tax evasion The illegal act of failing to accurately report income and/or deductions, and, in extreme cases, failing to pay taxes altogether.

tax avoidance The act of reducing taxes in ways that are legal and compatible with the intent of Congress.

Smart Money

Tax Tips That Pay Off

Paying taxes is no fun. Like many taxpayers, you may avoid tax planning for most of the year and only start looking for ways to reduce taxes as year-end approaches. Or you might think that only the very rich can benefit from tax avoidance strategies. However, almost all taxpayers can save money and avoid problems with the IRS with the following tips for year-round tax planning.

1. File accurate and complete returns. Check your completed return carefully before mailing it to the IRS. Always file joint returns with the same name first, include all social security numbers (yourself, your spouse, and any dependents over age one), use the right filing status, and take all allowed exemptions. Put forms and schedules in the designated order (by sequence number, *not* form number, for numbered forms, alphabetically for schedules). Check and recheck the arithmetic. Although these details may seem obvious, errors can delay refunds and result in fines or penalties plus interest (compounded *daily*) for underpayment of taxes.

2. Check withholding and make adjustments as required. At least once a year, check that enough is being withheld from your paycheck to avoid underwithholding penalties. Use last year's tax return and the W-4 form worksheet (available from your employer) to calculate the amount of withholding that equals about 100 percent of your prior year's tax or 90 percent of what you estimate you will owe in the current tax year. Adjust withholding and take all allowed exemptions and extra allowances for itemized deductions. If you usually get a refund, consider *reducing* your withholding. Although a refund seems like "found" money, you are actually making an interest-free loan to the government. Instead, set up an automatic savings plan at your bank so that you earn interest on those funds.

3. Defer income until next year. If you are self-employed, receive bonuses, or have income outside of a regular job (such as consulting), deferring income into the next tax year may keep you under the level where deduction and exemption phase outs begin or keep you from moving into a higher tax bracket. Your savings depends on your current and anticipated income and tax bracket.

4. Take all allowable deductions and time them carefully. Review a comprehensive list of deductions

make even more money. Deferring taxes is usually done through various types of retirement plans, such as individual retirement arrangements (IRAs), by investing in certain types of annuities, variable life insurance policies, or even Series EE savings bonds.

The fundamentals of tax planning include making sure you take all the deductions to which you are entitled and taking full advantage of the various tax provisions that will minimize your tax liability. Thus, comprehensive tax planning is an ongoing activity with both an immediate and long-term perspective. *It plays a key role in personal financial planning*—in fact, one of the major components of a comprehensive financial plan is a summary of the potential tax impacts of various recommended financial strategies. Tax planning is closely interrelated with many financial planning activities, including investment, retirement, and estate planning.

SOME POPULAR TAX STRATEGIES

Managing your taxes is a year-round activity. Because Congress considers tax law changes throughout the year, you may not know all of the applicable regulations until the middle of the year or later. Like other financial goals, tax strategies require frequent review and adjustment when regulations and personal circumstances change.

Tax planning can become very complex at times and may involve rather sophisticated investment strategies. In such cases, especially those involving large amounts of money, you should seek professional help. Many tax strategies, like those suggested in the *Smart Money* box, are fairly simple and straightforward and can be used by the average middle-income taxpayer. You certainly don't have to be in the top income bracket to enjoy the benefits of many (and perhaps most) of these tax-saving ideas and procedures. For example, the to be sure you haven't missed any. Accelerate and/or bunch deductions into one tax year to save taxes by increasing deductions or itemizing rather than using the standard deduction. For example, by making your fourth quarter estimated state tax payment before December 31 rather than on January 15 you can deduct it in the current taxable year. Grouping miscellaneous expenses and scheduling non-reimbursed elective medical procedures so that they fall into one tax year may push them above the required "floor" for deductions (2 percent of adjusted gross income [AGI] for miscellaneous expenses; 7.5 percent, for medical expenses). Expect your tax bracket to be lower next year? Increase discretionary deductions like charitable contributions this year (or, conversely, postpone them if you expect to be in a higher bracket next year).

5. Look at the tax implications of investment decisions. Keep tax consequences in mind whenever you sell securities—but *never allow tax considerations to dictate investment decisions.* Review your portfolio to see if you can sell securities to offset other gains or losses. For example, if you are in the 31 percent bracket and in April sold Stock A for a $4,000 long-term capital gain, sell Stock B, which you bought a year ago and whose prospects aren't good, for $3,500 below what you paid for it, and you'll offset $3,500 of the capital gain that would be taxed at 28 percent. Also consider waiting to sell a stock until it either qualifies for long-term capital gains treatment, or you can use it to offset gains or losses.

6. Use employee benefits that reduce income subject to withholding. Many companies offer flexible spending accounts (FSAs) for medical and dependent care expenses. The amounts you allocate for these expenses are not subject to federal, social security, or state taxes (except in New Jersey and Pennsylvania), resulting in tax savings of 25 to 40 percent or more on FSA dollars.

7. Contribute to tax-deferred retirement plans. Income on contributions to retirement plans such as employer-sponsored 401(k)s, Keogh and simplified employee pension (SEP) plans for the self-employed, and IRAs is tax-deferred. Also, IRA, Keogh, and SEP plan contributions reduce AGI; 401(k) contributions, like FSA dollars, reduce gross income. Fund these plans as early as possible during the year, so the money can accumulate tax-deferred income throughout the year. Dual income couples should coordinate retirement plan contributions. It is usually better for each spouse to contribute to his or her employer's plan, particularly where employers match a portion of 401(k) contributions.

interest income on Series EE (U.S. savings) bonds is free from state income tax, and the holder can elect to delay payment of taxes on the federal level until the earlier of the year the bonds are redeemed for cash or the year in which they finally mature. This feature makes Series EE bonds an excellent vehicle for earning tax-deferred income. Some other popular (and fairly simple) tax strategies follow.

Income Shifting. One way of reducing income taxes is to use a technique known as **income shifting.** Here the taxpayer shifts a portion of his or her income—and thus taxes—to relatives in lower tax brackets. This can be done by creating trusts or custodial accounts or by making outright gifts of income-producing property to family members. For instance, parents with $125,000 of taxable income (31 percent marginal tax rate) and $18,000 in corporate bonds paying $2,000 in annual interest might give the bonds to their 15-year-old child—with the understanding that such income is to be used ultimately for the child's college education. The $2,000 would then belong to the child, who would probably have to pay approximately $210 (.15 x [$2,000 – $600 minimum standard deduction]) in taxes on this income, and at the same time the parents' taxable income would be reduced by $2,000 (along with a reduction in their taxes of $620). Unfortunately, this strategy is not as simple as it might at first appear. The Tax Reform Act of 1986 specifies that the investment income of a minor (under the age of 14) is taxed at the same rate as the parents *to the extent that it exceeds $1,200.* For

income shifting A technique used to reduce taxes in which a taxpayer shifts a portion of income to relatives in lower tax brackets.

example, if a 5-year-old girl received $2,400 from a trust set up for her by her parents, the first $1,200 of that income (subject to a minimum $600 standard deduction) would be taxed at the child's rate and the remaining $1,200 would be subject to the parents' (higher) tax rate. These restrictions do not apply to children 14 and over, so it is possible to employ such techniques with older children (and presumably, with other older relatives, like elderly parents).

The reason income shifting is allowed in the first place is because there is a positive side to the practice. It is presumed that income shifting is done not only to reduce taxes, but also to build up a pool of savings for the purpose of meeting some specific future outlay such as a child's college education. According to what is known as the "fruit-of-the-tree" doctrine, individuals cannot give away or place in trust income (fruit) alone. Instead, they must also give away the income-producing property (fruit-bearing tree) as well. Additional tax implications of gifts to dependents are discussed in Chapter 15.

Tax Shelters. **Tax Shelters** are forms of investments that take advantage of certain *tax write-offs*. Some real estate (*income-generating* property) and natural-resource investments (oil and gas drilling) provide these desirable deductions.

The favorable write-offs come from deductions from gross income that are permitted by the IRS but do not involve an actual outlay of cash by the investor. In accounting terminology, these write-offs are called *depreciation, amortization,* or *depletion*. The presence of these noncash expenditures can lower the amount of taxes paid by taxpayers in certain income brackets. Tax-sheltered investments are generally considered to be *passive* investments; the amount of write-offs that can be taken is limited to the amount of income generated. There are a few exceptions, however. This rule does not apply to income-property investments of taxpayers with adjusted gross income under $100,000 and to certain oil and gas investments. Thus, if your income is under $100,000 a year and you own some rental property in which you actively participate, or you invest in an oil or gas drilling partnership, you may be able to benefit from all or most of the associated tax write-offs. Specifically, if your write-offs from these investments exceed the income they generate, you can use the excess write-offs *to shelter your other income*—the net result will be to reduce your taxable income and, therefore, the amount of taxes you have to pay. For example, you could invest in an apartment project that provided both an actual cash return of $5,000 and a depreciation deduction (from gross income) of $9,000. The net result of this investment would be to completely shelter the $5,000 cash income from taxes; even better, if you met the income limitations, you would have an additional $4,000 write-off ($9,000 − $5,000) that would reduce both your taxable income and tax liability.

With the exceptions noted above, the 1986 Tax Reform Act has pretty much eliminated tax-sheltered investments that rely heavily on tax write-offs as the major (or only) source of income. Today these investments must stand on their *investment,* not tax-shelter, merit. Two other noteworthy provisions relate to rental real estate. First, the passive investment limits do not apply if the taxpayer spends over half of his or her time and at least 750 hours per year managing the property. Also, the law provides that as much as $25,000 in write-offs from rental real estate could be used each year (to offset income from other sources) by people who "actively participate in the rental activity" and whose adjusted gross income is less than $100,000. This provision is phased out completely for adjusted gross incomes of $150,000 or more.

Tax-Free Income, or Tax Deferred? There are some investments that provide tax-free income; in most cases, however, the tax on the income is only deferred (or delayed) to a later day. Although there aren't many forms of tax-free investments left today, probably the best example would be the *interest* income earned on *municipal bonds*. Such income is free from federal income tax. No matter how much interest income you make, you don't have to pay any taxes on it. (Tax-free municipal bonds are discussed in Chapter 11.) Income that is **tax deferred,** in contrast, does not cause taxes to be paid now, but delays their payment to a future date. Until that time occurs, however, the advantage of these vehicles is that they allow you to *accumulate earnings* in a tax-free fashion. A good example of tax-deferred income would be income earned in an *individual retirement arrangement (IRA)*. See Chapter 14 for a detailed discussion of this vehicle.

Basically, any wage earner can open an IRA account and contribute up to $2,000 a year to the account. Of course, as noted earlier in this chapter, although any employed person can contribute to an IRA, only those people meeting certain pension and/or income constraints can deduct the annual contributions from their tax returns. If you fail to meet these restrictions, you can still have an IRA but you can't deduct the $2,000 annual contribution from your income. So why have an IRA? *Because all the income you earn in your IRA accumulates tax-free.* This is a *tax-deferred* investment, so you'll eventually have to pay taxes on these earnings, but not until you start drawing down your account. Thus, if you were in, say, the 31 percent tax bracket and could not write off your annual IRA deduction, you'd still be well advised to put $2,000 a year into an IRA to obtain the tax-deferred income feature. That is, if you could earn 12 percent before taxes on your investments, you could put $2,000 a year into fully taxable investments and end up with about $152,000 in 25 years. Or you could put the $2,000 each year into a tax-deferred IRA account and (given the same 12 percent rate of return) end up with approximately *$267,000* at the end of 25 years. You'll eventually have to pay taxes on your earnings when you start drawing down your IRA account, but you can't overlook the fact that the tax-deferred IRA investments result in fully *75 percent more income* (that is, $267,000 with the IRA versus $152,000 without). In addition to IRAs, tax-deferred income can also be obtained from certain types of pension and retirement plans and annuities. See Chapter 14 for more information on these financial products and strategies.

Concept Check

3-16. Differentiate between tax avoidance and tax evasion.

3-17. Explain each of the following strategies for reducing current taxes: (a) income shifting, (b) tax shelters, and (c) tax deferral.

3-18. Identify and briefly discuss at least six specific tax strategies that can be used by individuals to reduce their current taxes.

OTHER FORMS OF PERSONAL TAXES

LG6

In addition to federal income taxes, individuals must pay other types of taxes at the federal, state, and local levels. What other taxes might an employed homeowner have to pay? Spend a few moments answering this question before reading on.

Although the largest tax a person will normally pay is federal income taxes, there are other forms of taxes to contend with. For example, additional federal taxes may be levied on income as well as on specific types of transactions. At the state and local levels, sales transactions, income, property ownership, and licenses may be taxed. Because most individuals have to pay many of these other types of taxes, their impact on one's financial condition must be understood. Thus, a person saving to purchase a new automobile costing $15,000 should realize that the state and local sales taxes, as well as the cost of license plates and registration, may add another $1,300 or so to the total cost of the car.

OTHER FEDERAL TAXES

While income taxes are the single most important source of revenue, the federal government also raises funds through social security, excise, and gift and estate taxes. Next to income taxes, the most common form of tax is social security, which is paid by just about every gainfully employed individual except certain federal employees and some state and local government employees. None of the federal taxes described in the following sections, including social security, can be claimed as a deduction for federal income tax purposes.

Social Security Taxes. People probably pay more in social security taxes than in any other form of federal tax except income taxes. In fact, many families (especially those with incomes of less than $15,000 to $20,000 a year) actually pay more in social security taxes than they do in federal income taxes. As noted earlier in this chapter, social security taxes are paid at a uniform, stipulated

tax shelters Certain types of investments, such as real estate and natural resources, that provide noncash tax write-offs in the form of depreciation, amortization, or depletion.

tax deferred Income that is not subject to taxes immediately but which will be subject to taxes at a later date.

rate on a specified maximum amount of income earned from sources such as wages, salaries, bonuses, and commissions. The basis for determining the amount of social security taxes due is the total amount of gross earnings before any adjustments, deductions, or exemptions. In essence, *social security taxes are taken out of the first dollar you earn* and continue to be withdrawn up to a specified maximum amount of taxable income. Once you hit that maximum, your social security taxes stop for the year and begin again on January 1.

In 1994, with a social security tax rate of 7.65 percent and maximum taxable earnings of $60,600, the maximum tax was $4,636 (7.65% x $60,600). An additional 1.45 percent Medicare tax was charged on income over $60,600. The maximum wages to which the social security and Medicare tax apply are adjusted each year in response to changes in the cost of living. Note than an amount equal to the employee's contribution is also paid by the taxpayer's employer. In other words, the total amount of social security taxes paid for every wage earner amounts to twice the amount the employee pays (employers are subject to the same tax rates and taxable maximums as employees). Of course, if you earn less than the maximum taxable income, your social security benefits will also be less than the maximum. The social security tax rate, however, remains the same no matter how much or how little you earn. For example, if you earned only $20,000 in 1994, you would have paid social security taxes of only $1,530 (7.65% × $20,000). Keep in mind that the full amount of social security taxes is paid by each wage earner, regardless of what the spouse or any other household member pays.

On the other hand, if an individual works for more than one employer during the year and earns more than the wage base ($60,600 in 1994), he or she is entitled to a tax credit for the amount of overpayment. This credit can be claimed on your federal income tax return (see line 58 of the 1994 Form 1040).

Excise, Gift, Estate, and Other Taxes. In addition to income and social security taxes, the federal government receives revenue from the following types of taxes:

- *Excise taxes*: **Excise taxes** are added to the purchase price of certain luxury items and services, such as jewelry, automobiles, gasoline, telephone services, tobacco products, and liquor and paid at the time of purchase. As an example, new cars with a sale price over $32,000 are subject to a 10 percent excise tax on the amount paid in excess of $32,000.
- *Gift and estate taxes: Gift taxes* are levied by both federal and state governments, must be paid by the giver, and are based on the value of the gift. *Estate taxes,* also levied at the federal and state levels, are based on the estate's value upon the death of its owner and reduce the amount of inheritance passed on to the heirs. Chapter 15 on estate planning discusses these taxes in greater detail.
- *Other taxes:* Duties on imports, entrance fees to federal facilities such as parks and museums, and taxes on special types of transactions are still other types of federal taxation.

STATE TAXES

To raise revenue to finance their operations, state governments levy a variety of taxes. Probably the largest source of state revenue is the sales tax; other sources are income taxes, property taxes, and licensing fees.

- *State sales tax:* All states except a few apply statewide **sales taxes** to most consumer purchases, though some may exempt food, drugs, and/or services. While sales tax rates vary from state to state, most are in the 4 to 7 percent range. Because sales taxes are tied to purchases, there is really no practical way to avoid them. When making or budgeting for large purchases, you should recognize that sales taxes will add to their cost.
- *State income taxes:* Most states currently have personal income taxes, which range from about 3 to 11 percent of reported taxable income, that are either graduated tax rates that increase with taxable income or fixed rates that apply to all levels of income. Nearly all states follow the federal law in defining taxable income—though many provide for different exclusions and adjustments—although some states tax only certain types of income, such as interest, dividends, and capital gains. The calculation of state taxes is generally similar to that for federal income taxes, so that filing state tax returns is relatively easy. Like the federal government, most states withhold a portion of income from each paycheck. Many allow taxpayers to deduct federal taxes from taxable income before calculating their

state tax liability. (For federal tax purposes, persons who itemize can deduct the state income taxes they paid.)

- *State property taxes, licensing fees, and other taxes:* Although most states obtain the vast majority of their revenues from sales and income taxes, some also tax various forms of property, particularly automobiles and other motor vehicles. However, as a principal source of revenue, property taxes are levied primarily by local governments. State governments also obtain revenues from the sale of automobile licenses and by licensing certain professions. In addition, most states have excise taxes on gasoline, tobacco, liquor, and certain luxuries and gift and estate taxes similar to those levied by the federal government (see Chapter 15). Of these miscellaneous types of state taxes, only property taxes are deductible for federal income tax purposes.

LOCAL TAXES

Local governments, which include everything from cities and counties to school districts and stadium authorities, levy taxes to fund a variety of public services. Although the majority of local revenues come from property taxes, local governments often use income taxes, sales taxes, and licensing fees to add to their coffers.

- *Local property taxes:* **Property taxes** on real estate and other personal property, such as automobiles and boats, are primary sources of revenue to cities, counties, school districts, and other municipalities. Because, for most people, the home is the largest form of property ownership, real estate taxes are the dominant form of property taxes. Property taxes are typically collected by the county and then distributed among other governmental units—the city and school district, for example. The governmental unit to which taxes are paid determines the value of the taxed property. In general, the more expensive the home, the higher the real estate tax. If deductions are itemized, these taxes can be deducted when calculating federal income taxes. Further discussion of these taxes is included in Chapter 5 on housing.
- *Local income taxes:* Local governments—particularly larger cities in the eastern part of the United States—sometimes levy income taxes on all those employed within their boundaries. These taxes are similar to federal and state income taxes, but the rates are lower—usually about 1 to 2 percent but sometimes as high as 4 to 5 percent of taxable income (an exception is the District of Columbia, which has an income tax rate that rises above 10 percent). Most cities withhold income taxes, with final settlement made at the end of the year. These taxes are also a deductible itemized expense for federal income tax purposes.
- *Local sales taxes and licensing fees:* Many cities also have sales taxes. Licensing fees, such as building permits, also provide local governments with added revenue. In some states, a portion of the fees collected for automobile and other licenses represents a local licensing fee or property tax.

excise taxes Taxes levied at the point of sale on the purchase of certain luxury items and services, such as jewelry, automobiles, gasoline, and tobacco products.

sales taxes Taxes levied at the point of sale by state and local governments on most consumer purchases, though food, drugs, and/or services may be exempt.

property taxes Taxes typically levied by local and state governments on the value of real estate and certain other personal property in order to raise revenue needed to finance their operations.

SUMMARY

LG1. Discuss the basic principles of income taxes and determine your filing status. Because taxes have an impact on most individuals and families, a basic understanding of them is essential for effective financial planning and intelligent money management. The dominant tax in our country today is the federal income tax—a levy that provides the government with most of the funds it needs to cover its operating costs. The administration and enforcement of federal tax laws is the responsibility of the Internal Revenue Service (IRS), a part of the U.S. Department of the Treasury. Because the government operates on a pay-as-you-go basis, employers are required to withhold taxes from their employees' paychecks. The amount of taxes you owe depends on your filing status—single, married filing jointly, married filing separately, head of household, or qualifying widow(er) with dependent child—and the amount of taxable income you report.

LG2. Classify the various types of gross income, differentiate between itemized and standard deductions and exemptions, and calculate taxable income. Gross income includes active income (such as wages, bonuses, pensions, alimony), portfolio income (dividends, interest, and capital gains), and/or passive income (income derived from real estate, limited partnerships, and other tax shelters). You must decide whether to itemize your various deductions or take the standard deduction. Some allowable deductions for those who itemize include mortgage interest, medical expenses over 7.5 percent of AGI, and certain job-related expenses. To calculate taxable income, deduct allowable adjustments such as IRA contributions and alimony paid from gross income to get adjusted gross income (AGI) and subtract from AGI the amount of deductions and personal exemptions claimed.

LG3. Prepare a basic tax return using the appropriate tax forms and rate schedules. Once you determine your taxable income, you can find the amount of taxes owed using either the tax rate tables or, if your taxable income is over $50,000, the tax rate schedules. Tax rates vary with level of reported income and filing status. Personal tax returns are filed using one of the following forms: 1040EZ, 1040A, or 1040.

LG4. Explain who needs to pay estimated taxes, when to file your return, how to handle an audit, and where to get help with your taxes. Persons with income not subject to withholding may need to file a declaration of estimated taxes and make estimated tax payments on a quarterly basis. Returns must be filed on or before April 15 unless the taxpayer requests an automatic four-month filing extension. The IRS audits selected returns to confirm their validity by carefully examining the data reported in them. Assistance in preparing returns is available from the IRS, private tax preparers, and computer programs that can be used both for tax preparation and tax planning.

LG5. Implement a tax planning strategy. Effective tax planning is closely tied to other areas of financial planning. The objectives of tax planning are to reduce, shift, and/or defer taxes so the taxpayer gets maximum use/benefits from the money he or she earns. Some of the more popular tax strategies include shifting income to relatives in lower tax brackets, investing in real estate and other types of tax shelters, investing in tax-exempt municipal bonds, setting up individual retirement accounts, and using annuities and pension and retirement plans to generate tax-deferred income.

LG6. Describe the other major forms of personal taxes. In addition to income taxes, the federal government also levies social security taxes, excise taxes, and gift and estate taxes. Individuals also pay state and local taxes including sales taxes, property taxes, and various licensing fees.

FINANCIAL FACTS OR FANTASIES

Are the following statements financial facts (true) or fantasies (false)?

1. Every individual or married couple is required to file a federal income tax return regardless of the amount of income earned.
2. The amount of federal income tax withheld depends on both your level of earnings and the number of withholding allowances claimed.
3. Federal income taxes are levied against the *total* amount of money earned.
4. A tax credit is like a deduction or exemption in that it reduces your taxable income.
5. Tax avoidance is an illegal practice that could result in financial penalties and even prison sentences.
6. An easy way to earn tax-deferred income is to invest in Series EE savings bonds.

DISCUSSION QUESTIONS AND PROBLEMS

Discussion Question for Opening Profile

Summarize the Griffiths' tax preparation and planning strategies. Use the profile to give some examples of why it is important to include tax planning when managing your personal finances. What are some ways you can reduce your own tax liability?

1. Mary Parker is 24 years old, single, lives in an apartment, and has no dependents. Last year she earned $19,600 as a sales assistant for Texas Instruments; $1,800 of her wages were withheld for federal income taxes. In addition, she had interest income of $142. Estimate her taxable income, tax liability, and tax refund or tax owed.
2. Tina Marcelle received the following items and amounts of income during 1995. Help her calculate (a) her gross income and (b) that portion (dollar amount) of her income that is tax exempt.

Salary	$9,500
Dividends	800
Gift from mother	500
Child support from ex-husband	2,400
Interest on savings account	250
Rent	900
Loan from bank	2,000
Interest on state government bonds	300

3. If Jenny Perez is in the 31 percent tax bracket, calculate the tax associated with each of the following transactions:
   a. She sold stock for $1,200 that she purchased for $1,000 five months earlier.
   b. She sold bonds for $4,000 that she purchased for $3,000 three years earlier.
   c. She sold stock for $1,000 that she purchased for $1,500 eighteen months earlier.
4. Demonstrate the differences resulting from a $1,000 tax credit versus a $1,000 deduction for a taxpayer in the 28 percent tax bracket with $35,000 of pretax income.
5. ***Use Worksheets 3.1 and 3.2.*** John Otsubo graduated from college in 1994 and began work as a systems analyst in July 1994. He is preparing to file his income tax return for 1994 and has collected the following information:

Tuition scholarships and grants	$ 4,750
Scholarship, room, and board	1,850
Salary	13,650
Interest income	185
Deductible expenses, total	3,000
Income taxes withheld	1,600

   a. Prepare John's 1994 tax return, using the standard deduction amount given in Exhibit 3.4, a personal exemption of $2,450, and the tax rates given in Exhibit 3.5. Which tax form should John use, and why?
   b. Prepare John's 1994 tax return using the data in part (a) along with the following information:

IRA contribution	$ 1,000
Cash dividends received	150

   Which tax form should he use in this case? Why?
6. Milo Whitehead is married and has one child. He is currently in the process of putting together some figures so he can prepare their joint 1994 tax return. He can claim three personal exemptions (including himself). So far, he's been able to determine the following with regard to income and possible deductions.

Total unreimbursed medical expenses incurred	$ 1,155
Gross wages and commissions earned	38,820
IRA contribution	2,250
Mortgage interest paid	5,200
Capital gains realized	1,450
Income from limited partnership	200
Job expenses and other allowable deductions	875
Interest paid on credit cards	380
Dividend and interest income earned	610
Sales taxes paid	2,470
Charitable contributions made	1,200
Capital losses incurred	3,475
Interest paid on a car loan	570
Alimony paid by Milo to first wife	6,000
Social security taxes paid	2,750
Property taxes paid	700
State income taxes paid	1,700

Given the above information, how much taxable income will the Whiteheads have in 1994? (Note: Assume Milo is covered by a pension plan where he works, the standard deduction amounts in Exhibit 3.4 are applicable, and each exemption claimed is worth $2,450.)

CONTEMPORARY CASE APPLICATIONS

FPPC 3.1 The Aggarwals Tackle Their Tax Return

Sabash and Sue Aggarwal are a married couple in their early 20s living in Dallas. Sabash earned $30,000 in 1994 from his job as a sales manager with Carson Corporation. During the year, his employer withheld $2,900 for income tax purposes. In addition, the Aggarwals received interest of $350 on a joint savings account, $750 interest on tax-exempt municipal bonds, and a dividend of $400 on jointly owned stocks. At the end of 1994, the Aggarwals sold two stocks, A and B. Stock A was sold for $700 and had been purchased four months earlier for $800. Stock B was sold for $1,500 and had been purchased three years earlier for $1,100. Their only child, Rohn, age 2, received (as his sole source of income) dividends of $200 on stock of Kraft, Inc.

In spite of the fact that Sabash was covered by the Carson Corporation's pension plan, he planned to contribute $2,000 to an IRA for 1994. Following are the amounts of money paid out during the year by the Aggarwals:

Medical and dental expenses (unreimbursed)	$ 200
State and local property taxes	831
Interest paid on home mortgage	4,148
Charitable contributions	1,360
Total	$6,539

In addition, Sabash incurred some travel costs (not reimbursed) for an out-of-town business trip as follows:

Airline ticket	$250
Taxis	20
Lodging	60
Meals (as adjusted to 50% of cost)	36
Total	$366

Questions

1. Using the above information, prepare a joint tax return for Sabash and Sue Aggarwal for the year ended December 31, 1994, in a manner that will result in the smallest tax liability—that is, either itemize their deductions or take the standard deduction. (Note: Use Worksheet 3.2, Form 1040, and the tax rate schedule in Exhibit 3.5 to determine the Aggarwals' taxes. Assume the standard deduction amounts in Exhibit 3.4 are applicable and each exemption claimed is worth $2,450.
2. How much have you saved the Aggarwals as a result of your treatment of their deductions?
3. Discuss whether the Aggarwals need to file a tax return for their son.
4. Suggest some tax strategies that the Aggarwals might use to reduce their tax liability for next year.

FPPC 3.2 Joan Cavander: Bartender or Tax Expert?

Joan Cavander, who is single, is a bartender at the Twin Towers Supper Club in Atlanta. During the past year (1994), her gross income was $17,900 made up of wages and tips. She has decided to prepare her own tax return, because she cannot afford the services of a tax expert. After preparing her return, she has come to you for advice. The following is a summary of the figures she has prepared thus far:

Gross income:	Wages	$ 9,700
	Tips	8,200
Adjusted gross income (AGI)		$17,900
Less: Itemized deductions		2,300
		$15,600
Less:	Standard deduction	3,800
	Taxable income	$11,800

Joan believes that if an individual's income falls below $20,350, the federal government considers him or her "poor" and allows both itemized deductions and a standard deduction.

Questions

1. Calculate Joan Cavander's taxable income, being sure to consider her exemption. (Assume the standard deduction amounts in Exhibit 3.4 are applicable and each exemption claimed is worth $2,450.)
2. Discuss with Joan her errors in interpreting the tax laws, and explain the difference between itemized deductions and the standard deduction.
3. Joan has been dating Sam Haley for nearly four years, and they are seriously thinking about getting married. Sam has income and itemized deductions identical to Joan's. How much tax would they pay as a married couple (filing a joint return) versus the total amount the two paid as single persons (filing separate individual returns)? Strictly from a tax perspective, does it make any difference whether Joan and Sam stay single or get married? Explain.

GETTING A HANDLE ON YOUR FINANCIAL FUTURE

While some believe that a reasonable financial goal would be to minimize taxes paid, in actuality you should be trying to maximize your after-tax income. You can accomplish this by understanding how different sources of income are taxed. You should strive for the optimal combination of types of income that will minimize your taxes by making sure that you have taken advantage of all allowable deductions and exemptions in arriving at your tax liability.

If You Are Just Starting Out

For most of you just beginning your careers, your taxes are relatively simple. Most, if not all, of your gross income is in the form of wages and salaries, and the standard deduction is almost always greater than itemized deductions. As simple as this may be, there are a number of potential problems that could be avoided through good recordkeeping and sound tax planning.

Recordkeeping:

1. As you record your actual expenditures in your cash budget, also record which expenditures are tax deductible.
2. Set aside a certain day of the month to regularly update your records.
3. Keep track of cash contributions to charitable organizations, because these are easily forgotten.
4. Remember, a canceled check is not necessarily proof of payment to the IRS, so keep invoices and receipts as well.

Tax Planning:

1. Participate in your employer's 401(k) plan to reduce your gross income.
2. Pay for health and dependent care with pretax dollars through your employer's flexible spending plan.
3. If income limits allow, set up an IRA account.

If You Are Thirty-Something

As time goes by, your tax returns usually become more complex as your marital and family status evolve and you accumulate a wider variety of financial and personal assets. To minimize your tax burden, consider one of the following strategies: use deductions, credits, and income subject to preferential tax treatment to reduce your taxes; shift income to others; or defer taxes. These methods require careful planning as well as formalized recordkeeping.

Recordkeeping:

1. Keep all records of home improvement costs because, although they are not deductible, they add to the basis in the house and will reduce taxes due upon sale.
2. Keep good records of dividend and interest income. Check them against Form 1099 to ensure correct reporting.
3. Remember that the IRS can take as long as three years from the date of filing for an audit. Therefore, keep most of your tax records for at least that long.

Tax Planning:

1. Day-care expenses may be eligible for a child-care credit or could be paid through your employer's flexible spending plan.
2. Consider investments that receive preferential tax treatment, such as real estate or tax-free municipal bonds.
3. Use gifts and trusts to shift income to others in lower tax brackets.
4. Defer taxes by making pretax contributions to retirement plans or buying Series EE bonds and not claiming the interest as current income.
5. Invest in assets with low current income but high growth potential, such as common stocks.

Paul Larkin, who was introduced to you at the end of Chapter 1, would like your help in starting his financial plan. Review Paul's financial and personal information on pages 33-45 before answering the following questions.

1. Using the January 1, 1996 asset and liability information, develop a balance sheet for Paul Larkin. Assume he has no unpaid bills. On a balance sheet, assets are valued at their fair market value and liabilities are listed at their current outstanding balances. What is Paul Larkin's net worth?

2. Using the income and expenditure information for 1995, complete an income and expenditures statement for Paul. Use the "cash flow" concept for this financial statement including all money inflows as income and all outflows as expenditures. Did Paul have a cash surplus or a cash deficit in 1995? What impact did the 1995 cash surplus (deficit) have on the January 1, 1996 balance sheet?

   What is the result of including the money received from selling assets (Fidelity Select Energy Services mutual fund) as income? What is the result of including current savings (reinvested interest, dividends, capital gains distributions as well as contributions to employer-sponsored retirement accounts) as expenditures? What does an income and expenditures statement using the cash flow concept where all inflows and outflows are included show compared to a statement where investment inflows and savings are excluded?

3. Based on Paul's financial statements, calculate the following ratios:
   - Savings ratio
   - Liquidity ratio
   - Solvency ratio
   - Debt service ratio

4. Based on the information in the original case and in Paul's financial statements, list at least 3 positive and 3 negative aspects of Paul's current financial position.

After reading Chapters 1 and 2, you probably realize that Paul's financial goals are not defined well enough in the original case to serve as the basis for his financial plan and cash budget. Upon further review, Paul has restated his financial goals as follows:

- Pay off all his credit card balances within the next 2 years.
- Have liquid assets equal to 5 month's net salary within the next 3 years for an emergency fund.
- Buy a house within 2 years. Paul plans on using the inherited funds that are currently invested in the Fidelity Equity-Income II mutual fund for this goal.
- Save $7,000 for a down payment on a new car within 5 years.
- Continue contributing 7% of his gross salary to his 401(k) plan for retirement.
- Have enough accumulated in an account to provide his mother $5,000 a year during her retirement years. He expects she will retire in 15 years at age 65 and will live 20 years after retirement. He would like to have all the money accumulated by the time she retires.
- Establish a regular savings/investment program to accomplish these goals.

5. Using time value calculations, how much would Paul have to save this year to be on track in meeting his goals for:

- his emergency fund (Remember, Paul already has some funds in his money market account, money market mutual fund, and savings account. He does not want to consider the money in his checking account or cash on hand for this goal).
- the down payment for a new car.
- the fund for his mother's retirement years.

Assume Paul can earn 2% after inflation and taxes on his emergency fund and 5% after inflation and taxes on his car goal. In figuring the savings required for his mother's retirement fund, Paul assumes that he could earn 3% after taxes and inflation on the money once his mother retired. While he is accumulating the money before she retires, he feels he can take more risk and earn 6% after taxes and inflation.

FPPC

6. Prepare a cash budget for the year of 1996 using the income and expenditure data from the original case as well as the figures needed to meet his goals (from question 5). In addition, Paul would need to make monthly credit card payments totaling approximately $545 in order to pay off his current credit card debt within the next 2 years. (It is greater than the $465 a month you get when you divide his outstanding credit card debt by 24 because interest would continue to accrue until the debts were paid off.) Assume that income for 1996 will be the same as 1995 *except* that there will be no sale of assets.

7. Can Paul achieve all of his stated goals given his current income and expenditure patterns? If not, what recommendations would you make to help him achieve his goals?

8. If Paul and Christine are considering marriage, what would you recommend they do before marriage regarding their finances? What specific things do you know about them that could cause difficulties in marriage?

FPPC

9. Prepare a 1995 federal income tax return for Paul using the financial data in the original case. (HINT: Subtract the $2,580 he contributed to his 401(k) retirement plan from his gross salary before entering this income on the tax form. Also, remember that income earned on a 401(k) is tax-deferred.) Does Paul owe more taxes, or will he receive a refund? How much?

10. Assuming that 1996 will be similar to 1995 (except that there will be no sale of assets in 1996), should Paul make any adjustments to his withholding allowances? If yes, should he increase or decrease the number of withholding allowances claimed?

11. What is Paul's average tax rate in 1995? What is his marginal tax rate?

12. Approximately how much did Paul save in taxes by investing $2,580 in his 401(k) retirement account?

13. If Paul had contributed the $780 he spent on medical and dental expenses to a medical expense flexible spending account, how much would he have saved in federal income taxes?

14. Given Paul's goals and risk tolerances, what tax strategies would you recommend to help him reduce his tax liability in the future? Does he have enough money to implement the recommended tax strategies?

FPPC **15.** Since Paul and Christine have started talking about money and they are thinking about marriage in the future, they want to see if they would have paid more or less had they been married and filed a joint return for 1995 rather than filing two returns as singles. Use Paul's information from the case and question 9 along with the following information regarding Christine's 1995 income and expenditures to see if they would have experienced the "marriage tax penalty" if they had been married in 1995.

Christine's Income and Expenditures:

Salary	$39,000
Interest income	562
State and local income taxes paid	983
Federal income taxes withheld	5,775

What is the difference in their federal income tax liability as singles compared to marrieds?

Part 2

Managing Basic Assets

CHAPTER 4
MANAGING YOUR CASH AND SAVINGS

CHAPTER 5
MAKING HOUSING AND AUTOMOBILE DECISIONS

CHAPTER 4

MANAGING YOUR CASH AND SAVINGS

Don and Meredith's Money Management Procedures

The money management style of Don Roberts, 51, and Meredith Bell, 46, gives each considerable financial independence. Don has two grown sons from his first marriage, and their daughter Hannah is 12. "We both have financial backgrounds—Don has 26 years in real estate finance, and I was a corporate banker but now have my own editorial services business," Meredith explains. Don adds, "We confer on most major expenditure decisions but have our own checking accounts, divide household expenses, and make separate investment decisions."

At first, alimony, child support, and basic living expenses consumed most of their income. As their salaries grew, they lived primarily on Don's salary and saved Meredith's plus any bonuses. By saving steadily, they built college funds for the boys and a "nest egg" so that Don could start a real estate development firm in San Diego County. "Unfortunately, that venture failed," Don remarks. "We depleted most of our savings and retirement funds and had to start all over." Their priority now is saving for Hannah's college and their retirement. "She'll start college just before we want to retire, so we're accelerating our savings," Meredith says. Don resumed his real estate finance career and contributes the maximum to his employer's retirement plans. Meredith has a SEP (simplified employee pension) plan, and they have investment accounts for Hannah's college.

As experienced financial services consumers, Don and Meredith shop around for the best combination of convenience, service, and costs.

Learning Goals

LG1. *Understand the role of good cash management in the financial planning process.*

LG2. *Describe the new financial marketplace—traditional financial institutions, checking and savings products, and deposit safety.*

LG3. *Find the interest earned on your money using compound interest and future value techniques.*

LG4. *Develop a savings strategy that incorporates a variety of savings plans.*

LG5. *Open and use a checking account.*

LG6. *Select additional types of money management services that meet your needs.*

Don's account, a joint account that Meredith can use if necessary, is at the bank that offered the best terms when they wanted a home equity line. He keeps the minimum balance to avoid service charges. "The *annual* opportunity cost of leaving a $750 balance for one year is $37.50 (assuming I'd earn 5 percent interest on it). *Monthly* service charges start at $8, plus a per-check charge," he explains. "The choice is pretty obvious!"

When Meredith's bank increased its minimum balance requirement, she found a bank offering five years' free checking, with no minimum balance, for a $1,500 initial deposit. "Their service is great. I often use the ATM (automated teller machine) to get cash and bank by phone to check balances, which checks cleared, and transfer funds between savings and checking accounts." Both keep about one month's expenses in checking accounts and the rest, including an emergency fund of about six months' expenses, in money market mutual funds to earn interest on idle funds. "I get very nervous when that reserve dips below that level," Don comments. They are teaching Hannah about money management as well; she has her own savings account and saves half what she makes from her party-planning and babysitting jobs.

Like the Roberts-Bell family, you need to create your own savings plan and choose the best financial institutions. In Chapter 4 you will learn how to start.

THE ROLE OF CASH MANAGEMENT IN PERSONAL FINANCIAL PLANNING

LG 1

Cash management involves making sure that you have funds available for planned and unplanned expenditures and that your spending patterns are within budgetary limits. What methods do you currently use to make sure you can pay bills promptly and cover unexpected expenditures? Before reading on, spend a few moments answering this question.

This chapter is concerned with **cash management**—an activity that deals with the routine, day-to-day administration of cash and near-cash resources by an individual or family. We identified these resources in Chapter 2 as *liquid assets.* They are considered liquid because they are either held in cash or can be readily converted to cash with little or no loss in value. In addition to cash, there are several other kinds of liquid assets, including checking accounts, savings accounts, money market deposit accounts and mutual funds, and other short-term investment vehicles. Exhibit 4.1 briefly describes the more popular types of liquid assets and the representative rates of return they earned in early 1995. As a rule, near-term needs are met using cash on hand, and unplanned or future needs are met using some type of savings or short-term investment vehicle.

In personal financial planning, cash management is the way you make sure that funds are available for both household outlays and an effective savings program. The success of your financial plans depends on your faithfulness to established cash budgets. An effective way to keep your spending in line is to make all household transactions (even the allocation of fun money or weekly cash allowances) using a tightly controlled *checking account.* In effect, you should write checks only at certain times of the week or month and, more important, you should avoid carrying your checkbook with you when you might be tempted to write checks for unplanned purchases. If you are going shopping, establish a maximum spending limit beforehand—ideally, an amount consistent with your cash budget. Such a system not only helps you avoid frivolous, impulsive expenditures, but it also provides valuable documentation on how and where you spend your money. Then, if your financial outcomes are not consistent with your plans, you can better identify causes and initiate appropriate corrective actions.

Another aspect of cash management, establishing an ongoing savings program, is an important part of personal financial planning. Savings are not only a cushion against financial emergencies but also a way to accumulate funds to meet future financial goals. You may want to put money aside so you can go back to school in a few years to earn a graduate degree, or to buy a new home, or perhaps to take a luxury vacation—these are all examples of specific financial objectives that can be met through savings. There are many different ways to save; some are better suited to accumulating emergency funds, and others are more appropriate for building reserves for future expenditures. Clearly specifying the objectives of your savings program is a prerequisite to selecting appropriate savings vehicles.

Concept Check

4-1. What is cash management? What are its major functions?

4-2. Give two broad reasons for holding liquid assets. Identify and briefly describe the popular types of liquid assets.

THE NEW FINANCIAL MARKETPLACE

LG 2

Because of deregulation, today's financial markets and institutions are vastly different (and greatly improved) from what they were five to ten years ago. Many financial institutions provide a full menu of financial products and services. What are some of the financial products and services available from major financial institutions in your area? Spend a few moments listing them before reading on.

Prior to the 1970s, there was no real competition in the financial marketplace. The distinctions between various kinds of financial institutions were

EXHIBIT 4.1

Popular Liquid Assets

The wide variety of savings vehicles available makes it possible to meet just about any savings or short-term investment need.

Type	Representative Rates of Return (Early 1995)	Description
Cash	0%	Pocket money—the coin and currency in one's possession.
Checking Account	0–2.0%	A substitute for cash. Offered by commercial banks as well as other financial institutions such as savings and loans and credit unions.
Savings Account	2.0–4.0%	Money is available at any time but cannot be withdrawn by check. Offered by banks and other financial institutions.
Money market deposit account (MMDA)	2.5–4.0%	Primarily a savings vehicle that pays market rates of interest. Offers limited check-writing privileges and requires a fairly large (typically $1,000 or more) minimum deposit.
Money market mutual fund (MMMF)	3.5–5.5%	Savings vehicle that is actually a mutual fund (not offered by banks, S&Ls, and other depository institutions). Like an MMDA, it also offers check-writing privileges.
Certificate of deposit (CD)	4.5–6.5%	A savings instrument where funds are left on deposit for a stipulated period of time (one week to one year or more); imposes a penalty for withdrawing funds early. Market yields vary by size and maturity; no check-writing privileges.
U.S. Treasury bill (T-bill)	5.8–6.5%	Short-term, highly marketable security issued by the U.S. Treasury (originally issued with maturities of 13, 26, and 52 weeks); smallest denomination is $10,000.
U.S. savings bond (EE)	5.9%	Issued by U.S. Treasury; rate of interest is tied to U.S. Treasury securities. Long a popular savings vehicle (widely used with payroll deduction plans). Maturities are approximately five years; sold in denominations of $50 and more.

clear. Commercial banks offered checking accounts and short-term loans. Savings and loans offered savings accounts and real estate mortgage loans. Brokerage firms assisted in trading securities. And insurance companies offered life, disability, health, auto, and homeowner's insurance. This segmented market changed in the early 1980s with passage of the *Depository Institutions Deregulation and Monetary Control Act of 1980*. This important law, together with additional legislation passed in 1982, removed many restrictions on banks and savings institutions and allowed them to compete with each other and with nonbank financial institutions.

As a result of deregulation, the differences between financial institutions have blurred considerably. Many now offer the same services and compete directly for your business. For example, at many banks you can make securities transactions and buy mutual funds and insurance, while stockbrokers offer check-writing services, loans, and access to automatic teller machines. This trend continues as all types of financial service firms offer even broader product lines. Beginning in 1997, banks will be able to branch across state lines, and proposals under consideration in early 1995 would allow banks to diversify into new lines of business such as securities trading, real estate, and data processing. Today, it is indeed difficult to distinguish between the numerous providers of financial products and services.

Specialization within the financial institutions industry continues to decrease as many institutions offer similar services. For example, today it is difficult to tell a savings and loan from a commercial bank, because both offer so many of the same financial products and services. And in response to competition from nonfinancial institutions, many banks and S&Ls now offer help with personal financial planning, take deposits across state lines, sell insurance, and offer securities brokerage services.

cash management The routine, day-to-day administration of cash and near-cash resources by an individual or family.

Thus, the *financial services industry* as we know it today embraces all institutions that market various kinds of *financial products,* such as checking and savings accounts, credit cards, loans and mortgages, insurance, and mutual funds, and *financial services,* such as financial planning, taxes, securities brokerage, real estate, trusts, retirement, and estate planning. In effect, what used to be several distinct (though somewhat related) industries is now, in essence, one industry.

From the viewpoint of the individual consumer, today's financial marketplace is far superior to that of just ten years ago. Most noticeable are the wider array of financial products and services, and the more competitive rates of return. The price of these benefits appears to be today's generally higher costs of financial services.

TRADITIONAL FINANCIAL INSTITUTIONS: "BANKS"

In spite of the growing number of firms entering the financial services field, individuals and families continue to make the vast majority of their financial transactions at traditional financial institutions: commercial banks, savings and loan associations, savings banks, and credit unions. Although these are organized and regulated by different agencies, they are frequently referred to as "banks" due to their similar products and services. Compared to their nonbanking counterparts, probably the two biggest advantages these institutions have is that they are familiar and convenient. Further, while most people have checking and savings accounts, a much smaller number own stocks, bonds, or mutual funds. As a result, most people are not accustomed to dealing with brokerage firms and other types of financial service companies.

Commercial Banks. To millions of Americans, banking means doing business with a **commercial bank.** Of the four types of traditional financial institutions, commercial banks are by far the largest. In addition to checking accounts, commercial banks offer a full array of financial services, including a variety of savings vehicles, credit cards, several types of consumer loans, trust services, and such items as safe-deposit boxes, traveler's checks, and check-cashing privileges. It is little wonder that they are commonly called *full-service banks.*

Commercial banks are the only financial institutions that can offer *noninterest-paying checking accounts* (demand deposits)—a feature that in today's deregulated financial market provides little competitive advantage. Therefore, commercial banks also offer a variety of checking accounts that combine check-writing privileges with features of savings accounts. In addition, they offer several types of pure savings accounts. Most prevalent among these is the *regular savings account,* a basic savings account paying a minimum rate of interest. There is no limit on how much interest a bank can pay on regular savings accounts, so it clearly pays to shop around. However, most of these accounts still pay low (2 to 4 percent) interest rates. Whereas to many savers, regular savings accounts are simply a convenient way of accumulating money, for many others, they are the only savings or investment vehicle.

Commercial banks typically differentiate between their *special savings accounts* on the basis of deposit minimums. For higher minimums they offer a slightly higher rate of interest (.25 to .5 percent) than on accounts requiring lower or no minimum balance. If the account holder does not maintain the required minimum balance, the interest is usually paid on the account as if it were an account requiring no minimum balance.

In addition to special savings accounts, many banks offer *club accounts.* These accounts are established for a special purpose, such as saving money for Christmas shopping. They act as a budgeting device for the customer by requiring specified weekly or monthly deposits toward the particular savings goal—for example, $500 for Christmas shopping. To help club members keep track of scheduled deposits, banks often issue a coupon book showing the date and amount of each transaction. Club accounts generally pay less interest than regular savings accounts, because the bank incurs additional administrative costs to establish and maintain them.

With the variety of products and services and range of fees offered by commercial banks, choosing a bank is no simple matter. Many variables have to be considered.

Savings and Loan Associations. **Savings and loan associations (S&Ls)** are found in most parts of the country. One type of S&L is a *mutual association,* in which the depositors actually own the institution and the returns they receive technically are called *dividends* rather than *interest.* (Note: In finance, the word *mutual* indicates a type of cooperative ownership arrangement.) Although these payments are called dividends, they are treated as interest for all practical purposes. The other type of S&L is *stockholder owned*: Depositors in this case actually do receive interest on their deposits instead of dividends.

Regardless of their organizational structure, savings and loans are important because they channel people's savings into mortgage loans for purchasing and improving homes. Since deregulation, S&Ls have greatly expanded their product and service offerings. Although they still cannot offer noninterest-paying checking accounts (demand deposits), they do offer many of the same checking, savings, and lending products and services as commercial banks—in fact, it is difficult to differentiate between the two institutions. Typically savings deposits at S&Ls earn about .25 to .5 percent more than those at commercial banks. The availability of products and services at numerous branch offices and their attractive rates of interest contribute to the popularity of savings and loan associations.

Savings Banks. **Savings banks** are a special type of savings institution, similar to savings and loan associations and found primarily in the New England states. In addition to offering a number of different interest-paying checking accounts, they accept a variety of savings deposits on which they pay interest at a rate on par with that paid by savings and loans. Because most savings banks are *mutuals,* depositors are their actual owners. The savings bank accepts deposits and, after deducting the expenses of doing business, distributes the profits to the owners in the form of dividend payments, which are technically equivalent to interest payments. However, instead of distributing all profits, the mutual savings bank typically distributes only enough to provide depositors with a stated return of, say, 3.5 percent. It then reinvests any remaining profits in order to provide greater protection for depositors.

Credit Unions. A **credit union** is a special type of mutual association that provides financial products and services to specific groups of people who belong to a common occupation, religious or fraternal order, or residential area. Credit unions are owned (and, in some cases, operated) by their members. Although credit unions are used by over 64 million people, they are quite small when compared to commercial banks or S&Ls. A person who qualifies for membership in a credit union may buy a share by making a minimum deposit—often $5 or less. One *must* be a member—that is, have money on deposit—in order to borrow from a credit union. Because the credit union is run to benefit its members, the rate of interest it pays on savings is normally .5 to 1.5 percent above that paid by other savings institutions. Being a mutual association in which the savers own shares, credit unions technically pay dividends rather than interest on savings.

Most credit unions, in addition to offering different types of interest-paying checking accounts—called **share draft accounts**—offer a variety of savings accounts to their members. Savers often do not know the dividend rate until the end of the savings period, because the dividends paid in each period depend on the credit union's earnings for that period. Because credit unions not only pay a favorable return on members' savings but also allow them to borrow money at advantageous rates, they are attractive to many people.

commercial bank A financial institution that offers checking and savings accounts and a full range of financial products and services, including several types of consumer loans. It's the only institution that can offer noninterest-paying checking accounts (demand deposits).

savings and loan association (S&L) A financial institution that channels the savings of its depositors primarily into mortgage loans for purchasing and improving homes. Due to deregulation, however, S&Ls now offer a competitive range of financial products and services.

savings bank A type of savings institution, similar to an S&L and found mainly in the New England states, that is most often a mutual association owned by its depositors.

credit union A depositor-owned mutual association that offers different types of interest-paying checking (share draft) accounts, savings accounts, and loans to its members.

share draft account An account offered by credit unions that is similar to interest-paying checking accounts offered by other financial institutions.

THE GROWING MENU OF CHECKING AND SAVINGS PRODUCTS

People basically hold cash and other forms of liquid assets, like checking and savings accounts, for the convenience they offer in (1) making purchases; (2) meeting normal, recurring living expense and purchase requirements; and (3) providing a safety net (or cushion) to meet unexpected expenses or take advantage of unanticipated opportunities. As mentioned before, deregulation has resulted in greater competition among financial institutions, who now offer a wide array of products to meet every liquid-asset need.

Trying to compare the products of different financial institutions can be confusing. The federal *Truth-in-Savings Act (TISA) of 1993* helps consumers evaluate the terms and costs of banking products. Commercial banks, savings institutions, and credit unions must fully and clearly disclose fees, interest rates, and terms of both checking and savings accounts. The Act places strict controls on bank advertising and what constitutes a "free" account; for example, banks cannot advertise free checking if there are minimum balance requirements or per-check charges. Banks must use a standard *annual percentage yield (APY)* formula that takes compounding (discussed later) into account when stating the interest paid on accounts. This makes it easier for consumers to compare each bank's offerings. The law also requires banks to pay interest on a customer's full daily or monthly average deposit balance. No longer can banks pay interest only on the lowest daily balance or avoid paying any interest if the account balance falls below the minimum balance for one day. In addition, banks must notify customers 30 days before lowering rates on deposit accounts or certificates of deposit.

Let's now take a brief look at various types of checking and savings accounts. We will look at other short-term investment vehicles later in this chapter.

Checking Accounts. A checking account held at a financial institution is basically a **demand deposit,** meaning that the withdrawal of these funds must be permitted whenever demanded by the account holder. You put money into your checking account by *depositing* funds; you withdraw it by *writing checks.* As long as you have sufficient funds in your account, the bank, when presented with a valid check, must immediately pay the amount indicated by charging your account for the amount of the check. Money held in checking accounts is liquid and therefore can easily be used to pay bills and make purchases.

Regular checking is the most common type of checking account. It pays no interest, and any service charges that exist can be waived if you maintain a minimum balance (usually about $750 to $1,000). Technically, noninterest-paying regular checking accounts can be offered only by commercial banks. S&Ls, savings banks, and credit unions also offer checking accounts, but these must pay interest and, as such, are known as *NOW accounts* or, in the case of credit unions, *share draft accounts.* Because checks are generally accepted in paying bills and purchasing goods and services, demand deposit balances are considered a common and important type of cash balance. An important benefit of demand deposits is that using checks to pay bills provides a convenient payment record.

Savings Accounts. A savings account is another type of liquid asset that may be kept in commercial banks, savings and loan associations, credit unions, and many other types of financial institutions. Savings deposits are referred to as **time deposits,** because they are expected to remain on deposit for a longer period of time than demand deposits. Because generally higher interest rates apply to savings deposits, savings accounts are typically preferable to checking accounts when the depositor's purpose is to accumulate money for a future expenditure or maintain balances for meeting unexpected expenditures. Most banks pay higher interest rates on larger savings account balances. For example, a bank might pay 2.50 percent on balances up to $2,500, 2.75 percent on balances between $2,500 and $10,000, and 3.00 percent on balances over $10,000.

While financial institutions generally retain the right to require a savings account holder to wait a certain number of days before receiving payment of a withdrawal, most are willing to pay withdrawals immediately. In addition to withdrawal policies and deposit insurance, the stated interest rate and method of calculating interest paid on savings accounts are important considerations in choosing the financial institution in which to place savings.

Interest-Paying Checking Accounts. As a result of changes that took place in the late 1970s and early 1980s, depositors now have far greater flexibility in choosing how to satisfy their checking and cash balance needs. Beginning with the highly successfully money market mutual funds (MMMFs), a variety of new financial products were introduced, including money market deposit accounts (MMDAs) and NOW accounts. These last two are available at virtually every deposit-taking financial institution in the United States and are marketed under various names (Checkmatic Accounts, PrimeChecking, Preferred Checking, Premium Accounts, and so on).

Money market mutual funds. Starting from zero in the mid-1970s, money market mutual funds grew to over $615 billion in deposits in late 1994, making them the most successful type of mutual fund ever offered. (Mutual funds are discussed in greater detail in Chapter 13.) A **money market mutual fund (MMMF)** pools the funds of many small investors and purchases high-return short-term marketable securities offered by the U.S. Treasury, major corporations, large commercial banks, and various government organizations. The portfolio of a typical MMMF contains specialized short-term securities that mature in as little as one day to as long as one year. The securities are all highly liquid and marketable forms of debt that are sold in denominations of at least $10,000 and often as much as $250,000 or more. Because of their lofty minimum denominations, few people are able to buy these securities directly: However, they can do so indirectly through the purchase of MMMFs, many of which require low minimum deposits of as little as $500 to $1,000. The interest rate earned on an MMMF depends on returns earned on its investments, which fluctuate with overall credit conditions. MMMFs generally pay interest at rates considerably above (3.5 to 5.5 percent) those paid on regular savings accounts, although when short-term interest rates are generally low, as was the case in 1992 and 1993, the gap between them narrows (1 to 2 percent). Moreover, investors have instant access to their funds through check-writing privileges, although the checks often must be written for a stipulated minimum amount (usually $500). These checks look and are treated like any other check drawn on a demand deposit account except that, as with any other interest-bearing checking account, *you continue to earn interest on your money while the checks make their way through the banking system.*

Money market deposit accounts. **Money market deposit accounts (MMDAs)** were introduced in December 1982 and became extremely popular with depositors almost at once. They were created as a way of giving banks and other depository institutions a vehicle that would compete for deposits with money market mutual funds. MMDAs are popular with some savers and investors due to their convenience and safety because the deposits, unlike those in money funds, are *federally insured.* Most banks require a minimum MMDA balance of $1,000 to $1,500. Depositors can use check-writing privileges or automatic teller machines to access those accounts. A limited number—usually six—of checks and transfers can be made without charge each month, but a fee is charged on additional withdrawals. Although this feature obviously reduces the flexibility of these accounts, most depositors, who apparently look upon MMDAs as savings rather than convenience accounts, do not consider it a serious obstacle. Moreover, MMDAs pay the highest rate of any bank account on which checks can be written.

demand deposit An account held at a financial institution from which funds can be withdrawn (in check or cash) upon demand by the account holder; same as a *checking account.*

time deposit A savings deposit at a financial institution; so-called because it is expected to remain on deposit for a longer period of time than a demand deposit.

money market mutual fund (MMMF) A mutual fund that pools the funds of many small investors and purchases high-return short-term marketable securities offered by the U.S. Treasury, major corporations, large commercial banks, and various government organizations.

money market deposit account (MMDA) A savings account, offered by banks and other depository institutions, that is meant to be competitive with a MMMF.

negotiable order of withdrawal (NOW) accounts A checking account on which the financial institution can pay whatever rate of interest it deems appropriate (see p. 150).

NOW accounts. **Negotiable order of withdrawal (NOW) accounts** are checking accounts on which the financial institution can pay whatever rate of interest it deems appropriate. They were introduced on a limited basis in 1972 and made available to all depository financial institutions in 1980. Since the deregulation of interest rates in January 1986, the NOW account has become widely accepted as an "interest-paying checking account." Today there is no legal minimum balance for a NOW, but many institutions impose their own requirement, often between $500 and $1,000. Some have no minimum, paying interest on any balance in the account. Many institutions pay interest at a higher rate for all balances over a specified amount, such as $2,500. The higher rates of interest, however, can be misleading. As we will see later in this chapter, one of the major problems in the growth of these interest-paying checking accounts has been a rise in monthly bank *charges* that often has virtually wiped out any interest earned on all but the highest account balances. NOW accounts should be viewed primarily as *checking accounts* that can also serve as potentially attractive savings vehicles. In this capacity, they allow individuals and families to earn interest on balances that must be kept for transaction purposes anyway and would otherwise lie idle.

Asset Management Accounts. The new financial marketplace has greatly increased the number of banking service providers. No longer are banks and savings institutions the only ones that can offer traditional banking services. Perhaps the best example of this is the **asset management account (AMA),** or *central asset account.* First introduced in 1977 by the Wall Street brokerage firm Merrill Lynch, the AMA is a comprehensive deposit account that combines checking, investing, and borrowing activities. These accounts are offered primarily by brokerage houses and mutual funds. AMAs appeal to many investors because they can consolidate most of their financial transactions at one institution and on one account statement.

The typical AMA account includes a MMDA with unlimited free checking, a Visa or MasterCard debit card, use of automated teller machines (ATMs), and loan and brokerage accounts. Annual fees and account charges (such as a per-transaction charge for ATM withdrawals) vary, so it pays to shop around. AMAs pay higher interest rates on checking account deposits than banks, and they have increased in popularity as more institutions have lowered minimum balance requirements to $5,000. Their distinguishing feature is that they automatically "sweep" excess balances—for example, those over $500—into a higher-return MMMF daily or weekly. When the account holder needs funds to purchase securities or cover checks written on the MMDA, the funds are transferred back to the MMDA. If the amount of securities purchased or checks presented for payment exceeds the account balance, the needed funds are supplied automatically through a loan.

While the AMA is an attractive alternative to a traditional bank account, they have some drawbacks. Compared to a bank, there are fewer "branch" locations. (However, AMAs are affiliated with ATM networks, making it easy to withdraw funds.) ATM transactions are more costly, checks can take longer to clear, and you may not be able to get some bank services like traveler's and certified checks. AMAs are not covered by deposit insurance, although these deposits are protected by the Securities Investor Protection Corporation (SIPC) and the firm's private insurance.

HOW SAFE IS YOUR MONEY?

The 1980s and early 1990s were tumultuous times in the banking industry. The large number of bank failures, in both the savings and loan and commercial banking industries, raised concern about the strength of the deposit insurance system, and many banks merged. As a result, today many depositors remain justifiably concerned about the safety of their deposits. Deposit insurance provides protection for deposits up to specified limits. In addition, consumers should evaluate the financial condition of a bank before opening an account there and monitor it on a regular basis.

Almost all commercial banks, S&Ls, savings banks, and credit unions are *federally insured* by U.S. government agencies. The few that are not are usually insured through either a state-charted or private insurance agency. Most experts believe that these so-called *privately insured* institutions have less protection against loss than do the federally insured ones. Exhibit 4.2 lists the insuring agencies and maximum insurance amounts provided under the various federal deposit insurance programs.

Deposit insurance protects the funds you have on deposit at banks and other depository

EXHIBIT 4.2

Federal Deposit Insurance Programs

If you have your checking and savings accounts at a federally insured institution, you are covered by at least $100,000 of insurance as provided by one of the following federal insurance agencies.

Savings Institution	Insuring Agency	Amount of Insurance
Commercial bank	Federal Deposit Insurance Corporation (FDIC) through the Bank Insurance Fund (BIF)	$100,000/depositor
Savings and loan association	Federal Deposit Insurance Corporation (FDIC) through the Savings Association Insurance Fund (SAIF)	$100,000/depositor
Savings bank	Federal Deposit Insurance Corporation (FDIC) through the BIF	$100,000/depositor
Credit union	National Credit Union Administration (NCUA) through the National Credit Union Share Insurance Fund (NCUSIF)	$100,000/depositor

institutions against institutional failure. In effect, the insuring agency stands behind the financial institution and guarantees the safety of your deposits up to a specified maximum amount ($100,000 per depositor in the case of federal insurance). Actually, the deposit insurance is provided to each depositor and *not* on the deposit account. Thus, both the checking and the savings accounts of each depositor are insured and, *as long as the maximum insurable amount is not exceeded*, the depositor can have any number of accounts and still be fully protected. Each account in the financial institution, or any of its branches, will be fully covered regardless of number or type. This is an important feature to keep in mind, because many people mistakenly believe that the maximum insurance applies to *each* of their accounts and *certificates of deposit (CDs),* which are deposits that earn higher interest rates than passbook accounts because the depositor agrees not to withdraw the funds for a specified period of time. Not so. For instance, an individual with a total of $125,000 in two deposit accounts and one CD at a single commercial bank—for instance, a NOW account with a $15,000 balance at one branch, a MMDA with a $60,000 balance at the main office, and a $50,000 CD—is covered by only $100,000 of deposit insurance. Of course, if either the MMDA or CD were transferred to another bank or financial institution, it would be insured for up to $100,000 and the total amount in all the accounts would then be fully protected.

Now that banks are offering a greater variety of products, including mutual funds, it is very important to remember that *only deposit accounts, including certificates of deposit, are covered by deposit insurance. Securities purchased through your bank are not subject to any form of deposit insurance.*

While $100,000 in deposit insurance is quite a bit, it is possible to increase the amount of coverage if the need arises. Specifically, depositors who carefully follow federal guidelines can increase their coverage by opening accounts in multiple depositor names at the same institution. A married couple, for example, can obtain $500,000 in coverage by setting up *individual* accounts in the name of each spouse (good for $200,000 in coverage), a *joint* account in both names (good for another $100,000), and *separate trust or self-directed retirement (IRA, Keogh, etc.)* accounts in the name of each spouse (good for an additional $200,000). Note that in this case each depositor is treated as

asset management account (AMA) A comprehensive deposit account, offered primarily by brokerage houses and mutual funds, that combines checking, investing, and borrowing activities and automatically sweeps excess funds into short-term investments and provides loans when shortages exist.

deposit insurance A type of insurance that protects funds on deposit against failure of the institution. Insuring agencies include the *Federal Deposit Insurance Corporation (FDIC)* and the *National Credit Union Administration (NCUA).*

a separate legal entity and as such receives full insurance coverage—the husband alone is considered one legal entity, the wife another, and the man and wife as a couple a third. In addition, the trust and self-directed retirement accounts are also viewed as legal entities. However, all self-directed retirement accounts at one institution are grouped together and covered up to a maximum of $100,000.

Concept Check

4-3. Discuss the effect that deregulation has had on financial markets and institutions.

4-4. Briefly describe the basic operations and services provided by each of the following traditional banking institutions: (a) commercial bank; (b) savings and loan association; (c) savings bank; and (d) credit union.

4-5. Define and discuss (a) demand deposits; (b) time deposits; (c) interest-paying checking accounts.

4-6. Distinguish between a regular savings account, special savings account, and a club account.

4-7. Briefly describe the key characteristics of each of the following forms of interest-paying checking account: (a) money market mutual fund (MMMF); (b) money market deposit account (MMDA); (c) NOW account.

4-8. Describe the features of an asset management account (AMA), its advantages, and its disadvantages.

4-9. What role does the FDIC play in insuring financial institutions? What other federal insurance program exists? Explain.

4-10. Would it be possible for an *individual* to have, say, six or seven checking and savings accounts at the same bank and still be fully protected under federal deposit insurance? Explain. Describe how it would be possible for a *married couple* to obtain as much as $500,000 in federal deposit insurance coverage without going to several banks.

ESTABLISHING A SAVINGS PROGRAM

LG 3
LG 4

To get the most from your savings program, it is important to develop sound savings habits and understand your savings options. Before reading on, spend a few moments describing your savings program and the savings options that you have chosen to include in it.

An estimated 75 percent of American households have some money put away in savings. Clearly, saving money is considered an important activity by many individuals and families. The act of saving is a deliberate, well-thought-out activity designed to preserve the value of money, insure liquidity, and earn a high rate of return. Almost by definition, *smart savers are smart investors.* They regard saving as more than putting loose change into a piggybank; rather, they recognize the importance of saving and know that savings must be managed as astutely as any security. After all, what we normally think of as "savings" is really a form of investment—a short-term, highly liquid, fixed-dollar investment that is subject to minimum risk. Establishing and maintaining an ongoing savings program is a vital element of personal financial planning. To get the most from your savings, however, you must understand your savings options and how different savings vehicles pay interest.

STARTING YOUR SAVINGS PROGRAM

Careful financial planning dictates that a portion of your assets be held for the purposes of meeting liquidity needs and accumulating wealth. While opinions differ as to how much should be held as liquid reserves, the general consensus is that an amount equal to three to six months' after-tax income is best for most families. This means that if you take home $1,500 a month, you should have between $4,500 and $9,000 in liquid reserves. If your employer has a strong salary continuation program covering extended periods of illness and/or you have a sizable line of credit available, the lower figure is probably suitable; if you lack one or both of these, however, the larger amount is probably more appropriate.

A specific savings plan is needed to accumulate funds. In this regard, saving should be considered as important as any other budget activity, rather than an event that occurs only when income happens to exceed expenditures. Some people do this by arranging to withhold savings directly from their paychecks. This has been a common practice for many years with U.S. savings bonds purchase plans and credit union deposits. Today it is also possible to have funds regularly transferred to other financial institutions such as commercial banks, savings and loans, savings banks, and even money market mutual funds. Not only do direct deposit arrangements help your savings effort, they also enable your funds to earn interest sooner. The key to success is to establish a *regular* pattern of savings. You should make it a practice to set aside an amount that you can comfortably afford *each month,* even if it is only $50 to $100. (Keep in mind that earning 4 percent interest, a series of $100 monthly deposits will grow to over $36,500 in 20 years.) The *Smart Money* box on page 154 suggests several super savings strategies you can use to achieve your savings goals.

You must also decide which savings products best meet your needs. Many savers prefer to keep their emergency funds in a regular savings or money market deposit account at an institution with federal deposit insurance. Although these accounts are safe, convenient, and highly liquid, they tend to pay relatively low rates of interest. Other important considerations include your risk preference, the length of time you can leave your money on deposit, and the level of current and expected interest rates. Suppose one year from now you plan to use $5,000 of your savings to make the down payment on a new car, and you believe that interest rates will drop during that period. You should lock in today's higher rate by purchasing a one-year CD. On the other hand, if you are unsure about when you will actually need the funds or believe that interest rates will rise, you are better off with a MMDA or MMMF because the rates they pay change with market conditions and they allow you to access your funds at any time without penalty.

Because short-term interest rates generally fluctuate more than long-term rates, it is important to monitor interest rate movements, shop around for the best rates, and place your funds in savings vehicles that are consistent with your needs. When short-term interest rates drop sharply, as they did in the late 1980s and early 1990s, you won't be able to reinvest the proceeds from maturing CDs at comparable rates. You will need to reevaluate your savings plans and may choose to move funds into other savings vehicles that pay higher rates of interest—but may also be more risky.

Many financial planning experts recommend keeping a minimum of 10 to 25 percent of your investment portfolio in savings-type instruments in addition to the three to six months' holding of liquid reserves noted above. Thus, someone with, say, $50,000 in investments should probably have a minimum of $5,000 to $10,000—and possibly even more—in such short-term vehicles as MMDAs, MMMFs, or CDs. Also, at times the amount invested in short-term vehicles could well exceed the recommended minimum and approach 50 percent or more of the portfolio. This generally depends on expected interest rate movements. If interest rates are relatively high and you expect them to fall, you would invest in long-term vehicles in order to lock in the attractive interest rates. On the other hand, if rates are relatively low and you expect them to rise, you might invest in short-term vehicles so that you can more quickly reinvest them when interest rates rise. Clearly, the amount held in savings accounts and short-term vehicles—both for the purpose of maintaining liquid reserves and as a part of an investment portfolio—can be substantial.

FINDING INTEREST EARNED ON YOUR MONEY

Interest earned is the reward for putting your money in a savings account or short-term investment vehicle. Because with such accounts or securities there really is no other source of return, it is important for you to understand how interest is earned. Unfortunately, even in the relatively simple world of savings, all interest rates are not created equal.

The Matter of Compounding. Basically, interest can be earned in one of two ways. First, some short-term investments are sold on a *discount basis.* This means that the security is sold for a price that is lower than its redemption value, the difference being the amount of interest earned. Treasury bills, for instance, are issued on a discount basis. Another

Smart Money

Super Savings Strategies

Everyone agrees that it's important to save money, but Americans are notoriously poor savers. Our average personal savings rate is only about 5 percent of after-tax income. Saving money does not mean going on a "financial diet" and giving up everything you love. You'd be surprised how little items can add up! Here are tips to get you started.

1. **Make saving a habit.** Each time you are paid, take ten percent—or a lower amount if that is unrealistic for you—and put it into your savings account. Do the same thing for bonuses, tax refunds, and any extra income you receive.
2. **Exercise "selective frugality."** Take a good look at your spending habits and decide which things you really could live without. Often we don't realize how little expenses add up. Take lunch to work twice a week and save upwards of ten dollars—that's $520 in a year. Comparison shop before buying, use coupons, and eat out less. But be sure to bank the savings before you spend them.
3. **Set up payroll deductions.** Payroll deductions deposited directly into your savings account or into U.S. savings bonds are a painless way to save, because you never see the money. But don't "rob the piggybank" by dipping into the savings account or cashing the savings bonds.
4. **Bank your raises.** The next time you get a raise, try not to increase your spending accordingly. Deposit the net amount of your raise into your savings rather than checking account, so you won't think of it as available funds.
5. **Increase your income.** Work overtime, take on a second job, or run a business out of your home. Deposit all the pay for this work directly into your savings account.
6. **Continue making car payments.** When your car is paid off, make your car payment to your savings account. In a few years, you'll have enough stashed away to pay cash for a new car.
7. **Don't be afraid to invest.** Leaving your money in an account that earns low or no interest can cost you potential income. Try a short-term investment, so you'll be ready to change if interest rates improve; look into "no-load" funds (without initial sales charges) such as: taxable money funds, tax-exempt money funds, U.S. Treasury issues, and tax-exempt short term bond funds.
8. **Seek help from the experts.** Work with a financial planner at tax time and when you make any major purchases or divestitures. Invest $1,000 in a mutual fund with the advice of a money manager. (Remember, though, that with mutual funds you should invest for the long term and ignore short-term fluctuations.)
9. **Reinvest interest and dividends.** If you own CDs, let compounding work for you and allow interest to accrue rather than having it paid to you monthly. Use the dividends from stocks or mutual funds to purchase extra shares of the stock or funds.
10. **Make retirement plans.** Set up a 401(k) plan, tax-sheltered annuity plan, or tax-deductible Individual Retirement Arrangement. You don't pay taxes on earnings until you withdraw funds, and you get a tax deduction for the money you contribute to the plan.
11. **Don't forget to reward yourself occasionally.** Money should be enjoyed as well as spent. When you reach a savings goal, give yourself a treat. Or spend the money you saved by using coupons to buy something special. That little boost will make saving money a little easier.

Sources: Tershia d'Elgin, "How to Save $100," *Price Club Journal,* March 1993, p. 5 and "How to Save $1,000," *Price Club Journal,* March 1993, p. 6; Ann Perry, "Selective Frugality: Author Offers Tips for a Pain-Free Savings Plan," *San Diego Union-Tribune,* February 21, 1994, pp. C1–C2; "12 Super Savings Strategies," *San Diego Union-Tribune,* February 21, 1994, p. C1.

way to earn interest on short-term investments is by *direct payment,* such as what occurs when interest is applied to a regular savings account. Although this is a simple process, determining the actual rate of return can involve several complications.

The first of these relates to the method used to arrive at the amount and rate of **compound interest** earned annually: You have probably read or seen advertisements by banks or other depository institutions touting the fact that they pay daily, rather than annual, interest. To understand what this means, consider the following example. Assume you invest $1,000 in a savings account advertised as paying annual **simple interest** at a rate of 5 percent. With simple interest, the interest is paid on only the initial amount of the deposit. This means that if the $1,000 is left on deposit for one year, you will earn $50 in interest, and the account balance will total $1,050 at the end of the year. Note that in this case the **nominal (stated) rate of interest** is the same as the effective rate. In contrast, the **effective rate of interest** is the annual rate of return *actually earned* on the transaction. It is found in the following manner:

$$\text{Effective rate of interest} = \frac{\text{Amount of interest earned during the year}}{\text{Amount of money invested or deposited}}$$

In our example, because $50 was earned during the year on an investment of $1,000, the effective rate is $50/$1,000 = 5%, which is the same as the nominal rate of interest. (Note that in the above formula it is interest earned during the *year* that matters; thus, if you wanted to calculate the effective rate of interest on an account that you had for six months, you would have to double the amount of interest earned.)

But suppose you can invest your funds elsewhere at a 5 percent rate, *compounded semi-annually*. Because interest is applied to your account at midyear, this means you will earn *interest on interest* for the last six months of the year, thereby increasing the total interest earned for the year. The actual dollar earnings are determined as follows:

$$\begin{aligned}\text{First 6 months' interest} &= \$1{,}000 \times 0.05 \times 6/12 = \$25.00\\ \text{Second 6 months' interest} &= \$1{,}025 \times 0.05 \times 6/12 = \underline{25.63}\\ \text{Total interest} &= \underline{\underline{\$50.63}}\end{aligned}$$

Interest is being generated on a larger investment in the second half of the year, because the amount of money on deposit has increased by the amount of interest earned in the first half year ($25). Although the nominal rate on this account is still 5 percent, the effective rate is 5.06 percent ($50.63/$1,000). As you may have guessed, the more frequently interest is compounded, the greater the effective rate for any given nominal rate. These relationships are shown for a sample of interest rates and compounding periods in Exhibit 4.3. Note, for example, that with a 7 percent nominal rate, daily compounding adds one-fourth of a percent to the size of the total return—not a trivial amount.

Compound Interest Equals Future Value. Compound interest is the same as the *future value* concept introduced in Chapter 2. You can use the procedures described there to find out how much an investment or deposit will grow over time at a compounded rate of interest. For example, using the future value formula and the future value factor from Appendix A, you can determine how much $1,000 will be worth in four years if it is deposited into a savings account that pays 5 percent interest per year compounded annually like this:

$$\begin{aligned}\text{Future value} &= \text{Amount deposited} \times \text{Future value factor}\\ &= \$1{,}000 \times 1.216\\ &= \underline{\underline{\$1{,}216}}\end{aligned}$$

You can use the same basic procedure to find the future value of an *annuity,* except that you would use the future value annuity factor from Appendix B. For instance, if you put $1,000 a year into a savings account that pays 5 percent per year compounded annually, in four years you will have

compound interest When interest earned in each subsequent period is determined by applying the nominal (stated) rate of interest to the sum of the initial deposit and the interest earned in each prior period.

simple interest Interest that is paid on only the initial amount of the deposit.

nominal (stated) rate of interest The promised rate of interest paid on a savings deposit or charged on a loan.

effective rate of interest The rate of interest that is actually earned (charged) over the period of time funds are held (borrowed).

EXHIBIT 4.3

Nominal and Effective Rates of Interest with Different Compounding Periods

The effective rate of interest you earn on a savings account will exceed the nominal (stated) rate of interest if interest is compounded more than once a year (as are most savings and interest-paying accounts).

Nominal Rate	Effective Rate				
	Annually	Semiannually	Quarterly	Monthly	Daily
3%	3.00%	3.02%	3.03%	3.04%	3.05%
4	4.00	4.04	4.06	4.07	4.08
5	5.00	5.06	5.09	5.12	5.13
6	6.00	6.09	6.14	6.17	6.18
7	7.00	7.12	7.19	7.23	7.25
8	8.00	8.16	8.24	8.30	8.33
9	9.00	9.20	9.31	9.38	9.42
10	10.00	10.25	10.38	10.47	10.52
11	11.00	11.30	11.46	11.57	11.62
12	12.00	12.36	12.55	12.68	12.74

$$\text{Future value} = \text{Amount deposited yearly} \times \text{Future value annuity factor}$$
$$= \$1{,}000 \times 4.310$$
$$= \underline{\underline{\$4{,}310}}$$

How Much Interest Will You Earn? Before you open a deposit account, you should investigate several factors that determine the amount of interest you earn on your savings or interest-bearing checking account: frequency of compounding (discussed in the previous section), how the bank determines the balance on which interest is paid, and the interest rate paid. The more often interest is compounded, the higher your return. So look for a bank that uses daily or continuous (the most frequent compounding case) compounding. With regard to balances that qualify to earn interest, most banks now use the *actual balance,* or *day of deposit to day of withdrawal,* method. (Prior to the passage of the Truth-in-Savings Act in 1993, banks were able to pay interest on the lowest balance in the account during the payment period. This practice is no longer permitted.) The actual balance method is the most accurate and fairest, because it gives depositors both the highest interest earnings on their money and full credit for all funds on deposit.

As mentioned earlier, the Truth-in-Savings Act also standardized the way banks calculate the rate of interest they pay on deposit accounts. This makes it easy to compare each bank's *annual percentage yield (APY)* and to choose the bank offering the highest APY.

A VARIETY OF WAYS TO SAVE

Over the past decade or so, there has been a tremendous proliferation of savings and short-term investment vehicles, particularly for the individual of modest means. Savings and investing in short-term securities is no longer the easy task it once was, when the decision for most people boiled down to whether funds should be placed in a regular savings account or in Series E bonds. Today, investors can choose from savings accounts, NOW accounts, money market mutual funds and deposit accounts, certificates of deposit, Treasury bills, Series EE bonds, and asset management accounts. We examined several of these savings vehicles earlier in this chapter, including savings accounts, MMMFs, MMDAs, NOW accounts, and asset management accounts; accordingly, our attention here will center on the three remaining types of deposits and securities.

Certificates of Deposit. **Certificates of deposit (CDs)** differ from the savings instruments discussed earlier in this chapter in that CD funds must remain on deposit for a specified period of time, which can range from seven days to as long as seven or more years. Although it is possible to withdraw funds prior to maturity, an interest penalty usually makes withdrawal somewhat costly. While the bank or other depository institution is free to charge whatever penalty it likes, most result in a severely reduced rate of interest—typically a rate no greater than that paid on its most basic regular savings account. Since October of 1983, banks, S&Ls, and other depository institutions have been free to offer any rate and maturity CD they wish. As a result, today a wide variety of CDs are offered by most banks and depository institutions, though as a rule, most pay higher rates for larger deposits and longer periods of time. CDs are convenient to buy and hold because they offer attractive and highly competitive yields plus federal deposit insurance protection.

In addition to purchasing CDs directly from the issuer, they can be purchased from stockbrokers. **Brokered CDs** are simply certificates of deposit sold by stockbrokers. The brokerage house searches for the best deal (highest yield) it can get, and then sells these CDs to its customers. In essence, a bank or S&L issues the CDs, and the brokerage house merely sells (or places) them with the investing public. The minimum denomination is usually only $1,000, so they are affordable, and there's no commission to pay because the broker earns its commissions from the issuing bank or S&L. Brokered CDs are attractive for two reasons: First, you can sell them prior to maturity without a penalty, because the brokerage firms maintain active secondary markets; therefore, you can improve your liquidity. But remember, there are no guarantees here. The market always prevails, so if rates go up, the relative value of your CD falls and you don't earn the rate you started with. Second, you may be able to get higher yields—about .25 to .75 of a percent more—from brokered CDs than from your local bank. But be careful. The broker can always get higher yields by selling CDs issued by troubled financial institutions. Therefore, *buy a brokered CD issued only by a federally insured institution*—ask your broker, just to be sure.

U.S. Treasury Bills. The **U.S. Treasury bill (T-bill)** is considered the ultimate safe haven for savings and investments. T-bills are obligations of the U.S. Treasury issued as part of its ongoing process of funding the national debt. They are sold on a discount basis in minimum denominations of $10,000 followed by increments of $1,000 and are issued with three-month (13-week), six-month (26-week), and one-year maturities. The one- and six-month bills are auctioned off every Monday and one-year bills roughly every four weeks. They are backed by the full faith and credit of the U.S. government and pay an attractive and safe return that is free from state and local income taxes.

T-bills are almost as liquid as cash, because they can be sold at any time (in a very active secondary market) without any interest penalty. However, should you have to sell before maturity, you may lose some money on your investment if interest rates have risen, and you will have to pay a broker's fee as well. Treasury bills pay interest on a *discount basis* and as such are different from other savings or short-term investment vehicles—that is, their interest is equal to the difference between the purchase price paid and the worth at maturity. For example, if you paid $9,800 for a bill that will be worth $10,000 at maturity, you will earn $200 in interest ($10,000 − $9,800).

An individual investor may purchase T-bills directly through participation in the weekly Treasury auctions or indirectly through a commercial bank or a security dealer who buys bills for investors on a commission basis. Outstanding Treasury bills can also be purchased in the secondary market through banks or dealers. The biggest advantage to this approach is that the investor has a much wider selection of maturities from which to choose, ranging from less than a week to as long as a year.

It is relatively simple to buy T-bills directly. To participate in the weekly auction, all you need to do is submit a "tender" to the nearest Federal

certificate of deposit (CD) A type of savings instrument that is issued by certain financial institutions in exchange for a deposit; typically requires a minimum deposit and has a maturity ranging from seven days to as long as seven or more years.

brokered CD A certificate of deposit, typically with a $1,000 minimum denomination, that can be purchased with no commissions from a stockbroker and can be sold without penalty prior to maturity.

U.S. Treasury bill (T-bill) A short-term (three-month to one-year maturity) debt instrument issued by the U.S. Treasury in the ongoing process of funding the national debt.

Reserve Bank or branch specifying both the amount and maturity desired (tender forms are easy to fill out and readily available from commercial banks). The Treasury tries to accommodate individual investors through its *noncompetitive* bidding system, which most individual investors use because of its simplicity. In essence, all noncompetitive tender offers are awarded T-bills at a price equal to the average of all the accepted competitive bids. Thus, the investor is assured of being able to buy bills in the quantity desired while obtaining the benefit of an open auction system—and without going through the hassle of a competitive bid. On the downside, T-bills purchased through the noncompetitive bidding system are meant to be held to maturity and therefore lack the liquidity of bills that are acquired competitively.

Series EE Bonds. **Series EE bonds** are the well-known savings bonds that were first issued in 1941 and formerly called Series E bonds. They are often purchased through payroll deduction plans. Though issued by the U.S. Treasury, they are quite different from T-bills. In fact, perhaps their only similarity is that they are sold on a discount basis and are also free of state and local income taxes. These bonds are *accrual-type securities,* which means that interest is paid when they are cashed on or before maturity, rather than periodically over their lives. The government does make Series HH bonds available through the exchange of Series E or Series EE bonds; they have a ten-year maturity and are available in denominations of $500 to $10,000. Unlike EE bonds, HH bonds are issued at their full face value and pay interest semiannually at the current fixed rate of 4 percent.

Series EE bonds are backed by the full faith and credit of the U.S. government and can be replaced without charge in case of loss, theft, or destruction. They can be purchased at banks or other depository institutions, or through payroll deduction plans. Issued in denominations from $50 through $10,000, their purchase price is a uniform 50 percent of the face amount (thus, a $100 bond will cost $50 and be worth $100 at maturity).

The actual maturity date on EE bonds is unspecified, because the issues pay a variable rate of interest. The higher the rate of interest being earned, the shorter the period of time it takes for the bond to accrue from its discounted purchase price to its maturity value. As of May 1, 1995, there are new rules for saving bonds. All EE bonds held six months to five years—bonds can be redeemed any time after the first six months—earn interest at 85 percent of the average return on six-month Treasury bills. After five years, the rate of interest is 85 percent of the average return on five-year Treasury notes. Interest rates are calculated every six months in May and November and change in accordance with prevailing Treasury security returns. Current rates on Series EE bonds can be obtained from your bank or simply by calling 1-800-487-2663. (Note: For bonds purchased after May 1, 1995, the rates for the six-month period ending October 31,1995 were as follows: bonds held less than five years, 5.25 percent; bonds held five through 17 years, 6.31 percent. The long-term rate is quoted for reference only, because no bonds currently fall into this category.) Interest is credited every six months.

In addition to being exempt from state and local taxes, Series EE bonds provide their holders with an appealing tax twist: *Savers need not report interest earned on their federal tax returns until the bonds are redeemed.* Although interest can be reported annually (for example, when the bonds are held in the name of a child who has limited interest income), most investors choose to defer it. In effect, this means the funds are being reinvested at an after-tax rate equal to the bond's current rate.

A second attractive tax feature allows partial or complete tax avoidance of EE bond earnings when proceeds are used to pay educational expenses, such as college tuition, for the bond purchaser, a spouse, or other IRS-defined dependent. To qualify, the purchaser must be age 24 or older and as of 1994, have adjusted gross income below $56,200 for single filers and $91,850 for married couples. (These maximum income levels are adjusted annually.)

Concept Check

4-11. In general, how much of your annual income should you save in the form of liquid reserves? What portion of your investment portfolio should you keep in savings and other short-term investment vehicles? Explain.

4-12. Define and distinguish between the nominal rate of interest and the effective rate of interest. Explain why a savings and loan association that pays a nominal rate of 4.5 percent interest, compounded daily, on its savings accounts actually pays an effective rate of 4.6 percent.

4-13. What factors determine the amount of interest you will earn on a deposit account? Which combination provides the best return?

4-14. Briefly describe the basic features of each of the following savings vehicles: (a) certificates of deposit; (b) U.S. Treasury bills; and (c) Series EE bonds.

MAINTAINING A CHECKING ACCOUNT

FPPC

LG 5

Maintaining a checking account is both a safe way to hold money and a convenient way to pay for the goods and services consumed in everyday life. How frequently and for what purposes can you use a checking account? Spend a few moments answering this question before reading on.

Checking account balances are an important component of the money supply. They are a near-perfect substitute for cash and today are viewed by most people as absolutely essential. Checking accounts not only provide a safe and convenient way to hold money but also streamline point-of-sale purchases, debt payments, and other basic transactions. In one form or another (regular or interest-paying checking accounts), they can be maintained at commercial banks, S&Ls, savings banks, credit unions, and even at brokerage houses through asset management accounts. For convenience, we will focus our attention on commercial bank checking accounts, although our discussion applies to checking accounts maintained at other types of financial institutions as well.

OPENING AND USING YOUR CHECKING ACCOUNT

The factors that typically influence the choice of where to maintain a checking account are convenience, services provided, and cost. Many people choose a bank solely on the basis of such convenience factors as business hours, location, number of drive-in windows, and/or number and location of branch offices and automated teller machines (ATMs). Ease of access is obviously an important consideration because most people prefer to bank near their homes or places of employment. Services provided differ from bank to bank. Depending on their size, banks may rent safe-deposit boxes, provide for direct deposits and withdrawals, make loans, offer financial planning, and provide various types of bank card and check-cashing services.

Once you determine the banking services you need, you should evaluate the offerings of conveniently located financial institutions. In addition to convenience and availability of services, you should consider safety (deposit insurance and financial condition), interest rates, types of accounts (including special accounts that combine features such as credit cards, free checks, and reduced fees), structure and level of fees and charges, and quality of customer service. In today's competitive banking environment using the tips in the *Issues in Money Management* box on page 160 to investigate several banks can help you obtain the best services at minimum cost.

The Cost of a Checking Account. Free checking used to be fairly common but is not so today. One of the by-products of deregulation and the growth of interest-paying checking accounts has been a sharp increase in bank service charges. Today it is estimated that few, if any, banks and other depository institutions let you write as many checks as you wish free of charge. The rest levy monthly and/or per-check fees when your balance drops below a stipulated minimum, and some charge you for checking no matter how large a balance you carry in your account.

Usually you must maintain a minimum balance of $500 to $1,000 or more in order to avoid a service charge. While some banks use the *average* monthly balance in an account to determine whether to charge, the vast majority use the *daily* balance procedure. This means that if your account should happen to fall below the minimum balance just once during the month, you will be hit with the full service charge even if you keep an average

Series EE bond A savings bond issued in various denominations by the U.S. Treasury.

Issues in Money Management

Getting the Best Deal from Your Bank

Outraged by rising bank fees? That's not surprising; recently, they've risen faster than inflation. In fact, there is no limit on how often or how high banks can raise charges, and they can bill you for any services they choose. For instance, you may be charged when you deposit a check that's returned for insufficient funds, for using an ATM card, and sometimes even for not using an ATM card often enough. Because automated transactions are much more cost-effective, many banks now charge their customers if they use tellers or talk to customer representatives on the phone more than a few times a month.

How, then, should you go about finding a bank that will give you the conveniences you want with the fewest charges? Your first step should be to evaluate what services you actually need. Go back over account statements for several months, counting ATM transactions and looking for surcharges. If your bank balance fluctuates dramatically, you should look for an institution that uses a monthly average minimum, rather than charging you if your balance drops under its requirement for just one day. If you don't write many checks per month, look for a basic checking account, because the monthly fees are low.

Once you know your service needs, compare the rates, fees, minimum balances, and other conditions offered by several financial institutions. Look for an account with a high annual return, a low minimum balance, and perquisites such as free ATM services. If you may need to borrow money, find out whether your bank will give you a break on a mortgage or other loan.

Many banks now offer incentives for "relationship," or linked, accounts, so consider moving your checking, savings, and money market accounts to the same institution. If you have a certain minimum balance in your combined accounts, some banks will pay you a higher rate on a savings account or a CD. You may also qualify for a credit card with a reduced or no fee, or a low interest rate on the unpaid balance. Make sure your bank offers you the convenience of a single monthly statement that integrates all your account data, including the current value of CDs and mutual funds.

If the bank offers bank-by-phone privileges, clarify the kind of service and the fees. Some banks only provide an account balance or let you move money from a checking to a savings account. Others let you pay bills by calling in the information to the bank, which then sets up a transfer payment. Be forewarned: banks often charge a steep price for these services.

Don't forget to include a credit union in your search, because many offer free checking with low or no balance restrictions. Membership is restricted by affiliation, so you must find out if you are eligible.

One thing to remember is that if you are unhappy with a charge, say something to a bank representative. In today's competitive world, banks are eager for your business. If a valued customer complains about a $20-dollar bounced check fee, a bank will often drop the fee rather than risk losing the customer. You may be able to negotiate a better deal on your credit card rates and annual fees and get higher CD rates by bringing a competitor's rate to your bank's attention.

Last but not least, get the terms of your account agreements in writing.

Sources: Ellen Braitman, "Ten Things Your Banker Won't Tell You," *Smart Money*, August 1994, pp. 63–70; Helen Bond, "Three Steps to Lower Banking Charges," *Dallas Life*, August 7, 1994, p. 27; Vanessa O'Connell, "When It Pays to Wrestle with Your Banker," *Money*, September 1994, pp. 80–82; "10 Questions to Ask Your Bank," *Smart Money*, April 1993, p. 93.

balance that is three times the stipulated minimum. Let your balance fall $1 below the minimum on just one day out of the month, and you'll pay. Further, the amount of service charge you will pay will be quite substantial. If the daily balance falls below the minimum, you can expect to get hit in two ways: (1) with a base service charge of, say, $5.00 a month, and (2) with additional charges of, say, 25 cents for each check you write and 10 cents for each automatic funds transfer you make with your ATM card or bank-by-phone service. Using these fees as an illustration, assume you write 20 checks and make 7 ATM transfers in a given month. If your balance falls below the minimum, you will have to pay a service charge of \$5.00 + (20 × \$.25) + (7 × \$.10) = \$10.70.

In addition to the service charges levied on checking accounts, banks have increased most other check-related charges and raised the minimum balances required for free checking and waivers of specified fees. The charge on a returned check can be as high as \$15 to \$20, and stop payment orders typically cost \$10 to \$15. Some banks charge fees for ATM transactions, point-of-sale transactions made with an ATM card, or more than a specified number of bank-by-phone transactions. Most also charge for using the ATM of another bank that is a member of the same network.

The minimum balance and fee structure vary from bank to bank. Further, the service charges on regular checking accounts may be much less than on NOW accounts. Thus, if you intend to keep only a small amount in your checking account, you may be better off with a no-frills, regular checking account. All too often individuals find that the service charges they pay on their NOW accounts far exceed any interest they earn and that the net result is a very costly form of checking. It is not surprising, therefore, that many smart consumers today are using cost as the single most important variable in choosing where to set up a checking account.

Individual or Joint Account. Two people wishing to open a checking account may do so in one of three ways: (1) They can each open individual checking accounts (on which the other cannot write checks); (2) they can open a joint account that requires both signatures on all checks; or (3) they can open a joint account that allows either one to write checks (the most common type of joint account). One advantage of the joint account over two individual accounts is that it lowers the service charges. In addition, the account has rights of survivorship, which, in the case of a married couple, means that if one spouse dies, the surviving spouse, after fulfilling a specified legal requirement, can draw checks on the account. (If account owners are treated as tenants in common rather than having rights of survivorship, the survivor gets only his or her share of the account. Thus, when opening a joint account it is important to specify the rights preferred.) It is impossible to say what type of arrangement will be successful for a given couple. One financial expert recommends that couples experiment with different arrangements until they find the one most comfortable for them.

General Checking Account Procedures. Once you open a checking account, you should follow certain basic procedures. Always write checks in ink and include the name of the person being paid, the date, and the amount of the check—written in both numerals and words for accuracy. If these amounts don't agree, the *written* amount rather than the numbers is considered legally correct. The check should be signed the same as the signature card you filled out when you opened the account; otherwise, the bank may not accept it. It is also a good idea to note the check's purpose directly on the check—usually on the line provided in the lower left corner. This information is very helpful for both budgeting and tax purposes.

All checking account transactions—checks written, deposits, automated teller machine (ATM) transactions, point-of-sale debit purchases, and preauthorized automatic payments and deposits—should be entered in the **checkbook ledger** provided with your supply of checks. Then subtract the amount of each check, ATM cash withdrawal, purchase, or payment and add the amount of each deposit to the previous balance to keep track of your current account balance. Good transaction records and an accurate balance prevent overdrawing the account.

A deposit slip listing the currency, coins, and checks being deposited should accompany each deposit. These are generally included with your checks and are also available at your bank. Checks are listed by the *transit I.D. number* printed on the check, usually at the top right. You should also properly endorse all checks. Federal regulations require your endorsement to be made in black or blue ink, within 1½ inches of the check's trailing edge (left end of the check when viewed from the front) so as not to interfere with endorsements from the bank at which the check is deposited. (If you don't comply, you'll still get your money, but it may take longer.)

To protect against possible loss of endorsed checks, it is common practice to use a special endorsement, such as "Pay to the order of XYZ Bank," or a restrictive endorsement, such as "For

checkbook ledger A ledger, provided with a supply of checks, used to maintain accurate records of all checking account transactions.

deposit only." If the way your name is written on the check differs from the way you signed the signature card, you should sign your correct signature below your endorsement. In order to further ensure that the deposit is properly entered into your account, write your account number below your endorsement.

You can make deposits in several ways: at the bank during normal banking hours; at a remote banking facility, such as a drive-in window; at an **automated teller machine (ATM),** a type of remote computer terminal at which transactions can be made 24 hours a day, 7 days a week; in the bank's **night depository,** a protected type of mail slot on the exterior of the bank, in the special envelopes banks usually provide for after-hours deposits; or by mail in the self-addressed, sometimes postage-paid deposit envelopes often provided for this purpose. The use of ATMs, night depositories, and banking by mail is not advised when cash is being deposited because of the risk of an unaccountable loss.

When checks are deposited, a delay in funds availability may result due to the time required for them to clear. To avoid overdrawing your account, you should know your bank's "hold" policy on deposits. In 1988, the government established maximum funds availability delays on deposits. It generally takes between one and five business days for funds to become available. For example, on a check drawn on another local bank, funds must be made available no later than the second business day after deposit. An out-of-town check, however, may take up to five business days to clear. Longer holds—up to nine business days—can be applied by banks under special circumstances, such as when more than $5,000 is deposited into a given account in one day or when the depositor has repeatedly overdrawn his or her account within the immediately preceding six months.

Overdrafts. When a check is written for an amount greater than the current account balance, the result is an **overdraft.** Poor bookkeeping on the part of the account holder or a delay in the bank's receipt of a deposit can be the cause. If the overdraft is proven to have been intentional, the bank can initiate legal proceedings against the account holder. The action taken by a bank on an overdraft depends on the amount involved and the strength of its relationship with the account holder. In many cases, the bank stamps the overdrawn check with the words "insufficient balance (or funds)" and returns it to the party to whom it was written. This is often called a "bounced check." The account holder is notified of this action, and a penalty fee of $7 to $20 or more is deducted from his or her checking account. In addition, the depositor of a "bad check" may be charged as much as $10 to $15 by its bank, which explains why merchants typically charge customers who've given them bad checks $10 to $20 or more and often refuse to accept future checks from them.

When a strong relationship has been established between the account holder and the bank or arrangements have been made for **overdraft protection,** the bank will pay a check that overdraws the account. In cases where overdraft protection has not been prearranged but the bank pays the check, the account holder is usually notified by the bank and charged a penalty fee for the inconvenience. However, the check does not bounce, and the check writer's creditworthiness is not damaged.

There are several ways to arrange overdraft protection. Many banks offer an *overdraft line of credit,* which automatically extends a loan to cover the amount of overdrafts. In most cases, however, the loans are made only in specified increments, such as $50 or $100, and interest (or a fee) is levied against the loan amount, *not* the actual amount of the overdraft. This can be an expensive form of protection, particularly if you do not promptly pay such a loan. For example, if you had a $110 overdraft and the bank made overdraft loans in $100 increments, it would automatically deposit $200 in your account. If the bank charged 12 percent annually (or 1 percent per month) and you repaid the loan within a month, you would incur total interest of $2 [($200 × 12%)/12]. But remember you paid interest on $90 ($200 − $110) you didn't need; the annualized rate of interest on this overdraft loan is *21.8 percent* [($2/$110) × 12]. Another way to cover overdrafts is with an *automatic transfer program,* which automatically transfers funds from your savings to checking account in the event of an overdraft. Under this program, some banks charge both an annual fee and a fee on each transfer. Of course, the best form of overdraft protection is to employ good cash management techniques and regularly balance your checking account.

Stopping Payment. Occasionally it is necessary to **stop payment** on a check that has been issued because (1) checks or a checkbook are either lost or stolen; (2) a good or service paid for by check is found to be faulty (Note: Some states prohibit you from stopping payment on faulty goods or services); or (3) a check is issued as part of a contract that is not carried out. Payment on a check is stopped by notifying the bank. Normally the account holder must fill out a form indicating the check number and date, amount, and the name of the person to whom it was written. Sometimes stop-payment orders can be initiated by telephone, in which case a written follow-up is normally required. Telephone-initiated stop payments generally remain in effect for fourteen days and written ones for six months.

Once a stop-payment order has been issued, the bank tellers are told to refuse payment on the affected check. At the same time, the stop-payment information is placed in the bank's data processing system so that the check will be rejected if it is presented by another bank in the check-clearing process. Most banks require account holders who wish to stop payment to sign a statement relieving the bank of any liability if payment is erroneously made on the check in question. A fee ranging from $10 to $15 is usually charged to stop payment on a check.

MONTHLY STATEMENTS

Once each month, your bank will provide a statement that contains an itemized listing of all transactions (checks written, ATM transactions, debit purchases, automatic payments, and deposits made) within your checking account; also included are any service charges levied and interest earned, such as James Morrison's May 1995 bank statement shown in Exhibit 4.4. Many banks include canceled checks and deposit slips with the bank statement, although they are slowly (but surely) moving away from this practice. Of course, banks that do not return canceled checks and deposit slips will provide photocopies of them upon request, generally for a fee. You can use your monthly statement to verify the accuracy of your account records and to reconcile differences between the statement balance and the balance shown in your checkbook ledger. The monthly statement is also an important source of information for your tax records.

Account Reconciliation. You should reconcile your bank account as soon as possible after you receive your monthly statement. The **account reconciliation** process (or *balancing the checkbook,* as the process is also known) can uncover errors in recording checks or deposits, in addition or subtraction, and, occasionally, in the bank's processing of the checks. It can also help you avoid overdrafts, because it forces you to periodically verify your account balance. Discrepancies between the account balance reflected in your checkbook ledger and that shown in the bank statement can be attributed to one of four basic factors, assuming neither you nor the bank has made any errors.

1. Checks that you have written, ATM withdrawals, or other automatic payments subtracted from your checkbook balance have not yet been received and deducted by your bank and therefore remain outstanding.
2. Deposits that you have made and added to your checkbook balance have not yet been credited to your account.
3. Any service (activity) charges levied on your account by the bank have not yet been deducted from your checkbook balance.
4. Interest earned on your account (if it is a NOW or MMDA account) has not yet been added to your checkbook balance.

automated teller machine (ATM) A type of remote computer terminal at which customers of a bank or other depository institution can make basic transactions 24 hours a day, 7 days a week.

night depository A protected type of mail slot on the exterior of a financial institution that its customers can use to make after-hours deposits.

overdraft The result of writing a check for an amount greater than the current account balance.

overdraft protection An arrangement between the account holder and the depository institution wherein the institution automatically pays a check that overdraws the account.

stop payment An order made by an account holder asking the depository institution to refuse payment on an already issued check.

account reconciliation The process of verifying the accuracy of one's checking account records in light of the bank's records reflected in the monthly statement, which contains an itemized listing of all transactions within the checking account.

EXHIBIT 4.4

A Checking Account Statement

Each month you receive a statement from your bank or depository financial institution that summarizes the month's transactions and shows your latest account balance. Similar statements are also sent for savings accounts and interest-paying checking accounts such as NOWs and MMDAs. This sample statement not only shows the checks that have been paid but also lists all ATM transactions, point-of-sale transactions using the ATM card (the Interlink payments at Lucky Stores), and direct payroll deposits.

YOUR BANK #240
P.O. BOX 516 ANY CITY, USA 90000-0000

JAMES C. MORRISON
1765 SHERIDAN DRIVE
YOUR CITY, STATE 12091

N
21

CALL (800) 222-0000
24 HOURS/DAY, 7 DAYS/WEEK
FOR ASSISTANCE WITH
YOUR ACCOUNT.

PAGE 1 OF 1 THIS STATEMENT COVERS: 4/30/95 THROUGH 5/29/95

PREMIUM ACCOUNT

0123-45678

SUMMARY

PREVIOUS BALANCE	473.68	MINIMUM BALANCE	21.78
DEPOSITS	1,302.83+		
WITHDRAWALS	1,689.02-		
SERVICE CHARGES	7.50-		
DIRECT DEPOSIT DISCOUNT	1.00+		
NEW BALANCE	80.99		

CHECKS AND WITHDRAWALS

CHECK	DATE PAID	AMOUNT	CHECK	DATE PAID	AMOUNT
203	5/01	10.00	213	5/08	40.00
204	4/30	15.00	214	5/09	9.58
205	5/10	635.00	215	5/20	66.18
206	5/08	25.00	216	5/20	64.92
207	5/07	19.00	217	5/21	25.03
208	5/07	50.00	218	5/21	37.98
209	5/08	15.00	219	5/22	35.00
210	5/10	83.00	220	5/22	105.00
211	5/10	10.00	222*	5/22	100.00
212	5/08	70.00	223	5/21	40.00
			224	5/29	40.82

PREMIUM ACCOUNT FEE LESS $1.00 DISCOUNT	4/30	6.50

ATM TRANSACTIONS

INTERLINK PURCHASE #572921 ON 04/30 AT LUCKY STORE NO 043	5/01	50.00
WITHDRAWAL #08108 AT 00165A ON 05/04	5/06	20.00
INTERLINK PURCHASE #807409 ON 05/11 AT LUCKY STORE NO 056	5/13	12.51
WITHDRAWAL #01015 AT 00240C ON 05/17	5/17	20.00
WITHDRAWAL #04792 AT 00167C ON 05/20	5/20	20.00
WITHDRAWAL #04386 AT 00240D ON 05/21	5/21	40.00
INTERLINK PURCHASE #880318 ON 05/28 AT LUCKY STORE #043	5/29	30.00

DEPOSITS

	DATE POSTED	AMOUNT
AVS RNT CAR SYST PAYROLL G2 000000035382	5/03	618.69
AVS RNT CAR SYST PAYROLL G2 000000035382	5/17	83.39
AVS RNT CAR SYST PAYROLL G2 000000035382	5/17	600.75

ATM LOCATIONS USED

00165A: 249 PRIMROSE RD, ANY CITY, USA
00240C: 490 BROADWAY, ANY CITY, USA
00167C: 1145 BROADWAY, ANY CITY, USA
00240D: 490 BROADWAY, ANY CITY, USA

Take the following steps to reconcile your account:

1. Upon receipt of your bank statement, arrange all canceled checks in ascending numerical order based on their sequence numbers or issuance dates. (Note: Skip this step if your bank does not return canceled checks.)
2. Compare each check with the corresponding entry in your checkbook ledger to make sure no recording errors exist. (Note: If your bank does not return canceled checks, compare the bank statement information for each check with the corresponding entry in your checkbook ledger.) Place a checkmark in your ledger alongside each entry compared. Also, check off any other withdrawals, such as from ATMs, point-of-sale debit transactions, or automatic payments.
3. List the checks and other deductions (ATM withdrawals) still *outstanding*—that is, those deducted in your checkbook but not returned with your bank statement (see step 2). Total their amount.
4. Compare the deposit slips returned with the statement to deposits shown in your checkbook. Total the amount of deposits still *outstanding*—that is, those shown in your checkbook ledger but not yet received by the bank. Be sure to include all automatic deposits and deposits made at ATMs in your calculations.
5. *Subtract* the total amount of checks outstanding (from step 3) from your bank statement balance, and *add* to this balance the amount of outstanding deposits (from step 4). The resulting amount is your *adjusted bank balance.*
6. Deduct the amount of any bank service charges from, and add any interest earned to, your checkbook ledger balance. Make sure you include all service charges for the period, including those for returned checks, stop payments, and/or new checks ordered. The resulting amount is your *new checkbook balance.* This amount should equal your *adjusted bank balance* (from step 5). If it does not, you should check all addition and subtraction in your checkbook ledger, because you have probably made an error.

The reverse side of your bank statement usually provides a form for reconciling your account along with step-by-step instructions. Although a number of different approaches to reconciliation exist, the one described here is the most straightforward. Worksheet 4.1 includes an account reconciliation form, following these procedures, that was completed by James Morrison for the month of May 1995. The form can be used to reconcile regular checking accounts or any type of interest-paying checking account (like NOWs or MMDAs).

Tax Records. Your monthly bank statement is an important tax record. It can be reviewed along with your checkbook ledger to evaluate past income and expenditures. Although you may maintain accurate records of these items as part of your budgeting process, the statement can be used to provide proof of payment, which you might need if the Internal Revenue Service decides to audit your tax return. At the time a check is written, it is advisable to indicate its purpose both in the checkbook ledger and on the front of the check. Bank statements should be retained for a period of at least five years, because an audit can still be conducted several years after a tax return has been filed.

SPECIAL TYPES OF CHECKS

Because there is no way to be absolutely sure that a check is good, some type of verification is often necessary. This is common for large purchases or when the buyer's bank is not located in the area in which the purchase is being made. The most common instruments used to guarantee payment are *cashier's checks, traveler's checks,* and *certified checks.*

Cashier's Check. Anyone can buy a **cashier's check** from a bank. These checks are often used by people who do not have checking accounts. They can be purchased for about $5 and are occasionally issued at no charge to bank customers. In exchange for the amount of the check plus a service charge, the bank issues a check drawn on itself. In this way, the *bank* is now writing the check, *not* you—which is about the best assurance you can give that the check is good.

Traveler's Check. A number of large financial organizations—such as Citibank, American Express, MasterCard, VISA, and Bank of America—issue

> **cashier's check** A check payable to a third party that is drawn by a bank on itself in exchange for the amount specified plus, in most cases, a service fee (of about $5).

WORKSHEET 4.1

An Account Reconciliation Form—James Morrison's May 1995 Statement

James Morrison used this form to reconcile his checking account for the month of May 1995. Because line A equals line B, he has fully reconciled the difference between the $80.99 bank statement balance and his $339.44 checkbook balance. Accounts should be reconciled each month—as soon as possible after receipt of the bank statement.

CHECKING ACCOUNT RECONCILIATION

For the Month of May, 19 95

Accountholder Name(s) James Morrison

Type of Account Regular Checking

1. Ending balance shown on bank statement — $ 80.99

Add up checks and withdrawals still outstanding:

Check Number or Date	Amount	Check Number or Date	Amount
221	$ 81.55		$
225	196.50		
Lucky—5/28	25.00		
ATM—5/29	40.00		
		TOTAL	$ 343.05

2. Deduct total checks/withdrawals still outstanding from bank balance — $ 343.05

Add up deposits still outstanding:

Date	Amount	Date	Amount
5/29	595.00		
		TOTAL	$ 595.00

3. *Add* total deposits still outstanding to bank balance + $ 595.00

[A] **Adjusted Bank Balance (1 – 2 + 3)** $ 332.94

4. Ending balance shown in checkbook $ 339.44

5. Deduct any bank service charges for the period (–$7.50 + $1.00) – $ 6.50

6. Add interest earned for the period + $ 0

[B] **New Checkbook Balance (4 – 5 + 6)** $ 332.94

Note: Your account is reconciled when line A equals line B.

traveler's checks, which can be purchased at commercial banks and most other financial institutions in denominations ranging from $20 to $100. A fee of about 1.5 percent is charged on their purchase. If properly endorsed, traveler's checks are accepted by most U.S. businesses and can be exchanged for local currencies in most parts of the world. These checks are not valid unless properly countersigned by the purchaser, and because they are insured against loss or theft by the issuing agency, they provide a safe, convenient, and popular form of money for travel.

Certified Check. A **certified check** is made out to whoever is to be paid. The bank immediately deducts the amount of the check from your account and then stamps the check to indicate its certification. There is normally a charge of $10 to $15 or more for this service. In effect, the bank has guaranteed that because the funds are there to cover the check, the check is good. Because the bank has become the guarantor, it usually will not return the canceled check to you but will keep it for its own records.

Concept Check

4-15. What are the key factors to consider when opening a checking account? Discuss the advantages and disadvantages of individual versus joint accounts.

4-16. Is it possible to bounce a check due to insufficient funds when the checkbook ledger shows a balance available to cover it? Explain what happens when a check bounces. Is it possible to obtain protection against overdrafts?

4-17. Describe the procedure used to stop payment on a check. Why might one wish to initiate this process?

4-18. What type of information is found in the monthly bank statement, and how is it used? Explain the basic steps involved in the account reconciliation process.

4-19. Briefly define and differentiate between each of the following special types of checks:

a. Cashier's check
b. Traveler's check
c. Certified check

ADDITIONAL MONEY MANAGEMENT SERVICES

LG 6

In addition to various checking account services, banks and other depository institutions offer other services to their customers. What are some of the non-checking-related money management services available from these financial institutions? Before reading on, spend a few moments listing and briefly describing some of these services.

Banks and other depository institutions offer their customers a variety of additional convenient services. Many of these services rely on the use of current technology to transfer funds electronically. Regulation of electronic funds transfer system services protects consumers in a variety of ways. Safe-deposit boxes are another important bank service. Other money management services are also available.

ELECTRONIC FUNDS TRANSFER SYSTEMS

Electronic funds transfer systems (EFTS) use the latest telecommunications and computer technology to electronically transfer funds into and out of your account. For example, your employer may use EFTS to electronically transfer your pay from its bank account directly into your personal

traveler's check A check sold (for a fee of about 1.5 percent) by many large financial institutions, in denominations ranging from $20 to $100, that can be used for making purchases and exchanged for local currencies in most parts of the world.

certified check A personal check that is guaranteed (for a fee of $10 to $15 or more) by the bank on which it is drawn so that the funds are available for payment.

electronic funds transfer systems (EFTS) Systems that employ the latest telecommunications and computer technology to electronically transfer funds into and out of customers' accounts.

bank account at the same or another bank. This eliminates the employer's need to prepare and process checks and the employee's need to deposit them. EFTS include such services as automated teller machines and debit cards, pre-authorized deposits and payments, bank-by-phone accounts, and computer-based banking-at-home.

Automated Teller Machines and Debit Cards. Another form of EFTS uses specially coded plastic cards, called **debit cards,** to transfer funds. These cards are used to initiate the transfer of funds from the customer's bank account (a debit) to the recipient's account. Many people who were previously reluctant to use these cards now find them more convenient than cash and checks. Automated teller machine (ATM) cards are one type of debit card. VISA and MasterCard also issue debit cards linked to your checking account.

The ATM card has become a popular way to make banking transactions. Suppose you need cash at 1:30 a.m. Although no bank is open, you can go to an ATM machine and use your card to withdraw funds from your account. The *personal identification number (PIN)* issued with your card verifies that you are authorized to access the account. As noted earlier, ATMs are actually remote computer terminals that allow customers to make deposits, withdrawals, and other transactions, such as loan payments or transfers between accounts, 24 hours a day, 7 days a week. Most banks have ATMs outside of their offices, and some locate freestanding ATMs in shopping malls, airports, grocery stores, at colleges and universities, and other high-traffic areas to enhance their competitive position. If your bank belongs to an EFTS network, such as Cirrus, Star, or Interlink, you can get cash from the ATM of any bank in the United States that is a member of that network. You can also use your ATM card to make purchases from many types of retailers, who now have *point-of-sale terminals* that permit payment by ATM or other debit cards. Most banks charge a per-transaction fee of $2 to $4 for using the ATM of another bank, and some also charge for the use of the ATM card to pay certain merchants.

Debit card use is increasing because these cards are convenient for both retailers, who don't have to worry about bounced checks, and consumers, who don't have to write checks and can often get cash back when they make a purchase. First accepted by supermarkets, gas stations, and convenience stores, ATM and other debit cards can now be used at many retail stores, doctors' offices, fast food outlets, dry cleaners, and hair salons. Because most card issuers belong to regional or national networks, the cards are accepted in many states.

The convenience of debit cards may, in fact, be their biggest drawback: it can be easy to overspend. To avoid problems, make sure to record all debit card purchases immediately in your checkbook ledger and deduct them from your balance. Also, if there is a problem with a purchase, you can't stop payment—an action you could take if you had instead paid by check or credit card.

Pre-Authorized Deposits and Payments. Two related EFTS services are *pre-authorized deposits and payments*. They allow you to receive automatic deposits or make payments that occur on a regular basis. As an example, you can arrange to have your paycheck or monthly pension or social security benefits deposited directly into your account. Regular, fixed-amount payments, such as mortgage and consumer loan payments or monthly retirement fund contributions, can be pre-authorized to be made automatically from your account. You can also preauthorize regular payments of varying amounts, such as monthly utility bills. In this case, each month you would specify by phone the amount to be paid. Charges for pre-authorized payments may vary from bank to bank. Typically, customers must maintain a specified minimum deposit balance and pay fees averaging 25 to 50 cents per transaction. Not only does this system better allow the customer to earn interest on deposits used to pay bills, but it is a convenient payment mechanism that eliminates postage costs.

Bank-by-Phone Accounts. EFTS has also made it possible for bank customers to initiate a variety of banking transactions by telephone, either by calling a customer service operator who handles the transaction or using the key pad on a touchtone telephone to instruct the bank's computer. To use electronic phone banking, the customer first punches a secret code into the phone to access the accounts. The system then provides step-by-step instructions as to the appropriate codes to perform various transactions such as learning an account balance, finding out what checks have cleared, transferring funds to other accounts, and dispatching payments to participating merchants. The cost of these services varies depending on the type of service provided and the customer's level of bank balances. Bank-by-phone services typically charge customers who do not maintain adequate bank balances a monthly fee plus a specified amount for each transaction. In order to encourage electronic phone banking, many banks today charge no fee on basic account transactions. Some banks allow customers who do not maintain a minimum account balance to make a limited number of free operator-assisted transactions each month and charge fees only on additional transactions.

Computer-Based Banking-at-Home. A service that is now growing in popularity is banking at home via computer. With this service, a modem is used to telephonically link your personal computer to your bank's computer. This allows you to execute a number of transactions, such as paying bills electronically and transferring funds from one account to another, from your home at any time of the day or night. In addition, under this system you can request a current statement of your account to learn its balance and review recent transactions. Most systems also allow you to automatically dispatch fixed, regular payments, such as monthly mortgage payments or quarterly insurance premiums, and pay other bills. While a computer-based bank-at-home system doesn't replace the use of an ATM to obtain cash or deposit money, it can save both the time and the postage involved in paying bills.

The cost of most computer-based home-banking services is about $20 to $25 per month, which includes both the bank's fee and the cost of subscribing to an on-line computer information service such as Prodigy. (Note: The on-line service not only provides access to your bank, but also includes numerous other services, such as providing quotes on securities and life insurance rates along with a transaction capability; giving weather reports and news reports; and facilitating theater and airline ticket purchases as well as catalog purchases.) Such a system can pay for itself by allowing you to monitor and maintain your account balance above the minimum, thereby avoiding service and overdraft fees. However, in order to bank by computer you need a computer costing about $1,000—a cost that cannot be justified solely by its use for banking. On the other hand, if you already have a computer, home banking can be helpful because it gives you easy access to most of the data needed for budgeting and tax planning.

REGULATION OF EFTS SERVICES

The *Federal Electronic Fund Transfer Act of 1978* delineates your rights and responsibilities as an EFTS user. Under this law, you cannot stop payment on a defective or questionable purchase (however, individual banks and state laws have more lenient provisions). In the case of an error, you must notify the bank within 60 days of its occurrence on your periodic statement or terminal receipt. The bank must investigate and tell you the results within 10 days. The bank can then take up to 45 additional days to investigate the error, but it must return the disputed money to your account until the issue is resolved. If you fail to notify the bank within 60 days of the error, the bank has no obligation under federal law to conduct an investigation or return your money. In addition, it is very important that you notify the bank immediately about the theft, loss, or unauthorized use of your EFTS card. Notification within two business days after you discover the card missing limits your loss to $50. After two business days, you may lose up to $500 (but never more than the amount that was actually withdrawn by the thief). Additionally, if you do not report the loss within 60 days after your periodic statement was mailed, you can lose all of the money in your account. When reporting errors or unauthorized transactions, it is best to notify your bank by telephone and *follow up with a letter.* Keep a copy of the letter in your file.

This law also gives you some protection against being forced to use EFTS. Banks cannot require payments via EFTS, although they can encourage you to do so by offering a slightly lower interest rate. If you are required to receive wages or government benefits by EFTS, you must have the right to select the bank where the funds will be sent. Many state regulations offer additional consumer protection regarding your use of EFTS. However, your best protection is to carefully guard the personal identification number (PIN) used to access your accounts by EFTS. Do not write the PIN on your EFTS card, or on anything else for that matter. And be sure to check your periodic statements for possible errors or unauthorized transactions.

debit cards Specially coded plastic cards used to withdraw cash (an ATM card) or transfer funds from a customer's bank account to the recipient's account to pay for goods or services.

SAFE-DEPOSIT BOXES

A safe-deposit box is a rented drawer in a bank's vault. The annual rental fee depends on the box size. Small boxes can be rented for about $25 per year, while large ones may cost hundreds of dollars per year. When you rent a box, you receive one key to it, and the bank retains another key. The box can be opened only when both keys are used. This arrangement protects items in the box from theft and makes it an excellent storage place for jewelry, contracts, stock certificates, titles, and other special documents.

OTHER SERVICES

In addition to the numerous services described earlier in this chapter, banks also offer several other types of money management services. For example, bank trust departments provide investment and estate planning advice. They manage and administer the investments in a trust account or from an estate. Many banks today are broadening their range of services to include financial planning and investment brokerage services. One high growth area is mutual fund sales; in 1994, about 50 percent of all commercial banks offered mutual funds to their customers. Some of these mutual funds are from major mutual fund companies, while others are bank-sponsored funds. Often bank representatives will suggest mutual funds to customers as an alternative to CDs. However convenient it may be to purchase these securities through your bank, you should be sure to evaluate these funds carefully. Investigate the fund's performance and all fees and sales expenses, and compare these to other mutual funds before committing yourself. Many bank mutual fund customers are novice investors who are not aware that, unlike CDs, the return on these investments is not guaranteed. Remember, too, that mutual funds are not deposits and are therefore not covered by federal deposit insurance.

Concept Check

4-20. Briefly describe (a) banking at ATMs; (b) debit cards; (c) pre-authorized deposits and payments; (d) bank-by-phone accounts; and (e) computer-based banking-at-home.

4-21. What are you legal rights and responsibilities when using EFTS?

4-22. Describe briefly the following additional services that banks provide: (a) safe-deposit boxes, (b) trust services, and (c) mutual-fund sales.

SUMMARY

LG1. Understand the role of good cash management in the financial planning process. Cash management plays a vital role in personal financial planning. It involves the administration and control of liquid assets—cash, checking accounts, savings, and other short-term investment vehicles. With good cash management practices, you will have the necessary funds to cover your expenses and to establish a regular savings program.

LG2. Describe the new financial marketplace—traditional financial institutions, checking and savings products, and deposit safety. Financial deregulation has changed the financial marketplace by increasing the number and types of firms providing financial services. Individuals and families continue to rely heavily on traditional depository financial institutions—commercial banks, S&Ls, savings banks, and credit unions—for most of their financial services needs. These institutions provide regular checking accounts, savings accounts, and interest-paying checking accounts—money market mutual funds, money market deposit accounts, and NOW accounts. Asset management accounts offered by brokerage and mutual-fund companies combine checking, investment, and borrowing activities and pay higher interest on deposits than other types of checking accounts. Because of the large number of bank failures in the 1980s and early 1990s, you should make sure your bank has federal deposit insurance and is financially sound. Most traditional depository institutions are federally insured for up to $100,000 per depositor name.

LG3. **Find the interest earned on your money using compound interest and future value techniques.** Once you know the interest rate, frequency of compounding, and how the bank determines the balance on which interest is paid, you can calculate how much interest you will earn on your money. Compound interest is the same as future value. Future value and future value of an annuity formulas can be used to find out to what levels your savings will grow. The more frequently interest is compounded, the greater the effective rate for a given nominal rate of interest. Most banks now use the actual balance method to determine which balances qualify to earn interest; this is the most accurate and fairest method for depositors.

LG4. **Develop a savings strategy that incorporates a variety of savings plans.** Your savings strategy should include establishing a regular pattern of savings and having liquid reserves of about three to six months' after-tax income. The choice of savings products depends on your needs, your risk preference, the length of time you can leave money on deposit, and current and expected interest rate levels. You may wish to put some of your savings into vehicles that pay a higher rate of interest than savings or NOW accounts, such as certificates of deposit, U.S. treasury bills, and Series EE bonds.

LG5. **Open and use a checking account.** A checking account provides a convenient way to hold cash and pay for goods and services. The sharp increase in bank service charges makes it important to evaluate different types of checking accounts and their service charges, minimum balance requirements, and other fees. You should understand how to write and endorse checks, make deposits, keep good checking account records, prevent overdrafts, and stop payment on a check. The account reconciliation, or balancing, process confirms the accuracy of your account records and the monthly bank statement. Other special types of checks you may use occasionally include cashier's, traveler's, and certified checks.

LG6. **Select additional types of money management services that meet your needs.** In addition to checking and savings accounts, financial institutions provide other money management services. Electronic funds transfer systems (EFTS) use telecommunications technology to electronically transfer funds. Popular EFTS services include automated teller machines, debit cards, pre-authorized deposits and payments, bank-by-phone accounts, and computer-based banking-at-home. Safe-deposit boxes safely store valuables and important documents. Today many banks also provide financial planning and trust services, securities brokerage, and mutual-fund sales.

FINANCIAL FACTS OR FANTASIES

Are the following statements financial facts (true) or fantasies (false)?

1. An asset is considered liquid only if it is held in the form of cash.
2. Unlike money market mutual funds, money market deposit accounts are federally insured.
3. In all but a few cases, the nominal (stated) rate of interest on a savings account is the same as its effective rate of interest.
4. Interest paid on a deposit account can be calculated based on the lowest balance for the payment period.
5. U.S. savings bonds are not a very good way to save.
6. At most banks and other depository institutions, you will be hit with a hefty service charge if your checking account balance falls just $1 below the stipulated minimum amount for just one day out of the month.

DISCUSSION QUESTIONS AND PROBLEMS

Discussion Question for Opening Profile

How did Don and Meredith's family circumstances affect their money management? What can you learn from the way Don and Meredith adapted to the changes in their lives?

FPPC **1.** If you put $5,000 in a savings account that pays interest at the rate of 4 percent, compounded annually, how much will you have in five years? (Hint: Use the *future value* formula.) How much will you earn in interest over the five years? If you put $5,000 each year into a savings account that pays interest at the rate of 4 percent a year, how much would you have after five years?

2. You are getting married and are unhappy with your present bank. Discuss your strategy for choosing a new bank and opening an account, including what factors are important to you in selecting a bank, such as the type and ownership of new account(s), and bank fees and charges.

3. Bill and Betty Jacobs together earn approximately $42,000 a year after taxes. Through an inheritance and some wise investing, they also have an investment portfolio with a value of almost $90,000.

a. How much of their annual income do you recommend they hold in some form of savings as liquid reserves? Explain.

b. How much of their investment portfolio do you recommend they hold in savings and other short-term investment vehicles? Explain.

c. How much, in total, should they hold in short-term liquid assets?

4. Determine the annual net cost of the following checking accounts:

a. Monthly fee $5, 25¢ per check processing fee, average of 19 checks written per month.

b. Annual interest of 2.5 percent paid if balance exceeds $750, $8 monthly fee if account falls below minimum balance, average monthly balance $815, account falls below $750 in 4 months.

FPPC **5.** ***Use Worksheet 4.1*** Hun Park has a NOW account at the Third State Bank. His checkbook ledger lists the following checks:

Check Number	Amount
654	$206.05
658	55.22
662	103.00
668	99.00
670	6.10
671	50.25
672	24.90
673	32.45
674	44.50
675	30.00
676	30.00
677	111.23
678	38.04
679	97.99
680	486.70
681	43.50
682	75.00
683	98.50

In addition, he made the following withdrawals and deposits at an ATM near his home:

Date	Amount
11/1	$ 50.00 (withdrawal)
11/2	525.60 (deposit)
11/6	100.00 (deposit
11/14	75.00 (withdrawal)
11/21	525.60 (deposit)
11/24	150.00 (withdrawal)
11/27	225.00 (withdrawal)
11/30	400.00 (deposit)

Hun's checkbook ledger shows an ending balance of $286.54. He has just received his bank statement for the month of November. It shows an ending balance of $622.44; it also shows that he had interest earned for November of $3.28, had a check service charge of $8 for the month, and had another $12 charge for a returned check. His bank statement indicates the following checks have cleared: 654, 662, 672, 674, 675, 676, 677, 678, 679, and 681. ATM withdrawals on 11/1 and 11/14 and deposits on 11/2 and 11/6 have cleared; no other checks or ATM activities are listed on his statement, so anything remaining should be treated as outstanding. Use a checking account reconciliation form like the one in Worksheet 4.1 to reconcile Hun's checking account.

6. Suppose someone stole your ATM card and withdrew $650 from your checking account. How much money could you lose, according to federal legislation, if you reported the stolen card to the bank: (a) the day the card was stolen; (b) six days after the theft; and (c) 65 days after receiving your periodic statement?

CONTEMPORARY CASE APPLICATIONS

4.1 Susan Chan's Savings and Banking Plans

Susan Chan, a registered nurse earning $1,750 per month after taxes, has been reviewing her savings strategies and current banking arrangements to determine if she should make any changes. She has a regular checking account using the flat fee plan (described below), writes an average of 18 checks a month, and carries an average balance of $795 (although it has fallen below $750 in three months of the past year). Her only other account is a money market deposit account with a balance of $4,250. She tries to make regular monthly deposits of $50 to $100 but has only done so about every other month.

Of the many checking accounts Susan's bank offers, the three that best suit her needs are:

Regular Checking, per item plan: $3 per month service charge plus 35¢ per check.
Regular Checking, flat fee plan: Monthly fee of $7 regardless of the number of checks written. With either of these accounts, she can avoid any charges by keeping a minimum *daily* balance of $750.
Interest Checking: Monthly service charge of $7; interest of 3 percent, compounded daily (refer to Exhibit 4.3). With a minimum balance of $1,500, the monthly charge is waived.

Her bank also offers certificates of deposit for a minimum deposit of $500; the current interest rates are 3.5 percent for six months, 3.75 percent for one year, and 4 percent for two years.

Questions

1. Calculate the annual cost of each of the three accounts, assuming that Susan's banking habits remain the same. Which plan would you recommend, and why?
2. Should Susan consider opening the interest checking account and increasing her minimum balance to at least $1,500 to avoid service charges? Explain your answer.
3. What other advice would you give Susan about her overall savings strategy?

FPPC 4.2. Reconciling the Pattersons' Checking Account

Nick and Rosalyn Patterson opened their first checking account at The American Bank on September 14, 1995. They have just received their first bank statement for the period ending October 5, 1995. The statement and checkbook ledger are shown on page 174.

Questions

1. From this information, prepare a bank reconciliation for the Pattersons as of October 5, 1995, using a checking account reconciliation form like the one in Worksheet 4.1.
2. Given your answer to Question 1, what, if any, adjustments will the Pattersons need to make in their checkbook ledger? Comment on the procedures used to reconcile their checking account as well as on your findings.
3. If the Pattersons earned interest on their idle balances as a result of the account being a NOW account, what impact would this have on the reconciliation process? Explain.

Bank Statement

	NICK & ROSALYN PATTERSON **2128 E. 51ST ST.** **DETROIT, MICHIGAN**			**THE AMERICAN BANK** **800-000-0000** **STATEMENT PERIOD SEPT. 6 TO OCT. 5, 1995**	
	Opening Balance	**Total Deposits for Period**		**Total Checks/ Withdrawals for Period**	**Ending Balance**
	$0	**$569.25**		**$473.86**	**$95.39**
Date	**Withdrawals (Debits)**			**Deposits (Credits)**	**Balance**
Sept. 14				$360.00	$360.00
Sept. 23				97.00	457.00
Sept. 25	$ 45.20			9.25	421.05
Oct. 1				103.00	524.05
Oct. 1	3.00 BC				521.05
Oct. 2	65.90	$49.76	$45.00		360.39
Oct. 5	265.00				95.39

RT = Returned Check DM = Debit Memo BC = Bank Charges
FC = Finance Charges CM = Credit Memo

Checkbook Ledger

Check Number	Date 1995	Details	Check Amount	Deposit Amount	Account Balance
—	Sept. 14	Cash—gift from wedding		$360.00	$360.00
—	Sept. 24	Nick's wages from library		97.00	457.00
101	Sept. 24	Kroger—groceries	$ 45.20		411.80
102	Sept. 27	Michigan Bell Telephone bill	28.40		383.40
—	Oct. 1	Nick's wages for library work		103.00	486.40
103	Oct. 1	Univ. book store—college books	65.90		420.50
104	Oct. 1	Kmart—sewing material	16.75		403.75
105	Oct. 1	G. Heller—apartment rent	265.00		138.75
106	Oct. 2	Blue Cross—health insurance	17.25		121.50
107	Oct. 3	Kroger—groceries	49.76		71.74
108	Oct. 4	Cash, gas, entertainment, laundry	45.00		26.74
—	Oct. 5	Rosalyn's salary—Universal Corp.		450.00	476.74

GETTING A HANDLE ON YOUR FINANCIAL FUTURE

The major problem that most people face in implementing a cash management program is selecting the appropriate types of accounts and savings vehicles from a number of providers, including commercial banks, savings and loan associations, savings banks, credit unions, mutual funds, and brokerage firms. To do this properly requires some effort on the part of the consumer.

If You Are Just Starting Out

At this stage, you will be looking for institutions and establishing accounts. The following suggestions will help you make these decisions:

Checking:

1. Geographic convenience is usually the first consideration in choosing a transactions account. Determine if your needs are better suited by a provider close to work, school, or home.
2. Be aware of all of the services offered by your provider that you might need in the future.
3. Determine if there are service charges on the account and how they are applied.
4. From your monthly cash budget, decide which items could be paid by check and which could be paid with cash.
5. After setting up your transactions account, be sure to reconcile it every month. Use Worksheet 4.1.

Savings (Emergency Fund):

1. To determine how large an emergency fund you need, multiply your monthly take-home pay by a minimum of six months.
2. Check how interest is calculated on the account and how often it is credited.
3. Find out if there are any penalties or charges associated with the withdrawal of funds.
4. Be sure the account is federally insured.

If You Are Thirty-Something

Once you have become established in your career and have accumulated the necessary savings for emergencies, you can begin to concentrate more on your savings program, which is designed to meet your financial goals.

Savings Program:

1. Look into savings vehicles that you previously did not have the minimum amount to open the account. These may offer better returns.
2. Monitor the returns you are receiving on your existing accounts to be sure they are still consistent with your financial goals.
3. With increased knowledge and experience, you may find your attitude toward risk changing; if so, your savings vehicles should reflect this change.

Chapter 5

Making Housing and Automobile Decisions

A First Home for the Jameses

Terry and Sara James moved to Portland, Oregon from Dallas, Texas in 1991 because of its lifestyle, location—they love to windsurf *and* snow ski—and reasonable cost of living. They both found good jobs soon after the move: Terry, 30, designs computer workstation furniture and Sara, 29, teaches elementary school. "We rented a nice older home so we could settle in and learn about the city," Terry comments. "By 1993, low interest rates and an affordable housing market made the time right to buy a house."

The couple first analyzed their finances. "We had about $11,000 for the down payment and closing costs and didn't want to pay over one-third of our gross income for mortgage principal and interest, taxes, and insurance, so we set our top price at $130,000," explains Terry. "Then we met with a mortgage broker and prequalified (arranged a mortgage ahead of time). The broker prequalified us for $145,000, but we weren't comfortable with that much debt and stayed with our estimate." During prequalification, they discovered false entries on their credit report giving them bad references and had enough time to correct the problem.

Terry and Sara found a nice neighborhood with the older homes they liked. "It was a longer commute for me," says Sara. "But after looking elsewhere, we agreed on this area. Friends recommended a good realtor who showed us homes in our price range and style." After several weeks, they found just what they wanted:

Learning Goals

LG1. *Identify housing alternatives that meet your needs.*

LG2. *Evaluate the benefits and costs of home ownership and estimate how much you can pay for a home.*

LG3. *Assess the option of renting and perform a rent-or-buy analysis.*

LG4. *Describe the home-buying process.*

LG5. *Choose mortgage financing that meets your needs.*

LG6. *Implement a plan to choose and buy or lease an automobile.*

a bungalow built in 1926. Terry notes, "The original owner still lived there and maintained it beautifully, preserving its charm. It had only one bathroom and no fenced yard for our dog, but we decided we could deal with that. The price was right—$124,500; the property had been on the market for a while because there was a lien on it. Our agent advised us to offer $119,500, contingent upon getting the lien removed—which was easier than we expected. We did, it was accepted, and we were first-time homeowners!"

With mortgage rates so low, Terry and Sara chose a 30-year, 7.125% annual percentage rate, fixed-rate mortgage. They made a 5 percent ($5,975) down payment; because this was under 20 percent, they had to buy mortgage insurance. Other closing costs were around $4,000.

The Jameses' home-buying experience went very smoothly. "Our realtor and mortgage broker were on the ball," Sara says. "By prequalifying, we moved quickly to close the deal. There were no big surprises." Terry adds, "Staying under our budgeted amount gave us a greater comfort level at closing. Our maintenance estimates have been pretty accurate and repairs limited because the heating and electrical systems were updated around 1991. And we are paying much lower taxes because we can deduct the mortgage interest—a wonderful benefit." By planning ahead, Terry and Sara avoided the problems many first-time home buyers face. Chapter 5 provides you with the advice you need to have a positive experience like the Jameses when you buy a home or a car.

MEETING HOUSING NEEDS

LG1

A family's housing needs depend on such factors as age, income level, and number of children; these can be met in a variety of ways —from single-family homes to condos and apartments. What are your current as well as planned future housing needs, and what are the key factors shaping each of them? Before reading on, spend a few moments answering these questions.

Everybody's housing needs differ. Some people prefer quiet and privacy; others like the hustle and bustle of big-city life. Some demand to live within walking distance of work, shopping, and restaurants; others do not mind a 45-minute commute. Because you will have your own unique set of likes and dislikes, the best way to start your search for housing is to list your needs and then classify them according to whether their satisfaction is essential, desirable, or merely a "plus." Such a classification is important for three reasons. First, it serves to screen out housing that will not meet your minimum requirements. Second, it helps you recognize that you may have to make trade-offs, because you will seldom find any single home that meets all of your needs. Third, it can help you focus on those needs for which you are willing and able to pay.

ALTERNATIVE FORMS OF HOUSING

Because there are so many different types of residences, it is difficult to describe a "typical" home. We do know a few things, however, about what the "average" American home is like. Today's new home typically has at least three bedrooms and probably more than one bathroom; in addition, it will have at least a one-car garage or carport, a fireplace, and central heating and air conditioning. We also know something about home prices. For example, in early 1995, the median price for existing homes was about $110,400. However, as shown in Exhibit 5.1, prices varied widely from one part of the country to another. The stock of housing in America is nearly as diverse as its prices, consisting of not only single-family homes but also condominiums, cooperative apartments, manufactured homes, and numerous types of rental apartments and houses.

Single-Family Homes. The single-family, detached home remains the first choice in housing. Basically, such homes stand alone on their own legally defined lots. Sometimes homes are built side by side so that they share common side walls; these are known as *row houses* and are especially prevalent east of the Mississippi. As a rule, single-family homes offer their buyers privacy, prestige, pride of ownership, and maximum property control. In recent years, however, the cost of single-family residences—and especially residential lots—has increased dramatically. At the same time, the size of the average U.S. household has drastically decreased. These factors have led to smaller homes; to compensate for their smaller size, often luxurious amenities and features have been introduced. Higher costs and changing lifestyles also have led to alternative types of housing; thus, while the single-family, detached home is still the most popular type of residence, its dominant position is declining.

Condominiums. The term **condominium** or **condo** describes a form of ownership rather than a type of building. Condominiums can be apartments, townhouses, or cluster housing. The condominium buyer receives title to an individual unit and joint ownership in any common areas and facilities, such as lobbies, swimming pools, lakes, and tennis courts. Because buyers own their units, they arrange their own mortgages, pay their own taxes, and pay for maintenance and building services. They are typically assessed, on a monthly basis, a *homeowner's fee* to cover their proportionate share of common facility costs. Condominium owners belong to a *homeowners' association* that elects a board of managers to supervise the project's building and grounds. Condominiums generally cost less than single-family, detached homes because they are designed for more efficient land use and lower construction costs. Many home buyers are attracted to condominiums because they do not want the responsibilities of maintaining and caring for their property. Exhibit 5.2 lists some of the key things to check before buying a condominium.

Cooperative Apartments. An apartment in a building in which each tenant owns a share of the corporation that owns the building is known as a **cooperative apartment** or **co-op.** Residents lease their units from the corporation and are assessed

EXHIBIT 5.1

Selected Housing Prices around the United States (1995)

The price of housing varies widely from one location to another. For example, the median price of an existing home is $109,215 in Birmingham, Alabama, while in Washington, D. C., it is $167,613 and in San Diego, California, $178,704.

Location	Median Price: Existing	Median Price: New	Location	Median Price: Existing	Median Price: New
Albuquerque, NM	$118,212	$137,135	Milwaukee, WI	$119,396	$138,507
Atlanta, GA	99,622	115,575	Minneapolis-St. Paul, MN	105,249	122,090
Baltimore, MD	121,590	141,032	Nashville, TN	100,531	116,629
Baton Rouge, LA	83,268	96,581	Nassau-Suffolk County, NY	167,687	194,523
Birmingham, AL	109,215	126,697	New Orleans, LA	80,820	93,752
Boise, ID	106,688	123,764	New York, NY	180,841	209,777
Boston, MA	189,534	219,875	Newark, NJ	201,117	233,319
Charlotte, NC	108,520	125,911	Oklahoma City, OK	72,232	83,795
Chicago, IL	153,488	178,081	Orlando, FL	97,006	112,541
Cincinnati, OH	102,197	118,570	Philadelphia, PA	120,728	140,055
Cleveland, OH	97,690	113,325	Phoenix, AZ	96,855	112,351
Columbia, SC	88,216	102,326	Pittsburgh, PA	87,956	102,037
Columbus, OH	99,808	115,794	Portland, OR	121,579	141,040
Dallas, TX	102,137	118,499	Providence, RI	119,442	138,560
Denver, CO	127,624	148,048	Rochester, NY	88,930	103,156
Des Moines, IA	87,908	101,979	Saint Louis, MO	88,400	102,550
Detroit, MI	82,842	96,092	Salt Lake City, UT	108,469	125,849
Fort Worth, TX	89,560	103,895	San Antonio, TX	81,623	94,691
Hartford, CT	135,722	157,415	San Diego, CA	178,704	207,279
Honolulu, HI	372,166	431,636	San Francisco, CA	257,412	298,555
Houston, TX	84,848	98,441	Seattle, WA	149,477	173,372
Indianapolis, IN	97,173	112,729	Spokane, WA	102,332	118,693
Jacksonville, FL	87,068	100,999	Tampa, FL	82,636	95,852
Kansas City, MO	93,101	107,994	Tucson, AZ	86,314	100,133
Las Vegas, NV	119,543	138,710	Washington, DC	167,613	194,419
Los Angeles, CA	183,510	212,837	West Palm Beach, FL	128,095	148,576
Miami, FL	103,997	120,633	Wichita, KS	76,872	89,164

Source: Adapted from information in "The Top 145 Markets," *U.S. News & World Report*, April 10, 1995, pp. 80–83.

monthly in proportion to their ownership shares, which are based on the amount of space they occupy. The assessments cover the cost of service, maintenance, taxes, and the mortgage on the entire building. These are subject to change depending on the actual costs of operating the building and the actions of the board of directors, which determines the corporation's policies. Cooperative owners may find that the value of their ownership interest increases over time as a result of increased market values and a reduction in the outstanding loan balance. Because cooperative apartments are not profit-motivated, monthly assessments are likely to be lower than the rent on similar accommodations in a rental unit. Also, the cooperative owner receives the tax benefits resulting from interest and property taxes attributable to his or her proportionate ownership interest.

Manufactured Homes. **Manufactured homes** are partially or fully assembled, factory-produced housing units that can be transported to a desired location. They are placed on either a permanent or temporary foundation and then connected to

condominium (condo) A form of direct ownership of an individual unit in a multiunit project in which lobbies, swimming pools, and other common areas and facilities are jointly owned by all property owners in the project.

cooperative apartment (co-op) An apartment in a building in which each tenant owns a share of the corporation that owns the building.

manufactured home A partially or fully assembled, factory-produced housing unit that can be transported to a desired location, placed on either a permanent or temporary foundation, and then connected to utilities and used as a residence.

EXHIBIT 5.2

Things to Check before Buying a Condo

In the long run, it pays to carefully check out the various operating and occupancy features of a condo before you buy.

- Thoroughly investigate the reputation of the developer—through local real estate brokers, banks, or the Better Business Bureau—whether the building is brand new, under construction, or being converted.
- Read the rules of the organization.
- Investigate the condo homeowners' association, the restrictions on condo owners, and the quality of the property management.
- Check the construction of the building and its physical condition. If the building is being converted to condos, ask to see an independent inspection firm's report on the building's condition.
- Insist that any future changes in the building be put in writing.
- Talk to the occupants to see if they are satisfied with the living conditions.
- Determine how many units are rented; generally, owner-occupied units are better maintained.
- Determine if there is sufficient parking space.
- Watch for unusually low maintenance fees that will probably have to be increased soon.
- Consider the resale value.
- Compare the projected monthly homeowner's fees with those on similar buildings already in operation.

utilities. *Prefabricated homes* are manufactured in partially assembled sections at the factory, with final assembly on the owner's lot. Because they are mass-produced, their cost is considerably lower than comparable homes built on-site. Manufactured homes that are fully assembled at the factory are called *mobile homes*, although today they are rarely moved from their installed site. Most mobile home owners lease or purchase sites in mobile home parks. These homes range in size from 400 to 1,400 square feet and are typically sold with appliances, carpeting, curtains, and sometimes furniture. They cost about half as much as a similar-size home built on-site and have low maintenance costs. Although occasionally used as temporary housing, mobile homes provide *permanent residences* for many families, particularly retired persons. Nevertheless, the market price of mobile homes tend to decline over time, thus, they are not considered good investments.

Rental Apartments and Houses. All of the forms of housing discussed above represent different ways of achieving home ownership. However, for one reason or another, a large number of individuals and families choose to *rent* or *lease* their place of residence rather than own it. They live in apartments and other types of rental units ranging from duplexes, four-plexes, and even single-family homes to large, high-rise apartment complexes containing several hundred units. *Garden apartments* are usually built in groups of four to six units that may be either one or two stories and are separated by landscaped areas. *Efficiency apartments* are generally one-room apartments suitable for single people. *Townhouses* are two- or three-story apartments that usually have the bedrooms upstairs. All of these types of housing are popular and widely available.

The cost and availability of rental units vary from one geographic area to another. Unfurnished units, of course, rent for less than furnished ones. The U.S. Department of Housing and Urban Development (HUD) administers various programs that provide low-rent housing opportunities for people in lower income brackets. Because such a wide variety of rental units are available, people who wish to rent can usually find units that conform to their location, physical, and financial requirements.

Concept Check

5-1. In addition to single-family homes, what other forms of housing are available in the United States? Briefly describe the advantages and disadvantages of each.

5-2. Differentiate between a condominium and a cooperative apartment.

HOW MUCH HOUSING CAN YOU AFFORD?

FPPC 1

LG2

People buy homes for the emotional and financial payoffs they provide; accompanying these benefits are the costs of buying homes, such as down payments, closing costs, monthly mortgage payments, property taxes, and homeowner's insurance. What are the typical motives for buying a home, and what purchase and ownership costs must be considered when assessing its affordability? Spend a few moments answering these questions before reading on.

Spending many thousands of dollars to buy a home obviously involves a good deal of careful planning and analysis. Not only must you spend time deciding on the kind of home you want (its location, number of bedrooms, and so on), you must also consider its cost, what kind of mortgage to get, how large a monthly payment you can afford, what kind of homeowner's insurance coverage to have, and so forth. It should be clear that buying a home (or any other major, big-ticket item) touches on many of the elements in personal financial planning. The money you use for a down payment will likely be drawn from your *savings program*; the homeowner's policy you choose is a part of your *insurance planning*; and your monthly mortgage payments undoubtedly will have an enormous impact on your *cash budget* and *tax plans*.

Sound financial planning dictates caution when buying a home or any other major item. Spending too much for a home or automobile can have a detrimental effect not only on your budget and lifestyle, but also on your savings and investment plans, and possibly even your retirement plans. Knowing how much housing you can afford will go a long way toward helping you achieve your financial goals.

MOTIVES FOR OWNING A HOME

Whether it is a detached home or a condominium, home ownership is important to most people. It is preferred over renting for several reasons, the most important of which is probably the basic security and peace of mind derived from living in one's own home—pride of ownership, a feeling of permanence, and a sense of stability. This so-called "psychic reward" is the only reason that many people need to own a home. In addition to the emotional payoff, there's also a financial payoff from home ownership.

The Home as a Tax Shelter. Perhaps the biggest financial payoff from owning a home is the tax shelter it offers. You get a tax break from owning a home because you can deduct both the mortgage interest and the property taxes you pay when calculating your federal and, in most states, state income taxes. As explained in Chapter 3, mortgage interest (on mortgage loans up to a total of $1,000,000 taken out to buy, build, or improve a principal residence and second home, such as a vacation home, if any) and property taxes can be treated as a tax deduction. Such write-offs reduce your taxable income and thus the amount of taxes you pay. The only requirement is that you itemize your deductions. This tax break is so good that people who have never itemized usually begin doing so after they buy their first house. Also, keep in mind that for the first 15 to 20 years of ownership (assuming a 30-year mortgage) most of your monthly mortgage payment is made up of interest and property taxes—in fact, during the first 5 to 10 years or so, these could well account for *85 to 90 percent of your total payment.* This means you are allowed to write off nearly all of your monthly mortgage payment.

Here is how it works. Suppose you make mortgage payments of $1,000 a month of which $850 is interest and property taxes. That is about $10,000 a year in tax deductions. Assuming you are single with no other itemized deductions, that $10,000 will reduce your taxable income by an additional $6,200 ($10,000 minus your $3,800 standard deduction in 1994). If you are in the 28 percent tax bracket, such a tax deduction will reduce the amount of taxes you pay by an additional $1,736 ($6,200 × .28).

The Home as an Inflation Hedge. Another financial payoff is the **inflation hedge** allegedly

> **inflation hedge** An investment or asset that appreciates in value at a rate equal to or greater than the rate of inflation.

provided by home ownership. An inflation hedge is an investment or asset that appreciates in value at a rate equal to or greater than the rate of inflation. During both the 1970s and the mid-to-late 1980s, few inflation hedges could match the performance of home ownership. In fact, a home became one of the best investments you could make, because it generated a far better return than stocks, bonds, or mutual funds. Many people bought homes simply for their investment value. The rampant inflation and appreciation in home prices came to a halt in the early 1980s and again in the early 1990s. Although many real estate markets were strong in the late 1980s, housing values fell sharply during the recession of the early 1990s. In many areas of the country, sellers who had owned their homes for a short time were unable to sell them at a profit.

Today, housing prices in most parts of the country are increasing at a rate about equal to or slightly above the rate of inflation. As a result of this, and the fact that the inflation rate has declined dramatically, housing prices in most areas are rising at a much slower pace than in the past. Most experts believe that it will probably be a long time before we again see housing price increases that significantly outstrip the rate of inflation. Housing in the 1990s certainly does not appear to be the inflation hedge (or investment) that it once was.

THE COST OF HOME OWNERSHIP

While there definitely are some strong emotional and financial reasons for owning a home, there's still the question of whether or not you can afford to own one. Affordability is a two-edged sword: You must not only come up with the down payment and other closing costs but also meet the recurring cash-flow requirements associated with monthly mortgage payments and other home maintenance expenses. In particular, there are five items you should consider when evaluating the cost of home ownership and determining how much home you can afford: (1) the down payment, (2) points and closing costs, (3) mortgage payments, (4) property taxes and insurance, and (5) maintenance and operating expenses.

The Down Payment. The first hurdle is the **down payment.** Most buyers finance a major part of the purchase price of the home, but they are also required by lenders to invest money of their own, called *equity.* The actual amount of down payment required varies among lenders, mortgage types, and properties. To determine the amount of down payment that will be required in specific instances, lenders use the **loan-to-value ratio,** which specifies the maximum percentage of the value of a property that the lender is willing to loan. For example, if the loan-to-value ratio is 80 percent, the buyer will have to come up with a down payment equal to the remaining 20 percent. The loan-to-value ratio is normally based on the *greater of the market or appraised value.*

A property that is financed with a high loan-to-value ratio involves only a small percentage of borrower equity. For example, a mortgage that equals 90 to 95 percent of a property's purchase price is a high-ratio loan. It involves only 5 to 10 percent equity dollars; thus, if you buy a $100,000 home with a 95 percent loan-to-value ratio, you need to put down only $5,000 and can finance the other $95,000 through a mortgage.

Generally first-time home buyers must spend a number of years accumulating enough money to afford the down payment and other costs associated with the home purchase transaction. You can best accumulate these funds on a planned basis, using future value techniques (presented in Chapters 2, 11, and 14) to determine the monthly or annual savings (at a given rate of interest) necessary to have a stated amount by a specified future date. While detailed demonstration of this process is included in Chapter 11 (see Worksheet 11.1, B.), for now suffice it to say that a disciplined savings program is the best way to obtain the funds needed to purchase a home or any other big-ticket item requiring a sizable down payment or purchase outlay.

If you do not have enough savings to cover the down payment and closing costs, you can still consider several other sources. You may be able to obtain some funds by withdrawing (subject to legal limitations) your contributions from your company's profit-sharing or thrift plan. Your IRA is another option, although you must pay a 10 percent penalty (prior to age 59½) plus income taxes on any amount you withdraw. However, the higher tax deductions resulting from the mortgage interest may offset these costs.

Equity sharing is another down payment source that is becoming popular. It involves finding a partner who will provide all or part of the down payment in exchange for a specified percentage of the equity in the house, usually for a stated number of years. You may be able to arrange an equity sharing deal with a parent or a relative in exchange for monthly fair market rent and allowing them to take the tax deductions for their percentage of the depreciation, mortgage interest, and property taxes. Equity sharing consultants can be hired for a fee of about $200 to $500 to match prospective home buyers with an investor. The amount of the down payment, percentage of equity given to the investor, rent paid to the investor, interest payments, and term of the arrangement will vary depending upon the situation. Typically, equity-sharing contracts with nonfamily investors run from three to five years, at the end of which the owner can buy out the investor or extend the agreement. In such cases, the investors do not usually take the tax write offs but rather rely on the expected appreciation in the home's value for their return.

The Federal National Mortgage Association (known as "Fannie Mae") Community Home Buyer's Program assists buyers who haven't saved the 5 percent minimum down payment required on conventional loans. Its "3/2 Option" allows the borrower to obtain up to 2 percent of the 5 percent from a relative or from a public or nonprofit agency. This program is available from local lenders and is limited to home buyers with household incomes below a designated percent of the median amount in their area (115 percent in most areas but more in areas with high housing costs).

As a rule, when the down payment is less than 20 percent, the lender will require that the loan be made with **mortgage insurance,** which protects the lender from loss if the borrower defaults on the loan. Usually the mortgage insurance covers the lender's risk above 80 percent of the price of the house. Thus, with a 10 percent down payment, the mortgage will result in a 90 percent loan, and the mortgage insurance would cover 10 percent of the home's price. You will be charged a one-time fee of about .75 percent of the amount of the loan (paid at closing) plus an annual premium of about .25 to .5 percent (which is included in your monthly payments), until the loan balance is less than 75 or 80 percent of the appraised value of your home.

Points and Closing Costs. A second hurdle to home ownership relates to mortgage points and closing costs. **Mortgage points** are fees charged by lenders at the time they grant a mortgage loan. In appearance, points are like interest in that they are a charge for borrowing money. They are related to the lender's supply of loanable funds and the demand for mortgages; the greater the demand relative to the supply, the more points you can expect to pay. One point equals 1 percent of the amount borrowed. If you borrow $70,000, and loan fees equal 3 points, the amount of money you will pay in points will be $70,000 × .03 = $2,100.

Lenders typically use points as a way of charging interest on their loans. They can vary the interest rate along with the number of points they charge to create loans with comparable effective rates. For example, a lender might be willing to give you a 10 percent mortgage rather than an 11 percent one if you are willing to pay more points; that is, you take your pick: an 11 percent mortgage rate with 2 points or a 10 percent mortgage with 6½ points. If you choose the 10 percent loan, you will end up paying a lot more *at closing* (though the amount of interest paid *over the life of the mortgage* may be less).

Points increase the *effective rate of interest* on a mortgage. The amount you pay in points and the length of time you hold a mortgage determine the increase in the effective interest rate. For example, on a 9 percent, 30-year, fixed-rate mortgage, each point increases the annual percentage rate by about .11 percent if the loan is held for 30 years, .13 percent if held for 15 years, .20 percent if held

down payment A portion of the full purchase price provided by the purchaser at the time of purchase of a house or other major asset; often called *equity*.

loan-to-value ratio The maximum percentage of the value of a property that the lender is willing to loan.

mortgage insurance A type of insurance policy that protects the mortgage lender from loss in the event the borrower defaults on the loan; typically required by lenders when the down payment is less than 20 percent.

mortgage points Fees (each point equals 1 percent of the amount borrowed) charged by lenders at the time they grant a mortgage loan; they are related to the lender's supply of loanable funds and the demand for mortgages.

EXHIBIT 5.3

The Hidden Costs of Buying a Home: Closing Costs

The closing costs on a home mortgage loan can be substantial—as much as 5 to 7 percent of the price of the home. Except for the real estate commission (which is generally paid by the seller), the biggest share of the closing costs is charged to the buyer and must be paid—in addition to the down payment—at the time the loan is closed and title to the property is conveyed.

	Size of Down Payment	
Item	**20%**	**10%**
Loan application fee	$ 200	$ 200
Loan origination fee	800	900
Points	1,600	2,700
Mortgage insurance	—	675
Title search and insurance	500	550
Attorneys' fees	400	400
Appraisal fees	150	150
Home inspection	250	250
Mortgage tax	575	650
Filing fees	25	25
Credit reports	25	25
Miscellaneous	100	100
Total closing costs	$4,625	$6,625

Note: Typical closing costs for a $100,000 home—2 points charged with 20 percent down, 3 points with 10 percent down. Actual amounts will vary by lender and location.

7 years, and .40 percent if held 3 years. You pay the same amount in points regardless of how long you keep your home. Therefore, the longer you hold the mortgage, the longer the time period over which the points are amortized and the smaller the effect of the points on the effective annual interest rate.

According to recent IRS rulings, the points paid on a mortgage at the time a home is originally purchased are usually considered to be tax deductible. The same points are *not* considered tax deductible if they are incurred when *refinancing* a mortgage (unless they are paid in connection with the purchase or improvement of a home)—rather, the amount paid in points must be written off (*amortized*) over the life of the new mortgage loan.

Closing costs are all expenses (including mortgage points) that borrowers ordinarily pay at the time a mortgage loan is closed and title to the purchased property is conveyed to them. Closing costs are like down payments: They represent money you must come up with *at the time you buy the house.* Closing costs are made up of such items as (1) loan application fees, (2) loan origination fees, (3) points (if any), (4) title search and insurance, (5) attorneys' fees, (6) appraisal fees, and (7) other miscellaneous fees for things like mortgage taxes, filing fees, inspections, credit reports, and so on.

The loan application and origination fees are charges the lender makes for doing all the paperwork; the other charges are associated primarily with fulfilling the legal and credit requirements necessary to complete the home-purchase transaction. As Exhibit 5.3 shows, these costs can amount to 50 percent or more of the down payment. For example, with a 10 percent down payment on a $100,000 home, the closing costs, as shown in Exhibit 5.3, are nearly 70 percent of the down payment, or $6,625. A little simple arithmetic also indicates that this buyer will need nearly $17,000 to buy the house (the $10,000 down payment plus another $6,625 in closing costs).

Many first-time home buyers are shocked to find out how much they must pay in closing costs. In many instances, *sellers,* by custom or contract, will assume the responsibility for some of a buyer's mortgage points and other closing costs. Seldom, however, can a buyer escape all—or even most—of the expenses. At best, the seller will probably pick up just a small percentage (perhaps 10 to 15 percent) of the total amount of the closing costs, leaving the buyer to pay the rest.

EXHIBIT 5.4

Typical Principal and Interest Payment Patterns on a Mortgage Loan

For most of the life of a mortgage loan, the vast majority of each monthly payment goes to interest and only a small portion goes toward principal repayment. Over the 30-year life of the 9 percent, $80,000 mortgage illustrated here, the homeowner will pay more than $150,000 in interest.

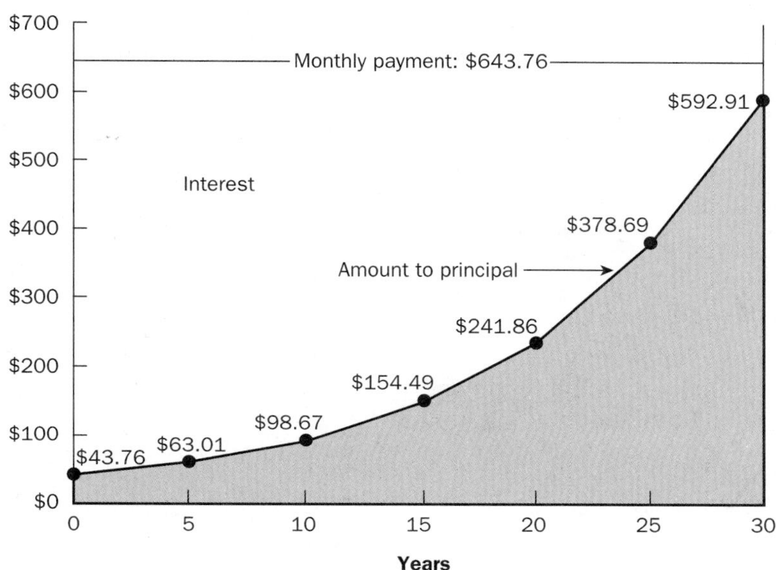

Note: Dollar amounts noted on graph represent the principal amount in the first scheduled payment of the given year.

Mortgage Payments. The monthly mortgage payment is determined using a fairly complex formula. Each monthly mortgage payment is made up partly of principal repayment on the loan and partly of interest charges. However, as Exhibit 5.4 shows, for most of the life of the mortgage the vast majority of each monthly payment goes to *interest.* The loan illustrated in the exhibit is an $80,000, 30-year, 9 percent mortgage with monthly payments of $643.76. Note that it is not until after the 22nd year of this 30-year mortgage that the principal portion of the loan payment exceeds the amount that goes to interest.

In practice, mortgage lenders and realtors use *comprehensive mortgage payment tables* to find monthly payments. These tables contain monthly payments for virtually every combination of loan size, interest rate, and maturity. Exhibit 5.5 provides an excerpt from one such comprehensive mortgage payment table (with values rounded to the nearest cent). It lists the *monthly payments* that would be associated with a $10,000 fixed-rate loan for selected maturities of 10 to 30 years and various interest rates ranging from 5 to 13 percent. It can be used to find the monthly payment for any size loan. Alternatively, many relatively inexpensive business calculators, such as the Texas Instruments BAII PLUS (which costs about $30) can be used to quickly and precisely calculate monthly mortgage payments.

Suppose you wish to use the mortgage payment tables to find the monthly loan payment on an $80,000, 9 percent, 30-year mortgage. To do this, simply divide the amount of the loan ($80,000) by $10,000 and then multiply this factor (8.0) by the payment amount shown in Exhibit 5.5 for a 9 percent, 30-year loan ($80.47):

$$\$80{,}000/\$10{,}000 = 8.0 \times \$80.47 \times \underline{\underline{\$643.76}}$$

closing costs All expenses (including mortgage points) that borrowers ordinarily pay at the time a mortgage loan is closed and title to the purchased property is conveyed to them.

EXHIBIT 5.5

A Table of Monthly Mortgage Payments (Monthly Payments Necessary to Repay a $10,000 Loan)

The monthly loan payments on a mortgage vary not only by the amount of the loan, but also by the rate of interest and loan maturity:

	Loan Maturity				
Rate of Interest	**10 Years**	**15 Years**	**20 Years**	**25 Years**	**30 Years**
5.0%	$106.07	$ 79.08	$ 66.00	$ 58.46	$ 53.68
5.5	108.53	81.71	68.79	61.41	56.79
6.0	111.02	84.39	71.64	64.43	59.96
6.5	113.55	87.11	74.56	67.52	63.21
7.0	116.11	89.88	77.53	70.68	66.53
7.5	118.71	92.71	80.56	73.90	69.93
8.0	121.33	95.57	83.65	77.19	73.38
8.5	123.99	98.48	86.79	80.53	76.90
9.0	126.68	101.43	89.98	83.92	80.47
9.5	129.40	104.43	93.22	87.37	84.09
10.0	132.16	107.47	96.51	90.88	87.76
10.5	134.94	110.54	99.84	94.42	91.48
11.0	137.76	113.66	103.22	98.02	95.24
11.5	140.60	116.82	106.65	101.65	99.03
12.0	143.48	120.02	110.11	105.33	102.86
12.5	146.38	123.26	113.62	109.04	106.73
13.0	149.32	126.53	117.16	112.79	110.62

Note: ***To use:*** (1) Divide amount of the loan by $10,000; (2) find the loan payment amount in table for specific interest rate and maturity; (3) multiply the amount from step 1 by the amount from step 2.
Example: The monthly payment for a $98,000, 9.5 percent, 30-year loan would be: (1) $98,000/$10,000 = 9.8; (2) payment associated with a 9.5 percent, 30-year loan, from table, is *$84.09*; (3) monthly payment required to repay a $98,000, 9.5 percent, 30-year loan is 9.8 × $84.09 = $824.08.

The resulting monthly mortgage payment would be $643.76. (*Note:* the more precise value found using a business calculator is $643.70.)

Obviously, the key issue with respect to mortgage payments is *affordability.* To ensure that the purchase of a home stays within your budget, you must determine the size of monthly mortgage payment you can afford. This, in turn, will determine how much you can borrow to finance the purchase of a home.

Affordability ratios. To obtain a mortgage, a potential borrower must be "qualified"—that is, demonstrate that he or she has an acceptable credit record and adequate income to comfortably make scheduled loan payments. Various federal and private mortgage insurers, as well as institutional mortgage investors, have certain standards they expect borrowers to meet to reduce the risk of default. Because of the influence these insurers/investors have on the mortgage market, their guidelines tend to be widely followed.

Probably the most important affordability guideline relates *monthly payments to borrower income.* This is done by comparing (1) the size of the monthly mortgage payment and (2) the borrower's total monthly installment loan payments (which would include payments not only on the mortgage, but also on automobile loans, furniture loans, and any other type of consumer installment loan) to monthly income. In this regard, the most widely followed ratios (for a *conventional mortgage*) stipulate that (1) monthly mortgage payments cannot exceed 25 to 30 percent of the borrower's monthly *gross* (before-tax) income and (2) the borrower's total monthly installment loan payments cannot exceed 33 to 38 percent of monthly gross income. Because both conditions stipulate a range, the lender has some leeway in deciding on the most appropriate ratio for a particular loan applicant.

Here is how these affordability ratios work. Assume your monthly income is $3,000. Using the lower end of the ranges (that is, 25 percent and 33 percent) for illustrative purposes, we see that this income level supports mortgage payments of $750 a month *so long as total monthly installment obligations do not exceed $1,000.* (These values were found as follows: $3,000 × .25 = $750 and $3,000 × .33 = $1,000.) Note that if your other monthly installment loan payments exceeded $250 (the difference between $1,000 and $750), your mortgage payment would have to be reduced accordingly. For instance, if you had $350 in other installment payments, your maximum monthly mortgage payment would be $1,000 − $350 = $650.

Determining the largest mortgage for which you qualify is just the first step, however. You also need to consider your lifestyle. Will taking on the responsibility of a mortgage require you to perhaps forgo some luxuries or radically change your spending habits? To see how buying a house affects your cash flow, you should revise your personal budget to include the costs of buying a home—monthly mortgage payments, utilities, maintenance, insurance, and so on. Only you can decide how much of your income you are willing to allocate to a mortgage. Trade-offs are typically involved; you may choose a lower-priced house with a smaller mortgage to maintain greater financial flexibility.

Property Taxes and insurance. Aside from loan costs, mortgage payments often include property tax and insurance payments. When this occurs, the monthly mortgage payment is made up of four parts. Part of the mortgage payment goes to (1) reduce the *principal* amount of the loan; (2) pay the *interest* on the loan; (3) pay property *taxes*; and (4) pay homeowner's *insurance*. Together, the mortgage payment consists of *p*rincipal, *i*nterest, *t*axes, and *i*nsurance (or **PITI** for short). Actually, that portion of the loan payment that goes for taxes and insurance is paid into an *escrow account*, where it accumulates over time. Then, once or twice a year, the lender draws funds from this account to pay required property taxes and homeowner's insurance premiums. Increases in tax rates and/or insurance premiums are passed on to the home buyer in the form of higher monthly loan payments.

Interestingly, some but not all lenders pay interest—typically at no higher than the regular savings rate—on escrow account balances. Generally, though, it is advisable for disciplined borrowers to negotiate with the lender to avoid paying into an escrow account. Such a strategy, if successful, gives you greater flexibility and an opportunity to earn a higher return on the funds that would otherwise be held in an escrow account.

Because they are local taxes levied to fund schools, law enforcement, and other local services, the level of **property taxes** differs from one community to another. And within a given community, individual property taxes will vary with the *assessed value* of the property—generally, the more expensive the home, the higher the property taxes, and vice versa. As a rule, annual property taxes vary from less than .5 percent to more than 2 percent of a home's approximate market value. Thus, the property taxes on a $100,000 home could vary from about $500 to more than $2,000 a year, depending on location and geographic area.

The other component of the monthly mortgage payment is **homeowner's insurance**. Its cost varies with such factors as the age of the house, location, materials used in construction, and geographic area. Homeowner's insurance is carried only on the replacement value of the home and its contents and not on the land. Annual insurance costs usually amount to approximately .25 to .5 percent of the home's market value or from $250 to $500 for a $100,000 house. The types, characteristics, and features of homeowner's insurance policies are discussed in Chapter 10.

Maintenance and Operating Expenses. In addition to the monthly mortgage payments, home buyers incur maintenance and operating expenses. Maintenance costs should be anticipated even on new homes. Painting, mechanical repairs, leak repairs, and lawn maintenance, for example, are inescapable facts of homeownership. Such costs are likely to be greater, though, for older, larger homes. Thus, while a large, established home may have an attractive purchase price, a new, smaller home may be the better buy in view of its lower maintenance and operating costs.

PITI Notation used to refer to a mortgage payment that includes stipulated portions of *p*rincipal, *i*nterest, property *t*axes, and homeowner's *i*nsurance.

property taxes Taxes levied by local governments on the assessed value of real estate for the purpose of funding schools, law enforcement, and other local services.

homeowner's insurance Insurance required by mortgage lenders that typically covers the replacement value of a home and its contents.

Another point to consider in the selection process is the cost of operating the home, specifically the cost of utilities, such as electricity, gas, water, and sewage. These costs have skyrocketed in the past 10 to 15 years and today represent a sizable component of homeownership costs. Because they are unavoidable and vary with geographic location, type of heating and air conditioning, size of home, amount of insulation, and other factors, you should get operating cost estimates when evaluating a particular home-purchase candidate.

PERFORMING HOME AFFORDABILITY ANALYSIS

To estimate the amount you can afford for a home, use Worksheet 5.1. This analysis determines the maximum home-purchase price using both your monthly income and down payment amount, after meeting estimated closing costs. In our example, the Renée and Pierre Goulet family had combined annual income of $48,400 and $22,500 available for a down payment and closing costs. They estimated monthly taxes and homeowner's insurance of $150 and expected the mortgage lender to use a 28 percent monthly mortgage-payment affordability ratio, to lend at an average interest rate of 9 percent on a 30-year mortgage, and to require a 10 percent minimum down payment. The Goulet's analysis showed that they can afford to purchase a home costing about $137,000. Their available monthly income (Item 13) rather than the amount available for making a down payment (Item 15) was the key determinant of the maximum affordable home-purchase price.

Exhibit 5.6 provides a quick way to estimate the size of the mortgage you can afford, based on different monthly mortgage payment and mortgage interest rate assumptions. First, determine the maximum monthly mortgage payment you can handle. Follow that line across to find the approximate size of the mortgage your payment will buy at each mortgage interest rate. (This figure assumes a 30-year, fixed-rate loan and does *not* include taxes and insurance.) For example, if you estimate that you have $1,000 available per month and the prevailing mortgage interest rate is 10 percent, you could afford a mortgage of about $114,000. Of course, the price of the home you could afford to buy also depends on the amount of cash you have available for making the down payment and paying closing costs.

Concept Check

5-3. Briefly describe the various motives for owning a home. Which one is most important to you? Which is least important?

5-4. What does the *loan-to-value ratio* on a home represent? Is the down payment on a home related to its loan-to-value ratio? Explain.

5-5. What are *mortgage points?* How much would a home buyer have to pay if the lender wanted to charge 2.5 points on an $85,000 mortgage? When would this amount have to be paid? What effect do points have on the mortgage's rate of interest?

5-6. What are *closing costs,* and what items do they include? Who pays these costs, and when?

5-7. What are the most common guidelines used to determine the amount of monthly mortgage payments one can afford?

5-8. Why is it advisable for the prospective buyer to investigate property taxes, insurance, maintenance, and operating expenses when shopping for a home? Explain.

THE OPTION OF RENTING

FPPC LG3

Buying a home may not be a viable option for some people. Due to financial constraints or personal lifestyle considerations, they decide to rent an apartment or house. What are some reasons you might choose to rent rather than buy, and what factors would be important to you in selecting a rental unit? Give some thought to these questions before continuing with the chapter.

Many people choose to rent rather than buy their home. For example, young adults usually rent for one or more of the following reasons: (1) They do not have the funds for a down payment and

WORKSHEET 5.1

Home Affordability Analysis for the Renée and Pierre Goulet Family

By using the following variables in the home affordability analysis form, the Goulet's estimate a maximum home purchase price of about $137,000: their combined annual income of $48,400; the $22,500 available for a down payment; closing costs along with estimated monthly taxes and homeowner's insurance of $150; the lender's 28 percent monthly affordability ratio; an average interest rate of 9 percent and expected loan maturity of 30 years; and a minimum down payment of 10 percent.

HOME AFFORDABILITY ANALYSIS*

Name: Renée and Peter Goulet   Date: December 12, 1995

Item	Description	Amount
1	Amount of annual income	$ 48,400
2	Monthly income (Item 1 ÷ 12)	$ 4,033
3	Lender's affordability ratio (in decimal form)	.28
4	Maximum monthly mortgage payment (PITI) (Item 2 × Item 3)	$ 1,130
5	Estimated monthly tax and homeowner's insurance payment	$ 150
6	Maximum monthly loan payment (Item 4 − Item 5)	980
7	Approximate average interest rate on loan	9%
8	Planned loan maturity (years)	30
9	Mortgage payment per $10,000 (using Item 7 and Item 8 and Table of Monthly Mortgage Payments in Exhibit 5.5)	$ 80.47
10	Maximum loan based on monthly income ($10,000 × Item 6 ÷ Item 9)	$ 121,785
11	Funds available for making a down payment and paying closing costs	$ 22,500
12	Funds available for making a down payment (Item 11 × .67)	$ 15,000
13	Maximum purchase price based on available monthly income (Item 10 + Item 12)	$ 136,785
14	Minimum acceptable down payment (in decimal form)	.10
15	Maximum purchase price based on down payment (Item 12 ÷ Item 14)	$ 150,000
16	Maximum home purchase price (lower of Item 13 and Item 15)	$ 136,785

*__Note:__ This analysis assumes that 1/3 of the funds available for making the down payment and paying closing costs are used to meet closing costs while the remaining 2/3 are available for a down payment. This assumption means that closing costs will represent an amount equal to 50 percent of the down payment.

closing costs; (2) they are unsettled in their jobs and family status; (3) they do not want the additional responsibilities associated with homeownership; (4) they may be able to later afford a nicer home by renting now, because housing market conditions or mortgage rates are currently unattractive but expected to improve in the near future. Monthly rent payments only pay for the use of the property and are *not* tax deductible. Those who choose to rent should be familiar with rental contracts and know how to compare the costs of renting versus buying.

EXHIBIT 5.6

How Much Mortgage Will Your Payment Buy?

This table provides a quick way to estimate the size of the mortgage you can afford based on the monthly mortgage payment and mortgage interest rate. It assumes a 30-year, fixed-rate loan. Remember that this amount is only for mortgage principal and interest; you must have funds available for paying taxes and insurance as well.

Monthly Mortgage Payment	Mortgage Interest Rate							
	6%	7%	8%	9%	10%	11%	12%	13%
$ 500	$ 83,396	$ 75,154	$ 68,142	$ 62,141	$ 56,975	$ 52,503	$ 48,609	$ 45,200
600	100,075	90,185	81,770	74,569	68,370	63,004	58,331	54,240
700	116,754	105,215	95,398	86,997	79,766	73,504	68,053	63,280
800	133,433	120,246	109,027	99,425	91,161	84,005	77,775	72,320
900	150,112	135,277	122,655	111,854	102,556	94,506	87,497	81,360
1,000	166,792	150,308	136,283	124,282	113,951	105,006	97,218	90,400
1,100	183,471	165,338	149,912	136,710	125,346	115,507	106,940	99,440
1,200	200,150	180,369	163,540	149,138	136,741	126,008	116,662	108,480
1,300	216,829	195,400	177,169	161,566	148,136	136,508	126,384	117,520
1,400	233,508	210,431	190,797	173,995	159,531	147,009	136,106	126,560
1,500	250,187	225,461	204,425	186,423	170,926	157,510	145,828	135,599

Note: ***To use:*** (1) Find the amount of monthly mortgage payment you can afford, to the nearest $100. Then find the current mortgage interest rate, to the nearest percent. The approximate mortgage amount will be at the intersection of the two columns. (2) To estimate the mortgage size if the interest rate ends in .5 percent, add the mortgage amounts for the lower and higher mortgage interest rates and divide by 2. (3) To estimate the mortgage size for a payment ending in 50, add the mortgage amounts for the lower and higher monthly mortgage payments and divide by 2.

Examples: (1) The estimated mortgage size if you have a monthly mortgage payment of $900 on a 30-year, 10 percent loan is $102,556. (2) To find the estimated mortgage size if you have a monthly mortgage payment of $900 and the mortgage interest rate is 9.5 percent, add the mortgage sizes for $900 at 9 percent and at 10 percent and divide by 2: [($111,854 + $102,556) ÷ 2] = $214,410 ÷ 2 = $107,205. (3) To find the estimated mortgage size if you have a monthly mortgage payment of $950 and the mortgage interest rate is 9 percent, add the mortgage sizes for $900 and $1,000 at 9 percent and divide by 2: [($111,854 + $124,282) ÷ 2] = $236,136 ÷ 2 = $118,068.

THE RENTAL CONTRACT

When you rent an apartment, duplex, house, or any other type of unit, you normally will be required to sign a **rental contract,** or **lease agreement.** Although oral agreements are generally binding, a written contract is a legal instrument that better protects both the *lessor* (the person who owns the property) and the *lessee* (the person who leases the property). Because the rental contract binds you—the lessee—to various actions, you should make certain that you fully understand it before signing it. As a rule, the contract specifies the *amount* of the monthly payment, the payment *date, penalties* for late payment, the *length* of the lease agreement, *deposit* requirements, the distribution of *expenses, renewal* options, and any *restrictions,* for example, on children, pets, subleasing to another tenant, or the use of facilities.

Most leases have a minimum term of either six months or one year and require payments at the beginning of each month. They initially require a deposit and/or payment of the last month's rent as security against damages and infringement of the lease agreement. In the absence of any serious damage, most of the deposit should be refunded to the lessee shortly after the lease expires; a portion of the deposit is sometimes retained by the lessor to cover the cost of cleaning and minor repairs, regardless of how clean and well-kept the unit is left. Because the landlord has control over the deposit, a written statement describing any damage in evidence *prior* to occupancy may help the lessee avoid losing the entire deposit. Renters should also clarify who bears expenses such as utilities and trash collection and exactly what, if any, restrictions are placed on the use of the property. It's also a good idea for renters to check the various renter-landlord laws in their states in order to fully understand their *rights,* as well as responsibilities.

THE RENT-OR-BUY DECISION

Today, about 36 percent of all U.S. families live in rented housing and about 64 percent own their own home. The economics of renting or buying a place to live depends, in large part, on three factors: (1) levels of housing prices and mortgage interest rates; (2) tax write-offs for home owners; and (3) the increase or decrease in home values over time.

Some people rent rather than buy because they either do not have the money for the down payment and closing costs, or their income is inadequate to safely make monthly mortgage payments. Others, however, rent because they prefer the greater mobility and not having to worry about maintenance and upkeep, or, for them, renting makes more economic sense than buying.

To choose the least-cost alternative, compare the cost of renting with the cost of buying, as illustrated by the rent-or-buy analysis in Worksheet 5.2 on page 193. Note that the calculations assume that if the residence is purchased, the homeowner will itemize deductions on his or her tax return. If instead the homeowner elects to take the standard deduction, the value of the two tax shelter entries in Worksheet 5.2 (marked with an asterisk) should be set equal to zero—and in that case, the attractiveness of buying is greatly diminished.

Assume that you must decide between renting an apartment for $650 a month or buying a similar-sized, $100,000 condominium. Purchasing the condo involves a $15,000 down payment, an $85,000, 9-percent, 30-year mortgage with monthly mortgage payments of $684 (from Exhibit 5.5), $4,500 in closing costs, and property taxes, insurance, and maintenance. With renting, the only costs would be the $650 monthly rental payment and an annual renter's insurance premium of $300. Assume that you will itemize deductions if you purchase the home and that you are in the 28 percent tax bracket. Substituting the appropriate values into Worksheet 5.2 and making the required calculations results in the total cost of each alternative. *Buying* is preferred over renting, because the total cost of renting is $1,974 ($8,100 − $6,126) a year more than the total cost of buying. Alternatively, of course, you could look for a less expensive apartment. If you could lower the rent by about $165 a month—that is, $1,974/12—renting would be preferred. Renting would also be better if you plan to take the standard deduction (rather than itemize) on your tax return, because the values of the entries on lines B.8. and B.9. would then equal zero, thus raising the cost of homeownership by about $2,700 a year.

The rent-or-buy decision cannot be made solely on the basis of numbers. You should also carefully consider both your personal situation and needs and the general condition of the housing market. If you think you may want to move to a different city in a few years or you are worried about job security, renting may make sense, even if the numbers favor buying. For some people, factors such as the need for privacy, the desire to personalize one's home, and the psychic satisfaction gained from homeownership outweigh the financial considerations. In some housing markets, a relative surplus of rental properties causes the cost of renting to be lower than the cost of owning a comparable house or condominium. It is a good idea to look at the rent-or-buy decision over a time horizon of several years, using different assumptions regarding rent increases, mortgage rates, home appreciation rates in the area, and the rate of return you can earn on the funds you can invest (if you rent) rather than use them to make a down payment (if you buy).

Concept Check

5-9. Why is it important to have a written lease? What should a rental contract include?

5-10. Discuss the relative advantages and disadvantages of renting a home. Does a homeowner have any advantage over a renter with respect to taxes? Explain.

rental contract (lease agreement) A legal instrument that protects both the lessor and the lessee from an adverse action by the other party; it specifies the *amount* of the monthly payment, the payment *date, penalties* for late payment, the *length* of the lease agreement, *deposit* requirements, the distribution of *expenses, renewal* options, and any *restrictions,* for example, on children, pets, subleasing, or the use of facilities.

THE HOME-BUYING PROCESS

LG4

Buying a house involves a process that begins with finding the right house at the right price and ends with closing the deal. Assuming that you are interested in buying a home, what steps would you use to effectively and efficiently achieve this goal? Before reading ahead, spend a few minutes responding to this question.

Buying a home usually requires a good deal of time, effort, and money. Learning about the available properties and their prices requires a systematic search and careful property analysis. Also, a buyer should have a basic understanding of the mortgage application process, real estate sales contracts, and other documents required to close a deal.

SHOP THE MARKET FIRST

Most people who shop the housing market rely on real estate agents for information, access to properties, and advice. Other sources of information, such as newspaper ads, are also widely used to identify available properties. Occasionally a person seeking to buy or rent property will advertise his or her needs and wait for sellers to initiate contact.

Buying a home involves many factors, both emotional and financial. Frequently, the emotional factors carry the greatest weight. As noted earlier, you must begin by figuring out what *you* require for your particular lifestyle in terms of living space, style, and special features. The location, neighborhood, and school district are usually important considerations as well. You should divide your list into the necessary features, such as the number of bedrooms and baths, and the optional—but desirable—features. And of course, affordability analysis is a critical component of your housing search.

However, once you start looking, you may find that you like a different house than you thought you originally wanted. For example, you may begin your search by looking for a one-story, contemporary ranch house with a pool, but fall in love with a two-story colonial with wonderful landscaping, no pool, and all the other features you want. It is a good idea to be flexible at first and look at a variety of homes in your price range; this can really help you define your wants and needs more clearly.

In some areas you can now use your computer or phone to help you with your housing search. For example, you may be able to access a real estate database. By specifying certain preferences—for example, location, price, size—buyers can get lists of properties that meet their needs. Other systems allow buyers to use a touch-tone phone to get a recorded description of homes listed by a particular agency or use an electronic kiosk to see and print descriptions and see color pictures of homes for sale.

If you already own a house but want or need a larger or different type of home, you can either trade up or remodel. You may choose to remodel if you like your neighborhood and can make the desired changes to your current home. In some cases, the cost to remodel will be less than the transaction costs of buying another house. The best remodeling projects are those whose costs you can recoup when you sell the house. Kitchen improvements, additional bathrooms, and family rooms tend to best enhance a home's market value. While a swimming pool may give you pleasure, you may not recover its cost when you sell the house.

It is highly unlikely that you will find the "perfect" home at the "perfect" price. You will have to make some compromises, and the greater your research and advance preparation, the better off you will be. This approach should help reduce the *buyer remorse* that often accompanies a major purchase. Soon after signing the sales contract, home buyers often question whether they did the right thing: Did I pay too much? Should I have negotiated harder? Is the location as good as I thought? Can I really afford the monthly payments? Can I manage without a pool/playroom/workshop? These feelings are normal and usually decrease once you move in. One way to reduce buyer remorse is to shorten, if possible, the time that elapses between signing the sales contract and closing the deal. The *Smart Money* box on page 194 provides further advice on how to avoid some common mistakes in the home-buying process.

Using an Agent. Most home buyers rely on real estate agents because they are in daily contact with the housing market. Once you describe your needs to an agent he or she can begin to search for appropriate properties. The agent also will help you negotiate with the seller, assist you in obtaining satisfactory financing, and, although not

WORKSHEET 5.2

Rent-or-Buy Cost Comparison

Using this procedure to make the rent-or-buy decision, you should *rent* if the total cost of renting is less than the total cost of buying, and *buy* if the total cost of renting is more than the total cost of buying. In this illustration, the rental option requires monthly payments of $650. The purchase option is a $100,000 condo, financed with a $15,000 down payment and an $85,000, 9-percent, 30-year mortgage, with additional closing costs of $4,500.

RENT-OR-BUY ANALYSIS			
A. COST OF RENTING			
1. Annual rental costs (12 × monthly rental rate of $ 650)		$ 7,800	
2. Renter's insurance		300	
Total cost of renting (line A.1 + line A.2)			$ 8,100
B. COST OF BUYING			
1. Annual mortgage payments (Terms: $ 85,000 , 360 months, 9 %) (12 × monthly mortgage payment of $ 684)	$ 8,208		
2. Property taxes (2 % of price of home)	2,000		
3. Homeowner's insurance (.5 % of price of home)	500		
4. Maintenance (.8 % of price of home)	800		
5. After-tax cost of interest on down payment and closing costs ($ 19,500 × 4.5 % after-tax rate of return)	878		
6. Total costs (sum of lines B.1 through B.5)		$ 12,386	
Less:			
7. Principal reduction in loan balance (see note below)	$ 558		
8. Tax savings due to interest deductions* (Interest portion of mortgage payments $ 7,650 × tax rate of 28 %)	2,142		
9. Tax savings due to property tax deductions* (line B.2 x tax rate of 28 %)	560		
10. Total deductions (sum of lines B.7 through B.9)		3,260	
11. Annual after-tax cost of home ownership (line B.6 – line B.10)		$ 9,126	
12. Estimated annual appreciation in value of home (3 % of price of home)		3,000	
Total cost of buying (line B.11 – line B.12)			$ 6,126

Note: Find monthly mortgage payments from Exhibit 5.5. An easy way to approximate the portion of the *annual* loan payment that goes to interest (line B.8.) is to multiply the interest rate by the size of the loan (in this case, $85,000 × .09 = $7,650). To find the principal reduction in the loan balance (line B.7), simply subtract the amount that goes to interest from total annual mortgage payments ($8,208 – $7,650 = $558).

*Tax-shelter items.

empowered to give explicit legal advice, help you prepare a real estate sales contract.

Most real estate firms belong to the local **Multiple Listing Service (MLS).** Basically, MLS compiles a list of properties for sale from information provided by the member firms in a given community or metropolitan area. A brief

Multiple Listing Service (MLS) An organization of real estate companies that compiles and updates weekly a list and brief description, including asking price, of all properties for sale by the member firms in a given community or metropolitan area.

Smart Money

How to Be a Savvy Home Buyer

Buying a home can be an enjoyable and exciting experience. Because it is also the largest single purchase you'll ever make, it can be an intimidating—and even scary—process as well. The following tips will help you feel more confident about embarking on your home-buying adventure:

1. Don't just think about your present needs. Many first-time buyers, especially those who are single and in their late 20s and early 30s, buy one-bedroom condominiums without considering that they are likely to marry and have families and will therefore require more space. Thinking ahead to accommodate future lifestyle changes will give you more flexibility.
2. Choose a reputable agent who knows the neighborhood where you're looking for a home. If you decide to look in a different area, ask to be referred to a new agent.
3. If you're a renter, the best time to close on a house is when your current lease expires. Unfortunately, though, it's not always possible to time a closing. Another option: sign a shorter lease, perhaps three to six months; go month-to-month; or have your landlord add an escape clause that allows you to get out of your lease with 30- or 60-days' notice.
4. Don't look at homes you can't afford; you will gain nothing, except feeling disappointed by the homes in your price range. When considering what's affordable, don't forget to factor in your debts, property taxes, insurance premiums, private mortgage insurance, the down payment, and maintenance and upkeep costs.
5. Avoid jumping at the first home you see. When you begin your search, look at five, ten, or even twenty houses. You will then have a more seasoned eye, and perhaps your priorities will have changed. Revisit your top three or four choices; you'll be better able to evaluate them and choose with confidence.
6. When you find a house that you love, spend some time in the neighborhood before buying to make sure that it's appropriate for you. Are the neighbors your age? Do many have children? Is it a transient neighborhood, or do families tend to stay for a long time? Are schools and shopping nearby? Are the streets clean and the walls graffiti-free? Is there a high crime rate?
7. Try to evaluate how easy it would be for you to resell the house. If you don't mind living in the evening flight path of the local airport, ask yourself if most potential buyers would. And even if you don't plan to have children, check out the quality of the local schools; that's often a key concern of home buyers.
8. Have the house thoroughly inspected before you buy. Don't rely on a realtor's estimate of repair costs. Get a licensed contractor's estimate, then add at least 10 percent to that figure. Most structural problems can be fixed, but major repairs of termite damage, the foundation, or the roof can be quite costly. Don't forget to evaluate the land on which the house is built.
9. Don't say no to a house that needs some cosmetic repairs. In fact, such a "fixer-upper" can be a good investment. It will be more reasonably priced than a home in mint condition, and by completing the work it needs (such as painting, carpeting, or landscaping) you will increase its value.
10. Avoid a bidding war. If another buyer makes a bid on the house you want, wait to see what happens, rather than creating a competition that allows the seller to drive up the price.
11. Read everything, including the seller's disclosure statement, reports on the property, and especially the sales contract—*before* you sign it! Ask your real estate agent to explain anything you don't understand, and get copies of everything you sign.

Sources: Adapted from Ilyce R. Glink, "Avoid Common Mistakes Made by Many First-Time Home Buyers," *San Diego Union-Tribune*, 24 April 1994, pp. H-7, 12; Dian Hymer, "Ten Common Pitfalls to Avoid When Buying a House," *San Diego Union-Tribune*, 25 April 1993, p. H-3; Dian Hymer, "Perseverance is Needed in Negotiating a Home Purchase," *San Diego Union-Tribune*, 24 April 1994, pp. H-6, 12.

description of each property and its asking price are included, and the list is updated weekly. As a rule, it is best to deal with a realtor that works for a MLS member firm; otherwise, you might lack access to a large part of the market.

Buyers should remember that *agents typically are employed by the sellers*. Unless you have agreed to pay a fee to the sales agent you are working with, that agent's primary responsibility, by law, is to sell listed properties at the highest possible prices. Further, because agents are paid only if they make a sale, some might pressure you to "sign now or miss the chance of a lifetime." You should avoid that type of agent. Select someone who will listen to your wants and then work to match you with the right property under terms that will benefit both the seller and you. Good agents recognize that their best interests are served when all parties to a transaction are satisfied. Depending on the geographic location, real estate commissions range from 5 to 6 percent for new homes and 6 to 7 percent for previously occupied homes. It is sometimes possible to negotiate a lower commission with your agent, or to find a discount broker or one who charges a flat fee. However, such commissions are paid only by the seller; the buyer pays the real estate agent nothing. Of course, because the price of a home is likely to be affected by the size of the real estate commission—indeed, many builders are believed to factor commission costs into the prices of their new homes—the buyer probably absorbs some or even all of the commission paid by the seller.

There are two other types of agents who can help you buy a house. A *buyer's broker*, as the term implies, is hired by the buyer to negotiate on his or her behalf, whereas the traditional agent represents the seller's interests. The commission to the buyer's broker is typically negotiated and may ultimately be paid by the seller. The *facilitator*, on the other hand, represents neither the buyer nor seller but is paid, typically by both parties, to serve as a neutral intermediary between them.

PREQUALIFYING AND APPLYING FOR A MORTGAGE

Before beginning your home search, it may be helpful to meet with one or more mortgage lenders and prearrange for a mortgage loan. **Prequalification,** as it is called, can work to your advantage. You will know ahead of time that you qualify for a specific mortgage amount (subject, of course, to changes in rates and other terms) and can therefore focus your search on homes within an affordable price range. Prequalification also provides estimates of the required down payment and closing costs for different types of mortgages. It identifies in advance of purchase any problems, such as credit report errors, that might arise as a result of your application, and allows you more time to correct them. Finally, prequalification enhances your bargaining power with the seller of a house you want by letting them know that the deal won't fall through because you can't afford the property or obtain suitable financing, and that the time required to close the sale should be relatively short.

There are many sources of mortgage loans, and you should begin investigating them while you are looking for your house. When you actually apply for a mortgage loan on a particular home, you will need to give the lender information on your income, assets, and outstanding debts. Documents the lender may request include proof of your monthly income (paycheck stubs, W-2 forms, and so on), statements showing all debt balances (credit cards, car and school loans, bank lines of credit, and so on), lists of financial assets such as savings accounts and securities, several months' bank account statements, and at least two years' income tax returns. We will cover financing your home in detail later in the chapter.

THE REAL ESTATE SALES CONTRACT

Once you select a home to buy, you must enter into a sales contract. State laws generally specify that in order to be enforceable in court, real estate buy-sell agreements must be in writing and contain certain information, including (1) names of buyer(s) and seller(s), (2) a description of the property sufficient to provide positive identification, (3) specific price and other terms, and (4) usually the signatures of the buyer(s) and seller(s). Real

prequalification The process of arranging with a mortgage lender, in advance of buying a home, to obtain the amount of mortgage financing the lender deems affordable to the homebuyer.

estate sales transactions often take weeks and sometimes months to complete. They involve a fair amount of legal work and therefore require expert assistance in preparation. Contract requirements help keep the facts straight and reduce the chance for misunderstanding, misrepresentation, or fraud.

Although these requirements fulfill the minimums necessary for court enforcement, in practice real estate sales contracts usually contain several other contractual clauses. Among these are provisions relating to earnest money deposits, contingencies, personal property, and closing costs. An **earnest money deposit** is the money you pledge when you make an offer, to show good faith. If, after you sign a sales contract, you withdraw from the transaction without a valid reason, you forfeit this deposit. A valid reason for withdrawal would be one stated in the contract as a contingency clause. With a **contingency clause,** you can condition your agreement to buy on such factors as the availability of financing, a termite or other physical inspection of the property, or the advice of a lawyer or real estate expert. Generally speaking, your lawyer should review and approve all agreements before you sign them.

CLOSING THE DEAL

After you obtain financing and your loan has been approved, the closing process begins. There are three important parts to a closing: (1) the RESPA statement, (2) the title check, and (3) the closing statement.

RESPA. Since 1974, closings on owner-occupied houses, condominiums, and apartment buildings of four units or fewer have been governed by the **Real Estate Settlement Procedures Act (RESPA).** This act (and its 1975 amended version) reduced closing costs primarily by prohibiting kickbacks made to real estate agents and others from lenders or title insurance companies in conjunction with closing services and by requiring advance disclosure of closing costs to buyers.

The specific requirements of RESPA are given in a U.S. Department of Housing and Urban Development booklet entitled *Settlement Costs and You: A HUD Guide for Homebuyers.* The law requires lenders to give a copy of this guide to potential borrowers. It can take much of the mystery out of the closing process. Although closing expenses still may climb into the thousands of dollars, homebuyers often can save significant amounts if they shop for financing, insurance coverages, and other closing items rather than merely accepting the costs quoted by any one lender or other provider of closing services.

Title Check. Numerous legal interests can exist in real estate simultaneously, for example, those of the owner(s), lender(s), lienholders (such as an unpaid roofing contractor), and easement holders. Before you take title to a property, therefore, you should make sure that the title is free of all liens and encumbrances (except those that are specifically referred to in the sales contract) and that the owners who are conveying title to you actually have the legal interest they claim.

Although it is up to you to question the quality of the title to the property you are buying, in most cases an attorney or title insurance company performs a **title check,** which consists of the necessary research of legal documents and courthouse records. The customary practices and procedures and the costs involved vary widely throughout the country. Regardless of the specific custom in your area, you should make some form of title check an essential part of your closing process.

Closing Statement. A **closing statement,** provided to both buyer and seller at closing, accounts for the monies that change hands during that procedure. The statement reconciles the borrower's and the seller's costs and shows how much the borrower owes and the seller receives from the transaction. Exhibit 5.7 on page 198 shows a simplified closing statement for both the borrower (buyer) and seller in a transaction involving the sale of a home for $100,000. In addition to the $100,000 purchase price, the borrower must pay 3 points on the $90,000 mortgage loan, plus a number of other charges, advance payments, reserve deposits with the lender, title charges, and recording fees—resulting in a gross amount due of $105,273.69. After subtracting the $3,000 earnest money deposit, the $90,000 of loan proceeds, and the county tax credit of $103.68, the borrower will have to pay $12,377.37 at closing. After charges are subtracted, including a $6,000 real estate commission, the sel-ler's mortgage payoff of $65,867.50, and the unpaid county taxes of $103.68 (to be paid by the seller), from the $100,000 sale price, the amount the seller will receive at closing is $27,048.32. Note that frequently the RESPA form developed by the U.S. Department of Housing and Urban Development is used. Before closing a home purchase transaction, you should be given an opportunity to review the closing statement and have your questions answered. Be sure to carefully and critically review the statement in order to make sure that it is accurate and consistent with the contractual terms of the transaction; if not, have the statement corrected before closing the deal.

Concept Check

5-11. Describe some of the steps that home buyers can take to improve the home-buying process and increase their overall satisfaction with their purchases.

5-12. What role does a real estate agent play in the purchase of a house? What is the benefit of the *Multiple Listing Service?* How is the real estate agent compensated, and by whom?

5-13. Why should you investigate mortgage loans and prequalify for a mortgage early in the home-buying process?

5-14. What information is normally included in a real estate sales contract? What is an *earnest money deposit?* What is a *contingency clause?*

5-15. Describe the steps involved in closing a home purchase transaction.

FINANCING THE TRANSACTION

FPPC

LG5

Obtaining adequate financing under reasonable terms at minimum cost is typically the most challenging aspect of the home-buying process. Once you've found the right home, what sources and types of mortgage financing would be available to you? Spend a few moments answering this question before reading on.

Often the success of a real estate transaction hinges on obtaining a mortgage with favorable terms. Earlier in the chapter, we saw that the mortgage terms can have a dramatic effect on the amount you can afford to spend on a home. A **mortgage loan** is secured by the property. This means that in the event of borrower default the lender obtains the legal right to liquidate the property to recover the funds it is owed. To obtain such a loan, you must be familiar with the available sources and types of mortgage loans. Additionally, it is useful to understand the economics of mortgage refinancing.

SOURCES OF MORTGAGE LOANS

The three major sources of home mortgages today are commercial banks, thrift institutions, and mortgage bankers or mortgage brokers. Some *credit unions* also make mortgage loans available to their members. During the past few years, *commercial banks*, formerly viewed primarily as short-term lenders, have become a major force in the residential mortgage market. Commercial banks also are an important source of **interim construction loans** used by persons who are building a home.

earnest money deposit Money pledged by a buyer to show good faith when making an offer to buy a home.

contingency clause A clause in a real estate sales contract that makes the agreement conditional on such factors as the availability of financing, property inspections, or obtaining expert advice.

Real Estate Settlement Procedures Act (RESPA) A law passed in 1974 that requires mortgage lenders to give potential borrowers a government publication that describes the closing process and to provide clear, advance disclosure of closing costs to home buyers.

title check The research of legal documents and courthouse records to verify that the title to a property is free of all liens and encumbrances and that the seller conveying title actually has the legal interest he or she claims.

closing statement A statement provided to both buyer and seller at closing that accounts for the monies that change hands during that procedure.

mortgage loan A loan secured by real property; in the event of borrower default the lender has the legal right to liquidate the property to recover the funds it is owed.

interim construction loan A loan that provides short-term financing while a home is being constructed.

EXHIBIT 5.7

A Simple Closing Statement

At the top in the borrower's (buyer's) statement, her charges, advance payments, reserve deposits with the lender, title charges, and recording fees are added to the $100,000 purchase price, and then the earnest money deposit, principal amount of the loan, and county tax credit are subtracted from the total to find the amount due from the borrower of $12,377.37. In the seller's statement, the total charges, mortgage payoff, and county tax credit to borrower are subtracted from the $100,000 sale price to find the $27,048.32 cash to be paid the seller.

A. Borrower's Statement		
Contract Price		$100,000.00
Plus: Charges		
Points (3% × $90,000)	$ 2,700.00	
Appraisal Fee	175.00	
Credit Report	84.00	
Tax Service	32.00	
Total		2,991.00
Plus: Advance Payments		
Interest to End of Month	$ 547.09	
Mortgage Insurance Premium	855.00	
Homeowner's Insurance Premium	347.00	
Total		1,749.09
Plus: Reserves Deposited with Lender		
Homeowner's Insurance (2 mos.)	$ 57.84	
Mortgage Insurance (2 mos.)	56.26	
County Property Taxes (2 mos.)	59.00	
Total		173.10
Plus: Title Charges		
Closing Fee	$ 103.50	
Title Insurance	245.00	
Total		348.50
Plus: Government Recording and Transfer Charges		
Recording Fees		12.00
GROSS DUE FROM BORROWER		$105,273.69
Less: Amounts Paid By or on Behalf of Borrower		
Earnest Money Deposit	$ 3,000.00	
Principal Amount of Loan	90,000.00	
County Tax Credit	(103.68)	
Total		(92,896.32)
AMOUNT DUE FROM BORROWER		$ 12,377.37
B. Seller's Statement		
Contract Sales Price		$100,000.00
Less: Charges		
Real Estate Commission	$ 6,000.00	
Closing Fee	103.50	
Title Insurance	535.00	
Affidavit of Value	2.00	
Termite Inspection	25.00	
1 year Home Warranty	315.00	
Total		(6,980.50)
Less: Payoff of Mortgage		(65,867.50)
Less: Credit to Borrower for County Taxes Owed		(103.68)
CASH TO SELLER		$ 27,048.32

These loans provide short-term financing during the construction period. After the home is completed, the homeowner obtains *permanent financing* (in the form of a standard, long-term, first mortgage loan) and uses it to repay the construction loan.

Thrift institutions include *savings and loan associations (S&Ls)* and *savings banks.* S&Ls either use customers' deposits to make loans or originate and sell loans to private investors. S&Ls concentrate on first mortgage loans on one-to-four-family houses, although some actively participate in the commercial real estate market as well. While their lending policies are dictated by regulators and mortgage market conditions, their terms are often more attractive than those of other mortgage lenders. Until recently, S&Ls were the largest source of home mortgages. Due to problems in the thrift industry, many homebuyers, concerned about having a long-term loan with an S&L that might not be around in a few years, have turned to other mortgage lenders.

Savings banks, 90 percent of which are located in the Northeast, direct a lot of their mortgage-lending money to their depositors. Because they are most often *mutual* organizations, and therefore depositor-owned, the terms of their mortgage loans tend to be slightly more favorable than those made by commercial banks and S&Ls.

Another way to obtain a mortgage loan is through a **mortgage banker** or **mortgage broker.** Both solicit borrowers, originate loans, and place them with mortgage lenders such as life insurance companies and pension funds. While *mortgage bankers* frequently use their own money to initially fund mortgages that they later resell, *mortgage brokers* take loan applications and then find lenders willing to grant the mortgage loans under the desired terms. Another difference is that mortgage bankers deal primarily in government-insured and -guaranteed loans, whereas mortgage brokers concentrate on finding conventional loans for consumers.

Using a mortgage broker. As a result of the S&L crisis and the increased number and complexity of types of mortgages, mortgage brokers have become a more important source of mortgage loans during recent years. Using a mortgage broker can save you the time and inconvenience of talking with a large number of lenders. In addition, brokers typically have computer programs that help you compare the effective costs of loans with different terms. Most brokers have ongoing relationships with many different types of lenders, thereby increasing your chances of finding a loan for which you qualify. Mortgage brokers frequently find loans for persons who would not qualify at a commercial bank or thrift institution. They can often cut through the red tape, act as the borrower's advocate to get more favorable terms, and reduce the amount of time required to close the loan.

For these reasons, a good mortgage broker can make the financing process much easier for homebuyers. However, not all mortgage brokers are competent; some have been known to misrepresent the services they can provide or recommend a loan that might not be best suited to its clients' needs. Before working with a particular mortgage broker, you should carefully investigate the firm and its reputation. Realtors, bankers, and other buyers can provide leads to good brokers. To help you get the best rate and terms, the broker should represent ten or more lenders, including some from other parts of the United States. Ask potential brokers how many of their loan applications are actually funded; about 70 percent or more should result in closings. If your state is one of the 30 that license mortgage brokers, be sure to choose one that is licensed and has been in business for several years. Many brokers are certified by the National Association of Mortgage Brokers, although this is not a requirement. You should also request a written estimate of closing costs; most competent brokers will provide this information and justify each cost.

Most mortgage brokers earn their income from commissions and origination fees paid by the lender. These lender costs are typically passed on to the borrower in the points charged on the loan. Borrowers may have to pay application fees of $300 to $500. They must also frequently pay processing and document preparation fees to the lender at closing. If a loan has no points, the buyer may have to pay a fee directly to the broker, which should be paid at closing. A broker that asks

mortgage banker A firm that solicits borrowers, originates primarily government-insured and -guaranteed loans, and places them with mortgage lenders; frequently uses its own money to initially fund mortgages it later resells.

mortgage broker A firm that solicits borrowers, originates primarily conventional loans, and places them with mortgage lenders; merely takes loan applications and then finds lenders willing to grant the mortgage loans under the desired terms.

for up-front fees and promises to find a loan is one to avoid. Rather than use a mortgage broker, you can shop for a mortgage on your own or with the assistance of your realtor, who is usually a knowledgeable source of information about various lenders and is legally prohibited from collecting fees or kickbacks for helping to arrange financing.

Seller Financing. One other important source of mortgage money is the seller of the property. Known as **seller financing,** this type of loan has long been in use, although it is most popular during periods of generally high interest rates. Seller financing can take one of two forms: balloon payments or buy-downs.

Balloon payments. If provided by the seller of an older home, seller financing will usually involve a **balloon payment,** which is a single, very large principal payment due at a specified future date. In this case, the seller of the home is a private party—the current owner, whose primary motivation is to sell the house. The balloon payment will be included in the transaction if the buyer does not have the money required for the down payment and/or does not want to commit to as large a mortgage loan as would otherwise be required. Under such circumstances, the buyer will look to the seller for financing.

Here is how it works. Suppose a potential buyer wants to purchase a $100,000 home that you have offered for sale; she has $15,000 available for a down payment, but because of high interest rates, does not wish to commit to a mortgage of more than $75,000. To sell the house, you agree to take a *note*, secured by a second mortgage, in the amount of $10,000. The note is set up so that it will mature (in full) in, say, five years; in addition, it will usually carry an interest rate that is at least a point or two below the market rate and will require monthly payments of *interest only* over the five-year term of the loan. In this case, the loan has only one principal (balloon) payment of $10,000, due at maturity. The buyer, of course, is hoping the interest rates drop within the five years so that the balloon payment note can be refinanced at a considerably lower rate.

A word of caution: Such forms of *creative financing* can cause serious problems for both the buyer and seller when interest rates fail to drop as expected or the buyer is simply unable to obtain alternative financing. The net result often is that the seller is left with a balloon-payment note that the buyer is unable to repay at its maturity.

Buy-downs. The other type of seller financing involves new homes and usually takes the form of a **buy-down.** In this case, a builder-developer will arrange with a financial institution (like an S&L) for mortgage financing at interest rates that are well below market rates—say, 8 percent financing on his homes at a time when the market rate of interest is around 9 or 9.5 percent. This obviously looks like a good deal, but how is this accomplished? Typically the builder/seller puts his money up front; in effect, he buys a reduced rate of interest by paying a specified number of points. In our example, the builder might have to pay 6 to 10 points to buy down the mortgage. Of course, such an arrangement can be costly and involve thousands of dollars. While the builder is trying to give the buyer the impression that he or she can finance a home bought from him at a special low interest rate, the fact is that the buyer will pay for the reduced interest in the form of a higher home-purchase price.

The intent behind buy-downs is to reduce the monthly mortgage payment—which can be accomplished even with a higher home price. Probably the most popular form of buy-down is the so-called "3–2–1 buy-down," meaning that the builder arranges a discount of 3 percentage points the first year, 2 percentage points the second year, and 1 point the third year. If the prevailing rate of interest is 9.5 percent, in a 3–2–1 buy-down on a 30-year mortgage the builder will arrange financing at 6.5 percent for year 1, 7.5 percent of year 2, 8.5 percent for year 3, and 9.5 percent for years 4 through 30. Thus, the monthly mortgage payments will start out low but will build up each year until the fourth year, when they will level off. For example, on a $70,000, 30-year mortgage loan, first-year payments would amount to around $442 a month; in the second year, they would jump to about $489; in the third, they would go up to around $536; and in the fourth and following years they would be up to about $583.

Buy-downs have received a lot of criticism because they tend to encourage homebuyers to overextend themselves and accept a larger mortgage loan than they can afford, especially under 3–2–1 type arrangements. In addition, the homeowner is often in for a big surprise when he has to sell his home after only three or four years. This occurs when the homeowner finds that the market value of his house is actually less than the amount he still owes on the mortgage. The reason, of course, is that the cost of the buy-down not only increased the price of the home, but it also added to the amount of the mortgage. Thus, a homebuyer, should exercise caution when considering a buy-down arrangement, or any other form of creative financing.

TYPES OF MORTGAGE LOANS

Knowing where to look for mortgage money is just the start. You also must choose the type of mortgage that is right for you. The mortgage market today is quite different from what it was 25 years ago. In 1970, for example, just a few basic types of mortgages were available. Today there is a full menu of mortgages; many financial institutions offer more than ten different kinds. Selecting the right mortgage obviously is an important aspect of buying a home.

Fortunately, personal computer programs are available for use in analyzing and comparing loan terms to choose those best for you. For example, *Managing Your Money* (see Chapter 2's box on using personal financial planning software) has a module that performs a rent-or-buy analysis as well as mortgage calculations. Another program, the *Home Buyers' Companion* (Parsons Technology; 1-800-223-6925; for Windows only), analyzes your home-buying options, costs, and mortgage alternatives. In many metropolitan areas you can purchase from a mortgage update service for about $20 a computer printout with the terms of the mortgages offered by lenders in your area. HSH Associates (1-800-873-2837) is a mortgage information service that covers the whole country. Its reports can be obtained in IBM-compatible disk form, together with software that can be used to compare different mortgage options. It is also possible to link your computer to a network of mortgage lenders; for a fee, a computer program will analyze your loan application and identify the best lenders in light of your individual circumstances.

The cost differentials among different types of mortgages can be substantial. It is not unusual to find differences of 2 full percentage points or more; for example, in early 1995 in a major market the quoted starting interest rate on one popular type of mortgage loan ranged from 4.10 to 6.75 percent, depending on the lender. Mortgage interest rates have always been a concern to homebuyers—a high interest rate can seriously affect your limits of affordability.

There is no single way to classify mortgages. For our purposes here, we will look at them in two ways: (1) terms of payment and (2) whether they are conventional, insured, or guaranteed. As far as terms of payment are concerned, there are literally dozens of different types of home mortgages from which to choose. For example, there are *graduated payment* and *growing equity* mortgages, in which the amount of the monthly mortgage payment gets progressively larger over time. With a *bi-weekly* mortgage, payments (equal to half of a regular monthly payment) are made every two weeks, rather than once a month. Because you make 26 payments (52 weeks ÷ 2), which is the equivalent of 13 monthly payments, the principal balance declines at a faster rate and you pay less interest over the life of the loan. For example, assume you qualify for a $100,000, 30-year mortgage with a 9 percent interest rate. You can either pay $805 monthly or $402.50 biweekly. The biweekly loan is paid off in the 21st year, saving you almost $62,000 in interest. However, with most 30-year mortgages you can make extra principal payments at any time, without penalty. Such a strategy may be better than committing to the biweekly mortgage, which frequently charges an extra processing fee.

Regardless of the type, mortgage loans made today are either fixed-rate mortgages or adjustable-rate mortgages. Because of their popularity, we now will take a closer look at these mortgages, their features, advantages, and disadvantages.

Fixed-Rate Mortgage. In spite of the fact that since mid-1975 a number of other types of mortgages have been developed, marketed, and

seller financing A type of loan provided either as a balloon payment by the seller of an older home or as a buy-down by a builder-developer of a new home to assist the buyer in purchasing their property; these incentives are commonly offered during periods of generally high interest rates.

balloon payment A single, very large mortgage principal payment due at a specified future date.

buy-down A type of seller financing made available by a builder-developer to a potential new-home buyer at below-market interest rates, often only for the first few years of the mortgage.

popularized, the **fixed-rate mortgage** today still accounts for a large portion of all home mortgages written. In this mortgage, both the rate of interest and the monthly mortgage payment are fixed over the full term of the loan. The most common type by far is the *30-year fixed-rate* loan. Because of the risks that the lender assumes in this type of mortgage, it is usually the most expensive form of home financing.

A variation of this standard fixed-rate loan that is gaining in popularity is the *15-year fixed-rate* mortgage. Its chief appeal is that it is repaid twice as fast (15 years versus 30) and yet the monthly payments don't increase significantly. Obviously, to pay off a loan in less time, the homeowner pays more each month. But the big (pleasant) surprise is that it does not take twice as large a monthly payment to pay off the loan in half the time; rather, the monthly payment on a 15-year loan is generally only about 20 percent larger than the payment on a 30-year loan. (Monthly mortgage payments on fixed-rate loans vary according to interest rates and loan terms, and these can be found by using the mortgage payment table in Exhibit 5.5.)

The basic features of 30- and 15-year fixed-rate mortgages are compared in the following table. In both cases, it is assumed that the purchaser borrows $80,000 at a 9 percent fixed rate of interest:

Type of Loan	Regular Payment	Term of Loan	Total Interest Paid over Life of Loan
Standard 30-year fixed rate	$643.76 per month	30 years	$151,754
15-year fixed rate	$811.44 per month	15 years	$ 66,059

Perhaps the most startling feature is the substantial difference in the total amount of interest paid. In effect, you can save *about $85,000* just by financing your home with a 15-year mortgage rather than a traditional 30-year one—not bad, considering it is only an $80,000 loan. Note that this amount of savings is possible even though monthly payments differ by about $168. In practice this difference would be even less, because 15-year mortgages are usually available at interest rates that are about half a percentage point below comparable 30-year loans. Thus, if the 30-year mortgage carried a 9 percent rate, you would expect the 15-year loan to be priced at, say, 8.5 percent. The monthly payments would then amount to only $788 rather than $811—a more realistic difference in monthly payments of *less than $150* ($788 − $644).

While the idea of paying off a mortgage in 15 years instead of 30 may seem like a good one, it is important to first consider how long you plan to stay in the house. If you plan to sell the house in a few years, paying off the loan faster may not make much sense. In addition, the tax deductibility of mortgage interest makes a mortgage one of the least expensive sources of borrowing. You should also determine whether you can earn a higher rate of return on the increase in the monthly payment for a 15-year mortgage than the rate of interest on the loan. If so, you would be better off investing the difference and taking a 30-year loan. You can also shorten the mortgage term by making extra principal payments on a regular basis or at times when you have extra funds, without committing to the shorter term.

Some lenders also offer other types of fixed-rate loans. The term of a *balloon loan* is frequently five, seven, or ten years. The interest rate is fixed, typically at .25 to .5 percent below the 30-year fixed rate. The monthly payments are the same as for a 30-year loan at the given rate. Unlike seller-financed balloon loans, which require payments of interest only, the monthly payments on these loans include principal and interest. When the loan matures, the remaining principal balance comes due and must be refinanced. Although the lower rate results in lower monthly payments, these loans have some risk, because it may be difficult to refinance them in the future, particularly if rates have risen.

Similar to the balloon loan but not involving refinancing risk is the *two-step loan.* This loan'sinitial rate is fixed for a set period, say five or seven years, typically at .25 to .5 percent *below* the 30-year fixed rate. At the end of the initial period (the first step), the loan converts to a fixed rate that is about .5 percent *higher* than the then-prevailing 30-year fixed rate for the remainder of the term (the second step), subject to a maximum rate increase of about 6 percent. If you plan to sell the house before the end of the first period—and most people move about every seven years—this loan may be a good option. You can save several thousand dollars in interest during the first step; however, if interest rates are higher when you reach the second step, your monthly payments will rise—often sharply.

Adjustable-Rate Mortgage. Another popular form of home loan is the **adjustable-rate mort-**

gage (ARM). Unlike the fixed-rate mortgage, the rate of interest, and therefore the size of the monthly payment, on an ARM is adjusted up and down in line with movements in interest rates. In essence, the rate of interest on the mortgage is linked to a specific *interest rate index* and adjusted at specific intervals (usually once or twice a year) in accordance with changes in the index. When the index moves up, so does the interest rate on the mortgage and, in turn, the size of the monthly mortgage payment. The new interest rate and monthly mortgage payment will then remain fixed until the next adjustment date, when the adjustment process will repeat itself.

The term of an ARM is set (usually at 30 years but sometimes at 15), while its interest rate and monthly payments are not. Because the size of the monthly payments will vary with interest rates, there is no way to tell what your future payments will be. However, because the borrower/homebuyer assumes most or all of the interest rate risk in these mortgages, the *initial* rate of interest on an adjustable-rate mortgage is normally well below—2 to 3 percentage points—the rate on a standard 30-year fixed-rate loan. Of course, whether or not the borrower actually will end up paying less interest depends on the behavior of market interest rates during the term of the loan.

Basic features. There are several basic features of an ARM that a homebuyer should understand. One is the **adjustment period,** which is the period of time between one rate/payment change and the next. Most ARMs have adjustment periods of six months or one year, though some have adjustment periods as short as three months and others as long as three or five years. Another feature is the **index rate,** which is meant to capture the movement in interest rates. Many lenders use an index rate that is based on the behavior of *six-month or one-year U.S. Treasury securities.* Others use the index rate based on *six-month CDs.* Another common index is the average cost of funds—as measured by rates paid on CDs, savings accounts, and other investments—to savings institutions, which is commonly measured by the *11th Federal Home Loan Bank District Cost of Funds.*

To determine the rate of interest on an ARM, lenders will add to the index a few percentage points called the **margin,** which is usually a fixed amount over the life of the loan. Thus, *the rate of interest on an ARM equals the index rate plus the margin.* This procedure is used in most cases not only to initially set up the loan but also to periodically adjust interest rates and monthly payments.

Consider a lender who uses an index rate that at inception of the loan equals 5.5 percent; if it charges a 2 percent margin, the loan will be set up initially as a 7.5 percent mortgage (5.5 percent + 2 percent = 7.5 percent). Because most ARMs are 30-year loans, the initial monthly payment is found like any other 7.5 percent, 30-year mortgage. For example, for a $65,000 loan, we can use Exhibit 5.5 to find its first-year monthly payment of $454.55. Assuming a one-year adjustment period, if the index rate rises to, say, 7 percent, the interest rate for the second year will be 9 percent (7 percent + 2 percent = 9 percent). The size of the monthly payment for the next 12 months will then be adjusted upward to about $521.90 and the process repeated each year thereafter until the loan matures.

To protect the borrower from extreme increases in interest rates and monthly payments, most adjustable-rate mortgages have **interest rate caps,** which place a limit on the amount the

fixed-rate mortgage The traditional type of mortgage, in which both the rate of interest and the monthly mortgage payment are fixed over the full term of the loan.

adjustable-rate mortgage (ARM) A mortgage on which the rate of interest, and therefore the size of the monthly payment, is adjusted up and down in line with movements in interest rates.

adjustment period In an adjustable-rate mortgage, the period of time between one rate/payment change and the next.

index rate An interest rate index that is meant to capture the movement of interest rates; used by mortgage lenders as a base rate for determining the rate of interest charged on ARMs.

margin The amount, typically up to a few percentage points, that is added to the basic index rate on an adjustable-rate mortgage loan to determine its prevailing rate of interest; it is usually fixed over the life of the loan.

interest rate cap A feature of an adjustable-rate mortgage loan that places a limit on the amount that the interest rate can increase each adjustment period (*periodic cap*) as well as over the life of the loan (*overall cap*).

interest rate can increase over a given period. There are two kinds: (1) *periodic caps*, which limit the interest rate increase from one adjustment to the next, and (2) *overall caps*, which limit the interest rate increase over the life of the loan. Many ARMs have both a periodic and an overall interest rate cap. Typically lenders cap annual rate adjustments at 1 to 2 percentage points and set lifetime interest rate caps at 5 to 6 percentage points. Some ARMs may include *payment caps*, which act to limit the monthly payment increase at the time of each adjustment to a certain amount—usually defined as a percentage of the previous payment. In other words, if your ARM has a 5 percent payment cap, that is the most your monthly payments can increase from one year to the next regardless of what happens to interest rates.

Beware of negative amortization. It is important to recognize that some ARMS are subject to **negative amortization**—an increasing principal balance resulting from the fact that the monthly loan payments are lower than the amount of monthly interest being charged. In other words, with some of these loans you can wind up with a larger mortgage balance on the next anniversary of the loan than on the last. This occurs either when the initial payment is intentionally set below the interest charge or when the ARM has interest rates that adjust monthly, although the actual monthly payment can be adjusted only annually. In this latter case, when rates are rising on these loans the current monthly payment can be less than the interest being charged, and the difference is added to the principal, thereby increasing the size of the loan. For example, assume the monthly payment on a 7.5 percent, 30-year, $80,000 loan is currently $560 and the loan's next annual adjustment is in ten months. If, as a result of rising interest rates, the applicable interest rate increases to 9 percent (that is, .75 percent per month), the monthly interest owed would be $600 (.75 percent × $80,000). Thus, negative amortization would occur in the amount of $40 per month ($600 interest − $560 monthly payment). If no other interest rate changes were to occur over the ten months remaining until the next annual adjustment, at that time the mortgage balance would be $80,400—the increase of $400 is attributable to the $40 per month negative amortization over the ten months. When considering an ARM, it is important to learn whether or not negative amortization can occur. Generally loans without the potential for negative amortization are available, although they tend to have slightly higher initial rates and interest rate caps.

Convertible ARMs. Since 1987, large lenders have offered **convertible ARMs,** loans that allow borrowers to convert from an adjustable-rate to a fixed-rate loan, usually at any time between the 13th and the 60th month. While these loans seldom provide the lowest initial rate, they allow the borrower, for a fee, to convert to a fixed-rate loan if interest rates decline. A conversion fee of around $500 is typical, and the fixed rate is normally set at .25 to .5 percent above the going rate on fixed-rate loans at the time you convert. Borrowers who like the generally low initial ARM rates and feel that interest rates will decline during the first 60 months or so of the loan may find the convertible ARM an attractive compromise between a fixed-rate and an adjustable-rate loan.

Choosing an index. When you select an ARM, it is important to understand the differences between the index rates. The index significantly affects the level and stability of your mortgage payments over the term of the loan. The one-year U.S. Treasury bill index is one of the most common indexes used by lenders, particularly in the eastern United States. Recently, some lenders have begun to use CD-based indexes. The 11th Federal Home Loan Bank District Cost of Funds is popular in the western United States, although the use of cost of funds indexes is gaining in other parts of the country as well.

The most important difference between the indexes is their volatility. Treasury bill rates are quite volatile because they respond to changes in the financial markets. CD rates also fluctuate considerably, because their issuers can quickly adjust them in response to changing market conditions. The 11th District Cost of Funds index is much less volatile because it represents an average of the cost of funds to S&Ls in the District. It tends to lag T-bill and CD rate movements, both up and down, and exhibits a fairly smooth pattern over time. To more fully understand how one particular index behaves relative to another, you may want to compare the index rates over the past several years.

So what does this mean for the homebuyer considering an ARM? If your mortgage is tied to a T-bill or CD index, you can expect sharper and more frequent upward and downward interest rate movements. On the other hand, cost of funds indexes move more slowly in both directions. To choose which is better for you, consider the annual rate cap on a particular mortgage, the relative level of interest rates, and your future interest rate expectations. If you have a low rate cap of about 1 to 2 percentage points and you think rates are going down, you may be comfortable with a T-bill or CD index.

Some lenders offer special first-year rates, called "teaser" rates, that are set below the index rate on the loan. You should be wary of lenders who advertise very low rates; ask them if the first-year rate is based on the index and then verify the rate for yourself. Be sure you can comfortably make the monthly mortgage payment when the interest rate steps up to the indexed rate.

Monitoring your mortgage payments. You should carefully monitor your mortgage over its life. Always verify the calculation of your loan payment when rate or payment adjustments are made. Recent government reports and consumer surveys estimate that errors may exist in 20 to nearly *80* percent of all ARMs. Most mistakes result from lender carelessness. To verify your payment amount, you need to know the index rate, the margin, and the loan formula used to make the adjustment; all are found in the loan agreement. The interest rates for the most commonly used indexes are readily available in the financial press and are frequently published weekly in the real estate section of most newspapers. The loan formula tells you when the rate is set—for example, 45 days before the adjustment date—and the margin on the loan. You can use a business/financial calculator to calculate the payment once you know the new rate, the number of years until the loan is paid off, and the current principal balance. If you suspect you are being overcharged, call your lender and ask for an explanation of the rate and payment calculations. Special mortgage checking services will review your ARM for a fee of about $70 to $100. These services may be useful if your mortgage is being serviced by a firm that is not the original lender, the lender does not satisfactorily answer your questions about the payment calculation, or your loan formula is particularly complicated.

Adjustable-rate mortgages are relatively complex and place the borrower or homebuyer at the mercy of the market. Their popularity is due not to their simplicity but to their low initial cost. Before using an adjustable-rate mortgage to finance your home purchase, you should take the time to understand all of the loan's terms and conditions.

Fixed-Rate or Adjustable-Rate? Fixed-rate mortgages are popular with homebuyers who plan to stay in their homes for at least five to seven years and want to know what their payments will be. Of course, the current level of interest rates and your expectation about future interest rates will significantly affect your choice of a fixed- or adjustable-rate mortgage. In 1984, when the average interest on a 30-year mortgage loan was a relatively high 13.76 percent, many people chose adjustable-rate mortgages in order to avoid being locked in to the then-prevailing high rates. In 1993, the interest rate on 30-year, fixed-rate loans averaged about 6.75 percent, its lowest level in 25 years. Many home buyers chose fixed-rate mortgages, and many homeowners with adjustable-rate mortgages refinanced them with fixed-rate loans to lock in the then-prevailing low rates. Even though adjustable-rate mortgages were being offered with initial rates as low as about 3.5 to 4.0 percent, the certainty of the fixed-rate loan had great appeal.

Historically, though, adjustable-rate mortgages have been less costly than fixed-rate mortgages. The starting rates for ARMs are set lower to induce borrowers to accept the risk that rates may rise. The future appeal of ARMs largely depends, of course, on future interest rates. Many financial experts recommend monitoring interest rates carefully and being prepared to convert or refinance an ARM to a fixed-rate loan when favorable market conditions exist. Some suggest that the initial interest rate on an ARM should be at least 2 percentage points below that of a comparable

negative amortization When the principal balance on a mortgage loan increases due to the fact that the monthly loan payment is lower than the amount of monthly interest being charged; some ARMs are subject to this undesirable situation.

convertible ARM An adjustable-rate mortgage loan that allows borrowers to convert from an adjustable-rate to a fixed-rate loan, usually at any time between the 13th and the 60th month.

fixed-rate loan in order to adequately compensate you for its greater risk. Again, it is important to consider how long you plan to be in your home; if you expect to move in a few years, the low starting rate on an ARM may allow you to afford a more expensive house.

Conventional, Insured, and Guaranteed Loans. A **conventional mortgage** is a mortgage offered by a lender who assumes all the risk of loss. To protect themselves on this type of mortgage, lenders usually require a down payment of at least 20 percent of the value of the mortgaged property. Of course, the down payment can be far less than this (sometimes 5 percent or less), but when this happens, the lender usually requires some form of mortgage insurance. Experience has shown that high borrower equity greatly lessens the chance of a mortgage default and a subsequent loss to the lender. However, such a high down payment requirement makes home buying more difficult for many families and individuals.

To promote homeownership, the federal government, through the Federal Housing Administration (FHA), offers lenders mortgage insurance on high loan-to-value ratio loans. The **FHA mortgage insurance** program helps people buy homes even when they have very little money available for a down payment and closing costs. In exchange for a mortgage insurance premium of 2.25 percent of the loan amount—which is paid by the borrower at closing or included in the mortgage—plus another .5 percent annual renewal fee, the FHA agrees to reimburse lenders in the event of buyer default for their losses up to a specified maximum amount. (Note: The renewal fee is paid for the life of the loan if the borrower's down payment is less than 5 percent, for 12 years if 5 to 10 percent, and for 7 years if over 10 percent.) The minimum required down payment on a FHA loan is 3 percent on the first $25,000 plus 5 percent on the amount over $25,000. Buyers cannot include closing costs in the mortgage amount. The interest rate on a FHA loan is generally about .5 percent lower than the rate on conventional fixed-rate loans. Affordability ratios are less stringent with FHA loans. In 1995, the maximum monthly mortgage payment ratio was 29 percent (of monthly *gross* income) and the maximum total monthly installment loan payment ratio was 41 percent (of monthly *gross* income). The maximum mortgage amount that the FHA can insure is based on the national median price of homes and varies depending on location; the maximum in early 1995 was about $153,000. As a result, the FHA program offers little benefit for people buying expensive homes. For those who plan to buy homes at equal to or below the median price, however, an FHA loan might be worth pursuing.

In addition to the FHA, a number of private companies insure low-down-payment mortgage loans for lenders. These plans, called **private mortgage insurance (PMI)** programs, work in a way similar to the FHA program, but their credit standards, insurable loan amounts, and insurance premiums are somewhat different. Their cost depends on the size of your down payment. Put down 10 percent on an $80,000 loan and you'll pay about .5 percent of the amount of the mortgage ($400) at closing and then about $20 per month; put down 5 percent on the same loan and you'll pay 1.25 percent ($1,000) at closing and about $30 per month; generally the monthly payment is made only during the first 7 to 9 years of a 30-year mortgage.

If you would like to buy a house, condominium, or cooperative but have only, say, 5 percent for a down payment, you should ask your real estate agent or mortgage lender whether you might qualify for either an FHA or PMI program. Both types of plans have helped millions of homebuyers.

Guaranteed loans are like insured loans, only better—if you qualify. **VA loan guarantees** are provided by the U.S. Veterans Administration to lenders who make qualified mortgage loans to eligible veterans of the U.S. Armed Forces and their unmarried surviving spouses. This program, however, does not require lenders or veterans to pay a premium for the guarantee. In many instances, an eligible veteran must pay only closing costs; in effect, under such a program, a veteran can buy a home with no down payment. (By the way, this can be done *only once* with a VA loan.) The mortgage loan—subject to a maximum—can amount to as much as 100 percent of a purchased property's appraised value. VA loans include a 2 percent funding fee (which is lower if the down payment is 5 percent or more) paid by the borrower at closing or included in the mortgage. The maximum interest rate is set by the VA and, like FHA loans, is usually about .5 percent below the rate of conventional fixed-rate loans. The maximum loan currently obtainable with a VA guarantee is $203,150. To qualify, the veteran's total monthly installment loan payment ratio can at maximum equal 41 percent (of monthly *gross* income). The VA loan guarantee is an important fringe benefit available to those who have served in the armed forces.

You should also check into the availability of other special mortgage loan programs sponsored by state and local public agencies. Like FHA and VA mortgage programs, these typically offer below-market interest rates and reduced down payment requirements.

REFINANCING YOUR MORTGAGE

Sometimes, after you've purchased a home and closed the transaction, interest rates on similar loans drop. If rates drop by 1 to 2 percent or more, you should consider the economics of refinancing. In the years between 1985 and 1988, and again from 1991 to 1994, many people who obtained mortgage loans during periods of high interest rates found refinancing attractive; loans with fixed rates as high as 13 percent could be refinanced for fixed rates as low as 6.75 percent. The decision to refinance should be made after carefully considering the terms of the old and new mortgages, the anticipated number of years you expect to remain in the home, any prepayment penalty on the old mortgage, and the closing costs associated with the new mortgage.

Worksheet 5.3 presents a form that can be used to analyze a potential refinancing. The data for the Philipatos family's analysis is shown. Their current 10-year-old, 12 percent mortgage, with original principal of $80,000, has a current balance of $74,250 and monthly payments of $823 per month for 20 more years. If they refinance the $74,250 balance at the prevailing rate of 9 percent over the remaining 20-year life of the current mortgage, the monthly payment would drop to $668. The Philipatos are very happy with their house and plan to live there for at least five more years. They will not have to pay any penalty for prepaying their current mortgage, and closing and other costs associated with the new mortgage are $2,400 after taxes. Substituting these values into Worksheet 5.3 reveals (in Item 7) that it will take the Philipatos 22 months to break even with the new mortgage. Because 22 months is considerably less than their anticipated minimum five years (60 months) in the home, the economics easily support refinancing their mortgage under the specified terms.

There are two basic reasons to refinance—to reduce the monthly payment or to reduce the total cost over the term of the loan. If a lower monthly payment is the objective, the analysis is relatively simple: determine how long it will take for the monthly savings to equal your closing costs (see Worksheet 5.3). If your objective is instead to reduce the total costs over the life of the loan, the analysis is more complex. The term of the new versus existing loan is a critical input. If you refinance a 30-year loan that has been outstanding ten years with another 30-year loan, you are actually extending the total maturity to 40 years; even with a lower interest rate, you may pay more interest. Therefore, you should refinance for a shorter-term loan, one that matures no later than the original loan. (The preceding example is prepared on this basis.) Many homeowners want to pay off their loans more quickly to free up funds to pay for their children's college education or for their retirement. By refinancing at a lower rate but continuing to make the same monthly payment, a larger portion of each payment will go toward the principal and the loan will be paid off more quickly. Alternatively, the borrower can make extra principal payments whenever possible. Paying only an additional $25 per month on a 30-year, 9 percent, $80,000 mortgage reduces the term to about 25 years and saves over $29,000 in interest.

Some people consider the reduced tax deduction associated with a smaller mortgage interest

conventional mortgage A mortgage offered by a lender who assumes all the risk of loss; typically requires a down payment of at least 20 percent of the value of the mortgaged property.

FHA mortgage insurance A program under which the Federal Housing Administration (FHA) offers lenders mortgage insurance on loans having a high loan-to-value ratio; its intent is to encourage loans to homebuyers who have very little money available for a down payment and closing costs.

private mortgage insurance (PMI) An insurance plan offered by a private company that insures low-down-payment mortgage loans for lenders.

VA loan guarantee A guarantee offered by the U.S. Veterans Administration to lenders who make qualified mortgage loans to eligible veterans of the U.S. Armed Forces and their unmarried surviving spouses.

WORKSHEET 5.3

Mortgage Refinancing Analysis for the Philipatos 

Using the form below, the Philipatos find that by refinancing the $74,250 balance on their 10-year-old, $80,000, 12-percent, 30-year mortgage (which has no prepayment penalty and requires payments of $823 per month) with a 9-percent, 20-year mortgage requiring $668 monthly payments and $2,400 in total after-tax closing costs, it will take 22 months to break even. Because the Philipatos plan to stay in their home for at least 60 more months, the refinancing is easily justified.

MORTGAGE REFINANCING ANALYSIS

Name: Demi and Nicholas Philipatos   Date: September 6, 1995

Item	Description		Amount
1	Current monthly payment (Terms: $80,000, 12%, 30 years)		$ 823
2	New monthly payment (Terms: $74,250, 9%, 20 years)		668
3	Monthly savings, pretax (Item 1 − Item 2)		$ 155
4	Tax on monthly savings [Item 3 × tax rate (28 %)]		43
5	Monthly savings, after-tax (Item 3 − Item 4)		$ 112
6	Costs to refinance:		
	a. Prepayment penalty	$ 0	
	b. Total closing costs (after-tax)	2,400	
	c. Total refinancing costs (Item 6a + Item 6b)		$ 2,400
7	Months to break even (Item 6c ÷ Item 5)		22

deduction as a disadvantage of refinancing. While the interest tax deduction may indeed be reduced as a result of refinancing, the important concern is the actual after-tax cash payments that must be made. In this regard, refinancing with a lower interest rate mortgage (with all other terms assumed unchanged) will always result in lower after-tax cash outflows, and is therefore economically appealing. Of course, as demonstrated in Worksheet 5.3, the reduction in after-tax cash outflows (that is, monthly savings) needs to be co paredto the refinancing costs in order to make the final refinancing decision.

Deciding which type of mortgage—fixed-rate or ARM—is best for you depends on market conditions and the length of time you plan to own your home. Because new mortgage products are offered regularly, you should carefully check out all your options prior to refinancing. Remember that in order to refinance, most lenders require that you have at least 20 percent equity in your home, based on current market appraisal. Be sure to check with your existing lender, because many financial institutions are willing to refinance their existing loans, often charging fewer points and lower closing costs than a new lender would charge.

Concept Check

5-16. Describe the various sources of mortgage loans. What role might a *mortgage broker* play in obtaining mortgage financing?

5-17. What is *seller financing?* Give examples of two forms of seller financing.

5-18. Briefly describe the two basic types of mortgage loans. Which has the lowest initial rate of interest? What is *negative amortization*, and which type of mortgage can experience it? Discuss the advantages and disadvantages of each mortgage type.

5-19. What factors should you take into account when deciding whether to refinance your mortgage to reduce the monthly payment? How can the refinancing decision be made?

BUYING OR LEASING AN AUTOMOBILE

FPPC

LG6

Though less expensive than housing, an automobile is a big-ticket purchase that requires careful consideration and deliberation. How would you go about carefull3y considering, analyzing, and financing the purchase of an automobile? Take a few moments to answer this question before reading on.

As a rule, a car is probably the first major expenditure that most people make. (While pickup trucks, minivans, sport utility, and similar vehicles are popular forms of transportation in many parts of the country, in the material that follows we will use the terms *automobile* or *car* to describe these and all other types of passenger vehicles.) An individual typically purchases an automobile every two to five years and pays anywhere from $1,000 to $30,000 (or more) for it, depending on its make, model, and age. The automobile purchase is second only to housing in terms of amount of money spent by the typical consumer. Because you will probably make an automobile-purchase decision many times during your life, a systematic approach to selection and financing can help you realize significant savings.

The automobile plays a major role in our society. It is an important factor in the economy, because the automobile industry provides hundreds of thousands of jobs and is a major consumer of raw materials produced by the steel and other vital industries. Although the primary motivation for automobile ownership is to provide transportation, automobiles are sometimes viewed as status symbols or purchased as part of a hobby or as an investment. There are a wide variety of models, styles, sizes, and colors. In addition to domestically produced automobiles, imported cars account for a large share of the American automobile market.

Before you buy a car (or make any major purchase), it is useful to spend some time researching the market and considering your personal needs. Many good sources of information about different types of cars, their prices, features, and reliability are available. Industry resources include manufacturers' brochures and dealer personnel. Car magazines, such as *Car and Driver, Motor Trend,* and *Road and Track,* and consumer magazines, such as *Consumer Reports* and *Consumers Digest,* regularly compare and rate cars. In addition, both consumer magazines and *Kiplinger's Personal Finance Magazine* publish annual buying guides that include comparative statistics and ratings on most domestic and foreign autos. *Consumer Reports* includes information on used cars in its guide, and it offers a fee-based service, called Consumer Reports Auto Price Service, that allows you to learn the list price and dealer's cost of a new car and the available options. This information should allow you to better negotiate with the dealer. You can even use your computer to analyze your options; programs such as *Car Buyers' Companion* (Parsons Technology, 1-800-223-6925; Windows version only) and *Popular Mechanics New Car Buyers' Guide 1995* (Books That Work; CD-ROM) provide information and price estimates on cars meeting criteria you specify and also help analyze financing options. The *Popular Mechanics* CD-ROM also provides color pictures and selected car reviews from the magazine.

CHOOSING THE CAR

Affordability. Before you shop for a car, you should determine how much you can afford to spend. This estimate should be stated on a monthly basis to be consistent with your cash budget. The amount you arrive at should result from a careful analysis of your available resources in view of other necessary expenses (including housing) and your transportation requirements. Once you have estimated the monthly amount available, you should evaluate the costs of owning or leasing various types of automobiles to select the one most suitable for you.

Operating Costs. The monthly out-of-pocket cost of operating an automobile consists of not only car payments, but also insurance, licenses, fuel, oil, tires, and other operating and maintenance outlays. Certain of these costs are *fixed* and remain so regardless of how much you drive; others are *variable* with the number of miles you drive. The biggest fixed cost is likely to be the *installment payments* associated with the loan or lease used to acquire the car; the biggest variable cost will probably be fuel. Another purchase cost is **depreciation,** which is the loss in value that occurs from driving the vehicle. In effect, depreciation is

EXHIBIT 5.8

Automobile Operating Costs

This car costs nearly $7,000 a year to operate; if it is driven about 12,000 miles a year, the car costs about 57 cents for every mile driven.

			Costs per Mile	
	Annual Costs*	**Monthly Costs***	**12,000 Miles/Year**	**25,000 Miles/Year**
Fixed Costs:				
Installment loan payments	$3,180	$265	$.265	$.128
Auto insurance	360	30	.030	.014
License plates and taxes	180	15	.015	.007
(1) Total fixed costs	$3,720	$310	$.310	$.149
Variable Costs:				
Fuel	$ 720	$ 60	$.060	$.060
Oil and tires	96	8	.008	.008
Repairs and maintenance	264	22	.022	.022
(2) Total variable costs	$1,080	$ 90	$.090	$.090
(3) Total out-of-pocket costs [(1) + (2)]	$4,800	$400	$.400	$.239
(4) Depreciation	$2,000	$167	$.167	$.080
Total operating costs [(3) + (4)]	$6,800	$567	$.567	$.319

*Annual and monthly *variable* costs are based on 12,000 miles/year.

the difference between the price you paid for the car and what you can get for it when you sell it. If you paid $15,000 for an automobile that can be sold three years later for $9,000, the car will cost you $6,000 in depreciation. While depreciation cost may not be a recurring out-of-pocket cost, it is nonetheless an important operating expense that should not be overlooked.

Exhibit 5.8 provides an example of what it might cost to operate a motor vehicle. Because the cost of operating an automobile varies with the year and make of the car, its mechanical condition, and even where you live, the figures in the exhibit should be viewed as only *representative* of the kinds of costs you can expect to incur. Note that the biggest cost component is the fixed out-of-pocket costs, followed by depreciation, and finally the variable costs. In total, this particular vehicle costs about $7,000 a year to operate, nearly $5,000 of which is annual out-of-pocket expenses. The figures are shown on an annual, monthly, and cost-per-mile basis. Clearly the more miles you drive each year, the lower the cost per mile. This is due to the fact that the *annual* fixed costs and depreciation (for a reasonable range of annual miles) do not change; thus, on a cost-per-mile basis these expenses go down with increased mileage. You should, of course, make sure that the expected (or actual) out-of-pocket operating costs of owning an automobile remain within budgeted amounts. (Note that for budgetary purposes depreciation can be ignored, because it does not represent an out-of-pocket expense in the normal sense.)

New, Used, or "Nearly New"? One decision you must make is whether to buy a new, used, or "nearly new" car. If you cannot afford to buy a new car, the decision is made for you. Some people always buy used cars, even though they can afford to buy a new car. Others pay more for a used luxury car, such as a Mercedes, than they would to purchase a new car of a less-expensive brand, such as a Chevrolet. The advantages of buying a used car are: (1) it is less expensive than a comparable new car; (2) it will not depreciate in value as quickly as a new car; and (3) because it is less expensive, the purchaser does not have to put down as much money as is required on a new car. Moreover, purchasing a used car less than 18 months old means saving the 20 to 25 percent depreciation in value typically experienced during the first 12 to 18 months of a car's life. The recent popularity of short-term car leases has increased the availability of late-model used cars. These are often well-priced, making them a good option to consider.

The main disadvantage of buying a used car is the uncertainty of its mechanical condition. Although it might look good, it could still have some mechanical problems requiring maintenance and repair expenditures in the near future. Even though according to a salesperson the car has low mileage and "has been driven only to and from church by a little old lady," you should have it checked by a reputable mechanic. The money spent on a thorough examination prior to its purchase could save hundreds of dollars and much aggravation later.

Purchasers of used cars have another means of protecting their investment in the *federal odometer disclosure law*. The penalties for violation of this law, which requires sellers to give buyers a signed statement attesting to the fact that the mileage shown on the odometer of their used cars is correct, are quite stringent. A seller of a used car should always be asked to provide such a statement.

Prior to purchasing either a new or used car, make certain you know what you want; if you have not done this, a slick auto salesperson may cause you to purchase a car you do not need. If you wish to buy a used car, you may prefer to shop for a car "for sale by owner" to avoid paying the added overhead charges of an auto dealer. Classified ads in local or nearby city newspapers provide an excellent source of information on used cars for sale. However, unlike cars purchased privately, those bought from dealers may have a warranty to protect you.

Another option is the "nearly new" car, usually a car used by the dealer with a few thousand miles on it or a rental car used for about four months or 10,000 miles. These cars may be a good value, come with good warranties, and are typically priced 20 to 40 percent below a comparable new car.

Size, Body Style, and Features. The size, body style, and features selected on a given automobile are largely dependent upon your motive for purchasing it. When considering these items, you should give some thought to their cost and effects, not only on performance, handling, and appearance, but also on fuel economy, reliability, repair problems, and the resale value of the car.

There is a great variety in the size and body style you can choose for your car. A two-passenger compact car may not be appropriate if you need the car for business. When determining size and body style, you should select from only those cars consistent with the primary use of the auto; you should not adapt your needs to fit the car. In most instances, there is also a direct relationship between size and cost: the larger the car, the more expensive it will be to purchase and to operate.

You can also select certain optional features providing a broad range of conveniences and luxuries—for a price. Most cars have at least some options. On new cars a window sticker details each option and its price, but on a used car only close observation serves to determine the options. Window stickers quite often list standard features that might be considered optional on some other models, and vice versa. When shopping for a new car, make certain you are comparing comparably equipped models.

By listing all options you want before shopping for a new car, you can avoid paying for features you really do not need. There are literally hundreds of options available ranging in price from a few dollars up to $1,000 or more including automatic transmission, a bigger engine, air conditioning, ABS brakes, radio or cassette or CD player, clock, power windows, power seats, electric door locks, rear window defroster, and special suspension. Other appearance-related options are two-tone or metallic paint, vinyl top, electric sunroof, whitewall tires, sport wheels, and various exterior trim packages.

Reliability and Warranties. The *reliability* of a car can be assessed by talking with friends owning similar cars and through objective assessments published in various consumer magazines and buying guides, such as *Consumer Reports*. The *warranty* offered by the manufacturer of new cars should also be studied and compared to that offered by other competing manufacturers. Significant differences may exist. It is important to read the warranty booklet included with a new car and make sure you understand the terms of the warranty. Most warranties are void if the owner

depreciation The loss in the value of an asset such as an automobile that occurs over its period of use; calculated as the difference between the price initially paid and the subsequent sale price.

has not performed routine maintenance or has somehow abused the car.

On all new cars, manufacturers in effect guarantee the general reliability and quality of construction for a specified period of time in a written warranty that obligates it to repair or replace, at little or no cost to the owner, any defective parts and flaws in workmanship. Today most new car warranties cover a minimum of the first three years of ownership or 36,000 miles, whichever comes first, and some provide coverage for as long as seven years or 70,000 miles. However, most warranties typically have limitations; for example, longer warranty periods may apply to only the engine and drive train. Auto manufacturers and private insurers also sell extended warranties and service contracts, sometimes called "buyer protection plans." Most experts consider these unnecessary and not worth their price given the relatively long initial warranty periods now being offered by most manufacturers.

Old Car: Trade-in or Sell? When buying a new or used car from a dealer to replace an old car, the question of a trade-in arises. Although trading-in is convenient, you are generally better off financially selling your old car outright. If you are willing to take the time you can usually sell your car above the wholesale price typically offered by a dealer on a trade-in.

Other Considerations. You should carefully consider fuel economy. When considering a new car, the *EPA (Environmental Protection Agency) mileage ratings* are especially useful. On new vehicles, manufacturers are required to post a sticker indicating the number of miles per gallon each model is expected to get (as determined through EPA tests) for both city and highway driving. The number of *safety features* built into the car should also be considered. These features are likely to be similar in new cars as a result of government regulations, but many features, such as airbags, may not be present in used cars. *Auto insurance costs,* which vary depending on make, model, safety features, and other factors (and are discussed in detail in Chapter 10), also should be assessed when considering automobile purchase alternatives.

THE PURCHASE TRANSACTION

Once you have determined the amount you can afford to spend and the features you desire, you are ready to begin shopping for a car. If you plan to purchase a new car, visit all dealers who have cars meeting your requirements. Look the cars over and ask questions—but don't make any offers until you have isolated two or three cars with the desired features that are priced within your budget. Also, if you can be flexible about the model and options you want, you can sometimes negotiate a better deal than if you have your heart set on a particular model and options. Comparison shopping is essential, because one dealer selling the same brand as another may give you a better deal. Watch out for the sales technique called "low-balling," where the salesperson quotes a low price for the car to get you to make an offer and then negotiates the price upward prior to your signing the sales contract.

Because lowballing, price haggling, and other high-pressure sales tactics often make car buying an unpleasant experience, many dealers during recent years have refocused their sales practices to emphasize customer satisfaction. Some manufacturers are offering firm prices so that if you buy today, you can be sure that no one will get a better deal tomorrow. Saturn dealers use this strategy, and other manufacturers offer "value pricing" on certain models equipped with popular options. More individual car dealers are also offering a one-price, no-haggling policy. However, you should still research prices, as described in the next section, because a set selling price does not guarantee the lowest cost. The markup on Saturns, for example, can be as high as 13 percent, compared to the industry average of 6.7 percent per car. Using the traditional negotiating approach may pay off. Today more dealers are following Saturn's approach of employing salaried "order takers" rather than commissioned salespeople.

Negotiating Price. The price you pay for a car, whether new or used, can vary widely. Not only must you choose among various makes and models, but there are also numerous options from which to choose; these differences often make comparisons difficult. The "sticker price" posted on a new car represents the manufacturer's *suggested* retail price for that particular car with the listed options. This price really means very little. The key to negotiating a good price is knowing the *dealer's cost* for the car. You can find out the dealer's invoice cost from reports in car buying guides available at your local bookstore or ordered from such services as AAA Auto Pricing Service, AutoIntelligence, AutoVantage, Car Bargains, *Consumer Reports* Auto Price Service, Fighting Chance, and Nationwide Auto Brokers. These reports show the base dealer's price plus the cost of each option for a specified make and model of auto. You can also use the sticker price and one of the annual consumer magazine car buying guides. For example, *Consumer Reports'* guide lists a cost factor for each car; multiplying this factor by the list price results in the approximate dealer's cost. If the cost factor for a 1996 Ford Taurus is .86 and the Taurus you want lists for $18,150, the dealer's cost is about $15,609 (.86 × $18,150). You should be aware, however, that the invoice price may not be what the dealer paid for the car; some dealers also get holdbacks or rebates from the manufacturer for each car sold.

Before making an offer, prepare a worksheet with the cost versus the list price for the exact car you want. This will help you avoid high-pressure salesmanship and being pushed to pay for options you don't want or need. Try to negotiate the lowest acceptable markup (3 to 4 percent for cars priced under $20,000; 6 to 7 percent for higher-priced models), push for a firm quote, and make it clear that you are comparison shopping. Don't let the salesperson pressure you into signing a sales contract or leaving a deposit until you are sure that you have negotiated the best deal. Good cost information will improve your bargaining position and possibly allow you to negotiate a price that is only several hundred dollars over the dealer's cost. To research used car prices, you can check one of the popular price guides—the National Automobile Dealers Association (NADA) *Official Used Car Guide*, the *Kelly Blue Book*, or *Edmund's Used Car Prices*—available at your library or bank, and the classified ads in your local newspaper.

If you want to avoid negotiating entirely, you can buy your car through a buying service. These include independent companies such as AutoAdvisor, AutoVantage, CarBargains, Car/Puter, and Nationwide Auto Brokers as well as services offered through credit unions, motor clubs, and discount warehouses like PriceCostco. The services vary in their approach and cost. They may either have an arrangement with a network of dealers to sell cars at a predetermined price over invoice (ranging from $200 for a domestic car to $1,200 or more for a luxury model), provide you with competitive bids from several local dealers, find the car you want and negotiate the price with the dealer, or take an order for a factory-built car. The price for these services ranges from about $35 for a PriceCostco membership to as much as $600. And the results vary, so you may want to compare prices and do some checking on your own. In general, you will get a good price through a service—although you can't assume that it will be the best price.

It is best not to discuss either your plan to finance the purchase or the value of your trade-in until you have settled the question of price. These should be separate issues. Salespeople will typically want to find out how much you can afford monthly and then offer financing deals with payments close to that amount. In the case of trade-ins, the dealer might offer you a good price for your old car and raise the price of the new car to compensate, or vice versa. The dealer may offer financing terms that sound attractive, but be sure to compare them to the cost of bank loans. Sometimes the price of the car is increased to make up for a low interest rate, or the attractive financing may apply only to certain models. If you are interested in dealer financing, make sure the monthly payment quoted by the dealer's finance manager is just for the loan. Learn and compare the annual percentage rate (APR) to the rate quoted on a bank loan. Frequently the financing charges include unneeded extras such as credit life insurance, accident insurance, an extended warranty, or service package. Once you understand price, you can negotiate intelligently.

Manufacturers and dealers frequently offer buyers special incentives such as rebates and cut-rate financing, particularly when car sales are slow. (Rebates should be deducted from the dealer's cost when you are negotiating the price.) You may be given a choice between a rebate and low-cost financing. To determine which is the better deal, calculate the difference between the monthly payments on a market-rate bank loan and the special dealer loan for the same term. Multiply the payment difference by the loan maturity, in months, and compare it to the rebate. For example, assume the dealer offers either a $1,000 rebate or a 5 percent interest rate on a $10,000, four-year loan. Your payments would be $230 with dealer financing and $254 on a 10 percent bank loan with similar terms. The payment savings over the life of the loan is $1,152 ($24 per month × 48 months), which is greater than the $1,000 rebate. In this case, you would be better off with the 5 percent loan.

Closing the Deal. Whether you are buying a new or a used car, to make a legally binding offer, you must sign a **sales contract** that specifies the offering price and all the conditions of your offer. The sales contract will also specify whether or not the offer includes a trade-in; when it does, the offering price will represent the amount in addition to the trade-in you are willing to pay. Because this agreement contractually binds you to purchase the car at the offering price, if accepted (and signed) by the dealer, you should be certain that you want and can afford the car prior to signing such an agreement. To show that you are making an offer in good faith, you may be required to include a deposit of $100 or more with the contract.

Once your offer has been accepted, you will need to complete the purchase transaction and accept delivery of the car. If you are not paying cash for the car, you can arrange financing through the dealer, at your bank, credit union, or a consumer finance company. The key aspects of these types of installment loans, which can be quickly negotiated if your credit is good, are discussed in Chapter 7. Prior to delivery, the dealer is responsible for cleaning up the car and installing any optional equipment. It is a good idea to make sure that all equipment you are paying for has been installed and the car is ready for use before paying the dealer. At the same time you pay, you should also receive title to the car.

LEASING YOUR CAR

Today, nearly 30 percent of all new-car buyers lease rather than buy their cars. When you **lease,** you receive the use of a car in exchange for making monthly lease payments over a specified period of time, usually two to five years. Leasing appeals to a wide range of car buyers, due in large part to rising new car prices and the elimination of the tax deduction for consumer loan interest. Although it is generally more economical to buy—and own—an asset over the long term, today many buyers lease their cars to lower the monthly payment, to obtain a more expensive car for the same monthly payment, and/or to minimize the down payment and preserve their cash.

With all the advertisements promising low monthly lease payments, it's easy to focus on only the payment. But with a lease you're not paying for the whole car, you're only paying for its use during a specified period. Leasing is a more complex arrangement than borrowing to buy a car, and until you understand how leasing works and compare the lease terms to bank financing, you really won't know if leasing is your best option.

The Leasing Process. The intitial step is the same for leasing and purchasing: research, comparison shop at several dealers, and find the desired car at the best price. Don't ask the dealer about leasing and any financing incentives until *after* you've negotiated the best price. Also compare the terms offered by at least one independent leasing firm. Just as with a purchase, try to negotiate lower lease payments; a payment reduction of $20 a month saves nearly $1,000 on a four-year lease. And don't reveal what you can afford to pay per month; such a disclosure can lead you to a poor lease deal. Once you agree on leasing terms, be sure to get everything in writing.

Nearly 80 percent of all customers choose the **closed-end lease,** often called the *walk-away lease* because at the end of its term you simply turn in the car, assuming you have neither exceeded the mileage limits nor abused the car. Under the less popular **open-end lease,** the estimated **residual value**—the remaining value of the car at the end of the lease term—is used to determine lease payments; if the car is actually worth less than this value at the end of the lease, you have to pay the difference.

One of leasing's commonly cited benefits is the absence of a down payment. However, today most leases ask for a "capital cost reduction," which is nothing more than a down payment. You should not be required to pay this, although doing so lowers the potential depreciation and therefore your monthly lease payments.

The lease payment calculation is based on four variables: (1) the **capitalized cost** of the car, the price of the car you are leasing; (2) the forecast *residual value* of the car at the end of the lease; (3) the **money factor,** or financing rate on the lease, which is similar to the interest rate on a loan; and (4) the lease term. The depreciation during the lease term (which is what you are financing) is the capitalized cost minus the residual value. Dividing the sum of the depreciation and the sales tax (on the financed portion only) by the number of months in the lease term and adding the lessor's required monthly return (at the money factor) results in the monthly payment. The lower the cost and higher the residual value, the lower your payment. Residual values quoted by different dealers often vary, so check several sources to find the highest residual value so you can minimize depreciation. The *Financial Shocks* box on page 216 describes how to avoid overpaying if you lease a car.

Lease terms typically run two to five years, but longer term leases have lower payments. Terminating a lease early is often difficult—and costly—so be reasonably certain that you can keep the car for the full lease term. The lease contract should outline all costs and additional fees associated with early termination. Early termination clauses also apply to cars that are stolen or totaled in an accident; some leases require "gap insurance" to cover the lost lease payments that would result from early termination caused by one of these events.

Recently some car dealers began offering **single-payment leases,** where the lessee pays the entire lease fee at the start of the lease term, instead of in monthly installments. All other terms and conditions are similar to regular lease contracts. First offered on luxury cars, single-payment leases are now available on many other models as well. This lease form can be cheaper than a traditional lease. For example, assume you have the choice of leasing a Mazda Miata for three years for $199 per month with $1,000 down or making one lease payment of $6,697. Your payments over the three-year lease term would be $7,164; with the down payment, your outlay totals $8,164—$1,467 more than the single-payment lease. Using advanced time value of money techniques, the single-payment lease results in an annual before-tax cost savings of about 15.5 percent. Of course, as with any lease you should negotiate the cost of the car before discussing the type of lease plan you want.

Under most leases, you are responsible for insuring and maintaining the car. At the end of the lease, you are obligated to pay for any "unreasonable wear and tear." A good lease contract should clearly define what is considered unreasonable. In addition, most leases require the lessee to pay a disposition fee of about $150 to $250 when the car is returned.

Most auto leases include a **purchase option**—a fixed price specified in the lease, the market price at the end of the lease term, or the residual value of the car—allowing the lessee to buy the car at the end of the lease term. A lower residual results in a lower purchase price but raises monthly payments. Experts recommend negotiating a fixed-price purchase option, if possible.

The annual mileage allowance—typically, about 12,000 to 15,000 miles per year for the lease term—is another important lease consideration. The lessee must pay typically between 8 and 15 cents per mile for additional miles. If you expect to exceed the allowable mileage, you should negotiate a more favorable rate for extra miles before signing the lease contract.

The Lease versus Purchase Analysis. To decide whether it is less costly to lease rather than

sales contract An agreement to purchase an automobile that states the offering price and all conditions of the offer; when signed by the buyer and seller, the contract legally binds them to its terms.

lease An arrangement in which the lessee receives the use of a car (or other asset) in exchange for making monthly lease payments for a specified period of time.

closed-end lease The most popular form of automobile lease, often called a *walk-away lease* because at the end of its term the lessee simply turns in the car, assuming the preset mileage limit has not been exceeded and the car hasn't been abused.

open-end lease An automobile lease under which the estimated *residual value* of the car is used to determine lease payments; if the car is actually worth less than this value at the end of the lease, the lessee must pay the difference.

residual value The remaining value of a leased car at the end of the lease term.

capitalized cost The price of a car that is being leased.

money factor The financing rate on a lease; similar to the interest rate on a loan.

single-payment lease A type of lease where the lessee pays the entire lease fee at the start of the lease term, instead of in monthly installments.

purchase option A fixed price specified in a lease at which the lessee can buy the car at the end of the lease term.

Financial Shocks

Don't Let Leasing Fraud Take You for a Ride

Would you pay more than sticker price for a car? Of course not! But an elderly Florida man arranged to lease a Honda Accord that cost $17,209 and trade in his old car, valued at $11,773. The lease payments should have been based on the $5,436 difference. But the dealer used a capitalized cost of $11,157, selling the car at well above sticker price and making about $5,700 in extra profit. In another case, a couple traded in their old car and negotiated a lease that reduced the $20,000 price of the leased car by the trade-in's $2,000 value. The lease contract that they signed, however, used $20,000 as the capitalized cost in the lease payment calculation. Because Florida's lease contract did not show the trade-in value or capitalized cost, the couple overpaid and essentially gave away their old car. And deceptive advertising and bait-and-switch tactics are also common. A New Jersey man was attracted by an ad for a Geo Prizm he could lease for $189 per month for three years, with no down payment. However, that deal was for a stripped-down version; the monthly cost for a Prizm with an automatic transmission was $250. He chose a Prizm with options package for a monthly cost of $210. Not until he got home and ran the numbers did he discover that his $210 payment worked out to a capitalized cost of $13,920—versus the *sticker* price of $13,325.

The rapid growth of leasing's popularity has, unfortunately, meant increased fraud as well. More than 50,000 deceptive leasing practice complaints were filed in 1994, leading many states—Connecticut, Florida, and Washington among them—to conduct major antifraud investigations.

The problem lies in the absence of auto lease disclosure laws; dealers have no obligation to reveal the capitalized cost or interest rate to consumers. (Some states are now considering laws to correct this.) Today car buyers enter the showroom knowing the car's invoice cost and negotiate hard for a good price. But most leasing customers focus on the monthly cost and fail to ask the amount of the capitalized cost the leasing company pays for the car or what interest rate is built into the payments. That's a big mistake because they can end up with a lease costing more than it should.

Because the lease contract doesn't have to show the car's price, dealers can inflate the car's capitalized cost. Also, large leasing companies often pay the dealer 5 to 10 percent above sticker price for the leased vehicle—apparently to allow greater flexibility to negotiate trade-ins. According to Florida's attorney general's office, this leads to the most common leasing fraud practice: lease payments based on 110 percent of sticker price, not the 90 percent the consumer expects. Capitalized costs of leased cars average 96.3 percent, versus 91.8 percent for purchased cars. Dealers argue that the leasing company—rather than you—is buying the car, so you don't need to know the price.

Savvy leasing customers know that's not true; the capitalized cost is a major part of the lease payment calculation. If the dealer won't disclose it, they go elsewhere. They insist on knowing the following eight figures: (1) list price for the car and options; (2) capitalized cost, which should be lower than list; (3) money factor, or financing rate, which is similar to the interest rate on a loan; (4) total interest paid; (5) total sales tax (which will be spread over your monthly payments); (6) residual value for which you can purchase the car at the end of the lease; (7) depreciation (the difference between the capitalized cost and residual value); and (8) lease term. The dealer can then show you how the monthly payment is calculated. For example, for a 24-month lease, it should be 1/24 of the total interest, 1/24 of the total depreciation, and 1/24 of the total sales tax. There may be an acquisition fee as well, but savvy customers negotiate the car's price as if they were buying, aren't pressured into signing on the spot, shop around for the best deal, and question any last-minute charges.

Sources: Ed Henry, "Leasing Scams that Can Take You For a Ride," *Kiplinger's Personal Finance Magazine*, February 1994, pp. 128–130; Douglas Lavin, "Cracking Down on Fraudulent Car Leases," *The Wall Street Journal*, September 28, 1994, pp. B1, B6; Douglas Lavin, "Driving a Hard Bargain," *Smart Money*, October 1994, pp. 104–109.

purchase a car, you need to use a **lease versus purchase analysis** to estimate the total cost of each alternative over equal time periods. Generally in this analysis the purchase is assumed to be financed with an installment loan with the same term as the lease. For example, assume that Mary Dixon is considering either leasing or purchasing a new car costing $13,000. The four-year closed-end lease she is considering requires a $1,000 down payment (capital cost reduction), a $200 security deposit, and monthly payments of $200, including sales tax. If she purchases the car, she will make a $2,600 down payment and finance the balance with a four-year, 8.5 percent loan requiring monthly payments of $255; in addition, she will have to pay 5 percent sales tax ($650) on the purchase, and she expects the car to have a residual value of $6,000 at the end of four years. Mary can earn 4 percent interest on her savings. After filling in Worksheet 5.4, Mary concludes that purchasing is better, because its *total cost* of $9,906 is $886 less than the $10,792 total cost of leasing—even though the monthly lease payment is $55 lower. Clearly, all else being equal, the least costly alternative is preferred.

If you are fortunate enough to have enough cash to buy your car, you may still want to consider leasing. Sometimes dealers offer such advantageous lease terms that you can come out ahead by investing the money you would pay for the car. To compare the total cost of a cash purchase, simply take the cost of the car, including sales tax, add to it the opportunity cost of using all cash, and deduct the car's value at the end of the lease or loan term. At 4 percent per year on her savings, Mary's total cost of the car is as follows: $13,650 cost + $2,184 lost interest (4 × .04 × $13,650) − $6,000 residual value = $9,834. In this case, she would be better off purchasing the car for cash than either leasing or financing the car.

Is leasing right for you? If you trade cars every two to four years and drive less than 12,000 to 15,000 miles a year, it may be better than purchasing. Use Worksheet 5.4 to find and compare the total cost of leasing to the total cost of purchasing. Or you can use Chart Software's *Expert Lease*, a DOS program, to analyze various lease versus purchase scenarios. Then consider the other factors described above. If you decide to lease, make sure that all terms are set forth in writing and that you understand everything in the lease agreement before signing it.

When the Lease Ends. At the expiration of the lease, you will be faced with a major decision. Should you return the car and walk away, buy the car, or even re-lease it for another year or more? If you turn in the car and move on to a new model, you may be hit with "excess wear and damage" and "excess mileage" charges and disposition fees. To minimize these, replace worn tires, get repairs done yourself, and document the car's condition before returning it. You may be able to negotiate a lower disposition fee. If you can't return the car without high repair charges or greatly exceeded mileage allowances, you may come out ahead by buying the car.

Whether exercising the purchase option makes sense depends on the residual value. Sometimes, with popular cars, the residual value in your lease agreement is below the car's market value. Buying the car makes sense; even if you want a different car, you exercise the purchase option and then sell the car in the open market and net $1,000 or more. If the reverse is true, and the residual is higher than the price of a comparable used car, just let the lease expire. Find your car's market value by looking in used-car guides and newspaper ads and compare it to the residual value. As for re-leasing, you need to analyze your options carefully, just as you did when you initially leased this car.

Concept Check

5-20. Briefly discuss how each of the following purchase considerations would affect your choice of a car.
- **a.** Affordability
- **b.** Operating costs
- **c.** New, used, or "nearly new" car
- **d.** Model and feature selection
- **e.** Reliability and warranty protection

5-21. Describe the purchase transaction process, including shopping, price negotiation, and closing the deal on a new car.

lease versus purchase analysis A procedure used to determine the total cost of leasing and the total cost of purchasing (using an installment loan) a car over equal time periods to choose the least costly alternative.

WORKSHEET 5.4

Comparing Mary Dixon's Automobile Lease versus Purchase Costs 

This worksheet demonstrates Mary Dixon's analysis of whether it is better to lease or purchase a new car costing $13,000. Under the lease, an initial payment of $1,200 ($1,000 down payment + $200 security deposit) and monthly payments of $200 are required over the four-year term of the closed-end lease. Purchasing requires a $2,600 down payment, sales tax of 5 percent ($650), and monthly payments of $255 over the four-year term. A 4-percent interest rate on savings and an estimated value for the car at the end of the four years of $6,000 is assumed. Because the total cost of leasing of $10,792 is greater than the $9,906 total cost of purchasing, Mary should purchase rather than lease the car.

AUTOMOBILE LEASE VERSUS PURCHASE ANALYSIS

Name: Mary Dixon Date: March 4, 1996

Item	Description		Amount
LEASE			
1	Initial payment:		
	a. Down payment (capital cost reduction):	$ 1,000	
	b. Security deposit:	200	$ 1,200
2	Term of lease and loan (years)*		4
3	Term of lease and loan (months) (Item 2 × 12)		48
4	Monthly lease payment		$ 200
5	Total payments over term of lease (Item 3 × Item 4)		$ 9,600
6	Interest rate earned on savings (in decimal form)		.04
7	Opportunity cost of initial payment (Item 1 × Item 2 × Item 6)		$ 192
8	Payment/refund for market value adjustment at end of lease ($0 for closed-end leases) and/or estimated end-of-term charges		$ 0
9	**Total cost of leasing (Item 1a + Item 5 + Item 7 + Item 8)**		$ 10,792
PURCHASE			
10	Purchase price		$ 13,000
11	Down payment		$ 2,600
12	Sales tax rate (in decimal form)		.05
13	Sales tax (Item 10 × Item 12)		$ 650
14	Monthly loan payment (Terms: 10,400, 48 months, 8.5%)		$ 255
15	Total payments over term of loan (Item 3 × Item 14)		$ 12,240
16	Opportunity cost of down payment (Item 2 × Item 6 × Item 11)		$ 416
17	Estimated value of car at end of loan		$ 6,000
18	**Total cost of purchasing (Item 11 + Item 13 + Item 15 + Item 16 − Item 17)**		$ 9,906

DECISION

If the value of Item 9 is less than the value of Item 18, leasing is preferred; otherwise the purchase alternative is preferred.

*This form is based upon assumed equal terms for the lease and the installment loan, which is assumed to be used to finance the purchase.

5-22. What are the advantages and disadvantages of leasing a car? Given your personal financial circumstances, if you were buying a car today would you probably pay cash, lease, or finance it, and why?

SUMMARY

LG1. Identify housing alternatives that meet your needs. A family's housing needs can be met in many different ways. In addition to single-family homes, there are condominiums, cooperative apartments, manufactured homes, and numerous types of rental apartments and houses. You should evaluate the advantages and disadvantages of each to choose the best one for your current lifestyle.

LG2. Evaluate the benefits and costs of home ownership and estimate how much you can pay for a home. In addition to the emotional rewards, other benefits of home ownership are the tax shelter and inflation hedge it provides. Home ownership costs include the down payment, points and closing costs, monthly mortgage payments, property taxes and insurance, and normal home maintenance and operating expenses. Any of these can amount to a considerable sum of money, and all of them should be carefully considered when using home affordability analysis to estimate how much you can afford to spend on a home.

LG3. Assess the option of renting and perform a rent-or-buy analysis. Many people rent because they cannot afford to buy a home; others choose to rent because renting is less costly and/or more convenient for their lifestyle and economic situation. The rental contract, or lease agreement, describes the terms under which you can rent the property: term, rent payment, restrictions, and so forth. Rent-or-buy analysis can help you choose the least costly alternative. You should also consider qualitative factors such as how long you plan to stay in an area and perform the analysis over a several-year time horizon.

LG4. Describe the home-buying process. Normally, people shopping for a home seek the help of a real estate agent to obtain needed information, access to properties, and advice; the agent earns a 5 to 7 percent commission, paid by the seller, when the transaction is closed. It's a good idea to prequalify for a mortgage before starting to look for a house. A real estate sales contract is used to confirm in writing all terms of the transaction between the buyer and seller. After a mortgage loan is approved, the loan is closed; this involves certain disclosures required by RESPA, a title check, and preparation of a closing statement that shows how much the borrower owes and the seller receives from the transaction.

LG5. Choose mortgage financing that meets your needs. Mortgage loans can be obtained from commercial banks, S&Ls, savings banks, and through a mortgage banker or mortgage broker. Seller financing is another important source of mortgage money. While there are many types of mortgage loans available, the most widely used are the 30- and 15-year fixed-rate mortgage and the adjustable-rate mortgage (ARM). Sometimes interest rates will drop a number of years after closing, and mortgage refinancing will become attractive. The refinancing analysis takes into account the difference in terms between the old and new mortgages, any prepayment penalty on the old mortgage, closing costs, and the number of years you plan to stay in the home.

LG6. Implement a plan to choose and buy or lease an automobile. The purchase of an automobile, usually the second largest expenditure a person will make, should be based on thorough market research and comparative shopping. Important purchase considerations include affordability, operating costs, new versus used or nearly new car, type of car and its features, and reliability and warranties. Knowing the dealer's cost is the key to negotiating a good price, and the economics of leasing versus purchasing the car with an installment loan should be considered once the price is set. The four components of the lease payment are the capitalized cost, residual value, money factor, and lease term. It's important to consider the other terms of the lease, such as annual mileage allowance and early termination penalties, before signing a lease contract.

FINANCIAL FACTS OR FANTASIES

Are the following statements financial facts (true) or fantasies (false)?

1. The most popular form of single-family housing is the condominium.
2. Mortgage insurance guarantees the lender that the loan will be paid off in the event of the borrower's death.
3. As a rule, the closing costs on a home are rather insignificant and seldom amount to more than a few hundred dollars.
4. The amount of money you earn has a lot to do with the amount of money you can borrow.
5. In an adjustable-rate mortgage, the size of the monthly mortgage payment will change periodically, along with prevailing mortgage interest rates.
6. For most people, an automobile will be their second largest purchase.

DISCUSSION QUESTIONS AND PROBLEMS

Discussion Question for Opening Profile
Describe the process the Jameses used to buy their first home. What are some problems homebuyers typically face? Discuss the strategies Terry and Sara used to bypass them.

1. How much would you have to put down on a house costing $100,000 if the house had an appraised value of $105,000 and the lender required an 80 percent loan-to-value ratio?
2. FPPC Using the maximum ratios for a conventional mortgage, how big a monthly payment could the Bacon family afford if their gross (before-tax) monthly income amounted to $4,000? Would it make any difference if they were already making monthly installment loan payments totaling $750 on two car loans?
3. How much might a home buyer expect to pay in closing costs on a $95,000 house with a 10 percent down payment? How much in total would the home buyer have to pay at the time of closing in the above transaction, taking into account closing costs, down payment, and a loan fee of 3 points?
4. FPPC Find the monthly mortgage payments on the following mortgage loans using the table in Exhibit 5.5:
   - **a.** $60,000/8.5 percent/30 years
   - **b.** $50,000/10 percent/20 years
   - **c.** $85,000/11.5 percent/15 years
5. FPPC ***Use Worksheet 5.1.*** Selma and Rodney Jackson wish to estimate the amount they can afford to spend to purchase their first home. They have a combined annual income of $37,500 and have $21,000 available to make a down payment and pay closing costs. The Jacksons estimate that homeowner's insurance and property taxes will be $125 per month. They expect the mortgage lender to use a 30 percent (of monthly gross income) monthly mortgage payment affordability ratio, to lend at an average interest rate of 9 percent on a 30-year mortgage, and to require a 15 percent down payment. Based on this information, use the home affordability analysis form in Worksheet 5.1 to determine the maximum-priced home the Jacksons can afford.
6. FPPC ***Use Worksheet 5.2.*** Rebecca Serra is currently renting an apartment for $625 per month and also pays $275 annually for renter's insurance. She just found a townhouse she can buy for $85,000. She has enough cash for a $10,000 down payment and $4,000 in closing costs. Her bank is offering 30-year mortgages at 9% per year. Rebecca estimated the following costs as a percentage of the home's price: Property taxes, 2.5%; homeowner's insurance, .5%; and maintenance, .7%. She is in the 28 percent tax bracket. Using Worksheet 5.2, calculate the cost of each alternative and recommend the less costly option to Rebecca.
7. FPPC What would the monthly payments be on a $75,000 loan if the mortgage were set up as
   - **a.** A 15-year, 10 percent fixed-rate loan?
   - **b.** A 30-year adjustable-rate mortgage in which the lender added a margin of 2.5 to the index rate (which presently stands at 6.5 percent)? Find the monthly mortgage payments for the first year only.

FPPC 8. ***Use Worksheet 5.3.*** Latha Yang purchased a condominium four years ago for $70,000. She has been paying $630 per month on her $60,000, 12 percent, 25-year mortgage. The current loan balance is $58,165. Recently interest rates have dropped sharply, causing Latha to consider refinancing the condo at the prevailing 9 percent rate. She expects to remain in the condo for at least four more years and has found a lender that will make a 9 percent, 21-year, $58,165 loan requiring $515 monthly payments. Although there is no prepayment penalty on her current mortgage, Latha will have to pay $1,500 in closing costs on the new mortgage. She is in the 15 percent tax bracket. Based on this information, use the mortgage refinancing analysis form (Worksheet 5.3) to determine whether Latha should refinance her mortgage under the specified terms.

9. Janet Forrester has an established budget in which she had allotted $500 a month to the out-of-pocket operating costs of a car. She is presently looking at a sporty model with monthly payments of $275; plates and taxes would amount to $360 a year, and car insurance $750 annually. Fuel is expected to cost about $60 for every 1,000 miles driven; because the car is under warranty, repairs, maintenance, tires, and oil are expected to amount to only $20 for each 1,000 miles. The car is expected to depreciate at the rate of about $2,500 a year. Given that Janet drives about 15,000 miles a year, find the total operating costs of this car on both an annual and a cost-per-mile basis (break the cost out by fixed, variable, and depreciation). Will she be able to stay within her budget with this car?

FPPC 10. ***Use Worksheet 5.4.*** Chris Svenson is trying to decide whether to lease or purchase a new car costing $12,000. If he leases, he will have to make a $400 security deposit and agree to make monthly payments of $285 over the 36-month term of the closed-end lease. If, on the other hand, he purchases the car, he will have to make an $1,800 down payment and will finance the balance with a 36-month loan requiring monthly payments of $340; in addition, he will have to pay a 6 percent sales tax ($720) on the purchase price, and he expects the car to have a residual value of $4,300 at the end of three years. Chris can earn 4 percent interest on his savings. Use the automobile lease versus purchase analysis (Worksheet 5.4) to find the total cost of both the lease and the purchase and recommend the best strategy to Chris.

CONTEMPORARY CASE APPLICATIONS

FPPC 5.1 Evaluating a Mortgage Loan for the Newtons

Farrah and Sam Newton, both in their early 30s, have been married for five years. Sam has an accounting degree and is presently employed as a senior cost accountant at an annual salary of $42,000. The Newtons have two children, ages 2 and 4. At present, they are renting a duplex but wish to buy a home in the suburbs of their rapidly developing city. They have decided that they can afford a $105,000 house and hope to find one with the features they desire in a good neighborhood.

The insurance costs on such a home are expected to be $500 per year, taxes are expected to be $1,000 per year, and annual utility bills are estimated at $1,200—an increase of $500 over those they pay in the duplex. The Newtons are considering financing their home with a fixed-rate, 30-year, 9 percent mortgage; also, the lender charges 2 points on mortgages with 20 percent down and 3 points if less than 20 percent is put down (the commercial bank with which the Newtons will deal requires a minimum of 10 percent down). Other closing costs are estimated at 5 percent on the purchase price of the home. Because of their excellent credit record, the bank will probably be willing to let the Newtons' monthly mortgage payments equal as much as 28 percent of their monthly gross income. Over the last four years, the Newtons have been saving for the purchase of a home and now have $24,000 in their savings account.

Questions

1. How much would the Newtons have to put down if the lender required a minimum 20 percent down payment? Could they afford it?
2. Given the Newtons want to put only $15,000 down, how much would closing costs be?

Considering only principal and interest, how much would their monthly mortgage payments be? Would they qualify for a loan using a 28 percent affordability ratio?

3. Using a $15,000 down payment on a $105,000 home, what would the Newton's loan-to-value ratio be? Calculate the monthly mortgage payments on a PITI basis.
4. What recommendations would you make to the Newtons? Explain.

FPPC 5.2 Julie's Rent-or-Buy Decision

Julie Brown is a single career woman in her late 20s. She currently rents an apartment in the fashionable part of town for $900 a month. After considerable deliberation, she is seriously considering the purchase of a luxury condominium for $125,000. She intends to put 20 percent down and expects that closing costs will amount to another $5,000; a commercial bank has agreed to lend her money at the fixed rate of 9 percent on a 15-year mortgage. Julie would have to pay an annual condominium owner's insurance premium of $600 and property taxes of $1,200 a year (she is presently paying renter's insurance of $550 per year). In addition, she estimates that annual maintenance and upkeep expenses will be about .5 percent of the price of the condo (which includes a $30 monthly fee to the property owners' association). Julie's income puts her in the 28 percent tax bracket (she itemizes her deductions on her tax returns), and she earns an after-tax rate of return on her investments of around 4 percent.

Questions

1. Given the information provided above, evaluate and compare Julie's alternatives of remaining in the apartment or purchasing the condo, using Worksheet 5.2.
2. Working with a friend who is a realtor, Julie has learned that luxury condos like the one she is thinking of buying are appreciating in value at the rate of 3.5 percent a year and are expected to continue doing so. Would such information affect the rent-or-buy decision made in Question 1? Explain.
3. Rework your calculations assuming that Julie does not itemize her deductions on her tax return but instead takes the standard deduction. Would that affect the rent-or-buy decision made in Question 1? Explain.
4. Discuss any nonquantitative factors that should be considered when making a rent-or-buy decision.
5. Which alternative would you recommend for Julie in light of your analysis?

FPPC 5.3 The McNeil's New Car Decision: Lease versus Purchase

Jim and Margaret McNeil, a dual-income couple in their late 20s, want to replace their seven-year-old car, which has 80,000 miles on it and needs some expensive repairs. After reviewing their budget, the McNeils conclude that they can afford auto payments of not more than $350 per month and a down payment of $2,000. They enthusiastically decide to visit a local Ford dealer after reading its newspaper ad offering a closed-end lease on a Ford Contour for a monthly payment of $245. After visiting with the dealer, test driving the car, and discussing the lease terms with the salesperson, they remain excited about leasing the car, but decide to wait until the following day to finalize the deal. Later that day the McNeils begin to question their approach to the new-car acquisition process, and they decide to carefully reevaluate their decision.

Questions

1. What are some of the basic purchase considerations the McNeils should take into account when choosing which new car to buy or lease? How can they get the information they need?
2. How would you advise the McNeils to research the lease versus purchase decision before visiting the Ford dealer? What are the advantages and disadvantages of each alternative?
3. Assume the McNeils can get the following terms on a lease or a bank loan available for the Ford, which they could buy for $15,000:

   Lease: 48 months, $245 monthly payment, one month's payment required as a security deposit, $350 end-of-lease charges; residual value of $6,775 is the purchase option price at the end of the lease.

   Loan: $2,000 down payment, $13,000 48-month loan at 10 percent interest requiring a monthly payment of $330. They assume the car's value at the end of 48 months will be the same as the residual value. Sales tax is 6 percent.

   If they choose the lease, they would earn a 4 percent return from investment of the down payment. They expect to drive about the same number of miles per year as they do now.

a. Use the format given in Worksheet 5.4 to determine which deal is better financially for the McNeils.

b. What other costs and terms of the lease option might affect their decision?

c. Based on the available information, should the McNeils lease or purchase the Ford, and why?

GETTING A HANDLE ON YOUR FINANCIAL FUTURE

As your income increases during your worklife, there will be an increased temptation to purchase more expensive and exotic consumer goods, automobiles, and homes with special features. You may feel that you have to have the latest HD-TV or newest compact disc player. You may want a sports car or to add on to your home.

The purpose of financial planning is to help you achieve these short-term and long-term goals. Even if you can afford certain luxuries, you should always properly evaluate the financing and operating costs of major purchases.

If You Are Just Starting Out

Your first major purchase will probably be an automobile. Decide what your needs are and be sure to include all operating costs in the decision-making process. In today's market, you might consider leasing as an option.

1. Review quality ratings of different automobiles to help focus your choices.
2. Decide on the amount you can afford to pay before you visit the showroom.
3. Consider purchasing a nearly new car that is still under factory warranty. Rental car companies are good places to find this type of deal.
4. Compare alternative financing options prior to talking with a dealer. The dealer will most likely try to finance your purchase through the dealership; this is not always the most advantageous avenue.
5. Once you have narrowed down your choices, check with your insurance agent for quotes on the different makes and models. You may be shocked at the differences.
6. Compare leasing to buying.

If You Are Thirty-Something

As you become established in your career, you may be looking to purchase a home and "settle down." Home buying is an involved process that can often take weeks or even months to finalize. These suggestions can help you in the selection and evaluation process:

1. Before you begin looking, decide what your needs are in terms of size and location.
2. Determine the amount of money you can afford based upon how much money you have for a down payment and closing costs as well as your income.
3. Don't forget the additional expenses of owning a home, such as property taxes and insurance.
4. If you are considering a home that is not newly built, ask to see the utility bills in order to accurately project this expense in your cash budget.
5. Make sure you are aware of any restrictive covenants in the deed as well as any easements.
6. If market interest rates decline about 2 percentage points, consider refinancing your home.
7. If you are considering buying a second home, keep in mind that generally second home purchases require a larger down payment, higher property taxes, and higher insurance premiums.

After reviewing his 1995 income and expenditures statement and his 1996 budget (constructed in Part 1, Questions 2 and 6), Paul has decided to make a few modifications in income, expenditures, and goals.

- Paul will accept a computer consulting job that will pay an additional $5,000 per year.
- He will be receiving a small tax refund in April, but he will need to reassess his tax situation for 1996 given the self-employment income from the consulting job.
- Paul will reduce his inventory of credit cards from seven to three cards.
- He will pay off all his new credit card purchases upon billing.
- He will make reductions in several monthly variable expenditures. The new budgeted amounts will be telephone ($45), groceries ($205), food away from home ($100), clothing ($75), appliance purchases ($50), entertainment ($100), gifts ($40/month January through October and $350/month November and December), and miscellaneous ($75).
- Paul will scale back some of his goals. At this time he feels he can save only $700 annually for a new car and only $1,500 annually for his mother's retirement. When his credit card debt is paid off, Paul will increase savings for these goals.

Assuming all of the above revisions start in January, 1996, Paul's budget deficit for 1996 should be reduced to approximately $15,000. He will reconsider other changes (such as his emergency fund goal, less expensive ways to pay off his credit card debt, and potential tax savings through purchasing a home this year rather than waiting two years) as the project progresses. He will continue to save $1,584 annually for his emergency fund goal.

1. In Part 1 of this project we found that Paul currently does not have 5 months net salary in liquid assets (money market accounts, money market mutual funds, and savings accounts) to meet his emergency fund goal. How many months of net salary does Paul currently have in these accounts? Evaluate Paul's current liquidity level and recommend to him whether his liquidity level is acceptable, whether he should designate some savings to increase his liquidity, or whether he should sell other assets and put the funds in one of these liquid accounts. Remember Paul's 1996 budget, tax considerations, his goals, and his risk tolerance when making your recommendation.

2. If you recommended that Paul designate savings to increase his emergency fund reserves, what type of account would you recommend for his emergency fund savings, assuming he wants to make monthly contributions to the account?

If you recommend that Paul sell another asset and put the funds in a liquid asset, what would you recommend selling, what would be the tax implications of that sale, and where would you put the funds?

FPPC **3.** Paul has just received his January, 1996 bank statement for his checking account. It contains the following information:

ending balance	$1,712.15
service charge	0.00
ATM fee	12.00

His checkbook ledger shows a final balance of $1,989.34. However, the following checks and deposits are still outstanding:

check #1506	$78.34
check #1510	75.00
deposit made on January 28	27.56
ATM withdrawal made January 30	20.00

Reconcile Paul's January bank statement. How much difference, if any, is there between the bank statement balance and the ending balance in his checkbook after reconciliation? If there is a large discrepancy, what practices should Paul improve so that he will have better control of this account?

4. Paul currently maintains a minimum balance checking account at Jefferson National Bank. However, Christine has suggested that Paul should consider a NOW account since he maintains a fairly high balance in his checking account. He would like to compare the following two accounts:

MINIMUM BALANCE ACCOUNT

- no service charge for accounts maintaining a minimum daily balance of $800 or more
- monthly service charge of $8 if the minimum daily balance falls below $800
- no interest paid
- ATM fee of $.25 per transaction at bank machines
- ATM fee of $1 per transaction at non-bank machines
- stop payment fee of $20
- insufficient funds fee of $20

NOW ACCOUNT

- no service charge for accounts maintaining a minimum daily balance of $1,250 or more
- monthly service charge of $10 if the minimum daily balance falls below $1,250
- 2.2% (annual percentage rate) interest is paid monthly on the average daily balance
- other fees are the same as on the minimum balance account

Paul reports that in an average month he writes 37 checks and makes 16 ATM transactions (11 at non-bank machines). He maintains an average daily balance in his checking account of $1,500, but the minimum daily balance falls to less than $1,250 (but more than $800) about 2 months a year. He has used the stop payment service only once in the past 5 years, and he has not bounced a check since he was in college.

Using the above information, compare the positive and the negative aspects of these two accounts. How much interest would Paul earn in a year with each account? What would the service charges and ATM charges be in a year with each account? Which one of these accounts would you recommend for Paul? What more could Paul do to lower his bank service charges?

5. In their recent discussions about money and marriage, Paul and Christine have mentioned opening a joint checking account before marriage. They have considered having a joint checking account (paying all their bills from that account) or perhaps maintaining their two individual accounts plus opening a joint account (from which only selected joint expenses would be paid). What are the pros and cons of opening a joint account? Would you recommend only one joint account, one joint plus two separate accounts, or no joint account at this time? If you recommend a joint account, should it be set up so both Paul and Christine must sign the check to make withdrawals or so only one signature is required?

6. Paul is currently maintaining four separate cash management accounts (checking, money market account, money market mutual fund, and savings account). What are the positive and the negative characteristics of each of these accounts? Would you recommend any changes? If yes, what changes and why?

7. Tower Software (Paul's employer) has just introduced a payroll savings plan where an employee can buy EE U.S. Savings Bonds each payroll period. Given Paul's financial situation and goals, would you recommend he sign up for this plan? If yes, why and how much money should he have deducted monthly from his paycheck to buy EE U.S. Savings Bonds? If no, why not?

8. Paul has been discussing his new-found interest in financial planning with Jack and Sarah Mathews, his friends that own the duplex he rents. One evening they dug out their most recent bank statement and asked Paul if their funds were covered by FDIC insurance. The following is a summary of their account balances:

Joint checking account	$ 3,045
Joint money market account	15,390
Joint certificates of deposit	95,336
Jack's IRA certificates of deposit	34,997
Sarah's IRA certificates of deposit	25,007

Assuming the bank is covered by FDIC insurance, how much of the Mathews funds in this bank are covered by FDIC insurance? What would you recommend to them as ways to get coverage on all of their funds if they want to leave all the money in this one bank? What could they do to get full FDIC coverage if they are willing to move some of the funds to another bank?

9. Jack and Sarah also purchased $15,000 of securities through their bank. Are these securities which are held jointly covered by FDIC insurance? Why or why not?

One of Paul's intermediate term goals is to buy a home. He had planned on waiting a couple of years, but the Mathews told him that there are significant tax advantages associated with home ownership. Given Paul's budget deficit, he wants to look at anything that could save him money. Paul has started house hunting and feels that he could find an acceptable property in the $100,000 price range. The lenders he has talked with typically require only a 10% down payment; however, Paul could make a larger down payment from his Fidelity Equity-Income II mutual fund. The after-tax rate of return on the Fidelity Equity-Income II fund is about 13 percent annually. He has shopped for home mortgages and narrowed his choices to the following:

30-YEAR FIXED-RATE MORTGAGE

- 8.5% interest with 1 discount point
- other closing costs and prepaids of $3,500 (includes a 1% loan origination fee)
- monthly payments

30-YEAR ADJUSTABLE-RATE MORTGAGE (ARM)

- 6.0% interest with 2 discount points
- other closing costs and prepaids of $3,250 (includes a 1% loan origination fee)
- 2.0% annual interest rate cap
- 6.0% overall interest rate cap

- indexed to 1-year Treasury Bill rates
- monthly payments

Paul expects to have the following changes in expenditures associated with the purchase and maintenance of this house:

- property taxes of 1.5% of the house value ($1,500/year)
- homeowners insurance of $675/year
- private mortgage insurance of $200/year (required if he makes a down payment of less than 20%)
- maintenance of 2.0% of the house value ($2,000/year)
- utility expenditures of $175/month

Paul expects to live in this house at least 5 years, and feels it will appreciate in value at 5 percent a year.

10. What are the positive and the negative aspects of making a larger-than-required down payment given Paul's financial circumstances? How much would you recommend Paul put down?

FPPC **11.** Compare and evaluate the two mortgages for Paul. Assuming Paul makes a 10% down payment on a $100,000 house, what would the front-end costs and the monthly payments be for principal and interest on each of the above two mortgages? How much could the monthly payments for principal and interest go up on the ARM after the first year? Over the life of the loan? What are the characteristics of the T-Bill index used on the ARM compared to other ARM indices? Keeping in mind his financial situation and risk tolerances, which mortgage would you recommend for Paul? Why?

FPPC **12.** In addition to an 8.5% fixed-rate mortgage with 1 discount point, the lender also offers an 8.8% fixed-rate mortgage with no discount points. Compare the difference in monthly payments and front-end costs for these two mortgage alternatives (assuming all else remains the same). How many months would Paul need to expect to keep the mortgage before it would be wise for him to consider paying the discount point? Which of these fixed-rate mortgages would you recommend for Paul? Why?

FPPC **13.** Will Paul be able to qualify for the 8.5% fixed-rate mortgage for $90,000 if the lender applies the following two affordability ratios:

a. monthly mortgage payments cannot exceed 28% of the borrower's monthly before-tax income, and

b. total monthly debt payments cannot exceed 34% of this same monthly before-tax income.

c. If not, can he qualify for the 6.0% adjustable-rate mortgage using these criteria?

In figuring if Paul will qualify, use all of his 1996 income *except* the dividend income and capital gains distributions from the Fidelity Equity-Income II mutual fund that he will have to sell to buy the new house and the prize money received from running in marathons. Remember that he has increased his gross income by taking on a new consulting job (see beginning of Part 2). Also use the minimum required payments for the revolving credit ($250) as part of the monthly debt payments. The amount of his monthly house payment will be the sum of the following:

- monthly payment for principal and interest
- 1/12 of the annual property taxes
- 1/12 of the annual homeowners insurance premium
- 1/12 of the annual private mortgage insurance premium

He is willing to sell all or part of his Fidelity Equity-Income II mutual fund to pay for the front-end costs.

14. Complete a rent/buy analysis for Paul assuming he would buy a $100,000 house with a 10% down payment using the 6.0% adjustable-rate mortgage with 1 discount point. Use the rental information from the original case and the marginal tax rate calculated in Part 1 of the project. Assume he will be able to itemize deductions, and be sure to include the discount points as part of the closing costs. Based on this analysis, should Paul continue renting or purchase a home? Why?

15. Using all the information you have to date, would you advise Paul to purchase a home now or to wait a couple of years? Why?

16. Paul has decided to defer the buy/rent decision until after he has looked at other areas of his financial plan (credit, insurance, and so forth). *However, his taxes and budget do need to be updated.

- Estimate Paul's 1996 federal income taxes considering that he will make $5,000 net consulting income. Don't forget his self-employment tax liability on this income.
- Update Paul's 1996 budget in light of the changes listed at the beginning of Part 2 and including changes just made in his emergency fund goal. Assume all changes were implemented in January of 1996.

Compare these two financial documents with those completed in Part 1 of the project. What changes have occurred in Paul's financial position?

*He has also decided *not* to increase the amount of liquid assets for his emergency fund either by monthly saving or by selling other assets until after he gets his credit under control. He does not feel he has the money to purchase EE U.S. Savings Bonds at this time either.

PART 3

CREDIT

CHAPTER 6

BORROWING ON OPEN ACCOUNT

Randy and Jan Learn the Meaning of Credit

"It's amazing how many banks will extend a $5,000 credit line to you when you buy a house," notes Randy Walker. "When a new furnace, air conditioning unit, and roof ate up our available credit, we just added more credit cards and kept on buying." In 1987, Jan decided to stay home when their first daughter was born, and then Randy was unemployed for eight weeks. "That *really* put us in a tail-spin," he recalls. "I was earning $30,000 a year with a monthly mortgage payment of $850, a car payment, and hardly any savings."

Soon the Walkers, who live in central Illinois, could barely cover the credit card monthly interest charges. "Our budget was so tight that even buying groceries was hard," Jan says. "We ignored the warning signs and continued using credit to get by. We were by no means disciplined with our spending." After weighing their options, they consulted an attorney. "We took his advice—to file bankruptcy—too quickly," Randy says regretfully. "We didn't expect much salary growth, so in October 1988, we filed Chapter 7 (liquidation) instead of Chapter 13 (debt restructuring). Knowing what we do now, we should have tried *everything possible*—like low interest loans from relatives or credit counselling—to resolve our situation before filing."

"The actual bankruptcy filing process was easy—perhaps too easy," Jan comments. "If someone had asked, 'Do you *really* know what you're getting into?' we might have taken another route." Because they had just enough

Learning Goals

LG1. *Describe the reasons for using consumer credit and identify its benefits and problems.*

LG2. *Develop a plan that will enable you to establish a strong credit history.*

LG3. *Distinguish among the different forms of open account credit: bank credit cards, other credit cards and charge accounts, and revolving credit lines.*

LG4. *Apply for, obtain, and manage open account credit.*

LG5. *Choose the right credit cards and recognize their advantages and disadvantages.*

LG6. *Avoid credit problems, protect yourself against credit card fraud, and understand the personal bankruptcy process.*

cash flow to pay their mortgage and car loan, they were able to "reaffirm" those loans at the time of filing and keep the assets.

When they were discharged from bankruptcy in June 1989, the Walkers vowed to take firm control of their personal finances. Randy studied personal finance magazines and books. For four years they had almost no credit availability, forcing them to manage their cash better, and Randy worked a second job for a while. They still had a few retail credit cards and reestablished their credit by charging small amounts that they paid off religiously. "But that black cloud of bankruptcy hung over us for what seemed like forever," Randy says. "In 1993, we got a secured MasterCard and managed our small debts to the point where the banks are again asking us to take their credit cards!"

The Walkers caution, "Say no to those offers! If you get in over your head, try *every other avenue* before filing for Chapter 7 bankruptcy. Develop financial discipline; if you can't pay cash, you probably don't need it!" Even though Randy's career and salary have advanced, they budget $100 per month for credit card purchases and really take a hard look at any purchases over $300. They are saving for retirement and now have a college fund for their two daughters. "Read all the personal financial books (like this one) you can and *take their advice*," they urge. "Study the following chapter, so you'll learn to manage your credit wisely and not get into trouble like we did."

THE BASIC CONCEPTS OF CREDIT

LG1
LG2

Consumer credit is a convenient and effective way to purchase a variety of goods and services. Results can be disastrous, however, if the use of credit is not kept to a manageable level. Stop for a moment to think of the ways you would use consumer credit. What steps would you take to make sure your use of credit doesn't get out of hand?

Just say "Charge it." With those two little words and a piece of plastic, you can buy gas for your car, have a gourmet meal at an expensive restaurant, or furnish an apartment. It happens *a couple hundred million times a day* across the United States. Credit, in fact, has become an entrenched part of our everyday lives, and we, as consumers, use it in one form or another to purchase just about every type of good or service imaginable. Indeed, because of the ready availability and widespread use of credit, our economy is often called a "credit economy." And for good reason: by year-end 1994, individuals in this country had run up about $900 *billion dollars* in consumer debt—and that *excludes* home mortgages.

Consumer credit is important in the personal financial planning process because of the impact it can have on (1) the attainment of financial goals, and (2) cash budgets. For one thing, various forms of consumer credit can help you reach your financial objectives by enabling you to acquire some of the more expensive items in a systematic fashion, and without throwing your whole budget into disarray. But there's another side to consumer credit: It has to be paid back! Unless credit is used intelligently, the "buy-now-pay-later" attitude can quickly turn an otherwise orderly budget into a budgetary nightmare and lead to some serious problems—even bankruptcy! So, really, the issue is one of moderation and affordability.

In today's economy, consumers, businesses, and governments alike use credit to make transactions. Credit helps businesses supply the goods and services needed to satisfy consumer demand. In addition, business credit provides higher levels of employment and helps raise our overall standard of living. Local, state, and federal governments borrow for various projects and programs that also increase our standard of living and create additional employment opportunities. Clearly, borrowing helps fuel our economy and enhance the overall quality of our lives. Consequently, consumers in a credit economy need to know how to establish credit and how to avoid the dangers of using it improperly.

WHY BORROW?

People typically use credit as a way to pay for goods and services that cost more than they can afford to take from their current income. This is particularly true for those in the 25-to-44 age group, who simply have not had time to accumulate the liquid assets required to pay cash outright for major purchases and expenditures. As people begin to approach their mid-40s, their savings and investments start to build up, and their debt loads, in turn, tend to decline.

People borrow for several major reasons:

- ***To avoid paying cash for large outlays.*** Rather than pay cash for large purchases, such as houses and cars, most people borrow a portion of the purchase price and then repay the loan on some scheduled basis. Spreading payments over time makes big-ticket items more affordable, and consumers get the use of an expensive asset right away. Most people consider the cost of such borrowing a small price to pay for the immediate satisfaction they get from owning the house, car, or whatever it happens to be. In their minds, at least, the benefits of current consumption outweigh the interest costs on the loan. Unfortunately, while the initial euphoria of the purchase may wear off over time, the loan payments remain for many years.
- ***To meet a financial emergency.*** For example, people may need to borrow to cover living expenses during a period of unemployment, or to purchase plane tickets in order to visit a sick relative. As indicated in Chapter 4, however, use of savings (not credit) is the ideal way to provide for financial emergencies.
- ***For convenience.*** Merchants as well as banks offer a variety of charge accounts and credit cards that allow consumers to charge just about anything—from gas and oil or clothes and stereos to doctor and dental bills and even college tuition.

EXHIBIT 6.1

Minimum Payments Mean Maximum Years

Paying off credit card balances at the minimum monthly amount required by the card issuer will take a long time and cost you a great deal of interest, as the following table demonstrates. The calculations are based on a minimum 3 percent payment and 17.5 percent annual interest rate.

Original Balance	Years to Repay	Interest Paid	Total Interest Paid as Percent of Original Balance
$5,000	18.4	$4,541	90.8%
4,000	17.2	3,595	89.9
3,000	15.7	2,649	88.3
2,000	13.5	1,703	85.2
1,500	11.9	1,230	82.0
1,000	9.8	757	75.7
500	6.1	284	56.8

Further, in many places—restaurants, for instance—using a credit card is far easier than writing a check. A credit card purchase provides a permanent, itemized record of the transaction that simplifies the budgeting process. Although such transactions often incur no interest (at least initially), these credit card purchases are still a form of borrowing, since payment is not made at the time of the transaction.

- ***For investment purposes.*** As we'll see in Chapter 12, it's relatively easy for an investor to partially finance the purchase of many different kinds of investment vehicles with borrowed funds.

IMPROPER USES OF CREDIT

Many people use consumer credit to live beyond their means. Overspending is the biggest danger in borrowing, especially because it's so easy to do. Once hooked on "plastic," people may use their credit cards to make even routine purchases and don't realize they have overextended themselves until it's too late. Overspenders simply won't admit that they're spending too much. As far as they're concerned, they can afford to buy all those things because, after all, they still have their credit cards and can still afford to pay the minimum amount each month.

Unfortunately, such spending eventually leads to mounting bills. And by making only the minimum payment, they pay a huge price in the long run. Look at Exhibit 6.1, which shows the amount of time and interest charges required to repay credit card balances if you make only a minimum payment of 3 percent of the outstanding balance. If you carry a $1,500 balance—just under the $1,700 national average—on a card that charges 17.5 percent annually, it would take you *almost 12 years* to retire the debt, and your interest charges would total *$1,230—82 percent of the original balance!* And some cards offer even lower minimum payments of 2 to 2.5 percent. While such small payments may seem like a good idea, clearly they do not work to your advantage and only increase the time and amount of interest required.

To avoid the possibility of future repayment shock, you should keep in mind the following types of transactions for which you should *not* (routinely, at least) use credit: (1) to meet basic living expenses; (2) to make impulse purchases, especially expensive ones; and (3) to purchase nondurable (short-lived) goods and services. Except in situations where credit cards are used occasionally for the sake of convenience (such as for gasoline and entertainment) and/or payments on recurring credit purchases are built into the monthly budget, a good rule to remember when considering the use of credit is that *the product purchased on credit should outlive the payments.*

Unfortunately, people who overspend eventually arrive at the point where they must choose to either become delinquent in their payments or sacrifice necessities, such as food and clothing. If payment obligations are not met, the consequences are likely to be a damaged credit rating, lawsuits, or even personal bankruptcy. Exhibit 6.2 lists some common signals that indicate it may be time to stop buying on credit. *Ignoring the telltale signs that you are overspending can only lead to more serious problems.*

EXHIBIT 6.2

Some Credit Danger Signs

If one or more of these signs exist, you should take them as an indication that it is time to proceed with caution in your credit spending. Revise and update your spending patterns, cut back on the use of credit, and be alert for other signs of overspending.

You may be headed for serious trouble if:

- You regularly use credit cards to buy on impulse.
- You postdate checks to keep them from bouncing.
- You regularly exceed the borrowing limit on your credit cards.
- You never add up all your bills, to avoid facing grim realities.
- You now take 60 or 90 days to pay bills you once paid in 30.
- You have to borrow just to meet normal living expenses.
- You often use one form of credit—such as a cash advance from a credit card—to make payments on other debt.
- You can barely make the minimum required payments on bills.
- You are using more than 20 percent of your take-home income to pay credit card bills and personal loans (excluding mortgage payments).
- You have no savings.
- You are so far behind on credit payments that collection agencies are after you.

ESTABLISHING CREDIT

The willingness of lenders to extend credit depends on their assessment of your creditworthiness—your ability to repay the debt on a timely basis. They look at a number of factors in making this decision, such as your present earnings and net worth. Equally important, they look at your current debt position and your credit history. Thus, it's worth your while to do what you can to build a strong credit rating.

First Steps in Establishing Credit. First, open checking and savings accounts. These signal stability to lenders and also indicate that you handle your financial affairs in a businesslike fashion. Second, use credit—open one or two charge accounts and use them periodically, even if you prefer paying cash. For example, get a Visa card and make a few credit purchases each month (don't overdo it, of course). You might pay an annual fee or interest on some (or all) of your account balances, but in the process, you'll become identified as a reliable credit customer. Third, obtain a small loan, even if you don't need one. If you don't actually need the money, put it in a liquid investment, such as a money market account or certificate of deposit. The interest you earn should offset some of the interest expense on the loan; you can view the difference as a cost of building good credit. (It goes without saying that you should repay the loan promptly, perhaps even a little ahead of schedule, to minimize the difference in interest rates—don't pay off the loan too quickly, though, as lenders like to see how you perform over an extended period of time.) Keep in mind, your ability to obtain a large loan in the future will depend in part on how you managed smaller ones in the past.

Build a Strong Credit History. From a financial perspective, maintaining a strong credit history is just as important as developing a solid employment record! Don't take credit lightly, and don't assume that getting the loan or the credit card is the toughest part. It's not. That's just the first step; servicing it (i.e., making payments) in a prompt and timely fashion—month in and month out—is the really tough part of the consumer credit process. And in many respects, it's the most important element of consumer credit, as it determines your creditworthiness. By using credit wisely and repaying it on time, you're establishing a *credit history* that tells lenders you're a dependable, reliable, and responsible borrower.

The consumer credit industry keeps very close tabs on your credit and your past payment performance (more on this when we discuss *credit bureaus* later in the chapter). So the better job you do in being a responsible borrower, the easier it will be to get credit when and where you want it. The best way to build up a strong credit history and maintain your creditworthiness is to *consistently* make payments *on time*, month after month. Being late occasionally—say, two or three times a year—might label you a "late payer." When you take on credit, you have an *obligation* to live up to the terms of the loan, including how and when the credit will be repaid.

If you foresee difficulty in meeting a monthly payment, let the lender know and usually some sort of arrangements can be made to help you through the situation. This is especially true with installment loans that require fixed monthly payments. If you have one or two of these loans and, for some reason or another, you encounter a month that's going to be really tight, the first thing you should try to do is get an extension on your loan. Don't just skip a payment, because that's going to put your account into a *late status until you make up the missed payment*—in other words, until you make a *double* payment, your account/loan will remain in a late status, subject to a monthly late penalty. The alternative of trying to work out an extension with your lender obviously makes a lot more sense. Here's what you do: explain the situation to the loan officer and ask for an extension of one (or two) months on your loan. In most cases, so long as this hasn't occurred before, the extension is almost automatically granted. The maturity of the loan is formally extended for a month (or two), and the extra interest of carrying the loan for another month (or two) is either added to the loan balance or, more commonly, paid at the time the extension is granted (such an extension fee generally amounts to a fraction of the normal monthly payment). Then, in a month (or two), you pick up where you left off and resume your normal monthly payments on the loan. This is the most sensible way of making it through those rough times since it doesn't harm your credit record. Just don't do it too often.

To summarize, here are some ways to build a strong credit history:

- Use credit only when you can afford it and only when the repayment schedule fits comfortably into the family budget—in short, don't overextend yourself.
- Fulfill all the terms of the credit.
- Be *consistent* in making payments *promptly*.
- Consult creditors immediately if you cannot meet payments as agreed.
- Be truthful when applying for credit. Lies are not likely to go undetected.

How Much Credit Can You Stand? Sound financial planning dictates that if you are going to use credit, you should have a good idea of how much you can comfortably tolerate. The easiest way to avoid repayment problems and ensure that your borrowing will not place an undue strain on your monthly budget is to *limit the use of credit to your ability to repay the debt!* A useful *credit guideline* (and one widely used by lenders) is to make sure your monthly repayment burden does not exceed 20 percent of your monthly *take-home pay*. Most experts, however, regard the 20 percent figure as the *maximum* debt burden and strongly recommend **debt safety ratios** closer to 10 to 15 percent. Note that the monthly repayment burden here is *exclusive* of your monthly mortgage obligation.

To illustrate, consider an individual who takes home $1,500 a month. Using a 20 percent ratio, she should have monthly consumer credit payments of no more than $300—that is, $1,500 × .20 = $300. This is the maximum amount of her monthly disposable income that she should have to use to pay off both personal loans and other forms of consumer credit (such as credit cards and education loans). This, of course, is not the maximum amount of consumer credit this person can have outstanding—in fact, her total consumer indebtedness can, and likely would, be considerably larger. The key factor is that with her income level, her *payments* on this type of debt should not exceed $300 a month. (Caution: This is not to say that credit terms should be lengthened just to accommodate this guideline; rather, in all cases, it is assumed that standard credit terms apply.)

Exhibit 6.3 provides a summary of low (10 percent), manageable (15 percent), and maximum (20 percent) monthly credit payments for a number of income levels. Obviously, the closer your total monthly payments are to your desired debt safety ratio, the less future borrowing you can undertake. Conversely, *the lower the debt safety ratio, the better shape you're in, creditwise, and the easier it will be for you to service your outstanding consumer debt.*

debt safety ratio The proportion of total monthly consumer credit obligations to monthly take-home pay.

EXHIBIT 6.3

Alternative Consumer Credit Guidelines Based on Ability to Repay

Using this credit guideline, the amount of consumer credit you should have outstanding depends on the monthly payment you can afford to make.

	Monthly Consumer Credit Payments		
Monthly Take-Home Pay	***Low* Debt Safety Ratio (10%)**	***Manageable* Debt Safety Ratio (15%)**	***Maximum* Debt Safety Ratio (20%)**
$ 500	$ 50	$ 75	$100
750	75	112	150
1,000	100	150	200
1,250	125	188	250
1,500	150	225	300
2,000	200	300	400
2,500	250	375	500
3,000	300	450	600

To find your debt safety ratio, simply use the following formula:

$$\text{Debt safety ratio} = \frac{\text{Total monthly consumer credit payments}}{\text{Monthly take-home pay}}$$

Thus, if you take home $1,360 a month and make total payments of $180 a month on outstanding consumer credit, you will have a debt safety ratio of $180/$1,360 = 13 percent, well within the manageable range.

The Special Credit Problems of Women. At one time, a woman stood very little chance of getting credit on her own. In most lenders' minds, she was too much of a risk; even if she was gainfully employed, she might become pregnant and lose her job. Today, the Equal Credit Opportunity Act (ECOA; discussed more fully later in the chapter) has removed most of these credit obstacles. Creditors cannot check into a woman's marital status or childbearing plans and, with two-income families, must consider the woman's income on the same basis as the man's, even if it's part-time employment.

Even with these and other protections, however, some women—especially those who are divorced or widowed—still have difficulty getting credit if they do not have their own credit history. The following steps can help overcome this problem:

- ***Use your own name when filing a credit application.*** Use your legal name, not a social title, such as Mrs. Thomas Watkins. A married woman can choose from several legal names; for example, if your maiden name is Joan Brown and you take your husband's name of Watkins, you can choose Joan Watkins or Joan Brown Watkins. *Use your legal name consistently* to build your own credit history.
- ***Make sure any information reported to the credit bureau is in your name as well as your husband's.***
- ***Consider retaining a credit file separate from your husband's*** when you marry, particularly if you have already established a good credit rating. You should notify creditors of your name change and intention to maintain your own file.

A Final Word of Caution. One of the real dangers of credit cards and other forms of open account credit is that they are so easy to use. Too many people tend to overlook the fact that they must eventually pay for the merchandise charged with their cards—but each time they make a transaction this way, they are incurring a liability to the issuer. Indeed, as the accompanying *Smart Money* box on page 238 illustrates, a growing number of people are learning this lesson the hard way! The bottom line is, if credit is used properly, it can go a long way in helping you manage your personal finances; misuse it and you are just asking for trouble.

Concept Check

6-1. Why do people borrow? What are some of the improper uses of credit? Are there any dangers associated with borrowing? Explain.

6-2. Describe the general guidelines lenders use to calculate an applicant's maximum debt burden. How can you use the *debt safety ratio* to determine whether your debt obligations are within reasonable limits?

6-3. What steps can you take to establish a good credit rating? What extra steps might be necessary for a woman?

TYPES OF OPEN ACCOUNT CREDITS

LG3

In open account credit, the consumer obtains a revolving line of credit—which may or may not involve the use of a credit card. What types of open account credit would be most appealing to you? Take a minute to think about this question before reading on.

Open account credit is a form of credit extended to a consumer in advance of any transactions. Typically, a retail outlet or bank agrees to allow the consumer to buy or borrow up to a specified amount on open account. Credit is extended as long as the consumer does not exceed the established **credit limit,** and makes payments in accordance with the specified terms. Open account credit issued by a retail outlet, such as a department store or oil company, is usually applicable only in that establishment or one of its locations. In contrast, open account credit issued by banks, such as *MasterCard* and *Visa* accounts, can be used to make purchases at a wide variety of businesses. In the remainder of this chapter, we will direct our attention to various types and characteristics of open account credit; in Chapter 7, we will look at various forms of single-payment and installment loans.

Having open account credit is a lot like having your own personal line of credit—it's there when you need it. But unlike most other forms of debt, consumers who use open account credit can generally avoid paying interest charges *if they promptly pay the full amount of their account balance.* For example, assume that in a given month you charge $75.58 worth of purchases on an open account at a department store. Sometime within the next month or so, you will receive a **credit statement** from the store that summarizes recent transactions on your account. Now, if there are no other charges and the total account balance is $75.58, you can (usually) avoid any finance charges by paying the account in full prior to the next billing date.

Open account credit generally is available from two broadly defined sources: (1) financial institutions and (2) retail stores/merchants. *Financial institutions* issue general-purpose credit cards as well as secured and unsecured revolving lines of credit and overdraft protection lines. Commercial banks have long been a major provider of consumer credit; and since deregulation, so have S&Ls and credit unions. Deregulation has also brought other financial institutions into this market—most notably, major stock-brokerage firms, consumer finance companies, and a growing list of commercial banks that have gone *interstate* to market their credit cards and other consumer credit products. *Retail stores and merchants* make up the other major source of open account credit. They provide credit to promote the sales of their products. Their principal forms of credit include open charge accounts and credit cards.

Of the various types of open account credit, the two biggest are *bank credit cards* and *retail*

open account credit A form of credit extended to a consumer in advance of any transaction; type of credit that accompanies charge accounts and credit cards.

credit limit A specified amount beyond which a customer may not borrow or purchase on credit.

credit statement A monthly statement that summarizes the transactions in a consumer credit account; includes a record of new charges, credits and payments, any interest charges, and the minimum monthly payment required on the account.

Smart Money

Don't Fall into the Credit Card Trap!

"Arlene B." is addicted to credit. When she maxed out one charge card, she simply got another, and then another. Soon, she had several gasoline company cards, department store cards, and six bank credit cards, and had run up massive debts on all of them. Whenever the real estate broker's sales were slow, she used credit to survive. She begged for cash advances on credit cards even though she was late with payments and borrowed against a home equity line. She couldn't stop running up debt, even though she knew she didn't have the money to pay a fraction of what she owed.

Surprisingly, there are many "debt junkies" like Arlene. According to Ruth Susswein, executive director of the Bankcard Holders of America, the average consumer has eight to ten credit cards, including two or three bank cards, and carries about $1,700 in debt on each of several cards. All too often, consumers lose track of their credit purchases and incur large debts without recognizing why they do so. Rather than adjust spending or increase income to live within their means, they borrow to cover living expenses. They search out new credit sources, both credit cards and loans, but don't evaluate the effect of such borrowing on their future financial condition.

Most financial planners agree that consumer debt plays a valuable role in personal financial planning. Credit cards are convenient; they let you take advantage of an extra few weeks to pay for purchases, earn rebates, or spread out repayment over a few months. Emergency situations are another time when borrowing is justified. But taking on debt without a known source of repayment is dangerous. Without proper management, your debt payments may become a permanent, rather than temporary, part of your financial picture.

Today there's another danger for credit addicts. More and more credit cards have finance charges based on variable interest rates that adjust with changes in market rates. In a period of rising interest rates, such as 1994, many consumers found that their total debt was considerably more than originally anticipated due to higher interest costs.

A surefire way to avoid getting stuck with higher interest payments is to pay your outstanding balances in full. That's a good idea anyway, according to financial advisers, because you can save more in interest than you would earn on an investment. For example, if you are in the 28 percent tax bracket, you'd have to earn *over 15 percent* on an investment to offset the cost of paying 11 percent interest on a credit card balance—and that's a very low interest rate today.

Of course, eliminating debt entirely is just not possible for many people. If this is true for you, get rid of as much debt as possible by curtailing credit purchases, carrying fewer cards, and possibly transferring balances to a lower-rate card. Work out a plan to make a certain minimum monthly payment—the more the better; don't stick to the card's low minimum requirement or you'll be paying off the debt for many years to come—and have the self-discipline to stick to it.

Most importantly, along with a plan to systematically pay down your credit card debt, you must fundamentally change your spending habits. Try not to use your charge cards while paying down your balance, and when you emerge (triumphantly) from debt, don't allow yourself to charge more than you can afford to pay. Runaway debt can ruin your future and leave you feeling anxious and ashamed. Unless you bring it under control, you will find it difficult to achieve other important financial goals, like saving for your children's education or your retirement.

Sources: Adapted from Deborah Lohse, "Start Slashing Your Credit-Card Costs to Avoid Sting of Rising Interest Rates," *The Wall Street Journal*, March 27, 1994, pp.C1, C15; Mark Schwanhausser, "The Debt Trap: Short-Term Fixes Turn into Long-Term Problems," *San Jose Mercury News*, November 13, 1994, p. 1D; Linda Stern, "2 Routes Can Lead out of Credit-Card Trap," *San Diego Union-Tribune*, February 14, 1994, p. C3.

charge cards. Together, there are about a billion of these cards outstanding today. Let's now take a closer look at the many forms of open account credit: bank credit cards, retail charge cards, 30-day charge accounts, travel and entertainment cards, prestige cards, affinity cards, secured credit cards, *debit cards*, and several kinds of *revolving lines of credit*, including overdraft protection lines, unsecured lines of credit, and home equity credit lines—all of which are available from banks and other financial services institutions.

BANK CREDIT CARDS

Probably the most popular form of open account credit is the **bank credit card** issued by commercial banks and other financial institutions—Visa and MasterCard are the two dominant types. These cards allow their holders to charge purchases worldwide at literally millions of stores, restaurants, shops, and gas stations, as well as at state and municipal governments, colleges and universities, medical groups, and mail-order houses. They can be used to pay for almost anything—groceries, doctor bills, college tuition, airline tickets, and car rentals. Thousands of banks, S&Ls, credit unions, brokerage houses, and other financial services institutions issue Visa and MasterCard, and each issuer, within reasonable limits, can set its own credit terms and conditions. In recent years, several more big-league players have entered the field. Sears introduced its Discover card (now owned by Dean Witter), American Express its Optima True Grace card, and AT&T its Universal card (which is actually just a special Visa or MasterCard).

FEATURES OF BANK CREDIT CARDS

Bank credit cards are issued by a third party—a bank or some other financial institution—and can be used to borrow money as well as buy goods and services on credit. Because of their potential for use in thousands of businesses and banks, they can be of great convenience and value to consumers. Individuals who use them, however, should be thoroughly familiar with their basic features.

Line of Credit. The **line of credit** provided to the holder of a bank credit card is set by the issuer for each card. It is the maximum amount that the cardholder can owe at any point in time. The size of the credit line depends on both the applicant's request and the results of the issuer's investigation of the applicant's credit and financial status. Lines of credit offered by issuers of bank cards can reach $10,000 or more, but for the most part they range from about $500 to $2,500. While the card issuers fully expect you to keep your credit within the specified limits, most won't take any real action unless you extend your account balance a certain percentage beyond the account's stated maximum. For example, if you had a $500 credit limit, you probably wouldn't hear a thing from the card issuer until your outstanding account balance exceeded $600; that is, 20 percent above the $500 line of credit. On the other hand, don't count on getting off scot-free, for an increasing number of card issuers are beginning to assess *over-the-limit* fees whenever you go over your credit limit (more on this later).

Cash Advances. In addition to purchasing merchandise and services, the holder of a bank credit card can also obtain a **cash advance** from any participating bank. Cash advances are loans on which interest begins to accrue immediately. They are transacted in the same fashion as merchandise purchases except that they take place at a commercial bank or some other financial institution and involve the receipt of cash (or a check) instead of goods and services. Another way to get a cash advance is to use the "convenience checks" you receive from the card issuer to pay for purchases. You can even use your credit card to draw cash from an ATM, any time of the day or night. Usually, the size of the cash advance from an ATM is limited to some nominal amount (perhaps $300), though the amount that you can obtain from the teller window at a bank is limited only by the unused credit in your account. Thus, if you've only used $1,000 of a $5,000 credit limit, you can take out a cash advance of up to $4,000.

Other Features. Bank credit cards sure aren't what they used to be! The fact is, credit cards today offer a lot more than just a convenient way of getting credit. Because the market has become so

bank credit card A credit card issued by a bank or other financial institution that allows the holder to charge purchases at any establishment that accepts it; can also be used to obtain cash advances.

line of credit The maximum amount of credit that a customer is allowed to have outstanding at any point in time.

cash advance A loan that can be obtained by a bank credit cardholder at any participating bank or financial institution; begins to accrue interest immediately and requires no formal application.

competitive, card issuers have had to offer all sorts of services and features (some would call them "gimmicks") in an attempt to get you to use their cards. One popular feature is the so-called *buyer protection plan,* which automatically protects most items of merchandise purchased with your credit card against loss, theft, or damage for up to 90 days. For example, if the purchased item breaks during the 90-day period, the card issuer will see that the item is replaced for free. Many of these plans also include an automatic extension of manufacturer's warranties, up to one additional year. Here's a list of some of the other services offered:

- High-value travel accident insurance
- Full-value auto rental insurance coverage
- 24-hour toll-free travelers' emergency message service
- Lost card registration
- Discounts on long-distance phone calls
- Price protection plans
- 24-hour toll-free customer service lines

While it is not clear just how valuable these services really are, one thing is sure: They do act to keep interest costs on credit cards very high. Make no mistake about it, one way or another, cardholders will end up paying for all these services!

Rebate (Co-branded) Credit Cards. The fastest-growing segment of the bank card market is the **rebate (co-branded) credit card,** which combines features of a traditional bank credit card with an incentive: either cash (Discover), merchandise rebates, airline tickets, or even investments. Over 50 million cardholders carry Visa or MasterCard rebate cards, and new types are introduced on a regular basis. There is even a Rolling Stones Visa or MasterCard, complete with the group's logo, that gives discounts at Camelot music stores and on Rolling Stones merchandise. Among the many incentive programs are:

- ***Frequent flyer programs.*** The cardholder earns free frequent flyer miles for each dollar charged on his or her credit card. These frequent flyer miles can then be used with airline-affiliated programs for free tickets, first-class upgrades, and other travel-related benefits. Examples include the Citibank American Airlines Advantage Visa or MasterCard, First Chicago's United Airlines Mileage Plus Visa or MasterCard, and American Express and Diners Club programs, with miles that can be used on one of several airlines.
- ***Automobile rebate programs.*** Ford, General Motors, and Volkswagen offer bank cards that allow the cardholder to earn annual rebates of 5 percent for new car purchases or leases, up to specified limits ($700 for Ford and Volkswagen, $500 for GM).
- ***Other merchandise rebates.*** An increasing number of companies are participating in bank card rebate programs, including Apple Computer (5 percent, up to $500 per year), Carnival Cruise Lines (3 percent, up to $400 per cruise), and Nordstrom Department Stores (1 to 5 percent rebate on purchases, plus other discounts). Most major oil companies now offer rebate cards where the cardholder earns credits applied to purchases of the company's gasoline. Several regional phone companies offer rebates on phone calls.
- ***Investment programs.*** The Edvance Card gives the cardholder a $50 U.S. Savings Bond for every $2,500 in charges, up to a maximum of 23 bonds per year.

Are rebate cards a good deal? Well, yes and no. You should evaluate these cards carefully by looking at your usage patterns and working out the annual cost of the cards before and after the rebate, to see if they make sense for you. Don't get so carried away with the gimmick that you lose sight of the total costs. Most incentive cards carry higher interest rates than regular bank cards. These cards work best for those who can use the rebates, charge a lot, and don't carry high monthly balances. For example, suppose you charge $2,200 a year on a GM rebate card and carry a monthly balance of $1,100. If the interest rate is 18 percent, the annual cost is about $198 and you earn a $110 rebate ($2,200 × .05) that reduces the cost to $88 if you use the rebate. Frequent flier cards are best for high volume chargers who do not carry balances. For example, with $25,000 in charges on American and United cards you earn one domestic coach ticket. If you pay in full each month and assume the ticket is worth $500, the net benefit after the $50 annual fee is $450. But if you only charge $2,200 and carry a $1,100 balance, the card costs $248 per year (assuming interest at 18 percent and a $50 annual fee) and earns less than 10 percent of a ticket. In that case, you would be better off with a low-rate card.

Interest Rates on Bank Card Charges. With very few exceptions, the *annual* rate of interest charged on bank credit cards ranges from about 14 to 21 percent; in fact, in late 1994, the national average was nearly 18 percent (17.74%, to be exact). However, some states have **usury laws** that limit these rates to something more like 12 to 15 percent. And the interest rate on merchandise purchases may differ from that on cash advances.

About 70 percent of all bank cards have variable interest rates tied to the **prime (or base) rate,** the rate a bank uses as a base for loans to individuals and small or midsize businesses. Most of these cards adjust the interest rate quarterly and have a minimum and maximum rate. If the issuing bank's terms are prime +9.4 percent, with a minimum of 12.9 percent and a maximum of 19.8 percent, and the prime rate is 7.5 percent, the interest on balances would be 16.9 percent. Some cards have rates as low as prime +2.5 percent, although they tend to adjust rates monthly. Bank cardholders should therefore be aware that general interest rate hikes will increase the interest they pay on outstanding balances.

Generally speaking, *the interest rates on credit cards are higher than any other form of consumer credit.* But more and more banks—even the bigger ones—now offer more competitive rates, especially to their better customers. Some offer a special low introductory rate for the first six months or a year. Moreover, a growing number of banks are willing to negotiate their fees as a way to retain their customers. Whether this trend will have any significant impact on reducing interest rates and fees remains to be seen, but at least most consumers would agree it is a step in the right direction.

Bank credit card issuers must disclose interest costs and related information to consumers *before* extending credit. In the case of purchases of merchandise and services, the specified interest rate is not normally applied to charges until after the **grace period.** During this short time period, usually 25 to 30 days, you can pay your credit card bill in full and avoid any interest charges. Once you carry a balance, the interest rate is usually applied to any unpaid balances carried from previous periods, as well as any new purchases made. Interest on cash advances, however, *begins the day the advance is taken out.*

Other Fees. In addition to the interest charged on bank credit cards, there are a few other fees you should be aware of. To begin with, many—though not all—bank cards levy *annual fees* just for the "privilege" of being able to use the card. In most cases, the fee is around $15 to $25 a year, though it can amount to much more for prestige cards. Sometimes, this annual fee will be waived in the first year, but you'll be stuck with it for the second and every other year you hold the card. As a rule, the larger the bank or S&L, the more likely it is to charge an annual fee for one of its credit cards. What's more, many issuers also charge a *transaction fee* for each cash advance; this fee usually amounts to about $2 per cash advance *or* 2 percent of the amount obtained in the transaction, whichever is more.

And now, more and more card issuers are coming up with new ways to sock it to you. The newest twist: late-payment fees and over-the-limit charges. If you're a bit late in making your payment, at some banks you'll be hit with a late-payment fee—which is really a redundant charge since you're already paying interest on the unpaid balance. In a similar fashion, if you happen to go over your credit limit, you'll get hit with a charge for that, too (again, this is on top of the interest you're already paying). Critics really dislike this fee because they maintain it's very difficult for cardholders to know when they've hit their credit ceilings. Regardless of when or why any of these fees are levied, the net effect is that *they add to the true cost of using bank credit cards.*

OTHER CREDIT CARDS AND CHARGE ACCOUNTS

In addition to bank cards, credit cards are issued by many retail companies. You should also be aware of several other kinds of credit cards and

rebate (co-branded) credit card A bank credit card that combines features of a traditional bank credit card with an additional incentive, such as rebates and airline mileage.

usury laws State laws governing interest rates on consumer and other types of credit.

prime (base) rate The rate of interest a bank uses as a base for loans to individuals and small to midsize businesses.

grace period A short period of time, usually 25 to 30 days, during which you can pay your credit card bill in full and not incur any interest charges.

charge accounts, including 30-day charge accounts, travel and entertainment cards, prestige cards, affinity cards, and secured credit cards.

Retail Charge Cards. **Retail charge cards** are the second largest category of credit card and are issued by department stores, oil companies, airlines, car rental agencies, and so on. These cards are popular with merchants because they build consumer loyalty and enhance sales; and consumers like them because they are a convenient way to shop. These cards carry a pre-set credit limit—a line of credit—that varies with the creditworthiness of the cardholder.

This form of credit is most common in department and clothing stores and other high-volume outlets, where customers are likely to make several purchases each month. Most large oil companies offer charge cards that allow customers to buy gas and oil products, but they're expected to pay for such purchases in full upon receipt of the monthly bill. To promote the sale of their more expensive products, oil companies frequently offer revolving credit for use in purchasing items such as tires, batteries, and accessories. Many families have—and regularly use—five or six different retail charge cards. Interest on most retail charge cards is fixed at 1.5 to 1.65 percent monthly, or 18 to 19.8 percent per year.

30-Day Charge Account. Commonly offered by certain types of businesses for the general convenience of their customers, the **30-day,** or **regular, charge account** requires the customer to pay the full amount billed within 10 to 20 days after the billing date. If payment is made within the specified period, no interest is charged; if received after the due date, however, an interest penalty is usually tacked on to the account balance. These accounts generally do not involve the use of a charge card. They are offered by various types of public utilities (such as gas and electric companies, telephone companies, and so on), as well as some doctors and dentists, drugstores, and repair services.

Travel and Entertainment Cards. **Travel and entertainment (T&E) cards** are similar to bank credit cards in that they enable holders to charge purchases at a variety of locations. While these cards used to be accepted primarily at travel- and entertainment-related businesses—like hotels, motels, airlines, and restaurants—they have now found their way into all sorts of establishments, from upscale department and clothing stores to gas stations and drugstores. These cards have annual fees of up to $300 just for the privilege of using them. In sharp contrast to retail and bank credit cards, however, most T&E cards do *not* carry an extended line of credit. Instead, the outstanding balances must be *paid in full* within either one or two billing periods for the account to remain current. *American Express* is, by far, the biggest issuer of this type of card (with over 36 million cardholders worldwide), followed by *Diners Club* (almost 7 million). However, these numbers are minute compared to the number of bank credit cards outstanding; there are over 375 million Visa cards and another 255 million or so MasterCards in circulation. T&E cards now offer frequent flier miles and other features, like Diners Club's collision coverage for car rentals and luggage insurance.

In 1994, American Express added a new twist to this segment of the market by introducing the *Optima True Grace* card. Like the regular American Express card, the Optima card is aimed at affluent cardholders who want not only convenience, but also a regular revolving charge account that carries with it a line of credit. Because the Optima True Grace card's outstanding balance does not have to be paid in full each month, it is, for all practical purposes, just another type of *bank credit card!* Its special feature is a 25-day interest-free grace period for all new purchases, whether or not you carry a balance. Most credit cards immediately charge interest on new purchases if the cardholder has an outstanding balance. However, this feature comes at a cost: the card's interest rate is higher than many other credit cards.

Prestige Cards. Not all credit cards are created alike. Some offer many more advantages and features than others. That's precisely what **prestige cards** are; they offer higher credit limits (up to $100,000 or more), worldwide travel services, and other features meant to attract the upscale cardholder. Such cards impose higher credit standards for qualification, along with higher annual fees. MasterCard, Visa, American Express, and Optima all offer prestige cards. MasterCard and Visa have their *Gold* cards, while American Express and American Express Optima each have two prestige cards—the *Gold* card and, the "ultimate" in credit cards, the *Platinum* card, available by invitation only.

Exhibit 6.4 on page 244 compares some of the major features of different bank and T&E cards.

Most of these cards are fully interchangeable, since they perform many of the same functions. Together these cards account for about 70 percent of all credit card activity, the balance of the transactions being made with retail charge cards.

Affinity Cards. Credit cards with a cause. That's the way to describe **affinity cards.** These cards are nothing more than standard bank Visa or MasterCards that are issued in conjunction with a sponsoring group—most commonly, some type of charitable, political, or professional organization. So named because of the bond between the sponsoring group and its members, affinity cards are sponsored by such nonprofit organizations as the American Heart Association, CARE, MADD, Easter Seals, the American Association of Individual Investors, the Sierra Club, and Special Olympics. In addition, they are issued by college and university alumni groups, labor organizations, religious and fraternal groups, professional societies, even airline frequent flyer programs. In many cases, all you have to do is support the cause in order to obtain one of these cards (as in the case of MADD or CARE). In other cases, you'll have to belong to a certain group in order to get one of their cards (for example, be a graduate of the school or member of a particular professional group to qualify).

Why even bother to carry one of these cards? Unlike traditional bank cards, affinity cards make money for the group backing the card, as well as for the bank, because the sponsoring groups receive a share of the profits (usually one-half to one percent of retail purchases made with the card). So, for the credit cardholder, it's a form of "painless philanthropy." But to cover the money that goes to the sponsoring organization, the cardholder usually pays higher fees and/or higher interest costs. In spite of this, some may view these cards as a great way to contribute to a worthy cause. Others, however, may feel it makes more sense to use a traditional credit card and then write a check to their favorite charity.

Secured Credit Cards. You may have seen the ad on TV, where the announcer says that no matter how bad your credit, you can still qualify for one of their credit cards. The pitch may sound too good to be true, and in some respects it is. For there's a catch. Namely, the credit is "secured," meaning you have to put up *collateral* in order to get the card! These are so-called **secured,** or **collateralized, credit cards** where the amount of credit is determined by the amount of liquid collateral you're able to put up. These cards are targeted at people with no credit or bad credit histories, who don't qualify for conventional credit cards. Issued as Visa or MasterCards, except for the collateral, they're like any other credit card. To qualify, a customer must deposit a certain amount (usually $500 or more) in a 12–18 month certificate of deposit, that the issuing bank holds as collateral. The cardholder then gets a credit line equal to the deposit. If the customer defaults, the bank has the CD to cover its losses. By making payments on time, it's hoped that these cardholders will establish (or reestablish) a credit history that may qualify them for a conventional (unsecured) credit card. Even though fully secured, these cards still carry annual fees and finance charges that are equal to, or greater than, those of regular credit cards.

retail charge card A type of credit card issued by retailers, airlines, and so on, that allows customers to charge goods and services up to a preestablished amount.

30-day (regular) charge account A charge account that requires customers to pay the full amount billed within 10 to 20 days after the billing date.

travel and entertainment (T&E) card A credit card, such as American Express or Diners Club, that is accepted by travel and entertainment-related establishments, as well as a growing number of other businesses and stores; these cards require the holder to pay current balances *in full.*

prestige card A type of bank or T&E card that offers higher credit limits, has stricter requirements for qualification, and generally offers more features than its "regular" counterpart.

affinity cards A standard bank credit card issued in conjunction with some charitable, political, or other sponsoring nonprofit organization; these cards are a source of revenue to the sponsoring group since they normally earn a small percentage of all retail transactions.

secured (collateralized) credit cards A type of credit card that's secured with some form of collateral, like a bank CD; with these cards, the amount of credit you get depends on how much collateral you can put up (also known as "collateralized" credit cards).

EXHIBIT 6.4

Major Credit Card Features

There are some important differences among the major credit cards, including the annual fee, maximum amount of credit available, required minimum monthly payment, and number of outlets that accept the card.

BANK CARDS	MasterCard[a]	Gold MasterCard[a]	VISA[a]	Premier VISA[a]	Discover Card	American Express Optima True Grace
Annual fee	$0–$50, as set by issuing bank	$0–$75, as set by issuing bank	$0–$75, as set by issuing bank	$0–$75, as set by issuing bank	$0	$25 (waived first year and if used three times per year thereafter)
Criteria	Set by issuing bank	Set by issuing bank	Set by issuing bank	Set by issuing bank	Varies by state	Minimum income of $20,000
Minimum credit	$200	$5,000	$200	$5,000	$1,000	Determined by credit department
Maximum credit	$10,000	$25,000	$10,000	$25,000	None	Determined by credit department
Minimum payment	Bank sets according to state regulations; expressed as a percentage of amount owed				Percentage of amount owed	Set by state law; expressed as percentage of amount owed
Individual receipts returned	No	No	No	No	No	Yes (photocopies)
Cash machine link	Yes	Yes	Yes	Yes	Yes	Yes
Cash advances available	Yes	Yes	Yes	Yes	Yes	Yes
Number of outlets that accept card	12,600,000 (worldwide)		12,000,000 (worldwide)		N/A	3,900,000 (worldwide)

T&E CARDS	American Express (Green)	American Express (Gold)	American Express (Platinum)	Citicorp Diners Club
Annual fee	$55	$75	$300	$80
Criteria	Minimum income of $15,000	Minimum income of $20,000	Minimum charged by holder must be $10,000 annually	Minimum income of $25,000
Minimum credit	None	$10,000	$10,000	None
Maximum credit	None	None	None	None
Minimum payment	Balance	Balance	Balance	Balance
Individual receipts returned	Yes (photocopies)	Yes (photocopies)	Yes (photocopies)	Only upon request
Cash machine link	Yes (bank checking)	Yes	Yes	Yes
Cash advances available	No	Yes	Yes	Yes
Number of outlets that accept card		3,900,000 (worldwide)		2,500,000 (worldwide)

[a]Data for MasterCard and VISA are meant to reflect the features that are typically found on the vast majority of these cards; unfortunately, more exact information is not available, as the cards are issued by thousands of financial institutions worldwide, and these institutions are mostly free to set their own standards.

DEBIT CARDS

It looks like a credit card, it spends like a credit card, it even has the familiar MasterCard and Visa credit card markings. But it's not a *credit* card—rather, it is a *debit* card. Simply put, a **debit card** provides direct access to your checking account and, as such, *works like writing a check*. For example, when you use a debit card to make a purchase, the amount of the transaction is charged directly to your checking account. Thus, using a debit card is not the same thing as buying on credit; it may appear that you are charging it, but actually you are paying with cash. Accordingly, there are no finance charges to pay.

Debit cards are becoming more popular, especially with consumers who want the convenience of a credit card but not the high cost of interest that comes with them. They are accepted at any establishment displaying the Visa or MasterCard logo but function as an alternative to writing checks. If you use a debit card to make a purchase at a department store or restaurant, the transaction will show up on your next monthly *checking account* statement. Needless to say, to keep your records straight, you should enter debit card transactions directly onto your checkbook ledger as they occur and treat them as withdrawals, or checks, by subtracting them from your checking account balance. Debit cards can also be used to gain access to your account through 24-hour teller machines or ATMs —which is the closest thing to a cash advance that these cards have to offer.

The big disadvantage of a debit card, of course, is that it does not provide a line of credit. In addition, it can cause overdraft problems if you fail to make the proper entries to your checking account or inadvertently use it when you think you are using a credit card. Also, some debit card issuers charge a per transaction fee or a flat annual fee; and even some *merchants* may charge you for using your debit card. On the plus side, a debit card does not carry with it the potential credit problems and high costs that credit cards do. Further, it is every bit as convenient to use as a credit card—in fact, if convenience is the major reason you use a credit card, you might want to consider switching to a debit card for at least some transactions, especially at outlets such as gas stations that give discounts for cash purchases and consider a debit card to be as good as cash.

Prepaid Cards. Tired of fumbling for change to buy a candy bar from a vending machine or to use a pay phone? Buy a **prepaid card** and your pockets won't jingle with coins anymore. These "smart cards" can now be used to purchase a variety of items—phone calls, meals in some employee cafeterias, vending machine snacks—and their use is increasing. You pay a fixed amount for the card, which is then stored on either a magnetic strip or rechargeable microchip. Each time you make a purchase, the amount is electronically deducted from the card. First used for public transportation fares in large cities, prepaid cards are now used by many companies. Indeed, you might be carrying one yourself, as they have become very popular on college campuses, where they're used to purchase meals, books, and other items. The popularity of these "electronic purses" is increasing, as consumers and merchants alike find them convenient.

REVOLVING CREDIT LINES

Revolving lines of credit are offered by banks, brokerage houses, and other financial institutions. These credit lines normally do not involve the use of credit cards. Rather, they are accessed by simply writing checks on common checking accounts or specially designed credit line accounts. They are a form of open account credit and often represent a far better deal than credit cards, not only because they offer more credit but also because they can be a lot less expensive. Also, according to the latest tax laws, there may even be a tax advantage to using one of these other kinds of credit! These lines basically provide their users with ready access to borrowed money (that is, cash advances) through revolving lines of credit. They are every bit as convenient as credit cards, since access is gained by simply writing a check. The three major forms of open (noncredit card) credit are: overdraft protection lines, unsecured personal lines of credit, and home equity credit lines.

Overdraft Protection. An **overdraft protection line** is simply a line of credit linked to a checking account that enables a depositor to overdraw his or her checking account up to a prede-

debit card A card used to make transactions for *cash* rather than credit; replaces the need for cash or checks by initiating charges against one's *checking* account.

prepaid card A plastic card with a magnetic strip or microchip that stores the amount of money the purchaser has to spend and deducts the value of each purchase; eliminates the need to use cash.

revolving line of credit A type of open account credit offered by banks and other financial institutions that can be accessed by writing checks against demand deposit or specially designated credit line accounts.

overdraft protection line A line of credit linked to a checking account that allows a depositor to overdraw the account up to a specified amount.

termined limit. These lines are usually set up with credit limits of $500 or $1,000, but they can be for as much as $10,000 or more. The consumer taps this line of credit by simply writing a check. If this check happens to overdraw the account, the overdraft protection line will automatically advance funds in an amount necessary to put the account back in the black. In some cases, overdraft protection is provided by *linking the bank's credit card to your checking account.* These arrangements act just like regular overdraft lines, except when the account is overdrawn, the bank automatically taps your credit card line and transfers the money into your checking account. It's treated as a cash advance from your credit card, but the end result is still the same as a regular overdraft protection line: it automatically covers overdrawn checks.

Unfortunately, you never know for sure just how much a given check will overdraw your account (if in fact it does). The reason is that unless you write very few checks, the balance shown on your checkbook ledger will seldom be the same as the amount shown by the bank. The way to handle this is to simply record the check in your checkbook ledger as you normally would, including the new balance after the check is written. If this overdraws your account—at least as far as your checkbook ledger is concerned—this will not be a problem, since you have an overdraft protection line to cover it. If it does in fact overdraw your account, the bank will notify you of this in a matter of days and inform you that it has advanced funds to your checking account. The amount of the advance will be shown on the notice and should immediately be entered into your checkbook ledger as a *deposit.*

Funds advanced from an overdraft protection line usually carry an interest rate of 12 to 15 percent, though rates as high as 18 to 20 percent are not all that uncommon. Once an advance is made, a monthly repayment schedule is set up for systematically repaying the loan, along with all interest charges—generally with monthly payments being spread out over a period of 18 to 36 months. A statement is sent out each month, along with the monthly check statement, summarizing any activity in the overdraft protection line (new advances, repayments, new balance, and amount of credit still available) and indicating the required monthly payment. Note that since there ordinarily is no limit on the number of times you can overdraw your account, the amount of the monthly payment will change every time the bank advances money to your account.

It should be clear that if you are not careful, you can quickly exhaust this line of credit by writing a lot of overdraft checks. As with any line of credit, there is a limit to how much you can obtain. You should be extremely careful with such a credit line and *under no circumstances take it as a license to routinely overdraw your account!* Doing so on a regular basis is a signal that you are probably mismanaging your cash and/or living beyond your budget. It is best to view an overdraft protection line strictly as an *emergency* source of credit—and any funds advanced should be repaid as quickly as possible.

Unsecured Personal Lines. Another form of revolving credit is the **unsecured personal credit line,** which basically makes a line of credit available to an individual on an as-needed basis. In essence, it is a way of borrowing money from a bank, S&L, credit union, savings bank, or brokerage firm any time you wish, without going through all the hassle of setting up a new loan. Here is how it works. Suppose you submit a loan application for a personal line of credit at your bank. Once you have been approved and the credit line established, you will be issued *checks* that you can write against it. Thus, if you need a cash advance, all you need to do is write a check (against your credit line account) and deposit it into your checking account. Alternatively, if you need the money to buy some high-ticket item—say, an expensive stereo system—you can just make the credit line check out to the dealer and, when it clears, it will be charged against your unsecured personal credit line as an advance. (These credit line checks look and "spend" just like regular checks and as such do not have to be channeled through your normal checking account.)

Personal lines of credit are usually set up for minimums of $2,000 to $5,000 and often amount to $25,000 or more. As with an overdraft protection line, once an advance is made, repayment is set up on a monthly installment basis. Depending on the amount outstanding, repayment is normally structured over a period of two to five years; to keep the monthly payments low, larger amounts of debt are usually given longer repayment periods. As a rule, these credit lines are set up with adjustable rates of interest so that the interest charged on advances varies with some benchmark rate, such as the prime rate—normally floating 2 to 4 percentage points above the prime/benchmark rate. Thus, if the prime rate goes up (or down) by, say, 1 percent, the cost of the credit line will also go up (or down) by the same 1 percent. Monthly statements are sent out that summarize the activity in the credit line and stipulate the required minimum monthly payment.

While these credit lines do offer attractive terms to the consumer, they do not come without their share of problems, perhaps the biggest of which is the ease with which cash advances can be obtained. In addition, these lines normally involve *substantial* credit limits and are about as easy to use as credit cards. This combination can have devastating effects on a family's budget if it leads to overspending or excessive reliance on credit. To be safe, these lines should be used only for emergency purposes or to make *planned credit expenditures.* In addition, systematic repayment of the debt should be built into the budget, and every effort should be made to ensure that the use of this kind of credit will not place undue strain on the family finances.

Home Equity Credit Lines. Here is a familiar situation. A couple buys a home for $75,000; some 15 years later, it is worth twice that much. The couple now has an asset worth $150,000 on which all they owe is the original mortgage, which may now have a balance of, say $50,000. The couple clearly has built up a substantial amount of equity in their home—$150,000 − $50,000 = $100,000. But how can they tap that equity without having to sell their home? The answer is to obtain a **home equity credit line.** Such lines are much like unsecured personal credit lines except that they are *secured* with a second mortgage on the home. Offered by most banks, S&Ls, major brokerage firms, and a growing number of credit unions, these lines of credit allow you to tap up to 100 percent of the equity in your home by merely writing a check.

While there are banks and financial institutions that do allow their customers to borrow up to 100 percent of the *equity* in their homes, the majority of the lenders set their maximum credit lines at 75 to 80 percent of the *market value* of the home, which sharply reduces the amount of money they'll lend. The typical home equity credit line has a minimum of $10,000 and an advance period of five to 20 years when you can tap into the line by writing checks or using a special credit card. At the end of the advance period, you must stop borrowing and begin to repay the principal and interest over a 10 to 20 year period. Of course, you can also pay off these lines earlier, and many consumers use them to good advantage by having the self-discipline to pay down the line quickly.

Here's how these lines work. The above couple has built up an equity of $100,000 in their home—equity against which they can borrow through a home equity credit line. Assuming they have a good credit record and using a 75 percent loan-to-market-value ratio, a bank would be willing to lend up to $112,500; that is, 75 percent of the value of the house is .75 × $150,000 = $112,500. Subtracting the $50,000 still due on the first mortgage, we see that our couple could qualify for a home equity credit line of a whopping $62,500. Note, in this case, that if the bank had been willing to lend the couple *100 percent of the equity* in their home, it would have given them a (much higher) credit line of $100,000, which is the difference between what the house is worth and what they still owe on it. Most lenders don't like to do this because it results in very large credit lines and, perhaps more important, it doesn't provide the lender with any cushion.

Home equity lines also have an interesting tax feature that you should be aware of—that is, the annual interest charges on such lines may be fully deductible for those who itemize. This is the only type of consumer loan that still qualifies for such tax treatment. According to the latest provisions of the tax code, a homeowner is allowed to *fully deduct the interest charges on home equity loans of up to $100,000,* regardless of the original cost of the house or use of the proceeds. Indeed, the only restriction is that the amount of total indebtedness on the house cannot exceed its fair market value—which is highly unlikely, since homeowners usually cannot borrow more than 75 to 80 percent of the market value of the house anyway. Thus, in our preceding example, the homeowners could take out the full amount of their

unsecured personal credit line A line of credit that is made available to an individual on an as-needed basis in the form of check-writing privileges against it.

home equity credit line A line of credit issued against the existing equity in a home.

EXHIBIT 6.5

Comparative Home Equity Credit Line Terms

Home equity credit lines are offered by a number of different types of financial services institutions, involve relatively large credit limits, and normally have rather generous repayment terms. This table shows representative terms, which typically vary by state.

Home Equity Credit Line Product	Minimum/ Maximum Credit Line	Maximum Percent of Equity Lent	Interest Rate Formula	Minimum Advances	Repayment Terms	Minimum Monthly Payments
Bank of America Home Equity Credit Line	$10,000/ $150,000	75%	One-month secondary market CD +3.5%	$500	10 years interest only, then becomes 15-year amortized loan	Interest only
Beneficial Home Equity Credit Line	$12,000/ $50,000	80% if first lien; 75% if second lien	Prime +4%	$5,000	In full in 10 to 30 years, depending on loan amount	Interest and principal, based on average daily balance
Citibank Equity Source Account	$15,000/ $500,000	75%; may vary by state	Prime + 0.5 to 1.25%, depending on customer balance relationship and origination fees	Varies by state	5 to 10 years interest only, then becomes amortized loan for balance of 30 year maximum term	Interest only
First Nationwide Bank Equity Reserve Account	$10,000/ $300,000	80%	Prime + 1.25%	None	In full in 15 years	Greater of interest only or $100
Merrill Lynch Equity Access	$15,000/ $2 million	75%; 70% for condominiums and co-ops	Prime + 1.5% if Merrill Lynch client; Prime + 1.75% otherwise	None	In full in 10 years	Interest only

credit line ($62,500), and every dime that they paid in interest would be tax deductible. If they paid, say, $7,500 in interest, and if they were in the 28 percent tax bracket, this feature would reduce their tax liability by some $2,100—($7,500 × .28)—given, of course, that they itemize their deductions.

Not only do home equity credit lines offer shelter from taxes, they're also among *the cheapest forms of consumer credit.* While other types of consumer credit may cost 15 to 18 percent or more, home equity lines can be had for 8.5 to 11 percent (these were representative rates in early 1995). To see what that can mean to you as a borrower, assume you have $10,000 in consumer debt outstanding. If you had borrowed that money through a standard consumer loan at, say, 16.5 percent, you'd pay interest of $1,650 per year—none of which would be tax deductible. But borrow the same amount through a home equity credit line at, say, 11 percent, and you'll pay only $1,100 in interest. That's all tax deductible though, so if you're in the 28 percent tax bracket, the after-tax cost to you would be $1,100 × (1 − .28) = $792. This is less than half the cost of the other loan! Which would you rather pay for a $10,000 loan, $1,650 or $792? That's really not a tough decision; but it does explain, in large part, why these lines have become so popular and are today the fastest growing form of consumer credit.

A home equity credit line may involve an extensive credit application process, including an appraisal of the property. In addition, there'll probably be some *closing costs* to pay when the line is set up (such closing costs are usually much lower than those on first mortgages, but they still can easily amount to $300 or $400, or more). It's not unusual, however, for lenders in highly competitive markets to offer home equity lines with *no fees* whatsoever. In essence, the lenders waive all appraisal fees, title insurance costs, and the like; thus, there are no closing costs on these lines. Once the credit line is set up, the homeowner receives a book of checks that can be used to obtain funds just like the checks used with unsecured personal lines. Repayment terms are flexible, with most lenders charging adjustable rates of interest and giving the borrower 10 to 15 years to repay. Monthly statements are sent out that recap the activity in the account and indicate the size of the monthly payment.

The terms of home equity credit lines can vary considerably, so it pays to shop around for the best deal. Be sure to compare application charges, annual fees, closing costs, size restrictions on the line, minimum advance, points, and, of course, interest rates. If you want the line for emergencies or don't intend to use it much, look for a line with no points and low or no fees, even if the interest rate is higher. If you do plan to borrow, the interest rate should be your main concern. Exhibit 6.5 provides a sample of home equity credit lines offered by a variety of financial institutions. What is perhaps most startling is the maximum amount of credit available under these lines. Note that $100,000 figures are not at all unusual. And it's precisely because of the enormous amount of money available that this form of credit should be used with caution. *The fact that you have the equity in your home does not mean that you have the cash flow necessary to service the debt that such a credit line imposes.* Remember that your house is the collateral. If you can't repay the loan, you could lose it! At the minimum, major expenditures should be made only after you have determined that you can afford the purchase and that the required monthly payments will fit comfortably within your budget. Also, if there are normal closing costs involved, don't even think about setting up a home equity line unless you've decided to actually use it—otherwise, it is too expensive to just have as a form of emergency credit.

Perhaps the biggest problem with this type of credit is the temptation to use the long-term repayment schedule that this type of credit offers to keep payments *artificially* low and, in so doing, purchase items whose lives will be nowhere near as long as that of the associated debt. For example, to use a 15-year second mortgage to buy a car with a 5-year life makes absolutely no sense! You will still be paying for the car 10 years after you have sold it. The fact is that if the only way you can afford the car is to buy it with 15 years of payments, you cannot afford it in the first place. Home equity credit lines can be an effective way of tapping the built-up equity in a home, but you should avoid using them to buy items you could not otherwise afford.

Concept Check

6-4. What is *open account credit?* Who are the main providers and what are the main categories of this form of credit?

6-5. What is a *line of credit?* Explain. Does a line of credit come with all types of credit cards?

6-6. How do bank credit cards and *travel and entertainment cards* differ? Comment on the following statement: "If used intelligently, bank credit cards can be quite useful."

6-7. What is the attraction of *rebate cards?* List and briefly describe some of the more popular services and features that are now being offered on bank credit cards.

6-8. Explain how you could use your credit card to obtain a *cash advance.* Does it make any difference whether you obtain the cash advance from an ATM or the bank's teller window?

6-9. How is the interest rate typically set on bank credit cards? In terms of interest rate, does it matter if you use your credit card to purchase merchandise or obtain a cash advance?

6-10. Many bank card issuers also impose different types of fees; briefly describe three of these fees. Do these fees have any impact on the true (effective) cost of using credit cards? Explain.

6-11. Explain the difference between a *retail charge card* account and a *30-day charge account.* What's a *secured credit card* and how does it differ from a *prestige card?*

6-12. What is a *debit card?* How is it similar to a credit card? How does it differ?

6-13. Describe how *revolving credit lines* provide open account credit. How would you obtain an advance from an *overdraft protection line?* What are the basic features of a *home equity credit line?*

OBTAINING AND MANAGING OPEN ACCOUNT CREDIT

LG4

Used wisely, open account credit is a useful way to purchase goods and services. To get such credit, you must submit an application to the lender, who then evaluates it based on certain credit criteria, including annual income, job history, and your loan payment record. Given your current personal situation, how do you think a lender would view your application for credit? Give some thought to this question before reading on.

Americans love to use their charge cards. In 1994 alone, they bought over $450 *billion* in goods and services on credit. And this figure is rising as more places accept "plastic," consumers find credit and debit cards more convenient than cash or checks, and the number of other benefits, like rebates and frequent flier miles, continue to grow.

For the sake of convenience, people often maintain a variety of open accounts. Nearly every household, for example, uses 30-day charge accounts to pay their utility bills, phone bills, and so on. In addition, most families have one or more retail charge cards, a couple of bank cards, and possibly a T&E card; some people, in fact, may have as many as 15 to 20 cards, or more. Today's average cardholder has 11 cards and about $3,300 in annual charges, with an average unpaid balance of about $1,700. And that's not all—Families can also have one or more revolving credit lines in the form of an overdraft protection, unsecured personal, and/or home equity line. When all these cards and lines are totaled together, a family conceivably can have tens of thousands of dollars of readily available credit. It is easy to see why consumer credit has become such a popular way of making relatively routine purchases. Although open account credit can increase the risk of budgetary overload, these accounts can also serve as a useful way of keeping track of expenditures.

OPENING AN ACCOUNT

Unlike many 30-day charge accounts, retail charge cards, bank credit cards, T&E cards, and revolving lines of credit all require *formal application procedures.* Let's look now at how you'd go about obtaining open account credit, including the normal credit application, investigation, and decision process. We'll couch our discussion in terms of credit cards, but keep in mind that similar procedures apply to other revolving lines of credit as well.

The Credit Application. With over a billion credit cards in the hands of American consumers, one would think that consumer credit is readily available. And it is—but you have to apply for it. Applications are usually available at the store or bank involved. Sometimes they can be found at the businesses that accept these cards or obtained on request from the issuing companies. Exhibit 6.6 provides an example of a bank credit card application. In this case, it is for either Visa or MasterCard. The information requested concerns personal/family matters, housing, employment and income, existing charge accounts, and credit references. This information is intended to provide the lender with insight about the applicant's creditworthiness. In essence, the lender is trying to determine whether the applicant has the *character* and *capacity* to handle the debt in a prompt and timely manner. When applying for credit, you should provide the information requested as accurately and thoroughly as possible, since it will be verified during the credit investigation process.

The Credit Investigation. Once the credit application has been completed and returned to the establishment issuing the card, it is subject to a **credit investigation.** The purpose is to evaluate the kind of credit risk you pose to the lender (the party issuing the credit or charge card). So be sure to fill out your credit application in a careful manner. Believe it or not, they really do look at those things. The key items lenders look at are how much money you make, how much debt you presently have outstanding and how well you handle it, and how stable you are (for example, your age, employment history, whether you own or rent a home, and so on). Obviously, the higher your income and the better your credit history, the greater the chances of having your credit application approved.

As a part of the investigation process, the lender will attempt to verify much of the information provided by you on the credit application—for obvious reasons, false or misleading information will almost certainly result in outright rejection of your application. For example, the lender will verify your place of employment, level of income, current debt load and debt service history, and so forth. Often, this can be done through one or two quick phone calls. If you've lived in the area for a number of years and have established relations

EXHIBIT 6.6

A Bank Credit Card Application

This credit application, like most, seeks information about the applicant's place of employment, monthly income, place of residence, credit history, and other financial matters that are intended to help the lender decide whether or not to extend credit.

WELLS FARGO BANK CREDIT CARD APPLICATION

NOTE: Your annual income must be at least $10,000 or $833 per month before taxes. Gold Card annual income must be at least $30,000 or $2,500 per month before taxes.

Check only one box for account you are requesting:
☐ MasterCard ☐ Visa ☐ Both MasterCard and Visa ☐ Gold MasterCard ☐ Visa Gold

Check only one box for type of interest rate you are requesting:
☐ Traditional (Fixed Rate) ☐ Proven Credit (Variable Rate)

Applicant may include spouse's income and still apply for an individual account if you live in a community property state. If married, you may apply for a separate account in your own name.

PLEASE TELL US ABOUT YOURSELF

First Name | Middle Initial | Last Name (Jr./Sr.) | Social Security Number – – | Date of Birth Mo. Day Yr.

Home Address: Number, Street Name (Apt #) | City | State | Zip | How long at Current Address: Yrs. Mos. | ☐ Own ☐ Parents ☐ Rent ☐ Other | Monthly Rent or Mortgage Payment $ | Home Phone Number ( )

Previous Address, If Less than 3 Years at Current Address: Number, Street Name (Apt #), City, State, Zip | Name & Phone of Friend/Relative Not Living with You ( )

Self-Employed: Must be in same business for 3 years and attach last 2 years' tax returns. Self-Employed ☐ Yes ☐ No | Employer/Business Name | Complete Business Address: Number, Street Name | City | State | Zip

Your Position | Business Phone | How Long Employed There Yrs. Mos. | Your Monthly Salary Before Taxes $

OTHER INCOME: You may include your spouse's income even when applying for an individual account in your name.
Note: You need not list income from alimony, child support, or separate maintenance payments unless you wish it considered. | Other Monthly Pre-tax Income $ | Source of Other Income

CO-APPLICANT INFORMATION

First Name | Middle Initial | Last Name (Jr./Sr.) | Social Security Number – – | Date of Birth Mo. Day Yr.

Co-Applicant's Monthly Salary Before Taxes. (If co-applicant's income is included under other income, do not enter here.) $

FINANCIAL DATA (PLEASE INDICATE OTHER ACCOUNTS YOU HAVE)

With Wells Fargo: ☐ Checking ☐ Savings ☐ IRA ☐ CD ☐ Money Market Account ☐ Loans ☐ None

Other Institutions: ☐ Checking ☐ Savings ☐ IRA ☐ CD ☐ Money Market Account ☐ Loans ☐ None

OVERDRAFT PROTECTION

☐ **Yes,** set up Overdraft Protection on my Wells Fargo checking account
#
and waive my first year membership fee. If applying for more than one card, please select only one for Overdraft Protection. ☐ Visa ☐ MasterCard

EXPRESS CARD LINKAGE

☐ **Yes,** link the following Express ATM card(s) to this credit card account.
#
#

SUPERCHECKS

☐ **Yes,** send me a FREE supply of SUPERCHECK checks. Please allow 2-3 weeks for delivery.

BALANCE CONSOLIDATION

☐ **Yes,** please send me a Balance Consolidation Form. I'd like to simplify my bill paying by consolidating my other credit card balances to my Wells Fargo credit card.

PAYMENT PROTECTION INSURANCE PLAN

☐ **Yes,** enroll me in the optional Payment Protection Insurance Plan. I have read and agree to the Benefits, Exclusions and Cost described in the Customer Disclosure. I understand the insurance cost is 60¢ per $100 per month of my insured month-ending balance. I authorize premiums to be billed to my account. (Only **one accountholder** may enroll.) Check which applicant is to be insured: ☐ Applicant ☐ Co-Applicant Initials ✗ ________

PLEASE READ AND SIGN BELOW

I certify that all information provided is true, correct, and complete and that I am at least 18 years old and/or legally able to enter into this contract. The Bank is authorized to verify or check any of the information given, and to obtain credit reports on me, and to make Overdraft Protection advances as needed. I authorize the Bank to obtain address information from the California Department of Motor Vehicles and waive the address confidentiality requirement of Section 1808.21 of the California Vehicle Code. I agree to be bound by the Terms and Conditions of the Customer Agreement and Disclosure Statement, which will be sent to me. The Bank will review this application in California and the contract is made in California. The Bank will determine the amount of credit extended. If the Bank is unable to issue the product(s) requested, I authorize the Bank to grant a different product or credit line. I understand and agree that each person signing will have full and equal access to any credit line extended and each will be individually and jointly liable for payment of all amounts owing on the account, even if only one of us uses the account. **I hereby stipulate to the terms of the Comprehensive Dispute Resolution Program described in the Customer Agreement and Disclosure Statement, including a non-jury trial or arbitration.**

I agree that information contained in this application or other information regarding my credit may be provided to affiliated companies of Wells Fargo Bank.

SIGN HERE

X
Applicant's Signature | Date | Driver's License # | Mother's Maiden Name

X
Co-Applicant's Signature | Date | Driver's License # | Mother's Maiden Name

with a local bank, a call to your banker may be all it takes to confirm your creditworthiness. If you haven't established such bank relations—and most young people have not—then the lender is likely to turn to the local credit bureau for a *credit report* on you.

credit investigation An investigation that involves contacting credit references or corresponding with a credit bureau in order to verify information on a credit application.

The Credit Bureau. Basically a **credit bureau** is a type of reporting agency that gathers and sells information about individual borrowers. If, as is often the case, the lender does not know you personally, it must rely on a cost-effective way of verifying your employment and credit history. It would be far too expensive and time-consuming for individual creditors to confirm your credit application on their own, so they turn to credit bureaus that maintain fairly detailed credit files about you. Information in your file comes from one of three sources: creditors who subscribe to the bureau, other creditors who supply information at your request, and publicly recorded court documents (such as tax liens or bankruptcy records).

Contrary to popular opinion, your credit file does *not* contain everything anyone would ever want to know about you—there's nothing on your lifestyle, friends, habits, religious or political affiliations. Instead, most of the information is pretty dull stuff, and covers such things as:

- Your name, social security number, age, number of dependents, and current and previous addresses
- Your employment record, including current and past employers, and salary data, if available
- Your credit history, including the number of loans and credit lines you have, number of credit cards issued in your name, your payment record, and account balances
- Public records data involving bankruptcies, tax liens, foreclosures, civil suits, and criminal convictions
- Finally, the names of firms and financial institutions that have recently requested copies of your file are also recorded

While one late MasterCard payment probably won't make much of a difference on an otherwise clean credit file, a definite pattern of delinquencies (consistently being 30 to 60 days late with your payments) or a personal bankruptcy certainly will. Unfortunately, poor credit traits will stick with you for a long time, since delinquencies will remain on your credit file for as long as seven years and bankruptcies for ten years. An example of an actual credit bureau report is provided in Exhibit 6.7. It demonstrates the kind of information you can expect to find in one of these reports.

Local credit bureaus (there are more than a thousand of them) are established and mutually owned by local merchants and banks. They collect and store credit information on people living within the community and make it available, for a fee, to members who request it. If the information requested can be transmitted over the phone or by fax, the cost of the inquiry is typically about $5 or $10. On the other hand, if the credit bureau must obtain, either through its own investigation or from another credit bureau, additional information in order to update the applicant's file, the cost of the report will be much higher. Local bureaus are linked together nationally through one of the "big three" national bureaus—Trans-Union, Equifax Credit Information Services, and TRW Credit Data—each of which provides the mechanism for obtaining credit information from almost any place in the United States, It's important to understand that credit bureaus merely collect and provide credit information. They do not analyze it, they do not rate it (or at lest they're not supposed to), and they certainly do not make the final credit decision.

Credit bureaus have been heavily criticized because of the large numbers of credit reporting errors and their poor record in correcting these errors on a timely and efficient basis. One 1991 survey of 161 randomly selected credit reports found that almost half had errors and about 20 percent had mistakes serious enough to jeopardize credit eligibility. And consumers were frustrated by the time-consuming process and credit bureaus' apparent "care less" attitude about their mistakes—as far as they were concerned, you were guilty until proven innocent. As a result, in recent years the major credit bureaus have taken a more consumer-oriented approach, greatly improving their customer service and dispute resolution procedures and making reports easier to read. Many of these changes were formalized by a 1995 amendment to the Fair Credit Reporting Act (described later in the chapter) that establishes industry guidelines for credit reporting procedures. Credit bureaus must provide low-cost copies of credit reports and have toll-free phone numbers. Disputes must be

> **credit bureau** An organization, typically established by local banks and merchants, that collects and stores credit information about individual borrowers and, for a specified fee, supplies it to financial institutions that request it.

EXHIBIT 6.7

An Example of a Credit Bureau Report

Displayed here is an actual credit report from a major credit reporting bureau. These reports have been revised to be easier to understand. Notice that in addition to some basic information, the report deals strictly with credit information—including payment records, past due status, and types of credit; also reported is a summary of any relevant public records (see item 1).

This is your consumer identification number. Please refer to this number when you call or write.

ID # XXXXXXXXXXXXX

MARY R. CONSUMER
1500 RAINBOW LANE
ANYTOWN, CA 90000-0000

ITEM	ACCOUNT NAME	DESCRIPTION	STATUS/PAYMENTS
1	*KEARNEY MESA MUN CT 8950 CLAIRMONT MESA BLVD SAN DIEGO,CA 92101 REFERENCE # 00	THE ORIGINAL AMOUNT OF THIS COURT ITEM IS $300. THE PARTY THAT BROUGHT THIS ACTION AGAINST YOU OR THE COURT REFERENCE NUMBER IS	THIS JUDGMENT WAS FILED IN 04/01/90 AND PAID IN FULL ON 06/20/90.
2	AMERICAN EXPRESS CO P O BOX 7871 SROC FORT LAUDERDALE,FL 33329 NATL CREDIT CARDS ACCT #	THIS CREDIT CARD ACCOUNT WAS OPENED 04/75 AND HAS 1 MONTH REPAYMENT TERMS. YOU HAVE CONTRACTUAL RESPONSIBILITY FOR THIS ACCOUNT AND ARE PRIMARILY RESPONSIBLE FOR ITS PAYMENT. THE HIGH BALANCE OF THIS ACCOUNT IS $72.	AS OF 06/92 THIS ACCOUNT IS PAID IN FULL AND ALL PAYMENTS HAVE BEEN PAID ON TIME.
***CREDIT LINE CLOSED - CONSUMER'S REQUEST - REPORTED BY SUBSCRIBER			
3	BANK OF BOSTON NA 15 WESTMINSTER STREET PROVIDENCE,RI 02903 BANKING ACCT #	THIS CREDIT CARD ACCOUNT WAS OPENED OVER 10 YEARS AGO AND HAS REVOLVING REPAYMENT TERMS. YOU ARE OBLIGATED TO REPAY THIS JOINT ACCOUNT. THE CREDIT LIMIT OF THIS ACCOUNT IS $2,100.	AS OF 02/89 THIS ACCOUNT IS PAID IN FULL AND ALL PAYMENTS HAVE BEEN PAID ON TIME.
4	COUNTRYWIDE FUND CORP 400 COUNTRYWIDE WAY SIMI VALLEY,CA 93065 UNDEFINED FIRM TYPE ACCT #	THIS CONVENTIONAL REAL ESTATE LOAN WAS OPENED 1993 AND HAS 30 YEAR REPAYMENT TERMS. YOU ARE OBLIGATED TO REPAY THIS JOINT ACCOUNT. THE ORIGINAL AMOUNT OF THIS ACCOUNT IS $350,000.	AS OF 01/94 THIS ACCOUNT IS CURRENT AND ALL PAYMENTS HAVE BEEN PAID ON TIME. YOUR BALANCE AS OF 12/31/94 IS $345,067. YOUR SCHEDULED MONTHLY PAYMENT IS $2,447. THE LAST PAYMENT REPORTED TO TRW WAS MADE ON DATE UNAVAILABLE. PAYMENT HISTORY: CCCCCCCCCCCC/CCCCCC

YOUR CREDIT HISTORY WAS REVIEWED BY:

THE FOLLOWING INQUIRIES ARE REPORTED TO THOSE WHO ASK TO REVIEW YOUR CREDIT HISTORY.

ITEM	ACCOUNT NAME	DATE	REMARKS
5	MOSSY DATSUN INC 2700 NATIONAL CITY BLVD NATIONAL CITY,CA 91950 AUTOMOTIVE	11/26/94	INQUIRY MADE FOR CREDIT EXTENSION, REVIEW OR OTHER PERMISSIBLE PURPOSE FOR UNSPECIFIED REPAYMENT TERMS. THE AMOUNT IS UNSPECIFIED.
6	FIRESTONE TIRE 6275 EASTLAND ROAD BROOK PARK,OH 44142 UNDEFINED FIRM TYPE	09/04/93	INQUIRY MADE FOR CREDIT EXTENSION, REVIEW OR OTHER PERMISSIBLE PURPOSE FOR UNSPECIFIED REPAYMENT TERMS. THE AMOUNT IS UNSPECIFIED.

resolved in 30 days and take the consumer's documentation into account, not just the creditor's. Better procedures are required to assure that reports are corrected properly and that errors do not reappear; and creditors are now liable—and can be sued by consumers—if they do not correct credit reporting errors.

Even with these changes, credit bureaus can still make mistakes. Unfortunately, when they do, it can mean *big* problems for you, because a credit report can affect whether or not you get credit! Millions of Americans have learned the hard way that their credit records are riddled with errors. You should ensure that your credit report accurately reflects your credit history. Here are some things you can do.

If you plan to take out a big loan—to finance, say, a new car—it might pay to get a copy of your credit report before you do anything. Knowing what kind of information credit agencies have collected on you—and whether or not it's correct—can save you a lot of time later. *It's especially important for young adults and married women to make sure that all accounts for which they are individually or jointly liable are listed in their credit files, as lenders are normally reluctant to consider applicants with little or no credit history.* As for errors, most people don't know there are any in their reports until it's too late. Particularly troubling is *adverse* information about you (i.e., that you're a deadbeat or don't pay your bills on time) that simply isn't true. Common inaccuracies include bad debts of another person with a similar name, tax liens or judgments that have been satisfied, and disputes with merchants that have been resolved.

It's not hard to get a copy of your credit report, and *most consumer advisors recommend you review your files at the major bureaus annually.* You can obtain a copy of your credit report by submitting a written request that includes your name, spouse's name, current and prior (five years') addresses, date of birth, Social Security number, and verification of this information such as a copy of a driver's license. You are entitled to one report every two years for a maximum fee of $3; fees for additional reports vary by state and range from about $3 to $8 for an individual report. If you've been denied credit within 60 days of your request, you are entitled to a free copy of your credit report. (TRW provides one free copy per year.) Most local credit bureaus are listed in the Yellow Pages of the phone book. The addresses to request credit reports and toll-free customer information phone numbers for the three national credit bureaus are provided below:

- Equifax Credit Information Services
  P.O. Box 105873
  Atlanta, GA 30348
  (800) 685-1111
- Trans-Union Corporation,
  Consumer Relations Center
  P.O. Box 390
  Springfield, PA 19064-0390
  (800) 851-2674
- TRW Information Systems,
  National Consumer Assistance Center
  P.O. Box 2350
  Chatsworth, CA 91313-2350
  (800) 392-1122

Once you receive your credit report, review it carefully. If you find any errors, send a letter describing the situation. Include the name of the creditor, the account number, the reason the information is wrong, and any available proof, such as a cancelled check showing payment was made. Request a copy of the corrected file to be sure the mistake is indeed corrected. If the creditor still disagrees with your claim, you can submit a 100-word statement that is included in your file.

You may see ads for credit repair bureaus who offer to fix your credit record for a fee. Most of these are bogus. This is one job you can—and should—do yourself.

The Credit Decision. Using the data provided by the credit applicant, along with any information obtained from the credit bureau, the store or bank must decide whether or not to grant credit. Very likely, some type of **credit scoring** scheme will be used to make the credit decision. By assigning values to such factors as your age, annual income, number of years on your present job, whether you rent or own your home and how long you have lived there, age of your car(s), number and type of credit cards you hold, level of your existing debts, whether or not you have savings accounts, whether you have a phone, and general credit references, an overall credit score for you can be developed. There may be 10 or 15 different factors or characteristics that are considered, and each characteristic will receive a score based on some predetermined standard. For example, if you're 24 years old, single, earn $22,000 a year (on a job that you've had for only two years) and rent an apartment, you might receive the following scores:

1. Age (under 25)	5 points
2. Marital status (single)	−2 points
3. Annual income ($20–25 thousand)	12 points
4. Length of employment (2 yrs. or less)	4 points
5. Rent or own a home (rent)	0 points
	19 points

Based on information obtained from your credit application, similar scores would be assigned to another seven to ten factors.

In all cases, the stronger your personal traits or characteristics, the higher the score you'll receive. For instance, if you had been 44 years old (rather than 24), you might have received 18 points for your age factor, being married rather than single would have given you 9 points, and earning $75,000 a year would obviously have been worth a lot more than earning $22,000! The idea is that the more stable you are *perceived* to be, the more income you make, the better your credit record, and so on, the higher the score you should receive. In essence, statistical studies have shown that certain personal and financial traits can be used to determine your creditworthiness. Indeed, the whole credit scoring system is based on extensive statistical studies, which identify the characteristics to look at and the scores to assign. It's all very mechanical: Assign a score to each characteristic, add up the scores, and, based on that total score, determine the creditworthiness of the applicant.

Generally, if your score equals or exceeds a predetermined minimum, you will be given credit; if not, credit will be refused. Sometimes borderline cases are granted credit on a limited basis. For example, a large department store that normally limits the outstanding balance on its revolving charge accounts to $500 might give a customer with a marginal credit score a revolving charge account with a $200 credit limit. Even when a formal credit scoring scheme is used, the credit manager or loan officer is normally empowered to offer credit if such action seems appropriate. Applicants who are granted credit are notified and sent a charge card and/or checks, along with material describing the credit terms and procedures.

COMPUTING FINANCE CHARGES

Because card issuers do not know in advance how much you will charge on your account, they cannot specify the dollar amount of interest you will be charged. But they can—and must, according to the Truth in Lending Act (defined later in this chapter)—disclose the rate of interest that they charge and their method of computing finance charges. The dollar amount of finance charges referred to above includes all interest and fees that must be paid in order to receive the loan. This is the **annual percentage rate (APR),** the true rate of interest paid over the life of the loan, and must be calculated in the manner outlined by law. Note that on open account credit, creditors cannot specify in advance the dollar amount of interest since they do not know how much will be purchased on the account. The annual percentage rate on these accounts can be stated, however, since there are no fees charged other than interest. Remember: It is your right as a consumer to be told the dollar amount of charges (where applicable) and the APR on any financing you consider.

The amount of interest you pay for open account credit depends in part on the method the lender uses to calculate the balances on which they apply finance charges. Most bank and retail charge card issuers use one of four variations of the **average daily balance (ADB) method,** which applies the interest rate to the average daily balance of the account over the billing period. According to Bankcard Holders of America, a non-profit consumer education organization, the most common method (used by an estimated 95 percent of bank card issuers) is the *average daily balance including new purchases*. The other techniques are aver-

credit scoring A method of evaluating an applicant's creditworthiness by assigning values to factors such as income, existing debts, and credit references.

annual percentage rate (APR) The actual or true rate of interest paid over the life of a loan.

average daily balance (ADB) method A method of computing finance charges by applying interest charges to the average daily balance of the account over the billing period, excluding purchases or returns made during that period.

EXHIBIT 6.8

Finance Charges for Different Balance Calculation Methods

The way a credit card issuer calculates the balance on which the consumer pays finance charges has a big effect on the amount of interest you actually pay, as the following table demonstrates.

A consumer starts the first month with a zero balance and charges $1,000, of which he pays off only the minimum amount due (1/36th of balance due). The next month, he charges another $1,000. He then pays off the entire balance due. This same pattern is repeated three more times during the year. The interest rate is 19.8%

Method	Finance charge
Average Daily balance (including new purchases):	$132.00
Average Daily Balance (excluding new purchases):	$ 66.00
Two-cycle Average Daily Balance (including new purchases):	$196.20
Two-cycle Average Daily Balance (excluding new purchases):	$131.20

Source: Courtesy of Bankcard Holders of America, Salem, Virginia.

age daily balance excluding new purchases, two-cycle average daily balance including new purchases and two-cycle average daily balance excluding new purchases. Balance calculations under each method are as follows:

- ***ADB including new purchases.*** For each day in the billing cycle, add the outstanding balance, including new purchases and subtracting payments and credits, then divide by the number of days in the billing cycle.
- ***ADB excluding new purchases.*** Same as first method, *excluding* new purchases.
- ***Two-cycle ADB including new purchases.*** Calculated like the first method, but using the average daily balance for both the current and previous billing cycles.
- ***Two-cycle ADB excluding new purchases.*** Same as the above two-cycle method, but *excluding* new purchases.

These different balance calculations can have a significant impact on finance charges, and you should be aware that the finance charges of two cards with the same APR but different methods of calculating balances may differ dramatically. It's very important to know the method your card issuer uses. Most banks compute finance charges for a one month period; however, Discover Card, Colonial National Bank, and Household Bank are among the larger issuers who use the *two-cycle average daily balance method*. As we can see from the comparisons in Exhibit 6.8, carrying a balance on a credit card can turn out to be very expensive.

Let's look at an example of how to calculate balances and finance charges under the most popular method, the *average daily balance including new purchases*. Assume that you have a LastBank Visa card with a monthly interest rate of 1.5 percent. Your statement for the billing period extending from October 10, 1995, through November 10, 1995—a total of 31 days—shows that your beginning balance was $582, you make purchases of $350 on October 15 and $54 on October 22, and you made a $25 payment on November 6. Therefore, the outstanding balance for the first five days of the period (October 11 through 15) was $582; for the next seven (October 16 through 22), $932 ($582 + $350); for the next 15 days (October 23 through November 6) it was $986 ($932 + $54); and the last four days, it was $961 ($986 less the $25 payment). We can now calculate the average daily balance using the procedure shown in Exhibit 6.9: the outstanding balances are weighted by the number of days that the balance existed and then averaged (divided) by the number of days in the billing period. By multiplying the average daily balance of $905.42 by the 1.5 percent interest rate, we get a finance charge of $13.81.

MANAGING CREDIT CARD ACCOUNTS

Congratulations! You have applied for and been granted a bank credit card and a retail card from your favorite department store. You carefully reviewed the terms of the credit agreement and

EXHIBIT 6.9

Finding the Average Daily Balance and Finance Charge

The average daily balance including new purchases is the method most widely used by credit card issuers to determine the monthly finance charge on an account:

	Number of Days (1)	Balance (2)	(1) × (2) (3)
	5	$582	$ 2,910
	7	932	6,524
	15	986	14,790
	4	961	3,844
Total	31		$28,068

$$\text{Average daily balance} = \frac{\$28,068}{31} = \$905.42$$

Finance Charge: $905.42 × .015 = $13.81

understand how finance charges are computed for each account. Now you must manage your accounts efficiently, using the monthly statement to help you make the required payments on time, and to track purchases and returned items.

The Statement. If you use a credit card, you will receive monthly statements similar to the sample bank card statement in Exhibit 6.10, showing billing cycle and payment due dates, interest rate, minimum payment, and all account activity during the current period. Retail charge cards have similar monthly statements, but without a section for cash advances. (Revolving line of credit lenders will also send you a monthly statement showing the amount borrowed, payments, and finance charges.) The statement summarizes your account activity: the previous balance (the amount of credit outstanding at the beginning of the month, not to be confused with past-due, or late, payments), new charges made during the past month (four in this case), any finance charges (interest) on the unpaid balance, the preceding period's payment, any other credits (such as those for returns), and the new balance (previous balance plus new purchases and finance charges, less any payments and credits).

Although merchandise and cash transactions are separated on the statement, the finance charge in each case is calculated at the rate of 1.5 percent per month (18 percent annually). Many card issuers charge a higher rate for cash advances. Note that the average daily balance method is used to compute the finance charge in this statement.

You should review your statements promptly each month. Save your receipts and use them to verify statement entries for purchases and returns *before* paying. If you find any errors or suspect fraudulent use of your card, first use the issuer's toll-free number to report any problems. Then follow up *in writing* within 60 days of the postmark on the bill.

Payments. Credit card users can avoid future finance charges by paying the total new balance shown on their statement each month. For example, if the $534.08 total new balance shown in Exhibit 6.10 is paid by the September 21, 1995 due date, no additional finance charges will be incurred. (The cardholder, however, will still be liable for the $4.40 in finance charges incurred to date.) If cardholders cannot pay the total new balance, they can pay any amount that is equal to or greater than the **minimum monthly payment** specified on the statement, usually a specified percentage of the new balance. They will, however, incur additional finance charges in the following month. This account has a minimum payment of 5 percent of the new balance, rounded to the

minimum monthly payment In open account credit, a minimum specified percentage of the new account balance that must be paid in order to remain current.

EXHIBIT 6.10

A Bank Credit Card Monthly Statement

Each month, a bank credit cardholder receives a statement that provides an itemized list of charges and credits, as well as a summary of previous activity and finance charges.

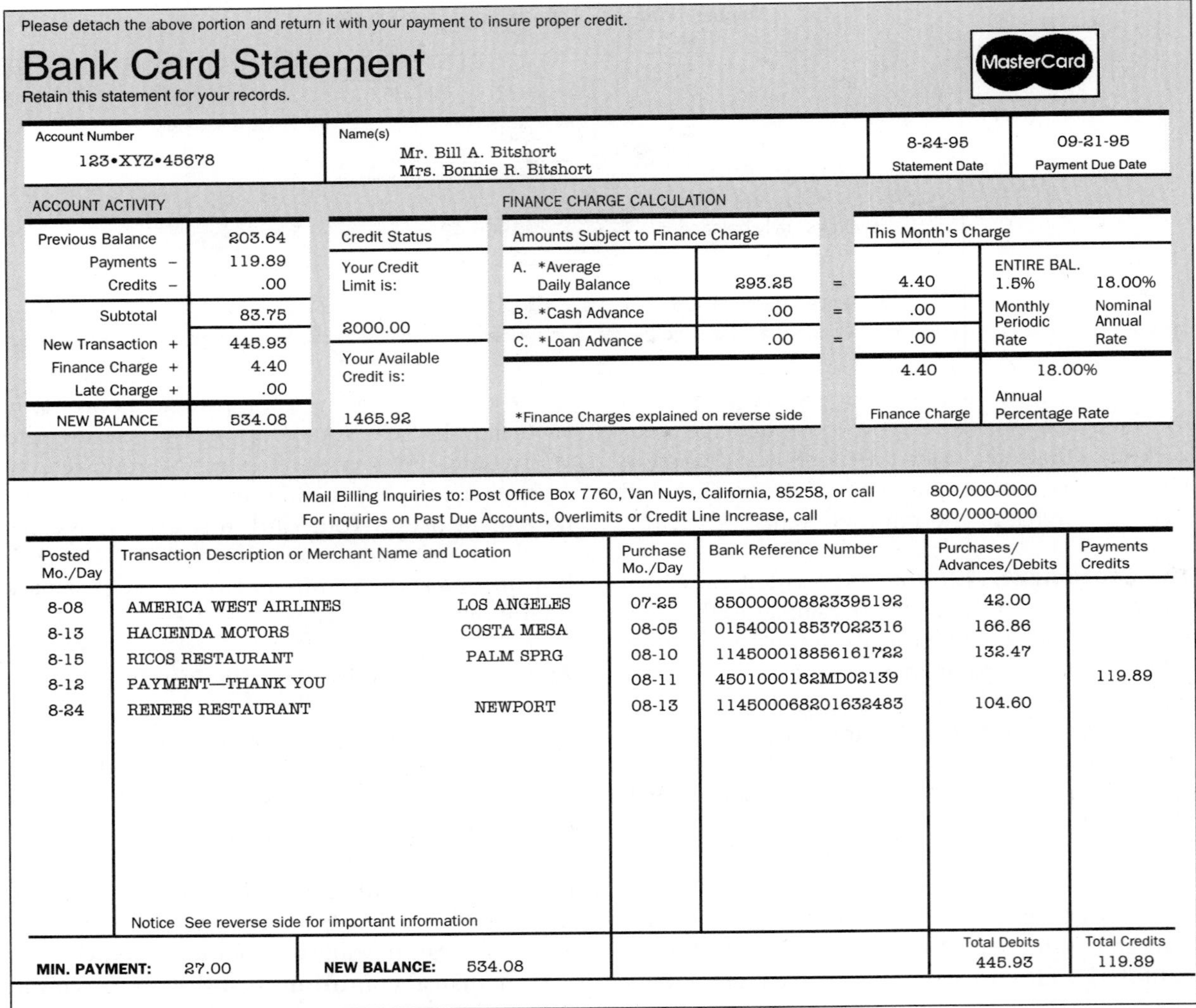

Please detach the above portion and return it with your payment to insure proper credit.

Bank Card Statement

Retain this statement for your records.

MasterCard

Account Number	Name(s)	Statement Date	Payment Due Date
123•XYZ•45678	Mr. Bill A. Bitshort Mrs. Bonnie R. Bitshort	8-24-95	09-21-95

ACCOUNT ACTIVITY

Previous Balance	203.64
Payments –	119.89
Credits –	.00
Subtotal	83.75
New Transaction +	445.93
Finance Charge +	4.40
Late Charge +	.00
NEW BALANCE	534.08

Credit Status	
Your Credit Limit is:	2000.00
Your Available Credit is:	1465.92

FINANCE CHARGE CALCULATION

Amounts Subject to Finance Charge			This Month's Charge		
A. *Average Daily Balance	293.25	=	4.40	ENTIRE BAL. 1.5% Monthly Periodic Rate	18.00% Nominal Annual Rate
B. *Cash Advance	.00	=	.00		
C. *Loan Advance	.00	=	.00		
*Finance Charges explained on reverse side			4.40 Finance Charge	18.00% Annual Percentage Rate	

Mail Billing Inquiries to: Post Office Box 7760, Van Nuys, California, 85258, or call 800/000-0000
For inquiries on Past Due Accounts, Overlimits or Credit Line Increase, call 800/000-0000

Posted Mo./Day	Transaction Description or Merchant Name and Location		Purchase Mo./Day	Bank Reference Number	Purchases/ Advances/Debits	Payments Credits
8-08	AMERICA WEST AIRLINES	LOS ANGELES	07-25	850000008823395192	42.00	
8-13	HACIENDA MOTORS	COSTA MESA	08-05	015400018537022316	166.86	
8-15	RICOS RESTAURANT	PALM SPRG	08-10	114500018856161722	132.47	
8-12	PAYMENT—THANK YOU		08-11	4501000182MD02139		119.89
8-24	RENEES RESTAURANT	NEWPORT	08-13	114500068201632483	104.60	
	Notice See reverse side for important information				Total Debits 445.93	Total Credits 119.89

MIN. PAYMENT: 27.00 NEW BALANCE: 534.08

nearest full dollar. As shown at the bottom of the statement, this month's minimum payment is $27: $534.08 × .05 = $26.70 = $27.00. If the new balance had been less than $250, the bank would have required a payment of $10 (which is the absolute minimum dollar payment), or of the total new balance, if less than $10. Cardholders who fail to make the minimum payment are considered in default on their account, and the bank issuing the card can take whatever action it deems necessary.

Returning Merchandise. When you return merchandise purchased with a credit card, the merchant will issue a *credit* to your account. The credit is transacted in the same fashion as a purchase and will appear on your statement as a *deduction* from the balance. If you purchase an item and have problems with it, you may not have to pay that part of your credit card bill if you have attempted in good faith to resolve the problem with the merchant. This protection is provided by the Fair Credit Billing Act, discussed later in the chapter. Of course, if the problem is resolved in the merchant's favor, you will ultimately have to pay.

Concept Check

6-14. Briefly describe the basic steps involved in opening a charge account; provide your answer from the customer's point of view. Describe *credit scoring* and explain how it's used (by lenders) in making a credit decision.

6-15. Describe the basic operations and functions of a *credit bureau*. What kind of information do they gather about you? Is there anything you can do if the information they have on file is wrong?

6-16. What is the *annual percentage rate (APR)?* Describe the most common method used to compute finance charges. What are the legal requirements with respect to disclosure of interest rates and charges?

6-17 The monthly statement is a key feature of bank and retail credit cards. What does this statement typically disclose? Why are merchandise and cash-advance transactions often separated on bank card statements?

USING CREDIT WISELY

LG5 LG6

With so many different types of credit cards to choose from, it's easier than ever to charge your purchases of goods and services. But such readily available credit can also lead to problems such as overspending and fraud. What do you perceive as the major advantage and disadvantage of credit cards, and what types of problems could arise when using them? Before reading on, give some thought to these questions.

Does it seem that every week there's at least one new credit card application in your mailbox? You're probably right; in 1994, one consumer credit group identified 25,000 different bank cards, with some banks having four or five versions. As the competition for your business intensifies, card issuers are continually coming up with attractive offers for a variety of credit cards. It's easy to be overwhelmed by all these choices. And although we've discussed how credit cards and revolving lines of credit can simplify your life financially, you can get into trouble unless you use them wisely. That's why you should shop around carefully to choose the right credit cards for your personal situation, understand the advantages and disadvantages that credit cards present, know how to resolve credit problems, and how to avoid the ultimate cost of credit abuse—bankruptcy.

SHOP AROUND FOR THE BEST DEAL

They say it pays to shop around, and when it comes to credit cards, that adage certainly applies. With all the fees and high interest costs, it pays to get the best deal possible. So, where do you start? Most credit experts suggest the first thing you should do is step back and take a look at yourself. What kind of "spender" are you, and how do you pay your bills? The fact is, no single credit card is right for everyone. If you pay off your card balance each month, you'll want a card that's different from the one that's best for someone who carries a credit balance from month to month, and may only pay the minimum due.

Regardless of which category you fall into, there are basically four card features to look for:

- Annual fees
- Rate of interest charged on account balance
- Length of the grace period
- Method of calculating balances

Now, if you normally pay your account balance in full each month, get a card with *no annual fees and a long grace period.* The rate of interest on the card is really irrelevant, since you don't carry account balances from month to month anyway.

In sharp contrast, if you don't pay your account in full, then look for cards that charge *a low rate of interest on unpaid balances.* The length of the grace period isn't all that important here, but obviously, other things being equal, you're better off with low (or no) annual fees. Sometimes, however, "other things aren't equal," in which case you have to decide between interest rates and annual fees. If you're not a big spender and don't build up big balances on your credit card (i.e., the card balance

EXHIBIT 6.11

Published Information about Bank Credit Card Terms

Information about low-cost credit cards is readily available in the financial media. Here's an example of what you can find in *Money* magazine. Notice the report has several categories for both standard and gold (premium) cards, for people who carry a balance or those who pay in full.

THE BEST CREDIT-CARD DEALS

Institution (state) Telephone	Rate	Annual fee	National average
Standard			**17.89%**
FOR PEOPLE WHO CARRY BALANCES			
Metropolitan Natl. (Arkansas) 800-883-2511	8.40%	$25	
Pulaski Bank & Trust (Ark.) 800-980-2265	8.75	35	
Federal Savings (Arkansas) 800-374-5600	8.90	33	
Simmons First Natl. (Ark.) 800-636-5151	9.75	35	
FOR PEOPLE WHO PAY IN FULL			
USAA Federal Savings (Texas) 800-922-9092	12.50%	$0	
Amalgamated[1] (Illinois) 800-365-6464	13.75	0	
AFBA Industrial (Colorado) 800-776-2265	14.50	0	
First Western (Pennsylvania) 800-837-6669	14.65	0	

Institution (state) Telephone	Rate	Annual fee	National average
Gold			**15.68%**
FOR PEOPLE WHO CARRY BALANCES			
Pulaski Bank & Trust[1] (Ark.) 800-980-2265	8.75%	$50	
Federal Savings (Arkansas) 800-374-5600	8.90	48	
Simmons First Natl.[2] (Ark.) 800-636-5151	9.75	50	
FOR PEOPLE WHO PAY IN FULL			
Amalgamated[1] (Illinois) 800-365-6464	12.25%	$0	
USAA Federal Savings (Texas) 800-922-9092	12.50	0	
Union Planters Natl.[1] (Tenn.) 800-628-8946	13.50	0	

Source and notes: *Bank Rate Monitor*, North Palm Beach, Fla. 33408. Rates for the credit cards are as of Nov. 29, 1994. All cards are variable rate. Selection is based on rates and annual fees. [1]Mastercard only [2]Visa only All others are MasterCard/Visa.

Source: *MONEY*, January 1995, p. 45.

rarely goes above $400 or $500), then *avoid* cards with annual fees and get one with as *low* a rate of interest as possible. (*Note:* The above situation would probably apply to most college students—or at least it should.) On the other hand, if you do carry big balances (say, $1,000 or more), then you'll probably be better off *paying an annual fee* (even a relatively high one) *to keep the rate of interest on the card as low as possible.* For example, your total yearly finance charges (including annual fees) will likely be *less* with a card that has, say, a $50 annual fee and an interest rate of 15 percent than one which has no annual fee but charges a higher (19 percent) rate of interest.

The bottom line is don't just take the first credit card that comes along. Instead, get the one that's right for you. To do that, call around to the various banks and financial institutions (that is, S&Ls and credit unions) in your area to get information about the credit terms on their cards—be sure to read the credit agreement carefully and ask about annual fees, grace periods, and interest rates. Also, if the local deals aren't all that great, you might want to consider cards that are offered nationally. Many banks market their cards throughout the United States, and it may pay to check them out. To help you do that, look to publications like *Money* magazine and *Kiplinger's Personal Finance* magazine. They regularly publish information about banks and other financial institutions that offer low-cost credit cards nationally, an example of which is provided in Exhibit 6.11.Or you can order a report of the best credit card deals around the country from Bankcard Holders of America ($4; 524 Branch Dr., Salem VA 24153, 703-389-5445) or RAM Research ($5; CardTrak Newsletter, Box 1700, Frederick, MD 21702; 800-344-7714).

ADVANTAGES AND DISADVANTAGES OF CREDIT CARDS

Both bank credit and retail charge cards can simplify your life, financially, if they are used properly.

Their most significant advantage is that by charging purchases, customers can delay payment until the end of the billing period. Note, however, that because of the high finance charges levied on balances carried from period to period, there is no real advantage to delaying payment beyond this point. Some of the basic advantages and disadvantages of using these cards follow.

Advantages. The major reasons to use credit cards include interest-free loans, simplified recordkeeping, returns and resolution of unsatisfactory purchase disputes, convenience, and use in emergencies.

- ***Interest-Free Loans.*** Many credit and charge cards provide short-term, interest-free loans on the purchase of goods or services. As discussed earlier, these *grace periods* generally cover a 25- to 30-day period of time during which you can pay your bill in full and not incur any interest charges (note that such grace periods do not apply to cash advances). Unfortunately, while most banks still offer grace periods, the trend is to shorten or eliminate such provisions. In addition, a growing number of card issuers are including purchases made during the current period when computing average daily balances. As a rule, you should use credit cards primarily to charge merchandise and services, and then pay the monthly statements in full to avoid any finance charges. If the card issuer does not offer a grace period, or includes current purchases in the average daily balance, the card should be used only in financial emergencies, since interest would be charged from the time of the transaction. Use of the card for any other purpose (such as for cash advances) signals poor personal financial management.
- ***Simplified recordkeeping.*** Both bank and retail credit cards provide detailed records of transactions in the form of monthly statements that consolidate records of purchases. No matter how many and varied the purchases made at a department store or the number of places where bank credit card transactions occur, the consumer receives only one statement from each card issuer that records them all. This greatly simplifies the record-keeping process and makes bill paying a lot easier.
- ***Returns and resolution of unsatisfactory purchase disputes.*** When you purchase an item on credit and later wish to return it, you need only have the store credit your retail or bank card account. Some stores only issue store credit, which can be used only at that retailer, to compensate customers who return items purchased for cash. Also, resolving any disagreement over goods or services purchased is easier if you charged them and have not yet paid for them. In that case, you have about 30 days to ensure that they are satisfactory; if not, you can refuse to pay that amount.
- ***Convenience.*** Many people use charge cards because they are convenient and eliminate the need to write a check each time a purchase is made. By charging all transactions during the month, the customer need write only one check to pay each card issuer's monthly bill. This can be a real time-saver for people who use their bank cards to make a large number of transactions at a variety of places or purchase many items at a given store during the month.
- ***Use in Emergencies.*** Finally, credit cards allow the cardholder to purchase needed items when sufficient cash is not available. With proper planning and budgeting, the consumer should be able to avoid running short of cash; however, charging a needed item because of a cash shortage may be justifiable in some situations. A tendency to run short of cash on a regular basis, however, signals the need to reevaluate one's budget.

Disadvantages. Banks credit and retail charge cards have two major disadvantages: (1) They offer the temptation to overspend, and (2) their high interest costs add to the price of the purchase.

- ***Tendency to overspend.*** People who don't use budgets tend to forget that what they charge must eventually be paid for. The credit card gives them a sense of buying power that may not be supported by their actual income; as a result, they often avoid paying the full amount of the bill. Because they can't cover their ever-increasing bills, they make only the minimum payments and thus incur costly finance charges.
- ***High interest costs on unpaid balances.*** The rate of interest charged on unpaid credit card balances is usually quite high. The typical 1.5 percent per month represents an 18 percent annual rate; and in a number of states, the APR can go as high as 21 percent (1.75 percent per month), or more. To make matters even worse, the interest paid on most forms of consumer loans—including all types of credit cards—is no

longer tax deductible, thanks to the Tax Reform Act of 1986 (see Chapter 3).

AVOIDING CREDIT PROBLEMS

By now it should be clear that open account credit can be a valuable technique for personal financial planning. As more places accept credit cards, the volume of credit card purchases has grown tremendously—and so has the level of credit card debt. It's not unusual to find people using credit cards to solve cash flow problems; even the most careful among us can occasionally find ourselves with mounting credit card debt, especially after the year-end holiday buying season. The real problems occur when the situation is no longer temporary and the debt continues to increase. If overspending is not curtailed, the size of the unpaid balance may place a real strain on the budget. Essentially, individuals who let their credit balances build up are *mortgaging their future.* By using credit, they are actually committing a part of their future income to make payments on the debt. Unfortunately, the more income that has to go just to make payments on charge cards (and other forms of consumer credit), the less there is available for other purposes.

The best way to avoid credit problems is to be disciplined when using credit. Reduce the number of cards you carry, and don't rush to accept all the tempting pre-approved credit cards that fill your mailbox. A wallet full of cards can work against you in two ways. Obviously, the ready availability of credit could tempt you to overspend and incur too much credit card debt. But there's another, less obvious, danger: when you apply for a loan, lenders look at the *total amount* of credit you have available as well as at the outstanding balances on your credit cards. If you have a lot of unused credit capacity, it may be harder to get a major loan because of lender concerns that you could become overextended.

So think twice before accepting a new credit card. You really don't need three or four bank cards. Two is the most financial advisors suggest you carry: perhaps one rebate card, if you charge enough to make the benefit worthwhile, and a low-rate card for purchases you have to repay over time. If the offer is really too attractive to pass up, then *replace one of your old cards.*

Suppose that, despite all your efforts, you find that your credit card balances are higher than you'd like and you anticipate having problems reducing them to a more manageable level. The first step is to stop making any new charges until you pay off the balances. Then commit to a repayment plan. One good strategy is to pay off the highest interest cards first, keeping the original payment rather than reducing it as your balance drops, or even better, pay more than the minimum—even if it's just $10. You'd be surprised how much difference this makes. You may also want to consider transferring your balances to a card with a low introductory rate and paying off as much as possible before the rate increases. Another option is to consolidate all your credit card debt and pay it off as quickly as possible using a lower-rate loan, such as a home equity line of credit. This can be a risky strategy, however. If you continue to be undisciplined about repaying your debts, you could lose your home. And clearing up your credit card balances may tempt you to start the credit card borrowing cycle all over again.

IMPORTANT CONSUMER CREDIT LEGISLATION

Just as you have an obligation to repay your debt in a prompt and timely fashion, lenders also have certain legal obligations they're expected to fulfill when they extend credit. Accordingly, when you apply for credit, it's in your best interest to be aware of the legal obligations of the issuing establishment. There is always a possibility that your rights will be violated. A number of important consumer protection laws affect the extension of credit. The major concerns of credit legislation have been credit discrimination (Equal Credit Opportunity Act); disclosure of credit information (Fair Credit Reporting Act); billing procedures, errors, and complaints, recourse on unsatisfactory purchases, (Fair Credit Billing Act); disclosure of finance charges, other fees, and credit terms and loss of credit card (Consumer Credit Protection [Truth in Lending] Act); and protection against collector harassment (Fair Debt Collection Practices). The key provisions of these acts are summarized in Exhibit 6-12.

CREDIT CARD FRAUD

Despite all the legislation, there are still people out there who are doing their very best to rip you off! And as far as your good credit is concerned, there's no better way to do that than through your credit card. In fact, plastic has become the vehicle of choice among crooks as a way of defrauding and

EXHIBIT 6.12

Major Consumer Credit Legislation

The following exhibit summarizes the provisions of the most important federal consumer credit protection laws.

Equal Credit Opportunity Act (ECOA) (1975, amended 1977)

- Credit discrimination on the basis of sex or marital status is illegal.
- Lenders may not ask questions about an applicant's sex, marital status, and childbearing plans.
- Lenders must view women's income the same as men's and to include alimony and child support as part of a woman's income.
- Credit discrimination based on race, national origin, religion, age, or the receipt of public assistance is illegal.
- If a husband and wife open a joint account or cosign a loan, the credit grantor must report the information to the credit bureau in the name of both parties.

Fair Credit Reporting Act (1971, amended 1994)

- Credit bureau reports must contain accurate, relevant, and recent information about the personal and financial situation of credit applicants.
- Only bona fide users of financial information may review credit files.
- Consumers who are refused credit or whose borrowing costs increase as the result of a credit investigation must be told why and given the name and address of the reporting credit agency.
- Consumers have the right to review their credit files personally and correct any inaccurate information.
- Credit bureaus must have toll-free phone numbers and provide consumers one low-cost report every two years.
- Disputes must be resolved in 30 days and consider the consumer's documentation.
- Credit bureaus must have formal procedures to correct reports.
- Creditors can be sued by consumers for not correcting credit reporting errors.

Fair Credit Billing Act (1975)

- At least 14 days prior to the payment-due date, creditors must mail bills that include all credits and refunds for the period in which they occurred.
- Customers must notify the creditor in writing of any billing errors within 60 days of the date they receive the statement.
- Credit issuers have 30 days to respond to customer inquiries about billing errors and 90 days to resolve the complaint, during which time creditors may not collect the bill or issue an unfavorable credit report.
- Credit cardholders may withhold payment for unsatisfactory goods or services charged to their accounts if, after good-faith attempts, they cannot satisfactorily work out their disagreement with the seller.
- Merchants may give cash discounts of any size to customers who pay cash instead of using credit.

Consumer Credit Protection Act (Truth in Lending) (1969, amended 1971 and 1982)

- Prior to extending credit, all lenders must disclose both the dollar amount of finance charges and the annual percentage rate charged (accurate to the nearest 0.25 percent), as well as other loan terms and conditions.
- Every credit card must contain some form of user identification—generally a picture or signature.
- The credit card owner's liability for a lost or stolen card is limited to a maximum of $50 per card.
- Companies may not send out unrequested credit cards (unsolicited credit card applications are allowed).

Fair Debt Collection Practices Act (1978)

- Credit customers must be informed in writing within five days of first contact by collector of the amount owed, to whom, and how to dispute the claim (written notice sent within 30 days).
- The collector must cease collection efforts until he sends the customer written verification of the debt. The customer can prevent a collector from communicating with him or her by notifying the collector in writing.
- Collectors may not (1) use abusive language, threaten the customer, or call at inconvenient times or at the place of work; (2) misrepresent themselves; (3) use unfair tactics in an effort to collect the debt; (4) contact anyone else about the customer's debt unless they are trying to locate him or her; and (5) collect an amount greater than the debt or apply payments to another disputed debt.

Fair Credit and Charge Card Disclosure Act (1988)

- Card issuers must provide full disclosure of all fees, grace periods, and other financial terms in unsolicited application invitations.
- Card issuers must notify you in advance when your account is about to be renewed.

stealing from both you and the merchants that honor credit cards. No doubt about it—credit card crime is big business, with losses of over $1 billion a year. Stolen account numbers (obtained by dishonest employees or even by thieves going through the trash to find discarded receipts) are the biggest source of credit card fraud. For all a crook needs to order merchandise or services over the phone is your account number. Even worse, a crook who also has your bank account number or home address may be able to get a credit card or open other types of charge accounts—*all in your name!*

Basically, "it's us against them," and the first thing you have to understand is that credit card you're carrying around is a very powerful piece of plastic. Be careful with it. You certainly can't count on retail merchants to protect you—in a recent test by *Money* magazine, only 5% of merchants checked signatures against the card and most accepted purchases made with borrowed cards. To reduce your chances of being defrauded, here are some suggestions you should follow:

- Never, ever, give your account number to people or organizations *who call you*—no matter how legitimate it sounds, if you didn't initiate the call, don't give out the information!
- It's okay to give your account number over the phone when ordering or purchasing something from a major catalog house, airline, hotel, and so on, but don't do it for any other reason.
- When paying for something *by check*, don't put your credit card account number on the check and don't let the store clerk do it—show the clerk a check guarantee card (if you have one), a driver's license, or some other form of identification.
- Don't put your phone number or address on credit/charge slips, even if the merchant asks for it—they're *not* entitled to it anyway; but if the clerk insists, just scribble down any number you want.
- When using your card to make a purchase, *always keep your eye on it* (so the clerk can't make an extra imprint); and if the clerk makes a mistake and wants to make another imprint, ask for the first imprint, and tear it up on the spot.
- Always draw a line on the credit slip through any blank spaces above the total, so the amount can't be altered.
- *Destroy* all carbons and old credit slips; and when you receive your monthly statement, be sure to *go over it promptly* to make sure there are no errors (if you find a mistake, call or send a letter immediately, detailing the error).
- If you lose a card or it's stolen, *report it to the card issuer immediately*—the most you're ever liable for with a lost or stolen card is $50 (per card), but if you report the loss *before* the card can be used, you won't be liable for any unauthorized charges (the phone number to call is listed on the back of your statement).
- Destroy old cards or those you no longer use.

BANKRUPTCY: PAYING THE ULTIMATE PRICE FOR CREDIT ABUSE

It certainly wouldn't be an overstatement to say that during the 1980s and early 1990s, *debt was in!* In fact, the explosion of debt that occurred since 1980 is almost incomprehensible. The national debt more than quadrupled, from less than a trillion dollars when the '80s began to about $4.5 trillion by early 1995. Businesses also took on debt at a rapid pace. And, not to be outdone, consumers were using credit like there was no tomorrow. Consumer installment debt rose precipitously as well, reaching almost $1 trillion by 1995. So it shouldn't be too surprising that when you couple this heavy debt load with a serious economic recession (like the one we had in 1990–91) and a very slow economic recovery from 1992 to 1993, you have all the ingredients of a real financial crisis. And that's just what happened as personal bankruptcies soared—indeed, nearly a million people a year filed for **personal bankruptcy** during that period.

When too many people are too heavily in debt, a recession (or some other economic reversal) can come along and push many of them over the edge. But let's face it, the recession is not the main culprit here, because the only way a recession can push you over the edge is if you're already sitting on it! The real culprit is excess debt. Some people simply abuse credit by taking on more than they can afford. Maybe they're pursuing a lifestyle beyond their means, or an unfortunate event—like the loss of a job—takes place. Whatever the cause, sooner or later, they start missing payments and their credit rating begins to deteriorate. Unless some corrective actions are taken, this is followed by repossession of property and, eventually, even bankruptcy. These people basically have reached the end of a long line of deteriorating financial affairs. Households that cannot resolve serious credit problems on their own need help from the courts. Two legal remedies that are widely used under such circumstances include (1) the Wage Earner Plan and (2) straight bankruptcy.

Wage Earner Plan. The **Wage Earner Plan** (as defined in *Chapter 13* of the U.S. Bankruptcy Code) is a workout procedure that involves some type of debt restructuring—usually by establishing a debt repayment schedule that's more compatible to the person's income. It may be a viable alternative for someone who has a steady source of income, not more than $750,000 in secured debt and $250,000 in unsecured debt, and a reasonably good chance of being able to repay the debts in three to five years. The majority of creditors must agree to the plan, and interest charges, along with late-payment penalties, are waived for the repayment period. Creditors usually will go along with this plan because they stand to lose more in a straight bankruptcy. After the plan is approved, the individual makes periodic payments to the court that in turn are used to pay off the creditors. Throughout the process, the individual retains the use of, and keeps title to, all of his or her assets.

Straight Bankruptcy. **Straight bankruptcy,** which is allowed under *Chapter 7* of the bankruptcy code, can be viewed as a legal procedure that results in "wiping the slate clean and starting anew." About 70 percent of those filing personal bankruptcy choose this route. However, straight bankruptcy does not eliminate all of the debtor's obligations, nor does the debtor necessarily lose all of his or her assets. For example, the debtor must make certain tax payments and keep up alimony and child-support payments but is allowed to retain certain payments from social security, retirement, veterans', and disability benefits. In addition, the debtor may retain equity in a home (up to $15,000), a car (up to $2,400), and other personal assets, such as clothing, books and tools of his or her trade. These are minimums as established by federal regulations; generally, state laws are much more generous with regard to the amount the debtor is allowed to keep. The choice of federal or state regulations would depend on the debtor's assets.

Other Bankruptcy Options. While most individual bankruptcies involve either straight liquidations or Wage Earner plans, several other options have been added recently. To begin with, the U.S. Supreme Court ruled that individuals can now file for reorganization under *Chapter 11* of the bankruptcy code—a type of bankruptcy which had previously been reserved mostly for businesses. Chapter 11 bankruptcy is for individuals who don't qualify for Chapter 13 reorganization—either because they exceed the debt limitations or do not have a regular source of income—but who want to try to restructure their debt. For these people, Chapter 11 is really the only alternative to straight bankruptcy. Like the Wage Earner Plan discussed above, Chapter 11 filers can restructure their debts, or a portion of them, to be repaid over time. The big difference is that in Chapter 11 bankruptcy, the creditors vote on—and can possibly block—the restructuring plan. This, of course, means the reorganization process can drag on for years and involve hefty legal fees. The second alternative now available is a so-called *"Chapter 20"* bankruptcy—its labeled as such because it combines parts of both Chapters 7 and 13. Although not actually a part of the bankruptcy code, this procedure allows individuals to wipe out their unsecured debt, as per Chapter 7, *and* then use Chapter 13 to restructure their secured debt, including mortgages and home equity loans and nondischargeable debts such as certain tax and child support payments.

USING THE SERVICES OF A CREDIT COUNSELOR

Filing for bankruptcy is a serious matter and should only be taken as a last resort. For one thing, it's going to stick with you for a long time (it will remain in your credit file for ten years) and certainly won't help your chances of getting credit in the future. It often makes a lot more sense to try and work problems out before they get so bad that bankruptcy is the only viable alternative. Some people can do that on their own but, in many cases, it may be a good idea to seek the help of a *credit counselor.*

personal bankruptcy A form of legal recourse open to insolvent debtors in which they may petition a court for protection from creditors and arrange for the orderly liquidation and distribution of their assets.

Wage Earner Plan An arrangement for scheduled debt repayment over future years that is an alternative to straight bankruptcy; used when a person has a steady source of income and there is a reasonable chance of repayment within three to five years.

straight bankruptcy A legal proceeding that results in "wiping the slate clean and starting anew"; where most of a debtor's obligations are eliminated in an attempt to put the debtor's financial affairs in order.

Issues in Money Management

Are Debt Counselors What They Appear to Be?

With consumer debt on the rise, many people who are struggling financially have turned to debt counselors for help. Groups such as the non-profit Consumer Credit Counseling Service (CCCS), which was started in the 1950s as an alternative to filing personal bankruptcy, begin by evaluating outstanding debt against income to determine if lifestyle or budget changes would be enough to solve the problem. When such changes are not enough, the credit counselor will help consolidate debts, work out deals with creditors to lower the amount a consumer owes, collect money for creditors and disburse it, and arrange a repayment plan that is within their client's means—all for a small fee, or without charge. Such groups continue to grow in popularity; in 1993, more than 645,000 debtors channeled $1.14 billion through CCCS's 1,100 offices in the United States, Canada, and Puerto Rico.

Recently, however, charges have been made that credit counselors may not provide the objective help that debtors need, and instead function primarily as bill collectors. While they advertise themselves as charitable organizations, these services are mostly funded by creditors, 31 percent of whom are credit-card issuers. It is easy to see why creditors subsidize them: credit counselors on average keep eight to 15 cents of every dollar they collect, whereas typical bill collectors keep more than twice as much. In addition, unsecured creditors get nothing when a debtor files for bankruptcy, making a partial payment arranged through a credit counselor attractive by comparison.

In March 1994, the Association of Independent Consumer Credit Counseling Agencies (AICCCA) filed suit in New York against the National Foundation for Consumer Credit Inc. (NFCC), the umbrella organization for the Consumer Credit Counseling Service. According to the suit, the NFCC fails to disclose the amount of revenue it receives from creditors, encourages debtors to get into repayment plans they can't afford and ultimately can't pay, and neglects to discuss the option of bankruptcy—even when it is in consumers' best interest.

Mona Jefferson, a 49-year-old insurance company manager and single mother, went to her local CCCS for help with $130,000 in bills arising from family medical expenses. The agency arranged to have interest charges dropped on a few accounts and set up a three-year debt-reduction plan, which required her to mail them a monthly check for $3,700 plus a $20 fee. However, they were only interested in her credit-card and credit-line debts. They did not provide much-needed budget advice or help with her high monthly mortgage payments and other secured debt. As a result, she could only make ten months' worth of payments and ended up filing for bankruptcy.

To avoid falling into such a trap, debtors should explore all their options before seeking the help of a credit counselor. First, advisors suggest, try contacting your creditors yourself; you can probably work out a deal on your own if you have few lenders and need only two to three months to catch up. If, however, you have six or more creditors, you should probably see a credit counselor. Make sure to ask your counselor for several debt-reduction options that are appropriate for your financial situation. More importantly, face up to credit and debt problems as soon as they occur, and do everything possible to avoid ruining your credit record.

Sources: Adapted from Laura Cianci, "Controversy Brews Over Free Credit Counselors," *Lexington Herald-Leader*, June 6, 1994, p. Business-2; Albert B. Crenshaw, "Bills, Bills, Bills: Overburdened Consumers Can Lighten Their Loads With Organization, Realistic Budgets and a Little Time," *Lexington Herald-Leader*, January 12, 1992, p. E1; Eric Tyson, "Debt Doctors: Angels of Mercy?" *Worth*, October 1994, p. 117.

Credit counselors work with a family in setting up a budget and may even negotiate with creditors to establish workable schedules for repaying outstanding debts. The counseling service will often go so far as to collect money from the debtor and distribute it to creditors. There are private firms that, for a fee, will act as intermediaries between borrowers and creditors and provide counseling services. These counselors generally attempt to reduce the size of payments, the size of outstanding debt, or both. However, their fees can run as

> **credit counselor** A professional financial advisor who assists overextended consumers in repairing budgets for both spending and debt repayment.

much as 20 percent of the amount owed. Another option is a nonprofit agency, such as those affiliated with the nationwide network of *Consumer Credit Counseling Services* (800-388-2227). You'll get many of the services that private agencies provide, at a lower cost. Of course, as with any financial advisor, you should check out a credit counselor's credentials, fees, services provided, and track record *before* using his or her services. Otherwise, you could find that credit counseling may not be the answer to your problems, as the *Issues in Money Management* box on page 266 demonstrates.

Concept Check

6-18. What are some of the key factors you should consider when choosing a credit card? Given your current spending habits, what types of cards would be best for you and why?

6-19. Describe briefly the advantages and disadvantages of using credit cards.

6-20. How does recent consumer credit legislation relate to (a) credit discrimination, (b) disclosure of credit information, (c) disclosure of finance charges, (d) loss of credit card, (e) errors, complaints, and recourse on unsatisfactory purchases, (f) protection against collector harassment, and (g) credit card renewal notices?

6-21. Discuss the steps you would take to avoid and/or resolve credit problems.

6-22. What's the biggest source of credit card fraud? List at least five things that you can do to reduce your chances of being a victim of credit card fraud.

6-23. Explain the conditions that might make bankruptcy necessary. Distinguish between a *Wage Earner Plan* and *straight bankruptcy*. How might you use the services of a credit counselor?

SUMMARY

LG1. Describe the reasons for using consumer credit and identify its benefits and problems. Families and individuals use credit as a way to pay for relatively expensive purchases and occasionally, to deal with a financial emergency; in addition, consumer credit is being used increasingly simply because it is so convenient. Finally, it is also used to partially finance the purchase of various types of investments. Unfortunately, while there are some definite positive aspects to the use of consumer credit, there are also some negatives, the most important being that it can be misused to the point where people live beyond their means by purchasing goods and services they simply can't afford. Such overspending can get so bad that it eventually leads to bankruptcy.

LG2. Develop a plan to establish a strong credit history. Establishing a strong credit history is an important part of personal financial planning. Opening checking and savings accounts, obtaining one or two credit cards and using them judiciously, and taking out a small loan and repaying it on schedule are ways to show potential lenders that you can handle credit wisely. Be sure to use credit only when you are sure you can repay the obligation, make payments promptly, and notify a lender immediately if you cannot meet payments as agreed. Using the debt safety ratio, you can calculate how much of your monthly take-home pay is going to consumer credit payments. One widely used credit capacity guideline is that total monthly consumer credit payments (exclusive of your mortgage payment) should not exceed 20 percent of your monthly take-home pay.

LG3. Distinguish among the different forms of open account credit: bank credit cards, other credit cards and charge accounts, and revolving credit lines. Open account credit is one of the most popular forms of consumer credit; it is available from various types of financial institutions, as well as all sorts of retail stores and merchants. The major types of open account credit include bank credit cards, retail charge cards, 30-day charge accounts, travel and entertainment cards, and various forms of revolving lines of credit.

Many bank cards offer an incentive such as rebates or merchandise discounts. Be sure to calculate the total cost of the card, based on your spending patterns, to determine whether these special cards make sense for you. Although credit cards account for a significant portion of consumer transactions, revolving lines of credit provide their users with ready access to borrowed money (by simply writing checks). Basically, there are three types of revolving credit lines: overdraft protection lines, unsecured personal lines of credit, and home equity credit lines.

LG4. Apply for, obtain, and manage open account credit. Most types of open account credit require formal application, which generally involves an extensive investigation of your credit background and an evaluation of your creditworthiness. This usually includes checking credit bureau reports. You should verify the accuracy of these reports on a regular basis and promptly correct any errors. The amount of finance charges, if any, due on consumer credit depends in large part on the technique used to compute the account balance; the average daily balance method is the most common today. Managing your accounts involves understanding the monthly statement and making payments on a timely basis.

LG5. Choose the right credit cards and recognize their advantages and disadvantages. With so many different types of credit cards available, it pays to shop around to choose the best credit card for your needs. You should consider your spending habits and then compare the fees, interest rates, grace period, and any incentives. If you pay your balance off each month, you will want a card with low annual fees; if you carry a balance, a low interest rate is your best bet. Advantages of credit cards include interest-free loans, simplified recordkeeping, ease of making returns and resolving unsatisfactory purchase disputes, convenience, and use in emergencies. The disadvantages are the tendency to overspend and high interest costs on unpaid balances.

LG6. Avoid credit problems, protect yourself against credit card fraud, and understand the personal bankruptcy process. Avoiding credit problems requires self-discipline. Keep the number of cards you use to a minimum and be sure you can repay any balances quickly. When credit card debt gets out of control, adopt a payment strategy to pay off the debt in as short a time as possible by looking for a low-rate card, paying more than the minimum payment, and not charging any additional purchases until the debt is repaid. Another option is a consolidation loan. To protect yourself against credit card fraud, don't give out your card number unnecessarily, destroy old cards and receipts, verify your credit card transactions, and report a lost card or suspicious activity immediately. A solution to credit abuse, albeit a drastic one, is personal bankruptcy. Those who file work out a debt restructuring program under Chapter 13's Wage Earner Plan or Chapter 7's straight bankruptcy. If you have serious problems managing personal credit, a credit counselor can help you learn to control spending and work out a repayment strategy.

FINANCIAL FACTS OR FANTASIES

Are the following statements financial facts (true) or fantasies (false)?

1. One of the benefits of using credit is that it allows you to purchase expensive goods and services by spreading the payments for them over time.
2. Excluding mortgage payments, most families should have no problem handling their credit so long as they limit their monthly credit payments to 30 percent of their take-home pay.
3. One of the major differences between bank credit cards and standard travel and entertainment (T&E) cards is that T&E cards do not come with credit lines.
4. You use a check rather than a credit card to obtain funds from an unsecured personal line of credit.

5. When you make application for credit, most big lenders will contact the local credit bureau, which decides whether or not you should receive the credit.

6. The best credit card for someone who does not pay their account balance in full each month is one that has a high interest rate but no annual fees.

DISCUSSION QUESTIONS AND PROBLEMS

Discussion Question for Opening Profile

Assume it is mid-1987 and you are Randy Walker. You barely have enough money for basic living expenses unless you charge almost everything, and as a result your personal debt is growing each month. Describe the steps you would take to analyze and resolve your credit situation.

1. After graduating from college last fall, Sarina Rao took a job as a consumer credit analyst at a local bank. From her work reviewing credit applications, she realizes that she should begin establishing her own credit history. Describe for Sarina several steps she could take to begin building a strong credit record. Does the fact that she took out a student loan for her college education help or hurt her credit record?
2. Joel Stern has a monthly take-home pay of $1,200; he makes payments of $250 a month on his outstanding consumer credit (excluding the mortgage on his home). How would you characterize Joel's debt burden? What if his take-home pay were $850 a month, and he had monthly credit payments of $90?
3. Calculate your own debt-safety ratio. What does it tell you about your current credit situation and your debt capacity? Does this information indicate a need to make any changes in your credit use patterns, and if so, what steps should you take?
4. Mary Maffeo has an overdraft protection line. Assume that her October 1995 statement showed a latest (new) balance of $862. If the line had a minimum monthly payment requirement of 5 percent of the latest balance (rounded to the nearest $5 figure), what would be the minimum amount she would have to pay on her overdraft protection line?
5. Don and Judy Summers have a home with an appraised value of $180,000 and a mortgage balance of only $90,000. Given that an S&L is willing to lend money at a loan-to-value ratio of 75 percent, how big a home equity credit line can Don and Judy obtain? How much, if any, of this line would qualify as tax deductible interest if their house originally cost $100,000?
6. Sally Rivera is a student at City Community College, and has a balance of $380 on her retail charge card; if the store levies a finance charge of 21 percent per annum, how much monthly interest will be added to her account?
7. Alan Bell recently received his monthly MasterCard bill for the period June 1–30, 1995, and wants to verify the monthly finance charge calculation, which is assessed at a rate of 17.4 per year and based on average daily balances including new purchases. His outstanding balance, purchases, and payments are as follows:

Previous balance:	$386
Purchases:	
June 4	137
June 12	78
June 20	98
June 26	75
Payments:	
June 21	35

What is his average daily balance and the finance charge for the period? (Use a table like the one in Exhibit 6.9 for your calculations.)

CONTEMPORARY CASE APPLICATIONS

6.1 The Dunnermans Seek Some Credit Card Information

Warren and Patricia Dunnerman are a newly married couple in their mid-20s. Warren is a senior at a state university and will graduate in the summer of 1996. Patricia graduated last spring with a degree in marketing and recently started working as a sales rep for the Alhambra Corporation. She supports both of them on her monthly salary of $1,500 after taxes. At present, the Dunnermans pay all of their expenses by cash or check. They would, however, like to use a bank credit card for some of their transactions. Because neither Warren nor Patricia is familiar with how to go about applying for a credit card, they approach you for help.

Questions

1. Advise the Dunnermans on how they should go about filing out a credit application.
2. Explain to them the procedure that the bank will probably follow in processing their application.
3. Tell them about credit scoring, and how the bank will arrive at a credit decision.
4. What kind of advice would you offer the Dunnermans on the "correct" use of their card? What would you tell them about building a strong credit record?

6.2 Nancy Starts Over After Bankruptcy

A year after declaring bankruptcy, and moving with her daughter back into her parents' home, Nancy Singh is about to get a degree in nursing. As she starts out on a new career, she also wants to start a new life—one built on a solid financial base. Nancy will be starting out as a full-time nurse at a salary of $31,000 a year, and plans to continue working at a second (part-time) nursing job at an annual income of $15,500. She will be paying back $24,000 in bankruptcy debts and wants to be able to move into an apartment within a year, then buy a condo or house in five years.

Nancy will not have to pay rent for the time she lives with her parents. And, she will have child care at no cost, which will continue after she and her daughter are able to move out on their own. While the living arrangement with her parents is great financially, the accommodations are "tight," and Nancy's work hours interfere with her parents' routines. Everyone agrees that one more year of this is about all the family feels it can take. However, before Nancy is able to make a move, even into a rented apartment, she will have to reestablish credit over and above paying off her bankruptcy debts. In order to rent the kind of place she'd like, she will need to have a good credit record for a year. In order to buy a home, she will need to sustain that credit standing for at least three to five years.

Questions

1. In addition to opening checking and savings accounts, what else might Nancy do to begin establishing credit with a bank?
2. While Nancy is unlikely to be able to obtain a major bank credit card for at least a year, how might she begin establishing credit with local merchants?
3. What's one way she might be able to obtain a bank credit card? Explain.
4. How often should Nancy monitor her credit standing with credit reporting services, like TRW?
5. What general advice would you offer with regard to getting Nancy back on track to a new life financially?

GETTING A HANDLE ON YOUR FINANCIAL FUTURE

The proper use of consumer credit can provide you with the ability to achieve your financial goals without jeopardizing your cash budget. The use of debt is not without its disadvantages, however. Easy credit can lead to impulse purchases, high interest charges, and if payments are not made on time, a poor credit rating. Remember that while credit will increase your purchasing power, it does not increase your ability to pay your bills. Credit is not an increase in income.

If You Are Just Starting Out

One of the most important things you can do when you are just starting out is to establish your credit. This can be accomplished by opening a checking and savings account and applying for a retail credit card.

Establishing Credit:

1. Don't write bad checks. Be sure to reconcile your statement as discussed in chapter 4.
2. If you are married, establish credit in your own name as well as jointly with your spouse.
3. Read the credit agreement carefully so that you understand all of the terms and conditions.
4. Avoid using firms that guarantee for a fee that they will get you a credit card regardless of your financial or credit history without thoroughly investigating the offer.

Managing your credit:

1. Pay off balances early if possible.
2. Try to keep your monthly debt repayment to no more than 20% of your monthly take-home pay.
3. Keep a list of your credit cards and their numbers so that you can report lost or stolen cards immediately.
4. Be sure you understand the method of calculating interest on unpaid balances. It does make a difference in the amount of interest you pay.

If You Are Thirty-Something

Once you have established your good credit, it is essential that you maintain it. You should use credit only when you can afford it and be sure to fulfill all of the terms. You might also want to investigate other types of credit at this stage. Some examples are overdraft protection on your checking account, unsecured personal lines of credit, and home equity lines of credit.

Maintaining your credit:

1. Periodically review your credit file to ensure its accuracy.
2. If your combined monthly payments become too much to handle, consider a bill consolidation loan coupled with the cancellation of most of your credit accounts.
3. Many retail stores will increase your credit limit when you reach your maximum if you are in good standing. This may encourage you to purchase more from that store, thereby increasing your debt.

Managing your credit:

1. Monitor your credit card usage. Consider canceling all credit cards that you have not used in six months.
2. Where possible, take advantage of the interest-free loan aspects of credit cards by paying the balance in full each month.
3. Watch for warning signs such as paying later each month or only paying the minimum required.
4. Note the cutoff dates for the billing cycle and make major purchases after that date to give you an additional billing cycle to pay for the purchase.

Chapter 7

USING CONSUMER LOANS

Financing the Cost of a College Education

"Looking back on the past 10 years, I wonder how I managed it all!" exclaims Andrea Taylor, a 49-year old psychotherapist who lives near Portland, Maine. A bitter divorce, when sons Daniel and Jonathan were 13 and 10, left the family emotionally and financially stressed. "It was really touch and go for a while," she recalls. "My income was small, and I got almost nothing from my ex-husband. My main concern was taking care of the kids, pulling us together as a family. Fortunately, I'd always had good 'money sense,' but my budgeting skills were really put to the test." She resisted taking out loans because basically she is "debt-averse," rarely carrying a balance on her credit cards—maybe for school clothes, Christmas shopping—and then repaying it in a few months.

However, she realized she'd have to borrow to send her sons to college. At the same time she decided to change careers. "It was truly terrifying to think about sending two boys to college *and* starting my graduate program in psychotherapy the same year Dan entered college. I had no one to fall back on; I was it! But for me, education was the top priority, so I used every possible financial resource." Both boys were able to finance about half of their college expenses with federal and college-sponsored grants; the other half was split between federal, college-sponsored, and home equity loans and personal funds—part-time and summer jobs and family savings. Andrea also received grants and no-interest loans for her program and worked while

Learning Goals

LG1. *Know when to use consumer loans and differentiate between the major types.*

LG2. *Identify the various sources of consumer loans.*

LG3. *Choose the best loans by comparing finance charges, maturity, collateral, and other loan terms.*

LG4. *Describe the features of, and calculate finance charges on, single-payment loans.*

LG5. *Evaluate the benefits of an installment loan and understand the terms of the loan purchase contract.*

LG6. *Determine the costs of installment loans and analyze whether it is better to pay cash or take out a loan.*

in grad school. She cashed in her teachers' retirement fund, which was earning only 1 or 2 percent, and refinanced her house to get a lower rate and pay off her home equity loan. "Funding our education was a family effort. We cut expenses drastically and took no vacations; the boys had no cars or computers. My aim was to keep our loans as small as possible," Andrea explains.

As a way to teach her sons about money, she made each responsible for some of his loans. She explained what their obligations were and made sure college was what they wanted, because they'd be repaying the loans for many years. When repayment began Andrea opted for a longer maturity and lower monthly payment—even though she'd pay more total interest—because Jonathan was still in college. She plans to repay the balance as soon as possible. Daniel started with a shorter maturity and higher payment but then consolidated his loan to lower payments and provide more cash for living expenses.

Andrea advises other families to be committed to your goal and communicate openly about financial realities. "I'm looking forward to 1996, when tuition payments end and I can start saving for retirement," she says. "I wish I could have done otherwise, but our education came first." Through sound personal financial planning and wise use of consumer loans, Andrea and her sons have improved their lives. Chapter 7 tells you what to look for if you, too, need to borrow to reach financial goals.

BASIC FEATURES OF CONSUMER LOANS

LG1
LG2

In addition to open account credit, consumers can also borrow money from banks and other financial institutions; these loans can be set up as either single-payment or installment loans, and they can be used to pay for just about any type of big-ticket item. Can you list some reasons why you might want to borrow money through a consumer loan? Take a few minutes before reading on to think about this question.

At several points in this book, we have discussed the different types of financial goals that individuals and families can set for themselves. These goals often involve substantial sums of money and may include such things as a college education, or the purchase of a new car. One way to reach these goals is to systematically save the money. Another is to use a loan to at least partially finance the transaction. Consumer loans are important to the personal financial planning process because of the help they provide in reaching certain types of financial goals. Working a major expenditure or purchase into a financial plan can be done just as easily with a consumer loan as it can by saving. The key, of course, is to successfully manage the credit by keeping the amount of debt used and debt-repayment burden *well within your budget!*

USING CONSUMER LOANS

As we saw in Chapter 6, the use of open account credit can prove helpful to those who plan and live within their personal financial budgets. More important to the long-run achievement of personal financial goals, however, are single-payment and installment consumer loans. These long-term liabilities are widely used to finance goods that are too expensive to buy from current income, to help with a college education, or to pay for certain types of nondurable items, like expensive vacations. Of course, the extent to which this type of borrowing is used must be dictated by personal financial plans and budgets.

These loans differ from open account credit in a number of ways, including the formality of their lending arrangements. That is, while open account credit results from a rather informal process, **consumer loans** are *formal, negotiated contracts* that specify both the terms for borrowing and the repayment schedule. In addition, whereas an open account credit line can be used over and over again, consumer loans are one-shot transactions that are made for specific purposes. Because there is no revolving credit with a consumer loan, there is no more credit available (from that particular loan) once it is paid off. Further, there are no credit cards or checks issued with this form of credit. Finally, while open account credit is used chiefly to make repeated purchases of relatively low-cost *goods and services,* consumer loans are used mainly to *borrow money* in order to have the funds to pay for big-ticket items.

DIFFERENT TYPES OF LOANS

While they can be used for just about any purpose imaginable, most consumer loans fall into one of the five following categories:

- ***Auto loans.*** Financing a new car, truck, or van is the single most common reason for borrowing money through a consumer loan. Indeed, auto loans account for about 35 percent of all consumer credit outstanding. Generally speaking, about 80 to 90 percent of the cost of a new vehicle (somewhat less with used cars) can be financed with credit; the buyer must provide the rest through a *down payment.* The loan is *secured* with the auto, meaning that the vehicle serves as **collateral** for the loan and can be repossessed by the lender should the buyer fail to make payments. These loans generally have maturities that run from 36 to 60 months, perhaps longer.
- ***Loans for other durable goods.*** Consumer loans can also finance other kinds of *costly durable goods,* such as furniture, home appliances, TVs, stereos, home computers, recreational vehicles, and even small airplanes and mobile homes. These loans are also secured by the item(s) purchased and generally require some down payment. Maturities vary with the type of asset purchased: 9- to 12-month loans are common for less costly items, such as TVs and stereos, whereas 7- to 10-year loans are the rule with mobile homes.
- ***Education loans.*** Getting a college education is another very important reason for taking out

a consumer loan. Such loans can be used to finance either undergraduate or graduate studies, and there are special government-subsidized loan programs available to both students and parents; we'll discuss student loans in more detail below.

- ***Personal loans.*** These loans are typically used for nondurable expenditures, such as an expensive European vacation or to cover temporary cash shortfalls. Many personal loans are made on an *unsecured* basis—that is, there is no collateral with the loan other than the borrower's good name.
- ***Consolidation loans.*** This type of credit is used to try and straighten out an unhealthy credit situation. When consumers overuse credit cards, credit lines, and/or consumer loans, and can no longer service the debt in a prompt and timely fashion, a consolidation loan may help control this deteriorating credit situation. By borrowing money from one source to pay off other forms of credit, borrowers can replace, say, five or six monthly payments that total $400 with one payment amounting to $250. *Consolidation loans are usually expensive, and people who use them must be careful to stop using credit cards and other forms of credit until they fully repay the loans. Otherwise, they may end up right back where they started.*

Student Loans. Today, the annual cost of a college education ranges from about $6,000 at a state school to well over $20,000 at most private colleges—and is rising at about 7 percent a year, well above the inflation rate. Many families, even those who started saving for college when their children were young, are faced with higher than expected bills. Fortunately, many different types of financial aid programs exist, including some federal programs described below, as well as state, private, and college-sponsored programs.

Certainly one of the most legitimate reasons for going into debt is to pay for a college education. While you could borrow money for college through normal channels—that is, take out a regular consumer loan from your bank and use the proceeds to finance an education—there are better ways to go about getting education loans. That's because the federal government (and some state governments) have available several different types of subsidized educational loan programs. The four federally sponsored programs are:

- Stafford Loans
- Perkins Loans
- Supplemental Loans for Students (SLS)
- Parent Loans (PLUS)

The Stafford and Perkins loans have the best terms and act as the foundation to the government's student loan program. SLS and PLUS are *supplemental loans* for students who demonstrate a need but, for one reason or another, do not qualify for Stafford or Perkins loans, or whose total need is not being met by the other types of aid they are receiving. While Stafford, Perkins, and SLS loans are made directly to students, PLUS loans are made to the parents or legal guardians of college students.

To see how student loans work, let's take a look at the Stafford loan program (except where noted, the other three federally subsidized programs have much the same standards and follow the same procedures as discussed here). Stafford loans carry very low, government-subsidized interest rates; most major banks, as well as some of the bigger S&Ls and credit unions participate in the program. Actually, the loans are made directly by one of the participating banks or financial institutions, though the student has no direct contact with the lending institution. Instead, the whole process—and it really is quite simple—begins with a visit to the school's financial aid office, where a financial aid counselor will help you determine your eligibility. To be eligible, you have to demonstrate a *financial need,* where the amount of your financial need is defined as the cost of attending school *LESS* the amount that can be paid by you or your family (in these programs, students are expected to contribute something to their educational expense, regardless of their income).

consumer loans One-time loans made for specific purposes using formally negotiated contracts specifying the borrowing terms and repayment.

collateral An item of value that is used to secure the principal portion of a loan.

personal loan A type of consumer loan typically used for the purchase of nondurable items or for covering a temporary cash shortfall.

consolidation loan A loan made from one source to pay off other, existing debts; used to reduce monthly debt-repayment burden.

In addition, you have to be making *satisfactory progress in your academic program* and you cannot be in default on any other student loans. In effect, so long as you can demonstrate a financial need, are making satisfactory academic progress, and are not a deadbeat, you'll probably qualify for a Stafford loan.

Now all you have to do to obtain a loan is complete a simple application form, like the one in Exhibit 7.1. The completed application is then submitted to *your school's financial aid office*. You do *not* have to deal with the bank (your school will submit all the necessary papers to the institution actually making the loan), and you will *not* be subject to any credit checks (although with SLS or PLUS loans, you may be subject to a credit judgment by the lender). There are specific loan limits with each of the four programs. For example, with Stafford loans, you can borrow up to $2,625 per academic year for first year studies, $3,500 for the second year, and $5,500 per academic year thereafter, up to a maximum of $23,000 for undergraduate studies. Graduate students can qualify for up to $8,500 per academic year. The maximum for both undergraduate and graduate loans is $65,000, combined. Should you require even more money—that is, if your financial need exceeds the maximum amount of a Stafford loan—you can also apply for an SLS loan. There's no limit on the *number* of loans you can have, only on the maximum dollar amount that you can receive annually from each program.

Each year, right on through graduate school, a student can take out a loan from one or more of these government programs. Over time, that can add up to a lot of loans and a substantial amount of debt—all of which has to be repaid. But here's another nice feature: In addition to carrying low (government-subsidized) interest rates, loan repayment does not begin until after you're out of school (for the Stafford and Perkins programs only—repayment on SLS and PLUS loans normally begins within 60 days of loan disbursement). In addition, interest does *not* begin accruing until you get out of school. Of course, while you're in school, the lenders will receive interest on their loans, but it's paid by the federal government! Once repayment begins, you start paying interest on the loans, which are amortized with monthly payments over a period of five to ten years. To help you service the debt, if you have a number of student loans outstanding, you can *consolidate* the loans, at a single blended rate, and extend the repayment period out to as far as 20 years. In addition, you can ask for either an *extended repayment* for a longer term of up to 30 years; a *graduated repayment schedule,* which will give you low payments in the early years and then higher payments later on; or an *income-contingent repayment plan,* with payments that fluctuate annually according to income and debt levels. But no matter what you do, *take the repayment provisions on these loans seriously, as defaults will be reported to credit bureaus and become a part of your credit file!*

In summary, here are some things about student loans to keep in mind:

- Check with your school's financial aid office to see what programs are available and then apply early.
- Stafford or Perkins loans have the best terms.
- Borrow no more than you need—remember, these loans are eventually going to have to be repaid.
- Consider work-study as an alternative to borrowing.
- Become aware of loan forgiveness programs for selected occupations (military, law enforcement, Peace Corps, and so on).
- Take the loan repayment provisions seriously —defaults aren't taken lightly and can cause serious credit problems for you.
- If you're having problems servicing the loans, contact the lender and see if some arrangements can be worked out (most lenders would rather work with you than have you default).

In addition to the government programs described above, there are other types of financial assistance that are available to help you finance a college education, as described in the *Financial Shocks* box on pages 278-279.

Single Payment or Installment Payments. Consumer loans can be broken into categories based on the type of repayment arrangement—single-payment or installment. **Single-payment loans** are made for a specified period of time

> **single-payment loan** A loan made for a specified period of time at the end of which payment in full is due.

EXHIBIT 7.1

The SNAP APP: A Student Loan Application Form

This is a standard application form for Stafford loans, and requests only the most basic information about the student borrower. It does not require information about a student's credit history, income level, and so on. The form is so simple, in fact, that the bottom half is the actual promissory note that the student is expected to sign.

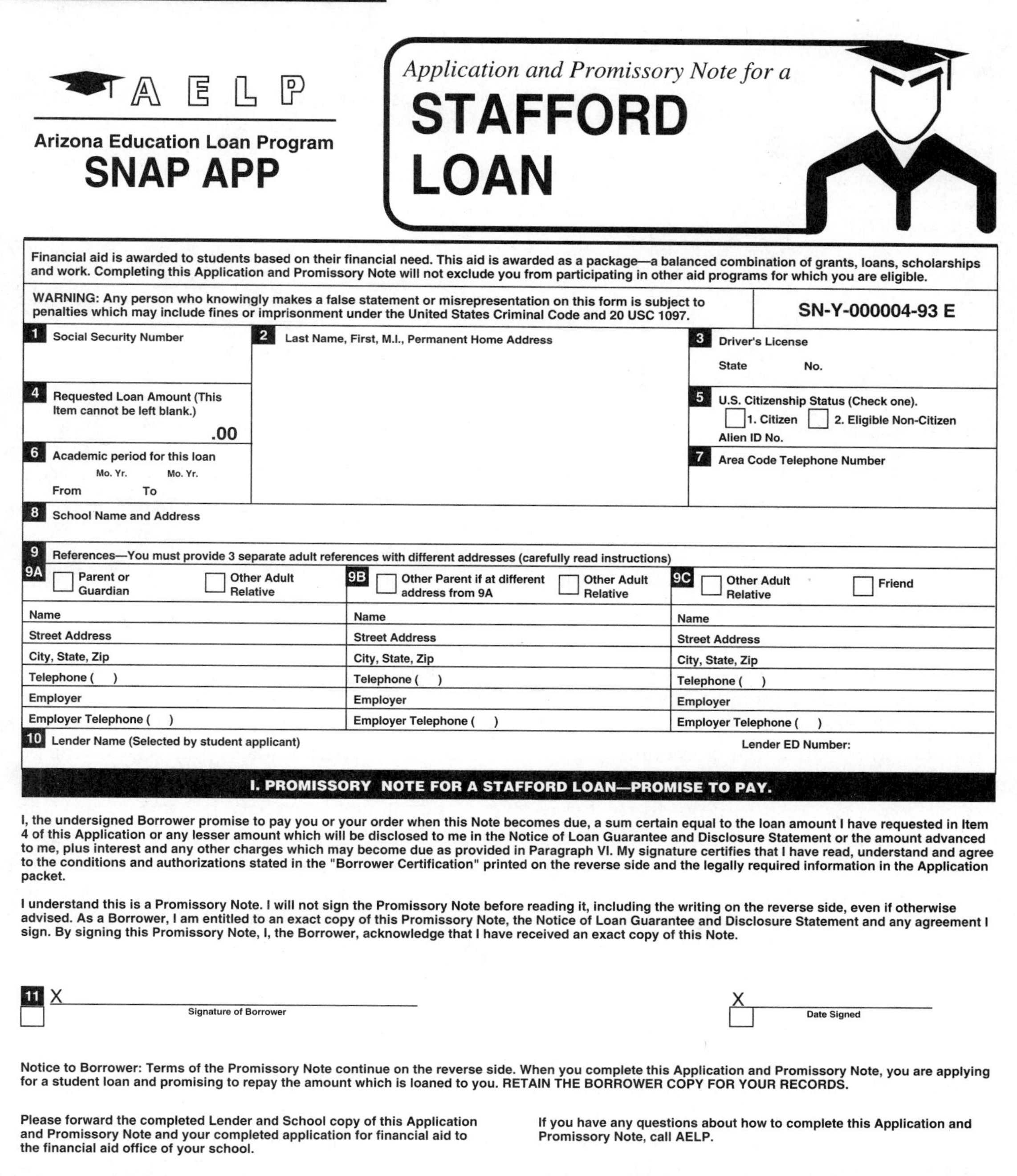

A E L P

Arizona Education Loan Program

SNAP APP

Application and Promissory Note for a

STAFFORD LOAN

Financial aid is awarded to students based on their financial need. This aid is awarded as a package—a balanced combination of grants, loans, scholarships and work. Completing this Application and Promissory Note will not exclude you from participating in other aid programs for which you are eligible.

WARNING: Any person who knowingly makes a false statement or misrepresentation on this form is subject to penalties which may include fines or imprisonment under the United States Criminal Code and 20 USC 1097.

SN-Y-000004-93 E

1 Social Security Number

2 Last Name, First, M.I., Permanent Home Address

3 Driver's License
State No.

4 Requested Loan Amount (This item cannot be left blank.)
.00

5 U.S. Citizenship Status (Check one).
☐ 1. Citizen ☐ 2. Eligible Non-Citizen
Alien ID No.

6 Academic period for this loan
Mo. Yr. Mo. Yr.
From To

7 Area Code Telephone Number

8 School Name and Address

9 References—You must provide 3 separate adult references with different addresses (carefully read instructions)

9A ☐ Parent or Guardian ☐ Other Adult Relative	9B ☐ Other Parent if at different address from 9A ☐ Other Adult Relative	9C ☐ Other Adult Relative ☐ Friend
Name	Name	Name
Street Address	Street Address	Street Address
City, State, Zip	City, State, Zip	City, State, Zip
Telephone ( )	Telephone ( )	Telephone ( )
Employer	Employer	Employer
Employer Telephone ( )	Employer Telephone ( )	Employer Telephone ( )

10 Lender Name (Selected by student applicant) Lender ED Number:

I. PROMISSORY NOTE FOR A STAFFORD LOAN—PROMISE TO PAY.

I, the undersigned Borrower promise to pay you or your order when this Note becomes due, a sum certain equal to the loan amount I have requested in Item 4 of this Application or any lesser amount which will be disclosed to me in the Notice of Loan Guarantee and Disclosure Statement or the amount advanced to me, plus interest and any other charges which may become due as provided in Paragraph VI. My signature certifies that I have read, understand and agree to the conditions and authorizations stated in the "Borrower Certification" printed on the reverse side and the legally required information in the Application packet.

I understand this is a Promissory Note. I will not sign the Promissory Note before reading it, including the writing on the reverse side, even if otherwise advised. As a Borrower, I am entitled to an exact copy of this Promissory Note, the Notice of Loan Guarantee and Disclosure Statement and any agreement I sign. By signing this Promissory Note, I, the Borrower, acknowledge that I have received an exact copy of this Note.

11 X ______________________ Signature of Borrower X ______________ Date Signed

Notice to Borrower: Terms of the Promissory Note continue on the reverse side. When you complete this Application and Promissory Note, you are applying for a student loan and promising to repay the amount which is loaned to you. RETAIN THE BORROWER COPY FOR YOUR RECORDS.

Please forward the completed Lender and School copy of this Application and Promissory Note and your completed application for financial aid to the financial aid office of your school.

If you have any questions about how to complete this Application and Promissory Note, call AELP.

Financial Shocks

College Financing 101: How to Pay for College

So you don't have sufficient resources to pay for a college education? Don't worry—you have plenty of company. As college costs rise, fewer people are paying cash up front for college. Planning ahead makes good sense, because you will probably need to use a combination of savings, current income, financial aid, and loans. On average, six out of 10 undergraduates at private two- and four-year colleges receive some form of need-based financial aid. The good news is that over $34 billion in federal, state, and institutional financial aid is available each year.

Financial aid comes in several forms: grants and scholarships, which are based on merit or financial need and do not have to be repaid; loans, which must be repaid, but often at low interest; and work-study programs, which provide jobs for students. There are also military programs such as the Reserve Officers' Training Corps (ROTC), which pay full tuition for two to four years plus a stipend in exchange for service after graduation.

The federal government provides 75 percent of all college funding, but most students end up combining federal and non-federal aid. The following is a review of non-federal sources of financial assistance:

GRANTS AND SCHOLARSHIPS

Most grants are offered by states, regions, colleges, and private organizations. If you look, you'll probably find a surprising number of resources in your own backyard. Talk to your high school counselor, read your local newspaper, and investigate local civic, religious, and professional groups. Many colleges award scholarships to attract students in underrepresented groups (determined by such factors as cultural background, gender, and residence). There are also obscure, highly specialized awards: if you play the bagpipes, you are eligible for a scholarship at the College of Wooster in Ohio, and if you live in Wheelock, Vermont, you qualify for an award from Dartmouth College. Scholarships offered by private foundations are catalogued in published directories such as *The Scholarship Book* by Daniel Cassidy (Prentice-Hall), and *Free Money For College* by Laurie Blum (Facts On File).

---

at the end of which payment in full (principal plus interest) is due. They generally have maturities ranging from 30 days to a year; rarely do these loans run for more than a year. Sometimes single-payment loans are made to finance purchases or pay bills when the cash to be used for repayment is known to be forthcoming in the near future; in this case, they serve as a form of **interim financing.** In other situations, single-payment loans are used by consumers who want to avoid being strapped with monthly installment payments and choose instead to make one large payment at the end of the loan. Often these loans are negotiated on short notice in order to meet some unexpected need.

Installment loans are repaid in a series of fixed, scheduled payments rather than in one lump sum. The payments are almost always set up on a monthly basis, with each installment being made up partly of principal and partly of interest. For example, out of a $75 monthly payment, $60 might be credited to principal and the balance to interest. These loans are typically made to finance the purchase of a good or service for which current resources are inadequate. The repayment period can run from six months to six years or more.

Installment loans have become a way of life for many consumers. They are popular because they provide a convenient way to "buy now and pay later" in fixed monthly installments that can be readily incorporated into a family budget. The process of using installment loans to finance purchases is often referred to as "buying on time."

Fixed or Variable Rate. The majority of consumer loans are made at fixed rates of interest—that is, the interest rate charged (as well as the monthly payment) remains the same over the life of the obligation. However, variable-rate loans are also being made with increasing frequency, especially on *longer-term installment loans*. As with an adjustable-rate home mortgage, the rate of inter-

LOANS

Although government loans generally carry the lowest rates, you can finance your education through a private lender. One of the largest is Knight College Resources, which offers the Achiever Loan; it can cover up to the full cost of a college education and must be repaid over 15 years. If you prefer to spread payments over a longer period, consider the Excel loan from the New England Education Loan Marketing Corporation (Nellie Mae). Repayment schedules depend on the amount of the loan; if you borrow over $20,000, you can pay it off over 20 years.

For many people, borrowing against their own resources may be a better bet. Home-equity loans are the most popular, because interest on the debt is tax-deductible. You can establish a home-equity line of credit and draw on it for college payments as needed. You can also borrow against your 401(k), pension, or profit-sharing plan. Be careful, though: the interest is not tax-deductible, and the loan must be paid back within five years. You will also be in hot water if you lose your job or quit while the loan is outstanding.

Other resources to tap include parents' and child's savings. Many students contribute toward the cost of their education by working during the summer and the school year, or living at home and commuting to school.

In some cases, it's better to borrow temporarily rather than dip into your assets. If your investment portfolio is earning 8 percent or 9 percent interest, take out student loans with a lower rate and let your investments grow; at the end of senior year, use the accumulated profits to pay off the loans.

Many colleges offer their own finance programs, such as a deferred payment plan or a discount rate for multiple siblings. You may be able to pay each year's tuition, room, and board in ten equal payments automatically deducted from your bank account, with no interest charged, or prepay the total undergraduate tuition at the rate in effect when the student enters (this generally doesn't cover room, board, or other fees).

Clearly, you can find many ways to pay for college. Start early, perform an organized, thorough search, and explore all viable possibilities. The more you try, the more likely you will be to get aid.

Sources: Adapted from John Beaver, "Help Yourself To College Aid," *Parade* Magazine, November 6, 1994, pp. 14, 16; B. J. Towe, "Coming Up With College Funds—Fast!" *Better Homes and Gardens,* October 1994, pp. 36–40; Grace W. Weinstein, "Here Come the College Bills. Now What?" *Kiplinger's Personal Finance Magazine,* August 1994, pp. 69–71.

est charged on such credit changes every 6 to 12 months in keeping with prevailing market conditions. If market interest rates go up, the rate of interest on the loan goes up accordingly, as does the monthly loan payment. These loans have periodic adjustment dates (6 to 12 months apart), at which time the interest rate and monthly payment are adjusted as necessary. Once an adjustment is made, the new rate remains in effect until the next adjustment date (sometimes the amount of the payments remains the same, but the number of payments changes). Many variable rate loans have caps on the maximum increase per adjustment period, and also over the life of the loan.

Variable rates can also be used with single-payment loans, but the mechanics are a bit different. That is, the rate charged is usually pegged to the *prime rate,* or some other "base" rate. It's meant to be reflective of the bank's cost of funds and moves in response to fundamental credit conditions in the market. Changes in the prime rate are widely reported in the media because of the wide-spread impact the prime has on the cost of borrowing.

Here's how it's used to set the interest rate on a single-payment loan. Instead of putting a single, specific rate on a loan, it might be quoted at, say, prime plus 3 points; under these conditions, if prime is 8 percent, the borrower starts with a rate

interim financing The use of a single-payment loan to finance a purchase or pay bills in situations where either the funds to be used for repayment are known to be forthcoming in the near future or permanent financing is to be arranged.

installment loan A loan that is repaid in a series of fixed, scheduled payments rather than a lump sum.

of interest of 8 + 3 = 11 percent. Then, if the prime rate changes, the rate of interest on the loan changes automatically, except that in this case the adjustment is made *immediately* (there are usually no adjustment dates with single-payment, variable-rate loans). The loan will then carry a new rate of interest that will remain in effect until the next change. At maturity, interest charges at the different rates will be totaled and added to the principal to determine the size of the (single) loan payment. Variable-rate loans are desirable *if interest rates are expected to fall* over the course of the loan; in contrast, fixed-rate loans are preferable *if interest rates are expected to rise*.

Regardless of whether the loans are fixed or variable, their cost tends to vary with market conditions. Generally, when interest rates move up or down in the market, so will the cost of consumer loans. Inevitably, there are going to be times when *the cost of credit simply becomes too high to justify borrowing* as a way of making major purchases. So when market rates start climbing, you should ask yourself whether the cost is really worth it; financially, you may be far better off delaying the purchase until rates come down.

WHERE CAN YOU GET CONSUMER LOANS?

Consumer loans can be obtained from a number of sources, including commercial banks, consumer finance companies, credit unions, savings and loan associations, sales finance companies, life insurance companies, possibly even pawnshops, or friends and relatives. *Commercial banks* dominate the field and provide nearly half of all consumer loans. Behind banks are *consumer finance companies* and then *credit unions;* together these three financial institutions account for about 75 percent of the consumer loan market! Interestingly, S&Ls are not much of a force in this market, and they're becoming even less so with the passage of time. The selection of a lender often depends on both the rate of interest being charged and the ease with which the loan can be negotiated. Exhibit 7.2 provides a summary of the types of loans, lending policies, costs, and services offered at the major providers of consumer loans.

Commercial Banks. Because they offer various types of loans at attractive rates of interest, commercial banks are a popular source of consumer loans. One nice thing about commercial banks is that they typically charge lower rates than most other lenders, in large part because they take only the best credit risks and are able to obtain relatively inexpensive funds from their depositors. The demand for their loans is generally high, and they can be selective in making consumer loans. Commercial banks usually lend only to customers with good credit ratings who can readily demonstrate an ability to make repayment in accordance with the specified terms. They also give preference to loan applicants who are account holders. The fact that an applicant is already a good customer of the bank enhances his or her chances of being approved for the requested financing. Although banks prefer to make loans secured by some type of collateral, they also make unsecured loans to their better customers. The interest rate charged on a bank loan may be affected by the loan's size, terms, and whether it is secured by some type of collateral.

Consumer Finance Companies. Sometimes called *small loan companies,* **consumer finance companies** make secured and unsecured (signature) loans to qualified individuals. These companies do not accept deposits but obtain funds from their stockholders and through open market borrowing. Because they do not have the inexpensive sources of funds that banks and other deposit-type institutions do, their interest rates are generally quite high. The actual rates charged by consumer finance companies are regulated by interest rate ceilings (or usury laws) set by the states in which they operate. The maximum allowable interest rate may vary with the size of the loan, and the state regulatory authorities may also limit the length of the repayment period. Loans made by consumer finance companies typically are for $5,000 or less and are secured by some type of collateral. Repayment is required on an installment basis, usually over a period of five years or less.

Consumer finance companies generally make small loans to high-risk borrowers. Of course, these loans are quite costly, but they may be the only alternative for people with poor credit ratings. Some people are attracted to consumer finance companies because of the ease with which they can obtain loans. Due to the high rates of interest charged, individuals should consider this source only after exhausting all others.

Credit Unions. Only members can obtain installment and single-payment loans from credit unions. Because they are nonprofit organizations with minimal operating costs, credit unions charge relatively low rates on their loans.

They make either unsecured or secured loans, depending on the size and type of loan being requested. The maximum allowable size of a loan is often set by regulatory agencies. In addition, the directors of a credit union frequently set their own in-house loan limits. Generally speaking, membership in a credit union provides the most attractive borrowing opportunities available, since their interest rates and borrowing requirements usually are more favorable than other sources of consumer loans. An added convenience of a credit union loan is that loan payments can often be deducted directly from payroll checks.

Savings and Loan Associations. Savings and loan associations (as well as savings banks) primarily make mortgage loans. However, they are also permitted to make loans on such consumer durables as automobiles, televisions, refrigerators, and other appliances. In addition, they can make certain types of home improvement and mobile-home loans, as well as some personal and educational loans. Among other things, financial deregulation has enabled S&Ls to enter the consumer loan market. Since 1982, federally chartered S&Ls have been allowed to invest a portion of their assets in consumer loans, although they have pulled back from these loans, as recent "S&L Bailout" legislation mandates that they direct more of their lending to home mortgages. As a rule, the rates of interest on consumer loans at S&Ls are fairly close to the rates charged by commercial banks, though if anything, they tend to be a bit more expensive. Like their banking counterparts, the rates charged on specific loans will, in the final analysis, depend on such factors as the type and purpose of the loan, the duration and type of repayment, and the overall creditworthiness of the borrower.

Sales Finance Companies. Businesses that sell relatively expensive items—such as automobiles, furniture, and appliances—often provide installment financing to purchasers of their products. Because dealers cannot afford to tie up their funds in installment contracts, they sell them to a **sales finance company** for cash. This procedure is often referred to as "selling paper," since merchants in effect sell their loans to a third party. When the sales finance company purchases these notes, customers are usually notified to make payments directly to it.

The largest sales finance organizations are the **captive finance companies** owned by manufacturers of big-ticket items—automobiles and appliances. General Motors Acceptance Corporation (GMAC) and General Electric Credit Corporation (GECC) are just two examples of captive finance companies that purchase the installment loans made by dealers of their products. Also, most commercial banks act as sales finance companies by buying paper from auto dealers and other businesses. The cost of financing through a sales finance company is generally a little higher than the rates charged by banks and S&Ls, particularly when you let the dealer do all the work in arranging the financing (dealers normally get a cut on the finance income, so it's obviously to their advantage to secure as *high* a rate of interest as possible). However, since the early 1980s, auto makers have been using interest rates on new-car loans as a marketing tool. They do this by dropping the rate of interest on car loans *(for selected models)* to levels that are well below the market—for example, not long ago, Ford and GM were offering 2.9 percent, two-year financing on some of their cars. In this way the auto manufacturers use these loan rates (along with rebates) to stimulate sales by keeping the cost of buying a new car down. Clearly, cutting the cost of borrowing for a new car can result in big savings!

consumer finance company A firm that makes secured and unsecured personal loans to qualified individuals; also called a *small loan company*.

sales finance company A firm that purchases notes drawn up by sellers of certain types of merchandise, typically big-ticket items.

captive finance company A sales finance company that is owned by a manufacturer of big-ticket merchandise. GMAC is a captive finance company.

EXHIBIT 7.2

The Major Sources of Consumer Loans

Banks, finance companies, and other financial institutions provide a full range of consumer credit to their customers. These institutions follow a variety of lending policies and lend money at different rates of interest.

	Commercial Banks	Consumer Finance Companies
Types of Loans	■ Single-payment loans ■ Installment loans ■ Passbook loans ■ Check-credit plans ■ Credit card loans ■ Second mortgages ■ Education loans	■ Installment loans ■ Second mortgages
Lending Policies	■ Seek customers with established credit history ■ Often require collateral or security ■ Prefer to deal in large loans such as auto, home improvement, and modernization, with the exception of credit card and check-credit plans ■ Determine repayment schedules according to purpose of loan ■ Vary credit rates according to the type of credit, time period, customer's credit history, and security offered ■ May require several days to process a new credit application	■ Often lend to consumers without established credit history ■ Often make unsecured loans ■ Often vary rates according to size of loan balance ■ Offer a variety of repayment schedules ■ Make a higher percentage of small loans than other lenders ■ Maximum loan size limited by law ■ Process applications quickly, frequently same day as application is made
Costs	■ Lower than some lenders because they: — Take fewer credit risks — Lend depositors' money, a relatively inexpensive source of funds — Deal primarily in large loans, which yield larger dollar income without raising administration costs	■ Higher than most because they: — Take greater risks — Must borrow and pay interest on money to lend — Deal frequently in small loans, which are costly to make and yield a small income
Services	■ Offer several different types of consumer credit plans ■ May offer financial counseling ■ Handle credit transactions confidentially	■ Provide credit promptly ■ Make loans to pay off accumulated debts willingly ■ Design repayment schedules to fit the borrower's income ■ Usually offer financial counseling ■ Handle credit transactions confidentially

Life Insurance Companies. Life insurance policyholders can often obtain loans from their insurance companies. Certain types of policies not only provide death benefits but also have a savings function, in which case they can be used as collateral for loans. *(Be careful with these loans, however, as they could involve a tax penalty if certain conditions are not met.* A detailed discussion of life insurance is presented in Chapter 8.) Life insurance companies are required by law to make loans against the **cash values**—the amount of accumulated savings—of certain types of life insurance policies. The rate of interest on this type of loan is stated on the policy, and it used to be set as low as 5 or 6 percent. The newer policies, however, carry loan rates that aren't set until the loans are made; that usually means borrowing money at or near prevailing market rates. While you will be charged interest for as long as the policy loan is outstanding, these loans do not have repayment dates—in other words, you do not have to pay them back. The reason for this is when you take out a loan against the cash value of your life insurance policy, you are really borrowing from yourself. Therefore, the amount of the loan outstanding, plus any accrued interest, will be deducted from the amount of cov-

EXHIBIT 7.2
Continued

Credit Unions	Savings and Loan Associations	Life Insurance Companies
■ Installment loans ■ Share draft credit plans ■ Credit card loans ■ Second mortgages	■ Installment loans ■ Home improvement loans ■ Education loans ■ Savings account loans ■ Second mortgages	■ Single or partial payment loans
■ Lend to members only ■ Make unsecured loans ■ May require collateral or cosigner for loans over a specified amount ■ May require payroll deductions to pay off loan ■ May submit large loan applications to a committee of members for approval ■ Offer a variety of repayment schedules	■ Will lend to all creditworthy individuals ■ Often require collateral ■ Loan rates vary depending on size of loan, length of payment, and security involved ■ As a result of the "S&L Bailout," are becoming less of a force in the consumer loan field	■ Lend on cash value of life insurance policy ■ No date or penalty on repayment ■ Deduct amount owed from value of policy benefit if death or other maturity occurs before repayment
■ Lower than most because they: — Take fewer credit risks — Lend money deposited by members, which is less expensive than borrowed money — Often receive free office space and supplies from sponsoring organization — Are managed by members whose services in most cases are donated — Enjoy federal income tax exemptions	■ Lower than some lenders because they: — Lend depositors' money, a relatively inexpensive source of funds — Secure most loans by savings accounts, real estate, or some other asset	■ Lower than many because they: — Take no risk — Pay no collection costs — Secure loans by cash value of policy
■ Design repayment schedules to fit borrower's income ■ Generally provide credit life insurance without extra charge ■ May offer financial counseling ■ Handle credit transactions confidentially	■ Often offer financial counseling ■ Specialize in mortgages and other housing-related loans ■ Handle credit transactions confidentially	■ Permit repayment at any time ■ Handle credit transactions confidentially

erage provided by the policy. The chief danger in life insurance loans is that they do not have a firm maturity date; consequently, borrowers may lack the motivation to repay them.

Friends and Relatives. Sometimes a close friend or relative will be willing to lend you money. In many cases, such loans are attractive because little or no interest is charged. The terms will, of course, vary depending on the financial needs of the borrower, but they should be specified in some type of loan agreement that states the costs, conditions, and maturity date of the loan, as well as the obligations of both borrower and lender. Not only does a written loan agreement reduce opportunities for disagreement and unhappiness, it also protects both borrower and lender should either of them die or other unexpected events occur. Still, *given the potential for disagreement and conflict inherent in this type of arrangement, borrowing*

cash value (of life insurance) An accumulation of savings in an insurance policy that can be used as a source of loan collateral.

Issues in Money Management

Take the Risk Out of Family Loans

When friends and family ask you to loan them money, how can you say no? Many people can't or don't want to. Indeed, family loans frequently provide down payments on first homes, seed money for new businesses, and emergency help during a financial crisis.

Although stories abound about relationships souring because of unpaid loans, many people are actually profiting financially from lending money to relatives—especially with interest rates on savings accounts at a two-decade low. There are also emotional rewards—loans give parents a way to help out their children in the here and now, rather than from the hereafter.

Nevertheless, such loans are a risky endeavor: accountants estimate that between 20 percent and 50 percent of loans between friends and relatives are never repaid, compared to the approximately 4 percent default rate on credit card debt.

The bottom line is that even if your borrowers are trustworthy, you must structure the loan carefully. Here are some guidelines:

1. **Lend only money you can afford to give away.** Be prepared, both financially and emotionally, for the worst-case scenario: that the loan won't be repaid. That way, if the worst indeed happens, you can call the loan a gift and go on with your life.
2. **Make the arrangement businesslike.** If friends or family are treating you like a bank, don't hesitate to act like one. Draw up a formal promissory note, on your own or with the help of an attorney. You can find samples at most banks or office-supply stores. The terms should be specific and agreed to by both parties. A businesslike agreement makes the transaction more formal and serious and alerts the borrower that repayment is expected. Another good reason to document your loan: if your relative does default, you'll need an enforceable loan document to deduct the loss on your income taxes.
3. **Charge interest if the loan won't be paid back immediately.** This is only fair to you. The best loans for both borrowers and lenders carry an interest rate higher than the lenders could find on savings instruments but lower than the borrowers could obtain from institutional lenders. Most people try to do their relatives a favor by charging a lower interest rate. Don't charge an unreasonably low rate, though; to discourage this practice, the IRS sets a minimum for what you must charge called the applicable federal rate (AFR), which fluctuates monthly. If you charge less than the AFR, you must pay tax on the interest you would have received had you charged the AFR.
4. **Both parties must understand that this is a loan, not a gift.** If this is not spelled out, the borrower may misinterpret the lender's repayment expectations or fail to give them priority; while one hears, "Pay me when you can," the other hears, "The loan will be paid off soon." A clear statement that you expect to be repaid will go a long way to ensure you will receive the money, experts say. Be specific about repayment terms, establishing weekly or monthly payments or a lump sum agreement.

Lastly, always remember that giving a loan is more than just lending money: it becomes an emotional issue that has the potential of threatening your closest relationships. A formal agreement will help you set some boundaries and prevent any misunderstandings you may later regret.

Sources: Adapted from Andrew Feinberg, "A Debt in the Family: Taking the Peril out of Playing Banker to Your Kin," *Worth*, June, 1994, pp. 119–120; Beth Kobliner, "Make Money Lending to Relatives," *Money*, February, 1994, p. 21; Alina Matas, "Lending Money to Family or Pals? Get It Down in Writing, Tactfully," *San Diego Union-Tribune*, July 11, 1994, p. C-3.

from friends or relatives is not advisable, and should be seriously considered only when there are no other viable alternatives, or perhaps if the terms of credit are so much better than those available from the more traditional sources. Indeed, as the *Issues in Money Management* box above suggests, a loan to or from a friend or family member is far more than a run-of-the-mill banking transaction: the interest is emotional, and the risks are the relationship itself!

As a last resort, you might even want to consider a *pawnshop*—if you have some sort of valuable asset (like a piece of jewelry, a musical instrument, or a CD player) that you can leave as collateral. Such establishments tend to proliferate during economically tough times, as an increasing number of people turn to them as a source of "financing." As long as you have an asset to pawn, you may be able to obtain a short-term, single payment loan from one of these shops. But bear in mind that the amount of money you will receive is likely to be only a small fraction of the perceived resale value of the asset you pawn. Moreover, the rate of interest charged on the loan can be extremely high, and the pawned asset can be sold if you do not repay the loan within the designated period of time.

Concept Check

7-1. Discuss the difference between *consumer loans* and open-account credit.

7-2. List and briefly discuss the five major reasons for borrowing money through a consumer loan.

7-3. Identify several different types of federally sponsored student loan programs. Briefly note some of the basic features of these programs and how they differ from regular consumer loans. As a college student, what aspects of these student loan programs appeal to you the most?

7-4. Define and differentiate between (a) fixed and variable rate loans and (b) a *single-payment loan* and an *installment loan*.

7-5. Compare the consumer lending activities of (a) *consumer finance companies* and (b) *sales finance companies*. Describe a *captive finance company*.

7-6. Discuss the role of (a) credit unions and (b) savings and loan associations in consumer lending. Point out any similarities or differences in their lending activities. How do they compare to commercial banks?

MANAGING YOUR CREDIT

LG3

The planned use of a consumer loan can be a good way to meet a given financial goal, as long as you carefully evaluate why you are borrowing and whether your current budget is adequate to repay the loan. What are some other factors and loan features to consider when choosing a loan? Give some thought to this question before proceeding.

Borrowing money to make major acquisitions—and, in general, using consumer loans—is a sound and perfectly legitimate way to conduct your financial affairs. Meeting a major financial goal by buying on credit can be worked into your network of financial plans, while servicing the debt can be factored into your monthly cash budget. Doing it this way certainly is far superior to borrowing in a haphazard manner, giving little or no consideration to debt repayment. When borrowing is well thought out in advance and *full consideration is given not only to the need for the asset or item in question but also to the repayment of the ensuing credit,* sound credit management is the result. And sound credit management underlies effective personal financial planning.

From a financial planning perspective, you should ask yourself two questions when considering the use of a consumer loan: (1) Does making this acquisition fit into your financial plans, and (2) does the required debt service on the loan fit into your monthly cash budget? If the expenditure in question will seriously jeopardize your financial plans and/or if the repayment of the loan is likely to place an undue strain on your cash budget, you should definitely reconsider the purchase! Perhaps it can be postponed, or you can liquidate some assets in order to come up with more down payment, or you may even have to alter some other area of your financial plan in order to work the expenditure in. Whatever route you choose, the key point is to make sure that it will be fully compatible with your financial plans and cash budget *before* the loan is taken out and the money spent.

SHOPPING FOR LOANS

Once you have decided to use credit, it is equally important that you shop around and evaluate the various costs and terms available. You may think that the only thing you need do to make a sound credit decision is determine which source offers the lowest finance charge. This could not be further from the truth—for as we'll see below, finance charges are just one of the factors to consider when shopping for a loan.

Finance charges. What's it going to cost me? For a lot of people, that's one of the first things they want to know when taking out a loan. And that's appropriate, because borrowers should know what they're going to have to pay to get the money. Lenders are required by law to clearly state all finance charges and other loan fees. Find out the effective (or true) *rate* of interest you're going to have to pay on the loan, and whether the loan carries a fixed or variable rate. Obviously, *so long as everything else is equal,* it's in your best interest to secure the least expensive loan. In this regard, ask the lender what the *annual rate of interest* on the loan will be, since it's easier (and far more relevant) to compare percentage rates on alternative borrowing arrangements than the dollar amount of the loan charges. This rate of interest is known as the *APR* (annual percentage rate) and includes not only the basic cost of money, but also any additional fees that might be required on the loan (APR will be more fully discussed later). Also, if it's a variable-rate loan, find out what the interest rate is pegged to, how many "points" are added to the base rate, how often the loan rate can be changed, and if rate caps exist. Just as important, how will the lender make the periodic adjustments—will the *size* of the monthly payment change, or the *number* of monthly payments? To avoid any future shock, it's best to find these things out before the loan is made.

Loan maturity. Try to make sure that the size and number of payments will fit comfortably into your spending and savings plans. As a rule, the cost of credit increases with the length of the repayment period. Thus, to lower your cost, you should consider shortening the loan maturity—but only to the point where doing so will not place an unnecessary strain on your cash flow. For while a shorter maturity may reduce the cost of the loan, it will also increase the size of the monthly loan payment. Indeed, finding a monthly loan payment that you will be comfortable with is a critical dimension of sound credit management. Fortunately, the personal computer provides an effective way of evaluating different loan configurations. Altering the loan maturity is just one way of coming up with an affordable monthly payment; with the aid of a personal computer, you can quickly run through all sorts of alternatives to find the one that will best fit your monthly budget.

Total cost of the transaction. When comparison shopping for credit, always look at both the total cost of the price of the item purchased *and* the price of the credit. Retailers often manipulate both sticker prices and interest rates, so you really will not know what kind of deal you are getting until you look at the total cost of the transaction. Along this line, comparing *monthly payments* is a good way to get a handle on total cost. It is a simple matter to compare total costs: Just add the amount put down on the purchase to the total of all the monthly loan payments; other things being equal, the one with the lowest total is the one you should pick.

Collateral. Make sure that you know up front what collateral (if any) you will have to pledge on the loan and what you stand to lose in case you default on your payments. Actually, if it makes no difference to you and if it is not too inconvenient, using collateral makes sense, since it may result in *lower* finance charges—perhaps half a percentage point or so.

Other credit considerations. In addition to the above guidelines, other questions that you should address include the following: Can you choose *a payment date* that will be compatible with your spending patterns? Can you obtain the loan *promptly and conveniently?* What are the charges for late payments, and are they reasonable? Will you receive a refund on credit charges if you prepay your loan? Or will you have to pay prepayment penalties? Taking the time to look around for the best credit deal will pay off not only in reducing the cost of such debt but also in keeping the burden of credit in line with your cash budget and financial plans. In the long run, you are the one who has the most to gain (or lose). Thus, *you* *should see to it that the consumer debt you undertake does in fact have the desired effects on your financial condition.*

KEEPING TRACK OF YOUR CREDIT

To stay abreast of your financial condition, it is a good idea to periodically take inventory of the consumer debt you have outstanding. You should do this a minimum of once a year, and ideally every three or four months. To take inventory of what you owe, simply prepare a list of all your outstanding consumer debt. Include *everything except your home mortgage*—installment loans, single-payment loans, credit cards, revolving credit lines, overdraft protection lines, and home equity credit lines.

You might find Worksheet 7.1 helpful in preparing a list of your debts. To use it, simply list the current monthly payment and the latest balance due for each type of consumer credit outstanding; then, total both columns to see how much you are paying each month and how large a debt load you have built up. Hopefully, when all the numbers have been totaled up, you will not be surprised to learn just how much you really do owe.

A way to quickly assess your debt position is to compute your *debt safety ratio* (we looked at this ratio in Chapter 6) by dividing the total monthly payments (from the worksheet) by your monthly take-home pay. If 20 percent or more of your take-home pay is going to monthly credit payments, you are relying too heavily on credit; in contrast, if your debt safety ratio works out to 10 percent or less, you are in a strong credit position. *Keeping track of your credit and holding the amount of outstanding debt to a reasonable level is the surest way to maintain your creditworthiness.*

Concept Check

7-7. What two questions should be answered before taking out a consumer loan? Explain.

7-8. List and briefly discuss the different factors that you should consider when shopping for a loan. How would you determine the total cost of the transaction?

SINGLE-PAYMENT LOANS

FPPC LG4

The cost of a single-payment loan depends not only on the stated rate of interest, but also on the type of interest used to calculate finance charges. In addition to the cost of the loan, what other loan provisions—like the need for collateral, the maturity of the loan, and the existence of a prepayment penalty—would be important to you? Stop to think about this question before going on.

A single-payment loan differs from other loans in that it is repaid in full with a single payment on a given due date. The payment usually consists of principal and all interest charges. Sometimes, however, interim interest payments may have to be made (for example, every quarter), in which case the payment at maturity is made up of principal plus any unpaid interest. Single-payment loans can be secured or unsecured and can be taken out for just about any purpose, from buying a new car to paying for a vacation. They are perhaps most useful when the funds needed for a given purchase or transaction are temporarily unavailable but are expected to be forthcoming in the near future. By helping you cope with a temporary cash shortfall, these loans can serve as a form of interim financing until more permanent arrangements can be made.

IMPORTANT LOAN FEATURES

The first thing you have to do when applying for either a single-payment or installment loan is submit a **loan application,** an example of which is shown in Exhibit 7.3 on pages 290-291. Basically, the loan application provides the lending institution with information about the purpose of the loan, whether it will be secured or unsecured, and the

loan application An application that provides a lender with information about the purpose of the requested loan, whether it will be secured or unsecured, and the applicant's financial condition.

WORKSHEET 7.1

Tracking Your Consumer Debt

A worksheet like this allows you to keep track of your outstanding credit along with your monthly debt service requirements. Such information is a major component of sound credit management.

AN INVENTORY OF CONSUMER DEBT

Name ______________________ **Date** ______________

Type of Consumer Debt	**Creditor**	**Current Monthly Payment***	**Latest Balance Due**
Auto loans	1.	$	$
	2.		
	3.		
Education loans	1.		
	2.		
Personal installment loans	1.		
	2.		
Home improvement loan			
Other installment loans	1.		
	2.		
Single-payment loans	1.		
	2.		
Credit cards (retail charge cards, bank cards, T&E cards, etc.)	1.		
	2.		
	3.		
	4.		
	5.		
	6.		
	7.		
Overdraft protection line			
Personal line of credit			
Home equity credit line			
Loan on life insurance			
Margin loan from broker			
Other loans	1.		
	2.		
	3.		
	Totals	$	$

$$\text{Debt safety ratio} = \frac{\text{Total monthly payments}}{\text{Monthly take-home pay}} \times 100 = \frac{\$\_\_\_\_}{\$\_\_\_\_} \times 100 = \_\_\_\_\%$$

*Leave the space blank if there is *no* monthly payment required on a loan (e.g., as with a single-payment or education loan).

financial condition of the borrower. The loan officer uses this document, along with other information (such as a credit report from the local credit bureau and income verification), to determine whether or not you should be granted the loan—here again, some type of *credit scoring* (as discussed in Chapter 6) may be used to make the decision. As part of the loan application process, you should also consider the various features of the debt, the three most important of which are loan collateral, loan maturity, and loan repayment.

Loan Collateral. Most single-payment loans are secured by certain specified assets. For *collateral,* lenders prefer to accept only items they feel will be readily marketable at a price sufficiently high to cover the principal portion of the loan—for example, an automobile, jewelry, or stocks and bonds. If a loan is obtained to purchase some personal asset, that asset may be used to secure it. In most cases, lenders do not take physical possession of the collateral but file a **lien,** which is a legal claim that permits them to liquidate the collateral in order to satisfy the loan in the event of borrower default. The lien is filed in the county courthouse and is a matter of public record. If borrowers maintain possession or title to *movable* property—such as cars, TVs, and jewelry—the instrument that gives the lenders title to the property in the event of default is called a **chattel mortgage.** If lenders hold title to the collateral—or actually take possession of it, as in the case of stocks and bonds—the agreement giving them the right to sell these items in case of default is a **collateral note.**

Loan Maturity. As indicated earlier, the maturity, or term, on a single-payment loan usually extends for a period of one year or less and very rarely goes out to two years or longer. When you request a single-payment loan, you should be sure that its term is long enough to allow you to receive the money needed for repayment but not any longer than necessary. Don't stretch the maturity out too far, since the dollar amount of the finance charges paid increases with time. Because the loan is retired in a single payment, the lender must be assured that you will be able to repay it even if certain unexpected events occur in the future. The term of your single-payment loan therefore must be reconciled with your budget, as well as your ability to pay. If the money you plan to use for repayment will be received periodically over the term of the loan, an installment type loan may be more suitable.

Loan Repayment. The repayment of a single-payment loan is expected to take place at a single point in time: on its maturity date. Occasionally the funds needed to repay this type of loan will be received prior to maturity. Depending on the lender, the borrower might be able to repay the loan early and thereby reduce the finance charges. Credit unions often permit early repayment of these loans with reduced finance charges. Commercial banks and other single-payment lenders, however, may not accept early repayments; or if they do, they will charge a **prepayment penalty** on them. This penalty normally amounts to a set percentage of the interest that would have been paid over the remaining life of the loan. The Truth in Lending Act requires lenders to disclose in the loan agreement whether or not, and in what amount, prepayment penalties are charged on a single-payment loan. *A borrower should understand this information prior to signing a loan agreement.*

Occasionally an individual will borrow money using a single-payment loan only to discover that he or she is short of money when the loan comes due—after all, making one big loan payment can cause a real strain on one's cash flow. Should this happen to you, don't just let the payment go past due; rather, *inform the lender in advance so that a partial payment, loan extension, or some other arrangement can be made.*

lien A legal claim that permits the lender, in the event of borrower default, to liquidate the items serving as collateral in order to satisfy the obligation.

chattel mortgage A mortgage on personal property given as security for the payment of an obligation.

collateral note A legal note that gives the lender the right to sell collateral in the event of the borrower's default on the obligation.

prepayment penalty A penalty sometimes charged by a financial institution for advance payment of a loan.

EXHIBIT 7.3

A Bank Loan Application

The loan application contains information about the person(s) applying for the loan, including source(s) of income, current debt load, and a brief record of employment.

WELLS FARGO BANK

INSTALLMENT LOAN APPLICATION

You may apply for an individual account regardless of your marital status. This application is:

☐ In your name only, or ☐ Joint with your spouse, or ☐ Joint with ______ (NAME), who is not your spouse.*

***Each of you must complete a separate application as if applying for separate credit. Submit both together.**

MARITAL STATUS: ☐ Married **(If married, complete information about your spouse)**
☐ Separated ☐ Unmarried (includes Single, Divorced, and Widowed)
List ages of all persons dependent on you for financial support: ______ AGE AGE AGE AGE

TYPE OF LOAN: ☐ Auto ☐ Personal ☐ Other (list) ______
Purpose of Loan: ______
Loan: $ ______ for ______ months. I prefer my payment due date to be ______.

APPLICANT / SPOUSE

APPLICANT	SPOUSE
FIRST NAME / MIDDLE INITIAL / LAST NAME / JR./SR.	FIRST NAME / MIDDLE INITIAL / LAST NAME / JR./SR.
SOCIAL SECURITY NO. ___ ___ ___ - ___ ___ - ___ ___ ___ ___	SOCIAL SECURITY NO. ___ ___ ___ - ___ ___ - ___ ___ ___ ___
DATE OF BIRTH Mo. / Day / Yr. · DRIVER'S LICENSE NUMBER · STATE	DATE OF BIRTH Mo. / Day / Yr. · DRIVER'S LICENSE NUMBER · STATE

STREET ADDRESS	TIME AT PRESENT RESIDENCE Yrs. ____ Mos. ____
CITY · STATE · ZIP CODE	HOME PHONE ( )
☐OWN ☐RENT ☐OTHER if other, please explain:	MONTHLY PAYMENT $
PREVIOUS RESIDENCE (if at current residence less than 3 years)	
CITY · STATE · ZIP CODE	TIME AT PREVIOUS RESIDENCE Yrs. ____ Mos. ____
NAME OF NEAREST RELATIVE NOT LIVING WITH YOU	HOME PHONE ( )
ADDRESS	
List any other names under which you or your spouse have obtained credit:	

APPLICANT'S EMPLOYMENT / SPOUSE'S EMPLOYMENT

APPLICANT'S EMPLOYMENT	SPOUSE'S EMPLOYMENT
CURRENT EMPLOYER · WORK PHONE ( )	CURRENT EMPLOYER · WORK PHONE ( )
EMPLOYER'S ADDRESS Street City State Zip	EMPLOYER'S ADDRESS Street City State Zip
POSITION · SELF-EMPLOYED Yes☐ No☐ · TIME THERE Yrs. ____ Mos. ____	POSITION · SELF-EMPLOYED Yes☐ No☐ · TIME THERE Yrs. ____ Mos. ____
PREVIOUS EMPLOYER (If at current employer less than 3 years)	PREVIOUS EMPLOYER (If at current employer less than 3 years)
POSITION · TIME THERE Yrs. ____ Mos. ____	POSITION · TIME THERE Yrs. ____ Mos. ____

APPLICANT'S INCOME / SPOUSE'S INCOME

APPLICANT'S INCOME		SPOUSE'S INCOME	
MONTHLY GROSS SALARY AND WAGES	$______	MONTHLY GROSS SALARY AND WAGES	$______
DIVIDENDS AND INTEREST	$______	DIVIDENDS AND INTEREST	$______
OTHER INCOME (describe)**	$______	OTHER INCOME (describe)**	$______

** Alimony or child support income needs to be listed only if you wish such income to be considered in loan qualification.

Ref. #: ______
Bank Rep: ______ Banknet ______ AU: ______
FOR BANK USE ONLY

EXHIBIT 7.3

Continued

BANKING RELATIONSHIPS

Wells Fargo Accounts: ☐ Checking Account: # ______ ☐ Savings Account: # ______
☐ Other Accounts: ______

Other Financial Institution Accounts:

☐ Checking ☐ Savings ☐ Other ______ Financial Institution: ______ Balance: $ ______
☐ Checking ☐ Savings ☐ Other ______ Financial Institution: ______ Balance: $ ______

CREDIT EXPERIENCE

List all open obligations (including spouse's) and credit references, including alimony, child support and other payment obligations. Indicate with an asterisk * any installment debts to be repaid from the proceeds of this loan.

Type of Loan:	Institution:	Approximate Balance:	Monthly Payment:
First Mortgage/Rent		$	$
Second Mortgage		$	$
Auto		$	$
Auto		$	$
VISA/MC		$	$
Credit Card		$	$
Credit Card		$	$
Line of Credit		$	$
Other		$	$

Has any applicant declared bankruptcy? ☐ Yes ☐ No If yes, when? ______ Has any applicant had any item repossessed? ☐ Yes ☐ No If yes, when? ______

List additional debts on a separate sheet

YES! I WANT THE CONVENIENCE OF EXPRESS TRANSFER!

I would like the monthly payment automatically deducted from my Wells Fargo account: # ☐☐☐☐-☐☐☐☐☐☐☐

Automatically transferred funds are for my monthly payments on the due date, so long as there are adequate funds on deposit or there is available credit in my account, until the final payment is billed by mail or until the Bank receives written notice to cancel. I understand the Bank reserves the right to terminate the automatic repayment plan without notice. Cancellation of the plan for any reason may affect the interest rate on my loan. I will see my loan documents for details.

LOAN PROTECTION PLAN®

Ensure you can continue to make your new monthly payment with the benefit of Wells Fargo Bank's Loan Protection Plan.® Your loan representative will explain the benefits and program eligibility. Enrollment is not required as a condition for obtaining the loan.

Initial the selected coverage best suited to you:

____ Joint Life & Single Disability (J) ____ Joint Life (7) ____ Single Life & Disability (K) ____ Single Life (6) ____ No Coverage Desired (2)

Note: Only life plans are available on variable rate and deferred first payment option loans.

LOAN DISBURSEMENT ORDER

How do you want to receive the loan proceeds? ☐ Deposit to Wells Fargo Account: # ______
☐ Other (describe) ______

Do you wish to finance the loan fee? (PLEASE INITIAL) ____ Yes ____ No

AGREEMENT

I certify that all information provided by me is true, correct and complete. I authorize you to make whatever inquiries about me you deem necessary and appropriate for the purpose of evaluating my credit application, including obtaining credit bureau reports and contacting my employer. I also authorize you to provide credit information about your credit experience with me to other creditors and credit reporting agencies. I authorize the Bank to obtain address information from the California Department of Motor Vehicles and waive the address confidentiality requirements of Section 1808.21 of the California Vehicle Code. Further, my signature below certifies that the benefits of the Loan Protection Plan® have been explained to me. If I have not elected to participate in either the credit life or disability plans, I understand I am waiving all rights under them during the life of my present monthly payment loan, even if it is revised or extended.

______ APPLICANT'S SIGNATURE ______ DATE ______ CO-APPLICANT'S SIGNATURE (Spouse's signature required only if spouse is a joint applicant) ______ DATE

SL-204 (9/92) Member FDIC

Under such circumstances, the lender will often agree to a **loan rollover,** in which case the original loan is paid off by taking out another loan. The lender will usually require that all the interest and at least part of the principal be paid at the time of the rollover. Thus, if you originally borrowed $5,000 for 12 months, the bank might be willing to lend you, say, $3,000 for another 6 to 9 months as part of a loan rollover. In this case, you'll have to "pay down" $2,000 of the original loan, along with all interest due. However, you can expect the interest rate on a rollover loan to go up a bit; that is the price you pay for falling short on the first loan. Also, you should not expect to get more than one, or at the most two, loan rollovers—a bank's patience tends to grow somewhat short after a while!

FINANCE CHARGES AND THE ANNUAL PERCENTAGE RATE

As indicated in Chapter 6, the Consumer Credit Protection Act, or Truth in Lending Act, requires lenders to disclose both the dollar amount of finance charges and the annual percentage rate (APR) of interest. A sample **loan disclosure statement** applicable to either a single-payment or installment loan is given in Exhibit 7.4. Note that such a statement discloses not only interest costs but also other fees and expenses that may be tacked on to the loan. Although disclosures like this allow you to compare the various borrowing alternatives, you still need to understand the methods used to compute finance charges, since similar loans with the same *stated* interest rates may have different finance charges and APRs. The two basic procedures used to calculate the finance charges on single-payment loans are the *simple interest method* and the *discount method.*

Simple Interest Method. Interest is charged only on the *actual loan balance outstanding* in the **simple interest method.** This method is commonly used on revolving credit lines by commercial banks, S&Ls, and credit unions. To see how it is applied to a single-payment loan, assume that you borrow $1,000 for two years at a 12 percent annual rate of interest. On a single-payment loan, the actual loan balance outstanding for the two years will be $1,000, because no payments will be made until this period ends. With simple interest, the finance charge, F_s, is obtained by multiplying the *principal* outstanding by the stated annual rate of interest and then multiplying this amount by the term of the loan:

$$F_s = P \times r \times t,$$

where

F_s = finance charge calculated using simple interest method
P = principal amount of loan
r = stated annual rate of interest
t = term of loan, as stated in years (for example, t would equal 0.5 for a 6-month loan, 1.25 for a 15-month loan, and 2.0 for a two-year loan)

Substituting $1,000 for P, .12 for r, and 2 for t in the equation, we see that the finance charge, F_s, on this loan equals some $240 ($1,000 × .12 per year × 2 years). Since the size of the loan payment with this type of credit arrangement is found by adding the finance charges to the principal amount of the loan, you would have to make a loan payment of $1,000 + $240 = $1,240 at maturity to retire this debt.

To calculate the true, or annual, percentage rate (APR) of interest on this loan, the average annual finance charge is divided by the average loan balance outstanding, as follows:

$$\text{APR} = \frac{\text{Average annual finance charge}}{\text{Average loan balance outstanding}}$$

The figure for the average annual finance charge is found by dividing the total finance charge by the life of the loan (in years). In our example, the result is $120 ($240/2). Because the loan balance outstanding remains at $1,000 over the life of the loan, the average loan balance outstanding is

loan rollover The process of paying off a loan by taking out another, usually with the requirement that all interest and part of the principal on the original loan be paid at the time of rollover.

loan disclosure statement A document that lenders are required to supply borrowers that states both the dollar amount of finance charges and the APR applicable to a loan.

simple interest method A method of computing finance charges in which interest is charged on the actual loan balance outstanding.

EXHIBIT 7.4

A Loan Disclosure Statement

The loan disclosure statement informs the borrower of all charges (finance and otherwise) associated with the loan and the annual percentage rate (APR). In addition, it specifies the payment terms as well as the existence of any balloon payments.

FEDERAL TRUTH IN LENDING ACT DISCLOSURES

ANNUAL PERCENTAGE RATE The cost of your credit as a yearly rate. %	
FINANCE CHARGE The dollar amount the credit will cost you. $	
AMOUNT FINANCED The amount of credit provided to you or on your behalf. $	
TOTAL OF PAYMENTS The amount you will have paid after you have made all payments scheduled. $	

e means an estimate

You have the right to receive at this time an itemization of the Amount Financed.
☐ I want an itemization. ☐ I do not want an itemization.

Your payment schedule will be:

Number of Payments	Amount of Payments	When Payments Are Due

Insurance: Credit life insurance and credit disability insurance are not required to obtain credit, and will not be provided unless you sign and agree to pay the additional cost.

Type	Premium	Signature
Credit Life		I want credit life insurance ____________ SIGNATURE
Credit Life and Disability		I want credit life and disability insurance ____________ SIGNATURE
Joint Credit Life		I want joint credit life insurance ____________ SIGNATURE
Joint Credit Life and Disability		I want joint credit life and disability insurance ____________ SIGNATURE

You may obtain property insurance from anyone you want that is acceptable to Bank One, Arizona, NA. If you get the insurance through Bank One, Arizona, NA, you will pay $______ for ______ months of coverage.

Security: You are giving a security interest in the property being purchased.

Filing Fees: $________________

Late Charge: If a payment is late, you will be charged $10 or 5% of the payment, whichever is less.

Prepayment: If you pay off early, you will not have to pay a penalty.

Assumption: Someone buying your house may, subject to conditions, be allowed to assume the remaining obligation on the original terms.

See your contract documents for any additional information about nonpayment, default, and any required repayment in full before the scheduled date.

Each undersigned acknowledges receipt of one copy of the above fully completed Disclosure Statement prior to consummation of the proposed transaction. Each undersigned further acknowledges this disclosure statement is not a commitment to extend credit, or to provide or acquire insurance.

DATED ________________, 19_____ (X) ______________________________ (DEBTOR'S SIGNATURE)

BANK ONE, ARIZONA, NA (X) ______________________________ (DEBTOR'S SIGNATURE)

BY________________________________ ______________________________

Source: Bank One, Arizona, NA.

$1,000. Dividing the $120 average annual finance charge by the $1,000 average loan balance outstanding, we obtain an APR of 12 percent. Thus, the APR and the stated rate of interest are equivalent: They both equal 12 percent. This is always the case when the simple interest method is used to calculate finance charges, *regardless of whether loans are single-payment or installment.*

Discount Method. With the **discount method**, total finance charges are calculated on the principal amount of the loan, and they are then subtracted from the amount of the loan. The difference between the amount of the loan and the finance charge is then disbursed (paid) to the borrower—in other words, finance charges are paid in advance and represent a discount from the principal portion of the loan. The finance charge on a single-payment loan using the discount method, F_d, is calculated in exactly the same way as for a simple interest loan:

$$F_d = F_s = P \times r \times t.$$

Using the above method, the finance charge, F_d, on the $1,000, 12 percent, two-year, single-payment loan is, of course, the same $240 we calculated earlier. However, in sharp contrast to simple interest loans, the loan payment with a discount loan is the original principal amount of the loan, *P*, since the finance charges on the loan are deducted from the loan proceeds. Thus, for the $1,000 loan above, the borrower will receive $760—which is found by subtracting the interest charges from the loan principal ($1,000 less $240)—and in two years, will be required to pay back $1,000.

To find the APR on this discount loan, substitute the appropriate values into the APR equation cited above. For this two-year loan, the average annual finance charge is $120 ($240/2). However, as explained above, since this is a discount loan, the borrower will receive only $760. And because this is a single-payment loan, the average amount of money outstanding is also $760. When these figures are used in the APR equation we find the true rate for this 12 percent discount loan is more like 15.8 percent ($120/$760). Clearly, the discount method yields a much higher APR on single-payment loans than does the simple interest method. Exhibit 7.5 contrasts the results from both methods for the single-payment loan example discussed here.

Concept Check

7-9. What is a *lien*, and under what circumstances is it part of a consumer loan?

7-10. Briefly describe and differentiate between (a) a *chattel mortgage* and (b) a *collateral note.*

7-11. When might you request a *loan rollover?*

7-12. Describe the two methods used to calculate the finance charges on a single-payment loan. As a borrower, which method would you prefer? Explain.

INSTALLMENT LOANS FPPC LG5 LG6

Installment loans are paid off with a series of payments over time; these payments, along with the accompanying finance charges, can be figured using either simple interest or add-on interest. Does it really make much difference which procedure is used? Give some thought to this question before reading on.

Installment loans (known as ILs for short) differ from single-payment loans in that they require the borrower to repay the debt in a series of installment payments (usually on a monthly basis) over the life of the loan. Installment loans are far more popular than single-payment loans—in fact, they rank as one of the most popular forms of consumer credit. Much of this popularity is, of course, due to the convenient way in which the loan repayment is set up; not surprisingly, most people find it easier on their checkbooks to make a series of small payments rather than one big one.

A REAL CONSUMER CREDIT WORK HORSE!

As a financing vehicle, there are few things that installment loans can't do—which explains, in large part, why this form of consumer credit is so widely used. ILs, in fact, account for nearly two-thirds of all consumer debt outstanding (excluding home mortgages). Installment loans can be used to

EXHIBIT 7.5

Finance Charges and APRs for a Single-Payment Loan ($1,000 Loan for Two Years at 12% Interest)

Sometimes what you see is not what you get—such as when you borrow money through a discount loan and end up paying quite a bit more than the quoted rate.

Method	Stated Rate on Loan	Finance Charges	APR
Simple interest	12%	$240	12.0%
Discount	12	240	15.8

finance just about any type of big-ticket item imaginable. New car loans are, of course, the dominant type of IL, but this form of credit is also used to finance home furnishings, appliances and entertainment centers, camper trailers and other recreation vehicles, even expensive vacations; and, of course, more and more college students are turning to this type of credit as the way to finance their education.

Not only can they be used to finance all sorts of things, they can also be obtained at many locations. You'll find them at banks and other financial institutions, as well as major department stores and merchants that sell relatively expensive products. Go into a home appliance store to buy a high-priced stereo and chances are you'd be able to arrange for IL financing right there on the spot. These loans can be taken out for just a few hundred dollars, or they can involve thousands of dollars—indeed, ILs of $25,000 or more are really not all that uncommon. What's more, they can be set up with maturities as short as six months to as long as seven to ten years, even fifteen years!

Most installment loans are secured with some kind of collateral—for example, the car or home entertainment center you purchased with the help of an IL will usually end up serving as collateral on the loan. Even personal loans that are used to finance things like expensive vacations can also be secured—in this case, the collateral could be securities, CDs, or some other type of financial asset. One fast growing segment of this market is, in fact, ILs secured by second mortgages. These so-called *home equity loans* are similar to home equity credit lines discussed in Chapter 6, except they involve a set amount of money loaned over a set period of time (often as long as 15 years), rather than a revolving credit line from which you can borrow, repay, and reborrow. Thus, if a borrower needs, say, $25,000 to help pay for an expensive new boat, he would simply take out a loan in that amount and secure it with a second mortgage on his home. For all practical purposes, this loan would be like any other IL in the sense that it's for a set amount of money and is to be repaid over a set period of time in monthly installments. In addition to their highly competitive interest rates, a big attraction of these loans is that the interest paid on them can still be used as a tax deduction. So, borrowers get a double whammy of *low interest rates and tax deductibility!* As with home equity lines, however, failure to repay could result in the loss of your home.

THE INSTALLMENT PURCHASE CONTRACT

All of the information relevant to a transaction that's being financed on an installment loan basis is included in the **installment purchase contract.** This agreement specifies the obligations of both the purchaser (borrower) and the lender. Although its form is likely to vary with the lender, it will probably contain four basic components: a sales contract, a security agreement, a note, and an insurance

discount method A method of calculating finance charges in which interest is computed, then subtracted from the principal, and the difference is disbursed to the borrower.

installment purchase contract An agreement that specifies the obligations of both the purchaser (borrower) and seller (lender), issued when a purchase transaction is being financed on an installment basis.

agreement. A sample installment purchase contract containing all four of these components is presented in Exhibit 7.6.

Security Agreement. The **security agreement** (or **security interest**) indicates whether the lender has control over the item being purchased. Although state laws determine whether or not the borrower retains legal title to the collateral, the lender files a lien on the collateral in order to make the security interest public. In either case, the lender retains control over the collateral. If default does occur, the lender can sell the collateral and use the proceeds to satisfy the unpaid balance on the loan and cover any costs incurred in this process. The lender must pay the borrower any excess funds obtained from the liquidation of the collateral. However, if a *deficiency* occurs—that is, if the proceeds from liquidation are *not* sufficient to satisfy the loan—the borrower may or may not be liable for the unsatisfied portion of the debt, depending on state law (in some states, the lender cannot turn to the borrower to make up the deficiency).

The Note. The formal promise on the part of the borrower to repay the lender is spelled out in the **note**. It states all the legal obligations of both borrower and lender and outlines all details concerning repayment, default, and disposition of collateral. The note is normally secured by the sales contract, or security agreement, which provides the lender with a security interest in the assets being acquired. It is the document that, when signed by both borrower and lender, legally binds the two parties to the terms and conditions stated therein. Although many of the detailed provisions of the note in Exhibit 7.6 are on the reverse side of the contract (not shown), the entire document, once signed, is considered to be the note.

Credit Life Insurance. Sometimes, as a condition of receiving an installment loan, a borrower is required to buy **credit life insurance** and possibly **credit disability insurance.** Credit life (and disability) insurance is tied to a particular IL and basically provides insurance that the loan will be paid off if the borrower dies (or becomes disabled) before the loan matures. In essence, these policies insure the borrower for an amount sufficient to repay the outstanding loan balance. The seller's (or lender's) ability to dictate the terms of these insurance requirements is restricted by law in some states. If this type of insurance is required as a condition of the loan, its cost must be added in the finance charges and included as part of the APR. From the borrower's perspective, credit life and disability insurance is NOT a very good deal: *it's very costly and really does little more than provide lenders with a very lucrative source of income.* Not surprisingly, because it is so lucrative, some lenders aggressively push it on unsuspecting borrowers and, in some cases, even require it as a condition for granting a loan. The best advice is to avoid it, if at all possible!

Special Features. In addition to the major points discussed above, installment purchase contracts often contain several other features that should be of interest to borrowers. These special features generally are contained in clauses to the sales contract and/or note that pertain to default, repossession, and balloon payment:

An **acceleration clause** allows the lender to demand immediate repayment of the entire amount of the unpaid debt in the event the purchaser defaults on loan payments. Although this clause is customary in installment loans, the lender is likely to allow a late payment or levy a penalty instead of calling the loan by exercising the acceleration clause.

Most installment purchase contracts contain *recourse clauses* that stipulate the action the lender

security agreement (security interest) In an installment purchase contract, a legal agreement that indicates whether or not the lender retains control over the item being purchased.

note In an installment purchase contract, the formal promise on the part of the borrower to repay the lender in accordance with the terms specified in the agreement.

credit life (or disability) insurance A type of life (or disability) insurance sold in conjunction with installment loans in which the coverage decreases at the same rate as the loan balance.

acceleration clause A clause in an installment loan contract that allows the lender to demand immediate repayment of the entire outstanding loan balance if the purchaser defaults on loan payments.

EXHIBIT 7.6

An Installment Purchase Contract

The installment purchase contract contains all the particulars of a given installment loan, including terms of payment, type and amount of credit insurance, financing arrangement, and other pertinent information.

RETAIL INSTALLMENT CONTRACT AND SECURITY AGREEMENT (Goods)

Date ______________, 19____

SELLER (CALLED "YOU")	BUYER (CALLED "I")
NAME ______________	NAME ______________
ADDRESS ______________	NAME ______________
CITY ________ STATE ______ ZIP ______	ADDRESS ______________
SALESMAN ______________	CITY ________ STATE ______ ZIP ______

ANNUAL PERCENTAGE RATE The cost of your credit as a yearly rate.	**FINANCE CHARGE** The dollar amount the credit will cost you.	**AMOUNT FINANCED** The amount of credit provided to you or on your behalf.	**TOTAL OF PAYMENTS** The amount you will have paid after you have made all payments scheduled.	**TOTAL SALES PRICE** The total cost of my purchase on credit, including my downpayment of $ __________
%	$	$	$	$

Terms

My payment schedule will be:

Number of Payments	Amount of Payments	When Payments Are Due
		, 19—— and same date of each following month

Security Agreement

Security: I gave you a security interest in the goods or property being purchased.
Late Charge: If I don't pay any payments in 10 days after it's due, I shall also pay 5% of that payment but not over $5.00.
Prepayment: If I pay off early, I may be entitled to a refund of part of the finance charge.
See the contract document for any additional information about nonpayment default; any required repayment in full before the scheduled date, and prepayment refunds.

Late Charges

DESCRIPTION OF GOODS	MANUFACTURER	MODEL NO.	RETAIL NO.	CASH SALE PRICE
				$
				$

Insurance

INSURANCE DISCLOSURE

NO INSURANCE IS REQUIRED FOR THIS SALE. I may buy any insurance from anyone I choose. Only if requested and for cost stated below, you or buyer of this contract will obtain insurance. Charges will be included in the Amount Financed. I understand this is the only insurance you offer and you (or buyer of this contract) expect to profit from its sale. I consent to this. The one Buyer signing this insurance Disclosure will be insured when coverage begins, unless a different Buyer's name appears here:

(WRITE "YES" OR "NO" AS DESIRED, DATE, AND SIGN, IF NONE DESIRED, SIGN BELOW.)

____ Credit Life* .... $______
____ Credit Disability* .... $______
____ Property insurance .... $______

DATE ______________ SIGNATURE ______________

NO INSURANCE DESIRED: ______________ SIGNATURE

ITEMIZATION OF AMOUNT FINANCED

Financing

Sales Tax (if any) $______

1. Cash Sale Price.................................$______
2. a. Cash Downpayment...................$______
   b. Trade-in...................................$______
   DESCRIPTION ______________
   Total Downpayment (a – b)........................$______
3. Unpaid Balance of Cash Sale Price (1 – 2)...........$______
4. Insurance (for term of credit)
   Credit life...................................$______
   Credit Disability.............................$______
   Property......................................$______
   Total Insurance Charges.......................$______
5. Amount Financed (3 – 4)..........................$______
6. Finance Charge...................................$______
7. Total of Payments (5 – 6)........................$______
8. Total Sale Price (1 – 4 – 6)....................$______
9. Payable in ________ monthly payments of $______ each beginning ______________ and continuing same day of each month until fully paid.

Note

PROMISE TO PAY. Instead of the Cash Price. I promise to pay the total Sale Price and I agree to pay you (or buyer of this contract) a Total of Payments in monthly payments in the amounts and on the dates stated above. I will pay at your business address, or other address given me. If more than one Buyer is named above, you may enforce this contract against all or any Buyers, but not in a combined amount greater than amount owed.

Prepayment Provision

PREPAYMENT. If I fully prepay before the final due date, the amount I owe will be reduced by (a) unearned Finance Charges computed at the Annual Percentage Rate shown above, the unpaid balances of Amount Financed scheduled for the time after prepayment to maturity, (b) unearned credit insurance charges determined by the "Rule of 78ths". and (c) unearned property insurance charges determined by assuming an equal part is carried each month.

FAILURE TO PAY. If I don't pay on time, all my payments may become due at once, and without notifying me before bringing suit, you may sue me for the total amount I owe, less the same unearned Finance Charges I would receive if I fully prepaid. You may also repossess the goods described above.

Acceleration Clause

SECURITY. You waive any security interest in my home that could result if the goods are installed.

NOTICE

ANY HOLDER OF THIS CONSUMER CREDIT CONTRACT IS SUBJECT TO ALL CLAIMS AND DEFENSES WHICH THE DEBTOR COULD ASSERT AGAINST THE SELLER OF GOODS OR SERVICES OBTAINED PURSUANT HERETO OR WITH THE PROCEEDS HEREOF. RECOVERY HEREUNDER BY THE DEBTOR SHALL NOT EXCEED AMOUNTS PAID BY THE DEBTOR HEREUNDER.

NOTICE TO THE BUYER: 1. Do not sign this agreement before you read it or if it contains any blank spaces. 2. You are entitled to an exact copy of this contract.

I HAVE READ AND RECEIVED A COMPLETED, READABLE, SIGNED COPY OF THIS CONTRACT.

SELLER: ______________ BUYER: ______________
By: ______________ BUYER: ______________

can take in case of default, such as wage garnishment and repossession. Some purchase agreements allow the lender to collect a portion of the purchaser's (borrower's) wages if he or she defaults on payments by garnishing the borrower's wages. **Garnishment** is a legal method of getting an employer to pay a portion of a borrower's wages to the lender. The borrower must, of course, be in default, and a court order must be issued enabling the employer to take such action. The Federal Garnishment Law specifically limits the amount of an employee's weekly wages that can be garnished to no more than the smaller of (1) 25 percent of take-home pay or (2) the amount by which weekly take-home pay exceeds 30 times the federal minimum hourly wage. Many state laws have completely prohibited garnishing or have placed severe restrictions on this practice.

The act of seizing collateral when the borrower defaults on a loan is termed **repossession.** In many states, the ability of the lender to repossess collateral is limited (and may even require a court order), but in others, collateral can be repossessed without notice and even "stolen," in effect, from the borrower. Quite often there are detailed procedures that the lender must follow when selling repossessed items in order to satisfy unpaid debts. The repossessed item is eventually sold at auction or by some other means, and the amount due the merchant or lender, along with legal and other expenses in connection with the repossession, is taken from the sale proceeds. If this amount is not enough to cover the loan, the customer may or may not be liable for the remaining portion.

Sometimes installment purchase agreements are set up in such a fashion that the final payment is considerably larger than the others. The Truth in Lending Act requires that any **balloon payment,** which is defined as a payment more than twice the size of the normal installment payment, be clearly identified as such. For example, if a loan required payments of $200 per month for 23 months followed by a final payment of $1,000 in the 24th month, the existence of the $1,000 balloon payment would have to be clearly disclosed. Because balloon clauses have been abused by some lenders and can place borrowers in an undesirable position, some states prohibit their use in loans. It is best not to enter into an agreement that includes such a clause, since balloon payments can cause real financial strain when they fall due. Only if you had adequate savings, or are expecting a known sum of money at some future date, could the use of a balloon payment be justified.

FINANCE CHARGES, MONTHLY PAYMENTS, AND APR

Earlier in this chapter, we discussed finance charges and annual percentage rates (APRs), and illustrated simple interest and discount methods of determining finance charges on single-payment loans. In this section, we look at the use of simple and add-on interest to compute finance charges and monthly payments for installment loans (technically, discount interest can also be used with ILs, but because this is rare, we ignore it here). For purposes of illustration, we will use a 12 percent, $1,000 installment loan that is to be paid off in 12 monthly payments. As in the earlier illustration for single-payment loans, interest is the only component of the finance charge; the presence of any other loan charges (such as credit life insurance, or title and notary fees) is ignored.

Using Simple Interest. When simple interest is used with ILs—and most major banks and S&Ls do use it on their installment loans—interest is charged only on the outstanding balance of the loan. Thus, as the loan principal declines with monthly payments, the amount of interest being charged decreases as well. Because finance charges change each month, the procedure used to find the interest expense is mathematically very complex. Fortunately, this problem is avoided in practice, because the convention in the industry is to use *finance tables* (or desktop computers). Essentially, the tables provide the *monthly payment* that would be required to retire an installment loan that carries a given simple rate of interest and has a given term to maturity. Because the tables have interest charges built right into them, the monthly payments cover both principal and interest. Exhibit 7.7 provides an excerpt from such a table for a variety of widely used interest rates and maturities.

The values in the table represent the monthly payments required to retire a $1,000 loan. Even though it's assumed you're borrowing $1,000, the table can be used with any size loan. For example, if you're looking at a $5,000 loan, just multiply the monthly loan payment from the table by 5—that is, $5,000/$1,000 = 5; or if you have, say, a $500 loan, multiply the loan payment by .5 ($500/$1,000 = .5).

EXHIBIT 7.7

A Table of Monthly Installment Loan Payments (to Repay a $1,000/Simple Interest Loan)

A table like this can be used to find the monthly payments on a wide variety of simple interest installment loans. While it's set up in reference to a $1,000 loan, with a little modification, it can easily be used with any size loan (the principal can be more or less than $1,000).

Rate of Interest	Loan Maturity						
	6 Months	12 Months	18 Months	24 Months	36 Months	48 Months	60 Months
7.5%	$170.33	$86.76	$58.92	$45.00	$31.11	$24.18	$20.05
8.0	170.58	86.99	59.15	45.23	31.34	24.42	20.28
8.5	170.82	87.22	59.37	45.46	31.57	24.65	20.52
9.0	171.07	87.46	59.60	45.69	31.80	24.89	20.76
9.5	171.32	87.69	59.83	45.92	32.04	25.13	21.01
10.0	171.56	87.92	60.06	46.15	32.27	25.37	21.25
10.5	171.81	88.15	60.29	46.38	32.51	25.61	21.50
11.0	172.05	88.50	60.64	46.73	32.86	25.97	21.87
11.5	173.30	88.62	60.76	46.85	32.98	26.09	22.00
12.0	172.50	88.85	60.99	47.08	33.22	26.34	22.25
12.5	172.80	89.09	61.22	47.31	33.46	26.58	22.50
13.0	173.04	89.32	61.45	47.55	33.70	26.83	22.76
14.0	173.54	89.79	61.92	48.02	34.18	27.33	23.27
15.0	174.03	90.26	62.39	48.49	34.67	27.84	23.79
16.0	174.53	90.74	62.86	48.97	35.16	28.35	24.32
17.0	175.03	91.21	63.34	49.45	35.66	28.86	24.86
18.0	175.53	91.68	63.81	49.93	36.16	29.38	25.40

In many respects, this table is just like the mortgage loan payment schedule introduced in Chapter 5, except we use much shorter loan maturities here than we do with mortgages.

Here's how to use the table in Exhibit 7.7. Suppose we want to find the monthly payment required on our $1,000, 12 percent, 12-month loan. Looking under the 12-month column and across from the 12 percent rate of interest, we find a value of $88.85; that is the monthly payment it will take to pay off the $1,000 loan in 12 months. When the monthly payments ($88.85) are multiplied by the term of the loan in months (12), the result will be total payments of $88.85 × 12 = $1,066.20. The difference between the total payments on the loan and the principal portion represents the *finance charges on the loan*—in this case, $1,066.20 − $1,000 = interest charges of $66.20.

Now from each monthly payment, a certain portion goes to interest and the balance is used to reduce the principal. Because the principal balance declines with each payment, the amount that goes to interest also *decreases* while the amount that goes to principal *increases.* Exhibit 7.8 illustrates this pattern. Note that since *monthly* payments are used with the loan, the interest column in Exhibit 7.8 is also based on a *monthly* rate of interest—that is, the annual rate is divided by 12 to obtain a monthly rate (12 percent per year/12 = 1 percent per month). This monthly rate is then applied to the outstanding loan balance to find the monthly interest charges in column 3. Because interest is charged only on the outstanding balance, *the annual percentage rate (APR) on a simple interest IL will always equal the stated rate*—in this case, 12 percent.

Add-on Method. A number of installment loans, particularly those obtained directly from retail merchants or made at finance companies and the like, are made using the **add-on method.**

garnishment Court-ordered payment of a portion of a defaulting borrower's wages to a lender.

repossession The act of seizing collateral when the borrower defaults on an installment loan.

balloon payment A final payment on an installment loan that is substantially larger than the normal installment payment.

add-on method A method of calculating interest by computing finance charges on the original loan balance and then adding the interest to that balance.

EXHIBIT 7.8

Monthly Payment Analysis for a Simple Interest Installment Loan (Assumes a $1,000, 12%, 12-Month Loan)

Part of each monthly payment on an installment loan goes to interest and part to principal. As the loan is paid down over time, less and less of each payment goes to interest, and more and more goes to principal.

Month	Outstanding Loan Balance (1)	Monthly Payment (2)	Interest Charges [(1) × 0.01] (3)	Principal [(2) − (3)] (4)
1	$1,000.00	$88.85	$10.00	$78.85
2	921.15	88.85	9.21	79.64
3	841.51	88.85	8.42	80.43
4	761.08	88.85	7.61	81.24
5	679.84	88.85	6.80	82.05
6	597.79	88.85	5.98	82.87
7	514.92	88.85	5.15	83.70
8	431.22	88.85	4.31	84.54
9	346.68	88.85	3.47	85.38
10	261.30	88.85	2.61	86.24
11	175.06	88.85	1.75	87.10
12	87.96	88.85	0.89	87.96
Total		$1,066.20	$66.20	$1,000.00

Note: Column 1 values for months 2 through 12 are obtained by subtracting the principal payment shown in column 4 for the preceding month from the outstanding loan balance shown in column 1 for the preceding month; thus, $1,000 − $78.85 = $921.15, which is the outstanding loan balance in month 2.

Add-on loans are very expensive; indeed, they generally rank as one of the most costly forms of consumer credit, with APRs that are often well above rates charged even on many credit cards. With add-on interest, the finance charges are calculated using the *original* balance of the loan, which are then added to the original loan balance. Thus, the amount of finance charges on an add-on loan can be found by using the familiar simple interest formula:

$$F = P \times r \times t.$$

Given the $1,000 loan we have been using for illustrative purposes, the finance charges on a 12 percent, one-year add-on loan would be

$$F = \$1{,}000 \times .12 \times 1 = \$120.$$

Compared to the finance charges for the same loan on a simple interest basis ($66.20), the add-on loan is a lot more costly, a fact that will also show up in monthly payments and APR. Keep in mind that both of these loans would be quoted as "12 percent" loans; thus, you may think you are getting a 12 percent loan, but looks can be deceiving—especially when you are dealing with add-on interest! So, when taking out an installment loan, make sure you find out whether simple or add-on interest is being used to compute finance charges. And if it's add-on you might want to consider looking elsewhere for the loan.

To find the monthly payments on an add-on loan, all you need to do is add the finance charge ($120) to the *original* principal amount of the loan ($1,000) and then divide this sum by the number of monthly payments to be made. In the case of our $1,000, one-year loan, this results in monthly payments of $93.33, found as follows:

$$\text{Monthly payments} = \frac{\$1{,}000 + \$120}{12} = \frac{\$1{,}120}{12} = \$93.33.$$

As expected, these monthly payments are much higher than the ones with the simple interest loan ($88.85).

Because the actual rate of interest with an add-on loan is considerably higher than the stated rate, we must determine the loan's APR. The procedure for finding the mathematically precise APR is highly complex and far beyond the scope of this book. Fortunately, there are several ways to approximate the APR on an add-on loan, the most accurate of which is the so-called **N-ratio method.** The N-ratio actually results in an APR that is remarkably close to the precise figure. This method uses the following formula to find the approximate APR:

$$\text{Approximate APR} = \frac{M(95N + 9)F}{12N(N + 1)(4P + F)}$$

where

APR = annual percentage rate of interest
M = number of payments in a year
N = number of loan payments scheduled over life of loan
F = total finance charges
P = principal amount of loan

To see how this formula works, let's return to our $1,000, 12 percent, one-year add-on loan. With this loan, $M = 12$, $N = 12$, $F = \$120$, and $P = \$1{,}000$. *The approximate APR in this case works out to be 21.4%:*

Approximate APR

$$= \frac{(12)[(95)(12) + 9](\$120)}{(12)(12)(12 + 1)[(4)(\$1{,}000) + \$120]}$$

$$= \frac{(12)(1149)(\$120)}{(12)(12)(13)(\$4{,}120)}$$

$$= \frac{\$1{,}654{,}560}{\$7{,}712{,}640} = 21.4\%.$$

As a matter of interest, the precise APR on this loan is 21.36 percent.

When viewed from an APR perspective, this 12 percent add-on loan turns out to be *very expensive,* as it has an actual rate of interest (21.4 percent) that is considerably higher than the quoted rate of 12 percent. (A rough but reasonably accurate rule of thumb is that the APR on an add-on loan is about *twice* the stated rate—thus, if the loan is quoted at an add-on rate of 9 percent, you're probably going to end up paying a true rate that's closer to 18 percent.) This is because when add-on interest is applied to an installment loan, the interest included in each payment is charged on the initial principal even though the outstanding loan balance is reduced as installment payments are made. A summary of comparative finance charges and APRs for this example is presented in Exhibit 7.9.

Under the Truth in Lending Act, the exact APR (accurate to the nearest 0.25 percent) must be disclosed to borrowers. Note that not only interest, but also any other fees required to obtain a loan are considered part of the finance charges and should be included in the computation of the APR.

Prepayment Penalties. Another type of finance charge often found in installment loan contracts is the **prepayment penalty,** an additional charge you owe if you decide to pay off your loan prior to maturity. When you pay off a loan early, you may find that you owe quite a bit more than you expected, especially if the lender uses the **Rule of 78s,** (or **sum-of-the-digits method**) to calculate the amount of interest and principal balance to date. You might think that paying off a $1,000, 12 percent, one-year loan at the end of six months would mean that you have paid about half of the principal and owe just $500 to the lender. Not so with a loan that uses the rule of 78s! This method charges more interest in the early months of the loan, on the theory that the borrower has use of more money in the early stages of the IL and should pay more finance charges in the early months of the loan and progressively less later. To see how this works, let's assume we want to pay off the $1,000, 12 percent, one-year add-on loan after six months. Using the Rule of 78s, of your $559.98 in payments (that is, 6 payments at $93.33 each = 6 × $93.33 = $559.98), just $472.29 went to principal—all the rest went to interest. As a result, even though you have made payments for half of the life of the loan, you still owe more than 50 percent of the principal. So, before signing the loan agreement, be sure to ask how the interest will be calculated, just in case you decide to prepay the loan.

BUY ON TIME OR PAY CASH?

Often when you buy a big-ticket item, you have little choice but to take out a loan to finance the purchase—the acquisition (perhaps it's a new car) is just so expensive that you cannot afford to pay

N-ratio method A formula used for estimating the annual percentage rate (APR) on an add-on loan.

prepayment penalty An additional charge you owe if you decide to pay off your loan prior to maturity.

Rule of 78s (sum-of-the-digits method) A method of calculating interest that charges more interest in the early months of the loan, on the theory that the borrower has use of more money in the early stages of the IL.

EXHIBIT 7.9

Comparative Finance Charges and APRs (Assumes a $1,000, 12%, 12-Month Installment Loan)

In sharp contrast to simple interest loans, the APR with add-on installment loans is *much higher* than the stated rate.

	Simple Interest	Add-on Interest
Stated rate on loan	12%	12%
Finance charges	$ 66.20	$ 120.00
Monthly payments	$ 88.25	$ 93.33
Total payments made	$1,066.20	$1,120.00
APR	12%	21.4%

cash. And even if you do have the money, you may still be better off using something like an IL *if the cash purchase would end up severely depleting your liquid reserves.* But don't just automatically take out a loan. Rather, take the time to find out if, in fact, that's the best thing to do. Such a decision can easily be made by using Worksheet 7.2. This worksheet considers the cost of the loan relative to the after-tax earnings generated from having your money in some type of short-term investment vehicle. A basic assumption here is that the consumer has an adequate level of liquid reserves, and that these reserves are being held in some type of savings account. (Obviously, if this is not the case, there's little reason to go through the exercise, since you have no choice but to borrow the money.) Essentially, it boils down to this: *If it costs more to borrow the money than you can earn in interest, then draw the money from your savings to pay cash for the purchase; if not, then consider taking out a loan.*

To see how this works, consider the following situation: You're thinking about buying a second car (a nice low-mileage used vehicle) and after the normal down payment, you still need to come up with $9,000. This balance can be taken care of in one of two ways: (1) You can take out a 36-month, 12 percent IL (according to Exhibit 7.7, the *Table of Monthly Loan Payments,* such an IL would have monthly payments of $33.22 × 9 = $298.98); or (2) you can pay cash for the car by drawing the money from a money fund (the fund currently pays 6 percent interest, and that's expected to hold for the foreseeable future). We can now use the worksheet to decide whether to buy on time or pay cash—the complete details of which are provided in Worksheet 7.2. In this case, we assume the loan is a standard IL, where the interest does not qualify as a tax deduction, and that you're in the 28 percent tax bracket. Note in the worksheet that by borrowing the money, you'll end up paying nearly $1,765 in interest (line 8), none of which is tax deductible. In contrast, by leaving your money on deposit in the money fund, you'll receive only $1,166 in interest, after taxes (see line 11). Taken together, we see the net cost of borrowing (line 12) is nearly $600—in essence, you'll be paying over $1,750 to earn less than $1,200, which certainly doesn't make much sense! Clearly, it's far more cost-effective in this case to *pay cash* for the car, for by doing so, you will save nearly $600.

While such a figure provides a pretty convincing reason for avoiding a loan, there may be occasions where the actual dollar spread between the cost of borrowing and interest earned is very small, perhaps only $100, or less (actually, if our example above had involved a home equity loan, where interest is tax deductible, the net cost of borrowing [line 12] would have dropped to $103). Being able to deduct the interest on a loan can lead to a relatively small spread, but it can also occur, for example, if the amount being financed is relatively small—say, you want $1,500 or $2,000 for a ski trip to Colorado. Under these circumstances, and so long as the spread stays sufficiently small, you may decide it's still worthwhile to borrow the money in order to maintain a higher level of liquidity. Although this course of action is perfectly legitimate when very small spreads exist, it makes less sense as the gap starts to widen.

WORKSHEET 7.2

To Borrow or Not to Borrow

Using a worksheet like the one shown here, you can decide whether to buy on time or pay cash by comparing the (after-tax) cost of interest paid on a loan with the after-tax interest income lost by taking the money out of savings and using it to pay cash for the purchase.

BUY ON TIME OR PAY CASH

Name John E. Jones **Date** February 28, 1996

■ **Cost of Borrowing**		
1. Terms of the loan		
a. Amount of the loan	$ 9,000.00	
b. Length of the loan (in years)	3 yrs.	
c. Monthly payment	$ 298.98	
2. Total loan payments made (monthly loan payment × length of loan in months) $ 298.98 per month × 36 months		$ 10,763.28
3. Less: Principal amount of the loan		$<9,000.00>
4. Total interest paid over life of loan (line 2 − line 3)		$ 1,763.28
5. Tax considerations:		
• Is this a home-equity loan (where interest expenses can be deducted from taxes)	☐ yes no ☒	
• Do you itemize deductions on your federal tax returns	☒ yes no ☐	
• If you answered yes to BOTH questions, then proceed to line 6; if you answered no to *either one or both* of the questions, then proceed to *line 8* and use *line 4* as the after-tax interest cost of the loan.		
6. What Federal Tax Bracket are you in? (use either 15, 28, 31, 36, or 39.6%)	— %	
7. Taxes saved due to interest deductions (line 4 × tax rate, from line 6: $_____ × ____%)		$ —
8. Total after-tax interest cost on the loan (line 4 – line 7)		$ 1,763.28
■ **Cost of Paying Cash**		
9. Annual interest *earned* on savings (Annual rate of interest earned on savings × amount of loan: 6 % × $9,000.00)		$ 540.00
10. Annual after-tax interest earnings (line 9 × [1 − tax rate] — e.g., 1 − 28% = 72%: $ 540.00 × 72 %)		$ 388.80
11. Total after-tax interest earnings over life of loan (line 10 × line 1-b: $ 388.80 × 3 years)		$ 1,166.40
■ **Net Cost of Borrowing**		
12. Difference in cost of borrowing vs. cost of paying cash (line 8 minus line 11)		$ 596.88

BASIC DECISION RULE: *Pay cash* if line 12 is positive; *borrow the money* if line 12 is negative.

Note: For simplicity, compounding is ignored in calculating *both* the cost of interest and interest earnings.

Concept Check

7-13. Briefly describe the basic features of an installment loan. What is a home equity loan and how are these loans similar to other installment loans? What are the major advantages and disadvantages of home equity loans?

7-14. Briefly describe an *installment purchase contract,* and define the four basic components such a contract is likely to contain.

7-15. Explain the purpose and describe the general content of the *note* that is ordinarily included as part of an installment purchase agreement.

7-16. Explain why a borrower is often required to purchase *credit life and disability insurance* as a condition for receiving an installment loan. Is this a good deal for the borrower?

7-17. Discuss each of the following features that may be included in an installment purchase agreement: (a) *acceleration clause,* (b) wage *garnishment,* (c) *repossession* feature, and (d) *balloon* clause.

7-18. Define simple interest as it relates to an installment loan.

7-19. Under what conditions does it make more sense to pay cash for a big-ticket item than to borrow the money to finance the purchase? Are there ever times when borrowing the money is the best course of action?

SUMMARY

LG1. Know when to use consumer loans and differentiate between major types. Single-payment and installment loans are formally negotiated consumer loan arrangements that are used mainly as a way to finance big-ticket items. Most of these consumer loans are taken out as auto loans, loans for other durable goods, education loans, personal loans, and consolidation loans.

LG2. Identify the various sources of consumer loans. Consumer loans can be obtained from a number of sources, including commercial banks (the biggest providers of such credit), consumer finance companies, credit unions, S&Ls, sales finance (and captive finance) companies, life insurance companies, and finally, as a last resort, your friends and relatives.

LG3. Choose the best loans by comparing finance charges, maturity, collateral, and other loan terms. Before taking out a consumer loan, you should be sure that the purchase is consistent with your financial plans and that you can service the debt without straining your budget. When shopping for credit, it's in your best interest to compare such loan features as finance charges (APRs), loan maturities, monthly payments, and collateral requirements and choose the loan with terms that are fully compatible with your financial plans and cash budgets.

LG4. Describe the features of, and calculate finance charges on, single-payment loans. In a single-payment loan, the borrower is obligated to make just one principal payment (at the maturity of the loan), though he/she may be required to make one or more interim interest payments. Such loans are usually made for a period of one year or less, and normally are secured by some type of collateral; a major advantage of the single-payment loan is that it doesn't require monthly payments and as such, won't tie up the borrower's cash flow. Finance charges can be calculated using either the simple interest method, which applies the interest rate to the outstanding loan balance, or the discount method, where the interest is calculated the same way as simple interest, but then deducted from the loan principal, resulting in a higher APR.

LG5. Evaluate the benefits of an installment loan and understand the terms of the loan purchase contract. In an installment loan, the borrower agrees to repay the loan through a series of equal installment payments (usually on a monthly basis) until the obligation is fully repaid; in this way, the borrower can come up with a loan-repayment schedule that fits neatly into his/her financial plans and cash budgets. This highly popular form of consumer credit can be used to finance just about any type of big-ticket asset or expenditure; and many of them are taken out as home equity loans in order to capture tax advantages. The main parts of the purchase contract are the sales contract, which sets forth the terms of the arrangement; the security agreement, giving the lender control of the item being purchased; the note, or formal promise to repay; and the insurance agreement, which specifies whether the borrower has to obtain credit life insurance.

LG6. **Determine the costs of installment loans and analyze whether it is better to pay cash or take out a loan.** Most single-payment loans are made with either simple or discount interest, whereas most ILs are made with either simple or add-on interest. So long as simple interest is used, the actual finance charge will always correspond to the stated rate of interest; in contrast, when discount or add-on rates are used, the APR will always be more than the stated rate. In the final analysis, whether or not it makes sense to borrow rather than pay cash comes down to a matter of which is the least costly alternative.

FINANCIAL FACTS OR FANTASIES

Are the following statements financial facts (true) or fantasies (false)?

1. Education loans not only carry low, subsidized interest rates, they also have repayment schedules that don't start until the student is out of school.
2. Consumer loans can be set up with fixed rates of interest or with variable loan rates.
3. The three biggest lenders in the consumer loan field are commercial banks, S&Ls, and credit unions.
4. Most single-payment loans are secured with some type of collateral and are usually relatively short in duration (i.e., they generally have maturities of one year or less).
5. A balloon payment on an installment loan gives the borrower the right to skip monthly payments by deferring them to the very end of the loan.
6. Given a choice, you should take a loan with add-on rather than simple interest.

DISCUSSION QUESTIONS AND PROBLEMS

Discussion Question for Opening Profile

Discuss Andrea Taylor's attitude toward debt and her use of consumer credit; contrast Andrea's use of debt with the Walkers (in Chapter 6). Describe her strategies for financing her family's education. How would you characterize Andrea Taylor's overall personal financial planning and money management?

FPPC 1. Assume you have been shopping for a new car and intend to finance it, in part, through an installment loan. The car you are looking for has a sticker price of $10,000. Big A Autos has offered to sell it to you for $2,500 down and finance the balance with a loan that will require 36 monthly payments of $253.12; Cars-Are-Us will sell you exactly the same vehicle for $3,000 down plus a 48-month loan for the balance, with monthly payments of $177.65. Which is the better deal? Explain?

2. Every six months, Keith Clark takes an inventory of the consumer debts he has outstanding. The latest tally showed the following list: He still owed $4,000 on a home improvement loan (monthly payments of $125); he was making $85 monthly payments on a personal loan that had a remaining balance of $750; he had a $2,000, secured single-payment loan that is due late next year; he had a $70,000 home mortgage on which he was making $820 monthly payments; he still owed $8,600 on a new-car loan (monthly payments of $205); he had a $960 balance on his Visa card (minimum payment of $40), a $70 balance on his Shell credit card (balance due in 30 days), and a $1,200 balance

on a personal line of credit ($60 monthly payments). Use Worksheet 7.1 to prepare an inventory of Keith's consumer debt. Find his debt safety ratio given that he has a take-home pay of $2,500 per month; would you consider this ratio good or bad? Explain.

FPPC **3.** Find the finance charges on a 14 percent, 18-month single-payment loan when interest is computed using the simple interest method. Find the finance charges on the same loan when interest is computed using the discount method. Determine the APR in each case.

FPPC **4.** Bill Withers has to borrow $4,000. First State Bank will lend him the money for 12 months through a single-payment loan at 13.5 percent discount; Home Savings and Loan will make him a $4,000 single-payment, 12-month loan at 15 percent simple. Where should Bill borrow the money? Explain.

FPPC **5.** Assuming that interest is the only finance charge, how much interest would be paid on a $500 installment loan to be repaid in six monthly installments of $87.02? If simple interest were charged at the annual rate of 15 percent on the outstanding balance, what would the APR be on this loan? Explain.

FPPC **6.** After careful comparison shopping, Chris Jenkins decided to buy a sporty new Nissan 240SX; with some options added, the car had a price of $17,000—including plates and taxes. Because he could not afford to pay cash for the car, he used savings and his old car as a trade-in to put $4,000 down and financed the rest with a $13,000, 48-month loan at a simple interest rate of 12½ percent.

- **a.** What will his monthly payments be? (Use the loan payment table in Exhibit 7.7.)
- **b.** How much total interest will Chris pay in the first year of the loan? (Use a monthly payment analysis procedure similar to the one in Exhibit 7.8.)
- **c.** How much interest will Chris pay over the full (48-month) life of the loan?
- **d.** What is the APR on this loan?

FPPC **7.** Stan Lee plans to borrow $5,000 and repay it in 36 monthly installments. This loan is being made at an annual add-on interest rate of 11½ percent.

- **a.** Assuming that the only component of the finance charge is interest, calculate this charge.
- **b.** Use your finding in part a to calculate the monthly payment on the loan.
- **c.** Use the N-ratio method to estimate the APR on the loan.

FPPC **8.** ***Use Worksheet 7.2 to help Sherman make this credit decision:***

- **a.** Consider the following situation: Sherman Jacobs wants to buy a home entertainment center. Complete with a big-screen TV, VCR, and sound system, the unit would cost $4,500. Sherman has over $15,000 in a money fund, so he can easily afford to pay cash for the whole thing (the fund is currently paying 5½ percent interest, and Sherman expects that yield to hold for the foreseeable future). To stimulate sales, the dealer is offering to finance the full cost of the unit with a 36-month installment loan at 9 percent, simple. Sherman wants to know: Should he pay cash for this home entertainment center or buy it on time? (Note: assume Sherman is in the 28 percent tax bracket and that he itemizes deductions on his tax returns.) Briefly explain your answer.
- **b.** Rework the above problem, assuming Sherman has the option of using a 48-month, 9.5 percent home equity loan to finance the full cost of this entertainment center. Again, use Worksheet 7.2 to determine if Sherman should pay cash or buy on time. Does your answer change (from the one you came up with in part a, above)? Explain.

CONTEMPORARY CASE APPLICATIONS

FPPC 7.1 Financing Marilyn's Education

At age 19, Marilyn Bronson is in the middle of her second year of studies at a community college in San Diego. She has done well in her course work; majoring in prebusiness studies, she currently has a 3.75 grade point average. Marilyn currently lives at home and works part-time as a filing clerk for a nearby electronics distributor. Her parents cannot afford to pay her tuition and college expenses—she is virtually on her own as far as college goes.

Marilyn hopes to transfer to the University of Texas next year. She has already been accepted and feels that she would get an excellent education there. After talking with her counselor, Marilyn feels that she will not be able to hold down a part-time job and still manage to complete her bachelor's degree program at Texas in two years. Knowing that on her twenty-second birthday she will receive approximately $30,000 from a trust fund left her by her grandmother, Marilyn has decided to borrow against the trust fund in order to support herself during the next two years. She estimates that she will need $20,000 to meet tuition, room and board, books and supplies, travel, personal expenditures, and so on during that period. Unable to qualify for any special loan programs, Marilyn has found two sources of single-payment loans, each requiring a security interest in the trust proceeds as collateral. The terms required by each potential lender are as follows:

a. California State Bank will lend $25,000 at 10 percent discount interest. The loan principal would be due at the end of two years.

b. National Bank of San Diego will lend $20,000 under a two-year note. The note would carry a 12 percent simple interest rate and would also be due in a single payment at the end of two years.

Questions

1. How much would Marilyn (a) receive in initial loan proceeds and (b) be required to repay at maturity under the California State Bank loan?
2. Compute (a) the finance charges and (b) the APR on the loan offered by California State Bank.
3. Compute (a) the finance charges and (b) the APR on the loan offered by the National Bank of San Diego. How big a loan payment would be due at the end of two years?
4. Compare your findings in Questions 2 and 3, and recommend one of the loans to Marilyn. Explain your recommendation.
5. What other recommendation might you offer Marilyn relative to the disposition of the loan proceeds?

FPPC 7.2 Glen Gets His Camaro

Glen Watson, a 27-year old bachelor living in Charlotte, North Carolina, has been a high school teacher for five years. For the past four months, he has been thinking about buying a Chevrolet Camaro, but feels he is not able to afford a brand-new one. Recently, however, a friend, John McKenzie, has offered to sell him his two-year-old, fully loaded Camaro Z-28. John wants $12,500 for his car, which has been driven only 8,000 miles and is in very good condition. Glen is eager to buy the car but has only $6,000 in his savings account at Tar Heel Bank. He expects to net $3,000 from the sale of his Chevrolet Cavalier, but this will still leave him about $3,500 short. He has two alternatives for obtaining the money:

a. Borrow $3,500 from the First National Bank of Charlotte at a fixed rate of 12 percent per annum, simple interest. The loan would be repaid in equal monthly installments over a three-year (36-month) period.

b. Obtain a $3,500 installment loan requiring 36 monthly payments from the Charlotte Teacher's Credit Union at a 6½ percent stated rate of interest. The add-on method would be used to calculate the finance charges on this loan.

Questions

1. Using Exhibit 7.7, determine the required monthly payments if the loan is taken out at First National Bank of Charlotte.
2. Compute (a) the finance charges and (b) the APR on the loan offered by First National Bank of Charlotte.
3. Determine the size of the monthly payment required on the loan from the Charlotte Teacher's Credit Union.
4. Compute (a) the finance charges and (b) the APR on the loan offered by the Charlotte Teacher's Credit Union.
5. Compare the two loans and recommend one of them to Glen. Explain your recommendation.

GETTING A HANDLE ON YOUR FINANCIAL FUTURE

Contemplating a consumer loan involves many questions. Should I pay on installments or with a single payment? Is the interest rate fixed or variable? Whatever answers you determine to these questions, the first should always be—does this purchase fit into my financial plan?

If You Are Just Starting Out

One of your first uses of consumer credit will probably be for the purchase of an automobile. Assuming that the purchase meets your financial goals, you must determine how much of a monthly payment you can afford and then calculate the maximum amount you can finance.

Points to Remember:

1. Before you go to borrow money for a major purchase, calculate your expected debt safety ratio to see if you will stay under 20 percent of your monthly take-home pay *with the new loan.*
2. Know the maximum amount you are willing to pay and the maximum length you are willing to finance something *before* you go shopping.
3. Separate the purchasing decision from the financing decision. Shop for the best price and then choose the best financing package.
4. Even if 100 percent financing is available, consider putting some of your own money into the purchase. This will reduce the payments and allow you to pay off the loan earlier, if you so choose.
5. Avoid financing automobiles for too long a period of time. You may find that when you go to trade for another the outstanding balance on your existing loan is greater than what the dealer will offer you in trade.
6. If you use single-payment loans, be sure to budget the principal repayment at the end of the term as well as periodic interest payments, if required.

If You Are Thirty-Something

As you get older you will probably be able to accumulate funds that could be used to make major purchases. You will probably be faced with the decision of whether or not to pay cash or to finance a purchase. The decision hinges on the opportunity cost of your investments and how you would finance the purchase. Generally, if it costs more to borrow the money than you can earn on your funds, you should pay cash. However, you would not want to deplete all of your liquid assets.

Points to Remember:

1. If you use the purchase as collateral be sure that the lender releases the lien on it after the loan is repaid.
2. Consider using single-payment loans as a source of interim financing when you know where the source of repayment is coming from.
3. You might want to consider using a *home equity installment loan* instead of a consumer loan for some of your major purchases. This may enable you to deduct the interest expense from your income taxes.
4. If you are able to pay off the loan early, do so. However, be aware of any prepayment penalties.
5. Be sure you include all relevant information on any loan applications you fill out, especially for the debts you owe, as they will be checked for accuracy.
6. Look for the wage assignment clause in any purchase agreement you sign in conjunction with your financing. In the event of default, this allows the lender to collect part of your wages *without* a court order.

One of Paul Larkin's original goals was to pay off all of his credit card debt within the next two years. However, because of his budget deficit, he now wants to take a comprehensive look at his credit situation before deciding on how to handle this debt.

1. Complete an inventory of consumer debt for Paul Larkin using the information in the original case. You will need to calculate the minimum monthly payments for each of the credit cards based on the January 1, 1996 outstanding balances. What is Paul's debt safety ratio? Evaluate his ability to handle this debt.
2. After reviewing the inventory of consumer debt, Christine suggested that Paul borrow enough from his Community Credit Union line of credit to pay off all of his credit cards. If Paul did this, what would the minimum monthly payment be on the line of credit? What would the monthly payment be if Paul wanted to pay the line of credit off within two years? Would you recommend that Paul use the line of credit to pay off the credit cards? Why or why not?
3. Assume Paul does pay off his credit cards using the line of credit, and now has decided to keep only three of his credit cards—the Dillards card plus two of the other cards. If Paul does pay his new charges off each month upon billing, which two cards would be best to keep? If Paul lets his balances revolve, which two cards would be best for him? Paul estimates that he would carry an average daily balance of $300 a month on each of the two cards. Which two cards would you recommend Paul keep? Why?
4. Before paying off the AT&T Universal MasterCard and the Optima True Grace cards, Paul reviewed the monthly transactions for the previous month. Calculate the finance charges on these two cards using the calculation methods stated in the original case.

AT&T Universal			**Optima True Grace**		
Date	**Transaction**	**Amount**	**Date**	**Transaction**	**Amount**
12/1	Beginning balance	$1,089	12/1	Beginning balance	$998
12/15	Purchase	135	12/6	Purchase	23
12/20	Payment	354	12/23	Purchase	116
12/30	Purchase	403	12/25	Payment	256

Payments on both of these cards were made before the due date for the billing cycle.

5. In reviewing the current charges on his GM Gold MasterCard, Paul noticed a charge for $126 that he did not make. According to federal legislation, what should Paul do to correct this billing error?
6. If the three credit cards Paul decides to keep were stolen and the following unauthorized charges were made before the cards were reported missing, what would be Paul's maximum liability, according to federal legislation?

Credit Card #1	$350
Credit Card #2	$ 25
Credit Card #3	$140

FPPC **7.** Christine (Paul's girl friend) would like to purchase a new home computer. She thinks the computer and printer she needs would cost about $3,500, but she is not sure if she should use cash or credit. The following loans are available:

General Telephone Credit Union	Ace Computer Company
13% stated interest rate simple interest loan 24 monthly payments	11.5% stated interest rate add-on interest loan 24 monthly payments

a. Compare the monthly payments, the total finance charges, and the APRs on the above loans. Which would you recommend as the best loan for Christine? Why?

b. (For students using the computer disk) Run the amortization table for the recommended loan. How much interest would be paid in the first year of this loan? During the second year?

c. Before Christine decides on using credit, she wants to compare the cost of using the loan you recommended with the cost of paying cash for the computer equipment. If she pays cash, she would withdraw funds from her General Telephone Credit Union Money Market Fund (currently earning 3.5%). Compare the relative cost of cash vs. credit. Which would you recommend for this purchase?

FPPC **8.** Jack and Sarah Mathews (Paul's landlords) have decided to loan their daughter and son-in-law $10,000 to help with the purchase of a new home. The Mathews plan to charge 8 percent simple interest for a 48-month period. How much would the monthly payments be on this loan? What would you recommend Jack and Sarah do to reduce the risks of making a family loan such as this?

PART 4

Part 4: Managing Insurance Needs

CHAPTER 8

INSURING YOUR LIFE

The Saunders Have a Couple Good Reasons to Buy Life Insurance

Like many couples, the birth of their first child made Dan and Joanna Saunders start to think about life insurance. "After all," says Dan, "who wants to talk about what to do if you die? And trying to sort through all the choices was really confusing." They knew they were underinsured but didn't know what type of coverage they needed, or where to get it at an affordable price. When their second child was born in 1993 and they moved to a larger house near Boston, they recognized it was time to get more financial protection.

Dan, who works in publishing, has $50,000 in group term life through his employee benefits program and also has a $100,000 whole life policy with New York Life. He's concerned because many publishers are downsizing, and if he's laid off, that coverage is gone. "But what's more important is that we don't even have enough life insurance to cover our new mortgage," he explains. "So we're looking into ways to increase our coverage so we can protect our assets and provide funds for our children, including college." One possibility is that Joanna, who is a partner in a retail store and doesn't have any coverage, can purchase group term life insurance through a trade association. The Saunders have also read about low-load life insurance, purchased directly from the company so that you don't have to pay sales commissions.

"Just after Carolyn was born, we were inundated with calls from insurance agents," says Joanna. "One told us that a permanent policy was best because it had a savings feature and that some time in the future, term insurance

Learning Goals

LG1. *Explain the role that insurance planning plays in personal financial planning and the relationship between risk and insurance.*

LG2. *Discuss the primary reasons for life insurance and identify those who need coverage.*

LG3. *Calculate how much life insurance you need.*

LG4. *Differentiate between the various types of life insurance policies and describe their advantages and disadvantages.*

LG5. *Recognize key life insurance policy provisions and features.*

LG6. *Choose the best life insurance policy for your needs at the lowest cost.*

would become too costly. Then he showed us reams of numbers indicating that our cash value would grow at 8 percent. Another said term life was the way to go. The premiums were lower and we'd do better taking the difference between what we'd pay in permanent and term premiums and investing it ourselves. We were confused!" Before they bought a policy, however, they decided to figure out how much additional life insurance they would need and what kind of policy to buy.

First, they figured out how much it would take to maintain their current standard of living, repay the mortgage, and have money for college and other expenses like child care. Next, they looked at the value of their assets, including the equity in their house and investment accounts, and other income sources, such as Social Security benefits. The bottom line was that they needed another $250,000 in insurance! "We've always been good savers," notes Dan. "So I'm leaning toward term insurance as the most cost-effective way to supplement the whole life policy I already have. And Joanna can get good rates on term insurance through her group."

It's easy, as the Saunders found, to put off buying life insurance, or to avoid it altogether, because you're not sure what to buy. In Chapter 8, we'll help you understand who needs life insurance, how much to buy, and how to select the best policies for your needs.

Sources: Based on information from Laura M. Holson and Liz Comte Reisman, "Lessons in Life," *Smart Money*, December 1994, p. 135; Jim Lowell, "Today's Best Choices in Life Insurance," *Your Money*, April/May 1994, pp. 46–49.

BASIC INSURANCE CONCEPTS

LG1

Sound insurance planning rests on a basic understanding of your exposure to risk and how insurance can protect you against those risks. Before reading on, give some thought to the different ways that insurance could help protect you personally. Why is it important to have adequate life insurance, and what role should life insurance play in your financial plans?

A key ingredient of every successful financial plan is adequate life insurance coverage. The overriding purpose of life insurance is *to protect your dependents from financial loss* in the event of your untimely death. Some types of life insurance also possess attractive investment attributes. In essence, life insurance provides an umbrella for your financial plans. It not only protects what you already have (like providing funds to pay off the mortgage on your home) but also helps to assure the attainment of unfulfilled financial goals (such as the future education of your children). Being informed about life insurance is clearly just as important to financial planning as being well versed about taxes and investments. As with any other aspect of financial planning, you want to get as much from your insurance dollar as possible.

Over a period of years, the difference between buying life insurance wisely and unwisely can easily add up to thousands of dollars in extra premiums and many times that amount in lost protection. Wide differences exist among the types of life insurance policies that are available, their costs, and the quality of the companies and the agents that sell them. This chapter shows how you can intelligently determine how much life insurance protection you and your family need and explains the different types of life insurance policies available today. Although the diversity of market offerings may seem overwhelming, you'll see that most policies, despite their different names, are essentially variations of several basic types.

INSURANCE PLANNING

For one reason or another, the financial goals that you've set for yourself may never be reached. While no one likes to think about the possibility of losing everything you have acquired and planned for, unforeseen emergencies do happen. A disaster —flood, earthquake, or fire—could destroy your home. If you have an accident or serious illness, or you die, your family could be left without adequate income. Or a dependent's health problems might result in substantial financial burdens.

Suppose you've worked hard to acquire a nice home, furnishings, and other assets, along with a comfortable standard of living for your family. Wouldn't you want to protect all this? This is where *insurance* comes into the financial planning process. Its basic purpose is *to protect your dependents from losing the things that you've already acquired, and to shield you and your family from an interruption in your expected earnings*. Insurance, in short, lends a degree of certainty to your financial plans.

Auto and homeowners insurance, for example, reimburse you for damage or destruction to existing assets. Life insurance is meant to replace income that would have been earned had premature death not occurred—income that can easily total \$2 to \$4 million over the course of a college graduate's career. In practical terms, this means providing funds so that the family can keep their home, maintain an acceptable lifestyle, and provide for children's education or other special needs. Disability insurance does the same should you become disabled, while hospitalization and medical insurance cover the additional expenses arising from being sick or in an accident. Insurance planning involves trying to anticipate the losses to which your assets and income could be exposed, and considers how you can protect against such losses by weaving insurance into your financial plans. To do so, you will have to make decisions about life, health, and property insurance.

THE CONCEPT OF RISK

In insurance, *risk* is defined as uncertainty with respect to economic loss. Whenever you and your family have a financial interest in something—whether it be your life, health, home, car, boat, or job—you face risk. You face the chance that your budget will be upset and that your net worth will perhaps be drastically reduced. Because of the devastating effect that losses can have on your financial well-being, you must devise ways to deal with risk. Obviously it makes sense to take steps *before* a loss occurs, as is done in *risk avoidance* and *loss prevention*. However, when losses do occur, you will need an economical way of covering them, which is what you obtain from *risk assumption* and *insurance*.

Risk Avoidance. Perhaps the simplest way to deal with risk is to avoid the act that creates it. As an example, people who are afraid they might lose everything they own because of a lawsuit resulting from an automobile accident could avoid driving. With respect to life and health risks, avid skydivers or bungee jumpers might want to choose another recreational activity!

Although **risk avoidance** can be an effective way to handle some risks, such action is not without its costs. For instance, the people who avoid driving suffer considerable inconvenience, and the retired skydiver may find he or she now suffers *more* stress, which can lead to different types of health risks. Risk avoidance is an attractive way to deal with risk only when the estimated cost of avoidance is less than the estimated cost of handling it in some other way.

Loss Prevention and Control. In a broad sense, **loss prevention** can be defined as any activity that reduces the probability that a loss will occur (such as driving within the speed limit). **Loss control,** in contrast, is any activity that lessens the severity of loss once it occurs (such as wearing a safety belt or buying a car with air bags). Loss prevention and loss control should be important parts of the risk management program of every individual and family. In fact insurance provides a reasonable means for handling risk only when people use effective loss prevention and control measures. For example, if everybody drove fast and recklessly, risk avoidance might be the only effective way to deal with the risk of an automobile accident because automobile, life, and health insurance would be too expensive to buy.

Risk Assumption. With **risk assumption,** you choose to accept and bear the risk of loss. Risk assumption can be an effective way to handle many types of potentially small exposures to loss when insurance would be too expensive (for example, the risk of having your *Personal Financial Planning* text stolen). It is also a reasonable approach in the face of very large exposures that you cannot ordinarily prevent, or against which you cannot secure insurance (nuclear holocaust, for instance). Unfortunately, people often assume risks because they are unaware of various exposures to loss or think that their insurance offers adequate protection when in fact it does not. Therefore, one objective of these three chapters on insurance is to help you recognize the loss exposures that you will face and provide you with an understanding of when risk assumption is the preferred manner for handling certain risks.

Insurance. Insurance permits society to reduce financial risks and share losses. Risk or uncertainty can be reduced because insurers are able to combine the loss experiences of large numbers of people and, with certain actuarial data, estimate the chance of loss faced by the insured population. This prediction then allows each person to contribute a relatively small amount (the insurance premium) to an insurance company in exchange for a promise that he or she will be reimbursed for covered losses. Insured individuals gain because they are able to transfer their risk to the insurer. The insurance company, in turn, can realize a gain if the amount of insured losses has been accurately estimated.

An insurance policy is a contract between you (the insured) and an insurance company (the insurer) under which the insurance company promises to pay for your losses according to the specified terms. From your perspective, *you are transferring the risk of loss to the insurance company*. The insurance company is willing to accept the risk because it hopes to make a profit by collecting premiums from a large number of insureds, investing the money, and paying out losses and expenses that are less than the premiums collected and investment earnings. Insurers can do this because they are able to combine many insureds into a "pool," for which losses are more predictable than for any one of the insureds individually.

The premiums you pay for insurance usually come out of your current income. Thus, the heart

risk avoidance Avoidance of an act that would create a risk.

loss prevention Any activity that reduces the probability that a loss will occur.

loss control Any activity that reduces the severity of loss once the loss occurs.

risk assumption The choice to bear or accept risk.

of the insurance decision is the comparison of the premiums you are willing (and able) to take from your current income relative to the need for, and the amount of, protection you will receive from the insurance that you buy. The decision is difficult, because you do not know for sure whether or not losses will occur, but only that you might suffer losses from certain unforeseen events. This discussion of risk and the following explanation of underwriting should help you to better understand the whole concept of insurance and the role that it can play in your financial planning. Later in this chapter we'll also provide some discussion of the factors to consider when making decisions about life insurance coverage.

UNDERWRITING

In all types of insurance, the company must decide whom it can insure and then determine the applicable rates. This function is called **underwriting.** Through underwriting, insurance companies try to guard against adverse selection, which happens when only high-risk clients apply for, and get, insurance coverage. Underwriters design rate-classification schedules so that people pay premiums commensurate with their chance of loss. The success of any insurance company is highly dependent on the quality of the work done here. If the underwriting standards are too high, people will be unjustly denied coverage, and insurance sales will drop. On the other hand, if standards are too low, many insureds will pay less than their fair share, and the insurance company's solvency could be jeopardized.

A basic problem facing underwriters is the choice of appropriate criteria to apply when they select and classify insureds. Since a perfect relationship does not exist between available criteria and loss experience, some people invariably believe that they are being charged more than they should be for their insurance. For example, a life insurance company may charge higher premiums to an applicant who is slightly overweight, even if he or she has no other health problems.

The life insurance underwriting process begins when the person desiring a policy submits an application. In addition to basic information (name, age, sex, occupation, type and amount of policy desired), a typical application asks questions like whether you have been denied insurance; engage in hazardous activities such as piloting a plane, scuba diving, hang gliding, or car or motorcycle racing; smoke cigarettes; had your driver's license suspended, have over three moving violations, or been charged with driving under the influence of alcohol or drugs. The next section is about your health: family health history, your height and weight, medical tests and treatment received within the past five years, any previous medical problems, whether or not you consulted a physician, and substance abuse problems. Most insurance companies require tests to rule out the HIV virus and drug abuse and obtain medical records from your personal physician.

All these factors are used to determine whether to accept you and what premium you qualify for. For example, someone in excellent health is considered "preferred" and pays the lowest premium. Other typical categories include standard, preferred smoker, and smoker. Those with special medical conditions—for example, high cholesterol or diabetes, fall into rated categories and pay considerably higher premiums if they are accepted.

All life insurance policies contain an incontestability clause that gives the insurance company one to two years to investigate all information provided by the insured in the application. If it discovers a material false statement during that period—for example, that you smoke when you said you didn't or failed to disclose a medical condition—the company can rescind the contract. After the elapsed period, the insurer cannot challenge the validity of the policy, regardless of whether the insured has died or is still living.

Notwithstanding incontestability, the insurance company can adjust the payment made under a policy at any time if the insured misstated his or her age or sex in the application. For example, assume that a male age 35 applied for a life insurance policy by mail and stated that he was a female age 35, because females of the same age pay lower premiums. When the insured dies and the company discovers the error, it would award a sum equal to the amount of insurance that the premiums paid would have purchased had the insurer known the applicant was male. Note that the policy is not voided but simply modified to conform to the facts.

Although historically insurers have assigned different rates to men and women, some states now have laws requiring that the same rates and underwriting standards apply to both males and females. Such laws illustrate the conflict between underwriting standards that seem to make sense based upon the insurers' actuarial tables and those that are considered fair by the general public and their elected representatives.

Underwriting is perhaps more of an art than a science. Insurers are always trying to improve their underwriting capabilities in order to set rates that will provide adequate protection against insolvency and yet be reasonable for most policyholders. From your standpoint, though, you should recognize that insurance companies often use very different underwriting standards and rate classification systems. Therefore, you can usually save money by shopping around for a company that has underwriting practices more favorable to your specific characteristics and needs. For instance, some life insurers offer discounts to nonsmokers and to people in better-than-average health. And many companies even offer discounts to those in preferred low-risk occupations, such as professionals and business executives.

Concept Check

8-1. Discuss the role that insurance plays in the financial planning process. Why is it important to have enough life insurance?

8-2. Define (a) *risk avoidance,* (b) risk assumption, (c) *loss prevention,* (d) *loss control,* and (e) *underwriting.* Explain their interrelationships, if any.

8-3. Explain the purpose of underwriting. What are some of the factors underwriters consider when evaluating a life insurance application?

HOW MUCH LIFE INSURANCE IS RIGHT FOR YOU? FPPC LG2 LG3

While there are many ways to determine the amount of life insurance that's right for you, probably the best is to base the decision on an assessment of your needs. Place yourself in the shoes of a married person with two young children. What kinds of financial needs and obligations would you want to cover with a life insurance policy? Take a moment to think about this question before reading on.

"Life Insurance is sold, not bought" is an axiom in the life insurance business. As a rule, people just don't get as strong an urge to buy life insurance as they might to buy a house, car, or new television set. Far too many people simply wait until an agent contacts them and then reluctantly accept "being sold." A partial explanation for this tendency to wait is that life insurance is intangible. Even after you purchase it, you can't see, smell, touch, or taste its benefits. In addition, although most people (especially family breadwinners) recognize they should buy life insurance, many believe it can be delayed another month—or two or three. The need is felt, but it is neither obvious nor pressing. But perhaps as much an explanation as anything else is the fact that the purchase of a life insurance policy is associated with something unpleasant—namely, death. People don't like to talk about death, or the things closely associated with it, so they all too often put off taking care of their life insurance needs. That's unfortunate, because life insurance does have definite benefits to offer, the most important being all the things that a family will still be able to buy after a loss occurs—things they very likely could not otherwise buy.

The point is not to push you to go out and stock up on as much life insurance as you can get, but rather to find out whether or not you do, in fact, need life insurance. If you do, you should give its purchase a high priority. Deciding whether or not, and in what amount, you need life insurance is an important issue.

WHO NEEDS LIFE INSURANCE?

The first question to ask about life insurance is if, in fact, you need it! The answer depends on many factors that we'll consider in this chapter, including your personal life situation and other financial resources. But many people just assume they need life insurance and lose sight of its major purpose:

underwriting With respect to insurance, the process of deciding who can be insured and determining the applicable rates.

to provide financial security for dependents. Other features, such as savings and tax benefits, are certainly valuable benefits, but they are secondary reasons to buy life insurance. If you have no dependents, you probably don't need life insurance. For example, buying life insurance on a child makes no sense—although agents may argue that it guarantees the child's insurability later should he or she develop health problems or that it provides savings for college. Actually, you can get better returns by investing what you would pay for insurance in higher-yielding savings vehicles.

Your life insurance needs change throughout your life. When you are single, you may not need any life insurance at all, unless you support parents or other relatives. Once you marry, the amount of insurance you provide for your spouse depends on his or her earning potential and the assets, such as a house, you want to protect. Insurance needs increase most when children enter the picture, because young families would suffer the greatest financial hardship from the premature death of a wage-earning spouse. As families build assets, their insurance needs may change, both in terms of the amount of insurance and types of policies that meet their objectives. Other life cycle changes affect insurance needs. For example, loss of a spouse through divorce or death may require additional life insurance on the surviving spouse; in contrast, once children finish college, insurance needs may drop. Whether you need more or less life insurance in later years depends on the availability of other financial resources, such as pension plans and investments, to provide for your dependents. This is why life insurance planning should occur within your overall personal financial planning framework.

CALCULATING YOUR INSURANCE NEEDS

Two techniques are commonly used to estimate an individual's life insurance needs: the *multiple earnings approach* and the *needs approach*. The **multiple earnings approach** gained its popularity based on simplicity rather than soundness. With this technique, you calculate the amount of life insurance to buy by simply multiplying your gross annual earnings by some arbitrarily selected number. Multiples of 3, 5, or even 10 times earnings are frequently used to find the amount of life insurance coverage needed. Life insurance agents have tables with multiples based on age, family situation, and gross annual pay. For example, the table might show that a married 35-year-old male with two children earning $40,000 a year should use a multiple of 8.7 times if he wants to replace 75 percent of this income. His total life insurance coverage, therefore, should amount to $40,000 × 8.7, or $348,000. This amount is then compared to the life insurance the person already has from existing individual policies or other sources. If the person has $50,000 from an employer's group life insurance policy and another $50,000 in death benefits from the company's pension plan, his remaining life insurance needs are $248,000 (that is, $348,000 − $50,000 − $50,000).

At best, this procedure should be used only to get a first, very rough approximation of life insurance needs. While it is simple to use, it fails to fully recognize the financial obligations and resources of the individual.

Most professional life insurance agents have abandoned the multiple earnings approach in favor of the **needs approach.** This method specifically considers the financial obligations that a person may have and the financial resources that are available, *in addition to life insurance.* Essentially, the needs approach involves three steps: (1) estimating the total economic resources needed; (2) determining all financial resources that would be available, including life insurance and pension plan death benefits already in force; and (3) subtracting the amount of resources available from the amount needed in order to determine the amount of *additional* life insurance required to provide for an individual's financial program.

When assessing economic needs, you must be sure to consider your particular family situation. Premature death will create greater financial hardship for certain types of families. For example, single parents, especially those with no additional resources (such as a divorced spouse who can take over in the event of premature death) typically need larger amounts of life insurance to provide for dependents. Two-income families that depend on a second income to make ends meet must insure both spouses adequately. "Blended" families that include children from prior marriages require more protection for the larger family unit in the event of one parent's death, and a parent may also need to provide coverage for dependent children not living with him or her. And families in the "sandwich" generation must protect both children and any elderly relatives they support from the severe financial impact caused by a wage-earning spouse's death. In each of these cases, adequate life insurance can provide financial security for dependents.

Assessing Economic Needs. The basic question asked in the needs approach is: What financial resources will the survivors need should the income producer die tomorrow? Although life insurance is often used in retirement planning, it primarily protects families from financial loss resulting from the death of an income producer. In this role, life insurance can provide money for the following financial needs: (1) family income, (2) additional expenses, (3) debt liquidation, (4) surviving spouse's income, (5) money for special requirements, such as the children's education, and (6) liquidity. For the well-heeled, the proceeds from a life insurance policy can also be used to pay estate taxes, thereby leaving intact all or most of the family estate. Such tax payments aside, let's look more closely at the six major financial needs of a typical family.

Family income. For most people with dependents, the principal financial need is to protect their families' incomes. If they die, they want to make sure that their families' ability to live comfortably is not seriously impaired. This may involve providing for elderly relatives or nonrelated dependents as well as dependent children. Perhaps the best way to estimate the amount of monthly income necessary to sustain a family is to develop a budget covering all expenses that are likely to be incurred. As discussed in Chapter 3, major items in most family budgets are housing costs; utilities; food; automobile expenses; medical and dental needs; clothing; life, health, property, and liability insurance; property taxes; recreation and travel; and savings.

One important question that you must face in developing a post-death family budget is, "What standard of living do I want my family to have?" While some feel a reduced level of consumption is in order, others want their families to maintain their present standard of living; still others would like to leave their families with the level of consumption that would have been achieved had the providers continued to live and work.

A final point to keep in mind concerning family income is that many families today depend on two incomes. Emphasis traditionally has been placed on insuring the family against the income loss of the father. But working mothers can also die unexpectedly. Therefore, to the extent that a family (with either one or two incomes) depends on the woman's income to make ends meet, *that income should be counted as part of the family income need.* Equally important, because the death of a working mother can have devastating effects on the family structure as well as the family budget, *her life should also be adequately insured.* In keeping with the growing importance of women in the work force, life insurance sales on the lives of women have increased dramatically in recent years. Whereas in 1965, only 10 percent of all policies were sold to women, by 1985 that number rose to 26 percent and in 1995 is approaching 40 percent.

Additional expenses. In most households, adult family members are responsible for performing many family and household services. Perhaps the most extreme example of such responsibilities is the homemaker not employed outside the home. Among the valuable services performed by the homemaker are child care, cooking, cleaning, and, of course, family taxi service! If the homemaker were to die, these services would represent new expenses to be paid out of the family's income. Such expenses could stretch the family budget to the breaking point and, thus, should be recognized when estimating insurance needs.

Pay off debts. In the event of their deaths, most breadwinners prefer to leave their families relatively debt-free. Therefore, to accomplish this objective a person must determine the average amount due for outstanding bills. Included in this amount would be the balances on installment loans, credit cards, department store accounts, and other similar obligations, as well as estimated funeral expenses. In addition, some heads of household will want to leave enough money to pay off their home mortgages and will include this amount in their debt-liquidation estimates. The debt-liquidation component of financial needs can be viewed as an estimate of the individual's average liabilities.

multiple earnings approach A method of determining the amount of life insurance coverage needed by multiplying gross annual earnings by some largely arbitrarily selected number.

needs approach A method of determining the amount of life insurance needed that considers the person's available financial resources (including life insurance), along with specific financial obligations.

Surviving spouse's income. Once children are on their own, the monthly household expenses should decrease substantially. Nevertheless, the surviving spouse may need monthly support for the remainder of his or her life. Therefore, the amount of income needed, as well as the duration of the survivor's life, needs to be estimated.

Special financial needs. In addition to the economic needs that have been discussed, some families would like to have the resources available to meet specific financial requirements, such as a college education fund for the children and/or surviving spouse, special care for a disabled or chronically ill dependent, an emergency fund for unexpected financial burdens, or, as previously mentioned, a fund for paying off the mortgage.

Liquidity. Often we may have assets but no cash. Real estate investors, for example, are notorious for owning several million dollars' worth of properties but bouncing checks for $100. Similarly, many farmers are land rich and cash poor. People who keep a very high percentage of their wealth in illiquid assets often need life insurance to provide enough cash to avoid estate shrinkage. The life insurance proceeds keep the mortgages paid and assets maintained until they can be sold in an orderly fashion at their fair market value.

Available Resources. After estimating the amount of financial needs your dependents must try to satisfy upon the death of an income provider, you should prepare a list of all available resources for meeting those needs. For most families, money from savings and social security survivor's benefits make up the largest non–life insurance financial resources. Additional resources include proceeds from company-sponsored group life insurance policies and the death benefits payable from accumulated pension plans and profit-sharing programs. Another important source is income that can be earned by the surviving spouse or children. If the surviving spouse is skilled and readily employable, his or her earnings could be a family's largest available resource. Also, many families have real estate (in addition to their home), jewelry, stocks, bonds, and other assets that can be liquidated to meet financial needs. After developing a complete list of available resources, you should make some reasonable estimate of their value. Although this step can be difficult due to the changing values of many of the assets, coming up with a set of reasonably accurate estimates is certainly within reach.

Needs Less Resources. The last step in determining the amount of life insurance required is to subtract the amount of available resources from the total needed to satisfy all of the family's financial objectives. If the amount of available resources exceeds the needs, no (additional) life insurance is required. If, as is the case in most families with children, the resources are less than the needs, that difference is the amount of additional life insurance necessary to provide the family with its desired standard of living.

Generally, insurance proceeds can be invested, until the money is actually needed, at a rate of return that exceeds taxes and inflation. This after-tax, after-inflation return may be 1 to 2 percent for reasonably conservative investments, and even higher for more risky investments.

By now you can see that insurance planning based on the needs concept can become quite complex. A competent financial planner or life insurance agent who understands the process can guide you through the planning stage. Virtually all life insurance companies today have computer programs set up to determine the life insurance requirements of families using the needs approach. Remember, though, that *life insurance needs are not static.* The amount and type of life insurance you need today probably will differ from the amount and type suitable for you five or ten years from now. Life insurance programs should be reviewed and adjusted (as necessary) at least every five years, or after major changes in the family have occurred (for example, the birth of a child or the purchase of a home).

THE NEEDS APPROACH IN ACTION

To illustrate how the needs approach can be used in insurance planning, consider the hypothetical case of Bill and Joan Benson. At the present time, the Bensons' primary desire is to have enough insurance on Bill's life to take care of Joan (age 35) and their two children (ages 6 and 8) should Bill die. Their priorities are to (1) leave the family debt free, (2) ensure an income for Joan and their children until the youngest child is age 18, (3) provide funds for Joan to make the transition from homemaker to gainful employment, and (4) establish a

WORKSHEET 8.1

Determining the Need for Life Insurance

A worksheet like this one can be used to determine your life insurance requirements according to the needs approach.

Insured's Name: Bill and Joan Benson Date: January 1996

				Totals
A. Family Income Needs				
1. Debt Liquidation:				
a. House mortgage	$65,000			
b. Other loans	$ 5,000			
c. Total debt (a + b)				$70,000
2. Final expenses				$15,000
3. Annual income needs:	**Period 1**	**Period 2**	**Period 3**	
a. Monthly living expenses	3,400	2,700	2,200	
b. Less: Social security survivor's benefits	2,435	0	1,100	
c. Less: Surviving spouse's income	0	2,250	0	
d. Less: Other pension benefits and income	0	0	900	
e. Net monthly income needed (a − b − c − d)	965	450	200	
f. Net yearly income needed (12 × e)	11,580	5,400	2,400	
g. Number of years in period	12	18	22	
h. Funding needed each period (f × g)	$138,960	$97,200	$52,800	
i. Total living needs (add line h for each period)				$288,960
4. Spouse reeducation fund				$ 25,000
5. Children's opportunity fund				$ 50,000
6. Other needs				$ 0
7. TOTAL INCOME NEEDS (add right column)				$448,960
B. Financial Resources Available				
1. Savings and investments	$65,000			
2. Group life insurance	$55,000			
3. Other life insurance	$ –			
4. Other resources	$ –			
TOTAL RESOURCES AVAILABLE (1 + 2 + 3 + 4)				$120,000
C. Additional Life Insurance Needed (A − B) (Note: no additional insurance is needed if number is negative.)				$328,960

fund that will permit the children to obtain college educations or begin careers. Because the Bensons know that insurance needs change, they believe a five-year planning horizon is appropriate. At the end of that period, the family's needs and resources will be reevaluated to see if their life insurance program warrants modification. Worksheet 8.1 will be used to calculate the life insurance needs of the Benson family.

Family Economic Needs. Since the Bensons use credit sparsely, their outstanding debts are limited to a mortgage (with a current balance of $65,000), an automobile loan ($4,000), and miscellaneous charge accounts ($1,000). The balances on these debts currently total $70,000. The mortgage is in its early years and will not be reduced significantly during the five-year planning period. Although the existing auto loan will be amortized, a new loan for

EXHIBIT 8.1

Approximate Monthly Social Security Survivor's Benefits

These benefits applied to the families of qualified wage earners who died in 1995; like other aspects of social security, the amount of monthly benefits depends in large part on the covered worker's level of income.

Approximate Monthly Survivors Benefits if the Worker Dies In 1995 and had Steady Earnings

Worker's Age	Your Family	Deceased Worker's Earnings In 1994				
		$20,000	$30,000	$40,000	$50,000	$60,600 Or More
35	Spouse and 1 child	$1,152	$1,542	$1,758	$1,940	$2,088
	Spouse and 2 children	1,426	1,800	2,051	2,264	2,435
	1 child only	576	771	879	970	1,044
	Spouse at age 60	549	735	838	925	995
45	Spouse and 1 child	1,150	1,540	1,750	1,914	2,006
	Spouse and 2 children	1,423	1,797	2,049	2,235	2,342
	1 child only	575	770	875	957	1,003
	Spouse at age 60	548	734	837	913	957
55	Spouse and 1 child	1,150	1,540	1,714	1,816	1,876
	Spouse and 2 children	1,422	1,797	2,001	2,120	2,189
	1 child only	575	770	857	908	938
	Spouse at age 60	548	734	817	866	894

Source: Social Security Administration

a replacement vehicle will probably be necessary. Bill therefore believes that $70,000 will be adequate to pay off these debts. In addition, the Bensons would like to have $15,000 available to pay estate administration expenses, taxes, and funeral costs. (These items are listed on lines 1 and 2 of part A of Worksheet 8.1.)

Bill and Joan have reviewed their budget and feel that the family's monthly living expenses would be $3,400 while the children are still living at home (12 years). During the period after both children leave home and until Joan retires at age 65 (18 years), the Bensons estimate her monthly living expenses to be $2,700 in current dollars. After Joan's retirement, they anticipate her living expenses to fall to $2,200 a month. The life expectancy of a woman Joan's age is 87 years, so the Bensons calculate that Joan will spend about 22 years in retirement. Because Joan and the children would be eligible for **social security survivor's benefits,** they include these benefits in their estimate of family income needs. Basically, survivor's benefits are paid to the dependents of deceased workers and are part of the social insurance provisions of the social security system. They are intended to provide basic (minimum) support to families faced with the loss of their principal wage earners. In addition to the elderly and disabled, the principal recipients of social security survivor's benefits include (1) unmarried children under age 18 (or 19 if still in high school), (2) nonworking spouses with children under age 16, and (3) surviving spouses age 60 and over.

Exhibit 8.1 lists some figures showing *approximate* monthly social security benefits available in 1995 to the survivors of qualified wage earners. Note that the level of benefits depends on the wage earner's age at death, earnings history, and the number of survivors. While these benefits used to be difficult to predict, the Social Security Administration now has an easy-to-use computer-based estimation system that will provide a fairly accurate estimate of the benefits your *survivors* would be entitled to receive if you die. To obtain this *Personal Earnings and Benefit Estimate Statement,* call the Social Security toll-free number, 1-800-772-1213, and request a short application form to fill out and send back in. (This statement is discussed in more detail in Chapter 14, and an actual sample is reproduced in Exhibit 14.6.)

Bill Benson knew about this program and applied for a statement of his own, which he recently received in the mail. Looking under the "Survivor's" portion of "Estimated Benefits," he learned that, based on his age (35) and recent income (he's close to the "high" level of earnings), his family would receive benefits of around $2,435 a month. Note that the Bensons would be entitled to the *maximum family benefits* which is paid to a surviving (nonworking) spouse with two or more minor children. However, when their youngest child reaches age 16, the benefits for Joan would cease, and each child's benefits also stop upon graduation from high school. Even so, because the worksheet we are using is an estimate, we will assume they receive $2,435 a month for the full 12 years (Period 1 of the worksheet).

Knowing what they'd receive from social security, they subtracted that amount from their target income (of $3,400 a month) to arrive at a *net monthly income* (line 3e on the worksheet). This is the amount of income they'll have to make up from some source other than social security to preserve their present standard of living. This is the basic income level they want to maintain until the youngest child has reached 18 years of age, a period of 12 years from now. Thus, they estimate that it should take about $138,960 to provide the family with $11,580 a year for 12 years. (See the Period 1 column of the worksheet.) Actually, given that money has a time value, it would take something *less* than the $138,960 to provide the needed income, but this complication can be ignored so long as we also disregard future inflation, which in fact would add to the amount needed. *In essence, since one element (inflation) will have at least a partially offsetting effect on the other (present value), we will ignore both of them in our calculation.* Because we're *estimating* future needs, there is little to be gained by trying to fine-tune these projections with even more estimates of future inflation rates and potential rates of return on invested capital!

A similar procedure is used to estimate available income for Period 2, the years after the children leave home and until Joan retires, and then, the years after Joan retires, Period 3. Period 2 is called the "Blackout Period," so named because it is a time during which the surviving spouse receives no social security benefits. However, Joan expects to work during this period, and feels she should be able to make a net monthly income of around $2,250 (in current dollars). That leaves her short about $450 a month, for a total need of $97,200 during the Blackout Period.

After retirement, the Bensons estimate that Joan's living expenses should drop even more (to around $2,200 a month). Because Joan will have worked for nearly 20 years, they think it is reasonable to assume she will earn retirement benefits of her own. But to be on the safe side, they estimate Joan's retirement benefits should amount to only $900 a month. In addition, once Joan reaches retirement age, she will once again be eligible for monthly social security benefits—which they estimate at about $1,100 a month. Based on this information, Joan will need a total of $52,800 to preserve her standard of living during retirement. Therefore, the Benson's total income needs over Joan's lifetime (Periods 1 through 3) are $288,960, shown as the total income needs (line 3i) on the worksheet.

Although Joan is trained as a stockbroker, because she will not go to work until both children are raised, they are concerned that her previous education may be somewhat out of date. Thus, they would like to have enough money to allow Joan to return to college for several years. They believe $25,000 should be sufficient for this purpose. Finally, both Bill and Joan want to guarantee that their children will have the money necessary for educational or other opportunities that may be available when they reach 18. To do this, they want to establish an opportunity fund of $50,000. The top part (Section A) of Worksheet 8.1 summarizes the Benson's economic needs. Note that they feel that the total amount necessary to meet their financial goals, should Bill die within the next five years, would be $448,960.

Available Financial Resources. Bill is employed as an assistant professor at a state university. Although the university has a retirement program, no preretirement survivor's benefits are available, other than social security. However, Bill is covered by an employer-sponsored group life insurance policy in the amount of one year's gross salary ($55,000). Also, the Bensons have roughly $65,000 in several mutual funds and a money market deposit account. These investments were obtained in part from an inheritance and from a $20,000 advance against Bill's textbook royalties.

Other potential resources, such as a promised gift of $20,000 from Joan's Aunt Sarah, a travel

social security survivor's benefits Benefits included in the social insurance provision of the social security system that are intended to provide basic support for families who have lost their principal wage earners.

accident life insurance policy with a $10,000 face value, and assorted personal property, are ignored in the planning process because of uncertainty as to either their amount or their availability. For example, Aunt Sarah may decide to donate the money to charity, or Bill may die from a cause unrelated to his travel insurance. Overall, then, the resources that the Bensons can count on to help achieve their economic objectives total $120,000, as summarized in the lower part (Section B) of Worksheet 8.1.

Additional Life Insurance Needed. As shown in the bottom line of Worksheet 8.1, the difference between the monies available and those that will be required is $328,960. This sum equals the amount of additional life insurance the Bensons will need on Bill's life to provide for the family's desired standard of living. Often the amount of the life insurance needed to fulfill a family's desired expenditures will exceed the family's willingness or ability for pay for it. Even after a careful search for the right type of policy at the best price, a family might decide they just cannot afford all of the insurance they would like. In these cases, a priority ranking of needs, coupled with a reassessment of available resources, is necessary. As an example, in the preliminary plans a college education fund might have been included while consideration was not given to income from employment of the surviving spouse or children. The family could decide, however, to let the children work their way through college and have the surviving spouse seek employment. Thus, ability and willingness to pay for life insurance can be adjusted to meet economic needs.

Concept Check

8-4. Explain the circumstances under which a single college graduate would or would not need life insurance. What life-cycle events would change this initial evaluation, and how might they affect his or her life insurance needs?

8-5. Discuss the two most commonly used ways to determine a person's life insurance needs.

8-6. Name and explain the most common economic needs that must be satisfied after the death of a family breadwinner.

WHAT KIND OF POLICY IS RIGHT FOR YOU?

LG4

Once you have determined how much *insurance to buy, the next thing you must do is decide on the* kind *of life insurance that's best for you. What factors would you want to consider when deciding on the type of life insurance policy to buy? Would you look for a good investment, or the most life insurance coverage for the money? Stop to think about these questions before going on.*

After you have determined the amount of life insurance necessary to meet your family's financial requirements, you must decide on the type of insurance contract that will best fit your needs. Generally speaking, most families can effectively satisfy their insurance needs through the use of one of the three basic types of life insurance: term life, whole life, or universal life insurance. Indeed, these three products account for 90 to 95 percent of all life insurance sales—with term life being the biggest seller, followed by whole life policies and then universal life. There are, of course, other types of life insurance policies available to consumers, but as we will see, most of these are simply modifications of these three types.

TERM INSURANCE

Under the provisions of a **term life insurance** policy, the insurance company agrees to pay a stipulated amount of money if the insured dies during the policy period. The period of coverage is often five years, with premiums payable annually, semiannually, or quarterly. Many other periods of coverage and payment plans are available. Term insurance is the purest form of life insurance in that it provides a stipulated amount of life insurance (that is, death benefits) and nothing more. There are *no* investment or savings features associated with it. Term insurance can be an economical way to purchase life insurance, on a temporary basis, for protection against financial loss resulting from death, especially in the early years of family formation.

Nearly all life insurance companies sell some form of term insurance. In addition, employer-sponsored group life insurance plans, and com-

EXHIBIT 8.2

Annual Renewable Term Life Insurance Premiums; $100,000 Policy, Preferred Nonsmoker Rates

When you buy term insurance, you are basically buying a product that provides life insurance coverage and nothing more. The following table shows rates for several age categories and selected policy years; actual premiums increase every year. As you can see, females pay less than males for coverage, and premiums increase sharply with age.

Policy Year	Age 25		Age 40		Age 60	
	Male	**Female**	**Male**	**Female**	**Male**	**Female**
1	$ 130	$ 119	$ 148	$ 139	$ 366	$ 252
5	169	147	252	219	927	562
10	218	187	426	368	1,702	1,080
15	196	176	647	507	2,666	1,313
20	279	259	1,258	1,054	4,574	2,989
Total Cost, 20 years	$3,777	$3,381	$9,871	$8,287	$38,457	$22,346

Source: A major life insurance company; January 1995 rates.

panies that sell directly to the public through the mail or newspaper and magazine advertisements, often offer term insurance at low rates. Unfortunately, in the past, many families, because of either lack of knowledge or poor advice, did not properly incorporate term life insurance into their insurance programs. As consumers have become more knowledgeable, however, term life insurance sales have increased accordingly. Today, in fact, term policies account for more than a third of all (group and individual) life insurance sales.

Types of Term Insurance. The most common types of term insurance are straight term and decreasing term. With regard to term policies, there are two important provisions that you should be aware of: renewability of the policy and its convertibility to a whole life policy.

Straight term. Policies written for a given number of years—for example, 1, 5, 10, or 20 years—are called **straight-term** (or level-term) **policies**. In such policies, the *amount* of life insurance coverage remains unchanged throughout the effective period of the policy. In contrast, the *annual premium* on a straight-term policy may increase each year, as with *annual renewable term policies,* or remain level throughout the policy period, as with *level-premium term policies.* Exhibits 8.2 and 8.3 list representative annual premiums for annual renewable term and level-premium term life policies, respectively. Note that annual renewable term policies start out with relatively low annual premiums, but they increase rapidly over time; in contrast, level-premium policies start out with higher annual premiums, but because they do not change over time, their total cost is actually considerably less than the cost of a renewable term policy. (In early 1995, the National Association of Insurance Commissioners approved a regulation requiring many insurers to increase reserves for policies with rates guaranteed for a long period. As states adopt this rule, level term premium policies will be more expensive.)

Decreasing term. Because the death rate increases for each year of life, the premiums on straight-term policies for each successive period of coverage will also increase. As an alternative to such a situation, some term policies *maintain a level premium* throughout all periods of coverage, but *the amount of protection decreases.* Such a policy is called a **decreasing-term policy,** since the

term life insurance Insurance that provides only death benefits, for a specified period of time, and does not provide for the accumulation of any cash values.

straight-term policy A term insurance policy that is written for a given number of years and whose coverage remains unchanged throughout the effective term; also called level-term policy.

decreasing-term policy A term insurance policy in which the protection decreases over the policy's life.

EXHIBIT 8.3

Level-Premium Term Life Rates; $100,000 Preferred Nonsmoker Policy

This table shows rates for $100,000 of level-premium term life insurance. Although level premium costs less than annual renewable term for the same time period, you must requalify at the end of each term to retain the low premium.

	5 Year		10 Year		15 Year		20 Year	
Age	**Male**	**Female**	**Male**	**Female**	**Male**	**Female**	**Male**	**Female**
25	$140	$132	$140	$132	$155	$140	$ 170	$162
30	143	132	143	132	155	141	176	164
35	149	134	150	136	172	152	202	181
40	185	159	196	166	216	187	267	230
50	344	271	380	298	450	344	565	419
60	599	365	650	404	N/A	N/A	1,075	645

Source: A major life insurance company; January 1995 rates.

amount of protection decreases over its life. Decreasing term is used when the amount of needed coverage declines over time. For example, decreasing-term policies are popular with homeowners who want a level of life insurance coverage that will decline at about the same rate as the balances on their home mortgages. Families with young children use these policies to ensure a sufficient level of family income while the kids are growing up. (As they grow older, the amount of coverage needed decreases until the last child becomes independent and the need expires.)

Renewability and Convertibility Provisions. The **renewability** provision allows the insured to renew his or her policy for another term of equal length, without having to show evidence of insurability. Renewal is at the option of the insured, but the premium increases to offset the greater chance of death at older ages. Generally, term policies may be renewed at the end of each term until the insured reaches age 65 or 70. If you buy term insurance, it's a good idea to obtain a *guaranteed renewable provision* in your policy. Otherwise, if you become uninsurable due to accident or illness during the policy period, you will lose your chance to renew your protection. Today, this valuable provision is standard in most term policies at no extra cost. Certainly, you *never* should buy a term policy that does not have guaranteed renewability. You should also be aware, that with a level-premium term policy you typically must requalify medically at the end of the guaranteed rate period to renew the policy at favorable rates. If you are in poor health, the guaranteed renewable provision simply allows you to continue the existing policy, but at much higher annual renewable term rates.

The **convertibility** provision allows the insured to convert coverage to a comparable whole life policy (discussed below) without evidence of insurability. The convertibility feature guarantees the insureds that (1) they will not lose their insurance protection at the end of the period and (2) upon conversion, they will have lifelong protection (as long as they pay their premiums, of course). The convertibility provision can be useful to persons who need a large amount of death protection at a relatively low cost, but who also want to continue their insurance coverage throughout their entire lives. This way, term coverage can be purchased to provide for a large amount of immediate death protection, and then later, when the insured has more income (and saving for retirement and liquidity for estate taxes become the more dominant issues), the policy can be converted to whole life. The convertibility option is standard with most of today's term policies.

You should note that many convertible policies place some limitation on when the conversion can take place. For example, a ten-year term policy may stipulate that the conversion has to be made before the end of the eighth year, or a term policy to age 65 may require conversion prior to age 61.

Advantages and Disadvantages of Term. Since term insurance offers an economical way to purchase a large amount of life insurance protection over a given (relatively short) period of time, it is particularly advantageous during the child-rearing years. And with the guaranteed renewable and convertible options, coverage can be continued throughout the insured's life, although, of course, the cost continually grows due to the increased chance of death. Indeed, increasing cost is the main disadvantage of term insurance and is a principal reason why people discontinue needed coverage.

Criticizing term insurance on the basis of increasing cost, however, is similar to finding fault with homeowners insurance for not paying for a loss caused by an automobile accident. Clearly, the purpose of homeowners insurance is not to provide automobile coverage, just as the purpose of a term policy is *not* to provide lifelong coverage. The objective of term insurance is to provide a large amount of protection for a limited period of time—something it accomplishes very well!

WHOLE LIFE INSURANCE

Few people ever outlive the need for some type of life insurance. Accordingly, **whole life insurance,** as the name implies, is designed to offer financial protection for the whole life of an individual. In addition to death protection, whole life insurance has a *savings* feature, called **cash value,** which results from the investment earnings on paid-in insurance premiums Thus, whole life provides not only insurance coverage but also a modest return on your investment! The idea behind cash value is to provide the insurance buyer with a tangible return while he or she also receives insurance coverage—the savings rates on whole life policies are normally *fixed* and *guaranteed* to be more than a certain rate (say, 4 to 6 percent). An illustration of how the cash value in a whole life policy builds up over time is provided in Exhibit 8.4. Obviously, the longer the insured keeps the policy in force, the greater the cash value. Whole life is available through several different payment plans, including continuous-premium, limited-payment, and single-premium, all providing for accumulation of cash values.

Life insurance companies set aside assets (that is, they "accumulate reserves") to pay the claims expected from the policies they issue. As time goes by, the cash value of a policy—the amount of assets allocated for each person insured—increases to reflect the greater chance of death that comes with age. If policyholders decide to cancel their contracts prior to death, that portion of the assets set aside to provide payment for the death claim is available to them. This right to a cash value is termed the policyholder's **nonforfeiture right.** Policyholders, by terminating their insurance contracts, forfeit their rights to death benefits. Correspondingly, the company must forfeit its right to keep all of the monies paid by these policyholders for the future death benefit it is no longer required to pay.

Types of Whole Life Policies. Although a wide variety of whole life policies exists, only the major ones—continuous-premium, limited-payment, and single-premium—are described here. To get a feel for the cost of these policies, look at the rates shown in Exhibit 8.5. By contrasting the premiums in this exhibit with those in Exhibits 8.2 and 8.3, you can readily see how much more expensive whole life is relative to term life. That is the price you pay for the savings/investment feature that comes with whole life.

Continuous-premium. Under a *continuous premium whole life* policy, or *straight life,* as it's more commonly called, individuals pay the level

renewability A provision in term policies that allows the insured to renew his or her policy for another term without proof of insurability. The best type of renewability, from the insured's viewpoint, is the *guaranteed renewable provision.*

convertibility A provision in term policies that allows the insured to convert the policy to a whole life policy providing the same death benefit without proof of insurability.

whole life insurance Life insurance that is designed to offer financial protection for the entire life of the insured; allows for the accumulation of cash values, along with providing stipulated death benefits.

cash value The accumulated refundable value of an insurance policy that is based on insurance premiums paid and investment earnings; can be used as a source of loan collateral.

nonforfeiture right A life insurance option that gives the policyholder the portion of those assets that had been set aside to provide payment for future death claims. This amount, the **cash value,** is given to the policyholder upon cancellation of the policy by the insured.

EXHIBIT 8.4

Illustration of the Cash Value and Pure Protection in a Whole Life Policy

Here is an example of the projected cash value for an actual $200,000 whole life policy issued by a major life insurer to a male, age 30. For each year of the illustration, the difference between the $200,000 death benefit and the projected cash value represents the *death protection* offered by the insurer.

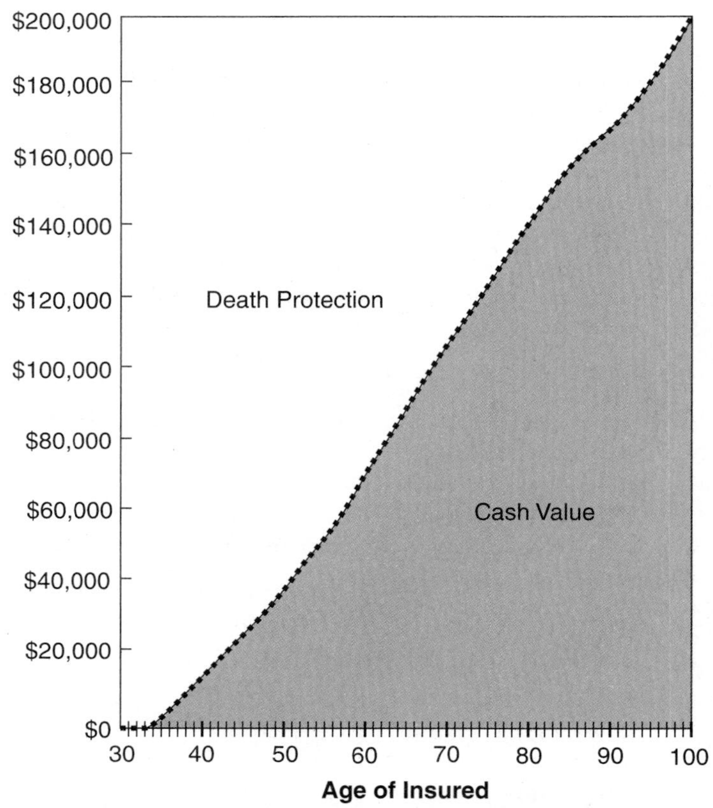

premium each year until they die or exercise a nonforfeiture right. The earlier in life the coverage is purchased, the lower the annual premium. This concept is often used as a selling point by some life insurance agents to convince younger persons to buy now. Their argument is that the sooner you buy, the less you pay. What they mean by this is what you pay *annually* rather than the total payments over the life of the policy. Of course, the sooner people purchase whole life, the longer they have coverage in force, but (all other things being equal) the *more* they pay in total.

While good reasons (such as securing needed protection, savings, and insurability) do exist for many young people to buy whole life, it should seldom be purchased by anyone simply because the annual premium will be less than if it is purchased at a later date. Of the variety of whole life policies available, continuous-premium/straight life offers the greatest amount of permanent death protection and the least amount of savings per dollar of premium paid. Since the emphasis of whole life insurance for most families is *death protection* rather than savings, the continuous-premium policy is usually the wisest choice when filling a permanent life insurance need.

Limited-payment. The *limited-payment whole life* policy offers coverage for the entire life of the insured but schedules the payments to end after a certain period of time. For example, 20-pay life, 30-pay life, paid-up age 55, and paid-up age 65 are types of frequently sold limited pay whole

EXHIBIT 8.5

Whole Life Insurance Annual Premiums; $100,000 Policy, Preferred Nonsmoker Rates

As with any life insurance product, the older you are, the more expensive it is to buy whole life. Also, whole life is more costly than term because you are getting an investment/savings account in addition to life insurance coverage, represented by the cash value column. Of course, the actual amount of cash value will depend on the actual dividend rate, which may be more or less than the current rate.

	Annual Premium		Premiums Paid through Year 20		Total Cash Value at Year 20*
Age	**Male**	**Female**	**Male**	**Female**	**Male/Female**
25	$ 988	$ 941	$19,760	$18,820	$ 30,894
30	1,233	1,188	24,460	23,760	38,971
35	1,473	1,438	29,460	28,760	46,223
40	1,833	1,788	36,660	35,760	55,980
50	2,816	2,666	55,425	52,425	76,225
60	4,291	3,899	85,820	77,980	112,765

*Guaranteed cash value plus annual dividends at the January 1995 rate of 6.8%

Source: A major life insurance company.

life policies. Under the 20-pay and 30-pay life contracts, the policyholder makes level premium payments for a period of 20 or 30 years, respectively. Under the premium schedule of paid-up at age 55, 65, or other stipulated-age policies, the policyholder makes premium payments until he or she attains the stated age. Of course, for any individual, the shorter the period of time over which premiums are payable, the larger the amount of the annual premium. Upon completion of the scheduled payments, the insurance remains in force at its face value for the remainder of the insured's life.

Some insurance companies emphasize the sale of limited-pay policies to the detriment of those who purchase them. In the sales presentation, considerable attention is focused on the "large" savings element that will develop and the fact that the policyholder is relieved of having to pay premiums for the entire life of the insured. However, this logic fails on two points. First, for most people, the primary purpose of whole life insurance is permanent protection against financial loss resulting from death—not the accumulation of savings. Second, even if people buy continuous-premium whole life policies, they need pay the premium only as long as they wish to keep the policies in force for their full face value. Policyholders may stop payment of premiums at any time after some nonforfeiture value has been accumulated. Rather than take this benefit in cash, they can convert the policies to ones that are paid up for some amount less than the original face value of the policy. (This is discussed in subsequent sections.)

The preceding discussion is not intended to imply that limited-payment policies are not desirable. Rather, the point is that if lifelong death protection is the primary aim of the life insurance policy, continuous-premium whole life should be purchased instead of a limited-payment policy. Since more continuous-premium whole life insurance can be purchased with the same number of dollars as limited-payment whole life, people who need whole life insurance are probably better off using continuous-premium life insurance so they can make the most of their insurance coverage. Once their insurance needs are reduced, they can convert the policy to a smaller amount of paid-up life insurance. On the other hand, if people have life insurance already in force that is sufficient to protect against income loss, they can use limited-payment policies as part of their savings or retirement plans.

Single-premium whole life. Continuous-premium and limited-payment whole life policies represent methods of acquiring life insurance on an installment basis. In contrast, a *single-premium whole life* policy is purchased with one cash premium payment at the inception of the contract that buys life insurance coverage for the rest of your life. The single-premium policy has only limited usefulness in the life insurance programs of most families. However, because of its investment attributes, single-premium life insurance, or SPLI for short, appeals to those looking for a *tax-sheltered investment vehicle*.

From an investment perspective, SPLI is attractive because, like any whole life insurance policy, interest/investment earnings within the policy build up on a tax-deferred basis. It also provides some life insurance coverage—usually just enough to qualify under IRS rules—but this amounts to an added bonus. (Of course, the death benefits from an SPLI policy are treated like those from any other life insurance policy and pass tax-free to the beneficiaries.) Minimum premiums usually run around $5,000, though most buyers today put in much more. Once the purchase is made, investment earnings start to build up tax-free.

There is a catch, however: Any cash withdrawals or loans taken against the SPLI cash value before you reach age 59½ will receive a double whammy from the IRS. First, they are likely to be treated as a gain, rather than a return of your premium payment, so they will be subject to income taxes. Second, the IRS will assess an additional 10 percent penalty against the withdrawal or loan. Because of these severe tax limitations, SPLI is ill-suited for young families with moderate incomes. The SPLI product is most appropriate for middle-aged purchasers who want to supplement their retirement plans and also need some additional life insurance protection.

Advantages and Disadvantages of Whole Life. The most noteworthy feature of whole life insurance is that premium payments contribute toward building an estate regardless of how long the insured lives. This feature results because the face value of the policy is paid upon death, or alternatively, because the cash value—which may be significant, as Exhibit 8.5 shows—may be borrowed against or withdrawn when the need for insurance protection has expired. A corresponding benefit of whole life (except single-premium) is that individuals who need insurance for an entire lifetime can budget their premium payments over a relatively long period, thus eliminating the problems of unaffordability and uninsurability often encountered with term insurance in later years.

Some people like whole life because the periodic payments force them to save regularly. And, of course, there's the favorable tax treatment afforded to accumulated earnings—as your earnings build up on a tax-sheltered basis, the underlying cash value of the policy also increases at a much faster rate than it would otherwise. Insurance experts will also point out that the whole life policy offers other potentially valuable options in addition to death protection and cash value. Some of these options include the continuation of coverage after allowing the policy to lapse because premiums were not paid (nonforfeiture option) and the ability to revive an older, favorably priced policy that has lapsed (policy reinstatement). These and other options will be discussed in a later section on insurance contract features.

The most frequently cited disadvantages of whole life insurance are that (1) it provides less death protection than term insurance, and (2) it provides lower yields than many other investment vehicles—returns on most whole life insurance policies are just not all that attractive. As with term insurance, the negative aspects of whole life often arise from misuse of the policy. In other words, a *whole life policy should not be used to obtain maximum return on investment*. However, if a person wishes to combine a given amount of death protection for the entire life of the insured (or until the policy is terminated) with a savings plan that provides a moderate tax-sheltered rate of return, whole life insurance may be a wise purchase.

One way to keep the cost down is to consider the purchase of *low-load* whole life insurance. Low-load products are sold directly by insurers to consumers, sometimes via a toll-free number, thereby eliminating sales agents from the transaction. With traditional whole life policies sold by an agent, between 100 and 150 percent of the first year's premium, and between 20 and 25 percent of total premiums paid over the life of the policy, are absorbed by sales commissions and marketing expenses. By comparison, only between 5 and 10 percent of low-load policies goes to cover marketing and selling expenses. As a result, cash values grow much more quickly. In one case, a 50-year-old male was able to purchase a low-load policy with a $500,000 death benefit for an annual premium of $7,500. Within five years, his cash surrender value was projected to be over $36,000, while a comparable, fully loaded policy was projected to produce only a $24,000 cash value.

EXHIBIT 8.6

Universal Life Insurance Annual Outlay; $100,000 Policy, Preferred Nonsmoker Rates

Universal life premiums are lower than whole life and can vary over the policy's life. After deducting the cost of the death benefit and any administrative fees from your annual contribution, the rest goes into an accumulation account and builds at a variable rate—in this example, the current rate is 7.4%. The guaranteed rate, however, is only 4%, so your actual cash value may be less.

	Annual Outlay		Premiums Paid through Year 20		Cash Surrender Value at Year 20*	
Age	Male	Female	Male	Female	Male	Female
25	$ 419	$ 358	$ 8,380	$ 7,160	$ 6,091	$ 5,048
30	505	425	10,100	8,500	8,137	6,176
35	644	534	12,880	10,680	11,235	8,453
40	841	682	16,820	13,640	15,107	11,399
50	1,469	1,146	29,380	22,920	25,168	20,074
60	2,598	1,992	51,960	39,840	36,638	32,633

*Based on January 1995 rate of 7.4%

Source: A major life insurance company.

UNIVERSAL LIFE INSURANCE

The stockbrokerage firm of E. F. Hutton, through its life insurance subsidiary, is generally credited with marketing the first universal life insurance policy in 1979. Today most life companies sell universal life insurance or similar policies. Basically, **universal life insurance** is a form of cash value insurance that combines *term insurance,* which provides the death benefits of the policy, with a tax-sheltered savings/investment account that pays interest usually at *competitive money market rates.* Exhibit 8.6 shows representative premiums and cash values for a $100,000 universal life policy.

The special aspect of a universal life policy is that the death protection (or pure insurance) portion and the savings portion are identified separately in its price. This is referred to as *unbundling.* Traditionally, for whole life insurance, you pay a premium to purchase a stated face amount of coverage in a policy with a *fixed cash-value schedule.* Not so with universal life. Here's what happens: When you make a premium payment on a universal life policy, part goes to pay administrative fees and the remainder is put in the cash value, or savings portion of the policy, where it earns a certain rate of return—this rate of earnings varies with market yields, but is guaranteed to be more than some stipulated minimum rate (say, 4 percent). Then, each month, the price of one month's term insurance is withdrawn from the cash value to purchase the required death protection. So long as there's enough in the savings portion to buy death protection, the policy will stay in force. Should the cash value grow to an unusually large amount, then the amount of insurance coverage will be increased for the policy to retain its favorable tax treatment (tax laws require that the death benefits in a universal life policy *must always exceed the cash value* by a stipulated amount).

The clear separation of the protection and savings elements in the universal policy has raised the question of whether or not this type of insurance is in fact whole life insurance. This question is important, because the accumulation of cash values in whole life policies arises partly from interest credited to them. Under present tax laws, *this accumulation occurs income tax–free as long as the cash value does not exceed the total premiums paid to the insurer.* However, if a whole life policy is surrendered for its cash value, and that cash value exceeds the premiums paid, then *the gain* is taxed. Through an Internal Revenue Service ruling and

universal life insurance A type of insurance contract that combines term insurance (death benefits) with a tax-deferred savings/investment account that pays competitive money market interest rates.

federal legislation, universal life insurance policies enjoy the same favorable tax treatment as do other forms of whole life insurance—that is, death benefits are income tax–free and, prior to the death of the insured, amounts credited to the cash value, including investment earnings, accumulate on a tax-deferred basis.

Basic Structure. Insurance companies sell a variety of policies under the heading of universal life. In spite of the different names, the basic structure of these policies is pretty much the same. The premium you pay for the policy, called the *annual contribution* or *annual outlay,* is deposited in an *accumulation account.* The insurer credits interest to the account at a current rate and deducts from it the cost of the death benefits (and other expenses). The size of the deduction for the death protection depends on the amount of term insurance to be purchased and the age of the insured. The crediting of interest and the deductions for expenses and insurance coverage usually occur monthly. Each year the policy is in force, the insurance company sends the insured an annual statement summarizing the monthly deductions and credits.

Within the basic structure of a universal life insurance policy, there are two types of death protection. The first type, known as Option A, provides a level death benefit. As the cash value increases, the amount of pure insurance protection *decreases.* The second type, Option B, provides a stated amount of insurance plus the accumulated cash value. Thus, the death benefit at any time varies with the rate of earnings on the savings plan and will increase along with the accumulated cash value.

The Flexibility Feature. A characteristic of universal life insurance that is important in your financial planning is its flexible nature. The annual premium you pay can be increased or decreased from year to year. This feature is based on the fact that the cost of the death protection *may be covered from either the annual premium or the accumulation account* (that is, cash value). Thus, as long as the accumulation account is adequate, you can choose to skip an annual premium and cover the cost of the death protection from the accumulation account. In addition, the death benefit can be increased or decreased, and you can change from the level benefit type of policy to the cash value plus a stated amount of insurance. Note, however, that evidence of insurability is usually required if the death benefit is to be increased.

This flexibility allows you to adapt the levels of death protection to your life-cycle needs. For example, you'll probably want to increase the death benefit when you have another child and, conversely, decrease it when your children are grown. If you get a divorce or your spouse dies, you can adjust the components of a universal life policy to better meet your current financial needs—say, decrease the death benefit and increase the tax-deferred savings portion—whereas with whole life, your policy is fixed.

Some Precautions. One of the attractions of a universal life insurance policy is the promise of the cash value being credited at the "current" rate of interest. For example, the *current* rate of interest may be 7.5 percent compared to a *guaranteed* minimum rate of 4 percent. Make it a point to find out just what current rate of interest is used to credit earnings to your accumulation account. A common rate is that of 90-day Treasury bills. Other rates, however, may be used. Another caution regarding universal life is that you may be attracted to the relatively low interest charge on loans that you can take from your cash value. However, the cash value that is equal to the loan is usually then credited with only the *guaranteed interest rate* of 4 to 4.5 percent.

Universal life's flexibility in making premium payments, while an attractive feature, is also one of its major drawbacks. A policyholder who economizes on premium payments in early years may find that he or she must pay higher premiums than originally planned in later policy years to keep the policy in force. Some policyholders buy universal life expecting their premiums to vanish once cash value builds to a certain level. As the *Financial Shocks* box on page 333 explains, many policyholders have seen their premiums reappear when interest rates fell below the rate in effect at the time they bought the policy.

You should also evaluate the charges or fees that the insurance company levies on its universal life policies. Ask the insurance agent about the front-end load or commission you'll have to pay on the first premium, the expense charge on each annual premium, investment expense charged by

Financial Shocks

"Vanishing Premiums" That Didn't

Imagine that you bought a universal life insurance policy during the late 1970s or mid-1980s, lured by the combination of a savings component and a death benefit, but especially by the promise of "vanishing premiums." Say you could buy a $500,000 policy for about $2,100—about half of the cost of a whole life policy. The illustration the sales agent showed you indicated that after six years of interest accumulating at only the current 9 percent rate, the investment earnings would cover the cost of the annual premium payments until you were 72. It sounded like a pretty good deal, so you bought the policy.

Then you watched interest rates plummet. The actual earnings on your policy's savings component fell far short of projections and weren't high enough to cover the premiums. In fact, your premiums never vanished—or if they did, they soon reappeared, sometimes at a higher rate than before. So you joined the ranks of the many universal life policyholders who must now make premium payments for years longer than expected. And if you tried to change or drop your universal life insurance packages altogether, you were hit by substantial surrender charges. Faced with the prospect of paying added premiums or losing their investments, policyholders began to complain. Some even sued their insurance companies for allegedly misleading them at the time of the sale.

Who is at fault in this crisis? Consumer advocates and regulators place the blame on unscrupulous agents who promised too much when they sold the policies. Often, buyers were shown impressive illustrations that used mountains of numbers to paint a glorious picture of cash piling up inside the policy, rendering it self-funding after the first several years. What many consumers didn't realize, however, was that these predicted payment deadlines weren't guaranteed and were contingent on the continuation of existing high interest rates.

Gene Grabowski, a spokesman for the American Council of Life Insurance, denies the charge that agents misled consumers. According to Grabowski, policies must be accompanied by a disclaimer that vanishing premiums and premium rates are not guaranteed, and that insurers are allowed to raise or reinstate premiums. However, many agents may have glossed over the risks involved, and many customers may have ignored disclaimers or did not understand the potential ramifications.

Because many policyholders are still unaware of this problem, some insurers are taking a proactive stance and confronting the "premium problem" head-on. Instead of waiting for customers to complain, Manufacturers Life Insurance Co. is dispatching agents to notify policyholders that they will have to pay unexpected premiums for years longer than expected. Customers have several options, including extending the premium-payment period or reducing the death benefit. Other firms are also taking steps to notify policyholders of vanishing premium problems.

What should you do if you have a vanishing-premium policy? Contact your agent and review the coverage, bearing in mind that agents stand to profit by selling new coverage. In about 90 percent of the cases, cautions New York insurance consultant Glenn S. Daily, it's more cost-effective for a policyholder to keep or modify an existing policy than to buy a new one.

Sources: Adapted from: Karen Slater Damato and Leslie Scism, "Insurer Warns of Premiums That 'Vanish'," *The Wall Street Journal*, June 30, 1994, pp. C1, C10; Kristin Davis, "Buying Life Insurance: What the Numbers Don't Show," *Worth*, June, 1994, pp. 49–52; Stuart Weiss, "Universal Life: Is It Time to Bail Out?" *Worth*, May 1993, pp. 102–103; David Wichner, "Vanishing Act? Cash Value Insurance Policies Being Gobbled By Interest Rates," *Phoenix Gazette*, June 28, 1993, p. E1.

the insurer in determining the "current" rate of return, and any other charges you may be assessed. Most states require that the insurance company issue an annual disclosure statement that spells out premiums paid, expenses and mortality costs, interest earned, and beginning and ending cash values.

OTHER TYPES OF LIFE INSURANCE

In addition to term, whole life, and universal life, several other types of life insurance policies are available, including variable life insurance, insurance on multiple lives, group life, credit life, mortgage life, industrial life insurance, special purpose policies, and deferred-premium life insurance. These policies serve very diverse needs. Some may help you meet specific needs, while others are simply more expensive alternatives to traditional types of life insurance.

Variable Life and Variable Universal Life Insurance. A basic feature of *whole* life insurance is that it combines insurance coverage and a savings account into one package. *Universal* life extends this concept by being a bit more aggressive with the savings component, and thereby offering the potential for slightly higher returns and a quicker build-up of the cash value. *Variable life* goes even further, as it allows the policyholder to decide on how to invest the money in the savings (cash value) component and as a result, offers the highest and most attractive level of investment returns—but unlike whole or universal life policies, *no minimum return is guaranteed*. In addition, as the name implies, the amount of insurance coverage provided will vary with the profits (and losses) generated in the investment account. Thus, in **variable life insurance** policies, the amount of death benefits payable are, for the most part, related to the policies' investment returns. Variable life insurance comes in two forms. *Straight variable life* has a fixed premium. The premiums on *variable universal life* are flexible; the policyholder can decide how much of the premium goes toward the death benefit, as with universal life. These policies also have high expenses; in addition to commissions, annual fees for servicing the insurance and managing the investment portfolios erode returns.

A variable life policy, in short, combines insurance protection with the ability to spread your money over a variety of different investment accounts, all in one convenient, tax-favored package. The investment accounts are set up just like *mutual funds,* and most firms that offer variable life policies let you choose from a full menu of different funds, ranging from money market accounts and bond funds to aggressively managed stock funds. As a policyholder, you can put your money in any one or more of the funds offered under the policy and can also freely move your money from one fund to another as market conditions dictate. Furthermore, like all life insurance products, variable policies offer attractive tax benefits: investment earnings can grow within the policy free of any current taxation; you can switch between funds with no tax consequences; and the policy's death benefit passes tax-free to your beneficiaries.

While all these features may sound great, it's important to keep in mind that if you want the benefits of higher investment returns, you must also be willing to assume the risks of reduced insurance coverage—bigger investment profits do, indeed, lead to more death benefits and an accelerated build-up in cash value, but investments can also end up losing money (sometimes in a big way), and that can lead to lower cash values and reduced insurance coverage (though it can never fall below the minimum death benefit stated in the policy). Clearly, *you should use extreme care when buying either form of variable life insurance.*

Insurance on Multiple Lives. Reflecting the rapid growth of two-income families, knowledgeable planners and agents are recommending **joint life insurance,** or "first-to-die" insurance, as it's frequently called. Joint life pays the full death benefit when the *first* spouse dies, and is appropriate where the death of either spouse would result in a loss of income that would jeopardize the family's lifestyle. This policy usually is about 10 to 25 percent cheaper than buying two policies with the same death benefit—one on each income provider. But what happens if both earners are killed in a common disaster, such as a car accident? This should not be a problem because most joint life policies have a *double indemnity* clause whereby twice the normal death benefit is paid to the beneficiaries.

Companies have developed a variety of joint policies tailored to different needs. Some policies allow the surviving party to convert the policy to one providing a death benefit to his or her beneficiary. Others insure nonrelated persons. These policies are ideal for business partners. If one dies, the insurance provides the funds for the remaining partner(s) to buy his or her share of the business.

In contrast, **survivorship insurance,** also known as "last-to-die" insurance, covers two parties who are usually married, but pays benefits only when the last surviving insured dies. This type of policy normally is used to help pay estate taxes. U.S. tax laws are set up so that estate taxes are minimal when one married partner dies and leaves his or her estate to the surviving spouse. When the surviving spouse dies, however, his or her estate may be subject to federal estate tax rates as high as

55 percent. Survivorship insurance immediately generates the dollars to pay such a tax. Because of certain exclusions allowed by the government, a family generally should not be concerned about estate taxes unless the total estate, including life insurance death benefits, exceeds $600,000.

Group Life Insurance. Under **group life insurance,** one master policy is issued, and each eligible member of the group receives a certificate of insurance. Group life is nearly always term insurance, and the premium is based on the characteristics of the group as a whole, rather than related to any specific individual. Group life insurance is often provided by employers as a fringe benefit for their employees. However, just about any type of group (be it a labor union, professional association, or alumni organization) can secure a group life policy, so long as the insurance is only incidental to the reason for the group.

Accounting for about 30 percent of all life insurance in force in the United States, group life insurance is one of the fastest-growing areas of insurance. Many group life policies now offer coverage for not only the group members but also their dependents. In addition, group life policies generally provide that if individual members leave the group, they may continue the coverage by converting their protection to individually issued whole life policies—such conversion normally does not require evidence of insurability so long as it occurs within a specified period of time. Of course, after conversion, the individual pays all premiums. Before buying additional coverage purchased through a group plan or converting a group policy to an individual one, it's important to compare rates. Often the premiums are more expensive than other readily-available sources of term insurance.

As noted in Chapters 1 and 2, the availability of group coverage through employee benefit programs should be considered when developing a life insurance program. However, because of its potentially temporary nature and relatively low face amount (often equal to about one year's salary), it should fulfill only low-priority insurance needs. Only in rare cases should a family rely solely on group life insurance to fulfill its primary income-protection requirements.

Credit Life Insurance. Banks, finance companies, and other lenders generally sell **credit life insurance** in conjunction with installment loans. Usually credit life is a term policy, of less than five years, with a face value that decreases at the same rate as the outstanding balance on the loan. Although liquidating debts upon the death of a family breadwinner is often desirable, the funds for this need should be fulfilled through an individual's term or whole life insurance program. Buying credit life insurance per se is one of the most expensive ways to buy life insurance and should be avoided. Further, contrary to popular belief, a lender cannot legally reject a loan just because the potential borrower chooses not to buy credit life insurance.

Mortgage Life Insurance. Mortgage life insurance is a form of term life insurance that's designed to pay off the mortgage balance on a home in the event of the death of the borrower. As in the case of credit life, this need can usually be met less expensively by shopping the market for a suitable decreasing-term policy. Credit life and mortgage life are relatively expensive, because

variable life insurance Life insurance in which the benefits payable to the insured are related to the returns being generated on the investments that support the policy's payment obligations.

joint life insurance Life insurance on two lives, but which pays only when the *first* person dies; also known as "first-to-die" insurance.

survivorship life insurance Life insurance that also covers two persons, but only pays when the *second* one dies; also known as "last-to-die" insurance.

group life insurance A type of life insurance that provides a master policy for a group and a certificate of insurance for each eligible member.

credit life insurance A type of term life insurance sold in conjunction with installment loans; the coverage decreases at the same rate as the loan balance.

mortgage life insurance A term insurance policy on the borrower's life that names the lender as beneficiary, allowing for the mortgage balance to be automatically paid off in the event of the borrower's death.

lenders are often influenced by the amount of sales commission they receive in selecting the insurers with whom they place the coverage. Also, as might be expected, an insurer who pays high commissions is frequently one who charges a high premium.

Industrial Life Insurance. **Industrial life insurance,** now called **home service life,** is a type of whole life insurance that is issued in policies with small face amounts, often $1,000 or less. It is sold by agents who call on policyholders weekly or monthly to collect the premiums. The term *industrial* arose because when these policies first became popular, they were sold primarily to low-paid industrial wage earners. Because of high marketing costs, industrial life insurance costs a good deal more per $1,000 of coverage than regular whole life policies. Even so, some insurance authorities believe that industrial life insurance offers the only practical way to deliver coverage to low-income families. Although many of the largest life insurance providers started out in this business, industrial/home service life today accounts for less than 1 percent of the total amount of life insurance in force in the United States.

Special-Purpose Policies. Certain types of policies frequently combine some form of term and whole life insurance for coverage on one or more family members. These policies have often been developed by life insurers because of the highly competitive nature of the life insurance business. You should try to determine whether such a policy truly meets your needs or is primarily a marketing gimmick. Although many of the special-purpose policies are sold under various company trade names, general designations are as follows: family plan policies, family income policies, family maintenance policies, and jumping juveniles.

One appealing feature of certain "family plans" is that they offer the guaranteed insurability of children. For instance, the policy might specify that when the children reach a certain age (say, 21 or 25), they can convert to a specified type of life insurance at a predetermined price regardless of their physical condition. Although special-purpose policies can fill some family needs, more than likely you'll find that these needs can be satisfied at less cost if you simply buy convertible-term or continuous-premium whole life as separate policies.

Deferred-Premium Life Insurance. Several life insurance companies actively market their products to college students. These companies recognize, though, that most college students have little money to spend on life insurance. Their answer is to sign students up for **deferred-premium life insurance,** whereby a modest amount of life insurance is actually *purchased with an interest-bearing debt obligation* that is later paid off through a series of deferred-premium payments. Apart from the fact that many college students do not have enough significant financial responsibilities to justify life insurance, these deferred-payment plans are generally undesirable because they place students in debt. Students who accept this type of payment plan generally are required to sign a legally binding installment loan contract. Although deferred-payment plans have some legitimate business and tax-planning uses, for the majority of college students their purchase is unwise.

Concept Check

8-7. What is term insurance? Describe some of the common types of *term life insurance* policies.

8-8. What are the advantages and disadvantages of term life insurance?

8-9. Explain how whole life insurance offers financial protection to an individual throughout his or her entire life.

8-10. Describe the different types of whole life policies. What are the advantages and disadvantages of *whole life insurance?*

8-11. What is *universal life insurance?* Explain how it differs from whole life, *variable life,* and variable universal life.

8-12. Why should the following types of life insurance contracts be avoided? (a) *credit life insurance,* (b) *mortgage life insurance,* (c) *industrial or home service life insurance,* and (d) *deferred-premium life insurance.*

8-13. Explain how *group insurance* differs from term insurance. What do employees stand to gain from group insurance?

KEY LIFE INSURANCE CONTRACT PROVISIONS

LG5

Because all life insurance contracts are not alike, it's a good idea to review the various provisions contained in your policy to make sure you're getting just what you want. For example, things like policy loans, dividend participation provisions, settlement options, and so forth, are spelled out in most life insurance policies. What features would you like to see in a life insurance policy? Give some thought to this question before reading on.

All life insurance contracts have various provisions that establish the rights and obligations of the policyholder and the insurance company. Standard or uniform life insurance policies do not exist, and the wording of policy provisions and features varies among companies and according to the state in which the policy is sold. Nevertheless, many elements are common to most life insurance contracts. They can be divided into two groups: (1) life insurance contract features and (2) other policy features.

LIFE INSURANCE CONTRACT FEATURES

The key features found in most life insurance contracts are (1) the beneficiary clause, (2) settlement options, (3) policy loans, (4) payment of premiums, (5) grace period, (6) nonforfeiture options, (7) policy reinstatement, and (8) change of policy.

Beneficiary Clause. All life insurance policies should have one or more beneficiaries. The **beneficiary** is the person who will receive the death benefits of the policy if the insured dies. Otherwise, death benefits are paid to the estate of the deceased and are subject to the often lengthy and expensive legal procedure of going through probate court. An insured person is able to name both a *primary beneficiary* and various *contingent beneficiaries.* The primary beneficiary will receive the entire death benefit if he or she is surviving when the insured dies. If the primary beneficiary does not survive the insured, the insurer will distribute the death benefits to the contingent beneficiary or beneficiaries. If neither primary nor contingent beneficiaries are living at the death of the insured, then the death benefits pass to the estate of the insured and is distributed by the probate court according to the insured's will or, if no will exists, according to state law.

When naming the beneficiary, the policyholder should make certain the identification is clear. For example, a man could buy a policy and simply designate the beneficiary as "my wife." However, if a subsequent divorce and remarriage were to occur, a controversy could arise as to which "wife" was entitled to the benefits. Similarly, if children are the intended beneficiaries, problems can arise when other children become part of the insured's family. For instance, if a man named "my children" as beneficiaries, would proceeds be payable only to his natural and legitimate children, or would his adopted, illegitimate, or stepchildren also share in the proceeds? Obviously, you should update your beneficiary if circumstances, such as marital status, change.

What if the insured and the primary beneficiary, such as a husband and wife, were to lose their lives in a common disaster, such as an airplane accident? According to state laws, the contingent beneficiary(ies) normally would receive the death benefits if the deaths are determined to be simultaneous. If the primary beneficiary were determined to have survived the insured, even by a matter of minutes, the death benefits may go to the primary beneficiary's estate, however. This means that the death benefit ultimately would end up in the hands of the primary beneficiary's selected heirs. Imagine what could happen in a common

industrial life insurance (home service life) A type of whole life insurance that is issued in policies with relatively small face amounts (usually $1,000 or less); formerly was offered to low-paid industrial workers.

deferred-premium life insurance Life insurance that allows for the deferral of premium payments; the payment deferral is accompanied by a signed promissory note.

beneficiary In life insurance, a person who receives the death benefits of an insurance policy upon the insured's death.

disaster for a married couple where both spouses have children by a previous marriage. The $500,000 death benefit from a deceased wife's insurance policy could wind up in the hands of her husband's children, with her own children receiving nothing, just because her husband survived her by a few minutes! Even for couples with no previous marriages, carefully laid plans to avoid estate taxes could be upset by a common disaster where the deaths were not quite simultaneous.

To combat the common disaster problem, the insured should use a *survival clause* on the beneficiary form. For instance, a woman could specify her primary beneficiary as "My husband, Alfred, if he survives me by 60 days." As contingent beneficiaries, she could then name, "My children, Betty and Carl, in equal shares." This simple survival clause should assure that death benefits will go to her children if both she and her husband are fatally injured in a common disaster, even though he might survive her by a short time.

In sum, make sure you have named both a primary and a contingent beneficiary in any life insurance policies you buy and that no mistake can be made in determining who the beneficiaries are. Also, be sure to use survival clauses where appropriate. Note, too, that the person you name as a beneficiary can be changed at any time as long as you did not indicate an *irrevocable beneficiary* when you took out the policy. Thus, if your wishes change, all you need do is notify the insurance company—easy to do but also easy to forget. Therefore, when you write the premium check each year, verify that your policy's named beneficiary is also your desired beneficiary. (Similarly, you should update any prescribed settlement options—discussed next—with desired changes.)

Settlement Options. Insurance companies generally offer several ways of paying life insurance policy death proceeds. The funds allocation decision may be permanently established before the insured's death or left up to the beneficiary when the policy matures. The most common **settlement option** is the lump-sum cash payment, chosen by about 98 percent of all policyholders. You should, however, know about several other options, including:

- ***Interest only.*** Policy proceeds are kept by the insurance company for a specified time period; the beneficiary receives interest payments, usually at some guaranteed rate. This option can be useful when there is no current need for the principal—for example, proceeds could be left on deposit until children go to college, with interest supplementing family income. Typically, however, interest rates paid by insurers are lower than other savings vehicles.
- ***Fixed-period payment.*** The face amount of the policy, along with interest earned, is paid to the beneficiary over a fixed time period. For example, a 55-year-old beneficiary may need additional income until social security benefits start.
- ***Fixed-amount payment.*** The beneficiary receives policy proceeds in regular payments of a fixed amount until the proceeds run out.
- ***Life income.*** The insurer guarantees to pay the beneficiary a certain payment for the rest of his or her life, based on the beneficiary's sex, age when benefits start, life expectancy, the policy face value, and interest rate assumptions. This option appeals to beneficiaries who don't want to outlive the income from policy proceeds and be dependent on others for support. An interesting variation of this settlement option is the *life-income-with-period-certain option,* whereby the company guarantees a specified number of payments that pass to a secondary beneficiary if the original recipient dies before the time period ends.

Policy Loans. An advance made by a life insurance company to a policyholder is called a **policy loan.** Such a loan is secured by the cash value of the life insurance policy. A provision in nearly all whole life policies grants this right. Although these loans do *not* have to be repaid, any balance plus interest on the loan remaining at the death of the insured is *subtracted from the proceeds of the policy.* The rate of interest charged on older policies is customarily 5 to 8 percent per annum, and it is stated in the policy. Newer policies, in contrast, offer either a fixed rate loan, with an interest rate normally set at about 8 percent, or a rate that varies with market interest rates on high-quality bonds. Some policies let the insured choose whether the loans will be at fixed or variable rates.

Policy loans should be taken out only in unusual circumstances because they can reduce death proceeds. One long-time advocate of whole life insurance has decried policy loans as "stealing from your widow." Although not all would agree

EXHIBIT 8.7

Various Nonforfeiture Options (For a 21-year-old Male; Dollar Amount of Benefits for Each $1,000 of Insurance)

Even if the insured stops making premium payments on his whole life policy, he still has certain benefits that he owns in the form of a specified amount of cash value or paid-up (whole life or term) insurance coverage.

End of Policy Year	Cash or Loan Value	Paid-up Insurance	Extended Term Insurance	
			Years	Days
1	$ 0.00	$ 0	0	0
2	0.00	0	0	0
3	4.79	15	1	315
4	16.21	48	6	161
5	27.91	81	11	15
6	39.91	113	14	275
7	52.20	145	17	158
8	64.78	176	19	157
9	77.66	206	20	342
10	90.84	236	22	29
11	104.33	265	22	351
12	118.13	294	23	231
13	132.25	322	24	54
14	146.69	350	24	191
15	161.43	377	24	290
16	176.47	403	24	356
17	191.79	429	25	28
18	207.38	454	25	42
19	223.22	478	25	36
20	239.29	502	25	13
Age 60	563.42	806	17	26
Age 65	608.49	833	15	272

Source: *Principles of Risk Management and Insurance* by George E. Rejda. Copyright © 1995 HarperCollins, p. 364. Reprinted by permission.

with this emotional assessment, life insurance is intended to provide basic financial protection for your dependents, and spending those proceeds prematurely is an unwise practice. On the other hand, because these loans are less expensive than borrowing from other financial institutions, they may appeal to those who wish to keep their borrowing costs low and are not bothered by the accompanying loss of death proceeds if the loans are not repaid. A word of caution: *Be very careful with these loans, because unless certain conditions are met, the IRS may treat them as withdrawals, meaning they could be subject to tax penalties.* If you're in any way unsure, consult your insurance agent or a tax advisor.

Payment of Premiums. All life insurance contracts have a provision that specifies when premiums are due. With most insurers, the policyholder may elect to pay premiums on an annual, semiannual, quarterly, or monthly basis. Some premium checks are mailed directly to the company; in other instances, a sales agent collects premiums from the policyholder. Another method of payment allows policyholders to pay premiums through an automatic deduction from their bank accounts. In the case of the death of a policyholder who has paid premiums more than one month in advance, many companies refund those premiums along with the policy death proceeds.

settlement option A specified way of paying the death proceeds from a life insurance policy, such as lump-sum cash payment, payments for a stated period, payments of a stated amount, or income for life.

policy loan An advance made by an insurer to a life insurance policyholder that is secured by the cash value of the policy.

Grace Period. The *grace period* permits the policyholder to retain full death protection for a short period of time (usually 31 days) after missing a premium due date. In other words, you won't lose your insurance protection just because you're a little late in making the premium payment. If the insured dies during the grace period, the face amount of the policy less the unpaid premium is paid to the beneficiary.

Nonforfeiture Options. As discussed earlier, a *nonforfeiture option* provides the policyholder with some benefits when a policy is terminated prior to its maturity. State laws require that all permanent whole life policies (and term contracts that cover a long period) contain a nonforfeiture provision. In addition to cash withdrawal, companies usually offer the two options—*paid up insurance* and *extended term*—described below. Exhibit 8.7 shows these options for a $1,000 whole life policy issued to a male, age 21.

- ***Paid-up insurance.*** The policyholder receives a policy exactly like the terminated one, except with a lower face value. In effect, the policyholder uses the cash value to buy a new, single-premium policy. As we see in Exhibit 8.7 a policy canceled after ten years has a cash value of $90.84 per $1,000 of face amount and buys $236 of paid-up whole life insurance. The $90.84 cash value continues to grow because of future interest earnings, even though the policyholder makes no further premium payments. This option is useful when a person's income and need for death protection declines—when they reach age 60 or 65, for example—yet they still want some coverage.
- ***Extended term.*** The insured uses the accumulated cash value to buy a term life policy for the same face value as the lapsed policy. The coverage period is based on the amount of term protection a single-premium payment (equal to the total cash value) buys at the insured's present age. If the insured in Exhibit 8.7 chooses this option at the end of 10 years, he'd receive $1,000 coverage for 22 years and 29 days. (This option usually goes into effect automatically if the policyholder quits paying premiums and gives no instructions to the insurer.)

Policy Reinstatement. While a policy is under the reduced paid-up option or the extended-term option, the policyholder may reinstate the original policy by paying all back premiums plus interest at a stated rate and providing evidence that he or she can pass a physical examination and meet any other insurability requirements. *Reinstatement* basically revives the original contractual relationship between the company and the policyholder. Most often the policyholder must reinstate the policy within a specified period (three to five years) after the policy has lapsed. However, before exercising a reinstatement option, a policyholder should determine whether buying a new policy (from the same or a different company) might be less costly.

Change of Policy. Many life insurance contracts contain a provision that permits the insured to switch from one policy form to another. For instance, policyholders may decide that they would rather have paid-up age 65 policies as opposed to their current continuous-premium whole life policies. A change of policy provision would allow this change without penalty. When policyholders change from high- to lower-premium policies, they may need to prove insurability. This requirement reduces the possibility of adverse selection against the company.

OTHER POLICY FEATURES

In addition to the key contractual features described in the preceding section, some other policy features that you should be aware of are (1) a multiple indemnity clause, (2) a disability clause, (3) guaranteed purchase option, (4) a suicide clause, (5) exclusions, (6) participation, and (7) living benefits.

Multiple Indemnity Clause. **Multiple** (most often double or triple) **indemnity clauses** double or triple the face amount of the policy if the insured dies as a result of an accident. This benefit is usually offered to the policyholder at a small additional cost. Many insurance authorities dismiss the use of a multiple indemnity benefit as irrational. This coverage should be ignored as a source of funds when programming insurance needs, since it provides no protection in the event of death due to illness.

Disability Clause. A **disability clause** in a life insurance contract may contain a waiver-of-premium benefit alone or coupled with disability income. A *waiver-of-premium benefit* excuses the payment of premiums on the life insurance policy if the insured becomes totally and permanently disabled prior to age 60 (or sometimes age 65). Under the *disability income portion,* the insured is granted not only a waiver of premium, but also receives a monthly income equal to $5 or $10 per $1,000 of policy face value. Some insurers will continue these payments for the life of the insured, while others will terminate them at age 65. Disability riders for waiver-of-premium and disability income protection are relatively inexpensive and can be added to most whole life policies, but generally not to term policies.

Guaranteed Purchase Options. The policyholder who has a **guaranteed purchase option** may purchase additional coverage at stipulated intervals without providing evidence of insurability. This option is frequently offered to under-40 buyers of a whole life policy. The increases in coverage usually can be purchased every three, four, or five years in amounts equal to the amount of the original policy or $10,000, whichever is lower. This option should be quite attractive to individuals whose life insurance needs and ability to pay are expected to increase over a 5- to 15-year period.

Suicide Clause. Nearly all life insurance policies have a *suicide clause* that voids the contract if an insured commits suicide within a certain period, normally two years, after its inception. In these cases, the company simply returns the premiums that have been paid. If an insured takes his or her own life after this initial period has elapsed, the policy proceeds are paid without question.

Exclusions. Although all private insurance policies exclude some types of losses, life policies offer very broad protection. In addition to the suicide clause, the only other common exclusions are aviation and war. In aviation exclusions, the primary types of losses not covered are those occurring when the insured is a relatively inexperienced private pilot or is flying in military aircraft. No restrictions apply to fare-paying passengers of commercial airlines. (Most life insurers accept without premium surcharge the pilots and crews of scheduled airliners.) War exclusions often are inserted in policies in anticipation of or during periods of combat. They typically provide that should the insured die as a result of war, a return of premiums with interest will be made. War exclusions are intended to guard against adverse selection, which could materially disrupt the mortality experience of the company and consequently its solvency. When the potential insured has a hazardous occupation or hobby, the company will either exclude coverage for that activity or charge an additional premium to cover the added risk exposure. Seldom, if ever, would a company be able to modify the premium charged or coverage offered should the insured take up, say, Formula One racing or hang gliding after a policy is issued.

Participating Policies. Many life insurance companies offer **participating policies,** which means that the policyholder is entitled to receive policy dividends that reflect the difference between the premiums that are charged and the amount of premium necessary to fund the actual mortality experience of the company. When the base premium schedule for participating policies is established, a company estimates what it believes its mortality and investment experience will be and then adds a generous margin of safety to these figures. The premiums charged the policyholder are based on these overly conservative estimates.

multiple indemnity clause A clause in a life insurance policy that typically doubles or triples the policy's face amount in the event of the insured's accidental death.

disability clause A clause in a life insurance contract that may contain either a waiver-of-premium benefit or a waiver of premium coupled with disability income.

guaranteed purchase option An option in a life insurance contract that allows the policyholder the right to purchase additional coverage, at stipulated intervals, without having to provide evidence of insurability.

participating policy A life insurance policy that pays dividends that reflect the difference between the premiums that are charged and the amount of premium necessary to fund the insurer's actual mortality experience.

When company experience is more favorable than estimated, a return of the overcharge is made to policyholders in the form of **policy dividends.** These policy dividends may be received as cash payments (which, since they are viewed as a return of premium, are not subject to taxation), left with the company to earn interest, used to buy additional paid-up coverage, or applied toward the next premium payment. The dividend option selected is purely a matter of the individual policyholder's preference. Note that it is advantageous to use the dividends to buy paid-up options when more insurance coverage is desired, since these additions are available at their *net* rates, meaning they contain no load for sales expenses and consequently provide an economical way to increase coverage.

Living Benefits. A number of major life insurers, including Aetna, John Hancock, and Prudential, now are offering so-called living benefits options with whole and universal life policies. *Living benefits* allow the insured to receive a percentage of his or her death benefits prior to death. Some insurers actually are offering this option free of charge to established policyholders if the insured suffers a terminal illness expected to result in death within a specified period, such as six months to a year, or to need expensive treatment, such as an organ transplant, to survive. For example, an insured dying of cancer received over $44,000 of a $45,000 whole life policy and used the money to retire mortgage and car loans. In this case, the insured died within two months. If the insured had been expected to live longer, he would have received a lower living benefit. In another case, a woman needing a liver transplant to survive used living benefits from her life insurance to cover the almost $200,000 not covered by health insurance. Doing so preserved her other financial resources and prevented even greater hardships later.

Some insurers are marketing a *living benefit rider,* which allows advances of a policy's death benefit, usually about 2 percent per month, to pay for long-term health care, such as nursing home expenses. This rider can cost an extra 5 to 15 percent of the normal life insurance premium and benefits are capped as a percentage of the death benefit. For example, a living benefit rider may cap benefits at 50 percent of the death benefit, so that an insured with a $100,000 policy could receive a maximum of $2,000 per month for 25 months. The remaining $50,000 death benefit would pass to the beneficiaries upon the death of the insured. While human interest stories have been written about dying persons who receive "peace of mind" because of living benefits, critics say that these options subvert the primary purpose of life insurance, which is to provide adequate cash payments to beneficiaries to cover expenses incurred and income lost because of an insured's death.

Concept Check

8-14. What is a *beneficiary?* A contingent beneficiary? Explain why it is essential to designate a beneficiary.

8-15. Explain the basic *settlement options* available for the payment of life insurance proceeds upon a person's death.

8-16. What do nonforfeiture options accomplish? Differentiate between paid up insurance and extended term options.

8-17. Explain the following clauses often found in life insurance policies: (a) *multiple indemnity clause,* (b) *disability clause,* and (c) suicide clause. Give some examples of common exclusions.

8-18. Describe what is meant by a *participating life insurance policy,* and explain the role of policy dividends in these policies.

BUYING LIFE INSURANCE

LG6

Buying the right life insurance policy to protect your dependents requires many steps, from assessing your financial needs to choosing a company. How would you determine the type of policy to buy and find the best one to meet your requirements? Spend a few moments considering these questions before proceeding.

Selecting a life insurance policy is a complex process. Before you begin looking for a policy, it's important to understand the competitive features of life insurance. Then you can estimate how much life insurance you need to cover your dependents' financial requirements. Next, you should evaluate the different types of policies available to meet your needs and familiarize yourself with the various provisions that life insurance contracts typically include. With this basic understanding of life insurance in mind, you can then shop the market for the insurance protection best suited for you.

The following section discusses three competitive features of life insurance: protection from creditors, medium for savings, and tax benefits. Then we'll review the needs concept and the types of policies you might want to consider. Finally, to help you shop wisely, we'll explain how to compare costs and provide criteria for selecting life insurance companies and agents that offer the kind of services you'd like.

COMPETITIVE FEATURES OF LIFE INSURANCE

In addition to the elements that make up the insurance contract and other policy features, the following competitive features of life insurance require discussion: (1) protection from creditors, (2) medium for savings, and (3) tax benefits.

Protection from Creditors. When an insured dies, all assets and liabilities are totaled, and the heirs receive what is left after all legitimate claims against the estate have been satisfied. However, the purchase of life insurance can be structured so that death benefits will be paid to a named beneficiary rather than the deceased's estate. This way the cash proceeds do not become a part of the estate. Even if the insured had more liabilities than assets, the proceeds would not be used to liquidate them. Similarly, creditors who have successfully secured judgments against persons with substantial accumulations of life insurance cash values often cannot levy any claim on those assets. State laws differ with respect to the rights of creditors to the death benefits or cash values of life insurance policies, but in nearly all cases, both can be better protected than such assets as stocks, bonds, mutual funds, and investment real estate.

Medium for Savings. In addition to protection from creditors, life insurance can be an attractive medium for savings for some people, particularly those who are looking for safety of principal. The financial returns on the savings element in life insurance policies are often contrasted with investments in stocks, bonds, mutual funds, and real estate. Granted, most variable life policies are more investment vehicles than they are life insurance products, and as such, they can legitimately be compared to other investment outlets. For other types of insurance, though, *the comparison is inappropriate*. Certainly, any time the purchase of life insurance is being considered primarily because of its tax-sheltered investment properties, that transaction should be evaluated relative to what you can earn (on an after-tax basis) from alternative investment vehicles. More often than not, you'll find that *better returns are available from alternative investments,* especially when you factor in load fees, steep surrender charges, and other expenses.

Even though there's been a lot of growth recently in variable life and universal life policies, these products still account for only a small segment of life insurance sales. By far, the biggest share of life insurance is sold for the insurance protection it provides—without question, that's why most people buy whole or universal life policies. It's the death protection they're after, and the savings feature is just a pleasant by-product. The savings feature is not something to be overlooked, but it's not the principal reason for purchase. In both whole and universal life insurance, the approach to investing the cash-value part of the policy is very much toward the safe, conservative side where stability of income and preservation of capital are the primary concerns of the money managers. Under these conditions, it doesn't make any sense to compare the returns on these accounts to stocks, long-term bonds, and other forms of investing. More appropriately, the returns on whole and universal life insurance cash values should be compared to savings accounts, money funds, U.S. Treasury bills, and the like. When that's done, you're likely to find that the returns on these insurance products stack up very well: indeed, they compare favorably in providing returns ranging from 3 to 6 percent for recently issued policies, especially when you consider these are tax-deferred returns.

Tax Benefits. Life insurance proceeds, as a rule, are not subject to state or federal *income* taxes. Further, if certain requirements are met, policy

> **policy dividends** Payments made to participating policyholders that represent a refund of overcharges which result from the insurance company's overestimation of its mortality experience.

proceeds can pass to named beneficiaries free of any *estate* taxes. Generally, though, to qualify for this estate tax exemption, the insureds must relinquish various "incidents of ownership" in their policies, including the right to change the beneficiary, to take the policy's cash surrender value, and to choose a settlement option. When the named beneficiary is a spouse, the sacrifice of these rights is unnecessary. In these cases, the life insurance proceeds typically can be excluded from estate taxes as part of the marital deduction.

An equally attractive benefit is that the *investment earnings* in whole, universal, and variable life products build up within the policy on a tax-deferred basis (this is called *inside build-up*). Such a feature means that the cash surrender value will build up much quicker than if you had to pay taxes annually on any investment earnings for the year.

Another tax advantage is that when cash values are withdrawn from an insurer, income taxes are payable only on the amount by which the cash value exceeds the total premiums that have been paid. In practice, this excess seldom results, because part of the premium that is paid is allocated to the death benefit cost incurred by the company during the time the policy is in force. Consequently, it does not become a part of the cash value of the policy. But, here again, *be very careful with cash withdrawals,* because in some cases, unless you're over age 59½, you may be hit with income tax on the withdrawal *plus* a good-sized tax penalty. The IRS rules governing cash withdrawals can get a bit complex (to say the least); and to make matters even worse, Congress has had a tendency lately to change things almost annually. The best course is to check with someone in the know (like a tax accountant) if you're in doubt.

REVIEW NEEDS AND COVERAGES

As discussed earlier, life insurance is used in a person's financial program to fill the gap between the resources that will be available after death and those that will be needed. In addition, some life insurance policies can effectively be used as a savings medium.

For most young families on limited budgets, death protection greatly exceeds their savings need. If you fall into this category, guaranteed renewable and convertible term insurance should account for the largest portion of your insurance protection. They provide the most coverage for the least cost while you build up your assets. Healthy older people with many other financial resources may wish to use term policies for specific coverage needs.

Most families also need some amount of permanent insurance and savings, which a continuous-premium whole life policy can satisfy. Some financial advisors recommend that you use cash value insurance to cover your *permanent need for insurance*—the amount your dependents will need regardless of the age at which you die. (Although term insurance is less expensive, you may not be able to buy term insurance as you get older, or it may be too expensive.) Such needs may include final expenses—funeral costs and estate taxes—and either the survivor's retirement need (period 3 in Worksheet 8.1) or additional insurance coverage, whichever is less. This amount is different for every person. Using these guidelines, the Bensons in our earlier example would need about $95,000 permanent and $240,000 term. Limited-payment, variable life, and single-premium policies should be purchased only when the primary goal is savings or additional tax-deferred investments and not protection against financial loss resulting from death.

Whole life or other cash value policies may make sense in several other situations. A family history of heart disease, cancer, or similar conditions may increase your risk of developing health problems and make it hard to qualify for term insurance at a later date. And if you are already over 50, term may be too expensive. Or perhaps you've "maxed" out your other tax-deferred savings options and want to buy cash value insurance to accumulate additional retirement funds. But before buying a cash value policy, remember that many of these policies don't start building cash value until after year 3 or 5 and may have surrender penalties for about 10 to 15 years. Dropping a cash value policy too soon means losing the heavy up-front fees as well as any long-term tax benefits. So analyze all the consequences if someone suggests replacing an existing cash value policy; it may be preferable to keep it and supplement your coverage with a new policy.

COMPARE COSTS

The cost of a life insurance policy varies considerably from company to company, even for the same amount and type of coverage. Compar

EXHIBIT 8.8

Term Premium Cost Comparisons; $250,000 Policy, Preferred Rates

The price of a term life policy varies considerably among companies. The following table shows the extremes a male in excellent health might find when comparing the 10-year cost of a $250,000 term life policy.

Age	Company	10-year Cost
25	A	$ 2,010
	B	2,230
	C	2,660
	D	7,500
35	A	2,630
	B	2,480
	C	3,380
	D	11,880
45	A	4,680
	B	4,330
	C	6,700
	D	24,130
55	A	9,300
	B	9,080
	C	16,590
	D	67,500

Source: Various publications.

ison shopping can save you thousands of dollars over the life of your policy, as Exhibit 8.8 clearly demonstrates.

Term life quote services can streamline the selection process for you by providing, free of charge, the names of about five companies offering the lowest-cost policies based on your specifications. For example, *Quotesmith* (800-556-9393), *Insurance Quote* (800-972-1104), *Life Quote* (800-521-7873), *TermQuote* (800-444-8376) and *SelectQuote* (800-343-1985) maintain databases of many companies and will also act as your agent to buy the policy if you wish. TermQuote also provides quotes for both term and permanent life insurance. For low-load policy quotes, contact *Wholesale Insurance Network* (800-808-5810). And don't overlook companies who sell directly to the public or offer low-load policies—for example, John Alden, Ameritas, Lincoln Benefit, and USAA—so that your policy dollars go toward your death benefit or cash account instead of the agent's commission. And if you smoke or have a health problem like high cholesterol or high blood pressure, spending time to check out several companies can really pay off. Some companies are more willing to accept these risks than others and may even give you preferred rates if within a certain time period you correct the problem. But until you do your homework, you won't know which policy offers you the coverage you need at the lowest cost; and keep in mind, sometimes an agent-sold policy may be cheaper than one you can buy directly.

It's not enough, however, to look at current rates. You'll need to ask how long rates are locked in and about guaranteed rates, the maximum you can be charged when you renew. Although a guaranteed policy may cost another $20 a year, you won't be hit with unexpected rate increases later. Know how long you need the coverage and find the best rates for the total period; low premiums for a five-year policy may jump when you renew for additional coverage. And be sure you are getting the features you need, like convertibility of term policies.

Finally, be sure that the policies you are comparing *are similar in terms of provisions and amounts.* In other words, you should not compare a $100,000 term policy from one company with a $150,000 universal policy from another. Instead, you should first decide how much and what kind of policy you want and then compare costs. For similar cash value policies, you may find it useful to compare interest-adjusted cost indexes that are often shown on policy illustrations. The *surrender cost index* measures the policy's cost if you

Smart Money

Getting the Most Out of Life (Insurance)

Consumers faced with a major purchase such as buying a house or a car aggressively hunt for bargains, armed with facts and worksheets and arguing over every last dollar. But when it comes to life insurance, the same people wait for an insurance agent to call them, then sit passively and let the agent make their decisions. This behavior is so typical that industry pros actually grow suspicious when a consumer takes the initiative. Says Steve Richter of Prudential Life, "If someone calls and says, 'I want to buy life insurance,' I wonder if they're on the way to the hospital in an ambulance."

It's understandable, of course, to avoid thinking about life insurance—it means confronting your eventual death and putting a monetary value on life. But treating life insurance like any other investment, analyzing your needs and researching the options, will improve your financial health. Here are some do's and don'ts to guide you:

1. *Remember your other financial goals.* Every dollar you spend on life insurance is one dollar less for disability insurance, your children's college education, or your retirement. Your life insurance should be an element of a well-conceived financial plan.
2. *Forget corporate loyalty.* Life insurance offered by your employer may be convenient, but it's not necessarily the best deal if you have to pay the premiums. With such a group policy, everyone, regardless of their health situation, has to be accepted, which drives up the cost.
3. *Don't get taken in by misleading policy illustrations.* When you shop for a cash-value policy, agents will give you an "illustration" that purports to show how your investment might perform over 20 to 50 years. But remember: *the policy's actual performance probably depends on what happens to interest rates or stock prices.* If the illustration you're shown is based on higher rates than prevail today, the estimates of your earnings could be off by a mile. The golden rule: stay away from any projection that is significantly better than the competition's.
4. *Don't buy cash-value insurance when a term policy is more appropriate.* If you're in your 20s to early 40s with a young family, you probably don't have much to spare for insurance premiums and can also afford to be more aggressive with your savings. Most important, you want the largest death benefit possible to protect your family if you were to die in the relatively near future—and that means term insurance is your best bet. Many agents try to sell you permanent because they make a much larger commission. In many cases, cash-value policies make sense only if you need tax-deferred savings vehicles.
5. *Pay premiums annually.* If you make several payments a year, the policy will cost more; the interest charge on these "fractional payments" is often 8 percent or higher.
6. *Don't buy what you don't need.* Insurance companies offer a host of extras that sound great but aren't worth the cost. An accidental-death rider, for example, costs an extra $50 a year and pays your survivors double the death benefit if you die in an accident. But it's silly to speculate on how you'll meet your end, especially since accidental death is relatively uncommon.
7. *Seek out a specialist.* If you have heart disease, diabetes, or some other "impaired risk," look for a company that handles many cases like yours. Their underwriters are trained to analyze the extent of a given condition and rate clients accordingly, rather than lumping them all into one group.
8. *Clean up your act.* You probably know that you can cut your insurance premium if you stop smoking and lose weight, but you may not realize just how much you can save. For instance, most insurance companies charge twice as much to insure a smoker.

Sources: Adapted from: Glenn S. Daily, "The Big Mistakes People Make When Buying Life Insurance," *Bottom Line/ Personal,* July 15, 1994, pp. 5–6; Laura M. Holson and Liz Comte Reisman, "Lessons In Life," *SmartMoney,* December 1994, pp. 130–139; Jane Bryant Quinn, "Traps May Lurk in Cash-Value Life Insurance," *San Diego Union-Tribune,* February 21, 1994, p. C-1.

surrender it at a certain point, typically 10 or 20 years, assuming premiums and dividends earn 5 percent interest. The *net payment cost index* is calculated in a similar manner but assumes that the policy is kept in force. For more tips on becoming a savvy insurance customer, consult the *Smart Money* box on page 346.

SELECT A COMPANY

The life insurance company should be selected before choosing an agent, because in the life insurance business many agents represent only one company. Consequently, before looking for an agent, you might want to develop useful criteria to screen companies. Usually they can be evaluated on the basis of their financial stability, reputation in the community and nation, the liberal/restrictive nature of their policy provisions, and whether they offer participating policies (if this feature is important to you). Other factors to consider, especially when choosing a company for cash value insurance, are performance of the company's investments (check the A.M. Best reference books in most libraries) and dividend history; how the insurer controls its costs (good signs are low agent and policyholder turnover); the level of commissions and other fees; and company ratings (discussed below).

In shopping around, you might find that one company is preferable for your term protection and another for your whole life needs. Age and size are useful indicators of the financial stability of life insurance companies. Unless a good reason exists to do otherwise, you should probably limit your choice of companies to those that have been doing business for 25 years or more and have annual premium volume in excess of $50 million. Although these criteria will rule out a lot of smaller firms, there'll still be plenty of companies left from which to choose.

STICK WITH HIGHLY RATED INSURERS

Since 1991, five major life insurers and several dozen smaller ones have collapsed, leaving as many as a million customers dependent on a state-by-state patchwork of guarantee funds that don't hold any money. Indeed, the recent financial difficulties of such large life insurers as Executive Life, First Capital Life, Fidelity Bankers Life, Monarch Life, and Mutual Benefit Life all demonstrate the need to carefully study the financial stability of life insurers offering policies to you. The above noted insurers all invested heavily in high-risk junk bonds and/or real estate that resulted in large losses in the reserve funds held to pay claims. When policyholders began to demand their cash values earlier than expected, regulators realized that the available funds were inadequate, so they seized the insurers' assets and began the insolvency process, known as *rehabilitation*. Most holders of life insurance policies and annuities issued by the insurers in rehabilitation received full benefits, with the exception of Executive Life annuity holders, who received about 70 percent of the promised benefit level. Nevertheless, policyholders of these troubled insurers were forced to deal with the uncertainty of whether they would receive full value on their policies, plus the inability to withdraw their cash values during moratoriums imposed by regulators.

Assuming you are not a trained financial analyst familiar with the subtleties of insurance accounting practices, how can you tell whether your insurer is on firm financial footing? Similarly, how can you compare the financial solvency of competing insurers when deciding which policy or annuity to buy? Fortunately, several private rating agencies are in the business of assessing the financial strength of insurers and can provide the information you need. There are three major rating agencies that study life insurers and assign letter grades for financial strength. These ratings are available to the public and can be acquired by written request from the rating company (they may even be available in major university or public libraries). These rating agencies include A.M. Best Company (Ambest Road, Oldwick, NJ 08858), Standard & Poor's Corporation (25 Broadway, New York, NY 10004), and Moody's Investor's Service (99 Church Street, New York, NY 10007). Also, at least once a year, Professor Joseph Belth of Indiana University compiles all of these ratings in his monthly publication, *The Insurance Forum* (P.O. Box 245, Ellettsville, IN 47429), which is available by subscription. Although the rating agencies have 19 or more letter grades that they assign, you should only consider insurers in the very top categories. The top three grades for A.M. Best are A++, A+, and A; for Moody's they are Aaa, Aa1, and Aa2; and for Standard and Poor's they are AAA, AA+, and AA.

EXHIBIT 8.9

Some Highly-Rated Life Insurers with Top Ratings for Financial Strength

These life insurers are among those receiving the top grade from at least two of the three of the leading rating agencies in 1994. These grades are designed to reflect each insurer's long-term ability to pay promised benefits to holders of insurance policies and annuities.

	Assigned Rating		
Company	**Best**	**Standard & Poor's**	**Moody's**
AIG Life Insurance Co.	A++	AAA	Aaa
Canada Life Assurance Co.	A++	AAA	Aa2
Guardian Life Insurance Company of America (NY)	A++	AAA	Aaa
Hartford Life Insurance Co.	A++	AAA	Aa2
ITT Hartford Life & Annuity	A++	AAA	N/A
John Hancock Mutual Life Insurance Company	A++	AAA	Aa2
Massachusetts Mutual	A++	AAA	Aa1
Nationwide Life Insurance Company (OH)	A++	AAA	Aa1
New York Life Insurance & Annuity Corporation (DE)	A++	AAA	Aaa
New York Life Insurance Company (NY)	A++	AAA	Aaa
Northwestern Mutual Life Insurance Company (WI)	A++	AAA	Aaa
State Farm Life Insurance Company (IL)	A++	AAA	Aaa
Sun Life Assurance of Canada	A++	AAA	Aa1
Sun Life Assurance of Canada-US	A++	AAA	Aa1
Teachers Insurance & Annuity Association of America (NY)	A++	AAA	Aaa
USAA	A++	AAA	Aa1

Sources: Adapted from Joseph M. Belth, "Financial Strength Ratings of Life Insurance Companies," *The Insurance Forum,* March/April 1995, pp. 154–173, and A. M. Best & Co. ratings as of November 30, 1994.

At this point, you may wonder how these rating agencies come up with such a letter grade. Generally, the rating agencies examine publicly available financial information and conduct an analysis of the insurer that ranges from debt structure to pricing practices and management strategies. The purpose is to assess *the insurer's ability to pay future claims to policyholders—or claims paying ability,* as it is also known. The insurer pays a fee for this service. The rating agencies then inform the insurer of the assigned rating and, with the exception of Moody's, will *not* publish it if the insurer requests that the rating be withheld. Obviously, an insurer receiving a low rating is more likely to suppress publication, something that should be viewed as a clear signal that here is an insurance company to *avoid!* Most experts agree that you should purchase only from insurers that (1) are assigned ratings by at least two of the major rating agencies, and (2) are consistently rated in the top two or three categories (say, Aaa or Aa1 by Moody's) by each of the major agencies from whom they received ratings. If you do not have access to the ratings, ask your agent how the company is rated by Best's, Moody's and S&P. Or you might want to refer to Exhibit 8.9, which provides a list of highly-rated life insurance companies.

SELECTING AN AGENT

Your selection of a life insurance agent is important because you will be relying on him or her for guidance with respect to some very important financial decisions. Do not assume that just because agents are licensed they are competent and will serve your best interests. Consider an agent's formal and professional level of educational attainment. Does the agent have a college degree with a major in business or insurance? Does the agent have a professional designation, such as Chartered Life Underwriter (CLU), Chartered Financial Consultant (ChFC), or Certified Financial Planner (CFP)? These designations are awarded only to those who meet certain experience requirements and pass comprehensive examinations in such fields as life and health insurance, estate and pension planning, investments, and federal income tax law. In addition, observe how an agent reacts to your questions. Does he or she use fancy buzzwords and stock answers or instead listen attentively and, after a period of thought, logically answer your questions? These and other personal characteristics should be considered. In most instances, you should talk with several agents before committing yourself and discuss the pros and cons of each agent with your spouse. Then, when you have decided, call and ask that agent to return for another visit.

When seeking a good life insurance agent, try to obtain recommendations from other professionals who work with agents. For example, bankers in trust departments, attorneys, and accountants who are specialists in estate planning are typically good sources. In contrast, be a bit wary of selecting an agent simply because of the agent's aggressiveness in soliciting your patronage.

Concept Check

8-19. "Besides the regular policy features, some important competitive features are often found in life insurance policies." Discuss some of these competitive features.

8-20. Briefly describe the steps to take when you shop for and buy life insurance.

8-21. Briefly describe the insurance company ratings as assigned by Best's, Moody's, and S&P. Why is it important to know how a company is rated? What ratings would you look for in a life insurance company? Explain.

SUMMARY

LG1. Explain the role that insurance planning plays in personal financial planning and the relationship between risk and insurance. Adequate life insurance coverage is vital to sound personal financial planning, as it not only protects that which you have already acquired, but also helps to assure the attainment of unfulfilled financial goals. The whole notion of insurance is based on the concept of risk and the different methods of handling it: risk avoidance, loss prevention and control, risk assumption, and insurance (a cost-effective procedure that allows families to reduce financial risks by sharing losses). Through the underwriting process, insurance companies decide who they consider an acceptable risk and the premiums to charge for coverage.

LG2. Discuss the primary reasons for life insurance and identify those who need coverage. Life insurance fills the gap between the financial resources available to your dependents if you should die prematurely and what they need to maintain their lifestyle. Some policies only provide a death benefit, while others also have a savings component. If you have children or elderly relatives who count on your income to support them, you should include life insurance as one of several financial resources to meet their requirements. If you have no dependents, however, you probably don't need life insurance. Your life insurance needs change over your life cycle and should be reviewed on a regular basis.

LG3. Calculate how much life insurance you need. There are a number of ways to determine the amount of life insurance that a family should have. Although the multiple needs approach is simple to use, most experts agree that the needs approach is the best procedure. It systematically considers such variables as family income, household and other expenses, debt liquidation, liquidity needs, and special requirements, which are then compared to the financial resources available to meet these needs.

LG4. Differentiate between the various types of life insurance policies and describe their advantages and disadvantages. The three basic types of life insurance policies are term life, whole life, and universal life; term life insurance basically provides a stipulated amount of death benefits, whereas whole life combines death benefits coverage with a modest savings program, and universal life packages term insurance with a tax-deferred investment account that pays competitive money market returns. Other types of life insurance include variable and variable universal life, joint life, survivorship life, group life, credit life, mortgage life, industrial life, and deferred-premium life insurance.

LG5. Recognize key life insurance policy provisions and features. Some important life insurance policy provisions that you should become familiar with are the beneficiary clause, settlement options, policy loans, payment of premiums, grace period, nonforfeiture options, policy reinstatement provisions, and insurability options. Other policy features include multiple indemnity and disability clauses, guaranteed purchase options, suicide clause and other exclusions, participation through policy dividends, and living benefits.

LG6. Choose the best life insurance policy for your needs at the lowest cost. To get as much coverage as possible from your insurance dollar, it is important that you not only compare costs but also buy the proper amount of life insurance and pick the right type of insurance policy. Beyond the provisions and cost of the insurance policy, you should also carefully consider the financial stability of the insurer offering the policy, paying special attention to the ratings assigned by major rating agencies.

FINANCIAL FACTS OR FANTASIES

Are the following statements financial facts (true) or fantasies (false)?

1. About the only way to protect you and your family from the risk of potential economic loss is to buy insurance.
2. The best way to find out how much life insurance you need is to multiply your annual earnings by 3.
3. Social security survivor's benefits should be factored into your life insurance plans if you have a dependent spouse and/or minor children.
4. Term insurance provides nothing more than a stipulated amount of death benefits and, as a result, is considered the purest form of life insurance.
5. Mortgage life insurance is a cost-effective way to assure that your mortgage will be paid off when you die.
6. Selecting an insurance company is the first thing you should do when buying life insurance.

DISCUSSION QUESTIONS AND PROBLEMS

Discussion Question for Opening Profile

Do you think the Saunders were right to delay buying life insurance until they had children? Evaluate their decision-making strategy. Do you agree with Dan's conclusion that they should buy term life? Why or why not? What guidelines would you suggest to help them shop for the right policy?

FPPC 1. ***Use Worksheet 8.1.*** Janna Meyers' 65-year old mother, who was recently widowed, now lives with Janna. Janna is 40, single, and earns $45,000 a year as a human resources officer for a bank, which provides life insurance coverage equal to one times salary. She owns a condo with a market value of $85,000 and a $50,000 mortgage. Other debts include a $5,000 car loan and $3,500 in various credit card balances. Her 401(k) plan has a current balance of $24,500, and she keeps $7,500 in a money market account for emergencies.

Janna is concerned that her existing insurance coverage from the bank may not be adequate to provide for her mother, who is in good health, if Janna should die. She estimates that her mother would need about $1,800 a year for living expenses, and her only income is $800 a month in Social Security survivor's benefits. Janna estimates that her final expenses would be about $5,000, that her mother would live another 20 years, and that she wants to provide a $15,000 contingency fund as well. Use Worksheet 8.1 to calculate Janna's total life insurance requirements and recommend the type of policy she should buy.

FPPC 2. ***Use Worksheet 8.1.*** Given your current personal financial situation, do you feel you need life insurance coverage? Why or why not? Use Worksheet 8.1 to confirm your answer and calculate how much additional insurance (if any) you might have to purchase.

3. Using the premium schedules provided in Exhibits 8.2, 8.3, and 8.5, how much in *annual* premiums would a 25-year-old male have to pay for $100,000 of annual renewable term, level-premium term, and whole life insurance (assume a 5-year term or period of coverage)? How much would a 25-year-old woman have to pay for the same coverage? Comment on your findings. Now, consider a 40-year-old male (or female): using annual premiums, compare the cost of ten years of coverage under annual renewable and level premium term options and straight life insurance coverage. Comment on your findings.
4. Monica and Manuel Cordero are a dual career couple who just had their first child. Manuel, age 29, already has a group life insurance policy but Monica's employer does not offer life insurance. A financial planner is recommending that the 25-year-old Monica buy a $250,000 whole-life policy with an annual premium of $1,670—the policy has an assumed rate of earnings of 8 percent a year. Help Monica evaluate this advice and decide on an appropriate course of action.
5. While at lunch with a group of co-workers, one of your friends mentions that he plans to buy a variable universal life policy because it provides a good annual return and is a good way to build savings for his 5-year-old's college education. Another colleague says that she is adding coverage through the group plan's additional insurance option. What advice would you give them.

CONTEMPORARY CASE APPLICATIONS

8.1 Judith Parker's Insurance Decision: Whole Life, Variable Life, or Term?

Judith Parker, a 38-year-old divorced mother of three children, ages 12, 10, and 4, works as a product analyst for Ralston Purina. Although she is covered by a group life insurance policy at work, she feels, based on some rough calculations, that she needs additional protection. David Dustimer, an insurance agent from Siegfried Insurance, has been trying to persuade Judith to buy a $150,000, 25-year limited-payment whole life policy. However, Judith favors a variable life policy. To further complicate matters, Judith's father feels that term insurance is more suitable to the needs of her young family. To resolve the issue, Judith has decided to consult Terry Patrick, a childhood friend who is now a professor of insurance at a nearby university.

Questions

1. Explain to Judith the differences among (a) a whole life policy, (b) variable life policy, and (c) a term policy.
2. What are the major advantages and disadvantages of each type of policy?
3. In what ways(s) is a whole life policy superior to either a variable or term policy? In what way(s) is a variable life policy superior? How about term insurance?
4. Given the limited information in the case, which type of policy would you recommend for Ms. Parker? Defend and explain your recommendations.

FPPC 8.2 The Sutters Want to Know When Enough Is Enough

Dave and Karen Sutter are a two-income couple in their early 30s. They have two children, ages 6 and 3. Dave's monthly take-home pay is $1,800 and Karen's is $2,100. The Sutters feel that because they are a two-income family, they both should have adequate life insurance coverage. Accordingly, they are presently trying to decide how much life insurance *each one of them* should carry.

To begin with, they would like to set up an education fund for their children in the amount of $80,000 to provide college funds of $10,000 a year—in today's dollars—for four years for each child. Moreover, in the event of either's death, they want the surviving spouse to have the funds to pay off all outstanding debts, including the $110,000 mortgage on their house. They estimate that they have another $15,000 in consumer installment loans and credit cards. They also project that if either of them dies, the other probably will be left with about $10,000 in final estate and burial expenses.

As far as their annual income needs are concerned, Dave and Karen both feel very strongly that each should have enough insurance to replace their respective current income levels until the youngest child turns 18 (a period of 15 years). Though neither Dave nor Karen would be eligible for social security survivor's benefits, because they both intend to continue working, both children would qualify, in the amount of around $1,100 a month. The Sutters have amassed about $75,000 in investments, and they have a declining-term life policy *on each other* in the amount of $85,000, which would be used to partially pay off the mortgage. Further, Dave has a $60,000 group policy at work and Karen a $90,000 group policy.

Questions

1. Assume that Dave's gross annual income is $30,000 and Karen's is $40,000. Their insurance agent has given them a multiple earnings table showing that the earnings multiple to replace 75 percent of their lost earnings is 8.7 for Dave and 7.4 for Karen. Use this approach to find the amount of life insurance each should have if they wanted to replace 75 percent of their lost earnings.
2. Use Worksheet 8.1 to find the additional insurance needed on both Dave's and Karen's lives. (Note: Because Dave and Karen hold secure, well-paying jobs, both agree they won't need any additional help once the kids are grown; each also agrees that he/she will have plenty of income from their social security and company pension benefits to take care of themselves in retirement. Thus, when preparing the worksheet, assume "funding needs" of zero in periods 2 and 3.)
3. Is there a difference in your answers to Questions 1 and 2? If so, why? Which number do you think is more indicative of the Sutter's life insurance needs?
4. Using the amounts computed in Question 2 (employing the needs approach), what kind of life insurance policy would you recommend for Dave? For Karen? Briefly explain your answers.

GETTING A HANDLE ON YOUR FINANCIAL FUTURE

The main purpose of life insurance is to protect your family against financial loss in the event of your untimely death. You should be aware that your life insurance needs change as your marital and family status evolve. Once your needs have been determined, you have to select the appropriate type of life insurance and select a company and agent. Remember, you should continually monitor your insurance needs and periodically review the financial ratings of the company to ensure its safety and soundness.

If You Are Just Starting Out

If you are single and have no desire to leave anything to anyone, your life insurance needs are probably zero. However, if you are married with no children and have a spouse who works, you would probably need to have enough life insurance to pay off all or the majority of your debts and provide for funeral expenses upon your death.

Points to Consider:

1. In determining the amount of insurance needed, do not forget to consider social security benefits in your calculations.
2. Review your employee benefits to determine if you have enough coverage through your employer.
3. Check the benefits associated with the professional organizations to which you belong or with your credit cards to see if there is any insurance coverage.
4. If you determine that you need additional insurance coverage, see how much money is available for life insurance premiums based upon your cash budget.
5. When shopping for life insurance, check whether or not your employer offers a group life policy and compare this to nongroup rates.
6. Most young couples, particularly those with children, find they can get the most insurance for their money with *term life insurance*. If you do select term life insurance, take out a policy that is renewable.

If You Are Thirty-Something

At the beginning of this stage of the life cycle you are probably at the peak of your life insurance needs. You usually have young children, a mortgage, car loans, and various other credit obligations.

Since your income has probably increased, you might be in a position to convert from term insurance to more permanent insurance to lock in the cost and to use the tax-deferred nature of policies that provide a savings or investment feature.

Careful monitoring is essential during this time to enable you to quickly adjust your coverage to meet your changing needs for life insurance protection.

Points to consider:

1. If you are vested in your employer's retirement plan, there may be death benefits provided that you should consider.
2. Choose your beneficiary wisely. If your spouse is not good at handling large sums of money or you want to make sure that the proceeds benefit your children, you might want to consider a life insurance trust.
3. If you are buying insurance that has a savings or investment feature, compare the rates of return to other investment alternatives.
4. Be sure to read the exclusions on the policy. For example, it may not pay if you are a pilot or passenger on a noncommercial airline.
5. You might want to consider a disability clause that provides for a waiver of premium in the event you become disabled.
6. You should generally avoid the use of credit life insurance associated with a loan. You can normally buy the coverage, if you need it, at a lower price.
7. If you want your home mortgage paid off upon your death, you should obtain a decreasing-term policy that corresponds with your declining balance.
8. Resist the temptation to continue paying for insurance that is no longer needed. Put the money in a savings or investment account.

Chapter 9

Insuring Your Health

The Hanson's "Self-Managed Care"

It's easy to take your health insurance plan for granted—until it isn't there anymore. That's what Bonnie and Jeff Hanson discovered in 1990 when Jeff left his job as an executive for a large software company to form a small personal finance software company with Bonnie in southern Connecticut. "We didn't realize how lucky we were," Jeff says. "Our health benefits were really generous; the company paid a large portion of the premiums and the policy picked up all other costs after we covered an annual deductible of $250 per family member. So we didn't think twice about seeing a doctor for even minor complaints." For the next year and a half, the Hansons (both in their late 40s) and their three children (ages 15, 12, and 10), continued with the group plan under federal COBRA legislation. "But when we paid the whole $480 monthly premium ourselves—that's $5,760 a year, and the costs were expected to rise even further—we were shocked at how much health insurance actually costs," recalls Bonnie. "So we sat down and figured out how we could reduce our premiums yet still protect ourselves."

Their first step was to establish their health care priorities. "We knew we couldn't afford the comprehensive coverage my former employer provided," Jeff says. "What we needed most was coverage for catastrophic illness, surgical procedures, and outpatient testing." They explored several options, including individual policies and group plans offered by trade

Learning Goals

LG1. *Discuss how the health care industry is changing and why it's important to have adequate health care insurance.*

LG2. *Differentiate between the major types of health care plans and identify the major private and public providers of health insurance and their programs.*

LG3. *Explain the basic types of medical expense coverage and policy provisions for medical expense plans.*

LG4. *Assess the need for and provisions of long-term care insurance.*

LG5. *Calculate your need for and provisions of disability income insurance.*

LG6. *Analyze your own health care insurance needs and shop for appropriate coverage.*

associations. By switching in 1992 to an insurance plan offered by an association of small businesses, the Hansons reduced their monthly premiums from $480 to about $300. "But that involved trade-offs," explains Jeff. "We opted to 'self-insure' for routine care by choosing a high deductible, $1,000, and later raised it to $2,000." They also chose a 50 percent copayment, which means they pay half the costs after the deductible, but out-of-pocket costs are capped at $7,000, and accidents and surgeon's fees are fully covered. "Although $7,000 seems like a lot, we decided we could live with it. With this policy, we have coverage for serious illness so we won't be ruined financially. And we've invested the money saved on premiums so that it's available to help with medical expenses."

The Hansons didn't stop there, however. "By taking a close look at how we used health care services, we found other ways to cut costs," says Bonnie. "We tracked our expenses to see how many were really necessary. As a result, we stopped running to the doctor for every sneeze or headache and handled many minor problems by phone. Our lifestyle now includes health-wise practices like regular exercise and low fat diets. We call our system 'self-managed care.'" In the chapter that follows, you will learn about the different kinds of health care plans, who provides them, and various coverage options, so that like the Hansons, you can evaluate and choose the right health insurance for your needs.

Source: Loosely adapted from information in Ed Henry, "Personal Finances," *Kiplinger's Personal Finance Magazine*, September 1993, p. 150.

THE NEED FOR HEALTH CARE INSURANCE COVERAGE

LG1

Health care insurance coverage is an essential element of the personal financial planning process because of the umbrella of protection it provides for your financial plans. What are your current health care coverage exposures and needs? Before reading on, take a few moments to list some of the potential health care needs and costs to which you are exposed.

Assume you have done everything possible to establish and implement fully operational personal financial plans. You have an effective budget, you keep track of expenditures, you have several ongoing investment and retirement plans, and so forth. Imagine what would happen to all of this if a member of your family or you became seriously ill. Without adequate health care insurance, all of your financial accomplishments and goals could be destroyed.

Consider the case of Paul Murphy, who fell off a ladder while painting his house and broke his leg and badly sprained his back. His five days in the hospital were followed by four weeks of recuperation and physical therapy treatments before Paul could return to work. In all, his medical and hospitalization costs—ambulance, X-rays, setting the fracture, traction for his back, hospital room, physical therapy, etc.—were over $8,500, in addition to $4,000 in lost pay.

Such expenses certainly would devastate most family budgets. That is why the next best thing to good health is probably a good health care insurance plan. If you ever have a serious illness or accident, you may discover that the road to recovery can involve not only the physical pain from sickness and injury, but also economic pain. The cost can easily run into the tens of thousands of dollars once you add up hospitalization and medical expenses as well as the loss of income while you recover. Clearly, without adequate health care insurance to pay expenses and disability income insurance to replace lost income, a person's economic health can suffer long after he or she has recovered physically.

AN INDUSTRY IN CHANGE

The health care field is undergoing rapid changes today as rising health care costs have prompted new ways of delivering health services. Only a few years ago, a consumer's basic choices were the doctor's office, a hospital, or a health maintenance organization (HMO). Today, you may also visit a *neighborhood emergency center* for minor emergencies on a walk-in, often 24-hour-a-day, basis, an ambulatory outpatient surgical center (both usually less costly than comparable in-hospital treatment), or an *individual practice association (IPA)* or *preferred provider organization (PPO)* for hospital and medical services. These and other new ways of providing health care are discussed later in this chapter.

Another ongoing change is the rising cost of health care, particularly hospital room charges, and the percentage of personal expenditures devoted to it. Total national private and public spending for health care in the mid-1990s was about *$1 trillion* and is projected to reach $1.8 trillion by the year 2000. Today about 17 percent of all of our personal expenditures in the United States are made on health care, an increase from less than 11 percent in 1980. Also, the rate of increase substantially exceeds that of the consumer price index (CPI). In early 1995, for example, medical care costs increased by almost 5 percent while the CPI rose at an annual rate of about 3 percent. And of the various costs that make up the medical care portion of the CPI, hospital expenses lead the list of price increases, rising an average of almost 10 percent a year since 1980. In 1992, the average cost to treat a patient in a community hospital was $820 per day. Physicians' fees, nurses' salaries, and other product and service costs essential to health care also have increased faster than the CPI, though not as fast as hospital charges.

Several major factors account for this phenomenon, chief among them probably being the aging U.S. population (which needs more health care), the government's Medicare and Medicaid programs, and the rapid growth in the broad base of private health plans. More than 87 out of every 100 noninstitutionalized Americans are now eligible for at least some cost reimbursement for losses resulting from illness or accident. In addition, technological advances in diagnosis and treatment techniques, new drug therapies, and major acquisitions of expensive new health care equipment and facilities by hospitals and clinics have pushed costs upward. A poor demand-and-supply distribution of health care facilities and services may be still another factor. Administrative costs, excessive paperwork, and insurance fraud also contribute to rising costs.

The implementation of managed care and cost containment programs (discussed later in this chapter) has slowed the rate of growth in health care costs somewhat. However, recent government efforts to reform the health care system and provide universal coverage failed (about 30 million Americans have no health insurance and another 20 million are underinsured). Unfortunately, no immediate relief is in sight. In light of these spiraling costs, the need for health care financing plans and insurance is greater than ever.

MAKING SENSE OF IT ALL

If we ranked consumer insurance programs on a complexity scale, life insurance would be at the "simple" end and health insurance at the other end. In all but rare instances, life insurance pays regardless of the cause of loss. What's more, the loss itself is seldom arguable, and the amount of the loss is the face amount of the policy (or some multiple thereof). In addition, each life insurance policy you own will pay regardless of any other policies you have; there are no deductibles, waiting periods, participation clauses, or chances of cancelation; and differences in policy provisions among leading insurers are relatively slight. In contrast, each of these issues is pertinent to health insurance coverages. Because of these complicating factors, designing the best way to meet your health care needs requires a truly systematic approach. You need to learn the different types and sources of health care plans, the types of medical expense coverages and policy provisions, and about long-term care and disability income coverages. Next, you need to inventory your needs and existing coverages. With that task completed, you then can shop the market for the right protection at the best price.

SORTING OUT YOUR HEALTH CARE COVERAGE OPTIONS

Although many of today's health care insurance policies provide much broader coverage than those offered in the past, the wide variety in quality of policies makes caution imperative when shopping among them. Health care coverage is provided through either private or government insurers and falls into two basic types of plans: traditional indemnity and managed care. These plans provide a wide variety of medical and surgical expense coverages. In addition, there are long-term care and disability income plans. Each coverage category has many different versions of policies. By understanding the basic features of each plan, you can make a wiser purchase decision.

Concept Check

9-1. Why should health care insurance planning be included in your personal financial plan?

9-2. What factors have contributed to today's high costs of health care?

TYPES AND SOURCES OF HEALTH CARE PLANS

LG2

You can obtain health care coverage in the form of an indemnity plan or a managed care plan from private insurance carriers, special organizations like HMOs, and several government agencies. What type of plan do you have, and from which of these broad groups of providers do you receive health care coverage? Spend a few moments answering these questions before reading ahead.

There are two types of basic health care coverage: an indemnity plan or a managed care plan—the fastest-growing segment of the health-care delivery industry. Both these plans provide financial aid for losses arising from illness or accidents and are available from several sources, including private insurance companies and managed care providers. Your plan may be a group plan through your employer or some other group or an individual plan purchased directly from the provider. Finally, government agencies also provide health care coverage. Let's now look more closely at the types of plans from which you can choose and who provides them.

TYPES OF HEALTH CARE PLANS

Most health care plans fall into one of two categories: traditional indemnity (fee-for-service) plans and managed care plans, which include health maintenance organizations (HMOs), preferred provider organizations (PPOs), and similar groups.

Traditional Indemnity (Fee-for-Service) Plans. Traditional **indemnity (fee-for-service) plans** were the dominant form of health care insurance as recently as 1988, when they accounted for 71 percent of all private health insurance plans. By 1993, this figure had dropped to 49 percent. With these plans, the person or organization from which you obtain the health care services is separate from the insurer. The insurer pays the provider or reimburses you for expenses. The insured usually has unlimited choices of doctors and hospitals. To receive payment, the policyholder submits claims for medical treatment. Reimbursement is typically 80 percent of eligible costs incurred after payment of a deductible, which can range from $100 to $2,000 or more. The lower your deductible, the higher your premium payment. The amount you receive may be based on 80 percent of the *usual, customary, and reasonable (UCR) charges*—what the insurer considers the prevailing fees within your area, not what your doctor or hospital actually charges. If your doctor charges more than the UCR, you may be responsible for the full amount of the excess. UCR charges vary significantly among insurers, so you may wish to compare your doctor's fees with what a plan pays. Some providers have indemnity plans where physicians who accept the insurance agree to accept the UCR payments set by the insurer.

Managed Care Plans. **Managed care plans** make up the fastest growing segment of the health care industry; in 1993 these plans enrolled about 51 percent of all Americans covered by health care insurance, and this percentage is increasing at a rapid pace. In a managed care plan, subscribers/users contract with and make monthly payments *directly to the organization that provides the health care service.* Insurance companies may not even be involved—although today most major insurance companies offer both indemnity and managed care plans. Although managed care plans take different forms, they share certain features:

- Members receive comprehensive health care services from a designated group of doctors, hospitals, and other providers, who must meet the managed care provider's specific selection standards.
- These plans use various strategies to provide cost-efficient medical care, such as controlling the amount of care provided and emphasizing prevention of illness.

The insured pays no deductibles and only a small fee, or copayment, for office visits; most medical services—including preventive and routine care that indemnity plans may not cover—are fully covered when obtained from plan providers. Examples of managed care plans are health maintenance organizations (HMOs), individual practice associations (IPAs), preferred provider organizations (PPOs), and other plans.

Health maintenance organization. Today about 50 million people in the United States belong to some form of **health maintenance organization (HMO).** Exhibit 9.1 shows the ten largest U.S. HMOs. The traditional HMO is often referred to as a *group HMO*, because a group of doctors employed by the HMO provide the health care services from a central facility. These HMOs have developed primarily in larger cities. Usually the doctors and the hospital are in the same complex.

An HMO provides comprehensive health care services to its members. The plan includes outpatient care, such as minor surgery, doctors' office visits, and X-ray and laboratory services; hospital inpatient care; surgery; maternity care; mental health care; and prescriptions. As a member of an HMO, you pay a monthly fee that varies according to the number of persons in your family. Also, you may pay $2 to $10 each time you use an outpatient service or need a prescribed drug. However, there are no other charges to worry about—there are no doctors' fees, X-ray charges, or other expenses to HMO members who use the facilities for their health care needs.

The primary purpose of HMOs is to reduce the costs of health care, both by using resources more efficiently and by practicing "preventive medicine"—most HMOs provide physical exams and sponsor pro-health activities such as smoking clinics, exercise programs, and so on. The advantage to members is that they are not faced with exclusions, deductibles, coinsurance, or filing insurance

EXHIBIT 9.1

Largest Health Maintenance Organizations

Today the ten largest health maintenance organizations (HMOs) in the United States provide health care services to over 25 million subscribers.

HMO company*	Year HMO started	No. of HMOs	No. of enrollees	Primary regions served
1. Kaiser Foundation Health Plan Inc.	1945	12	6,670,000	California
2. United HealthCare	1975	21	3,670,000	Midwest, South
3. CIGNA HealthCare	1929	44	3,500,000	All regions
4. U.S. Healthcare	1973	13	1,900,000	Northeast
5. The Prudential Health Care System	1973	50	1,800,000	All regions
6. FHP Health Care	1961	9	1,730,000	West, Midwest
7. Humana Inc.	1983	19	1,600,000	Midwest, South
8. Aetna Health Plans	1985	25	1,500,000	All regions
9. Health Systems International	1979	7	1,470,000	West Coast
10. PacifiCare	1978	6	1,400,000	California

*Rating based on membership

Source: John Sedgwick, "Welcome to the World of Managed Care." *Self,* April 1995, p. 197.

claims. The primary disadvantage is that members are not always able to choose their physicians. Also, because group HMOs practice in central facilities, members should be sure to ask about the benefits provided if they should need care outside the geographic area of their HMO.

Individual practice association. An **individual practice association (IPA)** is actually a variation of a standard HMO, because the financial and service arrangements are similar, with only the physical facility being different. As a member of an IPA, you prepay monthly and are entitled to a wide range of health care services. However, the services are *not provided from a central facility.* Physicians operate out of their own offices and from community hospitals that provide services to IPA members as well as others. IPAs appeal to people who would like some choice of physician. They also extend the advantages of an HMO into less populated regions where central facilities are not feasible.

Preferred provider organization. A **preferred provider organization (PPO)** has characteristics of both an IPA and an insurance plan. PPOs provide greater flexibility than traditional HMOs, offering comprehensive health care services to its subscribers within a network of physicians and hospitals. In addition, it provides insurance coverage for medical services not provided by the PPO network. A PPO, which can be administered by an insurance company or a provider group, contracts for services from designated physicians and

indemnity (fee-for-service) plan Health care insurance plan where the person or organization from which you get the health care services is separate from the insurer, who pays the provider or reimburses you for a percentage of expenses after a deductible. These plans provide unlimited choices of doctors and hospitals.

managed care plan Health care plan where subscribers/users contract directly with the provider organization, which furnishes comprehensive health care services for a fixed fee from a designated group of providers that meet stringent selection criteria. These plans emphasize cost control and preventive treatment.

health maintenance organization (HMO) An organization consisting of hospitals, physicians, and other health care personnel who have joined together in a central facility to provide necessary health care services to its subscribers.

individual practice association (IPA) A form of HMO where subscribers receive services from physicians operating out of their own offices and from community hospitals rather than from a central facility.

preferred provider organization (PPO) A health care provider that combines the characteristics of an IPA with an insurance plan to provide comprehensive health care services to its subscribers within a network of physicians and hospitals.

EXHIBIT 9.2

Health Care Insurance Benefits Paid, by Type of Insurer (Billions of Dollars)

Insurance companies pay out billions of dollars annually in health care benefits.

Year	Total*	Insurance companies	Self-insured and HMOs	Blue Cross/Blue Shield
1950	$ 1.3	$ 0.8	$ NA	$ 0.6
1955	3.1	1.8	NA	1.4
1960	5.7	3.0	NA	2.6
1965	9.6	5.2	NA	4.5
1970	17.2	9.1	NA	8.1
1975	32.1	16.5	NA	16.9
1980	76.3	37.0	16.2	25.5
1981	85.9	41.6	18.9	29.2
1982	97.1	49.2	21.6	32.2
1983	104.1	51.7	24.1	34.4
1984	107.5	56.0	26.1	34.7
1985	117.6	60.0	32.5	37.5
1986	128.5	64.3	36.8	40.6
1987	151.7	72.5	56.5	44.5
1988	171.1	83.0	62.8	48.2
1989	194.5	89.4	79.8	50.7
1990	208.9	92.5	93.4	55.9
1991	223.0	97.6	112.0	60.0
1992	246.4	104.8	132.1	63.1

*Totals do not add up because of duplication between insurance companies and self-insured/HMO plans.

Source: *Source Book of Health Insurance Data* (Washington, DC: Health Insurance Association of America, 1994 Edition), p. 38.

hospitals who agree to accept a negotiated fee schedule. You will benefit from the lower price if you use those physicians and hospitals. Like other forms of managed care, PPOs use techniques such as review of proposed treatment that emphasize efficient and cost-effective delivery of health care. Today, PPOs account for about 20 percent of health care plans.

Other managed care plans. In addition to the plans described above, there are two other managed care plans you may encounter. The **exclusive provider organization (EPO)** is a variation of a PPO. Like a PPO it contracts with providers to offer services to members at reduced cost, but only reimburses for use of affiliated providers. Plan members who use another provider must bear the entire cost. The **point-of-service (POS) plan** is a hybrid form of HMO that in 1993 accounted for 9 percent of all health care plans. A POS plan allows members to go outside the HMO network for care. Payment for non-affiliated physician services is similar to indemnity plan payments; the plan pays a specified percentage of the cost after satisfaction of an annual deductible. This plan is becoming more popular because it combines the features of the HMO with freedom of choice.

WHO PROVIDES HEALTH CARE INSURANCE?

The major providers of health care insurance include private companies—health care insurance companies, managed care organizations, and Blue Cross/Blue Shield plans, which may be purchased through a group or on an individual basis—and government agencies. In 1992, private health care insurance plans covered about 181 million people; over 80 million received all or part of their coverage from group plans.

As Exhibit 9.2 shows, insurers paid $246 billion in health care insurance benefits in 1992. Over $95 billion of these benefits were paid under group insurance plans. Exhibit 9.3 shows how premium volume for private insurers grew between 1950 and 1992 in relation to disposable personal income. In 1940 (not shown) only .42 percent of disposable personal income went for health care premiums; by 1970 this figure reached 2.8 percent and by 1992 had risen to 6.3 percent.

Until recently, there were clear distinctions among the private providers and the health care plans they offered. Today, however, these differences have blurred, and there are many organiza-

EXHIBIT 9.3

Health Care Insurance Premiums (Billions of Dollars)

The amount of money spent on health care insurance premiums has risen dramatically in dollar terms and—more important—as a relative amount of disposable personal income.

Year	Insurance companies	Self-insured and HMOs	Blue Cross/ Blue Shield	Net total all insurers*	Disposable personal income (billions)	Premiums as percentage of disposable personal income
1950	$ 1.3	$ NA	$ 0.7	$ 2.0	$ 207.5	1.0%
1955	2.7	NA	1.5	4.3	278.8	1.5
1960	4.7	NA	2.8	7.5	358.9	2.1
1965	7.4	NA	4.8	12.1	486.8	2.5
1970	11.5	NA	8.4	20.0	715.6	2.8
1975	20.8	NA	17.6	37.0	1,142.8	3.2
1980	43.7	17.3	26.3	84.7	1,914.3	4.4
1981	49.0	20.0	30.4	95.1	2,121.8	4.5
1982	58.3	22.9	34.3	109.5	2,261.4	4.8
1983	63.2	25.6	37.6	119.9	2,428.1	4.9
1984	70.4	28.6	40.0	127.6	2,668.6	4.8
1985	75.2	36.7	41.5	139.5	2,838.7	4.9
1986	75.5	40.6	43.5	143.4	3,013.3	4.8
1987	84.1	59.8	46.3	167.1	3,194.7	5.2
1988	98.2	71.1	51.2	189.9	3,548.2	5.4
1989	108.0	89.1	56.0	215.6	3,787.0	5.7
1990	112.9	103.9	62.6	235.8	4,050.5	5.8
1991	116.4	123.4	67.1	256.2	4,230.5	6.1
1992	125.0	143.9	70.9	281.3	4,500.2	6.3

*Premiums for the different types of insurers may sum to an amount greater than total premiums because of double counting.

Source: Adapted from *Source Book of Health Insurance Data* (Washington, DC: Health Insurance Association of America, 1994 Edition), pp. 41 and 96.

tions from which to choose the right plan for your particular needs.

Private Insurers. Health care coverage is sold by hundreds of private insurance companies, including such well-known names as Aetna, CIGNA, Equitable, John Hancock, Metropolitan Life, Prudential, and Travelers. Until recently, most private companies offered only traditional indemnity insurance. Today, they sell a variety of indemnity and managed care plans to both groups and individuals.

As noted earlier, managed care plans are offered by a variety of providers, including dedicated organizations that only provide managed care (such as Kaiser and FHP), and other firms (such as private insurers and Blue Cross/Blue Shield) that also offer indemnity plans. Managed care organizations can be nonprofit, like Kaiser, or for profit, like Humana. They may either own centralized hospital and doctors' office facilities that only serve members or operate as administrative organizations that arrange with individual hospitals and doctors—who also serve non-members—to provide services to plan members through IPAs, PPOs, or EPOs.

Blue Cross/Blue Shield. In a technical sense, **Blue Cross/Blue Shield plans** are not insurance policies but rather prepaid hospital and medical expense plans. Until recently, these plans were nonprofit health care service organizations; in June 1994, the national Blue Cross/Blue Shield Association announced that it would allow its 69 members to become for-profit corporations. This

exclusive provider organization (EPO) Health plan that reimburses members only if they use affiliated providers.

point-of-service (POS) plan Type of HMO that allows members to go outside the HMO network for care; the plan reimburses members for non-affiliated services at a specified percentage of the cost after satisfaction of an annual deductible.

Blue Cross/Blue Shield plans Prepaid hospital and medical expense plans under which health care services are provided to plan participants by member hospitals and physicians.

move was designed to make it easier for plans to obtain funding and compete more effectively in the health care field; about 12 plans indicated that they were considering the switch.

Blue Cross contracts with hospitals, who in exchange for a specified fee or payment agree to provide specified hospital services to members of groups covered by Blue Cross. Similarly, Blue Shield plans are contracts for surgical and medical services. These plans serve as intermediaries between groups who want these services and physicians who contractually agree to provide them. Today, about 52 Blue Cross and Blue Shield plans have combined to form one provider. Blue Cross/Blue Shield organizations compete for business with private insurance companies (many of which are nonprofit mutual insurance companies) and attempt to retain a portion of their income to finance growth.

Currently, about 67 million people are covered by some type of Blue Cross/Blue Shield protection, including 27 million in its own managed care programs. Because they are producer cooperatives, benefit payments are seldom made to the subscriber but rather directly to the participating hospitals and physicians.

Group versus Individual Health Care Insurance. You can purchase health care insurance from group plans, usually obtained through your employer but also available through trade or professional associations or from the provider in the open market as individual health care insurance.

Group health care insurance refers to health care contracts written between a group (usually an employer, union, credit union, college or university, or other organization) and the health care provider: a private insurance company, Blue Cross/Blue Shield plan, or managed care organization. Typically, group plans provide comprehensive medical expense coverage, and many also offer prescription drug, dental, and vision care services. The coverages of each specific plan are subject to negotiation between the group and the insurer, and the group may offer several types of plans.

If you go to work for an organization of more than just a few employees, you will probably be covered by some type of group health care plan. Today, about 40 percent of employers pay the total premium for basic health care coverage of employees; the rest require employees to pay a portion of the cost. Only 6 percent still pay the full cost of coverage for employees and their dependents; at most firms, employees pay all or part of the premiums for family coverage. Some groups choose to *self-insure*, which means that the employer or other group takes responsibility for full or partial payment of claims. The administration of a self-insured plan may be handled by the group itself or through an administrative agreement with an insurance carrier or a third-party administrator.

Because managed care programs help to control costs, fewer large employers are offering indemnity plans in their benefit packages—60 percent in 1994, down from 89 percent in 1988. About 50 percent offer a choice of indemnity or managed care plans. Typically, the employee can choose between several deductible levels for indemnity plan coverage and one or more managed care options. When a person leaves the group, existing group plan coverage can be continued for 18 months if the employee pays the full premiums plus an administrative fee. The employee can, within the 18 months, elect to convert to an individual plan, although the cost may be quite high. (Continuation of group coverage is discussed in more detail later in this chapter.)

At one time, group health care coverage was far superior to individual coverage, especially in terms of availability and cost to the employee. No one was denied coverage, regardless of health. Today, however, the differences between group and individual coverage have narrowed, and many of the advantages of group coverage have disappeared. To control rising medical costs, many employers no longer guarantee universal coverage but underwrite employee applications much the way insurers do. They may deny coverage for a medical condition that already exists and limit or charge more for specialized coverages. Employers are also shifting a larger percentage of the cost to employees, in the form of larger premium contributions, co-payments, and deductible amounts; some employers create different risk categories so that employees who have known health risks pay higher premiums.

Today, many people compare group and individual policies before deciding which coverage to buy. With the rise in corporate downsizings, employees may lose group benefits. As a result, many opt for individual coverage to prevent coverage lapses and avoid the difficulty of getting coverage later if health problems develop. Another advantage of individual coverage is the ability to tailor the coverage to the person's needs. In contrast, an individual under a group plan is entitled only to the benefits that are available in the master group plan. And although the protection afforded under many group plans is excellent, many families still need to supplement this coverage with an individual health care plan. This situation is especially true with respect to disability income insurance for upper-middle-income wage earners (discussed later in this chapter). However, unlike group life insurance (which is not recommended as a basis for a life insurance plan—see Chapter 8), group health care insurance can serve as the foundation on which a family builds its individual health care insurance program.

Government-Sponsored Health Care. Federal and state agencies also provide health care coverage. Social Security Administration programs provide a considerable amount of coverage for losses arising from illness and accidents as well as disability. *Workers' compensation* is a state program that covers medical expenses, rehabilitation, and disability income for job-related medical conditions. Let's take a closer look at social security and worker's compensation programs.

Social Security's Medicare program. Many people think of Social Security as primarily concerned with retirement benefits. But as its official name—*old-age, survivor's, disability, and health insurance (OASDHI)*—indicates, the program provides other coverage as well. Health benefits are provided under two separate programs: (1) *Medicare*, discussed below, and (2) disability income, discussed later in the chapter. (Although the Medicaid program also provides medical benefits and is partly funded by the federal government, it is not discussed here since it is a state-run public assistance program that provides benefits only to those unable to pay for health care.) All Social Security cash benefit programs automatically adjust payments periodically to reflect increases in the cost of living. These increased benefits depend, however, upon the government's ability to raise taxes—a subject of much heated debate in recent years.

Although **Medicare** is a health care plan primarily designed to help persons 65 and over meet their health care costs, it now also covers many persons under age 65 who are current recipients of monthly social security disability benefits. Funds for medicare benefits come from social security taxes paid by covered workers and their employers. Medicare has two primary components: (1) basic hospital insurance and (2) supplementary medical insurance.

- ***Basic hospital insurance.*** This coverage (commonly called *Part A*), provides inpatient hospital services—room and board and other customary inpatient services—for the first 90 days of illness, after a deductible ($716 in 1995) is applied for the first 60 days of illness. Coinsurance provisions, applicable to days 61 through 90 of the hospital stay, can reduce benefits further. Medicare also covers all or part of the cost of up to 100 days in post-hospital extended-care facilities such as nursing homes providing *skilled care*. (However, the most common types of nursing home care—*intermediate and custodial care*—are not covered under Medicare.) It also covers some post-hospital health services, such as intermittent nursing care, therapy, rehabilitation, and home health aid. Deductible and coinsurance amounts are revised annually to reflect changing medical costs.
- ***Supplementary medical insurance (SMI).*** The **supplementary medical insurance (SMI)** program (commonly called *Part B*) covers: (1) physicians' and surgeons' services; (2) home health service (visitation by a registered nurse); (3) medical and health services such as X rays,

group health care insurance A type of health care insurance consisting of contracts written between a group (employer, union, and so forth) and either a private insurance company, Blue Cross/ Blue Shield, or managed care organization.

Medicare A health care plan administered by the federal government to help persons age 65 and over, and others receiving monthly social security disability benefits, meet their health care costs.

supplementary medical insurance (SMI) A voluntary program under Medicare (commonly called *Part B*) that provides payments for extra services, such as physicians' and surgeons' services, home health service, and X-ray and laboratory services, and requires participants to pay premiums.

diagnostics, laboratory tests, rental of necessary durable medical equipment, prosthetic devices, and ambulance trips; and (4) limited psychiatric care. Unlike the basic hospital plan, SMI is a voluntary program financed by premiums paid by participants, which are then matched with government funds. SMI is open to nearly anyone age 65 or over who enrolls and pays the required monthly premiums ($46.10 in 1995), which are the same regardless of age, health status, or sex. With SMI, the insured pays 20 percent of costs after a $100 deductible and SMI pays 80 percent of *approved charges*—not 80 percent of whatever the physician bills, so actual payment may be substantially less than 80 percent of the total bill. In addition, neither Part A nor Part B of Medicare pays for prescription drugs taken outside of the hospital.

Although Medicare pays for many health care expenses for those over 65, there are still gaps in coverage. About 70 percent of Medicare enrollees supplement their benefits with private "Medigap" insurance policies.

Workers' compensation insurance. **Workers' compensation insurance** programs are mandated by every state and also the federal government to compensate workers for job-related illness or injury. Although workers' compensation legislation, benefit amounts, and payment periods differ in each state, benefits often include medical and rehabilitation expenses, disability income, and scheduled lump-sum amounts for death and certain injuries, such as dismemberment. These laws are designed to lighten the burden of job-related illness or injury to the worker. Employers bear the entire cost of worker's compensation plans in all states. Premiums are based on merit; employers who file the most claims pay the highest rates. Consequently, employers try to reduce accidents and injuries to keep premiums low. Self-employed persons who are covered under the law must make contributions for themselves and their employees. The four basic areas of coverage provided by worker's compensation insurance are:

- *Medical and rehabilitation expenses.* Pays hospital, surgical, and other related expenses, including prosthetic devices such as artificial limbs, needed to help employees recover and reenter the work force as quickly as possible. Some jurisdictions provide compensation to retrain seriously injured victims for new employment.
- *Disability income.* Pays a specified percentage of the covered person's predisability earned wages, up to some maximum amount, usually limited to one-and-a-half times the average weekly wage of workers within that state. The duration of disability payments varies from 50 weeks in some states to a lifetime in others.
- *Lump-sum payments.* Paid to employees who suffer dismemberment in work-related accidents or to their beneficiaries in the event of death.
- *Second-injury funds.* Relieve employers of the additional worker's compensation premium they might incur if they employ an already handicapped worker who is further injured on the job.

Other Sources of Health Care Coverage. Supplementing the traditional health care plans are several other sources of funds or services. As discussed in Chapter 10, both homeowner's and automobile insurance policies contain limited amounts of medical expense protection. Homeowner's policies cover accidents that happen around the home to people who are visiting you (although not to members of the insured household). Automobile policies may cover you if you are involved in an automobile accident regardless of whether you are in a car, on foot, or on a bicycle. Further, if someone negligently injures you, you have legal grounds on which to collect from that person or his or her liability insurer.

In addition to social security, various other government programs help pay medical expenses. Medical care is provided for people who have served in the armed services and were honorably discharged and for military personnel and their dependents. Public health programs exist to treat communicable diseases, handicapped children, and mental health disorders. In total, federal, state, and local government now spend well over $300 billion a year on health care expenses. When people—especially elderly and low-income—suffer accident or illness, often a government program is available to help out.

Concept Check

9-3. Describe the features of traditional *indemnity (fee-for-service) plans* and explain the key differences between them and *managed care plans.*

9-4. "Health maintenance organizations (HMOs) attempt to reduce the cost of health care to individuals and families through more efficient utilization of health care personnel and facilities, and by practicing preventive medicine." Explain basically how these organizations work. Contrast HMOs with IPAs and PPOs.

9-5. Who are the primary providers of health care insurance? Discuss the basics of the *Blue Cross/Blue Shield plans*.

9-6. What is *group health insurance?* Differentiate between group health care insurance and individual health care insurance.

9-7. What is the formal name used for social security? Briefly describe eligibility for and benefits of social security's *Medicare* program.

9-8. What is the objective of workers' compensation insurance statutes? Explain (a) lump-sum payments and (b) second-injury funds as they relate to workers' compensation.

MEDICAL EXPENSE COVERAGES AND POLICY PROVISIONS

LG3

Today's consumer can choose from a wide variety of medical expense insurance products to obtain precisely the type of protection desired. Are you familiar with any particular types of medical expense policy coverages? Make a list of these coverages and relate them to your health care needs before reading on.

Thus far, we have discussed the major types of health care insurance plans and their providers. Now we will examine the various types of medical expense coverage health insurance—hospital, surgical, physicians, major medical, comprehensive, and dental—and some typical provisions you will find in your medical expense plan. In addition, we will take a brief look at the cost containment provisions frequently included in these plans.

TYPES OF MEDICAL EXPENSE COVERAGES

Hospital Insurance. Hospital insurance policies reimburse you for the costs of hospital room (semiprivate) and board and other expenses incidental to hospitalization. In the United States, more people are covered by some type of hospitalization insurance than any other kind of private health care insurance. Basically, hospital insurance pays for a portion of (1) the per-day hospital room (semiprivate) and board charges, which typically include floor nursing and other routine services, and (2) ancillary expenses, such as use of an operating room, laboratory tests, X-ray examinations, and medicine received while hospitalized. Although a few hospital insurance policies will pay for an in-hospital private duty nurse, most will not. Some hospital plans simply pay a flat daily amount for each day the insured is in the hospital, regardless of actual charges. Numerous hospital plans now also offer reimbursement for some outpatient and out-of-hospital services, such as in-home rehabilitation or ambulatory center care, diagnostic and preventive treatment, and preadmission testing.

In most policies, hospital insurance is written to provide daily, semiprivate room and board charges for up to a specified number of days, such as 90, 120,or 360. The maximum reimbursement for ancillary expenses, in contrast, may be a stated dollar amount or sometimes a multiple of the daily room rate. In the first instance, frequently found maximums are $1,000, $2,000, and $5,000, whereas in the second, the multiple might be 15 or 20. Thus, if the room and board rate were $250 per day, applying this multiple would result in an ancillary expense limit of either $3,750 or $5,000.

Surgical Expense Insurance. *Surgical expense insurance* provides coverage for the cost of surgery in or out of the hospital. Most plans provide so-called *service benefits*, which offer reimbursement of surgical expenses that are "reasonable and customary." The insurer determines the level of

workers' compensation insurance A type of health care insurance, required by state and federal governments and paid for by employers, that compensates workers for job-related illness or injury.

Financial Shocks

Experimental Treatments: Who Pays?

Donna Rogers thought she had won her fight against breast cancer when, after surgery, chemotherapy, and radiation treatments, she was seemingly cancer-free. But two years later, cancer appeared in her hip. She had two options: continue with chemotherapy for the two years she was expected to live or undergo a new type of bone marrow transplant (BMT), a stem-cell transplant. She was accepted by the transplant program at the University of Colorado but then faced another, unexpected fight—against her health insurance provider, which refused to cover the $75,000 to $100,000 treatment. The company paid for BMTs for other forms of cancer but excluded the stem-cell procedure, considering it an experimental treatment not yet proven effective by widespread clinical trials.

Unfortunately, Rogers's experience is becoming all too typical, as insurance companies faced with skyrocketing health care costs refuse to pay for expensive new treatments. Patients with chronic fatigue syndrome or late-stage Lyme disease, for example, typically have trouble getting reimbursed for expensive antibiotics. And many insurers won't cover off-label uses of drugs (when a drug has been approved by the FDA, but not for your disease) on the grounds that in this context the drug is experimental.

At the heart of the issue lies a fundamental question: shouldn't a patient's course of treatment be determined by a qualified health care professional, and not by the courts, or by a claims agent whose loyalty is to an insurance company? Although most insurance policies clearly state that they don't cover experimental or investigative procedures, their definitions of the terms are vague. This leads to highly subjective and seemingly arbitrary decisions about coverage. Many patients feel betrayed, accusing their insurers of using a treatment's experimental status as an excuse not to pay. Insurers counter that they are protecting patients from dangerous and unproven medicine and keeping premium costs down. At the same time, though, denying

benefit that is reasonable and customary based upon a survey of surgical costs during the previous year. Most people who have such a policy also have had an experience where the insurer partially reimburses a medical bill because the reasonable and customary rate is less than the physician's actual bill. Nevertheless, service benefits generally cover most of the bill and should rise over time in an era of inflating medical costs.

Some plans still pay *scheduled benefits*, as opposed to service benefits. Under this type of plan the insurer will reimburse you up to a fixed maximum amount for a particular surgical procedure. For example, the policy might state that you would receive no more than $850 for an appendectomy or $700 for diagnostic arthroscopic surgery on a knee. Such scheduled benefits are often inadequate when compared with typical surgical costs; in 1993, the median cost for an appendectomy was $1,000 and for diagnostic arthroscopy, $845.

Surgical expense coverage usually will pay for almost any type of surgery that is required to maintain the health of the insured. In the event that a necessary surgical procedure is not named in the policy, the company will pay the amount listed for a comparable operation. Reimbursement for the cost of anesthetics and their administration is provided in most surgical expense policies. These benefits may also be covered in an "additional benefits" provision of a hospital insurance policy. Specific surgical expense policies may also allow payment for the nonemergency treatment of tumors and other afflictions using X-rays or radium. Some policies provide a limited diagnostic allowance for X-rays and lab fees. Surgical expense coverage is typically sold in conjunction with a hospital insurance policy either as an integral part of that policy or as a rider.

Certain surgical procedures may be excluded from reimbursement by the plan. Elective, cosmetic surgery, such as the proverbial "nose job" or "tummy tuck," normally is excluded. Cosmetic surgery following a deforming accident often is reimbursed, however. A more controversial area is exclusion of experimental surgery, especially certain types of organ transplants and experimental treatments for cancer or other diseases. If a high mortality rate is associated with such procedures, coverage may eliminate a patient's only hope for survival.

Many cases end up in expensive legal battles, with the courts ruling case-by-case and often siding with the patient's doctor. A California jury, for example, awarded $89 million to the family of a breast-cancer victim who died because her HMO refused to pay for a stem-cell BMT. For this reason, insurers are usually eager to settle such cases out of court.

The best idea for people who are about to undertake an expensive course of therapy is to try and prevent their insurance company from turning down their claim. To increase the odds of an insurance approval:

- *Request hospital pre-certification as soon as possible.* Ask the hospital to set a date for the procedure and give it to the insurer, thereby establishing a deadline by which the insurer must make a decision about coverage.
- *Ask your doctor or the hospital to send an information package to your insurer* with studies affirming the procedure's efficacy, safety, and acceptance in the medical community.
- *Find an advocate.* The Medical Care Ombudsman Program in Bethesda, Maryland, provides free assessment of treatment options from a volunteer group of respected doctors. Often, such powerful recommendations pressure insurers into paying.

If your insurance company denies you coverage and a court upholds the decision, there may still be a way for you to get the recommended treatment. You may be eligible for clinical trials of experimental new procedures performed at the National Institutes of Health in Bethesda, Maryland. There is no cost for treatment except transportation to the site. Some drug companies will provide a drug, proven effective in clinical trials but that has not yet received formal FDA approval, free to certain patients. You can raise funds privately in your community with help from the Organ Transplant Fund and the Children's Organ Transplant Association or your hospital. Finally, your employer may be willing to help pay for an experimental procedure outside of the group health benefits plan.

Sources: Adapted from Elizabeth Fenner, "A Mother Chooses Life," *Money*, September 1994, pp. 87–97; Melynda Dovel Wilcox, "Fighting For Your Life," *Kiplinger's Personal Finance Magazine*, November 1994, pp. 112–119.

insurers normally will seek to exclude them. The *Financial Shocks* box above addresses the issue of coverage for experimental treatments.

Physicians Expense Insurance. *Physicians expense insurance,* previously called *regular medical expense,* covers the cost of such services as physician fees for nonsurgical care in a hospital, including consultation with a specialist. Also covered are X-rays and laboratory tests performed outside of a hospital. Home, clinic, or doctor's office visits normally are not covered except through special provisions. Plans are offered on either a service (reasonable and customary) or scheduled benefit basis. Often, the first few visits with the physician for any single cause will be excluded. This exclusion serves the same purpose as the deductible and waiting period features found in other types of insurance.

Major Medical Insurance. **Major medical plans** provide broad coverage for nearly all types of medical expenses resulting from either illnesses or accidents. As the name implies, the amounts that can be collected under this coverage are relatively large. Lifetime limits of $100,000, $250,000, $1,000,000, or higher are common, while some policies have no limits at all. The trend in recent years has been toward higher benefit levels.

Major medical coverage was first offered in the early 1950s to supplement basic hospital, surgical, and physicians expense coverages. This basic concept still applies today. Because the other three hospital and physicians expense coverages meet the smaller health care costs, major medical is used to finance medical costs of a more catastrophic nature. Approximately three out of every four Americans are covered by some type of major medical health plan. The popularity of this insurance has grown more since inception than that of any

major medical plan An insurance plan designed to supplement the basic coverages of hospital, surgical, and physicians expenses; used to finance medical costs of a more catastrophic nature.

other kind of health insurance in history. Many people use major medical with a high deductible to protect against catastrophic illness. To give insureds an incentive to avoid unnecessary medical costs, major medical plans typically are written with provisions that limit payments to less than full reimbursement. These policy provisions are discussed in a subsequent section.

Comprehensive Major Medical Insurance. A **comprehensive major medical insurance** plan combines the basic hospital, surgical, and physicians expense coverages with major medical protection to form a single policy, usually with a low deductible. Comprehensive major medical insurance is frequently written under a group contract. However, some efforts have been made to make this type of coverage available on an individual basis.

Dental Insurance. *Dental insurance* covers necessary dental health care as well as some dental injuries sustained through accidents. (Accidental dental expenses for natural teeth are normally covered under standard surgical expense and major medical policies.) The coverage may provide for oral examinations, including X rays, cleanings, fillings, extractions, inlays, bridgework, dentures, oral surgery, root canal therapy, and orthodontics. Of course, dental policies vary with respect to the number of these items included within the coverage. Some dental plans contain provisions limiting reimbursement (particularly with regard to orthodontics) to a portion of the expenses incurred, and others have "first dollar protection"—they pay for all claims. Most present dental coverage is written through group insurance plans, although some companies do offer individual and family policies. However, because many types of dental insurance function more as budgeting devices than as true insurance, premiums are often relatively large in light of the dollar amount of coverage obtained.

Special Insurance Coverages You *Don't* Need. An examination of every type of health care insurance coverage available would fill a book twice the size of this one. However, the types of health care plans already discussed are sufficient to meet the protection needs of most individuals and families. Other popular coverages often are simply frills and gimmicks. These plans may be classified as accident policies, sickness policies, and hospital income policies. Sound insurance programming seldom dictates the purchase of these types of policies. Nevertheless, large-scale marketing efforts by some insurers, coupled with public misunderstanding, has brought about their proliferation. Hopefully, the following discussion will help you guard against a potentially unwise purchase.

Accident policies are those that pay a specified sum to an insured who is injured in a certain type of accident. The most common types of accident policies are those relating to travel accidents. These policies often are sold in conjunction with oil company and travel and entertainment credit cards or at airports. Their primary shortcoming is that the amount of the payment is not directly related to the amount of the loss. Also, as noted earlier, because only certain types of accidents are covered, it becomes impossible to structure a systematic insurance program using these coverages.

Sickness policies are similar in design and shortcomings to accident policies except that a named disease, as opposed to an accident, conditions the payment. Sickness policies may be written separately or in conjunction with accident policies. *Dread disease policies* are a popular version of sickness insurance. Today's renditions limit health care coverage to a specific type of disease or illness. Cancer policies appear to be the most common, with some organ transplant policies also being offered. Some states, such as New York, prohibit the sale of single dread disease policies; that is, such coverage can only be sold as part of other hospital, surgical, or accident policies.

Hospital income policies typically guarantee the insured a specific daily, weekly, or monthly amount as long as the insured remains hospitalized. However, they generally exclude illnesses that could result in extended hospitalization (for example, mental illness or from health conditions that existed at the time the policies were purchased). Several of these plans have been accused of returning in benefits only 10 to 20 cents of each $1 of premiums collected.

The basic problem with buying policies that cover only a certain type of accident, illness, or financial need is that major gaps in coverage will occur. Clearly, the financial loss can be just as great regardless of whether the insured falls down a flight of stairs or contracts cancer, lung disease, or heart disease. Most limited-peril policies should be used only to supplement a comprehensive insurance program if the coverage is not overlapping. Both dread disease and hospital income policies are frequently offered directly through television and newspaper advertisements.

POLICY PROVISIONS OF MEDICAL EXPENSE PLANS

To compare the health care coverages offered by different insurers, you need to evaluate whether they contain liberal or restrictive provisions. Generally, policy provisions can be divided into two groups: terms of payment and terms of coverage.

Terms of Payment. Four provisions govern how much your medical expense plan will pay. These include (1) deductibles, (2) the participation (coinsurance) clause, (3) the internal limits on the policy, and (4) the coordination of benefits clause, if any.

Deductibles. Because major medical insurance coverages are designed to supplement the basic hospital, surgical, and physicians expense coverages, those offered under an indemnity (fee-for-service) plan frequently have a relatively large *deductible,* typically $500 or $1,000. The **deductible** represents the initial amount *not* covered by the policy and therefore the responsibility of the insured. Comprehensive major medical plans tend to offer lower deductibles, sometimes $100 or less. Most plans currently offer a calendar-year, all-inclusive deductible. In effect, this allows a person to accumulate the deductible from more than one incident of use. Some plans also include a *carry-over provision* where any part of the deductible that occurs during the final three months of the year (October, November, and December) can be applied to the current year, and can *also* be included in the following calendar year's deductible. In a few plans, the deductible is on a per-illness or per-accident basis. Thus, if you were covered by this type of policy with a $1,000 deductible and suffered three separate accidents in the course of a year, each requiring $1,000 of medical expenses, you would not be eligible to collect any benefits from the major medical plan.

Participation (Coinsurance). Another feature of most major medical insurance policies is some type of **participation,** or **coinsurance, clause.** This provision stipulates that the company will pay some portion—say, 80 or 90 percent—of the amount of the covered loss in excess of the deductible rather than the entire amount. Coinsurance helps to reduce the possibility that policyholders will fake illness and to discourage them from incurring unnecessary medical expenses. Although comprehensive major medical plans normally have a participation clause, too, this clause often does not apply to expenses related to basic hospital, surgical, and physicians expense coverage.

Because major medical limits now go up to $1 million or more, many plans have a **stop-loss provision** that places a cap on the amount of participation required. Otherwise, a $1 million medical bill could still leave the insured with, say, $200,000 of costs. Often such provisions limit the insured's participation to less than $10,000, and sometimes as little as $2,000.

Internal limits. Most major medical plans are written with internal limits. **Internal limits** place constraints on the amounts that will be paid for certain specified expenses, even if the overall policy limits are *not* exceeded by the claim. Charges that are commonly subject to internal limits are hospital room and board, surgical fees, mental and nervous conditions, and nursing services. Providing internal or inside limits is similar in purpose to participation, or coinsurance, clauses. The insurer

comprehensive major medical insurance A health care insurance plan that combines, into a single policy, basic hospital, surgical, and physicians expense coverages with major medical protection.

deductible The initial amount *not* covered by an insurance policy and therefore the responsibility of the insured; it is usually determined on a calendar-year or on a per-illness, per-accident basis.

participation (coinsurance) clause A provision in many health insurance policies stipulating that the insurer will pay some portion—say, 80 or 90 percent—of the amount of the covered loss in excess of the deductible.

stop-loss provision A cap in a major medical insurance policy that limits the insured's payment under the participation, or coinsurance, clause to a specified amount, such as $10,000.

internal limits A feature commonly found in health insurance policies that places a constraint on the amount that will be paid for certain specified expenses, even if the overall policy limits are *not* exceeded by a given claim.

wants to give the insured an incentive not to incur unreasonably high medical expenses and to control costs, thereby keeping premiums down. Therefore, if an insured elects a highly expensive physician or medical facility, he or she will be responsible for paying the portion of the charges that are above a "reasonable and customary" level or beyond a specified maximum amount. The example in the following section illustrates how deductibles, coinsurance, and internal limits constrain the amount a company is obligated to pay under a major medical plan.

Major medical policy: an example. Assume that Frank Payne, a graduate student, has coverage under a major medical insurance policy that specifies a $500,000 lifetime limit of protection, a $1,000 deductible, an 80 percent coinsurance clause, internal limits of $350 per day on hospital room and board, and $2,000 as the maximum payable surgical fee. Assume further that he was hospitalized for 5 days at $500 a day and required an operation to remove a small tumor that cost $1,800. Other covered medical expenses incurred with the illness totaled $1,800. Therefore, he incurred total medical expenses of $6,100: $2,500 for hospital room and board, plus $1,800 for the surgeon, plus $1,800 for the other medical expenses.

Because of the coinsurance clause in the policy, however, the maximum the company has to pay is 80 percent of the covered loss in excess of the deductible. In the absence of internal limits, the company would pay $4,080 (.80 × [$6,100 − $1,000]). The internal limits further restrict the payment. Even though 80 percent of the $500-per-day hospital charge is $400, the most the company would have to pay is $350 per day. Therefore, the insured becomes liable for $250 ($50 per day × 5 days). The internal limit on the surgery is not exceeded, because after considering coinsurance, the insurer will have to pay $1,440 (.80 × $1,800), which is below the $2,000 internal limit. The company's obligation is reduced to $3,830 ($4,080 − $250), while the insured must pay a total of $2,270 ($1,000 deductible + .20[$6,100 − $1,000] coinsurance + $250 excess hospital charges). The lesson here is that although major medical insurance can offer very large amounts of reimbursement, you may still be left responsible for substantial payments.

Coordination of benefits. In contrast to most property and liability insurance coverages, which are discussed in Chapter 10, health care insurance policies are not contracts of *indemnity*. This means that insureds can collect multiple payments for the same accident or illness unless a **coordination of benefits provision** is included in their health care insurance policies. For example, many private health care insurance policies have coordination of benefits provisions with medical benefits paid under workers' compensation. In contrast, some companies widely advertise that their policies will pay claims regardless of how much other coverage the policyholder has. Of course, these latter types of insurance policies often cost more per dollar of protection. From the standpoint of insurance planning, the use of policies with coordination of benefits clauses can help you prevent coverage overlaps and, ideally, reduce your premiums.

Considering the complexity of medical expense contracts, the various clauses limiting payments, and the coordination of benefits with other plans, one might expect that insurers frequently pay only partial claims and sometimes completely deny claims. If you make a claim and do not receive the payment you expected, do not give up. Exhibit 9.4 provides some guidelines on how you might go about getting your health care insurance claims paid.

Terms of Coverage. A number of contractual provisions affect the value of a medical expense insurance contract to you. Some of the more important provisions address (1) the persons and places covered, (2) cancellation, (3) continuation of group coverage, (4) rehabilitation coverage, (5) preexisting conditions, (6) pregnancy and abortion, and (7) mental illness.

Persons and places covered. Some health care insurance policies cover only the named insured, while others offer protection to all family members. Of those that offer family coverage, some terminate benefits payable on behalf of children at age 18 and others continue them to age 24 as long as the child remains in school or is single. *If you are in this age group, you or your parents should check to see if you are covered under your parents' policy.* If not, sometimes by paying an additional premium, you can add such coverage. (Note: If a child is over the age stipulated in the policy, and if the additional premium to add the child to the family policy has not been paid, that individual could be without any health care insurance. If any-

EXHIBIT 9.4

How to Get Your Health Care Insurance Claims Paid

The following guidelines will help you cut through red tape to get your health care insurance claims paid.

1. *Double check your claim form for accuracy before filing.* Make sure all the information is complete and correct; with computer processing, a typographical error or missing item could delay or even reject your claim.
2. *File all claims promptly, even if you don't think you are covered.* You need to file claims, usually within six to 12 months of the date of service, to meet your annual deductible.
3. *If a claim is rejected, don't take "no" for an answer.* Find out exactly why the claim is denied and provide additional information if required. The reason may be simple—a misspelled name or transposed numbers, claims for two separate family members were filed on the same day, or several procedures for one person were included on a single claim. An incorrect diagnostic code may be at fault if your claim is denied due to "inappropriate service" or "unrelated diagnosis;" call your doctor to get it corrected.
4. *If your claim is not handled to your satisfaction, go directly to the company's claims supervisor or home office.* Sometimes a letter to the company president breaks the logjam. As a last resort, tell the company that you will file a complaint with the state insurance department—and do it if necessary.
5. *Keep good records of utilization review approvals for hospital admissions or medical procedures.* You are ultimately responsible for getting these approvals, so be sure to allow enough time before your hospitalization and request written confirmation.

Sources: Adapted from Janet Bodnar and Melynda Dovel Wilcox, "When Your Health Insurance Makes You Sick," *Kiplinger's Personal Finance Magazine*, October 1991, pp. 64–71; and Jane Bennett Clark, "Insurance Fumbles—and How to Recover," *Kiplinger's Personal Finance Magazine*, January 1995, pp. 124–125.

thing should happen to him or her—no matter how severe—the parents and/or child may have to bear the full cost of the illness or accident.) Some policies protect you only while you are in the United States or Canada; others offer worldwide coverage but exclude certain named countries.

Cancellation. Many health insurance policies are written to permit *cancellation* at any time at the option of the insurer. Some policies explicitly state this; others do not. To protect yourself against premature cancellation, you should buy policies that contain a provision that specifically states that the insurer will not cancel coverage as long as premiums are paid.

Continuation of group coverage. At one time, people who lost their jobs, or were temporarily laid off, could lose their group health care insurance coverage in addition to their salary. Because the lack of income and health care coverage could place an employee and his family in a precarious position, in 1986 Congress passed the *Consolidated Omnibus Budget Reconciliation Act* (*COBRA*). Under COBRA an employee who leaves the group voluntarily or involuntarily (except in the case of "gross misconduct") may elect to continue coverage for up to 18 months by paying premiums to his former employer on time (up to 102 percent of the company cost). All benefits previously available—except for disability income coverage—are retained, including hospital, surgical, major medical, dental, and vision coverages.

Similar continuation coverage is available for retirees and their families for up to 18 months or until they become eligible for Medicare, whichever occurs first. The dependents of an employee may be covered for up to 36 months under COBRA under special circumstances such as divorce or death of the employee. If the employee worked in a firm of less than 20 employees (minimum COBRA requirements) or after COBRA requirements expire, most states provide for conversion of the group coverage to an individual policy without evidence of insurability. Premium charges and benefits of the converted policy would be determined at the time of conversion. However, the most important aspect of the conversion feature is that group coverage can be changed to individual coverage regardless of the current health of the insured. Clearly, it is important to understand your continuation rights under COBRA as well as the laws of the state in which you are employed.

coordination of benefits provision A provision often included in health care insurance policies; it requires that benefit payments be coordinated in the event that the insured is eligible for benefits under more than one policy.

Rehabilitation coverage. In the past, health care insurance plans focused almost exclusively on reasonable and necessary medical expenses. If an illness or accident left an insured partially or totally disabled, no funds normally would be available to help the person retrain for employment and a more productive life. Now, though, many policies include expense reimbursement for counseling, occupational therapy, and even some educational or job-training programs. With this **rehabilitation coverage,** the goal is not to medicate but to rehabilitate. This is a good feature to look for in major medical and disability income policies.

Preexisting conditions. Most health care insurance policies that are sold to individuals (as opposed to group/employer-sponsored plans) contain **preexisting condition clauses.** This means that the policy might exclude coverage for any physical or mental problems that you had at the time you bought it. In some policies, the exclusion is permanent; in others, it lasts only for the first year or two that the coverage is in force. Group insurance plans may also have preexisting condition clauses, but these tend to be less restrictive than those in individually written coverages.

Pregnancy and abortion. Many individual and group health care insurance plans include special clauses that pertain to medical expenses incurred through pregnancy or abortion. The most liberal of these policies pay for all related expenses, including sick-leave pay during the final months of pregnancy. Other policies pay for medical expenses that result from pregnancy or abortion complications but not for routine procedure expenses. In the most restrictive cases, no coverage for any costs of pregnancy or abortion is granted.

In recent years, the federal government and many states have passed laws that require certain employer-sponsored group health care insurance programs to provide more liberal pregnancy and abortion reimbursement plans. Even in the absence of law, though, many employers are expanding their coverage for employees in this area. Because of adverse self-selection problems, individual health care insurance will continue to restrict this policy feature.

Mental illness. Mental illness and emotional disorders are perhaps America's most prevalent but least talked about health problems. The high-pressure "get ahead" lives that many people lead often give rise to drug and alcohol abuse, stress-related physical disability, and various forms of psychosis or neurosis. In addition, family problems, economic setbacks, and chemical imbalances within the body all can contribute to poor mental health. Yet, even though mental illness or emotional disorder at some time strikes one out of three families, many of those affected will not admit they need help.

Compounding this problem of denial is the fact that many health insurance coverages omit or offer reduced benefits for treatment of mental disorders. Both hospital insurance and major medical insurance often restrict the duration over which they will reimburse mental illness expenses. For example, one widely marketed health insurance policy offers hospital benefits that continue to pay as long as you remain hospitalized—except for mental illness. Under this policy, payment for mental illness is restricted to one-half the normally provided payment amounts and for a period not to exceed 30 days. Unfortunately, mental illness is the number one sickness requiring long-term hospital care.

As you can see, coverage for mental illness is an important type of insurance protection. Therefore, make sure you check your policies to learn how liberal—or how restrictive—they are with respect to this feature.

COST CONTAINMENT PROVISIONS FOR MEDICAL EXPENSE PLANS

Considering the continued, rapid inflation in medical costs, it's hardly surprising that insurers, along with employers that sponsor medical expense plans, are looking for ways to limit the costs incurred. During the past decade, various cost containment provisions have been added to almost all medical expense plans, both indemnity and managed care policies. Although the success of such provisions has been limited, you are likely to find them in your own health care insurance plan. Among these cost containment provisions are:

- *Pre-admission Certification.* The pre-admission certification provision requires you to receive approval from your insurer prior to entering the hospital for a scheduled stay. You normally will be asked to provide an estimate of the length of expected stay, as well as other details. Of course, such approval is not normally required for emergency stays.

- *Continued Stay Review.* This applies when you need to remain in the hospital for a period exceeding that approved by the insurer in your pre-admission certification. Once again, the insurer must be informed of your continued stay in advance for you to receive the normal reimbursement.
- *Second Surgical Opinions.* In spite of a physician's opinion, many types of recommended, nonelective surgeries are either unnecessary or can be delayed. Good medical practice may dictate a second surgical opinion in these cases. Most surgical expense insurance now provides for full reimbursement of the cost of second opinions. Indeed, many plans *require* second opinions on specific, nonemergency procedures and, in their absence, may reduce the surgical benefits paid.
- *Caseworker Assignment.* For major surgery or extensive stays of a seriously ill person, the family of that person often is not in a position to calmly and rationally discuss hospital and surgical expenses with doctors. Naturally, the family only wants the best for their kin without regard to cost. In these situations, some plans assign a medically trained caseworker to discuss procedures and costs with the physicians involved. This practice gives the insurer some check on the procedures, and resulting costs, prescribed by the attending physicians.
- *Waiver of Coinsurance.* More traditional medical insurance plans provide first-dollar coverage for hospital and surgical expenses incurred during a hospital stay. Outpatient surgery is reimbursed by the major medical plan, which normally means that the insurer will pay only 75 or 80 percent of total costs, thanks to the coinsurance clause. Because insurers can save money on hospital room and board charges by encouraging outpatient surgery, many now agree to waive the coinsurance clause and pay 100 percent of surgical costs for outpatient procedures. A similar waiver sometimes is applied to generic pharmaceuticals, which also are reimbursed via major medical coverage. Under one such plan, a patient had the choice of an 80 percent coinsured payment for a brand-name pharmaceutical that cost $22 or a 100 percent reimbursement for its $7 generic equivalent. Because the patient chose the generic pharmaceutical, both the insurer and insured saved money.

Concept Check

9-9. Differentiate between hospital and surgical expense insurance. Define and compare *service benefits* and *scheduled benefits* under surgical expense insurance.

9-10. What is a *major medical* plan? What are its common features? What is *comprehensive major medical insurance?*

9-11. Describe a *hospital income policy.* How does it differ from medical expense plans that offer hospital insurance?

9-12. Briefly describe the following policy provisions commonly found in medical expense plans: (a) deductibles, (b) coinsurance, (c) coordination of benefits, and (d) preexisting conditions.

9-13. Briefly describe the key provisions of the *Consolidated Omnibus Budget Reconciliation Act (COBRA)* as they relate to continuation of group coverage when an employee voluntarily or involuntarily leaves the group.

9-14. Explain the cost containment provisions now frequently found in medical expense policies. Why do insurers use the provision for second surgical opinions to save on medical costs?

rehabilitation coverage Insurance that covers the expenses of counseling, occupational therapy, and even some education or job training for persons injured or disabled by illness or accident.

preexisting condition clause A clause included in most individual health care insurance policies that permits permanent or temporary exclusion of coverage for any physical or mental problems that the insured had at the time the policy was purchased; this clause, if included, is much less restrictive in group policies.

LONG-TERM CARE INSURANCE

LG4

Illnesses or accidents suffered by a member of your family can result in expenses beyond those necessary for immediate medical treatment. Perhaps an elderly family member is too ill or too frail to take care of his or her personal needs. If that person requires special care at home or needs to enter a nursing home, who pays these extra expenses? Think about the best alternatives to provide "long-term care" before you read on.

Thanks to ever-improving health care and better knowledge about health risks, such as smoking and poor diet, our population is living longer and will continue to do so in the foreseeable future. Many people are living to very advanced ages. In fact, those age 85 and above are expected to comprise about 5 percent of the population by the year 2050, up from about 1 percent in 1990. People reaching advanced ages often become too frail to perform basic activities of everyday life, such as eating, bathing, and dressing. You probably know some elderly persons who needed either to enter a nursing home or to hire special care in their own home because they simply could not adequately care for themselves.

While no one likes to think about spending years in a nursing home, this possibility is more likely than ever with today's longer life expectancies. Even if you are still young, someone in your family may need long-term care. So it is important to understand how this coverage works, if it makes sense given your family situation, and how to choose an insurance policy.

Long-term care is the term often used to describe the delivery of medical and personal care, other than hospital care, to persons with chronic medical conditions resulting from either illness or frailty. The cost of such care can be very expensive. For instance, the cost of nursing home care averages $40,000 per year—$110 per day—but is as high as $70,000 per year in some major cities. By the year 2020, the U.S. Administration on Aging projects that over 2.7 million Americans will be confined to a nursing home. Considering the likelihood of advanced aging in the United States and the costs of adequate long-term care, we must ask ourselves, "Who will pay the price?"

FINANCING LONG-TERM CARE

Exhibit 9.5 shows how nursing home care, a major component of long-term care, has been financed in the United States in recent years. The primary parties financing nursing home care have been individuals and government programs such as Medicare and Medicaid, which pays benefits only to the indigent, as classified under the strict eligibility laws of your state. Medicaid benefits are tightly capped by law, and the current political environment appears to favor continued cutbacks in this program.

About 40% of all nursing home costs are paid out-of-pocket by individuals, as shown in Exhibit 9.5. Frequently, the persons receiving care cannot afford this expense, so the younger generation ends up footing the bill. Although the exhibit indicates that private insurance has not been much of a factor in the past, the market for it is developing and expanding rapidly as more people become aware of the reality and cost of long-term care. Major medical insurance plans exclude most of the costs related to long-term care, so a special policy is required. Fortunately, more than 100 insurers now offer long-term care insurance policies. In 1993, 3.4 million long-term care policies were in force.

LONG-TERM CARE INSURANCE PROVISIONS AND COSTS

Because the market for long-term care insurance is evolving, few experts are surprised at the wide range of policy provisions and premiums currently being offered. Because of substantial variation in product offerings, you must be especially careful to evaluate the important policy provisions. They include (1) type of care, (2) eligibility requirements, (3) services covered, (4) daily benefits, (5) benefit duration, (6) waiting period, (7) renewability, (8) preexisting conditions, and (9) inflation protection. Exhibit 9.6 summarizes the benefits typically offered by leading insurers under these and other provisions. Of course, policy provisions are important factors in determining the premium for each policy.

Type of Care. Some long-term care policies offer benefits only for nursing home care while

EXHIBIT 9.5

Who Pays the Nursing Home Bill?

Because very few people have private insurance coverage that pays nursing home costs, most of these bills are paid either out-of-pocket by patients and their families or by government programs.

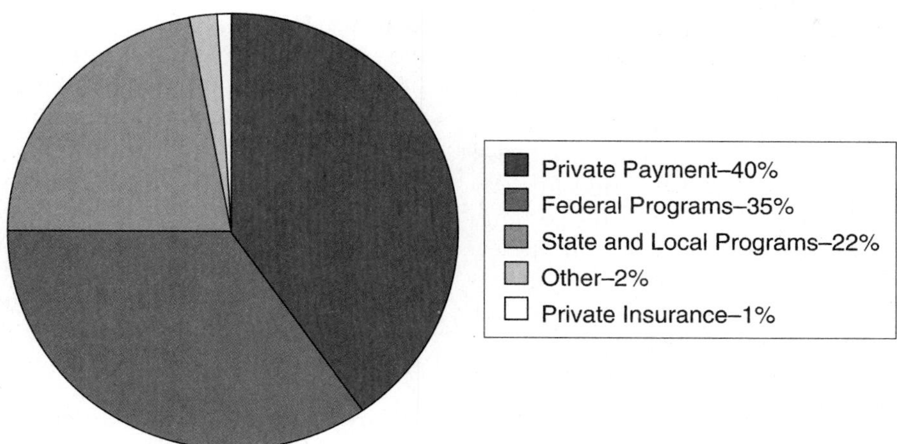

Source: *Source Book of Health Insurance Data* (Washington, DC: Health Insurance Association of America, 1994 Edition), p. 90.

EXHIBIT 9.6

Typical Coverages Offered in Long-Term Care Insurance Policies

Long-term care insurers offer a wide range of benefits in their policies.

Services covered	Skilled, intermediate, and custodial care Home health care Adult day care (often)
Daily benefit	\$50–\$250/day nursing home \$25–\$100/day home health care
Benefit eligibility	Physician certification/medically necessary
Maximum benefit period	5 years; unlimited
Alzheimer's disease coverage	Yes
Deductibility periods	0, 20, 30, 90, 100 days
Renewability	Guaranteed
Preexisting condition	6 months
Inflation consideration	Yes, for an additional premium
Age limits for purchasing	40–84

others pay only for services in the insured's home. Because you cannot easily predict whether or not a person might need to be in a nursing home, most financial planners recommend policies that cover both. Many of these policies focus on nursing home care, and any expenses for health care in the insured's home are covered in a rider to the basic policy.

long-term care The delivery of medical and personal care, other than hospital care, to persons with chronic medical conditions resulting from either illness or frailty.

Eligibility Requirements. Some very important provisions determine whether or not the insured will receive payment for claims. These are known in the industry as "gatekeeper" provisions. The most liberal policies state that the insured will qualify for benefits as long as his or her physician orders the care. A common and much more restrictive provision pays only for long-term care that is medically necessary for sickness or injury.

One common gatekeeper provision that falls between the previous two requires the insured's inability to perform a given number of "activities of daily living" (ADLs). The ADLs listed in most policies include walking, eating, dressing, bathing, getting in and out of bed, and using the toilet. Some policies recognize as ADLs certain cognitive abilities, such as normal short-term memory, but many policies do not. In the case of an Alzheimer's patient who remains physically healthy, inclusion of cognitive abilities as ADLs would be extremely important.

Services Covered. The better policies offer to pay for several levels of service, specifically skilled, intermediate, and custodial care. *Skilled care* is needed when a patient requires constant attention from a medical professional, such as a physician or registered nurse. *Intermediate care* occurs when medical attention or supervision is necessary, but not the constant attention of a medical professional. *Custodial care* provides for assistance in the normal activities of daily living, but medical attention or supervision is not required. A physician or nurse may be on call, however. In the past, many policies restricted services to skilled care only, thereby excluding intermediate and custodial care, which are the major services offered by nursing homes.

Daily Benefits. Long-term care policies reimburse the insured for services incurred up to a daily maximum. For nursing home care policies, the daily maximums generally range from $50 to $250 depending upon the amount of premium the insured is willing to pay. For combination nursing home and home care policies, the maximum home care benefit normally is half the nursing home maximum.

Benefit Duration. The maximum duration of benefits ranges from one year to the insured's lifetime. Lifetime coverage is very expensive, however. The consumer should realize that the average stay in a nursing home is about 19 months. Most financial planners recommend the purchase of a policy with a duration of three to six years to provide the insured with protection for a longer-than-average period of care.

Waiting Period. Even if the insured meets the eligibility requirements of his or her policy, he or she must pay long-term care expenses during the **waiting,** or **elimination, period.** Typical waiting periods are 20 to 100 days. While premiums are much lower for policies with longer waiting periods, the insured must have liquid assets to cover his or her expenses during that period. If the insured still is receiving care after the waiting period expires, he or she will begin to receive benefits for the duration of the policy as long as the eligibility requirements continue to be met.

Renewability. A **guaranteed renewability** provision assures continued coverage for your lifetime as long as you continue to pay the premiums. This clause does not assure a level premium over time, however. Nearly all policies allow the insurer to raise premiums if the claims experience for your peer group of policyholders is unfavorable. Watch out for policies with an **optional renewability** clause. These policies are renewable *only at the option of the insurer.*

Preexisting Conditions. Many policies include a preexisting conditions clause, similar to those explained earlier, ranging from 6 to 12 months. On the other hand, many policies have no such clause whatsoever, which effectively eliminates one important source of possible claim disputes.

Inflation Protection. Many policies offer riders that, for an additional premium, allow you to increase your benefits over time. Hopefully, this rider allows the insured to receive benefits roughly matching the rising cost of nursing home and home health care. Most inflation protection riders allow you to increase benefits by a flat amount, often 5 percent, per year. Others offer benefits linked to the rise in the consumer price index. Most policies do not allow increasing benefits for an entire lifetime, but discontinue inflation adjustments after either 10 or 20 years. Inflation protection riders are important, but expensive, adding between 25 and 40 percent to the basic premium for a long-term care insurance policy.

Premium Levels. Long-term care insurance is not inexpensive, and premiums vary widely between insurance companies. For example, one major insurer charges a healthy 60-year old $933 per year for a policy that pays for three years' care at $100 per day for nursing home care and $50 per day for home care, and has a 100-day waiting period and a 5-percent inflation rider. The same coverage costs a 55-year old $693 per year, and a 70-year old, $1,991 per year. Other companies could charge a 65-year old $2,200 per year or more for the same coverage. Clearly, before buying long-term care insurance, the consumer must carefully compare both the key provisions and the premiums quoted on policies offered by different insurers.

WHO NEEDS LONG-TERM CARE INSURANCE?

Although long-term care policies have improved in recent years and now offer broader coverages and more options, they are still expensive. And the odds of needing more than one year of nursing home care before you reach 65 are 1 in 33. On the other hand, the expense of a prolonged nursing home stay could cause severe financial hardship to your family. As a result, some children are either buying or sharing the cost of policies for their parents. Before buying one for yourself or a relative, you should ask the following questions:

- ***Do you have a lot of assets to preserve for your dependents?*** Because you must deplete most of your assets before Medicaid will pay for nursing home care, some financial advisors recommend that people over 65 whose net worth is over $100,000 and income exceeds $50,000 a year consider long-term care insurance—*if* they can afford the premiums. The very wealthy, however, may prefer to self-insure.
- ***Can you afford the premiums?*** Premiums of many good-quality policies can be 5 to 7 percent of annual income or more. Such high premiums may cause more financial hardship than the cost of the nursing home stay. You may be better off investing the amount you would spend in premiums so that it would be available for *any* future needs, including long-term health care.
- ***Is there a family history of disabling disease, or are you a woman?*** Either of these factors increases your odds of needing long-term care. Because women live longer, they are more likely to become disabled.
- ***Do you have family who can care for you?*** The availability of relatives or home health services to provide care can reduce the cost of long-term care.

If you decide that you or a relative should have long-term care insurance, make sure to buy from a financially sound company, based on ratings from the major ratings agencies, that has experience in this market segment. Here are some additional guidelines to help you choose the right policy.

- ***Buy the policy while you're healthy.*** Once you have a disease such as Alzheimer's or multiple sclerosis or have a stroke, you can't buy a policy. The best time to buy is when you're in your mid-50s or 60s.
- ***Buy the right types of coverage—but don't buy more coverage than you need.*** Your policy should cover several care levels, such as skilled, intermediate, and custodial, and also adult day centers and assisted living facilities. If you have access to family caregivers or home-health services, select a policy with generous home-health benefits; if not, opt for only nursing home coverage. To reduce costs, increase the waiting period before benefits start; the longer you can cover the costs yourself, the lower your premiums. You may also choose a

waiting (elimination) period The period of time, after the insured meets the eligibility requirements of his or her policy, during which he or she must pay long-term care expenses; after the waiting period expires, the insured will begin to receive benefits for the duration of the policy as long as the policy's eligibility requirements continue to be met.

guaranteed renewability Policy provision assuring continued insurance coverage for the insured's lifetime as long as he or she continues to pay the premiums. The insurer may raise premiums in the future, however, if the claims experience for the insured's peer group of policyholders is unfavorable.

optional renewability Contractual clause allowing the insured to continue insurance *only at the option of the insurer.*

shorter benefit payment period; three years is a popular choice, but the average nursing home stay is about two years. Lifetime coverage increases the premium for a 65-year old as much as 40 percent.

- ***Understand what the policy covers and when it pays benefits.*** The amounts paid, benefit periods, and the services covered vary among insurers. One rule of thumb is to buy a policy that covers 80 to 100 percent of current nursing home costs in your area. Some policies pay only for licensed health care providers, while others include assistance with household chores. Know how the policy defines benefit eligibility.

Concept Check

9-15. Why should a consumer consider purchasing a long-term care insurance policy?

9-16. Describe the differences between long-term care policies with respect to (a) type of care, (b) eligibility requirements, and (c) services covered. List and discuss some other important policy provisions.

9-17. Discuss some of the questions one should ask before buying long-term care insurance. What guidelines can be used to choose the right policy?

DISABILITY INCOME INSURANCE

FPPC LG5

When a family member becomes sick for an extended time period, the affect on the family goes beyond medical bills. If a major wage earner in your family was too ill to work, how long could you continue to pay your monthly bills? And what resources are available to cover living expenses? Consider these questions before proceeding.

The Health Insurance Association of America estimates that a 35-year-old worker has a 12 percent chance of becoming disabled for three months; this chance increases to 70 percent by age 55. Although these percentages are the same as the chance of dying, most Americans have life insurance but haven't taken steps to protect their family if a serious illness or accident prevented them from working for an extended time period.

The best way to protect yourself against the potentially devastating financial consequences of a health-related disability is with disability income insurance. **Disability income insurance** provides families with weekly or monthly payments to replace income when the insured is unable to work as a result of a covered illness, injury, or disease. Some companies also offer disability income protection for a homemaker-spouse; in that case, the coverage helps pay for the services that the spouse would normally provide.

The need for disability income coverage is great, yet generally ignored by the public. Although most workers receive some disability insurance benefits from their employer, in many cases the group plan falls short and pays only about 60 percent of their salary for a limited time period. The first step in considering disability income insurance is to determine the dollar amount your family would need (typically on a per-month basis) in the event an earner becomes disabled. Then you can buy the coverage you need or supplement existing coverage if necessary.

ESTIMATING YOUR DISABILITY INSURANCE NEEDS

The overriding purpose of disability income insurance is to replace all (or most) of the income—that is, earnings—that would be lost in the event you became disabled and physically unable to hold a job. In essence, it should enable you to maintain a standard of living at or near your present level. To help decide how much disability income insurance is right for you, you can use Worksheet 9.1 to estimate your monthly disability benefit needs (this is a procedure developed and recommended by the Consumer's Union of the United States, publishers of *Consumer Reports*). Here is all you have to do:

1. Disability benefits are generally, but not always, tax-free, so you need to replace only your take-home (after-tax) pay. (Note: Be sure to ascertain whether or not, and to what extent, your disability benefits are tax-free. Benefits from employer-paid policies are fully or partially taxable.) Estimate take-home pay roughly from your previous year's federal income tax return

WORKSHEET 9.1

Estimating Disability Income Insurance Needs

Using a worksheet like this makes the job of estimating disability benefit needs a lot easier.

DISABILITY BENEFIT NEEDS

Name(s) ______________________ Date ______________

1.	Estimate current monthly *take-home* pay		$ ______
2.	Estimate existing monthly benefits:		
	a. Social security benefits	$ ______	
	b. Other government benefits	______	
	c. Company benefits	______	
	d. Group disability policy benefits	______	
3.	Total existing monthly disability benefits (2a + 2b + 2c + 2d)		$ ______
4.	**Estimated monthly disability benefits needed ([1] − [3])**		$ ______

by subtracting the taxes paid, including social security taxes, from your gross earned income (salary only, because any interest and dividend income you now receive should continue). Divide this total by 12 to get your monthly take-home pay.

2. You may already have disability benefits from government or employer programs. Estimate the monthly amounts as follows:

a. The local social security office may help you estimate your social security benefits, but you can definitely get an estimate of your benefits by calling 1-800-772-1213 for a *Personal Earnings and Benefit Estimate Statement.* An insurance agent can also often help you make the estimate, because many insurance companies have a computer program that can easily calculate it. As of early 1995 the average social security disability benefit was around $1,600 a month for a wage earner with dependents. To be "disabled" under social security, however, you must be unable to do *any* job whatever. Benefits are payable only if your disability is expected to last at least one year (or to be fatal). Payments do not begin until you have been disabled for at least five months. The actual amount paid is a percentage of your previous monthly earnings, with some statistical adjustments. The percentage is higher for people with low earnings. A 35-year-old who earns $20,000 and has dependents would receive $1,152 per month; if he or she earned $40,000, the amount rises to $1,757 per month. Because the Social Security Administration generally has rejected 40 percent or more of the applicants for disability income coverage, many financial planners recommend that you assume *no* such benefits for purposes of estimating your need for private insurance coverage.

b. Other government programs that provide certain disability benefits, if you qualify, include armed services disability benefits, Veterans Administration pension disability benefits, civil service disability benefits, the Federal Employees Compensation Act, and state workers' compensation systems. There are also special programs for railroad workers, longshoremen, and people with black-lung disease.

c. Ask your company benefits supervisor to help you calculate the company benefits. In a few states (including California, Hawaii, New Jersey, New York, and Rhode Island, plus the Commonwealth of Puerto Rico),

disability income insurance Insurance that provides families with weekly or monthly payments to replace income when the insured is unable to work as a result of a covered illness, injury, or disease.

employers must provide a certain minimum level of benefits. However, the state-mandated *minimums* tend to be small, and benefits typically expire after 26 weeks in any 52-week period.

Ask first about sick pay or wage continuation plans (for all practical purposes, these are short-term disability income insurance). Then ask about any plans formally designated as disability insurance. For each benefit your employer offers, check on its tax treatment.

d. Your company may have sponsored a group disability insurance plan. A private insurer provides the coverage, and you pay for it, often through a payroll deduction. A major advantage of a group plan is that it is usually considerably less expensive than individual coverage, and may have less stringent enrollment requirements. A disadvantage is that if you change jobs, you may lose the coverage. The benefits from a group plan in which you pay the premiums are tax-free (unless paid through a flexible spending account).

3. Add up the monthly disability benefits to which you are already entitled.
4. Subtract your existing monthly disability benefits from your current monthly take-home pay. The result will show the monthly disability benefits you will need to maintain your present after-tax income. Note that investment income and spousal income (if he or she is presently employed) are ignored, because it is assumed that this income will continue and is necessary to maintain your current standard of living. If your spouse is presently unemployed but would enter the work force in the event you ever became disabled, his or her estimated monthly income (take-home pay) could be subtracted from item 4 of Worksheet 9.1 to determine your net monthly disability benefit needs.

DISABILITY INCOME INSURANCE PROVISIONS AND COSTS

The scope of your disability income coverage, as well as its cost, depends upon a number of contractual provisions. Although disability income insurance policies can be very complex, certain contractual provisions bear very close examination. These provisions include (1) definition of disability, (2) benefit amount and duration, (3) probationary period, (4) waiting period, (5) renewability, and (6) other provisions.

Definition of Disability. Disability policies specify the standards that must be met for you to receive benefits. The most liberal definition is one that considers you disabled if you cannot perform at least one primary duty of your own occupation. This is known as the *own occupation* (or "Own Occ") definition. With this definition, a professor who lost his voice, but still could get paid to write or do research, would receive full benefits because he could not lecture, a primary function of his occupation. With a *residual benefit option,* you would be paid partial benefits if you can only work part time or at a lower salary.

Many policies use a more strict definition based upon whether the insured can perform any occupation for which he or she is reasonably suited on the basis of education, training, or experience. Known as the *any occupation* (or "Any Occ") definition, the insurer has more leeway in determining whether or not the insured should receive benefits, so this type of policy is considerably less expensive.

A *presumptive disability* clause often is found in individual disability policies. This provision supersedes the previously discussed definition of disability when certain types of losses occur. Loss of both hands, sight in both eyes, and hearing in both ears are examples where the insured may be *presumed* totally disabled and may receive full benefits even though he or she still can be employed in some capacity.

Benefit Amount and Duration. Most individual disability income policies pay a flat monthly benefit, which is stated in the policy, while group plans pay a fixed percentage of gross income. In either case, insurers normally will not agree to amounts in excess of 60 to 70 percent of the insured's gross income. Insurers will not issue policies for the full amount of gross income because this would give some people an incentive to fake a disability (for example, "bad back"), thereby allowing them to collect more in insurance benefits than they normally would receive as take-home pay.

Monthly benefits can be paid for a few months or for a lifetime. If you are assured of substantial pension, social security, or other benefits at retirement, then you may want a policy that pays ben-

EXHIBIT 9.7

Disability Income Insurance Premium Costs

The cost of disability income insurance varies with the terms of payment as well as the length of the waiting period. Women pay substantially higher rates than men. This table shows premiums for basic disability income coverage for a 35-year-old that pays $2,000 per month in benefits, with guaranteed premiums to age 65. Any additional features, such as inflation riders, cost more.

Benefit Period	2 Years		5 Years		To Age 65		Lifetime	
Waiting Period	**Male**	**Female**	**Male**	**Female**	**Male**	**Female**	**Male**	**Female**
30 days	$698	$1,192	$922	$1,601	$1,284	$2,327	$1,402	$2,508
60 days	539	983	715	1,145	986	1,674	1,086	1,821
90 days	427	587	559	809	746	1,163	829	1,281
6 months	386	514	514	728	692	1,067	774	1,183
One year	358	464	475	660	638	972	718	1,086

Source: A major life insurance company, rates as of March 1995.

efits until age 65. Most people would not be assured of retirement benefits unless they were able to continue their occupations for many more years, however. Persons in this situation should consider a policy offering lifetime benefits. Many policies offer benefits for periods as short as 2 or 5 years. While these policies may be better than nothing, they do not protect against the major financial losses associated with long-term disabilities.

Probationary Period. Both group and individual disability income policies are likely to contain a probationary period, which is a time delay from the date the policy is issued until benefit privileges are activated. For example, a 30-day probationary period means the policy must be in force for 30 days before any benefits are available. Any disability stemming from an illness, injury, or disease that occurs during the probationary period is *not* covered—even if it continues beyond this period. The probationary period often runs from 7 to 30 days. The purpose of this feature is to keep costs down, thereby making these policies more affordable.

Waiting Period. The waiting, or elimination, period provisions in a disability income policy are similar to those discussed for long-term care insurance. Typical waiting periods are 30 days, 60 days, 90 days, six months, and one year. Insurers use these to omit coverage for the frequent small loss and to limit further the incentives for insureds to fake disabilities. As long as you have an adequate emergency fund to provide family income during the early months of disability, substantial savings of premium can be realized if you purchase a policy with a relatively long waiting period, as shown in Exhibit 9.7.

With most insurers, you effectively can trade off an increase in the waiting period from, say, 30 days to 90 days for an increase in the duration of benefits from five years to age 65. In fact, as Exhibit 9.7 shows, the premium charged by this insurer for a policy covering a 35-year-old male with a 30-day waiting period and two-year benefit period is about the same as one charged for benefits payable to age 65 with a six-month waiting period. Accepting this type of trade-off usually makes sense because the primary purpose of insurance is to protect against a catastrophic loss, rather than smaller losses that are better handled through proper budgeting and saving.

Renewability. Most individual disability income insurance is either *guaranteed renewable* or *noncancelable.* As with long-term care policies, guaranteed renewability assures that you can renew the policy until you reach the age stated in the clause, usually age 65. Premiums can be raised over time if justified by the loss experience of all those in the same class (usually based on age, sex, and occupational category). Noncancelable policies offer guaranteed renewability, but also guarantee that future premiums will remain the same as those stated in the policy at issuance. Because of this guarantee of future premiums, noncancelable policies generally are more expensive than those with only a guaranteed renewability provision.

Other Provisions. The purchasing power of income from a long-term disability policy that pays, say, $2,000 per month could be severely affected by inflation. In fact, a 3 percent inflation rate would reduce the purchasing power of this $2,000 benefit to less than $1,500 in 10 years. To counteract such a reduction, many insurers offer a *cost-of-living adjustment (COLA)*. With a COLA provision, the monthly benefit is adjusted upward each year, often in line with the Consumer Price Index, although these annual adjustments frequently are capped at a given rate, say 8 percent. While some financial advisors suggest buying COLA riders, others feel the 10 to 25 percent additional premium is not worth it with today's low inflation rate.

While the COLA provision only applies once the insured is disabled, the *guaranteed insurability option (GIO)* can allow you to purchase additional disability income insurance in line with inflation increases while you are still healthy. Under the GIO, the price of this additional insurance is fixed at the inception of the contract and you do not have to prove insurability.

A *waiver of premium* is standard in disability income policies. If you are disabled for a minimum period of time, normally 60 or 90 days, the insurer will waive any future premiums that come due while you remain disabled. In essence, the waiver of premium provides you with additional disability income insurance that just happens to be in the amount of your regular premium payment.

CURRENT TRENDS IN DISABILITY INSURANCE

Because big claims on certain policies—like those with "own occupation" disability definitions and those with noncancellable guarantees—have pushed rates up sharply, many insurers are phasing out these policies and offering basic coverage at more affordable rates. Buying a guaranteed renewable plan rather than a noncancellable guarantee, for example, will cost 15–20 percent less. Other policies offer incentives to return to some form of work by limiting own-occupation coverage to five years, after which time you must seek other work if you're able. You are buying protection for earnings, not a specific profession. Women and those in locations or professional groups considered high risk will be paying more. Most insurers no longer offer unisex rates and charge women, who file more claims, rates that average 25 percent—and sometimes as high as 50 percent—more than men's premiums. The data in Exhibit 9.7 shows the differential between male and female premiums.

Although you may get some disability insurance through your employer, it may not be adequate for your needs. Today, group disability coverage is becoming more restrictive because employers are trying to control costs as the work force ages and more claims are filed. As with other forms of health insurance, the specific policy provisions selected affect the premium cost of a disability income insurance policy. *Remember that disability income insurance is just one part of your overall personal financial plan.* You'll need to find your own balance between cost and coverage. Exhibit 9.8 provides some suggestions for buying the right policy.

Concept Check

9-18. What is disability income insurance? Explain the waiting period provisions found in such policies.

9-19. Describe both the liberal and strict definitions used to establish whether or not an insured is disabled. Why is benefit duration an important consideration when shopping for disability income coverage?

A GUIDE TO BUYING HEALTH CARE INSURANCE

LG6

The best way to buy health care insurance is to match your insurance needs with the various types of coverages available. What types of coverages would best meet your current health care insurance needs? Before reading on, spend a few moments relating available forms of health care insurance to your needs.

We have now reached the point where we should address the matter of how to systematically plan purchases of health care insurance. In many ways, the approach here is similar to that proposed for

EXHIBIT 9.8

10 Suggestions for Buying Disability Income Insurance

Here are 10 suggestions to help you put together the right disability income insurance policy for your needs.

1. *Start with your employee benefits;* you may be able to supplement a basic policy at group rates 15–35% below private rates. Also, women may get unisex rates. Understand what your group policy covers and how it defines disability. Group plans generally pay 60 percent of base salary and may be limited in both maximum payment and benefit period; you may need to fill in gaps with private insurance.
2. *Buy an individual policy if you think you won't quality later.* You can buy a small policy with a rider that allows you to buy more later.
3. *Get several price quotes;* rates vary considerably.
4. *Make sure that the insurance company is financially strong.*
5. *To reduce premiums and still get adequate coverage, lengthen waiting periods.* Going from 30 to 90 days can save 20 percent; to one year, 30 percent. Stretch the period for as long as possible based on your financial resources.
6. *A policy with benefits to age 65, not lifetime, saves 25 percent on a 40-year-old male's premium.* Once you reach retirement, you should be able to use other resources. (That's why it's important to consider disability just one part of your overall personal financial plan.)
7. *Consider including a residual benefit option.* This makes up the income shortfall if you only work part-time or in a lower-paying job.
8. *Decide if you want to pay more for "own occupation" coverage.* The premium increases about 10 percent; you'll have to decide if it's worth it, depending on your current occupation.
9. *Ask about discounted premiums.* Some companies offer 10 percent off if you provide copies of tax returns or prepay premiums.
10. *Include an exclusion for a recurring medical problem.* You can reduce your premium if you exclude problems like a bad back or knee.

Sources: Adapted from Mary Rowland, "Disability Insurance: Kicking the Tires," *Worth*, June 1993, pp. 93–96; Ellen E. Schultz, "Getting the Most from Your Group Disability Plan," *The Wall Street Journal*, October 21, 1994, p.C1; and Amey Stone, "Affordable Insurance that Works When You Can't," *Business Week*, August 29, 1994, pp. 88–89.

life insurance in Chapter 8. The primary difference is that with health care insurance you generally must consider a variety of both coverages and sources for your protection.

You should list your potential areas of loss; determine what types of coverages and other resources are available to you; and, to spot gaps in your present protection, subtract your coverages and resources from the amount of your potential losses. Once you have identified gaps in protection, you should structure a health care insurance plan that is best for you.

NEEDS

Most people need protection against two types of losses that can result from illness or accident: (1) expenses for medical bills, rehabilitation counseling, training and education, and, in some cases—such as loss of a homemaker—replacement services and (2) loss of income due to time spent away from work. The amount needed to pay medical expenses cannot be easily estimated, but in cases of long-term, serious illnesses, medical bills and related expenses can run into the hundreds of thousands of dollars. Thus, you should probably figure you face potential hospital, surgical, pharmaceutical, and other charges of at least $250,000 and, with a protracted disability, as high as $1 million. In contrast, the income need is relatively easy to calculate: it is simply a percentage of your (or your spouse's) current monthly earnings—most people believe that 60 to 75 percent is sufficient.

MATCHING NEEDS AND RESOURCES

In the next step of your health care insurance purchase planning, you should match your present resources against your needs. Exhibit 9.9 should help you perform this task. It sets forth a checklist for the sources and types of coverages you might already have. Among these resources you should rely most on social security, present group coverages, Blue Cross/Blue Shield, individual coverages, savings, and employer wage continuation plans. The remaining sources of recovery are less significant for planning purposes, because they typically restrict payments to specified types of illnesses or accidents.

EXHIBIT 9.9

A Checklist of Sources and Types of Coverages

Health care insurance can be obtained from a variety of providers, each offering various types of coverages.

Social Security
Disability income
Medicare (medical expenses)
Medicaid (medical expenses)

Workers' Compensation
Disability income
Medical expenses
Rehabilitation
Lump sum

Group Health Plans
Hospital expenses
Surgical expenses
Physicians expenses
Major medical
Comprehensive major medical
Pharmaceuticals
Chiropractic, optometry, etc.
Dental
Mental illness
Rehabilitation
Long-term care

Blue Cross/Blue Shield
Hospital expenses
Surgical expenses
Physicians expenses
Other expenses

Existing Individual Resources
Present individual coverages
Family dependency
Savings

Wage Continuation Plan (Employer)
Sick leave
Short-term disability
Long-term disability

Other Plans
Homeowner's medical expenses
Auto medical expenses
Negligence claim
Veterans' medical benefits
Indian health services
Public health clinics (for example, communicable diseases, maternal and child health, migrant health expense)

After you have identified your present coverages, you should examine them to learn their terms of payment and coverage. The key policy provisions that should most concern you will vary with the type of coverage—that is, medical expense, long-term care, or disability income plans. Use the previous discussions of provisions for each type of policy to evaluate your current coverage. If you find gaps for which you do not have adequate coverage or savings, you need to arrange ways in which to meet potential losses.

PREPARING A HEALTH CARE PLAN

Throughout this chapter, we have emphasized the need for good health insurance protection to cover the costs of illness or accident. However, a good health care plan encompasses much more than a means of financing medical expenses, replacement services, and lost income. It should also incorporate other means of risk reduction. Accordingly, recall from Chapter 8 that you can deal with risk in four ways: risk avoidance, loss prevention and control, risk assumption, and insurance. Although these four methods apply to all types of risk, each is especially useful in developing health care plans.

Risk Avoidance. Risk avoidance means avoiding the exposure that creates the potential for loss. For example, people who do not stand on the backs of chairs to reach into high places seldom fall off chairs; people who do not take illegal drugs never have to worry about disability from overdose; people who refuse to ride on motorcycles avoid the risk of injury from this relatively dangerous means of transportation; and people who do not smoke in bed will never doze off and start a fire in their house. Looking for ways to avoid exposure to loss is a good starting point for a health care plan.

Loss Prevention and Control. For many instances of illness or accidents, risk avoidance is not applicable. This is when you can turn to loss prevention.

Illness. Today, health care emphasizes prevention as well as treatment. Encouraging people to accept responsibility for their own well-being and to live healthier lifestyles can reduce high health care costs. In fact, life and health insurance company data as well as public health statistics show that smoking, alcohol and drug dependency, improper diet, inadequate sleep, and lack of regular exercise contribute to more than 60 percent of all diagnosed illnesses. Heart disease, cancer, tuberculosis, and mental disorders all have been positively linked to these forms of self-abuse. In contrast, the odds are overwhelming that if you maintain a basic program for fitness, you will miss fewer days of work, spend less on medical bills, and live a healthier and happier life.

Accidents. The National Safety Council reports that more than one-half of all automobile accidents could be prevented if motorists followed highway safety laws. Topping the list of violations is driving under the influence of alcohol and drugs (DUI). This unnecessary exposure to loss accounts for about half of all automobile fatalities; specifically, alcohol abuse is a leading cause of injury and death among college students and other young persons. (This toll on youth has prompted most states to raise the minimum legal drinking age.)

Further, accident data overwhelmingly document the loss prevention effectiveness of safety belts, shoulder straps, and child passenger seats. Smoke alarms, bathtub safety mats, and proper storage of chemicals, pesticides, cleaning fluids, and prescription drugs also pose easy and effective measures for reducing loss frequency and severity. In sum, regardless of whether you are at home, school, work, or play—or traveling in between—you should integrate accident prevention measures into your health care plans.

Risk Assumption. The next essential step in preparing a health care plan involves considering the risks you are willing to retain. Some risks pose relatively small loss potential and therefore can be budgeted for. Of course, this is a primary reason to choose insurance coverages that include deductibles and waiting periods, as it is more economical to pay small losses from savings than to pay higher premiums to insure them. Similarly, although you are wise to buy policies with high limits, few people are willing to pay the premium for 100 percent reimbursement of all losses above the deductible. To increase insurance affordability, most people assume part of the risk of large losses through participation or coinsurance, internal limits, and maximum aggregate limits. It is impossible to live in a world in which all of your risks are either avoided, prevented, or insured. Thus, before you buy health care coverages—or, for that matter, any type of insurance coverage—you should explicitly identify the types and amounts of risk that you are willing and able to bear.

SHOPPING FOR HEALTH CARE INSURANCE

We now return to the focus of this discussion. It is very important for you to recognize that a healthcare plan should incorporate methods of risk avoidance, loss prevention and control, and risk assumption. However, our goal throughout this chapter has been to give you a systematic way to decide what health insurance (or other health care financing plan—HMO, PPO, Blue Cross/Blue Shield, and so on) you should buy. To proceed, then, through this step of shopping for health care insurance, you need to consider three items: (1) cost of coverage, (2) selecting health insurance as an employee benefit, and (3) quality of agent and company.

Costs of Coverage. In some ways, shopping for health care insurance is like shopping for a car. Both are major purchases. It is likely that on a monthly basis, a family would spend as much or more for their medical insurance as they do on an auto loan payment. Today an individual can expect to pay $145 to $190 per month for a health care plan; a family, $329 to $500 per month or more. In addition, you would not simply compare, say, a major medical coverage from Blue Cross/Blue Shield to that of Prudential any more than you would blindly choose between a Chevrolet and a Ford. In each instance you need to size up competitive offerings on a feature-for-feature basis. (What size engines do the cars have? Does either have air conditioning, antilock brakes, a compact disc system, higher gas mileage, a longer warranty, or better styling?) Similarly, what provisions do available health care insurance policies contain? What are their definitions of an accident? What exclusions apply? What persons and places are covered? What are the applicable deductibles, methods of payment, duration of benefits, and participation percentages? Big cost differences exist among health care insurance coverages just as they do among different models of Chevrolets and Fords, but you can judge which is the best buy only after you have compared the costs of the coverages in relation to the features they offer.

Selecting Health Care Insurance as an Employee Benefit. As noted earlier, many people obtain health insurance coverage through their employer group. In some cases, the employer offers only one plan that it may pay entirely or partially. When this is the case, the employee should evaluate the plan's benefits and costs and decide whether to be part of the plan and whether additional private coverage is required to meet his or her needs.

The trend now, however, among medium and large employers is to offer employees a choice of fringe benefits (a *flexible-benefit plan* as discussed in Chapter 2). Many times the menu of benefits includes more than one health care insurance option so the employee can choose among a major medical plan, an HMO, and perhaps an IPA in addition to choosing the amount of life insurance, disability income insurance, and other benefits he or she might like. In a typical example, you could be given $350 a month to "spend" on any of the following benefits for you and your family: several forms of health care coverage (major medical: $200 deductible, $425; $500 deductible, $345; HMO, $422; IPA, $480; dental insurance, $55); disability income coverage, $28; several life insurance options for employee only (term life: $75,000, $11; $150,000, $21; accidental death for $500,000, $15). In this case, your benefit dollars from your employer would cover the least expensive health care coverage. The cost of any additional coverage you choose would be deducted from your paycheck.

After reviewing the menu, you see that your employer has given you enough ($350) to purchase the least expensive health care insurance policy for your family. If you want more comprehensive "first-dollar" health care coverage and/or any of the other coverages (dental, disability income, and life insurance), they will be paid by you through a deduction from your payroll check. Before making this decision, it is important that you review your insurance needs and carefully evaluate all of the coverage being offered. Compare the cost of coverage through your employer with that offered through private policies. Generally health care coverage is much more reasonably priced through group coverage, but disability income and life insurance may be less expensive through a private policy (especially for young workers). If your spouse is employed, then you should also evaluate his or her benefit package before making any decisions. Also, *remember that the purpose of insurance is to protect yourself against very large possible losses rather than to pay relatively small expenses.* Therefore, if your family depends on your income to live, don't select dental insurance *instead of* life and disability income coverage.

Another important area of group coverage is benefits paid to retirees. Because the number of companies providing health care benefits to retirees has decreased sharply—in 1993, only 35 percent of large companies offered such benefits—you may no longer be able to count on receiving employer-paid benefits once you retire. So it is important to know what your options are to assure you and your family continued health care coverage. At some companies retirees can pay a portion of the premium cost; others have dropped it altogether. You will need to consider COBRA coverage and look for group coverage through an HMO or professional organization, which is cheaper than private plans. Once you turn 65, Medicare will cover basic medical expenses, but you will probably want to supplement this coverage with one of the ten standard Medigap plans, which will cost from $600 to $2,500 per year for a 65-year old, depending on coverage.

Quality of Agent and Company. As with all types of insurance, you should buy your health care coverages from an agent who will listen to your needs and answer your questions with well thought out responses—not sales jargon and pressure—and from a company that is rated highly for financial soundness by at least two of the major rating agencies, as discussed in Chapter 8. Also, your health care insurer should be known to settle claims fairly and promptly. You should avoid companies with narrow and unusual, legalistic claims practices. Friends with claims-settlement experience and the consumer division of your state's department of insurance regulation can help you learn about an insurer's record for service after a loss. You should be just as concerned about the financial soundness and claims service of your group insurance underwriters as you would be when purchasing an individual health care policy.

CHOOSING A HEALTH CARE PLAN

Once you have familiarized yourself with the different health care plans, providers, and coverages and reviewed your needs, you must choose one or more plans to provide coverage for you and your dependents. We've already discussed how to do this for long-term care and disability income insurance, so here we will focus on health care insurance.

If you are employed, you should review the various health care plans your company offers. If you can't get coverage from an employer, get plan descriptions and policy costs from several providers, including a group plan from a professional or trade organization if available, for both indemnity and managed care plans. Then take your time and carefully read the plan materials to understand exactly what is covered, and at what cost. Next, add up what you have spent on medical costs over the past few years and what you might expect in the future, so you can see what your costs would be under various plans.

How do you find health care insurance if you have just graduated from college, don't yet have a job, and can no longer be covered by your parents' policy? Or maybe you are between jobs or need time to search out the best policy but don't want to be without protection. The *Smart Money* box on page 388 will help you with these situations.

You'll have to ask yourself some difficult questions to decide if you want an indemnity or managed care plan, and then to choose the particular plan:

- ***How important is cost compared to having freedom of choice?*** You may have to pay more to stay with your current doctor if he or she is not part of a managed care plan you are considering. It may be a difficult trade-off. Also, you have to decide if you can live with the managed care plan's approach to health care.
- ***Will you be reimbursed if you choose a managed care plan and want to see an out-of-network provider?*** For most people, the managed care route is cheaper, even if you only visit a doctor three or four times a year, because of indemnity plan "reasonable charge" provisions.
- ***What types of coverages do you need?*** Everyone has different needs; one person may want a plan with good maternity and pediatric care while another wants outpatient mental health benefits. Make sure the plans you consider offer what you want.
- ***How good is the managed care network?*** Look at the participating doctors and hospitals to see how many of your providers are part of the plan. Check out their credentials; a good sign is accreditation from the National Committee for Quality Assurance (NCQA). Are the providers' locations convenient for you? What preventive medical programs does it provide? Has membership grown? Talk to friends and associates to see what their experiences have been with the plan.
- ***How old are you and how is your health?*** Many financial advisors recommend buying the lowest-cost plan if you're young and healthy—which may be an indemnity plan with a high deductible.

Concept Check

9-20. Briefly discuss the procedures for (a) determining health care insurance needs, (b) matching needs and resources, and (c) preparing a health care plan.

9-21. Describe the role played in the process of preparing a health care plan by (a) risk avoidance, (b) loss prevention and control, and (c) risk assumption.

9-22. Describe the procedures used to evaluate and select health care insurance as an employee benefit.

9-23. Describe the following considerations that must be addressed when shopping for health care insurance: (a) costs of coverage and (b) quality of agent and insurance company.

Smart Money

Health Care Insurance Tips for the Recent Grad

In today's weakened economy, it may take students graduating from college six months to a year to find a job. As if that weren't enough of a problem, they must also worry about health care insurance—a topic they probably never considered before, because during college they were covered by the school or their parents' plans. However, this coverage ends once they graduate. Some cross their fingers and hope they don't get injured or sick before gaining employment. For those who find this strategy too risky or stress-inducing, there are other options.

Health care insurance providers offer short-term policies specifically designed to act as a bridge for college graduates seeking employment or people between jobs who hope to find work soon. The plans, from such companies as John Alden, Golden Rule, and Time Insurance, typically provide up to six months of major medical coverage for premiums as low as $20 a month (with a high deductible). The downside is that such plans don't cover preexisting conditions. On the other hand, they are easy to obtain, and no physical or waiting period is required; it is usually just a matter of filling out a brief form and mailing a check.

There are several issues besides price to consider when looking for a short-term policy. Some companies exclude expenses incurred outside the United States. Many will not write a second short-term policy if you don't find work by the time your policy expires. In addition, most companies require that you pay the premium for the entire coverage period at the outset. Seek out a plan that offers pro-rated refunds if you find a job and cancel your policy prematurely or that lets you pay monthly rather than all at once.

For recent graduates who fear their job search may last a year or more, standard, long-term, individual coverage would be a better bet. This coverage can be continued indefinitely and is good world-wide, but it's much harder to obtain than a short-term policy. Individual plans usually require a physical or "evidence of insurability," and the premiums cost a minimum of $100 to $200 per month. Group plans, which are often available through college alumni groups or religious and social organizations, are nearly as expensive but tend to offer more benefits for the cost.

A more expensive way for recent grads, especially those with preexisting conditions, to get insurance is to extend their coverage under a parent's group plan. The federal government's COBRA legislation requires companies to extend coverage for former dependents up to 36 months if they pay the full premium, which can run $150 to $300 a month. However, to qualify you must act fast; the deadline for signing up is 45 days from the existing policy's expiration date.

Whatever your situation, if you find yourself in need of health care insurance while you're looking for a job after graduation, don't just jump at the first policy you're offered. Take the time to shop around for the plan that best suits your needs.

Sources: Adapted from Stephen Frank, "Jobless Grads Need To Pick Health Plans," *The Wall Street Journal*, August 18, 1993, pp. C1 and C10; Amey Stone, "Health Insurance For Grads Getting On Their Feet," *Business Week*, July 18, 1994, p. 91.

SUMMARY

LG1. Discuss how the health care industry is changing and why it's important to have adequate health care insurance. The health care field is undergoing rapid changes today as rising health care costs have prompted new ways of delivering health services. The emphasis is on cost containment through managed care programs and preventive medicine Because of the high cost of health care, the potential for economic loss from illness or accident is large. Therefore, it is important to have adequate health care insurance coverage to protect you and your family.

LG2. **Differentiate between the major types of health care plans and identify the major private and public providers of health insurance and their programs.** In addition to the traditional indemnity health care insurance programs, a rapidly growing trend is for individuals/families to obtain health care services directly from specific provider groups under managed care plans. With these plans the subscribers/users contract with and make monthly payments to the organization that provides the health care services. The most common examples of these groups are health maintenance organizations (HMOs), individual practice associations (IPAs), and preferred provider organizations (PPOs).

There are several important private providers of health care coverage, including insurance companies, managed care organizations, and Blue Cross/Blue Shield. Today insurance companies and Blue Cross/Blue Shield also offer managed care programs. Health care insurance can be acquired through a group policy from an employer or other group and individual health insurance policies. Two government programs that provide health benefits are Social Security, which provides both medical insurance and long-term disability insurance, and workers' compensation for job-related injuries.

LG3. **Explain the basic types of medical expense coverage and policy provisions for medical expense plans.** The basic types of medical expense coverage are hospital insurance, surgical expense insurance, physicians expense insurance (that covers the costs of nonsurgical procedures), and major medical insurance (which covers all types of medical expenses). Some health insurers offer comprehensive major medical policies that combine basic hospital, surgical, and physicians expense coverages with a major medical plan to form a single policy, dental insurance, long-term care insurance (that covers out-of-hospital care for those with chronic illnesses), and disability income insurance (designed to replace wages lost due to illness or accident).

The most important provisions in medical expense insurance policies pertain to terms of payment, terms of coverage, and cost containment. How much your medical expense plan will pay depends on deductibles, participation (coinsurance), internal limits, and coordination of benefits. The terms of coverage encompass the persons and places covered, cancellation, continuation of group coverage, rehabilitation, preexisting conditions, pregnancy and abortion, and mental illness. Some of the more common cost containment provisions are pre-admission certification, continued stay review, second surgical opinions, caseworker assignment, and waiver of coinsurance.

LG4. **Assess the need for and provisions of long-term care insurance.** Long-term care insurance is necessary to cover nonhospital expenses, such as nursing home care or home health care, that can be caused by chronic illness or frailty. Terms of payment provisions include daily benefits, benefit duration, waiting period, and inflation protection. The availability of coverage depends upon provisions addressing type of care, eligibility requirements, services covered, renewability, and preexisting conditions.

LG5. **Calculate your need for and provisions of disability income insurance.** The loss of family income caused by the disability of a principal earner can be at least partially replaced by disability income insurance. Provisions pertaining to benefit amount and duration, waiting period, and cost-of-living adjustments define the terms of payment. Important coverage terms include the definition of disability, probationary period, renewability, guaranteed insurability, and waiver of premium. Because these policies are expensive, you should choose as long a waiting period as possible given your other available financial resources.

LG6. **Analyze your own health care insurance needs and shop for appropriate coverage.** From a health care insurance perspective, most people need protection from two types of losses: (1) the cost of medical bills and other associated expenses and (2) loss of income due to time away from work. The best way to buy health care insurance is to match your insurance needs with the various types of coverages available. When shopping for health care insurance, you should carefully consider the costs of coverage, the cost of health care insurance as an employee benefit, the quality of both the agent and the insurer or managed care provider, and your own medical needs and care preferences.

FINANCIAL FACTS OR FANTASIES

Are the following statements financial facts (true) or fantasies (false)?

1. Health care insurance coverage should be viewed as an essential component of your personal financial plans.
2. The difference between a health maintenance organization (HMO) and a preferred provider organization (PPO) is that the HMO offers a wider range of choices of physicians, hospitals, and so forth.
3. Hospital insurance is the most comprehensive type of medical insurance you can buy.
4. With health care insurance that covers the whole family, children may be included in the coverage up to age 24 as long as they are full-time students.
5. When a person is chronically ill and requires either nursing home care or home health care services, most of these expenses are absorbed by Medicare and private medical expense insurance.
6. The costs of coverage and the quality of the agent and insurance company are two important considerations when shopping for health care insurance.

DISCUSSION QUESTIONS AND PROBLEMS

Discussion Question for Opening Profile: Describe how the Hansons made health care planning part of their personal financial planning process and obtained coverage at a reasonable cost. What steps could you take to implement "self-managed care" and reduce your own health care insurance costs?

1. Susana Chang was seriously injured in a skiing accident and broke both her legs and an arm. Her medical expense bills were 5 days hospitalization at $800 per day, including room and other services; $4,300 in physician's fees (including the time she was in the hospital and 5 follow-up office visits); $320 in prescription medicines; and $1,200 for physical therapy treatments.
   a. If she has an indemnity plan with a $500 deductible that pays 80 percent of her charges and has a $5,000 stop-loss provision, how much will she have to pay out of pocket? (Assume that charges fall within the customary and reasonable payment amounts.)
   b. What would you estimate to be her out-of-pocket costs if she belonged to an HMO and used its providers? (The copayment for office visits is $12.)
   c. Monthly premiums are $155 for the indemnity plan and $250 for the HMO. If she had no other medical expenses for the year, which plan provides more cost-effective coverage for Susana?
2. Discuss the pros and cons of long-term care insurance. Does it make sense for anyone in your family at the present time? Why or why not? What factors might change this decision in the future?
3. FPPC ***Use Worksheet 9.1.*** John Fitzmorris, a 35-year old computer programmer, earns $48,000 a year,

and his monthly take-home pay is $2,500 a month. His wife Linda works part time at their children's elementary school but receives no benefits. John's employee benefit plan includes group disability income insurance with coverage for a total of 2½ years at $1,500 per month. The Fitzmorris family is concerned about their financial well-being if John were to be disabled for an extended period.

a. Use Worksheet 9.1 to calculate John's disability benefit needs assuming that he will not qualify for Social Security.

b. Based on your answer in part a., make some recommendations to John about the type and size of disability income policy he should buy, including a discussion of possible provisions he might want to include. Would you advise him to buy own occupation coverage or not, and why? What other factors should he take into account when choosing a policy?

FPPC **4.** ***Use Worksheet 9.1.*** Calculate your own disability income insurance need using Worksheet 9.1. Discuss how you would go about purchasing this coverage.

5. Given your current situation, discuss the factors that would be important to you in choosing a health care plan. What type of plan would you select, and why? What steps can you take to keep your health care costs down?

CONTEMPORARY CASE APPLICATIONS

9.1 Evaluating John's Health Care Coverage

John Lannefeld was a self-employed window washer earning approximately $400 per week. One day, while cleaning windows on the eighth floor of the First National Bank Building, he tripped and fell from the scaffolding to the pavement below. He sustained severe multiple injuries but miraculously survived the accident. He was immediately rushed to Mt. Sinai Hospital for surgery. He remained there for 60 days of treatment, after which he was allowed to go home for further recuperation. During his hospital stay, he incurred the following expenses: surgeon, $2,500; physician, $1,000; hospital bill, room and board, $250 per day; nursing services, $1,200; anesthetics, $300; wheelchair rental, $70; ambulance, $60; and drugs, $350. John has a major medical policy with LIC Corporation that has a $3,000 deductible clause, an 80 percent coinsurance clause, internal limits of $180 per day on hospital room and board and $1,500 as a maximum surgical fee. The policy provides no disability income benefits.

Questions

1. Explain the policy provisions as they relate to deductibles, coinsurance, and internal limits.

2. How much should John recover from the insurance company? How much must he pay out of his pocket?

3. Would any other policies have offered John additional protection? What about his inability to work while recovering from his injury?

4. Based upon the information presented, how would you assess John's health care insurance coverage? Explain.

FPPC 9.2 Benito and Teresa Get a Handle on Their Disability Income Needs

Benito Fernandez and his wife, Teresa, have been married for two years and have a one-year-old son. They live in Detroit, where Benito is a supervisor for Ford Motor Company. He earns $2,200 per month, of which he takes home $1,580. As an employee of Ford, he and his family are entitled to receive the benefits provided by the company's group health insurance policy. In addition to major medical coverage, the policy provides a monthly disability income benefit amounting to 20 percent of the employee's average monthly take-home pay for the most recent 12 months prior to incurring the disability. (Note: Benito's average monthly take-home pay for the most recent year is equal to his current monthly take-home pay.) In the instance of complete disability, Benito would also be eligible for social security payments of $700 per month.

Teresa is also employed. She earns $500 per month after taxes working part-time at a nearby grocery store. The store provides her with no benefits other than social security. In the event Benito became disabled, Teresa would continue to work at her part-time job. If she became disabled, social security would provide monthly income of $300. Benito and Teresa spend 90 percent of their combined take-home pay to meet their bills and provide for a variety of necessary items. They use the remaining 10 percent to fulfill their entertainment and savings goals.

Questions

1. How much, if any, additional disability income insurance does Benito require to ensure adequate protection against his becoming completely disabled?
2. Does Teresa need any disability income coverage? Explain.
3. What specific recommendations with respect to disability income insurance coverage would you give Benito and Teresa to provide adequate protection for themselves as well as their child?

GETTING A HANDLE ON YOUR FINANCIAL FUTURE

The rate of increase in health care costs in the United States is causing employers to implement cost-saving measures in their health insurance plans. In many cases, increased premiums are being shifted to employees. Currently, Congress is debating solutions to the "health care crisis" and proposing sweeping changes to the current health care system. These changes provide even more of an incentive for you to be sure that you do not have duplicate or inadequate health care coverage.

If You Are Just Starting Out

Just because you may be young and in good health does not mean you don't need health care insurance and disability income insurance. In fact, young people are more likely to have an accident resulting in a disability than they are to die of an illness or be killed in an accident.

Health Care Coverage:

1. To lower your health care premiums, consider increasing the deductible, coinsurance percentage, and/or the waiting period.
2. Learn how long your policy will pay benefits and how benefit payments are determined.
3. In a non-emergency situation, check in advance with your provider to determine whether or not the procedure or treatment will be fully covered by your insurance and if not, how much you will have to pay.
4. If you leave the country, you may not be covered by your current policy. You might need to purchase a supplemental policy for the duration of your travels.

Disability Income Coverage:

1. Be cautious when factoring social security benefits into your disability income requirements. Usually benefits are paid if you are disabled for at least one year or if the injury is terminal.
2. You need to know how disability is defined in your policy. If it says "any occupation," then it may not pay if you can be employed at all. If it says "your own occupation," then you would receive benefits even if you could be employed in another capacity.
3. For planning purposes, find out the waiting periods specified by your policy and whether or not your employer will keep you on payroll during that time.
4. To reduce the cost of private disability income insurance, consider a longer waiting period and invest the premium savings.

If You Are Thirty-Something

Changes in your marital and family status obviously greatly affect your health care coverage. More dependents on a policy usually translates into higher premiums.

Health Care Coverage:

1. Once your children reach a certain age or are no longer full-time students, they may not be covered by your health insurance. Don't let their coverage lapse.
2. Consider adding a dental policy for orthodontic and other costs.
3. Avoid the purchase of specialty insurance, such as cancer policies, because you may already have adequate coverage under your existing plan.
4. As you approach retirement, consider long-term care insurance to cover the costs of nursing home care.

Disability Income Coverage:

1. Make sure your policy is noncancelable and provides for future insurability so that you can increase your coverage as your income grows.
2. Consider adding a cost-of-living adjustment to your policy to offset the effects of inflation.
3. As you approach retirement, you may want to reduce and eventually cancel your disability income coverage, because many policies will not pay beyond age 65 anyway.

CHAPTER 10

PROTECTING YOUR PROPERTY

Bill Stanley Explains the Importance of Liability Insurance

In almost 30 years in the property and casualty insurance business—20 years as an agent—in Indianapolis, Bill Stanley (now 52 and retired) helped many clients define their insurance needs. "Let's face it," Bill says. "Who wants to think about a catastrophic loss from an auto accident, burglary, or fire? Most of us have few, if any, such losses. But you can't predict if *your* home or car will be badly damaged, or you'll be sued if you injure someone. If it happens, you'll be glad to have enough property and liability insurance."

But, Bill cautions: don't lose sight of *why* you buy insurance—*to protect against catastrophic losses* (losses that can bring financial ruin)—not just to pay for damage to your property. "That's one of the biggest mistakes you can make," Bill says. "Often buyers take a $250 or $500 deductible for physical damage to their car, to limit the 'pain' of wrecking their $14,000 Miata, and a $100,000 or $300,000 liability limit; that protects the other guy, so he can handle his own pain if he's crippled for life. The reality is, *if you're at fault, you (or your parents) can be financially crippled for life."* Bill recommends taking *the highest deductible you can afford.* "Losing $1,000 or $5,000 if you have an accident hurts but won't ruin you; if you're not at fault, you'll collect from the other party anyway. Liability coverage comes into play when the accident *is* your fault. Your loss isn't limited to what

Learning Goals

LG1. *Discuss the importance of having property and liability insurance and understand the basic principles of property insurance, including types of exposure, principle of indemnity, and coinsurance.*
LG2. *Identify the different coverages provided by a homeowner's insurance policy.*
LG3. *Select the right homeowner's insurance policy for your needs.*
LG4. *Analyze the different coverages in a personal automobile policy (PAP) and choose the most cost-effective policy.*
LG5. *Describe other forms of property and liability insurance.*
LG6. *Assess your property and liability insurance needs, choose a company and agent, and settle claims.*

you paid for the car—the sky's the limit. You can be sued for $1 million or more. These same principles apply to a homeowner's or renter's policy. Take as large a property deductible as possible and *at least* a $500,000 liability limit. Then take the money saved by raising your deductible and buy as much liability as you can afford! If you can, buy an umbrella policy (a policy that provides excess liability protection over your auto liability and homeowner's/renter's liability limits) as well."

Bill cites two examples that show the importance of liability coverage: "Two children, ages 9 and 11, were running at people in a shopping mall and caused a 78-year-old lady to fall and break her hip," he relates. "The parent was found negligent for failing to control her children's unruly behavior. The case was settled for $82,000, the costs of the injured's hospitalization, rehabilitation, and pain and suffering. The insured had sufficient liability limits, so the whole amount was covered. Another client hit another player in the head with his ball while golfing and caused permanent brain damage. He was found negligent and an out-of-court settlement was reached for $340,000. The insured had a $300,000 liability limit and felt he was not negligent; he forced the case into court, where the jury awarded the claimant $402,000. The insured had to take a second mortgage on his home to pay the rest of the judgment."

With Bill's advice in mind, let's now look at Chapter 10 for more information on ways to properly insure your property.

SOME BASIC PROPERTY INSURANCE PRINCIPLES

LG1

The effective use of property and liability insurance requires an understanding of the types of losses to which you are exposed and how to best cover them. Consider your present situation: What kinds of property losses are you exposed to at this point in your life? Do you think your exposure to loss will be any different in 10 or 15 years? Take a minute or two to think about these questions before reading on.

Suppose a severe storm destroyed your house. Could you afford to replace it? Most people could not. To protect yourself from this and similar types of property loss, you need *property insurance.* Also, every day you face the risk of negligence. For example, you might be distraught over a personal problem and unintentionally run a red light, seriously injuring a pedestrian. Because the consequences of this and other potentially negligent acts can cause financial ruin, appropriate *liability insurance* is essential. Property and liability insurance should be as much a part of your personal financial plans as life and health insurance. Such coverage protects the assets you have already acquired and ensures the achievement of your financial goals. In particular, **property insurance** guards against catastrophic losses of real and personal property caused by perils such as fire, theft, vandalism, wind storms, and many other calamities. **Liability insurance,** in contrast, offers protection against the financial consequences that may arise from certain types of legal actions.

Although people spend a lot of money for insurance coverage, few really know what they are getting for their premium dollars. Even worse, the vast majority of people are totally unaware of any gaps, overinsurance, and underinsurance in their property and liability insurance programs. Since such inefficient and inadequate insurance protection is completely at odds with the objectives of personal financial planning, you should become familiar with the basics of property and liability insurance.

The basic principles of property and liability insurance pertain to types of exposure, criteria for an insurable exposure, the principle of indemnity, and coinsurance. Each of these is discussed in the following sections.

TYPES OF EXPOSURE

Most individuals face two basic types of exposure: physical loss of property and loss through liability.

Exposure to Property Loss. The vast majority of property insurance contracts define the property covered directly in the policy and name the perils (causes of loss) for which insurance proceeds will be available. Some property contracts do offer protection on a more comprehensive basis, however, and limit coverage by excluding certain types of property and perils. These contracts impose two obligations on the property owner: (1) developing a complete inventory of the property in need of insurance coverage and (2) identifying the perils against which protection is desired.

Property inventory. Most people neither fully appreciate the value of all the property they own nor do they attempt to itemize their property for insurance purposes. Nevertheless, a property inventory should be prepared not only to help you select coverages but also to help you settle a claim if a loss occurs. All property insurance companies require you to show proof of loss when making a claim. Consequently, a prepared schedule of property owned, along with corresponding values at the time of inventory, can serve as evidence to satisfy the company.

Ordinarily, a family has a home, household furnishings, clothing and personal accessories, lawn and garden equipment, and motor vehicles (intended for road use), all of which need to be insured. Fortunately, the majority of automobile and homeowner's insurance policies provide coverage for these types of belongings. Many families also own such items as motorboats and trailers, various types of off-road vehicles, business property and inventories, jewelry, stamp or coin collections, furs, musical instruments, important papers and documents, antiques, paintings, bonds and other securities, and items of special value, such as expensive cameras, golf clubs, electronic recording and playing equipment, or citizen-band radios. Coverage for these belongings often must be specially arranged with the insurer. To help policyholders prepare inventories, many property insurance companies have easy-to-complete personal property inventory forms available. A partial sample of one such form is shown in Exhibit 10.1. In addition, people can

EXHIBIT 10.1

A Personal Property Inventory Form

Using a form like this will help you keep track of your personal property, including date of purchase, original price, and replacement cost. Note that this exhibit is only part of a 19-page homeowner's inventory record; this particular inventory record is put out by the *Personal Insurance Division of the Chubb Insurance Companies,* and includes not only household furnishings, but also clothing, electrical appliances, books and tools, electronic equipment, and various items of exceptional value, like china, antiques, fine art, jewelry, and so forth.

Living Room

Article	Qty.	Date Purchase	Purchase Price	Replacement Cost
Air Conditioners (Window)				
Blinds/Shades				
Bookcases				
Books				
Cabinets				
Carpets/Rugs				
Chairs				
Chests				
Clocks				
Couches/Sofas				
Curtains/Draperies				
Decks				
Fireplace Fixtures				
Hassocks				
Lamps/Lighting Fixtures				
Mirrors				
Musical Instruments				
Pictures/Paintings				
Records/Tapes				
Planters				
Stereo Equipment				
Tables				
Television Sets				
Wall Units				
Other				
Other				
Other				

Living Room

Stereo System

Brand	
Model	
Serial #	Date Purchased
Purchase Price $	Replacement Cost $

Stereo Receiver/Tuner

Brand	
Model	
Serial #	Date Purchased
Purchase Price $	Replacement Cost $

Turntable

Brand	
Model	
Serial #	Date Purchased
Purchase Price $	Replacement Cost $

Cassette Deck

Brand	
Model	
Serial #	Date Purchased
Purchase Price $	Replacement Cost $

Compact Disc Player

Brand	
Model	
Serial #	Date Purchased
Purchase Price $	Replacement Cost $

Source: Homeowner's Inventory, Chubb Insurance Companies, Personal Insurance Division, Warren, NJ 07060.

supplement inventory forms with photographs or videotapes of their belongings. For insurance purposes, a picture may truly be worth a thousand words. Regardless of whether the completed inventory forms are supplemented with photographs or videotapes, *every effort should be made to keep these documents in a safe place,* where they can't be destroyed—like a safe-deposit box. As added protection, you might even consider keeping a *duplicate copy* somewhere; for example, with a parent or trusted relative. Remember, you may need these photographs and inventories if something serious does happen and you have to come up with an authenticated list of property losses.

Identifying perils. Many people feel a false sense of security after buying insurance, because they believe that they are safeguarded against all contingencies. The fact is, however, that certain **perils** (defined as a cause of loss) cannot be reasonably insured against. For example, most homeowner's or automobile insurance policies limit or exclude coverage for flood, earthquake, mud slides, mysterious disappearance, war, nuclear radiation, and wear and tear. In addition, property insurance contracts routinely limit coverage on the basis of location of the property, time of loss, persons involved, and the types of hazards to which the property is exposed. These limitations are explained further in subsequent sections of this chapter.

Liability Exposures. Every day you face the risk that you might negligently cause property damage or bodily injury to someone else. For example, when golfing you might become impatient and tee off before the people in front of you are clearly out of range. If your ball struck one of them and you were found legally liable for that injury, a judgment ranging into the thousands, or in some cases millions, of dollars could be levied against you. Of course, a debt that size could force many families into financial ruin and even bankruptcy. Many different liability exposures are encountered every day. Driving a car, entertaining guests at home, and being careless in performing professional duties are some of the more common liability risks. However, even if you were never negligent and always prudent, you could still run the risk that someone might think that you were the cause of a loss and therefore bring a costly lawsuit against you.

Fortunately, *liability insurance* coverage is available to protect against losses resulting from each of these risks, *including the high legal fees required to defend yourself against suits that may or may not have merit.* It's important to include adequate liability insurance in your overall insurance program, either through your homeowner's and automobile policies or a separate umbrella policy. But before discussing the methods available for insuring against liability exposures, let's look at the ways in which legal liability arises.

Liability based on negligence. Legal definitions of negligence and liability have evolved over hundreds of years of court decisions and enactments of statutes, and these definitions are expected to continue to be modified as society's values change. In addition, specific rules of law vary not only over time but also in their interpretations depending on judges, juries, and locations throughout the country. Consequently, only a general overview of these concepts can be presented here.

A person is said to have performed a **negligent action** when his or her behavior has been inconsistent with the **reasonable person doctrine.** This doctrine holds that if a person fails to act in a reasonable manner—as would one with normal intelligence, perceptions, and experiences common to the community—that person is negligent. However, evidence that someone was negligent is only the first step in establishing liability. In addition, the defendant (the person accused of negligence) must be proven to have had a duty toward the plaintiff (the accuser) and to have caused the plaintiff a compensable loss as a result of a breach of that duty. Further, it must be shown that (physical or financial) injury to a person or damage to property actually occurred. If any of these elements is missing, the defendant is relieved from legal liability.

PRINCIPLE OF INDEMNITY

The **principle of indemnity** states that the insured may not be compensated by the insurance company in an amount exceeding the economic loss. Most property and liability insurance contracts are based on this principle. Recall from Chapters 8 and 9 that life and health insurance contracts, in contrast, are *not* specifically contracts of indemnity. Four important concepts that are related to the principle of indemnity are found in property and liability insurance: (1) insurable interest, (2) actual cash value, (3) subrogation, and (4) other insurance.

Insurable Interest. The concept of **insurable interest** means that the individuals who insure property must stand to lose something if that property is subject to loss and that they cannot receive more in payment than their financial interest in the property. For example, assume that John and Mary own equal shares in an apartment house that has a market value of $200,000 (excluding the value of the land, which is uninsurable). If the building is destroyed, the maximum the insurer will pay to each partner is $100,000, since that is the extent of either party's economic interest in the property. If these partners sell the property but forget to cancel their insurance policy, and the property is subsequently destroyed by fire, the insurance company will pay them nothing (since they had no interest in the property at the time of loss).

Ownership, however, is not the only way someone can develop an insurable interest in a property. For instance, an owner of a dry cleaning operation has a legal obligation to return the clothing received in the normal course of business. If a fire damages the clothing, the proprietor may be liable to customers for the value of the damaged clothing. Thus, the proprietor, although not the owner of the clothing, does have a legal obligation to maintain the clothing in good condition and may obtain insurance that will provide protection against this type of loss.

Actual Cash Value and Replacement Cost. The principle of indemnity also *limits the amount an insured may collect to the actual cash value of the property.* **Actual cash value** is defined as replacement cost less physical depreciation, although some insurers do guarantee replacement cost without taking depreciation into account—for example, most homeowner's policies will settle building losses on a replacement basis if the proper type and amount of insurance is purchased. But it is common practice in most other situations to deduct depreciation in order to obtain the actual cash value. If an insured property is damaged, the insurer is obligated to pay no more than what the property would cost new today (its replacement cost) less depreciation from wear and tear. For example, assume that fire destroys two rooms of furniture that have a replacement cost of $5,000. The actual age of the furniture was six years, and it was estimated to have a useful life of ten years. Therefore, at the time of loss the furniture was subject to an assumed physical depreciation of 60 percent (6 years ÷ 10 years) —in this case, $3,000. Since the actual cash value is estimated at $2,000 ($5,000 replacement cost minus $3,000 depreciation), the maximum the insurer would have to pay is $2,000. Note that the original cost of the property has no bearing on the settlement.

Subrogation. After an insurance company pays a claim, its **right of subrogation** allows it to request reimbursement from the person who caused the loss or from that person's insurance company. For example, assume that you are in an automobile accident in which the other party damages your car. You may collect from your insurer or the at-fault party's insurer but not from both (at least not for the same loss). If you receive payment from your

property insurance Insurance coverage that protects real and personal property from catastrophic losses caused by a variety of perils.

liability insurance Insurance that protects against financial losses arising from the insured's responsibility for property losses of or injuries to others.

peril A cause of loss.

negligent action An action that is deemed inconsistent with the reasonable person doctrine.

reasonable person doctrine A doctrine stating that if a person fails to act in a reasonable manner—as would someone with "normal" intelligence, perceptions, and experiences—he or she is guilty of negligence.

principle of indemnity An insurance principle stating that an insured may not be compensated by his or her insurer in an amount exceeding the amount of economic loss.

insurable interest A concept stating that individuals who insure property must stand to lose something if that property is subject to loss and that they cannot receive more in compensation than the extent of their legal interest in the property.

actual cash value A value assigned to an insured property that is determined by subtracting depreciation from replacement cost.

right of subrogation The right of an insurer who has paid a claim to request reimbursement from the person who caused the loss or that person's insurer.

insurance company, you must subrogate (transfer) to it your right to sue the other person. Clearly, to collect the full amount from both parties would leave you better off after the loss than before it. Such an action would violate the principle of indemnity. An important by-product of the subrogation clause is that it makes the party who caused the accident (or loss) ultimately responsible for paying the damages. In this way, the *insurance company* can go after the responsible party to collect its loss (the amount it paid out to you); and best of all, it's not your problem.

Other Insurance. Nearly all property and liability insurance contracts have an *other-insurance clause,* which also supports the concept of indemnity. This provision prohibits insured persons from insuring their property with two or more insurance companies and then collecting in full for a loss from all companies. The other-insurance clause normally states that if a person has more than one insurance policy on a property, each company is liable for only a pro rata amount of the loss based on its proportion of the total insurance covering the property. For example, assume that John and Mary in the earlier example purchased two policies of $200,000 each on their $200,000 building. If a total loss occurred, each company would pay 50 percent, because the ratio of the coverage purchased from each company to the total coverage on the property is one-half ($200,000/$400,000). Similarly, if each of *three* companies had issued a $200,000 policy, their individual shares would be one-third ($200,000/$600,000). Without this provision, insured persons could use duplicate property insurance policies to profit from their losses. In liability insurance policies, the other-insurance clause usually provides that if two (or more) policies cover the same exposure, only one of them will provide coverage until its limits are used up, after which the other will provide coverage above that amount up to no more than the amount of the allowable loss.

COINSURANCE

Coinsurance, a provision commonly found in property insurance contracts, requires policyholders to buy insurance in an amount equal to a specified percentage of the replacement value of their property, and, if that's not done, then the *policyholder* is required to pay for a proportional share of the losses. In essence, the coinsurance provision stipulates that if the property isn't properly covered, the property owner will become the "coinsurer" and bear part of the loss. If the stipulated amount of coverage (usually 80 percent of the value of the property) is obtained, then the policyholder will be reimbursed for covered losses dollar for dollar up to the amount of the policy limits. Otherwise, payment will be based on a specified percentage of loss. For example, assume that John and Mary's fire policy on their $200,000 apartment building contained an 80 percent coinsurance clause. This means that the policy limits must equal or exceed 80 percent of the value of their building. Further assume that they had run short of money and decided to save by buying a single $120,000 policy instead of a minimum of $160,000 (80% × $200,000) as required by the coinsurance clause. If a loss of any amount occurred, the company would be obligated to pay only 75 percent ($120,000/ $160,000) of it up to the amount of the policy limit. Thus, on damages of $40,000, the insurer would pay only $30,000 (75% × $40,000). Obviously, it is important that you closely evaluate the coinsurance clause of any property insurance policy in order to make sure that you will not have an unexpected additional burden in the event a loss does take place.

Concept Check

10-1. Briefly explain the fundamental concepts related to *property and liability insurance*.

10-2. Explain the *principle of indemnity*. Are there any limits imposed on the amount an insured may collect under this principle?

10-3. Explain the *right of subrogation*. How does this feature help lower insurance costs?

10-4. Describe how the *coinsurance* feature works.

HOMEOWNER'S INSURANCE LG2 LG3

Because your home is likely to be your biggest (and most expensive) possession, every effort should be taken to make sure that it's ade-

quately insured. What kinds of protection should you look for when insuring a home? Would you want the same protection if you were renting rather than buying a home? Give some thought to these questions before going on.

Although homeowner's insurance is often thought of as a single type of insurance policy, four different forms (HO-1, HO-2, HO-3, and HO-8) are actually available to homeowners, and two other forms (HO-4 and HO-6) are designed to meet the needs of renters and owners of condominiums (see Exhibit 10.2). An HO-4 renter's policy offers essentially the same broad protection as an HO-2 homeowner's policy, except that the coverage does not apply to the rented dwelling unit because tenants usually do not have a financial interest in the real property. All HO forms are divided into two sections. Section I applies to the dwelling, its contents, and accompanying structures; Section II deals with comprehensive coverage for personal liability and for medical payments to others. The forms differ in that the scope of coverage under Section I is least with an HO-1 policy and greatest with an HO-3 policy. HO-8 is a modified coverage policy for older homes. It is used by homeowners to insure houses that have market values well below their costs to rebuild. The coverage in Section II is the same for all forms.

In the following paragraphs, the important features of homeowner's forms HO-2 and HO-3 are emphasized because these are the most frequently sold policies. The coverage offered under these forms is basically the same; the differences lie only in the number of perils against which protection applies.

PERILS COVERED

As mentioned previously, a peril is defined as a cause of loss. Some property and liability insurance agreements, called *comprehensive* policies, cover all perils except those specifically excluded, while others name the perils covered individually. The latter type is called a **named peril policy.**

Section I Perils. The perils against which the home and its contents are insured are shown in Exhibit 10.2. The coverage on household belongings is the same for the HO-2 and HO-3 forms, but coverage on the house and other structures (for example, a detached garage) is comprehensive under HO-3 and named peril in HO-2. Whether homeowners should buy an HO-2 or an HO-3 form depends primarily on the amount they are willing to spend to secure additional protection. In some states, the premium differential is small, making an HO-3 policy the better buy. In other states, the HO-2 form has a substantially lower premium. Also, the size of the premiums for the HO-2 and HO-3 policies can differ substantially among insurance companies. Because of its more limited coverage, the purchase of an HO-1 is not recommended. (A special note on the HO-8 is presented later.)

Note in Exhibit 10.2 that the types of Section I perils covered includes just about everything from fire and explosions to lightning and wind damage, to theft and vandalism; unfortunately, these are all perils to which any homeowner is exposed. While the list of perils is quite extensive, there are a couple of types that are specifically excluded from most homeowner's contracts—in particular, *most policies (even HO-2 and HO-3 forms) exclude earthquakes and floods.* A major reason for this, of course, is the catastrophic nature of such events—that is, they can, and often do, cause widespread and very costly damage! In addition, many areas of the country simply are not susceptible to earthquakes and/or floods, and as a result, homeowners in those areas shouldn't have to pay for coverage they don't need. But even if you live in an area where the risk of an earthquake or flood is relatively high, you'll find your *standard homeowner's policy does not provide protection against these perils.* Fortunately, as we'll see later in this chapter, coverage for earthquakes and/or floods is available, but it's provided under a separate policy. Thus, if you live in an area where you need such coverage, you'll have to obtain it through some form of a rider or supplemental policy.

Section II Perils. The perils insured against under Section II of the homeowner's contract are

coinsurance In property insurance, a provision that requires a policyholder to buy insurance in an amount equal to a specified percentage of the value of their property, including improvements.

named peril policy An insurance policy that names the perils covered individually.

EXHIBIT 10.2

A Guide to Homeowner's Policies

The amount of insurance coverage you receive depends on the type of homeowner's (HO) policy you select. Insurance coverage can also be obtained for those who live in *rental units* (HO-4) or who own units in a *condominium* (HO-6).

Coverage	HO-1 (Basic Form)	HO-2 (Broad Form)	HO-3 (Special Form)
		Section I Coverages	
A. Dwelling	$15,000 minimum	$15,000 minimum	$20,000 minimum
B. Other structures	10% of A	10% of A	10% of A
C. Personal property	50% of A	50% of A	50% of A
D. Loss of use	10% of A	20% of A	20% of A
Covered perils	Fire or lightning Windstorms (including tornadoes) or hail Explosion Riot or civil commotion Aircraft Vehicles Smoke Vandalism or malicious mischief Theft Breakage of glass or safety glazing material (limit of $100) Volcanic eruption	Fire or lightning Windstorms (including tornadoes) or hail Explosion Riot or civil commotion Aircraft Vehicles Smoke Vandalism or malicious mischief Theft Breakage of glass or safety glazing material Falling objects Weight of ice, snow, or sleet Accidental discharge or overflow of water or stream Sudden and accidental tearing, cracking, burning, or bulging of a steam, hot water, air conditioning, or automatic fire protective sprinkler system, or appliance for heating water Freezing Sudden and accidental damage for artificially generated electrical current Volcanic eruption	Dwelling and other structures covered against risks of direct physical loss to property except losses specifically excluded Personal property covered by same perils as HO-2 plus damage by glass or safety glazing material, which is part of a building, storm door, or storm window
		Section II Coverages (Minimums)	
E. Personal liability	$100,000	$100,000	$100,000
F. Medical payments to others	$1,000 per person	$1,000 per person	$1,000 per person

the (alleged) negligence of an insured. As discussed earlier in this chapter, negligence is defined as failure to act in a reasonable manner. The coverage is called *comprehensive personal liability coverage,* because it offers protection against nearly any source of liability (major exclusions are noted later) resulting from negligence. It does not insure against other losses for which one may become liable, such as libel, slander, defamation of character, and contractual or intentional wrongdoings. For example, coverage would apply if you carelessly, but unintentionally, knocked someone down your stairs. If you purposely struck and injured another person, however, or harmed someone's reputation either orally or in writing, the homeowner's liability coverage would not protect you. An additional feature of Section II is the limited amount of medical coverage of persons other than the homeowner's family in certain types of minor accidents on or off the insured's premises. The basic purpose of this coverage is to help homeowners meet their moral obligations and also to help deter possible lawsuits. The limited medical payment coverage pays irrespective of negligence or fault.

EXHIBIT 10.2

Continued

HO-4 (Renter's—Contents, Broad Form)	HO-6 (Condominium Unit Owner's)	HO-8 (Older House Form)
Section I Coverages		
Not applicable Not applicable $6,000 minimum 20% of C	$1,000 minimum Not applicable $6,000 minimum 40% of C	Same as HO-1, except losses are paid based on the amount required to repair or replace the property using common construction materials and methods.
Same perils as HO-2 for personal property	Same perils as HO-2 for personal property	Same perils as HO-1, except theft coverage applies only to losses on the residence premises up to a maximum of $1,000; certain other coverage restrictions also apply.
Section II Coverages (Minimums)		
$100,000 $1,000 per person	$100,000 $1,000 per person	$100,000 $1,000 per person

PROPERTY COVERED

The homeowner's policy offers property protection under Section I for the dwelling unit, accompanying structures, and the personal property of homeowners and their families. Coverage for certain types of losses also applies to lawns, trees, plants, and shrubs. However, structures on the premises used for business purposes (except incidentally) are excluded from coverage, as are animals (pets or otherwise) and motorized vehicles not used in the maintenance of the premises. This latter exclusion means there is no coverage for motorcycles, autos, golf carts, or snowmobiles (an exception is small boats). Further, business inventory (goods held by an insured who is a traveling salesperson or other goods held for sale) is not covered. Even though business inventory is excluded, business property (such as books, typewriters, working materials, and microcomputers) is covered, up to a maximum of $2,500, while it is on the insured premises.

If you work at home, either full- or part-time, you may need to increase your policy's limits to protect your home office. This insurance is critical, because damage to your home ruins not only where you live but your source of income as well. In many cases, adding a rider to your homeowner's policy can increase your home-business limits to adequate levels for your computer and office equipment and also provide some additional limited liability coverage. The cost for these riders is low, about $10 to $40 per year, depending on how many coverages you include. If you need greater protection, you should investigate a separate business owner's policy that offers broader coverage for business liability, all risk protection for equipment, and business income protection if damage to your home results in lost income.

PERSONAL PROPERTY FLOATER (PPF)

As we will see later in this chapter, there are limits to the types and amounts of coverages provided. As a result, your homeowner's policy may offer less protection than you need for many expensive items of personal property. To overcome this deficiency, insurers have developed the **personal property floater (PPF),** which provides either blanket or scheduled coverage of such items. Essentially, *a PPF extends protection to items not adequately covered in a standard homeowner's policy.* It is often added as an endorsement to the homeowner's policy but may be a separate policy.

A blanket, or unscheduled, PPF provides comprehensive coverage for virtually all the insured's personal property. It offers the maximum protection available and typically covers not just named perils but "all risks of physical loss," except for those specifically excluded. Most notably these exclusions are for wear and tear, damage from insects or vermin, nuclear energy, and gradual deterioration.

In addition, many types of scheduled (that is, itemized) personal property floaters are available to supplement coverage under a homeowner's contract. These coverages are especially useful for property valued at more than the Schedule C limits on amounts payable and perils insured. Coverage under a scheduled personal property floater is extensive and guards against loss or damage to expensive belongings. Some of the more popular uses of PPFs are for furs, jewelry, photographic equipment, silverware, fine art and antiques, musical instruments, and stamp and coin collections. For example, you should itemize a diamond ring valued at $7,500, because it is worth more than the standard $1,000 Schedule C allowance for jewelry theft. By itemizing valuables, you are covered for loss or damage as well as theft. If you lose the ring down the drain or it gets mangled in the garbage disposal, you can collect from the insurance company. Generally, insurance companies require appraisals before scheduling items, to prove their value.

RENTER'S INSURANCE: DON'T MOVE IN WITHOUT IT

If you live in an apartment (or some other type of rental unit), you should be aware that while the building you live in very likely is fully insured, *your furnishings and other personal belongings are not.* Rather, as a renter (or even as the owner of a condominium unit), you need a special type of HO policy to obtain insurance coverage on your possessions. Consider, for example, the predicament of Lois Weaver. She never got around to insuring her personal possessions in the apartment she rented in Denver. One wintry night, a water pipe ruptured, and escaping water damaged her furniture, rugs, and other belongings. When the building owner refused to pay for the loss, Ms. Weaver hauled him into court—and lost. How could she have lost? Simple: *Unless a landlord can be proven negligent*—and this one wasn't—*he or she isn't responsible for a tenant's property.* The moral of this story is clear—once you've accumulated a good deal of personal belongings (from clothing and home furnishings to stereo equipment, VCRs, and TVs), you'd better make sure they are covered by insurance, even if you're only renting a place to live! Otherwise you risk losing everything you own. Apparently a lot of tenants don't realize that, as surveys show most of them are without insurance. And that's unfortunate, since insurance for tenants, or renters, is available at very reasonable rates. It's simply a scaled-down version of homeowner's insurance, wherein the contents of a house, apartment or cooperative unit are covered, but not the structure itself.

The policy is called Renter's Form HO-4. For owners of condominium units, there's one called HO-6; it's similar but includes a minimum of $1,000 in protection for any building alterations, additions, and decorations paid for by the policyholder. Both the HO-4 and HO-6 policies include liability coverage. Like regular homeowner's insurance, they protect you at home and away. For example, if somebody is injured and sues you, the policy would pay for damages up to a specified limit, generally

$100,000, although some insurers go as high as $500,000.

A standard renter's policy covers furniture, carpets, appliances, clothing, and most other personal items for their cash value at the time of loss. The cost of renter's insurance isn't high: Expect to pay $80 to $100 a year for about $8,000 in coverage, depending on where you live. For maximum protection, you can buy *replacement cost insurance* (discussed again later in this chapter), which pays the actual cost of replacing articles with comparable ones—though some policies limit the payout to four times the cash value. You'll pay more for this, naturally—perhaps as little as another 10 percent, or perhaps much more, depending on the insurer. Also, the standard tenants policy provides only limited coverage of such valuables as jewelry, furs and silverware. Coverage varies, although some insurers now pay up to $1,000 for the loss of watches, gems and furs, and up to $2,500 for silverware. For larger amounts, you need a separate policy or a supplement, called a *personal property floater*, as discussed earlier.

Renter's insurance pays for losses caused by fire or lightning, explosion, windstorms, hail, theft, civil commotion, aircraft, vehicles, smoke, vandalism and malicious mischief, falling objects, building collapse, and the weight of ice and snow. Certain damages caused by water, steam, electricity, appliances, and frozen pipes are covered as well. If your residence can't be occupied because of damage from any of those perils, the insurance will pay for any increase in living expenses resulting from, say, staying at a hotel and eating in restaurants. The liability coverage pays for damages and legal costs arising from injuries or damage caused by you, a member of your family or a pet, on or off your premises.

TYPES OF LOSSES COVERED

A person can suffer three different types of property-related losses when misfortune occurs: (1) the direct loss of property, (2) an indirect loss that occurs due to the loss of damaged property, and (3) extra expenses resulting from direct and indirect losses. The homeowner's insurance contract offers compensation for each of these types of loss.

Section I Coverage. When a house is damaged by an insured peril, the insurance company will pay reasonable living expenses that a family might incur while the home is being repaired. Also, in many instances the insurer will pay for damages caused by perils other than those mentioned in the policy if a named peril is determined to have been the underlying cause of the loss. Assume, for instance, that lightning (a covered peril) strikes a house while a family is away and knocks out all the power, which causes $400 worth of food in the freezer and refrigerator to spoil. The company will pay for the loss even though temperature change (the direct cause) is not mentioned in the policy.

Section II Coverage. In addition to paying successfully pursued liability claims against an insured, the homeowner's policy includes coverage for (1) the cost of defending the insured, (2) any reasonable expenses incurred by an insured in helping the company's defense, and (3) the payment of court costs. Since these three types of costs apply even in cases in which the liability suit is without merit, coverage in these areas is an added benefit that can save you thousands of dollars in attorney fees.

PERSONS COVERED

The homeowner's policy covers the persons named in the policy and the members of their families who are residents of the household. A person can be a resident of the household even while temporarily living away from home. For example, college students who live at school part of the year and at home during vacations are normally regarded as household residents. As such, their belongings (things like stereo equipment, TVs, personal computers, and microwave ovens) usually are covered by their parents' homeowner's policy, even though they may have them at school. But there could be limits and exceptions to the coverage, so check the policy to make sure what is and is not covered (for example, some companies may consider a student living off-campus to be independent and therefore ineligible for coverage under their parents' insurance).

The standard homeowner's contract also extends limited coverage to guests of the insured for

personal property floater (PPF) policy An insurance policy that provides coverage to expensive personal property not otherwise covered in a standard homeowner's policy.

property losses that occur at the insured house if the insured wants such coverage to apply. If the insured does not choose to file a claim for the guest's property loss, the guest will be reimbursed only if he or she can prove negligence on the part of the homeowner. If the home is financed, coverage for loss to the house will also apply to the mortgage lender, provided that the lender is named in the insurance policy.

LOCATIONS COVERED

While some insurance contracts have territorial exclusions, homeowner's policies offer coverage worldwide. Consequently, an insured's personal property is *fully covered* regardless of whether it is loaned to the next-door neighbor or kept in a hotel room in Outer Mongolia. The only exception is property left at a second home, such as a beach house or resort condominium—in which case, coverage is reduced to 10 percent of the policy limit, except while the insured is actually residing there. Homeowners and their families have liability protection for their negligent acts wherever they occur. This liability protection, however, does not include negligent acts involving certain types of motorized vehicles (like large boats and aircraft), or arising in the course of employment or professional practice. It does include golf carts (when used for golfing purposes) and recreational vehicles such as snowmobiles and minibikes, provided they are used on the insured premises.

LIMITATION ON PAYMENT

The insurable interest, actual cash value, subrogation, and other insurance features that restrict the amount paid under a property and liability insurance contract have already been described. In addition to these features, replacement cost, policy limits, and deductibles can also influence the amount an insurance company will pay for a loss.

Replacement Cost. The amount necessary to repair, rebuild, or replace an asset at today's prices is the **replacement cost.** The homeowner's coverage on a house and the accompanying structures is based on replacement cost coverage. This means that the insurer will repair or replace damaged items without taking any deductions for depreciation. Here is an illustration of a replacement cost calculation for a 2,400-square-foot home with a two-car garage:

Dwelling: 2,400 sq. ft. at $62 per sq. ft.	$148,800
Extra features: built-in appliances, mahogany cabinets, 3 ceiling fans	8,600
Porches, patios: back screened and trellised patio	2,700
Two-car garage: 900 sq. ft. at $24 per sq. ft.	21,600
Other site improvements: driveway, storage, landscaping	4,700
Total replacement cost	$186,400

The $186,400 represents the amount of money it would take *today* to fully replace the home in question. Keep in mind, however, that *for homeowners to be eligible for reimbursement on a replacement-cost basis, they must keep their homes insured for at least 80 percent of the amount it would cost to build them today exclusive of the value of the land.* In periods of inflation, homeowners must either increase their coverage limits on the dwelling unit every year or take a chance on falling below the 80 percent requirement. Alternatively, for a nominal cost, homeowners can purchase an *inflation protection rider,* whereby the amount of coverage is automatically adjusted for the effects of inflation. In essence, such a rider is used to continuously modify the coverage limits (replacement costs) of the home in keeping with prevailing inflation rates. At the same time, an inflation protection rider basically eliminates the chance of a coinsurance penalty. That is, if the 80 percent condition (referred to earlier) is not met, then the coinsurance penalty will kick in, in which case, the maximum compensation allowable for total or partial losses may be determined on an actual cash value basis and will be based on a specified percentage of loss.

Contrary to popular opinion, actual cash value and replacement cost need not bear any relationship to a home's market value. Because replacement cost and actual cash value relate only to the physical structure and do not consider the influence of location, a home's market value can be in excess of its replacement cost or below its actual cash value. Also, even if a home is in an excellent state of repair, its market value may be lessened because of functional obsolescence within the structure. In fact, the HO-8 homeowner's form was adopted in partial response to this problem. In many older neighborhoods, a 2,200-square-foot home might have a market value, excluding land, of, say, $60,000; the replacement cost, though, might be $160,000. Thus, to get good protection, a homeowner would have to buy a policy with limits of $128,000 (.80 × $160,000). This is expensive to the homeowner and creates moral hazard to the insurer. With the HO-8 policy, however, homeowners generally can get their property repaired in full up to the amount of their loss or up to the property's market value, whichever is less. This reduced limit saves the insured's premiums and reduces the risk that people will burn their houses down to make money on the insurance proceeds.

Although coverage on a house is often on a *replacement-cost basis,* standard coverage on the contents may be on an *actual cash value basis.* Therefore, depreciation is taken into account in calculating the amount of any payments made for losses to furniture, clothing, and other belongings. The depreciation amount is subtracted from the *current replacement cost* of the items—not from what may have been paid for the property several years ago. Thus, it is possible to collect more in insurance than the property's original price if the rate of inflation has exceeded the rate of depreciation.

Recently, many insurers have begun offering, for a slight increase in premium, replacement-cost coverage on contents. It seems likely that in the future the standard coverage on contents will become replacement cost rather than actual cash value. Because the additional premium required to buy replacement-cost coverage is generally small, you should seriously consider this option—as well as an inflation protection rider on the dwelling—when buying homeowner's insurance. As you can see, it's important to understand just what's included in replacement cost. The *Smart Money* box on page 408 will help you evaluate your policy and determine whether extra coverage if necessary.

Policy Limits. In Section I of the homeowner's policy, the amount of coverage on the dwelling unit (coverage A) establishes the amounts applicable to the accompanying structures (coverage B), the unscheduled personal property (coverage C), and the temporary living expenses (coverage D). Generally, the limits under coverages B, C, and D are 10, 50, and 10 to 20 percent, respectively, of the amount of coverage under A (see Exhibit 10.2). For example, if the house were insured for $150,000, the limits for coverages B, C, and D would be $15,000, $75,000, and $30,000, respectively (that is, 10% × $150,000; 50% × $150,000; and 20% × $150,000). Each of these limits can be increased if insufficient to cover the exposure. Also, for a small reduction in premium, some companies will permit a homeowner to reduce coverage on unscheduled personal property to 40 percent of the amount on the dwelling unit.

Remember that homeowner's policies usually specify internal limits for certain types of personal property as included under the coverage C category. These coverage limits are within the total dollar amount of coverage C, and they in no way act to increase that total. The limited dollar coverages for each reported loss are as follows:

From any covered peril

1. $200 on money, bank notes, bullion, gold other than goldware, silver other than silverware, platinum, coins, and medals
2. $1,000 on securities, accounts, deeds, evidences of debt, letters of credit, notes other than bank notes, manuscripts, passports, tickets, and stamps
3. $1,000 on watercraft, including their trailers, furnishings, equipment, and outboard motors
4. $1,000 on trailers not used with watercraft
5. $1,000 on grave markers

From theft only

6. $1,000 for loss by theft of jewelry, watches, furs, and precious and semiprecious stones
7. $2,000 for loss by theft of firearms
8. $2,500 for loss by theft of silverware, silver-plated ware, goldware, gold-plated ware, and pewterware; includes flatware, hollowware, tea sets, trays, and trophies made of or including silver, gold, or pewter

Some policies also offer $5,000 coverage for home computer equipment. You can increase these limits by purchasing higher Schedule C coverages.

In Section II, the standard liability limit (coverage E) is $100,000, and the medical payments portion (coverage F) normally has a limit of $1,000 per person. Additional coverages included in Section II consist of claim expenses such as court costs and attorney fees, first aid and medical expenses, including ambulance costs, and damage to others' property of up to $500 per occurrence.

Although these limits are the ones most commonly sold, most homeowners need additional protection, especially liability coverage. In these days of high damage awards by juries, a $100,000 liability limit may not be adequate—in fact, a greater amount is advisable for persons with higher incomes and net worths. The liability limit with most companies can be increased for only a nominal cost. For example, the annual premium difference between a $100,000 personal liability limit and a $300,000 limit is likely to be only $40 to $50! You can also increase personal liability coverage with an

replacement cost The amount necessary to repair, rebuild, or replace an asset at today's prices.

Smart Money

When Replacement Cost Insurance Is Not Enough

If you have a replacement-cost homeowner's policy, you may think that you're all set if disaster hits. But take a close look at your policy before assuming you can rebuild and refurnish your home to its existing condition. The large number of recent disasters—fires and earthquakes in California, floods in the Midwest, hurricanes in the Southeast and Hawaii—have made it painfully clear to homeowners that they should not skimp on insurance coverage.

Take, for example, the Malibu, California, couple who bought a small house in 1989 and added a second floor and more bedrooms and baths. They purchased additional replacement-cost insurance to cover the improvements. However, when fire destroyed the home in 1993, the insurance company's offer was $100,000 short of full replacement cost. Why? Because they had substantially underestimated the value of the home, and particularly its contents, whose coverage was limited to 50 percent of the policy's face value. Over the years they had acquired expensive furnishings, such as silver, china, and so forth, so that the 50 percent was not enough. And they confused "replacement cost" with the more expensive "*guaranteed* replacement cost" policy, which means you can rebuild your home at today's costs, regardless of policy value.

It's not unusual to find such gaps. Oakland, California, homeowners faced similar problems after the 1991 fires, as did the southeastern victims of Hurricane Andrew in 1992. Their so-called replacement-cost policies did not cover the costs to rebuild and refurnish. So it pays to examine your policy to see exactly what's covered and look for a better policy if necessary. Here are some situations where you may want extra coverage.

- ***Building code changes.*** Standard replacement-cost coverage generally does not include the cost of compliance with new building codes, although some policies may have it. This is a real problem with an older house, where the expense of rebuilding in accordance with new regulations (such as earthquake and energy codes) may far exceed what the insurer will pay to rebuild to prior condition. The solution is to get "law-and-ordinance" or "code-and-contention" coverage, which adds about 10 percent to premium costs.
- ***Valuable contents.*** While many homeowners assume that replacement cost means their contents are fully insured, a standard policy covers only 50 to 75 percent of policy's face value, regardless of the contents' actual value. If you have lots of valuable antiques, art works, jewelry, and so forth, protect additional contents with a special coverage rider for your policy.
- ***Zoning law changes.*** Changes in zoning laws since your house was built may not allow you to rebuild on the same site if your house is destroyed. Some who lost homes to the 1993 Southern California fires found their sites rezoned as hazardous areas; if it cost more to rebuild elsewhere, they had to pay the difference themselves. If you live in an area where this could be a problem, buy a policy that says you can rebuild the same house, regardless of cost, on any lot.
- ***Foundation damage.*** Another common assumption is that foundations are covered. But many policies don't cover them, because it was believed that foundations don't burn. The 1991 Oakland fires proved that wrong; many foundations melted from the heat. Earthquakes also damage foundations. So check that your policy includes damage to the foundation.

Clearly, the best policy is guaranteed-replacement-cost coverage, and it doesn't cost too much more. But you may not be able to buy it for some homes, such as older homes with special craftsmanship, those whose market value is less than the cost to rebuild, or very expensive homes. You can, however, get replacement-cost coverage—just make sure it covers *100 percent of rebuilding costs*. After the recent batch of hurricanes, fire, and ice storms, many homeowners discovered that the old 80 percent formula is no longer adequate. Although it's hard to figure out what 100 percent of replacement cost is, get estimates from several companies and compare them to see whether you have enough coverage.

Source: Elizabeth Razzi, "Home Insurance That Won't Let You Down," *Kiplinger's Personal Finance Magazine,* August 1994, pp. 43–46; Liz Comte Reisman, "Closing the Coverage Gap," *Smart Money,* November 1994, pp. 106–107.

EXHIBIT 10.3

Homeowner's Insurance Premiums

Homeowners insurance premiums vary depending on city and company. The following table compares the cost of an HO-3 guaranteed-replacement-cost policy with a $500 deductible for a $150,000 house and includes discounts for deadbolt locks, fire extinguishers, and a centrally-monitored security system.

	Insurance Company				
Location	**Allstate**	**Farmers***	**Nationwide**	**State Farm†**	**USAA#**
Anaheim, Cal.	$531	$250	$399	$ 327	$ 330
Atlanta	521	—	482	657	379
Birmingham, Ala.	465	374	680	544	700**
Des Moines	485	281	451	434	416**
Miami	—	—	779	1,068	1,073
Milwaukee	397	256	351	347	296
New Haven, Conn.	500	—	553	291	336
Philadelphia	558	—	761	726	555**
Richland, Wash.	301	240	286	354	324
Sacramento, Cal.	481	354	539	452	392
Wichita, Kan.	673	371	517	552	573**

— Not writing policies in this market. *Includes nonsmoker and new-home discounts, which are also available from other companies. †Figures are for HO-5 policies; State Farm doesn't offer guaranteed-replacement-cost coverage on HO-3 policies. #Sells homeowners insurance only to present and former U.S. military officers and their families. **USAA's guarantee is up to 125% of the dwelling amount and can be raised to 150% for an additional premium.

Source: Elizabeth Razzi, "Home Insurance that Won't Let You Down," *Kiplinger's Personal Finance Magazine*, August 1994, p. 46.

umbrella personal liability policy, discussed later in the chapter.

Deductibles. Each of the preceding limits on recovery constrains the maximum amount payable under the policy. In contrast, *deductibles* place constraints on what a company must pay for small losses. *Deductibles help reduce insurance premiums*, because they do away with the frequent small loss claims that are proportionately more expensive to administer. The standard deductible in most states is $250 on the physical damage protection provided in Section I. However, deductible amounts of $500 or $1,000 are available on an optional basis. The premium savings on policies with larger deductibles are often significant. For example, in some states an increase in the deductible from $250 to $500 results in an annual premium savings of about 10 percent, depending on the amount of coverage purchased. Homeowners should check with their insurance agents to see whether it is feasible to increase the deductible. Deductibles do not apply to the liability and medical payments coverage, since insurers want to be notified of all claims, no matter how trivial. If companies did not set this procedure, they could in some cases be notified too late to properly investigate and prepare adequate defenses for resulting lawsuits.

HOMEOWNER'S PREMIUMS

Perhaps it might be useful at this point to bring together the previous comments concerning the premiums on homeowner's insurance policies. Generally speaking, a homeowner's contract form is selected by the insured, and it usually provides physical damage coverage on the dwelling up to at least 80 percent of the cost to rebuild at today's prices. With the amount of coverage on the dwelling set, basic amounts of coverage apply to the other structures on the site, personal property, and loss of use. As you will recall, these other coverages are stated as a percentage of the amount of protection placed on the dwelling unit. As a standard provision, each of these property damage coverages is subject to a $250 deductible. Also included in the homeowner's policy are basic amounts of protection for liability losses ($100,000), medical payments to others ($1,000), and additional coverages, such as damage to property of others ($500). For this basic package of protection, an insurer will quote a premium. As Exhibit 10.3 shows, basic rates vary considerably based on insurer and location of the property.

As we have discussed, most people need to modify this basic package of coverages. Some will want to add an inflation rider and increase the coverage on their homes to 100 percent of the replacement cost. Also, changing the contents protection from actual cash value to replacement cost and scheduling some items of expensive personal property may be desirable. Most insurance professionals also advise homeowners to increase their liability and medical payments limits. Each of these changes will result in an additional premium charge.

At the same time, you may want to try to *reduce* your total premium by increasing the amount of your deductible, as discussed earlier. Since it is better to budget rather than insure small losses, larger deductibles are becoming more popular. Also, you may qualify for discounts for deadbolt locks, security systems, and other safety features such as smoke alarms and sprinkler systems. In sum, recognize that although the homeowner's policy is good protection for some people, most homeowners (and tenants) will need to modify the basic coverages offered. Thus, when you compare premiums among insurers, make sure the premiums quoted reflect the same additions to and subtractions from the standard coverages, limits, and deductible.

Concept Check

10-5. What are the perils against which most properties are insured under various types of homeowner's policies?

10-6. What types of property are covered under a homeowner's policy? When should you consider adding a *personal property floater (PPF)* to your policy? Are the following included in the coverage: (a) an African parrot, (b) a motorbike, (c) Avon cosmetics held for sale, and (d) Tupperware for home use?

10-7. Describe (a) types of losses, (b) persons, (c) locations, and (d) periods that are covered under a homeowner's policy.

10-8. Describe *replacement cost* coverage and compare this coverage to actual *cash value*. Which is preferable?

10-9. What are deductibles? Do they apply to either liability or medical payments coverage under the homeowner's policy?

AUTOMOBILE INSURANCE

LG4

Probably no asset involves more exposure to loss than the automobile. Stop for a moment to consider why it's so important to have adequate insurance coverage on your car. What are some of the different types of exposure to loss you face when you get behind the wheel of a car?

Another asset that provides major exposure to loss is the automobile. Damage to this asset as well as negligence in its use can result in significant losses. Each year U.S. motor vehicle accidents account for over 40,000 deaths, millions of disabling injuries, and economic loss of $90 billion or more. In addition, indirect monetary losses to society result from police and legal costs, as well as from the lost productive capacity of capital and human resources. Fortunately, from the standpoint of the individual, a big part of these costs can be protected against through insurance.

The major features of automobile insurance are discussed in the next several sections of this chapter. In the first of these sections, the coverages of a typical private passenger automobile policy are discussed. However, a number of states have legislatively provided for the modification of automobile insurance coverages through no-fault insurance. Therefore, following the section on the automobile policy is an explanation of how no-fault laws typically affect reimbursement for losses caused by automobile accidents. Next, auto insurance premiums and financial responsibility laws are discussed.

INSURANCE COVERAGE

The **personal auto policy (PAP)** is an easy-to-understand policy made up of six parts; the first four identify the coverages provided in the policy and are as follows:

- Part A: Liability coverage
- Part B: Medical payments coverage
- Part C: Uninsured motorists coverage
- Part D: Coverage for damage to your vehicle

You are almost sure to purchase liability, medical payments, and uninsured motorists protection. You may, however, choose *not* to buy protection against damage to your automobile if it is "worn" and of relatively little value. On the other hand, if you have a loan against your car, you will probably be *required* to have physical damage coverage—part D—at least equal to the amount of the loan. Let's now take a closer look at the coverage provided by parts A through D.

Part A: Liability Coverage. Most states require that you buy at least a minimum amount of liability insurance. As part of the liability provisions of PAP, the insurer agrees to (1) pay damages for bodily injury and property damage for which you become legally obligated due to an automobile accident, and (2) settle or defend any claim or suit asking for such damages. This provision for legal defense is quite important. It can mean a savings of thousands of dollars, since even a person who is not at fault in an automobile accident may be compelled to prove his or her innocence in court. Note, though, that the coverage is for a defense in civil cases only. It provides no defense against any criminal charges that may be brought against the insured as a result of an accident (such as a drunk driver who's involved in an accident).

In addition to providing reimbursement for bodily and property damages, the automobile liability portion of your insurance policy stipulates that certain supplemental payments may be made. Examples of supplemental payments include expenses incurred by the insurance company in settling the claim, and other reasonable expenses incurred by the insured at the request of the insurance company (for instance, food and travel expenses). Supplemental payments can also take the form of reimbursement for premiums spent on appeal bonds, bonds to release attachments of the insured's property, and bail bonds required of an insured as a result of an accident. The amount of these supplemental payments is not restricted by the applicable policy limits. In other words, the insurance company does not reduce your policy limits by the amount that it costs to protect you in these ways.

Policy limits. Although the insurance company provides both bodily injury and property damage liability insurance under part A, *there is likely to be a single dollar limit up to which it will pay for damages from any one accident.* Typical limits are $50,000, $100,000, $300,000, and $500,000. You'd probably be well advised to consider nothing less than $300,000 in such coverage in today's legal liability environment. Damage awards are increasing, and the PAP policy provides that the insurer's duty to defend you *ends when the coverage limit has been exhausted*; unfortunately, today it is very easy to "exhaust" $50,000 or $100,000. This means that *you* must bear any additional costs above the policy limit. So be sure to purchase adequate coverage—*regardless of the minimum requirements in your state.* Otherwise, you place your assets at risk.

Some insurers make so-called *split limits* of liability coverage available. For example, policy limits to protect individuals against claims made for **bodily injury liability losses** may be available in the following combinations: $10,000/$20,000; $25,000/$50,000; $50,000/$100,000; $100,000/$300,000; and $500,000/$1,000,000. The first amount in each combination is a limit per individual and the second a limit per accident. Thus, if you purchased the $50,000/$100,000 policy limits, the maximum amount *any one person* negligently injured in an accident could receive from the insurance company would be $50,000. Further, the total amount that the insurer would pay to *all injured victims* in one accident would not exceed $100,000. If a jury awarded a claimant $80,000, the defendant whose insurance policy limits were $50,000/$100,000 could be required to pay $30,000 out of his or her pocket ($80,000 award—$50,000 paid by insurance). For the defendant, this could mean loss of home, cars, bank accounts, and other assets. In many states, if the value of these assets is too little to satisfy a claim, the defendant's wages may be garnished (taken by the court and used to satisfy the outstanding debt).

The policy limits available to cover **property damage liability losses** are typically $10,000,

personal auto policy (PAP) A comprehensive automobile insurance policy developed in the 1970s to be easily understood by the "typical" insurance purchaser.

bodily injury liability losses A clause in a PAP that protects individuals against losses from bodily injury; may specify coverage as a combination of per-individual and per-accident limits.

property damage liability losses A provision in a PAP that covers damage to property on a per-accident basis.

$25,000, and $50,000. In contrast to bodily injury liability insurance limits, property damage policy limits are stated as a per-accident limit without specifying any limits applicable on a per-item or person basis.

Persons insured. There are two basic sets of definitions in the PAP that determines who is covered under the liability coverage: insured person and covered auto. Essentially, an *insured person* includes you (the named insured) and any family member, any person using a covered auto, and any person or organization that may be held responsible for your actions. The *named insured* is the person named in the declarations page of the policy. The spouse of the person named is considered to be a named insured if he or she resides in the same household. Family members are persons related by blood, marriage, or adoption who are residing in the same household. An unmarried college student living away from home usually would be considered a family member.

The named insured and family members have part A liability coverage regardless of the automobile they are driving. To have the liability coverage, however, other persons must be driving a covered auto and there must be reasonable belief that they are entitled to do so. *Covered autos* are the vehicles shown in the declarations page of your PAP, autos acquired during the policy period, any trailer owned, and any auto or trailer used as a temporary substitute while your auto or trailer is being repaired or serviced. An automobile that you lease for an extended time period can be included as a covered automobile.

When a motorist who is involved in an automobile accident is covered under two or more liability insurance contracts, the coverage *on the automobile* is primary and the other coverages secondary. For example, if Dan Slegal, a named insured in his own right, were involved in an accident while driving Deeann Bauer's automobile (with permission), a claim settlement in excess of the limits of Deeann's liability policy would be necessary before Dan's liability insurance would apply. If Deeann's insurance had lapsed, Dan's policy would then offer primary protection (but it would apply to Dan only and not Deeann).

Part B: Medical Payments Coverage. *Medical payments coverage* provides for payment to a covered person of an amount no greater than the policy limits for all reasonable and necessary medical expenses incurred within three years of an automobile accident. It provides for reimbursement even if other sources of recovery, such as health or accident insurance, also make payments. In addition, in most states the insurer reimburses the insured for medical payments even if the insured proves that another person was negligent in the accident and receives compensation from that party's liability insurer.

As with liability and uninsured motorists insurance, a person need not be occupying an automobile when the accidental injury occurs in order to be eligible for benefits. Injuries sustained as a pedestrian or on a bicycle in a traffic accident are covered, too. (Motorcycle accidents normally are not covered.) This insurance also pays on an excess basis. For instance, if you are a passenger in a friend's automobile during an accident and suffer $8,000 in medical expenses, you can collect under your friend's medical payments insurance up to his or her policy limits. Further, you can collect (up to the amount of your policy limits) from your insurer the amount in excess of what the other medical payments provide. Of course, you may also collect from the liability insurance of another person involved in the accident if that person can be shown to have been at fault. In addition, you may also be able to collect from your health insurance policy.

Policy limits. Medical payments insurance usually is available with per-person limits of $1,000, $2,000, $3,000, $5,000 or $10,000. Thus, an insurer conceivably could pay $60,000 or more in medical payments benefits for one accident involving a named insured and five passengers. Most families are advised to buy the $5,000 or $10,000 limit, because even though they may have an ample amount of other health insurance available, they cannot be certain that their passengers are equally well protected. Having automobile medical payments insurance also reduces the probability that a passenger in your auto will sue you and attempt to collect under your liability insurance coverage (in those states that permit it).

Persons insured. Coverage under an automobile medical payments insurance policy applies to the named insured and family members who are injured while occupying an automobile (whether owned by the named insured or not) or while struck by an automobile or trailer of any type. Also, it applies to any other person occupying a covered automobile.

Part C: Uninsured Motorists Coverage. **Uninsured motorists coverage** is available to meet the needs of "innocent" accident victims negligently injured by uninsured or hit-and-run motorists. Legislation requiring that uninsured motorists insurance be included in each liability insurance policy issued has been enacted in nearly all states. The insured is allowed, however, to reject this coverage in most of these states. In many states, a person may also collect if the negligent motorist's insurance company is insolvent. Under uninsured motorists insurance, an insured is legally entitled to collect an amount equal to the sum that could have been collected from the negligent motorist's liability insurance had such coverage been available, up to a maximum amount equal to the *uninsured motorists limit* stated in the policy.

Three points must be proven in order to receive payment through uninsured motorists insurance: (1) another motorist was at fault; (2) this motorist had no available insurance; and (3) damages were incurred. Property damage is not included in this coverage in most states. Therefore, under uninsured motorists coverage, you generally can collect only for losses arising from bodily injury. If the motorist and insurer cannot agree on the terms of the settlement of a claim under uninsured motorists coverage, the motorist can seek an attorney to negotiate the claim. If a mutually agreeable settlement still cannot be worked out, the insured has the right to have the case arbitrated by a neutral third party. In most cases, the accident victim and the insurer are then bound to accept the decision of the arbitrator. In addition to *uninsured* motorists, for a nominal premium you can also obtain protection for *underinsured* motorists—that is, for coverage when you're involved in an accident where the driver at fault has a liability limit much lower than you're entitled to. Under such coverage, your insurance company makes up the difference and then goes after the negligent driver for any deficiency.

Policy limits. Uninsured motorists insurance is available at minimum cost (usually less than $10 per year). It often is sold with basic limits of $10,000 to $20,000, with additional amounts available for a small increase in the premium. At the least, uninsured motorists insurance should be purchased at the minimum available limits. The cost of this coverage is very small compared to the amount of protection it provides.

Persons insured. The named insured, family members, and any other person occupying a covered auto are covered by the uninsured motorists protection.

Part D: Coverage for Physical Damage to a Vehicle. This part of the PAP provides coverage for damage to your auto. There are two basic types of coverage provided: collision and comprehensive (or "other than collision").

Collision insurance. **Collision insurance** is first-party property damage coverage that pays for collision damage to an insured automobile *regardless of fault.* The amount of insurance payable is the actual cash value of the loss in excess of a stated deductible. Remember that actual cash value is defined as replacement cost less depreciation. Therefore, if a car is demolished, an insured will be paid an amount equal to the car's depreciated value minus any deductible.

Lenders often require the purchase of collision insurance on cars they finance. In some cases—especially when the auto dealer is handling the financing—the lender will attempt to sell this insurance. Generally, the purchase of collision insurance, or any other type of automobile insurance, from car dealers or finance companies *should be avoided.* Rather, buy such insurance from your regular insurance agent and include it (collision insurance) as part of your full auto insurance policy (PAP). The fact is, a full-time insurance agent is better trained to properly assess and meet a motorist's insurance needs. Moreover, it is likely that the collision provisions of your insurance policy fully protect you even in a *rental car.* Thus, not only is rental car collision insurance expensive—it may also be unnecessary! Be sure to check your PAP to see what coverage it provides for rental cars.

Individuals who purchase collision insurance may select from one of several *deductibles* available—$50, $100, $250, or even $1,000. Significant premium savings often can be obtained

---

uninsured motorists coverage Automobile insurance that is designed to meet the needs of innocent accident victims who are involved in an accident in which an uninsured or underinsured motorist is at fault.

collision insurance Automobile insurance that pays for collision damage to an insured automobile regardless of who was at fault.

---

by increasing the amount of the deductible. For example, one large automobile insurance company reports that a $50 deductible on a relatively new car can be purchased for an annual premium of $177, whereas the $100 deductible costs $150. Thus, a motorist who buys the $50 deductible is paying $27 for this additional $50 worth of protection.

Comprehensive automobile insurance. **Comprehensive automobile insurance** protects against loss to an insured automobile caused by any peril (with a few exceptions) *other than collision.* As one might imagine this coverage offers broad protection and includes, but is not limited to, damage caused by fire, theft, glass breakage, falling objects, malicious mischief, vandalism, riot, and earthquake. Contrary to popular belief, theft of personal property kept or left in the insured automobile normally is not covered under the automobile insurance policy. (It may, however, be covered under the off-premises coverage of the homeowner's policy if the auto was locked at the time the theft occurred.) The maximum compensation provided under this coverage is the actual cash value of the automobile.

NO-FAULT AUTOMOBILE INSURANCE

The concept of **no-fault automobile insurance** is based on the belief that the current automobile insurance liability system should be replaced by a system that reimburses the parties involved in an accident without regard to negligence. The principle is, "My insurance policy should pay the cost of my injuries, and your insurance policy should pay the cost of yours," regardless of who is at fault in an accident. Under the concept of *pure* no-fault insurance, the driver, passengers, and injured pedestrians are reimbursed by the insurer of the car for economic losses stemming from bodily injury. The insurer thus does not have to provide coverage for claims made for losses caused to other motorists. Each insured party is compensated by his or her own company, regardless of which party caused the accident. In return, legal remedies and payments for pain and suffering are restricted.

Unfortunately, the advocates of no-fault forgot that liability insurance was never intended to serve as the primary system for compensating injured parties. Its sole purpose is to protect the assets of the insured, not to pay losses, per se. This same concept applies to all liability insurance. The coverages of medical payments, collision, and comprehensive insurance discussed earlier do serve this compensation purpose to a certain extent. In addition, families can and should purchase widely available life, health, and disability protection, which will protect them not only for losses resulting from automobile accidents but also for nearly all other types of economic losses resulting from accident or illness. In fact, the numerous cries that no-fault automobile insurance is needed so that people can be compensated for their losses incurred in automobile accidents have probably had more of a harmful effect on overall insurance planning, since they have detracted from public understanding of the need for full life and health insurance programming. After all, there is no reason to be more concerned about the person who is injured in an automobile accident than for the homeowner who sustains injury while repairing his or her house. Nevertheless, because some valid arguments have been put forth by proponents of no-fault insurance, many states have passed laws to modify the coverages offered by the family automobile policy. *No state has yet adopted a pure no-fault insurance plan,* though.

Basically, the various state laws governing no-fault insurance can be differentiated according to whether or not (1) no-fault and liability insurance is compulsory and/or (2) there are any restrictions on lawsuits. The laws of the separate states vary substantially as to both the amount of no-fault benefits provided and the degree to which the restrictions for legal actions apply. Most states provide from $2,000 to $10,000 in first-party benefits (often called *personal injury protection*) and restrict legal recovery for pain and suffering to cases in which medical or economic losses exceed some threshold level, such as $500 or $1,000. In all states, recovery based on negligence is permitted for economic loss in excess of the amount payable by no-fault insurance.

Overall, most of the no-fault laws that have been passed fell short of accomplishing the two objectives fundamental to no-fault insurance—that is, elimination of liability as a basis for recovery, and provision of adequate compensation for all accident victims. Further, the no-fault concept gained its largest public support because its advocates promised that it would contribute to lower insurance premiums. As might be expected, based on the laws now on the books, that has not always been

EXHIBIT 10.4

Comparative Auto Insurance Premiums

Average auto insurance rates vary all over the map. While the national average is about $730 per year, the annual rate in the most expensive state (New Jersey) is more than *twice* the cost for the same coverage in the least expensive state (North Dakota). There is also considerable variation *within* states; urban drivers typically pay more than rural ones. You might want to check the list to see where your state stands in terms of auto insurance costs.

Rank	State	Average Premium	Rank	State	Average Premium
33	Alabama	$ 604.07	42	Montana	$ 551.37
9	Alaska	873.87	48	Nebraska	494.85
16	Arizona	782.68	11	Nevada	853.93
38	Arkansas	565.35	22	New Hampshire	710.77
8	California	892.80	1	New Jersey	1,094.56
13	Colorado	804.17	19	New Mexico	727.43
5	Connecticut	1,002.84	7	New York	985.07
12	Delaware	813.00	45	North Carolina	528.43
6	District of Columbia	1,001.09	51	North Dakota	448.24
18	Florida	753.94	43	Ohio	550.52
25	Georgia	664.85	32	Oklahoma	604.38
2	Hawaii	1,078.32	29	Oregon	632.21
47	Idaho	513.32	20	Pennsylvania	721.50
27	Illinois	649.48	3	Rhode Island	1,034.46
35	Indiana	586.58	24	South Carolina	684.10
50	Iowa	467.45	49	South Dakota	484.96
46	Kansas	526.96	37	Tennessee	574.08
30	Kentucky	616.22	15	Texas	785.78
10	Louisiana	862.62	31	Utah	607.42
40	Maine	556.67	36	Vermont	577.94
17	Maryland	761.57	39	Virginia	564.07
4	Massachusetts	1,009.56	21	Washington	711.57
14	Michigan	788.26	23	West Virginia	696.89
26	Minnesota	656.87	41	Wisconsin	554.10
28	Mississippi	643.74	44	Wyoming	531.91
34	Missouri	600.64		Countrywide	730.39

Source: The National Association of Insurance Commissioners.

achieved. In those states with substantive laws, though, some efficiencies have been gained. Still, because only a few states have required first-party benefits of substantial size, most seriously injured accident victims will continue to turn to the liability system or their own life and health insurance coverages for large amounts of compensation.

AUTOMOBILE INSURANCE PREMIUMS

What you pay for car insurance depends on many things, including where you live, what kind of car you drive, what kind of coverage you have, the amount of your deductibles, and so forth. One thing is sure, the size of the typical car insurance premium is anything but uniform. The fact is, average auto insurance premiums—for basically the same coverage—vary all over the map, as shown in Exhibit 10.4. If you're fortunate enough to live in one of the low-premium states (say one of the bottom 20), you're probably *relatively* satisfied with the cost of your car insurance; on the other hand, if you're in one of the more expensive states (like New Jersey, California, Arkansas, or Pennsylvania), you may well be feeling the pinch of these high and, in many cases, rapidly increasing auto insurance rates. Indeed, residents in many of the high-premium states have begun to rally against these rates and are demanding—through their state legislators and/or the ballot box—a return to what they see as more reasonable premiums. This matter is highly emotional, because it hits the pocketbooks of so many

comprehensive automobile insurance Coverage that provides protection against loss to an insured automobile caused by any peril other than collision.

no-fault automobile insurance A concept of automobile insurance that favors reimbursement without regard to negligence.

consumers, and is likely to be with us for some time to come. In effect, you have the insurance companies on one side arguing why the rates are necessary and justified, and on the other, you have the consumers arguing that the rates are too high and going up too fast.

FACTORS AFFECTING PREMIUMS

With this perspective in mind, let's look now at how auto insurance premiums are set. Among the factors that influence automobile insurance rates are (1) rating territory, (2) the amount of use the automobile receives, (3) the personal characteristics of the drivers, (4) the type of automobile, and (5) the insured's driving record.

- ***Rating territory.*** The starting point for determining rates; because more accidents occur in some geographic areas than others, rates are higher where claims filed and average costs of resulting claims paid are highest, reflecting auto repair costs, hospital and medical expenses, jury awards, thefts, and vandalism in the locale. Even someone with a perfect driving record will be charged the rates in effect for the area where the automobile is principally garaged. Accordingly, Herbert Dennenburg, former insurance commissioner of Pennsylvania, stated that he had found a magic formula for reducing auto insurance premiums: "I moved from Philadelphia [a high-rate area] to Harrisburg [a low-rate area]." (Note that several jurisdictions prohibit the use of rating territories, age, and/or sex factors. The belief has been that these factors unfairly discriminate against the urban, the young, and the male.)
- ***Use of the automobile.*** Rates are lower for an insured automobile that is not customarily driven to work or driven fewer than 3 miles one way to work. If you drive more than 3 but fewer than 15 miles to work, you'll pay a slightly higher premium; the rate rises further if you drive more than 15 miles each way to work. Most insurers also look at total annual miles driven; obviously, the more miles you drive in a year, the more you can expect to pay in auto insurance premiums.
- ***Personal characteristics of drivers.*** Such things as the age, sex, and marital status of the insured affect automobile insurance premiums. Young drivers—generally, unmarried females age 24 or under and unmarried males age 29 or under—are placed in higher-rate categories than older individuals. Married males under age 25 also fall into a relatively high-rate category. Females over 24 and married females of any age are exempt from the youthful operator classification and pay lower premiums. Insurance companies base the premium differentials on the number of accidents involving these age groups. For example, drivers aged 20 to 24 make up only about 10 percent of the total driving population but are involved in nearly 20 percent of the auto accidents.
- ***Type of automobile.*** Automobiles may be classified as standard performance, intermediate performance, high performance, sports, and rear engine. Some states even rate four-door cars differently than two-door models. An automobile not classified as standard performance usually gets charged higher rates. Thus, if you are thinking of buying, say, a Corvette or a Nissan 300ZX, you'd better be prepared to handle some pretty hefty insurance rates.
- ***Driving record.*** The driving records—traffic violations and traffic accidents—of the insured and those who live with them affect premium levels. The more severe types of traffic convictions are for driving under the influence of alcohol or drugs (DUI), leaving the scene of an accident, homicide or assault arising out of the operation of a motor vehicle, and driving with a revoked or suspended driver's license, all of which, of course, will result in higher insurance premiums. In addition—on a less severe basis—any conviction for a traffic violation that results in the accumulation of points under a state point system may result in a *premium surcharge.* Included in this category are such moving violations as speeding, running a red light, failure to yield the right of way, and illegal passing, but not parking violations, improper registration, lack of an operator's license, or lack of a valid safety sticker. In most states, accidents that are determined to be the fault of the insured also incur points and a premium surcharge. In many states, a driver with lots of traffic violations is placed in an **automobile insurance plan** (formerly called an *assigned-risk plan*) that provides automobile insurance for those refused regular coverage. The automobile insurance plan generally offers less coverage for higher premiums. Even with the high premiums, however, insurers lost $2.3 billion on this type of business in a recent five-year period.

EXHIBIT 10.5

Types of Discounts Offered by Ten Leading Auto Insurers

Listed here are ten of the most common types of discounts offered by some of the leading auto insurers in the country. While most of these discounts apply to the total cost of the insurance, some apply to only a certain portion of the coverage (for example, the antitheft discount applies only to the cost of the comprehensive portion of the policy).

Type of Discount	No. of Companies Offering the Discount	Savings Offered
Driver's training	All 10	Range 5–40%; most commonly 10%; not available in all states
Good student	9 of the 10	Range 5–30%; commonly 25%
Student away at school	All 10	Some companies put policyholders in a lower-price bracket; others offer discounts, usually 10–40%
Carpool	All 10	Some companies put policyowners in a lower-price bracket; others offer discounts of 5–25%
Multicar	All 10	Range 10–25%; usually about 15%
Passive restraints	All 10	Range 5–60%; full front airbag discounts range from 40–60%
Antitheft devices	All 10	Range 5–20%; state laws in MI, RI, IL, MA, NY and KY mandate such discounts; however, some companies offer these discounts in other states, too
Mature driver	All 10	Range 5–20%; discounts may start at age 50; driving habits, employment, and retirement affect discount; some companies put policyholder into lower class
Farmer	7 of the 10	Range 10–30%; most commonly 10%; some companies put policyholder into a lower-price bracket
Defensive-driving course	All 10	Range 5–15%; not available in all states; some state laws mandate such a discount

Source: Adapted from George E. Rejda, *Principles of Insurance,* 4th ed. (New York: HarperCollins, 1992), p. 251.

DRIVING DOWN THE COST OF CAR INSURANCE

One of the best ways to reduce the cost of car insurance is to take advantage of the variety of discounts most auto insurers today offer. Taken together, such discounts can knock 5 to 50 percent off your annual premium. A summary of some of the discounts given by top auto insurance companies is provided in Exhibit 10.5. Some give overall *safe-driving* discounts, and most give youthful operators lower rates if they have had *driver's training*—some states, in fact, have laws that require insurers to offer lower premiums to *any driver*, young or old, who has taken driver's training. Youthful drivers may also receive *good student* discounts for maintaining a B average or by being on the dean's list at their school. Such student discounts, by the way, apply to both high school and college students. Nearly all insurance companies provide discounts to families with two or more automobiles, if each car is insured by the same company. Most insurers also offer discounts to owners who install *airbags* or *antitheft devices* in their cars. Likewise, *nonsmoker and nondrinker* discounts are offered by a number of insurers. There are even some companies that specialize in insuring certain portions of the population. For example, certain insurers accept only persons who are educators or executives and others only government employees. While not offering discounts in the normal sense, these companies frequently do have lower premiums because, through more selective underwriting, they are able to reduce losses and operating expenses.

Clearly, it's to your advantage to look for and use as many of these discounts as you can. Another very effective way to drive down the cost of car insurance is to *raise your deductibles* (as discussed earlier in this chapter). This often overlooked tactic can have a dramatic effect on the amount of insurance premium you pay. For example, the difference between a $100 deductible and a $500

automobile insurance plan An arrangement that provides automobile insurance to drivers who have been refused coverage under normal procedures; formerly called an *assigned-risk plan.*

EXHIBIT 10.6

Financial Responsibility Requirements by State

Most states have financial responsibility laws that require motorists involved in auto accidents to furnish proof of financial accountability up to certain minimum dollar amounts; as seen here, those financial liability limits vary by state.

State	Liability Limits[a]	State	Liability Limits[a]
Alabama	20/40/10	Montana	25/50/5
Alaska	50/100/25	Nebraska	25/50/25
Arizona	15/30/10	Nevada	15/30/10
Arkansas	25/50/15	New Hampshire	25/50/25
California	15/30/5	New Jersey	15/30/5
Colorado	25/50/15	New Mexico	25/50/10
Connecticut	20/40/10	New York	10/20/5[b]
Delaware	15/30/10	North Carolina	25/50/10
District of Columbia	25/50/10	North Dakota	25/50/25
Florida	10/20/10	Ohio	12.5/25/7.5
Georgia	15/30/10	Oklahoma	10/20/10
Hawaii	15/35/10	Oregon	25/50/10
Idaho	25/50/15	Pennsylvania	15/30/5
Illinois	20/40/15	Rhode Island	25/50/25
Indiana	25/50/10	South Carolina	15/30/5
Iowa	20/40/15	South Dakota	25/50/25
Kansas	25/50/10	Tennessee	20/50/10
Kentucky	25/50/10	Texas	20/40/15
Louisiana	10/20/10	Utah	20/50/15
Maine	20/40/10	Vermont	20/40/10
Maryland	20/40/10	Virginia	25/50/20
Massachusetts	15/30/5	Washington	25/50/10
Michigan	20/40/10	West Virginia	20/40/10
Minnesota	30/60/10	Wisconsin	25/50/10
Mississippi	10/20/5	Wyoming	25/50/20
Missouri	25/50/10		

[a]The first two figures refer to bodily injury liability limits and the third figure to property damage liability. For example, 10/20/5 means coverage up to $20,000 for all persons injured in an accident, subject to a limit of $10,000 for one individual, and $5,000 coverage for property damage.

[b]50/100 for wrongful death

Source: George E. Rejda, *Principles of Insurance,* 5th ed. (New York: HarperCollins, 1995), p. 211.

deductible may be as much as 30 percent on comprehensive coverage and 25 percent on collision insurance; request a $1,000 deductible and you may save as much as 45 to 50 percent on both comprehensive and collision insurance.

FINANCIAL RESPONSIBILITY LAWS

The annual losses from automobile accidents in the United States run into billions of dollars. For this reason, **financial responsibility laws** have been enacted in most states, whereby motorists are *required* to buy a minimum amount of automobile liability insurance. As the name implies, financial responsibility laws attempt to force motorists to be financially responsible for the damages they cause as a result of automobile accidents. A summary of the financial responsibility requirements in each of the 50 states and the District of Columbia is given in Exhibit 10.6.

Two basic types of laws compel motorists to assume financial responsibility. The first is one in which all automobile owners in a given state are required to show evidence that they have liability insurance coverage prior to obtaining registration for their motor vehicles. Until 1971 only three states had these compulsory liability insurance requirements. Today, more than 41 states have compulsory auto insurance laws whereby motorists are required to show evidence of insurance coverage *before* they can receive their license plates. Penalties for not having liability insurance include fines and suspension of their driver's license.

Under the second type of financial responsibility legislation, motorists do not have to show evidence of their insurance coverage until after they are involved in an accident. If they then fail to demonstrate compliance with the law, their registrations and/or driver's licenses are suspended. This law has been criticized on the grounds that it allows negligent motorists to have one "free" accident. Even though the motorists who are not financially responsible lose their driving privileges, the losses to their victims may remain uncompensated.

Concept Check

10-10. Briefly explain the major coverages available under the *personal auto policy (PAP)*. Which persons are insured under (a) *uninsured motorists coverage* and (b) automobile medical payments insurance?

10-11. Explain the nature of (a) automobile *collision insurance* and (b) automobile *comprehensive insurance*.

10-12. Define *no-fault auto insurance* and discuss its pros and cons.

10-13. Describe the important factors that influence the availability and cost of auto insurance.

10-14. Discuss the role of *financial responsibility laws* and describe the two basic types of laws currently employed.

OTHER PROPERTY AND LIABILITY INSURANCE

LG5

Besides homeowner's and automobile insurance, there are several other types of property insurance policies that you should be aware of. For example, you can increase your personal liability coverage with a personal liability umbrella policy, you can insure certain types of recreational vehicles, and you can even get repair insurance when you buy a car. Do you think there'll ever be a time when you'll find it necessary to use such policies? Take a minute to think about this question before reading on.

While homeowner's and automobile insurance policies represent the basic protection needed by most families, there are still other insurance contracts that some people may find appropriate. Among those discussed here are the umbrella personal liability policy, earthquake insurance, flood insurance, mobile-home insurance, boat insurance, recreational vehicle insurance, professional liability insurance, and group legal plans.

EARTHQUAKE INSURANCE

Although most people think of California when earthquakes are mentioned, areas in other states are also subject to this type of loss. At the present time, very few homeowners buy this coverage even though the premiums are relatively inexpensive. Surprisingly, a great number of Californians were without earthquake coverage when the major San Francisco quake occurred in 1989.

FLOOD INSURANCE

Before 1969, floods were regarded by most private insurers as an uninsurable peril because the risk could not be spread among enough people who were not located in flood-prone areas. But in 1969, the federal government established a subsidized flood insurance program in cooperation with private insurance agents, who can now sell this low-cost coverage to homeowners and tenants *living in communities that have been designated as part of the federal flood program*. In addition, the flood insurance program is encouraging communities to initiate land-use controls in order to reduce future flood losses.

UMBRELLA PERSONAL LIABILITY POLICY

Persons with moderate to high levels of income and net worth may find the **umbrella personal liability policy** useful. It provides added liability coverage for both homeowner's and automobile insurance as well as coverage in some areas not provided for in either of these policies. These

financial responsibility laws Laws that attempt to force motorists to be financially responsible for the damages they become legally obligated to pay as a result of automobile accidents.

umbrella personal liability policy An insurance policy that provides excess liability coverage for both homeowner's and automobile insurance as well as coverage in some areas not provided for in either of those policies.

policies are often sold with limits of $1 million or more. In addition, some provide added amounts of coverage for a family's major medical insurance.

Because middle- and upper-income individuals are often viewed as viable targets for liability claims, umbrella protection can provide a desirable, added layer of coverage. In addition, the premiums are usually quite reasonable for the broad coverage afforded ($100 to $300 a year for as much as $1 million in coverage). While the protection is written on a comprehensive basis, it does contain a number of exclusions of which purchasers should be aware. As a rule, in order to purchase a personal liability umbrella policy, the insured party must already have relatively high liability limits on their auto and homeowner's coverage; that is, generally speaking, insurance companies require the insured to have, say, $100,000 in liability limits on their auto and homeowner's policies *before* they'll even consider selling an umbrella policy to that party.

Do you need the extra protection an umbrella liability policy provides? Clearly, the answer is yes if you have sizable assets that could be used to pay a judgment against you and for which your homeowner's and automobile policies don't cover the value. But you may also need this coverage if you rent your home or have house sitters or unbonded hired help such as gardeners or babysitters, because you're responsible for any injuries they incur or may cause, or if you work from home and clients visit you at your home office.

OTHER FORMS OF TRANSPORTATION INSURANCE

In addition to automobile insurance, there are other types of vehicles you may wish to insure, such as mobile homes and recreational vehicles. You may also have a boat that requires a separate policy.

- ***Mobile home insurance.*** Several million mobile homes now serve as homes for young couples, transients (those whose jobs require that they constantly be on the move from one place to another), and retirees. Special insurance policies for mobile-home owners offer protection on a blanket basis against the same perils covered on an HO-2 form, plus personal property and personal liability coverage. Rates are typically higher for mobile homes because they present a greater exposure to wind and fire loss. Total losses on mobile homes occur much more frequently than they do for either wood or brick houses.
- ***Recreational vehicle insurance.*** Recreational vehicles may include all-terrain vehicles, antique automobiles, dune buggies, go-carts, minibikes, trail motorcycles, camping vehicles (both motorized and trailer type), snowmobiles, and customized vans. Complete coverage generally is available for these vehicles, including bodily injury and property damage liability, medical payments, physical damage, and theft. You may have to shop around for the policy that best fits your needs, since not all insurance companies write recreational vehicle coverage, more restrictions are likely to apply, and rates will vary substantially depending on driver's age, vehicle use, and policy owner's location. You should discuss with a property insurance agent how best to insure your recreational vehicle, giving particular attention to who and what are covered, as well as where and when coverage applies.

  Many types of recreational vehicles—including motorcycles and mopeds—can be insured under the personal auto policy through a Miscellaneous Type Vehicle Endorsement that provides the same protection for their recreational vehicles as for their private passenger automobiles.
- ***Boat insurance.*** Most people underinsure their boats, partly because homeowner's policies offer limited protection for boat owners. However, a homeowner's policy typically covers only boats less than 26 feet in length (or some other stipulated maximum) or those with motors under 25 horsepower, limits physical damage coverage to only a few perils, and, in most cases, caps reimbursement at $1,000. To get proper coverage, you need to add liability, physical damage and theft, and medical payments coverage through either a boat and motor endorsement on the homeowner's policy or a specially designed boat-owner's policy. The physical damage and theft coverage under boat policies can be either limited or comprehensive. Because physical damage and theft provisions of boat policies are not standardized, you should not assume that coverage exists for any given type of loss. Make certain that your insurance agent explains which coverage applies and which losses are not covered.

PROFESSIONAL LIABILITY INSURANCE

Malpractice suits against those in the medical profession have increased substantially in recent years—in fact, liability claims against nearly all types of professionals, including lawyers, architects, financial planners, and engineers, are also rising rapidly. Even worse, this lawsuit mentality is beginning to spread to nonprofessionals as well—for example, sales representatives and agents are increasingly being sued for alleged acts of "errors and omissions." While certain professions and lines of work are more susceptible to malpractice suits than others, each year it seems a wider and wider segment of the work force is becoming exposed to the threat of these suits. Thus, the need for professional liability insurance is rapidly increasing, but the cost of such coverage is simply going out of sight! The courts and juries are giving enormous awards, which in turn simply drives the insurance rates even higher. Thus, professional liability insurance is available, but because of the increasing number of claims, rates are skyrocketing, while stricter underwriting standards are being imposed by insurers.

GROUP PLANS

As a benefit to members of some groups (labor unions, credit unions, fraternal organizations, and various other organizations), group property and liability plans are being introduced. Unlike life and health insurance agreements, these plans are not true group plans because they do not issue a single master policy to the group. Instead, they are arrangements for mass marketing of homeowner's and automobile policies, and the policies are individually sold and issued. The primary benefit of group plans is that the lower marketing expense of the insurance company is passed along to the group members in the form of reduced premiums.

Some groups also have **group legal insurance.** These plans are fee-for-services agreements into which the group enters with a given law firm on behalf of its members. The plans typically cover only basic legal matters such as divorce, writing of wills, small claims settlement, and landlord-tenant problems. In some cases, the group member is entitled to lower charges on other legal services provided by the participating firm.

Concept Check

10-15. Briefly describe the following property and liability insurance coverages: (a) *umbrella personal liability policies,* (b) mobile-home insurance, (c) boat insurance, (d) earthquake insurance, and (e) flood insurance.

10-16. Briefly describe group property and liability insurance plans; how do they differ from group life and health insurance plans?

BUYING INSURANCE AND SETTLING CLAIMS

LG6

Buying property and liability insurance requires a decision on what kinds of protection you need. What factors would you consider in making this decision? How about when it comes to filing a claim with an insurance company—do you know what's involved in such a process and how to go about filing a claim? Take some time to think about these questions before going on.

When preparing to buy property and liability insurance, you should first develop an inventory of exposures to loss and arrange them from highest to lowest priority. Losses that lend themselves to insurance protection are those that seldom occur but have the potential for being substantial—for example, damage to a home and its contents or liability arising out of a negligence claim. Less important, but nevertheless desirable, is insurance to cover losses that could be disruptive to the financial plans of a family even though they would not result in insolvency. Such risks include physical damage to automobiles, boats, and other personal property

group legal insurance A type of insurance plan consisting of a fee-for-service agreement between a group and a law firm; typically covers only such basic legal matters as divorce, wills, and small claims settlement.

of moderate value. Lowest priority should be given to insuring exposures that can easily be covered by savings or from current income. *Low-dollar deductibles, for instance, usually serve only to increase premiums.* Likewise, personal property of minor value, such as an old auto (one that is not a collectible), normally does not merit coverage. In addition to inventorying exposures and deciding on appropriate coverage and deductibles, you should exercise care in selecting both the property insurance agent and the insurer. Also, a knowledge of the procedures involved in settling property and liability claims can help you obtain maximum benefits from policies when claims do arise.

PROPERTY AND LIABILITY INSURANCE AGENTS

Most property insurance agents can be classified as either captive or independent. A **captive agent** is one who represents only one insurance company and is more or less an employee of that company. Allstate, Nationwide, and State Farm are major insurance companies that market through captive agents. **Independent agents,** in contrast, typically represent between two and ten different insurance companies. These agents may place your coverage with any of the companies with which they have an agency relationship as long as you meet the underwriting standards of that company. Names of companies that may be familiar to you that operate through independent agents include Aetna, Hartford, and Travelers. It is difficult to generalize with respect to the superiority of agents. In some cases an independent agent will provide the best combination of low-cost insurance and good service, while in others the captive agent might be the better choice. Because of wide differences in premiums charged and services rendered, it usually does pay to shop around.

Property insurance agents should be willing to take the time to go over your total property and liability insurance exposures. As you should know by now, there is much more to the purchase of property insurance than simply signing a homeowner's and an automobile insurance application. Decisions must be made about types of property and uses, perils to be covered, limits, deductibles, and floater policies, as well as other items that have been discussed throughout this chapter. An agent should be willing to talk with clients about these items. In the property insurance industry, agents who meet various experiential and educational requirements, including passing a series of written examinations, qualify for the **Chartered Property and Casualty Underwriter (CPCU)** designation. Agents who have been awarded CPCUs have proven knowledge and experience in their field.

You may also want to investigate companies that sell directly to the consumer, through an 800 number. Generally, their premiums are lower. Examples of direct sellers are Amica, American Express, and USAA.

PROPERTY AND LIABILITY INSURANCE COMPANIES

Although the selection of an agent is probably the most important step in the purchase of property and liability insurance, you should also ask some questions about the company, including its financial soundness, claims-settlement practices, and the geographic extent of its operations (this could be important if you are involved in an accident 1,000 miles from home). As with any form of insurance, you should check the company's ratings (see Chapter 8) and stick with those rated in the top categories, such as those listed in Exhibit 10.7. The agent should be a good source of information about the technical aspects of a company's operations, whereas friends and acquaintances often can provide insight into its claims-settlement policy.

SETTLING PROPERTY AND LIABILITY CLAIMS

Generally speaking, insurance companies settle claims promptly and fairly, especially for life and health insurance coverages. In settling property and liability claims, though, some chance for claimant-insurer disagreement does exist. The following discussion reviews the claims-settlement process and the people who participate in it. First, however, let's consider what you should do immediately following an accident.

First Steps Following an Accident. After an accident, the names and addresses of all witnesses, drivers, occupants, and injured parties, along with the license numbers of the automobiles involved, should be recorded. Law enforcement officers as well as your insurance agent should be immediately notified of the accident. You should never admit liability at the scene of an accident or discuss it with anyone other than the police and your insurer.

EXHIBIT 10.7

Top-Rated Property and Casualty Insurers

These property and casualty insurers are among those receiving the top grade from at least two leading rating agencies in 1994.

Company	Assigned Rating		
	Best	**Standard & Poors**	**Moody's**
American Home Assurance	A++	—	Aaa
Employers Reinsurance	A++	AAA	—
Federal Insurance	A++	—	Aaa
General Reinsurance	A++	AAA	—
Government Employees Insurance Co. (GEICO)	A++	AAA	Aa1
National Union Fire Insurance	A++	—	Aaa
Safeco Insurance	A++	AAA	Aa1
United Services Automobile Insurance	A++	AAA	Aaa
USAA Casualty Insurance	A++	AAA	—

Source: "Ranking the 50 Largest Property and Casualty Insurers," *Financial World*, September 13, 1994, pp. 54–55.

Remember: Prior to the determination of who, if anyone, is legally liable for an accident, the requisites of liability must be established. Also, the duties of the police are to assess the probability of a law violation and maintain order at the scene of an accident—not to make judgments with respect to liability.

Steps in Claims Settlement. If you're involved in an accident, one of the first things you're going to have to decide is whether or not you even want to file a claim. Check the *Issues in Money Management* box on page 424 for advice on this matter.

Should you opt to file a claim, it'll probably involve the following steps. First, you must *give notice* to the company that a loss (or potential for loss) has occurred. Timely notice is extremely important because it leads to the second step, which is the *investigation of the claim.* To properly investigate a claim, insurance company personnel may have to talk to witnesses or law enforcement officers, gather physical evidence to determine whether the claimed loss is covered by the policy, and check to make sure that the date of the loss falls within the policy period. If you delay filing your claim, you hinder the insurer's ability to check the facts. *All policies specify the time period within which you must give notice.* Failure to report can result in your loss of the right to collect.

Third, you must *prove your loss.* This step usually requires you to give a sworn statement. When applicable, you must also show medical bills, an inventory and certified value of lost property (for example, a written inventory, photographs, and purchase receipts), an employer statement of lost wages, and, if possible, physical evidence of damage (X rays if you claim a back injury, a broken window or pried door if you claim a break-in and theft at your house). After you have submitted proof of loss, the insurer either (1) pays you the amount you asked for; (2) offers you a lesser amount; or (3) denies that the company has any legal responsibility under the terms of your policy. In the case of a disputed amount—when you are a named insured or covered family member—most policies provide for some form of claims arbitration. You hire a third party, the company hires a third party, and these two arbitrators together select one more person. When any two of the three arbitrators reach agreement, their decision binds you and the company to their solution.

When a company denies responsibility, you do not get the right of arbitration. In such an instance,

captive agent An insurance agent who represents only the company that employs him or her.

independent agent An insurance agent who may place coverage with any company with which he or she has an agency relationship as long as the insured meets that company's underwriting standards.

Chartered Property and Casualty Underwriter (CPCU) An agent who has met various experiential and educational requirements and passed a series of written examinations in the fields of property and liability insurance.

Issues in Money Management

To File, or Not to File—That Is the Question

Last winter, Gene Robbins was driving just 15 miles per hour, hit an ice patch, and skidded into a tree. His insurer paid the bill: $650 minus a $200 deductible. A few months later, the insurer paid $800 net when Gene's teenage son backed the same car into a neighbor's empty parked car, denting the door. Then Gene received his new insurance bill—with a 30 percent hike in premiums. That increase was a blow, especially since Gene already paid a bundle with a teenage driver in the house. Would he have been better off paying for the repairs himself and not making the claims? The answer is not as simple as it seems.

Too many claims in too short a time or for too much money can boost your premiums and jeopardize your coverage. But not filing might risk serious financial liability later. *Most experts advise that you not take any chances where there's potential liability for serious damage to someone else's property or any damage to a person.* But what about the gray areas, such as Gene experienced? He wasn't driving recklessly when he skidded, no one was in the car Gene's son hit, and repair costs were moderate. What's your best move in a similar situation?

Most insurers base increases on "chargeable" accidents, though definitions vary among companies and states. State Farm, for example, considers an accident chargeable when the company pays at least $400 to $600, depending on locale. Exceptions include when your legally parked car is hit, or the other driver gets a moving violation and you don't. All insurers get nervous when you file more than one claim in a short period—two claims in three years, or three in five, for example. Some companies raise rates according to simple formulas; for example, an extra 10 percent on your premium for your first accident with a chargeable claim, an additional 20 percent for a second chargeable claim within three years, up to 50 percent more for a third claim. Other companies forgive a first accident if you've been a customer for several years, but premiums could take a big leap—at least 40 percent, and as much as 100 percent—for a second incident within some specified period.

Companies typically won't cancel insurance policies because of accidents, as long as you pay the higher premiums. Even if you are among the few who are cut, someone will insure you, presuming you have a driver's license—but your claim record could get you turned down at a new company or at least cost higher rates. Ultimately, you may have to go to the automobile insurance plan or other high-risk pool, often at double the regular cost.

You should consult your agent to learn how your present insurer defines chargeable accidents and how much rates will rise under given circumstances. Ask how long rate hikes stay in force and what happens if the company finds you have avoided making claims (some insurers will cancel). If you don't like your insurer's rules, shop around with the same questions in hand to find a better deal. Also find out whether your agent is willing after an accident to help you figure whether filing a claim or paying the bill yourself will cost less.

Insurers stress that today's minor accident may turn into next year's personal injury lawsuit. If you don't file a timely claim, they say, you may jeopardize your coverage. Still, it can be tempting to settle on your own and not file under certain circumstances. If so:

- *Always report to your agent any accident involving another person or someone else's property.* Hopefully, the agent will help you decide the smart course to take.
- *Try to get a formal release (drawn up by an attorney and witnessed) from the other party, if any, indicating that he or she will not sue.* If you pay anything, be sure to get a release saying "paid in full." This isn't guaranteed protection, but it may help.

Source: Adapted from Margaret Daly, "Car Insurance—Is It Ever Smart Not to File a Claim?" Better Homes and Gardens, September 1987, pp. 91, 93.

the company is saying the loss does not fall under the policy coverage. You must then either forget the claim or bring in an attorney or, perhaps, a public adjustor (discussed next).

Claims Adjustment. Usually the first person to call when you need to file a claim is your insurance agent. If your loss is relatively minor, the agent can quickly process it. If it is more complex, your company will probably assign a claims adjustor to the case.

Adjustors. The **claims adjustor** works either for the insurance company, as an independent adjustor, or for an adjustment bureau. In any case, the adjustor is primarily looking out for the interests of the company—which might very well be to keep you, its customer, satisfied. However, many claimants think insurance companies have more money than they know what to do with and are out to collect all that is possible. Thus, the adjustor walks a fine line: He or she must diligently question and investigate, while at the same time offering service to minimize settlement delays and financial hardship. To promote your own interest in the claim, you should cooperate with the adjustor and answer inquiries honestly—while keeping in mind that the company writes the adjustor's paycheck.

Public adjustors and attorneys. To this point, we have been referring primarily to the claims that you collect from your own insurance company. In accidents in which a question of fault arises, you may have to file a claim against a negligent party's insurer. In these instances, the insurer will still use an adjustor, but this person will be looking out for the insurer's (and its policyholders') economic interests without any regard to keeping you satisfied. If you are not happy with the offered settlement, you might have to hire an attorney to negotiate the claim for you. Because the attorney will have a better understanding of the law and the legal provisions of your policy than you do, hiring one greatly improves your chances of collecting an amount you're entitled to. Keep in mind, however, that for their services, attorneys will often charge 25 to 50 percent of any amount they get for you (the exact amount of the fee is negotiable). Many times, though, the use of a costly attorney is worthwhile if you are not being treated fairly by the insurance company's adjustor.

Concept Check

10-17. Differentiate between *captive and independent insurance agents.* What characteristics should you look for when choosing both an insurance agent and an insurance company for purposes of buying property and/or liability insurance?

10-18. Briefly describe the key aspects of the claims-settlement process, explaining what to do after an accident, the steps in claim settlement, and the role and types of *claims adjustors.*

claims adjustor An insurance specialist, employed by an insurance company, an adjustment bureau, or self-employed, who investigates claims.

SUMMARY

LG1. **Discuss the importance of having property and liability insurance and understand the basic principles of property insurance, including types of exposure, principle of indemnity, and coinsurance.** Property and liability insurance protects against the loss of real and personal property that can occur from various types of perils. In addition, such insurance protects against loss from lawsuits based on negligence. The principle of indemnity limits the insured's compensation to the amount of economic loss. The coinsurance provision requires that the policyholder buy insurance coverage that equals a set percentage of the property's value to receive full compensation under the policy's terms for any loss.

LG2. **Identify the different coverages provided by a homeowner's insurance policy.** Most homeowner's insurance contracts are divided into two major sections. Section I covers the dwelling unit, accompanying structures, and the personal property of the insured. Section II pertains mainly to comprehensive coverage for personal liability and medical payments. The most commonly sold homeowner's policies (Forms HO-2 and HO-3) cover a broad range of perils, including damage from such occurrences as fire or lightning, windstorms, explosions, aircraft, vehicles, smoke, vandalism, theft, freezing, and so on. Personal property coverage is typically set at 50 percent of the coverage on the dwelling.

LG3. **Select the right homeowner's insurance policy for your needs.** Everyone should have some form of homeowner's insurance, whether you own a single family house, a condominium, or rent an apartment. Renter's insurance covers your personal possessions. Except for the house and garage, which are covered on a replacement basis, homeowner's or renter's insurance normally provides for the payment of all losses on an actual cash value basis, subject to applicable deductibles and policy limits. However, for an additional premium, you usually can obtain replacement-cost coverage on personal belongings. Within Section I, internal limits are set for various classes of property. You may wish to increase these limits if you have additional valuable property. One way to do so is with a personal property floater. Because the standard Section II liability limit is only $100,000, it's a good idea to buy additional liability coverage, generally available at minimal cost. To reduce premiums, choose a policy with a higher deductible.

LG4. **Analyze the different coverages in a personal automobile policy (PAP) and choose the most cost-effective policy.** Automobile insurance policies usually contain provisions that protect the insured from loss due to personal liability, medical payments, uninsured motorists, collision (property damage to the vehicle), and comprehensive coverage (which applies to nearly any other type of noncollision damage your car might suffer, such as theft or vandalism). The factors that influence the policy premium include where you live, type of car, how much you drive, and driving record. Most automobile insurers offer discounts for good driving records, safety and anti-theft devices, driver's training courses, and similar factors. Other ways to reduce premiums are through higher deductibles and eliminating collision coverage if your car is old.

LG5. **Describe other forms of property and liability insurance.** In addition to the major forms of homeowner's and automobile insurance, a variety of other property and liability coverages is available, including umbrella personal liability policies, mobile-home insurance, boat insurance, recreational vehicle insurance, earthquake insurance, flood insurance, and professional liability insurance.

LG6. **Assess your property and liability insurance needs, choose a company and agent, and settle claims.** Before buying property and liability coverage, you should evaluate your exposure to loss and determine the coverage needed. You should also carefully select both the insurance agent(s) and the insurance company in order to obtain appropriate coverage at a reasonable price; and—equally important—make sure that the agent and company you deal with have reputations for fair claims-settlement practices. Before filing a claim, you should decide whether the amount of damage warrants a claim. Document all claims properly and file promptly.

FINANCIAL FACTS OR FANTASIES

Are the following statements financial facts (true) or fantasies (false)?

1. Homeowner's insurance provides protection not only on the home itself but also on most of its contents.
2. If you rent an apartment, you don't need to worry about property insurance since your furniture and other personal belongings are already covered by the landlord's insurance policy.
3. Uninsured motorists coverage is available as part of most automobile insurance policies.
4. The type of car you drive really has very little to do with how much you will have to pay for automobile insurance.
5. As a rule, you must obtain an umbrella personal liability policy if you want liability coverage of $1 million or more.
6. Filing a property or liability claim is quick and easy to do: Just call your agent, supply a few basic details, and look for your check in a few days.

DISCUSSION QUESTIONS AND PROBLEMS

Discussion Question for Opening Profile

Discuss the purpose of carrying insurance. What does Bill Stanley recommend you focus on when determining insurance needs? Is this different from what you previously believed was the "reason" for having insurance?

1. Assume that Clayton Barrow had a property insurance policy of $100,000 on his home. Would a 90 percent coinsurance clause be better than an 80 percent clause in such a policy? Give reasons to support your answer.
2. Last year Steve and Jessica Morgan bought a home with a dwelling replacement value of $250,000 and insured it (via an HO-3 policy) for $210,000. The policy reimburses for actual cash value and has a $500 deductible, standard limits for Schedule C items, and no scheduled property. Recently burglars broke into the house and stole a two-year old television set with a current replacement value of $600 and an estimated life of eight years. They also took jewelry valued at $1,850 and silver flatware valued at $3,000.
   a. If their policy has an 80 percent coinsurance clause, do they have enough insurance?
   b. Using the Schedule C limits listed in the text on page 402, calculate how much the Morgans would receive if they filed a claim for the stolen items.
   c. What advice would you give the Morgans about their homeowner's coverage?
3. Patricia Murphy's luxurious home in the suburb of Broken Arrow, Oklahoma, was recently gutted in a fire. Her living and dining rooms were completely destroyed, and the damaged personal property had a replacement price of $27,000. The average age of the damaged personal property was 5 years, and its useful life was estimated to be 15 years. What is the maximum amount the insurance company would pay Patricia, assuming it reimburses on an actual cash-value basis?
4. Amy and Ed Barnow, both graduate students, moved into an apartment near the university. Amy wants to buy renter's insurance, but Ed thinks they don't need it because their furniture isn't worth much. Amy points out that they do have computer and stereo equipment. Help the Barnows resolve their dilemma, suggest a plan for deciding how much insurance to buy, and give them some ideas on finding a policy.
5. Jonathan Miller has a personal automobile policy with coverages of $25,000/$50,000 for bodily injury liability, $25,000 for property damage liability, $5,000 for medical payments, and a $500 deductible for collision insurance. How much will his insurance cover in each of the following situations? Will he have any out-of-pocket costs?
   a. He loses control and skids on ice, running into a parked car and causing $3,785 damage to the unoccupied vehicle and $2,350 to his own car.
   b. He runs a stop sign and causes a serious auto accident where two people are badly injured and win lawsuits against him for $30,000 each.
   c. Miller's wife borrows his car while hers is being repaired. She backs into a telephone pole and causes $450 damage to the car.

CONTEMPORARY CASE APPLICATIONS

10.1 The Salvatis' Homeowner's Insurance Decision

Phil and Anita Salvati, ages 30 and 28, respectively, were recently married in Chicago. Phil is an electrical engineer with Geophysical Century, an oil exploration company. Anita has a master's degree in special education and teaches at a local junior high school. After living in an apartment for six months, the Salvatis have negotiated the purchase of a new home in a rapidly growing Chicago suburb. Republic Savings and Loan Association has approved their loan request for $108,000, which represents 90 percent of the $120,000 purchase price. Prior to closing the loan, the Salvatis must obtain homeowner's insurance for the home. The Salvatis currently have an HO-4 renter's insurance policy, which they purchased from Phil's tennis partner, Kelly Duvall, who is an agent with Kramer's Insurance Company. In order to learn about the types of available homeowner's insurance, Phil has discussed their situation with Kelly, who has offered a variety of homeowner's policies for Phil's and Anita's consideration. He has recommended that the Salvatis purchase an HO-3 policy, since it would provide them with comprehensive coverage.

Questions

1. What forms of homeowner's insurance are available? Which forms should the Salvatis consider?
2. What are the perils against which the home and its contents should be insured?
3. Discuss the types of loss protection provided by the homeowner's policies under consideration.
4. What advice would you give the Salvatis regarding Kelly's suggestion? What coverage should they buy?

10.2 Auto Insurance for Marjorie Turner

Marjorie Turner of Phoenix, Arizona, is a divorced 40-year-old loan officer at the Frontier National Bank of Arizona with a 16-year-old son. She has decided to use her annual bonus as a down payment on a new car. One Saturday afternoon in late December, she visited Chuck Thomas's Auto Mall and purchased a new, fully equipped Pontiac for $15,000. To obtain insurance on the car, Marjorie called her agent, Jane Cunningham, who represents Farmers Insurance Company, and explained her auto insurance needs. Jane said she would investigate the various options for her. Three days later, Marjorie and Jane got together to look over the alternative coverages. Jane offered several proposals, including various combinations of the following coverages: (a) basic automobile liability insurance, (b) uninsured motorists coverage, (c) automobile medical payments insurance, (d) automobile collision insurance, and (e) comprehensive automobile insurance.

Questions

1. Describe the key features of these insurance coverages.
2. Are there any limitations on these coverages? Explain.
3. Indicate the persons who would be protected under each of these coverages.
4. What kind of insurance coverages would you recommend Ms. Turner purchase? Explain your recommendation.

GETTING A HANDLE ON YOUR FINANCIAL FUTURE

Proper selection and purchase of insurance policies for property loss and liability will provide you with financial peace of mind. As in the case of other expenditures, you should include this in your cash budget and arrange the premium payment dates, where possible, to fit your needs.

If You Are Just Starting Out

Whether you are still in school or you have just begun your career, you need to have property and liability insurance. While you probably have some type of automobile insurance, it may not be adequate in terms of the policy limits, and if you are renting an apartment, you may not have renter's insurance.

Homeowner's or Renter's Insurance

1. Make an inventory of your personal property.
2. Determine if your coverage on personal property is based on actual cash value or replacement costs.
3. If you live in an apartment or any other type of rental unit, make sure you have renter's insurance—this may apply to you even if you are still in school, as you may *not* be covered by your parents' homeowner's policy (check with their agent to find out).
4. Ask your agent to calculate the change in premium if you raise the deductible.
5. Secure quotes from several different agencies to determine the best coverage for your money.

Automobile Insurance

1. Before you buy an automobile, determine what the insurance costs would be on various makes and models.
2. Try to pay the premium in full once a year in order to get the lowest rate. Most insurance companies will charge an additional "service fee" for monthly or quarterly payments.
3. See if you can get a reduced rate if you have both your automobile and homeowner's (renter's) insurance with the same company.
4. Even though the premiums may remain the same, you might want to raise the deductible and increase your policy limits.

If You Are Thirty-Something

Even though your income is probably greater than when you first started out, you still need to exercise good judgment in your purchase of insurance. As your household expands, you accumulate more personal property that needs protection. As your insurance requirements increase, you should periodically shop your policies to find out the going rate.

Homeowner's or Renter's Insurance

1. If your policy does not have an inflation adjustment, you need to pay attention to increases in the prices of homes in your neighborhood and make appropriate adjustments in your coverage.
2. Remember that damage to trees and shrubs is usually covered by your policy.
3. Consider the installation of burglar alarms and fire/smoke detectors as a means of lowering your insurance premiums.

Automobile Insurance

1. As your children get older, be sure that they take driver's education courses.
2. Consider canceling your collision and comprehensive coverage if you have a relatively old automobile. Remember, the policy only pays for actual cash value.
3. Review your policy limits on liability to make sure that you have at least $250,000 per person and $500,000 per accident.
4. You should make sure that you have adequate policy limits for coverage of uninsured motorists.

Other Insurance

1. In order to protect yourself in your job, you should check to see if your employer has professional liability coverage for you. If not, you may want to secure this type of insurance. This is not just for physicians anymore. All types of professionals are targets of lawsuits.
2. As your assets grow, you need to review your personal umbrella liability policy to see if your limits need to be increased. Remember, the more assets you have, the more likely you are to be sued in the event of an accident.

After analyzing his credit situation in Part Three, Paul borrowed $11,149 from his credit union line of credit to pay off all his credit card balances. He has decided, at least for now, to pay $525 monthly on the line of credit so that the debt will be paid off in two years. His first monthly payment will be made January 28, 1996.

Paul must make his annual employee benefit insurance selections by January 15th. He would like to take this opportunity to do a comprehensive analysis of his insurance needs.

1. FPPC Use the needs approach to calculate the amount of insurance needed on Paul's life. Paul would like his mother to receive enough money from his life insurance to provide $75,000 for her retirement. He assumes that his debt and the final expenses associated with his death will be paid from the assets left in his estate.
2. Evaluate the group term life policy Paul currently has available through his cafeteria benefit plan. Should Paul select life insurance as part of his employee benefits? If yes, how much and what will it cost? If no, should he purchase a private policy? If you recommend he buy a private policy, how much and what type of policy should he purchase? Using the examples in the text, approximately how much would the additional recommended policy cost?
3. Recommend appropriate beneficiary and settlement options for Paul's policy(s).
4. Paul's employer also offers an accidental death policy as a choice in the fringe benefit package. Should Paul buy this coverage rather than the coverage discussed in Question 2? Should he purchase accidental death coverage in addition to the coverage discussed in Question 2? If yes, how much and what would it cost? If no, why not?
5. FPPC Evaluate the disability income policy offered as part of Paul's employee benefit plan. Assume that he does not want to rely on Social Security or other government programs in case of a disability. Considering that he does have 23 days of paid sick leave accumulated, would this policy provide the coverage Paul needs? Should Paul select this policy as part of his employee benefit plan or should he purchase a private policy? How much would the recommended coverage cost?
6. Evaluate the two medical insurance options now offered through Paul's employee benefit plan. Paul is healthy except for an occasional injury. Last year (which was a representative year) he had a general physical ($200) and went to the doctor four times for minor ailments ($75 per visit). In addition, Paul suffered two injuries while running, sending him to the emergency room once ($350) and to the doctor three times ($100 per visit). During the year, he had ten prescriptions filled (average cost of $20 per prescription). All of them were generic except for two. Paul feels this medical history is a good indicator of the upcoming year.

   If Paul were covered under the major medical plan, what is the *maximum* amount Paul would have to pay per year for covered expenses (assuming the covered expenses remain below the maximum limit)? How much would Paul have to pay out-of-pocket for covered expenses if he incurred the same medical care as last year?

What are the potential out-of-pocket costs under the HMO coverage? How much would Paul have to pay out-of-pocket if he experienced the same medical care expenses as last year?

What factors, other than out-of-pocket costs for covered expenses, should Paul consider when choosing between these two plans? Which coverage (the major medical policy or the HMO) would you recommend? How much would the premiums cost?

7. Dental insurance is also offered through Paul's cafeteria benefit plan. Over the past 5 years, Paul has incurred expenses of approximately $120 per year on semi-annual check-ups. In addition, he has had about $200 of dental work (fillings) done annually. Paul has been to the dentist recently and has been told that in addition to the normal annual expenditures he will probably need to have two porcelain crowns done this year ($650 each). Given his dental history and expectations for the upcoming year, should Paul select dental coverage as part of his employee benefit plan? Why or why not? If yes, how much will the premiums cost?
8. Review your recommendations in Questions 1 through 7. How much of the $200 provided by Paul's employer for employee benefits will he spend if he follows your recommendations? Will money need to be withheld from his monthly check to pay for excess premiums? Considering Paul's insurance needs as well as his over-extended budget, do you want to change any of your previous insurance recommendations? Why or why not? If yes, what are the revised recommendations?
9. Evaluate Paul's auto insurance policy. Is this coverage adequate for his insurance needs? Recommend any needed changes. Approximately how much would the recommended changes cost?
10. Does Paul need any other types of insurance coverage? If yes, what and why? About how much would it cost?
11. Revise Paul's budget to reflect the changes in expenditures resulting from your insurance recommendations as well as the debt consolidation (see beginning of Part Four). Assume all changes are effective in January, 1996 and that Paul pays premiums annually for all private insurance (not through his employer) except for his auto insurance which is paid semi-annually.
12. Paul's mother has recently asked him about long-term care insurance. Some of her friends have purchased this coverage, and she is not sure whether she needs long-term care protection or not. What type of information does Paul and his mother need to consider in deciding if she should buy long-term care insurance? If she decides to buy this type of insurance, what factors should she look for and compare in long-term care insurance policies?

PART 5

INVESTMENTS

CHAPTER 11

INVESTING IN STOCKS AND BONDS

Jeff Kaiser: A College Student with an Investing Habit

"I started investing when my dad gave me some stock the Christmas I was 11," says Jeff Kaiser, a 19-year old Midwestern college student majoring in finance. "At first, stocks seemed boring; kids that age want toys! As the prices of the stock grew, so did my interest. Then my dad offered to match my summer job savings, and we'd invest the money after vacation. Again, the stock went up and my portfolio grew. After that, I was hooked. Every summer I saved as much as possible and invested it."

Now Jeff has two primary investment goals. "First, I want a second source of income; with the increase in corporate downsizing, I want additional financial security," he explains. "I also believe that my generation should assume that social security may not be around when we retire, and we should start planning *now* to have other financial resources in our 'golden years.' My second and most important goal is to generate enough capital to have a career investing and speculating in stocks."

Because he is looking for capital appreciation more than income, Jeff invests in common stocks. When he is older he'll consider bonds for their conservative but relatively stable rate of return. "Most stocks I plan to hold for the long term (three to five years). But I also have about 10 percent in 'high flier' stocks I'm holding for the short term. These are fun to watch, and some have turned out well, like Semtech Corp. I purchased it at $1\frac{5}{8}$ not too long ago and now it's around $11\frac{1}{2}$."

Learning Goals

LG1. *Discuss the role that investing plays in the personal financial planning process.*

LG2. *Identify several different investment objectives—or reasons for investing.*

LG3. *Describe the various types of risks to which investors are exposed, as well as the sources of return.*

LG4. *Discuss the merits of investing in common stock, including the different types of stock and the various measures of performance.*

LG5. *Describe different types of bonds and note how these securities are used as investment vehicles.*

LG6. *Distinguish between preferred stocks and convertible securities, and note the investment merits of each.*

When looking at rate of return, Jeff aims for between 15 and 25 percent return on his portfolio as a whole, depending on the year. "That may seem high; but every year so far, I have gotten at least one 'double' or 'triple' and that makes returns like that fairly easy to reach—as long as I don't lose too much on any other holdings," he says.

Jeff's strategy is to focus mainly on stocks priced below $30, to get better growth. He's comfortable with a reasonable level of risk and invests in many technology stocks. "Evaluating investments is not an exact science, and everyone has their own special process," he comments. "When I learn about a company's new product or service, from things I read or see on television shows about new technologies, I speculate about how consumers will react. If I think it's a winner, I'll look into the company, its financial statements, market price, and any recent changes in top management. Then I make a judgment call, as to whether it has real growth potential."

Even though he's still in college, Jeff has made investing a habit. "Don't think it's too late to start or that you need a large sum of money to invest," he advises. "Some of my friends have been saving small sums of money at regular intervals. After a while they found they had a substantial amount to invest. Keep doing it for fifteen or twenty years and you'll easily build your net worth." In Chapter 11 you'll learn about stocks and bonds so that like Jeff, you, too, can start investing.

THE OBJECTIVES AND REWARDS OF INVESTING

LG1
LG2
LG3

Getting the most from your investment capital requires not only a clear understanding of your investment objectives, but also a familiarity with the concepts of risk and return. Assume you've just inherited some money and have decided to invest a big chunk of it (say, $40,000). What kind of investment characteristics would you look for when deciding where to put your money? Are dividends and current income important to you? How about capital appreciation? What kind of risk would you be willing to tolerate? These are important questions for an investor—stop to think about them before reading on.

People invest their money for all sorts of reasons. Some do it as a way to accumulate the down payment on a new home; others do it as a way to supplement their income; still others invest in order to build up a nest egg for retirement. Actually, the term "investment" means different things to different people. Millions of people *invest* regularly in such securities as stocks, bonds, and mutual funds; others *speculate* in commodities or options. **Investing** is generally considered to take more of a long-term perspective and is viewed as the process of purchasing securities wherein stability of value and level of return are somewhat predictable. **Speculating,** on the other hand, is viewed as a short-term activity that involves the buying and selling of securities in which future value and expected return are highly uncertain. Obviously, speculation is considered to be far more risky than investing.

At first, you will probably keep your funds in some form of savings vehicle (as described in Chapter 4). Once you have *sufficient savings*—for emergencies and other purposes—you can begin to build up a *pool of investable capital.* This often means making sacrifices and doing what you can to *live within your budget.* Granted, it's far easier to spend money than it is to save it, but if you're really serious about getting into investments, you're going to have to accumulate the necessary capital! In addition to a savings and capital accumulation program, it's also important to have adequate *insurance coverage* in order to provide protection against the unexpected (we discussed different kinds of insurance in Chapters 8, 9, and 10). For our purposes here, we will assume that you are adequately insured and that the cost of insurance coverage is built into your family's monthly cash budget. Ample insurance and liquidity (cash and savings) with which to meet life's emergencies are two *investment prerequisites* that are absolutely essential for the development of a successful investment program. Once these conditions are met, you are ready to start investing.

BUT HOW DO I GET STARTED?

Contrary to what you may believe, there is really nothing mystical about the topic of investments—in fact, so long as you have the capital to do so, it's really quite easy to get started in investing. The terminology may indeed seem baffling at times and some of the procedures and techniques quite complicated. But don't let that mislead you into thinking there is no room for the small, individual investor. Nothing could be farther from the truth! For as we will see in this and the next two chapters, individual investors have a wide array of securities and investment vehicles to choose from. Further, opening an investment account is no more difficult than opening a checking account.

How, then, do you get started? To begin with, you need some money—not a lot; perhaps $1,000 to $2,000 will do, though $5,000 to $10,000 would be even better (and remember, this is *investment capital* we're talking about here—money you've accumulated above and beyond any basic emergency savings). In addition to money, you need knowledge and know-how. You should never invest in something you are not sure about—that is the quickest way to lose money. Learn as much as you can about the market, different types of securities, and various trading strategies. This course you're taking on personal finance is a good start, but you may want to do more. For one thing, you can become a *regular* reader of publications such as *Money, The Wall Street Journal, Barron's,* and *Forbes* (these and other sources of information are reviewed in Chapter 12). Also, try to stay up with major developments as they occur in the market; start following the stock market, interest rates, and developments in the bond market.

We strongly suggest that, after you've learned a few things about stocks and bonds, you set up a portfolio of securities on paper and make *paper trades* in and out of your portfolio for six months to a year in order to get a feel for what it is like to make (and lose) money in the market. Start out with an imaginary sum of, say, $25,000 (as long as you are going to dream, you might as well make it worthwhile). Then keep track of the stocks and bonds you hold, record the number of shares bought and sold, dividends received, and so on. Throughout this exercise, be sure to use actual prices (as obtained from *The Wall Street Journal* or your local newspaper) and keep it as realistic as possible. If you are going to make mistakes in the market, you're much better off doing so on paper. Also, if your parents, relatives, and /or friends have done a lot of investing, talk to them! Find out what they have to say about investing, pick up some pointers and possibly even learn from their mistakes. Eventually you will gain a familiarity with the market and become comfortable with the way things are done there. When that happens, you will be ready to take the plunge.

At that point, you will also need a way to invest—more specifically, a broker and some investment vehicle in which to invest. As we will see in the next chapter the stockbroker is the party through whom you will be buying and selling stocks, bonds, and other securities. If your relatives or friends have a broker they like and trust, have them introduce you to him or her. Alternatively, visit several of the brokerage firms in your community; talk to one of their brokers about your available investment funds and your investment objectives.

As a beginning investor with limited funds, it is probably best to confine your investment activity to the basics. Stick to stocks, bonds, and mutual funds. Avoid getting fancy, and certainly *don't* try to make a killing each and every time you invest—that will only lead to frustration, disappointment, and very possibly, heavy losses. Instead, go for "relatively" high returns; for example, those that comfortably exceed what you can get from a savings account. Further, *be patient!* Don't expect the price of the stock to double overnight, and don't panic when things fail to work out as expected in the short run (after all, security prices do occasionally go down). Finally, remember that you do not need spectacular returns in order to make a lot of money in the market. Instead, be *consistent* and let the concept of compound interest work for you. Do that and you'll find that just $2,000 a year invested at the fairly conservative rate of 10 percent will grow to well over $100,000 in 20 years! While the type of security in which you invest is a highly personal decision, you might want to give serious consideration to some sort of mutual fund as your first investment (see Chapter 13). Mutual funds provide professional management and diversification that small-time individual investors can rarely obtain on their own.

THE ROLE OF INVESTING IN PERSONAL FINANCIAL PLANNING

Buy a car, build a house, enjoy a comfortable retirement—these are goals that we would all like to attain some day and are, in many cases, the centerpieces of well-developed financial plans. As a rule, a financial goal such as building a house is not something we pay for out of our cash reserves; the cost (even the down payment) is simply too great to allow for that. Instead, we must accumulate the funds over time, which is where investment planning and the act of investing enter into the personal financial planning process. By investing our money, we are letting it work for us.

It all starts with an objective—a particular financial goal that we would like to achieve in a certain period of time. Take the case of the Zacharys. Shortly after the birth of their first child, they decided to start building a college education fund. After performing some rough calculations, they concluded that they'd need to accumulate about $40,000 over the next 18 years in order to have the money for their daughter's education. Simply by setting that objective, the Zacharys created a well-defined, specific financial goal. The *purpose* is to meet the educational needs of their child, and the *amount* of money involved is $40,000 in 18 years. But how do they reach their goal? The first thing they must decide is where the money will come from. While part of it will come from the return (profit) on their investments, they still have to come up with the *investment capital*.

investing The process of placing money in some medium such as stocks or bonds in the expectation of receiving some future benefit.

speculating A form of investing in which future value and expected returns are highly uncertain.

Coming Up With the Capital. So far, the Zacharys know how much money they want to accumulate, and how long they have to accumulate it. The only other thing they need to determine at this point is the *rate of return* they feel they can earn on their money. Having taken a financial planning course in college, the Zacharys know that the amount of money they'll have to put into their investment program depends in large part on *how much they can earn from their investments*—the higher their rate of return, the less they'll have to put up. Let's say they feel comfortable using a 9 percent rate of return. That's a fairly conservative number, and they're reasonably certain they can reach that level of return, on average, over the long haul. It's important to use some care in coming up with a projected rate of return. Don't saddle yourself with an unreasonably high rate, since that will simply reduce the chance of reaching your targeted financial goal.

Probably the best way of arriving at a reasonable projection is to look at what the market has done over the past three to five years, and then use the average return performance over that period as your estimate—or, if you want to be a bit more conservative, knock a point or two off the market's return. To help you in this regard, take a look at the statistics that appear at the bottom of this page; they show the average annual returns on stocks, bonds, and U.S. Treasury bills over 5-, 10-, and 15-year holding periods.

Notice that, over the past 15 years, unless someone had put just about everything into short-term U.S. Treasury bills, generating an average return of around 9 to 10 percent (or even more) was well within the reach of most investors. Of course, there's no guarantee that these returns will happen again in the next 5 to 10 years, but at least the past does provide us with a basis—or "handle"—for making projections into the future.

Now, returning to our problem at hand, there are two ways of finding the amount of capital needed to reach a targeted sum of money: (1) you can make a lump-sum investment right up front and let that amount grow over time; or (2) you can set up a systematic savings plan and put away a certain amount of money each year. Worksheet 11.1 is designed to help you find the amount of investment capital you'll need to reach a given financial goal. It employs the *compound value* concept discussed in Chapter 2, and is based on a given financial target (line 1), and a projected average rate of return on your investments (line 2). Note thatyou can use the worksheet to find either a required lump-sum investment (part A), or an amount that will have to be put away each year in a savings plan (part B). For our purposes here, we'll assume the Zacharys have $4,000 to start with (this comes mostly from gifts their daughter received from her grandparents). Since they know they'll need a lot more than that to reach their target, the Zacharys decide to use part B of the worksheet to find out how much they'll have to save annually.

The first thing to do is find the future value of the $4,000 initial investment—the question here is: how much will that initial lump-sum investment grow to over an 18-year period of time? Using the compound value concept and the appropriate "future value factor" (from Appendix A), we see, in line 7, that this deposit will grow to some $18,880. So, that's nearly $19,000 of our targeted $40,000 that we already have covered. Thus, by subtracting the terminal value of the initial investment (line 7) from our target (line 1), we come up with the amount that must be generated from some sort of annual savings plan—see line 8. (*Note:* if you were starting from scratch, you'd enter a zero in line 5, and the amount in line 8 would be equal to the amount in line 1.) Again, using the appropriate future value factor (this time from Appendix B), we find the Zacharys will have to save $511 a year in order to reach their target of $40,000 in 18 years. That is, the $511 a year will accumulate to $21,120, which when added to the $18,880 that the initial $4,000 will grow to, equals the targeted $40,000. (By the way, they can also reach their target by making a lump-sum investment right up front of $8,475—try working out part A of the worksheet on your own, and see if you can come up with that number.)

Holding Periods	Stocks (as measured by the S&P 500)	High-grade Corp. Bonds	Stocks and Bonds Together	U.S. T-Bills	Stocks, Bonds, and T-Bills Combined
5 years: 1990–94	9.95%	8.40%	9.18%	5.05%	7.80%
10 years: 1985–94	14.86	11.62	13.24	5.91	10.79
15 years: 1980–94	14.25	11.48	12.86	7.58	11.10

WORKSHEET 11.1

Finding the Amount of Investment Capital FPPC

A worksheet like this one can be used to find out how much money you must come up with in order to reach a given financial goal. Note that this worksheet is based on the same future value concept we first introduced in Chapter 2.

DETERMINING AMOUNT OF INVESTMENT CAPITAL	
Financial goal: To accumulate $40,000 in 18 years for the purpose of meeting the cost of daughter's college education.	
1. Targeted Financial Goal (see Note 1)	$ 40,000
2. Projected Average Return on Investments	9.0%
A. Finding a Lump Sum Investment:	
3. Future Value Factor, from Appendix A ■ based on ______ years to target date and a projected average return on investment of ______	
4. Required Lump Sum Investment ■ line 1 ÷ line 3	$
B. Making a Series of Investments Over Time:	
5. Amount of Initial Investment, if any (see Note 2)	$ 4,000
6. Future Value Factor, from Appendix A ■ based on 18 years to target date and a projected average return on investment of 9%	4.72
7. Terminal Value of Initial Investment ■ line 5 × line 6	$ 18,880
8. Balance to Come from Savings Plan ■ line 1 − line 7	$ 21,120
9. Future Value Annuity Factor, from Appendix B ■ based on 18 years to target date and a projected average return on investment of 9%	41.3
10. Series of Annual Investments Required over Time ■ line 8 ÷ line 9	$ 511

Note 1: The "targeted financial goal" is the amount of money you want to accumulate by some target date in the future.

Note 2: If you're starting from scratch—i.e., there is *no* initial investment—enter zero in line 5, *skip* lines 6 and 7, and then use the total targeted financial goal (from line 1) as the amount to be funded from a savings plan; now proceed with the rest of the worksheet.

An Investment Plan Provides Direction. Now that the Zacharys know how much they have to save each year, their next step is to decide how they will save it. Probably the best thing to do in this regard is to follow some type of *systematic routine*—for example, building a set amount of savings each month or quarter into the household budget. But whatever procedure is followed, keep in mind that all we are doing here is accumulating the required investment capital. That money still has to be put to work in some kind of investment program, and that's where an investment plan comes into the picture. Basically, an **investment plan** is nothing more than a simple, preferably written, statement that explains how the accumulated investment capital will be invested for the purpose of reaching the targeted goal. In the example we've been using, the Zacharys' capital accumulation plan calls for a 9 percent rate of return as a target they feel they can achieve. Now they have to come up with a way of obtaining that 9 percent return on their money—meaning they have to specify, in general terms at least, the kinds of investment vehicles they intend to use. *When completed, an investment plan is a way of translating an abstract investment target* (in this case, a 9 percent return) *into a specific investment program.*

WHAT ARE YOUR INVESTMENT OBJECTIVES?

Some people buy securities for the protection they provide from taxes (that's what tax shelters are all about). Others want to have money put aside for that proverbial rainy day or, perhaps, to build up a nice retirement nest egg. Your goals tend to set the tone for your investment program, and they play a major role in determining how conservative (or aggressive) you're likely to be in making investment decisions. In a very real way, they provide a purpose for your investments. Given that you have adequate savings and insurance to cover any emergencies, the most frequent investment objectives are to (1) enhance current income, (2) save for a major purchase, (3) accumulate funds for retirement, and (4) seek shelter from taxes.

Current Income. The idea here is to put your money into investments that will enable you to supplement your income. In other words, it's for people who want to live off their investment income. A secure source of high current income, from dividends or interest, is the principal concern of such investors. Retired people, for example, often choose investments offering high current income—at low risk. Another common reason for seeking supplemental income is that a family member requires extended costly medical care. Even after insurance, such recurring costs can heavily burden a family budget without this vital income supplement.

Major Expenditures. People often put money aside, sometimes for years, in order to save up enough to make just one major expenditure, the most common ones being:

- Save up for the down payment on a home
- Have the money for a child's college education
- Build up some capital for going into business
- Pay for an expensive (perhaps once-in-a-lifetime) vacation
- Pay for most or all of the purchase of a very special, expensive item
- Accumulate funds for retirement (discussed in the following section)

Whatever your goal, the idea is to set your sights on something and then go about building your capital with that objective in mind. It sure makes the act of investing more pleasurable. Once you have a handle on how much money you're going to need to attain one of these goals (following a procedure like the one illustrated with *Worksheet 11.1*), you can specify the types of investment vehicles you intend to use. For example, you might follow a low-risk approach by making a single lump-sum investment in a bond that matures in the year in which you need the funds; or you could follow a more risky investment plan that calls for investing a set amount of money over time in something like a growth-oriented mutual fund (where there is little or no assurance of what the terminal value of the investment will be). Of course, for some purposes—such as the down payment on a home or a child's education—you will probably want to accept a lot less risk than for others, as the attainment of these goals should not be jeopardized by the types of investment vehicles you choose to employ.

Retirement. Accumulating funds for retirement is *the single most important reason for investing.* Too often, though, retirement planning occupies only a small amount of our time, since we tend to rely very heavily on employers and social security for our retirement needs. As many people learn too late in life, that can be a serious mistake. A much better approach is to review the amounts of income you can *realistically* expect to receive from social security and your employee pension plan, and then decide, based on your retirement goals, *whether or not they will be adequate to meet your needs.* You'll probably find that you'll have to supplement them through personal investing. Obviously, the earlier in life you make this assessment, the greater your opportunity to accumulate the needed funds. (Retirement plans are discussed in Chapter 14.)

Shelter from Taxes. As Chapter 3 explained, federal income tax law does not treat all sources of income equally. For example, if you own real estate—either directly or through some pooling arrangement—you *may* be able to take depreciation deductions against certain other sources of income, thereby reducing the amount of your final taxable income. This tax write-off feature can make real estate an attractive investment vehicle *for some investors,* even though its pretax rate of return may not appear very high. The goal of sheltering income from taxes was made considerably more difficult with the Tax Reform Act of 1986; even so, such a goal for some investors still goes hand in hand with the goals of saving for a major outlay or for retirement. Clearly, if you can avoid paying taxes on the income from an investment, you will, all other things considered, have more funds available for reinvestment during the period.

DIFFERENT WAYS TO INVEST

Once you've established your investment objectives, there are a variety of investment vehicles from which you can choose in order to fulfill those goals. Various types of investment vehicles are briefly described in the following paragraphs; many of these securities will be more fully examined later in this chapter and in Chapter 13.

Common Stock. *Common stocks* are basically a form of *equity*—meaning that, as an investment, they represent an ownership interest in a corporation. Each share of stock symbolizes a fractional ownership position in a firm; for example, one share of common stock in a corporation that has 10,000 shares outstanding would denote a 1/10,000 ownership interest in the firm. A share of stock entitles the holder to equal participation in the corporation's earnings and dividends, an equal vote, and an equal voice in management. From the investor's perspective, the return to stockholders comes from either dividends and/or appreciation in share price. Common stock has no maturity date and as a result, remains outstanding indefinitely.

Bonds. In contrast to stocks, *bonds* are *liabilities*—they're IOUs of the issuer. The bondholder actually loans money to the issuer. Governments and corporations issue bonds that pay a stated return, called *interest.* When an individual invests in a bond, he or she receives a stipulated interest return, typically paid every six months, plus the return of the principal (face) value of the bond at maturity. For example, if you purchased a $1,000 bond that paid 10 percent interest in semiannual installments, you could expect to receive $50 every six months (that is, 10% × $1,000 × .5 years) and at maturity recover the $1,000 face value of the bond. Of course, a bond can be bought or sold prior to maturity at a price that can differ from its face value since bond prices, like common stock prices, do fluctuate in the marketplace.

Preferreds and Convertibles. These are forms of hybrid securities in that each has the characteristics of both stocks and bonds; in essence, they are a cross between the two. *Preferred securities* are issued as stock and, as such, represent an equity position in a corporation. Unlike common stock, however, preferreds have a stated (fixed) dividend rate, payment of which is given preference over dividends to holders of common stock. Like bonds, preferred stocks are usually purchased for the current income (dividends) they pay. A *convertible security,* in contrast, is a special type of fixed-income obligation (bond or preferred stock) that carries a conversion feature permitting the investor to convert it into a specified number of shares of common stock. Convertible bonds, therefore, provide the fixed-income benefits of a bond (interest) while offering the price appreciation (capital gains) potential of common stock.

investment plan A statement, preferably written, that specifies how investment capital will be invested for the purpose of achieving a specified goal.

Mutual Funds. An organization that invests in and professionally manages a diversified portfolio of securities is called a *mutual fund*. A mutual fund sells shares to investors, who then become part-owners of the fund's securities portfolio. Most mutual funds issue and repurchase shares at a price that reflects the underlying value of the portfolio at the time the transaction is made. Mutual funds have become very popular with individual investors because they offer not only a wide variety of investment opportunities but also a full array of services that many investors find particularly appealing.

Real Estate. Investments in *real estate* can take many forms, ranging from raw land speculation to limited-partnership shares in commercial property. The returns on real estate can come from rents, capital gains, and certain tax benefits. Unfortunately, estimating both risk and return in a real estate venture can be difficult and usually requires expert advice, particularly with respect to income tax implications.

Commodities, Financial Futures, and Options. *Commodities* are contracts to buy/sell such things as cotton, corn, wheat, coffee, and cocoa, as well as other raw materials (like copper, silver, and oil), at some future date. *Financial futures* are just like commodities, except they apply to certain types of financial instruments, like stock prices, bond interest rates, even foreign currencies. Both commodities and financial futures are actively traded in what is known as the futures markets. Because they do not pay interest or dividends, the returns on commodities and financial futures contracts are derived solely from the change in the price of the underlying commodity or financial instrument. These are very risky investments, because losses can mount up quickly and, in a short period of time, far exceed the amount invested. In a similar fashion, *options* give the holder the right to buy or sell common stocks (and other financial instruments) at a set price, over a specified period of time. Again, to earn a positive return one must correctly anticipate future price movements in the underlying financial asset. In contrast to futures contracts, the price paid for an option is the maximum amount that can be lost; however, options have very short maturities, and consistent losses can quickly exhaust one's investment capital. Futures and options are often referred to as **derivative securities** to the extent that they derive their value from the price behavior of some underlying real or financial asset.

MARKET GLOBALIZATION AND THE ALLURE OF FOREIGN SECURITIES

In addition to all the securities and investment vehicles mentioned above, a growing number of American investors are turning to foreign markets as a way to earn attractive returns. Such securities became increasingly popular during the 1980s, and many investment advisors today recommend that investors put at least part of their capital into foreign securities. A good deal of this interest has come about as advances in technology and communications, together with the gradual elimination of political and regulatory barriers, has allowed investors to make cross-border securities transactions with relative ease. As such, not only are more and more Americans beginning to invest in foreign securities, but foreign investors are becoming major players in U.S. markets as well. The net result is a rapidly growing trend toward market globalization, whereby investing is practiced on an international scale rather than confined to a single (domestic) market.

Ironically, as "our world is becoming smaller," our universe of investment opportunities is growing by leaps and bounds. The fact is, all of the investment vehicles noted previously can also be found in every one of the major markets around the world. Stocks, bonds, convertibles, mutual funds, futures and options, even short-term securities like Treasury bills and CDs are actively traded not only in the United States but also in foreign markets.

Twenty years ago (in the early 1970s), our markets dominated the world; the U.S. stock market alone accounted for fully two-thirds of the world equity markets and our bond market was nearly as big. That's no longer true; by the early '90's, the U.S. share of the world equity market had plunged to 30 percent, and the U.S. bond market accounted for less than half of the world's supply of debt securities. Today, the world debt and equity markets are dominated by just six countries, which together account for about 80 percent of the total value of the world markets. These six countries are:

	Approx. Market Values	
Country	**Stocks**	**Bonds**
United States	$4.2 trillion	$6.9 trillion
Japan	$2.8 trillion	$2.7 trillion
United Kingdom	$1.1 trillion	$470 billion
Germany	$425 billion	$1.2 trillion
France	$420 billion	$760 billion
Canada	$260 billion	$510 billion

Clearly, the United States is still the biggest player, but as these numbers show, there are some very big markets that exist beyond our borders. And keep in mind, these are just the six biggest markets. In addition to these six, there are another half dozen or so markets, like Switzerland, Australia, Italy, Singapore, and Hong Kong, that are also regarded as *major world players*—not to mention a number of relatively small, *emerging markets,* like Mexico, South Korea, Thailand, and the Philippines. Thus, investors who confine all their investing to the U.S. markets are missing out on a big chunk of the worldwide investment opportunities. Not only that, they're missing out on some very attractive returns as well! For over the 15-year period from 1980 through 1994, the U.S. stock and bond markets provided the highest annual returns just *once*—in 1982. Indeed, more often than not, the returns in this country just don't stack up very well to those available in other markets.

So, if you're looking for better returns, you might want to give some thought to investing in foreign securities. There are several different ways of doing that. Without a doubt, from the perspective of an individual investor, the best and easiest way is through *international mutual funds* (we'll discuss such funds in Chapter 13). Mutual funds aside, you could, of course, buy securities directly in the foreign markets. *Investing directly* is not for the uninitiated, however. For while most major U.S. brokerage houses are set up to accommodate investors interested in buying foreign securities, there are still a lot of *logistical* problems that have to be faced. Fortunately, there is an easier way, and that is to buy *foreign securities that are denominated in dollars and traded directly on U.S. exchanges*. One such investment vehicle is an American Depositary Receipt (ADR). ADRs are just like common stock, except that each ADR represents a specific number of shares in a specific foreign company. Indeed, the shares of more than 1100 companies from some 50 foreign countries are traded on U.S. exchanges as ADRs—companies like Sony, Canon, NEC, Volvo, Unilever, and Cadbury Schweppes. They're a great way to invest in foreign stocks because ADRs are bought and sold, on American markets, just like stocks in U.S. companies—and their prices are quoted in dollars, not British pounds or German marks. Furthermore, all dividends are paid in dollars.

Whereas the temptation to go after higher returns may be compelling, there is one thing to keep in mind when investing in foreign securities—that is, whether investing in foreign securities directly or through something like ADRs, the whole process of investing involves a lot more risk. That's because *the behavior of foreign currency exchange rates plays a vital role in defining returns to U.S. investors*. For as the U.S. dollar becomes weaker (or stronger) relative to the currency in which the foreign security is denominated, the returns to U.S. investors, from investing in foreign securities, will increase (or decrease) accordingly. Currency exchange rates can, in fact, have a dramatic impact on investor returns and quite often can convert mediocre returns, or even losses, into very attractive returns—and vice versa. There's really only one thing that determines whether the impact is going to be positive or negative, and that's the behavior of the U.S dollar relative to the currency in which the foreign security is denominated. In effect, *a stronger dollar has a negative impact on total returns to U.S. investors, and a weaker dollar has a positive impact*. Thus, other things being equal, the best time to be in foreign securities is when the dollar is *falling,* because that *adds* to returns to U.S. investors.

THE RISKS OF INVESTING

When selecting investments, you should look not only at potential return, but also the possible risks and uncertainties associated with various investment outlets. Much like foreign securities are exposed to currency exchange risks, just about any type of investment vehicle is subject to one type of risk or another—some more than others. The basic types of investment risk are business risk, financial risk, market risk, purchasing power risk, interest rate risk, liquidity risk, and event risk. Obviously, other things being equal, you'd like to reduce your exposure to these risks as much as possible.

Business Risk. When you invest in a company, you may have to face up to the possibility that the issuing firm will fail, due either to economic or industry factors or, as is more often the case, to poor decisions on the part of management. In a

derivative securities Securities, such as futures and options, whose value is derived from (or linked to) the price behavior of an underlying real or financial asset.

general sense, this is **business risk** and it may be thought of as the degree of uncertainty surrounding the firm's earnings and subsequent ability to meet principal, interest, and dividend payments on time. Companies that are subject to high degrees of business risk generally experience wide fluctuations in sales, have widely erratic earnings, and can, in fact, end the year with substantial operating losses.

Financial Risk. **Financial risk** relates to the amount of debt used to finance the firm. Look to the company's balance sheet to get a handle on a firm's financial risk. As a rule, companies that have little or no long-term debt are fairly low in financial risk. This is particularly so if a company has a healthy earnings picture as well. The problem with debt financing is that it creates principal and interest obligations that have to be met regardless of how much profit the company is generating. As with business risk, financial risk can lead to failure (as in the case of bankruptcy), or a rate of return that is sharply below your expectations.

Market Risk. **Market risk** results from the behavior of investors in the securities markets. The fact is, prices of stocks and bonds will sometimes change even though business and financial risks, and other intrinsic factors, stay about the same. Such changes have little to do with the securities themselves but instead are due to changes in political, economic, and social conditions, and/or in investor tastes and preferences. Essentially, market risk is reflected in the *price volatility* of a security—the more volatile the price of a security, the greater its perceived market risk.

Purchasing Power Risk. Possible changes in price levels within the economy also result in risk. In periods of rising prices (inflation), the purchasing power of the dollar declines. This means that a smaller quantity of goods and services can be purchased with a given number of dollars. In periods of declining price levels, the purchasing power of the dollar increases. An awareness of **purchasing power risk** and changes in purchasing power allows investors to select investments that are best suited for a given price level environment. In general, investments whose values tend to move with general price levels (like stocks or real estate) are most profitable during periods of rising prices, whereas those providing fixed returns (like bonds) are preferred during periods of low inflation or declining price levels.

Interest Rate Risk. **Fixed-income securities,** which include preferred stocks and bonds, offer purchasers a fixed periodic return and, as such, are most affected by **interest rate risk.** As interest rates change, the prices of these securities fluctuate, decreasing with rising interest rates and increasing with falling rates. For example, the prices of fixed-income securities drop when interest rates increase, in order to provide purchasers with a rate of return that is competitive with those available from securities that offer higher levels of interest income. Changes in interest rates are the result of fluctuations in the supply of and/or demand for money. These fluctuations are caused by various economic actions of the government or the interactions of business firms, consumers, and financial institutions.

Liquidity Risk. The risk of not being able to liquidate an investment conveniently and at a reasonable price is called **liquidity risk.** The liquidity of a given investment vehicle is important because it provides investors with a safety valve just in case they ever have to get out. In general, investment vehicles traded in *thin markets,* in which supply and demand are small, tend to be less liquid than those traded in *broad markets*. However, to be liquid, an investment must be easily salable at a reasonable price. One can generally enhance the liquidity of an investment merely by cutting its price. For example, a security recently purchased for $1,000 would not be viewed as highly liquid if it could be sold only at a significantly reduced price, such as $500. Vehicles such as mutual funds, or the stocks and bonds of major companies listed on the New York Stock Exchange, are generally highly liquid; others, such as an isolated parcel of raw land in rural Georgia, are not.

Event Risk. More than just a buzz word used by the financial media, **event risk** is real, and it can have a direct and dramatic impact on investment return. Basically, it occurs when something substantial happens to a company and that event, in itself, has a sudden impact on the company's financial condition. Event risk goes beyond business and financial risk, and it doesn't necessarily mean the company or market is doing poorly. Instead, it involves an event that is largely (or totally) unexpected, and which has a significant and usually immediate effect on the underlying value of an investment. A good example of event risk was the recent action by the Food and Drug Administration to halt the use of silicone breast implants. The share price of Dow Chemical—the dominant producer of this product—was quickly affected (in a negative fashion) as a result of this single event! Event risk can take many forms, though, fortunately, its impact tends to be confined to certain companies, securities, or segments of the market.

THE RETURNS FROM INVESTING

Any investment vehicle—be it a share of stock, a bond, a piece of real estate, or a stock option—has just two basic sources of return: *current income* and/or *capital gains*. Some investments offer only one source of return (for example, options provide only capital gains), but most offer both income and capital gains, which together make up what is called the *total return* from an investment. Of course, where both elements of return are present, the relative importance of each will vary among investments. Whereas current income is more important with bonds, capital gains usually makes up a larger portion of total return in the case of common stocks.

Current Income. Current income is received with some degree of regularity over the course of a year, and may take the form of dividends on stock, interest from bonds, and rents from real estate. People who invest to obtain income look for investment vehicles that will provide regular and predictable patterns of income. Preferred stocks and bonds, which are expected to pay known amounts at specified times (quarterly or semiannually, for example), are usually good income investments.

Capital Gains. The other type of return available from investments is capital appreciation (or growth), which is reflected in an increase in the market value of the investment vehicle. Capital gains occur when you're able to sell a security for more than you paid for it, or when your security holdings go up in value. Investments that provide greater growth potential through capital appreciation normally have lower levels of current income, since the firm achieves its growth by reinvesting its earnings instead of paying dividends out to the owners. Many common stocks, for example, are acquired for their capital gains potential.

INTEREST-ON-INTEREST: AN IMPORTANT ELEMENT OF RETURN

Question: When does an 8 percent investment end up yielding only 5 percent? Answer: Probably more often than you think! Of course, it can happen when investment performance fails to live up to expectations. But it can also happen even when everything goes right. That is, so long as at least part of the return from an investment involves the periodic receipt of current income (such as dividends or interest payments), that income has to be *reinvested* at a given rate of return in order to achieve the yield you thought you had going into

business risk The degree of uncertainty associated with a firm's earnings and consequent ability to pay interest and dividends.

financial risk A type of investment risk associated with the mix of debt and equity financing used by the issuing firm.

market risk A type of investment risk associated with factors such as changes in political, economic, and social conditions and in investor tastes and preferences that may cause the market price of a security to change.

purchasing power risk A type of risk resulting from possible changes in price levels that can have a significant effect on investment returns.

fixed-income securities Securities such as preferred stocks and bonds that offer purchasers fixed periodic returns.

interest rate risk A type of risk resulting from changing market interest rates that mainly affects fixed-income securities.

liquidity risk A type of risk associated with the inability to liquidate an investment conveniently and at a reasonable price.

event risk The risk that some major, unexpected event will occur, leading to a sudden, substantial change in the financial condition of a firm; for example, a company could go through a leveraged buy-out, or the money manager of a highly successful mutual fund could quit.

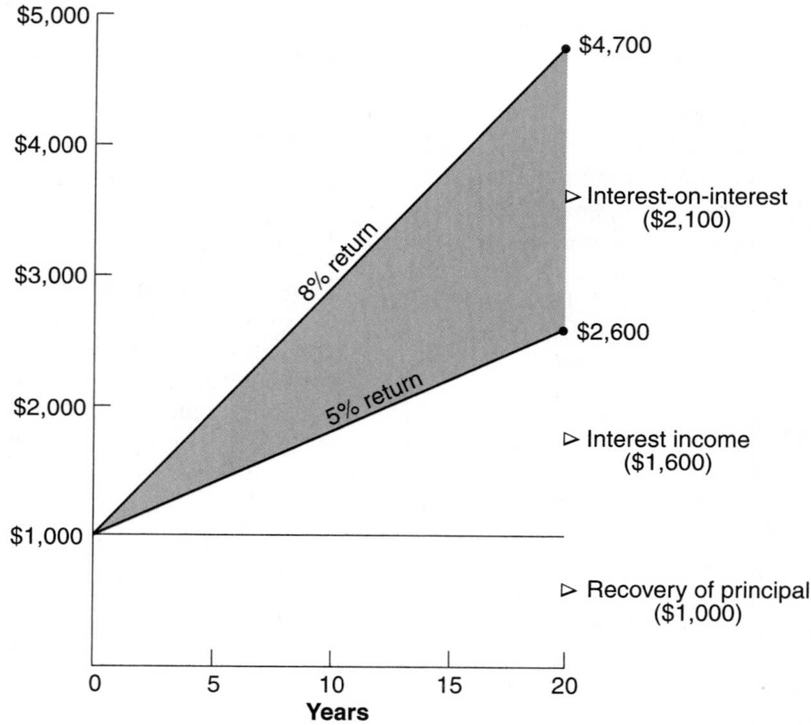

the investment. To see why that's so, consider an investor who buys an 8 percent U.S. Treasury bond and holds it to maturity, a period of 20 years. Each year the bondholder receives $80 in interest, and at maturity, the $1,000 in principal is repaid. There is no loss in capital, no default; everything is paid right on time. Yet this sure-fire investment ends up yielding only 5 percent. Why? Because the investor failed to reinvest the annual interest payments he was receiving. By not plowing back all the investment earnings, the bond-holder failed to earn any *interest-on-interest.*

Now take a look at the graph above. It shows the *three* elements of return for our 8 percent, 20-year bond: (1) the recovery of principal, or capital gains, if any is earned; (2) periodic interest income; and (3) the interest-on-interest earned from reinvesting the periodic interest payments. Observe that since the bond was originally bought at par ($1,000), you start off with an 8 percent investment. Where you end up depends on what you do with the profits (interest earnings) from this investment; that is, *whereas current income and capital gains make up the profits from an investment, interest-on-interest is a measure of what you do with those profits!* If you don't reinvest the interest income, you'll end up on the 5 percent line.

To move to the 8 percent line, you have to earn interest-on-interest from your investments. Specifically, since you started out with an 8 percent investment, that's the rate of return you have to earn when reinvesting your income. The rate of return you start with, in effect, is the required, or minimum, reinvestment rate. Put your investment profits to work at that rate and you'll earn the rate of return you set out to; fail to do so and your return will decline accordingly. And keep in mind that even though we used a bond in our illustration, so long as current income is part of an investment's return, *this same principle applies to any type of long-term investment vehicle.* It's just as relevant to common stocks and mutual funds as it is to long-term bond instruments. This notion of earning interest-on-interest is what the market refers to as a *fully compounded rate of return.* It's an important concept because you can't start reaping the full potential from your investments until you start earning a fully compounded return on your money.

Thus, if periodic investment income is involved, the reinvestment of that income and interest-on-interest are matters you're going to have to deal with. In fact, *interest-on-interest is a particularly important element of return for investment*

EXHIBIT 11.1

The Risk-Return Relationship

In the field of investments, there generally is a direct relationship between risk and return: The more risk you face, the greater should be the return you should expect to generate from the investment.

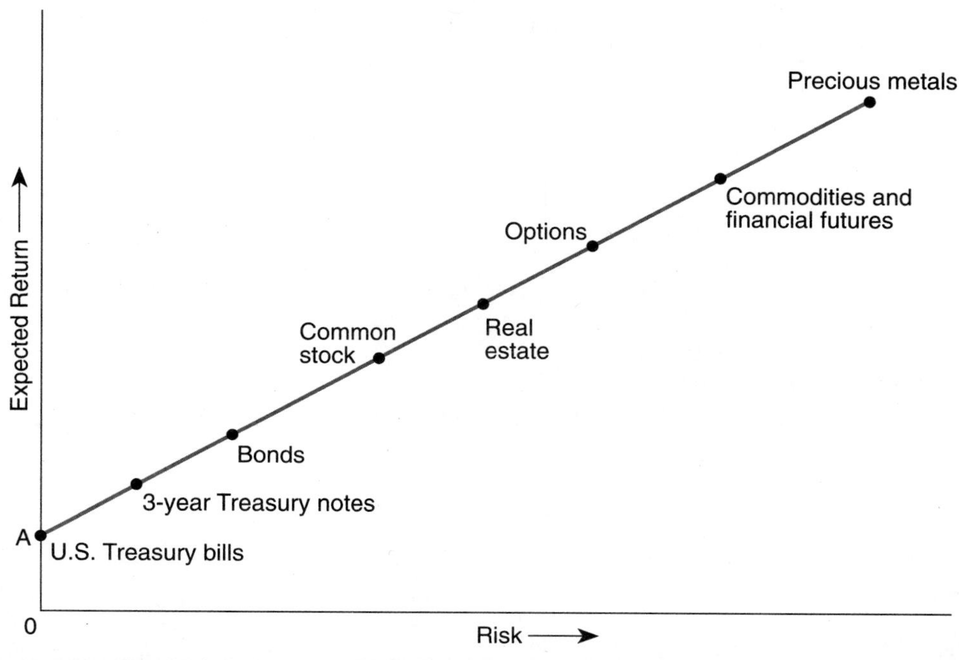

programs that involve a lot of current income. This is so because, in contrast to capital gains, current income has to be reinvested by the individual investor. (With capital gains, the investment vehicle itself is doing the reinvesting, all automatically.) It follows, therefore, that if your investment program tends to lean toward income-oriented securities, then interest-on-interest—and the continued reinvestment of income—will play an important role in defining the amount of investment success you have.

THE RISK-RETURN TRADE-OFF

The amount of risk associated with a given investment vehicle is directly related to its expected return. This is a *universal* rule of investing and means that if you want a higher level of return from your investment, you will probably have to accept a greater exposure to risk. Thus, investors should *expect* to be compensated for taking higher levels of risk by earning higher rates of return. Since most people are believed to be risk averse—they dislike taking risks—some incentive to taking risks must be offered. If a low-risk investment offered the same return as a high-risk one, investors would naturally opt for the former—or, put another way, investors would choose the investment with the least risk for a given level of return.

The direct relationship between risk and return is shown in Exhibit 11.1, which generalizes the risk-return trade-off for some popular investment vehicles. Note that it is possible to receive a positive return for zero risk, such as at point A; this is sometimes referred to as the **risk-free rate of return,** which is often measured by the return on a short-term government security, such as a 90-day Treasury bill.

risk-free rate of return The rate of return on short-term government securities, such as Treasury bills, that have no default risk or maturity premiums.

Equation 11.1

$$\text{Approximate yield} = \frac{\text{Average annual current income} + \left[\dfrac{\text{Future price of investment} - \text{Current price of investment}}{\text{Number of years in investment period}}\right]}{\left[\dfrac{\text{Current price of investment} + \text{Future price of investment}}{2}\right]}$$

$$= \frac{CI + \left[\dfrac{FP - CP}{N}\right]}{\left[\dfrac{CP + FP}{2}\right]}$$

where

CI = *average* annual current income (amount you expect to receive annually from dividends, interest, or rent)

FP = expected future price of investment

CP = current market price of investment

N = investment period (length of time, in years, that you expect to hold the investment)

WHAT MAKES A GOOD INVESTMENT?

In keeping with the above risk-return discussion, it follows that the value of any investment depends on the amount of return it is expected to provide relative to the amount of perceived risk involved. This basic rule applies to any type of investment vehicle, be it stocks, bonds, convertibles, options, real estate, or commodities. In this respect, they should all be treated the same.

Future Return. In the field of investments, the only return that matters is *the expected future return*. Except to the extent that they can help you get a handle on future income, past returns are of little value to investors—after all, it is not what the security did last year that matters, but rather, what it is expected to do next year.

Earlier, we defined returns as being made up of current income and capital gains. Thus, to get an idea of the future return on an investment, we must formulate expectations of its future current income and future capital appreciation. To illustrate, assume you are thinking of buying some stock in Rose Colored Glasses, Inc. (RCG). By reviewing several financial reports, you have come up with an estimate of the future dividends and price behavior of RCG as follows:

Expected average annual dividends, 1995–97	\$2.15 a share
Expected market price of the stock, 1997	\$75.00 a share

Since the stock is now selling for \$60 a share, the difference between its current and expected future market price (\$75–\$60) represents the amount of *capital gains* you can expect to receive over the next three years—in this case, \$15 a share. Thus, you have estimates of the stock's future *income stream* (from annual dividends and capital gains); what you need now is a way to measure *expected return*.

Approximate Yield. Finding the exact rate of return on this (or any) investment involves a highly complex mathematical procedure. However, you can obtain a reasonably close estimation of expected return by computing the investment's *approximate yield*. This measure is widely used by seasoned investors and results in a rate of return (yield) that is remarkably close to the exact figure; and it is relatively easy to use. Best of all, this barometer of return considers not only current income and capital gains, but interest-on-interest as well. As such, *approximate yield provides a measure of the fully compounded rate of return* from an investment and is the preferred way to measure expected return performance.

The method for finding the approximate yield on an investment is shown in Equation 11.1. If you briefly study the formula, you will see that it is really not as formidable as it may at first appear. All it does is relate (1) average current income and (2) average capital gains to the (3) average amount of the investment.

To illustrate, lets use the Rose Colored Glasses example again. Given the average annual dividends (*CI*) of $2.15, current stock price (*CP*) of $60, future stock price (*FP*) of $75, and an investment period (*N*) of 3 years (you expect to hold the stock through 1997), you can now use Equation 11.1 to find the expected approximate yield on this investment:

$$\text{Approximate yield} = \frac{\$2.15 + \left[\frac{\$75 - \$60}{3}\right]}{\left[\frac{\$60 + \$75}{2}\right]} = \frac{\$2.15 + \left[\frac{\$15}{3}\right]}{\left[\frac{\$135}{2}\right]} = \frac{\$2.15 + \$5.00}{\$67.50} = \frac{\$\,7.15}{\$67.50} = \underline{\underline{10.6\%}}$$

In this case, if your forecasts of annual dividends and capital gains hold up, an investment in Rose Colored Glasses should provide a return of around 10.6 percent per year.

Whether or not you should consider RCG a viable investment candidate depends on how this level of expected return stacks up to the amount of risk you must assume. Suppose you have decided that the stock is moderately risky. To determine whether the expected rate of return on this investment will be satisfactory, you can compare it to some benchmark. One of the best is the rate of return you can expect from a *risk-free* security such as a *U.S. Treasury bill.* The idea is that the return on a *risky* security should be greater than that available on a *risk-free* security (this is the concept underlying the graph in Exhibit 11.1). If, for example, U.S. T-bills are yielding, say, 4 or 5 percent, then you'd probably want to receive something like 12 to 15 percent for a moderately risky security like RCG. In essence, the 12 to 15 percent is your **desired rate of return**—it is the minimum rate of return you feel you should receive in compensation for the amount of risk you must assume. *An investment should be considered acceptable only if it's expected to generate a rate of return that meets (or exceeds) your desired rate of return.* In the case of RCG, the stock should *not* be considered a viable investment candidate, since it fails to provide the minimum or desired rate of return. In short, because of the risks involved with the stock, the amount of expected return falls short of the amount you deserve.

Concept Check

11-1. Briefly discuss the relationship between *investing* and personal financial planning. Do these two activities complement each other?

11-2. What's the difference between an *investment plan* and a capital accumulation plan? Are they in any way related?

11-3. Identify four major investment objectives. Why is it important to have one or more investment objective(s) when embarking on an investment program? Of the various investment objectives, which two (2) would *you* consider most important? Explain.

11-4. With so many different types of securities to choose from here in the United States, why would an American investor even want to consider investing in foreign markets? Identify two or three different ways of investing in foreign securities; as an individual investor, which approach would you find most appealing? Why are currency exchange rates so important to investors in foreign markets?

11-5. Describe the various types of risk to which investors are exposed. What is meant by the risk-return trade-off? What is the *risk-free rate of return*?

11-6. Briefly describe the two basic sources of return to investors. What is interest-on-interest, and why is it such an important element of return?

desired rate of return The minimum rate of return that an investor feels should be earned in compensation for the amount of risk assumed.

INVESTING IN COMMON STOCK

FPPC

LG4

Remember that money you inherited and decided to invest? Let's say you want to use part of it to buy some common stocks—a popular form of investing that offers attractive returns from both price appreciation and the receipt of dividends. What kinds of stocks (for example, blue chips, growth stock, and so on) would you be most interested in, and how w.ould you decide what price to pay for them? Give some thought to these questions before reading on.

Common stocks appeal to investors for a variety of reasons. To some, investing in stocks is a way to hit it big if the issue shoots up in price; to others, it is the level of current income they offer. In fact, given the size and diversity of the stock market, it is safe to say that no matter what the investment objective, there are common stocks available to fit the bill. Not surprisingly, common stocks are a popular form of investing, used by literally millions of individuals and a variety of financial institutions.

The basic investment attribute of a share of common stock is that it enables the investor to participate in the profits of the firm, which is how it derives its value. Every shareholder is, in effect, a part-owner of the firm and, as such, is entitled to a piece of its profit. However, this claim on income is not without its limitations, for common stockholders are really the **residual owners** of the company, meaning they are entitled to dividend income and a prorated share of the company's earnings only after all the other obligations of the firm have been met. Equally important, as residual owners, *holders of common stock have no guarantee that they will ever receive any return on their investment.*

COMMON STOCK AS A FORM OF INVESTMENT

The stock market can perform beautifully (like it did in 1991, when it went up some 20 percent), or it can produce very unspectacular returns—even big losses. 1994 was certainly a good example of an unspectacular year, as the market bounced up and down in reaction to a series of interest rate hikes by the Federal Reserve. As you can see in Exhibit 11.2, when all was said and done, the market did little more than move sideways, as it ended the year less than 100 points—or just 2.1%—above where it started; not exactly the kind of performance that draws investors to the stock market! But if you really want a year for the record books, there's probably no better example than 1987. Actually, the year started off very nicely as stock prices shot up in the first six months (incredibly, the market had gone up almost *30 percent* by midsummer), only to experience a terrible market crash on October 19, when stock prices, as measured by the Dow Jones Industrial Average, fell over 500 points on volume of over 600 million shares. October 19, 1987, was not just another bad day in the market—it was history! As far as the market was concerned, it was like no other day on record and hopefully, it's a situation that won't reoccur any too soon.

Fortunately, the October 19s of this world are the rare exception rather than the rule. And as a result, the stock market is not all risk and wild price volatility. There are also some pretty attractive rewards. Consider the fact that even though the last quarter of 1987 was a wild and woolly one, the market still ended the year on the plus side—if up by only a meager 2 percent. And in 1988, the market went up another 12 percent, followed by an even better 27 percent jump in market prices during 1989. Indeed, if you look at the eight years from August 1982 (which is generally regarded as the beginning of the great bull market of the 1980s) through July 1990 (which is about the time Iraq invaded Kuwait), you'll find the market went up an impressive 280 percent—and that's *after* factoring in the impact of the 1987 crash and another smaller market plunge that occurred in October 1989. Clearly, it's this kind of resiliency and overall market performance that explains the appeal of common stocks.

Issuers of Common Stock. Shares of common stock can be issued by any corporation in any line of business. But, although all corporations have stockholders, not all of them have publicly traded shares. The stocks of interest to us in this book are the so-called *publicly traded issues*—the shares that are readily available to the general public and that are bought and sold in the open market. Just about every facet of American industry is represented in the stock market. You can buy shares in public utilities, airlines, mining concerns, manufacturing

EXHIBIT 11.2

The Stock Market in 1994

As far as the stock market was concerned, 1994 was not exactly a stellar year! The 1994 market was really driven by the Federal Reserve Board, as that organization raised interest rates no less than six times during the year, with just about every rate hike resulting in a sharp drop in the Dow Jones industrial average. In spite of all the ups and downs, the market ended the year with the Dow at 3834.44, just 80.35 points (or 2.1 percent) above where the Dow opened in January (3754.09).

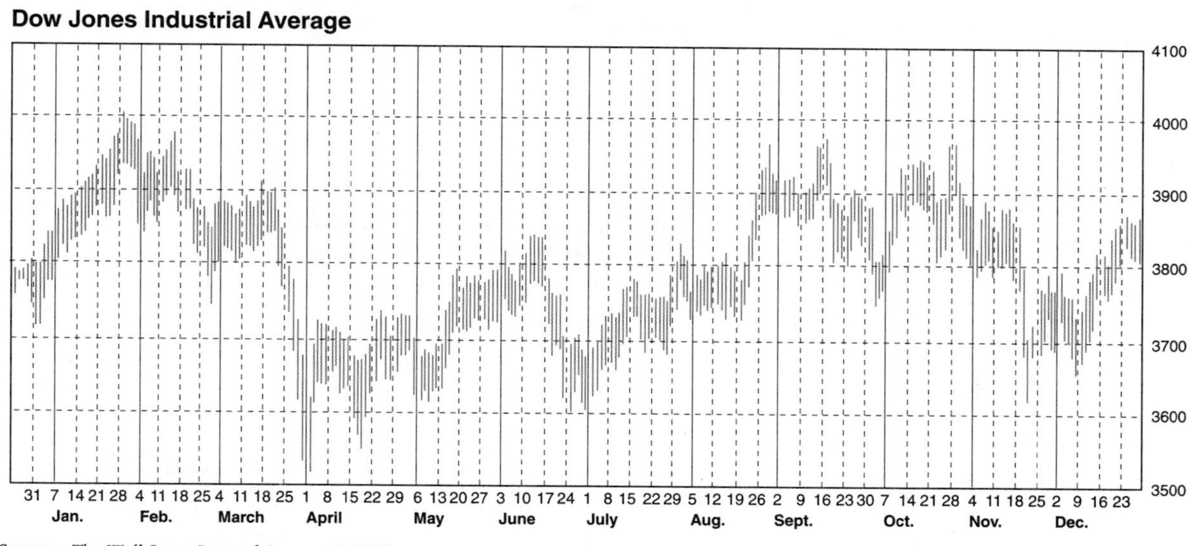

Source: *The Wall Street Journal,* January 3, 1995.

firms, and retail organizations, or in financial institutions like banks and insurance companies. The number of shares issued depends on the size of the firm and its financial needs.

Aside from the initial distribution of common stock when the corporation is formed, subsequent sales of additional shares may be made through a procedure known as a *public offering*. The corporation, working with its underwriter, simply offers the investing public a certain number of shares of its stock at a certain price. Exhibit 11.3 depicts the announcement for such an offering. Note in this case that OfficeMax is offering 35.7 million shares of stock (in both the United States and abroad) at a price of $19 per share. When issued, the new shares will be commingled with the outstanding shares (since they are all the same class of stock), and the net result will be an increase in the number of shares outstanding.

Voting Rights. The holders of common stock normally receive *voting rights,* which means that for each share of stock held, they receive one vote. In certain instances, common stock may be designated as nonvoting at the time of its issue, but this is the exception rather than the rule. Although different voting systems exist, the small stockholders need not concern themselves with them since, regardless of the system used, the chance that they will be able to affect corporate control with their votes is quite slim. Corporations have annual stockholders' meetings at which time new directors are elected and special issues are voted on. Since most small stockholders are unable to attend these meetings, they can use a proxy to assign their votes to another person, who will vote their stock for them.

residual owners Shareholders of the company, they are entitled to dividend income and shares of the company's profits only after all of the firm's other obligations have been met.

EXHIBIT 11.3

An Announcement of a New Common Stock Issue

Here the company is issuing nearly 36 million shares of stock at a price of $19 a share. For OfficeMax, that'll mean over $675 million in new capital! Note in this case, that in addition to offering the stock in the United States and Canada, there's 6.5 million shares being offered to *foreign investors*—which, by the way, is becoming increasingly common as more and more companies are going global in their search for capital.

This announcement is neither an offer to sell, nor a solicitation of an offer to buy, any of these securities. The offer is made only by the Prospectus.

November 10, 1994

35,700,000 Shares

Common Shares

Price $19 Per Share

Copies of the Prospectus may be obtained in any State or jurisdiction from such of the undersigned as may legally offer these securities in compliance with the securities laws of such State.

Number of shares being offered in the United States and Canada.

29,200,000 Shares

The above shares are being offered in the United States and Canada by the undersigned.

Donaldson, Lufkin & Jenrette
Securities Corporation

Morgan Stanley & Co.
Incorporated

William Blair & Company

Dean Witter Reynolds Inc.

McDonald & Company
Securities, Inc.

Number of shares being offered outside the United States and Canada.

6,500,000 Shares

The above shares are being offered outside the United States and Canada by the undersigned.

Donaldson, Lufkin & Jenrette
Securities Corporation

Morgan Stanley & Co.
International

William Blair & Company

Dean Witter International Ltd.

McDonald & Company
Securities, Inc.

Source: *Forbes,* December 19, 1994.

A **proxy** is merely a written statement assigning voting rights to another person.

BASIC TAX CONSIDERATIONS

Common stocks provide income in the form of dividends, usually paid quarterly, and/or capital gains, which occurs when the price of the stock goes up over time. As indicated in Chapter 3, from a tax perspective, it does make a difference how the investment income is earned. That is, whereas dividends are fully taxable at regular tax rates (up to 39.6 percent), capital gains are subject to a maximum tax rate of 28 percent. Thus, capital gains are subject to less tax than dividends, but that only applies to taxpayers in the maximum (31 percent or above) tax brackets. Of course, there is no tax liability on any capital gains until the stock is actually sold (*paper gains*—that is, any price appreciation that occurs on stock that you still own—accumulate tax-free). Taxes are due on any dividends and/or capital gains in the year in which the dividends are received and/or the stock is actually sold. Thus, if you received, say, $125 in dividends in 1995, you would have to include that income on your 1995 tax return.

Here is how it all works: Assume, for example, that you just sold 100 shares of common stock for $30 per share. Also assume that the stock was originally purchased two years ago for $20 per share and that during the current year you received $1.25 per share in cash dividends. For tax purposes, you would have a capital gain of $1,000—($30/share − $20/share) × 100 shares—and $125 in dividend income—$1.25/share × 100 shares. If you were in the 31 percent tax bracket, your dividends would be subject to a 31 percent tax rate (that is, $125 × .31 = $38.75 in taxes), but the capital gains you earned would be subject to a tax rate of only 28 percent—that is, $1,000 × .28 = $280 in taxes. Thus, you'd end up paying $318.75 ($38.75 + $280) in taxes. Whatever you are left with would represent your after-tax income—in this case, it would be $1,125 − $318.75 = $806.25.

TYPES OF DIVIDENDS

Corporations pay dividends to their common stockholders in the form of cash and/or additional stock. *Cash dividends* are the most common. Since firms can pay dividends from earnings accumulated from previous periods, stockholders may receive dividends *even in periods when the firm shows a loss.* Cash dividends are normally distributed on a quarterly basis in an amount determined by the firm's board of directors. For example, if the directors declared a quarterly cash dividend of 50 cents a share, and you owned 200 shares of stock, you would receive a check for $100.

A popular way of assessing the amount of dividends received is to measure the stock's dividend yield. Basically, **dividend yield** is a measure of common stock dividends on a relative (percent), rather than absolute (dollar), basis—that is, the dollar amount of dividends received is related to the market price of the stock. As such, dividend yield is an indication of the rate of current income earned on the investment dollar. It is computed as follows:

$$\text{Dividend yield} = \frac{\text{Annual dividends received per share}}{\text{Market price per share of stock}}$$

Thus, a company that annually pays $2 per share in dividends and whose stock is trading at $50 a share will have a dividend yield of 4 percent ($2/$50 = .04).

Occasionally the directors may declare a stock dividend as a supplement to or in place of cash dividends. **Stock dividends** represent new shares of stock issued to existing stockholders. Although they often satisfy the needs of some investors, stock dividends really have no value, since they represent the receipt of something already owned. For example, when a firm declares a 10 percent stock dividend, each shareholder receives one-tenth of a share of stock for each share owned—in other words, a stockholder with 100 shares of stock will receive 10 new shares. Since all stockholders receive a 10 percent increase in the *number* of shares they own, their proportion of ownership in

proxy A written statement used to assign a stockholder's voting rights to another person, typically one of the existing directors.

dividend yield The percentage return provided by the dividends paid on common stock; calculated by dividing the cash dividends paid during the year by the stock's market price.

stock dividends New shares of stock distributed to existing stockholders as a supplement to or substitute for cash dividends.

the firm remains unchanged. Moreover, the total market value of the shares owned is (roughly) the same after the stock dividend as before. Why is that so? Because the price of the stock will usually fall in direct proportion to the size of a stock dividend. Thus, in our example above, a drop in price will bring the total market value of 110 shares (after the stock dividend) to about the same as the total market value of the 100 shares that existed before the dividend. Clearly, under such circumstances, the investor is right back where he started from: he's received nothing of value. The shareholder who has received a stock dividend can, of course, sell the new shares in order to cash out the dividend. But then the value of the stocks owned by that shareholder will be reduced—granted, he'll then own the same number of shares as before the stock dividend, but they'll be worth less.

SOME KEY MEASURES OF PERFORMANCE

Professional money managers and seasoned investors tend to use a variety of financial ratios and measures when making investment decisions, particularly when common stock is involved. They look at such things as dividend yield (mentioned earlier), book value, return on equity, earnings per share, and price/earning multiples to get a feel for the investment merits of a particular stock. In short, they use these and other ratios to help them decide whether or not to invest in a particular stock. Fortunately, most of the widely followed ratios can be found in published reports (like *S&P Stock Reports* or *Value Line*), so you don't have to compute them yourself. Even so, if you're thinking about buying, or already have a position in common stock, there are a few measures of performance you'll want to keep track of.

Book Value. The amount of stockholders' equity in a firm is measured by **book value.** This is an accounting measure that is determined by subtracting the firm's liabilities and preferred stocks from the value of its assets. Book value indicates the amount of stockholder funds used to finance the firm. For example, assume Rose Colored Glasses (RCG) had assets of $5 million, liabilities of $2 million, and preferred stock valued at $1 million. The book value of the firm's common stock would be $2 million ($5 million—$2 million—$1 million). If the book value is divided by the number of shares outstanding, the result is *book value per share.* If RCG had 100,000 shares of common stock outstanding, its book value per share would be $20 ($2,000,000/100,000 shares). Because of the positive impact it can have on the growth of the firm, you'd like to see book value per share steadily increasing over time; also, look for stocks whose market prices are comfortably above their book values.

Net Profit Margin. As a yardstick of profitability, the **net profit margin** is one of the most widely followed measures of corporate performance. Basically, this ratio relates the net profits of the firm to its sales, providing an indication of how well the company is controlling its cost structure. The higher the net profit margin, the more money the company earns. Look for a relatively stable—or even better, an increasing—net profit margin.

Return on Equity. Another very important and widely followed measure, **return on equity** (or ROE, for short) reflects the overall profitability of the firm. It captures, in a single ratio, the amount of success the firm is having in managing its assets, operations, and capital structure. Return on equity is important because it has a direct and significant impact on the profits, growth, and dividends of the firm. The better the ROE, the better the financial condition and competitive position of the company. Look for a stable or increasing ROE, and watch out for a falling ROE, as that could spell trouble.

Earnings per Share. With stocks, the firm's annual earnings are usually measured and reported in terms of **earnings per share (EPS).** Basically, EPS translates total corporate profits into profits on a per-share basis and provides a convenient measure of the amount of earnings available to stockholders. Earnings per share is found by using the following simple formula:

$$\text{EPS} = \frac{\begin{matrix}\text{Net profit} \\ \text{after taxes}\end{matrix} - \begin{matrix}\text{Preferred} \\ \text{dividends paid}\end{matrix}}{\begin{matrix}\text{Number of shares of} \\ \text{common stock outstanding}\end{matrix}}$$

For example, if RCG reported a net profit of $350,000, paid $100,000 in dividends to preferred stockholders, and had 100,000 shares of common outstanding, it would have an EPS of $2.50 [($350,000 − $100,000)/100,000]. Note that preferred dividends are *subtracted* from profits since they have to be paid before any monies can be made available to common stockholders. The magnitude of earnings per share is closely followed by stockholders because it represents the amount that the firm has earned on behalf of each outstanding share of common stock. Here, too, look for a steady rate of growth in EPS.

Price/Earnings Ratio. When the prevailing market price of a share of common stock is divided by the annual earnings per share, the result is the **price/earnings (P/E) ratio,** which is viewed as an indication of investor confidence and expectations. The higher the price/earnings multiple, the more confidence investors are presumed to have in a given security. In the case of RCG, whose shares are currently selling for $30, the price/earnings ratio is 12 ($30 per share/$2.50 per share). This means that RCG stock is selling for 12 times its earnings. P/E ratios are important to investors because they provide a feel for the general expectations of the firm. They reveal how aggressively the stock is being priced in the market. Watch out for real high P/Es, since that could indicate the stock is being overpriced (and thus might be headed for a big drop in price). P/E ratios are not static, but tend to move with the market: when the market's soft, a stock's P/E will be low, and when things heat up in the market, so will the stock's P/E.

Beta. A stock's **beta** is an indication of its *price volatility;* it shows how responsive the stock is to the market. In recent years, the use of betas to measure the *market risk* of common stock has become a widely accepted practice, and as a result, published betas are now available from most brokerage firms and investment services. The beta for a given stock is determined by a statistical technique that relates the stock's historical returns to the market. The market (as measured by something like the S&P index of 500 stocks) is used as a benchmark of performance, and it always has a beta of 1.0. From there, everything is relative: low-beta stocks—those with betas of less than 1.0—have low price volatility (they're relatively price- stable), while high-beta stocks—those with betas of more than 1.0—are considered to be highly volatile. In short, the higher a stock's beta, the more risky it is considered to be. Stock betas can be either *positive* or *negative,* though the vast majority are positive, meaning that the stocks move in the same general direction as the market (that is, if the market is going up, so will the price of the stock).

Actually, beta is an *index* of price performance and is interpreted as a percentage response to the market. Thus, if RCG has a beta of, say, 0.8, it will rise (or fall) only 80 percent as fast as the market—if the market goes up by 10 percent, RCG will go up only 8 percent (10 percent × .8). In contrast, if the stock had a beta of 1.8, it would go up or down 1.8 times as fast—the price of the stock would rise higher and fall lower than the market. Clearly, other things being equal, if you're looking for a relatively conservative investment, you should stick with low-beta stocks; on the other hand, if it's capital gains and price volatility you're after, then go with high-beta securities.

PUTTING A VALUE ON STOCK

No matter what kind of investor you are or what your investment objectives happen to be, sooner or later you will have to face one of the most

book value The amount of stockholders' equity in a firm; determined by subtracting the company's liabilities and preferred stock value from the value of its assets.

net profit margin A key measure of corporate profitability that relates the net profits of a firm to its sales; it shows the rate of return the company is earning on its sales.

return on equity (ROE) ROE captures the overall profitability of the firm, as it provides a measure of the returns to stockholders; is important because of its impact on the growth, profits, and dividends of the firm.

earnings per share (EPS) The return earned on behalf of each share of common stock during a given 12-month period; calculated by dividing all earnings remaining after paying preferred dividends by the number of common shares outstanding.

price/earnings (P/E) ratio A measure of investors' confidence in and expectations for a given security; calculated by dividing the prevailing market price per share by the annual earnings per share.

beta An index of the price volatility imbedded in a share of common stock; provides a reflection of how the price of a share of stock responds to market forces.

difficult questions in the field of investments: *How much are you willing to pay for the stock?* In order to answer this question, you have to put a value on the stock. Measures such as book value, earnings per share, P/E multiples, and betas are a part of the *fundamental analysis* used to determine the underlying value of a share of stock. Basically, the notion of fundamental analysis is that the value of a stock depends on its expected stream of future earnings. Once you have a handle on the expected stream of future earnings, you can use that information in the *approximate yield* formula (Equation 11.1) to find the *expected rate of return on the investment.* If the expected return from the investment exceeds your desired or minimum rate of return, you should make the investment—in effect, you should be willing to pay the current or prevailing market price. Put another way, with fundamental analysis you are trying to determine whether or not you should pay the current or prevailing market price for the stock. If the return you expect from the investment (via Equation 11.1) is less than your desired rate of return, you should not buy the stock (at its current market price), since it is currently "over-priced" and, as such, you will not be able to earn your desired rate of return.

TYPES OF COMMON STOCK

Common stocks are often classified on the basis of their dividends or their rate of growth in EPS. Among the more popular types of common stock are blue-chip, growth, income, speculative, cyclical, defensive, mid-cap, and small cap stocks.

Blue-Chip Stocks. These are the cream of the common stock crop; **blue chips** are stocks that are unsurpassed in quality and have a long and stable record of earnings and dividends. They are issued by large, well-established firms that have impeccable financial credentials—firms like GE, Merck, Wal-Mart, and Coca-Cola. The companies hold important, if not leading, positions in their industries and frequently determine the standards by which other firms are measured. Blue chips are particularly attractive to investors who seek quality investment outlets that offer decent dividend yields and respectable growth potential. Many use them for long-term investment purposes, and, because of their relatively low risk exposure, as a way of obtaining modest but dependable rates of return on their investment dollars. They are popular with a large segment of the investing public and, as a result, are often relatively high priced, especially when the market is unsettled and investors become more quality-conscious.

Growth Stocks. Stocks that have experienced, and are expected to continue experiencing, consistently high rates of growth in operations and earnings are known as **growth stocks.** A good growth stock might exhibit a *sustained* rate of growth in earnings of 15 to 20 percent (or more) over a period during which common stocks are averaging only 5 to 6 percent. H&R Block, Microsoft, U.S. Healthcare, Blockbuster Entertainment, and Shering-Plough are all prime examples of growth stocks. These stocks normally pay little or nothing in dividends, since the firm's rapid growth potential requires that its earnings be retained and reinvested. The high growth expectations for those stocks usually cause them to sell at relatively high P/E ratios, and they typically have betas in excess of 1.0. Because of their potential for dramatic price appreciation, they appeal mostly to investors who are seeking capital gains rather than dividend income.

Income Stocks versus Speculative Stocks. Stocks whose appeal is based primarily on the dividends they pay out are known as **income stocks.** They have a fairly stable stream of earnings, a large portion of which is distributed in the form of dividends. Income shares have relatively high dividend yields and, as such, are ideally suited for individuals who are seeking a relatively safe and high level of current income from their investment capital. An added (and often overlooked) feature of these stocks is that, unlike bonds and preferred stock, holders of income stock can expect *the amount of dividends paid to increase over time.* Examples of income stock would include Duke Power, Baltimore Gas & Electric, PacifiCorp, U.S. West, Texaco, and Upjohn Co. Because of their low risk, these stocks commonly have betas of less than 1.0.

Rather than basing their investment decisions on a proven record of earnings, investors in **speculative stocks** gamble that some new information, discovery, or production technique will favorably affect the growth of the firm and inflate the price of its stock. For example, a company whose stock is considered speculative may have recently discovered a new drug or located a valuable resource such as oil. The value of speculative stocks and their P/E ratios tend to fluctuate widely as additional information with respect to the firm's future is received. The betas for speculative stocks are nearly always well in excess of 1.0. Investors in speculative stocks should be prepared to experience losses as well as gains, since *these are high-risk securities.* They include companies like Cisco Systems, Tyco Toys, Wall Street Deli, and Flightsafety International.

Cyclical Stocks or Defensive Stocks. Stocks whose price movements tend to follow the business cycle are called **cyclical stocks.** This means that when the economy is in an expansionary stage (recovery or expansion), the prices of cyclical stocks increase, and during a contractionary stage (recession or depression), they decline. Most cyclical stocks are found in the basic industries—automobiles, steel, and lumber, for example; these are industries that are sensitive to changes in economic activity. Investors try to purchase cyclical stocks just prior to an expansionary phase and sell just before the contraction occurs. Since they tend to move with the market, these stocks always have positive betas. Caterpillar, Georgia-Pacific, Allied Signal, Eaton Corp., and Premark International are all examples of cyclical stocks.

The prices and returns from **defensive stocks,** unlike those of cyclical stocks, are expected to remain stable during periods of contraction in business activity. For this reason, they are often called *countercyclical.* The shares of consumer goods companies, certain public utilities, and gold mining companies are good examples of defensive stocks. Because they are basically income stocks, their earnings and dividends tend to hold their market prices up during periods of economic decline. Betas on these stocks are quite low and occasionally even negative. Bandag, Loctite, Checkpoint Systems, and Humana are all examples of defensive stocks.

Mid-Caps and Small Caps. In the stock market, a stock's size is based on its market value—or, more commonly, on what is known as its *market capitalization* or *market cap.* A stock's market cap is found by multiplying its market price by the number of shares outstanding. Generally speaking, the market can be broken into three major components, or segments, as measured by a stock's market "cap":

Small Cap	Stocks with market caps of less than $500 million
Mid-Cap	Market caps of $500 million to $2–$3 billion
Large Cap	Market caps of more than $2–$3 billion

In addition to these three segments, there's another one reserved for the *really small* stocks, known as *micro-caps.* As the accompanying *Issues in Money Management* box explains, many of these stocks have market caps well below $100 million (some as low as $10 to $15 million), and should only be used by investors who fully understand the risks involved and can tolerate such risk exposure.

Of the 3 major categories above, the large cap stocks are the real biggies—the AT&Ts, GEs, and Exxons of the world. Many of these are considered to be blue-chip stocks, and while there are fewer large cap stocks than any other, these companies account for about 60 percent of the total value of U.S. equity markets. Just because they're big, however, doesn't mean they're better. Indeed, both the small and mid-cap segments of the market tend to outperform large stocks over time.

Mid-cap stocks are a special breed unto themselves and offer investors some very attractive return opportunities. They provide much of the

blue-chip stock A stock that is known to provide a safe and stable return; generally issued by companies that are expected to provide an uninterrupted stream of dividends and have good long-term growth prospects.

growth stock A stock whose earnings and market price have increased over time at a rate that is well above average.

income stock A stock whose chief appeal is the dividends it pays out; typically offers dividend payments that can be expected to increase over time.

speculative stock Stock that is purchased in the hope that its price per share will increase.

cyclical stock Stock whose price movements tend to parallel the various stages of the business cycle.

defensive stock Stock that tends to exhibit price movements that are contrary to movements in the business cycle; often called *countercyclical stock.*

Issues in Money Management

Micro-Cap Stocks Can Produce Big Bangs for the Hearty Investor

Is micro even better than small? It may be when it comes to stock capitalization. Micro-cap stocks—stocks with a total market capitalization of less than $100 million—earned about 20 percent average annual return for the past 20 years, according to Merrill Lynch Quantitative Analysis indexes. This exceeds the 17 percent returns of small-cap stocks ($100 million to $500 million), about 14 percent for mid-cap stocks ($500 to $2 to $3 billion), and 13 percent for larger firms ($2 to $3 billion and above).

But there's a catch to earning big rewards, and that is micro-cap investors must be daring and willing to commit for the long term. Because these stocks are more volatile and illiquid than those of larger firms, they aren't likely to provide steady or predictable results. Nor are they usually followed by analysts. You can make money if you get in early, look for small, undervalued companies with some sort of catalyst that will push the stock up, and the company performs as expected. On the flip side, many issues are very thinly traded and therefore hard to sell if it doesn't work out. Many financial advisors suggest diversifying a large-cap portfolio with micro-caps. Adding just 10 percent can boost your returns considerably, with minimal risk.

Although micro-caps floundered along with other stocks in early 1994, they bounced back later as investors were lured by the promise of high returns. Their low prices, together with the potential for strong earnings and growth at a time when interest rates are rising, made micro-caps especially attractive. In addition, the number of mutual funds that specialize in micro-cap stocks has grown considerably in recent years. As small cap stocks become more popular, micro-caps represent what micro-cap fund manager Chuck Royce dubs "the final frontier," offering opportunities similar to those of small caps 10 ago.

If you want to take the micro-cap route, be prepared to be your own stock analyst. You're unlikely to find much information on the stock and its performance in the financial press. So get out your calculator and run the numbers on companies like Interlinq Software, which makes mortgage lending software for financial institutions (market cap: $43 million); Checkmate Electronics, a manufacturer of magnetic-ink character readers ($38 million); Integracare, a rehabilitation services provider ($28 million); and Royal Grip, which makes golf club grips ($24 million). Check out the company's product lines, market niche, and management, as well as financial ratios. (One place to find names of actively traded small and micro-cap companies is *Business Week's* annual listing of the best small companies, published in May.)

Sources: Adapted from "The Best Small Companies," *Business Week*, May 23, 1994, pp. 100–101; Pam Black, "A Bigger Role for Small Fry in Your Portfolio?" *Business Week*, October 24, 1994, pp. 110–111; and Caitlin Mollison, "Micro Caps Can Spell Big Rewards for the Brave," *The Wall Street Journal*, September 19, 1994, pp. C1, C7.

sizzle of small-stock returns, but without all the price volatility. At the same time, because these are fairly good-sized companies, and many of them have been around for a long time, they offer some of the safety of the big, established stocks. Among the ranks of the mid-caps are such well-known companies as Justin Industries, Starbucks, Tyson Foods, International Dairy Queen, Tootsie Roll, Wendy's International, Briggs & Stratton, and Hormel, in addition to some not-so-well-known names. For the most part, while these securities offer a nice alternative to large stocks without all the drawbacks and uncertainties of small caps, they probably are most appropriate for investors who are willing to tolerate a bit more risk and price volatility.

Some investors consider small companies to be in a class by themselves. They believe these firms' stocks hold especially attractive return opportunities, which in many cases, has turned out to be true. Known as **small cap stocks,** these companies generally have *annual revenues* of less than $250 million, and because of their size, spurts of growth can have dramatic effects on their earnings and stock prices. ShowBiz Pizza Time, Mail Boxes Etc., President Riverboat Casinos, Checkers Drive-In Restaurants, Heartland Express, and Ben & Jerry's are just a few examples of some of the better-known small cap stocks. Now while some small caps (like Ben & Jerry's, for example) are solid companies with equally solid financials, that's definitely not the case with most of them! Indeed, because many of these companies are so small, they don't have a lot of stock outstanding, and their shares are not widely traded. In addition, small company stocks have a tendency to be "here today and gone tomorrow." While some of these stocks may hold the potential for high returns, investors should also be aware of the very high-risk exposure that comes with many of them.

INVESTING IN COMMON STOCK

The first step in investing is to know *where* to put your money; the second is to know *when* to make your moves. The first question basically involves matching your risk and return objectives with the available investment vehicles. As noted earlier, *a stock (or any investment vehicle for that matter) should be considered a viable investment candidate only so long as it promises to generate a sufficiently attractive rate of return* and, in particular, one that fully compensates you for any risks you have to take. Thus, if you're considering the purchase of a stock, you should expect to earn more than what you can get from T-bills or high-grade corporate bonds. The reason: stocks are riskier than bills or bonds, so you *deserve more return*. Indeed, if you can't get enough return from the security to offset the risk, then you shouldn't invest in the stock!

Selecting a Stock. Granted, you want an investment that provides an attractive rate of return—one that meets or exceeds your required return. So, how do you go about selecting such a stock? The answer is by doing a little digging and crunching a few numbers. Here's what you'd want to do: To begin with, find a company that you like and then take a look at how it's performed over the past three to five years. Find out what kind of growth rate (in sales) it has experienced, if it has a strong ROE and has been able to maintain or improve its profit margin, how much it has been paying out to stockholders in the form of dividends, and so forth. This kind of information is readily available in publications like *Value Line* and *S&P Stock Reports* (which we'll discuss in Chapter 12). The idea is to find stocks that are financially strong, have done well in the past, and continue to be market leaders, or hold prominent positions in a given industry or market segment. Looking at the past is only the beginning, however; for what's really important to stock valuation is the *FUTURE!* That is, as we discussed earlier in this chapter (see the section "What Makes a Good Investment?"), *the value of a share of stock at any point in time is a function of future returns, not past performance.*

So, let's turn our attention to be expected future performance of the stock. The idea is to assess the *outlook* for the stock, thereby gaining some insight about the benefits to be derived from investing in it. Of particular concern are future dividends and share price behavior. As a rule, it doesn't make much sense to go out more than two or three years because the accuracy of most forecasts begins to deteriorate rapidly after that point. Thus, using, say, a three-year investment horizon, you'd want to forecast annual dividends per share for each of the next three years, *plus* the future price of the stock at the end of the three-year holding period (obviously, if the price of the stock is projected to go up over time, you'll have some capital gains). You can try to generate these forecasts yourself or, you can look to a publication like *Value Line* and obtain the projections there (*Value Line* projects dividends and share prices five years into the future). Once you have projected dividends and share price, you can use Equation 11.1 to determine the expected return from this investment.

To see how that can be done, consider Intel Corp., the world's leading semi-conductor manufacturer. According to *Value Line,* the company has very strong financials: its sales have been growing at around 22 percent per year for the past five years, it has a net profit margin of more than 20 percent, and an ROE of just over 25 percent. Thus,

mid-cap stock A stock whose total market value—that is, number of shares outstanding × market price per share—falls somewhere between $500 million and $2 to $3 billion; these mid-sized companies are believed to offer attractive return potential without lots of price volatility.

small cap stock A stock with a total market value of less than $500 million that offers high growth and above average returns but at a cost of high risk.

historically, the company has performed very well and is definitely a market leader in its field. In early 1995, the stock was trading for $75 a share, and was paying annual dividends at the rate of about 25 cents a share. *Value Line* was projecting dividends to go up by about 15 cents a share for each of the next three to five years; also, they were estimating that the price of the stock should rise to about $125 within three years.

Using *Value Line* projections and given current dividends of 25 cents a share, we could expect dividends per share of 40 cents next year, 55 cents a share the year after (in year 2), and 70 cents per share in year 3—that is, if dividends do, in fact, grow by around 15 cents a year. Now, since Equation 11.1 uses "average annual current income" as one of its inputs, we'll use the midpoint of our projected dividends (55 cents a share) as a proxy for average annual dividends. In addition, given this stock is currently trading at $75 per share, has a projected future price of $125 a share, and we have a three-year investment period, we can use Equation 11.1 to find our expected return as follows:

$$\begin{aligned}\text{Approx Yield (Expected Ret.)} &= \frac{\$0.55 + \left[\dfrac{\$125 - \$75}{3}\right]}{\left[\dfrac{\$125 + \$75}{2}\right]}\\ &= \frac{\$0.55 + \$16.67}{\$100.00} = \underline{\underline{17.22\%}}\end{aligned}$$

Thus, if Intel stock performs as expected, it should provide us with a return of just over 17 percent. If that meets or exceeds our required rate of return (and it probably will), then the stock should be considered a viable investment candidate!

Timing Your Investments. Once you find a stock that you think will give you the kind of return you're looking for, you're ready to deal with the matter of timing your investment. So long as the prospects for the market and the economy are positive, the time may be right to invest in stocks. On the other hand, there are a couple of conditions when investing in stocks just doesn't make any sense at all. In particular, *don't* invest in stocks if:

- You feel *very strongly* that the market is headed down in the short run. If you're absolutely certain the market's in for a big fall (or will continue to fall, if it's already doing so), then wait until the market drops, and buy the stock when it's cheaper.
- You feel uncomfortable with the general tone of the market—it lacks direction, or there's way too much price volatility to suit you. This became a problem prior to and after the October 1987 crash, when computer-assisted trading started taking over the market. The result was a stock market that behaved more like a commodities market, with an intolerable amount of price volatility. When this happens, fundamentals go out the window, and the market simply becomes too risky. Do what the pros do, and wait it out on the sidelines.

Why Invest in Stocks? There are three basic reasons for investing in common stock: (1) to use the stock as a warehouse of value, (2) to accumulate capital, and/or (3) to provide a source of income. Storage of value is important to all investors, since nobody likes to lose money. However, some investors are more concerned about it than others and therefore put safety of principal first in their stock selection process. These investors are more quality-conscious and tend to gravitate toward blue chips and other nonspeculative shares. Accumulation of capital generally is an important goal to individuals with long-term investment horizons. These investors use the capital gains and/or dividends that stocks provide to build up their wealth. Some use growth stocks for such purposes; others do it with income shares; still others use a little of both. Finally, some people use stocks as a source of income; to them, a dependable flow of dividends is essential. High-yielding, good-quality income shares are usually their preferred investment vehicle.

Advantages and Disadvantages of Stock Ownership. Ownership of common stock has both advantages and disadvantages. Its advantages are threefold. First, the potential returns, in the form of both dividend income and price appreciation, can be quite substantial. The return performance of common stocks over the recent past, as well as over extended periods of time, has been noteworthy, to say the least! Second, many stocks are actively traded (there are literally thousands of such actively traded stocks) and as such they are a highly liquid form of investment—meaning they can be quickly bought and sold. Finally, they don't involve

EXHIBIT 11.4

Cash or Reinvested Dividends

Participating in a dividend reinvestment plan is a simple, yet highly effective way of building up capital over time. Over the long haul, it can prove to be a great way of earning a fully compounded rate of return on your money.

Situation: Buy 100 shares of stock at $25 a share (total investment $2,500); stock currently pays $1 a share in annual dividends. Price of the stock increases at 8 percent per year; dividends grow at 5 percent per year.

Investment Period	Number of Shares Held	Market Value of Stock Holdings	Total Cash Dividends Received
Take Dividends in Cash			
5 years	100	$ 3,672	$ 552
10 years	100	5,397	1,258
15 years	100	7,930	2,158
20 years	100	11,652	3,307
Participate in a DRP			
5 years	115.59	$ 4,245	$0
10 years	135.66	7,322	0
15 years	155.92	12,364	0
20 years	176.00	20,508	0

any direct management (or unusual management problems) and market/company information is usually widely published and easily available.

Risk, the problem of timing purchases and sales, and the uncertainty of dividends are all disadvantages of common stock ownership. Although potential common stock returns may be high, the risk and uncertainty associated with the actual receipt of that return is also great. Even though careful selection of stocks may reduce the amount of risk to which the investor is exposed, the risk-return trade-off cannot be completely eliminated. In other words, high returns on common stock are not guaranteed; they may or may not occur depending on numerous economic, industry, and company factors. The timing of purchases and sales is closely related to risk. Many investors purchase a stock, hold it for a period of time during which the price drops, and then sell it below the original purchase price—that is, at a loss. The proper strategy, of course, is to buy low and sell high, but the problem of predicting price movements makes it difficult to implement such a plan.

Be Sure to Plow Back Your Earnings. Unless you're living off the income, the basic investment objective with stocks is the same as it is with any other security: to earn an attractive, fully compounded rate of return. This requires regular reinvestment of dividend income. And there's no better way to accomplish such reinvestment than through a **dividend reinvestment plan (DRP).** The basic investment philosophy at work here is that if the company is good enough to invest in, it's good enough to reinvest in. In a dividend reinvestment plan, shareholders can sign up to have their cash dividends automatically reinvested in additional shares of the company's common stock —in essence, it's like taking your cash dividends in the form of more shares of common stock. The idea is to put your money to work by building up your investment in the stock. Such an approach can have a tremendous impact on your investment position over time, as seen in Exhibit 11.4.

Today, over 1,000 companies (including most major corporations) have DRPs in existence, and each one provides investors with a convenient and inexpensive way to accumulate capital. Stocks in

dividend reinvestment plan (DRP) A program offered by over 1,000 major corporations whereby stockholders can choose to take their dividends in the form of more shares of the company's stock, rather than cash; it provides a relatively painless way of earning a fully compounded rate of return.

most DRPs are acquired free of any brokerage commissions, and some plans even sell stocks to their DRP investors at below-market prices—often at discounts of 3 to 5 percent. In addition, most plans credit fractional shares to the investor's account. Shareholders can join these plans simply by sending in a completed authorization form to the company (one requirement: the shares must be registered in your name). Once you are in the plan, the number of shares you hold will begin to accumulate with each dividend date. There is a catch, however—that is, even though these dividends take the form of additional shares of stock, *reinvested dividends are taxable, in the year they're received,* just as if they had been received in cash.

Concept Check

11-7. From a tax perspective, would it make any difference to an investor whether the return on a stock took the form of dividends or capital gains? Explain.

11-8. What's the difference between a cash dividend and a *stock dividend*? Which would you rather receive?

11-9. Define and briefly discuss each of the following common stock measurements: (a) *book value,* (b) *ROE,* (c) *earnings per share (EPS),* (d) *price/earnings (P/E) ratio,* and (e) *beta.*

11-10. Briefly discuss some of the different types of common stock. Which type(s) would be most appealing to you, and why?

11-11. Under what conditions would a stock be considered a viable investment candidate? What are *dividend reinvestment plans,* and how do they fit into a stock investment program?

INVESTING IN BONDS FPPC

LG5

A bond is a fixed-income security that provides investors with a high, secure, and regular source of current income. Stop for a moment and give some thought to how you might be able to use bonds in your own investment program. Do you think you'd want to use them if you were an aggressive investor interested mostly in capital gains? Also, consider the question of what causes bond prices to change.

Bonds are a form of *debt capital,* meaning that they represent borrowed funds. Bonds are often referred to as *fixed-income securities* because the debt service obligations of the issuer are fixed—that is, the issuing organization agrees to pay a *fixed amount of interest periodically and to repay a fixed amount of principal* at or before maturity. Bonds normally have face values of $1,000 or $5,000, and maturities of 10 to 30 years.

WHY INVEST IN BONDS?

Like many other types of investment vehicles, bonds provide investors with two kinds of income: (1) They provide a generous amount of current income, and (2) they can often be used to generate substantial amounts of capital gains. The current income, of course, is derived from the interest payments received over the life of the issue. Capital gains, in contrast, are earned whenever market interest rates fall. A basic trading rule in the bond market is that interest rates and bond prices move in opposite directions: When interest rates rise, bond prices fall; and when they drop, bond prices rise. Thus, it is possible to buy bonds at one price and, if interest rate conditions are right, to sell them some time later at a higher price. Of course, it is also possible to incur a capital loss should market rates move against the investor. Taken together, the current income and capital gains earned from bonds can lead to attractive and highly competitive investor returns.

Bonds are also a versatile investment outlet. They can be used conservatively by those who seek high current income, or aggressively by those who actively go after capital gains. Bonds have long been considered an excellent way of getting high current income, but only since the advent of volatile interest rates have they also become recognized as trading vehicles—that is, as a way to earn fat returns from capital gains. Investors found that the number of profitable trading opportunities increased substantially as wider and more frequent swings in interest rates began to occur.

Finally, bond issues, being of generally high quality, can be used for the preservation and long-term accumulation of capital. In fact, many individuals, regularly and over the long haul, commit all or most of their investment funds to bonds because of this single attribute.

BASIC ISSUE CHARACTERISTICS

A bond is a negotiable, long-term debt instrument that carries certain obligations on the part of the issuer. Unlike the holders of common stock, bondholders have no ownership or equity position in the issuing firm or organization. This is so because bonds are debt, and bondholders, in a roundabout way, are only lending money to the issuer.

As a rule, bonds pay interest every six months. The amount of interest paid is a function of the **coupon,** which defines the annual interest that will be paid by the issuer to the bondholder. For instance, a $1,000 bond with an 8 percent coupon would pay $80 in interest every year—generally in the form of two $40 semiannual payments. The principal amount of a bond, also known as *par value,* specifies the amount of capital that must be repaid at maturity—thus, there is $1,000 of principal in a $1,000 bond. Of course, debt securities regularly trade at market prices that differ from their principal (or par) values. This occurs whenever an issue's coupon differs from the prevailing market rate of interest; in essence, the price of an issue will change until its yield is compatible with prevailing market yields. Such behavior explains why a 7 percent issue will carry a market price of only $825 when the market yield is 9 percent; the drop in price is necessary to raise the yield on this bond from 7 to 9 percent. Issues with market values lower than par are known as *discount bonds* and carry coupons that are less than those on new issues. In contrast, issues with market value in excess of par are called *premium bonds* and have coupons greater than those currently being offered on new issues.

Types of Issues. A single issuer may have many different bonds outstanding at a given point in time. In addition to their coupons and maturities, bonds can be differentiated from one another by the type of collateral behind them. In this regard, the issues can be viewed as having either junior or senior standing. *Senior bonds* are *secured* obligations, since they are backed by a legal claim, on some specific property of the issuer, that acts as *collateral* for the bonds. Such issues would include **mortgage bonds,** which are secured by real estate, and **equipment trust certificates,** which are backed by certain types of equipment and are popular with railroads and airlines. *Junior bonds,* on the other hand, are backed only with a promise by the issuer to pay interest and principal on a timely basis. There are several classes of *unsecured* bonds, the most popular of which is known as a **debenture.** Exhibit 11.5 shows the announcement for a recent Disney issue. Note that these are debenture bonds and even though there is *no collateral* standing behind them, Disney was still able to issue $300 million worth of these securities. But what really makes these bonds unusual is their maturity—that is, these are *100-year bonds that won't mature until the year 2093.* Now if these bonds stay out to maturity, Disney will have to pay almost $23 million a year, for each of the next 100 years, just in interest payments. Imagine, that means over the next century, Disney will pay out nearly $2.3 *billion* in interest payments alone—all on a $300 million loan.

Sinking Fund. Another provision that's important to investors is the **sinking fund,** which stipulates how a bond will be paid off over time. Not all bonds have these requirements, but for those that do, a sinking fund specifies the annual repayment schedule that will be used to pay off the issue and indicates how much principal will be retired each year. Sinking fund requirements generally begin one to five years after the date of issue and continue annually thereafter until all or most of the issue has been paid off. Any amount not repaid by maturity (which might equal 10 to 25 percent of the issue) is then retired with a single balloon payment.

coupon That feature on a bond that defines the annual interest income that the issuer will pay the bondholder.

mortgage bond A bond secured by real estate.

equipment trust certificate A bond secured by certain types of transportation equipment, like railroad cars and airplanes.

debenture An unsecured bond that is issued on the general credit of the firm.

sinking fund A provision in a bond that specifies the annual repayment schedule that will be used to pay off the issue, and the amount of principal that will be retired each year.

EXHIBIT 11.5

An Announcement of a New Corporate Bond Issue

On July 29, 1993, Walt Disney Co. issued a $300 million *unsecured* debenture bond, with a coupon of 7.55%. There's nothing unusual about that, except for the fact that this was a *100-year bond that won't mature until the year 2093*. Now, that's long-term—even for Mickey Mouse!

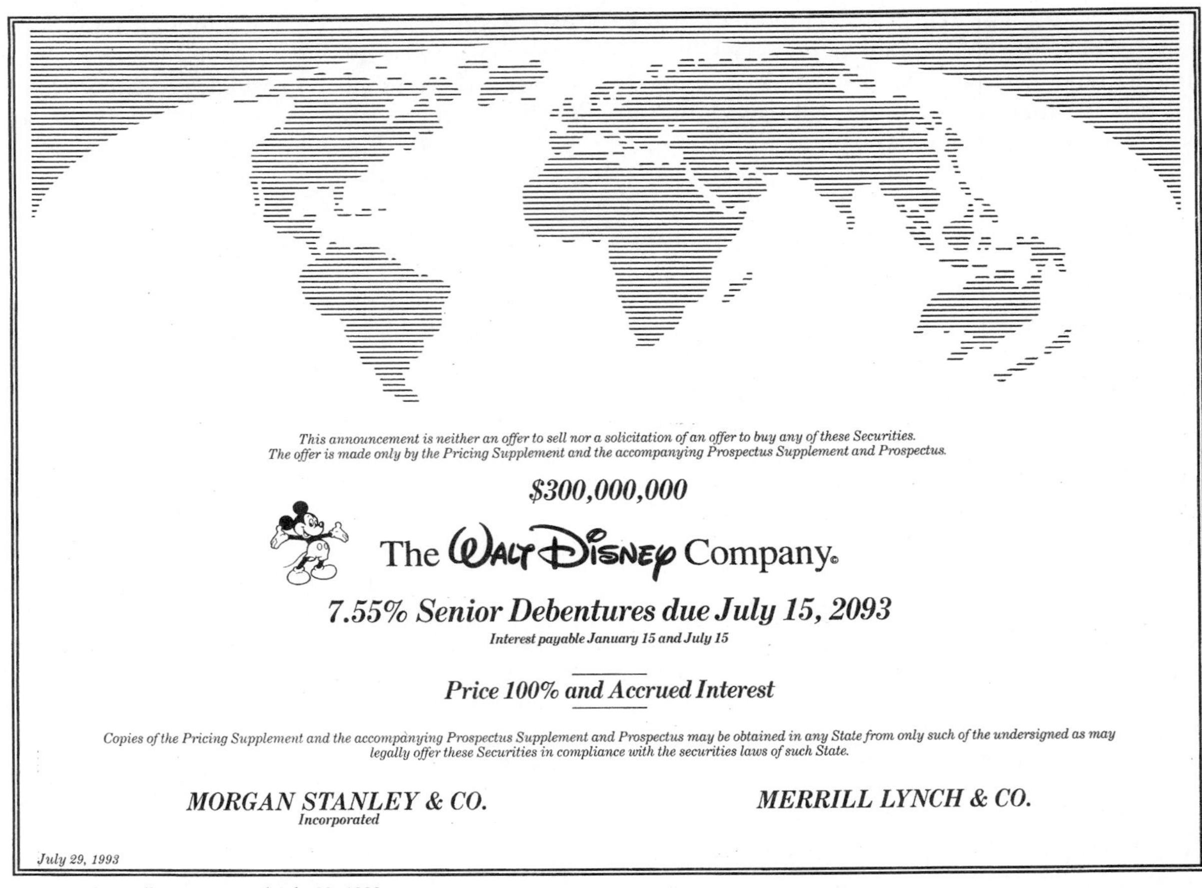

This announcement is neither an offer to sell nor a solicitation of an offer to buy any of these Securities.
The offer is made only by the Pricing Supplement and the accompanying Prospectus Supplement and Prospectus.
$300,000,000
The Walt Disney Company
7.55% Senior Debentures due July 15, 2093
Interest payable January 15 and July 15
Price 100% and Accrued Interest
Copies of the Pricing Supplement and the accompanying Prospectus Supplement and Prospectus may be obtained in any State from only such of the undersigned as may legally offer these Securities in compliance with the securities laws of such State.
MORGAN STANLEY & CO.
Incorporated
MERRILL LYNCH & CO.
July 29, 1993

Source: *The Wall Street Journal,* July 29, 1993.

Call Feature. Every bond has a **call feature,** which stipulates whether a bond can be called (that is, retired) prior to its regularly scheduled maturity date, and if so, under what conditions. As a rule, a bond cannot be called until it has been outstanding for five years or more. Call features are used most often to replace an issue with one that carries a lower coupon; in this way, the issuer benefits by being able to realize a reduction in annual interest cost. In an attempt to compensate investors who have their bonds called out from under them, a *call premium* (usually equal to about one year's interest) is tacked on to the par value of the bond and paid to investors, along with the issue's par value, at the time the bond is called. For example, if a company decides to call its 12 percent bonds some 15 years before they mature, it might have to pay $1,120 (a call premium of one year's interest—$120—would be added to the par value of $1,000) for every $1,000 bond outstanding.

While this might sound like a good deal, it's really not. Indeed, the only party that really benefits from a bond refunding is the issuer. The bondholder loses a source of high current income—for example, the investor may have a 12 percent bond called away at a time when the best he or she

EXHIBIT 11.6

The Reported Results of a Recent Treasury Note Auction

Treasury auctions are closely followed by the financial media; here, the results of a three-year Treasury note auction are reported. These auctions are highly competitive (the amount of bids submitted generally far exceeds the size of the issue) and as a result, the spread between the highest and lowest bid is quite small (here it amounts to just 2 basis points, or 2/100 of 1 percent—7.09 to 7.07 percent).

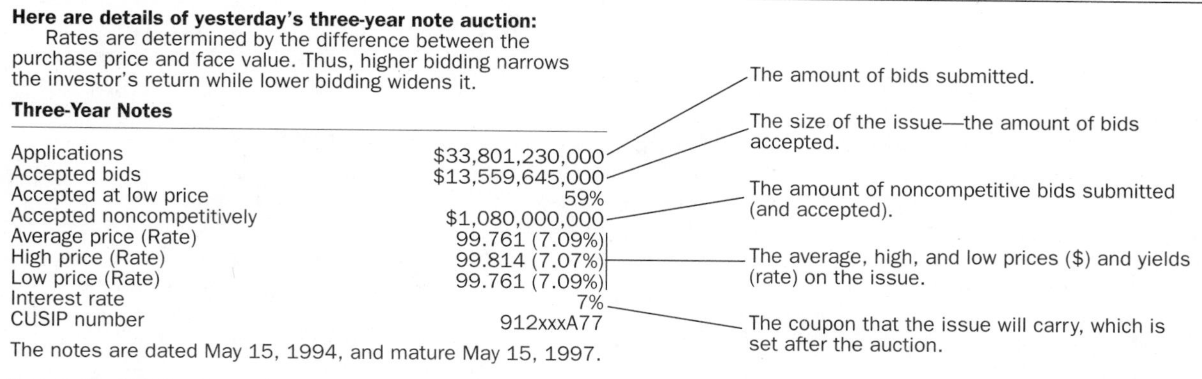

Here are details of yesterday's three-year note auction:
Rates are determined by the difference between the purchase price and face value. Thus, higher bidding narrows the investor's return while lower bidding widens it.

Three-Year Notes

Applications	$33,801,230,000
Accepted bids	$13,559,645,000
Accepted at low price	59%
Accepted noncompetitively	$1,080,000,000
Average price (Rate)	99.761 (7.09%)
High price (Rate)	99.814 (7.07%)
Low price (Rate)	99.761 (7.09%)
Interest rate	7%
CUSIP number	912xxxA77

The notes are dated May 15, 1994, and mature May 15, 1997.

The amount of bids submitted.
The size of the issue—the amount of bids accepted.
The amount of noncompetitive bids submitted (and accepted).
The average, high, and low prices ($) and yields (rate) on the issue.
The coupon that the issue will carry, which is set after the auction.

Source: *The Wall Street Journal.*

can do in the market is maybe 7 or 8 percent. To avoid this, stick with bonds that are either *noncallable* (these issues cannot be called/retired prior to maturity, for any reason), or that have long *call-deferment periods,* meaning they can't be called for refunding (or any other purpose) until the call-deferment period ends.

THE BOND MARKET

Today's bond market offers issues to meet just about any type of investment objective and to suit virtually any type of investor, no matter how conservative or aggressive. As a matter of convenience, the bond market is usually divided into four segments, according to type of issuer: Treasury, agency, municipal, and corporate.

Treasury Bonds. **Treasury bonds** (sometimes called *Treasuries* or *governments*) are a dominant force in the bond market and, if not the most popular, certainly are the best known. The U.S. Treasury issues bonds, notes, and other types of debt securities (such as the Treasury bills discussed in Chapter 4) as a means of meeting the ever increasing needs of the federal government. All Treasury obligations are of the highest quality (backed by the full faith and credit of the U.S. government), a feature that, along with their liquidity, makes them extremely popular with individual and institutional investors, both here and abroad. Indeed, the market for U.S. Treasury securities is the biggest and most active in the world! Every day, there's about $125 billion worth of Treasuries that change hands, as these securities are traded in all the major markets of the world, from New York to London to Tokyo. That's three quarters of a *trillion* dollars in bond trades—every week; to put that into perspective, in an average week, the New York Stock Exchange trades only about $35 billion worth of stocks.

Treasury notes carry maturities of two to ten years, whereas *Treasury bonds* have maturities of more than ten years—they go out as far as 30 years. Treasury notes and bonds are sold in $1,000 denominations (except two- and three-year notes,

call feature A feature often included in bond (or preferred stock) issues that allows the issuer to retire the security prior to maturity at some specified, predetermined price.

Treasury bond A federal government obligation that has a maturity of more than ten years and pays interest semiannually; also called a *government bond.*

Issues in Money Management

Buying Treasuries at the Auction— A Do-It-Yourself Approach to Investing

The largest issuer of debt securities in the world is the U.S. Treasury. Although the Treasury sells its bills, notes, and bonds primarily to institutional investors, individual investors can also buy from the Treasury through its *Treasury Direct* program. This program gives individual investors the opportunity to buy directly at the auction, *without having to pay any brokerage commissions.*

Treasury auctions are held on a regular basis throughout the year, with the dollar amount of securities to be sold announced four to six business days before the auction date. The securities are priced at the auction on the basis of competitive bids submitted by large institutional investors. Individual investors can participate in the auction by submitting *noncompetitive bids* (minimum investment requirements are as low as $1,000 to $10,000). Submitting a noncompetitive bid guarantees that you'll get all the securities you want, as *all noncompetitive bids are filled*—at the average of the high and low bids accepted at the auction.

Here's how it works: Suppose the Treasury announces its intention to sell, say, $15 billion worth of ten-year notes at its next auction. At auction, the Treasury may receive $35 to $40 billion in competitive bids (it always receives far more bids than it has securities to sell), and another $1 billion in small noncompetitive bids. The noncompetitive bids are filled first, so that leaves the Treasury with $14 billion worth of securities to be sold through competitive bidding. These bids are filled by accepting the highest price (lowest yield) first, and then accepting successively lower prices (higher yields) until the whole issue is sold—in this illustration, as is typical at most Treasury auctions, there will be a big chunk of the competitive bids that go unfilled. Usually the spread between the highest and lowest bids will be just a few basis points; for example, the competitive bids may range between 6.42 and 6.44 percent. If that's the case, then all noncompetitive bids would be filled at the *average* bid of, say, 6.43 percent. Once the auction is completed, the coupon on the Treasury note or bond will be set at or slightly *under* the range of bids—in this way, the issue price will be equal to or slightly less than par.

Suppose you want to purchase $15,000 of these ten-year notes for your personal portfolio. First, you must open a *Treasury Direct* account with the Federal Reserve by filling out a simple form (available from the nearest Federal Reserve bank or branch). Then you submit your application by completing a so-called *tender offer* (another very simple form, on which you indicate, among other things, that you want to make a *noncompetitive bid*), sending it in along with payment for the securities. After the auction, your Treasury Direct account will be credited with the purchase and a few days later, you'll receive a statement informing you of the terms of your purchase. The Treasury Direct program, although easy to use and understand, *is best suited for investors who plan to hold their securities to maturity.* Technically, these are "nonmarketable" securities, so to sell them, an investor must first transfer the securities to a bank or other financial institution—a process that might take a week or more.

Sources: Adapted from Tom Herman, "Buying Treasurys Without a Middleman," *The Wall Street Journal,* May 1, 1991, pp. C1, 15; Edward Giltenan, "Do-It-Yourself Treasurys," *Forbes,* November 14, 1988, p. 349; and Susan E. Kuhn, "The Tightwad Way to Tank Up on Treasuries," *Fortune,* June 18, 1990, p. 32.

which are sold in $5,000 minimums). The Treasury issues its notes and bonds at regularly scheduled auctions, the results of which are widely followed by the financial media (see Exhibit 11.6). Through this auction process, the Treasury establishes the initial yields and coupons on the securities it issues. These auctions are open to the public and as the *Issues in Money Management* box above explains, it's an easy and inexpensive way to buy Treasuries. All government notes and bonds today are issued as *noncallable* securities, and while interest income is subject to normal federal income tax, *it is exempt from state and local taxes.*

Agency Bonds. **Agency bonds** are an important segment of the U.S. bond market. Though issued by political subdivisions of the U.S. government, *these securities are not obligations of the U.S. Treasury.* They customarily provide yields comfortably above the market rates for Treasuries and

EXHIBIT 11.7

Table of Taxable Equivalent Yields

Tax-exempt securities generally yield less than fully taxable obligations, and, because of that, you have to be in a sufficiently high tax bracket (28 percent or more) to make up for the yield shortfall.

	To Match a Tax-Free Yield of:					
	5%	**6%**	**7%**	**8%**	**9%**	**10%**
Tax Bracket*	**You must earn this yield on a taxable investment:**					
15%	5.88	7.06	8.24	9.41	10.59	11.76
28	6.94	8.33	9.72	11.11	12.50	13.89
31	7.25	8.70	10.15	11.59	13.04	14.49
36	7.81	9.38	10.94	12.50	14.06	15.63
39.6	8.28	9.93	11.59	13.25	14.90	16.56

*Federal tax rates that were in effect on Jan. 1, 1994.

therefore, offer investors a way to increase returns with little or no real difference in risk. Some of the more actively traded and widely quoted agency issues include those sold by the Federal Farm Credit Bank, the Federal National Mortgage Association (or "Fannie Maes," as they are more commonly known), the Resolution Funding Corp., the Federal Land Bank, the Student Loan Marketing Association, and the Federal Home Loan Bank. Although these issues are not the direct obligations of the U.S. government, a number of them actually do carry government guarantees and thus effectively represent the full faith and credit of the U.S. Treasury. Moreover, some have unusual interest-payment provisions (interest is paid monthly in a few instances and yearly in one case), and in some cases, the interest in exempt from state and local taxes.

Municipal Bonds. **Municipal bonds** are the issues of states, counties, cities, and other political subdivisions, such as school districts and water and sewer districts. They are unlike other bonds in that their interest income is usually free from federal income tax (which is why these issues are known as *tax-free bonds*). Any capital gains that might be earned from municipals, however, is subject to the usual federal taxes. A tax-free yield is probably the most important feature of municipal bonds and is certainly a major reason why individuals invest in them. Exhibit 11.7 shows what a taxable bond (like a Treasury issue) would have to yield in order to equal the take-home yield of a tax-free municipal bond. It demonstrates how the yield attractiveness of municipal bonds varies with an investor's income level; clearly, the higher the individual's tax bracket, the more attractive municipal bonds become.

As a rule, the yields on municipal bonds are substantially lower than the returns available from fully taxable issues. Thus, unless the tax effect is sufficient to raise the yield on a municipal to a level that equals or exceeds the yields on taxable issues, it obviously doesn't make sense to buy municipal bonds. You can determine the return a fully taxable bond would have to provide in order to match the after-tax return on a lower-yielding tax-free issue by computing what is known as a municipal's *fully taxable equivalent yield:*

$$\text{Fully taxable equivalent yield} = \frac{\text{Yield of Municipal bond}}{1 - \text{Tax rate}}$$

For example, if a certain municipal bond offered a yield of 6 percent, an individual in the maximum 39.6 percent federal tax bracket would have to find a fully taxable bond with a yield of nearly 10

agency bond An obligation of a political subdivision of the U.S. government; typically provides yields above the market rates for Treasury bonds.

municipal bond A bond issued by state and local governments for the purpose of financing certain projects; interest income is usually exempt from federal taxes.

percent in order to reap the same after-tax return: that is, 6% ÷ (1 − .396) = 6% ÷ .604 = 9.93%.

Municipal bonds are generally issued as **serial obligations,** meaning that the issue is broken into a series of smaller bonds, each with its own maturity date and coupon rate. Thus, instead of the bond having just one maturity date 20 years from now, it will have a series of, say, 20 maturity dates over the 20-year time frame. Because there is such a diversity of municipal bonds available, investors must also be careful to assess their quality in order to ensure that the issuer will not default. Although it may not seem that municipal issuers would default on either interest or principal payments, it does occur! Investors should be especially cautious when investing in **revenue bonds,** which are municipal bonds that are serviced from the income generated from specific income-producing projects, such as toll roads. Unlike issuers of so-called **general obligation bonds**—which are backed by the full faith and credit of the municipality—the issuer of a revenue bond is obligated to pay principal and interest *only if a sufficient level of revenue* is generated. General obligation municipal bonds, however, are required to be serviced in a prompt and timely fashion regardless of the level of tax income generated by the municipality.

Caution should be used when buying municipal bonds because *some of these issues are tax-exempt and others are not.* One effect of the far-reaching 1986 Tax Reform Act was to change the status of municipal bonds used to finance nonessential projects, so that their interest income is no longer exempt from federal taxes. Such bonds are known as *taxable munies,* and they offer yields that are considerably higher than normal tax-exempt securities. Buy one of these issues and you'll end up holding a bond whose interest income *is fully taxable* by the IRS.

Corporate Bonds. The major nongovernmental issuers of bonds are corporations. The market for **corporate bonds** is customarily subdivided into several segments, which include *industrials* (the most diverse of the group), *public utilities* (the dominant group in terms of volume of new issues), *rail and transportation bonds,* and *financial issues* (banks, finance companies, and so forth). The corporate bond market offers the widest range of issue types. There are *first mortgage bonds, convertible bonds* (discussed in the next section) *debentures, subordinated debentures,* and *income bonds,* to mention just a few. Interest on corporate bonds is paid semiannually, and sinking funds are common. The bonds usually come in $1,000 denominations and are issued on a term basis with a single maturity date. Maturities usually range from 5 to 10 years, to 30 years or more. Many of the issues—particularly the longer-term bonds—carry call provisions that prohibit prepayment of the issue during the first five to ten years. Corporate issues are popular with individuals because of their relatively high yields.

The Special Appeal of Zero Coupon Bonds. In addition to the standard bond vehicles described above, investors can also choose from several types of *specialty issues*—bonds that, for the most part, have unusual coupon or repayment provisions. That's certainly the case with **zero coupon bonds,** which, as the name implies, are bonds that are issued without coupons. To compensate for their lack of coupons, these bonds are sold at a deep discount from their par values and then increase in value over time, at a compound rate of return, so that at maturity they are worth much more than their initial investment. Other things being equal, the cheaper the bond, the greater the return one can earn (for example, whereas a 10 percent bond might sell for $239, an issue with a 6 percent yield will cost a lot more—$417). Because they have no coupons, these bonds pay nothing to the investor until they mature. In this regard, zero coupon bonds are like the Series EE savings bonds that we discussed in Chapter 4. Strange as it may seem, this is the main attraction of zero coupon bonds. Since there are no interest payments, investors need not worry about reinvesting coupon income twice a year; instead, the fully compounded rate of return on a zero coupon bond is virtually guaranteed at the rate that existed when the issue was purchased. For example, in early 1995 good-grade zero coupon bonds with 20-year maturities were available at yields of around 8 percent; thus, for just a little over $200, investors could buy a bond that would be worth 5 times that amount, or $1,000, when it matures in 20 years. Best of all, they would be *locking in* an eight percent compound rate of return on their investment capital for the full 20-year life of the issue. Because of their unusual tax exposure (even though the bonds do not pay regular yearly interest, the IRS treats the annually accrued interest as taxable income), zeros should be used only in tax-sheltered investments, such as individual retirement accounts (IRAs), or be held by minor children who are likely to be taxed at low rates, if at all.

Zeros are issued by corporations, municipalities, and federal agencies; you can even buy U.S. Treasury notes and bonds in the form of zero coupon securities. Up until about ten years ago, major brokerage houses used to package U.S. Treasury securities as zeros and sell them to the investing public in the form of investment trusts. These units trusts were marketed under such names as *TIGRS, CATS,* and *LIONS* and became enormously popular with investors. Seeing this, the Treasury decided to eliminate the middleman and "issue" their own form of zero coupon bond, known as *Treasury STRIPS*, or *STRIP-Ts*, for short. When that happened, the market for CATS and other felines pretty much dried up. (There are some old issues still out there, but the new issue market for these securities has virtually disappeared.) Actually, the Treasury does not issue zero coupon bonds, but instead, *they allow government securities dealers to take regular coupon-bearing notes and bonds in stripped form,* which can then be sold to the public as zero coupon securities. Essentially, the coupons are *stripped* from the bond, repackaged, and then sold separately as zero coupon bonds. For example, a 20-year Treasury bond has 40 semiannual coupon payments, plus one principal payment—each of these 41 cash flows can be repackaged and sold as 41 different zero coupon securities, with maturities that range from six months to 20 years.

BOND RATINGS

Bond ratings are like grades: A letter grade assigned to a bond issue designates its investment quality. Ratings are widely used and are an important part of the municipal and corporate bond markets. The two largest and best known rating agencies are Moody's and Standard & Poor's. Every time a large, new corporate or municipal issue comes to the market, it is analyzed by a staff of professional bond analysts to determine its default risk exposure and investment quality. The financial records of the issuing organization are thoroughly worked over and its future prospects assessed. The result of all this is the assignment of a bond rating at the time of issue that indicates the ability of the issuing organization to service its debt in a prompt and timely manner. Exhibit 11.8 lists the various ratings assigned to bonds by each of the two major services. Except for slight variations in designations (Aaa versus AAA, for example), the meanings and interpretations are basically the same. Note that the top four ratings (Aaa through Baa; or AAA through BBB) designate *investment-grade* bonds—such ratings are highly coveted by issuers as they indicate financially strong, well-run companies. The next two ratings (Ba/B; or BB/B) are where you'll find most **junk bonds;** these ratings mean that while the principal and interest payments on the bonds are still being met, the *risk of default* is relatively high, as the issuers generally lack the financial strength found with investment-grade issues. While junk bonds—or *high yield bonds,* as they're also known—are popular with some investors, it should be understood that these are highly speculative securities. They may offer high rates of return, but they also involve substantial amounts of risks; in particular, there's a very real likelihood that the issue may encounter some difficulties.

Once a new issue is rated, the process doesn't stop there. For older, outstanding bonds are also regularly reviewed to ensure that their assigned ratings are still valid. Most issues will carry a single

serial obligation An issue, usually a municipal bond, that is broken down into a series of smaller bonds, each with its own maturity date and coupon rate.

revenue bond A municipal bond that is serviced from the income generated from a specific project.

general obligation bond A municipal bond that is backed by the full faith and credit of the issuing municipality rather than by the revenue generated from a given project.

corporate bond A bond issued by a corporation; categories include industrials, public utilities, railroad and transportation bonds, and financial issues.

zero coupon bond A bond that pays no annual interest but sells at a deep discount to par value.

junk bond Also known as *high-yield* bonds, these are highly speculative securities that have received low ratings from Moody's or Standard & Poor's; the low ratings mean that the issuers could have difficulty meeting interest and principal payments as they come due.

EXHIBIT 11.8

Moody's and Standard & Poor's Bond Ratings

Agencies like Moody's and Standard & Poor's rate corporate and municipal bonds; the ratings provide an indication of the bonds' investment quality (particularly with respect to an issue's default risk exposure).

Bond Ratings*		
Moody's	**S&P**	**Description**
Aaa	AAA	*Prime-Quality Investment Bonds*—This is the highest rating assigned, denoting extremely strong capacity to pay.
AaA A	AA A	*High-Grade Investment Bonds*—These are also considered very safe bonds, though they're not quite as safe as Aaa/AAA issues; double-A-rated bonds (Aa/AA) are safer (have less risk of default) than single-A-rated issues.
Baa	BBB	*Medium-Grade Investment Bonds*—These are the lowest of the investment-grade issues; they're felt to lack certain protective elements against adverse economic conditions.
Ba B	BB B	*Junk Bonds*—With little protection against default, these are viewed as highly speculative securities.
Caa Ca C	CCC CC C D	*Poor-Quality Bonds*—These are either in default or very close to it; these are often referred to as *Zombie Bonds.*

*Some ratings may be modified to show relative standing within a major rating category; for example, Moody's uses numerical modifiers (1, 2, 3), whereas S&P uses plus (+) or minus (−) signs.

rating to maturity, but it is not uncommon for some to undergo revision. Finally, although it may appear that the firm is receiving the rating, it is actually the individual issue that is being rated. As a result, a firm can have different ratings assigned to its issues; the senior securities, for example, might carry one rating and the junior issues a slightly lower rating. Most bond investors pay careful attention to ratings, since they can affect comparative market yields—specifically, the higher the rating, the lower the yield of an obligation, other things being equal. Thus, whereas an A-rated bond might offer a 9 percent yield, a comparable AAA issue would probably yield something like 8.5 to 8.75 percent.

BOND PRICES AND YIELDS

The price of a bond is a function of its coupon, maturity, and the movement of market interest rates. *When interest rates go down, bond prices go up, and vice versa.* The relationship of bond prices to market rates is captured in Exhibit 11.9. Basically, the graph serves to reinforce the *inverse* relationship between bond prices and market interest rates: Note that *lower* rates lead to *higher* bond prices. The exhibit also shows the difference between premium and discount bonds. A **premium bond** is one that sells for more than its par value, which occurs whenever market interest rates drop below the coupon rate on the bond; a **discount bond,** in contrast, sells for less than par, and is the result of market rates being greater than the issue's coupon rate. Thus, the 10 percent bond in our illustration traded as a premium bond when market rates were at 8 percent, but as a discount bond when rates stood at 12 percent.

When a bond is first issued, it is usually sold to the public at a price that equals, or is very close to, its par value. Likewise, when the bond matures—some 15, 20, or 30 years later—it will once again be priced at its par value. But what happens to the price of the bond in between is of considerable concern to most bond investors. In this regard, we know that the extent to which bond prices move depends not only on the *direction* of change in interest rates, but also on the *magnitude* of such changes; for the greater the moves in interest rates, the greater the swings in bond prices. But there's more, for bond prices will also vary according to the coupon and maturity of the issue—that is, bonds with *lower coupons* and/or *longer maturities* will respond more vigorously to changes in market rates and undergo *greater price swings.* It should be obvious, therefore, that if interest rates are moving *up,* the investor should seek high coupon bonds with short maturities, since this will

EXHIBIT 11.9

Price Behavior of a Bond with a 10 Percent Coupon

A bond will sell at its par value so long as the prevailing market interest rate remains the same as the bond's coupon (for example, when both coupon and market rates equal 10 percent). However, when market rates drop, bond prices rise, and vice versa; moreover, as a bond approaches its maturity, the price of the issue will always move toward its par value, no matter what happens to interest rates.

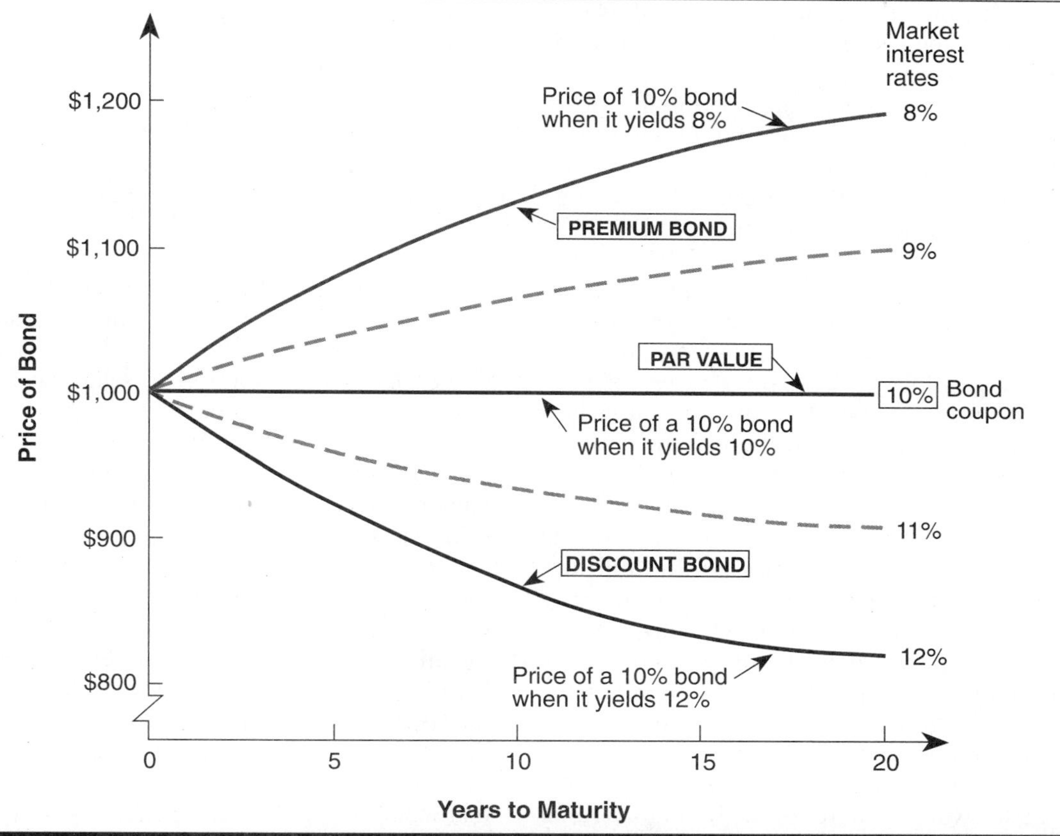

cause minimal price variation and *act to preserve as much capital as possible*. In contrast, if rates are heading *down*, that's the time to be in long-term bonds—if you're a speculator looking for lots of capital gains, then go with long-term, *low coupon* bonds, whereas if you're trying to lock in a high level of coupon (interest) income, then stick with long-term, *high coupon* bonds that offer plenty of call protection (which you can get from issues that are noncallable or have extended call-deferment periods).

Current Yield and Yield to Maturity. The *yield* on a bond is the rate of return that you would earn if you held the bond for a stated period of time. The two most commonly cited bond yields are current yield and yield to maturity. **Current yield** reflects the amount of annual interest income the bond provides relative to its current market price. The formula for current yield is

premium bond A bond that has a market value in excess of par; occurs when interest rates drop below the coupon rate.

discount bond A bond with a market value lower than par; occurs when market rates are greater than the coupon rate.

current yield The amount of current income a bond provides relative to its current market price.

$$\text{Current yield} = \frac{\text{Annual interest income}}{\text{Market price of bond}}$$

As you can see, the current yield on a bond is basically the same as the dividend yield on a stock. Assume, for example, that a 9 percent bond with a $1,000 face value is currently selling for $910. Since annual interest income would equal $90(.09 × $1,000) and the current market price of the bond is $910, its current yield would be 9.89 percent ($90/$910). This yield, which is commonly quoted in the financial press, would be of interest to investors seeking current income; other things being equal, the higher the current yield, the more attractive a bond would be to such an investor.

The annual rate of return that a bondholder would receive *if he or she held the issue to its maturity* is captured in the bond's **yield to maturity.** This measure captures two types of return: the annual interest income and the recovery of principal at maturity. If a bond is purchased at its face value, its yield to maturity will equal the coupon, or stated, rate of interest. If it is purchased at a discount, its yield to maturity will be greater than the coupon rate because the investor will receive, in addition to annual interest income, the full face value of the bond even though he or she paid something less than par—in effect, the investor will earn some capital gains on the investment. Of course, if the bond is purchased at a premium, the opposite will be true: The yield to maturity on the issue will be less than its coupon rate since the transaction will involve a capital loss—that is, the investor will pay more for the bond than he or she will get back at maturity.

You can find the yield to maturity of a bond by using the *approximate yield* formula introduced earlier in this chapter. In particular, by setting the future price (*FP*) of the investment equal to the bond's face value ($1,000), you can use the following version of the approximate yield equation to find the *approximate yield to maturity on a bond:*

$$\text{Approximate Yield to Maturity} = \frac{CI + \left[\dfrac{\$1{,}000 - CP}{N}\right]}{\left[\dfrac{CP + \$1{,}000}{2}\right]}$$

As you will recall, *CI* equals annual current income (or annual interest income, in the case of a bond), *CP* stands for current price (of the bond), and *N* is the investment period (the number of years to maturity). Assume, for example, that you are contemplating the purchase of a $1,000, 9 percent bond with 15 years remaining to maturity, and that the bond currently trades at a price of $910. Given *CI* = $90, *CP* = $910, and *N* = 15 years, the approximate yield to maturity on this bond will be

$$\text{Approximate Yield to Maturity} = \frac{\$90 + \left[\dfrac{\$1{,}000 - \$910}{15}\right]}{\left[\dfrac{\$910 + \$1{,}000}{2}\right]}$$

$$= \frac{\$90 + \left[\dfrac{\$90}{15}\right]}{\left[\dfrac{\$1{,}910}{2}\right]} = \underline{\underline{10.05\%}}.$$

This is above both the 9 percent stated (coupon) rate and the 9.89 percent current yield, since the bond is purchased at a discount from its face value. (Note that had the bond been selling at $1,090, it would have had a current yield of 8.26 percent and an approximate yield to maturity of 8.04 percent—both below the 9 percent coupon rate; such behavior would be due to the fact that the bond was selling at a premium price.)

Yield to maturity measures are used by investors to assess the underlying attractiveness of a bond investment. The higher the yield to maturity, the more attractive the investment, other things being equal. *If a bond provided a yield to maturity that equaled or exceeded an investor's desired rate of return, it would be considered a worthwhile investment candidate,* as it would promise a yield that would adequately compensate the investor for the level of risk involved.

Concept Check

11-12. What is the difference between a secured bond and an unsecured bond? Give a few examples of each. Briefly describe the following bond features: (a) *sinking funds,* (b) *call features,* and (c) *coupon.*

11-13. Are *junk bonds* and *zero coupon bonds* the same? Explain. What are the basic tax features of a tax-exempt *municipal bond*? Are there such things as *taxable* municipal bonds? Explain.

11-14. Illustrate why an investor in a high tax bracket would prefer municipal bonds to other investment vehicles.

11-15. Explain the system of bond ratings used by Moody's and Standard & Poor's.

11-16. What effects do current market interest rates have on the price behavior of outstanding bonds?

PREFERREDS AND CONVERTIBLES

LG6

While stocks and bonds are the most basic of investment vehicles, there are some securities—like preferred stocks and convertible bonds—that combine the features of both equity and debt issues. Can you think of some ways that preferred stocks are like common stocks? In what ways are they like bonds? How about convertibles? In what way are they like bonds? Like stocks? Think about these questions before going on.

Preferreds and convertibles are corporate securities that hold a position senior to common stock. Although preferred stocks are actually a form of equity, they, along with convertibles, are considered to be fixed-income securities because their level of current income is fixed. Convertible securities, issued initially as either bonds or preferred stocks, are subsequently convertible into shares of the issuing firm's common stock. Preferred stocks, in contrast, are issued and remain as equity. They derive their name in part from the preferential claim on income they command—that is, all preferred dividends must be paid before any payments can be made to holders of common stock.

PREFERRED STOCKS

Preferred stocks carry a dividend that's usually fixed, and which is paid quarterly and stated either in dollar terms or as a percent of par (or stated) value. They are considered *hybrid securities* because they possess features of both common stocks and corporate bonds. They are like common stocks in that they pay dividends, *which may be passed* when corporate earnings fall below certain levels. Moreover, preferreds represent equity ownership and are issued without stated maturity dates. They are, however, also like bonds in that they provide investors with a prior claim on income and assets, and the level of current income is usually fixed for the life of the issue. Most important, because these securities usually trade on the basis of the yield they offer to investors, they are viewed in the marketplace as fixed-income obligations and, as a result, are treated much like bonds.

Preferred Stock Features. Preferred stocks possess features that not only distinguish them from other types of securities, but also help to differentiate one preferred from another. For example, the amount of dividends that an issue pays is a common way of describing preferred stocks—thus, a company could have a "three dollar" preferred stock outstanding (meaning the issue pays $3 per share in annual dividends) and another issue of preferred that pays $4.75 a share in yearly dividends. These are two separate issues and they would trade at two different prices. Many preferred stocks today are issued with call features, which means they can be retired if the issuing company decides to do so, and some even have sinking fund provisions, indicating how they will be paid off over time (sinking fund preferreds, in effect, have implied maturity dates). In addition to these features, preferred stock investors should also determine whether the stock is "cumulative" or "noncumulative."

Cumulative versus noncumulative. Most preferred stocks are **cumulative,** which means that any dividends passed in previous periods must be paid in full prior to distributing any dividends to common stockholders—in essence, if the preferred stockholders do not receive any dividends, then

yield to maturity The annual rate of return that a bondholder, purchasing a bond today, would earn if he or she held it to maturity.

cumulative (preferred stock) A preferred stock feature requiring that any passed dividends must be paid prior to distributing any dividends to common stockholders.

neither do the common shareholders. For example, assume a firm has outstanding a *$4 preferred stock* (which means the stated dividend is $4 per year, or $1 per quarter) and that the last two quarterly dividends have not been paid. Before any dividends can be paid to the common stockholders, the preferred stockholders must be paid the $2 of past dividends *plus the current quarterly dividend of $1*. Had the preferred stock been *noncumulative,* only the current $1 dividend would have had to be paid prior to distributing any earnings to the common stockholders.

Investing in Preferreds. Most individuals invest in preferred stocks because of the high current income they provide in the form of annual dividends. Moreover, such dividend income is highly predictable even though it lacks legal backing and can be passed. It's not surprising, therefore, that dividend yield is viewed by many investors as the key ingredient in evaluating the investment appeal of most preferred stocks. *Dividend yield*—which is found by dividing annual dividend income by the market price of the stock—is a reflection of an issue's current yield and, as such, is used to assess preferred stock investment opportunities. Other things being equal, the higher the dividend yield, the more attractive the investment vehicle. For example, suppose a certain preferred stock pays a dividend of $2 per year and is currently priced at $20; this preferred would have a dividend yield of $2/$20 = 10%. Whether or not a 10 percent return from this preferred stock makes for a good investment depends on (1) the amount of risk exposure involved and (2) the kinds of returns you can generate elsewhere—in other words, if you can earn better than 10 percent on other similarly risky investments, then do it!

Once you invest in a preferred, you should keep your eyes on market interest rates, since preferred stock prices are closely related to prevailing market rates; after all, you are investing in a *fixed-income* security whose value is determined chiefly by dividend yield. When the general level of interest rates moves up, the yields on preferreds rise and their prices *decline* accordingly; in contrast, when rates drift down, the yields on preferreds decrease and their prices *rise*. Thus, like that of any fixed-income security, the price behavior of most good-grade preferred stocks is inversely related to market interest rates.

CONVERTIBLE SECURITIES

Convertible issues, more popularly known simply as *convertibles,* represent still another type of fixed-income security. Although they possess the features and performance characteristics of both fixed-income and equity securities, *convertibles should be viewed primarily as a form of equity*. Most investors commit their capital to such obligations not because of their attractive yields, but because of the potential price performance that the stock side of the issue offers. In short, convertible securities are popular with individual investors because of the *equity kicker* they provide. Not surprisingly, whenever the stock market is strong, convertibles tend to be strong, and vice versa. Irrespective of whether they're issued as *convertible bonds* (the most common type of convertible) or *convertible preferreds,* these securities are closely linked to the firm's equity position and are therefore usually considered interchangeable for investment purposes. Except for a few peculiarities, such as the fact that preferreds pay dividends rather than interest and do so on a quarterly rather than semiannual basis, convertible bonds and convertible preferreds are evaluated in pretty much the same way. The following discussion on convertible bonds, therefore, applies to convertible preferreds as well.

Issue Features. A convertible bond basically is issued as a *debenture* (that is, unsecured debt) but carries the provision that, within a stipulated time period, *it may be converted into a certain number of shares of the issuing company's common stock*. Generally, the investor merely trades in the convertible bond for a stipulated number of shares of common stock. Exhibit 11.10 provides the details of a recently issued convertible bond. Note that this obligation originally came out as a 5 percent debenture bond but in time, each $1,000 bond can be exchanged for (converted into) First Financial Management stock at $69 a share. Thus, *regardless of what happens to the market price of the stock,* the convertible bond investor can redeem each $1,000 bond for 14.5 shares of the company's stock: that is, $1,000/$69 = 14.50. If at the time of conversion the stocks are trading in the market at $125 a share, then the investor would have just converted a $1,000 bond into $1,812 worth of stock—which is the value of 14½ shares trading at $125 each.

EXHIBIT 11.10

A Newly Issued Convertible Bond

Investors who hold this First Financial Management bond can convert it, anytime prior to maturity, into the company's common stock at a stated price of \$69 per share, and in so doing, receive $14\frac{1}{2}$ shares of stock in exchange for each \$1,000 convertible bond they hold. Prior to conversion, the bondholders will receive annual interest income of \$50 for each bond.

This announcement is neither an offer to sell nor a solicitation of an offer to buy any of these Securities. The offer is made only by the Prospectus and the related Prospectus Supplement.

\$447,150,000

FFMC

First Financial Management Corporation

5% Senior Convertible Debentures Due 1999

Interest Payable December 15 and June 15

The Debentures are convertible into Common Stock of the Company at any time prior to maturity, unless previously redeemed, at a conversion price of \$69 per share, subject to adjustment in certain events.

Price 100% and Accrued Interest

Copies of the Prospectus and the related Prospectus Supplement may be obtained in any State from only such of the undersigned as may legally offer these Securities in compliance with the securities laws of such State.

MORGAN STANLEY & CO.
Incorporated

BEAR, STEARNS & CO. INC.

CS FIRST BOSTON

DEAN WITTER REYNOLDS INC. ***HAMBRECHT & QUIST*** *Incorporated* ***KIDDER, PEABODY & CO.*** *Incorporated*

MERRILL LYNCH & CO. ***MONTGOMERY SECURITIES***

SALOMON BROTHERS INC ***SMITH BARNEY INC.***

J. C. BRADFORD & CO. ***PIPER JAFFRAY INC.*** ***THE ROBINSON-HUMPHREY COMPANY, INC.***

December 21, 1994

Source: *The Wall Street Journal,* December 21, 1994.

The key element of any convertible issue is its **conversion privilege,** which stipulates the conditions and specific nature of the conversion feature. First, it states exactly when the bond can be converted. Sometimes, there will be an initial waiting period of six months to perhaps two years after the date of issue, during which time the issue cannot be converted. The *conversion period* then begins, after which the issue can be converted at any time. Technically it is the *bondholder* who has the right to convert the bond into common stock, but more commonly the issuing firm will initiate the conversion by calling the issue. From the investor's point of view, the most important item of information is the **conversion ratio,** which specifies the number of shares of common stock that the bond can be converted into. For example, a $1,000 convertible bond might stipulate a conversion ratio of 20, meaning that you can "cash in" one convertible bond for 20 shares of the company's stock.

Conversion Value. Given the significance of the price behavior of the underlying common stock to the value of a convertible security, one of the most important measures to a convertible bond investor is conversion value. In essence, **conversion value** is an indication of what a convertible issue would trade for *if it were priced to sell on the basis of its stock value.* Conversion value is easy to find: Simply multiply the conversion ratio of the issue by the current market price of the underlying common stock. For example, a convertible that carried a conversion ratio of 20 would have a conversion value of $1,200 if the firm's stock traded at a current market price of $60 per share (20 × $60 = $1,200). Unfortunately, convertible issues seldom trade precisely at their conversion value; rather, they invariably trade at **conversion premiums,** which means that the convertibles are priced in the market at more than their conversion values. For example, a convertible that traded at $1,400 and had a conversion value of $1,200 would have a conversion premium of $200 (that is, $1,400 − $1,200 = $200).

Investment Merits. Convertible securities appeal to investors who want *the price potential of a common stock along with the downside risk protection of a corporate bond.* This two-sided feature is critical with convertibles and is virtually impossible to match with straight common or straight debt. As a rule, whenever a convertible trades near or above its par value ($1,000), it will exhibit price behavior that closely matches that of the underlying common stock: If the stock goes up in price, so will the convertible, and vice versa. In fact, the price change of the convertible will *exceed* that of the common, because of the conversion ratio. For example, if a convertible carries a ratio of, say, 20, then for every point the common stock goes up (or down) in price, the price of the convertible will move in the *same direction by a multiple of 20.* Because of the obvious importance of the underlying common stock, investors should carefully consider this element before investing in convertibles. If the future prospects for a stock are promising, the convertible could turn out to be a good investment.

A final feature of convertible bonds is that the current income earned from interest payments normally exceeds the income from the dividends that would be received from a comparable investment in the underlying common stock. For example, a $1,000 convertible with an 8 percent coupon would yield $80 per year to the holder; if the convertible carried a conversion ratio of 20, and each share of stock paid $2.50 in dividends, an investment in 20 shares of the firm's stock would provide only $50 per year in dividend income. Thus, with convertibles it is possible to reap the advantages of common stock (in the form of potential upward price appreciation) and still generate improved current income.

conversion privilege The provision in a convertible issue that stipulates the conditions of the conversion feature, such as the conversion period and conversion ratio.

conversion ratio A ratio that specifies the number of shares of common stock into which a convertible bond can be converted.

conversion value A measure of what a convertible issue would trade for if it were priced to sell on the basis of its stock value; found by multiplying the conversion ratio by the current market price of the underlying common stock.

conversion premium The difference between a convertible security's market price and its conversion value.

Concept Check

11-17. What is preferred stock? Distinguish between a *cumulative preferred* and noncumulative preferred stock.

11-18. What is a convertible bond? Why do investors buy convertible securities?

11-19. Describe the *conversion privilege* of a convertible security. Explain how the market price of the underlying common stock affects the market price of the convertible bond.

SUMMARY

LG1. Discuss the role that investing plays in the personal financial planning process. Investing plays an important part in personal financial planning, as it is the vehicle through which many of your financial goals can be reached. Your investment activities should be based on a sound investment plan that is linked to an ongoing savings plan.

LG2. Identify several different investment objectives—or reasons for investing. Most people invest their money in order to enhance their current income, accumulate funds for a major expenditure, save for retirement, and/or shelter some of their income from taxes. These objectives can be achieved most effectively when you confine your investment activities to investment vehicles (from stocks and bonds to mutual funds and real estate) that are expected to provide satisfactory rates of return—that is, rates of return that provide adequate compensation for risk and that meet or exceed desired rates of return.

LG3. Describe the various types of risks to which investors are exposed, as well as the sources of return. While investing offers returns in the form of current income and/or capital gains, it also involves risk; the basic types of investment risk are business risk, financial risk, market risk, purchasing power risk, interest rate risk, liquidity risk, and event risk—all of which combine to affect the level of return from an investment.

LG4. Discuss the merits of investing in common stock, including the different types of stock and the various measures of performance. Common stocks are a popular form of investing that can be used to meet just about any investment objective—investors can choose from blue-chip, growth, income, speculative, cyclical or defensive, and small or mid-cap stocks; and if they're so inclined, they can even buy foreign stocks by investing in ADRs (American Depositary Receipts). Regardless of the type, the value of such stocks is based on various performance measures like net profit margin, ROE, earnings per share; price/earnings (P/E) ratio, beta, and approximate yield.

LG5. Describe different types of bonds and note how these securities are used as investment vehicles. Bonds are another popular form of investing; such securities are basically the publicly issued debt of corporations and various levels of government (from the U.S. Treasury and various agencies of the U.S. government to state and local—municipal—governments). Known as fixed-income securities, such obligations can be used to generate either current income or capital gains (as when market rates go down).

LG6. Distinguish between preferred stocks and convertible securities, and note the investment merits of each. Preferred stocks and convertible bonds combine the features of both equity and debt securities, and are also widely used by individual investors. Preferred stocks are like common stocks to the extent that they pay dividends, but they are also like bonds in that they provide investors with a fixed claim on assets and a fixed level of income; in contrast, convertible bonds are issued as debt securities but they carry a provision that allows their holders to convert the bonds into shares of common stock.

FINANCIAL FACTS OR FANTASIES

Are the following statements financial facts (true) or fantasies (false)?

1. You would have to save $2,500 a year in order to end up with a $25,000 nest egg in ten years.
2. Buying American Depositary Receipts is a great way to invest in foreign stocks.
3. A good investment is one that offers a positive rate of return.
4. You can get an idea of a stock's price volatility by looking at its beta.
5. When interest rates go down, bond prices also go down because such securities become less valuable.
6. Convertible bonds are so named because they can be exchanged for a set number of shares of common stock.

DISCUSSION QUESTIONS AND PROBLEMS

Discussion Question for Opening Profile

Discuss what has motivated Jeff to begin investing early and how his reasons might apply to you. What are some ways that you can begin investing *now?*

FPPC **1.** ***Use Worksheet 11.1.*** Sarah Shoen is a young career woman who's presently employed as the managing editor of a well-known business journal. While she thoroughly enjoys her job and the people she works with, what she would really like to do is open a bookstore of her own. In particular, she would like to open her store in about eight years, and she figures she'd need about $50,000 in capital to do so. Given she thinks she can make about 8 percent on her money, use Worksheet 11.1 to find the following:

a. How much would she have to invest today, in one lump sum, to end up with $50,000 in eight years?

b. If she's starting from scratch, how much would she have to put away annually to accumulate the needed capital in eight years?

c. How about if she already has $12,000 socked away; how much would she have to put away annually to accumulate the required capital in eight years?

d. Given Sarah now has a handle on how much she has to save, briefly explain how she could use an *investment plan* to help her reach her objective.

FPPC **2.** What makes for a good investment? Use the approximate yield formula (Equation 11.1) to rank the following investments according to their expected returns:

a. Buy a stock for $45 a share, hold it for three years, and then sell it for $75 a share (the stock pays annual dividends of $3 a share).

b. Buy a security for $25, hold it for two years, and then sell it for $60 (current income on this security is zero).

c. Buy a one-year, 12 percent note for $950 (assume the note has a $1,000 par value and that it will be held to maturity).

FPPC **3.** Selected financial information about Engulf and Devour, Inc. is provided as follows:

Total assets	$20,000,000
Total liabilities	$8,000,000
Total preferred stock	$3,000,000
Total annual preferred stock dividends	$240,000
Net profits after tax	$2,500,000
Number of shares of common stock outstanding	500,000 shares
Current market price of common stock	$50.00 per share
Annual common stock dividends	$2.50 a share

Using the above information, compute the following:

a. The stock's dividend yield

b. Book value per share

c. Earnings per share

d. P/E ratio

4. Assume you've just inherited $350,000 and you've decided to take a big chunk of it ($250,000 to be exact) and invest it in common stocks. Your objective is to build up as much capital as you can over the next 15 to 20 years, and you're willing to tolerate a "good deal" of risk.

   a. What *types* of stocks (for example, blue chips, income stocks, and so on) do you think you'd be most interested in and why? Come up with at least 3 different types of stocks and briefly explain the rationale for each.

   b. Would your selections change if you were dealing with a smaller amount of money—say, only $50,000? What if you were a more risk adverse investor?

5. Using the resources available at your campus or public library, select a company from *Value Line* that would be of interest to you. (*HINT:* pick a company that's been publicly traded for at least 10 to 15 years, and *avoid* public utilities, banks and other financial institutions.) Obtain a copy of the latest *Value Line* report on your chosen company. Using the forecasted data reported in *Value Line,* determine the following. (*Note:* Use a three-year holding period throughout this exercise.)

   a. What's the latest price of the stock you selected and how much is the stock currently paying in annual dividends?

   b. According to *Value Line,* what are the (approximate) projected dividends per share for each of the next three years; also, what's the (approximate) estimated price of the stock at the end of the three-year holding period?

   c. Use Equation 11.1 to find the expected return on this stock.

   d. If you were investing in this stock, what would you want to earn as a minimum/required rate of return? Briefly explain how you came up with that number.

   e. Would you consider this stock to be a worthwhile investment candidate? Explain.

6. An investor in the 28 percent tax bracket is trying to decide which of two bonds to select: one is a 7.5 percent U.S. Treasury bond selling at par and the other is a municipal bond with a 5.25 percent coupon, which is also selling at par. Which of these two bonds should the investor select? Why?

7. Describe and differentiate between a bond's (a) current yield and (b) yield to maturity. Why are these yield measures important to the bond investor? Find the approximate yield to maturity of a 20-year, 13 percent, $1,000 par value bond that is trading at a price of $850. What's the current yield on this bond?

8. Which of the following three bonds offers the highest current yield? Which one has the highest yield to maturity?

   a. A 9.5 percent, 20 year bond quoted at $97\frac{3}{4}$.

   b. A 16%, 15 year bond quoted at $164\frac{5}{8}$.

   c. A 5.25 percent, 18 year bond quoted at 54.

9. Find the conversion value of an issue that carries a conversion ratio of 24, given that the market price of the underlying common stock is $55 a share. Would there be any conversion premium if the convertible bond had a market price of $1,500? If so, how much?

10. A certain 6% convertible bond (maturing in 20 years) is convertible into 20 shares of the company's common stock. The bond has a par value of $1,000 and is currently trading at $800; the stock (which pays a dividend of 75 cents a share) is currently trading in the market at $35 a share. Use the above information to answer the following questions:

   a. What is the current yield on the convertible bond? What is the dividend yield on the company's common stock? Which provides more current income: the convertible bond or the common stock? Explain.

   b. What is the bond's conversion ratio? Its conversion price?

   c. What is the conversion value of this issue? Is there any conversion premium in this issue? How much?

   d. What is the approximate yield to maturity on the convertible bond?

11. Using the resources available at your campus or public library, work the following problems. (Note: Show your work for all your calculations.)

   a. Select any two *common stocks,* and determine the dividend yield, earnings per share, and P/E ratio for each.

   b. Select any two *bonds,* and determine the current yield and approximate yield to maturity of each.

   c. Select any two *preferred* stocks, and determine the current yield of each.

   d. Select any two *convertible debentures,* and determine the conversion ratio, conversion value, and conversion premium for each.

CONTEMPORARY CASE APPLICATIONS

11.1 The Torreses Struggle with Two Investment Goals

Like a lot of married couples, Steve and Barbara Torres are trying their best to deal with not one, but two very important investment objectives: (1) building up an *education fund* to put their two children through college; and (2) building up a *retirement nest egg* for themselves. Their children are now 10 and 12 years old, and the oldest will be starting college in six years. Steve and Barbara want to have $40,000 set aside *for each child* by the time each one starts college (so they have six years to go with one child and eight with the other). As far as their retirement plans are concerned, the Torreses both hope to retire at age 65, in 20 years. Both Steve and Barbara work, and together, they currently earn about $75,000 a year.

Six years ago, the Torreses started a college fund by investing $6,000 a year in short-term CDs. That fund is now worth $45,000—enough to put one of the kids through any one of the in-state colleges. In addition, they have $50,000, which they received from an inheritance, invested in several mutual funds, and another $20,000 in a tax-sheltered retirement account. Steve and Barbara feel they'll easily be able to continue to put away $6,000 a year for the next 20 years—in fact, Barbara thinks they'll be able to put away even more, particularly after the children are out of school. The Torreses are pretty conservative investors and feel they can probably earn about 8 percent on their money. (You can ignore taxes in this exercise.)

Questions

1. Using Worksheet 11.1, determine whether the Torreses have enough money *right now* to meet the educational needs of their children. That is, will the $45,000 they've accumulated so far be enough to put their children through school, given they can invest their money at 8 percent? Remember, they want to have $40,000 set aside for *each* child by the time each one starts college.
2. Regarding their retirement nest egg, assuming *no additions* are made to either the $50,000 they now have in mutual funds or the $20,000 in the retirement account, how much would these investments be worth in 20 years, given they can earn 8 percent? (*Hint:* See Appendix A.)
3. Now, if they can invest $6,000 a year for the next 20 years and apply that to their retirement nest egg, how much would they be able to accumulate given their 8 percent rate of return? (*Hint:* See Appendix B.)
4. How do you think the Torreses are doing with regard to meeting their twin investment objectives? Explain.
5. What recommendations would you make to them with regard to *where* they should invest their money—what kind of stocks, bonds, or other investment instruments do you think would be right for them?

11.2 Jill Decides to Try Her Hand at Investing

Jill Karras is a 26-year-old management trainee at a large chemical company. She is single and has no plans for marriage. Her annual salary is $34,000 (placing her in the 28 percent tax bracket), and her monthly expenditures come to approximately $1,500. During the past year or so, Jill has managed to save around $8,000, and she expects to continue to save at least that amount each year for the foreseeable future. Her company pays the premium on her $35,000 life insurance policy. Since Jill's entire education was financed by scholarships, she was able to save the money from summer and part-time jobs she held as a student. Altogether, she has a nest egg of nearly $18,000, out of which she would like to invest about $15,000. She will keep the remaining $3,000 in a money market account that pays 4.5 percent interest; she will use this money only in the event of an emergency. Although Jill can afford to take more risks than someone with family obligations, she does not wish to be a speculator; rather, she simply wants to earn an attractive rate of return on her investments.

Questions

1. What investment options are open to Jill?
2. What chance does she have of earning a satisfactory return on her investments if she invests her $15,000 in (a) blue-chip stocks, (b) growth stocks, (c) speculative stocks, (d) corporate bonds, or (e) municipal bonds?
3. Discuss the factors you would consider when analyzing these alternative investment vehicles.
4. What recommendation would you make to Jill with respect to her available investment alternatives? Explain.

GETTING A HANDLE ON YOUR FINANCIAL FUTURE

To provide you with direction toward achieving your financial goals, you need an investment plan. This is generally nothing more than a written statement of how the funds will be invested and then a selection of the appropriate investment vehicles in terms of risk and expected returns to achieve the targeted goal.

If You Are Just Starting Out

You may think that you are too young to start investing. However, as you learned with the time value of money, the sooner you start investing, the more your money can make for you.

Selecting Appropriate Investments:

1. The investment choice in many cases is dependent upon the priority of your financial goals. If the goal is extremely important and cannot be delayed, the investment should probably be low in risk.
2. Some investments require minimum dollar amounts to purchase. This may delay your investment and result in a lower rate of return than expected.
3. Research your investment choice thoroughly to be sure that it is consistent with your financial goals.
4. Monitor your investments' performances. If they are not meeting your expectations, consider changing your portfolio.

If You Are Thirty-Something

There are a number of changes that have probably occurred since you first started investing. First, you have become more knowledgeable about all the investment opportunities available. Second, your attitude toward risk may have changed with your increasing income generating additional investable funds. Third, your time horizon for many of your goals is getting shorter. All of these changes will necessitate a reevaluation of your financial goals and investments.

Investing in Common Stocks:

1. Carefully analyze the purchase in accordance with your financial goals. Don't buy a stock just because it has a recognizable name.
2. Don't buy on rumor or upon the release of favorable information. Remember that the price of a share of stock responds to unanticipated information. If the release of the news were expected, there might not be any change in the stock price.
3. Consider using dividend reinvestment plans, which allow purchases with no transaction costs and possible cash discounts.

Investing in Bonds:

1. Remember that when interest rates change, the longer the bond's maturity, the greater the price volatility.
2. The lower the coupon on the bond, the greater the price volatility with changes in interest rates. This means that zero coupon bonds have the greatest price risk.
3. Don't be deceived by the term "high yield" investment; this is just another way of describing junk bonds.
4. When purchasing corporate bonds, be sure to look at the bond rating. As a general rule, avoid any bond with a rating of less than Baa (or BBB)—unless you have a good understanding of the ins and outs of junk bonds.

Chapter 12

Making Securities Transactions

Steve and Kelly Start Building a Securities Portfolio

Steve and Kelly Stuart, both 26, began investing in 1992 after paying off their credit card debt. "We saved the amount of the monthly payment and bought bank CDs. As rates dropped, we turned to the stock market," says Steve. Kelly adds, "We keep a fairly detailed budget and save about 15 percent of our salaries, even though they aren't large—Steve's studying for a Ph.D. in chemistry and I design children's clothes—and we live in expensive New York City."

The Stuarts' long-term investment goal is saving for retirement; short-term, to buy a house in a few years. "As our parents near retirement, we see the importance of good planning and recognize that we are responsible for our future financial security," Steve explains. With many years for their portfolio to grow, they're buying stocks for capital appreciation and currently have a portfolio made up of 73 percent stocks (mostly small cap), 19 percent cash equivalents, 6 percent mutual funds, and 2 percent convertible bonds. "Our mix has become more aggressive over time," notes Steve. "We moved from a few blue-chip stocks and savings bonds to small cap stocks, mutual funds, and convertible bonds. Next is international mutual funds."

The Stuarts' investing styles differ. Steve likes individual stocks—"Investing is fun!"—while Kelly prefers the professional management of mutual funds. Although Steve chooses most of the stocks, the final selection is a team effort. They consult *Forbes, The Wall Street Journal,*

Learning Goals

LG1. *Distinguish between primary and secondary markets, as well as listed exchanges and the over-the-counter market.*

LG2. *Choose the right stockbroker to suit your needs.*

LG3. *Explain the process of buying and selling securities and recognize the different types of orders.*

LG4. *Discuss the essentials of and motivations for margin trading and short selling.*

LG5. *Improve your investing skills by using various forms of investment information.*

LG6. *Build an investment portfolio and manage your investments.*

Value Line, CNBC (a cable business network), and *Dow Jones News/Retrieval (DJN/R),* an on-line service. "*Forbes,* the *Journal,* and CNBC are great for general investment information," Kelly says. "*Forbes* has good suggestions for stocks and mutual funds. Then we go to *Value Line* and Standard & Poor's stock sheets for more details, followed by DJN/R for recent news and prices." Steve can access most of these sources through the university business library.

"We're long-term investors, but I monitor our holdings regularly," Steve says. "We note why we bought the company in the first place and watch to make sure nothing changes. Most of all, we try not to sell too early. If a stock dips, but the fundamentals are still good, we don't panic. If it goes up, we'll ride it for a while."

The Stuarts advise new investors to start early. "Your investments will probably grow faster than your salary, so with compounding your early efforts make the biggest difference," Kelly says. Steve adds, "Learn about the markets, read investment magazines or newspapers, watch business shows; you'll be more confident about your choices. College libraries in your area are a great—and cheap—source of investment information. But remember: you can always find a good and a bad opinion on any investment, so take everything with a grain of salt, and *make your own decisions.*" In this chapter, you'll learn about securities markets, brokers, securities transactions, information sources, and portfolio strategies so that you too can build your own portfolio.

SECURITIES MARKETS

LG1

Stocks, bonds, and other securities are traded in a highly efficient market network that includes both organized exchanges and over-the-counter (OTC) markets. Would it really make any difference to you, as an investor, if a security is traded on an organized exchange or in the OTC market? How does trading on an exchange differ from that in the OTC market? Take a few moments before reading on to think about these questions.

It takes more than money to be a successful investor. To carry out a successful investment program, you must understand the institutions, mechanisms, and procedures involved in making security transactions. We looked at some investment fundamentals, particularly with regard to stocks and bonds, in the preceding chapter. In this chapter, we will examine the different securities markets, sources of investment information, and ways to manage your investment holdings. Just as Steve and Kelly Stuart have discovered, *there is no substitute for being an informed investor.*

The term **securities markets** is generally used to describe the place where stocks, bonds, and other financial instruments are traded. The securities markets can be broken into two parts: the capital markets and the money markets. The *capital market* is where long-term securities (those with maturities of more than a year) are traded, while the *money market* is the marketplace for short-term, low-risk credit instruments with maturities of one year or less, like U.S. Treasury bills, commercial paper, negotiable certificates of deposit, and so on. Both types of markets provide a vital mechanism for bringing the buyers and sellers of securities together. Some of the more popular money market securities were discussed in Chapter 4, where we looked at short-term investment vehicles. This chapter considers the capital markets.

PRIMARY OR SECONDARY MARKETS

The securities markets can also be divided into primary and secondary segments. The *primary market* is the market where new securities are sold to the public—where one party to the transaction is always the issuer. The *secondary market,* in contrast, is where old (outstanding) securities are bought and sold—here the securities are "traded" between investors. A security is sold in the primary market just once, when it is originally issued by the corporation or some governmental body, like a state or municipality. Subsequent transactions, wherein securities are sold by one investor to another, take place in the secondary market. As a rule, when people speak of the securities markets, they are referring to the secondary market, since that is where the vast majority of security transactions take place.

Primary Markets. When a corporation sells a new issue, several financial institutions participate in the transaction. To begin with, the corporation will probably use an *investment banking firm,* which specializes in *underwriting* (selling) new security issues. The investment banker will give the corporation advice on pricing and other aspects of the issue and either will sell the new security itself or arrange for a *selling group* to do so. The selling group is normally made up of a large number of brokerage firms, each of which accepts the responsibility for selling a certain portion of the new issue. On very large issues, the originating investment banker will bring in other underwriting firms as partners and form an *underwriting syndicate* in an attempt to spread the risks associated with underwriting and selling the new securities.

A potential investor in a new issue must be provided with a **prospectus,** which is a document describing the firm and the issue. Certain federal agencies have the responsibility of ensuring that all information included within a prospectus is an accurate representation of the facts. Many times investors have trouble purchasing new security issues because all shares allocated to the stockbrokers have been sold—often prior to the official sale date. Also, if the new shares are sold using *rights or warrants,* the ability to purchase the new securities will be somewhat restricted, since only the holders of these rights or warrants can buy the stock.

Secondary Markets. The secondary markets permit investors to execute transactions between themselves—it's the marketplace where an investor can easily sell his or her holdings to someone else. Included among the secondary markets are the various *securities exchanges,* in which the buyers and sellers of securities are brought together. In addition, there is the **over-the-counter (OTC) market,** which is made up of a nationwide network of brokers and dealers who execute transactions in securities that are not listed on one of the exchanges. The **organized securities exchanges** typically handle transactions in the securities of larger, better-known companies, and the over-the-counter market handles mostly the smaller, lesser-known firms. The organized exchanges are well-structured institutions that bring together the market forces of supply and demand; the over-the-counter market is basically a mass telecommunications network linking buyers and sellers. Since most transactions of small investors are made in the secondary market, we will focus on it throughout this chapter.

ORGANIZED SECURITIES EXCHANGES

The forces of market supply and demand are brought together in organized securities exchanges. So-called **listed securities** are traded on organized exchanges and account for about 72 percent of the total dollar volume of shares traded in the stock market. All trading is carried out in one place (such as the New York Stock Exchange on Wall Street) and under a broad set of rules by people who are *members* of the exchange. Members are said to "own a seat" on the exchange, a privilege that is obtained by meeting certain financial requirements. Only the securities of companies that have met certain listing requirements are traded on the exchange, and those firms must comply with established regulations to ensure that they will not make financial or legal misrepresentations to their stockholders. Firms must not only comply with the rules of the specific exchange but also fulfill certain requirements as established by the Securities and Exchange Commission (SEC) which will be discussed later.

New York Stock Exchange. *The New York Stock Exchange (NYSE)* is the largest and most prestigious organized securities exchange not only in this country, but in the world. Known as "the big board," there are over *90 billion* shares of stock listed on it that, at year-end 1994, had a market value of around *$4 trillion.* Membership on the NYSE is limited to 1,366 seats. During this century, the cost of a seat has ranged from as little as $17,000 (in 1942) to over $1 million (in 1987); recently, seats were going for about $750,000. Most seats are owned by brokerage firms, the largest of which—Merrill Lynch—owns more than 20.

The NYSE has the most stringent listing requirements of all the organized exchanges. For example, in order to be listed, a firm must have at least 2,000 stockholders, each owning 100 shares or more. It must also have a minimum of 1.1 million shares of publicly held stock outstanding; have demonstrated pretax earning power of $2.5 million at the time of listing and of $2 million for each of the preceding two years; have $18 million in market value of publicly held shares; and must pay a listing fee. Firms that fail to continue to meet listing requirements can be *delisted.* More than 1,800 companies from around the world list their shares on the NYSE. All totaled, more than 2,300 different *stocks* (including a couple hundred *foreign* issues) and nearly 2,900 corporate *bonds* are traded on the NYSE.

American Stock Exchange. The *American Stock Exchange (AMEX)* is the second largest organized stock exchange in terms of the number of listed companies; when it comes to the dollar volume of trading, however, the AMEX is actually smaller than two of the *regional* exchanges (the Midwest and Pacific). Its organization and procedures are similar to those of the NYSE, though its membership costs and listing requirements are not as stringent. There are approximately 660 seats on

securities markets The marketplace in which stocks, bonds, and other financial instruments are traded.

prospectus A document made available to prospective security purchasers that describes the firm and a new security issue.

over-the-counter (OTC) market The market in which securities not listed on one of the organized exchanges are traded, usually those of smaller, lesser-known firms.

organized securities exchanges Exchanges where various types of securities are traded by (exchange) members for their own accounts and the accounts of their customers.

listed security A security that has met the prerequisites for, and thus is traded on, one of the organized securities exchanges.

the AMEX and over 1,000 listed stocks and 260 listed corporate bonds. The AMEX handles only about 2 percent of the share volume on *organized* security exchanges. In contrast, the NYSE handles around 86 percent of all common shares traded on organized exchanges, so the AMEX is nowhere near the New York exchange in terms of size or stature. Further, whereas the NYSE is home for many of the biggest and best-known companies in the world, firms traded on the AMEX are much smaller and, with few exceptions, would hardly qualify as "household names."

Regional Stock Exchanges. In addition to the NYSE and AMEX, there are a handful of so-called **regional exchanges.** The number of securities listed on each of these exchanges is typically in the range of 100 to 500 companies. As a group they handle perhaps 12 percent of all shares traded on organized exchanges. The best-known of these are the Midwest, Pacific, Philadelphia, Boston, and Cincinnati exchanges. These exchanges deal primarily in securities with local and regional appeal. Most are modeled after the NYSE, but their membership and listing requirements are considerably more lenient. Regional exchanges will often list securities that are also listed on the NYSE or AMEX in order to enhance their trading activity.

THE OVER-THE-COUNTER MARKET

Unlike an organized exchange, the over-the-counter (OTC) market is not a specific institution but, instead, exists as an intangible relationship between the buyers and sellers of securities. Securities traded in this market are sometimes called **unlisted securities.** It is the fastest-growing segment of the stock market, accounting for 28 percent of the total dollar volume of domestic shares traded, and today trades close to *35,000* issues. The market is linked together by a mass telecommunications network. Unlike those in the organized securities exchanges, the trades in the OTC market represent *direct* transactions between investors and securities dealers—that is, the investors buy from and sell to the securities dealers, whereas on the listed securities exchanges the broker acts as a middleman between buyers and sellers. All municipal bonds, along with most government and corporate bonds, as well as a numerical majority of common stocks are traded in the OTC market. Dealers make markets in certain securities by offering to either buy or sell them at stated prices.

Nasdaq. A part of the OTC market is linked through the *National Association of Securities Dealers Automated Quotation System (Nasdaq),* which provides up-to-date quotes and bid/ask prices on several thousand securities. (The **bid** and the **ask prices** represent, respectively, the highest price offered to purchase a given security and the lowest price at which the security is offered for sale. In effect, an investor pays the ask price when *buying* securities and receives the bid price when *selling* them.)

There are about 4,700 actively traded issues in the Nasdaq portion of the OTC market, and of these, about 2,600 are part of the so-called *National Market System (NMS).* The national market system is reserved for the biggest and most actively traded stocks; and, in general, for those stocks that have a *national following.* These securities are widely quoted, and the trades are executed about as efficiently here as they are on the floor of the NYSE. A number of large and well-known firms are found on the Nasdaq National Market System, including companies like Apple Computers, Intel, MCI, Lotus, Nordstrom, Microsoft, and Seagate Technology, as well as many big banks and insurance companies. Generally speaking, the big-name stocks traded on the Nasdaq/NMS receive about as much national visibility and are about as liquid as those traded on the NYSE. Indeed, because of this, *Nasdaq is now the second biggest market in the United States,* in terms of dollar volume of trading, and the third largest in the world!

The situation is considerably different, however, for OTC stocks that are not part of Nasdaq—the vast majority of the firms traded in the OTC market. These include the very small firms that may not even have much of a regional following, let alone a national constituency. These stocks are *thinly traded,* meaning there's not much of a market for them, and they often lack any measurable degree of liquidity. Many of these stocks appear in the so-called *pink sheets.* So named because of the color of paper used, the pink sheets are published daily and are available from brokers.

The companies who use pink-sheet listings are either unable or unwilling to meet the financial reporting requirements of the SEC. They cover a wide range, from new, rapidly growing firms to obscure but well-established firms that are closely held to companies on the verge of bankruptcy or penny stocks peddled by shady brokers. Although quotes on pink-sheet companies today are available electronically, prices are updated only when there's significant trading or when requested by traders making markets in pink-sheet stocks, so quotes may not be current. The quotes for these thinly traded securities reflect the value set by the market maker, not market forces. Because dealers mark up prices, often by large amounts, your final price may be much higher than the actual selling price, making it harder to earn a profit when you sell the stock. If you decide to buy a pink-sheet stock, make sure your broker is prepared to negotiate long and hard on your behalf.

FOREIGN SECURITIES MARKETS

In addition to those in the United States, there are organized securities exchanges in more than 30 other countries worldwide. Indeed, actively traded markets can be found not only in the major industrialized nations like Japan, Great Britain, Germany, and Canada, but also in emerging economies such as Mexico, Taiwan, Malaysia, and South Korea. The New York and Tokyo Stock Exchanges are the biggest in the world, while the London Stock Exchange is Europe's largest. Other major exchanges are located in Toronto, Sydney, Frankfurt, Paris, Zurich, Hong Kong, and Singapore. As these and other markets continue to develop, they'll open up opportunities not only for investors in those countries, but also for U.S. investors willing to go offshore in search of returns. At the same time, it's becoming increasingly clear that the U.S. securities markets can no longer be viewed in isolation, but rather, as a part of a worldwide network of securities markets.

REGULATING THE SECURITIES MARKETS

A number of laws have been enacted to regulate the activities of various participants in the securities markets and to provide for adequate and accurate disclosure of information to potential and existing investors. State laws, which regulate the sale of securities within state borders, typically establish procedures that apply to the sellers of securities doing business within the state. The most important and far reaching securities laws, however, are those enacted by the federal government:

- **Securities Act of 1933.** This act was passed by Congress to ensure full disclosure of information with respect to new security issues and to prevent a stock market collapse similar to that which occurred in 1929—1932. It requires the issuer of a new security to file a registration statement containing information about the new issue with the **Securities and Exchange Commission (SEC),** an agency of the U.S. government that was established to enforce federal securities laws.
- **Securities Exchange Act of 1934.** One of the most important pieces of securities legislation ever passed, it expanded the scope of federal regulation and *formally established the SEC* as the agency in charge of the administration of federal securities laws. The act gives the SEC power to regulate organized securities exchanges and the over-the-counter market by extending disclosure requirements to outstanding securities. It requires the stock exchanges as well as the stocks traded on them to be registered with the SEC. In essence, the Securities acts of 1933 and 1934 regulated not only securities exchanges and securities markets, but also the disclosure of information on both new and outstanding securities.
- **Investment Company Act of 1940.** This act protects those purchasing investment company

regional exchanges Organized securities exchanges (other than the NYSE and AMEX) that deal primarily in securities having a local or regional appeal.

unlisted security A security that is traded in the over-the-counter market; such a trade is made directly between the investor and the security dealer.

bid price The price at which one can sell a security.

ask price The price at which one can purchase a security.

Securities and Exchange Commission (SEC) An agency of the federal government that regulates the disclosure of information about securities and generally oversees the operation of the securities exchanges and markets.

(mutual fund) shares. It established rules and regulations for investment companies and formally authorized the SEC to regulate their practices and procedures. It requires the investment companies to register with the SEC and to fulfill certain disclosure requirements. The act was amended in 1970 to prohibit investment companies from paying excessive fees to their advisors as well as charging excessive commissions to purchasers of company shares. From the point of view of the individual investor, this act provides protection against inadequate or inaccurate disclosure of information, and against being charged excessive fees indirectly by the fund's advisors, and directly through the commissions paid to purchase company shares.

- **Other Significant Federal Legislation.** The *Maloney Act of 1938* provides for the establishment of trade associations for the purpose of self-regulation within the securities industry; this act led to the creation of the **National Association of Securities Dealers (NASD),** which is made up of all brokers and dealers who participate in the OTC market. The NASD is a self-regulatory organization that polices the activities of brokers and dealers in order to ensure that its standards are upheld. The SEC supervises the activities of NASD, thus providing investors with further protection from fraudulent activities. The *Investment Advisors Act of 1940* was passed to protect investors against potential abuses by investment advisors who sell their services to the investing public. The *Securities Investor Protection Act of 1970* created the SIPC (Securities Investor Protection Corp.), an organization that protects investors against the financial failure of brokerage firms, much like the FDIC protects depositors against bank failures (we'll examine the SIPC later in this chapter). The *Insider Trading and Securities Fraud Enforcement Act of 1988* toughened penalties for securities fraud and required brokerage firms to establish written policies to prevent trading abuses by their employees; it also made it easier for investors to bring legal action against brokers.

In addition to securities legislation, the *stock exchanges* themselves play important roles in monitoring and regulating the companies, brokerage firms, traders, and other parties that deal in listed securities. Likewise, most *brokerage firms* go to great lengths to prevent trading abuses by aggressively policing their own employees.

BULL MARKET OR BEAR?

The general condition of the market is termed *bullish* or *bearish,* depending on whether security prices are rising or falling over extended periods of time. Changing market conditions generally stem from changing investor attitudes, changes in economic activity, and certain governmental actions aimed at stimulating or slowing down the economy. Prices go *up* in **bull markets;** these favorable markets are normally associated with investor optimism, economic recovery, and governmental stimulus. In contrast, prices go *down* in **bear markets,** which are normally associated with investor pessimism and economic slowdowns. These terms are used to describe conditions in the bond and other securities markets as well as the stock market. For example, the bond market is considered bullish when interest rates fall, causing bond prices to rise; on the other hand, a bear market in bonds exists when bond prices fall (which occurs when rates rise). As a rule, investors are able to earn attractive rates of return during bull markets and only low (or negative) returns during bear markets. Market conditions are difficult to predict and usually cannot be identified until after they exist.

Over the past 50 or so years, the behavior of the stock market has been generally bullish, reflecting the growth and prosperity of the economy. Exhibit 12.1 shows the five biggest bull markets since the Second World War, the longest of which lasted 97 *months*—from June 1949 to July 1957. The most notorious of the five was surely the one which started in August 1982 and peaked in August 1987. This is the one that's associated with the big market crash of October 19, 1987, when in a *single day,* the market, as measured by the Dow Jones Industrial Average, dropped by a whopping 508 points! Actually, the market had started dropping in late August and by mid-October had already fallen some 400 points. Then came "Black Monday," when the market experienced its biggest and hardest crash in history, not only in absolute numerical terms (508 points), but also in percentage and dollar terms: in one day, the market fell nearly 23 percent and lost roughly half a *trillion* dollars in value. Fortunately, since late 1990, the market has once again become fairly bullish.

EXHIBIT 12.1

The Five Biggest Bull Markets since the Second World War (as Measured by Changes in the DJIA)

The prices of most stocks will go up in a bull market. Thus, it is hard to lose money—though not impossible, since not all stocks will appreciate in value during such markets. The most recent bull market started in November 1990 and was still going strong in early 1995.

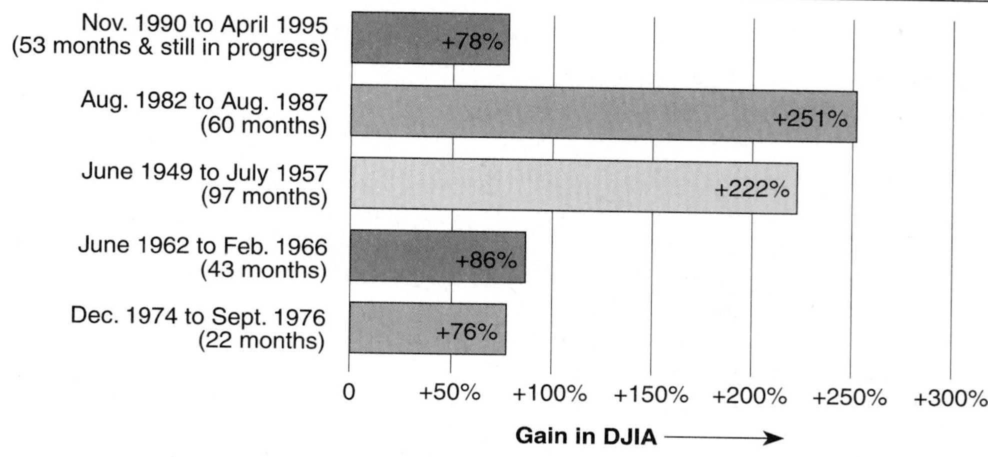

Concept Check

12-1. Explain what is meant by the *securities markets* and briefly describe the difference between the money market and the capital market.

12-2. How does a primary market differ from a secondary market? Give some examples of the types of securities found in the money market; in the capital market.

12-3. What are *organized securities exchanges*? What is the difference between the New York Stock Exchange and the American Stock Exchange? What are *regional exchanges*, and what role do they play?

12-4. Describe the operations of the *over-the-counter market*; compare and contrast it with organized securities exchanges. What are Nasdaq and the National Market System?

12-5. Explain the difference between a *bull market* and a *bear market*. How would you characterize the current state of the stock market? Are we in a bull market or a bear market?

12-6. Briefly summarize the key provisions of major securities legislation.

National Association of Securities Dealers (NASD) An agency made up of brokers and dealers in over-the-counter securities that regulates the operations of the OTC market.

bull market A condition of the market normally associated with investor optimism, economic recovery, and government stimulus; characterized by generally rising securities prices.

bear market A condition of the market typically associated with investor pessimism, economic slowdown, and government control; characterized by generally falling securities prices.

MAKING TRANSACTIONS IN THE SECURITIES MARKETS

LG2 LG3 LG4

Individual investors use the services of stock brokers to buy and sell securities in the marketplace. Stop for a moment to consider the different kinds of services offered by brokers. How great do you suppose the difference would be in the services and cost of a discount broker as opposed to a full-service broker?

In many respects, dealing in the securities markets almost seems like you are operating in another world—one with all kinds of unusual orders and strange-sounding transactions. Actually, making securities transactions is relatively simple once you understand the basics—in fact, you will probably find it is no more difficult than using a checking account! Indeed, while making money in the market isn't all that easy, making transactions is.

STOCKBROKERS

Stockbrokers, or **account executives,** as they're also called, purchase and sell securities for their customers. Although deeply ingrained in our language, the term "stockbroker" is really somewhat of a misnomer, as such an individual assists you in the purchase and sale of not only stocks but also bonds, convertibles, mutual funds, options, and many other types of securities. Brokers must be licensed by the exchanges on which they place orders and must abide by the strict ethical guidelines of the exchanges and the SEC. They work for brokerage firms and in essence are there to execute the orders placed. The largest stockbrokerage firm, Merrill Lynch, has brokerage offices in virtually every major U.S. city (and many foreign countries). Orders from these offices are transmitted by brokers to the main office of Merrill Lynch and then to the floor of one of the stock exchanges, or to the OTC market, where they are executed. Although the procedure for executing orders on organized exchanges differs a bit from that in the OTC market, you as an investor would never know the difference, since you would place your order with the broker in exactly the same fashion.

Selecting a Broker. It is important to select a broker *who understands your investment objectives, and who can effectively assist you in pursuing them.* If you choose a broker whose own disposition toward investing is similar to yours, you should be able to avoid conflict and establish a solid working relationship. It is probably best to ask friends, relatives, or business associates to recommend a broker. It is not important—and often even inadvisable—to know your stockbroker personally since most, if not all, of your transactions/orders will probably be placed by phone. In addition, a strict business relationship eliminates the possibility of social concerns interfering with the achievement of your investment objectives. This does not mean, of course, that your broker's sole interest should be commissions. Indeed, a broker should be far more than just a salesperson; for *a good broker is someone who's more interested in your investments than his or her commissions.* Should you find you're dealing with someone who's always trying to get you to trade your stocks, or who's pushing new investments on you, then by all means, dump that broker and find a new one!

Discount Brokers. Security transactions can also be made at **discount brokers.** Discount brokers tend to have low overhead operations and offer fewer customer services than full-service brokers. Those with the very lowest commissions, but who offer no other broker services, are called *deep discounters.* Other discount brokerages provide research and other services and charge higher commissions. Transactions are initiated by calling a toll-free number and placing the desired buy or sell order. The brokerage firm then executes the order at the best possible price and confirms the details of the transaction by mail. In order to discourage small orders, most discounters charge a minimum transaction fee ranging between $30 and $50. Depending on the size of the transaction, *discount brokers can save investors from 30 to 80 percent of the commissions charged by full-service brokers.* The investor who does not need the research and advisory help available from full-service brokers may find discount brokers especially attractive. Listed below are some major discount and full-service brokerage houses:

Discount Brokers

Brown & Company*
Charles Schwab
Fidelity Brokerage Services
Muriel Siebert & Company*
National Discount Brokers*
Quick & Reilly

(*Note:* Those firms marked with an * indicate bare-bones, deep-discount brokers.)

Full-Service Brokers

Dean Witter
Kemper Securities
Merrill Lynch
Paine Webber
Prudential Securities
Smith Barney Shearson

Brokerage Services. In addition to carrying out purchase and sale transactions for commission, full-service stockbrokers offer their clients a variety of other services. Selecting a good brokerage firm is just as important as choosing a good broker, since not all brokerage firms provide the same services. Try to select a broker with whom you can work and who is affiliated with a firm that provides the types of services you are looking for. Many brokerage firms, for example, provide a wide array of free information, ranging from stock and bond guides to research reports on specific securities or industries. Some have a research staff that periodically issues analyses of economic, market, industry, or company behavior and events, and relates them to its recommendations for buying or selling certain securities. As a brokerage firm client, you can expect to receive monthly bulletins discussing market activity and possibly even a recommended investment list. You will also receive an *account statement* describing all of your transactions for the period, commission charges, interest charges, dividends and interest received, the securities you currently hold, and your account balances.

Most brokerage offices provide up-to-the-minute stock price quotations and world news. Stock price information can be obtained either from the quotation board (a large screen that electronically displays all NYSE and AMEX security transactions within minutes of their occurrence) or from the computerized telequote system. World news, which can significantly affect the stock market, is obtained from a news wire service. Most offices also have a reference library the firm's clients can use.

Another valuable service offered by most major brokerage firms is the automatic transfer of surplus cash left in a customer's account into one of the firm's money funds, thereby allowing the customer to earn a reasonable rate of return on temporarily idle funds. Brokerage houses will also hold your securities for you, as protection against their loss; the securities kept in this way are said to be held in *street name*. Some of these services are also offered by discount brokerages.

Investor Protection. As a client, you are protected against the loss of securities or cash held by your broker by the **Securities Investor Protection Corporation (SIPC)**—a nonprofit corporation, authorized by the Securities Investor Protection Act of 1970 to protect customer accounts against the financial failure of a brokerage firm. Although subject to SEC and congressional oversight, the SIPC is *not* an agency of the U.S. government.

SIPC insurance covers each account for up to $500,000 (of which up to $100,000 may be in cash balances held by the firm). Note, however, that SIPC insurance does not guarantee that the dollar value of the securities will be recovered. It only insures that *the securities themselves will be returned*. So, what happens if your broker gives you bad advice, and as a result, you lose a lot of money on an investment? SIPC won't help you, as it's not intended to insure you against bad investment advice. Instead, if you have a dispute with your broker, first discuss the situation with the managing officer at the branch where you do your business. If that doesn't do any good, then write or talk to the firm's compliance officer and contact the securities office in your home state. If you still don't get any satisfaction, you may have to take the case to **arbitration,** a process whereby you and your broker present the two sides to the argument before an arbitration panel, which then makes a decision about how the case shall be resolved. If it's *binding* arbitration, and it usually is, you have no choice

stockbroker (account executive) An individual who buys and sells securities on behalf of clients and provides them with investment advice and information.

discount broker A broker with low overhead who charges low commissions and offers little or no services to investors.

Securities Investor Protection Corporation (SIPC) A nonprofit corporation, created by Congress and subject to SEC and congressional oversight, that insures customer accounts against the financial failure of a brokerage firm.

arbitration A procedure that's used to settle disputes between a brokerage firm and its clients; both sides of the "story" are presented to a board of arbitration, which makes a final and binding decision on the matter..

EXHIBIT 12.2

Broker Commissions on Common Stock Transactions

The amount of broker commissions paid on a common stock transaction obviously will vary with the market value of the transaction. You will pay a commission when you buy stocks and again when you sell them.

Value of Transaction	Fees for an Odd or Round Lot
Up to $2,500	$30 + 1.7% of the value of the transaction
$2,500 to $6,250	$56 + .66% of the value of the transaction
$6,250 to $20,000	$76 + .34% of the value of the transaction

Source: A major stock brokerage firm.

but to accept the decision—you cannot go to court to appeal your case. To make matters worse, many brokerage firms require you to resolve disputes by going to binding arbitration. Thus, before you open an account, check the brokerage agreement to see if it contains a binding arbitration clause.

Now, binding arbitration wouldn't be so bad if the track record were more evenly balanced. But until recently, most brokerage firms not only required investors to submit to binding arbitration, but also specified which arbitration panels could be used; not surprisingly, 90 percent of those panels were sponsored by the NASD or the NYSE. There was considerable controversy as to whether the panels, which prior to 1989 were often composed *entirely* of people with strong ties to the securities industry, were fair to investors. As a result of pressure from the SEC, and a July 1990 court decision in New York State, *many investors now have the option of using either securities industry panels or independent arbitration panels, such as those sponsored by the American Arbitration Association (AAA)*—which is considered more sympathetic towards investors. In addition, only one of the three arbitrators on a panel can be connected with the securities industry. Recently, the NASD and other securities organizations began encouraging investors to mediate disputes and voluntarily negotiate a settlement rather than immediately going into arbitration. Although *mediation* is not binding, it can further reduce costs and time for both investors and brokers. But probably the best way of avoiding either mediation or arbitration is to use care when selecting a broker in the first place, and then carefully evaluate the advice he or she offers.

Odd or Round Lots. Security transactions can be made in either odd or round lots. An **odd lot** consists of fewer than 100 shares of stock, while a **round lot** represents a 100-share unit or multiples thereof. The sale of 400 shares of stock would be considered a round-lot transaction, but the purchase of 75 shares would be an odd-lot transaction; trading 250 shares of stock would involve two round lots and an odd lot. Because the purchase or sale of odd lots requires additional processing and the assistance of a specialist (an *odd-lot dealer*), an added fee—known as an *odd-lot differential*—is tacked on to the normal commission charge, driving up the costs of these small trades. Indeed, the relatively high cost of an odd-lot trade is why it's best to deal in round lots whenever possible.

Brokerage Fees. Brokerage firms receive commissions for executing buy and sell orders for their clients. Brokerage commissions are said to be *negotiated,* which means that they are not fixed. In practice, however, most firms have *established* fee schedules that they use with small transactions (on larger, institutional trades, negotiation of commissions actually does take place). Although these fees are not really negotiated, they do differ from one brokerage firm to another; thus, it pays to shop around. Also if you're an "active trader," generating a couple thousand dollars (or more) in annual commissions, then by all means try to negotiate a

EXHIBIT 12.3

Comparison of Discount Brokers' Commissions

They say it pays to shop around and that piece of advice certainly applies when it comes to selecting a broker. Just look at the different commissions these brokers charge to execute essentially the same trade–to trade 500 shares of a $50 stock for example, ranges from $29 to $155 at the listed discont brokers, and as high as $449 at one of the major full-service brokers.

	Commission		
Firm	**100 shares at $50/share ($5,000)**	**500 shares at $50/share ($25,000)**	**1,000 shares at $5/share ($5,000)**
AccuTrade	$ 31	$ 110	$ 67
Brown & Co.	29	29	29
Charles Schwab	55	155	90
Fidelity	54	155	89
Jack White	36	48	63
National Discount Brokers	30	30	30
Olde Discount	40	100	53
Quick & Reilly	49	120	61
Average of 82 discount brokerage firms	43	95	68
Highest discount broker	83	248	135
Lowest discount broker	23	25	25
Major Full-Service Firm	111	449	223

Source: Adapted from Marie Swick, Jean Henrich, and Maria Crawford Scott, "The 1995 Discount Broker Survey: A Guide to Commissions and Services," *AAII Journal*, January 1995, pp. 12–16; and a major full-service stock brokerage firm.

reduced commission schedule with your broker. Chances are, they'll probably cut a deal with you—the fact is, brokers much prefer traders to buy-and-hold investors, since traders generate a lot more commissions.

The suggested fee schedule used by one large brokerage firm to set commissions on *common stock* transactions is given in Exhibit 12.2 Although this schedule does not specifically levy a premium on odd-lot transactions, the fixed-cost fee component does tend to raise their per share cost. (In addition to the fees shown in the schedule, some brokerage firms charge a differential of 12.5 cents per share on odd-lot transactions.) If the fee schedule in Exhibit 12.2 were used to calculate brokerage fees on the purchase of 80 shares of XYZ stock at $30 per share, the total value of the transaction would be $2,400 (80 shares × $30/share) and the brokerage fee would therefore be $30 + 1.7% (2,400) = $30 + $40.80 = $70.80; that amounts to about 3 percent of the value of the transaction. Generally speaking, brokerage fees on a round lot of common stock will amount to approximately 2 to 4 percent of the transaction value. (As a rule, at full-service brokerage firms, the broker gets to keep about 40 percent of the commission and the brokerage firm gets the rest.)

As the number of discount brokerage firms grows, there is greater variation in both fees charged and services offered. The way commissions are calculated also varies; some firms base them on the dollar value of the transaction, some on the number of shares, and some use both. Exhibit 12.3 compares commissions at eight discount and deep discount brokerage firms. The firms with higher commissions generally offer more services; for example, while most discounters offer sweep accounts, Brown & Co. does not. Many discounters charge clients extra for research services.

Brokerage commissions on bond transactions differ from those on stock transactions. Brokerage firms typically charge a minimum fee of $25 to $30, regardless of the number of bonds involved. For multiple bond transactions, the brokerage cost per $1,000 corporate bond typically amounts to around $10 (which is decidedly lower than that on a stock

odd lot A quantity of fewer than 100 shares of a stock.

round lot A quantity of 100 shares of stock, or multiples thereof.

EXHIBIT 12.4

Executing Trades in the Stock Market

Placing an order to buy or sell securities usually involves nothing more than a phone call to your broker. However, as we see here, there's a lot that goes on behind the scenes to execute that order—although it all happens very quickly and rather routinely.

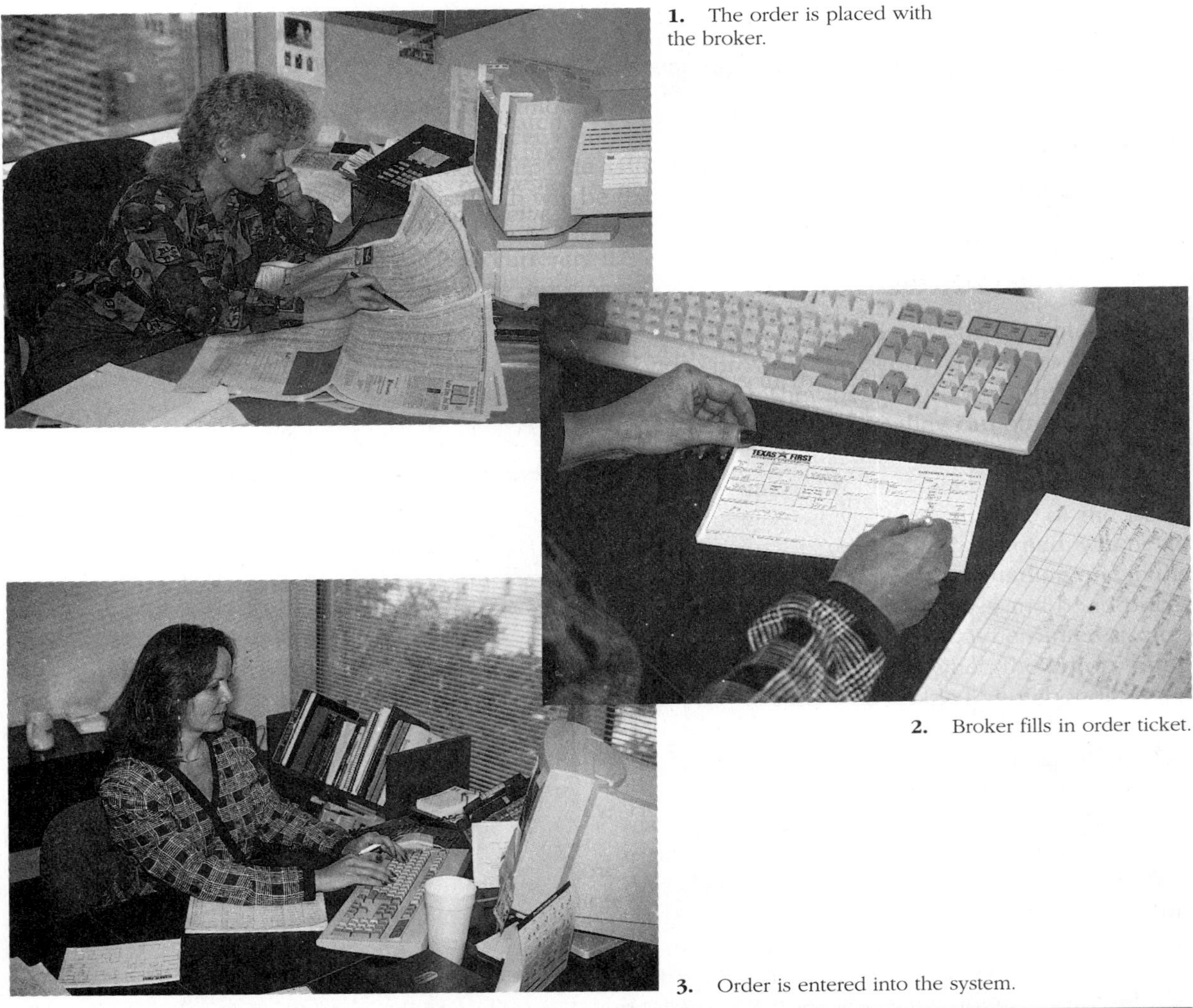

1. The order is placed with the broker.

2. Broker fills in order ticket.

3. Order is entered into the system.

transaction). The commission schedules for other securities, such as mutual funds and options, differ from those used with stocks and bonds (we will look at some of these in the next chapter).

The magnitude of brokerage commissions obviously is an important consideration when making security transactions, since these fees tend to raise the overall cost of purchasing securities and lower the overall proceeds from their sale.

EXECUTING TRADES

For most individual investors, a securities transaction involves placing a buy or sell order, usually by phone, and later getting a confirmation that it has been completed. They have no idea what happens to their orders. In fact, a lot goes on—and very quickly—once the order is placed. It has to, because on a typical day, the NYSE alone executes some 80,000 trades, and many thousands more occur on

EXHIBIT 12.4

Continued

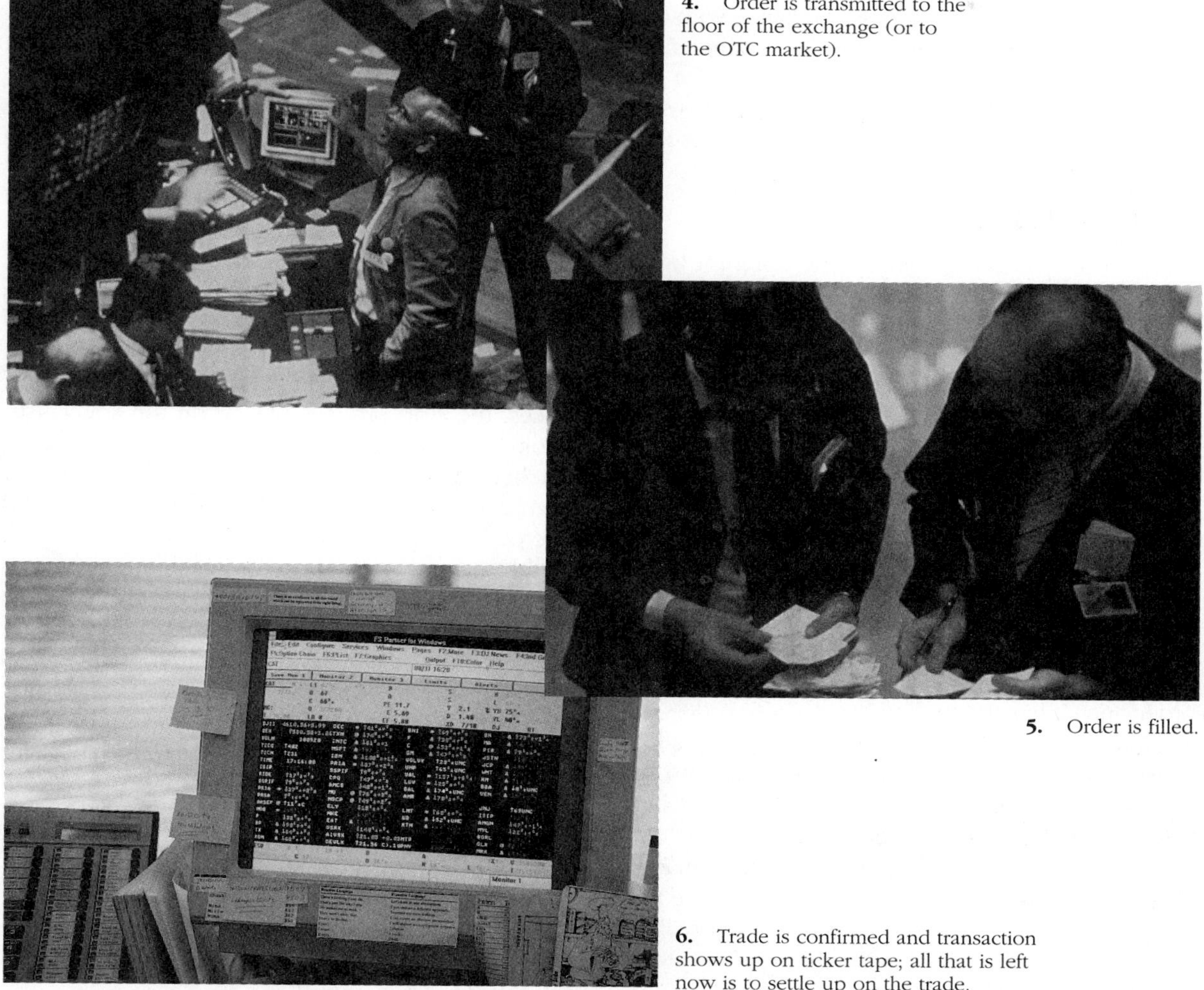

4. Order is transmitted to the floor of the exchange (or to the OTC market).

5. Order is filled.

6. Trade is confirmed and transaction shows up on ticker tape; all that is left now is to settle up on the trade.

Nasdaq, the AMEX, and the other exchanges. Exhibit 12.4 traces the steps in a typical securities transaction. In this case, the investor has placed a market order (which we will explain below) and as such, it should take *less than two minutes* to place, execute, and confirm the trade.

The process starts with a phone call to the broker, who then transmits the order via sophisticated telecommunications equipment to the stock exchange floor, or to the OTC market, where it is promptly executed. Confirmation that the order has been executed is transmitted back to the original broker and then to the customer. Once the trade takes place, the investor has three (business) days to "settle" his or her account with the broker—that is, to pay for the securities.

It's now possible to use your PC to execute on-line securities trades. The major on-line services—America Online, CompuServe, and Prodigy—have links to discount brokerages. Charles Schwab, Fidelity, and AccuTrade have their own software, so you can trade directly, without going through one of the subscription services. Your order goes by modem from your computer to the brokerage computer, which checks the type of order and confirms that it is in compliance with regulations. Then it is transmitted to the exchange floor or an OTC dealer for execution. The time for the whole process, including a confirmation that is sent back to your computer, is usually a minute or less.

TYPES OF ORDERS

Investors may choose from several different kinds of orders when buying or selling securities. The type of order chosen normally depends on the investor's goals and expectations with respect to the given transaction. The three basic types of orders are the market order, limit order, and stop-loss order.

Market order. An order to buy or sell a security at the best price available at the time it is placed is a **market order.** It is usually the quickest way to have orders filled, since market orders are executed as soon as they reach the trading floor. In fact, on small trades of less than a few thousand shares, it only takes about *15 to 20 seconds* to fill a market order once it hits the trading floor! These orders are executed through a process that attempts to allow *buy orders* to be filled at the lowest price and *sell orders* at the highest, thereby providing the best possible deal to both the buyers and sellers of a security. Because of the speed with which market orders are transacted, the investor can be sure that the price at which the order is completed will be very close to the market price that existed at the time it was placed.

Limit order. An order to buy at a specified price (or lower), or sell at a specified price (or above) is known as a **limit order.** The broker transmits a limit order to a *specialist* dealing in the given security on the floor of the exchange. The specialist makes a notation in his or her "book" indicating the limit order and limit price. The order is executed as soon as the specified market price is reached and all other such orders with precedence have been filled. The order can be placed to remain in effect until a certain date or until canceled; such an instruction is called a **good 'til canceled (GTC) order.** For example, assume that you place a limit order to buy 100 shares of a stock at a price of 20, even though the stock is currently selling at 20½. Once the specialist has cleared all similar orders received before yours, and the market price of the stock is still at \$20 or less, he or she will execute the order. Although a limit order can be quite effective, it can also cost you money! If, for instance, you wish to buy at 20 or less and the stock price moves from its current \$20.50 to \$32 while you are waiting, your limit order will have caused you to forgo an opportunity to make a profit of \$11.50 (\$32.00 − \$20.50) per share. Had you placed a market order, this profit would have been yours.

Stop-Loss Order. An order to sell a stock when the market price reaches or drops below a specified level is called a **stop-loss,** or **stop order.** Used to protect the investor against rapid declines in stock prices, the stop order is placed on the specialist's book and activated when the stop price is reached. At that point, the stop order becomes a *market order* to sell. This means that the stock is offered for sale at the prevailing market price, which could be *less* than the price at which the order was initiated by the stop. For example, imagine that you own 100 shares of DEF, which is currently selling for \$25. Because of the high uncertainty associated with the price movements of the stock, you decide to place a stop order at \$21. If the stock price drops to \$21, your stop order is activated and the specialist will sell all your DEF stock at the best price available, which may be \$18 or \$19 a share. Of course, if the market price increases, nothing will have been lost by placing the stop-loss order.

MARGIN TRADES: BUYING SECURITIES ON CREDIT

It is possible to borrow some of the money needed to purchase securities. *Buying on margin,* as it is called, is a common practice that allows investors to use borrowed money to make security transactions. Margin trading is closely regulated and is carried out under strict *margin requirements* set by the Federal Reserve Board. These requirements specify the amount of *equity* an investor must put up when buying stocks, bonds, and other securities. The most recent requirement is 50 percent for common stock, which means that at least 50 percent of each dollar invested must be the investor's own; the remain-

EXHIBIT 12.5

The Impact of Margin Trading on Investment Returns

The rate of return that an individual earns on his or her investment is affected, among other things, by the amount of margin being used; unfortunately, while margin trading can magnify returns, it will also magnify losses.

Transaction	Without Margin	With Margin
The Initial Investment		
Amount invested	$5,000	$2,500
Amount borrowed	0	2,500
Total purchase (100 shares @ $50)	$5,000	$5,000
Price *Increases:* Sell Stock for $70/Share One Year Later		
Gross proceeds (100 shares @ $60)	$7,000	$7,000
Less: Interest @ 9% of amount borrowed	0	225
Net proceeds	$7,000	$6,775
Less: Total investment	5,000	5,000
Net profit (loss)	$2,000	$1,775
Return on your investment (profit ÷ amount invested)	$2,000 / $5,000 = 40%	$1,775 / $2,500 = 71%
Price *Decreases:* Sell Stock for $30/Share One Year Later		
Gross proceeds (100 shares @ $40)	$3,000	$4,000
Less: Interest @ 9% of amount borrowed	0	225
Net proceeds	$3,000	$2,775
Less: Total investment	5,000	5,000
Net profit (loss)	($2,000)	($2,225)
Return on your investment (profit ÷ amount invested)	($2,000) / $5,000 = (40%)	($2,225) / $2,500 = (89%)

ing 50 percent may be borrowed. For example, with a 50 percent margin requirement, you could purchase $5,000 worth of stock by putting up only $2,500 of your own money and borrowing the remaining $2,500. Other securities besides stocks can be margined, and these have their own margin requirements; Treasury bonds, for example, can be purchased with a margin as low as 10 percent.

To make **margin purchases,** you must open a *margin account* and have a minimum of $2,000 in cash (or *equity* in securities) on deposit with your broker. Once you meet these requirements, the brokerage firm will loan you the needed funds (at competitive interest rates) and retain the securities purchased as collateral. You can also obtain loans to purchase securities from your commercial bank, but the Fed's margin requirements still apply, though they may be a bit more difficult to enforce. To see how margin trading works, assume that the margin requirement is 50 percent and that your brokerage firm charges 9 percent interest on margin loans (brokerage firms usually set the rate on margin loans at 1 to 3 points above prime, or at the prime rate for large accounts). If you want to purchase a round lot (100 shares) of Engulf & Devour, which is currently trading at $50 per share, you

market order An order to buy or sell a security at the best price available at the time it is placed.

limit order An order to either buy a security at a specified or lower price or to sell a security at or above a specified price.

good 'til canceled (GTC) order A limit order placed with instructions that it remain in effect indefinitely or until canceled.

stop-loss (stop) order An order to sell a stock when the market price reaches or drops below a specified level.

margin purchase The purchase of securities with borrowed funds, the allowable amount of which is limited by the broker and/or the Federal Reserve Board.

can either make the purchase entirely with your own money or borrow a portion of the purchase price. The cost of the transaction will be $5,000 ($50/ share × 100 shares). If you margin, you will put up only $2,500 of your own money (50 percent × $5,000) and borrow the $2,500 balance. Exhibit 12.5 compares the rates of return you would receive with and without the 50 percent margin. This is done for two cases: (1) a $20 per share increase in the stock price, to $70 per share, and (2) a $20 per share decrease in the stock price, to $30 per share. It is assumed the stock will be held for one year and all broker commissions are ignored.

As indicated in Exhibit 12.5, the use of margin allows you to increase the return on your investment when stock prices increase. Indeed, one of the major attributes of margin trading is that it allows you to *magnify your returns*—that is, you can use margin to reduce your equity in an investment and thereby magnify the returns from invested capital when security prices go up. The return on your investment when the stock price increases from $50 a share to $70 a share is 40 percent without margin and 71 percent with margin. However, when the stock price declines from $50 to $30 per share, the return on your investment will be a *negative* 40 percent without margin and a whopping *89 percent loss* with margin. Clearly, the use of margin magnifies losses as well as profits! If the price of the stock in our example continues to drop, you will eventually reach the point at which your equity in the investment will be so low that the brokerage house will require you to either provide more collateral or liquidate the investment. The risks inherent in buying on margin make it imperative that you thoroughly acquaint yourself with the risk-return trade-offs involved *before* using margin in your investment program.

SHORT SALES: THE PRACTICE OF SELLING BORROWED SECURITIES

Most security transactions are *long transactions;* they are made in anticipation of increasing security prices in order to profit by buying low and selling high. A **short sale** transaction, in contrast, is made in anticipation of a decline in the price of a security. Although not as common as long transactions, the short sale is often used by the more sophisticated investor to profit during a period of declining prices. When used by individual investors, most short sales are made with common stocks. When an investor sells a security short, the broker borrows the security and then sells it on behalf of the short seller's account—short sellers actually *sell securities they don't own.* The borrowed shares must, of course, be replaced in the future. If the investor can repurchase the shares at a lower price, a profit will result. In effect, the objective of a short sale is to take advantage of a drop in price by first selling high and then buying low (which, of course, is nothing more than the old "buy low, sell high" adage in reverse).

Short selling is perfectly legitimate; there's nothing illegal or unethical about it. Indeed, because the shares sold are *borrowed securities,* numerous rules and regulations protect the party that lends the securities and govern the short-sale process. One regulation, for example, permits stocks to be sold short only when the last change in the market price of the stock has been upward. Another safeguard is the requirement that all proceeds from the short sale of the borrowed securities be held by the brokerage firm—the short seller never sees any of this money! In addition, the short seller must deposit with the broker a certain amount of money (equivalent to the prevailing initial margin requirement) when the transaction is executed—so even a short-sale transaction involves an investment of capital.

A short-sale transaction can be illustrated with a simple example (and one that ignores brokerage fees). Assume that Patrick O'Sullivan wishes to sell short 100 shares of Advanced Buggy-Whips, Inc. at $52.50 per share. After Pat has met the necessary requirements (including making a margin deposit of $52.50 × 100 × 50% = $2,625), his broker borrows the shares and sells them, obtaining proceeds of $5,250 (100 shares × $52.50/share). If the stock price goes down as Pat expects, he will be able to repurchase the shares at the lower price. Now suppose the price drops to $40 per share, and he repurchases the 100 shares. Pat will make a profit, since he will have been able to replace the shares for $4,000 (100 shares × $40/share), which is below the $5,250 received when he sold the stock. His profit will be $1,250 ($5,250 − $4,000). If, on the other hand, the stock price rose to, say, $60 per share, and Pat repurchased the stocks at that price, he would sustain a loss of $750 ($52.50 − $60.00 = −$7.50 × 100 = −$750.00). Because of the high risk involved in short sales, you should thoroughly familiarize yourself with this technique and all its pitfalls *before* attempting to short sell any security.

Concept Check

12-7. What is a *stockbroker*? Why does the selection of a broker play such an important role in the purchase of securities?

12-8. "Stockbrokers not only execute buy and sell orders for their clients, they also offer a variety of additional services." Explain what some of these services are.

12-9. Describe the role that *discount brokers* play in carrying out security transactions. To whom are their services especially appealing? Explain.

12-10. What is the *SIPC*, and how does it protect investors? Does the SIPC protect investors against loss? Explain.

12-11. What is *arbitration*? Is that the same thing as mediation? Explain.

12-12. Name and describe three basic types of orders.

12-13. What are *margin* requirements? Why might an investor buy securities on margin?

12-14. What is a *short sale*? Explain the logic behind it.

BECOMING AN INFORMED INVESTOR

LG5

Basing investment decisions on sound information lies at the very heart of most successful investment programs. What do you think it takes to become an informed investor? What kinds of information do you think you should have, and where would you look for such information? Stop to think about these questions before reading on.

Face it: some people are more knowledgeable about investing than others. As a result, they may use certain investment vehicles or tactics that are not even in the vocabulary of others. Investor know-how, in short, defines the playing field. It helps determine how well you'll meet your investment objectives. Being knowledgeable about investments is important since one of the key elements in successful investing is *knowing how to achieve decent rates of return without taking unnecessary risks.*

There's no substitute for being informed when it comes to making investment decisions. While it can't guarantee success, it can help you avoid unnecessary losses—like the ones that happen all too often when people put their money into investment vehicles they don't fully understand. Such results aren't too surprising, since these investors violate the first rule of investing, which is: *Never start an investment program, or buy an investment vehicle, unless you're thoroughly familiar with what you're getting into!* Indeed, before making any major investment decision, you should thoroughly investigate the security and its merits. Formulate some basic expectations about its future performance, and gain an understanding of the sources of risk and return. This can usually be done simply by *regularly* reading the popular financial press and occasionally referring to other basic sources of investment information.

There are four basic types of investment information that you should try to follow:

- ***Economic developments and current events.*** To help you evaluate the underlying investment environment.
- ***Alternative investment vehicles.*** To keep you abreast of market developments.
- ***Current interest rates and price quotations.*** To enable you to monitor your investments and also stay alert for developing investment opportunities.
- ***Personal investment strategies.*** To help you hone your skills and stay alert for new techniques as they develop.

In the final analysis, the payoff of an informed approach to investing is both an improved chance of gain and a reduced chance of loss. While there are many sources of investment information, you, as a beginning investor, should concentrate on the more common ones, such as annual stockholders' reports, the financial press, brokerage reports, advisory services, and investment advisors.

short sale A transaction that involves selling borrowed securities with the expectation that they can be replaced at a lower price at some future date; generally made in anticipation of a decline in the security's price.

ANNUAL STOCKHOLDERS' REPORTS

Every publicly traded corporation is required to provide its stockholders and other interested parties with **annual stockholders' reports.** These documents provide a wealth of information about companies, including balance sheets, income statements, and other summarized statements for the latest fiscal year, plus a number of prior years. (The balance sheets and income statements for business firms are similar in form to the personal financial statements examined in Chapter 2.) Annual reports usually describe the firm's business activities, recent developments, and future plans and outlook. Financial ratios describing past performance are also included, along with other relevant statistics. In fact, annual reports provide a great deal of insight into the company's past, present, and future operations. You can obtain them for free directly from the companies, through a brokerage firm, or at most large libraries.

Here are some suggestions to help you get the most information when reading an annual report:

- ***Start with the Highlights or Selected Financial Data sections.*** These provide a quick overview of performance by summarizing key information, such as the past two years' revenues, net income, assets, earnings per share (EPS), and dividends. EPS have the most effect on the stock's price, so watch them closely.
- ***Read the chief executive's letter.*** But read it with a careful eye, looking for euphemisms like "a slowing of growth" for drop in earnings.
- ***Move on to the discussion of operations in Management's Discussion and Analysis.*** This section provides information on sales, earnings, debt, inventory levels, litigation, taxes, and so on.
- ***Review the financial statements, including the notes.*** These will tell you about the company's financial condition and performance. Look for trends in sales, costs, cash position, inventory, and net working capital.
- ***Read the auditor's report.*** This statement from the independent accountants who review the numbers has two paragraphs when everything is fine; a third paragraph or terms like "except for" or "subject to" means there may be problems that you need to understand.

THE FINANCIAL PRESS

The most common source of financial news is the local newspaper. The newspapers in many larger cities often devote several pages to business and financial information and, of course, big-city papers, like the *New York Times* and the *Los Angeles Times,* provide investors with an abundance of financial information. Other, more specific sources of financial news include *The Wall Street Journal, Barron's, Investor's Business Daily,* and the "Money" section of *USA Today*. These are all national publications that include articles on the behavior of the economy, the market, various industries, and individual companies. The most comprehensive and up-to-date coverage of financial news is provided Monday through Friday by *The Wall Street Journal. Barron's* concentrates on the week's activities as they relate to the financial markets and individual security prices. Other excellent sources of investment information include magazine-type publications such as *Money, Forbes, Fortune, Business Week, U.S. News and World Report, Smart Money, Worth,* and *Financial World*.

Economic Data. Summaries and analyses of economic events can be found in all the above sources. Economic data include news items related to government actions and their effects on the economy, political and international events as they pertain to the economy, and statistics related to price levels, interest rates, the federal budget, and taxes.

Market Data. Usually presented in the form of averages, or indexes, *market data* describes the general behavior of the securities markets. The averages and indexes are based on the price movements of a select group of securities over an extended period of time. They are used to capture the overall performance of the market as a whole. You would want to follow one or more of these measures *to get a feel for how the market is doing over time* and, perhaps, an indication of what lies ahead. The absolute level of the index at a given point in time (or on a given day) is far less important than *what's been happening to that index over a given period of time*. The most frequently cited market measures are those calculated by Dow Jones, Standard & Poor's, the New York Stock Exchange, the American Stock Exchange, and Nasdaq (for the OTC market). These measures are all intended to keep track of the behavior in the stock market, particularly stocks on the NYSE (the Dow, S&P, and NYSE averages all follow stocks on the big board). In addition, there are several averages and indexes that follow the action in other markets, including the bond, commodities, and options markets and even the markets for mutual funds, real estate, and collectibles. However, because all these other averages and indexes are not followed nearly as much as those of stocks, we will concentrate here on stock market performance measures.

Dow Jones Averages. The granddaddy of them all and the most widely followed measure of stock market performance is the **Dow Jones Industrial Average (DJIA).** Actually, the Dow Jones averages, which began in 1896, are made up of four parts: (1) an industrial average based on 30 stocks; (2) a transportation average based on 20 stocks; (3) a utility average based on 15 stocks; and (4) a composite average based on all 65 industrial, transportation, and utility stocks. The makeup of the 30 stocks in the DJIA does change a bit over time as companies go private, are acquired by other firms, or become less of a force in the marketplace; for example, in the past few years, Navistar International, Primerica, and USX Corporation were dropped from the DJIA and replaced with Caterpillar, Disney, and J. P. Morgan. The stocks are all picked from the NYSE, and while they are intended to represent a cross section of companies, there is a strong bias toward blue chips, which is one of the major criticisms of the Dow Jones Industrial Average. Critics also claim that an average made up of only 30 blue-chip stocks—out of some 2,300 issues—is hardly representative of the market. However, the facts show that as a rule, the behavior of the DJIA closely reflects that of other broadly-based stock market measures. Exhibit 12.6 lists the 30 stocks in the DJIA, along with some important dates in its life.

Standard & Poor's Indexes. The **Standard & Poor's (S&P) indexes** are similar to the Dow Jones averages to the extent that they both are used to capture the overall performance of the market. However, there are some important differences in the two measures. For one thing, the S&P uses a lot more stocks: the popular S&P 500 composite index is based on 500 different stocks, whereas the DJIA uses only 30 stocks. What's more, the S&P index is made up of all large NYSE stocks, as well as some major AMEX and OTC stocks, so there's not only more issues in the S&P sample, but also a greater breadth of representation. And finally, there are some technical differences in the mathematical procedures used to compute the two measures: the Dow Jones is an *average,* while the S&P is an *index.* In spite of these technical differences, however, the two measures are used in much the same way.

There are seven basic indexes: (1) an industrial index based on 400 stocks; (2) a transportation index of 20 stocks; (3) a public utility index of 40 stocks; (4) a financial index of 40 stocks; (5) a composite index for all 500 of the stocks used in the first four indexes; (6) the *MidCap 400,* and (7) the *SmallCap 600.* The MidCap index is made up of 400 medium-sized companies—those with market values that, for the most part, range from about $200 million to $2 billion, or more, while the SmallCap index consists of small companies, with market caps of around $200 million or less.

The S&P 500, like the DJIA, is widely followed by the financial media, and is reported not only in publications like *The Wall Street Journal* and *Barron's,* but also in most of the major newspapers around the country and other market outlets. The S&P has a much lower value than the DJIA—for example, in April 1995, the Dow stood at nearly 4,200, while the S&P index of 500 stocks was around 505. Now this does not mean that the S&P consists of less valuable stocks; rather, the disparity is due solely to the different methods used to compute the measures.

The NYSE, AMEX, and OTC Indexes. The most widely followed exchange-based indexes are those of the New York Stock Exchange (NYSE) and the American Stock Exchange (AMEX), and, for the

annual stockholders' report A report made available to stockholders and other interested parties that includes a variety of financial and descriptive information about a firm's operations during the past year.

Dow Jones Industrial Average (DJIA) The most widely followed measure of stock market performance; consists of 30 blue-chip stocks listed on the NYSE.

Standard & Poor's (S&P) indexes Indexes compiled by Standard & Poor's Corporation; similar to the DJIA but employ different computational methods and consist of far more stocks.

EXHIBIT 12.6

The Dow Jones Industrial Average

The DJIA is made up of 30 of the bluest of blue-chip stocks and has been closely followed by investors for the past 100 years or so.

The 30 Stocks in the DJIA:

Allied Signal	DuPont	Minnesota M&M
Aluminum Co. of Amer.	Eastman Kodak	Morgan, J. P.
Amer Express	Exxon	Philip Morris
American T&T	General Electric	Procter & Gamble
Bethlehem Steel	General Motors	Sears Roebuck
Boeing	Goodyear	Texaco
Caterpillar	IBM	Union Carbide
Chevron	International Paper	United Technologies
Coca-Cola	McDonalds	Westinghouse Electric
Disney	Merck	Woolworth

Some Important Dates for the Dow:

May 26, 1896	The Dow Jones Industrial Average makes its debut; originally made up of just 12 stocks (of the 12 stocks that originally made up the DJIA, only GE is still on the list).
January 12, 1906	Closes above 100 for the first time.
October 28, 1929	The infamous "1929 crash"; Dow drops 38.33 points in one day.
October 29, 1929	The Dow drops another 30.57 points—in just *two* days, the market value of stocks drops an incredible 25%; these two days are considered as the start of the Great Depression.
March 12, 1956	Closes above 500 for the first time.
November 14, 1972	Closes above 1000 for the first time.
December 6, 1974	Closes at 577.60 to end the worst bear market since the 1930s.
April 27, 1981	Closes at eight-year high of 1024.0.
August 12, 1982	Closes at 776.92, as the market bottoms out and the Great Bull Market of 1982–1987 is born.
August 25, 1987	Closes at 2722.42, the peak of the 1982–1987 bull market; in five years, the DJIA has gone up almost 2,000 points (250%).
October 19, 1987	The market crashes; the DJIA closes at 1738.74, for a record one-day drop of 508 points (23%).
October 21, 1987	Closes at 2027.85, as the market goes up nearly 290 points in the two days following the crash.
December 31, 1987	Closes *the year* at 1938.83, up 2% for the year, even after the crash.
December 31, 1988	Closes at 2168.57, up 12% for the year; the first time the market has ended the year above 2000.
April 27, 1989	Market moves to a post-crash high of 2433.10, which totally wipes out the loss of October 19, with about 200 points to spare.
July 16, 1990	Closes just short of 3,000, at 2,999.75; two weeks later, Iraq invades Kuwait and the market goes into a free-fall, tumbling to 2,365.10 by October 11.
April 17, 1991	Closes above 3,000 for the first time.
May 19, 1993	Closes above 3,500 for first time.
February 23, 1995	Closes above 4,000 for the first time.
June 16, 1995	Closes above 4,500 for the first time.

OTC market, the Nasdaq indexes. The **NYSE index** includes all the stocks listed on the "big board." In addition to the composite index, the NYSE publishes indexes for industrials, utilities, transportation, and finance subgroups.

The **AMEX index** reflects share prices on the American Stock Exchange. Made up of all stocks on the AMEX, it is set up in such a way that it directly captures the actual *percentage change* in share prices. For example, if the price change in AMEX stocks from one day to the next were +3 percent, the AMEX index would likewise increase by 3 percent over the previous day's value. Like the NYSE indexes, the AMEX index is often cited in the financial news.

Activity in the OTC market is captured by the **Nasdaq indexes,** which are calculated like the S&P and NYSE indexes. The most comprehensive of the Nasdaq indexes is the *OTC composite index,* which is calculated using more than 4,700 stocks traded on the Nasdaq system. The other five Nasdaq indexes are the industrial, insurance, bank, National Market composite, and National Market industrial. Although their degrees of responsiveness may vary, these indexes do tend to move in the same general direction over time. Because the *Nasdaq OTC composite index* is highly reflective of the price behavior of the smaller, more speculative stocks, it tends to be closely followed by investors and speculators interested in that market segment.

In addition to the major indexes described above, another measure of market performance is the **Wilshire 5000 Index.** Published by Wilshire Associates, Inc., the Wilshire 5000 is reported daily in *The Wall Street Journal* and in several other major publications. What makes this measure noteworthy is that unlike other major market indexes, the Wilshire 5000 is reflective of the *total market value* of the 5,000 most actively traded stocks. It's estimated that the 5,000 stocks included in this index account for about 98 or 99 percent of the total market value of all publicly traded stocks in this country. Thus, if you want an idea of the size of the U.S. stock market, just look at where the Wilshire 5000 stands; in April 1995, it stood at 4,962. Since this index is in billions of dollars, a measure of 4,962 translates into a total market value of some $4,962 billion—or, almost $5 trillion.

Industry Data. Local newspapers, *The Wall Street Journal, Barron's,* and various financial publications regularly contain articles and data about different industries. For example, Standard & Poor's *Industry Surveys* provides detailed descriptions and statistics for all the major industries; on a smaller scale, *Business Week* and other magazines regularly include indexes of industry performance and price levels. Other industry-related data can be obtained from industry trade associations, one example of which is the American Petroleum Institute.

Company Data. Articles about the performance and new developments of companies are included in local newspapers, *The Wall Street Journal, Barron's,* and most investment magazines. The prices of the securities of all listed companies and the most active over-the-counter stocks are quoted daily in *The Wall Street Journal, Investor's Business Daily,* and *USA Today,* and weekly in *Barron's.* Many daily newspapers also contain stock price quotations, though in the smaller ones the listing may be selective; in some cases, only stocks of local interest might be included.

Stock Quotes. To see how price quotations work and what they mean, consider the quotes that appear daily (M–F) in *The Wall Street Journal.* As we'll see, the quotations provide not only current prices, but a great deal of additional information as well. A portion of the NYSE stock quotations from *The Wall Street Journal* is presented in Exhibit 12.7. Let's use the Disney quotations for purposes of illustration. These quotes were published on Tuesday, April 4, 1995, and are for the trades that occurred on Monday, April 3. A glance at the quotations shows that stock prices are quoted in eighths of a dollar, with the fractions reduced to their lowest common denominator ($^2/_8$, $^4/_8$, and $^6/_8$ are expressed as $^1/_4$, $^1/_2$, and $^3/_4$, respectively). The first two columns, labeled "Hi" and "Lo," contain the highest and lowest price at which the stock sold during the preceding 52 weeks; Disney, for example, traded between 37$^3/_4$ and 56 $^1/_4$ during the 52-week period ending April 3, 1995. Listed to the right of the company's name is its *stock symbol* (Disney goes by the three-letter initial "DIS"); these stock symbols are the abbreviations used on the *market tapes* seen in brokerage offices and on CNBC/FNN television to identify specific companies. The figure listed right after the stock symbol is the cash dividend expected to be paid on each share during the year; this is followed by the dividend yield. (Note: Since Disney is expected to pay a cash dividend of $.36 a share, its dividend yield is 0.7 percent, which is found by dividing $.36 in dividends by the closing price of $54.63.) The next entry is the P/E ratio, which is the current market price divided by the per share earnings for the most recent 12-month period. Since it is believed to reflect investor expectations concerning the firm's future prospects, the P/E ratio is closely followed by investors as part of the stock-valuation process. Disney's P/E ratio was 24—which means the stock is trading at 24 times its earnings.

The daily volume follows the P/E ratio. Here, the sales numbers are listed in round lots (of 100 shares); thus the figure 15238 for Disney indicates that there were 1,523,800 shares of Disney stock traded on April 3. The next entries, in the "Hi," "Lo,"

NYSE index An index of the performance of all stocks listed on the New York Stock Exchange.

AMEX index An index of the performance of all stocks listed on the American Stock Exchange.

Nasdaq index An index, supplied by the National Association of Securities Dealers Automated Quotation, that tracks the performance of stocks traded in the OTC market.

Wilshire 5000 index An index of the total market value of the 5,000 most actively traded stocks in this country.

EXHIBIT 12.7

Listed Stock Quotes

This list summarizes one day's trading activity and price quotes for a group of stocks traded on the New York Stock Exchange. Common and preferred stocks are listed together and, except for a few minor differences, basically follow the same price quotation system.

		52 Weeks					Yld		Vol				Net	
		Hi	Lo	Stock	Sym	Div	%	PE	100s	Hi	Lo	Close	Chg	
		36 1/4	24	DillardStrs	DDS	.12	.4	12	7144	28 1/8	27 3/8	27 1/2	− 1/8	
		10 3/4	7 3/8	DimeBcp	DME		...	6	869	8 7/8	8 3/4	8 7/8	...	
	FO			DiMon wi			...	...	370	14 7/8	14	14 7/8	...	
		17 1/8	2 1/4	CG Dina	DIN	.28e	8.6	...	1854	3 3/8	3 1/8	3 1/4	− 1/4	
	n	13 1/8	1 3/8	CG Dina L	DINL	.28e	12.4	...	342	2 1/4	2	2 1/4	...	
		26 1/4	13 7/8	DiscountAuto	DAP		...	18	279	25	23 7/8	24 7/8	+ 7/8	
Disney common →		56 1/4	37 3/4	Disney	DIS	.36	.7	24	15238	54 7/8	53 3/4	54 5/8	+1 1/8	← Common stock quote
		31 7/8	22 1/2	DoleFood	DOL	.40	1.4	25	1227	29 3/8	28 5/8	29	...	
	s	28 1/2	16 3/16	♣ DirGen	DG	.20	.7	25	1002	27	26 3/8	27	+ 3/4	
	n	20 1/8	16 7/8	DominRes ubi	DOM	1.60e	8.5	...	299	19	18 3/4	18 3/4	− 1/8	
		42 1/2	34 7/8	DominRes	D	2.58	7.1	13	1482	36 1/4	35 7/8	36 1/8	+ 1/8	
		8 5/8	4 3/4	♣ Domtar g	DTC		...	...	373	8 1/4	8 1/8	8 1/4	− 1/8	
	s	26 1/4	20	♣ Donaldson	DCI	.28	1.1	19	78	25 1/8	24 3/4	25 1/8	+ 1/8	
		35 7/8	26 7/8	Donelley	DNY	.64	1.8	20	1844	35	34 3/8	35	+ 5/8	
		65 3/4	49 3/4	Dover	DOV	1.04	1.6	19	864	65 5/8	64 3/4	65 1/2	+ 3/4	
		79 1/4	58 5/8	DowChem	DOW	2.60	3.6	22	7593	73 1/4	72 3/8	72 1/2	− 3/4	
		40 3/8	28 1/8	♣ DowJones	DJ	.92f	2.5	20	544	37 7/8	37 1/2	37 1/2	− 3/8	
		21 5/8	14	DowneyFnl	DSL	.48	3.0	11	6	16	15 7/8	16	...	
		33 1/8	20 1/2	DrPepper	DPS		...	29	18	32 1/2	32 1/2	32 1/2	...	
		12 5/8	9 1/2	Dravo	DRV		...	dd	348	10 1/2	10 3/8	10 1/2	...	
		23 7/8	18 1/2	♣ DresserInd	DI	.68	3.2	19	2461	21 1/2	21 1/8	21 1/4	...	
		10 1/4	8 1/4	DreyfStrGvFd	DSI	.81	8.9	...	124	9 1/4	9	9 1/8	...	
		9 5/8	7 1/2	DreyfStrMunBd	DSM	.66	7.0	...	293	9 3/8	9 1/4	9 3/8	+ 1/8	
		10 5/8	8 1/4	DreyfusMuni	LEO	.73	7.3	...	684	10 1/4	10	10 1/16	− 1/8	
		62 3/8	50 3/4	DuPont	DD	1.88	3.1	15	16857	62 3/8	61	61	+ 1/2	
Dupont preferred →		72 1/2	56 3/4	DuPont pfB		4.50	7.2	...	15	62 5/8	62	62 1/4	− 1/4	← Preferred stock quote
	s	15 3/8	7 7/8	DuffPhelpsCp	DUF	.16	1.4	8	155	11 1/4	11 1/8	11 1/4	...	
		9 1/8	7 7/8	DuffphelpsUtil	DNP	.72	8.7	...	1611	8 1/4	8 1/8	8 1/4	+ 1/8	
		15 1/8	11 3/4	DuffPhelpsTF	DTF	.96	6.9	...	90	14	13 7/8	14	+ 1/8	
		13 1/2	10 1/4	DuffPhelpsBondTr	DUC	1.18a	9.3	...	242	12 3/4	12 5/8	12 3/4	...	
	n	12 3/4	7 5/8	DufPhipCr	DCR	.06e	.5	...	36	12 5/8	12 1/2	12 1/2	− 1/4	
		42 1/8	32 7/8	DukePwr	DUK	1.96	5.1	13	1571	38 3/4	38 1/4	38 1/2	+ 1/4	
		23 1/4	19 1/4	DukePwr pfA		1.59	7.2	...	16	22 1/4	22	22	− 1/4	
		28 3/8	23 1/8	DukePwr pfS		1.93	7.4	...	50	26 1/4	25 3/4	26 1/4	+ 3/8	
		28 1/4	23 1/4	♣ DukeRityInv	DRE	1.88	7.1	17	183	26 1/2	26 1/4	26 1/2	...	
		60 3/4	48 1/2	DunBradst	DNB	2.60	4.9	14	1597	52 7/8	52 1/2	52 3/4	+ 1/8	

Source: *The Wall Street Journal,* April 4, 1995, p. C4.

and "Close" columns, contain the highest, lowest, and last (closing) price, respectively, at which the stock sold on the day in question. Disney closed up $1\frac{1}{8}$ on April 3, which means that it had closed at $53\frac{3}{4}$ the day before.

The same quotation system is used for AMEX and Nasdaq *National Market* stocks. However, a slightly different procedure is used with OTC securities that are not part of the National Market System—that is, for many OTC stocks, only the dividend, volume, last price, and change in price are included in the quotes.

Preferred stocks are also listed with the common stock quotes. To find a preferred stock, just look for the letters "pf" or "pr" right after the company's name, as shown for the Dupont preferred in Exhibit 12.7. While a company may have any number of preferred issues outstanding, a quote will appear in the paper only if the stock actually traded on the day in question. Thus, whereas Dupont has two preferred issues outstanding, only one of them, *the \$4.50 preferreds,* traded on April 3. This particular preferred stock pays \$4.50 a year in dividends and based on the closing price for the day ($62^1/_4$), it is currently yielding 7.2 percent. Normally, it's the *annual dividend* that separates one preferred stock from another—for example, look at the two Duke Power issues: their annual dividends range from \$1.59 a share to \$1.93 a share. As for the rest of the quotation, you'll notice that preferred quotes are about the same as common stock quotes, except that the P/E ratios are left blank because they are irrelevant in the case of preferred stocks.

Bond Quotes. Exhibit 12.8 contains examples of both corporate and Treasury bond quotes; these quotes were also for trades that occurred on April 3, 1995. To understand the system used with NYSE listed corporate bonds, look at the first AT&T (ATT) issue. The row of numbers immediately following the company name gives the coupon and the year in which the bond matures; the "$7^1/_2$06" means that this particular bond carries a $7^1/_2$ percent annual coupon and will mature sometime in the year 2006. Such information is important, since it lets investors differentiate among the various bonds issued by the same corporation; notice that there were 12 different AT&T bonds listed on the day of this quote. The next column, labeled "Cur Yld," provides the *current yield* being offered by the issue at its *current market price.* Current yield is found by dividing the bond's annual coupon (here, 7.50%, or \$75.00) by the issue's closing price ($99^1/_8$, or \$991.25), which in this case amounts to 7.6 percent. The "Vol" column represents the actual number of bonds traded; there were 64 AT&T bonds traded on this day. Price information is contained in the last two columns. Unlike stocks, instead of high, low, and closing prices, bond quotes usually show just the closing price, along with the net change in the closing price from the day before. *All bonds are quoted as a percent of par,* meaning that a quote of, say, 85 translates into a price of 85 percent of the bond's par value. Since corporate bonds typically have par values of \$1,000, a bond quote of 85 means that the price is really \$850 (85% × \$1,000). Corporate bonds are also traded in fractions of $^1/_8$, but each fraction is worth 1.25 *dollars.* Thus, AT&T's closing price for the day was \$991.25, found by multiplying the quoted price by \$1,000, that is, $99^1/_8$ = 99.125% × \$1000 = \$991.25.

Convertibles are also listed along with other corporate bonds. They are easy to find—just look for the letters "cv" in the current yield column, such as in the case of the Alaska Air (AlskAr) $6^7/_8$ of 14 convertible in Exhibit 12.8. Except for the "cv" in the current yield column, all other aspects of the quote are exactly like that for any other listed bond. Also listed in Exhibit 12.8 are some zero coupon bonds issued by Allied Chemical Corporation (AlldC). Such bonds have the letters "zr" in place of their coupons; for example, with the Allied bonds, the "zr09" means the issue is a zero coupon bond that matures in 2009. Note that on April 3, this particular zero coupon bond traded at $32^1/_2$—in dollars, that means the bond was trading at \$325.00. That's what investors were paying in 1995, and, in return, they will receive about three times that amount (\$1,000) sometime in the year 2009.

U.S. Treasury (and agency) bond quotes are listed in thirty-seconds of a point. With government bonds, the figures to the right of the colon (:) show the number of thirty-seconds in the fractional bid or ask price. For example, look at the bid price of the $15^3/_4$ percent U.S. Treasury issue. It's quoted at 145:09 (bid), which translates to 145 $^9/_{32}$, or 145.28 of par. Thus, if you want to buy \$15,000 of this issue, you will pay \$21,792 (that is, \$15,000 × 1.4528). With \$15,000 to invest, you can only buy 10 bonds; with each bond trading at \$1,452.80, the number of bonds you can buy is \$15,000 ÷ \$1,452.80 = 10.32 bonds. Government bond listings include not only the coupon (see the "rate" column of the Treasury quotes in Exhibit 12.8) but also the year and *month* of maturity. When there is more than one date in the maturity column (see the $8^1/_4$ Treasury bond, with a maturity of 00–05), the second figure is the maturity date and the first indicates when the bond becomes freely callable. This bond matures in May 2005 and carries a call deferment provision through May 2000. If there is only one date, the bond is *non-callable.*

Treasuries are quoted in bid/ask terms; *bid* means what bond dealers are willing to pay (and how much you can sell them for) and *ask* is what they will sell the bonds for (or what it will cost you to buy). The "Yld" column is *not* the issue's current yield but the bond's *promised yield-to-maturity.*

BROKERAGE REPORTS

The reports produced by the research staffs of the major (full-service) brokerage firms provide still another important source of investor information. These reports cover a wide variety of topics, from economic and market analyses to industry and

EXHIBIT 12.8

Corporate and Treasury Bond Price Quotes

Both corporate and U.S. Treasury bonds are quoted as a percent of their par value. However, corporate bonds are quoted in eighths of a point, while Treasuries are quoted in 32's. Par for these bonds is normally $1,000, so each point in a bond quote is worth $10 (and each ⅛ of a point, $1.25). Thus, a quote of 89¼ is *not* $89.25, but $892.50 ($1,000 × .8925); likewise, a quote of 115 translates to $1,150 ($1,000 × 1.15).

CORPORATE BONDS

	Bonds	Cur Yld	Vol	Close	Net Chg.	
	AMR 9s16	9.0	78	99½	+ ¾	
	AMR 8.10s98	8.0	15	100⅝	− ⅛	
AT&T →	ATT 7½06	7.6	64	99⅛	− ⅛	← Corporate bond quote
	ATT 7¾07	7.7	105	100¾	+ ½	
	ATT 4¾98	5.1	23	93½	− ¼	
	ATT 4⅜96	4.5	25	96¾	...	
	ATT 4⅜99	4.9	17	90	+ ½	
	ATT 6s00	6.3	30	94¾	+ ⅝	
	ATT 5⅛01	5.8	40	88¼	− ¾	
	ATT 7⅛02	7.2	137	98⅜	+ ¼	
	ATT 8⅛22	8.1	222	99¾	...	
	ATT 8⅛24	8.2	15	99⅜	+ ¼	
	ATT 4½96	4.6	124	98¼	+ 7/32	
	ATT 6¾04	7.1	70	95	+ ⅜	
	Actava 9½98	10.1	35	94	− ¼	
	Actava 10s99	10.3	9	97	− ¼	
	Advst 9s08	cv	10	91½	+ ⅜	
Alaska Air →	AlskAr 6⅞14	cv	33	78¼	+ ¼	← Convertible bond quote
	AlskAr zr06		1	44½	...	
	AlbnyInt 5¼02	cv	16	87½	...	
	AlldC zr98	...	5	78½	+ ½	
Allied Chemical →	AlldC zr09	...	15	32½	− ⅜	← Zero coupon bond quote
	AExC 6⅛00	6.5	1	95⅜	− ⅞	
	Anhr 8⅝16	8.3	15	103½	+ ⅞	
	AnnTaylr 8¾00	8.8	23	98⅞	− ¼	
	Arml 11⅜99	11.3	100	100⅞	+ ⅞	
	Arrow 5¾02	cv	31	129½	− 1	
	Ashlnd 6¾14	cv	70	95	− 1	
	ARch 10⅞05	8.8	10	123½	+ 1⅞	
	AutDt zr12	...	34	43⅜	− ⅛	
	Avnet 6s12	cv	30	104¾	+ 1¼	
	BPAmer 7⅞02	7.7	6	101¾	+ ¾	
	Bally 10s06f	cv	10	84½	+ ½	
	BkNY 71½01	cv	10	166	+ 1¼	
	BellPa 7⅛12	7.8	15	91⅜	+ ⅜	
	BellPa 7½13	7.9	15	95	+ ½	
	BellsoT 8¼32	8.3	150	99⅝	+ ⅛	
	BellsoT 7⅞32	8.2	105	95⅞	+ 1¼	
	BellsoT 7s05	7.3	60	96½	+ ½	
	BellsoT 6¼03	6.8	5	92½	+ ½	
	BellsoT 6¾33	8.1	3	83¾	...	
	BergBru 6⅞11	7.8	5	87¾	+ 2¾	
	BstBy 9s97	9.0	6	100⅜	− ⅛	
	BstBuy 8⅝00	9.1	121	95¼	+ ¼	
	BethSt 8.45s05	9.0	25	93⅞	− ⅜	
	BethSt 8⅜01	8.8	5	95¼	− 1½	
	Bevrly 7⅝03	cv	40	96½	...	
	Boeing 8⅛96	8.3	2	101½	+ ½	
	BoisC 7s16	cv	112	97	− ¾	

TREASURY BONDS

Rate	Maturity Mo/Yr	Bid	Asked	Chg.	Ask Yld.	
11¾	Feb01	122:15	122:19	+ 7	6.99	
8	May01n	104:19	104:21	+ 12	7.05	
13⅛	May01	129:20	129:24	+ 7	7.05	
7⅞	Aug01n	104:00	104:02	+ 10	7.07	
8	Aug96-01	101:12	101:16	+ 2	6.83	
13⅜	Aug01	131:28	132:00	+ 16	7.05	
7½	Nov01n	102:02	102:04	+ 10	7.09	
15¾	Nov01	145:09	145:13	+ 20	7.04	← Treasury bond quote
14¼	Feb02	138:18	138:22	+ 14	7.05	
7½	May02n	102:09	102:11	+ 12	7.07	
6⅜	Aug02n	95:23	95:25	+ 13	7.12	
11⅝	Nov02	126:03	126:07	+ 19	7.11	
6¼	Feb03n	94:17	94:19	+ 12	7.16	
10¾	Feb03	121:08	121:12	+ 23	7.15	
10¾	May03	121:12	121:25	+ 16	7.16	
5¾	Aug03n	91:05	91:07	+ 13	7.16	
11⅛	Aug03	124:12	124:16	+ 15	7.18	
11⅞	Nov03	129:19	129:23	+ 14	7.19	
5⅞	Feb04n	91:17	91:19	+ 12	7.17	
7¼	May04n	100:17	100:19	+ 16	7.16	
12⅜	May04	134:03	134:07	+ 11	7.19	
7¼	Aug04n	100:16	100:18	+ 15	7.17	
13¾	Aug04	144:01	144:05	+ 13	7.19	
7⅞	Nov04n	104:26	104:28	+ 15	7.16	
11⅝	Nov04	130:04	130:08	+ 17	7.21	
7½	Feb05n	102:17	102:19	+ 14	7.13	
8¼	May00-05	103:29	104:01	+ 13	7.29	← Callable Treasury bond quote
12	May05	133:21	133:25	+ 22	7.23	
10¾	Aug05	125:05	125:09	+ 21	7.24	
9⅜	Feb06	116:00	116:04	+ 22	7.21	
7⅝	Feb02-07	101:02	101:06	+ 18	7.40	
7⅞	Nov02-07	103:10	103:14	+ 21	7.28	
8⅜	Aug03-08	106:09	106:13	+ 13	7.34	

Source: *The Wall Street Journal,* April 4, 1995, p. C16.

company reports, news of special situations, and reports on interest rates and the bond market. Reports on certain industries or securities prepared by the house's backoffice research staff may be issued on a scheduled basis and often contain lists of securities within certain industries classified as to the type of investment return they provide and the type of market behavior they are expected to exhibit. Also, brokerage houses often will issue lists of securities classified as either "buy" or "sell" depending on the research staff's analysis of their anticipated market behavior. Occasionally brokerage houses issue extensive analyses of specific securities, along with recommendations as to the type of investment returns expected and whether to buy or sell.

ADVISORY SERVICES

A number of subscription advisory services provide information and recommendations on various industries and specific securities. The services normally cost from $50 to several hundred dollars a year. Although these costs may be tax deductible, only the most active investors will find them worthwhile, since you can usually review such materials at your broker's office or university and public libraries. Probably the best known financial services are those provided by Standard & Poor's Corporation, Moody's Investors Service, and Value Line Investment Survey. Each offers an array of subscription services. Both Standard & Poor's and Moody's publish manuals containing historical facts and financial data on thousands of corporations, broken down into industry groups. Standard & Poor's publishes a monthly stock guide and bond guide, each of which summarizes the financial conditions of a few thousand issues; Moody's also publishes stock and bond guides. And a number of reports are also prepared on a weekly basis, like Standard & Poor's *Outlook*.

Separate reports on specific companies are another valuable type of subscription service. An example of one such stock report is given in Exhibit 12.9. This report, prepared by Standard & Poor's, presents a concise summary of a company's financial history, current finances, and future prospects; a similar type of report, with even more emphasis given to the security's investment merits and future prospects, is also available from *Value Line*. Recommended lists of securities, broken down into groups on the basis of investment objectives, constitute still another type of service. In addition to these popular subscription services, numerous *investment letters,* which periodically advise subscribers on the purchase and sale of securities, are available. Finally, by subscribing to weekly chart books, investors may also obtain graphs showing stock prices and volume over extended periods of time.

INVESTMENT ADVISORS

Successful investors often establish themselves as professional investment advisors. In this capacity, they attempt to develop investment plans consistent with the financial objectives of their clients. They may operate their own business, or be associated with large firms that employ research staffs and often publish various subscription materials. Many of the better-known investment advisors limit their practice to a select group of wealthy individuals who have similar investment objectives, while others accept clients with diverse goals. Professional advisors generally do not accept clients with investment assets of less than $50,000, and the more "elite" ones are likely to require considerably larger holdings. Annual fees for advisory services, which may involve the complete management of the client's money, are likely to range from about 1 percent to as much as 2 or 3 percent of assets under management.

There are several different ways you can obtain the services of a professional money manager: (1) you can hire an *independent investment advisor* (but they're usually pretty expensive and prefer to deal with well-heeled clients); (2) you can go to the *trust department of a major bank* (many offer their investment services to the general public at very reasonable costs, and you don't have to die or have a trust account to obtain such services—instead, all you have to do is enter into a simple *agency agreement*); (3) if you deal with a full-service brokerage firm, you can check with your broker to see if they offer fee-based *wrap accounts* (in these portfolio management accounts, your brokerage firm takes over the full-time management of your investments, in return for a flat annual fee—but watch out, that annual fee can get pretty hefty); or (4) you might consider the services of a *financial planner* (preferably a *fee-based* planner who has a strong track record in the field of *investments*). If you're thinking of using a professional money manager, the best thing to do is shop around—look at the kind of returns they've been able to generate (in good markets and bad), and don't overlook the

EXHIBIT 12.9

An S&P Stock Report

An S&P report like this one provides a wealth of information about the operating results and financial condition of the company and is an invaluable source of information to investors.

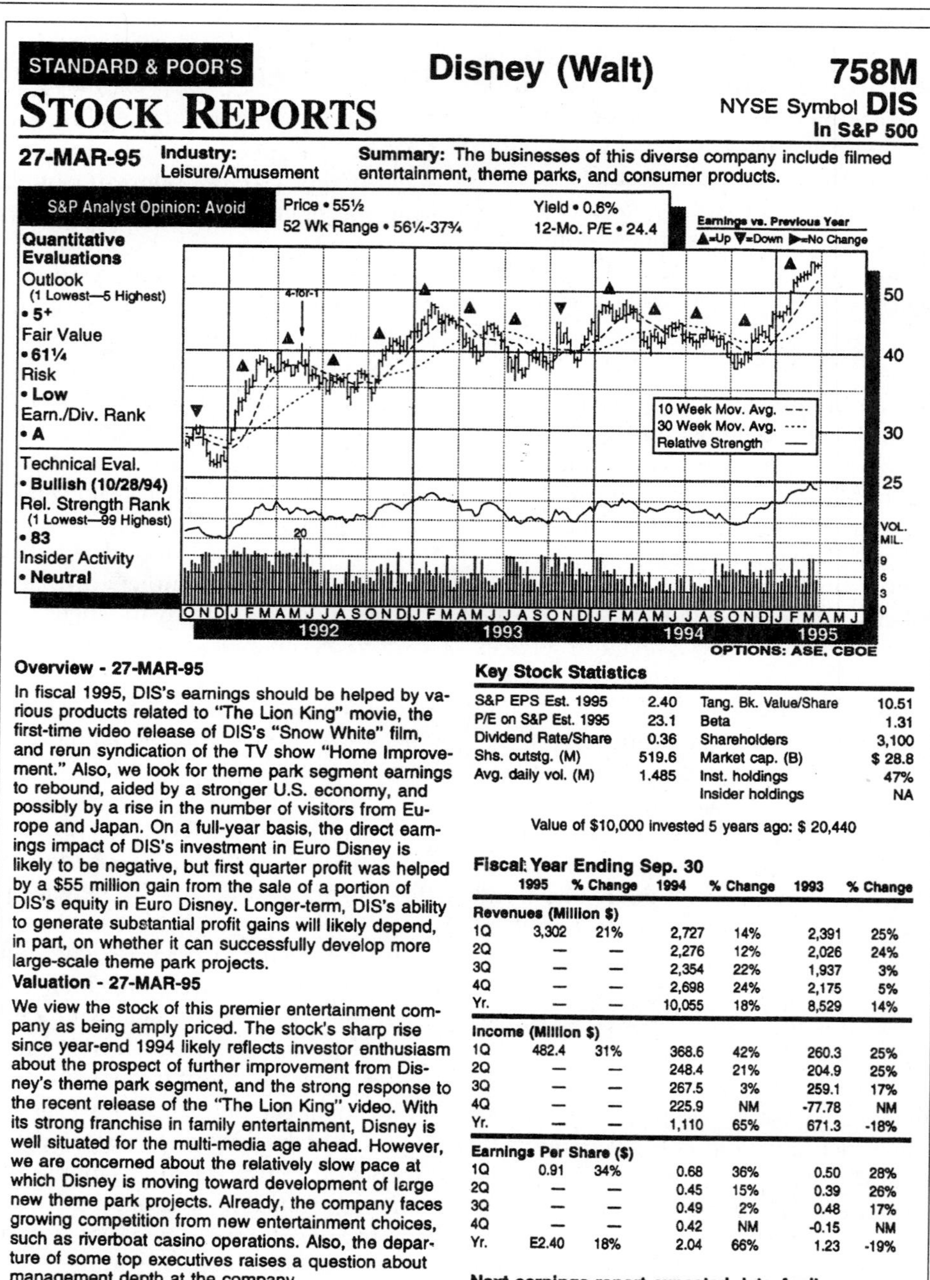

STANDARD & POOR'S

STOCK REPORTS

Disney (Walt)

758M

NYSE Symbol **DIS**

In S&P 500

27-MAR-95 **Industry:** Leisure/Amusement

Summary: The businesses of this diverse company include filmed entertainment, theme parks, and consumer products.

S&P Analyst Opinion: Avoid

Price • 55½ | 52 Wk Range • 56¼-37¾ | Yield • 0.6% | 12-Mo. P/E • 24.4

Quantitative Evaluations

Outlook (1 Lowest—5 Highest) • **5+**

Fair Value • **61¼**

Risk • **Low**

Earn./Div. Rank • **A**

Technical Eval. • **Bullish (10/28/94)**

Rel. Strength Rank (1 Lowest—99 Highest) • **83**

Insider Activity • **Neutral**

Overview - 27-MAR-95

In fiscal 1995, DIS's earnings should be helped by various products related to "The Lion King" movie, the first-time video release of DIS's "Snow White" film, and rerun syndication of the TV show "Home Improvement." Also, we look for theme park segment earnings to rebound, aided by a stronger U.S. economy, and possibly by a rise in the number of visitors from Europe and Japan. On a full-year basis, the direct earnings impact of DIS's investment in Euro Disney is likely to be negative, but first quarter profit was helped by a $55 million gain from the sale of a portion of DIS's equity in Euro Disney. Longer-term, DIS's ability to generate substantial profit gains will likely depend, in part, on whether it can successfully develop more large-scale theme park projects.

Valuation - 27-MAR-95

We view the stock of this premier entertainment company as being amply priced. The stock's sharp rise since year-end 1994 likely reflects investor enthusiasm about the prospect of further improvement from Disney's theme park segment, and the strong response to the recent release of the "The Lion King" video. With its strong franchise in family entertainment, Disney is well situated for the multi-media age ahead. However, we are concerned about the relatively slow pace at which Disney is moving toward development of large new theme park projects. Already, the company faces growing competition from new entertainment choices, such as riverboat casino operations. Also, the departure of some top executives raises a question about management depth at the company.

Key Stock Statistics

S&P EPS Est. 1995	2.40	Tang. Bk. Value/Share	10.51
P/E on S&P Est. 1995	23.1	Beta	1.31
Dividend Rate/Share	0.36	Shareholders	3,100
Shs. outstg. (M)	519.6	Market cap. (B)	$ 28.8
Avg. daily vol. (M)	1.485	Inst. holdings	47%
		Insider holdings	NA

Value of $10,000 invested 5 years ago: $ 20,440

Fiscal Year Ending Sep. 30

	1995	% Change	1994	% Change	1993	% Change
Revenues (Million $)						
1Q	3,302	21%	2,727	14%	2,391	25%
2Q	—	—	2,276	12%	2,026	24%
3Q	—	—	2,354	22%	1,937	3%
4Q	—	—	2,698	24%	2,175	5%
Yr.	—	—	10,055	18%	8,529	14%
Income (Million $)						
1Q	482.4	31%	368.6	42%	260.3	25%
2Q	—	—	248.4	21%	204.9	25%
3Q	—	—	267.5	3%	259.1	17%
4Q	—	—	225.9	NM	-77.78	NM
Yr.	—	—	1,110	65%	671.3	-18%
Earnings Per Share ($)						
1Q	0.91	34%	0.68	36%	0.50	28%
2Q	—	—	0.45	15%	0.39	26%
3Q	—	—	0.49	2%	0.48	17%
4Q	—	—	0.42	NM	-0.15	NM
Yr.	E2.40	18%	2.04	66%	1.23	-19%

Next earnings report expected: late April

Standard NYSE Stock Reports **March 31, 1995** Vol. 62/No. 63/Sec. 9

EXHIBIT 12.9

Continued

STANDARD & POOR'S
STOCK REPORTS

Disney (Walt)

758M
27-MAR-95

Business Summary - 27-MAR-95

Walt Disney Co. (formerly Walt Disney Productions) is engaged in the ownership and operation of theme parks and related businesses, and is a major supplier of filmed entertainment. Business segment contributions in fiscal 1994 (excluding an adverse impact from the Euro Disney project, of which DIS now owns approximately 39%) were:

	Revs.	Profits
Theme parks/resorts	34%	35%
Filmed entertainment	48%	44%
Consumer products	18%	22%

Theme parks/resorts include Disneyland in Anaheim, Calif., and the Orlando, Fla.-based Walt Disney World Complex, which contains the Magic Kingdom and resort hotels, Walt Disney Village, Epcot (Environmental Prototype Community of Tomorrow) Center and the Disney-MGM Studio Theme Park (opened to the public in May 1989). In April 1992, the Euro Disney theme park complex (originally 49% owned) opened near Paris, France. Euro Disney has been losing money, and a financial restructuring plan was implemented in 1994. Tokyo Disneyland, which has been open since April 1983, is owned and operated by Oriental Land Co., Ltd., pursuant to a licensing agreement with the company. DIS also earns royalties on certain revenues generated by the Tokyo park.

Filmed entertainment consists of the production and distribution of motion pictures for the theatrical, television, cable and home video markets. Movie financing has come, in part, from limited partnerships. The company also creates TV programming, owns a pay cable TV service called The Disney Channel, and owns a Los Angeles television station. Consumer products include licensing of products, a growing chain of retail stores, and publishing activity.

Important Developments

Mar. '95—DIS said that more than 20 million copies of The Lion King video have been purchased by consumers since its release in late February. Separately, development of a $3 billion Westcot project near Disneyland in California appears unlikely. However, DIS-related theme park expansion may soon be announced in Japan, where Oriental Land Co. owns and operates Tokyo Disneyland pursuant to a licensing agreement. Meanwhile, in fiscal 1995's first quarter, DIS's three business segments (excluding the direct impact of DIS's investment in Euro Disney) each had a profit increase of at least 20%, when compared to the year-ago level. Also, at December 31, 1994, DIS had cash and investments (excluding Euro Disney) totaling $2 billion. A portion of this may go toward additional repurchases of DIS common stock.

Capitalization

Total Debt: $3,665,400,000 (12/94).

Per Share Data ($) (Year Ended Sep. 30)

	1994	1993	1992	1991	1990	1989
Tangible Bk. Val.	9.92	8.68	8.24	6.80	5.96	4.95
Cash Flow	4.99	3.12	2.94	2.69	2.48	2.12
Earnings	2.04	1.23	1.52	1.20	1.50	1.28
Dividends	0.28	0.23	0.19	0.16	0.13	0.11
Payout Ratio	13%	19%	13%	13%	8%	8%
Prices - High	48⅝	48¾	45¼	32½	34⅛	34⅛
- Low	37¾	36	28½	23⅜	21½	16¼
P/E Ratio - High	24	40	39	27	23	27
- Low	19	29	19	20	14	13

Income Statement Analysis (Million $)

	1994	%Chg	1993	%Chg	1992	%Chg	1991
Revs.	10,055	18%	8,529	14%	7,504	21%	6,182
Oper. Inc.	3,412	32%	2,589	26%	2,047	14%	1,799
Depr.	1,608	56%	1,028	35%	760	-4%	795
Int. Exp.	172	-7%	184	21%	152	7%	142
Pretax Inc.	1,703	59%	1,074	-18%	1,302	28%	1,019
Eff. Tax Rate	35%	—	38%	—	37%	—	38%
Net Inc.	1,110	65%	671	-18%	817	28%	637

Balance Sheet & Other Fin. Data (Million $)

	1994	1993	1992	1991	1990	1989
Cash	187	363	765	886	820	381
Curr. Assets	NA	NA	NA	NA	NA	NA
Total Assets	12,826	11,751	10,862	9,429	8,022	6,657
Curr. Liab.	NA	NA	NA	NA	NA	NA
LT Debt	2,107	1,131	1,608	1,818	1,330	375
Common Eqty.	5,508	5,030	4,705	3,871	3,489	3,044
Total Cap.	8,554	6,834	7,201	6,443	5,822	4,482
Cap. Exp.	1,026	814	599	954	727	785
Cash Flow	2,719	1,700	1,576	1,431	1,362	1,167

Ratio Analysis

	1994	1993	1992	1991	1990	1989
Curr. Ratio	NA	NA	NA	NA	NA	NA
% LT Debt of Cap.	24.6	16.5	22.3	28.2	27.2	19.2
% Ret. on Assets	9.1	5.9	8.0	7.3	11.4	11.9
% Ret. on Equity	21.3	13.7	19.0	17.4	25.5	25.9

Dividend Data (Dividends have been paid since 1957.)

Amt. of Div. $	Date Decl.	Ex-Div. Date	Stock of Record	Payment Date
0.075	Jun. 28	Jul. 05	Jul. 11	Aug. 19 '94
0.075	Sep. 26	Oct. 07	Oct. 14	Nov. 18 '94
0.075	Nov. 21	Jan. 03	Jan. 09	Feb. 17 '95
0.090	Jan. 23	Apr. 07	Apr. 14	May. 19 '95

Data as orig. reptd.; bef. results of disc. opers. and/or spec. items. Per share data adj. for stk. divs. as of ex-div. date. E-Estimated. NA-Not Available. NM-Not Meaningful. NR-Not Ranked. Fiscal 1993 includes sizable restructu

Office—500 South Buena Vista St., Burbank, CA 91521. **Tel**—(818) 560-1000. **Chrmn, Pres & CEO**—M. D. Eisner. **EVP & CFO**—R. D. Nanula. **VP & Treas**—M. J. Montgomery. **Investor Contact**—W. M. Webb. **Dirs**—R. F. Bowers, R. E. Disney, M. D. Eisner, S. P. Gold, I. E. Lozano, Jr., R. A. Nunis, I. E. Russell, R. A. M. Stern, E. C. Walker, R. L. Watson, G. L. Wilson. **Transfer Agent & Registrar**—Co.'s office, North Hollywood, Cal. **Incorporated** in California in 1938; reincorporated in Delaware in 1987. **Empl**-65,000. **S&P Analyst:** Tom Graves, CFA

Issues in Money Management

Danger Signs on the Information Superhighway

There's a new way to reach your investment goals: on the information superhighway. Thanks to new technology, about 17 million investors meet in on-line investor's clubs by logging onto their computers. The three leading commercial on-line services (CompuServe, Prodigy, and America Online) as well as the Internet feature "investor bulletin boards," popular open forums organized by such topics as equities, bonds, annuities, and mutual funds. Investors can ask questions, offer tips on their favorite stocks or advice on investing strategies, or look for investment ideas.

For example, when 52-year-old Ruth Cinnamon's husband died, she inherited a large securities portfolio. A novice at investing, she lost about 25 percent of its value through poor decisions. This changed after she joined CompuServe and gained confidence from listening to investing forums and reading other members' posts. Gradually she began to make better investment choices and now feels in control of her portfolio. Small business owners Glenn and Robin Smith learned about mutual funds from Prodigy's MoneyTalk bulletin board. And Bruce and Rosa Longstreet use America Online for access to the financial press and other periodicals, as well as reports on various markets and economic indicators. Bruce looks not only for financial news but also business and economic trends.

But along with this wealth of information comes the potential for fraud. According to securities regulators in the United States and Canada, a growing number of hustlers and con artists use these bulletin boards to manipulate the price of small, thinly traded stocks called "penny stocks" that usually aren't listed on major exchanges. The perpetrator claims to have "inside information" or signs on with different names to create the appearance of a run on the stock. If even a fraction of a bulletin board's users acts on the tip, the price of the stock zooms skyward, and the schemer makes a quick buck by selling out. Other examples of misconduct include illegal promotions by phony or unlicensed brokers, pyramid schemes (electronic chain letters offering the chance to "get rich quick" in exchange for a small amount of money); and the promotion of dubious investments in diamond and gold mines and wireless cable.

In the past, these con artists peddled their scams by word of mouth or "cold calling." Now the computer lets them push their schemes anonymously and reach millions of people at once. And in all probability, they won't be caught; with the sheer volume of messages posted each day, regulators can do little more than scan for obscenity and profanity. In addition, prosecuting cyberspace crimes is tricky, raising questions of jurisdiction, privacy, and First Amendment rights. There is no legal precedent establishing liability. Nevertheless, the first legal actions against cyberscams were taken in July 1994, when New Jersey securities authorities filed cease-and-desist orders against the purveyors of two electronic pyramid schemes, and Missouri regulators stopped an unlicensed broker from hawking unregistered penny stocks.

Despite these dangers, computer bulletin boards can provide valuable investment tips if you take some precautions. Don't buy stocks you haven't researched, be especially careful when perusing messages in the low-priced stock sections, and don't assume that other people using the investor bulletin board have your best interests at heart. Most importantly, take all the information you receive with a big grain of salt, and remember that you're taking advice from people you don't know. After all, says Jack Rickard, editor of *Boardwatch Magazine,* a monthly devoted to on-line services, "If you see a tip, it may be from one of the top brokers in the country, or it could be from an 11-year-old kid."

Sources: Susan Brink, Anne Kates Smith, and Rita Rubin, "Information-Highway Robbery," *U.S. News & World Report,* July 11, 1994, p. 67; Jeff Dawson, "Online Investing: Real People Share the Secrets of their Success," *Mac Home Journal,* April 1995, downloaded from America Online April 17, 1995; Earl C. Gottschalk Jr., "Stock Hustlers Exploit On-Line Services," *The Wall Street Journal,* 21 June 1994, pp. C1, C24; Justin Martin, "Investors Go Online For Talk and Tips," *Fortune,* 12 December 1994, p. 48; Linda Stern, "On-line Fiscal Tips Can Be Out of Line," *San Diego Union-Tribune,* 11 July 1994, p. C-2.

matter of cost—find out up front how much you'll have to pay and what the fee is based on. Equally important, find out if the advisor has a specialty and if so, make sure it's compatible with your investment objectives; for example, don't go to a financial planner that specializes in high-risk limited partnerships if you're not interested in that kind of investment.

THE PC AS A SOURCE OF INVESTMENT INFORMATION

Today not only professional investors and money managers, but also individual investors use their PCs as part of the investment decision-making process. Indeed, a wide variety of software is now available on disks, CD-ROMs, or on-line that helps individual investors analyze and evaluate the investment merits of stocks and bonds. In addition, the PC can also manage and keep track of entire portfolios of securities.

With computerized databases, you can literally convert your computer to an on-line investment information library. These programs are revised frequently and give you immediate access to a vast array of historic and up-to-the-minute information on thousands of companies and securities, all sorts of financial information and financial ratios, and market performance data of stocks, bonds, and other securities—from yields and price/earnings multiples to market prices. For example, if you are thinking about buying a stock, you can access recent news stories about the company, its current financial statements, estimates of its future earnings, and even its current and past stock price and volume data.

Another source of electronic investment information that's becoming popular is on-line subscription services. At any time of day or night, subscribers can use their PC and a modem to dial into data services like *Dow Jones News/Retrieval* for stock quotes, financial data, and articles from *The Wall Street Journal* and *Barron's* or *TelScan Analyzer* to access market data, news wires, S&P MarketScope and company reports, investment newsletters, and other stock information. The features of the major commercial on-line services—America Online, CompuServe, Prodigy—and the Internet vary and increase frequently. They function as a conduit to other resources and typically provide stock quotes, market indexes, stock databases, economic indicators, mutual fund information, articles from business periodicals, electronic trading, and portfolio tracking. For example, through CompuServe you can access Value Line and Standard & Poor's databases (extensive financial and market information on many companies and securities), earnings projections for several thousand companies from the Institutional Brokers' Estimate System, and detailed financial statements filed with the Securities and Exchange Commission (SEC) by over 10,000 companies. America Online offers Hoover's Handbook with company profiles, Morningstar Mutual Fund Reports, and Decision Point Forum for technical analysis and market timing, with extensive chart libraries. The commercial services and the Internet also offer lively investor discussion groups and message boards where you can exchange ideas with other investors. Of course, as with any information source, you must be cautious before acting on any tips and do your own research first. The *Issues in Money Management* box on page 510 provides guidelines for venturing into "investing cyberspace."

To subscribe to one of these services, you pay a basic monthly fee that usually includes a certain number of hours usage and an hourly rate for additional hours. Some services charge extra for premium or expanded services such as specialized databases, order execution, and analysis software. Specialized services like Dow Jones News Retrieval also charge a one-time start-up fee.

In addition to on-line services, you can use one of the hundreds of investment programs that help you become a better investor. The latest programs are quite sophisticated and can create a portfolio and then test its composition to improve performance, help you fine-tune your asset allocation mix, examine all U.S. mutual funds to find your desired balance of risk and reward, or chart and analyze the trading pattern of any stock to find the right time to buy or sell. You can even program your computer to track a stock until it reaches your target P/E ratio and tells you it's time to buy.

Concept Check

12-15. Identify and briefly discuss the four basic types of information that you, as an investor, should try to follow.

12-16. Describe some of the major sources of investment information.

12-17. What role do market averages and indexes play in the investment process?

12-18. Describe some ways you can use your PC as an investment tool. What precautions should you take when using on-line information?

MANAGING YOUR INVESTMENT HOLDINGS

LG6

Developing a portfolio of securities is an important part of investing because a portfolio enables you to diversify your holdings. Why do you suppose diversification is such an important attribute? How would you go about building an investment portfolio? Give some thought to these questions before going on.

Actually, buying and selling securities is not difficult; the hard part is finding securities that will provide the kind of return you're looking for. Like most individual investors, in time you too will be buying, selling, and/or trading securities with ease. Eventually your investment holdings will increase to the point where you are managing a whole portfolio of securities. In essence, a **portfolio** is a collection of investment vehicles assembled to meet a common investment goal. For instance, Bill Hansen's investment portfolio is made up of 150 shares of Merck, 200 shares of Wal-Mart, and 10 Home Depot convertible bonds. But a portfolio is far more than a collection of investments! For a portfolio breathes life into your investment program; *it's an investment philosophy that provides guidelines for carrying out your investment program.* A portfolio, in effect, combines your personal and financial traits with your investment objectives to give some structure to your investments.

Seasoned investors often devote a good deal of attention to constructing diversified portfolios of securities. Such portfolios consist of stocks and bonds selected not only for their returns but also for their combined risk-return behavior. The idea behind **diversification** is that by combining securities with dissimilar risk-return characteristics, you can produce a portfolio of reduced risk and more predictable levels of return. In recent years, investment researchers have shown that you can achieve a measurable reduction in risk simply by diversifying your investment holdings. For the small investor with a moderate amount of money to invest, this means that *investing in a number of securities rather than a single one should be beneficial.* The payoff from diversification comes in the form of reduced risk without a significant impact on return. For example, Joan Rainer, who has $25,000 invested in Stock A, might find that by selling two-thirds of her holdings and using the proceeds to buy equal amounts of Stocks B and C, she will continue to earn the same level of return—say, 10 percent—while greatly decreasing the associated risk. Professional money managers emphasize the point that investors should not put all their eggs in one basket but instead should hold portfolios that are diversified across a broad segment of businesses.

BUILDING A PORTFOLIO OF SECURITIES

Developing a portfolio of investment holdings is predicated on the assumption that diversification is a desirable investment attribute that leads to improved return and/or reduced risk. Again, as emphasized earlier, holding a variety of investments is far more desirable than concentrating all your investments in a single security or industry (for example, a portfolio made up of nothing but auto stocks such as GM, Ford, or Chrysler would hardly be well diversified). Of course, when you first start investing, you will not be able to do much, if any, diversifying because of insufficient investment capital. However, as you build up your investment funds, your opportunities (and need) for diversification will increase dramatically. Certainly, by the time you have $5,000 to $10,000 to invest, you should start to diversify your holdings. To give you an idea of the kind of portfolio diversification employed by individual investors, take a look at the following numbers; they show the types of investments held by *average (small) investors:*

Type of Investment Product	Percent of Portfolio (March 1995)
Stocks and stock funds	41.2%
Bonds and bond funds	23.2
Short-term investments (CDs, money mkt. dep. accts., etc.)	34.2
Other (real estate and gold)	1.4
Total	100.0%

This portfolio, which is regularly up-dated, is used in *Money* magazine's *Small Investor Index* and reflects the portfolio holdings of a typical individual investor. Whether or not this is what your portfolio should look like depends on a number of factors, including your own needs and objectives.

Investor Characteristics. To formulate an effective portfolio strategy, begin with an honest evaluation of your own financial condition and family situation. Pay particular attention to such variables as:

- Level and stability of income
- Family factors
- Investment horizon
- Net worth
- Investor's experience and age
- Investor's disposition toward risk

These are the variables that set the tone for your investments. They determine the kinds of investments you should consider and how long you can tie up your money. For your portfolio to work, it must be tailored to meet your personal financial needs. Your income, family responsibilities, relative financial security, experience, and age all enter into the delicate equation that yields a sound portfolio strategy. For example, a married investor with young children probably would not be interested in high-risk investments until some measure of financial security has been provided for the family. Once that investor has ample savings and insurance protection for the family, he or she may be ready to undertake more risky ventures. On the other hand, a single investor with no family responsibilities would probably be better able to handle risk than one who has such concerns. Simply stated, an *investor's risk exposure should not exceed his or her ability to bear risk.*

The size and certainty of an investor's employment income has a significant bearing on portfolio strategy. An investor with a secure job is more likely to embark on a risk-oriented investment program than one with a less secure position. Income taxes bear on the investment decision as well. The higher an investor's income, the more important the tax ramifications of an investment program become. For example, municipal bonds normally yield about one-third less in annual interest than corporate bonds because the interest income on municipal bonds is tax-free. On an after-tax basis, however, municipal bonds may provide a superior return if an investor is in a tax bracket of 28 percent or higher.

An individual's investment experience also influences the appropriateness of the investment strategy. Normally, investors gradually assume levels of higher investment risk over time. It is best to "get one's feet wet" in the investment market by slipping into it gradually rather than leaping in head first. Investors who make risky initial investments very often suffer heavy losses, damaging the long-run potential of the entire investment program. A cautiously developed investment program will likely provide more favorable long-run results than an impulsive, risky one. Finally, investors should carefully consider risk. High-risk investments not only have high return potential but also a high risk of loss. Remember: By going for the home run (via a high-risk, high-return investment), the odds of striking out are much higher than by going for a base hit (a more conservative investment posture).

Investor Objectives. Once an investor has developed a personal financial profile, the next question is: "What do I want from my portfolio?" This seems like an easy question to answer. We would all like to double our money every year by making low-risk investments. However, the realities of the highly competitive investment environment makes this outcome unlikely, so the question must be answered more realistically. There generally is a trade-off between earning a high current income from an investment portfolio and obtaining significant capital appreciation from it. An investor must choose one or the other; it is difficult to have both. The price of having high appreciation potential in the portfolio is low current income potential. One must balance the certainty of high current income and limited price appreciation with the uncertainty of high future price appreciation.

The investor's needs may determine which avenue to choose. For instance, a retired investor whose income depends on his or her portfolio will probably choose a lower-risk, current income-oriented approach out of the need for financial survival. In contrast, a high-income, financially secure investor (a doctor, for instance) may be much more

portfolio A collection of securities assembled for the purpose of meeting common investment goals.

diversification The process of choosing securities having dissimilar risk-return characteristics in order to create a portfolio that will provide an acceptable level of return and an acceptable exposure to risk.

Smart Money

How to Build a Portfolio When You're Just Starting Out

You want to start an investment portfolio but only have a few hundred dollars to invest. Where do you start? Before you spend a penny you need to make sure you have set aside funds for emergencies. Then you need a long-term investment strategy that takes into account your overall goals and includes an appropriate mix of assets to reach them. Use this framework to guide your securities choices as you build a portfolio. Otherwise, you may end up with an assortment of investments that do not meet your needs. Of course, with limited funds, it will take a while to fully implement your game plan. So start with your largest asset category and then add the others as more investment funds become available.

No matter what asset allocation strategy you choose, you have several ways to make your portfolio grow. For example, you can buy a balanced or asset allocation mutual fund with an asset mix similar to yours. This conservative approach appeals to many novice investors and gives you instant diversification among asset classes with just one investment. Then keep adding to this fund until you have enough money—and investment experience—to move into specific fund categories or individual stocks. The main disadvantage to this approach is that you don't control the asset mix. If you are more daring, you can use a stock index fund as the core of your portfolio. This requires more risk tolerance, because you're starting with just common stocks, but the core fund itself is fairly conservative. Over time, you should be able to ride the market's ups and downs.

With either strategy, you then diversify into other investment categories to meet allocation goals. From a balanced fund, you'd buy a stock fund or individual stocks to increase your equity percent. With the core (index) approach, adding an intermediate bond fund creates your own balanced fund. Or you might buy small-cap or international funds. Don't agonize if you are a few percentage points from your plan; use the target percents as a general guide.

Building a portfolio of individual stocks takes more time and discipline than the fund route. Dividend reinvestment plans (DRIPs), offered by over 1,000 companies, are a way for an investor with limited funds to buy stocks and also keep expenses down. After you own at least one share of stock, you can reinvest dividends in more shares and buy stock directly from the company, usually without a fee. Because one-share transaction costs can be high, try Dean Witter's special one-share commission of 10 percent of the share price or organizations like First Share (1-800-683-0743) or the National Association of Investors Corp. (Box 220, Royal Oak, MI 48068). Be sure to study the shareholder information packages and DRIP prospectuses from companies that interest you. And diversify with shares in a variety of industries and economic sectors, and include growth, value, and income stocks. Your goal should be about 10 to 20 companies, but focus on quality, not quantity; four good stocks are better than 10 bad ones. Know whether you can buy more shares monthly or quarterly.

Remember to *invest regularly in your funds or stocks,* every month or pay period if possible. You'll be surprised how quickly your investments grow. And be patient; unless you hold your investments for a while, transaction costs and taxes will wipe out profits.

Sources: Adapted from Ellen C. Schultz, "How to Build a Stock Portfolio, Even If You Aren't a Moneybags," *The Wall Street Journal,* April 14, 1992, p. C1; and Maria Crawford Scott, "How to Implement Your Strategy If You Are Starting from Scratch," *AAII Journal,* February 1995, pp. 18–20.

willing to take on risky investments in the hope of improving his or her net worth. Likewise, a young investor with a secure job may be less concerned about current income and more able to bear risk. This type of investor will likely be more capital gains-oriented and may choose speculative investments. As an investor approaches age 60, the desired level of income likely rises as retirement approaches. The aging investor will be less willing to bear risk and will want to keep what he or she has, because these investments will soon be needed as a source of retirement income.

ASSET ALLOCATION AND PORTFOLIO MANAGEMENT

A portfolio must be built around an individual's needs, which, in turn, depend on income, family responsibilities, financial resources, age, retirement plans, and ability to bear risk. These needs shape one's financial goals. But to create a portfolio that is geared to those goals, you need to develop an **asset allocation** scheme. Basically, all that asset allocation involves is a decision on how to divide your portfolio among different types of securities. For example, what portion of your portfolio is going to be devoted to short-term securities, longer bonds and/or bond funds, and common stocks and/or equity funds? In asset allocation, emphasis is placed on *preservation of capital*. The idea is to position your assets in such a way that you can protect your portfolio from potential negative developments in the market, while still taking advantage of potential positive developments. Asset allocation is one of the most overlooked yet most important aspects of investing. Indeed, there's overwhelming evidence that, over the long run, the total return on a portfolio is influenced more by its assets allocation plan than by specific security selections.

Asset allocation deals in broad categories and *does not tell you which individual securities to buy or sell*. It might look something like this:

Type of Investment	Asset Mix
Short-term securities	10%
Longer bonds (7- to 10-year maturities)	25
Equity funds	65
Total portfolio	100%

As you can see, all you're really doing here is deciding how to cut up the pie. You still have to decide which particular securities to invest in. Once you've decided that you want to put, say, 25 percent of your money into intermediate-term (7- to 10-year) bonds, your next step is to select those specific securities. For ideas on how to start your own portfolio, even if you don't have a lot of money, see the *Smart Money* box on page 514.

Once you establish your asset allocation strategy, you should check it regularly for two reasons: first, to make sure that your portfolio is in fact approximately in line with your desired asset mix and second, to see if that mix is still appropriate for your investment objectives. Here are some reasons to reevaluate your asset allocation:

- A major change in personal circumstances—marriage, birth of a child, loss of a spouse from divorce or death, child graduating from college, loss of job, or family illness, for example—that changes your investment goals.
- The proportion of an asset rises or falls considerably, changing your target allocation for that class more than 10 percent.
- You're close to reaching a certain goal (such as saving for your child's college or for your retirement).

You may find that your portfolio requires *rebalancing* to bring it back into line or to reallocate assets. For example, suppose your asset allocation plan calls for 50 percent equities and the stock market falls so that stocks represent only 40 percent of your total portfolio. If you are still bullish on the market and stocks are still appropriate for your portfolio, you may view this as a good time to buy and, in so doing, bring your portfolio back up to 50 percent. If your personal goals change or you think the market may not recover in the near future, you may decide to change your percentages to hold fewer stocks. If you have achieved your goal of saving $80,000 for your son's college education and he starts next year, you may wish to move some funds into short-term vehicles. However, don't be too quick to rebalance; you must allow for some variation in the percentages, as market fluctuations make it impossible to maintain exact percentages. And don't forget the costs from commissions or sales charges and tax considerations such as capital gains.

Security selection and portfolio management are recurring activities that become an almost routine part of your investment program. You receive an interest or dividend check, and you have to find a place to put it; you add new capital to your investment program, or one of the Treasury notes you're holding matures, and you have to decide what to do with the money. These events occur with considerable regularity, so you're likely to be faced with a series of little (and sometimes not so little) investment decisions over time. This, in short, is portfolio management: the initial construction and ongoing administration of a collection of securities and investments.

Portfolio management involves the buying, selling, and holding of various securities for the

asset allocation A plan for dividing a portfolio among different classes of securities in order to preserve capital by protecting the portfolio against negative market development.

EXHIBIT 12.10

Four Model Portfolios

The type of portfolio you put together will depend on your financial and family situation as well as on your investment objectives. Clearly, what is right for one family may be totally inappropriate for another.

Family Situation	Portfolio
Newlywed couple:	70% in common stocks, with three quarters in mutual funds aiming for maximum capital gains and the rest in growth funds 30% in a money market fund or other short-term money market securities
Two-income couple:	50% in common stocks, with three quarters of that in blue chips or growth mutual funds and the remainder in more aggressive issues or mutual funds aiming for maximum capital gains 40% in discount Treasury notes whose maturities correspond with the bills for college tuition 10% in money market funds or other short-term money market securities
Divorced mother:	50% in money market funds or other short-term money market securities 50% in growth and income mutual funds
Older couple:	60% in blue-chip common stocks or growth mutual funds 30% in municipal bonds or short- and intermediate-term discount bonds that will mature as they start to need the money to live on 10% in CDs and/or money market funds

purpose of meeting a set of predetermined investment needs and objectives. To give you an idea of portfolio management in action, Exhibit 12.10 provides examples of four different portfolios, each developed with a particular financial situation in mind. Note in each case that the asset allocation schemes and portfolio structures change with the different financial objectives. The first one is the *newlywed couple;* in their late 20s, they earn $45,000 a year and spend just about every cent. They have managed to put away some money, however, and are quickly beginning to appreciate the need to develop a savings program. Next there is the *two-income couple;* in their early 40s, they earn $84,000 a year and are concerned about college costs for their children, ages 17 and 12. Next is the *divorced mother;* she is 34, has custody of her children, ages 7 and 4, and receives $28,000 a year in salary and child support. Finally, we have the *older couple;* in their mid-50s, they are planning for retirement in ten years, when the husband will retire from his $70,000-a-year job.

KEEPING TRACK OF YOUR INVESTMENTS

Keeping track of your investment holdings is essential to a well-managed securities portfolio. Just as you need investment objectives to provide direction for your portfolio, so too do you need to *monitor* it by keeping informed of what your investment holdings consist of, how they have performed over time, and whether or not they have lived up to your expectations. Sometimes investments fail to perform the way you thought they would. Their return may be well below what you would like, or perhaps you may even have suffered a loss. In either case, it may be time to *sell* the investment(s) and put the money elsewhere. A monitoring system for keeping track of your investments should allow you to identify such securities in your portfolio. In addition, it should enable you to stay on top of the holdings that are performing to your satisfaction. Knowing when to sell and when to hold can have a significant impact on the amount of return you are able to generate from your investments—certainly it will help you keep your money fully invested.

You can use something like Worksheet 12.1 to keep an inventory of your investment holdings. All types of investments can be included on this worksheet—from stocks, bonds, and mutual funds to real estate and savings accounts. To see how it works, consider the investment portfolio that has been built up over the last 15 years or so by John and Mary Maffeo, a two-income couple in their late 40s. As the figures in Worksheet 12.1 reveal, John and Mary hold common and preferred stock

WORKSHEET 12.1

A Worksheet for Keeping Tabs on Your Investment Holdings

A worksheet like this one will enable you to keep track of your investment holdings and identify investments that are not performing up to expectations.

AN INVENTORY OF INVESTMENT HOLDINGS

Name(s): John & Mary Maffeo **Date:** December 1995

Type of Investment	Description of Investment Vehicle	Date Purchased	Amount of Investment (Quote—$ Amount)	Amount of Annual Income from Dividends, Interest, Etc.	Latest Market Value (Quote—$ Amount)	Comments/ Planned Actions
Common stock	200 shares—Dillard Dept. Stores	3/5/85	24 1/4—$4,900	$72	27 3/4-$22,200	800 shs.
Common stock	300 shares—Calgene	10/12/88	8 3/4—$2,625	0	6 3/4—$2,025	SELL?
Common stock	400 shares—Pall Corp.	8/11/84	9 1/2—$3,800	$594	27—$48,600	1,800 shares!
Preferred stock	100 shares—Dupont pf 4.50	1/26/89	50 3/4—$5,075	$450	62 1/4—$6,225	
Corporate bond	$5,000—Pacific Telephone 7 1/4—08	8/19/82	75 1/2—$3,775	$363	94 3/4—$4,738	
Corporate bond	$7,000—Texaco 5 3/4—07	2/27/77	39 1/4—$2,748	$402	94 1/2—$6,615	
Treasury bond	$6,000—U.S. Treasury 7 1/2—99	10/4/92	62—$3,720	$450	102—$6,120	
Mutual fund	500 shares—Fidelity Magellan (growth)	6/16/76	7—$3,500	$3,120	72 1/2—$124,120	1712 shs.
Mutual fund	200 shares—Fidelity high-yield (bond)	1/17/79	6 1/2—$1,300	$246	12 1/4—$2,450	
Real estate	Four-plex at 1802 N. 75 Ave.	9/16/84	$140,000—$28,000	N/A	(est.) $250,000—$138,000	Time to sell?
Savings	1-year/6.5% CD at First National Bank	6/10/95	N/A—$10,000	$650	N/A—$10,000	
Savings	Money Fund at Paine Webber	3/13/83	N/A—$7,200	$340	N/A—$7,200	
	Totals		$76,643	$6,687	$378,293	

Instructions: List number of shares of *common and preferred stock* purchased as part of the description of securities held; then put the price paid *per share* under the "Quote" column and total amount invested (number of shares × price per share) under the "$ Amount" column. Enter the principal (par) value of all *bonds* held in place of number of shares: "$ Amount" column for bonds = principal value of bonds purchased × quote (for example, $5,000 × .755 = $3,775). List *mutual funds* as you did for stock. For *real estate,* enter total market value of property under "Quote" column and amount actually invested (down payment and closing costs) under "$ Amount." Ignore the "Quote" column for *savings* vehicles. For "Amount of Income" column, list *total* amount received from dividends, interest, and so on (for example, dividends per share × number of shares held). Under "Latest Market Value," enter market price as of the date of this report (for instance, in December 1995, Pall Corp. was trading at 27). The latest market value for *real estate* is entered as an *estimate* of what the property would likely sell for (under "Quote") and the *estimated* amount of equity the investor has in the property (under "$ Amount").

in four companies, three bond issues, two mutual funds, some real estate, and two savings accounts. In addition to the type and description of the investment vehicles, the worksheet contains the dates the investments were made (the purchase date is needed for tax purposes), the original amount of the investment, the amount of annual income currently being earned from it, and its latest market value.

Such a report would list all the investments John and Mary held as of December 1995, regardless of when they were purchased. In contrast, any securities/investments sold during the year (1995) would not be included. A report like this should be prepared at least once a year, and preferably every three to six months. When completed, it will provide a quick overview of your investment holdings and enable you to easily identify securities that are performing well and those that are not. Such information is invaluable in effectively managing an investment portfolio, as it lets you know where you stand at a given point in time. Note that the Maffeos earn almost $6,700 a year from their investments and that—thanks, in large part, to their investments in a couple of stocks and stock funds—their holdings have grown from around $75,000 to over $375,000! In fact, they have only one security that is not doing too well—Calgene Inc. All the rest are quite profitable.

Concept Check

12-19. Explain why it might be preferable for a person to invest in a *portfolio* of securities rather than in a single security. Be sure to mention risk and return in your response.

12-20. Briefly describe the concept of *asset allocation* and note how it works. Give an example of an asset allocation scheme. Discuss the role that asset allocation plays in the management of a portfolio.

12-21. What, if anything, is there to be gained from keeping track of your investment holdings?

SUMMARY

LG1. **Distinguish between primary and secondary markets, as well as listed exchanges and the over-the-counter market.** Stocks, bonds, and other long-term securities are traded in the capital, or long-term, markets. Newly issued securities are sold in the primary markets, while transactions between investors occur in the secondary markets. Listed securities are traded on organized exchanges, like the New York and American stock exchanges, as well as a number of smaller regional exchanges. In contrast, the over-the-counter (OTC) market handles the thousands of unlisted securities.

LG2. **Choose the right stockbroker to suit your needs.** Whether your broker is with a full-service or discount brokerage firm, he or she provides you with access to the securities market—in essence, brokers buy and sell securities for their customers. Full-service brokers offer a variety of other services, including research reports, investment advice, and sweep accounts. Many discount brokers now offer some of these same services. Choose a broker who understands your investment philosophy and goals and can help you achieve them.

LG3. **Explain the process of buying and selling securities and recognize the different types of orders.** The securities transaction process starts when you call and place an order with your broker, who then transmits it via sophisticated telecommunications equipment to the floor of the stock exchange or the OTC market, where it is promptly executed and confirmed. Investors can buy or sell securities in odd or round lots by simply placing one of the three basic types of orders: a market order, limit order, or stop-loss order.

LG4. **Discuss the essentials of and motivations for margin trading and short selling.** When you buy a security, you can pay cash for it or buy it on margin, where part of the cost of the security is paid with borrowed money. The objective of a margin transaction is to obtain magnified returns; however, losses are also magnified. An investor can also make money when the price of a security drops by short selling borrowed securities and then repurchasing them after they have dropped in price. If the price rises, however, the investor loses money.

LG5. Improve your investing skills by using various forms of investment information. Becoming an informed investor is essential to developing a sound investment program. Vital information about specific companies and industries, the securities markets, the economy, and different investment vehicles and strategies can be obtained from sources such as annual stockholders' reports, brokerage and advisory service reports, and the financial press. In addition, the personal computer is rapidly becoming a popular source of investment information.

Various averages and indexes, such as the Dow Jones Industrial Average, the Standard & Poor's Indexes, the NYSE, AMEX, and OTC (or Nasdaq) Indexes, and the Wilshire 5000 Index, provide information about daily market performance. These averages and indexes not only measure performance in the overall market, they also provide standards of performance for specific types of stocks such as transportation issues, banks, insurance companies, and public utilities.

LG6. Build an investment portfolio and manage your investments. Developing a well-diversified portfolio of investment holdings enables an investor to not only achieve given investment objectives, but also enjoy reduced exposure to risk and a more predictable level of return. To develop such a portfolio, the investor must carefully consider his or her level and stability of income, family factors, financial condition, experience and age, and disposition toward risk. Designing an asset allocation scheme, or mix of securities, that's based on these personal needs and objectives is also an important part of portfolio management. You should monitor your investment portfolio regularly to measure its performance and make changes as required by return data and life-cycle factors.

FINANCIAL FACTS OR FANTASIES

Are the following statements financial facts (true) or fantasies (false)?

1. Stocks listed on the New York Stock Exchange are traded in the over-the-counter market.

2. If you lose a lot of money because of a lousy investment recommended by your broker, you can recover all or most of your loss by filing a claim with the Securities Investor Protection Corporation.

3. You short sell a stock when you sell stock that doesn't belong to you.

4. Because they are so biased, you should pay little attention to annual stockholders' reports.

5. The MidCap 400 is a market index that's meant to reflect the market performance of medium-sized companies.

6. Coming up with a sound asset allocation plan is likely to have more of an impact on long-term return than the specific securities you hold in your portfolio.

DISCUSSION QUESTIONS AND PROBLEMS

Discussion Question for Opening Profile

Discuss Steve and Kelly Stuart's approach to investing, including how they select stocks. Do you think their portfolio is structured appropriately given their personal circumstances?

1. Barbara Moses has just purchased two different stocks. Her first transaction involved 100 shares of Xerox Corporation at $49.50 per share, and the second was 60 shares of Prime Computers at $15 per share. For each transaction, calculate the amount of brokerage commissions Barbara will have to pay, and express them as a percentage of the total cost of each stock. Use the brokerage fee schedule in Exhibit 12.2.
2. Assume Cecile Higgins places an order to buy 100 shares of Kodak; explain how the order will be processed if it is a market order. Would it have made any difference if it had been a limit order? Explain.
3. Helen Emerson wants to buy 300 shares of PepsiCo, which is currently selling in the market for $45 a share. Rather than liquidate all her savings, she decides to borrow through her broker. Assume the margin requirement on common stock is currently 50 percent and the brokerage firm charges 9 percent interest on margin loans. What would be the interest cost on the transaction if Helen sold the stocks at the end of one year? If the stock rises to $60 a share by the end of the year, show the kind of profit (in dollars) and return (in percentages) that Helen would earn if she makes the investment with 50 percent margin; contrast this to what she would make if she uses no margin.
4. Which of the following would offer the best return on investment? Assume you buy $5,000 in stock in all three cases; also, ignore interest costs in all your calculations.
   - **a.** Buy a stock at $80 without margin, and sell it at $120 one year later.
   - **b.** Buy a stock at $32 with 50 percent margin, and sell it one year later at $41.
   - **c.** Buy a stock at $50 with 75 percent margin, and sell it in one year at $65.
5. How much profit (if any) would Don Summers make if he short sold 300 shares of stock at $75 a share and the price of the stock suddenly tumbled to $60?
6. Using a resource like *The Wall Street Journal* or *Barron's*, find the latest values for each of the following market averages and indexes, and indicate how each has performed over the past six months:
   - **a.** DJIA
   - **b.** Dow Jones Utilities
   - **c.** S&P 500
   - **d.** NYSE Composite Index
   - **e.** AMEX index
   - **f.** Nasdaq Composite OTC index
   - **g.** MidCap 400
   - **h.** Wilshire 5000
7. Using the stock quotations in Exhibit 12.7, find the 52-week high and low for Dow Chemical. How much does the stock pay annually in dividends, and what is its latest dividend yield? How many shares of Dow Chemical changed hands (were traded), what was the closing price, and at what P/E ratio was the stock trading? According to the information in Exhibit 12.7, which of the Duke Power preferred stocks has the best dividend yield?
8. Using the bond quotes in Exhibit 12.8, how much would you have to pay for the following bonds? (Assume all the bonds have $1,000 par values.)
   - **a.** A 7⅛% AT&T bond that matures in 2002.
   - **b.** An 8⅜% Bethlehem Steel bond that matures in 2001.
   - **c.** A zero coupon Allied Chemical bond that matures in 1998.
   - **d.** An 11⅝% Treasury bond that matures in November 2004.

   How much annual interest income will you receive from each of these bonds, and which bond offers the highest current yield? Which has the lowest current yield?
9. Using the S&P report in Exhibit 12.9, find the following information as it pertains to Disney:
   - **a.** Amount of revenues (that is, sales) the company generated in 1994.
   - **b.** Latest annual dividends per share and dividend yield.
   - **c.** Earnings (per share) projections for 1995.
   - **d.** Number of common shares outstanding.
   - **e.** Book value per share and earnings per share in 1994.

   f. Where the stock is traded.
   g. Amount of long-term debt the company has.
   h. Given its beta, to approximately what price would this stock jump if the market went up by 15 percent over the next 12 months? (Assume the stock is currently priced at 55.)

10. ***Use Worksheet 12.1*** to help Rebecca and Andrew Cook, a married couple in their early 30s, evaluate their securities portfolio, which includes the following holdings:

   1. Adams Express (NYSE—stock symbol ADX): 100 shares bought in July 1991 for $18 per share.
   2. BankAmerica $2.04 *preferred stock* (NYSE—look for BankAmer pfL 2.04): 50 shares purchased in December 1992 for $19.25 per share.
   3. Bed Bath & Beyond (Nasdaq—stock symbol: BBBY): 150 shares purchased in 1993 at $19.50 per share; the stock pays no dividends.
   4. MBNA Corp. (NYSE; a bank holding company): 150 shares bought November 1993 for $23.25 per share; the stock split 3 for 2 in February 1994 and was paying a dividend of $0.72 per share after the split.
   5. A U.S. Treasury bond: $5,000 par value, 9³/₈% coupon, maturing in February 2006; purchased in April 1995, at 108.

   a. Based on the latest quotes obtained from *The Wall Street Journal*, or provided by your instructor, complete Worksheet 12.1.
   b. What's the total amount they invested in these securities, the annual income they receive, and the latest market value of their investments?

CONTEMPORARY CASE APPLICATIONS

12.1 The Gordons' Problem: What to Do with All That Money?

A couple in their early 30s, Allen and Sandra Gordon recently inherited $90,000 from one of their relatives. Allen earns a comfortable income as a sales manager for Smith and Johnson, Inc., and Sandra does equally well as an attorney with a major law firm. Since they have no children and do not need the money, they have decided to invest all of their inheritance in stocks, bonds, and perhaps even some money market instruments. However, they are not very familiar with the market, nor do they know how to go about selecting a broker. As a result, they turn to you for help.

Questions

1. In what markets and on what exchanges do you think most of the Gordons' transactions should take place?
2. What characteristics should the Gordons look for in a stockbroker? Take into consideration brokerage services and brokerage fees.
3. Construct an investment portfolio that you feel would be right for the Gordons; invest the full $90,000. Put *actual* stocks, bonds, preferreds, and/or convertible securities in the portfolio; also, if you like, you may put up to *one-third* of the money into short-term securities like CDs, Treasury bills, money funds, or MMDAs. Select any securities you want, so long as you feel they would be suitable for the Gordons. (Hint: you might want to refer back to Chapters 4 and 11 for some ideas.) Make sure the portfolio consists of *six or more different securities;* use the latest issue of *The Wall Street Journal* to determine the market prices of the securities you select. Show the amount invested in each security, along with the amount of current income (from dividends and/or interest) that will be generated from the investments. Briefly explain why you selected the particular securities for the Gordons' portfolio.

12.2 Steve Takes Stock of His Securities

Steve Harrington is 32 years old, single, and works as a research chemist for a major pharmaceutical firm. He is well paid and over time has built up a sizable portfolio of investments. He considers himself an aggressive investor and, because he has no dependents to worry about, likes to invest in high-risk–high-return securities. His records show the following:

1. In 1990, he bought 100 shares of *Reebok International* (an NYSE stock) at $14 a share; the stock paid a dividend of 30 cents a share in 1990.
2. In 1992 he bought 250 shares of *WD-40 Co.* (an OTC stock quoted on the Nasdaq National Market System) at $28 a share; at the time, the stock was paying annual dividends of $1.63 a share.
3. In 1991, Steve bought 400 shares of *Federal Home Loan Mortgage Corp.* (an NYSE stock) at $50; in 1992 the stock split 3 for 1 and the stock paid annual dividends of $2.20 a share.
4. In early 1994 he bought 200 shares of *SciClone Pharmaceuticals* (Nasdaq National Market System) at $7 a share; the stock was expected to pay no dividends in 1994.
5. Also in 1994, Steve bought 300 shares of *Tyco International* (an NYSE stock—stock symbol TYC) at $43 a share; at that time the stock paid an annual dividend of 40 cents a share.
6. He has $8,000 in a 4 percent money market mutual fund.

Every three months or so, Steve prepares a complete, up-to-date inventory of his investment holdings.

Questions

1. Use a form like Worksheet 12.1 to prepare a complete inventory of Steve's Investment holdings (Note: Look in the latest issue of *The Wall Street Journal* to find the most recent market value of the five *stocks* in Steve's portfolio.)
2. What is your overall assessment of Steve's investment portfolio? Does it appear that his personal net worth is improving as a result of his investments?
3. Based on the worksheet you prepared in Question 1, do you see any securities that you think Steve should consider selling?

GETTING A HANDLE ON YOUR FINANCIAL FUTURE

Once your goals have been established and you have decided on an investment plan, you are ready to implement the plan by purchasing and selling securities.

The proper selection of securities for your portfolio requires a thorough understanding of your personal investing characteristics, your financial goals, and a desired asset mix.

If You Are Just Getting Started

Since at this stage you probably have very little actual investment experience, you would more than likely select a full-service brokerage firm with access to the major markets and to financial research. This would give you access to investment recommendations to fit your risk and return requirements at the cost of higher commissions.

Selecting a Brokerage Firm:

1. Decide on the services you need to have available to you at this time and make a list so you can begin your evaluation of competing firms.
2. Ask the brokerage house about its research department in comparison with other firms. If you are paying for investment advice, you want to make sure it is good advice most of the time.
3. Look at the firm's commissions on various transactions. Even though technically commissions are negotiable, most firms have minimum charges on transactions, especially smaller ones.
4. Determine how the brokerage firm pays interest on cash balances. You want all of your money in an account that earns interest for **you.**
5. Examine the account agreement form and ask for clarification to any terms or provisions that you do not understand. Don't necessarily take the word of the account executive.

Selecting an Account Executive:

1. Select an account executive like you would any other professional. Ask your friends for references.
2. Arrange to meet in person with the account executive to discuss your goals and objectives.
3. If you walk in off the street, you will normally be assigned to whomever is "on duty" that day. This may be the most inexperienced member of the firm.
4. Regardless of how you first meet an account executive, if you do not feel comfortable with him or her, ask the office manager to assign you to someone else and start the interview process over again.
5. If you are still unsure about the account executive, you may want to contact the NASD to see if he or she has had any complaints filed against him or her.

If You Are Thirty-Something

As your portfolio grows, it should be monitored periodically to ensure proper performance and diversification of your investments. Studies have shown that the vast majority of your returns will come from being in the right asset class as opposed to the selection of specific securities so you should also review your asset allocation.

Determining Your Asset Allocation:

1. Identify asset classes that are suitable for achieving your financial goals.
2. Determine the weightings of the various asset classes based upon your time horizon and attitude toward risk.
3. Be sure your asset allocation reflects your particular financial objective. This means that you can have a different asset allocation for each goal.
4. Rebalance your portfolios when the allocation in any class exceeds its weight limit by, say, 5 to 10 percent..
5. Compare the advantages of rebalancing to the transactions costs. You would normally not rebalance more than once a quarter unless markets are extremely volatile.

Monitoring Your Account:

1. It is not necessary to follow your security prices every day. Although the more active you are in the market the more frequently you should monitor your securities.
2. Compare the change in your security's price to what has happened in the overall market over the same period of time. Try to determine if the change is due to market factors or firm specific factors.
3. To protect against sudden declines in the value of your securities consider using stop-loss orders.
4. Know which securities have gains and losses for year-end tax planning.
5. Keep a separate category for commissions paid on transactions and compare this with the profits on your trades. If the commissions equal or exceed your profits, you may be experiencing excessive trades . . . or excessive commissions.
6. If your selections are doing as well or better than the brokerage firm's selections, consider opening an account with a discount broker.

Chapter 13

Investing in Mutual Funds

Lori Rapuano's Mutually Rewarding Investments

Although Lori and Joe Rapuano discuss investment opportunities as a couple, it is Lori who manages their portfolio. "I've always been more interested in investing," says Lori, "even before my 1993 career change from insurance underwriter to financial consultant at a major brokerage firm. While I was growing up, my family included the kids in financial discussions, so I learned the value of investing and the limitations of savings accounts." The Rapuanos, who are in their mid-30s and live near Hartford, Connecticut, started investing about 10 years ago but at first didn't have any specific investment goals, other than capital appreciation. Today, their goals include sending their two children, ages 5 and 2½, to college and building retirement assets.

They separate their tax-deferred retirement funds from their regular account and invest each differently. "We are more cautious with our regular account, because we may need the funds for emergencies," explains Lori. "Also, Joe is considering graduate school, so we want a reasonable level of liquidity." Growth-oriented mutual funds form the core of their portfolios, which are well-diversified. In mid-1995, their regular portfolio included 21 percent cash, 4 percent municipal bonds, and 75 percent mutual funds: 45 percent of which was in balanced funds (stocks and bonds) and 55 percent divided among international bond, U.S. bond, and international stock

Learning Goals

LG1. *Describe the basic features and operating characteristics of a mutual fund.*

LG2. *Differentiate between open- and closed-end funds, and discuss the various types of fund loads and charges.*

LG3. *Discuss the types of funds available and the variety of investment objectives these funds seek to fulfill.*

LG4. *Identify and discuss the different kinds of investor services offered by mutual funds.*

LG5. *Gain an understanding of the variables that should be considered when selecting funds for investment purposes.*

LG6. *Identify the sources of return and calculate the rate of return earned on an investment in a mutual fund.*

funds. Their retirement accounts are 100 percent in mutual funds. About half of Lori's accounts are in equity funds, with a large percentage in international funds, and the rest is divided among bond and balanced (bonds and stocks) funds. Joe's retirement funds are allocated between U.S. and international equity mutual funds.

"We like mutual funds because they provide professional management and greater diversification than we could achieve on our own," comments Lori. Other fund features that appeal to the Rapuanos are automatic investment plans for monthly contributions, reinvestment of dividends, and the ability to switch within fund families without sales fees. They use Morningstar reports to research potential fund investments, as well as some brokerage firm reports. Lori bases her selection on the fund family's strength, the age of the fund, the fund's objectives, historical performance, management performance and longevity, and fee structure.

"As we've learned more about the capital markets, we're investing our long-term retirement funds more aggressively. I plan to add individual stocks to our portfolios soon," says Lori. "But we've done well with mutual funds—of course, there are always ups and downs—and they'll continue to have a prominent role among our investments." As you read the following chapter, you will learn how mutual funds can help you, too, reach your investing goals.

MUTUAL FUNDS: SOME BASICS LG1 LG2

Mutual funds are a very popular form of investing—they offer attractive levels of return from professionally managed, widely diversified portfolios of securities. Today, there are over 6,000 publicly traded mutual funds—enough to meet just about any investment need. Stop for a moment to think about mutual funds. Why would you want to invest in a mutual fund and what do they have to offer you as an investor?

For individual investors today, mutual funds are, without a doubt, the investment vehicle of choice. The fact is, more people invest in mutual funds than any other type of investment product. The reason they are so popular is that they offer not only a variety of interesting investment opportunities, but also a wide array of services that many investors find appealing. They provide an easy and convenient way to invest, and are especially suited to beginning investors and those with limited investment capital. A mutual fund is basically a financial services organization that receives money from its shareholders and then invests those funds in a diversified portfolio of securities. As such, an investment in a mutual fund represents an ownership position in a professionally managed *portfolio of securities;* when you buy shares in a mutual fund you become a part-owner of that portfolio. This concept underlies the whole mutual fund structure and is depicted in Exhibit 13.1.

THE MUTUAL FUND CONCEPT

The first mutual fund in this country was started in Boston in 1924; by 1940, there were 68 funds with $488 million in assets and nearly 300,000 shareholder accounts. That was only the beginning, however, as the growth in funds really took off in the late 1970s. Indeed, by 1995, assets under management had grown to over $2 *trillion,* as nearly 70 *million* investors held shares in over 6,000 publicly traded funds. The fund industry has grown so much, in fact, that it is now the second largest financial intermediary, behind only commercial banks (but not by much). We have reached the point where *there are more mutual funds in existence today than there are stocks on the New York and American stock exchanges, combined.*

Mutual fund investors come from all walks of life and all income levels. And they all share one common view: They've decided, for one reason or another, to turn the problems of security selection and portfolio management over to professional money managers. Questions of which stock or bond to select, when to buy, and when to sell have plagued investors for about as long as there have been organized securities markets. Such concerns lie at the very heart of the mutual fund concept and, in large part, are behind the growth in funds. The fact is, a lot of people simply lack the time, the know-how, or the commitment to manage their own securities. As a result, they turn to others. And more often than not, that means mutual funds.

Pooled Diversification. The mutual fund concept is based on the simple idea of turning the problems of security selection and portfolio management over to professional money managers. In essence, a mutual fund combines the investment capital of many people with similar investment goals, and invests the funds for those individuals in a wide variety of securities. (In an abstract sense, you might think of a mutual fund as the *financial product* that's sold to the public by an investment company. That is, the investment company builds and manages a portfolio of securities, and then sells ownership interests in that portfolio through a vehicle known as a mutual fund.) Investors receive shares of stock in the mutual fund and, through the fund, are able to enjoy much wider investment diversification than they could otherwise achieve. To appreciate the extent of such diversification, one need only look at Exhibit 13.2 on page 528. It provides a partial list of the securities actually held in the portfolio of a major mutual fund (actually, just one page of a 16 page list of security holdings). Observe that in November, 1994, this fund owned anywhere from 4,900 shares of one company (Ortel Corp.) to nearly 1.3 *million* shares of another (GE). Furthermore, note that within each industry segment, the fund diversified its holdings across a number of different stocks. Clearly, except for all but the super-rich, this is far more diversification than most investors could ever hope to attain. Yet each investor who owns shares in this fund is, in effect, a part owner of this diversified portfolio of securities.

Of course, not all funds are as big or as diversified as the one depicted in Exhibit 13.2. Even so,

EXHIBIT 13.1

The Basic Mutual Fund Structure

A mutual fund brings together the funds from numerous individual investors and uses this pool of money to acquire a diversified portfolio of stocks, bonds, and other securities.

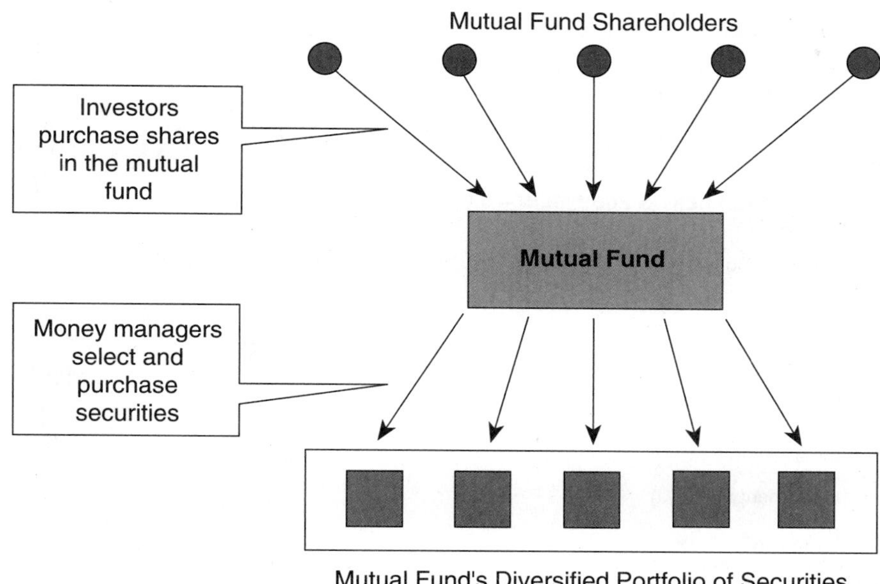

as the securities held by a fund move up and down in price, the market value of the mutual fund shares moves accordingly. When dividend and interest payments are received by the fund, they are passed on to the mutual fund shareholders and distributed on the basis of prorated ownership. For example, if you own 1,000 shares of stock in a mutual fund and that represents 10 percent of all shares outstanding, you would receive 10 percent of the dividends paid by the fund. When a security held by the fund is sold for a profit, the capital gain is also passed on to fund shareholders. The whole mutual fund idea, in fact, rests on the concept of **pooled diversification,** and works very much like insurance, whereby individuals pool their resources for the collective benefit of all the contributors.

WHY INVEST IN MUTUAL FUNDS?

Mutual funds can be used by individual investors in a variety of ways. Thus, whereas one investor may buy a fund because of the substantial capital gains opportunities it provides, another may buy a totally different fund not for its capital gains, but for its current income. Regardless of the kind of income a fund provides, individuals tend to use these investment vehicles for one or more of the following reasons: (1) to achieve diversification in their investment holdings; (2) to obtain the services of professional money managers; (3) to generate an attractive rate of return on their investment capital; and (4) for the convenience they offer.

Diversification. Certainly, as we saw above, diversification is a primary motive for investing in mutual funds. This ability to diversify, in effect, allows investors to sharply reduce their exposure to risk by indirectly investing in a number of different types of securities and/or companies, rather than just one or two. If you have only $500 to $1,000 to

pooled diversification A process whereby investors buy into a diversified portfolio of securities for the collective benefit of the individual investors.

EXHIBIT 13.2

A Partial List of Portfolio Holdings

The list of holdings in this one fund alone goes on for another 15 pages and includes stocks in hundreds of different companies. Certainly, this is far more diversification than most individual investors could ever hope to achieve.

COMMON STOCKS	Shares	Value (note 1) (000s)
HOLDING COMPANIES—0.4%		
Granite Industries BHD (a)	790,000	$ 1,855
Grupo Carso SA de CV Class A-1 (a)	893,800	10,052
Grupo Sidek SA de CV Class B Ord. (a)	155,500	664
		12,571
INDUSTRIAL MACHINERY & EQUIPMENT—3.6%		
Electrical Equipment—2.3%		
American Power Conversion Corp. (a)	105,600	1,703
General Electric Co.	1,268,300	58,342
Ortel Corp. (a)	4,900	127
Scientific-Atlanta, Inc.	223,800	4,420
Sensormatic Electronics Corp.	110,300	3,557
Star Paging International Holdings Ltd. (warrants) (a)	1,356,800	61
		68,210
Industrial Machinery & Equipment—0.9%		
Case Corp.	200,600	3,937
Caterpillar, Inc.	318,900	17,220
PRI Automation, Inc. (a)	127,700	2,139
Ultratech Stepper, Inc.	94,100	3,670
Vesco Instruments, Inc. (a)	48,800	537
		27,503
Pollution Control—0.4%		
Browning-Ferris Industries, Inc.	114,400	3,089
WMX Technologies, Inc.	338,200	8,708
		11,797
TOTAL INDUSTRIAL MACHINERY & EQUIPMENT		107,510
MEDIA & LEISURE—3.0%		
Broadcasting—1.4%		
Comcast Corp. Class A (Special)	158,200	2,511
Emmis Broadcasting Corp. Class A (a)	21,300	312
infinity Broadcasting Corp. (a)	114,400	3,432
Tele-Communications, Inc. Class A (a)	417,600	9,866

Source: Fidelity Growth Company.

invest, you obviously will not achieve much diversification on your own. However, if you invest that money in a mutual fund, you will end up owning part of a diversified portfolio made up perhaps of 100 or more securities.

Professional Management. Another major appeal of a mutual fund is the professional management it offers. Of course, management is paid a fee from the fund's earnings, but the contributions of a full-time expert manager should be well worth the cost. These pros know where to look for return, and how to avoid unnecessary risk; their decisions should result in better returns than the average investor can achieve.

Financial Returns. While professional managers *may* be able to achieve returns that are better than what small investors can generate, the relatively high purchase fees, coupled with the management and operating costs, tend to reduce the returns actually earned on mutual fund investments. However, the mutual fund industry has not attracted millions of investors because of the substandard returns they generate! Quite the contrary; over the long haul, mutual funds have been able to provide relatively attractive returns. Look at Exhibit 13.3. It shows the average return performance on a variety of different types of mutual funds and is indicative of the kind of returns investors were able to achieve during the ten-year period through December 1994.

EXHIBIT 13.3

The Comparative Performance of Mutual Funds (for the 10-year period through December 1994)

The type of fund you invest in has a lot to do with the kind of return you can expect. For example, had you put $10,000 in a typical International Stock fund in 1985, that investment would have grown to nearly $40,000 by 1994; in contrast, if you had invested that same amount of money in a government bond fund, it would have grown to only about $22,175 by year-end '94.

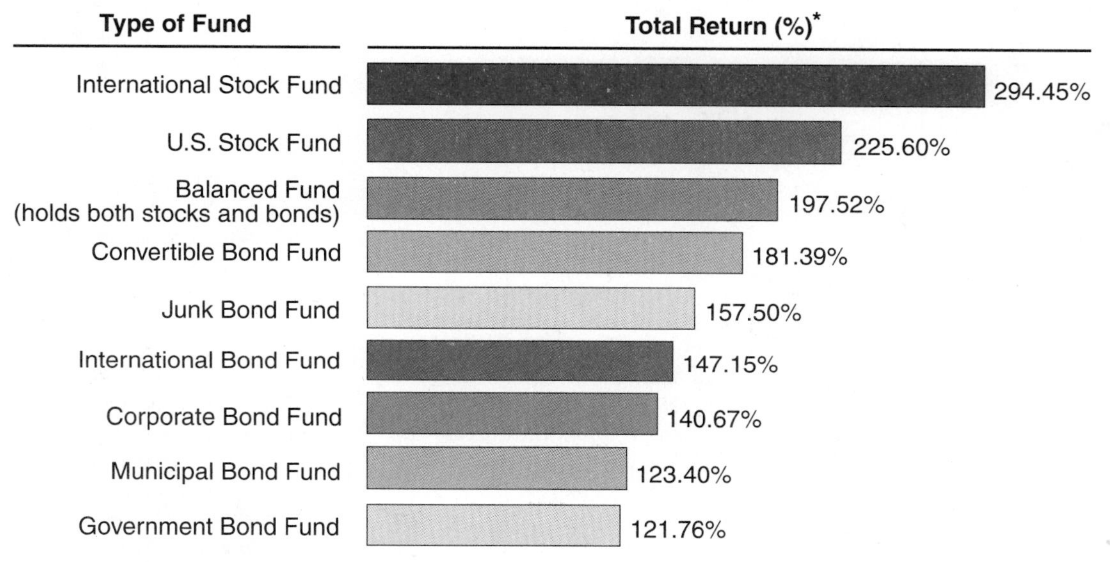

*Assumes reinvestment of all dividends and capital gains distributions.

Source: Morningstar's *Mutual Fund Performance Report,* February 1995.

With such return potential, it's easy to see why investors are so anxious to put their money into mutual funds—in many cases, it's probably safe to say that these returns are considerably better than what individual investors could have done on their own.

Convenience. The fact that mutual fund shares can be purchased through a variety of sources is still another reason for their appeal. Mutual funds make it easy to invest, and most do not require a great deal of capital to get started. They are relatively easy to acquire, they handle all the paperwork and recordkeeping, their prices are widely quoted, and it is usually possible to deal in fractional shares. Opening a mutual fund account is nearly as easy as opening a checking account. Just fill in a few blank spaces, send in the minimum amount of money, and you will be in business!

HOW MUTUAL FUNDS ARE ORGANIZED AND RUN

Although it's tempting to think of a mutual fund as a monolithic entity, that's really not accurate. Various functions—investing, recordkeeping, safekeeping and others—are split among two or more companies. Besides the fund itself, organized as a separate corporation or trust, here are the main players:

- The **management company** runs the fund's daily operations. These are the firms we know as Fidelity, Kemper, IDS, Dreyfus, Oppenheimer, and so forth, and they are the ones that create the funds in the first place. Usually, the management firm also serves as investment adviser to their clients.
- The **investment adviser** buys and sells the stocks or bonds and otherwise oversees the portfolio. Usually, there are three parties that

Issues in Money Management

Could Your Fund Go Under?

The 1990s were traumatic times for the nation's financial services industry. Savings and loans were already in trouble for fraud, mismanagement, and simply taking too many risks. The malaise also extended into the banking sector, and even some insurance companies were bogged down with junk bond-laden portfolios. One domino that did not fall, however, was the mutual fund sector. Obviously, you can lose money if your fund's stock or bond holdings decline in price, but there is little chance of loss stemming from fraud, scandal, or bankruptcy involving the fund management company itself. By transferring investment risk to shareholders, mutual fund companies sidestepped many problems that plagued their financial cousins.

In addition, the legal structure and heavy regulation of mutual funds offer key safeguards. A regular, open-end mutual fund is a separate corporation, or trust, owned by its shareholders, *not* by the firm that runs it. Consequently, the fund's assets *are placed in the custody of an independent third party, typically a trust or custodial bank.* "We do not have easy access to our shareholders' money," says Charles J. Tennes, a vice president with the GIT Investment Funds in Arlington, VA. "We have authority to buy and sell securities on their behalf, but the assets are held by someone else."

As another safeguard, each fund has a board of directors or trustees—at least 40 percent of whom must be independent of the management company—who monitor the management company. If the management firm was facing bankruptcy, the directors would liquidate or merge the fund, or find another outfit to run it. Shareholders elect and pay directors who can be sued for ignoring their fiduciary duties. Many independent directors are themselves fund shareholders.

As further protection, the management company and other affiliated parties can't engage in certain types of transactions with a fund. For example, the investment adviser cannot dump his or her holdings by selling them to the fund. Nor can the adviser affiliated with a brokerage charge the fund excessive commissions for conducting trades. These conflict-of-interest provisions are often considered the heart of the Investment Company Act of 1940.

Bob Pozen, general counsel and managing director of Fidelity Investments in Boston, believes there are other reasons for the lack of scandal in the mutual fund industry. First, he says, funds redeem investor shares upon demand, forcing funds to stick with liquid assets. Second, funds must value their holdings every day, a process known as marking-to-market. ". . . one of the big problems with insurance companies [was] that they didn't mark-to-market their assets daily. They were able to go a long time before anybody realized they had a problem," Pozen says. "You can't do that with mutual funds. You know the problems immediately."

Source: Adapted from Russ Wiles, "Checks and Balances: How Funds Are Organized," *Personal Investor,* September 1991, pp. 28-30.

participate in this phase of the operation: the *money manager,* who actually runs the portfolio and makes the buy and sell decisions; *security analysts,* who analyze securities and look for viable investment candidates; and *traders,* who try to buy and sell big blocks of securities at the best possible price.

- The **distributor** sells fund shares, either directly to the public or through certain authorized dealers (such as major brokerage houses and/or commercial banks). When you request a prospectus and sales literature, you deal with the distributor.
- The **custodian** physically safeguards the securities and other assets of a fund, without taking an active role in the investment decisions. To discourage foul play, an independent party (a bank, in most cases), serves in this capacity.
- The **transfer agent** keeps track of purchase and redemption requests from shareholders and maintains other shareholder records.

Each of these parties collects a fee for its services. However, actual ownership of a fund rests with the shareholders. With all the institutions—like banks, S&Ls, and insurance companies—that encountered serious financial problems in the recent past, one might be tempted to wonder if mutual funds are really all that safe. Well, as the *Issues in Money Management* box on page 530 reveals, because of all the safeguards, the chance of your losing any money from a mutual fund collapse is really quite low—almost nonexistent.

OPEN-END VERSUS CLOSED-END

While all mutual funds may be organized in pretty much the same way, there are some major differences that investors should be aware of. One way that funds differ is with respect to how they are structured. That is, funds can be set up either as *open-end companies,* which can sell an unlimited number of ownership shares, or as *closed-end companies,* which can issue only a limited number of shares.

Open-End Investment Companies. The term *mutual fund* is commonly used to denote an open-end investment company. Such organizations are the dominant type of investment company and account for well over 90 percent of assets under management. In an **open-end investment company,** investors actually buy their shares from, and sell them back to, the mutual fund itself. When they buy shares in the fund, the fund issues new shares of stock and fills the purchase order with these new shares. There is no limit to the number of shares the fund can issue, other than investor demand. Further, all open-end mutual funds stand behind their shares and buy them back when investors decide to sell. Thus, there is never any trading among individuals.

Both buy and sell transactions in a mutual fund are carried out at prices based on the current value of all the securities held in the fund's portfolio., This is known as the fund's **net asset value (NAV);** it is calculated at least once a day and represents the underlying value of a share of stock in a particular fund. NAV is found by taking the total market value of all securities held by the fund, subtracting any liabilities, and dividing the result by the number of shares outstanding. For example, if on a given day, the market value of all the securities held by the XYZ mutual fund equaled some $10 million, and if XYZ on that day had 500,000 shares outstanding, the fund's net asset value per share would amount to $20 ($10,000,000/500,000 = $20). This figure would then be used to derive the price at which the fund shares could be bought and sold.

Net asset value is included in the fund's quoted price and indicates the price at which an investor can *sell* shares. Consider, for example, *The Wall Street Journal* mutual fund quotations as shown on the next page.

The first price column is labeled "NAV." For example, Enterprise Capital Appreciation has a NAV $28.70 and an offer price of $30.13; that means the investor can *buy* shares in the fund at an offer price of $30.13 a share or *sell* them at the NAV of $28.70. (It's easy to remember which is the buy price and which is the sell price, because you, as the investor, always buy at the high price and sell at the low price.) The "NAV Chg." column shows the change in the price of the fund from one day to the next—here, the NAV of Enterprise Capital Appreciation went up 8 cents from the day before.

Closed-End Investment Companies. Whereas the term *mutual fund* is supposed to be used only with open-end funds, it is, as a practical matter, regularly used with closed-end investment companies as well. Basically, **closed-end investment companies** operate with a fixed number of shares outstanding and do *not* regularly issue new shares of stock. In effect, they have a capital structure like that of any other corporation, except that the corporation's business happens to be investing in marketable securities. Like open-end funds, closed-end investment companies have enjoyed remarkable growth in the past decade, or so. For while there were only 34 of these funds in existence in 1980, by year-end 1994, there were over 500 closed-end funds, with total net assets of $128 billion—still just

open-end investment company A company that can issue an unlimited number of shares which it buys and sells at a price based on the current market value of the securities it owns; also called a *mutual fund.*

net asset value (NAV) The price at which a mutual fund will buy back its own shares; NAV represents the current market value of all the securities the fund owns.

closed-end investment company An investment company that issues a fixed number of shares, which are themselves listed and traded on an organized securities exchange or in the OTC market.

The price you get when you **sell** shares (NAV)

The price you get when you **buy** shares (Offer Price)

	Fund	Inv. obj.	NAV	Offer Price	NAV Chg.	% Ret YTD	Max Initl. Chrg.	Total Exp. Ratio	
	Eaton V Traditional:								
	China p	ITL	13.20	13.86	–0.31	–25.3	4.750	2.4701	
	GovtObl p	BIN	10.46	10.98	–0.01	–1.8	4.750	1.5201	
	Growth p	GRO	7.35	7.72	–0.05	–7.9	4.750	0.9501	
	Inc Bos p	BHI	7.64	8.02	–0.01	–2.1	4.750	1.030	
	India p	ITL	9.93	10.43	–0.05	NS	4.750	NA	
	Invest p	S&B	6.66	6.99	–0.01	–3.4	4.750	0.9001	
	MunBond p	GLM	9.14	9.60	+0.01	–8.5	4.750	0.720	
	Spec Eq p	GRO	7.20	7.56	–0.02	–14.6	4.750	1.010	
	ST Trsy p	BST	57.37	57.37	...	+3.2	0.000	0.600	
	Stock p	G&I	11.29	11.85	–0.02	–7.7	4.750	0.960	
	Tot Rtn p	SEC	7.62	8.00	...	–12.7	4.750	1.3101	
	EclipBal	S&B	17.79	17.79	–0.01	–2.1	0.000	0.690	
	EclipEq	SML	12.12	12.12	–0.02	–9.2	0.000	1.120	
	Emerald Funds:								
	Balinst	S&B	9.49	NL	+0.02	NS	0.000	NA	
	EqA	GRO	10.48	10.97	+0.03	–9.5	4.500	0.860	
	Eqinst	GRO	10.51	NL	+0.03	NS	0.000	NA	
	FLTxEA	MFL	10.03	10.50	+0.04	–8.0	4.500	0.650	
	FLTxEI	MFL	10.03	NL	+0.03	NS	0.000	NA	
	MgdBdi	BND	9.59	NL	+0.02	NS	0.000	NA	
	SmCapl	SML	9.17	NL	–0.05	NS	0.000	NA	
	USGovA	BIN	9.75	10.21	+0.02	–3.5	4.500	0.640	
	USGovl	BIN	9.74	NL	+0.02	NS	0.000	NA	
	EmpBld	DNY	16.72	17.46	+0.01	–5.7	4.250	0.980	
	Endow	G&I	15.29	15.29	+0.03	–0.8	0.000	0.730	
	Enterprise Group:								
Enterprise Capital Appreciation →	CapA p	CAP	28.70	30.13	+0.08	–7.7	4.750	1.640	← A load fund that also charges a 12(b) - 1 fee (p)
	GvSec p	MTG	10.61	11.14	+0.02	–8.3	4.750	1.300	
	Gwth p	GRO	7.92	8.31	...	–4.1	4.750	1.600	
	Grinc p	G&I	17.01	17.86	+0.01	–2.9	4.750	1.500	
	HYBd p	BHI	10.72	11.25	...	–0.7	4.750	1.300	
	IntlGr p	ITL	16.64	17.47	–0.14	–4.6	4.750	2.000	
	SmCo	SML	4.98	5.23	–0.01	–5.9	4.750	NA	
	TE Inc p	GLM	12.72	13.35	+0.02	–6.8	4.750	1.250	
	Evergreen Funds:								
	Evergrn	GRO	13.51	NL	–0.05	–4.9	0.000	1.120	
	Found	S&B	12.14	NL	+0.03	–3.9	0.000	1.200	
	Glob RE	SEC	12.29	NL	–0.10	–16.7	0.000	1.560	
Evergreen Growth & Income →	GroInc	G&I	14.96	NL	–0.06	–2.9	0.000	1.260	← A true no-load fund
	Ltd Mkt	SML	19.32	NL	–0.06	–11.0	0.000	1.260	
	Mun CA	STM	9.82	NL	...	–1.9	0.000	0.520	
	MunlNat	ISM	9.42	NL	+0.02	–8.6	0.000	0.290	
	Retire	S&B	10.58	NL	...	–5.0	0.000	1.360	
	SI Mun	STM	9.98	NL	...	–1.6	0.000	0.580	
	Tot Rtn	EQI	17.06	NL	–0.03	–8.8	0.000	1.180	
	ExcelMld	SEC	3.18	3.33	...	–23.6	4.500	2.180	
	Excelsior Instl:								
	Balanced	...	6.95	6.95	...	NA	NA	NA	
	EqGrowth	...	6.81	6.81	–0.02	NA	NA	NA	
	Eqindex	...	7.04	7.04	+0.03	NA	NA	NA	
	ExcHY p	BHI	6.94	7.29	...	–3.5k	4.750	1.340	
	FAM Val	G&I	20.63	NL	–0.01	+1.1	0.000	1.390	
	FBL Series Fund:								
FBL Blue Chip →	BlChip t	G&I	18.31	18.31	–0.01	–2.3	0.000	1.830	← A fund with no initial load charge, but which has both a redemption fee & a 12(b)-1 fee (t)
	Growth t	G&I	12.44	12.44	–0.02	–7.1	0.000	1.600	
	HIGrBd t	BND	9.82	9.82	+0.01	–0.9	0.000	1.900	
	HIYldBd t	BHI	9.66	9.66	...	–3.0	0.000	2.000	
	Managed t	S&B	11.25	11.25	+0.02	–4.3	0.000	1.960	
	FFB Eq	CAP	9.88	10.35	+0.05	–7.0	4.500	1.250	
	FFBNJ	MNJ	9.96	10.43	+0.02	–6.9	4.500	0.140	
	FFB Lexicon:								
	CapApp	GRO	10.52	10.52	+0.04	–7.6	0.000	0.550	
	Fxinc	BIN	9.75	9.75	+0.01	–3.1	0.000	0.550	
	IntGv	BST	9.72	9.72	...	–2.1	0.000	0.550	
	SelValue p	G&I	11.47	11.47	+0.03	+1.8	0.000	0.390	
	SmCoGr	SML	10.19	10.19	–0.01	–13.7	0.000	0.430	
	FFTW Funds:								
	US Sht	BST	9.90	9.90	...	+3.5	0.000	0.480	
	WW Fxdin	WBD	9.37	9.37	+0.01	–1.8	0.000	0.870	
	WWShTmin	...	9.93	9.93	–0.01	NA	NA	NA	
	FGICShTmGv	BST	9.96	9.96	...	NS	0.000	NA	
	FMB Funds:								
	DivEC p	GRO	11.25	11.72	...	–2.4	4.000	1.500	
	DivE I	GRO	11.25	NL	...	–2.4	0.000	1.500	
	IntGC p	BST	9.66	9.96	...	–2.6	3.000	0.500	
	IntG I	BST	9.66	NL	...	–2.6	0.000	0.500	
	MITF p	IDM	10.03	10.34	+0.01	–2.5	3.000	0.350	
	MITF I	IDM	10.03	10.03	+0.01	–2.5	0.000	0.350	
	FPA Funds:								
	Caplt	GRO	19.23	20.57	–0.07	+3.0	6.500	1.030	
	Nwinc	BND	10.37	10.86	+0.01	+1.2	4.500	0.730	
FPA Paramount →	Parmt	G&I	13.96	14.93	...	+6.0	6.500	0.890	← A load fund—has a $6^1/_2$% front-end load
	Paren	G&I	21.22	22.70	–0.02	–3.4	6.500	1.020	
	Fairmt	CAP	22.31	NL	–0.21	–0.5	0.000	1.780	
	Fasclano	MID	17.52	NL	–0.07	–0.9	0.000	1.700	
	Federated Fortress:								
	AdjRt t	BST	9.36	9.36	...	–0.5	0.000	1.020	
	AmLdrFs	G&I	14.30	14.44	–0.01	–2.7	1.000	1.350	
Federated Fortress Bond Fund →	BondFd r	BND	8.98	9.07	...	–3.8	1.000	1.040	← A low-load fund with a redemption fee(r)
	EqincFS t	EQI	10.56	10.67	+0.01	–6.5	1.000	NA	
	GISI r	MTG	8.36	8.36	+0.02	–2.0	1.000	0.970	
Federated Fortress Municipal Income →	Muninc t	GLM	9.92	10.02	+0.03	–6.7	1.000	1.090	← A fund with a little of everything: a front-end load, back load, and 12(b)-1 fee(t)
	NYmunFS t	...	9.22	9.31	+0.03	NA	NA	NA	
	OHmunFS p	MOH	10.34	10.44	+0.03	–7.7	1.000	0.870	
	UtilFd r	SEC	11.75	11.87	...	–8.1	1.000	1.110	

Source: *The Wall Street Journal*, December 12, 1994.

a tiny fraction of the more than $2 trillion invested in open-end funds. Shares in closed-end investment companies are actively traded in the secondary market, just like any other common stock, but, unlike open-end funds, *all trading is done between investors in the open market*. The fund itself plays no role in either buy or sell transactions; once the shares are issued, the fund is out of the picture. By far, most closed-end investment companies are traded on the New York Stock Exchange, a few are on the American Exchange, and occasionally, some are traded in the OTC market or on some other exchange.

Many of the investment advisors that run closed-end funds (like Putnam, Dean Witter, Kemper, Nuveen, MFS, Scudder, and Templeton) also manage open-end funds, often with similar investment objectives. So, why would they do that? The answer is, because these are two different animals. While it may not appear so, there are some major differences between open- and closed-end funds. To begin with, because closed-end funds have a fixed amount of capital to work with, they don't have to worry about stock redemptions or new money coming into the fund. As such, they don't have to be concerned about keeping cash on hand to meet redemptions. Equally important, they can be more aggressive in their investment styles and invest in obscure yet attractive securities, even if they are not actively traded (since there'll be no pressure on the portfolio manager to cash-in these securities at inopportune times). And because they don't have new money flowing in all the time they don't have to worry about finding new investments. Instead, they can concentrate on a set portfolio of securities and do the best job they can in managing them. But that also puts added pressures on the money managers, since their investment styles and fund portfolios are closely monitored and judged by the market. That is, the share prices of closed-end companies are determined not only by their net asset values, but also by general supply and demand conditions in the market. As a result, depending on the market outlook and investor expectations, closed-end companies generally trade at a discount or premium to NAV. For example, a fund with a net asset value of $10 per share would be selling at a *discount* of $1 if it were trading at $9 and at a *premium* of $1 if it were quoted at a price of $11. Share price discounts can become quite large at times—for example, it is not unusual for discounts to amount to as much as 25 to 30 percent of net asset value. In contrast, price premiums occur less often and seldom exceed 10 to 15 percent.

TWO OTHER TYPES OF INVESTMENT COMPANIES

In addition to open- and closed-end mutual funds, there are two other types of investment companies that should be briefly discussed at this point. They are: (1) unit investment trusts, and (2) real estate investment trusts. The first type, a unit investment trust, is similar to open- and closed-end mutual funds to the extent that it, too, invests primarily in marketable securities, like stocks and bonds; real estate investment trusts, in contrast, invest primarily in various types of real estate or real estate-related types of investments, like mortgages.

Unit Investment Trust. A **unit investment trust** represents little more than an interest in an *unmanaged* pool of investments. In essence, a portfolio of securities is simply held in safekeeping for investors under conditions set down in a trust agreement. The portfolios usually consist of corporate, government, or municipal bonds, with tax-free municipal bonds and mortgage-backed securities being the most popular type of investment vehicle. There is *no trading* in the portfolios, and as a result, the returns, or yields, are fixed and usually predictable—at least for the short run. Unit trusts are like second cousins to mutual funds: Unlike conventional mutual funds, whose securities are actively traded, a trust sponsor simply puts together a portfolio of securities, and that's it. After the securities are deposited with a trustee, no new securities are added and, with rare exceptions, none are sold.

Various sponsoring brokerage houses put together these diversified pools of securities and then sell units of the pool to investors (each *unit* being like a share in a mutual fund). For example, a brokerage house might put together a diversified pool of corporate bonds that amounts to, say, $100 million. The sponsoring firm would then sell units

unit investment trust A type of investment vehicle whereby the trust sponsors put together a fixed/unmanaged portfolio of securities and then sell ownership units in the portfolio to individual investors.

in this pool to the investing public at a price of $1,000 per unit (a common price for these securities). The sponsoring organization does little more than routine recordkeeping, and it services the investments by collecting coupons and distributing the income (often on a monthly basis) to the holders of the trust units. Trusts appeal primarily to income-oriented investors who are looking for monthly (rather than semi-annual) income. But be careful, as these investments do have their dark sides. For one thing, they tend to be very costly and involve substantial up-front transactions costs. In addition, various strategies are used to artificially pump up yields and make returns look better than they really are; and contrary to what many investors believe (or are told), you *can* lose money on these things if premium-priced bonds in the trust are called for pre-payment.

Real Estate Investment Trusts. A **real estate investment trust (REIT)** is a type of closed-end investment company that invests money in mortgages and various types of real estate investments. A REIT is like a mutual fund in that it sells shares of stock to the investing public and uses the proceeds, along with borrowed funds, to invest in a portfolio of real estate investments. The investor, therefore, owns a part of the real estate portfolio held by the real estate investment trust. There are three basic types of REITs: those that invest in *properties,* such as shopping centers, hotels, apartments, and office buildings (the so-called *property,* or *equity,* REITs); mortgage REITs—those that invest in mortgages; and *hybrid* REITs, which invest in both properties and mortgages. Mortgage REITs tend to be more income oriented—they emphasize their high current yields (which is to be expected from a security that basically invests in debt). In contrast, while equity REITs may promote their attractive current yields, most of them also offer the potential for earning varying amounts of capital gains (as their property holdings appreciate in value). REITs must abide by the Real Estate Investment Trust Act of 1960, which established requirements for forming a REIT, as well as rules and procedures for making investments and distributing income. Since they are required to pay out nearly all of their earnings to the owners, they do quite a bit of borrowing to obtain funds for their investments (although, in today's market environment, they do try to keep the amount of leverage they employ at reasonable levels).

A number of insurance companies, mortgage bankers, commercial banks, and real estate investment companies have formed REITs, many of which are traded on the major securities exchanges. Like mutual funds, the income earned by a REIT is not taxed, but the income distributed to the owners is designated and taxed as ordinary income. Although the poor performance of REITs during the 1973 to 1975 recession caused them to fall into disfavor among investors, subsequent restructuring of their portfolios has rekindled a good deal of interest in this form of investing.

Indeed, in 1995, there were over 125 such investment companies. Some of the better known and more actively traded REITs include Federal Realty, Health Care Property Investors, New Plan Realty, Nationwide Health Properties, Washington REIT, and Weingarten Realty Investors. Your stockbroker should be able to give you advice with respect to REITs and help you select those that will be consistent with your investment objectives.

SOME IMPORTANT COST CONSIDERATIONS

When you buy or sell shares in a *closed-end* investment company, you pay a commission just as you would with any other listed or OTC common stock transaction. This is not so with *open-end* funds, however. In particular, the cost of investing in an open-end mutual fund depends on the types of fees and load charges that a fund levies on its investors.

Load Funds. Most open-end mutual funds are so-called **load funds,** since they charge a commission when the shares are purchased. Load charges can be fairly substantial and amount to as much as 7¼ percent of the *purchase* price of the shares. Normally there is no charge when you sell your shares. It is easy to find the amount of the load charge—it is part of the price quotation system and is found by taking the difference between the fund's offer price and its NAV. For example, refer back to the quote for the Enterprise Capital Appreciation fund. The difference between its offer price ($30.13) and NAV ($28.70) represents its load charge of $1.43 a share and is the commission you would pay for each share of Enterprise Capital Appreciation. This amounts to a load charge of 4.75 percent of the offer price—which you can calculate yourself by dividing the load charge (of $1.43) by the offer price (of $30.13), or just look in the quotations and refer to the next-to-last column marked, "Max. Initial Chrg," which provides front-end load charges in percentage terms.

Compared to what it costs to buy and sell common stock, the costs of many load funds are pretty steep, even after taking into account the fact that you normally pay no commission on the sale of most funds! Since 1992, the *maximum* load charge has been set at 7¼ percent of the purchase price. However, most mutual funds offer quantity discounts to investors who buy in large blocks (usually 1,000 or more shares). In addition, a growing number of so-called **low-load funds** charge commissions of only 1 to 3 percent; on the other hand, there's also an increasing number of **back-end load funds,** which charge a commission—or a so-called *redemption fee*—when you *sell* your shares.

No-Load Funds. Some open-end investment companies charge you nothing at all to buy their funds; these are known as **no-load funds.** It is easy to spot no-loads—just look for the letters "N.L." under the "Offer Price" column in mutual fund price quotes. For example, the Evergreen Funds shown in our illustrative quotes on page 532 are no-load funds. This means that the Evergreen Growth and Income fund can be *bought and sold* at its NAV price of $14.96 a share. Actually, there are relatively few pure no-loads left today, charging nothing to buy, sell, or hold their funds! Probably less than 30 percent of the funds sold today are true no-loads; all the rest charge some type of load or fee. Indeed, even funds that don't have front-end loads (and, thus, may appear as no-loads) can have back-end load charges that you'd have to pay when you sell your fund shares, or something called a 12(b)-1 fee, which you would pay for as long as you hold your shares.

12(b)-1 Fees. Also known as *hidden loads,* **12(b)-1 fees** have been allowed by the SEC since 1980, and were originally designed to help no-load funds cover their distribution and marketing expenses. Not surprisingly, their popularity spread rapidly among fund distributors, so that they are now used by many open-end mutual funds. The fees are assessed annually and can amount to as much as 1 percent of assets under management. In good markets and bad, they're paid, right off the top. And that can take its toll. Consider, for instance, $10,000 in a fund that charges a 1 percent 12(b)-1 fee. That translates into an annual charge of *$100 a year,* certainly not an insignificant amount of money. Always on the look-out for new ways to collect fees, the latest trend in mutual fund fees is the so-called *multiple class sales charge.* You'll find such arrangements at firms like American Capital, Dryfus, Merrill Lynch, MFS, Keystone, Smith Barney, Prudential, and others. The way it works is that the mutual fund will issue different classes of stocks on the same fund or portfolio of securities. Thus, rather than having just one class of stock outstanding, there might be three of them: Class A shares might have normal (relatively high) front-end loads; Class B stock might have no front-end loads, but substantial back-end loads along with a modest annual 12(b)-1 fee; and finally, Class C shares might carry maximum 12(b)-1 fees and nothing else. In other words, you choose your own poison.

To try and bring some semblance of order to fund charges and fees, in 1992, the SEC instituted a series of caps on mutual fund fees. Under the 1992 regulations, a mutual fund cannot charge more than 8½ percent in *total sales charges and fees,* and that includes front- and back-end loads, as well as 12(b)-1 fees. Thus, if a fund charges a 5 percent front-end load and a 1% 12(b)-1 fee, it can charge a maximum of only 2½ percent in back-end load charges—

real estate investment trust (REIT) A business that accumulates money for investment in real estate ventures by selling shares to investors; like a mutual fund, except REITs confine their investments to real estate and/or mortgages.

load fund A mutual fund on which a transaction cost (associated with the purchase of shares) is levied.

low-load fund A mutual fund in which commissions charged on purchases of shares range between only 1 and 3 percent of the purchase price.

back-end load fund A commission charged for redeeming mutual fund shares.

no-load fund A mutual fund on which no transaction fees are charged.

12(b)-1 fee A type of fee that's charged annually and which is supposed to be used to offset the promotion and selling expenses of a mutual fund; known as a *hidden load* because it's often used by funds as an indirect way of charging commissions.

otherwise, it will violate the 8½ percent cap. In addition, it set a 1 percent cap on annual 12(b)-1 fees and perhaps more significantly, stated that true "no-load" funds cannot charge more than 0.25 percent in annual 12(b)-1 fees (if they do, they have to drop the no-load label in their sales and promotional material).

Management Fees. The **management fee** is the cost you incur to hire the professional money managers to run the fund's portfolio of investments. These fees are also assessed annually and usually range from less than half a percent to 2½ percent of assets under management. All funds—whether they are load or no-load, open- or closed-end—have these fees; and like 12(b)-1 fees, they bear watching, since high management fees will take their toll on performance. As a rule, the size of the management fee is totally unrelated to the fund's performance—you'll pay the same amount whether it's been a winning year or a real loser. Expense ratios for individual funds are really quite easy to follow, since they are published each Monday in *The Wall Street Journal.* Take another look at the quotations on page 532—the last column in the exhibit is the "Total Expense Ratio." That figure represents the latest administrative, management, and 12(b)-1 fees levied by the fund in question. Note, in the quotations, that the Enterprise Capital Appreciation fund has an annual expense ratio of 1.64 percent of assets under management, whereas FFB Lexicon's Capital Appreciation fund has a ratio of only 0.55 percent. So, why the big difference? Probably, in large part, because Enterprise has an annual 12(b)-1 charge while FFB Lexicon does not.

Keeping Track of Fund Fees and Loads. Critics of the mutual fund industry have come down hard on the proliferation of fund fees and charges. Indeed, some would argue that all the different kinds of charges and fees are really meant to do one thing: confuse the investor. The fact is that a lot of funds were going to great lengths—lower a cost here, tack on a fee there, hide a charge somewhere else—to make themselves look like something they weren't. The funds were following the letter of the law, and, indeed, they were fully disclosing all their expenses and fees. The trouble was that the funds were able to neatly hide all but the most conspicuous charges in a bunch of legalese. Fortunately, steps have been taken to bring fund fees and loads out into the open.

For one thing, fund charges are more fully reported by the financial press. You don't have to look any farther than the *mutual fund quotations* found in *The Wall Street Journal* and most other major papers. For example, refer back to the quotations on page 532; notice the use of the letters "r," "p," and "t." If you see an "r" behind a fund's name, it means the fund charges some type of *redemption fee,* or back-end load, when you sell your shares; this is the case, for example, with the Federated Fortress Bond Fund. The use of a "p," in contrast, means the fund levies a *12(b)-1 fee,* which you'll have to pay, for example, if you invest in the Enterprise Capital Appreciation Fund. Finally, a "t" indicates funds that charge *both* redemption fees and 12(b)-1 fees; notice that's what you get with the Federated Fortress Municipal Income Fund. In fact, if you look closely at the quotations, you'll see that this Municipal Income fund not only levies redemption and 12(b)-1 fees *but also has a front-end load*—as indicated by the difference in its NAV and offer price. The point is: Don't be surprised to find load funds that also charge redemption and/or 12(b)-1 fees; and the same goes for no-load funds, as they're allowed to charge annual 12(b)-1 fees of 0.25 percent and still call themselves "no-load" funds. The quotations, of course, tell you only the *kinds* of fees charged by the funds; they don't tell you how much is charged. To get the specifics on the amount charged, you'll have to turn to the fund itself.

All (open-end) mutual funds are required to *fully disclose* their expenses in a standardized, easy-to understand format. Every fund prospectus must contain, right up front, a fairly detailed *fee table,* much like the one illustrated in Exhibit 13.4. Notice that this table has three parts. The first specifies all *shareholder transaction costs.* In effect, this tells you what it's going to cost to buy and sell shares in the mutual fund. The next section lists all the *annual operating expenses* of the fund. Showing these expenses as a percentage of average net assets, the fund must break out management fees, those elusive 12(b)-1 fees, and any other expenses. The third section provides a rundown of the *total cost over time* of buying, selling, and owning the fund. This part of the table contains both transaction and operating expenses and shows what the total costs would be over hypothetical 1-, 3-, 5-, and 10-year holding periods. To ensure consistency and comparability, the funds must follow a rigid set of guidelines when constructing the illustrative costs.

EXHIBIT 13.4

Mutual Fund Expense Disclosure Table

Mutual funds are now required by the SEC to make full disclosure of load charges, redemption fees, and annual expenses in a three-part table like the one shown here; and the table must be conspicuously placed in the front part of the prospectus, not hidden somewhere in the back.

Expenses and Cost of Investing in the Fund

The following information is provided in order to assist investors in understanding the transaction costs and annual expenses associated with investing in the Fund.

A. Shareholder Transaction Costs:

Sales Load on Purchases	2%
Sales Load on Reinvested Dividends	None
Redemption Fees or Deferred Sales Charges	None
Exchange (or Conversion Fees)	None

B. Annual Fund Operating Expenses:
(as a percentage of average net assets)

Management Fees	0.40%
12(b)-1 Fees	None
Other Expenses (estimated)	0.32%

C. Example of Fund Expenses Over Time:

You would pay the following total expenses over time on a $1,000 investment, assuming a 5% annual return, and a complete redemption of the investment at the end of each indicated time period:

1-year	3-years	5-years	10-years
$27	$43	$59	$108

Source: The prospectus of a major mutual fund.

BUYING AND SELLING FUNDS

Buying and selling shares of *closed-end investment companies* is no different from buying shares of common stock. The transactions are executed on listed exchanges or in the OTC market through brokers or dealers who handle the orders in the usual way. They are subject to the normal transaction costs; and because they are treated like any other listed or OTC stock, their shares can even be margined or sold short. The situation is considerably different, however, with *open-end funds.* There are several ways of acquiring such shares, depending on whether the fund is load or no-load. Regardless of type, however, the fund should provide you with a recent prospectus that explains its operations and other pertinent financial matters. Unfortunately, the prospectuses put out by a lot of mutual funds today are not as extensive as they used to be and in many cases, are little more than warmed over sales pitches. So be careful when using such information. Instead of, or in addition to, the fund's prospectus, ask for a copy of its *Statement of Additional Information,* which provides detailed information on the fund's investment objectives, portfolio composition, management, and past performance. Whether it's the prospectus or the fund's Statement of Additional Information, the bottom line is these publications should be required reading for anybody who's thinking about investing in a mutual fund. Note: The SEC is currently conducting a one-year (1995-96) test of a new, slimmed-down prospectus, tentatively called a *fund profile,* which is meant to provide, on one page and in simple, straightforward language, key information about a fund.

In the case of load funds, investors buy the stocks from a broker or through salespeople employed by the funds—not surprisingly, many of these funds carry the full $7\frac{1}{4}$ percent load charge, or something close to it. Most brokerage firms are authorized to sell shares in a variety of load funds, and this is the easiest and most convenient way of buying funds for investors who have established

management fee A fee paid to the professionals who administer a mutual fund's portfolio.

brokerage accounts. Sometimes, however, the fund may not be sold through brokerage houses, in which case the investor would deal directly with the fund's commissioned salespeople—individuals who are employed by the mutual fund for the sole purpose of selling its shares. If you happen to be interested in a no-load, or perhaps even a low-load fund, you may be pretty much on your own. You'll have to write or call the mutual fund directly (most have 1-800 numbers) in order to obtain information. You will then receive an order form and instructions on how to buy shares; no salesperson will ever call on you. To complete the transaction, you simply mail your check, along with the completed order form, to the mutual fund or its designated agent. Before you go through all that, however, check with your bank; if it's a major (good-sized) commercial bank, it may be authorized to sell a wide variety of mutual funds. Indeed, during the past few years, a lot of big mutual funds have made arrangements to sell their products through major banking and other financial institutions around the country—and at no added cost to you. Thus, you may be able to find just the fund you're looking for right in your local bank.

Selling shares in a fund is also a do-it-yourself affair, whether the fund is load or no-load. Because brokers and salespeople usually don't make anything on fund *sales,* they have little motivation to execute sell orders. As a result, you may find you'll have to redeem your fund shares by directly notifying the mutual fund (by mail) of your intention to sell. The fund then buys the shares back and mails you a check. But before selling your fund shares this way, check to see if the fund offers *phone switching*. This service is available from a number of investment companies, and it enables you to simply pick up the phone to move money from one fund to another—the only constraint is that the funds must be managed by the same investment company. Most companies charge little or nothing for these shifts, although funds that offer free exchange privileges often place a limit on the number of times you can switch each year. (We'll discuss this service in more detail later in the chapter when we cover *conversion privileges*.)

Concept Check

13-1. What is a mutual fund? Discuss the mutual fund concept; why are diversification and professional management so important?

13-2. Briefly describe how a mutual fund is organized. Who are the key players in a typical mutual fund organization?

13-3. Briefly define each of the following:
- **a.** *Closed-end investment company.*
- **b.** *Open-end investment company.*
- **c.** *Unit investment trust.*
- **d.** *Real estate investment trust.*

13-4. What is the difference between a load fund and no-load fund? Are there some advantages to either type? What is a *12(b)-1* fund? Can such a fund operate as a no-load fund?

13-5. Briefly describe a *back-end load*; a *low load*; a hidden load. How can you tell what kind of fees and charges a fund has?

TYPES OF FUNDS AND FUND SERVICES

LG3
LG4

Investors today can choose from a wide array of different types of mutual funds—indeed, no matter what your investment objective, the chances are you'll be able to find a fund to meet your needs. In addition, most mutual funds offer a full menu of investor services: everything from automatic reinvestment plans to retirement programs. As an investor, what type(s) of mutual fund(s) would you be most interested in? What types of investor services would you look for? These are important questions for mutual fund investors—stop to think about them before reading on.

Some mutual funds specialize in stocks and others in bonds; some funds have maximum capital gains as their investment objective, and some seek high income. Some funds thus will appeal to speculators and others primarily to income-oriented investors. Every fund has a particular investment objective, some of the more common ones being capital appreciation, income, tax-exempt income, preservation of investment capital, or some combination thereof. Disclosure of a fund's investment objective is required by the SEC, and each fund is expected to do its best to conform to its stated investment policy and objective. Categorizing funds according to their investment policies and objectives is widely practiced in the mutual fund industry, as it tends to reflect similarities not only in how the funds manage their money, but also in their risk and return characteristics. Some of the more popular types of mutual funds include growth, aggressive growth, equity-income, balanced, growth-and-income, bond, money market, sector, socially responsible, international, and asset allocation funds. Let's now take a look at the various types of mutual funds to see what they are and how they operate. After we do that, we'll look at the kinds of investor services these funds offer.

TYPES OF FUNDS

Growth Funds. The objective of a *growth fund* is simple—capital appreciation. Long-term growth and capital gains are the primary goals of such funds, and as a result they invest principally in common stocks that have above-average growth potential. Because of the uncertain nature of their investment income, growth funds are believed to involve a fair amount of risk exposure. They are usually viewed as long-term investment vehicles that are most suitable for the more aggressive investor who wants to build capital and has little interest in current income.

Aggressive Growth Funds. These are the so-called performance funds that tend to increase in popularity when the markets heat up. *Aggressive growth funds* are highly speculative investment vehicles that seek large profits from capital gains; in many respects, they are really an extension of the growth fund concept. Many are fairly small, with portfolios consisting mainly of high-flying common stocks. Also known as "Capital Appreciation" or "Small Cap" funds, they often buy stocks of small, unseasoned companies, stocks with relatively high price/earnings multiples, and stocks whose prices are highly volatile. Some of these funds even go so far as to use leverage in their portfolios (that is, they buy stocks on margin by borrowing part of the purchase price). All this is designed, of course, to yield big returns. However, aggressive growth funds are also highly speculative and are perhaps the most volatile of all the fund types. When the markets are good, these funds do well; when the markets are bad, they typically experience substantial losses.

Equity-Income Funds. *Equity-income funds* emphasize current income, which they provide by investing primarily in high-yielding common stocks. Capital preservation is also a goal of these funds, and so is some amount of capital gains, although capital appreciation is not their primary objective. They invest heavily in high-grade common stocks, some convertible securities and preferred stocks, and occasionally even junk bonds or certain types of high-grade foreign bonds. They like securities that generate hefty dividend yields, but also consider potential price appreciation over the longer haul. In general, because of their emphasis on dividends and current income, these funds tend to hold higher-quality securities that are subject to less price volatility than the market as a whole. They're generally viewed as a fairly low-risk way of investing in stocks.

Balanced Funds. *Balanced funds* are so named because they tend to hold a balanced portfolio of both stocks and bonds, and they do so for the purpose of generating a well-balanced return of both current income and long-term capital gains. In many respects, they're a lot like equity-income funds, except that balanced funds usually put much more into fixed-income securities; generally they keep at least 25 percent to 50 percent of their portfolios in bonds, and sometimes more. The bonds are used principally to provide current income, and stocks are selected mainly for their long-term growth potential. The funds can, of course, shift the emphasis in their security holdings one way or the other. Clearly, the more the fund leans toward fixed-income securities, the more income-oriented it will be. For the most part, balanced funds tend to confine their investing to high-grade securities. As such, they're usually considered to be a relatively safe form of investing, one where you can earn a competitive rate of return without having to endure a lot of price volatility.

Growth-and-Income Funds. Like balanced funds, *growth-and-income funds* also seek a balanced return made up of both current income and long-term capital gains, but they place a greater emphasis on growth of capital. Moreover, unlike balanced funds, growth-and-income funds put most of their money into equities—indeed, it's not unusual for these funds to have 80 percent to 90 percent of their capital in common stocks. They tend to confine most of their investing to high-quality issues, so you can expect to find a lot of growth-oriented blue-chip stocks in their portfolios, along with a fair amount of high-quality income stocks. One of the big appeals of these funds is the fairly substantial returns many of them have been able to generate over the long haul. But then, these funds do involve a fair amount of risk, if for no other reason than the emphasis they place on stocks and capital gains. Consequently, growth-and-income funds are most suitable for those investors who can tolerate their risk and price volatility.

Bond Funds. As their name implies, *bond funds* invest exclusively in various kinds and grades of bonds. Income is their primary investment objective, although they do not ignore capital gains. There are three important advantages to buying shares in bond funds rather than investing directly in bonds. First, bond funds generally are more liquid; second, they offer a cost-effective way of achieving a high degree of diversification in an otherwise expensive investment vehicle (most bonds carry minimum denominations of $1,000 to $5,000, or more); and third, bond funds will automatically reinvest interest and other income, thereby allowing the investor to earn fully compounded rates of return.

Although bond funds are usually considered to be a fairly conservative form of investment, they are not totally without risk, since the prices of the bonds held in the funds' portfolios will fluctuate with changing interest rates. Though many of the funds are basically conservative, a growing number are becoming increasingly aggressive—in fact, much of the growth that bond funds have experienced recently can be attributed to this new investment attitude. No matter what your tastes, you'll find there's a full menu of bond funds available, including:

- *Government bond funds,* which invest in U.S. Treasury and agency securities.
- *Mortgage-backed bond funds,* which put their money mostly into various types of mortgage-backed securities issued by agencies of the U.S. government (like GNMA issues). These funds appeal to investors not only because they provide diversification and a more affordable way to get into these securities, but also because they have a provision that allows investors (if they so choose) to reinvest the *principal* portion of the monthly cash flow, thereby enabling them to preserve, rather than consume, their capital.
- *High-grade corporate bond funds,* which invest chiefly in investment-grade securities rated triple-B or better.
- *High-yield corporate bond funds,* which are risky investments that buy *junk bonds* for the yields they offer.
- *Convertible bond funds,* which invest primarily in (domestic and possibly foreign) securities that can be converted or exchanged into common stocks; by investing in convertible bonds and preferreds, the funds offer investors some of the price stability of bonds, along with the capital appreciation potential of stocks.
- *Municipal bond funds,* which invest in tax-exempt securities, and which are suitable for investors looking for tax-free income. Like their corporate counterparts, municipals can also come out as either high-grade or high-yield funds. A special type of municipal bond fund is the so-called *single-state* fund, which invests in the municipal issues of only one state, thus producing (for residents of that state) interest income that is *fully* exempt from not only federal taxes, but state (and possibly even local/city) taxes as well.
- *Intermediate-term bond funds,* which invest in bonds with maturities of seven to ten years, or less, and offer not only attractive yields but relatively low price volatility as well; the shorter (two to five year) intermediate-term funds can also be used as substitutes for money market investments by investors looking for higher returns on their money, especially when short-term rates are way down (like they were in 1993).

Money Market Mutual Funds. From the introduction of the very first *money fund* in 1972, the concept of investing in a portfolio of short-term money market instruments caught on like wildfire. The reason for their popularity is really quite simple: money funds gave investors with modest amounts of capital access to the higher-yielding end of the money market, where many instruments require minimum investments of $100,000, or more. Today, there are about 900 money funds that, together, hold about half a trillion dollars in assets. Actually, there are several different kinds of money market mutual funds. **General-purpose money funds** essentially invest in any and all types of money market investment vehicles, from Treasury bills to corporate commercial paper and bank certificates of deposit. They invest their money wherever they can find attractive short-term returns. The vast majority of money funds are of this type. The **tax-exempt money fund** limits its investments to tax-exempt municipal securities with very short (30- to 90-day) maturities. Since their income is free from federal income tax, they appeal predominantly to investors in high tax brackets. **Government securities money funds** were established as a way of meeting investors' concern for safety. In essence, these funds eliminate any risk of default by confining their investments to Treasury bills and other short-term securities of the U.S. government or its agencies (such as the Federal National Mortgage Association).

Money funds are highly liquid investment vehicles and are very low in risk, since they are virtually immune to capital loss. However, the interest income they produce tends to follow interest rate conditions, and as such, the returns to shareholders are subject to the ups and downs of market interest rates. (Money funds were discussed more fully in Chapter 4, along with other short-term investment vehicles.)

Sector Funds. As its name implies, a *sector fund* restricts its investments to a particular sector of the market. In effect, these funds concentrate their investment holdings in the one or more industries that make up the targeted sector. For example, a *health care* sector fund would confine its investments to those industries that make up this segment of the market: drug companies, hospital management firms, medical suppliers, and biotech concerns. Its portfolio would then consist of promising growth stocks from these industries. The underlying investment objective of sector funds is *capital gains*. In many respects, they are similar to growth funds and thus should be considered speculative in nature.

The idea behind the sector fund concept is that the really attractive returns come from small segments of the market. Thus, rather than diversifying the portfolio across wide segments of the market, you should put your money where the action is. This notion may warrant consideration by the more aggressive investor who is willing to take on the added risks that often accompany these funds. Among the more popular sector funds are those that concentrate their investments in the so-called "glamour" industries: energy, financial services, gold and precious metals, leisure and entertainment, natural resources, electronics, chemicals, computers, telecommunications, utilities, and health care.

Socially Responsible Funds. For some, investing is far more than just cranking out some financial ratios. To these investors, the security selection process doesn't end with bottom lines, P/E ratios, growth rates, and betas; rather, it also includes the *active, explicit consideration of moral, ethical, and environmental issues*. The idea is that social concerns should play just as big a role in the investment decision as profits and other financial matters. Not surprisingly, there are a number of funds today that cater to such investors; known as **socially responsible funds,** they actively and directly incorporate morality and ethics into the investment decision. These funds will only consider socially responsible companies for inclusion in their portfolios—if a company doesn't meet certain moral, ethical, and/or environmental tests, they simply won't consider buying the stock, no matter how good the bottom line looks. Generally speaking, these funds abstain from investing in companies that derive revenues from tobacco, alcohol, or gambling; are weapons contractors; or operate nuclear power plants. In addition, the funds tend to favor firms that produce "responsible" products and/or services, have strong employee relations, have positive environmental records, and are socially responsive to the communities in which they operate. While these screens

general-purpose money fund A money market mutual fund that invests in virtually any type of short-term investment vehicle, so long as it offers an attractive rate of return.

tax-exempt money fund A money market mutual fund that limits investments to tax-exempt municipal securities with short maturities.

government securities money fund A money market mutual fund that limits its investments to short-term securities of the U.S. government and its agencies, thus eliminating any default risk.

socially responsible fund A type of mutual fund that puts social concerns on the same level of importance as financial returns, investing only in companies that meet certain moral, ethical, and/or environmental tests.

may seem to eliminate a lot of stocks from consideration, these funds (most of which are fairly small) still have plenty of securities to choose from, so it's not all that difficult for them to keep their portfolios fully invested. As far as performance is concerned, the general perception is that there's a price to pay for socially responsible investing in the form of lower average returns. That's not too surprising, however, for as you add more investment hurdles or screens, you're likely to reduce return potential. But for those who truly believe in socially responsible investing, perhaps they are willing to put their money where their mouths are!

International Funds. In their search for higher yields and better returns, American investors have shown a growing interest in foreign securities. Sensing an opportunity, the mutual fund industry was quick to respond with a proliferation of so-called **international funds**—a type of mutual fund that does all or most of its investing in foreign securities. Just look at the number of international funds around today versus a few years ago. In 1985, there were only about 40 of these funds; by 1994, that number had grown to over 350! The fact is, a lot of people would like to invest in foreign securities but simply don't have the experience or know-how to do so. International funds may be just the ticket for such investors, *provided they have at least a basic appreciation of international economics.* Since these funds deal with the international economy, balance of trade positions, and currency valuations, investors should have a fundamental understanding of what these issues are and how they can affect fund returns.

Technically, the term *international fund* is used to describe a type of fund that *invests exclusively in foreign securities,* often confining their activities to specific geographical regions (like Mexico, Australia, Europe, or the Pacific Rim). In addition, there's a special class of international funds, known as *global funds,* which invest not only in foreign securities, *but also in U.S. companies*—usually multinational firms. As a rule, global funds provide more diversity and, with access to both foreign and domestic markets, can go where the action is. Regardless of whether they're global or international (from here on out, we'll use the term "international" to apply to both), you'll find just about any type of fund you could possibly want in the international sector. There are international *stock* funds, international *bond* funds, even international *money market* funds; in addition, there are aggressive growth funds, balanced funds, long-term growth funds, high-grade bond funds, and so forth. Thus, no matter what your investment philosophy or objective, you're likely to find what you're looking for in the international area.

Basically, these funds attempt to take advantage of international economic developments in two ways: (1) by capitalizing on changing foreign market conditions, and (2) by positioning themselves to benefit from devaluation of the dollar. They do so because they can make money not only from rising share prices in a foreign market, but, perhaps just as important, from a falling dollar (which, in itself, produces capital gains to American investors in foreign securities and/or international funds). Many of these funds, however, will attempt to protect their investors from currency exchange risks by using various types of *hedging strategies.* That is, by using foreign currency options and futures (or some other type of derivative product), the fund will try to eliminate (or reduce) the effects of currency exchange rates. Some funds, in fact, do this on a permanent basis—in essence, these funds hedge away exchange risk so they can concentrate on the higher returns that the foreign securities themselves offer. Most others are only occasional users of currency hedges and will employ them only if they feel there's a real chance of a substantial swing in currency values. But even with currency hedging, international funds are still considered to be fairly high-risk investments and should only be used by investors who understand and are able to tolerate such risks.

Asset Allocation Funds. Studies have shown that the most important decision an investor can make is to decide where to allocate his or her investment assets. This is known as *asset allocation,* and, as we saw in Chapter 12, basically involves deciding how you're going to divide up your investments among *different types of securities.* For example, what portion of your money is going to be devoted to money market securities, what portion to stocks, what portion to bonds? Asset allocation deals in broad terms and does not address individual security selection. Even so, as strange as it may sound, asset allocation has been found to be a far more important determinant of total returns on a portfolio than individual security selection. Because a lot of individual investors have a tough time making asset allocation decisions, the mutual fund industry has, not surprisingly, created a product to do the job for them. Known as *asset allocation funds,* these funds spread investors' money across all different types of markets. That is, while most mutual funds concentrate on one type of investment—whether stocks, bonds, or money market securities—asset allocation funds put money into all these markets. Many of them also include foreign securities in their asset allocation scheme and some may even include inflation-resistant investments, like gold or real estate.

These funds are designed for people who want to hire fund managers not only to select individual securities for them, but also to make the strategic decision of how to allocate money among the various markets. Here's how many asset allocation funds work. The money manager will establish a desired allocation mix—it might look something like this: 50 percent of the portfolio goes to U.S. stocks, 10 percent to foreign securities, 30 percent to bonds, and 10 percent to money market securities. Securities are then purchased for the fund in this proportion, and the overall portfolio maintains the desired mix. Actually, each segment of the fund is managed almost as a separate portfolio, so securities within, say, the stock portion are bought, sold, and held as the market dictates. Now, here's what really separates asset allocation funds from the rest of the pack: *as market conditions change over time, the asset allocation mix will change as well.* Thus, if the U.S. stock market starts to soften, funds will be moved out of stocks to some other area; as a result, the stock portion of the portfolio may drop to, say, 35 percent and the foreign securities portion may increase to 25 percent. Of course, there's no assurance that the money manager will make the right moves at the right time, but that's the idea behind these funds.

Asset allocation funds are supposed to provide investors with one-stop shopping; that is, just find an asset allocation fund or two that fits your needs and invest in it (or them), rather than going out and buying a couple stock funds, a couple bond funds, and so on. The success of these funds rests not only on how good a security picker the money manager is, but also on how good a job he or she does in timing the market and moving funds among different segments of the market. The *Issues in Money Management* box on page 544 provides more information about the operations of these hot new investment products—and on the kind of performance they have been able to generate.

SERVICES OFFERED BY MUTUAL FUNDS

Many people are drawn to mutual funds because of their attractive returns. However, there are other reasons to invest in them, including their automatic investment and reinvestment plans, regular income programs, conversion privileges, and retirement plans. These are all examples of *mutual fund services* that many investors consider valuable—and, in fact, are sometimes the primary reasons for buying these funds.

Automatic Investment Plans. It takes money to make money, and for an investor that means being able to accumulate the capital to put into the market. Unfortunately, that's not always the easiest thing in the world to do. Enter mutual funds, which have come up with a program that makes savings and capital accumulation as painless as possible. The program is the **automatic investment plan** that allows fund shareholders to automatically funnel fixed amounts of money *from their paychecks or bank accounts* into a mutual fund. It's very much like a payroll deduction plan that treats savings a lot like insurance coverage—that is, just as insurance premiums are automatically deducted from your paycheck (or bank account), so too are investments to your mutual fund. This fund service has become very popular, as it allows shareholders to invest without having to think about it. Just about every major fund group offers some kind of automatic investment plan. To enroll, a shareholder simply fills out a form authorizing the fund to siphon a set amount (usually it has to be a minimum of $25 to $100 per period) from your bank account or paycheck at regular intervals—typically monthly or quarterly. Once enrolled, you'll be buying more shares in the fund(s) of your choice every month or quarter (most funds deal in fractional shares); of course, if it's a load fund, you'll still have to pay

international fund A mutual fund that does all or most of its investing in foreign securities; also includes *global funds,* a special type of international fund.

automatic investment plan A type of automatic savings program that enables an investor to systematically channel a set amount of money into a given mutual fund; it provides investors with a convenient way to accumulate capital.

Issues in Money Management

Asset Allocation Funds—So, What's in a Name?

Asset allocation funds seem to offer an unbeatable concept: they will divide your investment money among various asset classes—stocks, bonds, and cash; some also include foreign securities and gold. These funds became popular after the 1987 stock market crash. An offshoot of balanced funds, which maintain a fairly constant mix of stocks and bonds, the typical asset allocation fund has more asset classes and changes the mix as markets change. The idea is that being in several markets reduces risk, because markets generally move in different ways. Many use computer models to determine the best mix.

But is there a "typical" asset allocation fund? Actually, these funds are quite diverse. Some fund managers take a traditional balanced approach, with fairly constant percentages of stocks, bonds, and cash. "Tactical" asset allocators change the asset mix as they see fit. Some are market timers who move in and out of the market sectors and may at times be mostly in cash; others stay largely in stocks and use the fund's flexibility to change the equity percentage. Still other funds invest mostly in *other* mutual funds. For example, in February 1995, Flex-Fund Muirfield's holdings were 40 percent other funds, and Merriman Asset Allocation, 100 percent.

The latest twist in the asset allocation game are life-cycle funds, portfolios of stocks, bonds, and cash designed to match a particular investment time frame and risk tolerance. For example, as you approach retirement, Wells Fargo's Stagecoach program puts more of your assets into income investments. However, with other life-cycle funds, like those from T. Rowe Price and Vanguard, you decide which of several life cycle funds is right for you and when to move into another type.

So before you jump on the asset allocation bandwagon, you should ask yourself some questions about the funds and, most importantly, their performance records. First, is the fund actually an asset allocation fund? You can't assume that a fund called "asset allocation" is one! Be sure to read the fund's prospectus carefully for its investment strategy and portfolio holdings, look at its management style, and make sure its investment philosophy and risk profile match yours. Next, are these funds the best way to achieve your investment objectives? The rapid increase in asset allocation funds—there are now about 150 of them, and about half are less than three years old—means that few have much of a track record on which to base a decision. In fact, with only a few exceptions, even the older asset allocation funds can't match either the average mutual fund's performance or the market. For the period ending October 31, 1994, asset allocation funds earned annualized five year returns of 8.05 percent, compared to 8.39 for all funds and 10.14 for the S&P 500 Index. All things considered, you may be able to do better by managing your asset allocation strategy yourself.

Source: Adapted from Ellen Braitman and Emily Harrison, "What's in a Name?" *Smart Money,* April 1995, p. 105; Jeffrey Laderman, "Sometimes Diversity Is No Defense," *Business Week,* May 2, 1994, pp. 118–119; "Performance Close-Ups," *Morningstar Mutual Funds,* December 9, 1994, p. S3; and Amey Stone, "Does Your Lifestyle Demand a Lifestyle Fund?" *Business Week,* August 15, 1994, pp. 106–107.

normal sales charges on your periodic investments. To remain diversified, you can divide your money to as many funds (within a given fund family) as you like; and you can get out of the program anytime you like, without penalty, by simply calling the fund. Although convenience is perhaps the plans' chief advantage, they also make solid investment sense, as one of the best ways of building up a sizable amount of capital is to systematically add funds to your investment program over time. The importance of making regular contributions to your investment program cannot be overstated: it ranks right up there with compound interest!

Automatic Reinvestment Plans. This is one of the real draws of mutual funds, and it's a service that's offered by just about every open-ended mutual fund. Whereas automatic investment plans deal with money shareholders are putting into a fund, automatic *re*investment plans deal with the disposition of dividends and other distributions that the funds pay to their shareholders. Much like the dividend reinvestment plans we looked at with stocks, the **automatic reinvestment plans** of mutual funds enable you to keep all your capital fully employed. Through this service, dividend and/or capital gains income is *automatically used*

EXHIBIT 13.5

The Effects of Reinvesting Income

Reinvesting dividends and/or capital gains can have tremendous effects on one's investment position. This graph shows the results of a hypothetical investor who initially invested $10,000 and for a period of nearly 18 years reinvested all dividends and capital gains distributions in additional fund shares. (No adjustment has been made for any income taxes payable by the shareholder—which would be appropriate so long as the fund was held in, say, an IRA or Keogh account.)

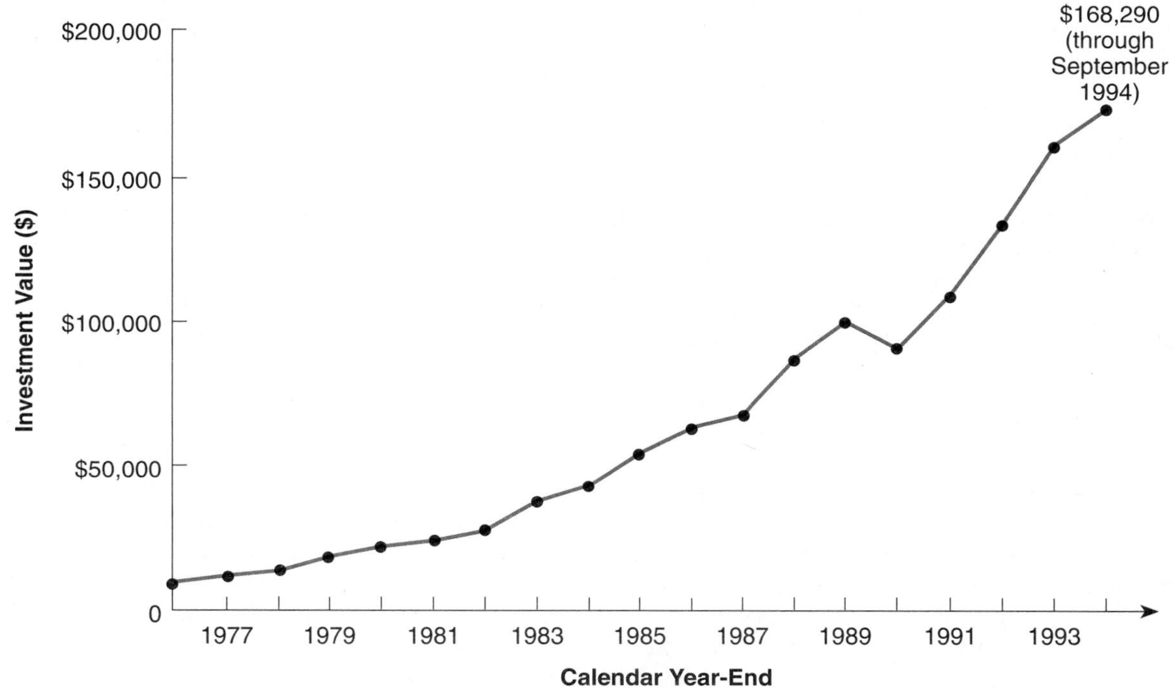

Source: *Morningstar Mutual Fund Values.*

to buy additional shares in the fund. Keep in mind, however, that even though you reinvest your dividends and capital gains, the IRS still treats them as cash receipts and taxes them in the year in which they are paid.

The important point is that by plowing back profits (reinvested dividends and capital gains distributions), the investor essentially can put his or her profits to work in generating even more earnings. Indeed, the effects of these plans on total accumulated capital over the long haul can be substantial. Exhibit 13.5 shows the long-term impact of one such plan. (These are the actual performance numbers for a *real* mutual fund—the Mutual Shares Fund.) In the illustration, we assume the investor starts with $10,000 and, except for the reinvestment of dividends and capital gains, *adds no new capital over time.* Even so, note that the initial investment of $10,000 grew to more than $168,000 over a nearly-18 year period (which, by the way, amounts to a compound rate of return of just over 17¼ percent). Clearly, so long as care is taken in selecting an appropriate fund, *attractive benefits can be derived from the systematic accumulation of capital offered by automatic reinvestment plans,* and as such, investors should seriously consider the idea of incorporating these plans into their mutual fund investment programs.

automatic reinvestment plan A plan frequently offered by mutual funds that allows share owners to elect to have dividends and capital gains distributions reinvested in additional fund shares.

Regular Income. While automatic reinvestment plans are great for the long-term investor, how about the investor who's looking for a steady stream of income? Once again, mutual funds have a service to meet this kind of need. It's called a **systematic withdrawal plan,** and it's offered by most open-ended funds. Once enrolled in one of these plans, you will automatically receive a predetermined amount of money every month or quarter.

To participate, shareholders are usually required to have a minimum investment of $5,000 to $10,000, and the size of the withdrawal must usually be $50 or more per month. Depending on how well the fund is doing, the income derived from the fund may actually be greater than the withdrawals, thus allowing the investor to not only receive regular income but also enjoy an automatic accumulation of *additional* shares in the plan. On the other hand, if the fund is not performing well, the withdrawals could eventually deplete the original investment.

Conversion Privileges. Sometimes investors find it necessary to switch out of one fund and into another; for example, their investment objectives may change, or the investment environment itself may have changed. **Conversion** (or **exchange**) **privileges** meet the needs of these investors in a convenient and economical manner. Investment companies that offer a number of different funds to the investing public—these are known as *fund families*—usually provide conversion privileges that enable shareholders to easily move from one fund to another; and as we saw earlier, this is usually done by phone (as in *phone switching*). The only limitation is that the investor must confine the switches within the same *family* of funds. For example, an investor can switch from a Dreyfus growth fund to a Dreyfus money fund, or to its income fund, or to any other fund managed by Dreyfus. With some fund families, the alternatives open to investors seem almost without limit; indeed, some of the larger families offer 20 or 30 funds (or more). One investment company (Fidelity) has over 200 different funds in its family, as it provides everything from high-performance stock funds to bond funds, tax-exempt funds, a couple dozen sector funds, and several dozen money funds.

Most fund families, especially the bigger ones, offer investors a full range of investment products, as they all try to provide one-stop mutual fund shopping. Whether you want an equity fund, a bond fund, or a money fund, these fund families have something for you. There are more than a hundred fund families in operation today, every one of which has some type of conversion privilege. Fifteen of the largest of these fund families are listed in Exhibit 13.6; note that, together, these 15 families have nearly $1.2 trillion in assets under management, and offer more than 1250 different mutual funds to the investing public. Conversion privileges are attractive because they permit investors to manage their holdings more aggressively by allowing them to move in and out of funds as the investment environment changes. Unfortunately, there is one major drawback; even though you never see the cash, the exchange of shares from one fund to another is regarded, for tax purposes, as a sale followed by a subsequent purchase of a new security. As a result, if any capital gains exist at the time of the exchange, the investor is liable for the taxes on that profit.

Retirement Plans. As a result of government legislation, self-employed individuals are permitted to divert a portion of their pretax income into self-directed *retirement plans*. And all working Americans, whether they are self-employed or not, are allowed to establish individual retirement accounts —note that IRAs can still be set up by anyone who is gainfully employed, although, as noted in Chapter 3, the tax deductibility of IRA *contributions* is limited to certain individuals. Today all mutual funds provide a special service that allows individuals to quickly and easily set up tax-deferred retirement programs as either IRA or Keogh accounts—or, through their place of employment, to participate in a qualified tax-sheltered retirement plan, like a 401(k), for example. The funds set up the plans and handle all the administrative details in such a way that the shareholders can take full advantage of available tax savings.

Concept Check

13-6. Briefly describe each of the following types of mutual funds:

- **a.** Aggressive growth funds
- **b.** Equity-income funds
- **c.** Growth-and-income funds
- **d.** Bond funds
- **e.** Sector funds
- **f.** *Socially responsible funds*
- **g.** *International funds*

EXHIBIT 13.6

All in the Family

Here's a list of 15 of the largest fund families, each one of which offers investors a full range of stock, bond, and money funds; these companies do everything they can to keep your money in the family.

Fund Families*	Asset Base (in billions)	No. of Stock, Bond Funds	No. of Money Funds	Total No. of Funds
Fidelity Distributors	$278.6	169	41	210
Vanguard Group	137.5	83	7	90
Merrill Lynch Funds	125.4	106	22	128
Capital Research & Management	112.1	32	2	34
Franklin/Templeton	90.3	93	17	110
Putnam Financial Services	63.0	80	4	84
Federated Investors	62.4	101	58	159
Dean Witter Reynolds	58.1	89	5	94
Smith Barney	55.0	57	6	63
Prudential-Bache	52.1	47	13	60
IDS Financial Services	47.1	33	2	35
T. Rowe Price Assocs.	39.9	77	7	84
Kemper Financial Services	39.4	26	4	30
Scudder	33.2	31	5	36
Oppenheimer Fund Management	29.3	36	2	38

*Number of funds, etc. as of late 1994/ early 1995; all these funds offer conversion privileges.

Source: Asset Base—*Investment Co. Institute;* No. of Funds—from various sources, including the funds themselves.

13-7. What is an asset allocation fund and how do these funds differ from other types of mutual funds?

13-8. If growth, income, and capital preservation are the primary objectives of mutual funds, why do we bother to categorize them by type? Do you think such classifications are helpful in the fund selection process? Explain.

13-9. What are fund families? What advantages do these families offer investors? Are there any disadvantages?

13-10. Briefly describe some of the investor services provided by mutual funds. What are *automatic reinvestment plans* and how do they differ from *automatic investment plans*? What is phone switching, and why would an investor want to use this type of service?

MAKING MUTUAL FUND INVESTMENTS

FPPC

LG5 LG6

While the mutual fund industry has made investing in funds as simple as possible, making a mutual fund investment decision is still not as easy as it may appear. For starters, with more than 6,000 funds to choose from, how do you select the one that's right for you, or the one that'll turn out to be a winner? Stop to think about this before reading on. How would you go about selecting a fund? What factors do you think are important in the fund selection process? How would you measure the performance of a mutual fund?

Suppose you are confronted with the following situation: You have money to invest and are trying to select the right place to put it. You obviously want to pick a security that meets your idea of acceptable risk, but also one that will generate an attractive rate of return. The problem is you have to make the selection from a list of over 6,000 securities. Sound like a "mission impossible"? Well, that's basically what the investor is up against when trying to select

systematic withdrawal plan A plan offered by mutual funds that allows shareholders to be paid specified amounts each period.

conversion (exchange) privileges A feature offered by many investment companies that allows investors to switch from one mutual fund to another within a specified family of funds.

a suitable mutual fund. But perhaps if the problem is approached systematically, it may not be so formidable a task. As we will see, it is possible to whittle down the list of alternatives by matching one's investment needs with the investment objectives of the funds.

THE SELECTION PROCESS

When it comes to mutual funds, one question that every investor has to answer is: Why invest in a mutual fund to begin with; why not just go it alone (that is, buy individual stocks and bonds directly)? For beginning investors, or investors with little capital, the answer is pretty simple—mutual funds provide far more diversification than they could ever get on their own, plus they get the help of professional money managers and at a very reasonable cost to boot. For more seasoned, better-heeled investors, the answers are probably a bit more involved. Certainly, the diversification and professional money management come into play, but there are other reasons as well. The competitive returns that mutual funds offer have to be a factor with many investors, and so do the services they provide. A lot of well-to-do investors have simply decided that they can get better returns over the long haul by carefully selecting mutual funds than trying to invest on their own. As a result, they put all or a big chunk of their money into funds. Many of these investors will use part of their capital to buy and sell individual securities on their own, and the rest will be used *to buy mutual funds that invest in areas that they don't fully understand or don't feel well-informed about*—for example, they will use mutual funds to get into foreign markets, as the way to buy mortgage-backed securities, to buy junk bonds (where diversification is so very important), or to buy value funds, because that's such a tricky and time-consuming way of investing.

Given the decision to use mutual funds has been made, the investor will then have to make the decision of which fund(s) to buy. The selection process itself (especially with regard to the *types* of funds purchased) obviously plays an important role in defining the amount of success one will have with mutual funds. It means putting into action all you know about funds in order to gain as much return as possible from an acceptable level of risk. Given that you have an asset allocation scheme in place and you are trying to select funds that are compatible to your targeted mix, the selection process begins with an assessment of your own investment needs; this sets the tone of the investment program. Obviously, what we want to do is select from those 6,000 or so funds the one or two (or three or four) that will best meet our total investment needs.

Objectives and Motives for Using Funds. Selecting the right investment means finding those funds that are most suitable to your investment needs. *The place to start is with your own investment objectives.* In other words, why do you want to invest in a mutual fund, and what are you looking for in a fund? Obviously, an attractive rate of return would be desirable, but there is also the matter of a tolerable amount of risk exposure. Face it: Some investors are more willing to take risks than others, and this is certainly an important ingredient in the selection process. More than likely, when you look at your own risk temperament in relation to the various types of mutual funds available, you will discover that certain types of funds are more appealing to you than others. For instance, aggressive growth or sector funds will probably *not* be attractive to individuals who wish to avoid high exposure to risk.

Another important factor in the selection process is the intended use of the mutual fund. That is, do you want to invest in mutual funds as a way of *accumulating capital* over an extended period of time, to *speculate* with your money in the hopes of generating high rates of return, or to *conserve your capital* by investing in low risk securities where preservation of capital is as, or more, important than return on capital. This is helpful information, since it puts into clearer focus the question of exactly what you are trying to do with your investment dollars. Finally, there is the matter of the types of services provided by the fund. If there are services you are particularly interested in, you should be sure to look for them in the funds you select. Having assessed what you are looking for in a fund, you now want to look at what the funds have to offer.

What Funds Offer. The ideal mutual fund would achieve maximum capital growth when security prices rise, provide complete protection against capital loss when prices decline, and achieve high levels of current income at all times. Unfortunately, this fund does not exist. Instead, just as each individual has a set of investment needs, each fund has its own *investment objective,* its own *manner of operation,* and its own *range of services.* These three parameters are useful in helping us to assess investment alternatives. But where does the investor look for such information? One obvious place is the fund's *prospectus* (or its Statement of Additional Information), where detailed information on investment objectives, portfolio composition, management, and past performance can be obtained. In addition, publications such as *The Wall Street Journal, Barron's, Money, Fortune,* and *Forbes* provide useful data and information concerning mutual funds. These sources provide a wealth of operating and performance statistics in a convenient and easy-to-read format. What's more, there are services available that provide background information and assessments on a wide variety of different kinds of funds. Among the best in this category are Morningstar's *Mutual Fund Values* (an excerpt of which is shown in Exhibit 13.7), Wiesenberger's *Investment Companies* (an annual publication with quarterly updates), *Donoghue's Mutual Funds Almanac* (a low-cost, annual publication that provides a variety of operating and performance statistics), *Value Line* (which produces reports similar to their stock reports, except they apply to mutual funds), and *Kiplinger's,* which provides individual *Mutual Fund Reports* that can be obtained at any time via a 1-800 number. In addition, there are *computer data bases* available that provide all sorts of performance statistics on floppy disks for easy use on home computers—for example, such quarterly- or annually-updated software is available, at very low cost, from Morningstar or the American Association of Individual Investors (AAII). Using sources like these, investors can obtain information on such things as investment objectives, load charges and annual expense rates, summary portfolio analyses, services offered, historical statistics, and reviews of past performance.

Whittling Down the Alternatives. At this point, fund selection becomes a process of elimination as investor needs are weighed against the types of funds available. A large number of funds can be eliminated from consideration simply because they fail to meet these needs. Some may be too risky; others may be unsuitable as a storehouse of value. Thus, rather than trying to evaluate 6,000 different funds, you can use a process of elimination to narrow the list down to two or three *types* of funds that best match your investment (and asset allocation) needs. From here, you can whittle the list down a bit more by introducing other constraints. For example, because of cost considerations, you may want to deal only in no-load or low-load funds (more on this below); or you may be seeking certain services that are important to your investment goals. Now we introduce the final (but certainly not the least important) element in the selection process: *the fund's investment performance.* Useful information includes (1) how the fund has performed over the past five to seven years; (2) the type of return it has generated in good markets as well as bad; (3) the level of dividend and capital gains distributions; and (4) the type of investment stability the fund has enjoyed over time (or put another way, the amount of volatility/risk in the fund's return). By evaluating such information, it is possible to identify some of the more successful mutual funds—the ones that not only offer the investment objectives and services you seek but also provide the best payoffs as well. And while you're doing this, you might want to keep in mind some of the fund facts noted in Exhibit 13.8 on page 551.

Stick With No-Loads or Low-Loads. There's a long standing "debate" in the mutual fund industry regarding load funds and no-load funds. The question is: Do load funds add value? And if not, then why pay the load charges? As it turns out, the results generally don't support load funds. Indeed, rather than producing superior returns, load fund returns, in general, don't seem to be any better than the returns from no-load funds and, in fact, in many cases, the funds with abnormally high loads and 12(b)-1 charges often produce returns that are far *less* than what you can get from no-loads! And, because of compounding, the differential returns tend to widen with longer holding periods. But that should come as no surprise, since big load charges and/or 12(b)-1 fees do nothing more than *reduce your investable capital* and therefore, reduce the amount of money you have working for you. In fact, the only way a load fund can overcome this handicap is to *produce superior returns*—which is no easy thing to do, year in and year out. Granted there are a handful of load funds that have produced very attractive returns over extended periods of time, but they are the exception rather than the rule.

EXHIBIT 13.7

Mutual Fund Information

Investors who want in-depth information about the operating characteristics, investment holdings, and market performance of mutual funds can usually find what they're looking for in publications like Morningstar's *Mutual Fund Values* (shown here) or Weisenberger's *Investment Companies.*

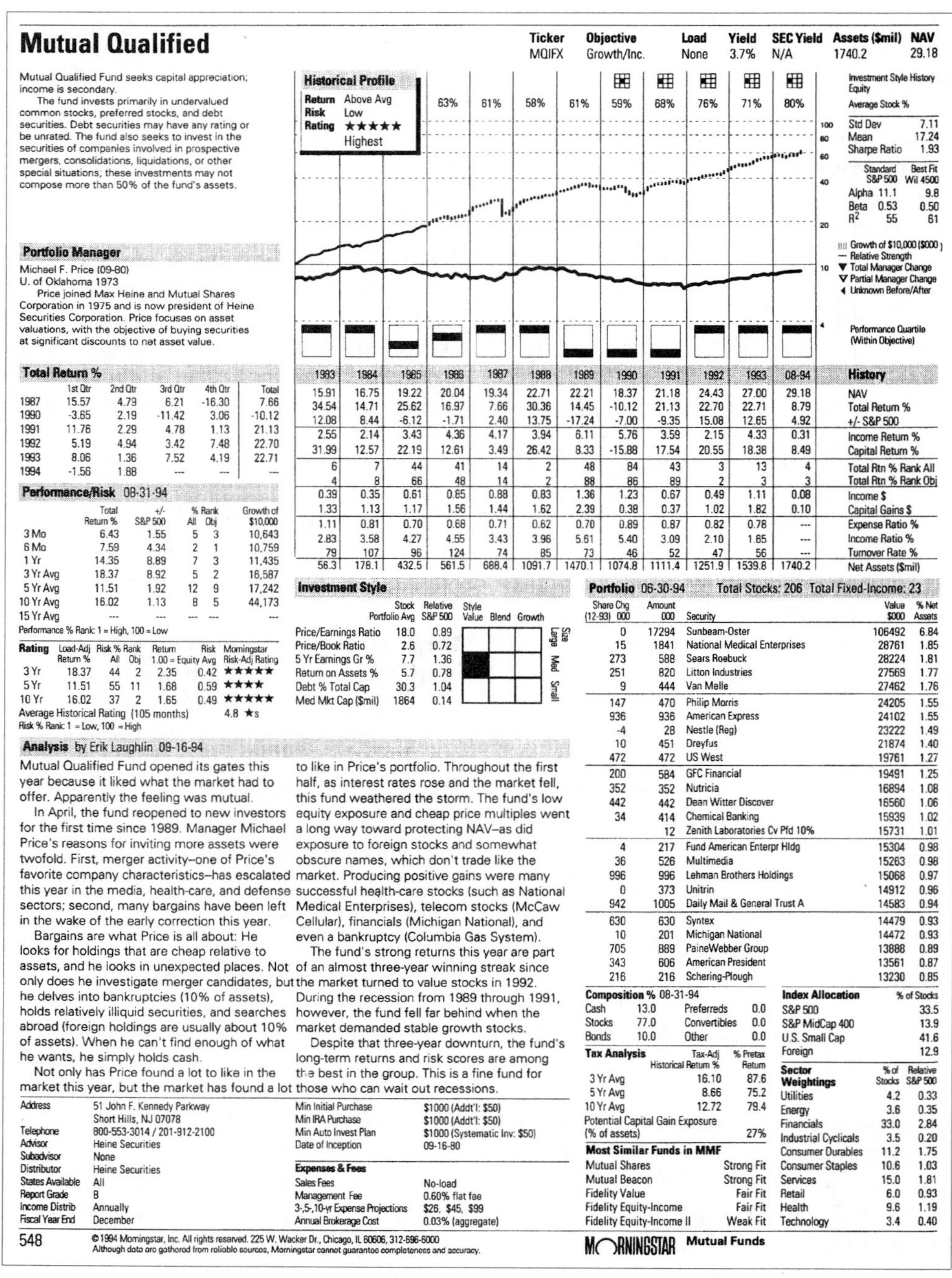

Mutual Qualified

Ticker	Objective	Load	Yield	SEC Yield	Assets ($mil)	NAV
MQIFX	Growth/Inc.	None	3.7%	N/A	1740.2	29.18

Mutual Qualified Fund seeks capital appreciation; income is secondary.

The fund invests primarily in undervalued common stocks, preferred stocks, and debt securities. Debt securities may have any rating or be unrated. The fund also seeks to invest in the securities of companies involved in prospective mergers, consolidations, liquidations, or other special situations; these investments may not compose more than 50% of the fund's assets.

Historical Profile
Return Above Avg
Risk Low
Rating ★★★★★ Highest

Std Dev	7.11
Mean	17.24
Sharpe Ratio	1.93

	Standard S&P 500	Best Fit Wil 4500
Alpha	11.1	9.8
Beta	0.53	0.50
R^2	55	61

Portfolio Manager

Michael F. Price (09-80)
U. of Oklahoma 1973

Price joined Max Heine and Mutual Shares Corporation in 1975 and is now president of Heine Securities Corporation. Price focuses on asset valuations, with the objective of buying securities at significant discounts to net asset value.

History	1983	1984	1985	1986	1987	1988	1989	1990	1991	1992	1993	08-94
NAV	15.91	16.75	19.22	20.04	19.34	22.71	22.21	18.37	21.18	24.43	27.00	29.18
Total Return %	34.54	14.71	25.62	16.97	7.66	30.36	14.45	-10.12	21.13	22.70	22.71	8.79
+/- S&P 500	12.08	8.44	-6.12	-1.71	2.40	13.75	-17.24	-7.00	-9.35	15.08	12.65	4.92
Income Return %	2.55	2.14	3.43	4.36	4.17	3.94	6.11	5.76	3.59	2.15	4.33	0.31
Capital Return %	31.99	12.57	22.19	12.61	3.49	26.42	8.33	-15.88	17.54	20.55	18.38	8.49
Total Rtn % Rank All	6	7	44	41	14	2	48	84	43	3	13	4
Total Rtn % Rank Obj	4	8	66	48	14	2	88	86	89	2	3	3
Income $	0.39	0.35	0.61	0.85	0.88	0.83	1.36	1.23	0.67	0.49	1.11	0.08
Capital Gains $	1.33	1.13	1.17	1.56	1.44	1.62	2.39	0.38	0.37	1.02	1.82	0.10
Expense Ratio %	1.11	0.81	0.70	0.68	0.71	0.62	0.70	0.89	0.87	0.82	0.78	---
Income Ratio %	2.83	3.58	4.27	4.55	3.43	3.96	5.61	5.40	3.09	2.10	1.65	---
Turnover Rate %	79	107	96	124	74	85	73	46	52	47	56	---
Net Assets ($mil)	56.3	178.1	432.5	561.5	688.4	1091.7	1470.1	1074.8	1111.4	1251.9	1539.8	1740.2

Total Return %

	1st Qtr	2nd Qtr	3rd Qtr	4th Qtr	Total
1987	15.57	4.79	6.21	-16.30	7.66
1990	-3.65	2.19	-11.42	3.06	-10.12
1991	11.76	2.29	4.78	1.13	21.13
1992	5.19	4.94	3.42	7.48	22.70
1993	8.06	1.36	7.52	4.19	22.71
1994	-1.56	1.88	---	---	---

Performance/Risk 08-31-94

	Total Return %	+/- S&P 500	% Rank All	% Rank Obj	Growth of $10,000
3 Mo	6.43	1.55	5	3	10,643
6 Mo	7.59	4.34	2	1	10,759
1 Yr	14.35	8.89	7	3	11,435
3 Yr Avg	18.37	8.92	5	2	16,587
5 Yr Avg	11.51	1.92	12	9	17,242
10 Yr Avg	16.02	1.13	8	5	44,173
15 Yr Avg	---	---	---	---	---

Performance % Rank: 1 = High, 100 = Low

Rating	Load-Adj Return %	Risk % Rank All	Risk % Rank Obj	Return 1.00 = Equity Avg	Risk 1.00 = Equity Avg	Morningstar Risk-Adj Rating
3 Yr	18.37	44	2	2.35	0.42	★★★★★
5 Yr	11.51	55	11	1.68	0.59	★★★★
10 Yr	16.02	37	2	1.65	0.49	★★★★★

Average Historical Rating (105 months) 4.8 ★s
Risk % Rank: 1 = Low, 100 = High

Investment Style

	Stock Portfolio Avg	Relative S&P 500
Price/Earnings Ratio	18.0	0.89
Price/Book Ratio	2.6	0.72
5 Yr Earnings Gr %	7.7	1.36
Return on Assets %	5.7	0.78
Debt % Total Cap	30.3	1.04
Med Mkt Cap ($mil)	1864	0.14

Portfolio 06-30-94 Total Stocks: 206 Total Fixed-Income: 23

Share Chg (12-93) 000	Amount 000	Security	Value $000	% Net Assets
0	17294	Sunbeam-Oster	106492	6.84
15	1841	National Medical Enterprises	28761	1.85
273	588	Sears Roebuck	28224	1.81
251	820	Litton Industries	27569	1.77
9	444	Van Melle	27462	1.76
147	470	Philip Morris	24205	1.55
936	936	American Express	24102	1.55
-4	28	Nestle (Reg)	23222	1.49
10	451	Dreyfus	21874	1.40
472	472	US West	19761	1.27
200	584	GFC Financial	19491	1.25
352	352	Nutricia	16894	1.08
442	442	Dean Witter Discover	16560	1.06
34	414	Chemical Banking	15939	1.02
	12	Zenith Laboratories Cv Pfd 10%	15731	1.01
4	217	Fund American Enterpr Hldg	15304	0.98
36	526	Multimedia	15263	0.98
996	996	Lehman Brothers Holdings	15068	0.97
0	373	Unitrin	14912	0.96
942	1005	Daily Mail & General Trust A	14583	0.94
630	630	Syntex	14479	0.93
10	201	Michigan National	14472	0.93
705	889	PaineWebber Group	13888	0.89
343	606	American President	13561	0.87
216	216	Schering-Plough	13230	0.85

Analysis by Erik Laughlin 09-16-94

Mutual Qualified Fund opened its gates this year because it liked what the market had to offer. Apparently the feeling was mutual.

In April, the fund reopened to new investors for the first time since 1989. Manager Michael Price's reasons for inviting more assets were twofold. First, merger activity–one of Price's favorite company characteristics–has escalated this year in the media, health-care, and defense sectors; second, many bargains have been left in the wake of the early correction this year.

Bargains are what Price is all about: He looks for holdings that are cheap relative to assets, and he looks in unexpected places. Not only does he investigate merger candidates, but he delves into bankruptcies (10% of assets), holds relatively illiquid securities, and searches abroad (foreign holdings are usually about 10% of assets). When he can't find enough of what he wants, he simply holds cash.

Not only has Price found a lot to like in the market this year, but the market has found a lot to like in Price's portfolio. Throughout the first half, as interest rates rose and the market fell, this fund weathered the storm. The fund's low equity exposure and cheap price multiples went a long way toward protecting NAV–as did exposure to foreign stocks and somewhat obscure names, which don't trade like the market. Producing positive gains were many successful health-care stocks (such as National Medical Enterprises), telecom stocks (McCaw Cellular), financials (Michigan National), and even a bankruptcy (Columbia Gas System).

The fund's strong returns this year are part of an almost three-year winning streak since the market turned to value stocks in 1992. During the recession from 1989 through 1991, however, the fund fell far behind when the market demanded stable growth stocks.

Despite that three-year downturn, the fund's long-term returns and risk scores are among the best in the group. This is a fine fund for those who can wait out recessions.

Composition % 08-31-94

Cash	13.0	Preferreds	0.0
Stocks	77.0	Convertibles	0.0
Bonds	10.0	Other	0.0

Index Allocation	% of Stocks
S&P 500	33.5
S&P MidCap 400	13.9
U.S. Small Cap	41.6
Foreign	12.9

Tax Analysis	Tax-Adj Historical Return %	% Pretax Return
3 Yr Avg	16.10	87.6
5 Yr Avg	8.66	75.2
10 Yr Avg	12.72	79.4
Potential Capital Gain Exposure (% of assets)		27%

Sector Weightings	% of Stocks	Relative S&P 500
Utilities	4.2	0.33
Energy	3.6	0.35
Financials	33.0	2.84
Industrial Cyclicals	3.5	0.20
Consumer Durables	11.2	1.75
Consumer Staples	10.6	1.03
Services	15.0	1.81
Retail	6.0	0.93
Health	9.6	1.19
Technology	3.4	0.40

Most Similar Funds in MMF

Mutual Shares	Strong Fit
Mutual Beacon	Strong Fit
Fidelity Value	Fair Fit
Fidelity Equity-Income	Fair Fit
Fidelity Equity-Income II	Weak Fit

Address	51 John F. Kennedy Parkway, Short Hills, NJ 07078
Telephone	800-553-3014 / 201-912-2100
Advisor	Heine Securities
Subadvisor	None
Distributor	Heine Securities
States Available	All
Report Grade	B
Income Distrib	Annually
Fiscal Year End	December

Min Initial Purchase	$1000 (Addt'l: $50)
Min IRA Purchase	$1000 (Addt'l: $50)
Min Auto Invest Plan	$1000 (Systematic Inv: $50)
Date of Inception	09-16-80

Expenses & Fees

Sales Fees	No-load
Management Fee	0.60% flat fee
3-,5-,10-yr Expense Projections	$26, $45, $99
Annual Brokerage Cost	0.03% (aggregate)

548

MORNINGSTAR Mutual Funds

Source: Morningstar, Inc., *Mutual Fund Values,* 1994.

EXHIBIT 13.8

Some Mutual Fund Facts That Every Investor Should Know

Mutual funds are meant to provide small investors with a simple, yet effective, way of buying into the stock and bond markets. Unfortunately, fund investing isn't always as simple as it looks. So, here are a few fund facts that every investor should keep in mind when making mutual fund investments.

- Even bad funds sometimes rank as top performers.
- Stock funds that get hit hard in market crashes aren't necessarily bad investments.
- Even great funds have bad years now and then.
- Most stock (and bond) funds fail to beat the market.
- You don't need a broker to buy mutual funds.
- A fund that doesn't charge a sales commission isn't necessarily a no-load fund.
- If you own more than a dozen different funds, you probably own too many.
- Mutual fund names are often misleading.
- Bond funds with high yields don't necessarily produce high returns.
- Money-market funds are *not* risk-free (you never know what kind of return you're going to earn with these things).
- If the market crashes, it will probably be too late to sell your fund shares (the damage will probably already have been done).
- Most mutual fund investors are wimps (because they put way too much into low-risk debt funds).

Source: Adapted from Jonathan Clements, "The 25 Facts Every Fund Investor Should Know," *The Wall Street Journal,* March 5, 1993, pp. C1, 19.

Obviously, it's in your best interest to pay close attention to load charges (and other fees) whenever you're considering an investment in a mutual fund. As a rule, to maximize returns, *you should seriously consider sticking to no-load funds, or low-loads* (funds that charge total load charges, including 12(b)-1 fees, of 3 percent or less). Or at the very minimum, you should consider a more expensive load fund *only* if it has a much better performance record (and offers more return potential) than a less expensive fund. There may well be times when the higher costs are justified, but far more often than not, you're better off trying to minimize load charges. That shouldn't be all that hard to do, however, as there are over a thousand no-load and low-load funds to choose from; and they come in all different types and sizes.

GETTING A HANDLE ON MUTUAL FUND PERFORMANCE

If you were to believe all the sales literature, you'd think there was no way you could go wrong by investing in mutual funds. Just put your money into one of these funds and let the good times roll! Unfortunately, the hard facts of life are that *when it comes to investing, performance is never guaranteed.* And that applies just as much to mutual funds as it does to any other form of investing. Perhaps even more so, because with mutual funds, the single variable that drives a fund's market price and return behavior is the performance of the fund's portfolio of securities.

Measuring Fund Performance. Basically, any mutual fund (or closed-end investment company) has three potential sources of return: (1) dividend income, (2) capital gains distribution, and (3) change in the fund's share price. Depending on the type of fund, some will derive more income from one source than another; for example, we would normally expect income-oriented funds to have higher dividend income than capital gains distributions. Mutual funds regularly publish reports that recap investment performance. One such report is *The Summary of Income and Capital Changes,* an example of which is provided in Exhibit 13.9. This statement, which is found in the fund's prospectus or annual report, gives a brief overview of the fund's investment activities, including expense ratios and portfolio turnover rates. Of interest to us here is the top part of the report (that runs from *Investment income to NAV at the end of the year*—lines 1 to 9); this is the part that reveals the amount of dividend

EXHIBIT 13.9

A Summary of Income and Capital Changes

The return on a mutual fund is made up of (1) the (net) investment income the fund earns from dividends and interest, and (2) the realized and unrealized capital gains the fund earns on its security transactions.

PER SHARE INCOME AND CAPITAL CHANGES (For a share outstanding throughout the year)

		1995	1994	1993
	INCOME AND EXPENSES			
	1. Investment income	$.76	$.88	$.67
	2. Less expenses	.16	.22	.17
	3. Net investment income	.60	.66	.50
Dividend Income →	4. Dividends from net investment income	(.55)	(.64)	(.50)
	CAPITAL CHANGES			
	5. Net realized and unrealized gains (or losses) on security transactions	6.37	(1.74)	3.79
Capital Gains Distribution →	6. Distributions from realized gains	(1.75)	(.84)	(1.02)
Change in NAV →	7. Net increase (decrease) in NAV*	4.67	(2.56)	2.77
	8. NAV at beginning of year	24.47	27.03	24.26
	9. NAV at end of year	$29.14	$24.47	$27.03
	10. Ratio of operating expenses to average net assets	1.04%	.85%	.94%
	11. Ratio of net investment income to average net assets	1.47%	2.56%	2.39%
	12. Portfolio turnover rate**	85%	144%	74%
	13. Shares outstanding at the end of year (000s omitted)	10,568	6,268	4,029

*Note: *Net increase (decrease) in NAV,* line 7 = line 3 − line 4 + line 5 − line 6; for example, the 1995 net increase in NAV was found as $.60 − .55 + 6.37 − 1.75 = $4.67.

***Portfolio turnover rate* relates the number of shares bought and sold by the fund to the total number of shares held in the fund's portfolio; a high turnover rate (for example, in excess of 100 percent) would mean the fund has been doing a lot of trading.

income and capital gains distributed to the shareholders, along with any change in the fund's net asset value.

Dividend income is the amount derived from the dividend and interest income earned on the security holdings of the mutual fund. When the fund receives dividends or interest payments, it passes these on to shareholders in the form of dividend payments. The fund accumulates all the current income it has received for the period and then pays it out on a prorated basis. Capital gains distributions work on the same principle, except that they are derived from the capital gains actually earned by the fund. This capital gains distribution applies only to *realized* capital gains—that is, where the securities holdings were actually sold and capital gains actually earned. *Unrealized* capital gains (or paper profits) are what make up the third and final element in a mutual fund's return, *for when the fund's securities holdings go up or down in price, its net asset value moves accordingly.*

A simple but effective way of measuring performance is to describe mutual fund returns in terms of the three major sources of return noted above — dividends earned, capital gains distributions received, and change in share price. These payoffs can be converted to a convenient return figure by using the standard *approximate yield* formula that was first introduced in Chapter 11. The calculations necessary for finding such a return measure can be shown by using the 1995 figures from Exhibit 13.9. Referring to the exhibit, we can see that this hypothetical no-load fund paid 55 cents per share in dividends and another $1.75 in capital gains distributions; also, it had a price at the beginning of the year (that is, at year-end 1994) of $24.47 that rose to $29.14 by the end of the year. Putting this data into the familiar approximate yield formula, we see that the hypothetical mutual fund provided an annual rate of return of 26.0 percent. This measure is simple to calculate, yet it captures all the important elements of mutual fund return.

$$\text{Approximate yield} = \frac{\text{Dividends and capital gains distributions} + \left[\dfrac{\text{Ending price} - \text{Beginning price}}{\text{1-year time period}}\right]}{\left[\dfrac{\text{Ending price} + \text{Beginning price}}{2}\right]}$$

$$= \frac{(\$.55 + \$1.75) + \left[\dfrac{\$29.14 - \$24.47}{1}\right]}{\left[\dfrac{\$29.14 + \$24.47}{2}\right]}$$

$$= \frac{\$2.30 + \$4.67}{\$26.80} = \frac{\$6.97}{\$26.80} = 26.0\%$$

What About Future Performance? There's no question that approximate yield is a handy measure of return. Unfortunately, looking at past performance is one thing, but how about the future? Ideally, we want to evaluate the same three elements of return over the future much like we did for the past. The trouble is, when it comes to the future performance of a mutual fund, it's extremely difficult—if not impossible—to get a handle on what the future holds as far as dividends, capital gains, and NAV are concerned. The reason: a mutual fund's future investment performance is directly linked to the future makeup of its securities portfolio—which is something that is impossible to predict. It's not like evaluating the expected performance of a share of stock, where you're keying in on one company. With mutual funds, investment performance depends on the behavior of many different stocks and bonds.

So, where do you look for insight into the future? Most market observers suggest you do two things. First, give careful consideration to the *future direction of the market as a whole*. This is important because the behavior of a well-diversified mutual fund tends to reflect the general tone of the market. Thus, if the feeling is that the market is going to be generally drifting up, that should bode well for the investment performance of mutual funds.

Second, take a good hard look at the past performance of the mutual fund itself, as that's a good way to get an indication of how successful the fund's investment managers have been. In essence, the success of a mutual fund rests in large part *on the investment skills of the fund managers*. So when investing in a mutual fund, look for consistently good performance, in up as well as down markets, over extended periods of time (five to seven years, or more). Most important, check to see if the same key people are still running the fund. Although past success is certainly no guarantee of future performance, a strong team of money managers can have a significant bearing on the level of fund returns. Put another way, when you buy a mutual fund, you're buying a formula (investment policy + money management team) that has worked in the past, in the expectation that it will work again in the future.

Concept Check

13-11. What are the most common reasons for purchasing mutual funds? Is financial return important to mutual fund investors? Explain.

13-12. Briefly describe the steps in the mutual fund selection process. Why is it important to have a clear understanding of what your own investment objectives and motives are?

13-13. Why does it pay to invest in no-load funds rather than load funds? Under what conditions might it make sense to invest in a load fund?

13-14. Identify three potential sources of return to mutual fund investors, and briefly discuss how each could affect total return to shareholders. Which would you rather have: $100 in dividend income or $100 in capital gains distribution? $100 in realized capital gains or $100 in unrealized capital gains? Explain.

13-15. How important is the general behavior of the market in affecting the price performance of mutual funds? Why is a fund's *past* performance so important to the mutual fund selection process? Does the *future* behavior of the market matter any in the selection process? Explain.

SUMMARY

LG1. Describe the basic features and operating characteristics of a mutual fund. Mutual fund shares represent ownership in a diversified, professionally managed portfolio of securities; many investors who lack the time, know-how, or commitment to manage their own money turn to mutual funds as an investment outlet. By investing in mutual funds, shareholders benefit from a level of diversification and investment performance they might otherwise find difficult to achieve.

LG2. Differentiate between open- and closed-end funds, and discuss the various types of fund loads and charges. Investors can buy either open-end funds, which have no limit on the number of shares they may issue, or closed-end funds, which have a fixed number of shares outstanding and which trade in the secondary markets like any other share of common stock. There is a cost, however, to investing in mutual funds. That is, investors face a full array of loads, fees, and charges, including front-end loads, back-end loads, annual 12(b)-1 charges, annual management fees, and so forth. Some of these costs are one-time charges (like front-end loads), but others (like 12(b)-1 and management fees) are paid annually.

LG3. Discuss the types of funds available and the variety of investment objectives these funds seek to fulfill. Each fund has an established investment objective that determines its investment policy and identifies it as a certain type of fund. Some of the more popular types of funds include growth funds, aggressive growth funds, equity-income funds, balanced funds, growth-and-income funds, bond funds, money funds, sector funds, socially responsible funds, asset allocation funds, and international funds. The different categories of funds have different risk-return characteristics and are important variables in the fund selection process.

LG4. Identify and discuss the different kinds of investor services offered by mutual funds. In addition to their investment returns, many investors buy mutual funds to take advantage of the various investor services they offer, such as automatic investment and reinvestment plans, systematic withdrawal programs, low-cost conversion and phone-switching privileges, and retirement programs.

LG5. Gain an understanding of the variables that should be considered when selecting funds for investment purposes. The fund selection process generally starts by assessing our own needs and wants; this sets the tone for our investment program and helps us decide on the types of funds to look at. Next, we take a look at what the funds have to offer, particularly with regard to the fund's investment objectives and investor services—here, we narrow down the alternatives by aligning our needs with the types of funds available. From this list of funds, we then introduce the final selection tests: fund performance and cost—other things being equal, looking for high performance and low costs.

LG6. Identify the sources of return and calculate the rate of return earned on an investment in a mutual fund. The investment performance of mutual funds is largely a function of the returns the money managers are able to generate from their securities portfolios; generally speaking, strong markets translate into attractive returns for mutual fund investors. Mutual funds have three basic sources of return: (1) dividends; (2) capital gains distributions; and (3) changes in the fund's NAV (as accruing from unrealized capital gains). The approximate yield measure recognizes these three elements and provides a simple yet effective way of measuring the annual rate of return from a mutual fund.

FINANCIAL FACTS OR FANTASIES

Are the following statements financial facts (true) or fantasies (false)?

1. Unlike what happened with banks and S&Ls, there's virtually no chance that you will ever lose any money from the financial failure of a mutual fund.
2. When a mutual fund is open-ended, it means there's no limit to how high the price of its stock can go.
3. Phone switching is a service that enables you to move your money from one fund to another, so long as you stay within the same family of funds.
4. The two principle sources of return to mutual fund investors are dividends and interest income.
5. A REIT (real estate investment trust) is a type of open-end mutual fund that enables individuals to directly invest in income-producing property and other forms of real estate.
6. The principle investment objective of an equity-income fund is capital gains and as a result, these funds invest very heavily in growth-oriented common stocks.

DISCUSSION QUESTIONS AND PROBLEMS

Discussion Question for Opening Profile

How do mutual funds fit into Lori Rapuano's investment objectives? List some reasons why she prefers to buy mutual funds rather than individual stocks. Evaluate her overall investment strategies.

1. Contrast *mutual fund ownership* with the *direct investment in stocks and bonds*. Assume your class is going to debate the merits of investing through mutual funds versus investing directly in stocks and bonds. Develop some pro and con arguments on each side of this debate and be prepared to discuss them in class. If you had to choose one side to be on, which would it be? Explain.
2. Using the mutual fund quotes on page 532, how much would you have to pay to buy each of the following funds, and how much would you pay (in dollars and percentage terms) in front-end load charges with each of these funds?
   - **a.** Fairmont Fund (Fairmt).
   - **b.** FPA Capital Fund (Capit).
   - **c.** Eaton V. Total Return Fund (Tot Rtn).
   - **d.** Federated Fortress Utility Fund (UtilFd).
   - **e.** FBL High Yield Bond Fund (HiYlBd).

   How much would you receive for each if you were selling these funds? Which of the five funds listed above have 12(b)-1 fees? Which ones have redemption fees? Are any of them no-loads? Which fund has the highest return to date? Which has the lowest?
3. Let's imagine that you've just inherited $20,000 from a rich uncle. Now you're faced with the problem of trying to decide how to spend it. You could make a down payment on a condo, or, better yet, on that Corvette that you've always wanted. Or, you could spend your windfall more profitably by building a mutual fund portfolio. Let's say that after a lot of soul searching, you decide to do the latter: build a mutual fund portfolio. Your task at hand is to develop a $20,000 mutual fund portfolio—use actual funds and actual quoted prices, invest as much of the $20,000 as you possibly can, and be specific! Briefly describe the portfolio you ended up with, including the investment objectives you are trying to achieve.
4. For each pair of funds listed below, select the one that would be the *least* risky; briefly explain your answer.
   - **a.** Growth versus growth-and-income
   - **b.** Equity-income versus high-grade corporate bonds
   - **c.** Intermediate-term bonds versus high-yield municipals
   - **d.** International versus balanced
5. What investor service is most closely linked to the notion of a fund family? If a fund is *not* part of a family of mutual funds, can it still offer a full range of investor services? Explain. Using something like *The Wall Street Journal,* or perhaps your local newspaper, find a couple examples of fund families; list some of the mutual funds they offer.
6. Using a source like *Barron's, Forbes, Money,* or perhaps even *Morningstar* (if it's readily available

to you), select five mutual funds—(a) a growth fund, (b) a balanced fund, (c) a sector fund, (d) an international fund, and (e) a high-yield corporate bond fund—that you feel would make good investments. Briefly explain why you selected each of the funds.

FPPC 7. About a year ago, Dave Kidwell bought some shares in the Hi-Flyer Mutual Fund. He bought the stock at $24.50 a share, and it now trades at $26.00. Last year the fund paid dividends of 40 cents a share and had capital gains distributions of $1.83 a share. Using the approximate yield formula, what rate of return did Dave earn on his investment? Would he have made a 20-percent rate of return if the stock had risen to $30 a share?

FPPC 8. A year ago, the Really Big Growth Fund was being quoted at an NAV of $21.50 and an offer price of $23.35; today it's being quoted at $23.04 (NAV) and $25.04 (offer). Use the approximate yield formula to find the rate of return on this load fund, given it was purchased a year ago and its dividends and capital gains distributions over the year totaled $1.05 a share.

FPPC 9. Listed below is the per-share performance record of Mountain States Growth-and-Income fund for 1994 and 1995.

	For the Years Ending	
	1995	**1994**
1. Investment income	$1.98	$1.90
2. Expenses	.59	.55
3. Investment income–net	1.39	1.35
4. Dividends from investment income–net	(.83)	(1.24)
5. Realized and unrealized gain (loss) on investment–net	8.10	9.39
6. Distributions from realized gain on investments–net	(2.42)	(3.82)
7. Net increase (decrease) in net asset value	6.24	5.68
Net asset value:		
8. Beginning of year	58.60	52.92
9. End of year	$64.84	$58.60

Use this information to find the rate of return earned on Mountain States in 1994 and in 1995. What is your assessment of the investment performance of Mountain States G&I for the 1994–95 period?

CONTEMPORARY CASE APPLICATIONS

13.1 Dave's Dilemma: Common Stocks or Mutual Funds?

Dave Brubaker has worked in the management services division of Ace Consultants for the past five years. He currently earns an annual salary of about $45,000. At 33, he is still a bachelor and has accumulated about $40,000 in savings over the past few years. He keeps his savings in a money market account, where it earns about 4.5 percent interest. Dave is contemplating withdrawing $30,000 from this account and investing it in common stock. He feels that such an investment can easily earn more than 4.5 percent. Marlene Anson, a close friend, suggests that he invest in mutual fund shares. Dave has approached you, his broker, for advice.

Questions

1. Explain to Dave the key reasons for purchasing mutual fund shares.
2. What special fund features might help Dave achieve his investment objectives?
3. What type(s) of mutual fund(s) would you recommend to Dave?
4. What recommendations would you make with respect to Dave's dilemma about whether to go into stocks or mutual funds? Explain.

13.2 Janet Perry Ponders Mutual Funds

Janet Perry is the director of a major charitable organization in the Raleigh-Durham area of North Carolina. A single mother of one young child, she earns what could best be described as a modest income. Since charitable organizations are not notorious for their generous retirement programs, Janet has decided it would be best for her to do a little investing on her own. She would like to set up a program that enables her to supplement her employer's retirement program and at the same time, provide some funds for her child's college education (which is still some 12 years away). Although her income is modest, Janet feels that with careful planning, she could probably invest about $250 a quarter (and, with luck, maybe increase this amount over time). She presently has about $15,000 in a bank savings account which she would be willing to use to kick off this program. In view of her investment objectives, she is not interested in taking a lot of risk. Because her knowledge of investments extends to savings accounts, series EE bonds, and a little bit about mutual funds, she approaches you for some investment advice.

Questions

1. In view of Janet's long-term investment goals, do you think mutual funds are an appropriate investment vehicle for her?
2. Do you think she should use her $15,000 savings to start off a mutual fund investment program?
3. What type of mutual fund investment program would you set up for Janet? Include in your answer some discussion of the types of funds you would consider, the investment objectives you would set, and any investment services (like withdrawal plans) you would seek. Would taxes be an important consideration in your investment advice? Explain.

GETTING A HANDLE ON YOUR FINANCIAL FUTURE

Sound investment planning is essential to achieving your financial goals. However, many investors find the search for appropriate investments too time consuming or they do not feel comfortable analyzing all the financial data necessary to make an appropriate investment decision. If this sounds like your attitude, then mutual funds are right for you.

If You Are Just Starting Out

For the beginning investor, mutual funds are a particularly helpful instrument because they offer professional management, the opportunity to earn an attractive rate of return, and a convenient means of investing with relatively small amounts of capital.

Choosing a Mutual Fund

1. Decide on your investment objectives and make a list of mutual funds that meet them. For example, if you prefer lower risks, then equity-income, growth-and-income, or balanced funds may be right for you.
2. Screen the funds and eliminate those which do not offer the services you require.
3. Review the performance figures of the funds you have selected. Rank them from best performing to worst over the last year, five years, and ten years.
4. Find out if there has been a recent change in the investment manager. This could affect the investment strategy of the fund.
5. Check the prospectus for transactions costs and operating expenses.
6. Select the fund(s) that are most appropriate.

If You Are Thirty-Something

As your financial resources and investment experience increase, you may begin to experiment with alternative strategies and vehicles.

Points to Consider

1. Be sure to keep your mutual fund portfolio diversified. This will help you maintain returns even during low or volatile periods in the market.
2. If you feel more confident, consider investing in higher risk funds like global or high yield funds.
3. As you evaluate changing your mutual fund portfolio, be sure to factor in any sales. Also, don't forget that profits from exchanges between funds must be reported to the IRS, which could affect the advantages of making the switch.
4. If you live in a state with high taxes, investigate tax-free funds. These funds invest in municipal bonds with tax-exempt interest which helps reduce tax obligations.
5. Don't forget to monitor your fund(s) performance. Some clues that it might be time to sell-out of a fund are—major change in investment objectives, three or more years of poor performance in comparison with similar funds, and the departure of a high-profile, successful fund manager.

1. Using the asset values and the interest rates given in the original case, and assuming constant balances were maintained all year, how much annual interest and dividend income would Paul receive in 1996 from his (ignore compounding)
   - minimum balance checking account at Jefferson National Bank?
   - money market account at Jefferson National Bank?
   - money market fund with Fidelity?
   - savings account at Community Credit Union?
2. In Part Two, Questions 4 and 6, you made recommendations concerning changes in Paul's cash management accounts. How much annual interest and dividend income would he receive in 1996 if he follows your recommendations from these two questions? (ignore compounding)
3. Using the dividend income and current values from the original case, what was the current dividend yield in 1995 on the
   - Physician's Corporation of America (PCAM) stock?
   - Fidelity Equity-Income II mutual fund?
   - Janus mutual fund?
   - Janus Venture mutual fund?
4. Calculate the approximate annual yield from the purchase date until January 1996 for the PCAM stock and the Fidelity Equity-Income II mutual fund using the data in the original case and ignoring commissions. Physician's Corporation of America has never paid dividends. Assume that the dividends and capital gains distributions paid by Fidelity Equity-Income II in 1995 were typical of those paid over the years in which this investment was owned. Compare the annual yield on these investments to the yield on Paul's less risky cash management accounts. Did the PCAM stock and the Fidelity Equity-Income II fund provide an adequate yield for the risk taken?
5. Track the net asset value (NAV) of Fidelity Equity-Income II, Janus Fund, and Janus Venture over a two-week period. Also track the Dow Jones Industrial Average and the Standard & Poor's 500 over this same period.
6. From looking at the mutual fund listings in *The Wall Street Journal*, what type of funds are Fidelity Equity-Income II, Janus Fund, and Janus Venture? Do any of these funds charge front-end loads, 12(b)-1 fees, and/or redemption fees? If there is a front-end load, what percentage load is charged? What are their total expense ratios? What are their year-to-date yields as well as their 1-year and 5-year average annual yields? How do these three funds rank over the 1-year and 5-year time periods?
7. Track the closing price for Physicians Corporation of America (PCAM) in *The Wall Street Journal* or any daily newspaper that lists Nasdaq stocks. Also track the Nasdaq Composite Index. Do this over the same two-week period in which you track Paul's mutual funds.
8. From the Nasdaq listing in *The Wall Street Journal,* what was PCAM's 52-week high and low, is it currently selling at prices near its 52-week high, how many shares traded the first day PCAM was tracked, what is the stock's P/E ratio?
9. Paul would like to update his investment knowledge on the stock and mutual funds he currently owns. Use reports available in the library (*Standard & Poor's Stock Report* or *Value Line*) or other sources mentioned in your text to learn more about PCAM. Use *Morningstar's Mutual Fund Values, Wiesenberger's Investment Companies, Value Line's Mutual Fund Reports,* or other sources mentioned in the text to learn more about Paul's three mutual funds. Write a paragraph evaluating each of these four investments. Are they good investments for Paul given his goals and risk tolerance?

10. What specific type(s) of risk are Paul's cash management accounts exposed to? What types of risk are his stock and mutual fund investments subject to?

FPPC 11. Paul is considering selling his shares of Fidelity Equity-Income II in order to buy a house, pay off his line of credit (previously credit card debt), and perhaps increase his emergency fund balance. If he sold all his Fidelity Equity-Income II at the current value listed in the case, how much would his before-tax capital gain be on these shares? Given his marginal tax bracket (Part Two, Question 16), approximately how much would he have to pay in federal income taxes on this transaction?

12. Refer to Paul's most recent budget (Part Four, Question 11), tax estimate (Part Two, Question 16), and his original balance sheet (Part One, Question 1). Also review your cash management recommendations (Part Two, Questions 1, 2, 4, and 6), your housing recommendations (Part Two, Questions 10 through 15), and the latest information on his line of credit that he used to pay off his credit card debt (beginning of Part Four) as well as all the information you have gathered in Part Five concerning his Fidelity Equity-Income II mutual fund investment. Keeping Paul's goals and risk tolerance in mind, what would you recommend Paul do with his shares of Fidelity Equity-Income II? Justify your recommendation.

FPPC 13. Paul is considering selling his shares of PCAM and investing this money in other stocks or bonds. If Paul sold all his PCAM stock at the current value listed in the original case and paid $107 in commissions when he sold and $74 in commissions when he purchased the shares, how much would his before-tax capital gain be on these shares? Approximately how much would he have to pay in federal income taxes on this transaction?

FPPC 14. Paul is considering reinvesting the funds from the PCAM sale in one of the following two stock investments. What is the current dividend yield on each of these investments? What would the approximate annual yield be on each given the following assumptions? He plans to keep the investment 5 years.

	Blue-chip stock	Aggressive growth stock	PCAM
Current market value	$34.25	$22.87	$26.75
Annual dividend income	1.75	0.50	0.25
Market value in 5 years	43.50	41.00	50.00

FPPC 15. Paul is also considering investing the PCAM proceeds in a corporate bond that is currently selling at discount for $5,250. It has a face value of $6,000, matures in 5 years, and has an AA rating from Moody's. It pays annual interest of $250. What is the current yield on this bond investment? What is the yield-to-maturity on this bond?

16. Given Paul's marginal tax rate, would a tax-free AA municipal bond with a current yield of 4.5% provide a higher after-tax current yield than the corporate bond in Question 15?

17. An acquaintance of Paul thought that he should invest in the aggressive growth stock (from Question 14) on margin. Would you recommend that Paul buy stock on margin? Why or why not?

18. Which investment would you recommend for Paul—keep the PCAM or buy the blue-chip stock, the aggressive growth stock, the corporate bond, the municipal bond or something else? Remember his goals and tolerance for risk as well as brokerage commissions and tax consequences when making the recommendation. Justify your recommendation.

FPPC 19. Look at your recommendations from Questions 12 and 18. Revise Paul's balance sheet, budget, and tax estimate to reflect any changes assuming Paul follows your recommendations.

PART 6

RETIREMENT AND ESTATE PLANNING

CHAPTER 14

MEETING RETIREMENT GOALS

Annabelle Reitman's Retirement Financing

Dr. Annabelle Reitman, 58, only began thinking seriously about retirement when her daughter entered college in 1989. "I wanted to retire at 59 and knew that I hadn't saved enough. But as a single parent, my first responsibility was to provide for my daughter and send her to college," she explains. "Only then could I think about retirement and how to afford the things I enjoy, like travel. Financially, I had to supplement my retirement benefits." So several years ago, while still directing a career development program at a Washington, D.C. university, she and a partner formed a firm specializing in career development training and school-to-work transition programs.

But in late 1994, the university offered an early retirement plan—a year's salary, paid over three years. "I researched it thoroughly, talking to benefits counselors and analyzing my current and future income sources," Annabelle recalls. "Because it provided enough income to cover me while I hopefully build my business, I accepted the offer." For three years, she will have the salary payout and a monthly payment from a university-funded retirement program (that continues for life). She also arranged to work at an antique store once a week, for little extras. At 59½, she can tap into a supplemental retirement annuity (SRA), which she funded with pre-tax dollars, and an individual retirement arrangement (IRA), started when her contributions were tax deductible, without tax penalties. She does not plan to use either until she's 60½, when the

Learning Goals

LG1. *Recognize the importance of retirement planning and identify the three biggest pitfalls to good planning.*
LG2. *Establish retirement goals and estimate your future income needs.*
LG3. *Explain the eligibility requirements and benefits of the Social Security program.*
LG4. *Differentiate among the different types of basic and supplemental employer-sponsored pension plans.*
LG5. *Describe the various types of self-directed retirement plans.*
LG6. *Choose the right type of annuity for your retirement plan.*

salary payout ends. At either 62 or 65, she is also eligible for Social Security retirement benefits.

Annabelle has invested her two university retirement funds conservatively, with 55 percent in fixed income and 45 percent in equities. The SRA has mutual funds, including some global funds for diversification. "I can change the SRA investments and manage them carefully," she says. "When interest rates fall, I move some money from fixed income securities to stocks. I wanted a more aggressive plan for my credit union IRA, which was performing poorly, so I withdrew the funds and invested in several individual stocks that could provide an inflation hedge."

How has Annabelle adjusted to her new life? "So far, so good," she reports. "The first year is the most important time to establish your new life. Remember to consider both financial and emotional needs. Plan to get out and do things; develop new interests and stay active." She also advises to start saving early. "Like most people, I thought I had plenty of time when I was younger. I also lacked the financial resources to fund my plans. Invest directly from your paycheck—even if it's just $25. Make it a habit; you won't miss it. I used part of every raise to increase my SRA contribution. I was amazed at how quickly it grew." The following chapter explains how to assess your own retirement needs and develop a plan, so like Annabelle, you too will be ready for retirement—even if it starts unexpectedly.

AN OVERVIEW OF RETIREMENT PLANNING FPPC LG1 LG2

Retirement planning is a key element in the financial planning process; to be effective, however, it should begin relatively early in life and involve a strategy of systematically accumulating retirement funds. Stop for a moment and think about how you intend to plan for retirement. At what age do you want to retire? What size nest egg do you want at retirement, and how do you intend to reach that goal?

Do you know your life expectancy? Well, if you're in your late teens or early 20s, you'll probably live another 50 or 60 years. While this prospect may sound delightful, it also brings into focus the need for careful retirement planning. After all, you may only work for about 40 of those years—perhaps less—and spend 10, 20, or more years in retirement. The challenge, of course, is to do it in style—and that is where retirement planning comes into play! But to enjoy a comfortable retirement, you must start *now*. For one of the biggest mistakes that people make in retirement planning is waiting too long to begin. Yet the longer you wait, the harder it will be to reach the kind of retirement income you would like.

Even those who have started their retirement savings may not be doing enough. In a recent Equitable Life survey of 30–48 year-olds with median incomes of $69,000, the average retirement goal was $830,000. However, the typical 41-year-old had saved *less than one year's salary,* and most of that was invested in fixed income investments earning about 6 percent. Investment firm T. Rowe Price estimates that a 48-year-old needs $330,000—and a 38-year-old, $489,000—in tax-deferred retirement plans for every $10,000 of annual income needed from age 65 to 90, assuming 4 percent inflation and 7 percent average annual investment returns.

Clearly, accumulating adequate retirement funds is a daunting task that takes careful planning. Like budgets, taxes, and investments, retirement planning is vital to your financial well-being and is a critical link in your personal financial plans. Yet it's difficult for most people under the age of 30 to develop a well-defined set of retirement plans. There are just too many years to go until retirement and too many uncertainties to deal with: inflation, social security, family size, the type of pension you'll receive—if any—and how much money you will have when you're ready to retire. However, it's just this kind of uncertainty that makes retirement planning so important. To cope with uncertainty, you must plan for a variety of outcomes, and monitor and modify your plans as your hopes, abilities, and personal finances change.

ROLE OF RETIREMENT PLANNING IN PERSONAL FINANCIAL PLANNING

The financial planning process would be incomplete without *retirement planning*. Certainly there is no financial goal more important than achieving a comfortable standard of living in retirement. In many respects, retirement planning captures the very essence of financial planning. It is forward looking (perhaps more so than any other function of financial planning), has an impact on both your current and future standard of living, and, if successful, can be highly rewarding and make a significant contribution to net worth.

Okay, it's important; so, where do you start? Well, like most aspects of financial planning, you need a goal or an objective—that is, the first step in retirement planning is to set *retirement goals* for yourself. Take some time to define the things you want to do in retirement, the standard of living you hope to maintain, the level of income you would like to receive, and any special retirement goals you may have (like buying a retirement home in Arizona, or taking an around-the-world cruise). Such goals are important because *they give direction to your retirement planning*. Of course, like all goals, they are subject to change over time as the situations and conditions in your life change. Once you know what you want out of retirement, the next step is to establish the *size of the nest egg* you're going to have to build in order to achieve your retirement goals. In essence, how much money will you need to retire the way you would like?

The final step is to formulate an *investment program* that will enable you to build up your required nest egg. This usually involves creating some type of systematic savings plan (putting away a certain amount each year) and identifying the types of investment vehicles that will best meet your retirement needs. This phase of your retirement program is closely related to two other aspects of financial planning—investment and tax planning. Investments and investment planning (see Chapters 11 through 13) are the vehicles through which to build retirement funds. They comprise the active, ongoing part of retirement planning in which you manage and invest the funds you have set aside for retirement. It is no coincidence that a major portion of most individual investor portfolios is devoted to building up a pool of funds for retirement. Taxes and tax planning (see Chapter 3) are also important, since one of the major objectives of sound retirement planning is to legitimately shield as much income as possible from taxes and, in so doing, maximize the accumulation of retirement funds.

THE THREE BIGGEST PITFALLS TO SOUND RETIREMENT PLANNING

Human nature being what it is, people often get a little carried away with the amount of money they want to build up for retirement. Face it, having a nest egg of $3 or $4 million would be great, but it's beyond the reach of all but a tiny fraction of the population. Besides, you don't need that much to live comfortably in retirement anyway. So, set a more realistic goal. But when you set that goal, remember: It's not going to happen by itself; you have to do something to bring it about. And this is precisely where things start to fall apart. Why? Because when it comes to retirement planning, people tend to make three big mistakes:

- They start too late.
- They put away too little.
- They invest too conservatively.

Many people in their 20s, or even 30s, find it hard to put money away for retirement. More often than not, that's because they have more pressing financial concerns to worry about—like buying a house, retiring a student loan, or paying for child care. The net result is that retirement planning is put off until later in life; in many cases, until they're in their late 30s or 40s. Unfortunately, the longer people put it off, the less they're going to have in retirement. Or, it means they're not going to be able to retire as early as they'd hoped. Even worse, once people start a retirement program, they tend to be too skimpy and put away too little. While this, too, may be due to pressing family needs, all too often it boils down to lifestyle choices. They'd rather spend for today than save for tomorrow. As a result, they end up putting, maybe, $1,000 a year into a retirement plan when, with a little more effective financial planning and family budgeting, they could easily afford to save two or three times that amount.

On top of all this, most people tend to be far too conservative in the way they invest their retirement money. Too often, people fail to achieve the full potential of their retirement programs because they treat them more like savings accounts than investment vehicles! The fact is, they place most, if not all, of their retirement money into *low yielding,* fixed-income securities, like CDs and Treasury notes. While you should *never speculate* with something as important as your retirement plan, you do not have to totally avoid risk. There's nothing wrong with following an investment program that involves a *reasonable* amount of risk, so long as it results in a correspondingly higher level of return. Caution is fine, but being overly cautious can be very costly in the long run. Indeed, a low rate of return can have an enormous effect on the long-term accumulation of capital and, in many cases, may mean the difference between just getting by or enjoying a comfortable retirement.

All three of these pitfalls become even more important when we introduce *compound* interest. Why is that so? Because *compounding essentially magnifies the impact of these mistakes.* To illustrate, consider the first variable—starting too late. If you were to start a retirement program at age 35, by putting away $2,000 a year, it would grow to more than $150,000 by the time you're 65, when invested at an average rate of return of 6 percent. Not a bad deal, considering your total out-of-pocket investment over this 30-year period is only $60,000. But look at what you end up with if you start this investment program ten years earlier, at age 25: That same $2,000 a year will grow to over $300,000 by the time you're 65. Think of it—for another $20,000 ($2,000 a year for an extra ten years), you can double the terminal value of your investment! Of course, it's not the extra $20,000 that's doubling your money; rather, it's *compound* interest that's doing all the work!

And the same holds true for the rate of return you earn on the investments in your retirement account. Take the second situation above—starting a retirement program at 25. Earning 6 percent means a retirement nest egg of over $300,000; increase that rate of return to 10 percent (a reasonable investment objective), and your retirement nest egg will be worth nearly $900,000! You're still putting in the same amount of money, but because your money is working harder, you end up with a much bigger nest egg. Of course, when you seek higher returns (as you would when you go from 6 to 10 percent), that generally means you also have to take on more risks. But that may not be as much of a problem as it appears, because in retirement planning, the one thing you have on your side is time (unless you start your plan very late in life). And the more time you have, the less of a burden risk becomes. That is, the more time you have, the easier it is to recover from those temporary market setbacks.

On the other hand, if you simply cannot tolerate the higher risks that accompany higher returns (and, certainly, some people cannot), then stay away from the higher-risk investments! Rather, stick to safer, lower-yielding securities and find some other ways to build up your nest egg. For instance, contribute more each year to your plan and/or extend the length of your investment period. The only other option—and not a particularly appealing one—is to accept the fact that you will not be able to build up as big a nest egg as you had thought and, therefore, will have to accept a lower standard of living in retirement. Finally, all else being the same, it should be clear that the more you sock away each year, the more you're going to have at retirement. That is, put away $4,000 a year, rather than $2,000, and you are going to end up with twice as much money at retirement.

The combined impact of these three variables is seen in Exhibit 14.1. Note that it's really the combination of these three factors that determines the amount you will have at retirement. Thus, you can offset the effects of earning a lower rate of return on your money by increasing the amount you put in each year and/or by lengthening the period over which you build up your retirement account—meaning you start your program earlier in life (or work longer and retire later in life). In essence, the table shows that *there are several different ways of getting to roughly the same result;* that is, knowing the kind of nest egg you'd like to end up with, you can pick the combination of variables (period of accumulation, annual contribution, and rate of return) that you're most comfortable with.

RETIREMENT GOALS

People have all sorts of retirement goals. Playing more golf, fishing, traveling, or pursuing a favorite hobby are just a few examples. To have the income to realize these goals, people should consider the age at which they will retire and what their financial position is likely to be at that time.

Age at Retirement. Estimating when you are likely to retire is important, because it lets you know how much time you have to save for retirement. Several years ago, it was not uncommon for workers to retire at age 60, or even 55. But the last couple of years have seen a trend toward later retirement. Some people now remain in the work force until age 70 or longer. If you think that a *shorter* working career is for you, then you must take the steps to put more money aside each year for retirement than others who plan to work for as long as they are physically and mentally capable.

Financial Position and Goals. Your financial position at retirement depends not only on your retirement plans but—perhaps even more so—on your choice of career and lifestyle. Remember that the quality of your life and lifestyle goals must be chosen on the basis of projected income and expenditures. Devoting some income toward retirement is essential to economic security in old age. You must be careful, therefore, not to satisfy low-priority, short-run desires at the expense of high-priority, long-run objectives.

ESTIMATING INCOME NEEDS

Retirement planning would be much simpler if we lived in a static economy. Unfortunately (or perhaps fortunately), we don't, and as a result, both your personal budget and the general economy are subject to considerable change over time, making accurate forecasting of retirement needs difficult at best. Even so, it is a *necessary task,* and one that you can handle in one of two ways. One strategy is to plan for retirement over a *series of short-run time frames.* A good way to do this is to state your retirement income objectives as a percentage of your present earnings. For example, if you desire a retirement income equal to 80 percent of your final take-home pay, you can determine the amount necessary to fund this need. Then, every three to five years, you can revise and update your plan.

Alternatively, you can follow a *long-term* approach in which you actually formulate the level of income you would like to receive in retirement, along with the amount of funds you must amass to achieve that desired standard of living. Rather than

EXHIBIT 14.1

Building Up Your Retirement Nest Egg

The size of your retirement nest egg will depend on when you start your program (period of accumulation), how much you contribute each year, and the rate of return you earn on your investments. As seen in this table, you can combine these variables in a number of different ways to end up with a given amount at retirement.

	Amount of Accumulated Capital from							
	Contribution of $2,000/yr. at These Average Rates of Return				Contribution of $5,000/yr. at These Average Rates of Return			
Accumulation Period*	**4%**	**6%**	**8%**	**10%**	**4%**	**6%**	**8%**	**10%**
10 yrs. (55 yrs. old)	$ 24,010	$ 26,360	$ 28,970	$ 31,870	$ 60,030	$ 65,900	$ 72,440	$ 79,690
20 yrs. (45 yrs. old)	59,560	73,570	91,520	114,550	148,890	183,930	228,810	286,370
25 yrs. (40 yrs. old)	83,290	109,720	146,210	196,690	208,230	274,300	365,530	491,730
30 yrs. (35 yrs. old)	112,170	158,110	226,560	328,980	280,420	395,290	566,410	822,460
35 yrs. (30 yrs. old)	147,300	222,860	344,630	542,040	368,260	557,160	861,570	1,355,090
40 yrs. (25 yrs. old)	190,050	309,520	518,100	885,160	475,120	773,790	1,295,260	2,212,900

*Assumes retirement at age 65; parenthetical figure, therefore, is the age at which the person would start his or her retirement program.

addressing the problem in a series of short-run plans, this approach goes 20 or 30 years into the future—to the time when you will retire—to determine how much saving and investing you must do today to achieve your long-run retirement goals.

Of course, if conditions and/or expectations change dramatically, it may be necessary to make corresponding alterations to your long-run retirement goals and strategies. For example, pension plans and retirement plan accounts may get ignored during a divorce process. There is a tendency at such times to focus on meeting current needs, with less attention paid to how the involved parties will cover retirement needs. Yet getting part of some types of plans from a former spouse may require a special court order, so it is important to consider retirement assets when negotiating the divorce settlement. After the divorce, you will need to reevaluate your retirement planning to assure that it will provide adequate funds, taking into account any changes resulting from the settlement.

Determining Future Retirement Needs. To illustrate how future retirement needs and income requirements can be formulated, let's consider the case of Jack and Lois Winter. In their mid-30s, they have two children and an annual income of about $60,000 before taxes. Up to now, Jack and Lois have given only passing thought to their retirement. But even though it's still some 30 years away, they recognize it's now time to give some serious consideration to their situation to see if they will be able to pursue a retirement lifestyle that appeals to them. Worksheet 14.1 provides the basic steps to follow in determining retirement needs. This worksheet shows how the Winters have estimated their retirement income and determined the amount of investment assets they must accumulate to meet their retirement objectives.

Jack and Lois began their calculation by determining what their *household expenditures* will likely be in retirement. Their estimate is based on maintaining a "comfortable" standard of living—one that will not be extravagant yet will allow them to do the things they would like in retirement. A simple yet highly effective way to derive an estimate of expected household expenditures is to base it on the current level of such expenses. Assume the Winter's annual household expenditures (excluding savings) currently run about $42,000 a year—this information can be readily obtained by referring to their most recent income and expenditures statement. Making some obvious adjustments for the different lifestyle they will have in retirement—their children will no longer be living at home, their home will be paid for, and so on—the Winters estimate that they will be able to achieve the standard of living they'd like in retirement at an annual level of household expenditures equal to about 70 percent of the current amount. Thus, *in terms of today's dollars,* their estimated household expenditures in retirement will be $42,000 × .70 = $29,400. (This process is summarized in steps A through D in Worksheet 14.1.)

WORKSHEET 14.1

Estimating Future Retirement Needs

This worksheet will help you define your income requirements in retirement, the size of your retirement nest egg, and the amount that you must save annually to achieve your given retirement goals.

PROJECTING RETIREMENT INCOME AND INVESTMENT NEEDS

Name(s) Jack & Lois Winter Date June 1996

I.	**Estimated Household Expenditures in Retirement:**	
A.	Approximate number of years to retirement	30
B.	*Current* level of annual household expenditures, excluding savings	$ 42,000
C.	Estimated household expenses in retirement *as a percent* of current expenses	70%
D.	Estimated annual household expenditures in retirement (B x C)	$ 29,400
II.	**Estimated income in Retirement:**	
E.	Social security, annual income	$ 13,000
F.	Company/employer pension plans, annual amounts	$ 9,000
G.	Other sources, annual amounts	$ 0
H.	Total annual income (E + F + G)	$ 22,000
I.	Additional required income, or *annual* shortfall (D – H)	$ 7,400
III.	**Inflation Factor:**	
J.	Expected average annual rate of inflation over the period to retirement	5%
K.	Inflation factor (in Appendix A): Based on 30 years to retirement (A) and an expected average annual rate of inflation (J) of 5%	4.32
L.	Size of inflation-adjusted annual shortfall (I x K)	$ 32,000
IV.	**Funding the Shortfall:**	
M.	Anticipated return on assets held *after* retirement	10%
N.	Amount of retirement funds required—size of nest egg (L ÷ M)	$ 320,000
O.	Expected rate of return on investments *prior* to retirement	8%
P.	Compound interest factor (in Appendix B): Based on 30 years to retirement (A) and an expected rate of return on investments of 8%	113.3
Q.	Annual savings required to fund retirement nest egg (N ÷ P)	$ 2,824

Note: Parts I and II are prepared in terms of current (today's) dollars.

Estimating Retirement Income. The next question is: Where will they get the money to meet their projected household expenses of $29,400 a year? They have addressed this problem by estimating what their *income* will be in retirement—again *in terms of today's dollars*. Their two basic sources of retirement income are social security and employer-sponsored pension plans. Based on today's retirement tables they estimate that they will receive about $13,000 a year from social security (as we'll see later in this chapter, you can now receive an estimate directly from the Social Security Administration of what your future social security benefits are likely to be when you retire) and another $9,000 from their employer pension plans, for a total projected income of $22,000. When this is compared to their projected household expenditures, it is clear that the Winters will be facing an annual shortfall of $7,400 (see steps E through I in Worksheet 14.1). This is the amount of retirement income that they must come up with; otherwise, they will have to reduce the standard of living they hope to enjoy in retirement.

At this point, we need to introduce the *inflation factor* to our projections in order to put the annual shortfall of $7,400 in terms of retirement dollars. Here we make the assumption that both income and expenditures will undergo the same average rate of inflation, causing the shortfall to grow by that rate over time. In essence, 30 years from now, the annual shortfall is going to amount to a lot more than $7,400. How large it will grow to will, of course, be a function of what happens to inflation. Assume that the Winters think inflation, on average, over the next 30 years will amount to 5 percent. Using the compound value table from Appendix A, we find that the *inflation factor* for 5 percent and 30 years is 4.32; multiplying this inflation factor by the annual shortfall of $7,400 gives the Winters an idea of what that figure will be by the time they retire: $7,400 × 4.32 = $31,970, or nearly $32,000 a year (see steps J to L in Worksheet 14.1). Thus, based on their projections, the shortfall will amount to $32,000 a year when they retire 30 years from now. This is the amount they will have to come up with through their own supplemental retirement program.

Funding the Shortfall. The final two steps in this estimating process are (1) to determine *how big the retirement nest egg must be* in order to cover the projected annual income shortfall and (2) to determine *how much to save each year* in order to accumulate the required amount by the time the Winters retire. To find out how much money they are going to have to accumulate by retirement, they must estimate the rate of return they think they will be able to earn on their investments *after* they retire. This will tell them how big their nest egg will have to be by retirement in order to eliminate the expected annual shortfall of $32,000. Let's assume this rate of return is estimated at 10 percent, in which case the Winters must accumulate $320,000 by retirement. This figure is found by *capitalizing* the estimated shortfall of $32,000 at a 10 percent rate of return: $32,000 ÷ .10 = $320,000 (see steps M and N). Given a 10 percent rate of return, such a nest egg will yield $32,000 a year: $320,000 × .10 = $32,000. And so long as the capital ($320,000) remains untouched, it will generate the same amount of annual income for as long as the Winters live and can eventually become a part of their estate.

Now that the Winters know how big their nest egg has to be, the final question is: How are they going to accumulate such an amount by the time they retire? For most people, that means setting up a *systematic savings plan* and putting away a certain amount *each* year. To find out how much must be saved each year to achieve a targeted sum in the future, we can use the table of annuity factors in Appendix B. The appropriate interest factor is a function of the rate of return one can (or expects to) generate and the length of the investment period. In the Winters' case, there are 30 years to go until retirement, meaning the length of their investment period is 30 years. If they feel they will be able to earn an average rate of return of 8 percent on their investments over this 30-year period, they will want to use an 8 percent, 30-year interest factor; from Appendix B, we see that this equals 113.3. Because the Winters must accumulate $320,000 by the time they retire, *the amount that they will have to save each year* (over the next 30 years) can be found by *dividing* the amount they need to accumulate by the appropriate interest factor; that is, $320,000 ÷ 113.3 = $2,824 (see steps O to Q in Worksheet 14.1).

The Winters now know what they must do to achieve the kind of retirement they want: Put away $2,824 a year and invest it at an average annual rate of 8 percent over the next 30 years. If they can do that, they will have their $320,000 retirement nest egg in 30 years. How they actually invest their money so as to achieve the desired 8 percent rate of return will, of course, be a function of the investment vehicles and strategies they use. All the worksheet tells them is how much money they will need, not how they will get there; it is at this point that investment management enters the picture.

The procedure outlined here admittedly is a bit simplified and does take a few shortcuts, but considering the amount of uncertainty imbedded in the long-range projections being made, it does provide a viable estimate of retirement income and investment needs. The procedure certainly is far superior to the alternative of doing nothing! One important simplifying assumption in the procedure, though, is that it ignores the income that can be derived from the *sale of a house.* The sale of a house not only offers some special tax features for older people (see Chapter 3) but can generate a substantial amount of cash flow as well. Certainly, if inflation does occur in the future (and it will!), it will very likely drive up home prices right along with the cost of everything else. A lot of people sell their homes around the time they retire and either move into smaller houses (often in Sun Belt retirement communities) or decide to rent in order to avoid all the problems of homeownership. Of course, the cash flow from the sale of a house can have a substantial effect on the size of the retirement nest egg. However, rather than trying to factor it into the forecast of retirement income and needs, we suggest that you *recognize* the existence of this cash flow source in your retirement planning, and consider it as a cushion against all the uncertainty inherent in retirement planning projections.

COMPUTER-BASED RETIREMENT PLANNING

Most fully integrated financial planning software packages like those mentioned in Chapter 2—*Managing Your Money, Quicken,* and *WealthBuilder*—contain retirement planning programs that perform the same basic forecasting functions as those in Worksheet 14.1. In essence, you answer a few key questions about expected inflation, desired rate of return on investments, and current levels of income and expenditures, and the computer determines the size of any income shortfall, the amount of retirement funds that must be accumulated over time, and different ways to achieve the desired retirement nest egg. There are also lower-cost programs offered by mutual fund companies—Fidelity's *Retirement Thinker,* T. Rowe Price's *Retirement Planning Kit,* and Vanguard's *Retirement Planner*—that focus more on early planning rather than budgeting or portfolio management.

As with any software, you should consider the features of each to find which works best for you. An attractive feature of most of these programs is the ability to easily run through a series of "what if" exercises. By just punching a few buttons, you can change one or more key variables to see how they impact the size of your retirement nest egg and the amount of money you must put away annually. For example, you can find out what would happen if you failed to achieve the desired rate of return on your investments. In addition to this important retirement planning function, such software often allows you to track various retirement accounts to readily see how your performance is stacking up to your retirement goals—whether you are ahead of schedule, and, if not, what you can do to get back on track. Thus, modern, computer-based retirement planning assists you not only in establishing retirement goals and plans, but also in keeping track of your progress toward those objectives. However, as with other areas of financial planning, you should reevaluate your retirement needs whenever the underlying assumptions change—for example, if your personal circumstances change (job loss, divorce, and so on) or inflation rises.

SOURCES OF RETIREMENT INCOME

As Exhibit 14.2 reveals, the three principal sources of income for retired people are social security, assets (income-producing types such as savings, stocks, and bonds), and pension plans. For the average retiree, these categories will account for 82 percent of total retirement income. Just about every retired worker receives social security income, about 65 to 85 percent obtain at least some of their income from savings and/or investment assets, and, surprisingly, only about half (40 to 55 percent) receive benefits from some type of employer-provided pension plan. However, keep in mind these are *sources* of retirement income and not dollar amounts. The *amount* of income retired individuals will receive will, of course, vary from amounts that are barely above the poverty line to six-figure incomes. The amount received in retirement depends on a number of variables, the most important of which is the

EXHIBIT 14.2

Sources of Income for the Average Retiree

Note that *government assistance* (which is made up mostly of Social Security benefits) is the single largest source of income for the average U.S. retiree. That is more than the average retiree receives from company pension plans *and* personal wealth/investment assets, combined—which does not say much for the savings habits of Americans.

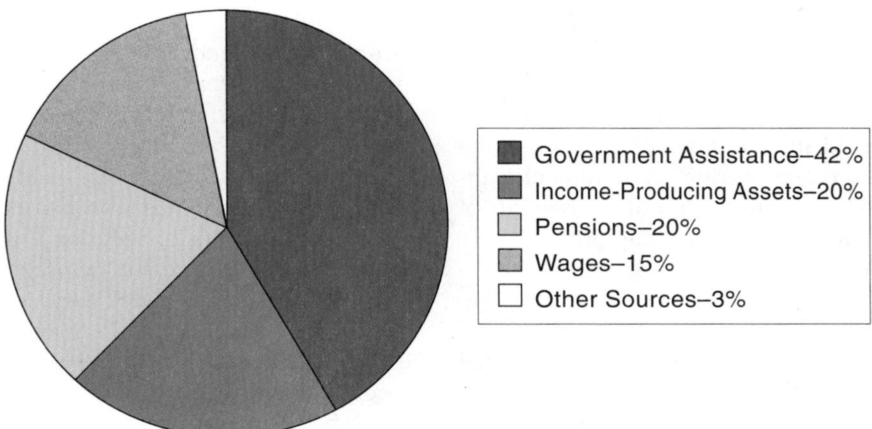

Source: Stephen M. Pollan and Mark Levine, "Retirement Isn't Just Obsolete, It's Unaffordable," *Worth,* December 1994/January 1995, p. 69.

level of preretirement earnings. Obviously, the more individuals make before they retire, the more they will receive in social security benefits and from company-sponsored pension plans—and, very likely, the greater the amount of income-producing assets they will hold. In this chapter, we will examine social security and various types of pension plans and retirement programs. In addition, we will look briefly at an investment vehicle that is designed especially for retirement income: the *annuity.*

Concept Check

14-1. Discuss the relationship of retirement planning to financial planning; does investment and/or tax planning have a role in retirement planning? Identify and briefly discuss each of the steps in the retirement planning process.

14-2. Identify and briefly discuss the three biggest mistakes that people tend to make when setting up retirement programs. Which of these three do you think is most important? Explain. What role does compound interest play in all this?

14-3. How do retirement goals and income needs fit in the retirement planning process? Discuss briefly the advantages of using a PC for retirement planning.

14-4. What are the most important sources of retirement income for most people?

SOCIAL SECURITY

LG3

Social security is an important source of income for retired people; however, if it's the only *source, the retiree is likely to find that his or her standard of living will be considerably less than expected. Do you feel social security will be around when you're ready to retire, and, assuming it is, how much do you think you'll receive in monthly benefits? What portion of your total retirement income do you think will come from social security benefits? Take a few minutes before reading on to consider these questions.*

The Social Security Act of 1935 was a piece of landmark legislation. Not *only* did it create a basic retirement program for working Americans at all income levels, it also established a number of other social programs, all of which are administered under the auspices of the *Old Age, Survivor's, Disability, and Health Insurance (OASDHI) program.* Some of the other services include supplementary security income (SSI), medicare, unemployment insurance, public assistance, welfare services, and provision for black lung benefits. This chapter gives primary attention to the old age and survivor's portion of the act, since it has a direct bearing on retirement planning. The disability and health/medicare benefits of social security are discussed in Chapter 9.

BASIC CONCEPTS

To fully appreciate the underlying merits of Social Security as a retirement program, you need to understand (1) its financing, (2) its solvency, and (3) its investment attributes.

Financing. The cash benefits provided by Social Security are derived from the payroll taxes (FICA) paid by covered employees and their employers. As pointed out in Chapter 3, the tax rate in 1995 was 7.65 percent—this is the amount that was paid by the employee and an equal amount was paid by the employer. Self-employed people are also covered by Social Security, and in 1995 they had to pay the total rate of 15.3 percent (that is, 7.65% × 2); and of course, since there are no employers to share the burden, self-employed people have to pay the full amount themselves. Regardless of whether the individual is an employee or self-employed, the indicated tax rate stays in effect only until the employee reaches a maximum *wage base,* which increases each year. For 1995, basic social security taxes were paid on the first $61,200 of wages earned, or self-employed income. Thus, the maximum social security tax paid by an *employee* in 1995 was $4,682 ($61,200 × .0765) and for the *self-employed,* $9,364 ($61,200 × .153). Note that starting in 1991, a second tax was added to cover the rising costs of medicare. Now, once the Social Security wage base is passed, the new, higher medicare wage base kicks in and employees are subject to a tax rate of 1.45 percent *on all earnings* over $61,200, while the added earnings of the self-employed are taxed at the rate of 2.9 percent.

Solvency. A lot of people fear that Social Security will run out of money by the time they are ready to collect their benefits. This is because a larger percentage of our population will be elderly in future years than has been the case in the past. For instance, as shown in Exhibit 14.3, the percentage of persons age 65 or over is expected to increase to 20.1 percent by the year 2030, up from just 5.4 percent in 1930 and 11.3 percent in 1980. This trend means that *retirement benefits will be mushrooming at the very same time that proportionately fewer people will be available in the work force to support those collecting Social Security.* For example, whereas in 1955, when there were seven workers supporting each person on Social Security, it is estimated that by the year 2000 there will be only two workers for each Social Security beneficiary.

While Congress has long been aware of the existence of this problem, it only took action recently to slowly raise the retirement age from 65 to 67, beginning in 2000. As the current legislation stands, by the year 2027 a person will have to wait until age 67 in order to collect full Social Security benefits. At the same time, the penalty for early retirement (age 62) is being increased substantially. Whereas today an individual can retire at age 62 and collect 80 percent of the full benefits, in the future that person will collect only *70 percent* of the full benefits upon early retirement. This revised penalty structure will be fully phased in by the year 2027.

Investment Attributes. If you are like most people, you probably wonder what Social Security holds for you. First, you might ask "Will there be any money left when I get to retirement age?" As discussed here, the probability that Social Security will have funds to pay out benefits is as close to 100 percent as any future economic plan can be—at least for the next 30 or 40 years. As a second concern, you might wonder, "What kind of investment return will I get on my contributions? Wouldn't I be better off to invest the money myself?" This type of question can be answered in terms of (1) Social Security as an investment and (2) expected rates of return under Social Security.

To begin with, Social Security should not be viewed as an investment. It is properly viewed as a social insurance system: an insurance system that insures covered workers and their families against poverty resulting from retirement, death, disability,

EXHIBIT 14.3

The Growing Importance of the Senior Citizen

As the population grows older, the demands and pressures on the integrity of the Social Security system will increase accordingly.

Year	Percent of Population 65 and Over	Year	Percent of Population 65 and Over
1930	5.4	1990	12.5
1940	6.8	2000	12.8
1950	8.1	2010	13.4
1960	9.2	2020	16.3
1970	9.8	2030	20.1
1975	10.3	2040	20.7
1980	11.3`	2050	20.4

Source: Adapted from U.S. Bureau of the Census, *Statistical Abstract of the United States,* 114th edition, Washington, D.C., Table No. 16, p. 16.

or health problems. If you die or become disabled at age 30 and have a spouse and two small children, your family could be eligible for monthly Social Security payments that would total more than $150,000—even if, up to that point, you had paid less than $10,000 in taxes. Similarly, you might retire and live for another 15, 20, or even 30 years. It makes no difference to Social Security. You will continue to draw benefits even though they could easily exceed the amount you paid into the system. On the other hand, you might pay Social Security taxes for 40 years and then die (without dependents) the day you retire—and not collect a penny. An insurance system works only when some participants collect less than they pay in—otherwise no one could collect more. This principle holds regardless of whether we are talking about private life insurance, homeowner's insurance, automobile insurance, or the retirement, life insurance, and disability coverage offered by Social Security.

Many critics have complained that the investment yields on Social Security could easily be exceeded through comparable investments in stocks, bonds, or real estate. Even if this claim were true, it would be irrelevant. The fact is that after allowing for all of the cash and noncash (for example, medicare) benefits of Social Security, the relatively safe nature of the benefits, and a moderate premium for the risk reduction features of the program, *the expected value of most workers' benefits far exceeds the expected value of their tax payments into the system*.

WHO IS COVERED?

Legislation enacted by Congress several years ago extended coverage of Social Security to just about all gainfully employed workers. There are now only two major classes of employees exempt from *mandatory* participation in the Social Security system: (1) federal *civilian* employees who were hired before 1984 and are covered under the Civil Service Retirement System; and (2) employees of state and local governments who have chosen not to be covered (though the vast majority of these employees are covered through *voluntary participation* in Social Security). In addition, certain marginal employment positions, such as newspaper deliverypersons under age 18 and full-time college students working in fraternity and sorority houses, are also exempt. But by far, the largest number of workers in these excluded classes are employees of state and local governments. These groups are not forced to participate because the federal government is not empowered to impose a tax on state and local governments—although once in the program, these employees have to stay in, as they no longer have the option of voting to leave.

WHEN ARE YOU ELIGIBLE FOR BENEFITS?

Social Security payments are not paid automatically to eligible individuals (or their dependents). An application for benefits must be filed with the Social

Security Administration, which then determines the applicant's eligibility for benefits based on whether he or she has had enough quarters (three-month periods) of participation in the system. To qualify for full retirement benefits, nearly all workers today must be employed in a job covered by Social Security for at least 40 quarters, or ten years. These quarters need not be consecutive. Once this 40-quarter requirement is met, the worker becomes fully insured and remains eligible for retirement payments even if he or she never works again in covered employment. Note, however, that when yearly covered wages are computed, zeros are inserted for years in which no Social Security taxes were paid—which substantially reduces the size of future monthly benefit payments.

The surviving spouse and/or dependent children of a *deceased worker* are also eligible for monthly benefits if the worker was fully insured at the time of death or, in some special cases, if certain other requirements are met. Workers may be considered fully insured if they had six quarters of coverage during the three-year-period preceding the time of death.

SOCIAL SECURITY RETIREMENT BENEFITS

Basic Social Security benefits that are important to retired people and their dependents include (1) old-age benefits and (2) survivor's benefits. Both of these programs provide extended benefits to covered workers and/or their spouses; the major provisions of each of these programs is briefly described in the material that follows.

Old-Age Benefits. Workers who are fully covered (that is, who have worked the required 40 quarters under Social Security) may receive old-age benefits for life once they reach the age of 65 (or higher age after 2000, as stated above). In addition, workers who elect to retire early—at age 62—will receive *reduced benefits,* currently, 80 percent of the full benefits; this amount is scheduled to gradually decline by the year 2027 to only 70 percent of the full amount. If the retiree has a spouse 65 or older, the spouse may be entitled to benefits equal to one-half of the amount received by the retired worker. The spouse may also elect early receipt of reduced benefits at age 62.

In the case of two-income families, both the husband and wife may be eligible for full Social Security benefits. When they retire, they can choose to receive their benefits in one of two ways: each can (1) take the full benefits to which each is entitled from his or her account, or (2) take the husband and wife benefits of the higher-paid spouse. If each takes his or her own full share, there are no spousal benefits; if they take the husband and wife benefits of the higher-paid spouse, they effectively receive 1.5 shares. Obviously, two-income couples should select the option that provides the greatest amount of benefits (the amount of Social Security benefits will be described later).

Survivor's Benefits. If a covered worker dies, the spouse can receive survivor's benefits from Social Security. These benefits include a small lump-sum payment of several hundred dollars, followed by monthly benefit checks. The lump-sum amount is paid automatically upon application. In order to be eligible for monthly payments, the widowed spouse generally must be at least 60 years of age, or have a dependent and unmarried child of the deceased worker in his or her care. (To qualify for *full* benefits, the surviving spouse must be at least 65 years of age; reduced benefits are payable between ages 60 and 65.) If the children of a deceased worker reach age 16 before the spouse reaches age 60, the monthly benefits cease and do not resume until the spouse turns 60. This period of time during which survivor's benefits are not paid is sometimes called the *widow's gap.* (As we saw in Chapter 8, Social Security survivor's benefits play a key role in life insurance planning.)

HOW MUCH ARE MONTHLY SOCIAL SECURITY BENEFITS?

The amount of Social Security benefits to which an eligible person is entitled is set by law and defined according to a fairly complex formula. Until recently, it was difficult to predict your future benefits. In 1988, however, the Social Security Administration introduced a computerized benefits estimation service. Under this program, you provide the Social Security Administration with some basic information about yourself, and it provides you with something called a *Personal Earnings and Benefit Estimate Statement*. To get one of your own, simply call their toll-free number (1-800-772-1213); you'll then receive a short questionnaire asking for a few basic facts, including your name, social security number, date of birth, previous and current year's earnings, and the age at which you plan to retire. About four to six weeks after you mail the form, you'll receive a personalized statement just like the one shown in Exhibit 14.4. This report lists the year-by-year Social Security earnings you've been credited with, and shows (in today's dollars) what benefits you can expect under three scenarios: (1) if you retire at age 62 and receive 80 percent of the full benefit (or less, depending on your age); (2) the full benefit at age 65 to 67 (depending on your year of birth); and (3) the increased benefit (of up to 8 percent per year) that's available if you delay retirement until age 70. The statement also estimates what your children and surviving spouse would get if you die, and how much you'd receive monthly if you became disabled. This statement is a valuable financial planning tool and is something that every working American should obtain—also, it's a good idea to get an updated report every five years or so.

Using information provided by Social Security, we can describe the *current level of benefits* (for someone who retired in 1995); this is done in Exhibit 14.5 on page 578. The benefits *as of 1995* are for a retired worker, a retired worker and (nonworking) spouse, and a two-income couple for low, medium, and high career income levels (a *high* income worker is one whose annual earnings equaled or exceeded the maximum Social Security tax base). Bear in mind the figures listed in the exhibit represent amounts that the beneficiaries will receive in the *first year* of their retirement. Those amounts will, of course, be adjusted upward each year with subsequent increases in the cost of living.

Retired Social Security recipients (aged 65 to 69) have their benefit payments *reduced* if they earn an annual income (in 1995) in excess of $11,280; this same earnings limitation is $8,160 for retirees between age 62 and 65. (Note that these earnings limitations rise annually with wage inflation.) The applicable rule states that for Social Security recipients aged 65 to 69, each $3 earned in excess of the stipulated threshold results in a $1 reduction in benefits; and for those under age 65, there's a $1 loss in benefits for each $2 in excess earnings. However, the earnings limitation ceases at age 70; thus, anyone 70 or older will receive full Social Security benefits regardless of how much they earn. In contrast, *unearned income such as interest, dividends, and rent may be of an unlimited amount without a corresponding benefits reduction*. The fact that benefits are subject to reduction with earned income, but not with unearned income, is one of the most criticized features of Social Security.

Taxes on Benefits. No longer are Social Security benefits a source of tax-free income. In 1984, Congress passed legislation to tax the benefits paid to "upper-income beneficiaries." Specifically, as the law presently stands, *Social Security retirement benefits are subject to federal income taxes if the beneficiary's annual income exceeds one of the following base amounts:* $25,000 for a single taxpayer, $32,000 for married taxpayers filing jointly, and zero for married taxpayers filing separately. In determining the amount of income that must be counted, the taxpayer starts with his or her *adjusted gross income* as defined by the pres-ent tax law (see Chapter 3) and then adds all nontaxable interest income (such as income from municipal bonds) plus a stipulated portion of the Social Security benefits received. Thus, if for single taxpayers the resulting amount is between $25,000 and $34,000, 50 percent of Social Security benefits are taxable. If income exceeds $34,000, 85 percent of Social Security benefits is subject to income tax. If the combined income of married taxpayers filing joint returns is between $32,000 and $44,000, 50 percent of the Social Security benefits is taxable. The percentage of benefits taxed increases to 85 percent when their combined income exceeds $44,000.

SOCIAL SECURITY AND RETIREMENT PLANNING

No one can accurately predict the amount of Social Security benefits that will be paid 30 or 40 years from now. For retirement planning purposes, however, it seems reasonable to expect Social Security will provide the average retired wage earner (who is married) with perhaps 40 to 60 percent of the wages that he or she was earning in the year before retirement. This, of course, assumes that the retiree has had a full career working in covered employment. Social Security therefore should be viewed as *a foundation for your retirement income*. By itself, *it is insufficient to allow a worker and spouse to maintain their preretirement standard of living*. For people who earn in excess of the wage base, a lower percentage of total preretirement wages will be replaced by Social Security. Consequently, it's

EXHIBIT 14.4

Personal Earnings and Benefit Estimate Statement

The Social Security Administration keeps a lifetime record of your earnings; thus when you apply for benefits, it checks your earnings record to see if you've worked long enough to qualify, and then it determines the amount of your monthly benefits. The statement shown on this and the facing page, prepared by the Social Security Administration, is intended to provide an estimate of what one's future benefits are likely to be (*Note*: statement *excludes* record of Medicare credit).

Facts About Your Social Security

The Facts You Gave Us

Your Name .... I. M. Somebody
Your Social Security Number 000-00-0000
Your Date of Birth .... Feb. 23, 1942
1994 Earnings .... Over $60,600
1995 Earnings .... Over $61,200
Your Estimated Future Average Yearly Earnings .... Over $61,200
The Age You Plan to Retire 65

We used these facts and the information already on our records to prepare this statement for you. When we estimated your benefits, we included any 1994 and 1995 earnings you told us about. We also included any future estimated earnings up to the age you told us you plan to retire.

If you did not estimate your future earnings, we did not project any future earnings for you.

Your Social Security Earnings

The chart below shows the earnings on our Social Security record. It also estimates the amount of Social Security taxes you paid each year to finance benefits under Social Security and Medicare. We show earnings only up to the maximum amount of yearly earnings covered by Social Security. These maximum amounts are also shown on the chart. The chart may not include some or all of your earnings from last year because they may not have been posted to your record yet.

Years	Maximum Yearly Earnings Subject To Social Security Tax	Your Social Security Taxed Earnings	Estimated Social Security Taxes You Paid
1937–1955	$ 3,000–4,200	$ 0	$ 0
1956	4,200	18	0
1957	4,200	369	8
1958	4,200	45	1
1959	4,800	1,645	41
1960	4,800	889	26
1961	4,800	259	7
1962	4,800	566	17
1963	4,800	1,840	66
1964	4,800	4,800	174
1965	4,800	4,800	174
1966	6,600	6,600	254
1967	6,600	6,600	257
1968	7,800	0	0
1969	7,800	0	0
1970	7,800	7,053	296
1971	7,800	7,800	358
1972	9,000	9,000	414
1973	10,800	10,800	523
1974	13,200	13,200	653
1975	14,100	14,100	697
1976	15,300	15,300	757
1977	16,500	16,500	816
1978	17,700	17,700	893
1979	22,900	22,900	1,163
1980	25,900	25,900	1,315
1981	29,700	29,700	1,588
1982	32,400	32,400	1,749
1983	35,700	35,700	1,927
1984	37,800	37,800	2,041
1985	39,600	39,600	2,257
1986	42,000	42,000	2,394
1987	43,800	43,800	2,496
1988	45,000	45,000	2,727
1989	48,000	48,000	2,908

EXHIBIT 14.4

Continued

Years	Maximum Yearly Earnings Subject To Social Security Tax	Your Social Security Taxed Earnings	Estimated Social Security Taxes You paid
1990	51,300	51,300	3,180
1991	53,400	53,400	4,085
1992	55,500	55,500	4,246
1993	57,600	57,600	4,406
1994	60,600	60,600	4,636
1995	61,200	61,200	4,682

Your Social Security Credits

To qualify for benefits, you need credit for a certain amount of work covered by Social Security. The number of credits you need will vary with the type of benefit. **Under current law, you do not need more than 40 credits to be fully insured for any benefit.** (See "How You Earn Social Security Credits" on the reverse side.)

Our review of your earnings, including any 1994 and 1995 earnings you told us about, shows that you now have **at least 40 Social Security Credits.**

Estimated Benefits

Retirement

You must have 40 Social Security credits to be fully insured for retirement benefits. Assuming that you meet all the requirements, here are estimates of your retirement benefits based on your past and any projected earnings. The estimates are in today's dollars, but adjusted to account for average wage growth in the national economy.

If you retire at 65, your monthly benefit in today's dollars will be about $1,470

The earliest age at which you can receive an unreduced retirement benefit is 65 **and 4 months.** We call this your full retirement age. If you work until that age and then retire, your monthly benefit in today's dollars will be about....................$1,500

If you continue to work and wait until you are 70 to receive benefits, your monthly benefit in today's dollars will be about....................$2,080

Survivors

If you have a family, you must have 31 Social Security credits for certain family members to receive benefits if you were to die this year. They may also qualify if you earn 6 credits in the 3 years before your death. The number of credits a person needs to be insured for survivors benefits increases each year until age 62, up to a maximum of 40 credits.

Here is an estimate of the benefits your family could receive if you had enough credits to be insured, they qualified for benefits, and you died this year:

Your child could receive a monthly benefit of about....................$840

If your child and your surviving spouse who is caring for your child both qualify, they could each receive a monthly benefit of about $840

When your surviving spouse reaches full retirement age, he or she could receive a monthly benefit of about $1,120

The total amount that we could pay your family each month is about $1,960

We may also be able to pay your surviving spouse or children a one-time death benefit of....................$255

Disability

Right now, you must have 31 Social Security credits to be insured for disability benefits. And, **20 of these** credits had to be earned in the **10 year period immediately before you became disabled.** If you are blind or received disability benefits in the past, you may need fewer credits. The number of credits a person needs to be insured for disability benefits increases each year until age 62, up to a maximum of 40 credits.

If you were disabled, had enough credits, and met the other requirements for disability benefits, here is an estimate of the benefits you could receive right now:

Your monthly benefit would be about $1,105

You and your eligible family members could receive up to a monthly total of about....................$1,655

If You Have Questions

If you have any questions about this statement, please read the information on the reverse side. If you still have questions, please call **1-800-537-7005.**

EXHIBIT 14.5

Selected Monthly Social Security Retirement Benefits

The Social Security benefits listed here are initial, *first-year benefits*. As time passes, the beneficiary will receive correspondingly higher benefits as the cost of living goes up. For example, the maximum benefit payable to someone who retired in 1980 was $572 a month; by 1995 those benefits had grown to almost $1,200 a month.

	Career Earnings Level		
I. Latest Benefits (1995)	**Low**	**Medium**	**High**
Retired worker, age 65	$761	$1,111	$1,199
Retired worker, age 62	609	889	959
Family benefits:			
Retired worker and spouse, both 65	$1,141	$1,666	$1,798
Retired worker and spouse, both 62	913	1,333	1,438
Two-income couple[a]			
Both retire at 65	$1,522	$2,222	$2,398
Both retire at 62	1,218	1,778	1,918

[a]*Both* in the same career income category and *both* eligible for normal benefits at their career income levels.

Source: *Understanding Social Security,* Social Security Administration, 1995, p. 34.

essential that average and upper-middle-income families plan to supplement their Social Security retirement benefits with income from other sources. Two popular sources are pensions and retirement programs, and annuities. These topics are discussed in the next two sections.

Concept Check

14-5. What benefits are provided under the Social Security Act, and who is covered? Describe the basic operations of the Social Security system.

14-6. Discuss the old-age and survivor's benefits provided to retirees and their dependents under the Social Security program.

14-7. Does Social Security coverage relieve you of the need to do some retirement planning on your own? Explain. What is a Personal Earnings and Benefit Estimate Statement, and how would such a statement help you in your retirement planning?

PENSION PLANS AND RETIREMENT PROGRAMS

LG4 LG5

There are two basic types of retirement programs: employer-sponsored and self-directed. Together, these programs can provide the funds needed for an active and comfortable retirement. If you're covered by a company-sponsored pension plan, why would you need to open a self-directed retirement program? Try to answer this question before going on.

Accompanying the expansion of the Social Security system has been a corresponding growth in employer-sponsored pension and retirement plans. In 1940, when the Social Security program was in its infancy, fewer than 25 percent of the work force had the benefit of an employer-sponsored plan. Today, better than 50 percent of all wage and salaried workers (in both the private and public sectors) are covered by some type of employer-sponsored retirement or profit-sharing plan.

In 1948, the National Labor Relations Board (NLRB) ruled that pensions and other types of insurance programs are legitimate subjects for collective bargaining. In response, many employers established new pension plans or liberalized the provisions of existing ones to meet or anticipate union demands. Qualified pension plans (discussed later) allow firms to deduct for tax purposes their contributions to employee retirement programs. Nor are these contributions included in employees' taxable income; as a result, the participants are able to build up their own retirement funds on a tax-deferred basis. Eventually, of course, when the funds are paid out as benefits, the employees will have to pay taxes on this income.

But, government red tape has taken a toll on pension plans. In particular, the **Employee Retirement Income Security Act** (sometimes referred to as **ERISA** or the *Pension Reform Act*) of 1974, established to protect employees participating in private employer retirement plans, has actually led to a reduction in the number of new retirement plans started among firms, especially the smaller ones. Indeed, the percentage of workers covered by company-sponsored plans has fallen dramatically since the late 1970s. It's estimated that today, *in the private sector,* only about 45 percent of all full-time workers are covered by company-financed plans—even worse, only about 35 percent of the part-time labor force is covered. In contrast, there has been a significant increase in salary-reduction forms of retirement plans (discussed later). In addition to ERISA, the widespread availability of Keogh plans, individual retirement arrangements (IRAs), and other programs has lessened the urgency of small firms (and bigger ones as well) to offer their own company-financed pension plans.

EMPLOYER-SPONSORED PROGRAMS: BASIC PLANS

Employers can sponsor two types of retirement programs—*basic plans,* in which employees automatically participate after a certain period of employment, and *supplemental plans,* which are mostly voluntary programs that enable employees to increase the amount of funds being set aside for retirement. We will look first at some of the key characteristics of basic plans. Apart from financing, there are certain features of employer-sponsored pension plans that you should become familiar with, including participation requirements, contributory obligations, benefit rights, retirement age, and methods of computing benefits.

Participation Requirements. In most pension plans, employees must meet certain criteria before they become eligible for participation. Most common are requirements relating to years of service, minimum age, level of earnings, and employment classification. Years of service and/or minimum-age requirements are often incorporated into retirement plans in the belief that a much greater labor turnover rate applies to both newly hired and younger employees. Therefore, to reduce the administrative costs of the plans, employees in these categories are often excluded from participation.

What's Your Contribution? Whether or not you, as an employee, have to make payments toward your own pension depends on the type of plan you're in. If you belong to a **noncontributory pension plan,** the employer pays the total cost of the benefits—you don't have to pay a thing. Under a **contributory pension plan,** the cost is shared by both the employer and the employee. Today the trend is toward contributory plans. In addition, nearly all plans for employees of federal, state, and local governments require a contribution from the employee. In contributory plans, the employee's share of the costs is frequently between 3 and 10 percent of annual wages and is typically paid through a payroll deduction. Probably the most common arrangement is for the employer to match the employee's contribution such that the employee puts up half the annual contribution and the employer puts up the other half. When employees who have participated in a contributory retirement plan terminate employment prior to retirement they are legally entitled to some benefit, based on the amount of their own contributions. Usually this benefit is a cash lump sum, but in some cases it can be taken as a monthly payment at retirement. Whether departing employees receive any benefit from the *employer's* contributions depends on the plan's benefit rights.

Vested Interest: A Right to the Benefits. Not everyone who participates in a pension plan will earn the right to receive retirement benefits. Pension plans impose certain criteria that must be met before the employee can obtain a nonforfeitable right to a pension, known as **vested rights.** Prior to 1974,

Employee Retirement Income Security Act (ERISA) A law passed in 1974 to ensure that workers eligible for pensions actually receive such benefits; also permits uncovered workers to establish individual tax-sheltered retirement plans. Also known as the *Pension Reform Act.*

noncontributory pension plan A pension plan in which the employer pays the total cost of the benefits.

contributory pension plan A pension plan in which the employee bears a portion of the cost of the benefits.

vested rights Employees' nonforfeitable rights to receive benefits in a pension plan based on their own and their employer's contributions.

employers often required workers to be employed for 25 years or more before vesting would occur. An employee who left before completing this period of employment (and plenty did) would lose all the employer-sponsored pension benefits previously earned. Because of the high mobility of labor and capital, many workers at retirement faced the prospect of having no pension. One of the principal purposes of the Pension Reform Act of 1974 (ERISA) was to eliminate this unfair practice (which indirectly contributed to the social problem of low incomes among the aged). ERISA required covered employers to grant employees vested rights after no more than 10 years of employment (when there was no partial vesting prior to 10 years of service), or alternatively, 15 years, where partial vesting began after five years.

While ERISA was certainly a step in the right direction, even better vesting requirements came in 1986 with the Tax Reform Act. A provision of that act accelerated the vesting period so that, as it now stands, *full vesting* rights are required after only five to seven years of employment. More specifically, companies must now choose between two vesting schedules. One, the so-called *cliff vesting,* requires full vesting after no more than five years of service—but you obtain no vesting privileges until then. It's sort of a "zero-one" proposition: there are no vesting privileges at all for the first five years, and then all of a sudden you're fully vested. Once vested, you're entitled to everything that's been paid in so far (your contributions *plus* your employer's) and everything that will be contributed in the future. Under the alternative procedure, the so-called *graded schedule,* vesting takes place gradually over the first seven years of employment. At the minimum, after three years you would have a nonforfeiture right to at least 20 percent of the benefits, with an additional 20 percent each year thereafter until you're 100 percent vested after seven years. Note, however, that these are minimum standards, and employers can grant more favorable vesting terms.

To illustrate the vesting process, assume that a medium-sized firm offers a plan in which full vesting of benefits occurs after five years. The plan is contributory, with employees paying 3 percent of their salaries and the employer paying an amount equal to 6 percent of the salaries. Under this plan, employees cannot withdraw the contributions made by the employer until they reach retirement. The plan provides annual benefits in the amount of $11 per year of service for each $100 of an employee's final monthly earnings—the amount earned during the final month in the employ of the firm. Therefore, an employee who worked a minimum of five years for the firm would be eligible for a retirement benefit from that company even if he or she left the company at, say, age 30. However, because of inflation, the value of the benefit for a worker who left the firm long before retirement age would be very small. Consequently, the employee might be better off simply withdrawing his or her own contributions (which always vest immediately) and terminating participation in the plan at the same time he or she leaves the employer. Of course, any worker who leaves the firm prior to accumulating five years of service would be entitled only to a return of his or her own contributions to the plan (plus nominal investment earnings).

Retirement Age. Nearly all retirement plans specify when an eligible employee is entitled to benefits—in most cases, at age 65. Often pension plans also provide an early retirement age. In these cases, employees may begin receiving reduced benefits prior to the normal retirement age. Many retirement plans for public employees also give workers the option of retiring after a stated number of years of service (say, 30 or 35) at full benefits, regardless of their age at the time. In the past, the trend in pension plans was toward earlier permissible retirement ages. However, now that many have begun to argue in favor of increasing the age for mandatory retirement (that is, letting people work longer), it is expected that there will be little motivation to further reduce the normal retirement age.

Defined Contributions or Defined Benefits. The method used to compute benefits at retirement is spelled out in detail in every retirement plan. The two most commonly used methods are the defined contribution plan and the defined benefits plan. A **defined contribution plan** specifies the amount of contribution that the employer and employee must make. At retirement, the worker is awarded whatever level of monthly benefits those contributions will purchase. While factors such as age, income level, and the amount of contributions made to the plan have a great deal to do with the amount of monthly benefits received at retirement, probably no variable is more important than the level of *investment performance* generated on the contributed funds. A defined contribution plan promises nothing at retirement except the returns that the fund managers have been able to obtain. The only thing that's defined is the amount of contribution that the employee and/or employer have to make (generally stated as a percent of the employee's income). The benefits at retirement depend totally on investment results. Of course, there's a certain standard of care that's followed by the investment managers, so there is some protection provided to the plan participants (indeed, most of the investing is confined to high-quality investment vehicles). But even so, that still leaves a lot of room for variability in returns. There'll be a big difference in retirement benefits for someone who's in a fund that's earned 6 percent versus someone else who's in a fund that's earned 12 percent.

Under a **defined benefits plan,** the formula for computing benefits, not contributions, is stipulated in the plan provisions. These benefits are paid out regardless of how well (or poorly) the retirement funds are invested. If investment performance falls short, the employer has to make up the difference to come up with the benefits agreed to in the plan. This type of plan allows employees to determine before retirement how much their monthly retirement income will be. Often the number of years of service and amount of earnings are prime factors in the formula. For example, a worker might be paid 2.5 percent of his or her final three-year average annual salary for each year of service. Thus, the *annual* benefit to an employee whose final three-year average annual salary was $65,000 and who was with the company for 20 years would be $32,500 (2.5% × $65,000 × 20 years). Other types of defined benefits plans may simply pay benefits based on (1) a consideration of earnings excluding years of service, (2) a consideration of years of service excluding earnings, or (3) a flat amount with no consideration given to either earnings or years of service. Many defined benefits plans also increase retirement benefits periodically to help retirees keep up with the cost of living. In periods of high inflation, these increases are essential to maintain retirees' standards of living.

Regardless of the method used to calculate benefit amounts, the employee's basic concern should be with the percent of final take-home pay that the plan is likely to produce at retirement. A pension is usually thought to be good if, when combined with Social Security, it will result in a monthly income of 70 to 80 percent of preretirement net earnings. To reach this goal, however, today's employees must take some responsibility, because there's a growing trend for *companies to switch from defined benefits plans to defined contributions programs.* Whereas in 1975, about 85 percent of all plans were defined benefits plans, today fewer than half are. Companies don't like the idea of being faced with undefined future pension liabilities—after all, the pension/retirement payments that don't come from investment earnings have to be made up from company earnings, and that means lower profits. So a lot of firms are avoiding these problems by gradually changing over to defined contributions plans—indeed, there are *far more* defined contribution plans in existence today than there are defined benefits plans. And in cases where the firms are sticking with their defined benefits plans, the benefits are often so meager that they don't come close to the desired 70 to 80 percent income target. (Some of the defined contributions plans don't either.) In either case *the employee is being forced to assume more responsibility for assuring the desired level of postretirement income.* The logic from the company's perspective is that if obtaining a comfortable standard of living in retirement is a worthwhile objective, the employee should be willing to help achieve it. That might mean participating in a company-sponsored supplemental retirement plan and/or possibly even setting up your own self-directed program (we'll look at both supplemental and self-directed plans later).

Funding Procedures. Pension plans must provide for the financing of benefits that will be paid out to retired workers. An **unfunded pension plan**

defined contribution plan A pension plan that specifies the amount of contributions that both employer and employee must make; it makes no promises concerning the size of the benefits at retirement.

defined benefits plan A pension plan is which the formula for computing benefits is stipulated in its provisions, thus allowing the employee to determine prior to retirement how much his or her retirement income will be.

unfunded pension plan A pension plan in which the employer must make payments to retirees from current income, because the plan itself has insufficient assets to cover existing liabilities.

allows the employer to make payments to retirees from current income. One expert has called unfunded pensions "owe as you go" plans. This name really is appropriate, since employers accumulate liabilities throughout the working careers of their employees but do not necessarily put any assets aside to offset them. In the past, only a minority of employees have been covered under unfunded pension plans, and they have received a good deal of unfavorable publicity as being too risky for employees. Consequently, ERISA sets forth minimum funding standards for pension plans. **Funded pension plans** formally establish charges against current income to allow for pension liabilities as they accrue. The amount of liability that arises under the plan each year is determined by actuarial computations. (An *actuary* is an expert in calculating risks and premiums for insurance.) These computations take into account such factors as mortality rates among workers and retirees, actual and potential investment earnings, labor turnover, normal and early retirement ages, and salary levels.

Funding of pension plans represents an attempt to minimize the risk that benefits will not be available to an eligible employee upon retirement. Nonetheless, the unfunded plan of a large, solvent government unit or corporate employer sometimes can offer a better guarantee of payment than the funded plan of a financially weak firm. ERISA requirements attempt to control the lack of adequate funding in funded plans.

Qualified Pension Plans. The Internal Revenue Code permits a corporate employer making contributions to a **qualified pension plan** to deduct from taxable income its contributions to the plan. As a result, the employees on whose behalf the contributions are made do not have to include these payments as part of their taxable income until the benefits are actually received. Further, in contributory plans, *the employee can also shelter his or her contributions from taxes.* In other words, such contributions are not counted as part of taxable income in the year in which they are made, but instead act to reduce the amount of taxable income reported to the IRS, and therefore lead to lower taxes for the employee. Still another tax advantage of these plans is that any and all investment income is allowed to accumulate tax free; as a result, investment capital can build up quicker. Yet, in spite of all these tax benefits, a lot of firms still believe that the costs of regulation exceed any benefits that might result and therefore choose to forgo the procedures required for having a plan qualified. Probably the biggest disadvantage of nonqualified pension plans from the employee's perspective is that any contributions made to *contributory* plans are fully taxable and as such, are treated just like any other type of income.

EMPLOYER-SPONSORED PROGRAMS: SUPPLEMENTAL PLANS

In addition to basic retirement programs, many employers offer supplemental plans. These plans are often *voluntary* and enable employees to not only increase the amount of funds being held for retirement but also enjoy attractive tax benefits. Essentially, there are three types of supplemental plans: profit-sharing, thrift and savings, and salary reduction plans.

Profit-Sharing Plans. Profit-sharing plans permit employees to participate in the earnings of their employer. A **profit-sharing plan** may be qualified under the IRS and become eligible for essentially the same tax treatment as other types of pension plans. An argument in support of the use of profit-sharing plans is that they encourage employees to work harder because the employees benefit when the firm prospers. Whether these types of plans accomplish this goal is debatable. One advantage of profit-sharing plans from the firm's viewpoint, however, is that they do not impose any specific levels of contribution or benefits on the part of the employer. When profits are low, the employer makes a proportionately smaller contribution to the plan; when profits are high, the firm pays proportionately more.

In order to provide reasonable returns, many employers establish minimum and maximum amounts to be paid as contributions to profit-sharing plans, regardless of how low or high corporate earnings are. Contributions to profit-sharing plans can be invested in certain types of fixed-interest products, stocks and bonds, or, in many cases, securities issued by the employing firm itself. Employees who receive the firm's securities may actually benefit twice. When profits are good, larger contributions are made to the profit-sharing plan *plus* the price of the shares already owned is likely to increase. A number of big-time, major firms offer *voluntary profit-sharing plans* that invest heavily in their own stock. It's not unusual in many of these cases for long-term career employees to accumulate several hundred thousand dollars worth of the company's stocks. And we're not talking about highly paid corporate executives here; rather, these are just average employees who had the discipline to consistently divert a portion of their salary to the company's profit-sharing plan. There is a very real and important downside to this practice, however—that is, if the company should hit on hard times, not only could you face salary cuts (or even worse, the loss of a job), but the value of your profit-sharing account very likely would take a big tumble as well.

Thrift and Savings Plan. **Thrift and savings plans** were established to supplement pension and other fringe benefits. Most plans require the employer to make contributions to the savings plan in an amount equal to a set proportion of the amount contributed by the employee. For example, an employer might match an employee's contributions at the rate of 50 cents on the dollar up to, say, 6 percent of salary. An employee making $20,000 a year could pay $1,200 into the plan annually, and the employer would kick in another $600. These contributions are then deposited with a trustee, who invests the money in various types of securities, including stocks and bonds of the employing firm. With IRS-qualified thrift and savings plans, the *employer's* contributions and earnings on the savings are not included in the *employee's* taxable income until he or she withdraws these sums. Unfortunately, this attractive tax feature does not extend to the employee's contributions, and as a result, any money put into one of these savings plans is still considered to be part of the employee's taxable income—subject to regular income taxes.

Thrift and savings plans usually have more liberal vesting and withdrawal privileges than pension and retirement programs. Often the employee's right to the contributions of the employer becomes nonforfeitable immediately upon payment, and the total savings in the plan can be withdrawn by giving proper notice. Those employees who terminate participation in such a plan, however, are frequently prohibited from rejoining it for a specified period, such as one year. An employee who has the option should seriously consider participation in a thrift plan, since the returns are usually pretty favorable—especially when you factor in the added kicker provided by the *employer's* contributions.

Salary Reduction Plans. Another type of supplemental retirement program—and certainly the most popular as judged by employee response—is the **salary reduction plan** or the so-called **401(k)** plan as its more popularly known. While our discussion here will center on 401(k) plans, similar programs are available for employees of public, nonprofit organizations; known as *403(b) plans,* they offer many of the same features and tax shelter provisions as 401(k) plans.

Today, more and more companies are cutting back on their contributions to traditional (defined benefit) retirement plans and are turning, instead, to 401(k) plans, a type of defined contribution plan. Almost 90 percent of all companies with over 200 employees now offer 401(k) plans. Assets of these plans more than doubled from 1988 to 1994, when they topped $500 billion—and they are expected to reach $1 trillion by the year 2000. But while an estimated 65 percent, or more, of eligible employees participate, most contribute only half of the maximum allowed.

A 401(k) plan basically gives the employee the option to divert a portion of his or her salary to a company-sponsored, tax-sheltered savings account. In this way, the earnings diverted to the savings

funded pension plan A pension plan that formally establishes charges against current income to allow for pension liabilities as they accrue in order to minimize the risk that benefits will be unavailable to an eligible employee upon retirement.

qualified pension plan A pension plan that meets specified criteria established by the Internal Revenue Code.

profit-sharing plan An arrangement in which the employees of a firm participate in the company's earnings.

thrift and savings plan A plan established by an employer to supplement pension and other fringe benefits, in which the firm makes contributions in an amount equal to a set proportion of the employee's contribution.

salary reduction, or **401(k), plan** An agreement under which a portion of a covered employee's pay is withheld and invested in an annuity or other qualified form of investment; the taxes on both the contributions and the account earnings are deferred until the funds are withdrawn.

plan accumulate tax free. Taxes must be paid eventually, but not until the employee starts drawing down the account at retirement, presumably when he or she is in a lower tax bracket. In 1995, an individual employee could put as much as $9,240 (up to 15% of salary, to this maximum) into a tax-deferred 401(k) plan—the annual dollar cap increases yearly, as it's indexed to the rate of inflation. (The contribution limits for a 403(b) plan are currently set at a maximum of $9,500 a year and won't be indexed to inflation until 401(k) contributions attain parity with these plans.)

To see how such tax-deferred plans work, consider an individual who earned, say, $60,000 in 1995, and would like to contribute the maximum allowable—$9,240—to the 401(k) plan where she works. Doing so reduces her taxable income to $50,760 and, assuming she's in the 28 percent tax bracket, lowers her federal tax bill by some $2,587 (i.e., $9,240 × .28). Such tax savings will offset a good portion—28 percent—of her contribution to the 410(k) savings plan. In effect, she will add $9,240 to her retirement program with only $6,653 of her own money; the rest will come from the IRS via a reduced tax bill! Further, all the *earnings* on her savings account will accumulate tax free as well.

These plans are generally viewed as highly attractive *tax shelters* that offer not only substantial tax savings but also a way to save for retirement. As a rule, so long as you can afford to put the money aside, *you should seriously consider joining a 401(k)/403(b) plan if offered at your place of employment.* This is especially true today because the restrictions placed on IRAs by the Tax Reform Act of 1986 mean these plans may be the only avenue you have for setting up a supplemental tax-sheltered retirement program. But there's more: A special attraction of 401(k) plans is that the firms offering them can sweeten the pot by matching all or a part of the employee's contributions. Presently, about 85 percent of the companies that offer 401(k) plans have some type of matching contributions program, often putting up 50 cents (or more) for every dollar contributed by the employee. Such matching plans provide both tax and savings incentives to individuals and clearly enhance the appeal of 401(k) plans.

401(k) plans offer participants several investment options, such as equity and fixed income mutual funds, company stock, and fixed interest vehicles such as *guaranteed investment contracts* (discussed later). The typical 401(k) has about five choices, and some plans have as many as ten or 12. Today the trend is toward giving plan participants more options and providing seminars and other educational tools to help employees make informed retirement plan decisions. While it is clearly better to have a wider range of investment alternatives, at the same time it makes it more difficult to choose the right ones for your needs. And as the *Smart Money* box on page 586 notes, it's important to know just who's managing your 401(k) plan's money. You may be surprised to learn that, more often than not, it's *you*.

The GIC in a 401(k). Look inside most 401(k) plans and you'll find something called a **guaranteed investment contract** (or **GIC,** for short). In fact, GICs are more widely used in 401(k) plans than any other investment vehicle—in 1995, *about 50 to 55 percent of all 401(k) money was invested in GICs.* And yet most people do not have the foggiest idea of what these things are. That's because we usually run into GICs at our place of employment, where they're offered as one of the investment choices in company-sponsored 401(k) plans (they are also available in other company-sponsored retirement programs, especially profit-sharing plans).

Guaranteed investment contracts are sold by insurance companies (and a handful of banks). They're a type of investment product whereby an insurance company accepts a deposit in return for paying a fixed rate of interest over a set period of time (usually from one to five years, and sometimes as long as ten years). In many respects, a GIC looks and acts very much like a bank CD. The big attraction of these fixed-rate investments is twofold: First, they usually pay a fixed rate of interest that's ½ to 1½ points over yields in the Treasury market; and second, the principal is *not* subject to fluctuation, like it is with stocks and bonds (at least not with fixed-rate GIC's). Essentially, the insurance company that issues the GIC invests the funds in various types of securities (ranging from mortgages and real estate to agency bonds—and, yes, even junk bonds). It then pays whatever competitive rate it wants to in order to land the business—that is, in most cases, the GIC is *not* backed by a specific, dedicated portfolio of securities. But what about the "guarantee" in a GIC: doesn't that mean anything? Well, contrary to what most people think, GICs are **NOT** backed by some form of federal insurance or any other type of government guarantee. They're guaranteed by the insurance company that sold the contract—the only *guarantee* in these contracts is that the insurance company promises to pay a fixed rate of interest over the life of the GIC. And that guarantee, of course, is only as good as the insurance company that issued the contract! The bottom line is if you're thinking of putting some of your 401(k) money into a GIC, find out how the issuer is rated by Best's, Standard & Poor's, and/or Moody's.

EVALUATING EMPLOYER-SPONSORED PENSION PLANS

When you participate in a company-sponsored pension plan, you're entitled to certain benefits in return for meeting certain conditions of membership—which may or may not include making contributions to the plan. Whether your participation is limited to the firm's basic plan or includes one or more of the supplemental programs, *it's vital that you take the time to acquaint yourself with the various benefits and provisions* of these retirement plans. And be sure to familiarize yourself not only with the basic plans (even though participation is mandatory, you ought to know what you're getting for your money), but also with any (voluntary) supplemental plans that you may be eligible to join.

So, how should you evaluate these plans? Most experts agree that while there are many aspects that go into a typical company-sponsored pension plan (some of which are a bit complex and difficult to evaluate), you can get a pretty good handle on essential plan provisions and retirement benefits by taking a close look at these features:

- ***Eligibility requirements***—precisely what are they, and if you're not already in the plan, when will you be able to participate?
- ***Defined benefits or contributions***—which are defined? If it's the benefits, exactly what formula is used to define them? Pay particular attention to how Social Security benefits are treated in the formula. If it's a defined contributions program, do you have any control over how the money is invested? If so, what are your options?
- ***Vesting procedures***—does the company use a cliff or graded procedure, and precisely when do you become fully vested?
- ***Contributory or noncontributory***—if the plan is contributory, how much comes from you and how much from the company; and what is the total of this contribution, as a percent of your salary? If it is noncontributory, what is the company's contribution, as a percent of your salary?
- ***Retirement age***—what is the normal retirement age, and what provisions are there for *early retirement?* What happens if you leave the company before retirement? Are the pension benefits *portable*—that is, can you take them with you if you change jobs?
- ***Voluntary supplemental programs***—how much of your salary can you put into one or more of these plans, and what, if anything, is *matched* by the company? Remember, these are like defined contributions plans, so there's nothing guaranteed as far as benefits are concerned.

Getting answers to these questions will help you determine where you stand and what, if any, improvements need to be made in your retirement plans. As part of this evaluation process, you should try to work up, as best as you can, *a rough estimation of what your benefits are likely to be at retirement*—you're going to have to make some projections about future income levels, investment returns, and so on, but it's an exercise well worth taking (before you start cranking out the numbers, however, check with the people who handle employee benefits at your place of work; they'll often give you the help you need). Then, using a procedure similar to what we did with Worksheet 14.1, you can estimate what portion of your retirement needs will be met from your company's basic pension plan. If there's a shortfall—*and there likely will be*—it will indicate the extent to which you need to participate in some type of company-sponsored supplemental program, such as a 401(k) plan, or (alternatively) how much you're going to have to rely on your own savings and investments to come up with the kind of standard of living you're looking for in retirement. *Such insights will enable you to more effectively dovetail the investment characteristics and retirement benefits of any company-sponsored retirement plans*

guaranteed investment contract or **GIC** An investment product, offered mostly by life insurance companies, that promises to pay a set rate of interest to investors over the life of the contract; found mostly in 401(k) and other company-sponsored retirement plans, the only guarantee they carry is that of the company that sold the contract.

Smart Money

Are You Ready to Manage Your 401(k) Plan?

As more companies switch from traditional employer-funded, professionally managed defined-benefit pension plans to defined-contribution plans, the odds increase that you will have to manage your own plan—401(k) at private firms and the similar 403(b) for nonprofit and public employees. And you are not alone if you worry about choosing the right investments for your own plan. It is a big job, and how much you have at retirement depends not only on the amount you invest but also whether you are a successful investor, or make a lot of mistakes.

Until recently, the average 401(k) plan offered about three investment options: perhaps a guaranteed investment contract (GIC), the company's stock, and a mutual fund. But new regulations protect companies against lawsuits over poor 401(k) performance if they offer at least three different investment options in addition to company stock, provide information about investment options so participants can make informed decisions based on risk-return features, report performance frequently, and allow employees to change plan investments more often. Experts predict that soon about half of major company 401(k) plans will offer 10 or more fund choices. But with more investment choices, it's easy to become confused about the best way to manage your retirement plan investments.

One of the biggest mistakes people make with their 401(k), according to many investment advisers, is investing much too conservatively. Even though retirement is years away for most 401(k) investors, the GIC is the most popular plan investment. Yet these investments, while safe, do nothing to compensate for inflation's erosion of returns. Jonathan Pond, president of Financial Planning Information of Boston, notes that a professional pension fund manager who invested this way would risk a jail sentence. The typical pension plan has about 60 percent of its assets in equities for dividend growth, capital appreciation, and an inflation hedge. Investors who argue that equities are too risky for retirement money should remember that they are investing for the long term and can ride out market ups and downs. Just look at historical returns from about 1947 to 1993: equities' annual returns averaged over 11 percent, while long-term corporate bonds earned about 5 percent and U.S. Treasury Bills, just under 4½ percent. That's a big difference, especially when you include compounding. Another common mistake is buying too much company stock. Investing in only one stock, especially when you also work for the company, can be risky; advisers suggest limiting company stock to 10 to 25 percent of your 401(k). Also, be sure to invest as much as you can in your 401(k), which is one of the few ways to save tax-deferred. And with most employers matching at least a portion of your contributions, you'd be foolish not to max them out.

What do financial planning experts suggest as an ideal 401(k) plan? Obviously, this depends on your age, circumstances, retirement goals, and plan offerings. They recommend following the lead of the pension funds and investing heavily in common stock and changing the percent and type of equities as you move through different life stages. You should also coordinate your 401(k) plan (and your spouse's) with your other investments so that you have an appropriate balance overall. Do not view your plan as a separate investment and ignore it when looking at your portfolio's asset mix, or you could find yourself with too many assets in one category.

In your 20s? Start your plan now and save whatever you can—especially if your employer matches contributions—even if you can't manage the maximum. Concentrate on growth-oriented equities, up to 100 percent of your plan, while you're young. As you move through your 30s, diversify into international equities and move a portion, say 30 percent, into fixed income investments. During your 40s and 50s, shift into more conservative equity and fixed income investments as you near retirement. However, many advisers recommend keeping a reasonably high portion in equities to hedge against inflation, *even after you retire;* today's longer life expectancy means you will probably live for quite a while past age 65.

Sources: Adapted from Earl C. Gottschalk, Jr., "On Your Own," *The Wall Street Journal,* December 9, 1994, p. R19; Ed Henry, "Charting a Course for Your 401(k)," *Kiplinger's Personal Finance Magazine,* March 1994, pp. 95–102; Penelope Wang, "ABC's of 401(k) Investing," *Money,* February 1995, pp. 144–145; and Gordon Williams, "Fiddling with 401(k)s," *Financial World,* February 1, 1994, pp. 64–68.

you're entitled to with the savings and investing that you do on your own.

SELF-DIRECTED RETIREMENT PROGRAMS

In addition to participating in company-sponsored retirement programs, individuals can also set up their own tax-sheltered retirement plans. There are two basic types of self-directed retirement programs: *Keogh* and *SEP plans,* which are for self-employed individuals, and *individual retirement arrangements (IRAs),* which can be set up by just about anybody.

Keogh and SEP Plans. **Keogh plans** were introduced in 1962 as part of the Self-Employed Individuals Retirement Act, or simply the Keogh Act. Keogh plans allow self-employed individuals to set up tax-deferred retirement plans for themselves and their employees. Like contributions to 401(K) plans, payments to Keogh accounts may be taken as deductions from taxable income. As a result, they reduce the tax bills of self-employed individuals. The maximum contribution to this tax-deferred retirement plan is $30,000 per year or 20 percent of earned income, whichever is less. (Technically, the rules allow 25 percent contributions *based on net income after Keogh contributions*—which works out to 20 percent of earned income. For example, the maximum contribution on $150,000 of earned income is $30,000, which results in a net income after Keogh contributions of $120,000; thus, the $30,000 contribution is equivalent to 25 percent of the $120,000 base, or 20 percent of $150,000.)

Any individual who is self-employed, either full- or part-time, is eligible to set up a Keogh account. Not only can self-employed businesspeople or professionals use Keoghs, they can also be used by individuals who hold full-time jobs and "moonlight" on a part-time basis—for instance, the engineer who has a small consulting business on the side or the accountant who does tax returns in the evenings and on weekends. If the engineer, for example, earns $10,000 a year from his part-time consulting business, he can contribute 20 percent of that income ($2,000) to his Keogh account and, in so doing, reduce both his taxable income and the amount he pays in taxes. Further, he is still eligible to receive full retirement benefits from his full-time job, as well as having his own IRA (though, as we'll see below, contributions to his IRA probably will not qualify for tax shelter). The only catch to Keogh accounts is that the individual must be self-employed—that is, the income must be derived from the net earnings (after all expenses except taxes and retirement contributions) of a self-employed business.

Keogh accounts can be opened at banks, insurance companies, brokerage houses, mutual funds, and other financial institutions. Annual contributions must be made at the time the respective tax return is filed or by April 15th of the following calendar year (for example, you have until April 15, 1996, to make the contribution to your Keogh for 1995). While a designated financial institution acts as custodian of all the funds held in a Keogh account, *the actual investments held in the account are under the complete direction of the individual contributor.* These are self-directed retirement programs where the *individual* decides which investments to buy and sell (subject to a few basic restrictions).

The income earned from the investments must be reinvested in the account and it, too, accrues tax free. All Keogh contributions and investment earnings must remain in the account until the individual turns 59½, unless he or she becomes seriously ill or disabled—early withdrawals for any other reason are subject to 10 percent tax penalties. However, the individual is *not required* to start withdrawing the funds at age 59½; the funds can stay in the account (and continue to earn tax-free income) until the individual is 70½, at which time the individual *must* begin withdrawing funds from the account. In fact, so long as the income from self-employment continues, an individual can continue to make tax-deferred contributions to a Keogh account until reaching the maximum age of 70½. Of course, once he or she starts withdrawing funds from a Keogh account (upon or after turning 59½), all such withdrawals are treated as ordinary income and subject to the payment of normal income taxes. Thus, the taxes on all contributions to and earnings from a Keogh account will eventually have to be paid, a characteristic of any tax-*deferred* (as opposed to tax-*free*) program.

Keogh plan An account to which self-employed persons may make payments, up to the lesser of $30,000 or 20 percent of earned income per year, that may be taken as deductions from taxable income; the earnings on such accounts also accrue on a tax-deferred basis.

A program that's similar in many respects to the Keogh account is something called a *Simplified Employee Pension Plan*—or SEP-IRA for short. It's aimed at small-business owners, particularly those with *no employees,* who want a plan that is simple to set up and administer. SEP-IRAs *can be used in place of Keoghs* and while they are simpler to administer and have the same dollar annual contribution cap ($30,000), their contribution rate is less generous; you can put in only 15 percent of earned income for a SEP-IRA, versus 20 percent for a Keogh.

Individual Retirement Arrangements (IRAs). Some people mistakenly believe that an IRA is a specialized type of investment. It is not. Actually, an **individual retirement arrangement (IRA),** or individual retirement *account,* as its more commonly known, is virtually the same as any other investment account you open with a bank, credit union, stockbroker, mutual fund, or insurance company. The form you complete designates the account as an IRA and makes the institution its trustee. That is all there is to it.

Basically, any gainfully employed individual can have an IRA account, though as we saw in Chapter 3, the *annual contributions* of only certain individuals qualify as tax deductions. Specifically, in order to be able to use your annual IRA contributions as a tax deduction, one of the following two conditions has to be met: (1) Neither you nor your spouse can be covered by a company-sponsored pension plan, or (2) your adjusted gross income has to be less than $40,000 (for married couples) or $25,000 (for singles). Translated, this means your IRA contributions would fully qualify as a tax deduction if you were covered by a company-sponsored pension plan but your adjusted gross income fell below the specified amounts (of $40,000 for joint filers and $25,000 for singles), *or* if you (or your spouse) weren't covered by a company-sponsored pension plan, no matter how much your adjusted gross income was. (Note that the income ceilings are phased out, so that people with adjusted gross incomes of $40,000 to $50,000 [or $25,000 to $35,000] who are covered by employer pension plans, are still entitled to prorated *partial deductions*.)

The annual contribution limits to IRAs are $2,000 for an individual and $2,250 for an individual and nonworking spouse. If both spouses work, each can contribute up to $2,000 to his or her own IRA. If the contributions qualify as tax deductions (as per the two conditions noted above), then the amount of the IRA contributions can be shown on the tax return as a deduction from taxable income —which, of course, will also reduce the amount of taxes that have to be paid. And understand that even if you don't qualify for a tax deduction, *you can still contribute up to the maximum of $2,000 a year to an IRA account;* the only difference (and it's a big one) is that these nondeductible contributions will have to be made with after-tax income.

As with Keoghs and 401(k) programs, the taxes on all the *earnings* from an IRA account are deferred until you start drawing down the funds, and this provision applies regardless of your income or whether you're already covered by a pension plan at your place of employment! You can deposit as much or as little as you want (up to the ceilings), and there are no percentage of income limitations—thus, if your earned income is only, say, $1,800, you can contribute all of it to your IRA.

IRAs are like Keogh and SEP plans in that they are *self-directed accounts*—meaning you are free, to make just about whatever investment decisions you want. Actually, as with any investment, an individual can be conservative or aggressive in choosing securities for an IRA (or Keogh), though the nature of these retirement programs generally favors a more conservative approach. In fact, conventional wisdom favors funding your IRA (and Keogh) with *income-producing assets;* this would also suggest that if you are looking for capital gains, it is best to do so *outside* your retirement account. The reasons are two-fold: (1) Growth-oriented securities are by nature *more risky,* and (2) you *cannot write off losses* from the sale of securities held in an IRA (or Keogh) account. This does not mean, however, that it would be altogether inappropriate to place a good-quality growth stock or mutual fund in a Keogh or IRA—in fact, many advisors contend that growth investments should always have a place in your retirement account due to their often impressive performance and ability to counteract inflation. Such investments may pay off handsomely, since they can appreciate totally free of taxes.

In the end, of course, *it is how much you have in your retirement account that matters rather than how your earnings were made along the way.* Also, regardless of what type of investment vehicle you use, keep in mind that once you place money in an IRA, it's meant to stay there for the long haul. For like most tax-sheltered retirement programs, there are severe restrictions on when you can withdraw the funds from an IRA. Specifically, except in the case of permanent disability, any funds withdrawn from an IRA prior to age 59½ are subject to a 10 percent tax penalty, on top of the regular tax paid on the withdrawal. (Note, however, that you can avoid the 10 percent tax penalty and still start withdrawals before age 59½ by setting up a systematic withdrawal program that essentially pays you equal amounts over the rest of your life expectancy; obviously, unless you have a substantial amount of money in your IRA, the annual payments under this program are likely to be pretty small.) In addition, when you move your IRA account to a new firm (this is known as a "roll-over"), the transfer is subject to a *20 percent withholding tax* if the proceeds from the transfer are paid to you directly—the rule is very clear on this: If you take possession of the funds (even for just a few days), you will be hit with the withholding tax. Thus, the best way to handle IRA roll-overs is to *arrange for the transfer of funds from one firm to another.*

Prior to the Tax Reform Act of 1986, IRAs had become immensely popular. By 1985 over 40 million Americans held IRAs, with an estimated worth of nearly $250 billion! The tax overhaul bill, however, sharply curtailed the tax-shelter feature of IRAs, and as a result, these accounts lost a lot of their appeal. Annual contributions plunged from $40 billion in 1986 to $8.2 billion by 1992, as most people who no longer qualified for tax-sheltered contributions simply quit putting their money into IRAs. And those who continued to make contributions even though they were nondeductible got hit with horrendous record-keeping requirements and a complex IRS tax form, *Form 8606* (for "Nondeductible IRA Contributions") that must be filed with federal tax returns. It's pretty clear that Congress wanted to sharply curtail the use of IRAs; this was very unfortunate, since most retirement experts agreed that the original IRA concept was a great one. Not only have investors stopped adding to IRAs, but also many have neglected the billions of dollars they previously invested. As of late 1993, an estimated $250 billion languished in banks and credit unions, mostly invested in money market accounts and CDs, which for several years has earned very low returns.

So, should you contribute to an IRA or not? Obviously, if you qualify for *fully deductible* contributions (as per the two provisions spelled out above) you should seriously consider making the maximum payments allowable. There are no special record-keeping requirements or forms to file, and for these individuals, the IRA continues to be an excellent vehicle for sheltering some of their income from taxes. But if your contributions don't qualify for full deductibility, the prevailing sentiment seems to be to avoid nondeductible IRAs; for not only is the paperwork burdensome, but some equally attractive alternatives are available for sheltering your income. As a starter, find out if the company you work for has a 401(k)—or 403(b)—plan in existence and if so, use it. Or you might want to consider parking your money in a *tax-sheltered annuity* (discussed later in this chapter). It offers basically the same advantages as a nondeductible IRA, with the added kicker that there's no limit as to how much you can put in each year (remember, you can only put $2,000 a year into an IRA).

GOVERNMENT INFLUENCE ON PENSION PLANS

The two major areas of government influence on pension plans are the Internal Revenue Code (IRC) requirements for plan qualification, and the rules and regulations established by the Employee Retirement Income Security Act of 1974 (ERISA). The major stipulations of the IRC were discussed earlier in the chapter. At this point, we will look at the most important features of ERISA. As the name implies, the act's primary objective is to increase the probability that employees who are covered by a retirement plan throughout their working careers will in fact receive benefits upon retirement. ERISA covers nearly all of the pension and retirement plans created by private employers engaged in interstate commerce. It does not cover plans sponsored by government, charitable organizations, or firms exclusively involved in intrastate commerce. The law regulates only plans that are in existence. It does not require firms to begin a retirement plan for

individual retirement arrangement (IRA) A retirement plan, open to any working American, to which a person may contribute a specified amount each year (up to $2,000 in the case of an individual taxpayer); while annual contributions to IRAs may or may not be tax deductible, the earnings from all IRAs do accrue on a tax-deferred basis. Also known, more popularly, as an individual retirement *account*.

their employees, nor does it prohibit them from discontinuing an existing plan (as many have done to avoid the myriad ERISA rules and regulations). Similarly, ERISA does not force companies to pay any minimum amounts to employees, other than those specified in the plans.

ERISA basically prescribes minimum standards with which covered plans must comply. These standards apply to plan provisions, funding, and administration. Among the major items treated are vesting, eligibility for participation, definition of service, minimum funding requirements, disclosure to participants, and employer fiduciary responsibility. Another important provision establishes the **Pension Benefit Guarantee Corporation (PBGC).** The purpose of this organization is to guarantee eligible workers that certain benefits will be payable to them even if their employer's plan has insufficient assets to fulfill its commitments. The funding for the PBGC comes from charges that are levied against all employers regulated by ERISA. In essence, the PBGC provides plan termination insurance to covered employees. Although the implementation of ERISA has not been free of problems, most observers agree that this law is a good start in ensuring that employees who have earned pensions will, in fact, receive them.

Concept Check

14-8. Which basic features of employer-sponsored pension plans should you be familiar with? Explain.

114-9. Discuss the distinguishing features of (a) *funded,* (b) *qualified,* (c) *defined benefit,* and (d) *contributory pension plans.* Under which procedure will you become fully vested most quickly—cliff or graded vesting? Explain.

14-10. What is the difference between a *profit-sharing plan* and a *salary reduction, or 401(k), plan*? Are these basic or supplemental plans?

14-11. What is a *guaranteed investment contract,* and who are the primary issuers? Briefly describe the investment features of a GIC. Where and how does a GIC obtain its guarantee?

14-12. Why is it important to evaluate and become familiar with the pension plan(s) and retirement benefits offered by your employer? Identify and briefly discuss at least six different plan provisions that you feel would be important in such an evaluation.

14-13. Briefly describe the tax provisions of *401(k) plans* and *IRAs.* Would you describe these plans as tax-deferred or tax-free programs? Explain. Describe and differentiate between *Keogh plans* and *individual retirement arrangements (IRAs).*

14-14. Describe *ERISA,* and discuss its influence on pension plans. What does *PBGC* stand for, and what function does this organization serve?

ANNUITIES

An annuity is a type of investment that systematically pays out benefits, usually over an extended period of time. They're widely used as a supplemental source of income by people in retirement, so it is important to consider the kind of return you'll get on your investment. You can choose a fixed-rate *annuity, with returns closely linked to money market yields, or a* variable-rate *annuity that allows you to aggressively play the stock and bond markets. What kind of annuity would you find most attractive? What would you see as the advantages and disadvantages of each type? Give some thought to these questions before reading on.*

The number of annuity contracts in force with U.S. life insurance companies has grown tremendously in the past 10 to 15 years. This growth has resulted primarily from greater public awareness of annuities, due to the increased marketing efforts of life insurance companies. In addition, the surge in retirement programs has contributed to the growth of annuities and so have the tax laws, which treat annuities as tax-sheltered investment vehicles—in fact, the demand for these products has been greatly heightened in recent years as changes in the tax laws have made annuities one of the few tax shelters left to investors. Stripped down, annuities represent little more than an agreement to make contributions now (or in installments) in return for a series of payments later—for a fixed number of years, or for life.

THE ANNUITY PRINCIPLE

An annuity is just the opposite of life insurance. As we pointed out in Chapter 8, life insurance is the systematic accumulation of an estate which is used for protection against financial loss resulting from premature death. In contrast, an **annuity** is the systematic *liquidation* of an estate in such a way that it provides protection against the economic difficulties that could result from outliving personal financial resources. The period during which premiums are paid for the purchase of an annuity is called the **accumulation period;** correspondingly, the period during which annuity payments are made is called the **distribution period.**

Under a pure life annuity contract, a life insurance company will guarantee regular monthly payments to an individual for as long as he or she lives. These benefits are composed of three parts: principal, interest, and survivorship benefits. The *principal* consists of the premium amounts paid in by the *annuitant* (person buying the annuity) during the accumulation period. *Interest* is the amount earned on these funds between the time they are paid and distributed. The interest earnings on an annuity accrue (that is, accumulate) tax-free. The portion of the principal and interest that has not been returned to the annuitant prior to death is the **survivorship benefit.** These funds are available to those members of the annuity group who survive in each subsequent period. By using mortality tables and estimated investment returns, life insurance companies can calculate for a group of annuitants of a given age the amount of monthly payment they can guarantee to each individual without prematurely depleting the total amounts that have accumulated. Consequently, the risk of outliving one's income is eliminated.

CLASSIFICATION OF ANNUITIES

Annuities may be classified according to several key characteristics, including the way the premiums are paid, the disposition of proceeds, inception date of benefits and the method used in calculating benefits. Exhibit 14.6 presents a chart of this classification system.

Single Premium or Installments. There are two ways to pay the premiums when you purchase an annuity contract: you can make a large single (lump-sum) payment right up front or pay the premium in installments. The **single-premium annuity contract** usually requires a minimum investment of anywhere from $2,500 to $10,000, with $5,000 the most common figure. These annuities have become very popular recently, primarily because of the attractive tax features they offer investors. Also, they are often purchased just before retirement as a way of creating a future stream of income. Sometimes the cash value of a life insurance policy will be used at retirement to acquire a single-premium annuity. This is a highly effective use of a life insurance policy: You get the insurance coverage when you need it the most (while you're raising and educating your family) and then a regular stream of income when you can probably use it the most (after you've retired).

While the majority of *group* annuity policies are funded with single premiums, many *individuals* still buy annuities by paying for them in installments. With these so-called **installment-premium annuity contracts,** set payments, starting as low as $100,

Pension Benefit Guarantee Corporation (PBGC) An organization established under ERISA that guarantees to eligible workers payability of certain pension benefits regardless of the employer's ability to fulfill its commitments.

annuity An investment product sold by life insurance companies that provides a series of payments over time.

accumulation period The period during which premiums are paid for the purchase of an annuity.

distribution period The period during which annuity payments are made to an annuitant.

survivorship benefit On an annuity, the portion of premiums and interest that has not been returned to the annuitant prior to his or her death.

single-premium annuity contract An annuity contract that is purchased with a lump-sum payment.

installment-premium annuity contract An annuity contract that is purchased through periodic payments made over a given period of time.

EXHIBIT 14.6

Different Types of Annuity Contracts

The different types of annuity contracts vary according to how you pay for the annuity, how the proceeds will be disbursed, how earnings accrue, and when you will receive the benefits.

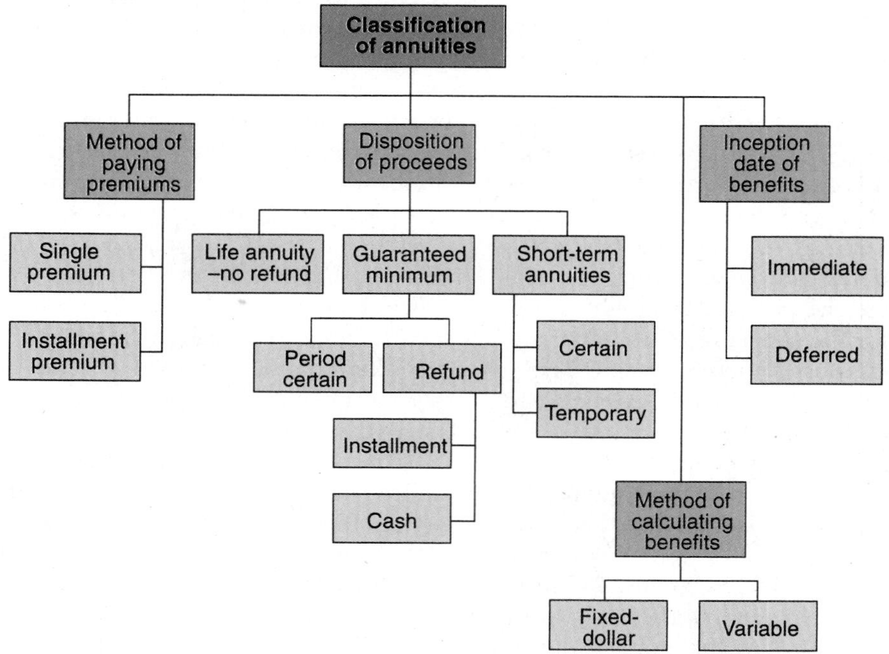

Source: Adapted from Robert I. Mehr, *Life Insurance: Theory and Practice,* rev. ed. (Dallas: Business Publications, 1977), p. 85.

are made at regular intervals (monthly, quarterly, annually) over an extended period of time. Sometimes, these annuities are set up with a fairly large initial payment (of perhaps several thousand dollars), followed by a series of much smaller installment payments (of, say, $250 a quarter). There are even plans that combine the features of both single-premium and installment-premium annuities. Known as *flexible plans,* they start out with a sizable initial investment, very much like single-premium annuities, except that the investor can put more money in later, *as desired*. In this type of contract, which is common with variable annuities, the individual is under no obligation to make future set payments at set intervals.

Installment-premium contracts also carry an important *life insurance provision,* which stipulates that if an annuitant dies before the distribution period begins, the annuitant's beneficiaries will receive the market value of the contract or the amount invested, whichever is greater (note that single-premium annuities contain similar life insurance provisions, so long as the payout of benefits is deferred to some future date). In addition, the annuitant can terminate an installment-premium contract at any time, or simply stop paying the periodic installments and take a paid-up annuity for a reduced amount. One potential advantage of purchasing an installment-type annuity early is that the scheduled benefits are based on mortality rates in effect when the contract is purchased. Even if the mortality rate improves, as it normally does with the passage of time, the annuitant will not be required to pay the higher premium stipulated in contracts issued later on.

Disposition of Proceeds. All annuities revolve around the basic pay-now, receive-later concept. As such, they allow individuals to prepare for future cash needs, like planning for retirement, while obtaining significant tax benefits. When it comes to the distribution of an annuity, you can either take a lump-sum payment, or, as is more often the case, you can *annuitize* the distribution by systematically parceling out the money into regular payments over a defined, or open-ended, period of time. Since most people choose to annuitize their proceeds (which is conceptually the way an annuity should be used), let's look at the most common annuity disbursement options:

- ***Life annuity with no refund (straight life).*** The annuitant receives a specified amount of income for life, whether the disbursement period turns out to be one year or 50 years. The estate or family receives no refunds when the annuitant dies. This results in the largest monthly payments of any distribution methods, because the issuer (a life insurance company) does not have to distribute the principal, if any, to the annuitant's heirs. This option is not widely used by individuals but may be found in group annuity contracts.
- ***Guaranteed-minimum annuity.*** A beneficiary also may become eligible for benefits. This annuity can take two forms. With a **life annuity, period certain,** the annuitant gets a guaranteed monthly income for life and the insurance company agrees to pay the monthly benefits for at least a minimum number of years (five or ten, for example). If the annuitant dies soon after the distribution begins, his (or her) beneficiaries receive the monthly benefits for the balance of the "period certain." With a **refund annuity,** if the annuitant dies, the designated beneficiary receives monthly payments (or in some cases, a lump-sum cash refund) until the total purchase price of the annuity has been refunded.
- ***Annuity certain.*** This pays a set amount of monthly income for a specified number of years, thereby filling a need for monthly income that will expire after a certain length of time. An annuitant selecting a ten-year annuity certain receives payments for ten years after retirement, regardless of whether he or she lived two or twenty more years. For example, a widow, age 52, could use a ten-year annuity certain contract to provide income until she reaches age 62 and can apply for Social Security benefits.
- ***Temporary life annuity.*** This annuity continues benefits for a specified period only if the annuitant survives, so it provides a larger monthly income than the annuity certain. If the above widow had chosen a ten-year temporary life annuity but died at age 60, no further payments would be made under the contract. It's most appropriate for those who have no beneficiaries or who need the added income.

Immediate versus Deferred Annuity. An annuitant usually has the choice of receiving monthly benefits immediately upon buying an annuity or of deferring receipt for a number of years. Logically, the first type is called an immediate annuity and the latter a deferred annuity. An **immediate annuity,** purchased with a single premium, is most often used in conjunction with the cash value or death proceeds of a life insurance policy to create a stream of cash receipts needed for retirement or to support a widow and/or dependent children.

life annuity with no refund (straight life) An option under which an annuitant receives a specified amount of income for life regardless of the length of the distribution period; in turn, no payments or refunds are made to the person's family or estate upon his or her death.

guaranteed-minimum annuity An annuity that provides a guaranteed minimum distribution of benefits.

life annuity, period certain A type of guaranteed-minimum annuity in which the annuitant is guaranteed a stated amount of monthly income for life and the insurer agrees to pay that amount for a minimum number of years regardless of whether or not the annuitant survives.

refund annuity A type of guaranteed-minimum annuity that provides that upon the annuitant's death, monthly payments will be made to the designated beneficiary until the total purchase price of the annuity has been refunded.

annuity certain An annuity that provides a specified amount of monthly income for a stated number of years without consideration of any life contingency.

temporary life annuity An annuity in which benefits continue for a specified period, only for as long as the annuitant survives.

immediate annuity An annuity in which the annuitant begins receiving monthly benefits immediately; often purchased with a single premium.

A **deferred annuity,** in contrast, can be bought with either a single payment or through an installment plan. This contract is quite flexible and can be issued with numerous options for both paying the premiums and receiving the proceeds. The big advantage of a deferred annuity is that your savings can build up over time free of taxes. With no taxes to pay, you have more money working for you and, as such, can build up a bigger retirement nest egg (of course, you'll have to pay taxes on your earnings eventually, but not until you start receiving payments from your annuity). Most annuities purchased under group contracts are immediate annuities, whereas those purchased by individuals are usually of the *deferred* type. In fact, because of their attractive tax features, a lot of people buy deferred annuities—and especially single-premium deferred annuities—more as a tax-sheltered *investment vehicle* than anything else.

Fixed versus Variable Annuity. When you put your money into an annuity, the premium is invested on your behalf by the insurance company, much like a mutual fund invests the money you put into it. From the time you pay the annuity premium until it is paid back to you as a lump sum or as an annuitized monthly benefit, you'll earn a rate of return on your investment. How that rate of return is figured determines whether you own a fixed or variable annuity. In a **fixed-rate annuity** the insurance company safeguards your principal and agrees to pay a guaranteed minimum rate of interest over the life of the contract—which often amounts to little more than prevailing money market rates that existed at the time you bought the contract. These are conservative, very low-risk annuity products that essentially promise to return *the original investment plus interest* when the money is paid out to the annuitant (and/or any designated beneficiaries). Unlike bond mutual funds, fixed annuities do not fluctuate in value when interest rates rise or fall; as such, your principal is secure at all times. However, contrary to what many people think, these annuities are *not* backed by a specific, dedicated portfolio of securities (like mutual funds are). Rather, they are backed by the insurance company's "general account," which often consists of a wide variety of investment vehicles; and when it comes to the rate of interest paid on the annuity, *the insurance company can pay whatever they want,* as they are in no way required to pay the rate they earn on their general account! With fixed annuities, once a distribution, or payout, schedule has been selected, the annuitant knows right up front what the (minimum) monthly benefit will be, as that's guaranteed by the annuity contract. These *interest-earning annuities,* as they're also called, are ideally suited for the cautious investor who likes the secure feeling of knowing what his or her monthly cash flow will be.

Imagine an investment vehicle that lets you move between stocks, bonds, and money funds and, at the same time, accumulate profits tax-free. That, in a nutshell, is a variable annuity. With a **variable annuity** contract, the amount that's ultimately paid out to the annuitant varies with the investment results obtained by the insurance company—*nothing* is guaranteed, not even the principal! When you buy a variable annuity, you decide where you want your money invested, based on your investment objectives and tolerance for risk: You can usually choose from stocks, bonds, money market securities or some combination thereof. Insurance companies typically offer five or six stock and bond funds, as well as money market investments for short-term safety; some companies even offer a relatively exotic fleet of alternatives, ranging from zero coupon bonds to real estate and foreign securities. As an annuity holder, you can stay put with a single investment for the long haul, or, as with most variable annuities, you can aggressively play the market by switching from one fund to another. Obviously, when the market goes up, investors in variable annuities do well; but, as many people learned in the market crash of October 1987, the returns on these policies can also go DOWN—and sometimes, in a very big way.

Because the payoff from a variable annuity depends to such an extent on the fate of the markets, the annuitants take a chance that their monthly income will be less than anticipated. Of course, most people who participate in variable annuity plans fully expect to be able to outperform fixed annuities. But that doesn't always happen, as we saw in the 1970s when a sluggish stock market led to variable annuity payments that were well below the amounts paid on corresponding fixed-rate plans. Annuitants, however, do have some control over this type of risk exposure, since they can choose to go with high- or low-risk investment vehicles and in so doing, influence the certainty of return. In effect, if you go with an account that stresses high-risk securities, you should expect a good deal of

EXHIBIT 14.7

Lump-Sum Costs Necessary for Funding Payments of $100 a Month

Annuity costs vary not only by the type of annuity and the sex and age of the beneficiary but also by the company selling the contract. Clearly, it pays to shop around: What it would cost a 55-year-old male to buy $100 a month through a life annuity contract from Company 2 would cost nearly 27 percent more if the same type of contract were bought from Company 3.

	Life Annuity With No Refund					
	Male			Female		
Company	55	65	75	55	65	75
1	$13,110	$11,170	$8,510	$13,930	$12,280	$9,700
2	11,820	10,250	8,010	12,450	11,140	8,980
3	15,020	11,970	8,420	16,510	13,440	9,580
4	12,900	10,960	8,480	13,660	11,860	9,270

	Life Annuity—10 Years Certain					
	Male			Female		
Company	55	65	75	55	65	75
1	$13,400	$11,840	$10,170	$14,070	$12,660	$10,770
2	12,050	10,800	9,390	12,560	11,440	9,870
3	N/A	N/A	N/A	N/A	N/A	N/A
4	13,190	11,570	9,940	13,790	12,200	10,300

uncertainty in return—the potential for high return might be there, but so is the chance for loss. If you're uncomfortable with that, then stick to annuities that offer safer investment choices (like zero coupon bonds or Treasury securities). Also, although there's nothing to prohibit you from staying with market-sensitive variable annuities during both the accumulation and distribution periods, in most cases you can convert to a fixed annuity at distribution. What you do, in effect, is use the cash value in your variable annuity to buy a paid-up fixed annuity. In this way, you use a *variable annuity during the accumulation period* to build up your capital as much as possible, and then switch to a *fixed annuity for the distribution period* to obtain a certain, well-defined stream of future income. While variable annuities have a lot to offer, they're not for everyone; take a look at the *Issues in Money Management* box on page 596—it will help you decide if these annuities are right for you.

SOURCES AND COSTS OF ANNUITIES

Annuities are administered by life insurance companies, and for that reason, it should come as no surprise that they're also the leading sellers of these financial products. In addition, annuities can also be purchased from stock brokers, mutual fund organizations, banks, and financial planners. When you buy an annuity, the cost will vary considerably with the age of the annuitant at issue, the age of the annuitant when payments begin, the method used to distribute benefits, the number of lives covered, and the sex of the annuitant. Exhibit 14.7 presents the lump-sum costs of several leading companies for two types of immediate annuities. Note the substantial differences that exist among the companies' premium. These differences confirm the

deferred annuity An annuity in which benefit payments are deferred for a certain number of years; purchased with either a lump-sum payment or in installments.

fixed-rate annuity An annuity in which the insurance company safeguards your principal and agrees to pay a guaranteed rate of interest on your money; in addition, the (minimum) monthly benefit is set by the contract.

variable annuity An annuity in which the monthly income provided by the policy varies according to the actual investment experience of the insurer.

Issues in Money Management

Are Variable Annuities Right for You?

Although they have been around over 40 years, variable annuities are enjoying renewed popularity. One reason is that the annuity's income grows tax-free, just like an IRA or 401(k). Unlike IRAs and 401(k)plans, however, there is no limit on the amount invested in a variable annuity, nor must you withdraw funds at 70½. The typical annuity offers an average of eight subaccounts (mutual-fund-like portfolios), including several types of stock funds, from small-caps to international, several fixed income accounts; some even have asset allocation funds. Sponsors have improved annuity performance to compete with mutual funds.

On the other hand, annuity deposits are not tax-deductible like 401(k) and some IRA contributions. As with any tax-deferred investment, you owe ordinary income taxes plus a 10 percent penalty on funds withdrawn before age 59½. So you had better be sure that you will not need the money you invest in annuities until then. Their high fees can erode investment returns, and tax penalties and surrender charges could cancel out tax benefits. Some mutual fund companies now offer no-load annuities without up-front sales or back-end surrender charges. However, these may have above-average annual fees.

There are some other facts that you should know before buying a variable annuity. For example, your heirs may wind up with a large tax bill if you die with money left in the annuity account. Any capital gain on your original investment is taxable. (Mutual fund gains, on the other hand, pass to your heirs at the market value at the time of transfer, so no taxes are due.) The "guaranteed death benefit" component of an annuity, which the salesperson may tout, is not life insurance but insurance against loss of your original investment. If you die before you earn it back, your heirs recoup the original principal. How much you earn still depends on market performance.

Choosing the right annuity can be difficult, because many annuity salespeople tend to gloss over details and provide only performance statistics that work to the annuity's advantage. For example, a salesperson might boast that the annuity was the star performer in the prior year—but omit the fact that the other funds in the annuity performed poorly. Or he or she could emphasize the annuity's high returns—returns that may not include high annual fees that greatly reduce that return. And if your annuity is part of your employer's retirement plan, do not assume that the annuities have been screened for quality. Typically, they are not endorsed by your employer. Also, remember that your employee retirement funds are already tax-deferred, so you can invest in mutual funds rather than the annuity, with its extra fees.

Are annuities right for you? Because of their high fees, investing in variable annuities makes sense only if you have maxed out contributions to other tax-deferred plans and can leave the money for 10 to 15 years. If you decide to investigate annuities, start with the number of subaccounts—the more categories and funds within each category, the better. They should match your investment style and goals; for example, not all annuity contracts offer broad diversification or specialty funds. Next, evaluate performance. A wide selection of funds does you no good if they perform poorly. Growth-oriented funds have performed best, providing the high returns needed to cover expenses. Weigh fees against performance but look twice before investing in an annuity that charges over 2.1 percent. Seek out those with solid performance, low expense ratios, and no front-end or surrender charges. Several annuities may offer the same fund portfolios, so check Morningstar's monthly *Variable Annuity/Life Performance Report* to find the lowest-cost annuity with that subaccount.

Sources: Adapted from Kristin Davis, "Annuities: Picking Your Way Through the Jungle," *Kiplinger's Personal Finance Magazine,* October 1994, pp, 55–63; Ellen E. Schultz, "Five Sad Variable-Annuity Facts Your Salesman Won't Tell You," *The Wall Street Journal,* April 13, 1995, p. R13; and Amey Stone, "Variable Annuities: More Choices, More Fans," *Business Week,* June 27, 1994, p. 104–105.

need to shop around before making an annuity purchase. Note, too. that in every category the cost to females is higher than the cost to males, due to the lower mortality rates among women. The differences in life expectancy for males and females can be seen in Exhibit 14.8. Mortality differences notwithstanding, legislation is pending that would exclude sex as a criterion for annuity rate making.

EXHIBIT 14.8

Life Expectancies of American Men and Women (Latest Available Statistics, 1990)

Life expectancy measures the number of years a person has left to live—for example, on average, a 20-year-old has a little over 56 years remaining. Note, however, that life expectancy varies by age, sex, and race.

AGE IN 1990 (years)	EXPECTATION OF LIFE IN YEARS				
		White		Black	
	Total	Male	Female	Male	Female
At birth	75.4	72.7	79.4	64.5	73.6
5	71.2	68.5	75.0	61.0	70.0
10	66.3	63.5	70.1	56.1	65.1
15	61.3	58.6	65.2	51.3	60.2
20	56.6	54.0	60.3	46.7	55.3
25	51.9	49.3	55.4	42.4	50.6
30	47.2	44.7	50.6	38.2	45.9
35	42.6	40.1	45.8	34.1	41.3
40	38.0	35.6	41.0	30.1	36.8
45	33.4	31.1	36.2	26.2	32.4
50	29.0	26.7	31.6	22.5	28.2
55	24.8	22.5	27.2	19.0	24.2
56	24.0	21.7	26.4	18.4	23.4
57	23.2	21.0	25.5	17.8	22.7
58	22.4	20.2	24.7	17.1	22.0
59	21.6	19.4	23.8	16.5	21.2
60	20.8	18.7	23.0	15.9	20.5
61	20.1	18.0	22.2	15.4	19.8
62	19.4	17.3	21.4	14.8	19.1
63	18.6	16.6	20.6	14.3	18.5
64	17.9	15.9	19.8	13.7	17.8
65	17.2	15.2	19.1	13.2	17.2
70	13.9	12.1	15.4	10.7	14.1
75	10.9	9.4	12.0	8.6	11.2
80	8.3	7.1	9.0	6.7	8.6
85 and over	6.1	5.2	6.4	5.0	6.3

Source: U.S. Bureau of the Census, *Statistical Abstract of the United States,* (114th edition) Washington, D.C., 1994, Table No. 116, p. 88.

In addition, just like mutual funds, there are some annual fees you should be aware of. In particular, be prepared to pay insurance fees of 1 percent or more—and that's on top of annual management fees of perhaps 1 to 2 percent paid on variable annuities. That's a total of 2 to 3 percent taken right off the top, year after year. And then there's also a *contract charge* (or maintenance fee) that's deducted annually to cover various contract-related expenses; these fees usually run from about $30 to $60 per year. Obviously, these fees can drag down returns and reduce the advantage of tax-deferred income. Finally, as we'll see later, most annuities charge hefty penalties for early withdrawal, meaning in order to get out of a poorly performing annuity, you'll have to forfeit a chunk of your money.

THE INVESTMENT AND INCOME PROPERTIES OF ANNUITIES

One of the major attributes of most types of annuities is that they are a source of income that cannot be outlived. While individuals might create a similar arrangement by simply living off the interest or dividends from their investments, they would find it difficult to engage in the systematic liquidation of their principal in a manner that would be timed to closely (or exactly) coincide with their death. Also viewed very positively is the fact that the income earned in an annuity is allowed to accumulate tax-free; thus, it provides a form of *tax-sheltered investment.* Actually, the income from an annuity is *tax-deferred,* meaning that taxes on the earnings will have to be paid when the annuity is liquidated.

EXHIBIT 14.9

The Comparative Returns of Variable Annuities versus Mutual Funds

Variable annuities are structured and operate very much like mutual funds and, as such, you'd expect their performance to be comparable. As we see here, that's not always the case.

Variable Annuity or Mutual Fund Category	Average Annual Return (Over 5-year Period ending 3/31/95)	
	Variable Annuities	**Mutual Funds**
Aggressive Growth and Small Cap	14.09%	13.19%
Growth	10.19	10.95
Growth & Income and Equity Income	10.31	9.90
U.S. Diversified Equity Average	**10.66**	**11.04**
International Stock—Europe, Foreign, Pacific, and World	4.54	6.07
Equity Average	**9.63**	**10.12**
Balanced and Asset Allocation	8.53	9.12
Corporate Bond—High Quality and General	7.17	8.08
Government Bond—Adjustable Rate Mortgage, Mortgage, Treasury, and General	7.21	7.55
Taxable Fixed-Income Average	**7.23**	**7.75**

Source: Morningstar, Inc., 225 Wacker Drive, Chicago, IL 60606. 312-696-6100

While shelter from taxes is an attractive investment attribute, there is a hitch. You may be faced with a big tax penalty if you close out or withdraw money from an annuity before it's time. Specifically, the IRS treats annuity withdrawals like withdrawals from an individual retirement arrangement, meaning that except in cases of serious illness, *anybody who takes money out before reaching 59½ will incur a 10 percent tax penalty.* Thus, if you're under 59½ and in the 28 percent tax bracket, you'll end up paying a 38 percent tax rate on any funds withdrawn from an annuity. (The IRS views withdrawals *entirely as taxable income* until the account balance falls to the amount of original paid-in principal—after which any further withdrawals would be tax-free.) Short of some type of serious illness, about the only way to tap your account penalty-free before you're 59½ is to *annuitize.* Unfortunately, the annuity payments must be spread out over your estimated remaining life span, which means the size of each monthly payment could end up being pretty small. Because of this threat of a tax penalty, the purchase of an annuity should always be considered as a long-term investment. Assume it's a part of your retirement program (that's the way the IRS looks at it) and that you're getting in for the long haul, because it's not that easy to get out before you turn 59½.

From an investment perspective, the returns generated from an annuity can, in some cases, prove to be a bit disappointing. For instance, as we discussed above, the returns on *variable annuities* are tied to returns in the money and capital markets, but even so, they are still no better than what you can get from other investment vehicles—and, as you can see in Exhibit 14.9, they are often lower, due in part to higher annuity fees. Also, the differential returns aren't due to tax features, since in both cases returns were measured on a before-tax basis. But the fact is the returns from annuities are tax-sheltered so that makes those lower returns look a lot more attractive. Even so, if you're considering a variable annuity, go over it much the same way you would a traditional mutual fund: Look for superior past performance, proven management talents, moderate expenses, and the availability of attractive investment alternatives that you can switch in and out of.

As far as *fixed-rate annuities* are concerned, while many of them advertise high rates of return, a close look at the fine print reveals that such rates are guaranteed only for the first one to five years, after which time they drop to something closer to money market yields—or less. True, there are minimum guaranteed rates that the annuities have to stand behind, but these are usually so low that they're really not much help. Investors generally have little choice but to accept the going rate or surrender the policy. Surrender can be painful, however, not only because of IRS penalties, but also because of the hefty *surrender fees* that are found on many of these contracts (these fees often amount to 5 to 10 percent of the account balance in the first year and then gradually decline to zero over a seven- to ten-year period).

It's possible to get around a surrender fee if the annuity has a *bailout* clause. Such a provision allows you to withdraw your money, free of any surrender fees, if the rate of return on the annuity falls below a certain level (say, a point or so below the initial rate). But you have to act fairly quickly, since the bailout provision may only exist for a limited period of time. Of course, even if you exercise a bailout provision, you may still have to face a tax penalty for early withdrawal—unless you transfer the funds to another annuity through what is known as a *1035 exchange*.

How Good Is the Insurance Company? One final point: If you're seriously considering buying an annuity, make sure you carefully read the contract and see what the guaranteed rates are, how long the initial rate applies, and if a bailout provision exists. Just as important, since *the annuity is only as good as the insurance company that stands behind it,* check to see how the company is rated by Best's, Standard & Poor's and/or Moody's. As we saw in Chapter 8, the life insurance industry has gone through some rough times, and dozens of insurance companies have gone under, jeopardizing more than 500,000 annuity holders. It's important to make sure that the insurance company itself is financially sound before buying one of its annuity products. After all, there is no FDIC or some other federal agency to step in and pick up the pieces. Recall in Chapter 8, we provided a list of some of the stronger life insurance companies; *that same list can be used to check out the issuer of a fixed or variable annuity.* You can also do the checking yourself by referring to Best's, Standard & Poor's, or Moody's. These independent rating agencies provide quality ratings (on hundreds of insurance companies) that are much like those found in the bond market and are meant to reflect the financial strength of the firm. Letter grades are assigned on the principle that the stronger the company, the lower the risk of loss—accordingly, if security is important to you, stick with insurers that carry one of the top ratings (A++ or A+ for Best's; AAA or AA for S&P; and Aaa or Aa for Moody's); see Chapter 8 for more discussion on these insurance ratings and how they work.

Concept Check

14-15. What is an *annuity*? Briefly explain how an annuity works, and also how it differs from a life insurance policy. Differentiate between a *single-premium annuity* and an *installment-premium annuity*.

14-16. Briefly explain the four procedures that are most widely used in the distribution of annuity proceeds. Which one results in the highest monthly payment?

14-17. Describe and differentiate among (a) an *immediate annuity*, (b) a *deferred annuity*, (c) a *straight life annuity*, and (d) a *refund annuity*.

14-18. What is a *fixed-rate annuity*, and how does it differ from a *variable annuity*? Does the type of contract (whether it's fixed or variable) have any bearing on the amount of money you'll receive at the time of distribution? Explain. Which type of contract would probably be most suitable for someone who wants a minimum amount of risk exposure? What's the purpose of a bailout provision in a fixed-rate annuity?

14-19. Explain how the purchase of a variable annuity is much like an investment in a mutual fund. Do you, as a buyer, have any control over the amount of investment risk to which you're exposed in a variable annuity contract? Explain.

14-20. How do variable annuity returns compare to mutual fund returns? Can you offer any logical reasons as to why there would be any difference in comparable returns? Explain.

14-21. Briefly explain why annuities are a type of tax-sheltered investment. Is there anything you have to give up in order to obtain this tax-favored treatment (Hint: age $59^{1}/_{2}$)?

14-22. Why is it important to check the financial ratings of an insurance company when buying an annuity? Why should you look at past performance when considering the purchase of a variable annuity?

SUMMARY

LG1. **Recognize the importance of retirement planning and identify the three biggest pitfalls to good planning.** Retirement planning plays a vital role in the total personal financial planning process. It employs many of the same basic principles and concepts of effective financial planning, including the establishment of financial goals and strategies, the use of savings and investment plans, and the use of certain insurance products, like annuities. The three biggest pitfalls to sound retirement planning are starting too late, not saving enough, and investing too conservatively.

LG2. **Establish retirement goals and estimate your future income needs.** Rather than address retirement planning in a series of short-run (three- to five-year) plans, it's best to take a long-term approach and look 20 to 30 years into the future, to determine how much saving and investing you must do today to achieve the retirement goals you've set for tomorrow. Implementing a long-term retirement plan involves determining future retirement needs, estimating retirement income from known sources (like social security and company pension plans), and deciding on how much to save and invest each year in order to build up a desired nest egg.

LG3. **Explain the eligibility requirements and benefits of the Social Security program.** Social Security forms the basic foundation for the retirement programs of most families; except for a few exempt classes (of mostly government employees), almost all gainfully employed workers are covered by social security. Upon retirement, covered workers are entitled to certain monthly benefits, as determined mainly by the employee's earning history and age at retirement.

LG4. **Differentiate among the different types of basic and supplemental employer-sponsored pension plans.** Employer-sponsored pension and retirement plans provide a vital source of retirement income to many individuals. Such plans can often spell the difference between enjoying a comfortable standard of living in retirement or a bare subsistence. With *basic* retirement programs, all employees participate after a certain period of employment. These plans can be defined-contribution or defined-benefit plans. There are also several forms of *supplemental* employer-sponsored programs, including profit-sharing plans, thrift and savings plans, and perhaps the most popular of all, salary reduction plans like the so-called 401(k) plans.

LG5. **Describe the various types of self-directed retirement plans.** In addition to company-sponsored retirement programs, individuals can also set up their own self-directed tax-sheltered retirement plans; it is through such plans that most individuals can build up the nest egg they will need to meet the retirement objectives they have set for themselves. The basic types of self-directed retirement programs are Keogh and SEP plans for self-employed individuals, and IRAs, which can be set up by any salary or wage earner.

LG6. **Choose the right type of annuity for your retirement plan.** Annuities are also an important source of income to retired people. Basically, an annuity is an investment vehicle that allows investment income to accumulate tax-deferred and provides for the systematic liquidation (payout) of all invested capital and earnings over an extended period of time. A wide variety of annuities exists, including single payment and installment-premium, fixed and variable, immediate and deferred. Different payout options also exist.

FINANCIAL FACTS OR FANTASIES

Are the following statements financial facts (true) or fantasies(false)?

1. The three biggest mistakes that people make in retirement planning are: they start too late, they try to sock away too much, and they invest their retirement funds too aggressively.
2. In order to receive maximum social security retirement benefits, a worker must retire before his or her 65th birthday.
3. Social security retirement benefits should be sufficient to provide retired workers and their spouses with a comfortable standard of living.
4. Because participation in a company's basic pension plan is mandatory, you're entitled to immediate vesting of all contributions.
5. Your contributions to an IRA account may or may not be tax deductible, depending in part on your level of income.
6. Since an annuity is only as good as the insurance company that stands behind it, you should check the company's financial rating before buying an annuity.

DISCUSSION QUESTIONS AND PROBLEMS

Discussion Question for Opening Profile
Describe Annabelle Reitman's general approach to retirement planning. What steps did she take to prepare for early retirement? If Annabelle had come to you for advice on her retirement program when she was 45, what would you have told her?

1. Alana Lopez, a 25-year-old branch banking officer at First State Bank, understands the importance of starting to save for retirement early. She has designated $2,000 per year for her retirement funds and assumes she will retire at age 65.

a. How much will she have if she invests in CDs and similar money market instruments that earn 4 percent on average?

b. How much will she have if she invests in equities instead and earns 10 percent on average?

c. Alana is urging her friend, Mark Randolph to start his plan right away, as he is 35. What would his nest egg amount to if he invested in the same manner as Alana and he, too, retires at age 65?

2. ***Use Worksheet 14.1*** to help Al and Linda Chung, who would like to retire while they are still relatively young—in about 20 years. Both have promising careers, and both make good money. As a result, they are willing to put aside whatever is necessary to achieve a comfortable lifestyle in retirement. Their current level of household expenditures (excluding savings) is around $60,000 a year, and they expect to spend even more in retirement; they think they'll need about 125 percent of that amount (note: 125 percent equals a multiplier factor of 1.25). They estimate that their social security benefits will amount to $15,000 a year in today's dollars and they will receive another $25,000 annually from their company pension plans. They feel that future inflation will amount to about 3 percent a year; in addition, they think they will be able to earn about 12 percent on their investments prior to retirement and about 8 percent afterward. Use Worksheet 14.1 to find out how big their investment nest egg will have to be and how much they will have to save annually in order to accumulate such an amount within the next 20 years.
3. Many critics of the social security program feel that participants are getting a substandard investment return on their money. Discuss why you agree or disagree with this point of view.

4. Use Exhibit 14.5 to determine the amount of social security retirement benefits that Elwood Cheeseater would receive annually if he had a high level of career earnings, is age 62, and has a dependent wife. If Elwood also receives another $47,500 a year from a company pension and some tax-exempt bonds that he holds, will he be liable for any tax on his social security income? Explain.
5. Ashante Martin has just graduated from college and is considering job offers from two companies. Although the salary and insurance benefits are similar, the retirement programs are not. One firm offers a 401(k) plan that matches employee contributions with $.25 for every $1 contributed by the employee, up to the $9,240 limit. The other has a contributory plan that allows employees to contribute up to 10 percent of their annual salary through payroll deduction and matches it dollar for dollar. The plan vests fully after five years. Because Ashante is unfamiliar with these plans, explain the features of each for her so that she can make an informed decision.
6. Joe Ramirez is an operations manager for a large manufacturer. He earned $45,000 in 1995 and plans to contribute the maximum allowed to the firm's 401(k) plan. Assuming that Joe is in the 28 percent tax bracket, calculate his taxable income and the amount of his tax savings. How much did it actually cost Joe on an after-tax basis to make this retirement plan contribution?
7. At what age would you like to retire? What type of lifestyle do you envision (for example, where do you want to live, do you want to work part-time, and so on)? Discuss the steps you think you should take so that you can realize this goal.

CONTEMPORARY CASE APPLICATIONS

14.1 Comparing Pension Plan Features: Which Plan Is Best?

Mary Carpenter and Ellen Shoemaker are neighbors in Kansas City. Mary works as a systems engineer for United Foods Corporation, Topeka Foods Division, while Ellen works as an executive assistant for U.S. Steel and Castings. Both are married, have two children, and are well paid. Before Mary and Ellen joined their respective companies, there had been some employee unrest and strikes. To counteract these problems, their firms had developed job enrichment and employee motivation programs. Of particular interest are the portions of these programs that deal with pensions and retirement.

Topeka Foods has a contributory plan under which 5 percent of the employees' annual wages is deducted to meet the cost of the benefits. An amount equal to the employee contribution is also contributed by the company. The plan uses a seven-year graded vesting procedure; it has a normal retirement age of 60 for all employees and the benefits at retirement are paid according to a defined contribution plan.

Although U.S. Steel and Castings has a minimum retirement age of 60, it provides for an extension period of five to six years before compulsory retirement. Employees (full-time, hourly, or salaried) also must meet participation requirements. Further, in contrast to the Topeka plan, the U.S. Steel and Castings program has a noncontributory feature. Annual retirement benefits are computed according to the following formula. 1 percent of the employee's final annual salary for each year of service with the company is paid upon retirement. The plan vests immediately.

Questions

1. Discuss the basic features of the retirement plans offered by Topeka Foods and U.S. Steel and Castings.
2. Which plan do you think is more desirable considering the basic features, retirement age, and benefit computations, as explained?
3. Explain how you would use each of these plans in developing your own retirement program.
4. What role, if any, could the purchase of annuities play in these retirement programs? Discuss the pros and cons of using annuities as a part of retirement planning.

FPPC 14.2 Evaluating Tanya Birch's Retirement Prospects

Tanya Birch is 57 years old and has been widowed for 13 years. Never remarried, she has worked full-time since her husband died—in addition to raising her two children, the youngest of which is now finishing college. Forced back to work in her 40s, her first job was in a fast-food restaurant. Eventually, she upgraded her skills sufficiently to obtain a supervisory position in the personnel department of a major corporation, where she is now earning $48,000 a year.

While her financial focus for the past 13 years has, by necessity, been on meeting living expenses and getting her kids through college, she feels she can now turn her attention to her retirement needs. Actually, Tanya hasn't done too bad in that area either. Due to some shrewd investing of the proceeds from her husband's life insurance policy, Tanya has accumulated the following investment assets:

Money market securities, stock, and bonds	$48,600
IRA and 401(k) plans	$33,500

Other than the mortgage on her condo, the only other debt she has is $7,000 in college loans.

Tanya would like to retire in eight years, and recently hired a financial planner to help her come up with an effective retirement program. He has estimated that in order for her to live comfortably in retirement, she'll need about $30,000 a year (in today's dollars) in retirement income.

Questions

1. Use Exhibit 14.5 to estimate the amount of annual income Tanya can expect from social security.

2. After taking into account the income she'll receive from social security and her company-sponsored pension plan, the financial planner has estimated that Tanya's investment assets will have to provide her with about $12,000 a year in order for her to meet the balance of her retirement income needs. Assuming a 6 percent *after-tax* return on her investments, how big of a nest egg will she need to earn that kind of income?

3. Given she can invest the money market securities, stocks, and bonds (the $48,600) at 5 percent after-taxes, and the amount she's presently accumulated in her tax-sheltered IRA and 401(k)—the $33,500—at 9 percent, how much will her investment assets be worth in eight years, when she retires?

4. Tanya's employer matches her 401(k) contributions dollar for dollar, up to a maximum of $3,000 a year. If she continues to put $3,000 a year into that program, how much more will she have in eight years, given a 9 percent rate of return?

5. What would you advise Tanya about her ability to retire in eight years, as she hopes to?

GETTING A HANDLE ON YOUR FINANCIAL FUTURE

"If I'd known I was gonna live this long I'd have taken better care of myself." Like the lyrics from this country and western song, many of you will not have taken adequate steps to take care of yourself financially in retirement. This is usually due to the fact that there appear to be more pressing needs with which you are currently faced and, as such, there is a natural tendency to focus on short-run financial goals. This results in a delay in the implementation of plans to achieve long-term goals, such as retirement planning.

If You Are Just Getting Started

The earlier you begin setting aside funds, the easier it will be to achieve your financial goals. However, in many cases, younger people have an aversion to planning for retirement. This could be because of the emphasis on youth, a fear of growing old, or the fact that there are too many current concerns to worry about something that will not happen for possibly another 40 years.

Reviewing Employer-Sponsored Retirement Plans:

1. You need to know the participation requirements to determine when and if you would be eligible.
2. Determine if it is contributory and if so, how much of your money goes into the plan.
3. You need to know the vesting requirements on the plan.
4. Determine at what age you can retire.
5. If you leave prior to retirement, can you get your money out of the plan?
6. If your employer offers a 401(k) plan, determine if it provides a matching contribution.
7. If your employer offers a defined contribution plan where you select the investment options, analyze very carefully the performance of the options over time before you make your selection.

Using Other Retirement Programs:

1. Consider opening an IRA account and making monthly contributions instead of waiting until the last minute to make a lump-sum contribution. Remember that you do not have to put in exactly $2,000 in an IRA.
2. If you are considering the purchase of an annuity, investigate the issuer. The annuity's promise to pay is only as good as the financial capability of the issuer.
3. If you are self-employed, consider opening a Keogh plan to provide for a tax-deferred retirement vehicle that would allow you to contribute up to $30,000 a year subject to a limitation of 20 percent of earnings.
4. As an alternative to the Keogh, consider a SEP-IRA, which also allows contributions of up to $30,000 but limited to 15 percent of earnings.

If You Are Thirty-Something

You will probably change jobs a number of times during your working life. As such, you may find that your retirement planning will become more complicated. Even if you are vested in your pension plan, most of them are not portable.

The worst possible situation, however, is when you change jobs so frequently that you never become vested in any retirement plan.

Evaluating the Impact of Job Changes:

1. Assuming that a change in job will not alter your anticipated retirement date or your expenditures in retirement, estimate the impact of the change on the portion of your retirement income coming from your employer's pension plan. If there is to be a shortfall, you need to increase your personal savings and investment to meet this need.
2. Be sure if you change jobs late in your career that you will be able to work long enough to be vested in the plan. If not, try to negotiate a higher salary or a deferred compensation agreement where payments would be made after retirement.
3. Explore the possibilities with your employer of earning income after retirement in the form of a consulting contract, if you would otherwise not be eligible for retirement benefits.

Selecting Retirement Options and Beneficiaries:

1. If you are single at retirement with no heirs, you would probably choose the straight life payment option that will provide the greatest payment during your life but cease at your death.
2. If you are single and have heirs, you might choose the guaranteed payout option that provides some minimum payout in the event that you died soon after beginning to receive retirement or annuity benefits.
3. If you are married and your spouse also has a retirement benefit you would want to determine how much additional income each would need upon the death of the other and choose the payment option that would maximize current income while providing for the other at the death of one of the spouses.
4. If you do not need all of the retirement income from your various sources at the time of retirement, postpone receiving those funds that have survivorship options such as IRAs and let them increase in value until needed.

1. Paul currently has $13,816 vested in his company's 401(k) plan. If he were to change jobs, he could either withdraw this money and use it as he wishes or he could roll it over into an IRA. If Paul did not use the money (not in an IRA), how much money would Paul have left after paying the early withdrawal penalty and federal income taxes? If Paul rolled the 401(k) money into an IRA, how should the transaction be handled so that he could avoid the 20% federal withholding on rollovers?
2. FPPC Paul is currently contributing 7% of his gross salary to his 401(k) plan, and his employer is matching $0.50 for every $1.00 that he contributes. Assuming Paul stayed with Tower Software, these contributions continued (at the same dollar level) over the next 35 years, and the account averaged an annual return of 9%, how much money would be in Paul's 401(k)—including these contributions plus the $13,816 that is currently in the account?
3. FPPC How much would be in the 401(k) after 35 years if Paul increased his contributions to 15% of his gross salary? Remember that Tower Software matches only the first 7% of contributions. Assume everything else is the same as in Question 2.
4. If Paul were going to increase the amount of retirement savings, would you recommend putting more money into his 401(k) or putting the increased contributions into an IRA? Justify your recommendation.
5. FPPC Referring to Paul's most recent budget (Part Five, Question 19 or Part Four, Question 11), would you recommend that he increase or decrease his contributions to his 401(k) at this time? If you recommend a change, revise Paul's budget to reflect that change.
6. FPPC Using the answer to Question 2 as the amount in Paul's retirement account when he reaches retirement, how much could Paul withdraw from this account at the end of each year if he wanted to make 25 withdrawals and the account earned 5% annually over this 25-year period?
7. Review what you learned about Janus Fund and Janus Venture mutual funds in Part Five, Questions 3, 5, 6, 9, and 10. Would you recommend Paul leave his 401(k) money in these funds or move some or all of it into the Guaranteed Investment Contract offered under the plan? Justify your recommendation.
8. FPPC The Mathews (Paul's landlord friends) have asked him for help in determining how much they should be saving for their retirement. One of Jack and Sarah Mathews' long-term goals is to retire in 12 years when Jack is 65. Their current living expenses are approximately $65,000 (excluding savings), but they feel they would be able to live during retirement on about 75% of their current living expenses. Assuming they continue to work for their current employers, they expect to receive approximately $1,200 a month from Jack's retirement plan and about $700 a month from Sarah's employer plan. They will also receive a net income of approximately $1,500 per month from their rental property. They have decided they do not want to count on any Social Security benefits when calculating their retirement needs. Calculate Jack and Sarah's retirement income and investment needs assuming an average rate of inflation of 5%, a 5% return on investments after retirement, and an 8% return on investments prior to retirement.
9. FPPC After looking at the required savings from the previous analysis, Jack and Sarah would like to consider Social Security benefits. Recalculate their retirement needs including Social Security benefits. They estimate Jack's monthly benefit would be $1,111 and Sarah's would be $761.

Chapter 15

Preserving Your Estate

Pauline Victor: A Willing Executor

Helping her father Jack with his financial affairs for several years prior to his death made Pauline Victor the logical choice to be executor of his estate. "I was familiar with his assets and also knew how he wanted things done," she says. "That saved a lot of time. And as a stockbroker, I could handle the financial end of things."

Jack's estate was sizable, but his will was simple. Pauline's mother died in 1983, so except for a $5,000 bequest for a grandson, all assets were to be divided equally between Pauline and her sister Marilyn. The estate included a house, securities, and insurance. "Dad left a letter of instructions that summarized his assets, so I knew exactly where everything was," she explains. "I found two life insurance policies I didn't know existed. He also made some suggestions as to how Marilyn and I might divide personal items." After discussions with her sister, Pauline put the house on the market. Each sister owned a house, and the cash proceeds were more useful. Then they went through the furnishings. "Fortunately, we had no problems dividing them up," notes Pauline. "I know some families with several children plus adult grandchildren who have haggled endlessly over possessions. It can be a mess, and even now they still hold grudges. I'm glad we didn't have to deal with that."

Settling the estate was easier for the Victor family as Minnesota residents. That state is one of

Learning Goals

LG1. *Describe the role of estate planning in personal financial planning and identify the four steps involved in the process.*

LG2. *Recognize the importance of preparing a will and other documents to protect you and your estate.*

LG3. *Explain how trusts are used in estate planning.*

LG4. *Determine whether a gift will be taxable and use planned gifts to reduce estate taxes.*

LG5. *Calculate federal and state taxes due on an estate.*

LG6. *Use effective estate planning techniques to minimize estate taxes.*

15 whose rules for probate (the process of settling an estate) keep court involvement to a minimum. This allowed Pauline to settle the estate in nine months. "As executor of an estate, particularly a sizable one like Dad's, you play many roles," she recalls. "I had to inventory the assets and determine their value. Then I had to pay any debts and taxes. Because the estate was over $600,000, we owed federal estate taxes, but, I let an accountant deal with tax issues."

She was able to get advice from her dad's former law partners, who also drew up required documents. By doing most of the legwork herself—filing papers, taking them to be notarized—she avoided unnecessary legal fees. Insurance turned out to cause the most problems. Pauline found nine policies in his safe, two of which still named her mother as beneficiary. It took months to establish Pauline and Marilyn as legal heirs. "I learned how important it is to review not only your will but also all other documents relating to assets that will become part of an estate, any time there is a change in marital status."

While administering an estate may be a daunting job, Pauline says, "If you're organized, take things a step at a time, and seek professional help when necessary, it's not as difficult as it seems." Reading Chapter 15 will help you plan your own estate and know what's required if a relative or friend asks you to be executor.

Sources: This is a "composite" profile made up from information in Lois Forer, "Where There's a Will . . . ," *Woman's Day,* March 15, 1995, pp. 104–107, and Ed Henry, "When the Executor Is You," *Kiplinger's Personal Finance Magazine,* February 1995, pp. 107–110.

PRINCIPLES OF ESTATE PLANNING

LG1

The overriding objective of estate planning is to ensure the orderly transfer of as much of one's estate as possible to heirs and/or designated beneficiaries. Do you need estate planning? How about your parents? Before reading on, spend a few moments assessing the importance of estate planning by you and by your parents.

Like it or not, no one lives forever. Although this thought may depress you, its reality certainly warrants your attention. Unless you develop plans and take action during your lifetime to accumulate, preserve, and upon your death, distribute your wealth, chances are that your heirs and beneficiaries will receive only part of your estate—the rest will go (often unnecessarily) to taxes and various administrative costs. This process, called *estate planning,* requires knowledge of wills, trusts, and taxes. Understanding these components and their interrelationships will help you to minimize estate shrinkage after your death, while still achieving your lifetime personal financial goals. Also, keep in mind that not only wealthy people but also individuals of modest or moderate means need to plan their estates.

Estate planning can be defined as a goal-oriented activity that uses tax-minimization techniques to provide the greatest possible financial security for an individual and his or her heirs or beneficiaries. It is closely related to both insurance and retirement planning. Certainly the most important reason for buying life insurance is to provide for your family in the event of your premature death. Likewise, one of the principal challenges of effective retirement planning is to achieve a comfortable standard of living in retirement while at the same time *preserving* as much of your accumulated wealth as possible. This not only reduces the chances of you (or your spouse) outliving your financial resources but also leaves money for your estate that can be passed on to your heirs and designated beneficiaries in accordance with your wishes. Another aspect of financial planning that is important to estate planning is *taxes.* As with other financial planning activities, one of the major objectives of estate planning is to eliminate or minimize tax exposure. Doing so, of course, will increase the amount of your estate that ultimately will be passed on to your heirs and beneficiaries.

Estate planning is very goal-oriented. The goals that usually motivate people to engage in estate planning include securing enough capital to meet college education costs and other special needs; ensuring financial security for family members in the event of the death of the head of household; taking care of oneself and one's family during a long-term disability; and providing for a comfortable retirement.

Planning occurs in every estate. Some planning is controlled by the estate owner and/or his or her professional counselors. Other planning—uncontrolled by the estate owner—is done by the federal and state governments. This *uncontrolled planning* occurs when the estate owner forfeits the right to arrange for the disposition of assets and the minimization of tax and other estate settlement costs. Individuals who wish to plan their estates must systematically uncover problems in a number of important areas and provide solutions for them. Exhibit 15.1 itemizes the major types of problems along with their associated causes or indicators. These problems can be minimized or eliminated by maximizing the after-tax return on personal and business investments while minimizing the forces of estate impairment, such as taxes and administrative costs. Techniques for accomplishing this objective are discussed in later sections.

WHO NEEDS ESTATE PLANNING?

Estate planning is indicated when there is a need for either "people planning" or "asset planning."

People Planning. *People planning* means anticipating the psychological and financial needs of those people and organizations you love and providing enough income or capital or both to ensure a continuation of their way of life. People planning also means keeping Mother's cameo brooch in the family and out of the pawnshop or preserving the business that Granddad started in the early 1900s. People planning is especially important to those individuals with (1) children who are minors; (2) children who are exceptionally artistic or intellectually gifted; (3) children or other dependents who are emotionally, mentally, or physically handicapped; and (4) spouses who cannot or do not want to handle money, securities, or a business.

EXHIBIT 15.1

Potential Estate-Planning Problems and Major Causes or Indicators

A number of problems can arise during the settlement of an estate that could have been prevented through careful estate planning. The first step toward prevention of problems is an awareness and understanding of their major causes or indicators.

Problem	Major Cause or Indicator
■ Excessive transfer costs	Taxes and estate administrative expenses higher than necessary.
■ Lack of liquidity	Insufficient cash. Not enough assets that are quickly and inexpensively convertible to cash within a short period of time to meet tax demands and other costs.
■ Improper disposition of assets	Beneficiaries receive the wrong asset or the proper asset in the wrong manner or at the wrong time.
■ Inadequate income at retirement	Capital insufficient or not readily convertible to income-producing status.
■ Inadequate income, if disabled	High medical costs, capital insufficient or not readily convertible to income-producing status, difficulty in reducing living standards.
■ Inadequate income for family at estate owner's death	Any of the above causes.
■ Insufficient capital	Excessive taxes, inflation, improper investment planning.
■ Special problems	A family member with a serious illness or physical or emotional problem, children of a prior marriage, beneficiaries who have extraordinary medical or financial needs, business problems, or opportunities.

Minor children cannot legally handle large sums of money or deal directly with real estate or securities. Custodial accounts, guardianships, or trusts are necessary for providing administration, security, financial advice, and the legal capacity to act on behalf of minors. Few children are exceptionally artistic or intellectually gifted, but those who are often need—or should have—special (and often expensive) schooling, travel opportunities, or equipment. Emotionally, mentally, or physically handicapped children (and other relatives) may need nursing, medical, or psychiatric care. Clearly, outright gifts of money or property to those who cannot care for themselves are foolishly inappropriate. These individuals may need more (or less) than other children. An individual who gives all of his or her children equal shares may not be giving them equitable shares.

How many of us have handled hundreds of thousands of dollars? Think of the burden we place on others when we expect a spouse who cannot—or does not want to—handle such large sums of money or securities to do so with what may be his or her only assets. The bottom line of "people planning" is that one engages in the process for only one reason—because one cares. Sometimes "spend it" is the best planning under the circumstances.

Asset Planning. From the standpoint of wealth alone, estate planning is essential for anyone—single, widowed, married, or divorced—with an estate exceeding $600,000. When a closely held business is involved, estate planning is essential in order to stabilize and maximize the asset- and income-producing value, both during the owner's lifetime and at the owner's death or disability. Likewise, estate planning is essential to avoid the special problems that occur when an estate owner holds title to property in more than one state, such as incurring attorneys' fees in each state or being taxed on the same assets by more than one state.

The estate planning process gets more complicated if you are part of a blended family or have special requests. As the *Financial Shocks* box on page 610 explains, with careful planning you can be sure that your assets go to the desired beneficiaries.

WHY DOES AN ESTATE BREAK UP?

Quite often, when people die, their estates die with them—not because they have done anything wrong but because they have not done *anything*. There are numerous forces that, if unchecked, tend to shrink an estate, reduce the usefulness of its assets,

> **estate planning** A goal-oriented activity that uses tax-minimization techniques to provide the greatest possible financial security for an individual and his or her heirs or beneficiaries.

Financial Shocks

Where There's a Will, There's a Way

Picture these scenarios: (1) Your second husband has no children but agrees to make your three children from your first marriage his beneficiaries. You die at age 60, leaving him a $2 million estate. But when he dies after a lengthy illness 15 years later, only $50,000 remains for the kids. (2) Or your wife remarries after you die. Although she promised to leave what she inherited from you to your children, she instead leaves it to the children she has with her second husband.

As more people become part of "blended" families (those created by remarriage after divorce or death of a spouse), estate planning becomes extremely complicated—and doubly necessary. Like the situations described above, unless you plan carefully, your assets may not be distributed according to your original wishes. This is especially critical when children are involved, regardless of their ages. And if you should put off writing a will, the courts will divide your possessions, based on your state laws. Typically, a spouse will receive anywhere from 25 to 50 percent and is free to do whatever he or she wishes with the bequest. If you've remarried, you may want to leave more than the statutory percentage of your estate to your children. This requires a will and, in many cases, special arrangements called trusts.

Admittedly, many of us have an emotional block when it comes to writing a will; after all, who wants to face their eventual demise? At the very least, it's an anxiety-producing situation. If the estate is being divided between your current spouse and children of a previous marriage, tension may be even greater. Your goals—providing for your current spouse's financial security and for your children, and minimizing taxes—may conflict. For example, if you arrange for your spouse to receive income from certain investments, your children have to wait until the spouse dies—which may be a long time—to inherit those assets. This can create friction among family members. You also should word wills carefully. For example, a widow left everything to "my beloved son, his lovely wife, and their children," but did not list them by name. The son and the wife later divorced, and he remarried a woman his mother didn't like as much. Because the widow did not change her will to specifically name the first wife and the grandchildren, the new spouse eventually inherited a sizable portion of the widow's estate, even though that was not the original intention.

In circumstances like these, good financial and legal advice can help you clearly define your intentions, look at things reasonably objectively, and balance conflicting interests. Trusts—special arrangements that allow you to shift assets out of your estate and into the control of a trustee—are usually the best way to handle these situations to everyone's benefit. For example, you can set up a marital trust for your spouse that provides annual income; upon his or her death, the remaining principal goes to your children. Trusts can protect your children's or grandchildren's inheritance by holding assets on their behalf. Liz Van Vallin changed her estate plan when she and her first husband divorced 11 years ago. To make sure that the boys' inheritance would stay out of her ex-husband's control, she set up a trust, to be created upon her death, to hold the boys' assets until they reached a given age. A close friend agreed to serve as trustee and carry out Liz's instructions with regard to the use of trust funds to support and educate her children.

Sources: Louis S. Richman, "Who Will Inherit Your Wealth?" *Fortune,* December 26, 1994, pp. 125–128; Gregory Spears, "Estate-Planning Musts for Blended Families," *Kiplinger's Personal Finance Magazine,* December 1994, pp. 91–96; Amey Stone, "Your Kids, Your Will—and Your Second Spouse," *Business Week,* May 2, 1994, pp. 130–131.

and frustrate the objectives of the person who built it. These include death-related costs, inflation, lack of liquidity, improper use of vehicles of transfer, and disabilities.

Death-Related Costs. When someone dies, the estate incurs certain types of death-related costs. For example, medical bills relating to a final illness and funeral expenses are good examples of *first-level death-related costs*. Most people also die with some current bills unpaid and some outstanding long-term obligations, such as mortgages, business loans, and installment contracts. Unpaid income taxes as well as property taxes also constitute debts often payable by the deceased's estate. *Second-level death-related costs* consist of the fees of attorneys, appraisers, and accountants along with probate expenses—so-called administrative costs, federal estate taxes, and state death taxes (some states have both inheritance and estate taxes).

Inflation. Death-related costs are only the tip of the estate-impairment iceberg. Failure to continuously reappraise and rearrange an estate plan to counter the effects of inflation can impair the ability of assets—liquid, real and personal property, or investments—to provide steady and adequate levels of financial security.

Lack of Liquidity. Insufficient cash to cover death costs and other estate obligations has always been a major factor in estate impairment. Sale of the choicest parcel of farmland or a business that has been in the family for generations, for instance, often has undesirable psychological effects on the heirs. The outcome can be a devastating financial and emotional blow.

Improper Use of Vehicles of Transfer. Assets are often put into the hands of beneficiaries who are unwilling or unable to handle them. Because of improper usage of vehicles of transfer, property often passes to unintended beneficiaries or to the proper beneficiaries in an improper manner or at an incorrect time. For example, spendthrift spouses or minors may be left large sums of money outright in the form of life insurance, through joint ownership of a savings account, or as the beneficiaries of an employee fringe benefit plan.

Disabilities. A prolonged and expensive disability of a family wage earner is often called a *living death*. Loss of income due to disability is frequently coupled with a massive financial drain caused by the illness itself. The financial situation is further complicated by inadequate management of currently owned assets. This not only threatens the family's financial security but also diminishes the value of the estate at an incredible speed.

WHAT IS YOUR ESTATE?

Your *estate* is your property—whatever you own. Your **probate estate** consists of the real and personal property that you own in your own name that can be transferred at death according to the terms of a will or under *intestate* laws if you have no valid will. A distinction must be made between the probate estate (a property law concept that essentially encompasses assets passing by will) and the gross estate (a tax law term that may encompass a considerably larger amount of property). Your **gross estate** includes all the property subject to federal estate taxes at your death, both probate and nonprobate. Life insurance, jointly held property with rights of survivorship, and property passing under certain employee benefit plans are common examples of nonprobate assets that might be subject to federal (and perhaps state) estate taxes.

In addition, you may provide for property that is not probate property and will not be part of your estate for federal estate tax purposes yet will pass to your family and form part of their financial security program. There are two types of such assets. One is *properly arranged* life insurance. For instance, you could give assets to your daughter to allow her to purchase, pay the premiums for, and be the beneficiary of a policy on your life. At your death, the proceeds would not be included as part of your estate. The other type of financial asset that falls into this category is social security. Payments to a surviving spouse and minor children generally are neither probate assets nor subject to any federal (or state) estate taxes. Because of the freedom from administrative costs and taxes, this category of assets provides unique and substantial estate-planning opportunities.

THE ESTATE-PLANNING PROCESS

The estate-planning process consists of a number of important steps. First, comprehensive and accurate data on all aspects of the family must be gathered. Exhibit 15.2 summarizes the types of factual data required by professionals to prepare detailed estate plans. Next, the data gathered must be categorized into general problem areas, and estate transfer costs must be estimated. With this information, the estate plan is then formulated and preparations made for its implementation. The objective of estate plans, of course, is to maximize the usefulness of people's assets during their lives and to achieve

probate estate The real and personal property owned by a person that can be transferred at death according to the terms of a will or under *intestate* laws in the absence of a valid will.

gross estate All property—both probate and nonprobate—subject to federal estate taxes at a person's death.

EXHIBIT 15.2

Factual Data Required in Estate Planning

The first step in developing an effective estate plan is to gather comprehensive and accurate data on all aspects of the family. The types of factual data required by professionals are listed below.

Personal data:	Names, addresses, phone numbers, family consultants Family birthdates, occupations, health problems, support needs Citizenship, marital status, marital agreements, wills, trusts, custodianships, trust beneficiary, gifts or inheritances, social security numbers, education, and military service
Property (except life insurance or business):	Classification, title, indebtedness, basis, date and manner of acquisition, value of marketable securities, and location
Life insurance:	Insured, kind of policies, amounts, insurance company, agents' names and addresses
Health insurance:	Medical expense insurance: insurance company, policy benefits Disability income
Business interest:	Name, address, ownership Valuation factors: desired survivorship control; name, address, and phone number of business attorney and accountant
Employee benefits:	
Family income:	Income of client, spouse, dependent children, income tax information
Family finances:	Budget information, investment preferences Ranking of economic objectives, capital needs, other objectives
Income and capital needs:	Retirement: Age, required amount, potential sources Disability: Required amount, sources Death: Expected sources of income
Liabilities:	Classification of liabilities, creditors, amounts, whether insured or secured
Factors affecting plan:	Gift propensity, charitable inclinations, emotional maturity of children, basic desires for estate distribution
Authorization for information:	Life insurance
Receipt for documents:	Personal and business
Observations from interview:	

Source: Copyright © 1995 by The American College, Bryn Mawr, PA. Adapted from Confidential Personal and Financial Data form. *Advanced Estate Planning Course*. All rights reserved.

their personal objectives after their deaths. The final steps in the estate-planning process involve testing and implementing the proposed plan.

Once the plan has been implemented, it is important to keep in mind that it is good only for as long as it fits the needs, desires, and circumstances of the parties involved. As these elements change, the estate plan must also be modified. Marriage or remarriage, divorce, the birth of a child, a change of job or location, and substantial changes in income, health, or living standards are the types of events that indicate a need for a review. Even if none of these occur, a review of life insurance needs should automatically be scheduled at least once every two years and a full estate audit made at least once every three to five years (or whenever there has been a major change in the federal or state death tax laws). Because of the general complexity of the laws relating to estate transfer, the assistance of estate planners, life insurance professionals, chartered financial consultants (ChFCs), certified financial planners (CFPs), accountants, and attorneys is often necessary in the planning and evaluation process. Due to the individual nature of estate planning, more specific guidelines cannot be included in this chapter.

Concept Check

15-1. Discuss the importance and goals of estate planning. Explain why estates often break up. Distinguish between the *probate estate* and the *gross estate*.

15-2. Briefly describe the steps involved in the estate-planning process.

WILLS

LG2

A will is a legal document that specifies the details of how an individual wishes to dispose of his or her estate. Have you prepared a will?

Spend a few moments listing reasons why you have or have not yet prepared a will before reading ahead.

A **will** is a written, legally enforceable expression or declaration of a person's wishes concerning the disposition of his or her property upon death. Unfortunately, about half of all Americans do not have wills. The importance of a valid will can be illustrated by looking at what happens when a person dies without one.

ABSENCE OF A VALID WILL: INTESTACY

Intestacy describes the situation that exists when a person dies without a valid will. State intestacy laws "draw the will the decedent failed to make" to determine the disposition of the probate property of persons who have died intestate. These statutes enumerate certain preferred classes of survivors. Generally, the decedent's spouse is favored, followed by the children and then other descendants. If the spouse and children or other descendants, such as grandchildren or great-grandchildren, survive, they will divide the estate, and other relatives will receive nothing. If no spouse, children, or other descendants survive, the deceased's parents, brothers, and sisters will receive a share of the estate.

The disposition of a typical intestate estate can be illustrated with a simple example. Assume an individual died without a valid will. That individual's separately owned property would be distributed as shown in Exhibit 15.3 after deduction of debts, taxes, and state family exemptions. If the deceased left no spouse, child, parent, sibling, grandparent, uncle, aunt, or descendant of any of the above, the state normally would take all of the property. Where property goes to the state due to the absence of a will, the property is said to *escheat to the state*. If a person without relatives dies with a valid will, his or her property will probably go to friends or to charity, rather than to the state. Aside from having lost control of the disposition of the property, the person who dies intestate also forfeits the privileges of naming a personal representative to guide the disposition of the estate, naming a guardian for persons and property, and specifying which beneficiaries would bear certain tax burdens. In addition, estate planning and a valid will may minimize the amount of estate shrinkage through transfer taxes. The importance of a valid will—regardless of the size of an estate—must not be overlooked in the personal financial planning process.

PREPARATION OF THE WILL

A will allows a person, called a **testator,** to determine the disposition of property at his or her death. A key characteristic of a will is that it can be changed or revoked at any time prior to the testator's (will owner's) death. Upon the death of the testator, it becomes operative and applies to the situation that exists at that time. Will preparation, or drafting, varies with respect to difficulty and cost depending on individual circumstances. In some cases a two-page will costing $150 may be adequate, while in others a complex document costing $1,500 or more may be necessary. A will must not only effectively accomplish the objectives specified for distribution of assets but also take into consideration income, gift, and estate tax laws. Often a knowledge of the corporate, trust, real estate, and securities laws is required as well. Note that a will, important as it is, may be ineffective or misstate the testator's estate plan if it does not consider and coordinate assets passing outside its limits.

Information Requirements. A properly prepared will should (1) provide a plan for distributing the testator's assets in accordance with his or her wishes, the beneficiaries' needs, and federal and state dispositive and tax laws; (2) consider the changes in family circumstances that might occur after its execution; and (3) be unambiguous and complete in describing the testator's desires. By following these general guidelines, the testator generally can develop a satisfactory will.

Use of an Attorney. *Will drafting, no matter how modest the size of the estate, should not be attempted by a layperson.* The complexity and interrelationships of tax, property, domestic relations,

will A written and legally enforceable document that expresses how a person's property should be distributed upon his or her death.

intestacy The situation that exists when a person dies without a valid will.

testator A person whose will directs the disposition of property at his or her death.

EXHIBIT 15.3

Distribution of a Typical Intestate Estate

If an individual dies intestate—without a valid will—the estate will be distributed according to preestablished state statutes or guidelines.

Decedent Dies Leaving	Distribution*	
Spouse and children or their descendants	Spouse receives one-third	Children receive two-thirds divided equally
Spouse and one child or child's descendants	Spouse receives one-half	Child receives one-half
Spouse but no children or their descendants, and decedent's mother or father survives	Spouse receives $10,000 plus one-half of balance	Father and mother or surviving parent (if one is already deceased) receive one-half of balance
Spouse but no children or their descendants, and no parent survives	Spouse reveives $10,000 plus one-half of balance	Brothers and sisters receive one-half of balance divided equally
Spouse but no children or their descendants, and no parent, brother, sister, niece, nephew, grandparent, uncle, or aunt survives	Spouse receives all	
Child or children but no spouse		Child or children receive all divided equally
No spouse and no children or their descendants, and decedent's mother or father survives		Mother and father receive all
No spouse and no children or their descendants, and no parent of the decedent survives		Brothers and sisters receive all divided equally

*Because intestate laws vary from state to state, the actual distribution of assets may differ from what is shown here.

Source: Courtesy of Stephen R. Leimberg, Esq., Bryn Mawr, PA.

and other laws make the homemade will a potentially dangerous document. Nowhere is the old adage, "He who has self for attorney has fool for client," more true, and few things may turn out more disastrous in the long run than the do-it-yourself will.

COMMON FEATURES OF THE WILL

Although there is no absolute format that must be followed in will preparation, most wills contain eight distinct parts: (1) introductory clause, (2) direction of payments, (3) dispositive provisions, (4) appointment clause, (5) tax clause, (6) common disaster clause, (7) execution and attestation clause, and (8) witness clause. Generalized examples of each of these clauses are briefly illustrated and described as follows. *These must be tailored to individual needs and circumstances by an attorney familiar with the testator's own situation.*

Introductory Clause. An introductory clause, or preamble, would normally take the following form:

> I, John Steven Fabian, of the city of Chicago, state of Illinois, do, hereby make my last will and revoke all wills and codicils made prior to this will.

The declaration of residence that is included here helps to determine the county that will have legal jurisdiction and be considered the testator's domicile for tax purposes. The portion of the clause related to revocation nullifies old and forgotten wills and *codicils*—legally binding modifications of an existing will.

Direction of Payments. The clause related to directing the estate with respect to certain payments of expenses is typically formulated along the following lines:

> I direct payment out of my estate of all just debts and the expenses of my last illness and funeral.

In many states, the rights of creditors are protected by law and such a clause is largely useless.

Dispositive Provisions. Three examples of dispositive clauses follow:

> I give and bequeath to my wife, Sally Warren Fabian, all my jewelry, automobiles, books, and photography equipment, as well as all other articles of personal and household use.
>
> I give to the Chicago Historical Society the sum of $100,000.

> All the rest, residue, and remainder of my estate, real and personal, wherever located, I give in equal one-half shares to my children, Charles Elliot and Lara Sue, their heirs and assigns forever.

The first type of clause disposes of personal effects. A testator may make a detailed and specific list of personal property and carefully identify each item, and to whom it is given, as an informal guide to aid the executor in dividing up the property. Such a list generally should not appear in the will itself, because it is likely to change frequently. The second type of clause, called a **pecuniary legacy**, passes money to a specified party. The correct title of a charity should be ascertained by direct and discreet inquiry. Note that the popular name is seldom the correct or full legal name. The third clause describes the distribution of residual assets after specific gifts have been made. Anti-lapse statutes provide that bequests to close relatives (as defined in the statute) who die before the testator will go to the relative's heirs unless the will includes other directions. Bequests to nonrelatives who predecease the testator will go to the other residual beneficiaries.

Appointment Clause. Examples of appointment clauses, which are typically included to appoint *executors* (the decedent's personal representatives), guardians, and trustees, as well as their successors, follow:

> I hereby nominate as the Executor of this Will my beloved wife, Sally Warren Fabian, but if she is unable or unwilling to serve then I nominate my brother, Winston James Fabian. In the event both persons named predecease me, or shall cease or fail to act, then I nominate as Executor in the place of said persons, the Northern Trust Bank of Chicago, Illinois.
>
> If my wife does not survive me, I appoint my brother, Eugene Lawrence Fabian, Guardian of the person and property of my son, Charles Elliot, during his minority.

The first clause is used to appoint executors and alternates, whose responsibility it is to administer the estate of the deceased. The second clause is used to appoint a guardian. In many states, the surviving parent of an unmarried minor child can appoint a guardian for the child and the inherited property. Often, the surviving parent is not allowed to become sole guardian of the property of a minor child.

Tax Clause. An example of a tax clause follows:

> I direct that there shall be paid out of my residuary estate (from that portion which does not qualify for the marital deduction) all estate, inheritance, and similar taxes imposed by a government in respect to property includable in my estate for tax purposes, whether the property passes under this will or otherwise.

In the absence of a specified provision in the will, so-called **apportionment statutes** of the testator's state will allocate the burden of taxes among the beneficiaries. The result may be an inappropriate and unintended reduction of certain beneficiaries' shares or adverse estate tax effects. Earlier statutes tended to charge death taxes on the residual of the estate, but today the trend is toward statutes that charge each beneficiary based on his or her share of the taxable estate. Because the spouse's share and the portion going to a charity are deducted from the gross estate before arriving at the taxable estate, neither is charged with taxes.

Simultaneous Death Clause. A sample of the type of clause often included within the will to give direction in the event of simultaneous death follows:

> If my wife and I shall die under such circumstances that there is not sufficient evidence to determine the order of our deaths, then it shall be presumed that she survived me. My estate shall be administered and distributed in all respects in accordance with such assumption.

The assumption that the spouse survives is used mainly to permit the marital deduction, which offers a tax advantage. Other types of clauses are similarly designed to avoid double probate of the same assets—duplication of administrative and probate costs. Such clauses require that the survivor live for a certain period, such as 30 or 60 days, in order to be a beneficiary under the will.

Execution and Attestation Clause. An example of the execution and attestation clause follows:

> In witness thereof, I have affixed my signature to this, my last will and testament, which consists of five (5) pages, each of which I have initialed, this 15th day of September, 1996.
>
> *John Steven Fabian*

pecuniary legacy A type of clause in a will that passes money to a designated party.

apportionment statutes State laws that allocate the burden of taxes among the beneficiaries in the absence of a specific provision in the will.

Every will should be in writing and signed by the testator at its end as a precaution against fraud. Many attorneys suggest that the testator also initial each page after the last line or sign in a corner of each page.

Witness Clause. The final clause, which helps to affirm that the will in question is really that of the deceased, is similar to the following:

> Signed, sealed, and published by John Steven Fabian, the testator, as his last will, in the presence of us, who, at his request, and in the presence of each other, all being present at the same time, have written our names as witnesses.

One must have the minimum number of witnesses required by the state where the will is being executed (signed). Most states require two witnesses; some require three. The law of most states requires witnesses to sign in the presence of one another, after they witness the signing by the testator. Their addresses should be noted on the will. If the testator is unable to sign his or her name for any reason, most states allow the testator to make a mark and to have another person (properly witnessed) sign for him or her.

REQUIREMENTS OF A VALID WILL

To be valid, a will must be the product of a person with a sound mind; there must have been no *undue influence* (influence that would remove the testator's freedom of choice); the will itself must have been properly executed; and its execution must be free from fraud.

Mental Capacity. In order to be judged mentally competent, testators must have (1) a full and intelligent knowledge of the act in which they are involved, (2) an understanding of the property they possess, (3) a knowledge of the dispositions they want to make of it, and (4) an appreciation of the objects they desire to be the recipients of their bounty. Generally, such capacity is presumed; clear and convincing proof of mental incapacity is required to set aside a will, and the burden of proof is on the contestant.

Freedom of Choice. A will is considered invalid if it can be shown that the testator was subject to the undue influence of another person at the time the will was made and executed. Threats, misrepresentations, inordinate flattery, or some physical or mental coercion employed to destroy the testator's freedom of choice are all types of undue influence.

Proper Execution. To be considered properly executed, a will must meet the requirements of the state's wills act or its equivalent. It must also be demonstrable that it is in fact the will of the testator. Most states have statutes that spell out (1) who may make a will—generally any person of sound mind, age 18 or older (age 21 in some states); (2) the form and execution a will must have—most states require a will to be in writing and signed by the testator at the logical end, preferably in black ink; and (3) requirements for witnesses. If at all possible, somebody other than a beneficiary should sign as a witness, because in a few states this could result in the disinheritance of that beneficiary. Many states have now provided for a *self-proving* will. For example, in Pennsylvania, if a testator's signing of the will is witnessed by two individuals who sign in the presence of each other and of a notary, those witnesses do not have to appear at the probate of the will. This saves time, money, and often a great deal of inconvenience to the executor.

CHANGING OR REVOKING THE WILL: CODICILS

A will is inoperative until the testator's death and therefore can be changed at any time as long as the testator has mental capacity. Wills should be revised periodically if there is a significant change in the testator's (or the beneficiaries') health or financial circumstances; if births, deaths, marriages, or divorces alter the operative circumstances; if the testator moves to a state other than where the will was executed; if an executor, trustee, or guardian can no longer serve; or if substantial changes occur in the tax law. An existing will can be either changed or revoked, although in certain states a so-called *right of election* (explained later) exists. By reviewing your will regularly, you can be sure that it accurately reflects your current wishes.

Changing the Will. In order to change an existing will, a **codicil,** which is a simple and convenient legal means of modifying an existing will, is drawn up. It is used when the will needs only minor modifications and is often a single-page document that reaffirms all the existing provisions in the will except the one to be changed. The codicil should be executed in accordance with the same formalities as a will and should be typed, signed, and witnessed in the same manner. Where substantial changes are required, a new will is usually preferable to a codicil. In addition, if a gift in the original will is removed, it may be best to draw a new will and destroy the old even if substantial changes are not required. This may help to avoid offending the omitted beneficiary. Sometimes, however, the prior will should not be destroyed even after the new will has been made and signed. If the new will fails for some reason (because of the testator's mental incapacity, for example), the prior will may qualify. Also, a prior will could help to prove a "continuity of testamentary purpose"—in other words, that the latest will (which may have provided a substantial gift to charity) continued an earlier intent and was not an afterthought or the result of an unduly influenced mind.

Revoking the Will. A will may be revoked either by the testator or automatically by the law. A testator can revoke a will by (1) making a later will that expressly revokes prior wills; (2) making a codicil that expressly revokes all wills earlier than the one being modified; (3) making a later will that is inconsistent with a former will; and (4) physically mutilating, burning, tearing, or defacing the will with the intention of revoking it. The law automatically modifies a will under certain circumstances, which vary from state to state but generally revolve around (1) divorce, (2) marriage, (3) birth or adoption, and (4) murder. In many states, if a testator becomes divorced after making a will, all provisions in the will relating to the spouse become ineffective. If a testator marries after making a will, the spouse receives that portion of the estate that would have been received had the testator died without a valid will—unless the will gives the spouse a larger share. If a testator did not provide for a child born or adopted after the will was made (unless it appears that such lack of provision was intentional), the child receives that share of the estate not passing to the testator's spouse that would have been given to him or her had the deceased not had a will. Finally, almost all states have some type of *slayer's statute* forbidding a person who participates in a willful and unlawful murder from acquiring property as the result of the deed.

Right of Election. Many states provide still another way to change a will: through the **right of election** the survivor has a right to "take against the will"—to take a specified portion of the probate estate regardless of what the will provides. Most states give this right only to surviving spouses, while at least one state extends a similar right to the testator's children. One state, for example, allows a surviving spouse to take at least that share that would have been allowed had the deceased died without a valid will. This right is generally forfeited by a spouse who deserted the testator.

SAFEGUARDING THE WILL

In most cases, the original of the will should be kept in a safe and accessible place at home, with copies in a safe-deposit box and with the attorney who drafted it. The original will should *not* be placed in the testator's safe-deposit box because the box would be "frozen" upon his or her death, making it difficult to begin estate administration procedures. Although some authorities and many attorneys recommend leaving the original of a will with the attorney who drafted it, this may make it awkward for the executor to choose his or her own attorney, a right that most states give the executor regardless of who drew the will or what the will states about who should be the estate's counsel. Further, it may discourage the estate owner from changing the will or engaging a new attorney even if he or she moves out of the state in which the will is drawn.

Worksheet 15.1 contains an executor's checklist of documents and information that should be kept in a safe-deposit box. If each spouse has a separate safe-deposit box, the couple may want to keep their wills in each other's boxes. Some states provide for *lodging* of the will, a mechanism for filing and safekeeping it in the office of the probate court (also called *orphan's* or *surrogate's court*). In those states, this procedure satisfies the need to safeguard the will.

LETTER OF LAST INSTRUCTIONS

People frequently have thoughts they want to convey and instructions they wish to have carried out

codicil A document that legally modifies an existing will without revoking it.

right of election The right of a surviving spouse to take a specified portion of the probate estate regardless of what the will provides.

WORKSHEET 15.1

An Executor's Checklist of Items to Keep in a Safe-Deposit Box

This checklist itemizes the various documents and information that the executor may need to effectively carry out the terms of the will. These items should be kept in a safe-deposit box.

Executor's Checklist

Name (Testator) ______________________ Date ______________

_____ 1. Birth Certificates
_____ 2. Marriage Certificates (Including Any Prior Marriages)
_____ 3. Your Will (and Spouse's Will) and Trust Agreements
_____ 4. Listing of Life Insurance Policies or Certificates
_____ 5. Your Social Security Numbers
_____ 6. Military Discharge Papers
_____ 7. Bonds, Stocks, and Securities
_____ 8. Real Estate Deeds
_____ 9. Business (Buy-Sell) Agreements
_____ 10. Automobile Titles and Insurance Policies
_____ 11. Property Insurance Policies
_____ 12. Letter of Last Instructions
_____ 13. Additional Documents

List all checking and savings account numbers, including bank addresses and location of safe-deposit boxes:

______________ ______________ ______________

______________ ______________ ______________

List name, address, and phone number of property and life insurance agents:

______________ ______________ ______________

______________ ______________ ______________

List name, address, and phone number of attorney and accountant:

______________ ______________ ______________

______________ ______________ ______________

List name, address, and phone number of (current or past) employer. State date when you retired if applicable. Include employee benefits booklets:

______________ ______________ ______________

______________ ______________ ______________

List all debts owed to *and* owed by you:

______________ ______________ ______________

______________ ______________ ______________

List the names, addresses, telephone numbers, and birth dates of your children and other beneficiaries (including charitable beneficiaries):

______________ ______________ ______________

______________ ______________ ______________

Source: Stephen R. Leimberg, Herbert Levy, Stephen N. Kandell, Morey S. Rosenbloom, and Ralph Gano Miller, *The Tools and Techniques of Estate Planning,* 9th ed. (Cincinnati: National Underwriter Company, 1992). Reprinted with permission of the publisher.

that cannot properly be included in their wills. These suggestions or recommendations should be included in a **letter of last instructions** in the form of an informal memorandum separate from the will. (Note: No bequests should be made in this letter of last instructions, because such documents have no legal standing.) Usually it is best to make several copies of the letter and keep one at home and the others in the hands of the estate's executor or attorney to be mailed or delivered to beneficiaries at the appropriate time.

A letter of last instructions might provide directions with respect to (1) location of the will and other documents; (2) funeral and burial instructions (often a will is not opened until after the funeral); (3) suggestions or recommendations as to the continuation, sale, or liquidation of a business (it is easier to freely suggest a course of action in such a letter than it is in a will); (4) personal matters that the testator might prefer not to be made public in the will, such as statements that might sound unkind or inconsiderate but would prove of great value to the executor (for example, comments about a spendthrift spouse or a reckless son); (5) legal and accounting services (executors are free, however, to choose their own counsel—not even testators can bind them in that selection); (6) an explanation of the actions taken in the will, which may help avoid litigation (for instance, "I left only $1,000 to my son, Ramon, because . . ." or "I made no provisions for my oldest daughter, Melissa, because . . ."); and (7) suggestions on how to divide up the personal property.

Administration of an Estate. When people die, they usually own property and owe debts. Often they will have claims (accounts receivable) against other persons. A process of liquidation, called the **probate process**, similar to that which occurs when a corporation is dissolved, must take place. In this process, money owed the decedent is collected, creditors (including the tax authorities) are satisfied, and what remains is distributed to the appropriate individuals and organizations. A local court generally supervises the probate process through a person designated as an **executor** in the decedent's will, or if the decedent died intestate (without a valid will), through a court-appointed **administrator**.

An executor or administrator, who is sometimes also referred to as the decedent's personal representative, must collect the assets of the decedent, pay debts or provide for the payment of debts that are not currently due, and distribute any remaining assets to the persons entitled to them by will or by the intestate law of the appropriate state. Estate administration is important for many reasons. Bank accounts and other contracts could not be collected without such a formal process because there would be no one who legally could bring suit or be entitled to give a release of liability. Also, title to real estate could not be made marketable because there would be no insurance against the existence of a creditor with claims against the property. Due to the importance of the estate administration process, you should select executors who are not only familiar with the testator's affairs but also can handle effectively the responsibilities of being an executor as the *Issues in Money Management* box on page 620 explains.

OTHER IMPORTANT ESTATE PLANNING DOCUMENTS

In addition to your will and the letter of last instructions, you should have several other documents to protect yourself and your family: a power of attorney, a living will, and a durable power of attorney for health care.

Power of Attorney. If you were incapacitated by a serious illness, a *power of attorney* would allow you to name as your agent the person you consider best suited to take over your financial affairs—perhaps a spouse or other relative. Although this is a simple document, it transfers enormous power to your designated appointee. So be sure that you can

letter of last instructions An informal memorandum separate from the will and containing suggestions or recommendations for carrying out the decedent's wishes.

probate process The court-supervised process of liquidation that occurs when a person dies; it consists of collecting money owed the decedent, paying his or her debts, and distributing the remaining assets to the appropriate individuals and organizations.

executor The personal representative of an estate designated in the decedent's will.

administrator The personal representative of the estate appointed by the court if the decedent died intestate (without a valid will).

Issues in Money Management

Estate Executors Inherit Many Responsibilities

If a relative or close friend asked you to be the executor of their will, you would probably accept without hesitation. You might not realize, however, exactly how much work you have committed to do.

An executor's responsibilities depend on the laws of the state where the deceased lived, the value of the estate, and whether the person died with or without a valid will. Generally, an executor compiles all the assets belonging to the deceased and determines their value, pays all debts, settles taxes, and takes the estate through *probate* (the legal process of distributing the deceased's assets). In some cases, the executor must defend claims against the estate or pursue claims on its behalf. Just keeping track of the money flow can be difficult, particularly if there are assets held in trust in addition to estate funds. Altogether, it may take a full year of wrestling with paperwork, tracking down assets, and filing papers.

Unfortunately, taxes often complicate matters further. An executor may face six or more sets of tax returns, including the deceased's state and federal income tax along with taxes on the trusts of the deceased. There are also federal estate taxes to pay on estates valued at more than $600,000.

Problems may also arise with the distribution of assets, particularly if the will is vague and there is animosity among family members. Heated disagreements may occur over the distribution of personal possessions such as furniture and jewelry. Often, family members pressure the executor to begin distributing assets before the estate is settled. But if there is not enough money left in the estate to cover all the bills and taxes, the executor is liable and may end up paying from his or her own pocket.

Executors usually feel a great psychological burden trying to live up to the trust the deceased placed in them. Perhaps just as difficult is the legal burden they shoulder. A revision of the "prudent investor" law, now being enacted in many states, sets forth investment standards for estate executors. Executors must create a diversified investment portfolio, taking into account inflation, taxes, and the future needs of the trust's beneficiaries. If they fail to invest the estate's funds wisely, they can be held liable and risk being sued for damages. The prudent investor law allows executors greater control over their investment choices, benefiting those who are experts in money management. The good news for those lacking such expertise is that the law allows trustees to delegate the management of trust money, whereas before they could do so only if the will specifically authorized it.

Indeed, executors should not be shy or feel guilty about delegating their authority to financial and legal professionals. An attorney can help file the will, send necessary notices, and assist with paperwork. At the very least, they can clearly explain to you exactly what is expected of you as an executor. You may also appoint a professional money manager familiar with estate administration to handle investment decisions.

Ideally, you should approach estate executorship as a shared task. Your role as someone close to the deceased who is sensitive to the beneficiaries' needs is invaluable. It is crucial that you maintain good records and communicate with the beneficiaries, keeping them informed about your progress in settling the estate. At the same time, you serve the estate's best interest by entrusting areas in which you lack expertise to well-chosen professionals.

Sources: Adapted from Lynn Asinof, "Handling an Estate Without Inheriting Trouble," *The Wall Street Journal*, July 15, 1994, pp. C1, C15; ibid, "Revised Standards May Make It Easier To Choose a Trustee for Your Estate," *The Wall Street Journal*, January 16, 1995, pp. C1, C21; Emily Harrison, "Dear Prudents . . . Named As a Trustee In a Friend's Will? New Laws May Make the Job More Complex," *SmartMoney*, February 1995, p. 70.

rely on the person you choose to manage your finances responsibly. If you have investments, your power of attorney should include language that covers powers of investment on your behalf. You may want to clear your power of attorney with the mutual funds and brokerage firms where you have accounts.

Living Will and Durable Power of Attorney for Health Care. Another important aspect of estate planning involves determining the medical care you wish to receive, or *not* to receive, if you become terminally ill. Two documents to achieve this are the *living will* and the *durable power of attorney for health care*. The **living will** states, in very precise terms, the treatments that you want and to what degree you wish them continued. You must be as specific as possible so that your wishes are clear; otherwise, a living will might be put aside because it is too vague. For example, you should define what you mean by "terminal illness." Each state has its own form for a living will, and you can usually complete them yourself.

Many experts prefer the **durable power of attorney for health care** instead of the living will; some advise having both to reinforce each other. Through the durable power of attorney for health care you authorize an individual to make health care decisions for you if you are unable to do so, either temporarily or permanently. Unlike the living will, it applies in any case where you cannot communicate your wishes, not just when you are terminally ill. You can limit the scope of the durable power of attorney and include specific instructions as to the desired level of medical treatment. You should spend some time making these decisions and then review your ideas and philosophy concerning these matters with your family and the person you designate before signing such a document. These documents, copies of which should be with your agent and your doctor, can make it easier for your family to deal with these difficult issues.

WHAT ABOUT JOINT OWNERSHIP?

Many people take title to property jointly either through a joint tenancy or as tenants by the entirety. These two forms of joint ownership have the following characteristics:

1. The interest of a decedent passes directly to the surviving joint tenant (that is, to the other joint owner) by operation of the law and is free from the claims of the decedent's creditors, heirs, or personal representatives.
2. A **joint tenancy with right of survivorship** may consist of any number of persons regardless of whether they are related by blood or marriage. A **tenancy by the entirety**, on the other hand, can exist only between husband and wife.
3. In the case of joint tenancy, each joint tenant can unilaterally sever the tenancy. This is not the case with a tenancy by the entirety, which can be severed only by mutual agreement or terminated by divorce or conveyance by both spouses to a third party. In some states a tenancy by the entirety can exist only with respect to real property, while others do not recognize such tenancies at all.
4. The co-owners have equal interests.

The advantage of joint tenancy, the more common form of joint ownership, is that it offers a sense of family security, quick and easy transfer to the spouse at death, exemption of jointly owned property from the claims of the deceased's creditors, and avoidance of delays and publicity in the estate-settlement process. The key disadvantage of joint tenancy is that the *jointly owned property cannot be controlled by a will* and therefore does not permit the first joint owner to die to control the property's disposition and management upon his or her death. Another disadvantage is that higher potential tax costs are often incurred in both the creation and the severance of a joint tenancy. For example, a father who purchases and pays for property and places it in his own and his daughter's name is making a gift to her. Upon the termination of the tenancy, if the daughter receives the entire proceeds (for example, upon the sale of a jointly owned home), the father is making a second gift to her. In both situations, he will have gratuitously transferred an interest to her that she did not have before. Fortunately, because federal gift tax law does not tax most interspousal transfers, the problem will not arise on a federal level between a married couple (although

living will A document that states, in very precise terms, the treatments that a person wants and to what degree he or she wishes them continued if he or she becomes terminally ill.

durable power of attorney for health care A document that authorizes another individual to make health care decisions for a person if he or she is unable to do so.

joint tenancy with right of survivorship A type of ownership by two or more parties, with the survivor(s) continuing to hold all such property on the death of one or more of the tenants. Each joint tenant can unilaterally sever the tenancy.

tenancy by the entirety A form of ownership by husband and wife recognized in certain states in which the property automatically passes to the surviving spouse. Tenancy can be severed only by mutual agreement, divorce, or conveyence by both spouses to a third party.

many states do tax such unintentional gifts). Although the property passes to the surviving spouse tax-free, larger estate taxes could be due when the second spouse dies—if the estate is worth more than $600,000. Because most people believe the advantage of joint ownership of major assets, such as a home or automobile, far outweigh the potential disadvantages, it is commonly utilized by married couples.

You should also be familiar with two other forms of ownership: *tenancy in common* and *community property.*

Tenancy in Common. A third common form of co-ownership is called **tenancy in common.** There is no right of survivorship, and each co-owner can leave his or her share to whomever he or she desires. Thus, the decedent owner's will controls the disposition of the decedent's partial interest in the asset. If the decedent dies without a will, the intestate succession laws of the state where the property is located will determine who inherits the decedent's interest. Tenancy in common interests can be unequal; a property owned by three co-owners could be apportioned such that their respective shares are 50 percent, 30 percent, and 20 percent of the property.

Community Property. Just as tenancy by the entirety is a special form of marital property co-ownership found only in common law states (that is, states that trace their property law to England), community property is a form of marital property co-ownership based on Roman law and found primarily in the southwestern states which had a Spanish or French influence.

Community property is all property acquired by the effort of either or both spouses during marriage while they are domiciled in a community property state. For example, wages and commissions earned and assets acquired by either spouse while living in a community property state are automatically owned equally by both spouses, even if only one was directly involved in acquiring the additional wealth. Property acquired before marriage or by gift or inheritance can be maintained as the acquiring spouse's separate property.

By agreement, which typically must be in writing to be enforceable, the couple can change community property into separate property, and vice versa. Each spouse can leave his or her half of the community property to whomever he or she chooses. Thus, there is no right of survivorship inherent in this form of ownership.

Concept Check

15-3. What is a *will?* Why is it important? Describe the consequences of dying intestate.

15-4. Describe the basic clauses that are normally included as part of a will.

15-5. Indicate any requirements that exist with respect to who may make a valid will.

15-6. How can changes in the provisions of a will be made legally? In what two ways can a will be revoked?

15-7. Indicate what is meant by each of the following: (a) intestacy, (b) codicil, (c) right of election, (d) lodging of the will, and (e) letter of last instructions.

15-8. What is meant by the *probate process?* Who is an executor, and what role does the executor play in estate settlement?

15-9. Define and differentiate between *joint tenancy with right of survivorship* and *tenancy by the entirety.* Discuss the advantages and disadvantages of joint ownership. How does *tenancy in common* differ from joint tenancy?

15-10. Describe briefly the importance of the following documents for estate planning: (a) power of attorney, (b) living will, and (c) durable power of attorney for health care.

TRUSTS

LG3

A trust is a legal relationship that facilitates the transfer of property, and/or the income from that property, to another party or parties. Why do you think trusts are frequently employed in the estate-planning process? Before reading ahead, spend a few moments speculating as to the potential estate-planning benefits of trusts.

A **trust** is a relationship created when one party, the **grantor** (also called the *settlor* or *creator*), transfers property to a second party, the **trustee,** for the benefit of third parties, the **beneficiaries,** who may or may not include the grantor. The property placed in the trust is called *trust principal* or *res* (pronounced "race"). The trustee holds the legal title to the property in the trust and must use the property and any income it produces solely for the benefit of trust beneficiaries. The trust generally is created by a written document. The grantor spells out the substantive provisions (such as how the property in the trust is to be allocated and how income is to be distributed), as well as certain administrative provisions. A trust may be *living* (created during the grantor's life) or *testamentary* (created in a will). It may be *revocable* or *irrevocable*. Property placed into a revocable trust can be regained and the terms of the trust altered or amended. Property placed into an irrevocable trust cannot be recovered by the grantor during its term. Although trusts were once considered estate-planning techniques only for the wealthy, today they can be valuable for those of more modest means as well. This change is attributed to rising real estate values during the 1970s and 1980s and the bull markets of the 1980s and 1990s. Also, as people live longer and marry more than once, they need ways to protect and manage assets. Let's now look at how trusts are used to solve various estate-planning problems.

PURPOSES OF TRUSTS

Trusts are designed for any number of reasons. The most common motives are to (1) attain income and estate tax savings and (2) manage and conserve property.

Income and Estate Tax Savings. Under certain circumstances, the burden of paying taxes on the income produced by securities, real estate, and other investments can be shifted from a high-bracket taxpayer to a trust itself or to its beneficiary, both of whom are typically subject to lower income tax rates than the grantor. However, the Tax Reform Act of 1986 severely limits the ability of a person to shift income in this manner. Specifically, with certain types of trusts, the beneficiary must be over 14 years of age; otherwise the income from the trust will be taxed at the same rate as the beneficiary's parents. In addition to possible income tax benefits, impressive *estate tax* savings are also possible, because the appreciation in the value of property placed into such a trust can be entirely removed from the grantor's estate and possibly benefit several generations of family members without incurring adverse federal estate tax consequences.

Management and Conservation of Property. Minors, spendthrifts, and mental incompetents need asset management for obvious reasons. However, busy executives and others who cannot or do not want to take the countless hours necessary to learn to handle large sums of money and other property often utilize trusts to relieve themselves of those burdens. The trustee assumes the responsibility for managing and conserving the property on behalf of the beneficiaries. The use of independent trustees is frequently employed by members of Congress, presidents, and other government officials to avoid potential conflicts of interest regarding investments. These are often called *blind trusts* because the official will not be informed as to the trust's investments during his or her term of office. In some cases, management by the trustee is held in reserve in case a

tenancy in common A form of joint ownership under which there is no right of survivorship, and each co-owner can leave his or her share to whomever he or she desires.

community property A form of joint ownership wherein all property acquired by the effort of either or both spouses during marriage while they are domiciled in a community property state is automatically owned equally by both spouses.

trust A relationship created when one party, the *grantor*, transfers property to a second party, the *trustee,* for the benefit of third parties, the *beneficiaries,* who may or may not include the grantor.

grantor A party (first party) in a trust relationship who transfers property to a second party for the benefit of third parties, who may or may not include the first party.

trustee An organization or individual hired by the *grantor* to manage and conserve her or his property for the benefit of the *beneficiaries.*

beneficiary An individual who receives benefits—income or property—from a trust or from the estate of a decedent.

EXHIBIT 15.4

Six Popular Trusts

Trusts can be used to shift assets (and thus appreciation) out of one's estate while retaining some say in how they will be used in the future. The drawback is that trusts can be cumbersome, and there are fees associated with their establishment. Here are brief descriptions of six popular trusts.

- **Credit Shelter Trust:** Most common trust for estate planning; couples with over $600,000 in assets can gain full use of each partner's $600,000 estate tax exemption. Assets are divided; when the first spouse dies, $600,000 of assets goes into a trust that bypasses the second estate. Typically the second spouse receives rights to the trust's income, and in emergencies, principal.
- **Qualified Terminable Interest Property (QTIP) Trust:** Usually set up in addition to a *credit shelter trust* to ensure that money stays in the family; it receives some or all of the assets in the estate over $600,000. (Assets left to a spouse who remarries could be claimed by the new spouse.) The survivor receives all income from the property until death, at which point the assets go to a third person. Estate taxes are due on trust assets when the second spouse dies. Also useful for couples with children from prior marriages.
- **Minor's Section 2503(c) Trust.** Set up for a minor, often to receive tax-free gifts. However, assets must be distributed by the time the child turns 21.
- **Crummey Trust:** Used to make $10,000 tax-free gifts to children; unlike a *minor's section 2503(c) trust*, these funds do not have to be distributed at age 21. However, the beneficiary can withdraw some interest or principal for a limited time (say, 30 days per year).
- **Charitable Lead (or Income) Trust:** Pays some or all of its income to a charity for a period of time (either 20 years or less, or someone's lifetime). Then the property is distributed to noncharitable beneficiaries. Grantor gets immediate income tax deduction based on expected future payout to charity.
- **Charitable Remainder Trust:** Similar to a *charitable lead trust*, except that income goes to taxable beneficiaries and principal to a charity when the trust ends.

healthy and vigorous individual is unexpectedly incapacitated and becomes unable or unwilling to manage his or her assets.

SELECTING A TRUSTEE

Five qualities are essential in a trustee. He or she must (1) possess sound business knowledge and judgment, (2) have an intimate knowledge of the beneficiary's needs and financial situation, (3) be skilled in investment and trust management, (4) be available to beneficiaries (specifically, this means the trustee should be young enough to survive the trust term), and (5) be able to make decisions impartially. A corporate trustee, such as a trust company or bank that has been authorized to perform trust duties, may seem best able to meet these requirements. A corporate trustee is likely to have investment experience and will not impose the problems created by death, disability, or absence. Unlike a family member, a corporate trustee can be relied on to be impartial and obedient to the directions of the trust instrument. Such objectivity has added value if there are several beneficiaries. On the other hand, a corporate trustee may charge high fees or be overly conservative in investments, impersonal, or lacking in the familiarity with and understanding of family problems and needs. Often a compromise is suggested: the appointment of one (or more) individual(s) and a corporate trustee as co-trustees.

COMMON TYPES AND CHARACTERISTICS OF TRUSTS

Although there are various types of trusts, the most common are the living trust, the testamentary trust, and the irrevocable life insurance trust, each of which is described below. Exhibit 15.4 describes six popular trusts.

Living Trust. A **living (inter vivos) trust** is one created during the grantor's lifetime. It can be either revocable or irrevocable and can last for a limited period or continue long after the grantor's death.

Revocable living trust. The grantor reserves the right to revoke the trust and regain the trust property in a **revocable living trust.** For federal income tax purposes, grantors of these trusts are treated as owners of the property in the trust—in other words, just as if they held the property in their own names. Therefore, they are taxed on any income produced by the trust. Three basic advantages of revocable living trusts are often cited. The first is that management continuity and income flow are assured even after the death of the grantor. No probate is necessary, because the trust continues to operate after the death of the grantor just as it did while he or she was alive. A second advantage is that the burdens of investment decisions and management responsibility are assumed by the trustee. A good example of this can be found in the case of individuals who want to control investment decisions and management policy as long as they are alive and healthy but who set up a trust to provide backup help in case they become unable or unwilling to continue managing their assets. A final advantage of the revocable living trust is that its terms and the amount of assets placed into it do not become public knowledge. Unlike the probate process, the public has no right to know the terms or conditions of a revocable living trust. Disadvantages of such trusts include the fees charged by the trustee for management of the property placed into the trust as well as the legal fees charged for drafting the trust instruments.

Irrevocable living trust. Grantors who establish an **irrevocable living trust** relinquish title to the property they place in it as well as the right to revoke or terminate it. Such trusts have all the advantages of revocable trusts as well as the potential for reducing taxes. Disadvantages of such a trust relate to the fees charged by trustees for management of assets placed in it, the gift taxes on assets put into it, the grantor's complete loss of the trust property and any income it may produce, and the grantor's forfeiture of the right to alter the terms of the trust as circumstances change.

Living trusts and pour-over wills. A will can be written so that it "pours over" designated assets into a previously established revocable or irrevocable living trust. The trust may also be named beneficiary of the grantor's insurance policies. The **pour-over will** generally contains a provision passing the estate—after debts, expenses, taxes, and specific bequests—to the specified trust. The pour-over will assures that the property left out of the living trust, either inadvertently or deliberately, will make its way into the trust (pour over into it). The trust contains provisions as to how those assets (together with insurance proceeds payable to it) will be administered and distributed. Such an arrangement provides for easily coordinated and well-administered management of estate assets.

Testamentary Trust. A trust created by a deceased's will is called a **testamentary trust.** Such a trust comes into existence only after the will is probated. No tax savings are realized by the grantor with this type of trust, because there is no divestiture of property until his or her death.

Irrevocable Life Insurance Trust. A wealthy individual can establish an **irrevocable life insurance trust** where the major asset of the trust is life insurance on the grantor's life. To avoid having the proceeds of the policy included in the grantor's estate, the policy is usually acquired by the independent trustee. The terms of the trust make it possible for the trustee to use the proceeds to pay the grantor's estate taxes and/or to take care of the grantor's spouse or children.

Concept Check

15-11. Describe the basic trust arrangement, and discuss purposes for which trusts are typically established. What essential qualities should a trustee possess?

15-12. What is a *living (inter vivos) trust?* Distinguish between a revocable living trust and an irrevocable living trust.

15-13. Explain what is meant by each of the following: (a) grantor, (b) trustee, (c) beneficiary, (d) pour-over will, (e) testamentary trust, and (f) irrevocable life insurance trust.

living (inter vivos) trust A trust created during the grantor's lifetime.

revocable living trust A trust in which the grantor reserves the right to revoke it and regain the trust property.

irrevocable living trust A trust in which the grantor relinquishes title to the property placed in it as well as the right to revoke or terminate it.

pour-over will A provision in a will that provides for the passing of the estate—after debts, expenses, taxes, and specific bequests—to the specified trust.

testamentary trust A trust created by a decedent's will.

irrevocable life insurance trust An irrevocable trust, typically established by a wealthy individual, where the major asset in the trust is life insurance on the grantor's life.

EXHIBIT 15.5

*Unified Rate Schedule for Federal Gift and Estate Taxes**

The schedule below defines the amount of federal gift and estate taxes that would have to be paid with gifts/estates of different sizes. Actually, estates of $600,000 or less pay no federal tax, although anything over that amount is currently taxed at 37 to 55 percent.

Amount with Respect to Which the Tentative Tax is to Be Computed	Tentative Tax
Not over $10,000	18% of such amount
Over $10,000 but not over $20,000	$1,800 plus 20% of the excess of such amount over $10,000
Over $20,000 but not over $40,000	$3,800 plus 22% of the excess of such amount over $20,000
Over $40,000 but not over $60,000	$8,200 plus 24% of the excess of such amount over $40,000
Over $60,000 but not over $80,000	$13,000 plus 26% of the excess of such amount over $60,000
Over $80,000 but not over $100,000	$18,200 plus 28% of the excess of such amount over $80,000
Over $100,000 but not over $150,000	$23,800 plus 30% of the excess of such amount over $100,000
Over $150,000 but not over $250,000	$38,800 plus 32% of the excess of such amount over $150,000
Over $250,000 but not over $500,000	$70,800 plus 34% of the excess of such amount over $250,000
Over $500,000 but not over $750,000	$155,800 plus 37% of the excess of such amount over $500,000
Over $750,000 but not over $1,000,000	$248,300 plus 39% of the excess of such amount over $750,000
Over $1,000,000 but not over $1,250,000	$345,800 plus 41% of the excess of such amount over $1,000,000
Over $1,250,000 but not over $1,500,000	$448,300 plus 43% of the excess of such amount over $1,250,000
Over $1,500,000 but not over $2,000,000	$555,800 plus 45% of the excess of such amount over $1,500,000
Over $2,000,000 but not over $2,500,000	$780,800 plus 49% of the excess of such amount over $2,000,000
Over $2,500,000 but not over $3,000,000	$1,025,800 plus 53% of the excess of such amount over $2,500,000
Over $3,000,000	$1,290,800 plus 55% of the excess of such amount over $3,000,000

*Taxable gifts/estates between $10,000,000 and $21,040,000 are subject to an additional 5% tax that takes back the benefit of the unified credit and the lower marginal rates.

GIFT TAXES

LG4

Sometimes, even when you give money away, *you may end up having to pay taxes on at least part of the gift. Why do you think a tax may be levied on gifts you make? Try to answer this question before reading ahead.*

Federal tax law provides for a **gift tax** on certain gifts made during one's lifetime as well as an **estate tax** on "deathtime" gifts. Both lifetime and deathtime gifts are considered cumulatively and are subjected to the integrated progressive tax rate schedule shown in Exhibit 15.5. The tax on gifts is imposed on the right to transfer property and is measured by the value of the property transferred. The *donor* is primarily liable for the tax; a gift tax return must be filed by the donor and is due when his or her income tax return is filed. The graduated table of rates in Exhibit 15.5 is used for *both* gift and estate tax purposes and is known as the **unified rate schedule.** These rates are applied to *all* taxable gifts—whether made during the donor's life or after his or her death—after making a number of adjustments and computations. Thus, ignoring the annual exclusion for the moment, the following situations would produce the same total transfer taxes, that is, gift taxes plus estate taxes:

1. Fred gives his daughter a $2,000,000 taxable gift and dies in poverty several years later. Gift taxes equal $588,000.
2. Mary gives her son a $1,000,000 taxable gift. She dies several years later and leaves him another $1,000,000. The total transfer taxes are $588,000: gift taxes of $153,000 plus estate taxes of $435,000.
3. Frank dies leaving his daughter a $2,000,000 estate. The estate tax equals $588,000.

TRANSFERS SUBJECT TO GIFT TAX

Almost all property can be the subject of a transfer on which the gift tax must be paid. There is no tax on services that one person performs for another, nor is the rent-free use of property a taxable transfer. A tax may be payable on cash gifts, gifts of personal or real property, and both direct and indirect gifts. For example, if a father makes the mortgage payments on his adult son's home, the payment is an indirect gift from father to son. In fact, almost any shifting of financial advantage in which the recipient does not provide full consideration in money or money's worth may be considered a gift. For example, suppose your father gave you a summer home valued at $75,000 in exchange for $25,000. This type of transaction is called a "bargain sale." The $50,000 excess value received over the consideration paid is treated as a gift. Of course, if you gave no consideration for the property, its market value ($75,000) would represent the amount of the gift.

WHEN IS A GIFT MADE?

The question of when a gift is made is important, because it determines (1) when the gift must be reported and the gift tax, if any, paid and (2) the date at which the value of the gift is measured. Usually a gift is considered to be made *when the donor relinquishes dominion and control over the property or property interest transferred.* For example, if a mother places cash in a bank account held jointly with her son, no gift is made until the son makes a withdrawal. Until that time, the mother can completely recover the entire amount placed in the account. Therefore, when parents place property into a revocable trust for their children, no gift occurs, because they have not relinquished control over the assets placed in it. However, if they later make the trust irrevocable and thereby relinquish their right to revoke the gift, the transfer will be considered a completed gift.

DETERMINING THE AMOUNT OF A TAXABLE GIFT

All that is transferred by an individual is not necessarily subject to a gift tax. Annual exclusions, gift splitting, charitable deductions, and marital deductions are all means of reducing the total amount for tax purposes.

Annual Exclusions. Almost all gifts are subject to the gift tax, but for the reason of administrative convenience, certain transfers, or gift equivalents, are not counted. The gift tax law eliminates from the computation of taxable gifts transfers by a donor of amounts up to $10,000 per calendar year to each of any number of donees. For example, a person could give gifts of $10,000 each to 30 donees for a total of $300,000 without paying any gift tax. Further, the ability to give tax-free gifts of $10,000 per donee regenerates *annually.* This **annual exclusion** is available only for gifts that the donee has the *immediate and unrestricted right* to use, possess, or enjoy upon receipt.

Gift Splitting. **Gift splitting** is permitted to equate the tax treatment of married taxpayers residing in common law states with the tax treatment of married taxpayers in community property states. When a spouse earns a dollar in a community property state, such as California or Texas, half of that dollar is deemed to be owned by the other spouse immediately and automatically. If a gift is made of that dollar, each spouse is considered to have given 50 cents. Similarly, in common law states, such as Colorado, New York, and Pennsylvania, federal law provides that a married donor, with the consent of his or her spouse, can elect to treat gifts as if they were made one-half by each spouse. Because of this gift-splitting option, if a wife transfers $20,000 to her son and the required consent is given by her husband, for tax computation purposes her gift will be viewed as $10,000 and her husband will be considered to have given the other $10,000. As a result of the split, the total amount will be entirely gift tax free, because a

gift tax A tax levied by the federal government on the value of certain types of gifts made during the giver's lifetime.

estate tax A tax levied by federal and/or state governments on the value of certain types of gifts (or an estate) made upon the giver's death.

unified rate schedule A graduated table of rates applied to all taxable gifts after a number of adjustments and computations; used for *both* federal gift and estate tax purposes.

annual exclusion An amount up to $10,000 annually for gifts to each donee that is eliminated from the computation of a donor's taxable gifts.

gift splitting A method of reducing gift taxes whereby a gift given by one spouse, with the consent of his or her spouse, can be treated as if each had given one-half of it.

$10,000 annual exclusion is allowed to each spouse. The wife could give $20,000 to any number of donees and, by splitting the gift with her husband, avoid the tax on the entire gift. This tax reduction technique is available even if one spouse makes all the gifts and the other spouse gives nothing. It is also available to spouses in community property states who make gifts of their separately owned property. Gift splitting is allowed, however, only for gifts from married couples to third parties.

Charitable Deductions. There is no limit on the amount that can be given gift tax free to a qualified charity (one to which deductible gifts can be made for income tax purposes). Therefore, people could give their entire estates to charity and receive gift tax deductions for the total amount. There would be no federal gift taxes regardless of the type or amount of assets transferred.

Marital Deductions. Federal law permits an unlimited deduction for gift tax and estate tax purposes on property given or left to a spouse who is a U.S. citizen. Spouses who are not U.S. citizens are allowed a $100,000 per year marital deduction for gifts and no marital deduction for estates unless the property is left in a special trust, the Qualified Domestic Trust (QDT). (This provision is designed to prevent tax-avoidance if the noncitizen spouse returns to his or her native country, where the bequest would not be taxed.) To receive the marital deduction the QDT must have at least one U.S. citizen trustee. Distributions of trust assets (but not income) to the surviving spouse result in estate tax; any trust assets remaining at the surviving spouse's death will be taxed.

REASONS FOR MAKING LIFETIME GIFTS

There are several tax-oriented reasons why estate planners recommend gift giving.

- *Gift exclusion:* A single individual can give any number of donees up to $10,000 each year entirely gift tax-free, with no tax costs to either the donee or the donor. If the donor is married and the donor's spouse consents, the gift tax-free limit will be increased to $20,000 even if the entire gift is made from the donor's assets.
- *Gift tax exclusion:* Regardless of a gift's size—and even if it is made within three years of the donor's death—it typically will not be treated as part of the donor's gross estate. However, the taxable portion of lifetime gifts (technically called *adjusted taxable gifts*) pushes up the rate at which the donor's estate will be taxed. Fortunately, property that qualifies for the annual exclusion is not taxable and therefore is both gift and estate tax-free. Estate tax savings from this exclusion can be significant.
- *Appreciation in value:* The appreciation on a gift, from the time it is made, is excluded from the donor's estate unless the gift is, for some reason, includable in the estate. For instance, if the donor retained the right to receive all the dividends for life, the entire value of the gift as of the date of the decedent's death would be brought back into the estate. Suppose Larry gives his son Steve a gift of stock worth $25,000. At the time of Larry's death two years later, the stock is worth $60,000. The amount subject to transfer taxes will be $15,000, the amount of the gift that exceeded the $10,000 annual exclusion at the time the gift was made.
- *Payment limit:* Because of the credit that can be used to offset otherwise taxable gifts, gift taxes do not have to be paid on gifts totaling $600,000 or less. Once this credit is taken, it cannot offset the taxes generated by future lifetime (or deathtime) gifts.
- *Impact of marital deduction:* The transfer tax marital deduction allows one spouse to give the other spouse an unlimited amount of money or other property entirely tax-free without reducing the $600,000 total that can be transferred to others tax-free.

Concept Check

15-14. Answer and/or describe the following as they relate to federal gift taxes: (a) what is a gift? (b) when is a gift made? (c) annual exclusion, (d) gift splitting, (e) charitable deduction, (f) marital deduction, (g) application of the tax rate, and (h) payment of the gift tax.

15-15. Discuss the reasons estate planners cite for making lifetime gifts. How and in what ways might gift giving help reduce estate shrinkage?

ESTATE TAXES AND PLANNING

LG5 LG6

Estate taxes may be generated when property is transferred at time of death, so one of the goals of effective estate planning is to minimize the amount of estate taxes paid. Are you aware of any strategies frequently used to plan for estate tax minimization? If so, spend a few moments listing them before reading on.

The federal estate tax is levied on the transfer of property at death. The tax is measured by the value of the property that the deceased transfers (or is deemed to transfer) to others. The parenthetical phrase "deemed to transfer" is important, because the estate tax applies not only to transfers that a deceased actually makes at death but also to certain transfers made during the person's lifetime. In other words, to thwart tax-avoidance schemes, the estate tax is imposed on certain lifetime gifts that in essence are the same as dispositions of property made at death.

While most gifts made during one's life are not part of the decedent's gross estate, there are some exceptions. A major exception pertains to life insurance given away within three years of the owner's death. It will be included in the owner's gross estate at the value as of the date of death. Thus, if the former owner is also the insured, the gross estate will include the proceeds (paid out amount) of the policy. For example, two and a half years before his death, Max gives his son Eric a $1 million dollar term insurance policy on Max's life. At the time of the gift, Max was in good health and the *cash value* of the policy was less than the $10,000 annual exclusion amount for gifts. Therefore, no gift tax return had to be filed. Because Max died within three years of gifting the life insurance policy, the $1 million proceeds amount is included in his gross estate for estate tax purposes. Had Max outlived the transfer by more than three years, the proceeds would not have been included in his gross estate.

COMPUTATION OF THE FEDERAL ESTATE TAX

There are five stages to computing federal estate taxes. The first involves determining the *gross estate*, the total of all property in which the decedent had an interest and that is required to be included in the estate. Second, the *adjusted gross estate* is determined by subtracting from the gross estate any allowable funeral and administrative expenses, debts, certain taxes, and losses incurred during administration. Third, the *taxable estate* is calculated by subtracting any allowable marital deduction or charitable deduction from the adjusted gross estate.

The computation of the *estate tax payable before credits* is the fourth stage. After determining the value of the taxable estate, any "adjusted taxable gifts"—which include certain taxable lifetime transfers not included in the deceased's gross estate—are added to the taxable estate. The unified rate schedule—the same one applicable to gift taxes that was shown in Exhibit 15.5—is then applied to determine a *tentative estate tax*. After this tentative tax is found, any gift taxes the decedent paid on certain gifts are subtracted. The result is the *estate tax payable before credits*.

The final stage involves the determination of the *net federal estate tax payable*. Certain credits are allowed against the estate tax payable, which result in a dollar-for-dollar reduction of the tax: (1) unified tax credit, (2) state death tax credit, (3) credit for tax on prior transfers, and (4) credit for foreign death taxes. After reducing the estate tax payable for any eligible credits, the net federal estate tax is payable by the decedent's executor, generally within nine months of the decedent's death. Worksheet 15.2 can be used to estimate federal estate taxes. The exhibit depicts the computations for a hypothetical situation involving the death in 1995 of a widow who left a gross estate of $1,500,000. This worksheet is useful in following the flow of dollars from the gross estate to the net federal estate tax payable.

The maximum tax rate on estates is 55 percent. The **unified tax credit** is currently $192,800, making the amount that passes tax-free $600,000. Using Exhibit 15.5, you can determine the tentative tax on an estate. For a $600,000 taxable estate, no tax is owed because the unified credit for each estate is

unified tax credit The credit that can be applied against the tentative gift or estate tax; the unified credit is currently $192,800, which absorbs all of the tentative tax on taxable transfers up to $600,000.

WORKSHEET 15.2

Computing Net Federal Estate Tax Payable

This worksheet is useful in determining *net federal estate tax payable.* Note that taxes are payable at the marginal tax rate applicable to the total taxable estate (line 5), which is the amount that exists before the tax-free exemption is factored in.

Computing Net Federal Estate Tax Payable

Name Mary Widow Date 1995

Line	Computation	Item	Amount	Total Amount
1		*Gross estate*		$1,500,000
	Subtract sum of:	(a) Funeral expenses	$ 5,000	
		(b) Administrative expenses	30,000	
		(c) Debts	20,000	
		(d) Taxes	5,000	
		(e) Losses	—	
2	Result:	*Adjusted gross estate*		$1,440,000
	Subtract sum of:	(a) Marital deduction	—	
		(b) Charitable deduction	—	
3	Result:	*Taxable estate*		$1,440,000
4	Add:	*Adjusted taxable gifts*		$ 0
5	Result:	*Tentative tax base*		$1,440,000
6	Compute:	*Tentative estate tax*[a]	$530,000	
7	Subtract:	Gift taxes payable on post-1976 gifts	—	
8	Result:	*Estate tax payable before credits*		$ 530,000
9	Subtract sum of:	(a) Unified tax credit	$ 192,800	
		(b) State death tax credit[b]	60,560	
		(c) Credit for tax on prior transfers	—	
		(d) Credit for foreign death taxes	—	$ 253,360
10	Add:	*15% Excess accumulations tax*		$ 0
11	Result:	*Net federal estate tax payable*		$ 276,640

[a]This value was calculated using the unified rate schedule presented in Exhibit 15.5 as follows: $448,300 + [($1,440,000 − $1,250,000) × .43] = $448,300 + ($190,000 × .43) = $448,300 + $81,700 = $530,000.

[b]Line 9(b) was determined from Exhibit 15.6 in the same fashion as line 6.

Source: Stephen R. Leimberg, et al. *The Tools and Techniques of Estate Planning,* 9th ed. (Cincinnati: The National Underwriter Company, 1992). Reprinted with permission of the publisher.

$192,800. A taxable estate of $700,000 would pay estate taxes of $37,000.

Worksheet 15.2 factors this unified credit into the calculation of line 9a. The $192,800 value shown on that line, which is the unified tax credit, represents the amount of tax that *would* be due on the first $600,000 of the taxable estate. It thus reduces the amount of federal estate taxes due. The value shown on line 9a will, of course, be the same for all estates: $192,800. Obviously, if line 9a is equal to or greater than line 8, the estate will owe no federal taxes.

STATE DEATH TAXES

More individuals are subject to state *death taxes* than are liable for federal estate taxes. This is because (1) federal laws permit certain deductions, such as the marital deduction, that many state laws do not and (2) the amount of property exempted from tax under federal law is larger than that exempted by the laws of most states. The four basic types of state death taxes are the state inheritance tax, state estate tax, credit estate tax, and the credit pickup estate tax.

Inheritance Tax. An **inheritance tax** is a common type of state death tax. It is a tax on the right to receive a decedent's property. Sixteen states currently have inheritance taxes. The amount of the tax depends on the value of the property received and the relationship of the beneficiary to the deceased. In most states, beneficiaries are divided into categories. The lowest rates and largest exemptions are allocated to lineal descendants—that is, those beneficiaries most closely related to the deceased. For example, in Pennsylvania, property left to a child of the deceased is taxed at 6 percent, while the same property left to a cousin is subject to a 15 percent rate. Real property left to a spouse is exempt from state inheritance taxes, while the same property transferred to siblings is subject to a 15 percent tax.

Estate Tax. A *state estate tax,* like the federal estate tax, is imposed on the deceased's right to transfer property and is measured by the value of the entire property transferred. Five states currently impose an estate tax.

Credit Estate Tax. The **credit,** or **gap, estate tax** is designed to bridge the gap between the state's inheritance and estate taxes and the maximum state death tax credit allowed against the federal estate tax (see line 9b of the form for computing the net federal estate tax payable in Worksheet 15.2). The credit tax is best illustrated by a simple example. If a deceased's taxable estate for federal estate tax purposes is $700,000, a credit of up to $18,000 against the federal tax is allowed for taxes paid to the state as death taxes. Exhibit 15.6 can be used to calculate the maximum federal estate tax credit for state death taxes. The amount of any state death taxes paid may be subtracted from the federal tax, provided, however, that the maximum to be subtracted does not exceed the maximum shown in the exhibit. If the state's death taxes amount to only $8,000, an additional tax—a $10,000 credit estate tax—is imposed such that the total state death tax is increased to $18,000, the maximum amount of credit allowed by the federal government for state death taxes.

Credit Pickup Estate Tax. About half of the states have no separate inheritance or estate tax but simply collect the amount that is allowed as the state death tax credit against the federal estate tax (line 9b). This is sometimes referred to as the *pickup tax*. Because the state collects only the federal credit amount (see Exhibit 15.6), which in turn reduces dollar for dollar the federal estate taxes, this type of estate tax costs the decedent's estate nothing. It simply shifts money from the federal to the state treasury.

Other Factors Affecting the Amount of State Death Taxes. Other factors that affect the amount of state death taxes include (1) state exemptions and deductions, (2) multiple state taxation, and (3) tax rates.

Exemptions and deductions. Not all property is subject to taxation. Generally, states exempt property transferred to the United States, to the state itself, and to certain charitable organizations. Most states exempt property passing to a surviving spouse. Some states either totally or partially exempt life insurance proceeds unless payable to or for the benefit of the estate or its creditors. All states allow deductions for administrative costs, debts, funeral and last-illness expenses, and certain property taxes that are unpaid at the time of the deceased's death.

Multiple taxation. Many individuals have summer and winter homes or land and other property in states other than where they live. Although most estates are taxed by only one state, in certain situations an estate or its beneficiaries may be liable for the taxes of more than one state. The right of a state to impose a death tax depends on the type of property involved. The general treatment of the major types of property is as follows:

- *Real estate.* Land and permanent buildings can be taxed only by the state in which the property is located.
- *Tangible personal property.* Cars, boats, and household goods can be taxed only in the state in which they are situated. A boat, for example, is taxed where it is permanently docked. Its

inheritance tax A state death tax on the right to receive a decedent's property; the amount is based on the value of the property received and the beneficiary's relationship to the deceased.

credit (gap) estate tax A tax designed to bridge the gap between a state's inheritance and estate taxes and the maximum state death tax credit allowed against the federal estate tax.

EXHIBIT 15.6

Federal Estate Tax Credit for State Death Taxes

Credit is given on federal estate tax returns for state death taxes paid up to certain maximum amounts as specified in the table below.

Taxable Estate	Maximum Tax Credit
Not over $150,000	8/10ths of 1% of the amount by which the taxable estate exceeds $100,000
Over $150,000 but not over $200,000	$400 plus 1.6% of the excess over $150,000
Over $200,000 but not over $300,000	$1,200 plus 2.4% of the excess over $200,000
Over $300,000 but not over $500,000	$3,600 plus 3.2% of the excess over $300,000
Over $500,000 but not over $700,000	$10,000 plus 4% of the excess over $500,000
Over $700,000 but not over $900,000	$18,000 plus 4.8% of the excess over $700,000
Over $900,000 but not over $1,100,000	$27,600 plus 5.6% of the excess over $900,000
Over $1,100,000 but not over $1,600,000	$38,800 plus 6.4% of the excess over $1,100,000
Over $1,600,000 but not over $2,100,000	$70,800 plus 7.2% of the excess over $1,600,000
Over $2,100,000 but not over $2,600,000	$106,800 plus 8% of the excess over $2,100,000
Over $2,600,000 but not over $3,100,000	$146,800 plus 8.8% of the excess over $2,600,000
Over $3,100,000 but not over $3,600,000	$190,800 plus 9.6% of the excess over $3,100,000
Over $3,600,000 but not over $4,100,000	$238,800 plus 10.4% of the excess over $3,600,000
Over $4,100,000 but not over $5,100,000	$290,800 plus 11.2% of the excess over $4,100,000
Over $5,100,000 but not over $6,100,000	$402,800 plus 12% of the excess over $5,100,000
Over $6,100,000 but not over $7,100,000	$522,800 plus 12.8% of the excess over $6,100,000
Over $7,100,000 but not over $8,100,000	$650,800 plus 13.6% of the excess over $7,100,000
Over $8,100,000 but not over $9,100,000	$786,800 plus 14.4% of the excess over $8,100,000
Over $9,100,000 but not over $10,100,000	$930,800 plus 15.2% of the excess over $9,100,000
Over $10,100,000	$1,082,800 plus 16% of the excess over $10,100,000

registry and location for insurance purposes are examined to determine its legal location.

- *Intangible personal property.* Securities such as stocks, bonds, notes, and mortgages may, in the absence of interstate agreements, be taxed by several states. Generally, intangible personal property is taxed only by the state of the deceased's domicile. Unfortunately, if a deceased has residences in more than one state or does not clearly establish his or her state of domicile, two or more states can impose death taxes on the same intangible personal property.

Tax rates. The rates at which transfers or receipts of property are taxed vary widely from state to state. Some states have graduated rates similar to the federal tax, while others, such as Pennsylvania, have flat rates that do not grow with the size of the estate. In fact, because the impact of state death taxes can be so significant, many individuals go "domicile shopping" at retirement to find a state with favorable rates, exemptions, and deductions.

ESTATE PLANNING TECHNIQUES

The federal and state tax laws described in the preceding paragraphs provide both problems and opportunities for the estate planner. Estate shrinkage can be minimized and financial security maximized by judicious use of certain tax-oriented arrangements and maneuvers. Techniques of estate planning can be summarized by the three *D's:* divide, defer, and discount.

Dividing. Each time a new tax-paying entity can be created, income taxes will be saved and estate accumulation stimulated. Some of the more popular techniques are:

1. *Giving income-producing property to children, either outright or in trust.* Because each child can receive a specified amount of unearned income each year, some income tax savings may be realized each year even by persons who are not in high tax brackets.
2. *Establishing a corporation.* Incorporation may permit individuals in high tax brackets, such as

doctors or other professionals, to save taxes by accumulating income in a manner subject to relatively lower income tax rates.

3. *Properly qualifying for the federal estate tax marital deduction.* This marital deduction allows an individual to pass—estate tax-free—unlimited amounts to a spouse, taking full advantage of both spouses' unified credits. Properly qualifying in some estates may mean something less than fully qualifying. In other words, there are circumstances in which an advisor may properly recommend passing a lower amount of property than the maximum marital deduction amount, that is, an individual's entire estate to the surviving spouse.

Deferring. Progressive tax rates (rates that increase as the income or size of the estate increases) penalize taxpayers whose maximum earnings (or estates) reach high peaks. This hinders the job of gaining and retaining financial security. There are devices, however, that help minimize the total tax burden by spreading income over more than one tax year or deferring the tax to a later period so that the taxpayer can invest the tax money for a longer period of time. Examples include:

1. Nonqualified deferred-compensation plans for selected individuals in corporate businesses, as well as private contractors.
2. Making installment sales instead of cash sales so that the taxable gain can be spread over several years.
3. Private annuities, which are arrangements whereby one person transfers property to another, usually a younger family member. This recipient promises in return to pay an annuity to the original owner for as long as he or she lives. The income tax attributable to such an annuity can thereby be spread over a number of years. Furthermore, the property transferred is not part of the transferor's estate.
4. Qualified pension and profit-sharing plans that allow tax deferral on the income and gains from investments.
5. Government Series EE bonds, because their earnings can be treated as taxable income at maturity rather than yearly as earned.
6. Stocks that pay no or low dividends but provide high price appreciation as a result of investing retained earnings in profitable projects.
7. Life insurance policies in which lifetime growth is not taxed and death values are income tax-free. If the insured survives, earnings inherent in policy values become taxable only as received: thus, the tax on any gain can be deferred over a lifetime.
8. Depreciable real estate that yields high write-offs in years when the estate owner is earning high levels of taxable *passive* income.
9. Installment payment of federal estate taxes applicable to a business interest. Payments can be spread over as many as 14 years with only the interest being paid on the unpaid tax during the first 4 years.

Discounting. Even after everything has been done to accumulate an estate and reduce the income and estate tax burdens on it, there may still be a tax payable. But there are two instruments that make it possible to, in effect, pay estate taxes at a discount: flower bonds and a special type of life insurance policy.

Flower bonds, although no longer issued by the federal government, can be acquired by anyone —even the terminally ill—in the secondary market with the assistance of a stockbroker. They are redeemed by the government at par in payment of the federal estate tax; therefore, whenever they can be purchased at a price substantially below their par value, the result is a "discount" in the estate taxes. Such savings are reduced, however, by inclusion of the bond at par in the gross estate of the deceased and by their low (3.5 to 5 percent) yield.

Life insurance, one of the primary tools of estate planners, can be purchased by a person other than the insured or the insured's spouse, or by a trust, for an annual premium of from 3 to 6 percent of the face (death) value of the policy. If proper arrangements are made, the proceeds of such insurance will pass to the decedent's beneficiaries free of income tax, estate tax, inheritance tax, and probate costs. Such proceeds may be used to pay death taxes, debts, and other probate and administrative costs. Life insurance proceeds can also be used to pay family expenses, special needs (such as college costs), mortgage balances, and other major expenditures. What's more, life insurance acts as an attractive form of loan collateral in the case of whole life and universal life policies. As pointed out in Chapters 7 and 8, some lending institutions and other creditors require borrowers to obtain life insurance in an amount sufficient to repay them in the event borrowers die prior to fully repaying their loans.

Concept Check

15-16. Explain the following as they relate to federal and/or state estate taxes: (a) general nature of the estate tax, (b) computation of the federal estate tax, (c) state inheritance tax, (d) state estate tax, (e) credit estate tax, (f) credit pickup estate tax, (g) amount of exemptions and deductions, (h) multiple taxation, and (i) state death tax rates.

15-17. The techniques of estate planning can be summarized by the three *D's:* divide, defer, and discount. Describe and discuss each of the three *D's* and their associated strategies.

SUMMARY

LG1. Describe the role of estate planning in personal financial planning and identify the four steps involved in the process. Estate planning involves the accumulation, preservation, and distribution of an estate in a manner that will most effectively achieve an estate owner's personal goals. The four major steps to estate planning are (1) gathering data, (2) identifying possible problems, (3) formulating a plan and preparing for its implementation, and (4) testing and implementing the plan (subject to periodic reviews and revisions, as necessary).

LG2. Recognize the importance of preparing a will and other documents to protect you and your estate. Important privileges are forfeited when a person dies without a valid will, including the right to decide how property will be distributed at death and the opportunity to select who will administer the estate and who will bear the burden of estate taxes and administrative expenses. The will should provide a clear and unambiguous expression of the testator's wishes, be flexible enough to encompass possible changes in family circumstances, and give proper regard to minimizing federal and state death taxes. A will is valid only if properly executed by a person of sound mind. Once drawn up, wills can be changed by codicil or fully revoked by a later will. The executor, named in the will, is responsible for collecting the decedent's assets, paying his or her debts and taxes, and distributing any remaining assets to the beneficiaries in the prescribed fashion.

Other important estate planning documents include the letter of last instructions, power of attorney, living will, and durable power of attorney for health care.

LG3. Explain how trusts are used in estate planning. The trust relationship arises when one party, the grantor, transfers property to a second party, the trustee, for the benefit of a third party, the beneficiary. While there are a variety of different types of trusts, each is designed primarily for one or more of the following reasons: to save income and estate taxes, to provide asset management to avoid probate, and/or to conserve property.

LG4. Determine whether a gift will be taxable and use planned gifts to reduce estate taxes. Gifts of cash, financial assets, and personal or real property made during the donor's lifetime are subject to federal taxes. A gift of $10,000 per year to each recipient is excluded from the donor's gift tax calculation. Donations to qualified charities and gifts between spouses are also excluded from the gift tax.

LG5. Calculate federal and state taxes due on an estate. Federal estate taxes are essentially a levy on the transfer of assets at death. They are unified (coordinated) with the gift tax—which imposes a graduated tax on the transfer of property during one's lifetime—so that the rates and credits are the same for both. Once federal estate taxes are computed, certain credits are allowed, and the resulting amount is payable in full generally within nine months of the decedent's death. States also impose taxes on estates.

LG6. **Use effective estate planning techniques to minimize estate taxes.** The three *D's* of estate planning—divide, defer, and discount—are found, to one extent or another, in most well-defined estate plans. Dividing involves the creation of new tax entities; deferring gives an individual the use of money that would otherwise have been paid in taxes; and discounting involves paying estate taxes with "discounted" dollars.

FINANCIAL FACTS OR FANTASIES

Are the following statements financial facts (true) or fantasies (false)?

1. Estate planning is one of the key elements of personal financial planning.
2. The wealthy are the only ones who have to worry about making out wills.
3. Due to recent changes in the law, a person no longer has to be mentally competent in order to draw up a valid will.
4. Once a will is drawn up, it is a relatively simple matter to make minor changes to it.
5. In order for a living trust to be legally enforceable, it must be irrevocable.
6. There are no federal estate taxes on estates of up to $600,000.

DISCUSSION QUESTIONS AND PROBLEMS

Discussion Question for Opening Profile

Discuss how Pauline Victor approached her duties as executor of her father's estate. What were her principal duties, and what advantages did she have in taking on the role?

1. Generate a list of estate planning objectives that apply to your personal family situation, including your parents. Be sure to consider the size of your potential estate and both people planning and asset planning.
2. Renée and Steve Burrows are in their mid-30s and have two children ages 8 and 5. They have combined annual income of $95,000 and own a house in joint tenancy with a market value of $310,000, on which they have a mortgage of $250,000. Steve has $100,000 in group term life insurance and an individual universal life policy for $150,000. However, the Burrows have not yet prepared their wills. Steve plans to do one soon, but they think that Renée doesn't need one because the house is jointly owned. As their financial planner, explain why it is important for both to draft wills as soon as possible.
3. Prepare a basic will for yourself, using the guidelines presented in the text; also prepare your brief letter of last instructions.
4. Your brother has asked you to be executor of his estate. What qualifications do you need, and would you accept the responsibility?
5. Joe Phillips, 48 and a widower, and Amy Parsons, 44 and divorced, were married five years ago. Joe has two children and Amy has one from their prior marriages. Their estate totals $1.4 million, including a house valued at $475,000, a vacation home in the mountains, investments, antique furniture that has been in Amy's family for many years, and jewelry belonging to Joe's first wife. Discuss how they could use trusts as part of their estate planning, and suggest some other ideas for them to consider when writing their wills and related documents.
6. FPPC ***Use Worksheet 15.2.*** When Jim Levitt died at age 75, he left an estate valued at $1,650,000 to his wife and children, after a $10,000 bequest to the local hospital. The death-related costs included $6,800 funeral expenses, $40,000 administrative expenses, and $12,500 in miscellaneous debts. Using Worksheet 15.2 and Exhibits 15.5 and 15.6, calculate the net federal estate tax payable on his estate.

CONTEMPORARY CASE APPLICATIONS

15.1 A Long Overdue Will for Kris

Kris Pappadopolus, a Greek national, migrated to the United States during the late 1950s. A man of many talents and deep foresight, he has during his stay in the United States built a large fleet of ocean-going oil tankers. Now a wealthy man in his 60s, he resides in Palm Springs, Florida, with his second wife, Veronica, age 35. He has two sons, who are both high school seniors. For quite a while, Kris has considered preparing a will in order to ensure that his estate will be aptly distributed if some unforeseen tragedy or natural cause takes his life. A survey of his estate—all legally owned by him—reveals the following:

Ranch in Amarillo, Texas	$ 500,000
Condominium in San Francisco	200,000
House in Palm Springs	600,000
Franchise in ice cream stores	2,500,000
Stock in Seven Seas International	5,000,000
Shares in Fourth National Bank	1,000,000
Corporate bonds	3,000,000
Other assets	200,000
Total assets	$13,000,000

In addition to $1 million for their education and welfare, he would like to leave each of his sons 20 percent of his estate. He wishes to leave 40 percent of the estate to his wife. The rest of the estate is to be divided among relatives, friends, and charitable institutions. He has scheduled an appointment for drafting his will with his attorney and close friend, Leonard Wiseman. Kris would like to appoint Leonard and his cousin, Plato Jones, as coexecutors of his estate. If one of them predeceases Kris, he would like his bank, Fourth National Bank, to act as coexecutor.

Questions

1. Does Kris really need a will? Explain why or why not? What would happen to his estate if he were to die without a will?
2. Explain to Kris the common features that need to be incorporated into a will.
3. Is a living trust an appropriate part of this estate plan? How would a living trust change the nature of Kris's will?
4. What are the options available to Kris if he decides to change or revoke the will at a later date? Is it more difficult to change a living trust?
5. What duties will Leonard Wiseman and Plato Jones have to perform as coexecutors of Kris's estate?

FPPC 15.2 Estate Taxes on Philip Colburn's Estate

Philip Colburn of Arlington Heights, Delaware, was 65 and in good health in 1988. He and his wife, Delores, who predeceased him, had been married for 35 years. They had an adult son who had been made sole beneficiary of their estate. When Philip retired as chairman of the Vilanto Corporation in 1988, his net worth (estate) was valued at $1 million. The value had increased 20 percent by 1995, when Philip died. Funeral costs amounted to $10,000, and the cost of administering the estate was $50,000. Miscellaneous debts totaled $10,000. These items were the only applicable deductions from his gross estate. Philip left $75,000 of his estate to his alma mater. Four years prior to his death, he had made adjusted taxable gifts (gifts above the annual exclusion which are not included in his gross estate) of $160,000. No gift taxes were paid or payable on any of these gifts. A state death tax credit was also available to the estate. Assume that current estate tax laws permit an unlimited marital deduction when applicable. Using Worksheet 15.2 as a guide to the calculations, answer each of the following questions.

Questions

1. Compute the value of Philip's gross estate at the time of his death.
2. Determine the total allowable deductions.
3. Determine the taxable estate at Philip's death.
4. Calculate (a) the tentative tax base, (b) the tentative estate tax (using Exhibit 15.5), and (c) the estate tax payable before credits.
5. Determine the value of the net federal estate tax payable on Philip's estate.
6. Comment on the estate shrinkage experienced on his estate. What might have been done to reduce this shrinkage? Explain.

GETTING A HANDLE ON YOUR FINANCIAL FUTURE

Estate planning is one of the most complex areas of personal financial planning, especially for the wealthy or families with children from previous marriages (his, hers, and ours). The ability to achieve your financial goals through managing your estate can be accomplished under normal circumstances through the creation of a valid will, the proper titling of property, the creation of a trust, and the use of gifts. It should allow you to direct the distribution of your property according to your desires. If properly constructed and implemented, an estate plan should preserve assets by reducing taxation and other expenses associated with the settlement of the estate.

If You Are Just Starting Out

Regardless of your age or financial condition, unless you want the state to decide how your assets are distributed upon your death, you need to have a valid will.

Things to Consider when Drafting a Will:

1. Decide on a personal representative to ensure proper administration of your estate. This may or may not be a family member, and your decision will probably depend on the complexity of your estate.
2. If you have minor children, you need to name a guardian to raise your children in the event of the death of both spouses.
3. If you don't want your life to be sustained by artificial means, you need to consider using a living will and/or a durable power of attorney for health care to specify under what conditions treatment can be made.
4. Consider leaving a letter of last instructions attached to your will to give your heirs more personal instructions concerning an explanation of assets, location of documents, or burial.
5. If you move to another state, you should have a new will prepared to reflect the laws of your new state and to establish it as your domicile.
6. Remember that if you die without a will (intestate) you have no control over how your assets will be distributed.

If You Are Thirty-Something

Many of you will find that your estate planning needs can no longer be met by a simple will due to changes in your marital and family status and increases in your wealth.

Estate Planning Techniques:

1. Consider gifting assets with high growth potential to children so that further increases in value will occur outside of your estate.
2. If you are a highly paid professional, you might want to incorporate to save on current taxes and provide for growth in your estate.
3. Although the marital deduction allows you to transfer to your surviving spouse all of your estate tax-free, this may not be the best thing to do. You might want to establish a credit shelter trust and a qualified terminable interest property (QTIP) trust to take advantage of both spouses' $600,000 exclusion.
4. Remember that while assets that are jointly owned may be transferred without a will, they may not be exempted from inclusion in the taxable estate of the deceased.
5. To take advantage of an income tax deduction as well as estate tax savings, the very wealthy sometimes donate property to charity and continue to receive the benefits of the property until the death of the last beneficiary. This is accomplished through the use of a charitable remainder trust.
6. If you inherit property that you do not need or cannot use, consider using a disclaimer. This refusal to accept property will result in its distribution to an alternative beneficiary and could result in estate tax savings.
7. If you have a business interest, the estate taxes can be paid over 14 years to reduce the possibility that the business would have to be sold to pay the federal estate tax.

1. Referring to Paul's most recent balance sheet (Part 5, Question 19), would Paul's estate be subject to federal estate taxes if he were to die? If yes, what steps should be taken to reduce estate taxes?
2. Which of Paul's assets would be probate and which would be non-probate assets?
3. Since Paul currently does not have a will, how would his estate be distributed if he were to die? Use Exhibit 15.3 to answer this question unless you know your own state laws.
4. Should Paul have a will written? Why? If yes, what should be included in his will?
5. What other estate planning documents should Paul consider having? Why?
6. Paul has considered saving for his mother's retirement in her name rather than in his own name. Since the contributions to this account (currently $1,500 a year) would be considered a gift to his mother, would Paul have to pay gift taxes on this gift?

TABLE OF FUTURE VALUE FACTORS

Instructions: To use this table, find the future value factor that corresponds to both a given time period (year) and an interest rate. To illustrate, if you want the future value factor for 6 years and 10 percent, move across from year 6 and down from 10 percent to the point at which the row and column intersect: 1.772. Other illustrations: For 3 years and 15 percent, the proper future value factor is 1.521; for 30 years and 8 percent, it is 10.062.

	Interest Rate											
Year	**2%**	**3%**	**5%**	**6%**	**8%**	**9%**	**10%**	**12%**	**15%**	**20%**	**25%**	**30%**
1	1.020	1.030	1.050	1.060	1.080	1.090	1.100	1.120	1.150	1.120	1.250	1.300
2	1.040	1.060	1.102	1.120	1.166	1.190	1.210	1.254	1.322	1.440	1.562	1.690
3	1.061	1.090	1.158	1.190	1.260	1.290	1.331	1.405	1.521	1.728	1.953	2.197
4	1.082	1.130	1.216	1.260	1.360	1.410	1.464	1.574	1.749	2.074	2.441	2.856
5	1.104	1.160	1.276	1.340	1.469	1.540	1.611	1.762	2.011	2.488	3.052	3.713
6	1.126	1.190	1.340	1.420	1.587	1.670	1.772	1.974	2.313	2.986	3.815	4.827
8	1.172	1.260	1.477	1.590	1.851	1.990	2.144	2.476	3.059	4.300	5.960	8.157
10	1.219	1.340	1.629	1.790	2.159	2.360	2.594	3.106	4.046	6.192	9.313	13.786
12	1.268	1.420	1.796	2.010	2.518	2.810	3.138	3.896	5.350	8.916	14.552	23.298
15	1.346	1.560	2.079	2.390	3.172	3.640	4.177	5.474	8.137	15.407	28.422	51.185
20	1.486	1.810	2.653	3.210	4.661	5.600	6.727	9.646	16.366	38.337	86.736	190.047
25	1.641	2.090	3.386	4.290	6.848	8.620	10.834	17.000	32.918	95.395	264.698	705.627
30	1.811	2.420	4.322	5.740	10.062	13.260	17.449	29.960	66.210	237.373	807.793	2619.936
35	2.000	2.810	5.516	7.690	14.785	20.410	28.102	52.799	133.172	590.657	2465.189	9727.598
40	2.208	3.260	7.040	10.280	21.724	31.410	45.258	93.049	267.856	1469.740	7523.156	36117.754

Note: All factors to nearest 1/1000 as shown to agree with Chapters 2 and 4 of text.

TABLE OF FUTURE VALUE OF ANNUITY FACTORS

Instructions: To use this table, find the future value of annuity factor that corresponds to both a given time period (year) and an interest rate. To illustrate, if you want the future value of annuity factor for 6 years and 10 percent, move across from year 6 and down from 10 percent to the point at which the row and column intersect: 7.716. Other illustrations: For 3 years and 15 percent, the proper future value of annuity factor is 3.472; for 30 years and 8 percent, it is 113.282.

	Interest Rate											
Year	**2%**	**3%**	**5%**	**6%**	**8%**	**9%**	**10%**	**12%**	**15%**	**20%**	**25%**	**30%**
1	1.000	1.000	1.000	1.000	1.000	1.000	1.000	1.000	1.000	1.000	1.000	1.000
2	2.020	2.030	2.050	2.060	2.080	2.090	2.100	2.120	2.150	2.200	2.250	2.300
3	3.060	3.090	3.152	3.180	3.246	3.270	3.310	3.374	3.472	3.640	3.813	3.990
4	4.122	4.180	4.310	4.380	4.506	4.570	4.641	4.779	7.993	5.368	5.766	6.187
5	5.204	5.310	5.526	5.630	5.867	5.980	6.105	6.353	6.742	7.442	8.207	9.043
6	6.308	6.460	6.802	6.970	7.336	7.520	7.716	8.115	8.754	9.930	11.259	12.756
8	8.583	8.890	9.549	9.890	10.637	11.030	11.436	12.300	13.727	16.499	19.842	23.858
10	10.950	11.460	12.578	13.180	14.487	15.190	15.937	17.549	20.304	25.959	33.253	42.619
12	13.412	14.190	15.917	16.870	18.977	20.140	21.384	24.133	29.001	39.580	54.208	74.326
15	17.293	18.600	21.578	23.270	27.152	29.360	31.772	37.280	47.580	72.035	109.687	167.285
20	24.297	26.870	33.066	36.780	45.762	51.160	57.274	72.052	102.443	186.687	342.945	630.157
25	32.030	36.460	47.726	54.860	73.105	84.700	98.346	133.333	212.790	471.976	1054.791	2348.765
30	40.567	47.570	66.438	79.060	113.282	136.300	164.491	241.330	434.738	1181.865	3227.172	8729.805
35	49.994	60.460	90.318	111.430	172.314	215.700	271.018	431.658	881.152	2948.294	9856.746	32422.090
40	60.401	75.400	120.797	154.760	259.052	337.870	442.580	767.080	1779.048	7343.715	30088.621	120389.375

Note: All factors to nearest 1/1000 as shown to agree with Chapters 2 and 4 of text.

TABLE OF PRESENT VALUE FACTORS

Instructions: To use this table, find the present value factor that corresponds to both a given time period (year) and an interest rate. To illustrate, if you want the present value factor for 25 years and 7 percent, move across from year 25 and down from 7 percent to the point at which the row and column intersect: .184. Other illustrations: For 3 years and 15 percent, the proper present value is .658; for 30 years and 8 percent, it is .099.

	Interest Rate											
Year	**2%**	**3%**	**5%**	**7%**	**8%**	**9%**	**10%**	**12%**	**15%**	**20%**	**25%**	**30%**
1	.980	.971	.952	.935	.926	.917	.909	.833	.870	.893	.800	.769
2	.961	.943	.907	.873	.857	.842	.826	.797	.756	.694	.640	.592
3	.942	.915	.864	.816	.794	.772	.751	.712	.658	.579	.512	.455
4	.924	.888	.823	.763	.735	.708	.683	.636	.572	.482	.410	.350
5	.906	.863	.784	.713	.681	.650	.621	.567	.497	.402	.328	.269
6	.888	.837	.746	.666	.630	.596	.564	.507	.432	.335	.262	.207
8	.853	.789	.677	.582	.540	.502	.467	.404	.327	.233	.168	.123
10	.820	.744	.614	.508	.463	.422	.386	.322	.247	.162	.107	.073
12	.789	.701	.557	.444	.397	.356	.319	.257	.187	.112	.069	.043
15	.743	.642	.481	.362	.315	.275	.239	.183	.123	.065	.035	.020
20	.673	.554	.377	.258	.215	.178	.149	.104	.061	.026	.012	.005
25	.610	.478	.295	.184	.146	.116	.092	.059	.030	.010	.004	.001
30	.552	.412	.231	.131	.099	.075	.057	.033	.015	.004	.001	•
35	.500	.355	.181	.094	.068	.049	.036	.019	.008	.002	•	•
40	.453	.307	.142	.067	.046	.032	.022	.011	.004	.001	•	•

*Present value factor is zero to three decimal places.

Note: All factors to nearest 1/1000 as shown to agree with Chapters 2 and 4 of text.

TABLE OF PRESENT VALUE OF ANNUITY FACTORS

Instructions: To use this table, find the present value of annuity factor that corresponds to both a given time period (year) and an interest rate. To illustrate, if you want the present value of annuity factor for 30 years and 7 percent, move across from year 30 and down from 7 percent to the point at which the row and column intersect: 12.409. Other illustrations: For 3 years and 15 percent, the proper present value of annuity factor is 2.283; for 30 years and 8 percent, it is 11.258.

	Interest Rate											
Year	**2%**	**3%**	**5%**	**7%**	**8%**	**9%**	**10%**	**12%**	**15%**	**20%**	**25%**	**30%**
1	.980	.971	.952	.935	.926	.917	.909	.893	.870	.833	.800	.769
2	1.942	1.913	1.859	1.808	1.783	1.759	1.736	1.690	1.626	1.528	1.440	1.361
3	2.884	2.829	2.723	2.624	2.577	2.531	2.487	2.402	2.283	2.106	1.952	1.816
4	3.808	3.717	3.546	3.387	3.312	3.240	3.170	3.037	2.855	2.589	2.362	2.166
5	4.713	4.580	4.329	4.100	3.993	3.890	3.791	3.605	3.352	2.991	2.689	2.436
6	5.601	5.417	5.076	4.767	4.623	4.486	4.355	4.111	3.784	3.326	2.951	2.643
8	7.326	7.020	6.463	5.971	5.747	5.535	5.335	4.968	4.487	3.837	3.329	2.925
10	8.983	8.530	7.722	7.024	6.710	6.418	6.145	5.650	5.019	4.192	3.570	3.092
12	10.575	9.954	8.863	7.943	7.536	7.161	6.814	6.194	5.421	4.439	3.725	3.190
15	12.849	11.938	10.380	9.108	8.560	8.061	7.606	6.811	5.847	4.675	3.859	3.268
20	16.352	14.878	12.462	10.594	9.818	9.129	8.514	7.469	6.259	4.870	3.954	3.316
25	19.524	17.413	14.094	11.654	10.675	9.823	9.077	7.843	6.464	4.948	3.985	3.329
30	22.396	19.601	15.373	12.409	11.258	10.274	9.427	8.055	6.566	4.979	3.995	3.332
35	24.999	21.487	16.378	12.948	11.655	10.567	9.844	8.176	6.617	4.992	3.998	3.333
40	27.356	23.115	17.159	13.332	11.925	10.757	9.779	8.244	6.642	4.997	3.999	3.333

Note: All factors to nearest 1/1000 as shown to agree with Chapters 2 and 4 of text.

ANSWERS TO FINANCIAL FACTS OR FANTASIES

Chapter 1
1. Fact
2. Fantasy
3. Fact
4. Fantasy
5. Fantasy
6. Fantasy

Chapter 2
1. Fantasy
2. Fact
3. Fact
4. Fantasy
5. Fantasy
6. Fantasy

Chapter 3
1. Fantasy
2. Fact
3. Fantasy
4. Fantasy
5. Fantasy
6. Fact

Chapter 4
1. Fantasy
2. Fact
3. Fantasy
4. Fantasy
5. Fantasy
6. Fact

Chapter 5
1. Fantasy
2. Fantasy
3. Fantasy
4. Fact
5. Fact
6. Fact

Chapter 6
1. Fact
2. Fantasy
3. Fact
4. Fact
5. Fantasy
6. Fantasy

Chapter 7
1. Fact
2. Fact
3. Fantasy
4. Fact
5. Fantasy
6. Fantasy

Chapter 8
1. Fantasy
2. Fantasy
3. Fact
4. Fact
5. Fantasy
6. Fantasy

Chapter 9
1. Fact
2. Fantasy
3. Fantasy
4. Fact
5. Fantasy
6. Fact

Chapter 10
1. Fact
2. Fantasy
3. Fact
4. Fantasy
5. Fact
6. Fantasy

Chapter 11
1. Fantasy
2. Fact
3. Fantasy
4. Fact
5. Fantasy
6. Fact

Chapter 12
1. Fantasy
2. Fantasy
3. Fact
4. Fantasy
5. Fact
6. Fact

Chapter 13
1. Fact
2. Fantasy
3. Fact
4. Fantasy
5. Fantasy
6. Fantasy

Chapter 14
1. Fantasy
2. Fantasy
3. Fantasy
4. Fantasy
5. Fact
6. Fact

Chapter 15
1. Fact
2. Fantasy
3. Fantasy
4. Fact
5. Fantasy
6. Fact

Credit List

Exhibit 1.7 ACCRA; P.O. Box 6749, Louisville, KY 40206-0749

Chapter 2 Opening Profile San Diego Union-Tribune

Worksheet 2.1 Reprinted by permission from the 1989 issue of *Changing Times Magazine*. Copyright © 1989 The Kiplinger Washington Editors, Inc.

Exhibit 5.1 Adapted from *U.S. News & World Report*, April 10, 1995

Exhibit 6.8 Bankcard Holders of America

Exhibit 6.11 Reprinted from the January 1995 issue of MONEY by special permission; copyright 1995, Time Inc.

Exhibit 8.7 From PRINCIPLES OF RISK MANAGEMENT AND INSURANCE, 5th Edition, by George E. Rejda. Copyright © 1995 by HarperCollins College Publishers. Reprinted by permission.

Exhibit 9.1 This table originally appeared in Self Magazine.

Exhibit 10.3 Reprinted by permission from the August 1994 issue of *Kiplinger's Personal Finance Magazine*. Copyright © 1994 The Kiplinger Washington Editors, Inc.

Exhibit 10.5 From PRINCIPLES OF RISK MANAGEMENT AND INSURANCE, 4th Edition, by George E. Rejda. Copyright © 1992 by HarperCollins College Publishers. Reprinted by permission.

Exhibit 10.6 From PRINCIPLES OF RISK MANAGEMENT AND INSURANCE, 5th Edition, by George E. Rejda. Copyright © 1995 by HarperCollins College Publishers. Reprinted by permission.

Exhibit 11.2 Reprinted by permission of The Wall Street Journal, © 1995 Dow Jones & Company, Inc. All Rights Reserved Worldwide.

Exhibit 12.4 1, 2, 3 and 6 photographed by The Dryden Press with permission of Trade Star Investments, Inc., Fort Worth, Texas branch office; 4. © Les Stone/Sygma; 5. © Rick Maiman/Sygma.

Exhibit 12.7 Reprinted by permission of The Wall Street Journal, © 1995 Dow Jones & Company, Inc. All Rights Reserved Worldwide.

Exhibit 12.8 Reprinted by permission of The Wall Street Journal, © 1995 Dow Jones & Company, Inc. All Rights Reserved Worldwide.

Exhibit 12.9 Reprinted by permission of Standard & Poor's, a division of The McGraw-Hill Companies.

UNF 13A Reprinted by permission of The Wall Street Journal, © 1994 Dow Jones & Company, Inc. All Rights Reserved Worldwide.

Exhibit 13.8 Reprinted by permission of The Wall Street Journal, © 1993 Dow Jones & Company, Inc. All Rights Reserved Worldwide.

Worksheet 15.2 The Tools and Techniques of Estate Planning, 9th edition, by Stephan R. Leimberg, et al., Copyright 1992, The National Underwriter Company. Reprinted with permission of the publisher.

Exhibit 15.5 Copyright ©1995 by The American College. Reprinted with permission.

Exhibit 15.6 Copyright ©1995 by The American College. Reprinted with permission.

Trademarks

UNIX™ is a registered trademark of AT&T.

Windows® is a registered trademark of Microsoft Corporation.

Macintosh® is a registered trademark of Apple Computer, Inc.

Quicken® is a registered trademark of Intuit.

Managing Your Money® is a registered trademark of MECA Software, Inc.

WealthBuilder™ is a registered trademark of Reality OnLine Inc.

TaxCut® is a registered trademark of MECA Software, Inc.

TurboTax®/MacInTax® are registered trademarks of Intuit.

Personal Tax Edge™ is a registered trademark of Parsons Technology.

Car Buyer's Companion™ is a registered trademark of Parsons Technology.

Popular Mechanics New Car Buyer's Guide 1995™ is a registered trademark of Books That Work.

Retirement Planning Thinkware™ is a registered trademark of Fidelity Investments.

Retirement Planner® is a registered trademark of Caplife.

Index

D

T

Bold indicates key terms